1995

NORTH AFRICAN HANDBOOK

With Andalucía – Moorish Southern Spain

SECOND EDITION

Editors ***Anne and Keith McLachlan***
Cartographer ***Sebastian Ballard***

The wind passes like a caress over the waves of
the desert sand
And the caravan leaves no more trace than a bird's
wing in the air or a fish in the water.
Let us flee the crowd, for in the multitude there
is no salvation,
Let us beware of taking root like a tree.

The Camel Track, *a traditional Arab song, translated by Alberto Denti di Pirajno*

TRADE & TRAVEL
Handbooks

Trade & Travel Publications Ltd
6 Riverside Court, Lower Bristol Road, Bath BA2 3DZ, England
Telephone 01225 469141 Fax 01225 469461

ISBN 0 900751 58 4 ISSN 0968-7459

CIP DATA: A catalogue record for this book is available from the British Library

In North America, published by

PASSPORT BOOKS
a division of *NTC Publishing Group*

4255 West Touhy Avenue
Lincolnwood (Chicago), Illinois 60646-1975, USA

ISBN 0-8442-8978-7

Library of Congress Catalog Card Number 94-66056

WARNING: While every endeavour is made to ensure that the facts printed in this book are correct at the time of going to press, travellers are cautioned to obtain authoritative advice from consulates, airlines, etc, concerning current travel and visa requirements and conditions before embarking. The publishers cannot accept legal responsibility for errors, however caused, that are printed in this book.

Maps – Publisher's note: a number of frontiers in the area covered by this Handbook are disputed and the subject of territorial claims by various countries in the region. Neither the coloured nor the black and white maps in this book are intended to have any political significance or purport to show authenticated international boundaries.

Cover illustration by Suzanne Evans

Printed and bound in Great Britain by Clays Ltd., Bungay, Suffolk

CONTENTS

TRADE & TRAVEL *HANDBOOKS*

"A travel guide business that looks set to sweep the world."
The Independent

*"The **India Handbook** (formerly the South Asian Handbook) has reminded me of how much I do not know about the sub-continent!"*
Mark Tully, BBC India correspondent

"More info - less blah."
Readers's letter, Germany

"By far the best, most comprehensive guides: in a class of their own. Unreservedly recommended - a Handbook will pay for itself many times over."
Journey Latin America

"On Bible thin paper with distinctive covers. The miraculous result is that they are, at the same time, sturdy, exhaustive and light-weight."
Fort Lauderdale Sun Sentinel

"Mines of information and free of pretentiousness: make other guidebooks read like Butlins brochures."
Bookshop review

"Accurate and reliable down to the minutest detail. Amazingly so."
Reader's letter, Canada

"By far the most informative guide to Burma published in recent years. Miraculously, the information appears to be up-to-date, rare for books in this genre."
Far Eastern Economic Review

PREFACE

The ***North African Handbook*** is unique in combining geographical coverage of Morocco, Mauritania, Algeria and Tunisia in North Africa with the historically closely related regions of Moorish Spain to give a unitary view of the western Arab world and the Islamic lands of south west Europe. A second link is also explored between the Maghreb countries and the more easterly lands of North Africa, including Libya, Egypt and Sudan. The traveller can thus enjoy making the archaeological, architectural and cultural connections across the great swathe of the western and southern Mediterranean lands that benefited from the glittering fusion of Islamic and European civilizations.

This edition has been extended geographically to include greater details of sites in Andalusian Spain, Moorish and otherwise, together with information on the under-rated but excellent city of Cádiz. New data on travel has been assembled on a number of splendid extensions to the more well trodden routes for travellers. In particular, there is a wealth of new material to guide the reader to the Western Desert areas of Egypt, where the wonderful city of Alexandria, the coastal towns of El-Alamein, Marsa Matruh and the little visited southern oasis of Siwa are all situated. The visitor's guide to Islamic Cairo has been entirely reshaped and updated for this edition and organized with a new map and a series of suggested routes. In Sudan, our information on the capital and travel beyond Khartoum is extended to take account of the new realities in that country. In Morocco, where value for money for the traveller is greatly increasing, where a better organized and a more relaxed atmosphere is now apparent, a considerable revision of information has been incorporated. Opportunities for adventure travel in the southern region are noted and new places for the more sedentary visitor are included.

The variety of existing attractions in Andalucía and North Africa is already considerable. Topographically, the region offers a magnificent range of environments from the high mountains of the Sierra Nevada and the High Atlas to the great coastal plains of the Sahel of Tunisia and the inland flat desert lands of Libya and Egypt. There are seas of sand dunes now more accessible to the visitor in most countries of the region together with the remote black basalt moonscapes of the interior of the great deserts in Libya. Adventure travel in four wheel drive vehicles in the most distant parts of the Sahara, including the areas of important pre-historic cave painting, is now possible for the more determined spirits.

The popular press has made overmuch of the political difficulties facing the countries of North Africa. Reality is that, while there are obvious constraints on travel, for example to Libya because of the continuing embargo on air traffic, most countries remain open to foreign visitors and risks are comparatively minimal. In Egypt, the problems faced by travellers are slight. Indeed in that country and others within the ***North African Handbook*** region the very fact of the hostile press reaction to news means that those Westerners who do venture there find an uncluttered landscape but a very warm welcome. In general, the hardy traveller will find conditions on the ground entirely friendly, except in Algeria, where the situation is still in flux and about which the traveller should take advice before venturing.

Readers should be aware that the political situation in North Africa has become more stable for all countries other than Algeria in the recent past. Marrakech, in Morocco, was the venue for the international Gatt meeting in March/April 1994, underlining the growing strategic and economic importance of that country.

Particular credits are given to a number of contributors, notable are Rowland Mead, whose travels throughout Andalucía have given added spice and data on that area; St John Gould, whose expertise on central and southern Morocco has been used to the full this year; Dr Charles Gurdon and his colleagues in Sudan and Egypt who have also provided major additions to the current text; Stefano Ciarli who has travelled widely in Tunisia for the **Handbook** and substantial revisions in that country result from this effort. The volume could not be so well informed without the constant help of our many friends and correspondents throughout the region and in UK. From the long list of informants perhaps most gratitude should be allotted this year to Abdollilah Bennis at the Embassy of Morocco, Dr Mohammed Chatou of ISESCO, Diana Stone of the Anthropology Department and George Joffé of the Middle East Centre at the School of Oriental and African Studies, University of London.

The authors' thanks are due to those travellers listed below who have written to us in the course of the last year with information and advice. Jill Chapman of Leicestershire; Jacki Cooper of Bath; A J Allan of London; Rodney Brookes, Tokoroa, New Zealand; Philip Geroge, Weymouth; Anne Lévesque, Inverness, Nova Scotia; Kathleen Mitchiner, Alexandria, Egypt; Fiona Moffitt, Cairo, Egypt; Dr Ian Wilson, London; Charlie Nurse, Cambridge.

Anne & Keith McLachlan
The Editors, London

THE EDITORS

Anne McLachlan

Anne McLachlan has travelled extensively for many years in North Africa, the Middle East and the Mediterranean, living for a time in Turkey, Iran and Spain. Frequent travel to the North African region has given a broad perspective. Recent visits include a return to southern Morocco to look in detail at the Anti-Atlas, Sous valley and Draa areas; off the beaten track in the Saharan area of Tunisia; and two fact-finding journeys to Egypt. The first, voyaging by land, air and water to the key sites of Aswan (one of her favourite places) and Luxor and the second, returning to her well-trodden paths in Cairo and the Nile Delta, and extending to Alexandria, the Egyptian Mediterranean coast and a foray south to the oasis of Siwa.

Iberia is her second home where she lives for part of each year in Andalucía, the heart of Moorish Spain, with easy access to Morocco and the countries of Maghrebi North Africa.

Keith McLachlan

Keith McLachlan has been a professional observer and traveller in the area covered by this ***Handbook*** for many years. He made his first trans-Saharan voyage as early as 1958, travelling from Al-Khoms on the Mediterranean across the mountains and deserts deep into southern Libya. Since then he has visited each of the countries of North Africa on a regular basis, spending long periods each year in travel. Recently he has journeyed to Libya, Morocco, Egypt and Tunisia gathering material for the ***Handbook***.

His position as professor at the School of Oriental and African Studies involves him in regular research visits to North Africa and he has a long acquaintance with the quirks of travel in this area. He also advises North African governments on their international border disputes and has a constant professional involvement in problems of oil and economic development in the region.

MAP SYMBOLS

International Border

Disputed Border

State / Province Border

Main Road (National Highway) R 15

Other Road

Jeepable Road, Track, Trek, Path, Ferry

Railway, Station T

Contours (approx)

River *River Nile*

Fortified Wall

Built Up Area

Lake, Reservoir

Salt Lake

National Park, Garden, Stadium

Sand Bank, Beach

State, Regional Capital

Other Towns

Bus Station B

Car Park P

Hospital H

Key Numbers 27

Airport

Bridge

Mountain

Oasis

National Park, Wildlife Park, Bird Sanctuary

Church / Cathedral

Mosque

NAH0

INTRODUCTION AND HINTS

Contents

General note The advice given below represents a regional summary of more detailed information provided in the *Information for visitors* section of each country entry.

Before you go

Documents

● **Passports**
All foreign tourists are recommended to have a passport that is valid for the whole of the period of stay. This avoids unnecessary contact with the bureaucracy. Many countries require visas. Details are given in each country section.

● **Special permits**
Certain zones, particularly adjacent to borders and in areas of conflict have restricted access and travel there is permitted only with military approval. Details of sensitive areas are given in the relevant country section.

● **Identity & membership cards**
If you are in full-time education you will be entitled to an International Student Identity Card (ISIC), which is distributed by student travel offices and travel agencies in 77 countries. The ISIC gives you special prices on all forms of transport (air, sea, rail etc) and access to a variety of other concessions and services. Contact ISIC, Box 9048, 1000 Copenhagen, Denmark, T (+45) 33939303.

Health

See main section, page 19

Money

● **Travellers' cheques**
Travellers' cheques can be honoured in

Exchange Rates (1 July 1994)

	US$	£	Ffr	DM	Ptas
Algeria (Dinar)	38.33	58.96	7.02	24.03	0.29
Andalucía (Peseta)	131.55	202.32	24.08	82.50	1.00
Egypt (Pound)	3.38	5.20	0.62	2.12	0.25
Gibraltar (Pound UK)	0.65	1.00	0.12	0.41	0.05
Libya (Dinar)	0.31	0.48	0.06	0.20	0.002
Mauritania (Ouguiya)	122.08	187.76	22.35	76.55	0.92
Morocco (Dirham)	9.01	13.86	1.65	5.65	0.07
Sudan (Pound)	35.04	53.90	6.42	21.98	0.27
Tunisia (Dinar)	1.00	1.54	0.18	0.63	0.008

most banks and *bureaux de change*. US$ are the easiest to exchange particularly if they are well-known like Visa, Thomas Cook or American Express. There is always a transaction charge so it is a balance between using high value cheques and paying one charge and carrying extra cash or using lower value cheques and paying more charges. A small amount of cash, again in US$, is useful in an emergency.

Some countries eg Egypt have a fixed exchange rate – wherever the transaction is carried out. Other countries have a varied exchange rate and, to a greater or lesser degree, a black market. See the appropriate country sections and be sure you know what you are doing before you get involved.

What to take

Travellers tend to take more than they need though requirements vary with the destination and the type of travel that is to be undertaken. Laundry services are generally cheap and speedy. A travelpack, a hybrid backpack/suitcase, rather than a rigid suitcase, covers most eventualities and survives bus boot, roof rack and plane/ship hold travel with ease. Serious trekkers will need a framed backpack.

Clothing of light cotton or cotton/polyester with a a woollen sweater for evenings, more northern regions, higher altitudes and the clear desert nights. Comfortable shoes with socks as feet may swell in hot weather. Modest dress for women including (**see page** 12) a sunhat and headscarf. See hints in country sections.

- **Checklist:**

Air cushions for hard seating
Bumbag
Earplugs
Eye mask
Insect repellent and/or mosquito net, electric mosquito mats, coils
Neck pillow
International driving licence
Photocopies of essential documents
Short wave radio
Spare passport photographs
Sun hat
Sun protection cream
Sunglasses
Swiss Army knife
Tissues/toilet paper
Torch
Umbrella (excellent protection from sun and unfriendly dogs)
Wipes (*Damp Ones*, *Baby Wipes* or equivalent)
Zip-lock bags

Those intending to stay in budget

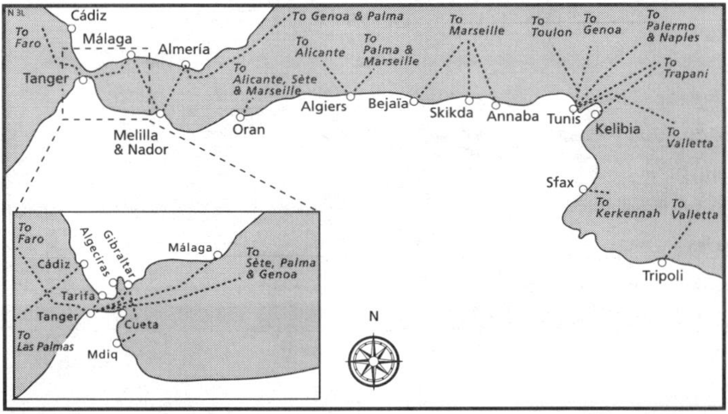

accommodation might also include:

Cotton sheet sleeping bag
Money belt
Padlock (for hotel room and pack)
Soap
Student card
Towel
Toilet paper
Universal bath plug

- **Health kit**

Antiacid tablets
Anti-diarrhoea tablets
Anti-malaria tablets
Anti-infective ointment
Condoms
Contraceptives
Dusting powder for feet
First aid kit and disposable needles
Flea powder
Sachets of rehydration salts
Tampons
Travel sickness pills
Water sterilizing tablets

Getting there

Air

It is possible to fly direct to several destinations within the countries of the Handbook (other than Libya which is currently suffering a UN embargo on international flights) from Europe, from the Middle East and most adjacent African countries and additionally into Morocco from USA, Canada and Brazil and into Egypt from USA. More details are given in the **Information for Visitors** sections. General airline restrictions apply with regard to luggage weight allowances before surcharge; normally 30 kg for first class and 20 kg for business and economy class. An understanding of the term 'limited' with regard to amount of hand luggage varies greatly. The major destinations are the national capitals and, particularly in Morocco and Tunisia, the tourist airports. The scheduled flying times from London are Khartoum 7 hrs, Cairo 5 hrs, Rabat 2½ hrs, Tanger 2 hrs, Tunis 2½ hrs, Málaga 2 hrs and from Paris are Nouakchott 5 hrs, Algiers 2½ hrs. Package tours which frequently offer cheaper flight-only deals generally operate smaller planes which take longer.

- **Discounts**

It is possible to obtain significantly cheaper tickets by avoiding school vacation times, by flying at night, by shopping around and by booking early to obtain one of the quota of discounted fares. Group discounts apply in many instances.

- **Airline security**

International airlines vary in their arrangements and requirements for secu-

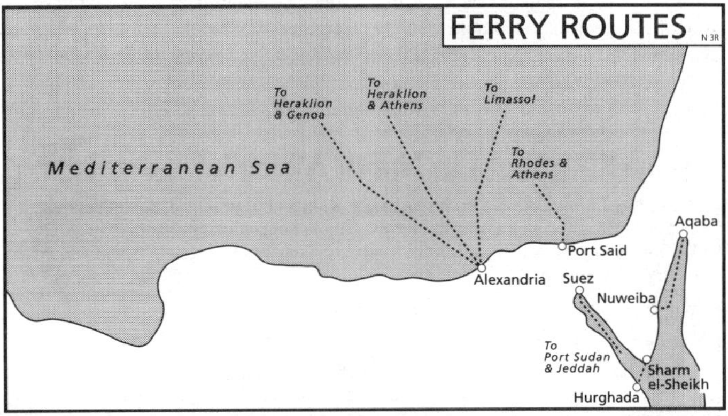

rity over electrical items such as radios, tape recorders and lap-top computers (as does the interest of the customs officials on arrival and departure). Check in advance if you can, carry the items in your hand luggage for convenience and have them wrapped for safety but available for inspection. Note that internal airlines often have different rules from the international carriers.

Sea

Ferries Numerous ferries operate across the Mediterranean carrying both vehicles and foot passengers. Prices vary according to the season. Details are given in the country sections along with rail and road entry points.

There are no regular passenger liners operating to North Africa but it is possible to travel on passenger-carrying cargo ships though you would need to be patient to reach your destination. Accommodation costs make this option very expensive compared to air travel. ABC Containerline, NSB and Mediterranean Shipping Co embarking from Felixstowe and Polish Ocean Lines embarking from Antwerp call in at Alexandria, Port Said or Damietta. Polish Ocean Lines from Hamburg call in at Casablanca while H W Janssen and Transeste from Felixstowe call in at Algeciras. In many cases the number of passengers is very limited and in all cases places would only be available for the trip to North Africa if all cabins had not been taken for the round trip. Full details are available from John Alton at Weider Travel, Charing Cross Shopping Concourse, The Strand, London WC2N 4HZ, T 071 8366363, Tx 918791.

● **Note**

In this Handbook, further details on air links to and from each country, arrival and departure regulations, airport taxes, customs regulations and security arrangements for air travel are outlined in the relevant *Information for visitors* sections.

When you arrive

Appearance

There is a natural prejudice in all countries against travellers who ignore personal hygiene and have a generally unkempt appearance. Observation of the local people will show, where they can afford it, their attention to cleanliness and neatness. The men attend the office in suits with a white shirt and tie or a newly pressed native garment and the women beneath their veil are very well dressed. All persons other than manual workers will be fully dressed. Scantily clad visitors, other than round the hotel pool, show insufficient consideration for their host country. In a hot climate it is eminently sensible and certainly more comfortable to copy the locals and cover

the body. In Spain there are fewer restrictions about clothing, in places nude sunbathing is tolerated, but at the other extreme some restaurants will not serve informally clad men.

Bargaining

Bargaining is expected in the bazaars. Start lower than you would expect to pay, be polite and good humoured, enjoy the experience and if the final price doesn't suit – walk away. There are plenty more shops. Once you have gained confidence, try it on the taxi drivers and when negotiating a room.

Beggars

Beggars are a fact of life. It is unlikely that they will be too persistent. Have a few very small coins ready. You will be unable to help many and your donation will most probably be passed on to the syndicate organizer! In the most visited areas of Morocco the tourist police move the mobile beggars on.

Confidence tricksters

The most common'threat' to tourists is found where people are on the move, at ports and railway and bus stations, selling 'antiques', 'gems' and offering extremely favourable currency exchange rates. Confidence tricksters are, by definition, extremely convincing and persuasive. Be warned – if the offer seems too good to be true that is probably what it is.

Courtesy

Politeness is always appreciated. You will notice a great deal of hand shaking, kissing, clapping on backs on arrival and departure from a group. There is no need to follow this to the extreme but handshakes, smiles and thank yous go a long way. Be patient and friendly but firm when bargaining for items and avoid displays of anger. Be very careful never to criticize as officials, waiters and taxi drivers can understand more than you think. See page 34 on how to deal with the bureaucracy. **However** when it comes to getting onto public transport, forget it all – the description 'like a Cairo bus' will need no explanation.

Drugs

Ignore all offers of drugs. The Rif area of Morocco is one area particularly noted for this. It is more than likely that the 'pusher', if successful, will report you to the police.

Firearms

Firearms including hunting guns may not be taken into any of the countries covered in this book without prior permission.

Mosques

Visitors to mosques (where permitted) and other religious buildings will normally be expected to remove their shoes and cover-all garments will be available for hire to enable the required standard of dress to be met.

Personal security

Travellers in North Africa and Andalucía are unlikely to experience threats to personal security. On the contrary, followers of Islam are expected to honour the stranger in their midst. However basic common sense is needed for the protection of personal property, money and papers. Use hotel safes for valuable items as hotel rooms cannot be regarded as secure and when travelling, carry valuables as close to the body as possible, and where convenient, in more than one place. External pockets on bags and clothing should never be used for carrying valuables. Bag snatching and pick pocketing is more common in crowded tourist areas, most reports of losses coming from Spain. It is obviously unwise to lay temptation in the way of a man whose annual income is less than the cost of your return airfare. **NB**: it is wise to keep a record of your passport number, travellers' cheques number and air ticket number somewhere separate from the actual items.

Police

Report any incident which involves you or your possessions. An insurance claim of any size will require the backing of a police report. If involvement with the police is more serious, for instance a driving accident, remain calm, read the section on how to deal with the bureaucracy (see page 34) and contact the nearest consular office without delay.

Prisoners Abroad

Prisoners Abroad, a UK charity, was formed to help people who fall foul of the law in foreign countries, where sentencing can be much harsher than at home. If you or a friend do get into trouble, you can contact Prisoners Abroad at 72-82 Rosebury Ave, London EC1R 4RR, T 071 833 3467, F 071 833 3467 (F +4471 833 3467 if outside the UK).

Tipping

Tipping in Egypt is a way of life – everyone expects a coin for services rendered or supposed. Many get no real wage and rely on tips. In Algeria, on the contrary, the practice is not widespread. In hotels and restaurants the service has probably been included so a tip to the waiter is an optional extra. It does no harm to round up the taxi fare, and a handful of small coins eases the way. Check in the relevant country section for what is expected.

Women travelling alone

Women face greater difficulties than men or couples. Young Muslim women rarely travel without the protection of a male or older female, hence a single Western woman is regarded as strange and is supposed to be of easy virtue – a view perpetuated by Hollywood. To minimise the pestering that will certainly occur, dress modestly, the less bare flesh the better, (see page 27), steadfastly ignore rude and suggestive comments directed at you but aimed at boosting the caller's ego, avoid any behaviour which would aggravate the situation, and keep a sense of humour. Single men often attract greater attention from customs officials and are more liable to receive unwelcome propositions.

Where to stay

Hotels

There is a very wide range of accommodation in North Africa. In the major cities and the popular tourist resorts, the top quality hotel chains are represented. The best offer top class accommodation with the full range of personal and business facilities while the cheapest are spartan and most frequently sordid. Availability of accommodation for visitors varies from country to country. While Andalucía, Egypt, Morocco and Tunisia are organized in this respect, the traveller in Libya, Algeria, Mauritania and Sudan will experience greater problems in finding a place to lay his head. The peak season when there is greatest pressure on accommodation varies on the country and the latitude and the relevant country section gives details.

Prices for the top class hotels are on a par with prices in Europe while medium range hotels are generally cheaper in comparison. In almost every case, the advertised room price, that charged to the individual traveller, is higher than that paid by the package tourist and it may be worth bargaining. The 6 categories used in this Handbook are based on the price of a good double room in high season. Normally the following facilities will be available and are therefore not repeated in the descriptions. Hotels are graded as accurately as possible by cost converted to American dollars. Our hotel price range is based on a double room with bath/shower in high season and includes any relevant taxes and service charges but no meals.

Abbrevations in the listings: a/c = air conditioning, T = telephone, Tx = Telex, F = Facsimile. Bath denotes bath and/or shower).

AL US$90+ This is an international class luxury hotel as found in the capital, large cities and major tourist centres. Good management ensures that all facilities for business and leisure travellers are of the highest international standard.

A US$75-90 An international hotel with choice of restaurants, coffee shop, shops, bank, travel agent, swimming pool, some business facilities, some sports facilities, air conditioned rooms with WC, bath/shower, TV, phone, minibar, daily clean linen.

B US$60-75 Offers most of the facilities in **A** but without the luxury, reduced number of restaurants, smaller rooms, limited range of shops and sport. Offers pool and air conditioned rooms with WC, shower/bath.

C US$40-60 These are the best medium range hotels found in the smaller towns and less popular areas of larger cities. Usually comfortable, bank, shop, pool. Best rooms have air conditioning, own bath/shower and WC.

D US$20-40 Might be the best you can find in a small town. Best rooms may have own WC and bath/shower. Depending on management will have room service and choice of cuisine in restaurant.

E US$10-20 Simple provision. Perhaps fan cooler. May not have restaurant. Shared WC and showers with hot water (when available).

F under US$10 Very basic, shared toilet facilities, variable in cleanliness, noise, often in dubious locations.

Ungraded hotels – too primitive to reach the standard of **F** – but may be cleaner and more interesting than **F**.

Camping

Provision varies. It is permitted at certain hostels; enlightened countries have both government and private sites, often with guards; beach camping depends on location and/or gaining permission. Often the difference between a cheap hotel and paying for a campsite is minimal. Assess the security of any site you choose and where possible ask permission to avoid any unpleasantness.

Youth hostels

These are found in most North African countries as part of the International Youth Hostel Federation. They differ according to location and size, provide a common room, sleeping provision in dormitories, a self-catering kitchen and often budget meals. There is no maximum age limit, persons under 15 should be accompanied by an adult and in some hostels only male guests are accepted. Length of stay is limited to three days. Most hostels are open 1000-1200 and 1700-2200. Prices are given in the country sections.

Food and drink

Food

Restaurants Given the variations in price of food on any menu our restaurants are divided where possible into three simple grades – ♦♦♦ expensive, ♦♦ average and ♦ cheap. Bearing in mind the suggestions in the Health section (**page 22**) on food best avoided in uncertain conditions, a wide choice still remains. Forget the stories of sheep's eyes and enjoy the selection of filling, spicy and slightly unusual meals. For the less adventurous, Western style food (other than pork) can be found in most hotels.

Drink

The most common drink is tea without milk, in a small glass, probably with mint. Coffee is generally available too. Bottled soft fizzy drinks are found even in small settlements and are safer than water. Alcohol is officially forbidden in Sudan and Libya but other countries sell beer and local wine. Where available imported wine and spirits are very expensive. Andalucía, of course, produces sherry. **Bottled water** is an essential part of every traveller's baggage.

Water

Be prepared for shortage or restriction of water, never regard tap water safe to drink except in Andalucía. Bottled water is cheap and easily available. See Health, page 22.

Getting around

Air

Domestic airlines link the main towns and run to published but infinitely variable schedules. They are especially recommended to cover the considerable distances in Algeria and to avoid hot dusty rides to sites like Abu Simbel. Safety records vary. See country sections for times and availability.

Road

Conditions vary from excellent dual carriageways to rural roads and unnerving one vehicle wide and farflung roads which are a rough, unsurfaced *piste*. Problems include blockage by snow in winter, floods in spring and sand at any time.

Buses, the main mode and cheapest means of transport, link nearly all the towns. Air-conditioned coaches connect the biggest cities and keep more strictly to the timetable. Smaller private vehicles require greater patience and often work on the 'leave when full' principle. Book in advance wherever possible. Orderly queues become a jostling mass when the bus arrives. Inner city buses are usually dirty and crowded and getting off can be more difficult than getting on. Sorting out the routes and the fares makes taking a taxi a better option.

Taxis The larger, long distance taxis are good value, sometimes following routes not covered by service buses and almost always more frequent. They run on the 'leave when full' principle and for more space or a quicker departure the unoccupied seats can be purchased. In general these taxis are 25% more expensive than the bus. Inner city taxis are smaller, may have a working meter, and can also be shared.

Car hire

Cars can be hired, with considerable ease in Andalucía, with great difficulty in Sudan and Mauritania and, depending on availability, quite easily in the other countries. They are not cheap and the condition of the vehicles other than in Spain often leaves much to be desired. The problems of driving your own or a hired car are two fold – other drivers and pedestrians.

Hitch-hiking

This is really only a consideration in outlying places not served by the very cheap public transport. Here, eventually, a place on a truck or lorry will be available, for which a charge is made.

Train

Rail networks are limited, are slow and generally more expensive than the alternative – the bus. First class is always more comfortable; offering air-conditioning and sometimes sleeping accommodation, cheaper carriages can be crowded and none too clean. Train travel offers the advantage of views available only from the track.

Communications

Language

While Arabic is the official language in all the countries of North Africa, many people have as their first language one of the many dialects. French is widely spoken in Morocco, Algeria, Tunisia and Mauritania and in all tourist areas some English or French will be understood. Spanish is useful not only in Andalucía but also in parts of Morocco. See Language for Travel, page 52 for a simple vocabulary.

Short wave radio guide

The BBC World Service (London) broadcasts throughout the region. Frequencies are shown in the accompanying table.

Country	KHz	Transmission times (GMT) Summer	Winter
Spain and Gibraltar	17705	0800-1615	0900-1615
	15070	0900-1830	0900-1830
	12095	0900-2030	0900-2030
Algeria, Morocco and Tunisia	17705	0900-1615	0700-1615
	15070	0700-2315	0700-2030
	12095	1500-2315	1500-2315
Egypt (North)	1323/227m MW	0300-2315	0300-2315
Egypt (South), Libya and Sudan	21470	0430-1615	0430-1615
	17640	0800-1515	0800-1515
	15070	0600-2030	0600-2030
	12095	0400-0730	0400-0730
	12095	1600-2215	1600-2030
Mauritania	17790	0700-1530	0700-1530
	15400	0430-1130	0445-1130
	15400	1500-2315	1500-2315
	15070	1500-2315	1500-2030

Weights and Measures

Metric	British and US
Weight:	
1 kilogram (kg) = 2.205 pounds	1 pound (lb) = 454 grams
1 metric tonne = 1.102 short tons	1 short tonne (2,000lb) = 0.907 metric ton
= 0.984 long ton	1 long tonne (2,240lb) = 1.016 metric tonnes
Length:	
1 millimetre (mm) = 0.03937 inch	1 inch = 25.417 millimetres
1 metre = 3.281 feet	1 foot (ft) = 0.305 metre
1 kilometre (km) = 0.621 mile	1 mile = 1.609 kilometres
Area:	
1 hectare = 2.471 acres	1 acre = 0.405 hectare
1 square km (km^2) = 0.386 sq mile	1 square mile (sq mile) = 2,590 km^2
Capacity:	
1 litre = 0.220 Imperial gallon	1 Imperial gallon = 4.546 litres
= 0.264 US gallon	1 US gallon = 3.785 litres
(5 Imperial gallons are approximately equal to 6 US gallons)	
Volume:	
1 cubic metre (m^3) = 35.31 cubic feet	1 cubic foot (cu ft) = 0.028 m^3
= 1.31 cubic yards	1 cubic yard (cu yd) = 0.765 m^3

HEALTH INFORMATION

CONTENTS

The following information has been prepared by Dr David Snashall, Senior Lecturer in Occupational Health, United Medical Schools of Guy's and St Thomas' Hospitals and Chief Medical Officer, Foreign and Commonwealth Office, London.

The traveller to North Africa is inevitably exposed to health risks not encountered in North America or Western Europe. Despite the countries being part of Africa where one expects to see much tropical disease this is not actually the case, although malaria remains a problem in some areas. Because much of the area is economically under-developed, infectious diseases still predominate in the same way as they did in the West some decades ago. Andalucía, at least the more prosperous coastal strip and large towns, presents less in the way of health hazards and has better health services than the countries south of the Mediterranean. There are obvious health differences between each of the countries of North Africa and in risks between the business traveller who tends to stay in international class hotels in large cities and the backpacker trekking through the rural areas. There are no hard and fast rules to follow; you will often have to make your own judgements on the healthiness or otherwise of your surroundings.

There are many well qualified doctors in the area, a large proportion of whom speak English or French but the quality and range of medical care is extremely variable from country to country and diminishes very rapidly away from big cities. In some countries, such as Mauritania, there are systems and traditions of medicine rather different from the Western model and you may be confronted with unusual modes of treatment based on local beliefs. At least you can be reasonably sure that local practitioners have a lot of experience with the particular diseases of their region. If you are in a city it may be worthwhile calling on your Embassy to obtain a list of recommended doctors.

If you are a long way from medical help, a certain amount of self medication may be necessary and you will find that many of the drugs that are available have familiar names. However, always check the date stamping and buy from reputable pharmacists because the shelf life of some items, especially vaccines and antibiotics is markedly reduced in hot conditions. Unfortunately many locally produced drugs are not subjected to quality control procedures and can be unreliable. There have, in addition, been cases of substitution of inert materials for active drugs.

With the following precautions and advice you should keep as healthy as usual. Make local enquiries about health risks if you are apprehensive and take the general advice of European and North American families who have lived or are living in the area.

Before you go

Take out medical insurance. You should have a dental check up, obtain a spare glasses prescription and, if you suffer from a longstanding condition such as diabetes, high blood pressure, heart/lung disease or a nervous disorder, arrange for a check up with your doctor who can at the same time provide you with a letter explaining details of your disability (in

English and French). Check the current practice for malaria prophylaxis (prevention) for the countries you intend to visit.

For a simple list of 'Health Kit' to take with you, see page 11.

Inoculations

Smallpox vaccination is no longer required. Neither is cholera vaccination, despite the fact that the disease is endemic in Mauritania and Algeria and also occurs in Morocco and Tunisia. Yellow fever vaccination is only required for Mauritania although in the other countries, particularly Algeria and Libya, you may be asked for a certificate if you have been in an area (Sub-Saharan Africa for example) affected by yellow fever immediately before travelling to North Africa. Cholera vaccine is not effective which is the main reason for not recommending it but occasionally travellers from South America, where cholera is presently raging, or from parts of South Asia where the disease is endemic may be asked to provide evidence of vaccination. The following vaccinations are recommended:

Typhoid (monovalent): one dose followed by a booster in one month's time. Immunity from this course lasts 2-3 years. Other injectable types are now becoming available as are oral preparations marketed in some countries.

Poliomyelitis: this is a live vaccine, generally given orally and the full course consists of three doses with a booster in tropical regions every 3-5 years.

Tetanus: one dose should be given with a booster at 6 weeks and another at 6 months and 10 yearly boosters thereafter are recommended.

Children: should, in addition, be properly protected against diphtheria, whooping cough, mumps and measles. Teenage girls, if they have not yet had the disease, should be given rubella (German measles) vaccination. Consult your doctor for advice on BCG inoculation against tuberculosis. The disease is still common in the region. North Africa lies mainly outside the meningitis belt and the disease is probably no more common than at home so vaccination is not indicated except during an epidemic.

Infectious hepatitis (jaundice)

This is common throughout North Africa. It seems to be frequently caught by travellers probably because, coming from countries with higher standards of hygiene, they have not contracted the disease in childhood and are therefore not immune like the majority of adults in developing countries. The main symptoms are stomach pains, lack of appetite, nausea, lassitude and yellowness of the eyes and skin. Medically speaking there are two types: the less serious, but more common, is hepatitis A for which the best protection is careful preparation of food, the avoidance of contaminated drinking water and scrupulous attention to toilet hygiene. Human normal immunoglobulin (gammaglobulin) confers considerable protection against the disease and is particularly useful in epidemics. It should be obtained from a reputable source and is certainly recommended for travellers who intend to live rough. The injection should be given as close as possible to your departure and, as the dose depends on the likely time you are to spend in potentially infected areas, the manufacturer's instructions should be followed. A new vaccination against hepatitis A is now generally available and probably provides much better immunity for 10 years but is more expensive, being 3 separate injections.

The other more serious version is hepatitis B which is acquired as a sexually transmitted disease, from a blood transfusion or injection with an unclean needle or possibly by insect bites. The symptoms are the same as hepatitis A but the incubation period is much longer.

You may have had jaundice before or you may have had hepatitis of either type before without becoming jaundiced, in which case it is possible that you could be immune to either hepatitis A or B. This immunity can be tested for before you travel. If you are not immune to hepatitis B already, a vaccine is available (3 shots over 6 months) and if you are not immune to hepatitis A already then you should consider vaccination (or gamma globulin if you are not going to be exposed for long).

Meningitis

This is a 'significant risk' in Mauritania and Sudan. Protection against meningococcal meningitis A and C is conferred by a vaccine which is freely available.

AIDS

In North Africa AIDS is probably less common than in most of Europe and North America but is presumably increasing in its incidence, though not as rapidly as in Sub-Saharan Africa, South America or South East Asia. Having said that, the spread of the disease has not been well documented in the North African region; the real picture is unclear. The disease is possibly still mainly confined to the well known high risk sections of the population i.e. homosexual men, intravenous drug abusers, prostitutes and children of infected mothers. Whether heterosexual transmission outside these groups is common or not, the main risk to travellers is from casual sex, heterosexual or homosexual. The same precautions should be taken as when encountering any sexually transmitted disease. In some of these countries there is widespread female prostitution and a higher proportion of this population is likely to be HIV antibody positive. In other parts, especially high class holiday resorts, intravenous drug abuse is prevalent and in certain cities, homosexual, transsexual and transvestite prostitution is common and again this part of the population is quite likely to harbour the HIV virus in large measure. The AIDS virus (HIV) can be passed via unsterile needles which have been previously used to inject an HIV positive patient but the risk of this is very small indeed. It would, however, be sensible to check that needles have been properly sterilized or disposable needles used. The chance of picking up hepatitis B in this way is much more of a danger. Be wary of carrying disposable needles yourself. Custom officials may find them suspicious. The risk of receiving a blood transfusion with blood infected with the HIV virus is greater than from dirty needles because of the amount of fluid exchanged. Supplies of blood for transfusion are now largely screened for HIV in all reputable hospitals so the risk must be very small indeed. Catching the AIDS virus does not necessarily produce an illness in itself; the only way to be sure if you feel you have been put at risk is to have a blood test for HIV antibodies on your return to a place where there are reliable laboratory facilities. The results may not be ready for many weeks.

Common problems

Altitude

Mountain sickness is hardly likely to occur in North Africa, even in the High Atlas. A not-too-rapid ascent is the sure way to prevent it. Other problems experienced at moderate altitude are: sunburn, excessively dry air causing skin cracking, sore eyes (it may be wise to leave your contact lenses out, especially in windy and dusty areas) and stuffy noses. Many travellers, as long as they are physically fit, enjoy travelling in the mountains where it is generally cooler and less humid and there are fewer insects.

Heat and cold

Full acclimatisation to high temperatures takes about two weeks and during this period it is normal to feel a degree of apathy, especially if the relative humidity is high. Drink plenty of water (up to 15 litres a day are required when working physically hard in hot, dry conditions), use salt on your food and avoid extreme exertion. Tepid showers are more cooling than hot or cold ones. Large hats do not cool you down but prevent sunburn. Remember that, especially in the mountains, there can be a large and sudden drop in temperature between sun and shade and between night and day so dress accordingly. Clear desert nights can prove astoundingly cold with a rapid drop in temperature as the sun goes down. Loose fitting cotton clothes are still the best for hot weather; warm jackets and woollens are essential after dark in some desert areas, and especially at high altitude.

Insects

These can be a great nuisance. Some, of course, are carriers of serious diseases such as malaria and yellow fever. The best way of keeping insects away at night is to sleep off the ground with a mosquito net and to burn mosquito coils containing Pyrethrum. Aerosol sprays or a 'flit' gun may be effective as are insecticidal tablets which are heated on a mat which is plugged into the wall socket (if taking your, own check the voltage of the area you are visiting so that you can take an appliance that will work. Similarly check that your electrical adaptor is suitable for the repellent plug).

You can use personal insect repellent, the best of which contain a high concentration of Diethyltoluamide. Liquid is best for arms and face (take care around eyes and make sure you do not dissolve the plastic of your spectacles). Aerosol spray on clothes and ankles deters mites and ticks. Liquid DET suspended in water can be used to impregnate cotton clothes and mosquito nets. Wide mesh mosquito nets are now available impregnated with an insecticide called Permethrin and are generally more effective, lighter to carry and more comfortable to sleep in. If you are bitten, itching may be relieved by cool baths and anti-histamine tablets (care with alcohol or driving) corticosteroid creams (great care – never use if any hint of sepsis) or by judicious scratching. Calamine lotion and cream have limited effectiveness and anti-histamine creams have a tendency to cause skin allergies and are therefore not generally recommended. Bites which become infected (commonly in dirty and dusty places) should be treated with a local antiseptic or antibiotic cream such as Cetrimide as should infected scratches. Skin infestations with body lice, crabs and scabies are unfortunately easy to pick up. Use Gamma benzene hexachloride for lice and Benzyl benzoate for scabies. Crotamiton cream (Eurax) alleviates itching and also kills a number of skin parasites. Malathion lotion 5% is good for lice but avoid the highly toxic full strength Malathion used as an agricultural insecticide.

Intestinal upsets

Practically nobody escapes this one so be prepared for it. Some of these countries lead the world in their prevalence of diarrhoea. Most of the time intestinal upsets are due to the insanitary preparation of food. Do not eat uncooked fish or vegetables or meat (especially pork), fruit with the skin on (always peel your fruit yourself) or food that is exposed to flies. Tap water is generally held to be unsafe or at least unreliable throughout North Africa with the exception of large cities in Morocco. Tap water in Andalusian cities is also usually safe. Filtered or bottled water is generally available. If your hotel has a central hot water supply this is safe to drink after cooling. Ice for drinks should be made from boiled water but rarely is, so stand your glass on the ice cubes, instead of putting them in the drink. Dirty water should first be strained through a filter bag (available from camping shops) and then boiled or treated. Bringing the water to a rolling boil at sea level is sufficient but at high altitude you have to boil the water for longer to ensure that all the microbes are killed. Various sterilising methods can be used and there are proprietary preparations containing chlorine or iodine compounds. Pasteurized or heat treated milk is now widely available as is ice cream and yoghurt produced by the same methods. Unpasteurized milk products including cheese and yoghurt are sources of tuberculosis, brucellosis, listeria and food poisoning germs. You can render fresh milk safe by heating it to 62°C for 30 minutes followed by rapid cooling or by boiling it. Matured or processed cheeses are safer than fresh varieties.

Diarrhoea is usually the result of food poisoning, occasionally from contaminated water (including seawater when swimming near sewage outfalls). There are various causes – viruses, bacteria, protozoa (like amoeba) salmonella and cholera organisms. It may take one of several forms coming on suddenly, or rather slowly. It may be accompanied by vomiting or by severe abdominal pain and the passage of blood or mucus when it is called dysentery. How do you know which type you have and how do you treat it?

All kinds of diarrhoea, whether or not accompanied by vomiting, respond favourably to the replacement of water and salts taken as frequent small sips of some kind of rehydration solution. There are proprietary preparations consisting of sachets of powder which you dissolve in water or you can make your own by adding half a teaspoonful of salt (3.5 grams) and 4 tablespoonfuls of sugar (40 grams) to a litre of boiled water. If you can time the onset of diarrhoea to the minute, then it is probably viral or bacterial and/or the onset of dysentery. The treatment, in addition to rehydration, is Ciprofloxacin 500 mgs every 12 hours. The drug is now widely available as are various similar ones.

If the diarrhoea has come on slowly or intermittently, then it is more likely to be protozoal i.e. caused by amoeba or giardia and antibiotics will have no effect. These cases are best treated by a doctor, as is any outbreak of diarrhoea continuing for more than 3 days. If there are severe stomach cramps, the following drugs may help: Loperamide (Imodium, Arret) and Diphenoxylate with Atropine (Lomotil).

The lynchpins of treatment for diarrhoea are rest, fluid and salt replacement, antibiotics such as Ciprofloxacin for the bacterial types and special diagnostic tests and medical treatment for amoeba and giardia infections. Salmonella infections and cholera can be devastating diseases and it would be wise to get to a hospital as soon as possible if these were suspected. Fasting, peculiar diets and the consumption of large quantities of yoghourt have not been found useful in calming travellers diarrhoea or in rehabilitating inflamed bowels. Oral rehydration has on the other hand, especially in children, been a lifesaving technique. As there is some evidence that alcohol and milk might prolong diarrhoea, they should probably be avoided during and immediately after an attack. There are ways of preventing travellers diarrhoea for short periods of time when visiting these countries by taking antibiotics but these are ineffective against viruses and, to some extent, against protozoa, so this technique should not be used other than in exceptional circumstances. Some preventives such as Enterovioform can have serious side effects if taken for long periods.

Malaria

This disease occurs in all the regions covered by this book, with the exception of Tunisia and Andalucía. The disease is, however, only common in Mauritania and Libya with some limited transmission occurring, seasonally in coastal Morocco, Central Algeria and bordering the Nile Valley in Egypt. Despite being nowhere near so common as in Sub-Saharan Africa, malaria remains a serious disease and you are advised to protect yourself against mosquito bites as described above and to take prophylactic (preventive) drugs where and when there is a risk. Start taking the tablets a few days before exposure and continue to take them six weeks after leaving the malarial zone. Remember to give the drugs to babies and children and pregnant women also.

The subject of malaria prevention is becoming more complex as the malaria parasite becomes immune to some of the older drugs. This phenomenon, at the time of writing, has not occurred in North African countries other than Mauritania and so the more traditional drugs can be taken with some confidence. Protection with Proguanil (Paludrine) 2 tablets per day, or Chloroquine 2 tablets per week will suffice and at this dose will not cause any side effects. In Mauritania where there is Chloroquine resistance, both drugs should be taken. You will have to find out locally the likelihood of malaria and perhaps be prepared to receive conflicting advice on how to prevent yourself from catching it. You can catch malaria even when taking prophylactic drugs, although it is unlikely. If you do develop symptoms (high fever, shivering, severe headache, sometimes diarrhoea) seek medical advice immediately. The risk of the disease is obviously greater the further you move from the cities into rural areas with limited facilities and standing water.

Psychological disorders

First time exposure to countries where sections of the population live in extreme poverty or squalor and may even be starving can cause odd psychological reactions in visitors. So can the incessant pestering, especially of women which is unfortunately common in some of these countries. Simply be prepared for this and try not to over react.

Snake and other bites & stings

If you are unlucky enough to be bitten by a venomous snake, spider, scorpion, lizard, centipede or sea creature try (within limits) to catch the animal for identification. The reactions to be expected are fright, swelling, pain and bruising around the bite, soreness of the regional lymph glands, nausea, vomiting and fever. If in addition any of the following symptoms supervene, get the victim to a doctor without delay: numbness, tingling of the face, muscular spasms, convulsions, shortness of breath or haemorrhage. Commercial snake bite or scorpion sting kits may be available but are only useful for the specific type of snake or scorpion for which they are designed. The serum has to be given intravenously, so is not much good unless you have had some practice in making injections into veins. If the bite is on a limb, immobilise it and apply a tight bandage between the bite and body, releasing it for 90 seconds every 15 minutes. Reassurance of the bitten person is very important because death by snake bite is in fact very rare. Do not slash the bite area and try and suck out the poison because this kind of heroism does more harm than good. Hospitals usually hold stocks of snake bite serum. Best precaution: do not walk in snake territory with bare feet, sandals or shorts.

If swimming in an area where there are poisonous fish such as stone or scorpion fish (also called by a variety of local names) or sea urchins on rocky coasts, tread carefully or wear plimsolls. The sting of such fish is intensely painful and this can be helped by immersing the stung part in water as hot as you can bear for as long as it remains painful. This is not always very practical and you must take care not to scald yourself but it does work. Avoid spiders and scorpions by keeping your bed away from the wall and look under lavatory seats and inside your shoes in the morning. In the rare event of being bitten, consult a doctor.

Sunburn and heat stroke

The burning power of the sun in North Africa is phenomenal, especially at high altitude. Always wear a wide-brimmed hat and use some form of sun cream or lotion on untanned skin. Normal temperate zone suntan lotions (protection factor up to 7) are not much good. You need to use the types designed specifically for the tropics or for mountaineers or skiers with a protection factor (against UVA) between 7 and 15. Certain creams also protect against UVB and you should use these if you have a skin prone to burning. Glare from the sun can cause conjunctivitis so wear sunglasses, especially on the beach.

There are several varieties of heat stroke. The most common cause is severe dehydration. Avoid this by drinking lots of non-alcoholic fluid and adding some salt if you wish.

Other afflictions

Athletes foot and other fungal infections are best treated by exposure to sunshine and a proprietary preparation such as Tolnaftate.

Dengue fever is not common in North Africa but there have been cases of this virus transmitted by mosquito bites producing severe headache and body pains. There is no treatment: you must just avoid mosquito bites.

Filariasis causing such diseases as elephantiasis occurs in Mauritania and again is transmitted by mosquito.

Hydatid disease is quite common in Egypt and Algeria but can be avoided by keeping well clear of dogs, which is good advice in any case.

Intestinal worms do occur in insanitary areas and the more serious ones, such as hook-worm, can be contracted by walking bare foot on infested earth or beaches.

Leishmaniasis causing a skin ulcer which will not heal is also present in most of the North African countries. It is transmitted by sand flies.

Prickly heat is a common itchy rash avoided by frequent washing and by wearing loose clothing. It can be helped by the regular use of talcum powder to allow the skin to dry thoroughly after washing.

Schistosomiasis (bilharzia) occurs particularly in Egypt and Morocco and can easily be avoided because it is transmitted by snails which live in fresh water lakes so do not swim in such places or in canals.

Rabies is endemic throughout North African countries. If you are bitten by a domestic animal try to have it captured for observation and see a doctor at once. Treatment with human diploid vaccine is now extremely effective and worth seeking out if the likelihood of having contracted rabies is high. A course of anti-rabies vaccine might be a good idea before you go.

When you return home

Remember to take your anti-malarial tablets for 6 weeks. If you have had attacks of diarrhoea, it is worth having a stool specimen tested in case you have picked up amoebic dysentery. If you have been living rough, a blood test may be worthwhile to detect worms and other parasites.

Further health information

The following organisations give information regarding well-trained English speaking physicians throughout the world: International Association for Medical Assistance to Travellers, 745 Fifth Avenue, New York, 10022; Intermedic, 777 3rd Avenue, New York, 10017.

Information regarding country by country malaria risk can be obtained from the World Health Organisation (WHO) or the Ross Institute, The London School of Hygiene and Tropical Medicine, Keppel Street, London WClE 7HT which publishes a strongly recommended book entitled *The Preservation of Personal Health in Warm Climates*. The organisation MASTA, (Medical Advisory Service to Travellers Abroad), also based at The London School of Hygiene and Tropical Medicine, T 071 6314408, Tx 8953474, F 071 4365389, will provide country by country information on up-to-date health risks.

Further information on medical problems overseas can be obtained from Dawood, Richard (ed), *Travellers Health, How to Stay Healthy Abroad*, Oxford University Press, 1992, costing £7.99. We strongly recommend this revised and updated edition, especially to the intrepid traveller heading for the more out of the way places.

General advice is also available in *Health Advice for Travellers* published jointly by the Department of Health and the Central Office of Information (UK) and available free from your Travel Agent.

REGIONAL INTRODUCTION

Contents

TRAVELLING IN ISLAMIC COUNTRIES

The people of North Africa principally follow Islam, which is similar to Judaism and Christianity in its philosophical content and Muslims recognise that these three revealed religions (religions of the book *Ahl Al-Kitab*) have a common basis. Even so, there are considerable differences in ritual, public observance of religious customs and the role of religion in daily life. When travelling through Islamic countries it as well to be aware that this is the case. The Islamic revivalist movement has in recent years become strongly represented in North African countries, particularly in Algeria and Sudan, though it is important elsewhere too.

Travel, tourism and foreign workers are common throughout the region so that the sight of outsiders is not unusual. Tourists attract particular hostility, however. They are seen as voyeuristic, short-term and unblushingly alien. Tourists have become associated with the evils of modern life – loose morals, provocative dress, mindless materialism and degenerate/Western cultural standards. In many cases these perceptions are entirely justified and bring a sense of infringed Islamic values among many local people, most of whom are conservative in bent. Feelings are made worse by apparent differences in wealth between local peoples whose per head income ranges from US$5,310 in Libya to US$650 in Sudan and foreign tourists living on an average of US$17,500 per head in the industrialized states. Tourists, whose way of life for a few weeks a year is dedicated to conspicuous consumption, attract dislike and envy. Muslims might wonder why a way of life in Islam, seen as superior to all other forms of faith, gives poor material rewards vis-à-vis the hordes of infidels who come as tourists.

The areas where sensitivity can best be shown are:

The dress code

Daily dress for most North Africans is governed by considerations of climate and weather. Other than labourers in the open, the universal reaction is to cover up against heat or cold. The classic case is Libya, where the traditional dress, the *barakan*, is a successor of the Roman toga made up of five or more metres length by two metre width of woven wool material which wraps round the head and body. For males, therefore, other than the lowest of manual workers, full dress is normal. Men breaching this code will either be young and regarded as of low social status or very rich and Westernized. When visiting mosques (where this is allowed), *medressa* or other shrines/tombs/religious libraries, men wear full and normally magnificently washed and ironed traditional formal wear. In the office, men will be traditionally dressed or in Western suits/shirt sleeves. The higher the grade of office, the more likely the Western suit. At home people relax in loose *jallabah*. North Africans will be less constrained on the

THE PRACTICE OF ISLAM: LIVING BY THE PROPHET

Islam is an Arabic word meaning 'submission to God'. As Muslims often point out, it is not just a religion but a total way of life. The main Islamic scripture is the Koran or Quran, the name being taken from the Arabic *al-qur'an* or 'the recitation'. The Koran is divided into 114 *sura*, or 'units'. Most scholars are agreed that the Koran was partially written by the Prophet Mohammad. In addition to the Koran there are the hadiths, from the Arabic word *hadith* meaning 'story', which tell of the Prophet's life and works. These represent the second most important body of scriptures.

The practice of Islam is based upon 5 central tenets, known as the Pillars of Islam: Shahada (profession of faith), Salat (worship), Zakat (charity), *saum* (fasting) and Haj (pilgrimage). The mosque is the centre of religious activity. The 2 most important mosque officials are the *imam* – or leader – and the *khatib* or preacher – who delivers the Friday sermon.

The **Shahada** is the confession, and lies at the core of any Muslim's faith. It involves reciting, sincerely, 2 statements: 'There is no god, but God', and 'Mohammad is the Messenger [Prophet] of God'. A Muslim will do this at every **Salat**. This is the daily prayer ritual which is performed 5 times a day, including sunrise, midday and sunset. There is also the important Friday noon worship. The Salat is performed by a Muslim bowing and then prostrating himself in the direction of Mecca (Arabic *qibla*). In hotel rooms throughout the Muslim world there is nearly always a little arrow, painted on the ceiling – or sometimes inside a wardrobe – indicating the direction of Mecca and labelled qibla. The faithful are called to worship by a mosque official. Beforehand, a worshipper must wash to ensure ritual purity. The Friday midday service is performed in the mosque and includes a sermon given by the *khatib*.

A third essential element of Islam is **Zakat** – charity or alms-giving. A Muslim is supposed to give up his 'surplus' (according to the Koran); through time this took on the form of a tax levied according to the wealth of the family. Good Muslims are expected to contribute a tithe to the Muslim community.

The fourth pillar of Islam is **saum** or fasting. The daytime month-long fast of Ramadan is a time of contemplation, worship and piety – the Islamic equivalent of lent. Muslims are expected to read one-thirtieth of the Koran each night. Muslims who are ill or on a journey have dispensation from fasting, but otherwise they are only permitted to eat during the night until "so much of the dawn appears that a white thread can be distinguished from a black one".

The **Haj** or Pilgrimmage to the holy city of Mecca in Saudi Arabia is required of all Muslims once in their lifetime if they can afford to make the journey and are physically able to. It is restricted to a certain time of the year, beginning on the 8th day of the Muslim month of Dhu-l-Hijja. Men who have been on the Haj are given the title *Haji*, and women *hajjah*.

The Koran also advises on a number of other practices and customs, in particular the prohibitions on usury, the eating of pork, the taking of alcohol, and gambling.

The application of the Islamic dress code varies across North Africa. It is least used in the larger towns of Morocco but closely followed in the rural towns of Egypt.

beach where Bermuda shorts and swimming trunks are the norm, especially in the Maghreb states.

For women the dress code is more important than for men. Quite apart from dress being tell-tale of social status among the ladies of Fes or Alexandria or of tribal/regional origin, decorum and religious sentiment dictates full covering of body, arms and legs. The veil is increasingly common for women moving in public as a reflection of growing Islamic revivalist views. There are many women who do not conform, including those with modern attitudes towards female emancipation, professional women trained abroad and, remarkably, many Berber women or women with genuinely nomadic or semi-nomadic lives such as the Touareg. The religious minorities – Copts in Egypt and Jews in Morocco, for example – do not wear the veil. Jewellery (see page 44) is another major symbol in women's dress especially heavy gold necklaces (see the Dar Cherait Museum at Tozeur in Tunisa for an excellent set of displays of women's dress, see page 566).

The role of dress within Islamic and social codes is clearly a crucial matter for the people of North Africa. While some latitude in dress is given to foreigners, good guests are expected to conform to the broad lines of the practice of the house. Thus, except on the beach or 'at home' in the hotel (assuming it is a tourist rather than local establishment), modesty in dress pays off. This means jeans or slacks for men rather than shorts together with a shirt or tee-shirt. In Islamic places such as mosques or *medressa*, hire *jallabah* at the door. For women, modesty is slightly more demanding. In public wear comfortable clothes that at least cover the greater part of the legs and arms. If the opportunity arises to visit a mosque or *medersa* open to tourists such as the Grand Mosque in Kairouan, *jallabah* and slippers are available for hire at the doors. Elsewhere full covering of arms and legs and a head scarf is necessary. Offend against the dress code – and most Western tourists in this area do to a greater or lesser extent – and risk antagonism and alienation from the local people who are increasingly fundamentalist in their Islamic beliefs and observances.

Forbidden places

Do not enter mosques at all in Morocco. In other countries do not enter mosques during a service. In other places dedicated to religious purposes behave with decorum – refrain from shouting, unseemly laughter and take photographs only when permitted. Outsiders have spent much time and ingenuity in penetrating Islam's holiest shrines. In North Africa this is not worth the effort since the most interesting sites are open to visitors in any case, except in Morocco. People who are clearly non-Muslim will be turned away by door keepers from places where they are not wanted. Those who try to slip past the guardians should be sure they can talk their way out of trouble !

Good manners

Islam has its codes of other practices and taboos but few will affect the visitor unless he or she gains entry to local families or organisations at a social level. A few rules are worth observing in any case by all non-Muslims when in company with Muslim friends. (i) Do not use your left hand for eating since it is ritually unclean. If knives and forks are provided, then both hands can be used. (ii) Do not accept or ask for alcohol unless your host clearly intends to imbibe. (iii) If eating in traditional style from a common dish, use your right hand only and keep your feet tucked under your body away from the food. (iv) Never offer pork or its derivatives to a Muslim visitor. Buy *hallal* meat killed in accordance with Muslim ritual and/or provide a non-meat dish. Do not provide alcoholic drink.

Religious festivals and holidays

The Islamic year (Hejra/Hijra/Hegira) is based on 12 lunar months which are 29 or 30 days long depending on the sighting of the new moon. The lengths of the months vary therefore from year to year and from country to country depending on its position and the time at sunset. Each year is also 10 or 11 days shorter than the Gregorian calendar. The Islamic holidays are based on this Hejarian calendar and determining their position is possible only to within a few days.

Ramadan is a month of fasting (see below). The important festivals which are public holidays (with many variations in spelling) are *Ras el Am*, the Islamic New Year; *Eïd al-Fitr* (also called Aïd es Seghir), the celebration at the end of Ramadan; Eïd al-Adha (also called Aïd el Kebir), the celebration of Abraham's willingness to sacrifice his son and coinciding with the culmination of the Haj in Mecca; *Mouloud*, the birthday of the Prophet Mohammad.

The day of rest for Muslims is Friday. Observance of Friday as a religious day is general in the public sector though privately owned shops may open for limited hours. The main exception is tourism where all systems remain operative other than in Libya and areas of Algeria. Holy days and feast days are taken seriously throughout the North African region.

Approximate dates for 1995:

1 Feb	Beginning of Ramadan
4 Mar	End of Ramadan
10 May	Festival of Sacrifice
31 May	Islamic New Year (Anno Hegira 1416)
9 Aug	Prophet's Birthday

Ramadan, the 9th month of the Muslim calendar, is a month of fasting for Muslims. The faithful abstain from eating between dawn and sunset for the period until an official end is declared to the fast and the start of the festival of the Eïd Al-Fitr. During the fast, especially if the weather is difficult or there are political problems affecting the Arab world, people can be depressed or irritable. The pace of activity in official offices slows down markedly. Travellers have to manage in these conditions by leaving even more time to achieve their aims and being even more patient than usual. If you have a choice, stay out of North Africa during Ramadan and the Eïd Al-Fitr. Travel, services and the atmosphere are all better at other times of year. Travel facilities immediately before and immediately after Ramadan are often very congested since families like to be together especially for the Eïd Al-Fitr.

POLITICAL RISKS FOR TRAVELLERS

Political risks are not necessarily higher in North Africa than in other parts of the 'developing world' but they do exist. To an extent the situation of security in each state in the area is tolerable for the individual traveller for most of the time. The following section gives a brief résumé of the situation in the countries covered by the Handbook and what signs of difficulty can be spotted to give advance warning of problems.

Checklist

Be prepared for a real threat to personal safety and/or disruption of travel/banking/commercial services if:

1. There are truck loads of armed police parked in side streets near the main thoroughfares, *suqs*, mosques, schools and universities.
2. Traffic is very light and the streets clear of pedestrians.
3. Armoured vehicles are seen or heard moving in urban areas.
4. The local radio/TV plays non-stop martial music or its normal programmes are disrupted.
5. Shooting/explosions can be heard, however distant.
6. Streets are thronged by chanting or stone-throwing groups.

What to do if unrest occurs

It is wise in circumstances of political uncertainty for a foreigner to be very

discreet:
1. Stay in your hostel or hotel.
2. If the telephones are working, get in touch with your embassy or consulate so that your location is known.
3. Conserve any rations you might have.
4. Do not join in any action by locals. Your motives could be misunderstood.
5. Make contact in your hostel or hotel with other foreigners so that you can form a mutual-assistance group.
6. Listen carefully to the advice given by local hostel or hotel officials.

There is no real science for assessing political risks. Any traveller who intends to be travelling in North Africa for a protracted period should check with his/her national authorities on the advisability of visiting the area. In the UK, the relevant Foreign and Commonwealth Office T 071 2333000 desk will give you the latest assessment from their embassies overseas. If you are deeply concerned, where possible phone your national embassy direct and ask for the press/information officer. Otherwise, take an interest in trends in the countries you intend to visit before leaving home. Some newspapers can be very helpful in this area notably the *Financial Times*, *Le Monde*, and the *International Herald Tribune*. Otherwise be aware of the key risks for the individual countries using the thumb-nail political assessment below. A summary of what professional risk assessors thought likely is given below :

Political risk in North Africa Jan 1994
Relative scores for stability out of 100: the more points, the less the risk

USA	84
Morocco	72
Egypt	70
Tunisia	70
Libya	68
Algeria	56
Sudan	27
Mauritania	N/A

Source: International Country Risk Guide

Key factors affecting political risks

Much of North Africa is at risk of sudden and violent change because governments are either entirely unrepresentative of the people or have only partial political legitimacy. Most authorities are repressive in policies, relying on secret police, threats against their opponents or even crude tactics of imprisonment and torture. There is thus a constant undercurrent of repressed political strife within North African communities, though each country is different in situation and practice.

Algeria

Algeria faces a set of economic and political changes in the years ahead in a process that could be difficult and at times violent. The conservative elements in the régime have been in power for some 30 years and, despite their failures, are loath to give up authority and privilege. They wish to control transition to a democratic structure, which is a contradiction. Particularly they do not wish to see the secular and socialist traditions of the party which won the struggle for Independence against France put aside by an incoming government of Islamic fundamentalists. The fundamentalists meanwhile clearly have a sense of moral victory in view of the régime's cancellation of the spring elections in 1992 and represent a strong and well organized political opposition which uses violent confrontation as a tool in its attempt to take over power. Meanwhile, other forces for change – intellectual, political and social in origin – create further elements of ferment.

Algeria's political uncertainties are made worse by its economic problems. Living standards are depressed and welfare is deteriorating as the government struggles with the difficulties of high foreign debts, poor oil revenues and low domestic output. The combination of economic and political problems will make Algeria relatively unstable. Violence is already considerable, directed against the régime and the security forces but also specifically against 'foreigners' and 'those from the West'. Precipitate alterations in the political climate are likely and travellers should as a matter of course check with their government agencies before entering the country.

Egypt

The large and complex organisations of state and society in Egypt make generalisations difficult. It is currently clear that the government faces great political problems. The opposition, principally a long established Islamic revivalist group known as *Ikhwan Al-Musalmin* (Muslim Brotherhood), is large and well organized. In addition to the assassination of President Sadat in 1981, it is claimed that Islamic fundamentalists have murdered a number of leading individuals within the régime and there have been attacks on tourists. The government has held elections of sorts and has a political mandate on that basis, but the régime is unpopular at a variety of levels. The economy is not performing well and the expulsion of Egyptians from employment in the Gulf states, particularly Iraq, is still widely felt. There is no sense among Egyptians that the economic struggle against rising population numbers is being won, while external threats to reduced flows of Nile water adds to tensions. The close association of the régime with the USA and the history of links with Israel since the Camp David accords, distances the government from mass opinion. Yet the régime has its supporters through the co-option of the military and many senior Egyptian families. A deeply conservative streak runs through the population and a feeling that Egypt should look, as the régime does, first to Egyptian interests rather than 'Islamic' or 'Arab' ideals.

The support for the régime from the USA has a strong positive side. Aid and food supply are guaranteed within limits so that the population can be fed and the state kept on an economic even keel. Care for foreign visitors by the régime is vital to keep the tourist industry alive though the opposition has at times deliberately targeted tourist facilities to make a political point. Egypt is a large country and 'troubles' tend on most occasions to be regional rather than national. A day's rioting in Giza will leave the Upper Nile and Sinai untouched. Similarly, some towns are far more fundamentalist inclined than others with Assuit and Qena being noted for their Islamic revivalist sentiment.

Although Egypt has a troubled history of foreign relations in the 1950s-1970s, it is now comparatively stable. Travellers should check with their national authorities before departure for Egypt.

Libya

Libya is a political oddity. In a general sense there are few domestic risks to the stability of the régime. There is negligible organized political opposition. Colonel Ghadhafi has a certain populist appeal which should not be underestimated. The security services and Colonel Ghadhafi's bodyguard battalions are relatively very powerful. The main risks in Libya are that Colonel Ghadhafi, who is the undisputed and sole centre of power, is removed by natural or other means or that there is a palace coup d'état. The Libyan state is so bound with personalities and so weak in national institutions that change could bring comparative anarchy for a period.

The main risks for foreigners are from capricious alterations in Libyan government policies on visas, internal movements and taxation on foreigners. Decisions are taken overnight by the ruling personalities and implemented without due notification to the public. A second area of risk is the actions of foreign governments against Libya. Libya is believed in some Western countries to be involved in state terrorism. The Lockerbie incident is currently at the centre of attention but other issues of a similar kind also exist. The bombing of Tripoli by the USA in 1986 was not notified in advance while the cessation of international air traffic in 1992 was. Measures of this latter kind are more of an inconvenience to travellers than an absolute block. But the tensions that go with failures in diplomatic relations mean that foreign visitors should be highly sensitive to personal risks. Care in taking photographs and asking questions needs to be doubled in Libya. Some European governments and the US administration advise their nationals to take care when visiting Libya but the realities on the ground suggest that travellers are suffering no problems other than those arising through the UN embargo on air transport to/from Libya.

Mauritania

The political fate of Mauritania is closely linked to that of its neighbours, particularly Morocco and the issue of the Western Sahara. A continuing weakness of Polisario will diminish strains on Mauritania from the threat of Saharois ascendancy. Internally, Mauritania is in the course of democratisation which seems to be partially succeeding. The main coastal sites offer the traveller only problems normal in developing countries. Inland, security is less absolute.

Morocco

It is an irony that the monarchy in Morocco is in its way far more legitimate as a government than other so-called popular régimes in the region. The king stands as a successor to a powerful tradition of leadership within Islam. The issue of fundamentalism in Islam has less damaging and possibly less serious implications in Morocco than elsewhere in the region. The king transcends the sectional interests of Arabs and Berbers and has separate lines of appeal to the common man and the bourgeoisie. Morocco is none the less politically a vigorous country and opposition movements are also strong. In so far as the king is able to co-opt powerful political interests to his side or to balance rival factions one against the other, he survives. He has acute dilemmas which are causes of instability. The question of the Western Sahara is unsettled, awaiting a UN referendum to gauge self-determination by the inhabitants of the area. Any hint of a loss of the area would be unsettling. The king has to co-operate with the industrialised countries, notably the USA, in order to secure arms, financial aid and diplomatic support. Yet the USA has policies towards the Arabs, including the Iraqis, which are deeply unpopular with the Moroccan masses. Similarly, the régime has to maintain good relations with Western Europe to ensure the flow of investment funds and tourists at a time when some European countries are pursuing policies against their Moroccan migrant workers. Within Morocco, government success or otherwise in job-creation and lifting the standard of living, while also managing to keep foreign creditors and the demands of the IMF satisfied, creates constant strains.

Deep tensions exist, therefore. Riots over costs of food occurred in 1984. There were (mainly orderly) mass street demonstrations in major cities in 1990 at the time of the UN Desert Storm operation against Iraq in Kuwait. Several assassination attempts have been made against the king, though some years ago. Morocco can thus be described as being in a state of stable equilibrium but one where, because of the key role of one individual, the king, rapid change is always possible. In sum, the political risk for the traveller in Morocco is comparatively small if the guidelines above are followed.

Tunisia

Tunisia is wracked by many of the problems experienced in Algeria – transition from an established highly centralized and increasingly unrepresentative régime to new structures which have a stamp of democratic legitimacy but at a time when Islamic revivalism is deeply affecting society. The current régime has established itself, though at the expense of becoming more hardline against the Islamic groups. It is in control of the fundamentalists to a large extent and seems to have been accepted fairly widely by the population at large. The government's economic difficulties are substantial but are being handled well, assisted by acting as a gateway to Libya during that country's international isolation. The government has repaired its relations with the USA and Europe in the wake of the Gulf Crisis and is experiencing a return of its important tourist trade. Overall, Tunisia seems to have survived a difficult few years and has remained for the most part a pleasant, mannerly and cultured society with a fair prospect for political stability. The future is inevitably slightly uncertain, however, since changes in adjacent states could adversely affect Tunisia. For the traveller, Tunisia is less immediately threatening than Algeria since the Tunisians generally recognize their dependence for jobs and income on tourism and will be most unlikely to attack foreigners.

Sudan

Sudan, of all the states of North Africa, is the most politically unreliable. In addition to the war between N and S which ebbs and flows depending on the fortunes of the fighting, the drought and the season, the country is deeply weakened by a capricious and unpopular Islamic government. There is a sense of defeat and depression in almost all aspects of the nation's political and economic life. Uncertainties over the survivability of the government, the cohesion of the state and the weakness of the country's institutions gives a poor basis for future stability. Economic problems are severe. Food supply cannot be guaranteed except in the capital. The balance of payments crisis is chronic and apparently beyond cure. Foreign aid is hindered by political disagreements with donor countries and failures in internal distribution systems. With these and many other problems, Sudan must be rated a poor political risk. Many European and American states discourage their citizens from visiting Sudan except on urgent business.

For the experienced traveller, Sudan can be managed once a visa has been acquired. Extreme sensitivity to the political climate is advised even for the hardened backpacker. Change, possibly violent change, is possible at any time. Keep in close touch with Sudanese friends and with your embassy so that you know what is going on. Travel up country with care. There is a large scale aid and humanitarian relief infrastructure in parts of the country which can serve as a reference point in cases of emergency.

HANDLING THE LOCAL BUREAUCRACY/ POLICE/SECURITY

Spain is a member of the European Community and in most respects administration, public management and the ethics of government are similar to those found in much of the rest of Europe. The traveller in Andalucía should be conscious that Spain has characteristics of its own that require careful thought. The causes for Spanish eccentricities are not hard to find. Spain was isolated from Western Europe throughout much of the 19th century, suffered a fascist dictatorship in the first part of the 20th century and only emerged as a fast developing state in the 1960s and 1970s. It became a democracy only in the 1970s. The forces for centralisation are powerful but offset by strong identities of the regions. Loyalties at times can be confused. While the idea of an integrated European community has attractions to many of the Spanish, old habits die hard and national self-assertion is never far below the surface.

North Africa shares a number of historical roots with Spain through the Arab conquest, the period of the Moorish kingdoms and simple geographical proximity. There are, none-the-less, enormous differences between Spain's European and Christian traditions and the contemporary history of North Africa. North Africa is Islamic in religion, oriental in civilisation and despotic in political tradition. Governments rule by fear, a culture of populism and political manipulation. They are changed most often by force and violence (See political risks, **page 30**). Travellers in North Africa should remember these facts in dealing with the local civil and military administrations.

Travellers will not be put off by these 'facts of life'. It is important, though, to adapt to the local ethos and to learn to live with it wherever you are. The quality of the civil service varies greatly throughout the region:

Civil Service in Spain & North Africa

The higher the score the better the service

USA	100
Spain	65
Morocco	55
Tunisia	50
Egypt	40
Algeria	35
Libya	35
Mauritania	35
Sudan	30

There are a number of quite clear rules in handling situations in these areas:

Avoid trouble The main areas of difficulty affect relations with the bureaucrats, police and other officials. To avoid trouble bear in mind:

(i) **Documents**: do not lose your passport and ensure that all travel documents are in order. Passports are lost but they are also traded for cash/drugs and officials can be very unsympathetic. Long and often expensive delays can occur while documents are replaced, especially in Libya where there is no diplomatic help for US, British, Venezuelan and several other nationals. Keep all forms such as landing cards and currency documents together with bank receipts for foreign exchange transactions. Spain is much less of a problem in this respect.

(ii) **Prices**: understand what prices are being asked for taxis, meals and hotels. Do not accept 'favours', like 'free lunches' they do not exist. In Tunisia and Morocco, for example, shop owners will attempt to give you gifts. At best these are used as a lever to get you buy other items expensively or can lead to disputes over alleged non-payment for goods. It is also a matter of discretion how you handle friendly relations with locals who invite you home for a meal/visit. In Libya, only hospitality will be involved and the same will largely be true in Algeria, Egypt and Sudan. But in Morocco and Tunisia in particular, commercial or other motives might arise in the form of pressure to buy a carpet, to deal in drugs or to pledge help for a visa to Europe. Be genial but firm in these situations. Or use local ways out – promise to look at the matter *ba'd bokhra enshallah*, ie later!

(iii) **Drugs**: do not get involved in buying and selling drugs. It is an offence in all the countries in this Handbook to handle drugs. Penalties can be severe including jail sentences in dismal prison conditions. In Morocco especially *agents provocateurs* can sell drugs and then inform the police.

(iv) **Politics**: keep clear of all political activities. Nothing is so sensitive in North Africa as opposition to the régimes. By all means keep an interest in local politics but do not become embroiled as a partisan. The *mokharbarat* (secret services) in North Africa are singularly unforgiving and unbridled in taking action against political dissent.

(v) **Black Market**: make use of black mar-

ket currency only when it is private and safe. Some countries such as Libya and Algeria have tight laws against currency smuggling and illegal dealing.
(vi) **Driving**: keep to driving regulations and have an appropriate international licence. Bear in mind that the incidence of traffic accidents in Andalucía and North Africa is high and that in the latter area personal rescue in the event of an accident can be protracted and not necessarily expert.
(vii) **Antiquities**: trading in antiquities is everywhere illegal. Most items for sale such as 'Roman lamps' and ancient coins are fakes. Real artifacts are expensive and trading in them can lead to confiscation and/or imprisonment.

Keep cool Remain patient and calm whatever the provocation. Redress against officials in North Africa (and Andalucía will seem very little different in this respect) is next to impossible. Keep the matter from becoming serious by giving no grounds for offence to officials. Be genial and low key. Aggression and raised voices do little to help. Where you feel you are right, be smilingly persistent but not to the point of a break down in relations.

Get help Getting help can often be cheap or free. Start off with agencies used to foreigners, namely travel agents, airline offices and hotels. They will have met your problem before and might offer an instant or at least painless solution on the basis of past experience. They will know the local system and how it works. They act as free translators. Friends who are either locals or who live locally can act as translators and helpers. They will often have networks of family and acquaintances to break through the bureaucratic logjams. Last, and only last, turn to your embassy or consulate. Embassies are there principally to serve the needs of the home country and the host government, not the demands of travellers, though they have ultimate responsibility for official travel documents and, at their own discretion, for repatriation in cases of distress. Treat embassy and consular officials calmly and fairly. They have different priorities and do not necessarily feel themselves to be servants for travellers in trouble.

WILDLIFE

The area covered by the book divides itself into two climatic regions, the Mediterranean and the Desert, with transitional areas between the two extremes. Within these zones, however, is a wide variety of habitats. The sea areas may be enclosed like the Mediterranean, or subject to tidal influences, as in Morocco and the Atlantic coast of Andalucía. Coastal wetlands include deltas, salt marsh and estuaries, while inland lakes and reservoirs provide freshwater sites. The *maquis* and the *garrigue* contrast with the agricultural areas, while mountain ranges such as the Atlas provide their own climate, delaying flowering and shortening seasons. Even the desert areas provide contrasts with the sands (*erg*), gravels (*reg*) and rock (*hammada*) interspersed with the occasional oasis.

Many of the habitats mentioned above are under threat, either from pollution, urbanisation, desertification or advanced farming techniques. Fortunately, in some countries such as Spain, Morocco and Tunisia, the conservation movement is gaining pace and many National Parks and Nature Reserves have been created and programmes of environmental education set up. In other countries, regrettably, wildlife is still regarded as a resource to be exploited, either for food or sport.

In both the Mediterranean and Desert regions, wildlife faces the problem of adapting to drought and the accompanying heat. The periods without rain may vary from four months on the shores of the Mediterranean to several years in some parts of the Sahara. Plants and animals have, therefore, evolved numerous methods of coping with drought and water loss. Some plants have extensive root systems; others have hard, shiny leaves or an oily surface to reduce water loss through transpiration. Plants such as the **broom** have small, sparse leaves, relying on stems and thorns to attract sunlight and produce food. Animals such as the **addax** and **gazelle** obtain all their moisture requirements from vegetation and never need to drink, while the **ostrich** can survive on saline water. Where rain is a rare occurence, plants and animals have developed a short life cycle combined with years of dormancy. When rain does arrive, the desert can burst into life, with plants seeding, flowering and dispersing within a few weeks or even days. Rain will also stimulate eggs to hatch which have lain dormant for years. Many animals in the desert areas are nocturnal, taking advantage of the cooler night temperatures, their tracks and footprints revealed in the morning. Another adaption is provided by the **sandfish**, which is a type of skink (lizard) which 'swims' through the sand in the cooler depths during the day. Perhaps the most remarkable example of adaption is shown by the **camel** (**see box, page** 388). Apart from its spreading feet which enable it to walk on sand, the camel is able to adjust its body temperature to prevent sweating, reduce urination fluid loss and store body fat to provide food for up to 6 months.

Mammals

Mammals have a difficult existence throughout the area, due to human disturbance and the fact that many of the species are not well adapted to drought. Many have, therefore, become nocturnal and their presence may only be indicated by droppings and tracks. Some mammals common in Northern Europe can, nevertheless, be seen in the Mediterranean environments and these include **fox**, **rabbit**, **hare**, Red, Fallow and Roe **deer** and at least 3 species of **hedgehog**. Despite widespread hunting, **wild boar** are common wherever there is enough cover in deciduous woodlands. **hyenas** and **jackals** still thrive in many areas of North Africa, but the attractive **fennec**, whilst still fairly common in Tunisia and Northern Algeria, is frequently illegally trapped. Typical woodland species include the **red squirrel** (the grey variety from North America has not been introduced), **garden dormouse**, which readily hibernates in houses in Andalucía, **pine** and **beech martens** and the **polecat**. The cat family, once common, is now rare, but the **lynx** hangs on in some areas, including two small populations in Southern Spain. The **leopard**, formerly common in North Africa, is now extremely rare, but is occasionally seen in some isolated regions, to the panic of local people. Two North African species, the **genet** and the **mongoose**, have been introduced to Andalucía to aid rodent control and the latter in particular thrives in the *maquis* and *garrigue* habitats. There are at least three species of **gazelle** in North Africa, the Dorcas Gazelle preferring the steppes, the Mountain Gazelle inhabiting locations over 2000 metres especially where there is juniper forest, and the Desert Gazelle locating in the *reg* of the northern Sahara. The latter is often hunted by horse or vehicle, its only defence being its speed. There are over 30 species of **bat** in the area, all but one – the Egyptian Fruit Bat – being insectivorous. Recent ringing has shown that bats will migrate according to the season and to exploit changing food sources. Many species of bat have declined disastrously in recent years due to the increased use of insecticides and disturbance of roosting sites. Desert rodents include the large-eyed **sand rat**, the **gerbil** and the **jerboa**. Many, sadly, find themselves in pet shops. On the bright side, one can mention the *Centro de Rescate de la Fauna Sahariana* in Almería, Spain (**see page** 111), which specializes, with considerable success, in breeding threatened Saharan species and returning them to the wild.

Reptiles and amphibians

Tortoises are widespread in North Africa and Andalucía. The best distributed is **Hermanns tortoise** which can reach a maximum size of 30 cm. **Pond terrapins** are small fresh water tortoises and can be found in all the Mediterranean habitats. Both tortoises and terrapins are taken in large numbers for the pet trade. There are over thirty species of lizard in the area, the most common being the **wall lizard**, which often lives close to houses. **Sand racers** are frequently seen on coastal dunes, while **sand fish** and **sand swimmers** take advantage of deep sand to avoid predators and find cooler temperatures in the desert *reg*. The **ocellated lizard** is impressive in size, growing to 20 cm and can be found in Andalucía and North West Africa. The **waran** (or Egyptian Monitor), seen in the more easterly areas, can grow to over a metre in length. **Geckoes** are plump, soft-skinned, nocturnal lizards with adhesive pads on their toes and are frequently noted near houses. The **chameleon** is a reptile with a prehensile tail and a long sticky tongue for catching insects. Although basically green, it can change colour to match its surroundings. **Snakes** are essentially legless lizards. There are some thirty species in the Mediterranean areas alone, but only the viperine types are dangerous. These can be identified by their triangular heads, short plump bodies and zig-zag markings. The **horned viper** lies just below the surface of sand, with its horns projecting, waiting for prey. **Sand boas** stay underground most of the time, while other species twine themselves around the branches of trees. Most snakes will instinctively avoid contact with human beings and will only strike if disturbed or threatened. For what to do if you are bitten by a snake, **see page 24**.

Marine life

The Mediterranean is a land-locked sea and it is only in the extreme west near the Straits of Gibraltar that there is any significant tidal range. Without strong tides and currents bringing nutrients, the Mediterranean is somewhat impoverished in terms of marine life. Fish and shell fish, nevertheless, have figured prominently in the diet of the coastal people for centuries, with **sardines**, **anchovies**, **mullet**, **sole**, **squid** and **prawns** being particularly popular. **Tuny** and **swordfish** are also widely caught. Overfishing, leading to the depletion of stocks, has become increasingly problematic. Marine mammals, such as the **common dolphin** and **porpoise** are frequently seen in the Straits of Gibraltar. Some whales are occasionally found in the western Mediterranean, having strayed through from the Atlantic. These are most likely to be **minke** or **fin whales**.

Butterflies and moths

Because of the lack of vegetation on which to lay eggs, butterflies are scarce in the steppe and desert areas. Andalucía and the Mediterranean fringe of North Africa, in contrast, are often rich in species, some quite exotic. The life cycle – mating, egg production, caterpillar, pupa, butterfly – can be swift, with some species having three cycles in one year. some of the butterflies are large and colourful, such as the **swallowtail** and the **two pasha**. The most common butterflies in the early spring are the **painted ladies**, which migrate from North Africa northwards, often reaching as far as Britain. Other familiar species include the **Moroccan orange tip**, **festoon**, **Cleopatra** and **clouded yellow**. Moths are also widely represented, but as they are largely nocturnal they are rarely seen. Day flying moths include the **Burnet** and **hummingbird hawk moths**. The largest moth of the area is the **giant peacock moth**, with a wingspan of up to 15 cm.

Birds

Neither the Mediterranean nor the Desert areas are particularly rich in resident bird species, but both can be swollen temporarily by birds on passage. Four categories of birds may be noted. Firstly, there are the **resident** birds which are found throughout the year, such as the crested lark and the Sardinian warbler. Secondly, there are the **summer visitors**, such as the swift and swallow, which spend the winter months south of the Equator. **Winter visitors**, on the other hand, breed in Northern Europe but come south to escape the worst of the winter and include many varieties of wader and wildfowl. **Passage migrants** fly through the area northwards in spring and then return southwards in increased numbers after breeding in the autumn. Small birds tend to migrate on a broad front, often crossing the desert and the Mediterranean Sea without stopping. Such migrants include the whitethroat, plus less common species such as the nightjar and wryneck. Larger birds, including Eagles, Storks and Vultures, must adopt a different strategy, as they depend on soaring, rather than sustained flight. As they rely on thermals created over land, they must opt for short sea crossings. One route uses the narrow Straits of Gibraltar, while the more easterly route follows the Nile Valley, Turkey and the Bosphorus. A third, lesser-used, route runs via Tunisia, Malta and Sicily, where birds run the gauntlet of the guns of so-called 'sportsmen'.

Within North Africa and Andalucía there are a number of typical habitats with their own assemblage of birds. The Mediterranean itself has a poor selection of sea birds, although the rare Audouins gull always excites 'twitchers'. Oceanic birds such as gannets and shearwaters, however, enter the Mediterranean during the winter. Wetland areas, such as the Coto de Doñana in Andalucía (see page 172) and Lake Ichkeul in Tunisia (see page 529) contain numerous varieties of the heron family such as the night heron and squacco heron, while spoonbill, ibis and both little and cattle egrets are common.

Flamingoes breed in a number of locations when conditions are right. Waders such as the avocet and black winged stilt are also typical wetland birds. The wetland species are augmented in the winter by a vast collection of wildfowl. Resident ducks, however, are confined to specialities such as the white-headed duck, marbled teal and ferruginous duck. On roadsides, the crested lark is frequently seen, while overhead wires often contain corn buntings, with their jangling song, and the colonial bee-eaters. Mountain areas are ideal for searching out raptors. There are numerous varieties of eagle, including Bonelli's, booted, short toed and golden. Of the vultures, the griffon is the most widely encountered. The black kite is more catholic in its choice of habitat, but the Montagu's harrier prefers open farmland.

The desert and steppe areas have their own specialist resident birds which have developed survival strategies. Raptors include the long-legged buzzard and the lanner, which prefer mountain areas. Among the ground-habitat birds are the Houbura bustard and the cream coloured courser. Duponts lark is also reluctant to fly, except during its spectacular courtship display. The trumpeter finch is frequently seen at oases, while the insectivorous desert wheatear is a typical bird of the *erg* and *reg* regions.

Finally, mention must be made of the **Nile Valley** (see page 769). Essentially a linear oasis stretching for hundreds of kilometres, it provides outstanding bird watching, particularly from the slow-moving cruise boats, which are literally 'floating hides'. Apart from the wide range of herons and egrets, specialities include the African skimmer, Egyptian geese, pied kingfisher and white pelican. Even the tombs and monuments are rewarding for the ornithologist, yielding Sakar falcons, Levant sparrowhawks and the black shouldered kite.

TRAVEL AND SURVIVAL IN THE DESERT

Travellers and the nature of deserts

For those travellers staying in well regulated accommodation in good hotels, the realities of the desert can be disguised for as long as electricity and pure water supplies are sustained. Much of the information in the following section can thus be ignored, though not with total impunity. Trips into the desert even by the most careful of tour operators carry some of the hazards and a knowledge of good practice might be as helpful on the beach or tourist bus as for the full-blooded desert voyager.

There is a contemporary belief that the problems of living and travelling in deserts have been solved. Much improved technology in transport together with apparent ease of access to desert areas has encouraged these comfortable ideas. The very simplicity of the problems of deserts, lack of water and high temperatures, make them easy to underestimate. In reality, deserts have not changed and problems still arise when travelling in them, albeit with less regularity than twenty or so years ago. One aspect of the desert remains unchanged – mistakes and misfortune can too easily be fatal.

Desert topography is varied. Excellent books such as Allan JA & Warren A (1993) *Deserts: a conservation atlas*, Mitchell Beazley, show the origins and constant development of desert scenery. In North Africa, desert and semi-desert is the largest single surface area and so has an importance for travellers rarely met with elsewhere. Its principal features and their effects on transport are best understood before they are met on the ground. The great *ergs* or sandseas comprise mobile dunes and shifting surface sands over vast areas. Small mobile *barkhans*, which are crescent shaped, can often be driven round on firm terrain but the larger transverse and longitudinal dunes can form large surfaces with thick ridges of soft sand. They constantly change their shape as the wind works across them. While not impassible, they can be crossed only slowly and with difficulty. The major sand seas such as those at Calanscio, Murzuq, and Brak should be treated as no-go areas for all but fully equipped and locally supported expeditions. Similar conclusions apply to the extensive outcrops of rocky desert as exemplified by the Jabal As-Sawda in Libya or the rougher parts of the S Atlas zones of Algeria and Morocco. The *wadi* beds which penetrate much of the Sahara, *serirs* and gravel plains provide good access for all-terrain vehicles.

The main characteristic of the desert is its **aridity**. Aridity is calculable and those navigating deserts are advised to understand the term so that the element of risk can be appraised and managed with safety. CW Thornthwaite's aridity index shows water deficiency relative to water need for a given area. There is a gradient from N to S throughout the region, of rising temperatures, diminishing rainfall and worsening aridity. Aridity of the desert is thus very variable, ranging from the Mediterranean sub-tropical fringe to a semi-arid belt to the S and a fully arid desert interior. In basic terms, the further S you are the more dangerous the environment. Do not assume that conditions on the coast properly prepare you for the deep S. The Sahara is also very varied in its topography, climate and natural difficulties posed for the traveller. Rapid transition from rough stone terrain to sand sea to salt flat has to be expected and catered for.

For practical purposes, aridity means

very high temperatures. The world's highest temperatures are experienced in the Sahara – over 55°C. Averages in the S desert run in summer at more than 50°C in the shade at midday. In full sun very much higher figures are reached. High temperatures are not the only difficulty. Each day has a large range of temperature, often of more than 20°C, with nights being intensely cold, sometimes below freezing. In winter, air temperatures can be very low despite the heat of the sun and temperatures drop very rapidly either when the sun goes down or when there is movement from sunlight to shade, say in a deep gorge or a cave.

Increasing aridity means greater **difficulty in water availability**. Scientists define the problem in terms of water deficits. North Africa as a whole and the deep Sahara in particular are very serious water deficit areas. Surface waters are lacking almost everywhere except in the case of the Nile in Egypt and Sudan. Underground water is scarce and often available only at great depths. Occasional natural seepages of water give rise to oases and/or palmeries. They are, however, rare. Since water is the key to sustaining life in deserts, travellers have always to assume that they must be self-sufficient or navigate from one known water source to another.

Isolation is another feature of the Sahara. Travellers' tales tend to make light of the matter, hinting that bedouin Arabs will emerge from the dunes even in the most obscure corner of the desert. This is probably true of the semi-desert and some inland *wadi* basins but not a correct assumption on which to build a journey in the greater part of the Sahara. Population numbers in the desert are very low, only one person per 20 km sq in Al-Kufrah in SE Libya, for example, and most of these are concentrated in small oasis centres. All-weather road systems are gradually being extended into and through the Sahara but they represent a few straggling lines across areas for the most part without fixed and maintained highways. The very fact that oil exploration has been so intense in the Sahara has meant that the surface of the desert is criss-crossed with innumerable tracks, making identification of all routes other than black top roads extremely difficult. Once off the main roads, travellers can part from their escorts and find no fixed topography to get them back on course. Vanishing individuals and vehicles in the Sahara are too frequent to be a joke. To offset this problem read on.

The most acute difficulty with off-road emergencies is finding the means of raising assistance because of isolation. Normal preventative action is to ensure that your travel programme is known in advance by some individual or an institution to whom regular check-in is made from points on the route. Failure to contact should automatically raise the alarm. Two vehicles are essential and often obviate the worst problems of break-down and the matter of isolation. Radio communication from your vehicle is an expensive but useful aid if things go wrong.

Bear in mind the enormous distances involved in bringing help even where the location of an incident in the desert is known. Heavy rescue equipment and/or paramedical assistance will probably be 500 km or more distant. Specialist transport for the rescuers is often not instantly available, assuming that local telecommunications systems work and local administrators see fit to help.

Living with the climate

Living with desert environments is not difficult but it does take discipline and adherence to sensible routines at all times. It is an observed fact that health problems in hot and isolated locations take on a greater seriousness for those involved than they would in temperate climates. It is still common practice with

Western oil companies and other commercial organisations regularly engaged at desert sites to fly ill or injured persons home as a first measure in the knowledge that most will recover more rapidly without the psychological and environmental pressures of a desert site. Most health risks in the desert are avoidable. The rules, evolved over many years, are simple and easy to follow:

1. Allow time to acclimatise to full desert conditions. Conserve your energy at first rather than acting as if you were still in a temperate climatic régime. Most people take a week or more to adjust to heat conditions in the deep Sahara.

2. Stay out of direct sunlight whenever possible, especially once the sun is high. Whenever you can, do what the locals do, move from shade to shade.

3. Wear clothes to protect your skin from the sun, particularly your head and neck. Use a high Sun Protection Factor (SPF) cream, preferably as high as SPF15 (94 per cent) to minimize the effects of Ultraviolet-B. Footwear is a matter of choice though many of those from the temperate parts of the world will find strong, light but well ventilated boots ideal for keeping sand, sun, venomous livestock and thorns off the feet. Slip on boots are best of all since they are convenient if visiting Arab encampments/housing/religious sites, where shoes are not worn.

4. Drink good quality water regularly and fully. It is estimated that 10-15 litres per day are needed by a healthy person to avoid water deficiency in desert conditions, even if there is no actual feeling of thirst. The majority of ailments arising in the desert relate to water deficiency and so it is worth the small effort of regular drinking of water. Too much alcoholic drink has the opposite effect in most cases and is not, unfortunately, a substitute for water!

5. Be prepared for cold nights by having some warm clothes to hand.

6. Stay in your quarters or vehicle if there is a **sand storm**.

7. Refrain from eating dubious foods. Deserts and stomach upsets have a habit of going hand in hand – 'gyppy-tummy' and 'Tripoli-trots' give a taste of the problem! Choose hot cooked meals in preference to cold meats and tired salads. Peel all fruit and uncooked fresh vegetables. Do not eat 'native' milk-based items or drink untreated water unless you are absolutely sure of its good quality.

8. Sleep off the ground if you can. There are very few natural dangers in the desert but scorpions, spiders and snakes are found (but are rarely fatal) and are best avoided.

Transport and common sense in the desert

The key to safe travel in desert regions is reliable and well equipped transport. Most travellers will simply use local bus and taxi services. For the motorist, motorcyclist or pedal cyclist there are ground rules which, if followed, will help to reduce risks. In normal circumstances travellers will remain on black top roads and for this need only a well prepared 2 wheel drive vehicle. Choose a machine which is known for its reliability and for which spares can be easily obtained. Across the whole of North Africa only Peugeot and Mercedes are found with adequate spares and servicing facilities. If you have a different type of car/truck, make sure that you take spares with you or have the means of getting spares sent out. Bear in mind that transport of spares to and from Libya and Sudan might be tediously long. Petrol/benzene/gas is everywhere available though diesel is equally well distributed except in the smallest of southern settlements. 4 wheel drive transport is useful even for the traveller who normally remains on the black top highway. Emergencies, diversions and unscheduled visits to off the road sites become less of a problem with all-terrain vehicles. Off the road, 4 wheel drive is essential, normally with 2 vehicles travelling together. A great variety of 4 wheel drive vehicles are in use in the region, with Toyota and Land Rover probably found most widely.

All vehicles going into the S areas of North Africa should have basic equipment as follows:
1. Full tool kit, vehicle maintenance handbook and supplementary tools such as clamps, files, wire, spare parts kit supplied by car manufacturer, jump leads.
2. Spare tyre/s, battery driven tyre pump, tyre levers, tyre repair kit, hydraulic jack, jack handle extension, base plate for jack.
3. Spare fuel can/s, spare water container/s, cool bags.

For those going off the blacktop roads other items to include are:
4. Foot tyre pump, heavy duty hydraulic or air jack, power winch, sand channels, safety rockets, comprehensive first aid kit, radio-telephone where permitted.
5. Emergency rations kit/s, matches, Benghazi burner (see page 44).
6. Maps, compasses, latest road information, long term weather forecast, guides to navigation by sun and stars.

Driving in the desert is an acquired skill. Basic rules are simple but crucial.
1. If you can get a local guide who perhaps wants a lift to your precise destination, use him.
2. Set out early in the morning after first light, rest during the heat of the day and use the cool of the evening for further travel.
3. Never attempt to travel at night or when there is a sandstorm brewing or in progress.
4. Always travel with at least 2 vehicles which should remain in close visual contact.

Other general hints include not speeding across open flat desert in case the going changes without warning and your vehicle beds deeply into soft sand or a gully. Well maintained corrugated road surfaces can be taken at modest pace but rocky surfaces should be treated with great care to prevent undue wear on tyres. Sand seas are a challenge for drivers but need a cautious approach – ensure that your navigation lines are clear so that weaving between dunes does not disorientate the navigator. Especially in windy conditions, sight lines can vanish, leaving crews with little knowledge of where they are. Cresting dunes from dip slope to scarp needs care that the vehicle does not either bog down or overturn. Keep off salt flats after rain and floods especially in the winter and spring when water tables can rise and make the going hazardous in soft mud. Even when on marked and maintained tracks beware of approaching traffic. One of the editor's friend's car was hit by the only vehicle which passed him that day on a 500 km drive in S Libya!

Emergencies

The desert tends to expose the slightest flaw in personnel and vehicles. Emergency situations are therefore to be expected and planned for. There is no better security than making the schedule of your journey known in advance to friends or embassy/consulate officials who will actively check on your arrival at stated points. Breakdowns and multiple punctures are the most frequent problem. On the highway the likelihood is always that a passing motorist will give assistance, or a lift to the nearest control post or village. In these situations it is best simply remain with your vehicle until help arrives making sure that your are clear of the road and that you are protected from other traffic by a warning triangle and/or rocks on the road to rear and front.

Off the road, breakdowns, punctures and bogging down in soft sand are the main difficulties. If you have left your travel programme at your last stop you will already have a fall back position in case of severe problems. If you cannot make a repair or extricate yourself, remain with your vehicle in all circumstances. Unless you can clearly see a settlement (not a mirage) stay where you are with water, food and shelter. The second vehicle can be used to search for help but only after defining the precise location of the incident. In the case of getting lost, halt, conserve fuel while you attempt to get a bearing on either the topography or the planets/stars and work out a traverse to bring you back to a known line such as a highway, mountain ridge or coastline. If that fails, take up as prominent a position as possible for being spotted from the air. Build a fire to use if and when y ou hear air activity in your vicinity. Attempt to find a local source of water by digging in the nearest wadi bed, collecting dew from the air at night. If you have fuel to spare it can be used with great care both as a means of attracting attention and a way of boiling untreated water. A *Benghazi burner* , two crude metal cones welded together to give a water jacket and space for a fire in the centre can achieve this latter purpose. As ever in North Africa, be patient and conserve your energy.

THE JEWELLERY OF NORTH AFRICA

North Africa today boasts a distinctive culture whose abundance of styles of dress and adornment almost defies description. The dynamic history of the region has produced imaginative traditionial designs mixed with foreign elements leading to a range of decoration few regions in the world can rival. Influences from the Phoenicians, Greeks and Romans, Arabs and Andalusians have each contributed subtly to the immense range of jewellery found in this part of the world.

Although some urban dwellers have adopted Western attitudes to dress and decoration, at times of festivals and especially for marriage ceremonies, traditional dress and elaborate jewellery that has changed little since the Middle Ages is still worn. The increase of tourism, while in some cases destroying traditional values, is in fact promoting and preserving crafts, especially jewellery making, by providing an eager and lucrative market for ornaments that was rapidly declining. Unfortunately, with the changes of cultural values, changes in fashion and style also occur and in North Africa large quantities of old, exquisite silver jewellery have been destroyed to provide raw materials for new pieces.

Throughout North Africa there is a division of tastes and wealth between towns where gold is favoured and the countryside where silver predominates. Basically, traditional styles continue to be popular and, especially in the Maghreb, jewellery tends to become more traditional the further south one

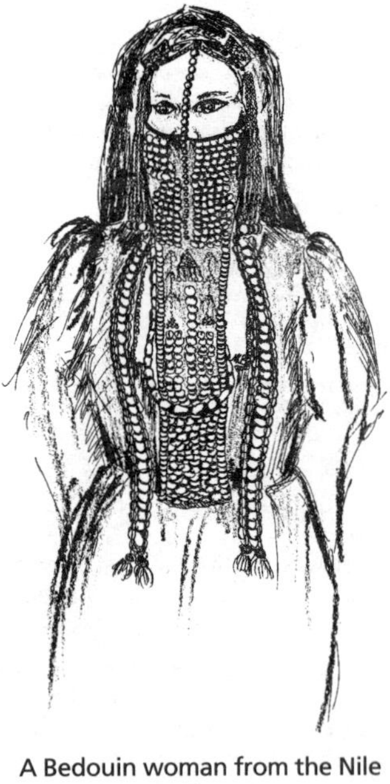

A Bedouin woman from the Nile

goes. A general shift can be discerned away from silver towards gold, especially in Egypt, where it is now believed to be a better investment.

Despite a whole field of inspiration being forbidden to Muslim jewellers, that of the human form, they developed the art of decorating jewellery in ways that eventually merged to become a distinctive 'Islamic' style. Using floral (arabesque), animal, geometric and calligraphic motifs fashioned on gold and silver with precious and semi-precious gems, coral and pearls they worked their magic.

According to Islamic law, silver is the only pure metal recommended by the Prophet Mohammad. For the majority of Muslims this sanction is felt to apply only to men who do not, as a rule, wear any jewellery other than a silver wedding ring or seal ring.

Every town has its own jewellery *suq* with larger centres providing a greater range of jewellery. There is almost always a distinction between the goldsmiths and the silversmiths and there are also shops, designated in Egypt by a brass camel over the door, which produce jewellery in brass or gold plate on brass for the cheap end of the market.

The tourist industry keeps whole secions of the jewellery business in work, especially in Egypt where designs which have a historical base – the **Scarab**, the **Ankh** (the symbol of eternal life), the **Eye of Horus**, **Nefertiti's head** and **heiroglyphic cartouches** – predominate. The jewellery spans the entire range of taste and quality from the very cheap mass-produced pendants to finely crafted very expensive pieces. The jewellers also sell a great number of silver pieces in the cheaper end of the tourist market which is very popular as 'ethnic' jewellery. Gold and silver jewellery is usually sold by weight and, although there might be an addi-

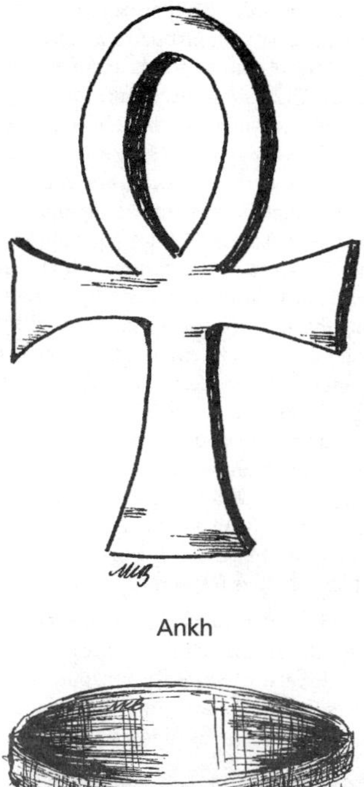

Ankh

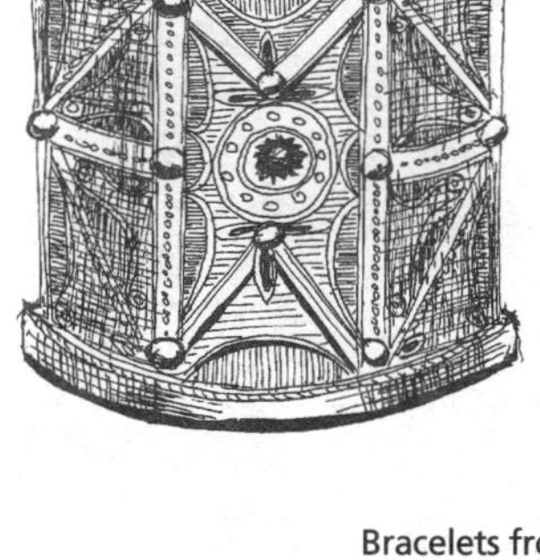

Bracelets from the Maghreb

tional charge for more intricate craftmanship, this means the buyer must judge quality very carefully.

The **earring** is by far the most popular and convenient ornament throughout North Africa. It appears in an infinite variety of styles with the crescent moon shape being the most common. This is closely followed by the **bracelet** or **bangle** which is also very much part of a woman's everyday wardrobe.

Most of the jewellery is worn both as an **adornment** and as an indication of social status or rank. It generally has some symbolic meaning or acts as a charm. Jewellery is usually steeped in tradition and is often received in rites of passage like puberty, betrothal and marriage. In North Africa, women receive most of their jewellery upon marriage. This is usually regarded as their sole property and is security against personal disaster.

One of the many styles of Khamsa or Hand of Fatima

Many of the **symbols** recurrent in North African jewellery have meanings or qualities which are thought to be imparted to the wearer. Most of the discs appearing in the jewellery represent the moon which is considered to be the embodiment of perfect beauty and femininity. The greatest compliment is to liken a woman to the full moon. Both the moon and the fish are considered as fertility symbols. The cresent is the symbol of Islam but its use actually predates Islam. It is the most common symbol throughout the region and acquires greater Islamic significance with the additon of a star inside. Other symbols frequently seen are the palm and the moving lizard both of which signify life and the snake which signifies respect.

Amulets are thought to give the wearer protection from the unknown, calamities and threats. They are also reckoned to be curative and to have power over human concerns such as longevity, health,

North African anklets or *Khul-Khal* (always worn in pairs)

wealth, sex and luck. Women and childen wear amulets more frequently as their resisitance to evil is considered to be weaker than that of a man.
The most popular amulets are the *Hirz*, the Eye and the *Khamsa* or hand. The *Hirz* is a silver box containing verses of the Koran. Egypt in particular has a pre-occupation with the Eye as an amulet to ward off the 'evil eye', usually modelled on the Eye of Horus which, as with most symbols in Ancient Egyptian jewellery, has always had mystical connotations. The *Khamsa* is by far the most widespread of the amulets. It comes in a multitude of sizes and designs of a stylized hand and is one of the most common components of jewellery in the region. This hand represents the 'Hand of Fatima', Mohammad's favourite daughter. Koranic inscriptions also form a large section of favoured pendants and are usually executed in gold and also heavily encrusted with diamonds and other precious stones.

Silver fibula from Algeria, inset with coral

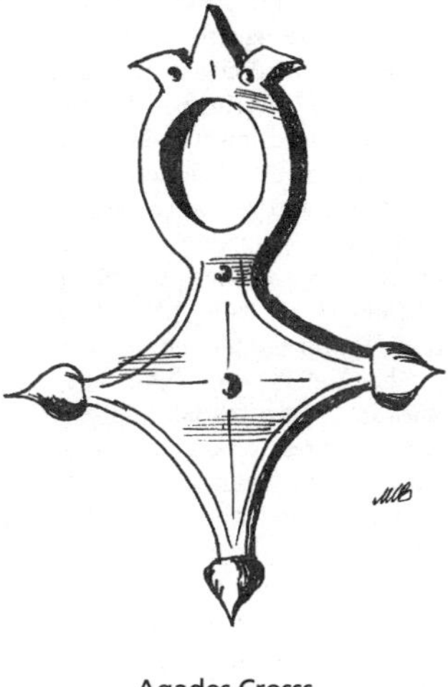

Agades Crosss

Coins or *mahboub* form the basis of most of the traditional jewellery, from the veils of the bedouins of the Nile Delta and the bodices of the women from the Egyptian oases to the spectacular festival and marriage ensembles worn in the Mahgreb. Each area, village or tribe has its own unique and extraordinary dress of which jewellery, be it hundreds of coins or huge amber beads, forms a fundamental part.

Among the more interesting items are **anklets** called *khul khal*, worn in pairs and found in a great variety of styles. In Egypt they are mostly of solid silver fringed with tiny bells. Fine examples are expensive due to their weight. They are losing popularity among the younger generation as they are cumbersome to wear with shoes and because of their undertones of subservience and slavery. It is still possible to see them being worn by married women in the remoter villages of Egypt.

Characteristic **Libyan** jewellery is gold plated silver though both silver and gold are common. The predominant motif, a tiny version of the **'Hand of Fatima'**, appears on every piece. In **Tunisia** and other countries of the Maghreb, look out for **fibulae** and **pectorals** used to secure women's capes. They occur in various styles and are usually of silver, sometimes inlaid with coral. The 2 most distinctive styles of jewellery in **Algeria** belong to the Kabyles of the High Atlas and coastal plain and to the Saharan tribes like the Touareg. Kabyle jewellery is distinguished by its colourful **enamelling** in bright yellow, violet and turquoise, while that of the Touareg is generally made of leather and engraved silver. The most well known **Touareg** piece is the **Agades Cross** (*tanaghilit*) which comes in many variations of the basic style. **Moroccan** jewellery, especially that of Fes and Tanger, shows a clear Andalusian influence in the intricate flowing **floral/leafy patterns**. Floral networks of filigree enhanced with enamelling are a speciality of Essaouira, while more geometric designs are found in Meknes.

Today the main jewellery bazaars in North Africa are **Khan el-Khalili** in Cairo (**see page** 732), **Suq al-Mushir** in Tripoli (**page** 615) and **Souk el-Berka** in Tunis, (**page** 507). In Algeria the suqs of Tamanrasset, Bou Saada Ghardaïa and Biskra have good jewellery. In Morocco **Essaouira** and the Imperial cities are all jewellery centres and **Tiznit** is the place to find Berber jewellery.

Marie-Claire Bakker contributed the text and illustrations for this section.

DRESS IN NORTH AFRICA

First time visitors to the countries of North Africa will be fascinated by the variety and colour of the garments worn as 'everyday' wear. This section, contributed by Jennifer Scarce, Curator of Eastern Cultures, National Museums of Scotland, sketches in the background and attempts an explanation of what is being worn and why.

The dress traditions of North Africa are striking and colourful evidence of a rich cultural heritage. Here, as in all societies, dress is a powerful form of cultural expression, a visual symbol which reveals a wealth of information about the wearer. Dress also reflects historical evolution and the cumulative effects of religious, ethnic and geographical factors on a society.

It is hardly surprising that the many influences which have shaped North African history have produced an equally diverse dress culture in which elements from antiquity, the Islamic world and Europe are found. The heritage from earlier times is a rich blending of decorative motifs and drapery. Carthaginian material culture drew upon local tradtions of colourful geometric ornament, which is still seen in Berber clothing and textiles, and luxury goods from Egypt. Greek and Roman fashions have survived in the striking dress of the inhabitants of the deserts and mountains of Morocco, Algeria and Tunisia where draped and folded garments are fastened with elaborate jewelled pins (See Jewellery **page** 44) and buckles. The Arabs introduced a different dress tradition, influenced by the styles of Egypt and Syria. Here the main features were loose flowing robes and cloaks, wrapped turbans and headcovering which combined a graceful line, comfort and modest concealment. The establishment of Islamic cities encouraged a diverse range of professions and occupations – civil and religious authorities, merchants, craftsmen – all with their distinctive dress. Within cities such as Fes, Marrakech, Algiers and Tunis specialist trades in textiles, leather and jewellery supported dress production. Widening political and commercial relations stimulated new elements in dress. Jewish and Muslim immigrants from Andalucía in the 15th century introduced styles influenced by Spanish tradition which survived in the full-skirted tight-waisted dresses of Moroccan Jewish women.

The Ottoman Turks introduced another feature into city dress, in the form of jackets, trousers and robes of flamboyant cut and lavishly embroidered decoration. Finally European fashion, with emphasis on tailored suits and dresses entered the North African scene.

One of the more rewarding pleasures of a visit to North Africa is the opportunity to see the intricate pattern of mixed dress styles which reflect an adjustment to economic and social change.

The widest range is seen in urban environments where European styles mingle with interpretations of local dress and the clothing of regional migrants. Men have adopted European dress in varying degrees. The wardrobes of civil servants, professional and business men include well-cut sober coloured European suits, which are worn with toning shirts, ties and smart shoes. Seasonal variations include fabrics of lighter weight and colour and short-sleeved shirts and 'safari' jackets. Casual versions of this dress code, including open-necked shirts, are seen in more modest levels of urban society. Blue jeans, blouson jackets, T shirts and trainers may be worn equally by manual workers and students.

Men's city dress alternates between European and local garments according to taste and situation. Traditional dress is based on a flexible combination of loose flowing garments and wraps which gives considerable scope for individuality. One of the most versatile garments is the ***jallabah***, an ankle length robe with long straight sleeves and a neat pointed hood, made in fabrics ranging from fine wool and cotton in dark and light colours to rough plain and striped homespun yarn. Elegant versions in white may be beautifully cut and sewn and edged with plaited silk braid. A modern casual version has short sleeves and a V-shaped neck and is made of poly-cotton fabric in a range of plain colours. Professional men may change from a suit into a *jallabah* at home, while working class men may wear a plain or striped *jallabah* in the street over European shirt and trousers.

The more traditional interpretation of dress can be seen in the medinas. Here the *jallabah* is worn with the hood folded at the the back or pulled up and draped over the head. In the past a fez or turban was worn under the hood and a white cotton high-necked shirt with long sleeves and loose white trousers gathered just below the knee were worn under the *jallabah*. In Tunisia and Algeria trousers of a more exaggerated voluminous style were worn as a result of Ottoman Turkish influence.

A handsome and dignified garment worn by high ranking state and religious officials is the *caftan*, another long robe with very wide sleeves and a round neck. The cut and detail, such as the use of very fine braid around the neck and sleeves and along the seams, are more formal than those of the *jallabah*. The modern *caftan* has narrower sleeves and is worn in public by men of an older and more conservative generation.

Headcoverings are a revealing indication of status and personal choice. A close fitting red wool felt pillbox cap, a *fez* or *chechia*, was normally worn alone or neatly wrapped with a turban length. Such caps were a major product of the souk of Tunis and were widely exported. Currently they are seen more often on older men both in traditional and European dress.

Footwear is a distinctive product of North Africa's longstanding leather industry. Shoes, usually in bright yellow or white, are made of fine leather. They are close fitting, have a long pointed toe and are worn with the back folded under at the heel. Traditional dress may be completed with the addition of drapery. Examples include the selham or burnous, a wide semicircular cloak with a pointed hood and the ksa, a length of heavy white woollen cloth which is skilfully folded and wrapped around the head and body in a style resembling that of the classical Roman toga.

Women's town dress is also a mixture of traditional and modern European forms and depends on wealth, status and personal taste. In the larger cities where women are employed in business and professions, European clothes are worn, cleverly accessorised with scarves and jewellery. Longer skirts and long-sleeved blouses are worn, being a more modest form of European dress.

Traditional dress is remarkably enduring especially in the cities of Morocco among women of all classes. The most important garments are the *caftan* and *jallabah* of the same basic cut and shape as those for men. The *caftan*, as worn in the past by wealthy women, was a sumptuous garment of exaggerated proportions made of rich velvet or brocaded silk embroidered with intricate designs in gold thread. The modern *caftan* is usually made of brightly coloured and patterned light-weight fabric and edged with plaited braid. The shape is simple and unstructured with a deep slit at each side from waist to hem. Variations can be found in texture and colour of fabric, changes in proportions of sleeves and length of side slits. The *caftan* in its many variations is always worn as indoor dress and can suit all occasions. Traditionally it is worn as an everyday garment belted over a long underskirt. A light shawl may be draped around the neck and the hair tied up with a patterned scarf. Women who normally wear European dress to work often change into a *caftan* at home. Very chic versions of the *caftan*, combined with modern hairstyles and accessories, are worn as evening wear at private and official functions.

Outdoor dress varies across North Africa and Morocco and Tunisia offer different solutions to the traditional requirements of modesty and concealment. Moroccan women wear a long straight *jallabah*, in a variety of materials and colours and usually slit from knee to ankle, over a *caftan*. There are 2 versions of the hood, a small one neatly folded at the back which functions more as a collar, or a large one which is pulled tightly over the face over a rectangular veil which conceals nose, mouth and chin. This traditional outdoor dress is worn with backless soft leather slippers or European sandal style shoes. In comparison the Tunisian outdoor dress is less structured and may be worn over European clothes. Here the basic garment is the *sifsari*, a length of white fabric which is folded in half and secured around the waist. The top half is then pulled up over the head and draped according to the required degree of facial concealment.

While the balance between contrasting dress codes is subject to subtle changes of emphasis in everyday life, the rituals of **marriage** still require a conspicuous display of traditional dress, jewellery and cosmetics for both bride and female guests. The city of Fes offers one of the most distinctive wedding ceremonies where the bride, robed in layers of magnificent brocaded garments and shawls and adorned with a gold crown hung with strings of pearls and with intricate patterns drawn with henna on her hands, is transformed into a splendid icon.

Regional dress, though less varied than in the past, is a striking visual record of the complex ethnic patterns and harsh living conditions of the rural areas. Particularly in Morocco, the tradition of the Berber tribes both settled and nomadic, is still retained in their handsome and brilliantly coloured draped garments. Extremes of heat and cold mean that adjustable layers of loose clothing and protective headgear such as a swathed turban or a straw hat are essential.

In rural areas the men's hooded *jallabah* is the most common, usually of homespun wool in unbeached white, blue or beige and brown stripes. It may be worn over another *jallabah*. Head coverings may be a closefitting knitted cap, a loosely wrapped white turban, or a tall pointed hat with a wide flat brim plaited from reeds, palm fibre or dried grass. Berber men used to drape a *haik*, a heavy cloak in coarse plain or striped wool, over their garments. In the south, the Touareg men still wear brilliant blue robes and conceal their heads and faces with turbans and veils as an extreme precaution against the sun, wind and sand.

Women's dress is considerably more varied and depends on a combination of colourful drapes. The basic garment of the Berber women is an *izar*, a long straight piece of cotton or wool in a series of colours ranging from white or black through to vivid reds, purples and yellows. The *izar*, worn over a *caftan*, is folded in half to envelope the body and is fastened at the shoulders with heavy silver pins or brooches. (See Jewellery, **page 44**). It can then be further draped, belted and adorned according to local usage. Striped woollen cloaks may be worn over the *izar*. Large turbans bound with cords and scarves, elaborately plaited and coiled hair, and much chunky silver jewellery traditionally complete this form of dress. Some of the most spectacular examples of Berber female dress are seen among the tribes in the High Atlas mountains, where heavy striped cloaks, are worn together with towering head-dresses adorned with skeins of wool and silk threaded with silver chains and pendants. The effect is completed by boldly tattooed and rouged faces.

Other easily identifiable forms of regional dress include the large black *haiks* with which women in the south conceal themselves and the red and white striped skirts and shawls and large straw hats of the country women of Chaouen in Morocco.

In their different ways, **state ceremonies** and tourism encourage the survival of local dress. The soldiers guarding the tomb of King Mohammed V in Rabat wear a dashing scarlet uniform based on Turkish style jackets and trousers worn with a swirling *burnous*. In Tunisia officials wear traditional dress on state occasions, thus supporting the makers of *chechias* and other garment makers.

In tourist areas doormen, porters and waiters are garbed in white *jallaba* and scarlet *fez,* watersellers in traditional dress and gaily decorated broad-brimmed hats roam the streets, displays of Berber dancing are arranged and tourists are encouraged to purchase 'local garments' and participate in versions of local festivals. The souks in these resorts are festooned with *caftans* and leather slippers.

At another level, North Africa's impressive cultural heritage is taken very seriously and many museums have displays of traditional dress which can be enjoyed by both local and foreign visitors (See Dar Cherait Museum, Tozeur,see **page 566**).

LANGUAGE FOR TRAVEL – ARABIC, FRENCH AND SPANISH

Arabic It is impossible to indicate in the Latin script how Arabic should be pronounced so we have opted for a very simplified transliteration which will give the user a sporting chance of uttering something that can be understood by an Arab. An accent has been placed to show where the stress falls in each word of more than two syllables.

For both Spanish and French the gender of nouns has been given in brackets. In Spanishmasculine is *el* and feminine *la* with plurals *los* and *las*. In French the plural of both *le* (masculine) and *la* (feminine) is *les*.

Spanish is spoken more or less as it appears. Bear in mind that *z*, and *c* before *e* and *i* are a soft *th*, *h* is silent, *ll* is pronounced *y* as in million, *ñ* as *ny* in onion and *v* almost like the English *b*. The people of Andalucía speak quickly and rarely find time to finish off the end of a word, but treat all attempts to speak their language with patience and good humour.

French unlike Spanish, does not have the final letter of the word pronounced unless accented as in *marché*.

Numbers

ARABIC NUMERALS

١	1	١٠	10	١٩	19	٨٠	80
٢	2	١١	11	٢٠	20	٩٠	90
٣	3	١٢	12	٢١	21	١٠٠	100
٤	4	١٣	13	٢٢	22	٢٠٠	200
٥	5	١٤	14	٣٠	30	٣٠٠	300
٦	6	١٥	15	٤٠	40	٤٠٠	400
٧	7	١٦	16	٥٠	50	١٠٠٠	1000
٨	8	١٧	17	٦٠	60		
٩	9	٧١	18	٧٠	70		

	Arabic	French	Spanish
0	sífr	zéro	cero
1	wáhad	un (m) une (f)	uno (m) una (f)
2	tnéen	deux	dos
3	taláata	trois	tres
4	árba	quatre	cuatro
5	khámsa	cinq	cinco
6	sítta	six	seis
7	sába	sept	siete
8	tamánia	huit	ocho
9	tíssa	neuf	nueve
10	áshra	dix	diez
11	ahdásh	onze	once
12	itnásh	douze	doce
13	talatásh	treize	trece
14	arbatásh	quatorze	catorce
15	khamstásh	quinze	quince
16	sittásh	seize	dieciséis
17	sabatásh	dix-sept	diecisiete
18	tmantásh	dix-huit	dieciocho

	Arabic	French	Spanish
19	tissatásh	dix-neuf	diecinueve
20	ishréen	vingt	veinte
30	tlaatéen	trente	treinta
40	arba'éen	quarante	cuarenta
50	khamséen	cinquante	cincuenta
60	sittéen	soixante	sesenta
70	saba'éen	soixante-dix	setenta
80	tmanéen	quatre-vingts	ochenta
90	tissa'éen	quatre-vingt dix	noventa
100	mía	cent	cien
200	miatéen	deux cents	doscientos
300	tláata mia	trois cents	trescientos
1000	alf	mille	mil

Greetings

	Arabic	French	Spanish
Hello!	assálamu aláikum	bonjour	buenos días
How are you?	keef hálek?	comment ça va?	¿como está?
Well!	kwáyes	très bien	muy bien
Good bye!	bisaláma	au revoir	adíos
Go away!	ímshi, barra	allez vous en!	¡márchese!
God willing!	inshállah	si Dieu le veut	si Dios quiere
Never mind	ma'lésh	ne t'inquiète pas	no se preocupe
Thank God!	hamdulilláh!	Dieu merci!	¡Gracias a Dios!
Yes/no	naam, áiwa/la	oui/non	sí/no
Please	min fádlek	s'il vous plaît	por favor
Thank you	shukran	merci	muchas gracias
OK	kwáyes	d'accord	vale
Excuse me	ismáh-lee	excusez-moi	perdón

Days

	Arabic	French	Spanish
Sunday	al-áhad	dimanche	domingo
Monday	al-itnéen	lundi	lunes
Tuesday	at-taláta	mardi	martes
Wednesday	al-árba	mercredi	miércoles
Thursday	al-khemées	jeudi	jueves
Friday	al-júma	vendredi	viernes
Saturday	as-sébt	samedi	sábado

Food

	Arabic	French	Spanish
banana	mouz	banane (f)	plátano (m)
beer	bírra	bière (f)	cerveza (f)
bread	khubz	pain (m)	pan (m)
breakfast	futóor	petit déjeuner (m)	desayuno (m)
butter	zíbda	beurre (m)	mantequilla (f)
cheese	jíbna	fromage (m)	queso (m)
coffee	qáhwa	café (m)	café (m)
dessert	hélwa	dessert (m)	postre (m)
dinner	ásha	dîner (m)	cena (f)
drink	mashróob	boisson (f)	bebida (f)
egg	baid	oeuf (m)	huevo (m)
fish	sámak	poisson (m)	pescado (m)
food	akl	nourriture (f)	comida (f)
fruit	fawákih	fruit (m)	frutas (f)

	Arabic	French	Spanish
lemonade	gazóoza	limonade (f)	limonada (f)
lunch	ghàda	déjeuner (m)	comida (f)
meat	láhma	viande (f)	carne (f)
menu (fixed price)	ká'ima	menu (à prix fixe)	menu (del día) (m)
milk	lában	lait (m)	leche (f)
olive	zeitóon	olive (f)	olivo (m)
restaurant	restaurán	restaurant (m)	restaurante (m)
salt	méleh	sel (m)	sal (m)
soup	shórba	potage (m)	sopa (f)
sugar	súkar	sucre (m)	azúcar (m)
tea (tea bag)	shay (shay kees)	thé (m)	té (m)
water (bottled)	móyyah (botri)	l'eau (f) (en bouteille)	agua (f) (embotellada)
wine	khamr	vin (m)	vino (m)

Travel

	Arabic	French	Spanish
airport	al-matár	aéroport (m)	aeropuerto (m)
arrival	wusóol	arrivée (f)	llegada (f)
bicycle	bisiclét/darrája	vélo (m)	bicicleta (f)
birth (date of)	youm al-meelád	date de naissance(f)	fecha de nacimiento (f)
bus	autobées	autobus (m)	autobús (m)
bus station	mahâttat al-autobées	gare routière (f)	estación de autobuses (f)
car	sayára	voiture (f)	coche (m)
car hire	sayárat-ujra	location de voitures (f)	alquilar de coches
customs	júmruk/gúmruk	douane (f)	aduana (f)
departure	khuróoj	départ	salida (f)
duty (excise)	daréebat	droit (m)	derechos (m)
duty free	bidóon daréeba	hors-taxe	libre de impuestos
engine	motúr	moteur (m)	motor (m)
fare	ujrat as-safr	prix du billet (m)	precio del billete (m)
ferry (boat)	má'diya	ferry/bac (m)	barca (f)
garage	garáge	garage (m)	taller (m)
here/there	héna/henák	ici/là	aquí/allí
left/right	yesáar/yeméen	à gauche/droite	a la izquierda/derecha
left luggage	máktab éeda al-afsh	consigne (f)	consigna (f)
map	kharéeta	carte (f)	mapa (m)
oil (engine)	zeit	huile (f)	aceite (m)
papers (documents)	watá'iq	papiers d'identité(m)	documentación (f)
parking	máwkif as-sayyarát	parking (m)	aparcamiento (m)
passport	jawáz	passeport (m)	pasaporte (m)
petrol	benzéen	essence (f)	gasolina (f)
port	méena	port (m)	puerto (m)
puncture	tókob	crevaison (f)	pinchazo (m)
quickly	sarée'an	vite	de prisa
railway	as-sikka al-hadeedíya	chemin de fer (m)	ferrocarril (m)
road	trik	route (f)	carretera (f)
slowly	shwai shwai	lentement	despacio
station	mahátta	gare (f)	estacíon de trenes (f)
straight on	alatóol	tout droit	todo recto
surname	lákab	nom de famille (m)	apellido (m)
taxi	taxi	taxi (m)	taxi (m)

	Arabic	French	Spanish
taxi rank	maháttat at-taxiyát	station de taxis (f)	parada de taxis (f)
ticket	tázkara	billet (m)	billete (m)
ticket (return)	tázkara dhaháb wa-eeyáb	billet de retour (m)	billete de ida y vuelta (m)
what time is it?	is-sa'a kam?	quelle heure est-il?	¿qué hora es?
train	tren	train (m)	tren (m)
tyre	itár	pneu (m)	neumático (m)
visa	fisa, ta'shéera	visa (m)	visado (m)

Common words

	Arabic	French	Spanish
after	bá'ad	après	después
afternoon	bá'ad az-zohr	après-midi	tarde (f)
Algeria	Aljazáyer	Algérie (f)	Argelia (f)
America	Amréeka	Amérique (f)	América (f)
and	wa	et	y
bank	bank	banque (f)	banco (m)
bath	hammám	bain (m)	baño (m)
beach	sháti al-bahr	plage (f)	playa (f)
bed	seréer	lit (m)	cama (f)
before	qabl	avant	antes de
Belgium	Belg	Belgique (f)	Bélgica (f)
big	kebéer	grand	grande
black	áswad	noir	negro
blue	ázrag	bleu	azul
camp site	mukháyyam	terrain de camping (m)	camping (m)
castle	kál'ah	château (m)	castillo (m)
cheap	rakhées	bon marché	barato
chemist shop	saidalíya	pharmacie (f)	farmacia (f)
church	kenéesa	église (f)	iglesia (f)
closed	múglaq	fermé	cerrado
cold/hot	bárid/sukhna	froid/chaud	frío/caliente
consulate	consulíya	consulat (m)	consulado (m)
day/night	youm/lail	jour (m)/nuit (f)	día (m)/noche (f)
desert	sahra	désert (m)	desierto (m)
doctor	tebeeb	médecin (m)	médico (m)
Egypt	Masr	Egypte (f)	Egipto (m)
embassy	sifára	ambassade (f)	embajada (f)
England	Ingiltérra	Angleterre (f)	Inglaterra (f)
enough	bás	assez	bastante
entrance	dukhóol	entrée (f)	entrada (f)
evening	mássa	soir (m)	tarde (f)
exchange (money)	tabdéel	change (m)	cambio (m)
exit	khuróoj	sortie (f)	salida (f)
expensive (too)	kteer	cher (trop)	caro (demasiado)
film	feelm	pellicule (f)	pélicula (f)
forbidden	mamnóoh	défendu	prohibido
France	France/Francia	France (f)	Francia (f)
full	melyán	complet	lleno
Germany	Almáni	Allemagne (f)	Alemania (f)
good (very good)	táyeb, kwáyes	bien (très bien)	bien (muy bien)
great	ákbar	formidable	magnífico
green	khádra	vert	verde
he/she	húwa/híya	il/elle	él/ella
house	mánzel	maison (f)	casa (f)

	Arabic	**French**	**Spanish**
hospital	mustáshfa	hôpital (m)	hospital (m)
hostel	bait ash-shebáb	auberge (f)	hostal (m)
hotel	fúnduq/hotéel	hôtel (m)	hotel (m)
how far to..?	kam kilometri...	... est à combien de km?	¿Cuántos km a..?
how much?	bikám	c'est combien?	¿cuánto es?
I/you	ána/inta	je/vous	yo/usted
information	malumát	renseignements (m)	información (f)
is there/are there?	hinák	y a-t-il un ..?	¿hay un ..?
Italy	Itálya	Italie (f)	Italia (f)
key	miftáh	clef (m)	llave (f)
later	ba'déen	plus tard	más tarde
Libya	Líbiya	Libye (f)	Libia (f)
light	nour	lumière (f)	luz (f)
little	sghéer	petit	pequeño
market	sook	marché (m)	mercado (m)
me	ána	moi	me
money	flóos	argent (m)	dinero (m)
more/less	áktar/akál	plus/moins	más/menos
morning	sobh	matin	mañana (f)
Morocco	al-Maghreb	Maroc	Marruecos (m)
mosque	mesjéed	mosquée (f)	mezquita (f)
near	karéeb	près	cerca
Netherlands (Dutch)	Holánda	Pays-Bas (m) (hollandais)	Países Bajos (m) (holandés)
newspaper	jaréeda	journal (m)	periódico (m)
new	jedéed	nouveau	nuevo
not	mush	ne...pas	no
now	al-án	maintenant	ahora
oil (heating)	naft	mazout (m)	aceite combustible(m)
open	maftooh	ouvert	abierto
pharmacy (see chemist)			
photography	taswéer	photographie (f)	fotografía (f)
police	bulées/shurta	gendarmerie (f)	policia (f)
post office	máktab al-baréed	poste	correos (m)
price	si'r	prix (m)	precio (m)
red	áhmar	rouge	rojo
river	wádi, wed	rivière (f),fleuve (m)	río (m)
roof	sat'h	toit (m)	techo (m)
room	górfa	chambre (f)	habitación (f)
sea	bahr	mer (f)	mar (f)
shop	dukkán	magasin (m)	tienda (f)
shower	doosh	douche (f)	ducha (f)
small	sghéer	petit	pequeño
Spain	Espánya	Espagne (f)	España (f)
square	maidán	place (f)	plaza (f)
stamp	tábi'	timbre poste (m)	sello (m)
street	shári	rue (f)	calle (f)
Sudan	as-Sóodan	Soudan (m)	Sudán (m)
Switzerland	Esswízi	Suisse (f)	Suiza (f)
synagogue	kenées	synagogue (f)	sinagoga (f)
telephone	teleefóon	téléphone (m)	teléfono (m)
today	al-yóom	aujourd'hui	hoy
toilet	tualét	toilette (f)	servicio (m)
tomorrow	búkra	demain	mañana
tower	qasr	tour (f)	torre (m)
Tunisia	Toónis	Tunisie (f)	Túnez (m)

	Arabic	French	Spanish
United States	al-wilayát al-muttáhida	Etats-Unis (m)	Estados Unidos (m)
washbasin	tusht	évier (m)	lavabo (m)
water(hot)	móyya (sukhna)	eau (chaude)	agua (caliente) (f)
week/year	usboo'/sána	semaine (f)/an (m)	semana (f)/año (m)
what?	shenu?	quoi?	¿qué?
when?	ímta?	quand?	¿cuándo?
where (is)?	wain?	oú (est)?	¿dónde (está)?
white	ábyad	blanc	blanco
why	laih	pourquoi	¿por qué?
yellow	ásfar	jaune	amarillo
yesterday	ams	hier	ayer

THE HISTORY OF NORTH AFRICA

The Sahara began to dessicate some 10,000 years ago and divided the Caucasoid populations of North Africa from the Negroid populations of West and Equatorial Africa. The original agricultural mode of production which had been the basis of settlement there was gradually replaced by nomadic pastoralism which, by around 4000 BC, had become the preserve of two groups, the Libyan-Berbers in the E part and the ancestors of the modern Touareg in the W. North African populations, all classified as part of the Hamito-Semitic group which stretched E into Arabia, soon became sub-divided into the Berbers in the W, the Egyptians in the E and the Nilo-Saharians and Kushites to the S in what today is Sudan.

Pharaonic Egypt

The key to the development of a complex civilization lay in the water and soils of the Nile valley. By 3000 BC, the Nile was supporting a dense sedentary agricultural society which produced a surplus and increasingly allowed socio-economic specialisation. This evolved into a system of absolute divine monarchy when the original 2 kingdoms were amalgamated by the victory of King Menes of Upper Egypt who then became the first Pharaoh. Pharaonic Egypt was limited by an inadequate resource base, being especially deficient in timber. Although it was forced to trade, particularly with the Levant (Eastern Mediterrean), it never became a major seafaring nation. Equally, the growing desertification of Libya meant that its influence never extended W. Instead, the Egyptian Empire sought control up the Nile valley, towards Kush (or Nubia) which it conquered as far S as the Fourth Cataract by 1500 BC. It also expanded E into the Levant, until it was restrained by the expanding civilisations of the Fertile Crescent after 2300 BC.

By 1000 BC, Pharaonic Egypt was being pressured from all sides. The Hyksos threatened the Delta from the Mediterranean, whilst the Lebu from Libya began to settle there too. They eventually created the 21st (Sheshonnaq) dynasty of the New Kingdom in 912 BC which, for a short time, extended its power E as far as Jerusalem. In the 7th century BC, however, Egypt was conquered by its Kushitic imitators to the S in the Nubian kingdom under King Piankhy who founded the 25th Pharaonic dynasty.

The Nubians were expelled some years later by the Assyrians, but their conquest marked the end of the greatness of Pharaonic Egypt. Thereafter, Egypt was to be a dependency of more powerful states in the Middle East or the Mediterranean. The rulers of Nubian Kush in their turn, having been expelled from Egypt, looked S from their new capital at Meroe – to which they had moved as a result of the subsequent Persian conquest of Egypt in 525 BC and later Persian attempts to conquer Kush. Kush became, instead, the vehicle of transmission of iron-working technology and of Egyptian concepts of divine political organisation southwards as well.

Greeks and Phoenicians

In North Africa, Egypt's failure to expand westward permitted other developments to occur. The North African coastal area became the arena for competition between those Mediterranean civilizations which had acquired a naval capacity – the Greeks and the Phoenicians. Indeed, this became the future pattern and resulted in the history of the region being described in the terms of its conquerers.

We do know, however, that the Greek and Phoenician settlements on the coast provoked a response from the nomadic communities of the desert – the Garamantes around the Fezzan in Libya, the Nigritae around Tuwat in modern Algeria and the Pharusii who were located in the Western Sahara. These communities appear to have specialized in warfare based on charioteering and they began to raid the new coastal settlements. At the same time, they also controlled trans-Saharan commerce – one of the major reasons why the Phoenicians, at least, were so interested in North Africa. As a result, they also engaged in trade with the new coastal communities, particularly those created by the Phoenicians. Other invasions also took place, this time of northeast Africa from Southern Arabia, bringing Arab tribes into Africa. The new Arab invaders spread rapidly into modern Ethiopia and Eritrea.

The Greeks had begun to colonize the Egyptian and eastern Libyan coastline as part of their attempt to control Egyptian maritime trade. Cyrene, the first of 5 Greek colonies in Cyrenaica in Libya, was founded about 625 BC and, a little earlier, 3 Phoenician colonies were created in Western Libya, on the coast of what is today Tripolitania – hence the name – in order to exploit new commercial opportunities, for the Phoenicians were first-and-foremost traders. More important, however, was the major Phoenician settlement at Carthage, on the coast of Northern Tunisia, close to the modern capital of Tunis, which was founded in 814 BC, in order to control access to Sicily.

Greeks and Phoenicians competed for control of the coastal areas in Libya and

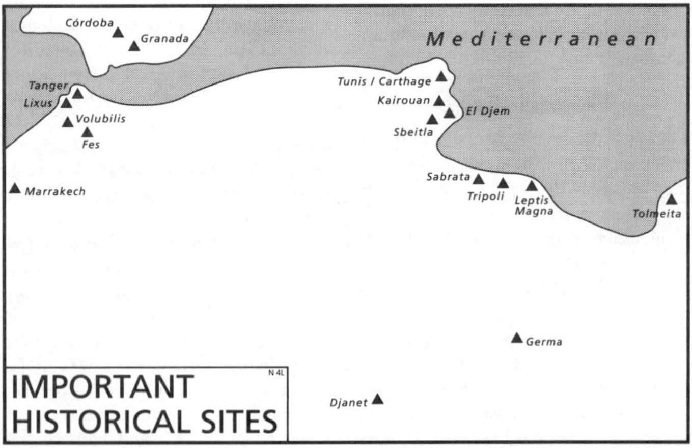

eventually created an uneasy division of the region between themselves. The Greeks took over Egypt after the creation of the Ptolemaic kingdom on the death of Alexander the Great in 323 BC and incorporated Cyrenaica into the new kingdom. The Phoenicians, by now being harried in their original Lebanese home base of Tyre by the Assyrians and Persians, created a new and powerful maritime commercial empire based on Carthage, with outlying colonies to the W, right round to the Atlantic coast at Lixus (Larache).

The Roman Empire

Control of North Africa passed on once again, this time to the rapidly expanding city-state of Rome. Control of the Ptolemaic kingdom of Egypt passed to Rome because of Roman interest in its agricultural produce and Egypt became a province of Rome in 30 BC. Cyrenaica had become a Roman province in 74 BC. Conflict with Carthage had begun much earlier because of its interest in Sicily which, for Rome, was of vital strategic importance. Although Carthage was expelled from Sicily in 201 BC, Rome still feared Carthaginian power and the city was eventually razed to the ground in 146 BC, after 3 years of warfare. The fertile plains around the city, a hinterland which had been its agricultural base and part of the Carthaginian Empire, were then converted into the Roman province of Africa.

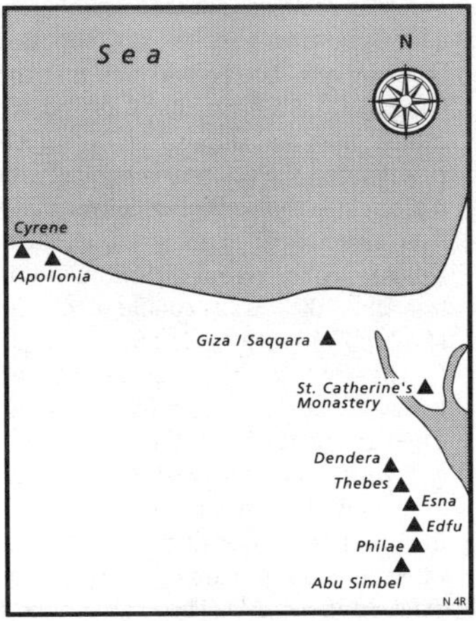

The difficult problem of border security for Roman administrators was solved by creating the **limes**, a border region along the desert edge which was settled with former legionaries as a militarized agriculturalist population. Thus, although the border region was permeable to trade, resistance to tribal incursion could be rapidly mobilized from the resident population, while regular forces were brought to the scene. The limes spread W from Egypt as far as the Moroccan Atlantic coast. In S Tunisia, the limes were reinforced by a ditch – the *fossia regia*.

By the beginning of the Christian era, North Africa had been organized into 4 Roman provinces: Proconsular Africa, Numidia, Mauritania Caesariana and Mauritania Tingitania. It had also become a major source of food for Rome and a major centre of Roman culture as the sedentary Berber populations themselves were Romanised. North Africa had, in short, ceased to be culturally part of Africa and was, instead, now part of the Mediterranean world. In addition to the commercial and cultural interpenetration of North Africa and Rome, this cultural interaction was intensified by 2 other factors. First, the region had long been in contact with Greek culture and, indeed, through the Phoenicians, with the culture of the Levant. Secondly, as a result of the destruction of the Kingdom of Judea in 70 AD, large numbers of Jews migrated into North Africa and Judaism intermixed with Berber culture to a significant extent, as contemporary Jewish traditions in Morocco and Tunisia make clear.

Christian North Africa

North African Christianity became the major focus of the development of Christian doctrine. The Coptic Church became the major proponent of Monophysitism after the Council of Chalcedon in 451 AD; Donatism dominated Numidia; and Tunisia was the home of the greatest of the early Christian fathers, St. Augustine. At the same time, official Christianity in Egypt – the Melkite Church – combined with the Coptic Church to convert areas to the S of Egypt to Christianity.

Political evolution, however, did not mirror the growth of Christian influence. In the 5th century, as the Roman Empire crumbled, North Africa was invaded by a Teutonic tribe based in Spain, the Vandals, who by 429 AD, had conquered as far as E Cyrenaica.

Byzantine control, of Tunisia at least, was restored by the Emperor Justinian and his general, Belisarius, in 533 AD. However it was unpopular, not least because of the onerous taxation system necessary to cover Byzantium's heavy military expenditure as it tried to confront the Sassanids in Asia as well as maintain its position in the Mediterranean. Hence when, a little more than a century later, Byzantine rule in Africa was threatened by the expansion of Islam, there was little enthusiasm to support its continuation in Northern Africa.

The Islamic period

In 642 AD, 10 years after the death of the Prophet Mohammad, Arab armies, acting as the vanguard of Islam, conquered Egypt. To secure his conquest, the Arab commander, Amr bin al-As, immediately decided to move W into Cyrenaica where the local Berber population submitted to the new invaders. Despite a constant pattern of disturbance, the Arab conquerers of Egypt and their successors did not ignore the potential of the region to the S. Nubia was invaded in 641-42 AD and again ten years later. Arab merchants and, later, bedouin tribes from Arabia were able to move freely throughout the S. However, until 665 AD, no real attempt was actually made to complete the conquest, largely because of internal problems within the new world of Islam. Then, after 2 feints SW towards the Fezzan, an army under Uqba bin Nafi conquered Tunisia and set up the first Arab centre there at Kairouan in 670 AD. Four years later, the Arabs in Kairouan were able to persuade Kusayla, the leader of the Berber confederation which spread right across Tunisia and modern Algeria as far as the Muluwiya river in Morocco, to convert to Islam. Shortly afterwards, Uqba bin Nafi, in a famous expeditionary raid to scout the unsubmitted areas to the W, swept across North Africa along the northern edge of the Sahara desert as far as the Atlantic coast of Morocco, into the land of the Sanhadja Berbers who dominated the major Western trans-Saharan trade routes.

These early conquests were ephemeral, being based on 2 mistaken assumptions. The first was that the new conquerers could afford to ignore the isolated Byzantine garrisons along the North African coast, because they would eventually collapse due to their isolation. The Byzantine navy, in fact, supplied them by sea. The second was that the Ommayyad Arab commanders and administrators now imposed on North Africa ignored the promises of equality of treatment given to Berber converts and thus encouraged a major rebellion, led by Kusayla. Arab control of Kairouan was lost and the Arab conquest of the Maghreb had to be undertaken again.

The first Arab move was against Kusayla, who was killed in 688 or 689 AD. Then after a further delay caused, once again, by unrest in the Levant, a new army moved northwards against Byzantine centres in Carthage and Bizerta, where the last remaining garrison was defeated in 690 AD. The Arab conquest came up against determined Berber resistance, this time in the Algerian Aurés where the core of the Berber Zenata confederation was led by al-Kahina, a Judaized or Christianised Berber priestess. Once again the Arabs retreated to Cyrenaica, returning to the attack only in 693 AD. In 697 AD, al-Kahina was killed and her forces defeated in a battle at Tubna in the Aurés which marked the start of a permanent Arab presence in North Africa.

The city of Tunis was founded to prevent further Byzantine encroachment at neighbouring Carthage and, under Musa bin Nusayr, Arab armies swept westwards to conquer Tanger in 704 AD. There they came to terms with the sole remaining Byzantine governor in North Africa, Julian of Ceuta, a Christian potentate who paid tribute to the new Muslim governor of neighbouring Tanger, Ziyad bin Tariq, in order to be confirmed in his post. Seven years later, Ziyad, with help from Julian who had maintained links with the Visigoth rulers of Spain, organized the Muslim invasion of the Iberian peninsula, starting at Gibraltar. By 732 AD, Muslim forces had conquered virtually all of Spain and Portugal and had even crossed the Pyrenees. The Muslim advance was stopped at or near to Poitiers by Charles Martel and, although, for the next 4 years, large parts of Provence were ravaged by marauding Muslim armies, the Muslim presence in Europe effectively ceased at the Pyrenees.

The early Islamic period

Despite their victory, the Ommayyads soon became very unpopular in North Africa where the egalitarian and revolutionary doctrines of the *kharejite* movement – that the caliphate should be elective, that a caliph who failed to uphold Islamic principle could be dismissed by the Muslim community and that sin automatically disqualified those involved from being considered to be Muslims – began to take root. Kharejite missionaries arrived in Kairouan in 719 AD and, within 30 years, the Berbers had become such enthusiastic supporters that they launched a rebellion against the Ommayyads at Tanger in 739-40 AD.

Although the rebellion was crushed, *kharajism* survived and, given the difficulties facing the Ommayyads in the Middle East where they were threatened by a new opposition, North Africa was left to its own devices. Ibadi kharajism gained the upper hand in Tripolitania and Sufri kharajism became dominant in southern Tunisia, while the core of Tunisia was left in the hands of the Fihrids, an Ommayyad Arab military caste now effectively abandoned by the Ommayyad caliphate in Damascus. The Ibadis eventually expanded their control throughout Tunisia and forced the Sufris westwards in 758 AD.

In 750 AD, the Ommayyad caliphate was destroyed by the Abbasids who rejected Ommayyad ideas of Arab superiority and supported the early Shi'a schismatic movement against the Sunni Muslim majority. Eight years later, the new Abbasid caliphate reconquered the old Arab province of Ifriquiya (modern Tunisia), but was unable to extend its authority further westward. In any case, the Abbasids did not have the resources to maintain a close control on such far-flung provinces and, by 800 AD, the Abbasid caliph in Baghdad, Harun al-Rashid allowed his governor in Ifriquiya, Ibrahim bin al-Aghlab, virtual autonomy. In effect, therefore, the Aghlabids became an independent dynasty in Tunisia until their downfall in 909 AD. The Aghlabids brought prosperity and high culture to Tunisia and, in 827 AD, began the Muslim conquest of Sicily.

The Aghlabids had to share North Africa with 3 other separate political authorities. After being expelled from Tripolitania, the Ibadis set up a separate state under Ibn Rustam at Tahert in central Algeria, which maintained close links with the Ibadi centre of Basra in southern Iraq. The Sufri Berbers of the Banu Midrar established their own state, based on their control of trans-Saharan trade, at Sijilmassa in southern Morocco. In the heartland of Morocco the Idrisids appeared, a new dynasty which, although not kharejite in belief, nevertheless was able to capture Berber support by claiming to be directly descended from the Prophet Mohammad. But, because they had supported a Shi'a rebellion against the Abbasids (who, once they had won control of the caliphate, rapidly abandoned Shi'ism in order to gain support for the Sunni majority) they had been forced to flee westwards into North Africa, an area outside Abbasid control. The founder of the dynasty, Idris bin Abdullah, arrived there in 788 AD. His son, Idris II, founded Fes in 809 AD and the dynasty survived until it was crushed by the Fatimids in 921 AD. Nonetheless, the Idrisids are the original founders of the modern Moroccan state and thus still have an influence even today.

The great dynasties and their successors

The failure of the Abbasid caliphate to retain control of North Africa paved the way for a series of local dynasties to take control.

(1) The Fatimids The first of the great dynasties that was to determine the future of North Africa did not, however, originate inside the region. Instead it used North Africa as a stepping stone towards its ambitions of taking over the Muslim world and imposing its own variant of Shi'a Islam. North Africa, because of its radical and egalitarian Islamic traditions, appears to have been the ideal starting point. The group concerned were the Isma'ilis who split off from the main body of Shi'a Muslims in 765 AD.

The Fatimids took control over what had been Aghlabid Ifriquiya, founding a new capital at Mahdia in 912 AD. Fatimid attention was concentrated on Egypt and, in 913-14 AD, a Fatimid army temporarily occupied Alexandria. The Fatimids also developed a naval force and their conquest of Sicily in the mid-10th century provided them with a very useful base for attacks on Egypt.

After suppressing a kharejite-Sunni rebellion in Ifriquiya between 943 AD and 947 AD, the Fatimids were ready to plan the final conquest of Egypt. This took place in 969 AD when the Fatimid general, Jawhar, finally subdued the country. The Fatimids moved their capital to Egypt, where they founded a new urban centre, al-Qahira (from which the modern name, Cairo, is derived) next to the old Roman fortress of Babylon and the original Arab settlement of Fustat.

The Fatimids' main concern was to take control of the Middle East. This meant that Fatimid interest in North Africa would wane and leave an autonomous Emirate there which continued to recognize the authority of the Fatimids, although it abandoned support for Shi'a Islamic doctrine.

(2) The Hillalian invasions Despite Fatimid concerns in the Middle East, the caliph in Cairo decided to return North Africa to Fatimid control. Lacking the means to do this himself, he used instead 2 tribes recently displaced from Syria and at that time residing in the Nile Delta – the Banu Sulaim and the Banu Hillal – as his troops. The invasions took place slowly over a period of around 50 years, starting in 1050 or 1051 AD, and probably involved no more than 50,000 individuals.

The Banu Sulaim settled in Cyrenaica, although, 2 centuries later, factions of the tribe also moved westwards towards Tripolitania and Tunisia. The Banu Hillal continued westwards, defeating and destroying the Zirids in a major battle close to Gabés in 1052.

The Hillalian invasions were a major and cataclysmic event in North Africa's history. They destroyed organized political power in the region and ensured the break up of the political link between Muslim North Africa and the Middle East. They also damaged the trading economy of the region. There was a major cultural development too for the Hillalian invasions, more than any other event, ensured that Arabic eventually became the majority language of the region.

(3) Egypt after the Fatimids Fatimid power in Egypt did not endure for long. They were forced to rely on a slave army recruited from the Turks of Central Asia and from the Sudanese. They found it increasingly difficult to control these forces and, eventually, became their victims. In 1073 AD, the commander of the Fatimid army in Syria, which had been recalled to restore order in Egypt, took power and the Fatimid caliph was left only with the prestige of his office.

What remained of the Fatimid Empire was now left virtually defenceless towards the E and the Seljuk Turks, who were already moving W, soon took advantage of this weakness. They were spurred on by the growth of Crusader power in the Levant and, after this threat had been contained, Egypt soon fell under their sway. Control of Egypt passed to Salah ad-Din ibn Ayyubi in 1169 AD and, for the next 80 years, the Ayyubids ruled in Cairo until, they in their turn, were displaced by their Mamluk slaves.

The first Mamluk dynasty, the Bahri Mamluks, were excellent administrators and soldiers. They expanded their control of the Levant and the Hijaz and extended their influence into Nubia. They cleared the Crusaders out of the Levant and checked the Mongol advance into the Middle East in the 1250s. They also improved Egypt's economy and developed its trading links with Europe and Asia. Indeed, the fact that the Mamluks were able to control and profit from the growing European trade with the Far East via Egypt was a major factor in their economic success.

In 1382 AD, the Bahri Mamluks were displaced from power by the Burgi Mamluks. Their control of Egypt was a period of instability and decline. The Ottoman Turks, in a swift campaign in 1516-17, eliminated them and turned Egypt into a province of the Ottoman Empire.

(4) The Almoravids The power vacuum left in the wake of the Hillalian invasions was filled by religious revivalism amongst the Lamtuna tribe, under the influence of a religious scholar, Abdullah ibn Yasin. He transformed the lackadaisical religious observance into a dynamic, inspiring, fully integrated and committed Islamic community. He called his new community the *dar al-murabitun* – the House of the people of the *ribat* (the Muslim equivalent of a monastic retreat, dedicated to preparation for *jihad*), now corrupted to 'Almoravid'.

Religious committment spurred them on. Ibn Yasin was succeeded by Yusuf Ibn Tashfin who led the Almoravids to victory over most of western North Africa as far as Algiers and over the southern half of Spain between 1060 AD and the end of the century. The Almoravids managed, however, to offend established religious leaders and the *Sufi* orders (mystical religious orders) of North Africa by their religious intolerance and rigidity. They also failed to check Christian expansionism in Spain. As a result, when a major rebellion against their authority began close to their capital of Marrakech in 1125 AD, it was not long before they were overthrown.

(5) The Almohads The Almohads (from *al-muwahhidun* – the unitarians) also began as a religious revivalist movement, this time amongst the Masmouda Berbers of the High Atlas close to Marrakech. They were inspired by a religious leader from the Hargha tribe of the Masmouda, located in the Anti-Atlas mountains, Muhammad ibn Tumart, who was born in 1080 AD. He studied in Spain and the Middle East before returning to Morocco, where he sought support for a revivalist movement designed to purify Islamic doctrine and practice.

The Almohads were organized on a tribal basis and, when Ibn Tumart died in 1130 AD, the most capable tribal leader, Abd al-Mumin, took over. In 1145 AD Abd al-Mumin crushed the Almoravids and, 2 years later, occupied the 2 leading cities of Fes and Marrakech, the latter of which became the Almohad capital.

The Almohads first moved against the Christian *Reconquista* in Spain, where they held the Christian advance towards Granada and Sevilla, although the ruler of Murcia managed to remain independent until 1172 AD. The more important move was against the growing threat of the Normans in the central Mediterranean. By 1160 AD, the Almohads had expelled the Normans from North Africa and had united the region under a single political authority.

The Almohad state was sapped by its essentially tribal political structure. In 1207 in Ifriquiya, the son of the Almohad governor, Abu Hafs Umar, a close associate of Ibn Tumart, created an independent Hafsid state which governed Tunisia until the Ottoman occupation in the 16th century. In a similar fashion, control of the Central Maghreb devolved on the Banu Zayyan clan of the Banu Abd al-Wad in 1233 AD. However it was the Banu Marin, who created the Marinid state in Morocco, who sealed the fate of the Almohads. The Banu Marin were a Zenata Berber tribe of pastoralists located in the lower Moulouya valley and around Figuig.

(6) The successor states The disappearance of the Almohads brought the era of the great unifying North African dynasties to an end. Thereafter power would reflect the division of the region, rather than its unity. There would also be a change in direction and influence, for now Christianity and Europe would increasingly dominate the North African horizon, as would the Mediterranean as a zone of conflict. Yet the experience of the Fatimids, the Hillalian invasions, the Almoravids and the Almohads did leave an important monument behind.

The Marinids Marinid expansionism was related to 2 factors: first a desire to take complete control of Trans-Saharan trade, for the Moroccan route was losing importance to those routes to the East, and, second, to counter growing Christian influence in Spain and in the Mediterranean. In 1291 AD, during the Marinid period, Castilla and Aragón came to an agreement to divide the North African world between them, in terms of commercial and diplomatic penetration. Castilla concerned itself exclusively with Morocco, while Aragón, by now the dominant trading power in the western Mediterranean, handled the Hafsids and the Zayyanids. The Marinids feared that they would not be able to exclude direct Castillian interference nor protect the remnants of the Muslim Empire in Spain. Indeed, all that was left was the Nasrid state in Granada which had been founded in 1238 AD and was to provide a final flowering of Islamic art in Spain. The Nasrid state was a useful buffer for the Marinids, although the Nasrids themselves were very ambivalent about Marinid support and often allied themselves with Christian powers for protection.

In the end, the Marinid state could not support such expansionist policies and their internal quarrelling made them easy prey for Portuguese aggressiveness. When Portugal occupied Ceuta in 1415 AD, Marinid prestige immediately declined and over the next 50 years the situation worsened as the Marinids faced threats from the Portuguese and their successors, the Wattasids (their former viziers).

They also had to face a new development in Morocco, the rapid growth of the Sufi cults which had developed in power and prestige after the discovery of the tomb of Idris II in 1437 AD. Political legitimisation now increasingly became a function of Sharifian descent (genealogical descent from the Prophet Mohammad) or of attachment to a Sufi order. The Marinids and the Wattasids failed both tests and, when the Portuguese occupied Ksar al-Kabir in 1458 AD, Tanger in 1471 AD, Larache in 1473 AD and Azzemour in 1486 AD, the final collapse of the dynasty was merely a matter of time. The Marinid role as defenders of the state had been taken up by Sharifian and *Sufi* groups. It was the latter who ultimately took over the state.

The Hafsids The new Hafsid state saw itself as the legitimate successor to the Almohads and its ruler as caliph. The claim was widely accepted, even in the Middle East, because the foundation of the Hafsid state coincided with the Mongol invasions which destroyed Baghdad and the last vestiges of the Abbasid caliphate in 1250 AD. But in reality, the Hafsid state lacked the social and political cohesion of its predecessor. Thus its long history was marked by the constant interplay of internal conflict between different members of the Hafsid family and with Arab and other tribal leaders who sought supreme power. Like the Marinid state, it also had to integrate increasing numbers of Muslims and Jews emigrating from al-Andalus.

It had to deal with an ever greater Christian threat. This came in 2 forms: direct aggression, such as the 8th crusade, led by the French King Louis IX, which beseiged Tunis unsuccessfully in 1270 AD, and commercial penetration. In the early part of the 13th century, the great Italian trading cities of Pisa, Genoa and Venice, together with the French of Provence, obtained trading and residence rights in Ifriquiya. The most important example of commercial penetration came from Aragón. The Aragonese had created a major trading empire in the Western Mediterranean and, after 1246 AD, Aragón had an ambassador in Tunis, the Hafsid capital. This was followed by mercantile representation after 1253 AD. After Aragón annexed Sicily in 1282 AD, this commercial hegemony was backed by military dominance as well.

By 1318 AD Aragonese influence was on the wane and Hafsid fortunes revived. The Hafsid state was, nonetheless, a Mediterranean state rather than one with its attention directed towards Africa or the Middle East. Its finances increasingly depended on piracy. By the end of the 15th century Hafsid influence had declined once again. Spain, the new threat to the Mediterranean Muslim world, annexed Tripoli in Libya and Bejaïa in Western Algeria in 1510 AD, as the first move in a widening penetration into the Maghreb. The Hafsids lingered on until 1574 AD, when the Ottoman Turks destroyed their state.

The Zayyanids The Zayyanid state, based at Tlemcen, was always a buffer between the Hafsids and the Marinids. It suffered from internal struggles for leadership among the 3 Zenata tribes that dominated it; it controlled a major trans-Saharan trade route; and it was dominated, first by the Marinids and later by the Hafsids. The Zayyanids, like the Hafsids, could not resist the Ottoman invasion of North Africa and disappeared at the start of the 16th century.

The Ottomans in North Africa

The arrival of the Ottomans in North Africa was the last invasion of the region before the colonial period began in the 19th century.

Events in Morocco

The 16th century was dominated by events outside the Ottoman sphere of control. The Marinid state in Morocco eventually collapsed when confronted with a Sharifian Dynasty, the Saadians, who conquered Marrakech in 1525 and Fes 29 years later. They were able to resist too close an Ottoman embrace, particularly after Portuguese influence was eliminated. Morocco became, under the Sadis, a powerful Muslim state entering into close relations with other nations, even in Europe, where a close relationship developed with Elizabethan England.

The Saadian dynasty fell into decline and political power in Morocco was seized by a series of powerful **Sufi** orders. The result was the growth of a series of petty states ultimately overwhelmed by the Alawite Dynasty. The Alawites were a Sharifian community that had been living in Sijilmassa since the 13th century.

Mawlay Isma'il, who reigned until 1727, set the Alawite state on firm foundations. He removed the European presence from the Moroccan coastline, except in Ceuta and Melilla, and forced back Turkish incursions from the E. He based his claim to power on his Sharifian status, a claim which has been astutely exploited by his predecessors to underpin their legitimacy, even when much of Morocco – the **bilad as-siba** – lay outside the area under their control – the **bilad al-makhzan**. The Alawite success was to be enduring, for the dynasty still rules Morocco today.

During the remainder of the 18th century, the Alawites concentrated on retaining their power. The Sultanate had to ensure that Turkish ambitions to expand into eastern Morocco were curbed and come to terms with the growth of European power. By the start of the 19th century, the Sultanate abandoned its traditional support for corsairing, banned in 1817, just one year after the last Christian slaves had been released. A few years later came France's invasion of Algeria and, in 1844, Morocco was defeated by French troops pursuing the great Algerian resistance leader, the Emir Abd al-Qadir. The defeat was a tremendous shock to Morocco, as its leaders realised they could no longer ignore the European threat. From their base in Tanger, the European consuls made ever greater demands on the Sultanate for commercial contact and, in 1856, Britain and Morocco signed an open-door treaty.

Spain, still present in her enclaves of Ceuta and Melilla, resented British influence over the Sultanate and 4 years later, on the pretext of tribal incursions into its territory, successfully fought a short border war with Morocco. Although the Sultanate survived, in 1880 it was forced to permit extra-territorial rights to Moroccan citizens employed by the European powers – the so-called 'protégé' system.

By the start of the 20th century, events accelerated as Morocco incurred foreign debt and mortgaged its customs revenues to pay off the loans. France, at that stage, began a slow penetration into Moroccan territory. Touat was occupied in 1902, Casablanca in 1907 and Fes in 1911. In every case, furious tribal resistance to French moves only provoked further French advances. Spain, too, began to move into Northern Morocco, a zone allocated to her by a secret agreement with France in 1904. The Treaty of Fes of 1912 instituted a Franco-Spanish 'protectorate' over the state.

The Ottoman occupation

The Ottoman occupation of North Africa was a by-product of Ottoman-Venetian competition for control of the Mediterranean, itself part of the boundless expansionism of the Ottomans once they had conquered Constantinople in 1453. The Ottoman attack was two-pronged, involving their newly acquired maritime power to establish a foothold and then backing it up with the janissary, land based forces that formed the empire's troops. The decrepit Mamluk Dynasty in

Egypt fell to the Ottomans in 1517 and a new, centralized Ottoman administration was established there.

Ottoman interests were soon attracted westward and a maritime campaign was launched on the North African coastline. It was carried out mainly by privateers, attracted both by the religious confrontation between Christian powers in Southern Europe and Islam in North Africa and by the growing practice of corsairing. In the wake of the *Reconquista* in 1492, Spain began to prepare for a veritable crusade against North Africa. Two years later Spain and Portugal, with Papal blessing, divided their future spheres of influence in North Africa between them and, 3 years later, the Spanish occupation began with the conquest of Melilla.

The Ottoman moves on North Africa were precipitated by the privateering activities of the Barbarossa brothers, Uruj and Khayr al-Din. The Ottomans eventually occupied Tunis permanently in 1574. Before this, however, they had gained a hold over Libya. Khayr al-Din Barbarossa occupied Tajura, on the coast close to Tripoli, in 1531 and was consequently able to threaten the precarious hold of the Knights of the Order of St John of Jerusalem on Tripoli itself. They had just occupied Tripoli and Malta at the request of Charles V of Spain, but were forced out of Tripoli altogether by the Ottomans in 1551. For 270 years North Africa, except for Morocco, was an Ottoman preserve.

The Barbary regencies

Direct control from Istanbul did not last long. The North African coastline was divided into a series of administrative units, with power divided between the bashas, sent from Istanbul, the deys who were in charge of the permanent janissary garrisons and, in Algiers at least, the taifa, the captains of the corsairing privateers that continued to operate.

Tripoli

At the beginning of the 18th century, the final formal links with Istanbul were broken. In 1711 a dynasty was founded in Tripoli by Ahmad Karamanli, who seized power in the temporary absence of the Ottoman governor and then massacred the leaders of the janissaries. The new autonomous government eventually controlled Tripolitania and the coastal regions of Cyrenaica. After a tussle for influence in Tripoli between Britain and France, the Ottoman Empire re-occupied the Regency of Tripoli and ejected the Karamanlis in 1835.

Algiers

In Algeria, the Ottomans organized a military administration which soon forced the Spanish out of their enclaves at Wahran (Oran) and Tlemcen. This new Ottoman possession suffered from continual struggles between the janissaries and the *taifa*. In 1671, the *taifa* turned on the janissaries, assassinating the *agha*. In his place they elected a *dey* who shared formal power with the Sultan's *basha*. Algiers, too, had effectively broken away from Istanbul's control.

The Regency of Algiers became a major corsairing centre during the 18th century. The more powerful European states expressed their displeasure by raiding North African corsairing ports, while their weaker colleagues bought immunity by paying tributes.

In 1827, the Dey of Algiers, enraged at the insolence of the French consul during an argument over debt, struck him with a fly whisk. In 1830 Charles X, the last Bourbon ruler of France, casting around for some way of distracting the military elite from threatening his régime's survival, recalled the incident of the insult to French dignity and ordered the invasion of Algiers. After an unopposed landing at Sidi Fredj, close to Algiers, the city was occupied without a fight and the Regency of Algiers came to an end.

Tunis

Once the Spaniards had been driven out of Tunisia and the remnants of the Hafsid dynasty had been eliminated, the Ottoman commander, Sinan Pasha, organized an administration similar to that in Algiers. By 1591, a system of janissary leadership through the *dey* was imposed on the Ottoman-appointed *basha* but rural administration was entrusted to another official, the *bey*, a post which soon rivalled the power of the *dey*. In 1702 the two offices were combined. After defeating an attempt by the Regency of Algiers to conquer Tunisia in 1705, Husayn bin Ali became bey and initiated the Husaynid Dynasty that ruled Tunisia until 1957. Following his accession to power, Tunisia effectively became independent of Istanbul and was known as the Regency of Tunis.

By the 19th century, the rule of the *bey* had become corrupt, and remote. European interference in Tunisian affairs had became more intrusive resulting in a growing European population which enjoyed extra-territorial rights under the 'Capitulations' system, and European consuls who became ever more powerful. Domestic unrest increased and in 1860, the *bey*, in desperation, granted Tunisians the Arab world's first constitution, the *Destour*. By 1868 the economic crisis had worsened and European powers insisted on a debt commission being instituted to handle Tunisia's finances in order to ensure repayment.

In 1878, the Congress of Berlin decided that Tunisia should fall under French influence. Then, in 1881, on the grounds that the Khroumir border tribe had been raiding into French-controlled Algeria, France invaded Tunisia and, in a rapid campaign, took control of the country.

Egypt and Sudan

In Egypt, the newly centralized Ottoman administration soon found itself struggling against the unreconstructed remnants of Mamluk society, with the province frequently splitting into 2 units, each controlled by a different section of the Mamluk dynasty. By 1786, the Ottomans had destroyed the Mamluk factions and restored central control. In 1798, Napoleon's army conquered Egypt, delivering a profound cultural shock to the Muslim world by demonstrating, in the most graphic manner, the technological superiority of Europe. In 1805 Muhammad Ali was appointed governor and lost no time in breaking away from the Ottoman Empire to found a new dynasty, the *khedivate*, which remained in power until a revolution in 1952.

Muhammad Ali sought to modernize Egypt and to expand its power. He brought in European military advisers, destroyed the remnants of the old political elite in Egypt and instituted wide-ranging economic reforms. In the Sudan, Muhammad Ali's Egypt was more successful; after the initial invasion in 1820, some 40 years were spent consolidating Egyptian rule, although, in 1881, the experiment failed.

By that time, Egypt itself had succumbed to the financial pressures of its modernisation programme. Borrowings from Europe began, with the inevitable consequence of unrepayable debt. In addition, Britain realized the potential importance of Egypt for access to its Indian Empire, particularly after the Suez Canal was opened in 1869. A debt administration was instituted in 1875, under joint British and French control. In 1881 AD, a nationalist officers' rebellion against what they saw as excessive European influence in the *khedivate*, provoked a British take-over which lasted until 1922. Following General Gordon's death in Khartoum and the consequent British campaign against the Mahdist state in the Sudan, which culminated in the Battle of Omdurman in 1898, Britain instituted an Anglo-Egyptian condominium over Sudan.

Colonialism in North Africa

The colonial experience throughout North Africa took many different forms. It was to involve 4 European states: Britain in Egypt and, after WWII, in part of Libya; Italy in Libya up to WWII, together with residual interests in Tunisia; Spain in northern Morocco and in the Sahara desert to the S of the country; and, of course, France, which controlled Tunisia, Algeria and most of Morocco, as well as the southern part of Libya after WWII. Colonialism was to take different forms, as well. In Algeria and Libya full colonial occupation was instituted, with a degree of integration into the administration and political structures of the metropolitan power. In Egypt, Tunisia and Morocco, a form of protectorate was instituted whereby the colonial power was present as a tutor, with the object of modernising political structures and the economy before restoring full Independence.

Colonialism in Egypt and Sudan

The British occupation of Egypt introduced a régime which, as the well known historian Ira Lapidus said 'managed the Egyptian economy efficiently but in the imperial interest'. Railways were built and widespread irrigation was introduced; the population virtually doubled inside 35 years; private property was increasingly concentrated in the hands of a new elite; and the foreign debt was repaid. Industrialisation was, however, neglected and Egypt became ever more dependent on cotton exports for revenue.

Social and political relations were not so smooth. The British occupation of Egypt coincided with a wave of Islamic revivalism. At the same time, a secular nationalist tradition was developing in Egypt which crystallized into a political movement at the end of the 19th century and was stimulated by Egyptian resentment at British demands on Egypt during WWI.

After 3 years of agitation Britain granted limited independence in 1922. It retained control of foreign affairs, foreigners in Egypt, the Sudan and the Egyptian army although some of these controls were abandoned in 1936. By the end of WWII, this complex political system had outlived its usefulness. In 1950, Egypt unilaterally abrogated the Canal Zone Treaty. After 2 years of guerrilla warfare and a military coup in Cairo which ended the *khedivate*, Britain finally agreed to abandon its position in the Canal Zone and its remaining hold over Egypt in 1952.

In Sudan, following the Battle of Omdurman in 1898 and the institution of the Anglo-Egyptian Condominium – in which Britain retained the upper hand – the administration was reformed and the economy stimulated. Care was taken to defuse religious antagonism although Mahdism was suppressed. In 1916, the autonomous Sultanate of Darfur was integrated into the Anglo-Egyptian administration.

With the beginning of the *Wafd*-led agitation for Independence in Egypt in 1919, the British authorities in Khartoum reduced Egyptian influence in the administration of Sudan. At the end of 1923, the Egyptian army in Sudan was ordered out and a minor pro-Egyptian rebellion by Sudanese troops was crushed. Remaining Egyptian administrative officials were removed and Britain's control of Sudan was complete.

By the end of WWII, in which Sudan was more directly involved than Egypt because of the Italian presence in Abyssinia, it had become clear that the British presence in Sudan could not endure for long. Indeed, moves towards Sudanese Independence went hand-in-hand with developments in Egypt and internal self government was introduced in 1952. By late 1955, it had become evident that full Independence was inevitable and on January 1, 1956, the British and Egyptian flags were lowered for the last time.

The colonial period in Libya

The re-imposition of Ottoman rule in Libya in 1835 marked an end to the corsairing economy of the Regency of Tripoli. Ottoman control was never fully applied throughout the country.

The Sanusi Order, which was named after its Algerian founder, Sayyid Muhammad bin Ali al-Sanusi was an Islamic revivalist movement. It chose the Sahara for its arena and settled amongst the Cyrenaican tribes, where it was welcomed for its piousness and for its ability to arbitrate tribal disputes. Later on, the Order also coordinated tribal resistance throughout the Sahara to French colonial penetration. The Order also began to control the eastern trade routes across the Sahara and, as a result, effectively became, an autonomous government of the central Saharan region. In Cyrenaica its power was so great that, outside the major urban settlements such as Benghazi, the Ottomans accepted it as the de facto government and a Turkish-Sanusi condominium developed.

The Ottoman administration in Tripoli had to cope with continuing European pressure, particularly from Italy and Malta. British and French influence led to the end of the slave trade towards the end of the 19th century, while the economy of Tripoli became increasingly integrated into the global economy of the Mediterranean region. By the start of the 20th century Italy's intention to colonize Tripolitania, Cyrenaica and the Fezzan became clear.

Fighting broke out between tribes backed by dissident Ottoman officers and the Italian army. The outbreak of WWI allowed the Ottoman Empire to provide military aid to the resistance and eventually a peace agreement was signed between Italy and the Sanusi at Akrama in Apr 1917. In 1922, with the Fascists in power, Italy again decided to occupy Libya. The second Italo-Sanusi war was between the Italians and the bedouin of Cyrenaica, for resistance in Tripolitania and the Fezzan was quickly broken. The ferocious struggle continued to 1930 when the last remnants of resistance were wiped out and Italy finally occupied the vast Libyan desert hinterland.

The Fascist victory was short-lived, for the Italian army was forced out of Libya during WWII and British military administrations took over in Cyrenaica and Tripolitania with the French in Fezzan. Under the Italians, Libya had acquired the basic elements of a communications infrastructure and some modernisation of the economy. It had also acquired a 50,000 strong Italian settler population, a substantial portion of whom remained until they were expelled by the Ghadhafi régime in 1970.

The situation of Libya posed problems. By the end of WWII it had acquired strategic significance for Britain and, after the Cold War began, for the USA as well. Britain had promised Cyrenaica that Italian control would never be restored. A series of proposals were made including Soviet Union trusteeship over Libya and the Bevin-Sforza Plan, whereby Britain would take a mandate for Cyrenaica, Italy for Tripolitania and France for the Fezzan for a period of 10 years, after which the country would be granted Independence. These were clearly unacceptable to the Libyans themselves, and the whole issue was dropped in the lap of the newly created United Nations in 1949.

The United Nations' special commissioner was able to convince all the Libyan factions that the only solution was a federal monarchy, bringing the provinces of Cyrenaica, Tripolitania and the Fezzan together under the Sanusi monarchy of Sayyid Idris. In Dec 1951, the independent Kingdom of Libya came into being.

Colonialism in the Maghreb

Algeria

The French conquest of Algiers in 1830

drew the army ever further into the interior. French forces fanned out westward, and came into contact with the forces of the Amir Abd al-Qadir, who had created a major tribal confederacy to resist further French advances. In 1847, after a brutal campaign of repression under General Bugeaud and a short border war with Morocco, culminating in the Moroccan defeat at the battle of Isly in 1844, Abd al-Qadir was forced into exile. By that time French forces had conquered the eastern region around Constantine and were moving into the vast reaches of the Sahara.

Settler colonisation was encouraged and soon there was a substantial European population living in Algeria with an administration tied into that of France. Emperor Napoleon III's attempt to create a pattern of indirect administration which would allow Algerian society to survive its colonial experience collapsed in 1871 and by the end of the 19th century Algeria was fully integrated into France from an administrative point of view.

Algeria was required to contribute heavily to the French war effort in WWI, particularly in the provision of manpower. This led to demands for a reform of the relationship between Algeria and France. In the event, the French government reneged on promises to reform it had made during the war. The 1930s were a period of political stagnation and economic deprivation, as the Great Depression hit North Africa. The result was massive rural depopulation and severe economic hardship which resulted in serious famine. Some minor reforms were introduced but there was no evidence at all that real change would ever occur.

WWII changed the picture, for France's defeat at the hands of the Germans destroyed the myth of French invincibility. The disappointment of Algerians who had served during the hostilities and returned home expecting radical change, resulted in the development of a new strand in Algerian nationalism. Many of its founding members had also had experience of army service in French colonies. They envisaged a secret organisation that would launch a guerrilla campaign against the French presence in Algeria and thereby obtain popular support.

The War of Independence raged for the next 8 years. Although the French army eventually contained the war within Algeria, the measures it used only stimulated popular support for Independence and for the FLN that they had been designed to crush. At the same time, settler anxieties over the vacillations of governments in Paris led to a combined army-settler revolt in Algiers in 1958 which brought General Charles de Gaulle to power in France. De Gaulle eventually accepted the Evian Accords which, in 1962, gave Algeria complete Independence.

Tunisia

In the immediate aftermath of the installation of the French Protectorate, Tunisian resistance was confined to tribal groups in the S of the country. Opposition to colonial occupation gradually began to gather strength reflecting popular opposition to the growing and predominantly Italian European settler colony in Tunisia, a colony totalling around 100,000 people and controlling some 800,000 ha of Tunisia's best agricultural land.

The opposition was led by a young, French-trained lawyer, Habib Bourguiba, who wanted a far more radical approach towards the French presence. In 1934, Habib Bourguiba took over the movement, now renamed the neo-Destour. French reaction to this radicalisation was very repressive until WWII when Tunisia was eventually occupied by Allied forces. In the wake of the war, it became clear that some concessions to nationalist sentiment would have to be made.

Before this was done, France tried to

enforce its position in Tunisia by requiring the Bey to accept the idea of 'co-sovereignty', whereby France would gain permanent rights to Tunisian territory. Following this attempt by France in 1950 to gain a firmer foothold inside North Africa, the nationalist movement under Habib Bourguiba took on the characteristics of a mass movement. As a result, Habib Bourguiba was able to negotiate autonomy for Tunisia in 1955 and in 1956, when Morocco was granted Independence, Tunisia soon followed suit.

Morocco

Colonialism came to Morocco far later than it did to its 2 Maghrebi partners. Indeed, the colonial period only lasted 44 years in Morocco and the country was not fully pacified until 1934, just 22 years before Independence was granted. In addition, the initial colonial experience was less severe in Morocco than in either Tunisia or Algeria, largely because it was carefully controlled by one man, Marshall Hubert Lyautey. Apart from a short break during WWI, he remained in charge of Morocco until his final recall in 1925. Lyautey was determined to preserve traditional Moroccan political institutions whilst modernising them and tried to avoid major violence in pacifying tribal rural Morocco, preferring instead a mixture of coercion and persuasion.

Northern Morocco, was occupied by Spain and the Spanish army experienced serious difficulties in controlling the Rif. In 1921, a major anti-colonial war broke out under Abd al-Karim, which eventually required a combined Franco-Spanish army of 500,000 to suppress it in 1926.

In the aftermath of the Rif War, the first stirrings of nationalist resistance appeared. The movement sprang into public prominence in 1930. WWII and the Allied occupation of Morocco in 1942 had ended the myth of French omnipotence and in 1944, with secret support from the Sultanate, **Istiqlal**, a movement demanding full Independence, was formed.

Riots in Casablanca in 1947 persuaded Sultan Mohammed V openly to support Istiqlal; which he did during a speech in Tanger. Popular support for Independence and for the Sultan as the symbol of Morocco's political integrity burgeoned, and in March 1956, Morocco became an independent state. Spain hurried to follow the French example, retaining control only of its towns on Morocco's Mediterranean coast, the enclave of Sidi Ifni (which it abandoned in 1969) and the colony of the Western Sahara which, it claimed, had never formed part of Morocco historically.

Mauritania

Until 1960, Mauritania had had no independent national existence. Instead it was traditionally divided between the nomadic populations of the Sahara desert and the sedentary populations of the Senegal river valley. Population pressures in the Sahara had, however, consistently forced excess population northwards into Morocco. Indeed, as with the Lamtuna in the 11th century, these northward migrations could have profound political significance, for it generated the empire of the Almoravids. The Zenata Berber tribes of the Sahara were intermingled from the 13th century onwards with Arab migrants, particularly the Banu Hassan. These Arab tribes effectively Arabised the Saharan populations and gave them their characteristics as the Moors of Mauritania. By the 17th century, the Arab tribes dominated their Berber neighbours and in 1674, the latter were symbolically subjugated to their Arab victors as *Zawaya* tribes.

For the history of the region after Independence, see individual country entries: (Morocco, see page 202; Mauritania, page 371; Algeria, page 410; Tunisia, page 491; Libya, page 608; Egypt, page 694; and Sudan page 896).

ANDALUCIA

Contents

Maps

Introduction

The name Andalucía is properly applied to the area of Iberia occupied by the Muslims in the period from 711 AD for approximately 5 centuries. Because Arab rule encompassed all of Iberia immediately after the conquest, indeed, pushing deep into France before being reversed at the battle of Poitiers in 732, the term Andalucía can in a historical sense loosely be applied to almost any area of Spain. The longest and most concentrated rule of the Moors was in the S. This lasted until the fateful battle of Navas de Tolosa in 1212, after which the residual territories under Muslim rule broke up to leave only the Kingdom of Granada as an effective independent state until 1492. Present day Andalucía takes in this area of the S which was longest and most thoroughly under Arab control.

Basics

OFFICIAL NAME Comunidad Autónoma de Andalucía (Autonomous Community of Andalucía).

REGIONAL FLAG Rectangular with 3 equal horizontal fields green, white, green.

OFFICIAL LANGUAGE Castilian Spanish.

OFFICIAL RELIGION None.

INDICATORS *Population* 6.86 mn. *Urban population* 80%. *Religion* Roman Catholic 97.0%. *Birth rate* 10.7 per 1,000. *Death rate* 8.2 per 1,000. *Life expectancy* 74 (men)/80 (women).

Environment

Land

Andalucía is some 103,000 sq km in area, about 20.5% of Spain, larger than Austria or Ireland and well over half the size of Tunisia.

Borders Andalucía comprises 8 administrative provinces – Almería, Cádiz, Córdoba, Granada, Huelva, Jaén, Málaga and Sevilla – and is the largest region of Spain. It is bounded to the N by the Sierra Morena and its adjacent E ranges, the Sierra Madroña and Sierra Aguila, and ends in the E in the coastal basins of Almería and Garrucha. In the W, Andalucía borders with the Portuguese Algarve, a cultural extension of Moorish Spain, and is elsewhere bounded by the Atlantic Ocean. To the S, the Mediterranean Sea coastline defines the region along the Costa del Sol. Gibraltar remains as a small appendage to Andalucía and is heavily dependent upon it to maintain its population and standard of living.

Main Regions The region naturally falls into 4 large zones, (1) the N moun-

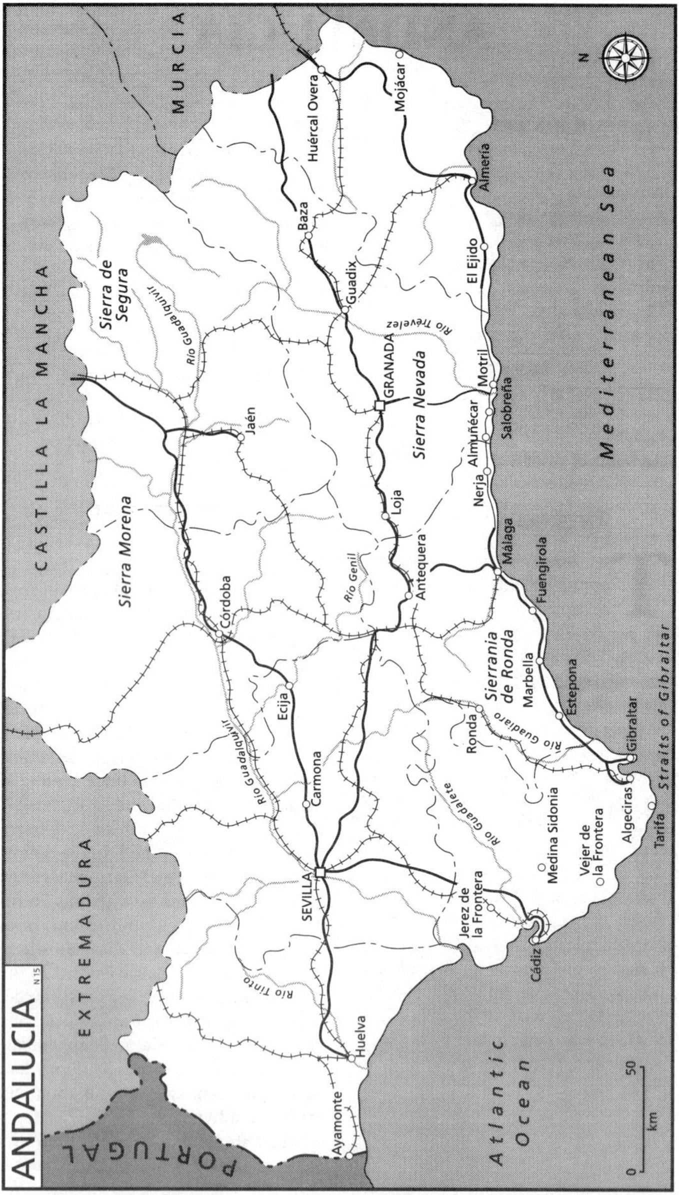
ANDALUCIA
N 15
PORTUGAL
EXTREMADURA
CASTILLA LA MANCHA
MURCIA
Sierra Morena
Sierra de Segura
Río Guadalquivir
Río Guadalquivir
Río Tinto
Río Genil
Río Trevélez
Sierra Nevada
Sierrania de Ronda
Río Guadiaro
Río Guadalete
Huércal Overa
Mojácar
Baza
Almería
Guadix
El Ejido
GRANADA
Motril
Salobreña
Almuñécar
Jaén
Nerja
Loja
Málaga
Antequera
Fuengirola
Córdoba
Marbella
Estepona
Ecija
Ronda
Gibraltar
Carmona
Algeciras
Medina Sidonia
Tarifa
SEVILLA
Vejer de la Frontera
Jerez de la Frontera
Cádiz
Huelva
Ayamonte
Atlantic Ocean
Mediterranean Sea
Straits of Gibraltar
N
0 50 km

tains dominated by the Sierra Morena, (2) the valley of the Guadalquivir and its delta (see page 143), (3) the southern sierras running in a broken chain from the Sierra del Aljibe above Jimena de la Frontera to the magnificent Sierra Nevada in the E and (4) the Mediterranean coastal plain, narrow and discontinuous except around Málaga and Almería, known as the Costa del Sol, see page 108. The region is above all mountainous with more than 75% of land over 1,000m, which in part explains the stronger survival of Moorish culture in this area than in the rest of Spain.

The Guadalquivir (from the Arabic *Wad Al-Kebir*) valley and the delta are flatlands, rich in alluvial soils and with abundant water for irrigation. Much of the delta itself, with its triangular limits set by the towns of Sevilla, Cádiz and Huelva, is only comparatively recently reclaimed from marshes to permanent agriculture. Some remote spots and designated National Parks such as the Parque Nacional de Doñana, remain as wild marshlands which conservationists are currently fighting to protect against encroachment. The delta is open to Atlantic influences and is temperate and oceanic rather than Mediterranean in outlook. The Guadalquivir valley gradually narrows in width E of the delta with Córdoba located in its own embayment in the upper valley: this terminates in the N around the town of Andújar. The area around Málaga on the other hand, representative of the Mediterranean coastlands between Gibraltar and Punta Sabinal, is one of mountains and steep sided narrow valleys, altogether without extensive plains. Granada is even more a mountainous retreat sitting in one of a series of upland basins like Antequera and Ronda in the Sierra Nevada. In the N, the sierras above the plain of the Guadalquivir belong to the high Castilian plateau and only the S facing slopes are attached to Andalucía: to the N and E the region rapidly blends into the *meseta* of European Spain.

There is great variety within the boundaries of Andalucía both in topography and lifestyle. Local loyalties are powerful and each subdistrict, town and village has a distinct microclimate, aspect and history giving it a unique flavour quite apart from the broader zones we have defined above. The break up of Arab Andalucía into fragmented kingdoms under the stress of the Castilian Reconquista still finds reflections in local allegiances and customs.

Rivers Andalucía, with its exposure to the Atlantic, is for the most part and in most years well watered, and carries a rich range of surface waters. The Guadalquivir is the dominant river system. It drains the entire area with the exception of the generally short, S flowing rivers which descend rapidly to the Mediterranean. The tributaries from the N are trapped wherever possible as reservoirs such as the Embalse de Bambézar on the Río Bambézar above Palma del Río.

Reservoirs are also a prominent feature of the long left bank tributaries which drain the Sierra Nevada ranges, though severe strains were felt in 1992 during the Expo at Sevilla when adjacent districts suffered water rationing in order to keep Sevilla supplied. Drainage in the Guadalquivir delta is artificially enhanced to prevent the river shifting its course and to enable land to be reclaimed for agriculture. The river is navigable as far E as Sevilla itself. Complex man-made salt pan areas exist throughout the delta region, for example near San Fernando.

The smaller valleys on the S side of the Sierra Nevada ranges have a charm of their own. They have pockets of intensive cultivation such as the vineyards of the Casares valley above Estepona (see page 136), the citrus plantations on the Guadiaro N of Sotogrande and the olive groves of the Ojén valley near Marbella (see page 135). Moorish water systems for town supply and irrigation are visible in the form of aqueducts and small reservoirs, with those in the Alhambra being the most sophisticated.

Climate

Andalucía extends 400 km from W to E and an average of 225 km from S to N. Altitudes vary from sea-level to 3,481m in Mulhacén in the Sierra Nevada. The region is a meeting place for the climatic influences of the Atlantic, the Mediterranean/Sahara and continental Europe. Variety and variability of weather result from these opposing influences.

The high mountains of the Sierras above Jimena and Ubrique reach 1,654m in Pinar and, like the Sierra Nevada itself, fall into the warm temperate climatic type. The lower mountainous knots of the Sierras between Antequera and Jaén reach altitudes of more than 2,000m and have a sub-Mediterranean climate in consequence though less extreme in winter and with shorter-lived snow cover and more dry days (over 40 on average) than the Sierra Nevada. The rest of the highlands above 500m to both N and S of the River Guadalquivir enjoy a marginal Mediterranean climatic régime with 40-75 rainfree days per year on average.

The Guadalquivir valley has 3 gentle climates, with the W lowlands below Sevilla the warmest and driest (125-150 rainfree days). Sevilla is somewhat wetter (100-120 rainfree days) and slightly E of the city, as altitudes increase, there is a further transition to a modified Mediterranean climate of 75-100 rainfree days per year. The coastlands of the Mediterranean Sea experience climates that also vary from W to E. The Gibraltar to Málaga coast is heavily influenced by the Atlantic and has only 40-75 rainless days. E of Málaga there is a rapid change to a drier régime with up to 200 rainfree days on average. All the Andalusian coast has average temperatures above 10°C in Jan. All areas have rain in winter while the high sierras are subject to long periods of snow.

Andalucía is a main routeway between the Atlantic and the Mediterranean and has a generally westerly set of winds in winter, often bringing rain. Local winds are also important and, in addition to onshore/off-shore breezes during the course of the day, the *levante* blows in from the E, causing mists along the coast as it mixes with cooler and wetter air. A strong *sirocco* wind blows up from North Africa bringing airborne sand, high temperatures and low relative humidity, usually for short periods.

Land use

Land use is highly polarized in Andalucía. The Mediterranean coastal rim is densely used for farming, settlement and tourism but rising altitudes a few km inland bring extensive farming and only modest use of land for tourism. The sierras have extensive land use but the lowlands of the Guadalquivir valley and the low plateaux of the W produce cereals and are planted with orchards. Andalucía is not entirely typical of land use overall in Spain, having excellent forests and rich farmlands.

Land use 1991 (%)

	Spain	Andalucía
Arable and orchard	40.8	19.0
Pastures and rough grazing	20.4	47.0
Forest and woodland	31.4	15.0
Other uses	7.4	19.0
Total	100.0	100.0

Source: *Encyclopaedia Britannica*, Authors

Land Tenure The Spanish S is a region of large farms and estates, especially in areas away from the Mediterranean coast. Farm holdings are managed in areas of more than 10,000 ha under orcharding, forestry and livestock ranches. The Guadalquivir lowlands and some of the intermediate altitude plateau farms are middle ranking *fincas* or private farms. Elsewhere, farms are often no more than small holdings used for self-sufficiency and some small scale commercial cropping. For the traveller, there is plenty of opportunity to buy fresh produce in season at the roadside from privately-run stands and kiosks for very reasonable prices. Oranges, lemons, vegetables and even potatoes are sold in this way. Stringent rules against trespass on farmland, particularly for hunting, are in evidence and areas marked either with the sign *coto privado de caza* (hunting by licence), or with a small rectangle carrying a black and a white triangle, are to be treated as private land. Similarly there are large areas of land still under military administration in Andalucía indicated by the warning *zona militar* and these are best avoided.

Potential The region's potential has scarcely been touched except for coastal tourism where that is, arguably, over-developed. The Moorish areas are scarcely exploited except at Granada and even there attention is concentrated on the Alhambra and Generalife areas. Most other castles, monuments and other remains are under-valued and visited infrequently. There is therefore enormous scope for the traveller to both escape the tourist throngs and see some excellent sites throughout the region. The landscapes of the sierras are now accessible on narrow but well-maintained roads throughout the year and offer a seasonal variety of quiet and unruffled progress. Spring in the coastal sierras is enlivened by a profusion of flowers and the passage of migrant birds from the large griffon vulture to the small warblers, including the nightingale (see below). Andalucía is not without its constraints on growth and development, not least in shortages of water and the ill thought out mass tourist development of the past. Very large parts of the region are, however, virgin territory and the discerning traveller will find much to enjoy.

Flora and fauna

There are over 5,000 species of flowering plants and over 400 species of birds, nearly half of which breed in the area. Part of the explanation for this rich diversity of wildlife lies in the variety of habitat available, which includes semi-desert in the E, wetlands such as the incomparable **Coto Doñana**, the highest mountains in mainland Spain, forests and farmland. The original Mediterranean forests were destroyed in prehistoric times and these have been replaced by cork oaks, pine woods and *maquis*. The coastline, too, provides contrasts, with dunes, cliffs and salt marsh. The almost land-locked Mediterranean is virtually tideless, but W of Gibraltar, the tidal estuaries and beaches provide yet another environment.

Spring is undoubtedly the best season for **wild flowers**. Many of the meadows, which have never known herbicides, are a riot of colour. The 'painted fields' between Vejer and Tarifa are covered with mallows, convolvulus, lupins, clover, irises and squills. In the *maquis* areas, cistuses, rock roses and aromatic herbs are abundant. A wide range of orchids can be found in all the habitats, but particularly on the limestone soils.

Mammals include 3 African species – the genet, the mongoose and the Barbary macaques of Gibraltar. On the Coto de Doñana red deer, fallow deer and wild boar are common, the Spanish lynx less so. Eleven varieties of bat may be encountered, including Daubenton's bat, which has been known to drink from swimming pools. The garden dormouse will readily enter houses.

Reptiles and **amphibians** are well represented, with many types of frog and toad, pond tortoise and terrapin. Lizards, geckoes and sand racers are common, as is the huge occelated lizard which has been known to eat a fully grown rabbit. Of the 7 common species of snakes, only the viperine water snake found in a few of the rivers is poisonous, but being only 300 mm long avoids humans.

Of the plethora of **insects**, the butterflies stand out. As well as the common painted ladies, Moroccan orangetips and speckled woods, there are the more exotic swallowtails, cleopatras and two-tailed pashas.

It is undoubtedly the **birds** which attract most naturalists to Andalucía. In John Gooder's book *Where to Watch Birds*, 12 outstanding sites are mentioned in Spain, and of these half are in Andalucía. The birds of prey are the most spectacular. Of the 3 species of vulture, the griffon vulture remains common, while there are 5 species of eagles plus buzzards, kites, harriers and kestrels. The migration of these raptors at Tarifa or Gibraltar in the spring or autumn, when literally thousands can be swirling around in the thermals, can be a memorable sight. Storks are common in the W of the region, nesting on church towers and pylons, while flamingoes are increasing their breeding sites, now locating at the Coto Doñana, Fuente de Piedra and Cabo de Gata.

Farmland, *maquis* and forest are all rich in birdlife. Overhead wires provide perches for woodchat shrikes, rollers, bee eaters and corn buntings, while dense scrub is the home of nightingales and Cetti's warbler. Even urban habitats have their attractions, with pallid swifts whirling around half-finished apartment blocks and the well-watered lawns of villas providing perfect conditions for blackbirds and, in winter, robins.

Andalucía had a particularly bad reputation for cruelty to animals, indiscriminate shooting and the liming and trapping of birds. This has begun to change in recent years. There is now a network of National Parks and Nature Reserves, some, indeed, with hides, wardens, trails and information centres. Young people, in particular, have a much more educated approach to conservation.

People

Spain had a total population estimated at 39 million in mid 1992. The total has grown slowly in the last decade at 0.4% per year. Andalucía fits the national model, with a total population of 6.9 million.

Present-day Andalucía remains a racial mixture of Spanish Latin origins and Arab semitic. Accurate statistics are altogether lacking concerning the relative proportions of Arabs and people of other origins in the population, given the conversion before the Reconquista of Jews and Christians to Islam and the later conversion of Jews and Muslims to Christianity after the Reconquista. Suffice to say that the population differs from the rest of Spain in many aspects of language and culture as a result of its unique ethnic evolution and experience. The high incidence of Arabic origin place names, such as Almería for example, is a daily testimony to the former Arab influence. Additions of foreign elements arising from the long connection between Cádiz and the Spanish colonial empire are also to be discerned. Most mixed of all is Gibraltar, where its role on the Straits and as an imperial garrison for Great Britain ensured that elements of African, European and Mediterranean races intermingled – Arabs, Levantine Jews, Genoese, Spanish and many others.

Population distribution

Andalucía is heavily urban, with more than 80% of people living in towns and cities. Sevilla has a population of 659,126, the fourth largest in the country, while the populations of the other provincial capitals cover a wide range: Málaga 590,000, Córdoba 300,000, Granada 265,000, Cádiz 158,000, Almería 155,000, Huelva 128,000 and Jaén 105,000. In effect, the population clusters along the Mediterranean coast and in the cities of the Guadalquivir valley including Cádiz,

Huelva, Jerez and Córdoba. The sierras are very lightly populated, having some scattered hill communities and occasional larger village-towns such as Jimena de la Frontera and Casares. Rural depopulation is a continuing feature of the region. Gibraltar's population of 30,000 is found entirely in Gibraltar town, though recent suburban developments adjacent to the marina are growing rapidly. The British military establishment in Gibraltar is rapidly being run down.

Population densities

Spain as whole has a density of 205 people per sq km. Andalucía has an average of 79 people per sq km, a misleading figure given the contrast between the densely settled lowlands and the empty uplands.

Age groups

Andalucía fits the pattern of Western Europe in its age distribution with 20% between 0-14 years, 67% between 15-64 years and 13% 75 and over. The over 75 group is growing quickly while the crude birth rate is falling quite rapidly. It was 21 per thousand in 1965 but down to 10 per thousand by 1991, while the crude death rate is stable at 9 per thousand. Longevity is at the Western European average of 77 years. Literacy rates are high at 95% for men and 93% for women. Spain has only recently emerged as an industrial power and regionally Andalucía has benefited from an expansion of tourism only in the last 30 years. Its living standards have not yet adjusted to the Western European norm with income per head for Spain reported at US$12,450 in 1991, with Andalucía at approximately US$10,000 per head. In rural areas and in the poorer suburbs there is still an element of poverty brought on by protracted unemployment.

History

The Moors

Early invaders In 711 **Tarik** crossed the Straits from North Africa with a force of several thousand Berbers and defeated the Visigothic ruler, King Roderic, by the Rio Guadalete near Tarifa. Within the decade the invaders conquered most of the peninsula which became part of the vast Muslim empire known as al-Andalus. The overthrow of the **Ommayyad Dynasty** by the **Abbasids** in 750 (see History of North Africa, page 61) had important consequences for al-Andalus. The sole surviving Ommayyad prince, **Abd Al-Rahman**, escaped to Córdoba where he established an independent Caliphate of al-Andalus, which survived for 300 years. Córdoba became one of the largest, wealthiest and most cultured cities in the western world. A power-struggle within the régime led to civil war after 1008 and the last of the Ommayyad caliphs was expelled in 1031.

Al-Andalus split up into a number of petty principalities or *taifas*. The rulers of several of the *taifas* were patrons of high culture and art and thereby played a crucial role in the transmission of Greek thought, via Arabic, to Europe at the start of the Renaissance.

The *taifas* were, however, caught between the expanding Christian powers and the Islamic revivalism of the **Almoravid** rulers of Morocco, who particularly objected to the taifa rulers' payment of tribute to the Christians. In 1086 Almoravid troops crossed the Straits to help the *taifas* defeat Castilla. The newcomers then overthrew the taifa rulers and re-established unity in al-Andalus. The defeat of the Almoravids in 1145 by the **Almohads**, led to fresh invasions, both from the Christian kingdoms and from Africa. The high-point of Almohad power in al-Andalus was reached around 1200 with a series of attacks on Castilla and Aragón.

The Spanish Inquisition

The Spanish Inquisition, established in 1480 by Fernando and Isabel under authority from the Pope, was to meet the threat seemingly posed by *conversos* (Jews forcibly converted to Christianity) suspected of secret observance of Judaism. Later attention was turned to the *Moriscos* (converted Muslims) and native Spanish heretics. Its authority did not extend to non-Christians. The Inquisition, with powers to investigate and try suspects, worked through tribunals in the principal towns and was controlled by an Inquisitor General appointed by the monarch. The harshest tribunal was in Sevilla, seen as a hot-bed of *conversos*, where 20,000 cases were tried between 1481 and 1524.

Each region was visited annually by an Inquisitor who published an Edict of Faith, a type of questionnaire for all adult Christians, covering their beliefs and requiring them to report known heretics. Those accused of serious crimes were imprisoned to await investigation and trial which could take years. The accusers were never named, but the prisoner could produce a list of his enemies whose evidence was then supposedly ignored.

Although there were controls on interrogation methods, three forms of torture were allowed – the rack, the hoist and the water torture. Those who confessed were given lighter sentences. Various fates awaited those found guilty – absolution, fines, flogging, galley-service, confiscation of property or being burned at the stake. As a consolation, those who confessed after being sentenced to death were strangled before being burned.

About 5,000 people were executed up to 1530, thereafter the Inquisition's ferocity declined and between 1560-1700 only 500 death sentences were passed from 50,000 cases. The Inquisition was abolished in 1820.

The Reconquista Although the power of the Christian kingdoms in Castilla, Aragón and Portugal had grown steadily since the collapse of the Caliphate of Córdoba, the decisive period of expansion occurred after the defeat of the Almohads by Castilla at Las Navas de Tolosa in 1212. With the Almohads threatened by dissent in the Maghreb most of al-Andalus was lost including Córdoba in 1236 and Sevilla in 1248. Only Granada survived as a Muslim kingdom, protected behind a chain of castles and paying heavy tribute to Castilla. The decline of **Marinid** power in Morocco after 1415 left Granada without allies. The marriage of Isabel of Castilla and Fernando of Aragón in 1469 united the two Christian kingdoms and paved the way for the final assault on Granada, culminating in a 9 month siege in 1491. In Jan 1492 Boabdil (see page 86) surrendered the keys of the city.

Although Muslims were promised the right to practise their religion the expulsion of the Jews in 1492 indicated religious intolerance in Spain. Forcible mass baptism of Muslims began in 1499, provoking a quickly suppressed rebellion. Muslims in Granada had the choice of conversion or emigration on unfavourable terms (children and property to be left behind). In 1502 the same policy was extended to Castilla and in 1525 to Aragón. Many 'converted' Muslims, known as Moriscos, practised their faith in secret. In 1609 Philip III expelled all Moriscos. The 300,000 people who left included many of the country's finest craftsmen and artisans. Thus the 780 year long Muslim presence in Iberia came to an end, commemorated now only in its legacy in the Spanish language, in Spanish place names and in the few remaining examples of its architectural greatness.

Modern history

While 19th century Spain was a backward agricultural society, the early 20th century saw increased conflict, the rise of revolutionary anarchism particularly in Andalucía, the growth of Catalan nationalism, greater military influence in politics and a brutal colonial war in Morocco. Violence increased until, in 1923, **General Prima de Rivera** seized power and dissolved parliament. Primo resigned in 1929 and **King Alfonso XIII**, who had supported Primo, called local elections in 1931 as the first step back to parliamentary government. The main towns voted overwhelmingly for Republican and Socialist candidates and Alfonso left the country. A republic was proclaimed and Republican and moderate Socialist leaders were released from prison to form a government. Two features of the new constitution were particularly controversial: home rule for Catalonia and the Basque country which was opposed by Spanish nationalists and the army; separation of the Church and the State which antagonized many Catholics. A mild land reform and other social policies stirred up right-wing hostility. Disputes between Socialists and Republicans led to their defeat in the 1933 election and the coming to power of the right who reversed earlier reforms. Left-wing groups rose in revolt in 1934 and were brutally put down by **General Franco** and the Spanish Foreign Legion. The Feb 1936 elections were held in an atmosphere of extreme tension, with the victory of the left-wing parties united in the Popular Front followed by the formation of a minority Republican government and growing violence as Socialists and Anarchists seized land while right-wing leaders plotted with army officers to seize power.

The military rising on 18 July 1936 failed in the main cities but succeeded in the Catholic North. In Andalucía and Catalonia workers seized land and factories. General Franco borrowed planes from Hitler to transport his best Spanish troops, then stationed in Morocco, into Andalucía to crush the revolt before marching them N towards Madrid. With the accidental death of General Sanjurjo, Franco became leader of the rebel (Nationalist) forces.

The Civil War was prolonged with Franco receiving troops from Germany and equipment from Italy while the Republicans, refused assistance from France and Britain, turned to the USSR for arms. Republican resistance collapsed in March 1939. Franco's revenge was harsh and many were executed or sent to labour camps.

Between 1939 and 1975 Franco ruled as dictator, all political parties and unofficial unions were banned, the press was tightly controlled and parliament acted as a rubber stamp. From the mid-1950s with the help of American money, tourism and remittances, the economy improved and Spanish society gradually changed. The ribbon development along the Andalusian coast dates from this period.

Juan Carlos, grandson of Alfonso XIII, became King at Franco's death and successfully steered Spain towards parliamentary democracy. The centrist UDC party won the elections in 1977 and drafted a new constitution. The **PSOE** (Partido Solcialista Obrero Español) led by Felipe González took over in 1982.

Since 1982, under González's leadership, Spain has joined the EU and NATO and has enjoyed rapid economic growth accompanied by improvement in the infrastructure and large scale foreign investment. Tight control of government spending has brought down inflation at the cost of increased unemployment and the hostility of the PSOE's former allies in the unions. After the ambitious spending in 1992 on projects such as Expo in Sevilla and the Barcelona Olympics, the collapse of a major bank in Dec 1993 indicated that the boom years were over.

Modern Andalucía

Government

The Kingdom of Spain, according to the 1978 Constitution is a 'parliamentary monarchy' in which sovereignty 'resides in the people'. Parliament contains 2 Chambers, the Congress of Deputies with 350 members elected by proportional representation and the Senate with 208 elected members (4 from each province) and 49 appointed members. The main political parties are the socialist PSOE, the conservative Popular Party and the left-wing United Left.

Although the Constitution emphasises the 'indissoluble unity of the Spanish nation', it also guarantees the 'right of autonomy of the nationalities and regions'. Andalucía is one of the 17 autonomous communities with its own assembly elected for a 4 year term and its own government (Junta de Andalucía) with powers over local functions including town-planning, housing and tourism. It has benefited financially from the policies of the PSOE. Felipe González and several other leading figures in the national government are from Andalucía which is one of the PSOE's strongholds, the party controlling the Junta de Andalucía and the larger towns.

Gibraltar is a democratically self-governing colony of the UK though its territory is claimed by Spain, for which the dispute over the Rock is long-running and bitterly contested. Border controls continue to exist between Spain and Gibraltar.

Economy

Agriculture

Despite the advent of mass tourism and a degree of industrialization in the region, farming is still the economic backbone of Andalucía. The variety and mildness of the climate combined with reliable rainfall and generous surface water flows provide a considerable, albeit increasingly overstretched, irrigation potential. Irrigated lands provide a series of world famous products – Sevilla's oranges, lemons, the grapes for wine and sherry from Jerez, the olive crop, the largest in the world – in addition to a great range of vegetables, cotton and fruits. Away from the lowlands, farming is hard and until recent years the mainly self-sufficient cultivators and herders of the sierras were very poor, eking a living from thin soils. The poorer, mainly higher, environments have now been abandoned as families move to employment in the towns and tourist complexes. Livestock is important, Andalucía producing cattle in great numbers for meat and milk as well as specimens for bull fighting. Most farms keep sheep and, despite conservation laws, flocks of goats still graze (often over-graze) the hillsides. There are approximately 800,000 cattle, 4 million sheep and 2.25 million pigs in Andalucía.

The most flourishing sector of farming is that of the private estates, generally in large holdings. Average farm sizes of commercial enterprises on the lowlands are in the region of 1,000 ha and on the uplands more than 5,000 ha with a large range of sizes in both areas. In the Mediterranean coastlands the farms are small and intensively cultivated on the **huerta** model, inherited from a Moorish tradition, in which horticultural techniques are used to produce high quality and high value crops for the local markets and for export. The citrus, vine and olive areas use similar techniques but for virtual monocultures over fairly wide areas. New plantings of orange and lemon groves are to be seen, developing the specialisms introduced by the Moors centuries ago. Olive cultivation is tending to decline as a result of competition from cheaper producers in North Africa. Spain has the world's third largest grape harvest with 6,481,000 tonnes produced in 1990. Andalucía is well known for table grapes but has few remarkable wines and vintages, except for those of Jerez where the bulk are converted into sherry (see box, page 175), much for export. A fall in the popularity of sherry in the UK has adversely affected the prosperity of the Jerez farming region. The main national crops in which Andalucía has an approximate 20% share are barley 9.4 million tonnes, grapes 6.5 million tonnes, and olives 2.2 million tonnes.

Energy/petroleum

Spain is able to produce little of her energy requirements. It has some poor quality coal available in Asturias providing 36 million tonnes per year but is otherwise import-dependent. Total consumption of coal in 1989 was 45.8 million tonnes. Imports of crude oil run at 50 million tonnes per year against domestic output of 7 million tonnes. Andalucía itself has no coal but an active subsidized oil refining industry is located at Algeciras, exporting oil products as well as supplying the domestic market. A major experiment in the use of wind-generated electricity can be seen between Algeciras and Tarifa on the heights immediately inland from the Straits of Gibraltar. Many propeller-type generators have been installed to catch the strong winds funnelling in from the Atlantic.

Economic plans

Regional development plans exist as master plans for each of the sub-districts within Andalucía. They are mainly indicative land use plans for urban areas provided to act as guide lines for the control of building permissions. There is great variation in the scope and level of enforcement of the provisions of the local plans. In very recent years, local authorities have become more conscious of the need to improve and protect the environment to prevent the complete destruction of the coast through the over-building of hotels and tourist sites. The controls are belated and much of the coast is already severely blighted by ill-considered property development, much of it incomplete, and by the crowding of properties onto the beaches. National laws protecting beaches are gradually taking hold and might save some residual areas from encroachment.

Industry

Industry is an important element of the economy in Andalucía. The major centre is in Sevilla, where there is a highly diversified industrial manufacturing base including food processing, textiles, light engineering and energy-related plants. Elsewhere in the urban centres of the Guadalquivir – Cádiz, Chiclana, San Fernando and, to a smaller extent, Córdoba – there are food processing and packing plants and other smaller industries which service the thriving agricultural sector. In Málaga there are breweries and consumer goods industries together with plants making items for the tourist sector. The tourist industry is large. Spain as a whole earned US$18.6 billion from tourism in 1990, approximately one tenth of this in Andalucía. Gibraltar is gradually developing an economy based on international financial services.

Economic trends

Andalucía experienced a boom in land prices, wages and employment in the 15 years to 1991. This trend was generated by confidence in the newly democratic structures of the state and its accession to the EU. Large flows of foreign finance came to Spain and much of it was invested in projects and properties on the Mediterranean coast, especially in Andalucía. The E area of the Andalusian Mediterranean coast grew more rapidly than the W until the opening of the border with Gibraltar in 1985, after which there was a rapid catching up process, since N Europeans could now enter Spain via Gibraltar airport.

Main Economic Indicators

Given that Andalucía is an integral part of Spain, exact provincial figures are generally lacking. The following table shows the best available estimates.

ECONOMIC INDICATORS

	1989	1990	1991
GDP Spain (Ptas '000 billion)	42.3	44.1	44.9
GDP Andalucía (Ptas '000 billion)	6.3	6.6	6.6
Imports (Ptas '000 billion)	8.5	8.9	9.7
Exports (Ptas '000 billion)	5.3	5.6	6.2
Balance of trade (Ptas '000 billion)	-2.7	-2.8	-2.7
Inflation (1985=100)	128.2	136.8	144.9
Public debt (US$ billion)	152.0	198.0	229.0

Source: IBRD, IMF, *Encyclopaedia Britannica*

THE MOUNTAIN CITIES AND KINGDOMS

CONTENTS

MAPS

Granada

Population 265,000 *Alt* 689m.

Granada is not to be missed and a visit there should not be rushed. The capital of the Province of Granada, it stands on the Rio Genil (which flows W eventually joining the Guadalquivir in Sevilla) and the Rio Darro which runs down from the mountains to join the Genil. Constructed on and around 3 hills, the city's impressive Moorish architectural heritage contrasts with the sprawling new development of tower blocks. It is situated 67 km N of Motril on the Mediterranean coast (see page 116) and 93 km S of Jaén (see page 143) in a fertile upland valley, the **Vega de Granada**. The lofty peaks of the **Sierra Nevada**, the highest mountains in Europe S of the Alps, snow-covered for most of the year, lie 30 km to the SE and act as an imposing backdrop to the town. The **Solynieve** (literally sun and snow) ski resort is situated here, open from Dec to mid-May. In addition to visitors coming to absorb the atmosphere of the **Alhambra**, the **Generalife** and the **Albaicín**, Granada can be a useful base for both skiers and sunseekers, which accounts for the city's immense popularity and often over-crowded streets.

WARNING Avoid walking alone in the Sacromonte hills and the narrow streets NE of Plaza Nueva after dark since pick-pockets can be a problem.

ACCESS The national airport is 17 km W of the city, but shuttle buses connect it to the town centre at Plaza Isabel la Católica, T 278677, costs 300 Ptas. Bus number 11 runs a circular route connecting the reasonably central train station on Avda Andaluces and the bus station on Camino de Ronda to the town centre. Once in the town, it is easiest to travel on foot around the lower part of the city since many of the major places of interest are close together and parking can be very difficult.

Things to see

Moorish past As the last stronghold of the Moors in Andalucía, Granada is richly endowed with reminders of its Arab occupiers. Even the city's name is thought to be derived from the Moorish word *karnattah* and not, as might be expected, the Spanish word *granada* though both mean pomegranate, the fruit which has now been adopted as the town's symbol.

The most famous landmark of Granada's Moorish heritage is the Al-

CLIMATE: GRANADA

	Jan	Feb	Mar	Apr	May	Jun	Jul	Aug	Sep	Oct	Nov	Dec	Av/Tot
Max (°C)	12	14	17	20	23	30	34	33	30	23	17	12	22
Min (°C)	2	3	5	7	10	15	17	17	15	10	6	3	9
Rain (mm)	54	49	62	53	44	8	3	8	25	49	48	70	473

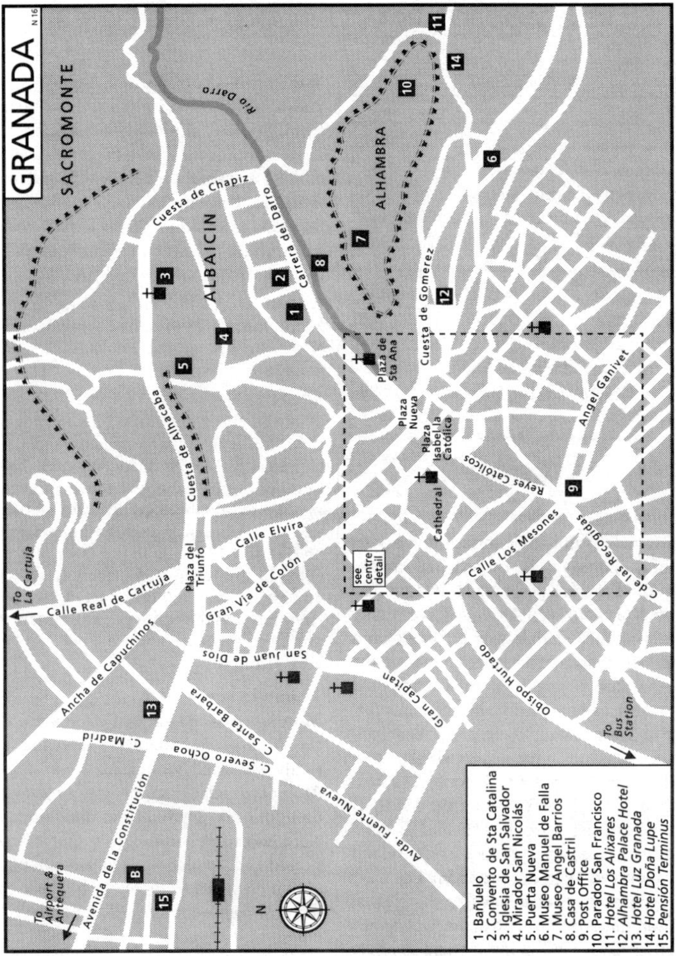

hambra, built by the **Nasrids** who moved to the city from Jaén in 1246 and established a dynasty which lasted for 250 years, gradually disintegrating as a result of internal strife until the reign of **Muley Hassan**. The jealousy of Hassan's wife Ayesha over his relationship with Zoraya, a Christian convert to Islam, led to a feud causing Ayesha to flee to **Guadix** (see page 96) with the heir Abu Abdallah (better known as **Boabdil**). He was proclaimed king there in 1482 and, known as *El Rey Chico*, Boabdil eventually overthrew both his father and his uncle to become the last King of Granada. However, after falling into Spanish hands twice, he ceded the city, the Moors' last Andalusian possession,

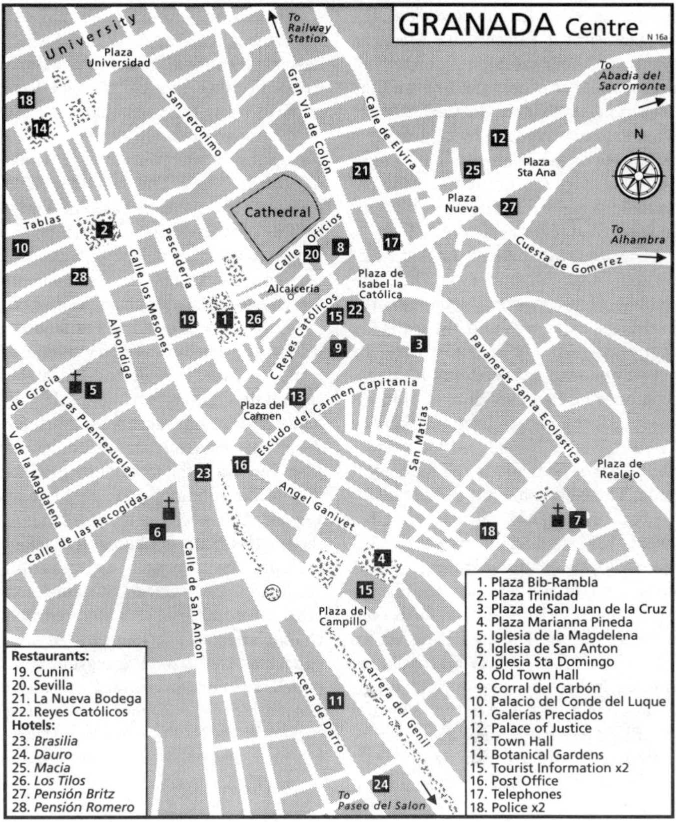

to the Catholic Kings. He is said to have asked for the Alhambra's main entrance in the **Torre de los Siete Suelos** (The Seven Storey Tower), through which he left, to be sealed up after him before he retreated to the hilly **Alpujarras**.

The **Alhambra** (*Qalat Alhamra* – Red Palace, named after the red soil in the area) is best avoided during the summer season when water is less plentiful, the gardens are not at their best and it can be almost impossible to see past the crowds of tourists. However it is better to see it in summer than not at all since, as the saying goes, "*quien no ha visto Granada, no ha visto nada*" (the person who has not seen Granada has seen nothing)! If visiting in summer you should arrive very early or take advantage of the floodlit evening visits, but do bear in mind that it will take several hours to make even a rapid tour and on a busy day several hours in the queue to get in. Take something to drink while you are waiting in the queue. The entrance at the **Puerta de las Granadas** (Gate of the Pomegranates) is off the steep Cuesta de Gomérez.

Within the coolness of its thick walls, shady trees, and fountains the area of the

Alhambra is divided into 4 sections: the **Alcázar** (Royal Palace), the **Alcazaba** (Fortress), the **Generalife** (Summer Palace) with its beautiful gardens, and the 16th century **Palacio de Carlos V** for which space was made by destroying a large area of the original Alhambra. In addition there is a church and the extremely popular *Parador San Francisco* in what used to be a convent.

The 9th century **Alcazaba** is the oldest part of the Alhambra and the foundations of the warriors' quarters, the baths, the dungeons and the stalls are still visible but the major part of the actual building was destroyed by Napoleon once he had used it to station his troops. Here you can climb the **Torre de la Vela** (Watch Tower) and look across the whole of Granada to the Sierra Nevada. The view is magnificent.

The present **Alcázar** was built between 1333 and 1391 under Yusuf I (1334-54) who had the **Patio de Arrayanes** (Court of Myrtles) built and his son, Mohammed V (1334-91), who is responsible for the well known **Patio de los Leones** (Court of Lions). Having fallen into decline over the centuries, serious restoration work began in the 1860s and is still underway, so some areas may be closed to the public. Although its exterior is simple, the interior is highly intricate with a variety of ornamented ceilings, although it should be noted that the decor never includes figures which are forbidden by Islam. It is composed of courtyards enclosed by extremely delicate archways and cooling fountains and water channels drawn off the nearby Genil and Darro rivers. Water is cleverly used as the central theme throughout the area with the many pools mirroring the surrounding carvings.

The **Patio de Arrayanes**, which is reached after passing through the **Mexuar** courtyard near the entrance, is named from the Arabic for the neat myrtle hedges along the sides of the narrow pool which runs down its centre. Leading off it is the **Sala de la Barca** which has an exceptional, restored *artesonado* wooden ceiling, thought by some to be in the form of a boat, although the name of the room probably derives from a corruption of the Arabic word *baraka* (blessing or luck). The Sala de la Barca leads into the adjacent **Salón de Embajadores** (Ambassadors' Hall) by far the largest room in the palace with a ceiling soaring to a height of 20m. Here foreign emissaries were received and **Columbus** is said to have met **King Fernando** to discuss his travels to the New World.

Beyond the **Sala de los Mozárabes** (Mozárabes Gallery) are the royal apartments focused around what must be, despite its relatively small dimensions (28m by 15m), the most photographed area of the Alhambra, the **Patio de los Leones**. You need to be there out of season to obtain a photograph which excludes the crowds. This beautiful, cunningly constructed courtyard contains a central pool of water, fed by 4 channels from the surrounding area and supported by 12 small grey lions. The patio is surrounded by arches resting on 124 marble pillars, each with a different capital. To the N of this courtyard which has been described as a representation of paradise itself, is the beautifully decorated **Sala de las Dos Hermanas** (Two Sisters Gallery) which was possibly part of the harem and is named after the twin slabs of white marble in its pavement. To the S is the **Galería de los Abencerrajes** (Abencerrajes Gallery). In the fountain at its centre, it is said that members of a noble family were beheaded by the ruler of the time as part of an internal feud, although there may be no more to this tale than the red streaks to be seen in the marble there! All around are *azulejos* (tiles) inscribed with verses from the Koran, while the flowing water channels and shrubbery also contribute to the cool atmosphere making this area a special delight to visit in the summer.

Take coffee in the *Parador San Francisco* as a chance to see the interesting courtyards of fountains and flowers within the converted convent – and as a rest during an arduous visit.

Generalife On the top of the hill above the Alhambra is the Generalife summer palace whose name is derived from the Arabic *Gennat-al-Arif* (Garden of the Architect). The construction is

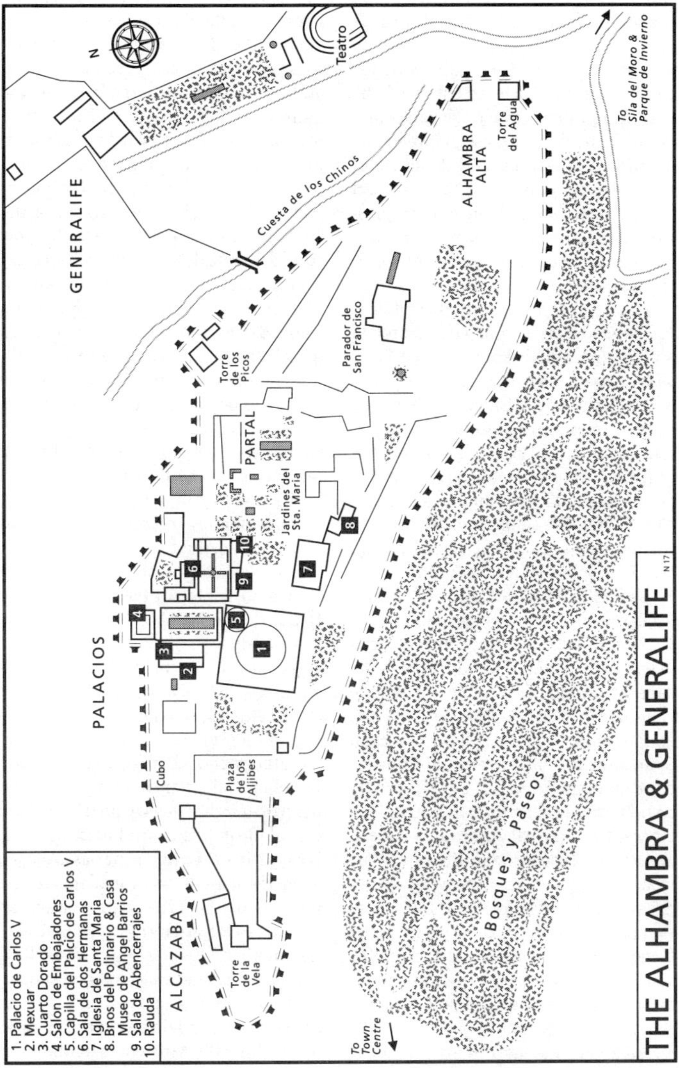

thought to date back to the middle of the 13th century. Although it underwent alterations following the fall of Granada, these were carried out by Arab workers. Direct access to it from the Alhambra is now possible via the bridge which crosses the Cuesta del Rey Chico. A shady avenue of cypress trees leads to the entrance of the Generalife which is notable for the lush greenery of the beautiful gardens around the palace and the extremely clever use of water, its sounds, its reflections and the effect of light playing upon it. The **Corte del Canal de Agua** is one of the most impressive features, where you will discover fountains arranged to form a magnificent archway.

The central area of the Generalife, surrounded by trees and with an arched wall on one side, is known as the **Patio de la Acequia**. The other main courtyard is the **Patio de los Cipreses** where the ancient trees are said to have been the setting for romantic intrigues over the centuries, most notably an affair between Boabdil's wife and a nobleman. The Generalife must not be missed whatever the season but especially if you are visiting in the heat of summer.

The Alhambra area (open winter 0900-1645, summer 0900-1845), T 220912, has floodlit evening sessions in summer. Ticket offices are at both the Alhambra and Generalife entrances. Combined ticket 600 Ptas, for the Generalife only, 225 Ptas. The disabled, Spanish senior citizens and children under 8 may enter free. A 2-day ticket may be better value. The walk from Granada city centre to the Alhambra area is steep and tiring. Instead take the No 2 bus from the city centre. If arriving by car, drive to the very top of the hill where there is an extensive car park next to the Generalife entrance. Avoid the unofficial, but very aggressive, parking attendants and also the persistent 'flower sellers'.

Albaicín The narrow streets of the old Arab quarter were occupied by the Moors as a ghetto until the 16th century and some of its original character remains today, although the mosques here have been replaced by churches. It is best reached by taking the Carrera del Darro from the Plaza Nueva (with good views to the Alhambra on the right) then striking off left up the Cuesta del Chapiz or the Calle de Zafra to ramble along the narrow cobbled streets and alleys through tiny plazas past Moorish ramparts and cisterns and the traditional Arab *cármenes* (a combination of houses and gardens). The oldest traces of the city's previous occupants are the now ruined **Puente del Cadi** (Judge's Bridge) over the Darro and the privately owned 11th century **Bañuelo** (Arab Baths) on Carrera del Darro which were restored in 1928 (ring for entry, tips appreciated). Open Mon-Sat 1000-1400. The nearby **Convento de Santa Catalina** dates from 1520 and is built around an older Moorish tower. The main mosque in the area now has the **Iglesia de San Salvador** built on its site, but the original *patio arabe* was fortunately preserved. The best views of the Alhambra and the distant Sierra Nevada are obtained from the *mirador* at the top of the hill beside the **Iglesia de San Nicolás** (Bus No 12).

Once up here the **Puerta Nueva** gateway is nearby to the N. From here W, parallel with Cuesta de la Alhacaba, are some 13th century Moorish walls, marking the oldest area of Moorish Granada. Near the W end is the **Convento de Santa Isabel** on Calle San Juan de los Reyes, named after the Queen who received the city at Boabdil's capitulation in 1492. Beyond it on Callejón de las Monjas, formerly part of the convent, are the remains of the 15th century Moorish palace of Dar al-Horra built for Boabdil's mother Ayesha la Horra whose feud with her husband was largely responsible for the Moors' loss of Granada. The style of the surviving tower and patio overlooking the Albaicín is reminiscent of the Alhambra itself. It is currently closed until further notice for restoration.

Corral del Carbón (Charcoal House) is interesting in that it is the oldest surviving Moorish building in Granada. It was originally a Moorish inn of a type widespread in the early 14th century before being successively adapted as a granary, a theatre, a centre for charcoal sellers and now craft shops. Very few of the inns of this era have survived, although there is the remains of one in Córdoba. Open Mon-Fri 1000-2000, Sat 1000-1400. Admission free.

Alcaicería (Silk Market) is located near the Cathedral on Calle Zacatín, since the original bazaar was adjacent to the mosque whose remains lie beneath the Christian building. It is unfortunate that very little of the original market remains following a fire in 1843 although restoration work has been carried out, reviving some of the original atmosphere but substituting expensive gift shops for the Moorish bazaars.

Other places of interest

The **Cathedral**, built on the foundations of a mosque, took 181 years to complete, hence the style ranging from the original Gothic to the later Baroque façade (contributed by Alonso Cano together with some paintings inside). It is said by some to be one of Spain's finest Renaissance churches with the domed **Capilla Mayor** designed by Diego de Siloé being regarded as its most innovative feature. Hours and admission as for Capilla Real.

The **Capilla Real** adjacent to the Cathedral was built for the Catholic Kings, begun in 1506 and completed in 1521 in order that they might be buried in Granada. The whole building is a flamboyant monument to the pair and contains their tombs together with those of their daughter **Juana la Loca** (the Mad) and her unfortunate husband **Felipe el Hermoso** (the Fair). Various features such as Juan de Zagala's *reja* (screen) and Bigarny's altar table make the Capilla Real more outstanding than the Cathedral itself. An additional highlight is the sacristy containing Queen Isabel's private art collection including several masterpieces and her rather magnificent royal jewels. Open Mon-Sat 1030-1300 and 1530-1800. Admission 150 Ptas, free Sun mornings.

Opposite the entrance to the Capilla Real in Calle Oficios is the arched marble doorway of the old **town hall**, behind which lies a *medresa* (Koranic school) which was founded by Yusuf I in 1349, attached to the mosque on the site of the Cathedral. A beautifully carved **Arabian Room** can be found on the other side of its patio, although little remains of the original Arab construction. Admission free.

The **Palacio de Carlos V** is regarded as being the most beautiful surviving Renaissance building in Spain. However its square, solid presence in the midst of the subtle Moorish splendours of the Alhambra is certainly incongruous. Begun in 1526, although it was largely completed by the early 17th century, the work was then abandoned for a long period and the buildings allowed to fall into decay. The finishing touches on the palace were only added this century once the restoration work had begun. The circular courtyard inside the palace has been used as a bullring and an arena and is now the site of the International Music and Dance Festival (see Festivals, see page 92). The building also houses 2 museums (see Museums, see page 92). Admission details as for the Alhambra.

Sacromonte and its gypsy caves which have been inhabited for hundreds of years are reached via the Albaicín. Be warned that the current residents' income is now derived largely from unsuspecting tourists visiting the area who are treated to rather amateurish *flamenco* dancing and fortune telling and more professional pocket-picking. However if you carry only a small amount of money and find a Spanish acquaintance to accompany you, the experience will be very interesting. Real *flamenco* dancing can be found in town for a price.

Not far from the university outside the city to the N on Calle Real de Cartuja is **La Cartuja**, an impressive Carthusian monastery in the Ainada Mar (Fountain of Tears) area of Granada where the Arabs once built their summer residences. This building took over 300 years to complete and is a mixture of styles spanning the period resulting in an overall impression of rather jumbled opulence. The extravagant 18th century baroque sacristy constructed of brown and white marble and stucco is its most notable feature and has been described as a 'Christian Alhambra'. It is open daily Mar-Sep 1030-1300 and 1600-1900, Oct-Feb 1030-1300 and 1530-1800. Admission 150 Ptas, free Sun mornings.

Museums

NB: many museums are now free for EU citizens. Produce your passport to gain this admission.

Casa Museo Federico García Lorca 17 km to the W of the city in Fuentevaqueros was the home of the dramatist and poet shot down by right-wing Nationalists in 1936. Ureña Buses go here approx hourly from Avda Andaluces by train station. Open 1000-1300 and 1800-2000 during summer and 1000-1300 and 1600-1800 during winter. Closed Mon. Admission 150 Ptas.

Casa Museo Manuel de Falla in Antequeruela Alta was the composer's home. Open 1000-1500. Closed Mon. Admission 150 Ptas.

The **Museo Angel Barrios** was the home of this 20th century guitarist inside the Alhambra grounds and contains information about his life. Open 1500-1800. Closed Sun and fiestas. Admission 150 Ptas.

Museo Arqueológico de la Casa de Castril, is in the 16th century Casa de Castril on Carrera del Darro and contains Greek and Roman sculpture, ceramics and coins. Open Tue-Sat 1000-1400. Admission 150 Ptas. T 225640.

Museo Bellas Artes (Fine Art Museum) is on the upper floor of the Palacio de Carlos V. Open Tue-Fri 1000-1400, Sat 1000-1300. Admission 150 Ptas.

Museo Hispano Musulmán (Hispano-Islamic Museum) is on the ground floor of the Palacio de Carlos V and contains many items from the Alhambra, most notably a spectacular 15th century vase, together with Moorish ceramics, stucco, carvings etc. Open Mon-Fri 1000-1400, Sat 1000-1300. Admission 150 Ptas. T 226279.

Festivals

A fiesta on the first 2 days of Jan celebrates the end of the Reconquista and the arrival of the victorious **King Fernando** and **Queen Isabel** in Granada. In early Feb the *Romería Popular de San Cecilio*, the city's patron saint, takes place – a pilgrimage to **Sacromonte Abbey** in his honour. During *Semana Santa* at Easter, the traditional processions take place and special viewing stands are set up in Plaza del Carmen. May begins with *Las Cruces de Mayo* when the squares and patios are decorated with floral crosses. In Jun, to mark Granada's major festival, *Corpus Christi*, there are bullfights and other celebrations. At the end of Jun or beginning of Jul the **International Music and Dance Festival** takes place in the Palacio de Carlos V, information from Calle Ancha de Santo Domingo, T 225201. 29 Sep is the occasion for another ***romería popular***, this time to the Hermitage of **San Miguel Alto**, and the last Sun in Sep is the *Fiesta de Nuestra Señora de las Angustias* (Our Lady of Sorrows). In Nov the **International Jazz Festival** takes place.

Local information

Price guide:			
AL	US$90+	D	US$20-40
A	US$75-90	E	US$10-20
B	US$60-75	F	under US$10
C	US$40-60		

Accommodation: **AL** ***Alhambra Palace***, Calle Peña Parida 2, T 221468, F 226404, up near the Alhambra, luxury in a pseudo-Moorish style, 130 rm, a/c, garden, TV, parking, shops; **AL** ***Luz Granada***, Avda de la Constitución 18, T 204061, F 293150, 173 rm, central, good views, a/c, TV, garage, disco; **AL** ***Parador San Francisco***, La Alhambra, T 221440, F 222264, magnificent and luxurious accommodation in a converted convent inside the Alhambra complex, 39 rm, book well in advance especially in summer, parking, TV, gardens, restaurant.

A ***Los Alixares***, Avda Alixares del Generalife s/n, T 225506, F 224102, 150 rm, modern, parking, pool, a/c, lovely views; **A** ***Brasilia***, Calle Recogidas 7, T 258450, 68 rm, functional accommodation, garage, central; **A** ***Hotel Washington Irving***, Paseo del Generalife, T 227550, F 228840, old fashioned grandeur, named after a visitor to Granada who wrote the *Tales of the Alhambra*, a/c, shops, parking; **A** ***Dauro***, Acera del Darro 19, T 222156, F 228519, 36 rm, garage, modern, TV, central, no restaurant.

C ***Macia***, Plaza Nueva 4, T 227535, F 223575, central; **C** ***Los Tilos***, Plaza Bib-Rambla 4, T 266712, central, slightly noisy.

D ***Doña Lupe***, Avda de los Alixares 51, T 221473, F 266801, excellent value near Alhambra.

● Pensiones

C ***Pensión Suecia***, Calle Molinos 2, F 266801, quiet, relatively near the Alhambra, heavily used by tour parties.

D ***Pensión Residencia Britz***, Cuesta de Gomérez 1, T 223652, noisy but convenient for the Alhambra; **D** ***Pensión Romero***, Calle Sillería de Mesones 1, T 266079, convenient, slightly noisy location near Plaza de la Trinidad.

E ***Pensión Terminus***, Avda Andaluces 10, T 201423, noisy area by train station. Cheap, *huéspedes* (guestrooms) are around Plaza Trinidad, try **E** ***Marquez***, T 275013, Calle Fabria Vieja, some rm have bath, quiet, secure, clean; and on same street **E** ***Europa*** and **E** ***Sevilla*** not so good as *Europa*; on Calle Laurel de los Tablos are **E** ***Reina*** and **E** ***Lima***.

Towards the river Genil on and around Calle San Antón are a number of other pensiones in the **C** and **D** categories which may be worth trying, including ***Pensión Paris***, Calle San Antón 3, T 263622 and ***Pensión Consul***, Calle San Antón 34, T 259857.

● Youth hostel

Camino de Ronda 171, T 222638, 78 beds, meals provided, swimming pool, in a sports complex on the edge of town, suitable for wheelchair users, bus No 11 300m, reservations essential; ***Camino de Fuente***, 18779 Viznar, T 543307, F 543448, 108 beds, 12 km from Granada in woodland setting, facilities for disabled.

● Camping

Sierra Nevada, Ctra de Madrid 107, T 270956, large top grade site near town with modern facilities and pool, open Mar-Oct; ***Los Alamos***, Ctra Nacional 342, Km 290, T 275743, pool, open Apr-Oct; ***María Eugenia***, Ctra Nacional 342, Km 286, T 200606, pool, 4 km further out, open all year; ***El Ultimo***, Ctra Huétor-Vega Km 22, T 123069, open all year. All sites on bus routes.

● Places to eat

Price guide:
♦♦♦Expensive; ♦♦average; ♦cheap.

♦♦♦ ***Cunini***, Calle Pescadería 14, T 263701, sea food, very expensive; ***Mirador de Morayma***, Vacas 2, T 228290, beautiful setting in the Albaicín with Andalusian dishes; ***Sevilla***, Calle Oficios 12, beside the Cathedral, T 221223, Andalusian dishes.

♦♦***Alcaicería***, Calle Oficios 8, regional cuisine aimed at tourists; ***MacDonalds***, Calle Recogidas 25, T 264140, for American fast food at a Spanish pace; ***Seís Peniques***, Plaza de los Tiros, T 226256, regional and international.

♦***La Nueva Bodega***, Calle Cetti Merién 3, T 222401, cheap and cheerful at the bar; ***Pizzería Burguer Goffi***, Calle Pedro Antonio de Alarcón, fast food and takeaways; ***Reyes Católicos***, Placeta Sillería 3, T 223928, friendly service and a range of fixed price *menús*; ***Casa Cepilla***, Plaza Pesciaderia 18, good value *menú del día*, rec. **Tea shops** on Plaza Nueva, try ***As-sirat***, Caldereria Nueva 5, wide selection, pleasant atmosphere.

● Banks

Are all closed on Sat from 15 Jun-15 Sep.

Numerous banks in Plaza Isabel la Católica and along Gran Vía de Colón, including foreign banks.

● Consulates

Germany, Avda Constitución 20, 2°; **Belgium**, Calle Recogidas 66, 1°A, T 251631; **France**, Carlos Pareja 5, T 261447; **Italy**, Doctor Martín Lagos, T 261361.

● Entertainment and cuisine

The former includes bullfights, especially during Corpus Christi and in autumn, the box office is on Calle Escudo del Carmen, open evenings only. Popular and reliable *flamenco* at ***Jardines Neptuno*** on Calle Arabia from 2200 daily, book in advance, entrance including drink, 2500 Ptas. Several other flamenco displays along Camino del Sacromonte. Those in the actual caves are heavily tourist-orientated. *Tapas* bars offer some local atmosphere in Campo Príncipe and along Calle Acera del Darro, Calle Martínez de la Rosa and Calle Gran Capitán. Typical dishes are *tortilla Sacromonte* (omelette with potatoes, peas, peppers, brains in batter and testicles, all finely chopped!), *habas con jamón* (beans with ham) and fried fish and seafood.

● Garages/petrol

On Ctra de la Sierra, Avda de la Constitución, Camino de Ronda, Avda de Ancha de Capuchinos.

● Handicrafts

Include rugs, marquetry, copper goods and *fajalauza* ceramics featuring blues and greens using traditional Arab techniques.

● Hospitals

Cruz Roja (emergencies), Calle Escoriaza 8, T 222024. ***General Hospital***, Avda Coronel Muñoz, T 276400. ***Hospital Clínico***, Avda Dr Olóriz, T 270200.

● Post Office

Correos in Puerta Real. Open Mon-Fri 0800-2100, Sat 0800-1400. Telegrams Mon-Fri 0800-2100, Sat 0900-1700, Sun 0900-1400.

● Telephones

Local code: 958. Calle Reyes Católicos 55. Open Mon-Sat 0900-1400 and 1700-2200.

● Travel agents

Bonanza, Calle Reyes Católicos 30, T 223578; ***Ecuador***, Calle Angel Ganivet 8, T 223567; ***Marsans***, Gran Vía de Colón 20, T 222088; ***Sacromonte***, Calle Angel Ganivet 6, T 225598.

● Tourist information

The main tourist office in splendid new accommodation in the Corral de Carbón opens weekdays 1000-1400. There is also a provincial tourist office at Plaza de Mariana Pineda 10, T 226688, open all year Mon-Fri 1000-1300 and 1630-1900, Sat 1000-1300.

● Transport

Local Bus No 2 from Plaza Bibataubín or Carrera del Genil beside *Galerías Preciados* for the Alhambra; No 8 for La Cartuja and No 12 for the Albaicín, both leave from beside the Cathedral; No 11 (circular) for the stations and town centre. Free bus maps are available from the tourist information office and *bonobús* tickets for 10 journeys can be bought in advance from tobacconists and kiosks for 450 Ptas.

Car hire **Atesa**, Plaza de Cuchilleros 1, T 224004; **Avis**, Calle Recogidas 31, T 252358; **Europcar**, Avda del Sur 12, T 295065; **Hertz**, Calle Luis Braille 7, T 251682. **Coche caballo** available near *Correos* on Calle de los Mesones. Fix the price before setting off.

Cycle hire From ***Ski 3*** shop at Ctra de Sierra Nevada 46, T 210211, approx 1,500 Ptas per day.

Taxi **Radio Taxi** T 201461, **Tele Taxi** T 280654.

Air National flight tickets and information from Iberia, Plaza Isabel la Católica 2, T 227592 and T 203322. Two flights per day to **Madrid** and **Barcelona** for transit to international destinations and flights each week to **Valencia** (3), **Palma de Mallorca** (3), **Las Palmas** (2) and **Tenerife** (1).

Train The train station is on Avda Andaluces T 271272. Additional RENFE office at Calle Reyes Católicos 63, T 223119. Three trains per day run to **Madrid** and **Sevilla**, and 1 to **Algeciras**, **Córdoba** and **Málaga**.

Road The main intercity bus company serving all major towns in Andalucía and the coast is Alsina Graells at Camino de Ronda 97, T 251358, to Málaga 1,015 Ptas, to Seville 2,050 Ptas. Long distance coaches are run by Bacoma at Avda de Andaluces 10, T 284251. There are daily buses to **Algeciras** (2), **Barcelona** (4), **Córdoba** (7) and **Sevilla** (8).

Excursions from Granada

Motril (see page 116), **Salobreña** (see page 117), and **Almuñécar** (see page 118), on the Mediterranean coast 70-90 km S, are all feasible for daytrips via Alsina Graells buses.

The **Sierra Nevada** (see page 85), snow-capped in winter, provides a striking backdrop for Granada. There are 2 main peaks which rise above the general plateau level, Veleta and Mulhacén, the latter at 3,390m is the highest mountain in Spain. Despite its proximity to the Mediterranean, the height of the Sierra Nevada ensures good skiing conditions from Dec-Apr. A purpose-built resort, **Sol y Nieve** boasts 48 km of downhill piste, 18 lifts and tows, a children's ski school and a growing *après ski*. The area is patronized by the Spanish royal family and Sol y Nieve will host the Alpine World Ski championships in 1995. The ski station is open all winter, for a recorded update on snow, weather and access T 249119 or for general information, Sierra Nevada Centro Turistica, T 249100. Summer activities include mountain walking, hang gliding and horse riding. The Sierra Nevada is also outstanding for wildlife. Its habitats include agricultural valleys, pine woods, meadows and bare rock slopes. Birds and alpine flowers are particularly good.

ACCESS is by black top road from Granada, journey time 35 mins. Check if the road is open on T 480153, information in Spanish and English. Autocares Bonal run a daily service to the Sierra Nevada, leaving at 0900 and returning at 1700, with tickets available at the Bar El Ventorillo beside the Palacio de Congresos on Paseo del Violón on the far bank of the Rio Genil. Departure point changes periodically, so check with the tourist office or on T 273100. The road S from Veleta into the **Alpujarras** (see page

Caves – The Troglodyte Tendency

There is a long history of cave-dwelling in Andalucía. Caves at **Boquete de Zafarraya** (Málaga), **Pinar** (Granada) and **Vera** (Almeria) show evidence of Neanderthal man, possibly dating back 85,000 years. Relics include bones, tools, ceramics and cooking implements. The caves at **Nerja** (Málaga) show that after the last Ice Age, Cro-Magnon man inhabited the caves of Andalucía. It is something of a surprise, however, to learn that today there are still nearly 35,000 cave dwellers in Andalucía, the largest proportion of them in the **Guadix** area of Granada province. In most cases, these are not natural caves, but dwellings which have been excavated by man in the brown Pliocene clay of the area. The custom is believed to date originally from the 16th century when the *Moriscos* were fleeing from the persecution of Philip II. Today, the Andalusian government has recognized the situation and embarked on a cave improvement programme.

The better caves in the Guadix area have 7 or 8 rooms, electricity, sewage disposal, television and even a cave garage. Many of these troglodytes have resisted the pressure to be rehoused in high rise flats: (where would they keep their donkey?). After all caves do not leak or collapse; they are quieter than apartment living; the temperature is a constant 17°C throughout the year, extra room is easily available.

The caves have title deeds like normal houses and are bought and sold in the same way. Community life is often good, with caves converted into discos, bars and churches. It is often thought that most cave-dwellers are gypsies, but this is not the case. The most famous gypsy troglodytes are those of the **Sacromonte** district of Granada, but in fact most of these have been rehoused in apartments and only return to their caves at night to fleece the *flamenco*-seeking tourists.

See also Matmata troglodytes, page 577.

87) is unsurfaced but passable in summer by the adventurous and those with 4 wheel drive vehicles.

• **Accommodation** During the skiing season accommodation is quite expensive, whilst many of the hotels close from Jun to Nov. The few which stay open all year may halve their prices during the summer. **AL** ***Mélia Sierra Nevada***, Pradollano s/n, luxury with indoor pool, T 480400, F 480458. **A** ***Parador Sierra Nevada***, Ctra de Sierra Nevada Km 35, small, modern, open all year, T 480400, F 480458. Cheaper accommodation is provided by the ***Albergue Universitario***, where the bus will drop passengers off.

• **Youth hostel** *Estación de Pradollano*, 18196 Sierra Nevada, T 480305, 104 beds, cafeteria and sauna, Granada 35 km.

Guadix

(Known as *Wadi-Ash* to the Moors who occupied it until 1489), 58 km E on the N-342, is accessible by train (the station is a 20 min walk from the town) or Autedia buses in Calle Rector Marín Ocete,10. About half the population here live in well-furnished caves dug out of the soft tufa rock of the hillside. It is thought this troglodyte community, similar to others found in North Africa (see Tunisia, page 577 and Libya, page 636) was established following the Christian Reconquista of Spain, when fear of Philip II caused local Moors to seek safety underground. However there are a few surface buildings worth noting, especially the ruined 9th century Moorish Alcazaba with magnificent views over the cave-dwellers' quarter of the town. The cathedral is similar to that at Granada, but is mainly interesting for the fact that it is built on the site of a mosque.

GRANADA TO JAEN

Those travelling N from Granada to Jaén and with a serious interest in Moorish remains, should take the slower, more westerly, N432. At 52 km N of Granada is the small town of **Alcalá la Real**, dominated by its 11th century hilltop castle, the Forteleza de la Mota built when the town was known to the Moors as *Al-Kalaat Be Zayde*. The site includes an impressive church built on the foundations of a mosque and a Moorish Tower of Homage, which today houses a museum containing archaeological remains including Roman, Moorish and Christian artefacts. Coins, skeletons, pottery and weapons are all carefully displayed. Skilful restoration work is being carried out, including re-roofing the church. The guide has a key and will deserve a tip. Access is easy – just drive from the town centre to the top of the hill, where there is well-landscaped parking. The views from the castle over the surrounding olive groves and mountains are stupendous making this a highly recommended diversion. Overnight accommodation, however, is restricted to the *Pensión Zacatín*, Pradillo 1, T 580568. **Alcaudete**, 24 km further N, has a ruined and neglected Moorish castle, which is best seen from the road. The castle in **Martos** on the N321, captured from the Moors in 1225, is also ruined. For details of Jaén, see page 143.

GRANADA TO ANTEQUERA

Santa Fé in the plains 8 km W of Granada on the N-342 is a town which acquired its grid pattern streets and intersecting main thoroughfares when it was established in 1491 as an encampment for the Christian armies under the Catholic Kings during the Siege of Granada and its subsequent fall in 1492. The original settlement was composed of tents until, as the story goes, a fire began in Queen Isabel's tent while she was praying and the whole area was razed to the ground. Unfortunately for the defending Nasrids, they suspected this was a trick and did not attack, leaving Fernando and Isabel the opportunity to order the rapid construction of a permanent settlement on the site.

The other historical event which is celebrated here are the **Capitulaciones de Santa Fé** or Agreements reached between the Catholic Kings and Christopher Columbus in Apr 1492 in which the explorer was promised certain privileges if his voyage of discovery should prove successful; this paved the way for his subsequent discovery of the New World and explains why the town is sometimes called the 'Cradle of America'.

Alhama de Granada lies 53 km SW of Granada via the GR-430. This town, occupying a central position in the old Moorish kingdom, was a vital 'key' to the rest of the area when it was taken by the Christians in 1482. It is well worth a detour if you have time in order to appreciate the splendid views and see the 12th century hot Moorish baths in the depths of the *Hotel Balnearia*. The local spa is still in use for the treatment of rheumatic problems. No access by train.

Loja is a white village on the River Genil with the impressive Los Infiernos Falls to the E of the town and the Iznájar Reservoir to the W. It played a significant military role during the Reconquista and was finally captured from the Moors by Fernando and Isabel in 1488, when King Boabdil was captured by them for the second time. The walls of the 9th century Moorish **Alcazaba** fortress (a national monument) still dominate the town although they are best seen from a distance. The *mirador* on the old road above Loja provides a good vantage point. To the W there is an Arab bridge over the Genil, which dates back to the time of the Caliphate of Córdoba and still carries traffic.

Archidona is the next small town reached by continuing W on the N-342, or by train although the station is way out of town. The main attraction is its 18th century octagonal main square, but the surrounding hills contain a significant reminder of the area's Moorish past in the shape of a church high in the Sierra de Archidona. The **Santuario de la Virgen de Gracia** is signposted up a very steep, narrow tarmac road from the town. It was originally a 9th century mosque, Moorish settlement having been established in the area under Emir Abd Al-Rahman in AD 756. Following the reconquest of Archidona in 1462 the mosque was converted into a Christian church, although there may have been a church on the site prior to the arrival of the Moors, since the 3 arches inside the door are Visigothic. The mosque's *mihrab* was converted by the Christians into an altar to the Virgen de Gracia, the local patron saint whose fiesta is celebrated on Aug 14. Restoration work began in 1988. Open Nov-Jan 0900-1400 and 1500-1900, Feb-Apr 0800-1400 and 1600-2000 May-Aug and Sep-Oct 0700-1400 and 1700-2200. Admission free. There is very limited parking at the summit.

Nearby are the scant remains of an Arab fortress, the scene of much fighting amongst various factions of the occupying Moors and later between the Moors and Christians during the Reconquista. Local legend claims that a Moorish girl from Archidona fell in love with a Christian youth and that, knowing there could be no future for them, the pair jumped to their deaths from the peak of the distinctive **Peña de los Enamorados** (Lovers' Rock).

Antequera

Pop 41,000 *Alt* 512m *Best seasons* Spring and autumn.

Antequera is a small town in the Province of Málaga, 45 km N of the Mediterranean coast and **Málaga** itself. It is situated in a fertile valley in the foothills of the **Sierra de Chimenea** mountain range.

ACCESS Air The nearest airport is in Málaga 45 km away. **Train** From the train station in Avda Estación walk past the Campsa petrol station via Calle Cruz Blanca and Calle Lucena to the central

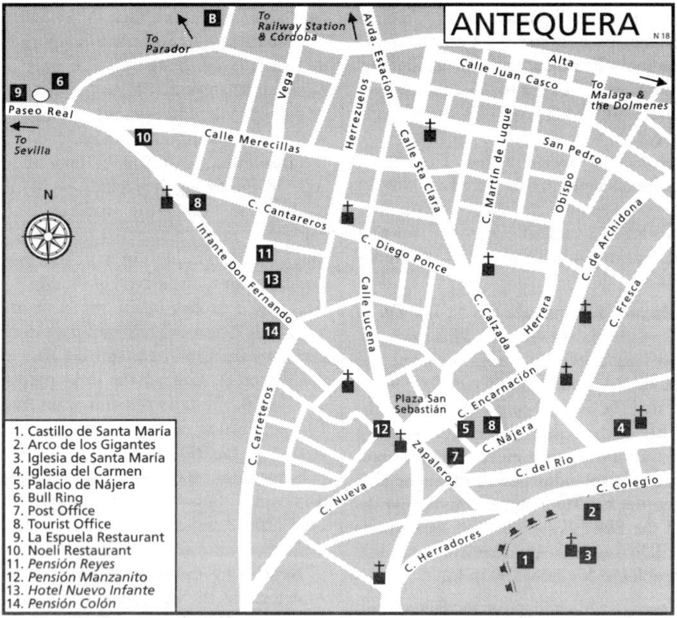

Plaza San Sebastián. Taxis await the trains. **Road** From the bus station on Paseo García del Olmo it is downhill to town via the nearby bullring, turning left onto the Alameda de Andalucía.

Things to see

Moorish past The Moorish remains at the top of the hill which overlooks the town can be reached on foot or by car (small parking area beneath the walls). The **Castillo de Santa María**, is a Moorish alcazaba built in the 14th century over the remains of a Roman castle. The most impressive features are the 2 towers, the 13th century Torre de Homenaje (Tower of Homage) and earlier Torre Blanco (White Tower). Both are undergoing restoration and should not be entered without the guide (if you can find him). The castle was captured from the Moors by a royal prince, the future King Fernando I of Aragón, in a Christian victory of such significance that he was henceforth known as *el de Antequera*. The courtyard of the alcazaba now consists of well-kept gardens with welcome shade, while the walls provide panoramic views over the town and surrounding hills. Admission free. Also on the hilltop is the **Arco de los Gigantes**, a type of triumphal arch built in 1585 for Philip II, but believed to incorporate stone from older monuments. Close to the arch is the church of **Santa María la Mayor**, with an ornate façade and restored Mudéjar ceilings. Today it functions as an art restoration centre, where students can learn stone masonry and the treatment of iron and woodwork. A display in the nave shows future restoration plans for Antequera's monuments.

Other places of interest

Antequera was originally a prehistoric site prior to successive occupation by the Romans, Arabs and Christians and its Megalithic **dólmenes**, a National Monument on the NE outskirts of the town off the road to Granada are some of the oldest and best preserved burial chambers in Europe. The **Cueva de Menga**, the oldest, dates back to 2500 BC with huge, roughly-cut stone slabs from a location 8 km away forming the roof. The nearby **Cueva del Viera**, discovered in 1905, is slightly less ancient and slightly smaller while the domed ceiling of the **Cueva de Romeral** c 1800 BC, 3 km N, is regarded as one of the earliest examples of Spanish architecture. Menga and Viera can be reached on foot by following signs for Granada from town. The local bus also runs this way. Open Tue-Fri 1000-1400 and 1500-1700, Sat and Sun 1000-1400. Admission is free. Romeral is a few km further along the main road on a rough track off left in the grounds of a sugar refinery. The cave itself is on the far side of the train line. Open Tue 1600-1800, Wed-Sat 0930-1430 and 1615-1830, Sun 1000-1400. Admission is free but the guardian will appreciate a tip.

Singilia Barba The recently excavated Roman ruins of Singilia Barba 6 km W of Antequera on the old road to Sevilla have revealed a cemetery, theatre, houses and many Roman artefacts. The area is privately owned, but the Town Hall in Antequera may be able to arrange a visit.

There are over 20 churches and convents in Antequera. The 16th century **Iglesia del Carmen** is noted for its Mudéjar woodwork ceiling, chiaroscuro panel and altars. The **Iglesia Encarnación** also has a Mudéjar ceiling, while the 17th century **Iglesia Los Remedios** is dedicated to Antequera's patron saint.

Museums

Ancient mansions are much in evidence in Antequera, including the Renaissance style **Palacio de Nájera** on Plaza Coso Viejo which now houses the **Museo Municipal** with its life-size bronze figure known as the *Efebo de Antequera* from 1 AD. Open Tue-Fri 1000-1330, Sat 1000-1300, Sun 1100-1300. Admission 100 Ptas. The **Museo Taurino** at the **Plaza de Toros** is open 1830-2100. Admission free.

Festivals

The *Carneval* is celebrated in Feb with satirical songs and fancy dress; traditional Catholic Easter processions take place during the *Semana Santa* celebrations; the *Feria de Primavera* (Spring Fair) at the end of May is seen as a practice for the *Real Feria de Agosto* (Royal Aug Fair) during the third week of Aug marked by bullfights; during the *Fiesta de Nuestra Señora de los Remedios*, 8 Sep, Antequera's patron saint is paraded through the streets.

Local information

● Accommodation

A *Parador de Antequera*, Calle García del Olmo s/n, T 2840261, F 2841312, 55 rm, pool, parking, restaurant, garden, TV, avoid during spring and Aug fairs if you want any sleep.

B *La Sierra*, Ctra Málaga-Madrid Km 583, T 2845410, restaurant, parking, TV, laundry, several km from town; **B** *Nuevo Infante*, Calle Infante Don Fernando 5, 2°, T 2700293, excellent new apartment style accommodation, garage, quiet, central, bar.

C *Lozano*, Póligono Industrial A6-A7, T 2842712, TV, good restaurant, several km from town near the dólmenes.

● Pensiones

D *Pensión Bella-Vista*, Cuesta de Archidona 27, T 2841997, off the Málaga-Granada road; **D** *Pensión Manzanito*, Plaza de San Sebastián 5, T 2841023, showers, in one of the main squares; **D** *Pensión Reyes*, Calle Tercia 4, T 2841028, restaurant, central but quiet; **D** *Pensión Colón*, Calle Infante Don Fernando 29, T 2844516, renovated, central. This about sums up the available accommodation here.

● Youth hostel

None in Antequera. Nearest is Málaga.

● Camping

The site at **El Torcal** does not figure in the official list for Andalucía, but is regarded as legitimate by the Antequera authorities, who are happy to advertise it. Located at Rio de la Villa, on the slopes of El Torcal.

● Places to eat

♦♦♦*Parador de Antequera*, Paseo García de Olmo, T 2840261, pricey but good. ♦♦ *La*

Espuela, Ctra de Córdoba s/n, Plaza de Toros, T 2702676, T 2702633, new restaurant inside the bullring, atmospheric, Andalusian cuisine; ***Mesón-Bar Noelía***, Alameda de Andalucía 12, T 2845407, functional but good; ***Reyes***, Calle Tercia 4, T 2841038. ♦***Bar Madroña***, Calle Calzada 31, T 2840014; ***Manzanito***, Plaza San Sebastián 4, T 2841023; ***Toril***, Calle Toril 3-5, T 2843184, lively.

● Banks
There are numerous banks in Calle Infante Don Fernando, though many do not open on Sat in summer.

● Entertainment, craft and cuisine
The 19th century bullring is used mainly during the *Feria de Primavera* and *Feria Real* (see Festivals). A **flamenco singing contest** also takes place during the former while more of the art can be seen during the *Noche Flamenco de Santa María* in Aug. A **flea market** is held in Avda de la Estación on Sun mornings. **Gastronomic specialities** include *porra antequerana* (fritters), *pío* (bread soaked in gravy), Antequeran *gazpacho* and *bienmesabe* (a dessert created by nuns).

● Garages/petrol
In Plaza de la Constitución near the bullring, Avda de la Estación.

● Hospitals
Casa de Socorro, Calle Picadero, T 2844411; *Cruz Roja*, Calle Infante Don Fernando s/n, T 2842283.

● Post Office
Correos, Calle Nájera s/n, near Museo Municipal, T 2842083. Mon-Fri 0800-1500, Sat 0900-1300. Telegrams by telephone, T 2222000.

● Sport
Gliding centre, contact Town Hall, T 2844211.

● Telephones
Local code: 95. All numbers have a 2 prefix. There is no *locutorio* but there are plenty of public telephones on Calle Infante Don Fernando and Alameda de Andalucía.

● Travel agents
Viajes Ibermar, Infante Don Fernando 49; *Viajes Toral*, Plaza Pintor Cristobal Toral 2, T 2840112.

● Tourist information
Plaza Coso Viejo, inside Palacio de Nájera, T 2842180. Open Tue-Fri 1000-1330, Sat 1000-1300, Sun 1100-1300. Also Oficina Municipal, Edificio San Luis, Calle Infante Don Fernando, T 2700405. Open daily 1000-1400 and 1700-2000.

● Transport
Local Car hire Autos Malu, c/o Viajes Toral, Plaza Pintor Cristóbal Toral, T 2840112; **Rentacar** Antequera, San Agustín 4, T 2702892. **Taxi** T 2841008, T 2841076.

Air National and international flights from **Málaga**.

Train The major train junction is at **Bobadilla Estación** several km W of **Antequera**. Only 3 trains per day visit **Antequera**, 2 go direct to **Sevilla**. For **Cádiz** change at **Dos Hermanas**, for other locations change at **Bobadilla**. RENFE office, Divina Pastora 8, reservations on T 2844068.

Road Bus station on Paseo García del Olmo, T 2841957. Local tickets from Ranea SA (to **Teba** and **Archidona**) and Casado SA upstairs, including 5 per day to **Bobadilla** train junction. Intercity routes downstairs, Alsina Graells, T 2841365. Frequent service to **Málaga**, **Sevilla** and **Granada**. No buses to **Ronda**.

Antequera to Ronda

Teba on the C-341 is a walled Moorish town on a hilltop above the Rio Almargen and is the first interesting stop after Antequera W on the train line towards Ronda, also accessible by bus from Antequera. Lord James of Douglas died here in 1330 in a battle against the Moors, despite being accompanied by a casket containing Robert the Bruce's heart. The heart has since been repatriated to Scotland and a monument erected here in Scottish granite. The large **Castillo de la Estrella** was built by the Moors.

Excursions

El Torcal de Antequera, 16 km S, is a nearby National Park in a mountain setting. To reach it by car, take the C-3310 towards Villanueva de la Concepción, turning off right after about 12 km towards the *refugio* (mountain hut) complete with bar, at the foot of the mountain which reaches 1,369m at its highest point. Buses towards Villanueva de la Concepción are infrequent and drop you at the turn off with several km still to walk. The best options are hitchhiking or a taxi. From the *refugio* there are 2 circular routes marked with arrows. With the aid of substantial footwear, the yellow circuit can be walked in under 1 hr, while the red path takes 2 hrs. El Torcal is noted for the eerie atmosphere created by its limestone and marble rocks which have been eroded by the wind and slightly acidic water into strange and tortuous shapes, known to geologists as 'karstic scenery'. The reserve covers 21 sq km. However it is also worth visiting for its marvellous views over the mountains and down to the Mediterranean as well as to appreciate its flora and fauna, especially in spring. Bird watchers might see booted and short-toed eagles, blue rock thrushes and black wheatears, while there is an abundance of reptiles including the rare green-eyed lizard. Keen naturalists should, however, avoid the weekends, when large numbers of Spaniards will ensure that any self-respecting fauna remains well hidden.

A guided tour operator, Sondytour, offers specialized tours to all local monuments. For further information T 2700405, open daily 1000-1400 and 1600-1800.

Laguna de la Fuente de Piedra, located close to the town of the same name, lies just off the N334 to the W of Antequera. In winter this saline lagoon extends up to 14,000 ha. In summer, however, the heat and wind induce high levels of evaporation. Until the 1950s it was used as a *salinera* producing salt commercially, today it is famous for its Greater Flamingoes and is fully protected by AMA, the environment department of the Andalucian Regional government, who have made it into a full scale nature reserve with a warden, conservation centre and hides. The breeding success of the flamingoes depends entirely on the amount of winter rain. In 1990, for example, after a wet winter, the flamingoes produced 10,400 chicks. In 1993, on the other hand, the lake had dried out by Easter, and the flamingoes dispersed to other areas. Other breeding birds include Gull Billed Terns, Black Winged Stilts, Avocets, Kentish Plovers and the rare White Headed Duck.

ACCESS Drive through the town of Fuente de Piedra, cross the railway and take a track to the left of a rubbish dump to a small hill on the top of which is the conservation centre. The best viewing time is in the early morning before the heat haze develops. A walk round the lagoon will take about 3 hrs.

• **Accommodation** There are 2 adequate pensiones and one small hotel, all located in the village on the Sevilla-Málaga road, while there is an excellent camp site close by.

Ronda

Pop 33,000 *Alt* 750m *Best seasons* Spring and autumn.

Ronda, a charming town 75 km W of Antequera and 100 km N of Algeciras, should be a priority for any traveller in S Andalucía. It is located on a plain in the Serranía de Ronda mountains, the town being cut in half by a most spectacular gorge – **El Tajo** – some 120m deep. It has a more extreme climate than the coast, with colder winters (snow is not uncommon) and very hot summers when midday temperatures can average 33°C.

History

Ronda has a long and fascinating history. The Iberians named it Arunda; then the Romans changed it to Munda. It enjoyed prosperous times during the Moorish occupation which lasted for more than 8 centuries. The Moors fortified it so well that it took 38,000 troops to capture it for the Christians in 1485. What remained of the Moorish Alcazaba was destroyed by the French during the Peninsular War in 1809. Ronda also saw plenty of action during the Civil War, when representatives from both sides were thrown into the Tajo. In the early years of this century Ronda was a popular retreat for British officers based in Gibraltar. Now the British come on coaches from the Costa, but this does not seem to spoil the essential charm of the town.

ACCESS Air The nearest airport is at Málaga, some 122 km E. **Train** The train station is located a short walk away (10 mins) on the N edge of the town in Avda Andalucía. **Road** Ronda is at the centre of a network of roads, the one S to San Pedro de Alcántara and the Costa del Sol being particularly well-engineered and scenic. The **bus** station is in the N of the town in Plaza Concepción García Redondo just 5 mins walk from the centre.

Things to see

Moorish past The **Puente Arabe**, a carefully restored Moorish bridge, can be found at an even lower level than the **Puente Romano**. From this low level it is interesting to see the different styles used to bridge this ravine. From here one can reach the **Baños Arabes** (Moorish Baths) dating from the 14th century. Af-

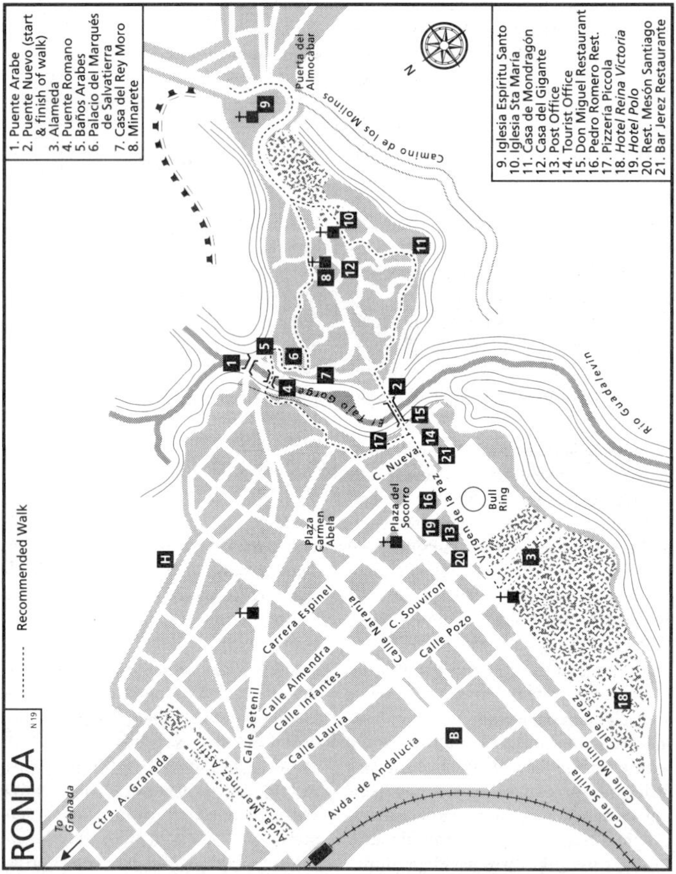

ter a period involving minor renovations the site is now open on an occasional basis. There is no entrance fee, but equally there are no brochures available nor are the various parts of the baths labelled. 'Guides' who lurk around the *cuidad* can be hired to provide information. It is to be hoped that with a further application of funds this neglected asset can be turned into a major tourist attraction.

The **Minarete de San Sebastián** is a 14th century example of the Nasrid style of architecture. In the walls nearby further evidence of Ronda's Moorish history is to be found in the Arab **Puerta del Almocábar**, a horseshoe arch with 2 matching towers. Of the 3 recorded original Moorish gates into the city, this is the only one remaining. One of the others once stood in Plaza del Campillo.

The **Iglesia de Santa María la Mayor** was originally a 13th century mosque, which was re-built by the Christians but retains much of the Moorish architecture. It has a late Gothic nave and Baroque choir stalls, while the frontal balcony facing the square provided a position for dignitaries to watch bullfights before the main bullring was built. One of the mosque's original Moorish horseshoe arches can still be seen.

The **Casa de Mondragón** is an Arab palace built by Abomelic, King of Ronda, in 1314. It was later adapted for the use of Ferdinand and Isabel. There are other Renaissance additions, but the rear Mudéjar patio has been retained. Entrance 200 Ptas, open 0800-1500. The **Casa del Gigante** is another 14th century Moorish palace, with decorative features claimed to date alongside those of the Alhambra (see page 87).

Other places of interest

The **Alameda** is a shady park with a small aviary. At the far end is a *balcón* giving magnificent views over the gorge and the surrounding countryside. Bird watchers are in their element here as the cliff boasts breeding peregrine falcons, blue rock thrushes, alpine swifts and choughs (see Wildlife, page 36).

The **Plaza de Toros** in Ronda, built 1785, is said to be the oldest in Spain. It holds only 5,000. Used as setting for film 'Carmen'. Ronda is the home of the modern form of bullfighting (on foot) which was perfected by the Romero family.

The **Casa del Rey Moro**, despite its name, was largely built in the early 19th century. It has a footpath cut in the rocks to the bottom of the gorge, said to have been used by Christian slaves to bring water to their Moorish masters!

The **Puerta de Carlos V**, the other gate in the original city walls, dates from the 16th century. Alongside the ramparts is the **Iglesia del Espíritu Santo**, a 15th century Catholic church built in the time of Ferdinand.

Museums

There is a small **Museo Taurino** under the Plaza de Toros, and whatever one's feelings about bullfighting, this is a fascinating place. Open summer 1000-1400 and 1600-1900, winter 1000-1400. Admission is 200 Ptas. Tickets can be obtained from the shop next to the bullring entrance.

The new **Museo Arqueológico** is housed in the Casa de Mondragón.

Suggested route

A convenient start is at the main bridge, the **Puente Nuevo** (2), which links the *ciudad viejo* (old town) with the *mercadillo* (new town). It was completed in 1793, but only after its architect fell to his death inspecting his work! Proceed through the Plaza de España, past the bullring and into the **Alameda** (3). Returning via the Plaza de Toros, go to Plaza de España and down Calle Villanueva. Take the first right into Los Remedios. After 200m , any alleyway to the right will bring you into a series of beautifully terraced gardens, known as **La Mina** (this does not have a number!), affording stupendous views of El Tajo. Emerging from the gardens, cross the gorge by the old bridge, the **Puente Romano** (4), originally a Roman bridge re-built in 1616. From here a path leads to the **Baños Arabes** (5). Return to Calle Santo Domingo and climb the steep hill past the **Palacio del Marqués de Salvatierra** (6), an ornate, privately owned 18th century building with handsome balconies of typical Ronda wrought ironwork. To the right is the **Casa del Rey Moro** (7).

At the top the hill, near a cluster of antique shops, is Calle Armiñán, the main road through the town. Turn left and follow this road to the old city walls marking the edge of the town, passing on the way the free-standing **Minarete de San Sebastián** (8). Note the 2 gates in the city walls and the **Iglesia del Espíritu Santo** (9). Continue back into town, turning left into the old quarter via Plaza Duquesa de Parcent. This charming square, also known as Plaza de la Cuidad, with well-kept gardens and trees, is flanked by a number of interesting buildings. The 18th century barracks is now the Town Hall; the site of the old Moorish fortress is now a boys' school; there are also 2 small convents and the law courts. The crowning glory of the square, however, is the church of **Santa María la Mayor** (10). The **Casa de Mondragón** (11) is nearby.

Proceed from here to Plaza del Gigante, which takes its name from the **Casa del Gigante** (12) which is located there. This is the best preserved Arab house to be seen in Ronda, distinguished by a gigantic figure depicted on one wall. Unfortunately the interior is closed to visitors. Continue to Plaza del Campillo, where there are views down steep slopes to the valley. Return to the Puente Nuevo via Calle Tenorio. This route should be followed using one of the town plans which can be obtained from the tourist office, in the Plaza de España.

TOURIST GUIDES There is a lively tourist guide business. For an informative tour of Ronda's historic sites, phone José Paez Carroscosa, T 2873468. **NB**: unofficial guides may fasten on to tourists while they are sightseeing, impart a few words of wisdom and then demand money. Don't get involved!

Festivals

These include *Semana Santa*; the *Feria de Mayo* in May celebrating the Reconquista; *Corpus Christi* in May/Jun when flowers cover the ground in the Alameda; the Pedro Romero Festival in early Sep with *corridas goyescas* (special bullfights in Goyaesque attire). There is also an International Folk Festival in Sep and a flamenco festival on the last Sat in Aug as part of the *Feria de Ronda*.

Local information

● Accommodation

A *Reina Victoria*, Calle Jerez 25, T 2871240, beautifully located Edwardian hotel built by the English, 88 rm, one rm is a small museum dedicated to the German poet Rainer María Rilke, good views, pool, garage.

B *Don Miguel*, Calle Villanueva 8, T 2877722, adjacent to gorge, comfortable, clean, excellent restaurant, garage; **B** *Polo*, Calle Mariano Souvirón, T 2872447, 33 rm, restaurant, convenient for the town centre.

D *Royal*, Calle Virgen de la Cruz, T 2871141, rec.

● Pensiones

C *Andalucía*, Martinez Astern 19, opposite railway station, clean, with bath, highly rec; **C** *El Tajo*, Calle Doctor Cajal 7, T 2876236, garage, modern, rec.

D *Pensión Biarritz*, Calle Almendra 7, T 2872910, clean, good beds, budget accommodation; **D** *Pensión Ronda Sol*, Calle Almendra 11, rm with bath, T 2874497; **D** *Casa de Huespedes La Española*, off Plaza España, rms with bath, clean, great views over Tajo.

Travellers wishing to stay in a nearby village could consider **D** *Moneda* Calle Luis Armiñán, Gaucín, T 2151156. **Gaucín**, which lies 37 km S of Ronda on the C341, was a favourite stop for British officers en route from Gibraltar to Ronda.

● Camping

There are no official camp sites in the vicinity of Ronda, the nearest being on the Costa del Sol and the Parque Natural Sierra de Grazalema to the W.

● Places to eat

The better restaurants in Ronda serve the traditional food of the area, including *cocidos* and game dishes. ◆◆◆ ***Don Miguel***, Plaza de España. T 2871090, probably the best food in Ronda, certainly the best view, with its terrace overlooking the bridge and gorge, some average priced meals; ***Pedro Romero***, Virgen de la Paz, T 2871061, located by the bull ring, regional decor. ◆◆ ***Bar Restaurante Jerez***, Paseo de Blas Infante 2, T 2872098, by the bullring, happily caters for both tourists and locals with average costs; ***Pizzería Piccola***, Calle Villanueva, T 2873943, one of the few restaurants in Ronda serving international food, nice atmosphere and good views over the Tajo; ***Restaurante Mesón Santiago***, Calle Marina 3, T 2871559, traditional Ronda restaurant with attractive patio dining area and cheap to average prices; ***Hermanos Andrades***, Calle Los Remedios 1, good value. ◆ ***Restaurante Flores***, Virgen de la Paz 9, T 2871040, popular with tourists, reasonable *menú del día* at 800 Ptas; ***Cervecería El Patio***, Calle Carrera Espinel 100, T 2871015, patio dining area; ***Rico, La Ibense***, Calle Espinel 42, icecreams and snacks. Restaurant at railway station is good. Try also the café at the bus station for a small snack and a large slice of Spanish life.

● Banks

The main bank in the town is the Caja de Ahorros de Ronda in Calle Virgen de la Paz opposite the bullring, numerous banks elsewhere in town. Normal banking hours. There are also a few establishments offering change facilities in the bullring area.

● Garages/petrol

Filling stations are hard to find. One is located on the S edge of the town on the Marbella road, the other on the N bypass. There are several garages located on the El Fuerte industrial estate.

● Hospitals

Hospital Comarcal, Ctra del Burgo, T 2871540; **Emergencies**: *Clinica Espinillo*, T 2871773.

● Post Office

Correos, Virgen de la Paz, 20, T 2876391. Open Mon-Fri 0800-1500, Sat 0900-1300.

● Shopping

Ronda's function as a regional centre means that it does not go out of its way to cater for tourists. The main pedestrianized shopping street is the Calle de la Bola (shown on maps as Carrera Espinel) which runs E from the bullring for approx 1 km. Regional specialities include saddlery, wrought ironwork and antiques. There is a **street market** held on Sundays at the Barrio de San Francisco near the S walls of the old town. Shops on Calle Nueva sell equipment for camping.

● Telephones

Local code: 95(2). *Locutorios* on Calle de la Bola and Calle El Niño.

● Tourist Information

Plaza de España 1, T 2871272.

● Transport

Local Bicycle hire Biciserrania, opposite bus station. **Car hire** Local firms only, **Francisco Sánchez**, Los Remedios 26, T 2871343; **Velesco**, Calle Lorenzo Borrego 11, T 2872722. **Taxis** The main taxi rank is in the Plaza Carmen Abela; **Radio Taxi**, T 2872316.

Train Station in Avda Andalucía, T 2871673. **Ronda** is on the line from **Bobadilla** to **Algeciras**. Five trains a day run in each direction, including 2 *expresos*. You should change at **Bobadilla** for **Málaga**. The line W runs through a number of towns and villages, including **Gaucín** **(see page 106)**, **Castellar de la Frontera** **(see page 106)** and **San Roque**, but the timetable should be checked carefully to see where each train stops.

Road Bus Most routes are operated by the Portillo company. There are 3 buses a day directly to **Málaga**, one to **La Línea** and 3 to **Cádiz** (one of which proceeds to **Jerez**). The most direct and frequent buses link with **Marbella** and these can be boarded in the Plaza de España. Services to the *pueblos blancos*, typical Andalusian hill villages in which the residents paint their houses white, to the W of Ronda involve complicated connections and careful planning.

RONDA TO ALGECIRAS

La Jimera de Líbar is set back off the C-341 on the right, 20 km SW of Ronda. Without turning off the main road, you can see the church tower which is worth noting since it was originally a minaret, converted into its present role following the Reconquista.

Gaucín, 7 km S of **El Colmenar** station, has a ruined 13th century Moorish castle, **El Castillo del Aguila**, so called for its eagle's views to Gibraltar and Africa. Guzmán el Bueno of Tarifa died here in 1309 while attempting to capture the fortress. Just N of the station is **Cortes de la Frontera Nature Reserve**, home of the wild Spanish goat.

Jimena de la Frontera, 23 km further down the C-341, is one of the more beautiful *pueblos blancos* notable for its ruined Moorish castle which was recaptured by the Christians in 1434. One clear reminder of its strong fortifications is the triple gateway at the entrance to the castle, although little else remains. The station is inconveniently several km out of town.

Castellar de la Frontera, on a side road 22 km S on the C-3331, adjacent to the Guadarranque reservoir, is 7 km uphill from the station at **Almoraima**. Abandoned in the 1970's (the inhabitants moving down to a new village), it has a large Moorish castle which is like a miniature town inside. Although little appears to have altered since it was captured from the Moors in 1434, the area is now rather incongruously occupied by German hippies.

One of the most interesting ways to do this journey is by train. Trains leave Ronda at 0702, 0725, 1141, 1623, 1947 and 2030, take almost 2 hrs and cost 600 Ptas. The railway runs adjacent to the Río Guadiaro which has cut some spectacular ravines, through a series of small tunnels between which are tantalizing views of the river and the mountainside. It travels on through the milk producing areas of San Pablo and Los Angeles, from where the fortress of Jimena de la Fron-

Cork In The Bottle

The native evergreen Cork Oak *Quercus suber*, which flourishes on the gentle hillslopes of the SW corner of Iberia is highly prized for its commercial value. It is instantly recognised by its orange-brown smooth trunk where the 'bark' has been gently stripped away from the ground up to its main branches.

It takes 20 years for a sapling to mature and thereafter the dead outer layer of 'bark' can be harvested every 7 years. As these trees can live for 300-400 years it is a good investment. The cork men from Cádiz province search all over Andalucía for suitable trees to cut and even villa owners with 3 or 4 trees may find themselves the subject of negotiations.

The cylinders of cork are removed in the summer and taken to processing plants (such as those near Castellar and San Roque). After boiling to dissolve the tannic acid and soften the material the rough outer layers are taken off and the sheets are left to mature.

Cork is, of course, best known for its use as a stopper in wine bottles, a practice introduced in the 17th century, thereby revolutionising the storage of wines. Cork, however, has many other uses. Its lightness, buoyancy, and resistance to burning means that it makes excellent material for insulation. It is also used for floor tiles, fishing floats and formerly for cricket balls. Furthermore, there is evidence that the ancient Egyptians, seeking comfort to the end, used this most versatile of materials for lining coffins.

tera can be seen. Griffin vultures are common here and down towards San Roque storks' nests adorn the electricity cable towers alongside the line. Alight at sleepy San Roque with its smart new station for the infrequent bus to La Linea and Gibraltar or continue down to the terminus at Algeciras. The train is slow, the stops are frequent but the experience of Spanish life both from the window and inside the train is not to be missed.

Algeciras

This is a busy container port in the Province of Cádiz. It is ugly and polluted, notable chiefly for its position at the end of the train line from Madrid and its proximity to Morocco. It has views across the Algeciras Bay to Gibraltar and the equally uninspiring town of **La Linea**, and across the Straits to Morocco. The recent opening of the long-awaited Algeciras bypass has helped to relieve the town's traditional traffic congestion. As a major embarkation point for Tanger and Ceuta with frequent daily ferries to both, Algeciras becomes congested during the summer months as migrant Algerian and Moroccan workers return home from France, Belgium and the Netherlands. Tickets available at the port, on embarkation from Trasmediterránea, Recinto del Puerto, T 663850. Refuse unofficial offers of tickets. See page 355 for further information.

Moorish past

The town's name is derived from the Moorish *el Gezira el-Khadra* (Green Island). The Moors landed here when they first invaded Iberian soil in 711 under their commanders Musa and Tarik. The 'Pillars of Hercules' at either side of the Straits of Gibraltar are named after the Moorish leaders: Jebel Tarik (Gibraltar) on the European coast after the general who led the invasion and Jebel Musa on the African coast after Musa Ibn Nusayr his lieutenant.

A major Christian victory was achieved by Alfonso XI in 1344. Participation in this assault was referred to by a character in Chaucer's *Canterbury Tales* as an indication of his knightly valour. A few decades later, in 1379, Algeciras was destroyed during a Moorish raid and had to be reconstructed by Carlos III. Consequently the Moorish names are the only remaining traces of the centuries they spent in the town.

Local information

● Accommodation

Although there are hotels here, most notably the luxurious but faded **A** ***Reina Cristina***, Paseo de la Conferencia, T 602622, F 603323, those interested in the Moorish past would do far better to travel W to **Tarifa** (**see page 183**) to seek accommodation and visible reminders of Andalucía's heritage.

THE MEDITERRANEAN HUERTAS

CONTENTS

MAPS

ALMERIA

The Province of Almería is the most easterly of the provinces of Andalucía. It is also the driest and least populated with only 400,000 people living in its 8,000 sq km. The scenery is varied with barren semi-desert, mountains, impressive cliffs and remote coves, but also vast areas of '*plasticultura*' (see page 116). Despite the airport at Almería, neither residential nor hotel tourism has made much progress here, especially when compared with the Costa del Sol. One has the distinct feeling that much of the area has more in common with North Africa than with mainland Europe. The huerta – a fertile, irrigated region – was introduced when the Moors brought their agricultural expertise to the S Iberian peninsula. Almería continues to be a source of much of Spain's agricultural produce today.

The City with 145,000 inhabitants is also a busy port, with ferry links to Melilla, Genoa and Palma. The old part of the town lies between the Moorish castle and the port, while the modern town centre focuses on the tree-lined Paseo de Almería. Recent development is spreading E along the coast. Almería's population has fluctuated, with a peak of 300,000 under the Moors in the 14th century.

Almería's climate is the driest and sunniest in Andalucía. Humidity is low

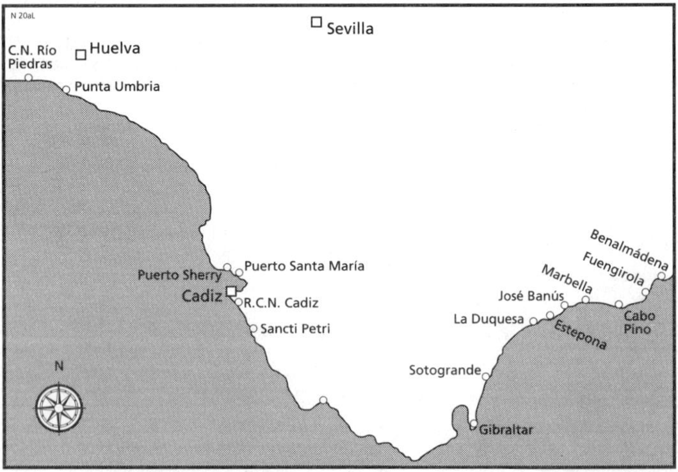

Pleasure Craft Harbours Of Andalucia

	Berths	Harbour/entrance width/depth	Anchorage	Services
GARRUCHA	221	170m/14m	sandy	WEFITRC
SAN JOSE	243	35m/6m	sandy	WE ITRC
CLUB DE MAR ALMERIA	185	300m/10m	stone & mud	WEFITRCMS
AGUADULCE	764	60m/6m	stone & sand	WEFITRCMS
ROQUETAS DE MAR	183	90m/4m	mud	WEFIT CMS
ALMERIMAR	1100	140m/2m	sand	WEFITRCMS
ADRA	120	65m/7m	mud	WE IT CMS
MOTRIL	168	92m/11m	muddy	WE ITRCMS
PUNTA DE LA MONA	227	45m/4m	rocky	WEFITRCMS
CALETA DE VELEZ	200	80m/5m	sand	CMS
EL CANDADO	215	30m/3m	sand & mud	WE TR M
R.C. MEDITERRANEO	20	70m/8m	mud & stone	WE TRC
BENALMADENA	961	180m/5m	sand	WEFITRCMS
FUENGIROLA	226	70m/4m	mud & sand	WE ITRCMS
CABO PINO	169	60m/4m	sand	WEF CMS
MARBELLA	377	20m/4m	sand	WEF CMS
JOSE BANUS	915	80m/7m	sand	WEFITRCMS
ESTEPONA	443	80m/5m	rocky	WE ITRCMS
LA DUQUESA	328	70m/7m	sandy	WEFIT CMS
SOTOGRANDE	545	80m/5m	sandy	WEFITRCMS
R.C.N. ALGECIRAS	70	40m/9m	sandy	WE ITR
CLUB NAUTICO BARBATE	105	150m/5m	mud & sand	WE R MS
C.N.SANCTI PETRI	250	100m/2m	mud	WEFI R
R.C.N. DE CADIZ	200	80m/8m	mud	WEFITRC S
SANTA MARIA	200	100m/5m	mud	WE ITRCMS
SHERRY	753	100m/4m	sandy	WEFITRCMS
R.C.N. HUELVA	400	river/12m	muddy	ITRCMS
PUNTA UMBRIA	175	river/1m	muddy	ITRC
RIO PIEDRAS		50m/1m	sandy	ITRCMS
C.N. SEVILLA	52	river/2m	mud & sand	WE ITRCMS

Key Water, **E**lectricity, **F**uel, **T**elephone, **R**amp, **C**rane, **M**echanic, **S**hop.

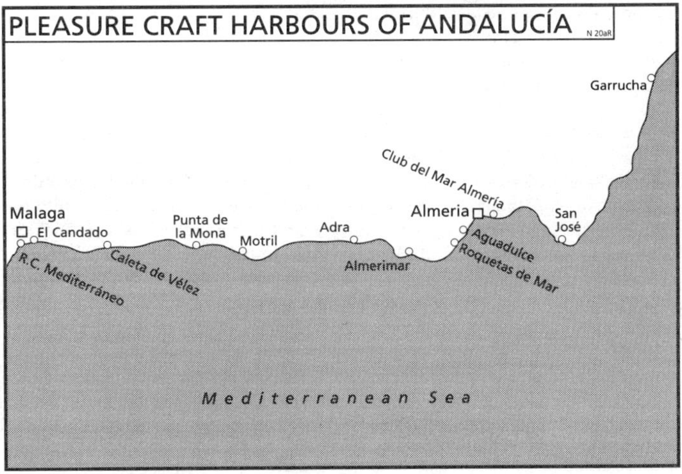

and hours of sunshine high. Cloud and rain are restricted to a mere 17 days a year. The highest temperature recorded is 38°C.

ACCESS Almería can be approached by road, train, ferry and air. **Air** The airport is 8 km from the city on the N-344 Almería-Níjar motorway. Buses leave every 30 mins for town centre. **Train** The train station is on the Ctra de Ronda near to the port. **Road** The bus station is 200m N of it in Plaza de Barcelona.

Things to see

Moorish past The **Alcazaba** is the largest Moorish castle in Andalucía and its hill site dominates the city of Almería. Although it can be easily seen from most parts of the city, it can be quite complicated to find the entrance. The historic parts of the city are clearly signposted, but the streets in the old part are narrow and confusing, so obtain a town plan from the Tourist Office first. Approach via the Cathedral and Calle Almanzor. If you are lost, you will find the local inhabitants very helpful. There is limited parking at the entrance of the Alcazaba and also in the nearby Plaza Vieja.

The Alcazaba has had a chequered history, reflecting that of the town itself. Its most glorious period was during the 11th century during the reigns of Jayran, Zuhayr and Almotacin, but it has also experienced periods of total neglect. The origins of the Alcazaba date back to 955, when the Caliph Abd Al-Rahman III gave the city the classification of 'Medina' and ordered the construction of the fortress. Although in the beginning the Alcazaba served as the headquarters of the governors and Muslim kings and in later times as the residence of the Christian rulers, it was always first and foremost a military base. This use, combined with the effects of the earthquake of 1522 plus subsequent renovations has substantially altered the original appearance.

It consists of 3 defensive compounds, all containing construction from different periods of history. The first compound was organized into a complex defence system including towers and ziz-zag ramps. This compound originally served as a military camp and a constant supply of fresh water was brought by windmills from wells below. Today it is a garden with attractive areas of flowing water. The ramparts eventually arrive at the **Wall of the Watch** which served as a bell tower. From here the massive wall stretches away to the NE, spanning a deep valley and up to the Mount of San Cristóbal with another tower and large statue. This wall reminds visitors inevitably of the Great Wall of China. The second compound served as a residence for the Muslim kings and Governors and also housed their guards and servants. Within the compound are the remains of watermills, a mosque (converted into a Mudéjar-style shrine by the Catholic Kings), some Muslim houses and military baths in the Roman style. Archaeological work is continuing in this compound. The third compound is entirely post-Muslim. After the reconquest of Almería, the Catholic Kings ordered the construction of a castle in the westernmost and highest part of the Alcazaba. Entrance was by a bridge over a

CLIMATE: ALMERIA

	Jan	Feb	Mar	Apr	May	Jun	Jul	Aug	Sep	Oct	Nov	Dec	Av/Tot
Max (°C)	16	16	18	20	22	26	29	29	27	23	19	17	22
Min (°C)	8	9	11	13	15	18	21	22	20	16	12	10	16
Rain (mm)	31	21	21	28	18	4	0	6	16	25	27	36	233

moat protected by 3 semicircular towers. The interior courtyard is dominated by the **Homage Tower**. Two other buildings are the **Windmill Tower** and the **Gunpowder Tower**. From these are excellent views over the city, the port and the gypsy area below the castle known as **La Chanca**. Open 1000-1400 and 1630-2000. Entrance fee 250 Ptas, free for EU citizens with proof of identity.

Other places of interest

The **Cathedral** is a large, uninspiring structure begun in 1524 on the site of an old mosque, but most of the work was carried out in the 17th century. It was built for defence against attacks by Berber pirates, as well as worship. It consequently has massive stone walls and small high windows. Inside is an altar designed by Ventura Rodríguez and paintings by Alonso Cano. Open 0830-1200 and 1730-2000.

Centro de Rescate de la Fauna Sahariana (Sahara Wildlife Rescue Cen-

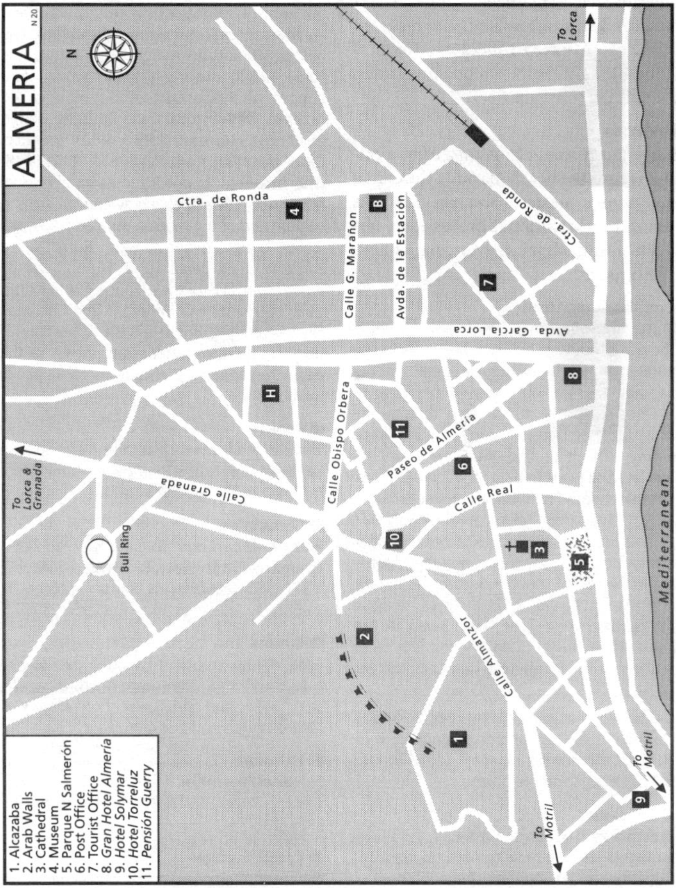

tre). This is located in the valley behind the Alcazaba and was established in 1971 with help from the World Wildlife Fund to save Saharan species in danger of extinction. The venture has been extremely successful. The centre is not generally open to the public, but it is possible to obtain a permit from the organization's headquarters close to the Tourist Office.

Museums

The Museo de Almería in Calle Jávier Sanz, which contained largely archaeological displays, has now been replaced by the new **Museo Arqueológico** on Ctra Ronda 13, T 225058. For opening times, consult the tourist office.

Festivals

Early Jan *Romería Virgen del Mar*, a pilgrimage to the beach marking the end of the winter fiestas; *Semana Santa* is marked by traditional processions; last week of Aug, *Virgen del Mar*; end of Dec, *winter fiestas*.

Local information

● Accommodation

There is a variety of hotels available, including traditional hotels in Almería itself without package tourists, but likely to be noisy, or alternatively in the surrounding resorts with wider facilities. Decent cheap accommodation is very difficult to find. **AL** ***Gran Hotel Almería***, Avda Reina Regente 8, T 238011, comfortable, located between the town and port, a/c rm, TV, garage, disco, pool; **A** *Solymar*, Ctra de Málaga 110, T 234622, good location overlooking the fishing port and the Moorish castle, excellent but expensive restaurant, guests might be worried by the gypsy re-housing portacabin site just 100m away! **A** ***Torreluz***, Plaza Flores, T 234799, this is in fact a series of 4 hotels offering various prices and facilities.

B *Costasol*, Paseo de Almería 58, T 234011, convenient for bus and train stations; **B** *Indalico*, Calle Dolores Sopeña 4, T231111, central but noisy location, garage.

● Pensiones

D *Estación*, Calzada de Castro 37, T 267239, a modest pensión close to both the train and bus stations; **D** *Maribel*, Avda Lorca 153, T 235173, adequate accommodation in a handy central position; **D** *Nixar*, Calle Antonio Vico, 14, T 237255, clean, 38 rm, some with bath.

● Youth hostel

Isla Fuerte Ventura, 04007 Almería, T 269788, 173 beds, meals available, suitable for wheelchair users.

● Camping

La Garrofa, Ctra Motril-Almería Km 108, T 235770, open all year round.

● Places to eat

There are plenty of eating places in Almería, but except in the major hotel restaurants, there are few concessions to international food. The best restaurants are either on, or just off, the Paseo de Almería, the N end of which has a good range of *tapas* bars suited to more limited budgets. ♦♦♦*Anfora*, Calle González Gerbín 25, T 231374, specializes in local produce; *Club de Mar*, Calle Muelle 1, T 255048, wharfside setting, good international cuisine. ♦♦There is little available between the top and bottom end of the market. ♦those on a more limited budget might consider ***Buffet Libre Almería***, Calle Jerez 10, T 260137, eat as much as you like for the set price; ***Hong Kong***, Calle Hermanos Machado 2, T 264338, basic Chinese cuisine. There are also a number of bar-restaurants offering cheap *menús* of the day in the Parque de Nicolás Salmerón opposite the port.

● Banks

There are branches of all the main Spanish banks in the town centre. Opening hours Mon-Fri 0900-1400, Sat 0900-1300.

● Consulates

France, Avda Cabo de Gata 81, T 252284; **Germany**, Hotel Satellite Park, Aguadulce, T 340555; **Netherlands**, Reyes Católicos 26, T 268504; **UK**, contact Málaga T 952 217571.

● Cuisine

Local dishes to look for include *gachas* (hot clam stew), *trigo* (stew with grains of wheat, pork, beans and herbs) and *choto al ajo y en ajillo* (kid with garlic or garlic sauce).

● Hospitals

Hospital Provincial, T 230604 and T 241455; *Cruz Roja*, T 222222. **Emergencies**: T 257198.

● Petrol/Garages

Peugeot: Talleres Sur Padre Santaella, 8,

T 238101; **Ford**: Pareje de los Callejones, Km 117, Ctra Nacional 340, T 233478; **Renault**: Ctra N-340, T 259312.

● Post Office

Correos, Plaza J Casinello 1, Paseo de Almería, T 237207.

● Shopping

The commercial centre of Almería is in the Paseo de Almería, the Puerta de Purchena, the Calle de las Tiendas and the surrounding area. Handicraft items which are typical of the area include ceramics and pottery, *jarapas* (rough cloth made with rags and strips), bedspreads and blankets, esparto grass and basketwork and small carved marble goods.

● Telephones

Local code: 951. Calle Navarro Rodríguez 9. Open Mon-Sat.

● Travel agents

Viajes Alysol, Paseo de Almería 34, T 237622; *Viajes Indamar*, Paseo de Almería 73, T 237883; *Viajes Rossell*, Calle Reina Regente, T 237477; *Viajes Sur*, Paseo de Almería 4, T 244677.

● Tourist information

This is located in Calle Hermanos Machado in the Edificio Multiple (Multiple Ministries Building), T 230858. The staff are multilingual and extremely helpful. This should be the first stop for all first-time visitors to Almería.

● Transport

Local **Car Hire** **Avis**, Canónigo Molina Alonso, T 252578; **Budget**, Plaza Marqués de Herida 7, T 258347; **Europcar**, Calle Rueda López 23, T 234966; **Hertz**, Avda Cabo de Gata 1, T 243329.

Taxis **Teletaxi**, T 251111; **Radio Taxi**, T 226161; **Taxis Nocturnos**, T 235757.

Air Information, T 221954. In addition to international charter flights, there are internal connections with **Madrid**, **Melilla** and **Barcelona**. *Iberia* have an office in town at Paseo de Almería 44, T 230933. Buses to airport every 30 mins between 0700 and 2130 during week and every 45 mins Sat and Sun.

Train It is difficult to mistake the RENFE station on Ctra de Ronda, T 251122, with its restored Gothic-style frontage and ultra-modern extension. There are 4 *talgos* (fast trains, **see page 193**) a day to **Madrid** and other connections with **Barcelona**, **Granada** and **Valencia**. An over-night train goes to **Córdoba** and **Sevilla**. RENFE also have an information office in the town centre, Calle Alcalde Muñoz T 231207.

Road **Bus** Plaza de Barcelona, T 210029. The bus station is a modern building with a cafetería and comfortable waiting room. There are daily national connections to **Madrid**, **Barcelona**, **Algeciras**, **Málaga**, **Granada** and **Sevilla**. Locally, there are 5 buses a day to **Berja**, 7 to **Adra** and 2 daily to **Cabo de Gata**, **Níjar**, **Mojácar** and **Tabernas**. There are hourly buses to the resorts of **Aguadulce** and **Roquetas de Mar**. Timetables are more easily obtained from the Tourist Office than the bus station, although they are displayed on the wall there.

Sea Car ferries run to **Melilla**, the Spanish enclave in North Africa, on Tue, Thur and Sat leaving at 1400, the voyage takes just over 6 hrs. **Aucona-Transmediterránea**, Parque Nicolás Salmerón 28, T 236356.

Excursions from Alméria

Mini Hollywood Take the N-324 N following the course of the Rio Andarax through a fascinating area of semi-desert, with bare mountain slopes showing rock structure, dried-up river beds and flat-topped plateaux giving a lunar landscape. This is the Sierra Alhamilla. Turn right at the junction with the N-340 and almost immediately on the right hand side of the road is **Mini Hollywood**. This is a relic of the golden age of the 'spaghetti western' films, such as *A Fistful of Dollars* and *Indiana Jones*, which were made in this area in the 1960s and 1970s. The film makers were attracted by the arid scenery, reminiscent of the American mid-west, plus the clear air and almost unbroken sunshine all of which were ideal for shooting. The film makers have now moved on but the sets remain, with bars, a bank, stables and Red Indian encampments. Cowboys enact shoot outs and stunts. Open 0900-1800 in winter, 0900-2100 in summer. Admission: adults 575 Ptas, children 300 Ptas.

Tabernas lies 2 km beyond Mini Hollywood and is dominated by a conical hill capped with a small Moorish castle. The town itself has little of interest. There is no Tourist Information Office and although the *Ayuntamiento* (Town hall) is willing to help, there is a total lack of information about the castle. It is best approached by heading for the Municipal Sports Stadium and taking the wide but rough track to the summit. There has been some recent half-hearted restoration work on the castle, but one is left with the feeling that the town could make more of this asset.

• **Accommodation** There are no hotels in Tabernas, but 3 *pensiones* are located on the N-340 which bypasses the town. **D** *Hermanos García* is probably the best of the 3, but possibly over-priced. A return route to Almería could be made by encircling the Sierra Alhamilla and passing through the village of **Níjar**, noted for its ceramics and *jarapas* cloth.

EAST OF MOJACAR

The N-344 E is undergoing improvements and is already of motorway standard as far as the airport. Shortly after this, fork right to **Cabo de Gata**, a village which takes its name from the vast area of succulents growing around it. Between the village and the headland of the same name is an expanse of salt marsh and lake which is part of the **Níjar-Cabo de Gato Nature Reserve**, which actually has, unusually for Spain, observation hides and a warden. Breeding birds include black-winged stilts, avocets and godwits. There can be as many as 1,000 greater flamingoes in the summer, while wildfowl numbers in the winter are high. The road continues to the Cabo de Gata headland with its lighthouse. This area is also part of the nature reserve and is noted for migratory birds, while the clear waters around the point are favoured by scuba divers. The road now becomes narrow with hairpin bends, but stupendous views. It eventually moves inland to rejoin the N-344, but returns to the coast again at **Carboneras** where a new marina is under construction. To the W of the town is a huge cement works, but further E is a small fishing port and an unspoiled resort area. There are half a dozen pensiones here. D *Felipe*, T 454015 has the best facilities while E *La Marina*, T 454070 is the cheapest. From Carboneras the N-341 continues N to Mojácar 22 km away.

A quick return route from Mojácar to Almería would be to head inland to the N-340 via Tabernas and the N-324; alternatively nearer the coast on the N-344 diverting to Níjar en route.

Mojácar

There are 2 parts to Mojácar – Old Mojácar and Mojácar Playa. The former is more interesting as it is a hill village with a distinctly Moorish flavour, with its cube-like white houses, Arab gateway and the original Moorish street pattern. Until quite recently, the women half-covered their faces with *cobijas* (triangular shawls) and drew *indalos* on their doors to keep away bad luck. *Indalos* are stick-like figures holding an arc above their heads, thought to have originated in neolithic times in the caves at Vélez-Blanco.

The Moors stoutly defended Mojácar against the armies of the Catholic Kings, who eventually allowed them to keep their customs provided they swore allegiance to the Christian crown. Mojácar, said to be the birthplace of Walt Disney, prospered during the early years of the 20th century and in the 1920s it had a population of 9,000, but after the Civil War ended the population shrank to 400! Its recovery began in the 1960s, when it was discovered by an intellectual set. In 1969 it was declared 'Spain's Prettiest Village'. An English travel company was then largely responsible for developing Mojácar Playa and the boom was well underway. Today Mojácar has a population of 5,000 people, half of whom are foreign residents, mainly British. A long-established English language magazine is produced monthly.

Local information

● Accommodation

There are 4 good hotels in Mojácar, but little for the tourist on a budget. **A** *Parador Reyes Católicos*, Playa, T 478250, F 478183, 98 rm, modern building in landscaped grounds, on seafront, pool, tennis, garage.

B *Continental*, Playa el Palmeral, T 478225, F 475136, excellent, beach, a/c, all facilities.

C *El Moresco*, Avda Horizion, T 478025, 147 rm, open all year round, good views, garden, indoor and outdoor pools, disco, a/c, 147 rm.

D *El Torreón*, Calle Jazmin, T 475259, offers cheap winter rates; **D** *Provenzal*, Playa del Descargador, T 478308, has the best facilities, including garage, of all Mojácar's rather expensive *pensiones*.

● Camping

El Cantal de Mojácar, Ctra Nacional 340, Desvío Vera-El Cantal, T 478204, restaurant.

● Places to eat

The vast range of eating places reflects Mojácar's international character. ♦♦♦ *Palacio*, Plaza del Cano, good reputation, nouvelle cuisine and traditional; *Bistro Breton*, Playa Mojácar, T 478008, French cuisine, closed Thur; *La Lubina*, Pueblo Indalo, T 458376, terrace, fish dishes; *Tito's*, Playa de la Ventanicas, T 478711, beach-side, specializes in fish. ♦♦ *Saturno*, Avda Mediterráneo, T 478202, good *tapas*.

● Travel agents

Indalo, Ctra Carboneras, T 478283; *Solar*, Urb Gaviota, T 478700; *Aysol*, Urb El Cruce, T 478175.

● Tourist information

Plaza Nueva, T 475162, very helpful, bus timetables posted on the window when closed on Sat afternoon and Sun.

Excursion from Mojácar

Garrucha across the Rio de Aguas is noted for its magnificent sandy beaches and large pleasure craft harbour. The road continues to **Vera** (naturist area with a hotel and camping facilities) and **Cuevas del Almanzora** on the W bank of Rio Almanzora which offers caves (of course) and a Gothic cathedral.

ALMERIA TO EL EJIDO

The N-340 initially hugs the coast using a series of recently constructed tunnels until, after 8 km, **Aguadulce** is reached. This is a sedate and mature holiday resort with a huge pleasure craft harbour, a wide range of hotels and apartment blocks, mostly low-rise. It has the usual entertainment of a holiday resort, but nothing of historical interest. Buses run hourly to Almería. Board at the bus station as there are no stops in the town.

From Aguadulce leave the N-340 and follow the coast road to **Roquetas de Mar**. This was originally a small agricultural village and fishing port. The port still operates, but with the addition of berths for pleasure craft. There are a number of fish restaurants adjacent to the port, but these are surprisingly expensive, considering their location. The main development at Roquetas is 3 km to the S, where a new resort has been built, tailor-made for the package tour industry.

● Accommodation Hotels include **B** *Playadulce*, Avda El Palmeral, T 341274; **D** *Alis*, Avda Mediterráneo, T 320375; **D** *Playamar*, Pez Espada, T 320250; and **E** *Playalinda*, Playa Serena, T 323111. In the **older part of town** are **C** *El Faro* Puerto de Roquetas, T 321015, pricy for a *pensión* but it has an interesting location by the port; and **C** *Los Angeles*, Estación 2, T 320125.

● Sport Golf: there is an 18 hole golf course in Roquetas, Golf Playa Serena, T 322055. Equipment can be hired. Closed Mon. **Sailing**: see above.

The route continues W running mainly between *plasticultura* and the coastal dunes, lagoons and salt marshes. This area is now an official nature reserve and bird watchers will be delighted with the breeding avocets, black-winged stilts, little terns and kentish plover plus a range of wildfowl in the winter, including the rare White Headed Duck. The road continues through the plastic until, below on the left, one looks down on the brand new resort of **Almerimar**. This consists of a

Plasticultura – Life And Death In The Greenhouse

Plasticultura began in the 1970s, transforming an arid, stony wilderness into an area of intensive, continuous farming. The crops are grown in low plastic greenhouses, helped by continual sunshine and water pumped from underground. Crops such as melons, lettuces, tomatoes, beans, aubergines and peppers, are grown throughout the year and transported by refrigerated lorry to the cities of N Europe. The business is immensely profitable, but not without its problems. Depression and suicide rates are high amongst the workers, many of whom are now recruited from Africa. The water table has inevitably lowered, so that some wells are 100 m deep, and water supply in other nearby areas is affected. Discarded heavy-duty plastic is difficult to dispose of and presents an environmental hazard.

small number of hotels and apartment blocks, a marina for over 1,000 craft and a Gary Player-designed golf course. The whole complex seems under siege from the acres of plastic surrounding it.

- **Camping** *Mar Azul*, Urb Almerimar, well equipped site right on beach.

The road then moves inland to **El Ejido**, the centre of the *plasticultura* industry. A surprising number of maps and brochures do not show El Ejido, but it has now grown to a population of over 40,000, making it the second largest town in the province. Whereas mass tourism has steadfastly refused to take off in Almería, *plasticultura* has brought prosperity to the area. Travellers will, therefore, be glad to leave the endless acres of unattractive plastic and head back E along the N-340 to Almería or carry on W to Adra and Motril.

Motril

Motril is located on the short Granada province section of the Andalusian coast where the E-W coast route meets the N-S Granada road. It is 115 km W of Almería and 3 km inland, separated from its port by sugar cane fields. Motril has a population of 45,000, making it the second largest town in Granada province. Its main industries are based on agricultural produce, especially sugar cane, and were developed initially by the Larios gin family. The town's climate is mild in winter and hot in summer, but it is slightly wetter than the neighbouring coastal area owing to the proximity of the Sierra Nevada mountains.

ACCESS Road This is entirely by road, the nearest railway stations being at Málaga and Almería. The N-340 coast road bypasses Motril, but buses stop in the town. The bus station is not centrally placed and is difficult to find, particularly as it is not shown on the official town plan. When you leave your bus you will find yourself on Calle Cruces. Turn right down the street and bear left into Calle Nueva to reach the town centre.

Things to see

Motril has little to interest the tourist, as its inhabitants will readily agree, but visitors will hardly fail to notice the **Iglesia Mayor de la Encarnación**, which is located in a tree-lined avenue at the entrance to the town. Construction began in 1510 and shows a variety of styles including mudéjar, baroque and gothic. The church also doubled as a fortress against Berber pirates, so the overall effect is rather austere.

Festivals

The main local festival of Motril's patron saint, the *Virgen de la Cabeza* takes place on 15 Aug. The **Santuario de la Virgen de la Cabeza** around which this fiesta is based in built on the site of an Arab castle which was occupied by Boabdil's mother (see Granada, **page 86**).

Local information

● Accommodation

There is a poor selection of accommodation in Motril itself, but the choice is widened by considering the nearby coastal resorts of **Calahonda** and **Torreneuva**. Note that the best hotel in Motril, the *Costa Andaluza*, is currently closed. **C** ***Los Balandros***, Ctra Nacional 340 Km 336, T 835740, on the coast road, 7 km out of town in the small resort of Torrenueva, pleasant gardens.

D *Alborán*, Varadero Carrera de Mar, T 601370; **D** *La Campaña*, Calle Princesa 22, T 600007, central location, would suit travellers on a limited budget; **D** *Tropical*, Avda Rodríguez Acosta 23, T 600450, 21 rm, restaurant, good central location and facilities.

● Camping

Don Cactus, Ctra Motril-Almería Km 11, T 623109, top category, open throughout the year. There are 2 2nd category sites at Playa Poniente.

● Places to eat

None of the following is especially recommended, but if you need a meal while in Motril, these are possibilities. ♦♦♦*La Caramba*, Avda de Salobreña 19, T 602578, closed Wed; *Tropical*, in the hotel, closed Jul, traditional fish and seafood. ♦♦*Mesón El Rincón de David*, Avda Rodríguez Acosta 22, T 605686, specializes in ham and cheese dishes, regional wines. ♦out of Motril, most of the bargain restaurants are on the seafront at nearby Torrenueva beach. They all tend to specialize in seafood and shellfish and include *Nueva Torre*, *El Cordobés* and *Torre Mar*.

● Banks

There are branches of all the major Spanish banks and local savings banks in Motril, mainly in the area of Avda Acosta and Calle Hernández Velesco.

● Chemists

Fernández Sáez, Plaza Burgos 6.

● Garages

Renault: Avda Rodríguez Acosta; **Ford**: Ctra Almería; **Citroën**: Avda Salobreña; **Peugeot**: Ctra Almería.

● Post Office

Correos, Calle San Rafael.

● Telephones

Local code: 95(2). There are various telephone cabins around town.

● Travel agents

Jumantur, Calle Cuevas 1, T 630416.

● Tourist information

There is no office in Motril, but the *Ayuntamiento* produce a brochure in Spanish entitled *Motril, Costa Tropical* which includes a useful town plan. It is stocked by some travel agents.

● Transport

Local Car hire Autos Joya, Calle Cuevas 7, T 823007. **Taxis** can be found in Avda Andalucía and Plaza Aurora.

Road Bus to reach the bus station, take Calle Nueva out of the town centre, fork right into Calle Cruces and the bus station is on the left opposite Calle Ancha. This is a 10 min uphill walk out of town, but necessary if you need to book a ticket. The main bus company in this area is Alsina Graells with the following daily services: 8 buses each way along the coast, 10 to **Granada**; 3 long distance coaches to **Sevilla** via **Córdoba** and 1 to **Jaén** and **Cádiz** and 2 to **Madrid**.

Salobreña

Salobreña is a small resort with some Moorish remains 4 km W of Motril. It is in 2 parts, an old hill village and a modern beach development. The older part has the most spectacular location on the Granada coast, and has a long and interesting history. Its golden age was in the 8th century when it was one of Granada's 30 districts and an area of some agricultural and industrial importance.

The newer coastal area of Salobreña is a purpose-built tourist development, but is inoffensive, well-planned and consists mainly of low-rise apartment blocks. The main hotel accommodation is found close to the coast road.

Things to see

Moorish past During the Nasrid period (1166-1247) Salobreña was used by Granada's royal families for summer holidays. The Catholic Kings took over the town in 1489 and this was followed a year later by a mudéjar uprising. The highest point of old Salobreña is capped by the **Castillo**, built by the Moors and remodelled by the Christians. Despite some damage by earthquakes, it remained the most important fortress in the W of the province of Granada. It is kidney-shaped and consists of 2 enclosures, one of which contained the prison. A large flattened tower contained the armoury, while another tower protected the entrance. The **Tower of Homage** is of square construction and contains 2 large rooms on 2 storeys. The windows have decorated arches, and Moorish ceramics and glass have been found on the site. To reach it, follow the signs marked 'Castillo' through the narrow roads and alleyways. Open daily 1000-1300 and 1600-2100. Entrance fee 100 Ptas.

Other places of interest

The **Iglesia** is also worth a visit. It is located on the E side of the Castillo at a lower level. It was constructed in the first half of the 16th century in mudéjar style on the site of a former mosque and was extensively restored in the 17th and 18th centuries. As with many churches in this area, it has 3 naves separated by square pillars. The sculptures inside date from the 17th century.

Festivals

Easter week is marked by traditional *Semana Santa* processions; end Jul *Fiesta de San Juan y San Pedro*. Aug sees exhibitions and talks as part of a *Cultural Week*; the *Fiesta de Nuestra Señora del Rosario* takes place in the first week of Oct.

Local information

● Accommodation

C *Salobreña*, Ctra Nacional 340 Km 326, T 610261, 151 rm, marvellous position on a spur overlooking old Salobreña, pool, tennis, parking, garden.

D *Salambina*, Ctra Nacional 340 Km 328, T 610037, good views overlooking the hill village and the coast, restaurant expensive.

● Pensiones

There are a number of cheaper *pensiones*, both on the sea front and in the old town, including **D** *Pensión Palomares*, Calle Fábrica Nueva 48, T 610181, acceptably clean and welcoming; **D** *Mari Tere*, Ctra de la Playa 94, T 610126 very handy for the sea, and **D** *Pérez*, Avda del Cristo 28, T 610231.

● Camping

El Peñón, Paseo Maritímo, 2nd category beach-side site.

● Places to eat

There is a variety of eating places in Salobreña to suit all pockets. ♦♦♦*Mesón Duran*, Ctra Málaga Km 341, international cuisine, sea views. ♦*Chiringuitos* on the beach, such as *Tres Hermanos* and *Flores* provide good, cheap, fish dishes; *Mesón la Bodega*, Plaza de Goya, has atmosphere along with sherry from the barrel and a *menú del día* at 950 Ptas.

● Tourist information

The office is located in Plaza de Goya and has a helpful brochure on Salobreña, but only in Spanish!

● Transport

Road Bus These stop at the town entrance just off the coast road. There are 8 local buses a day in each direction, hourly to **Motril**, 7 buses a day to **Granada** and less frequent connections to **Almería**, **Málaga** and **Sevilla**.

Almuñécar

This town is almost at the border with Málaga province, 17 km W of Salobreña. The town has a long history and was probably founded by the Phoenicians, while there are the remains of a Roman aqueduct on the outskirts of the town. The **Castillo de San Miguel** is a fortress which dominates the town and although it has Moorish origins, it is largely of more recent construction during the time of Charles V, and serves today as the local cemetery.

Laurie Lee in *As I Walked Out One Midsummer Morning* described Almuñécar in withering terms at the start of the Civil War, when he was rescued from its rather stony beach by a British destroyer. Today, he would be surprised at Almuñécar's development as the largest holiday resort on Granada's Costa Tropical, although its expansion will probably be limited in the future by its distance from the nearest airport at Málaga 76 km W.

ACCESS Road The **bus** station is on the left as one enters the town from the Málaga road. Between 8 and 10 buses a day link Alumñécar with the nearby coastal towns. There are long distance coaches to Sevilla and Córdoba, while 8 buses a day go to Granada. The main **taxi** rank is next to the bus station.

● Accommodation

There is a variety of accommodation available, but nothing in the luxury category. The largest hotel is the **B** ***Helios***, Plaza de San Cristóbal, T 634459, pool, garage, suitable for wheelchair users.

Smaller is **C** ***La Najarra***, Calle Guadix, T 630873, F 630191, pool, no restaurant; **D** ***Goya***, Avda General Galindo, T 630550.

● Camping

El Paraiso, Taramay, T 632370, beach location, suitable for wheelchair users.

Nerja

Nerja is located on the coast approximately half way between Málaga (50 km) and Motril, built on a low cliff littered with sandy coves. Sheltered by the mountains, Nerja has a mild winter climate and hot summers, which has encouraged residential tourism in recent years. For centuries the inhabitants eked a living by making silk, growing sugar cane and fishing. The mass tourism which began in the 1970s has not really spoiled Nerja and it has more charm than most of the resorts along the Costa del Sol. The main attraction within Nerja is the **Balcón de Europa**, a promenade jutting into the sea giving delightful views along the coast. Beware, however, of the inflated prices in the cafés and bars around the Balcón.

ACCESS Road This is entirely by road, the nearest airport and railway stations being in Málaga. Buses arrive on the main road N of the town, the Avda de Pescia, or at the bus station on Calle San Miguel.

Moorish past Nerja started life as the Moorish settlement of *Narixa*, suggesting reliable spring waters. Unfortunately, an earthquake in 1884 destroyed much of the town and no Moorish constructions survived. However it is an excellent base to explore **La Axanquía**. Although there are no grand Moorish remains, this whole region is alive with Muslim atmosphere (see excursions, **page 121**).

Festivals Carnival for 3 days in Feb

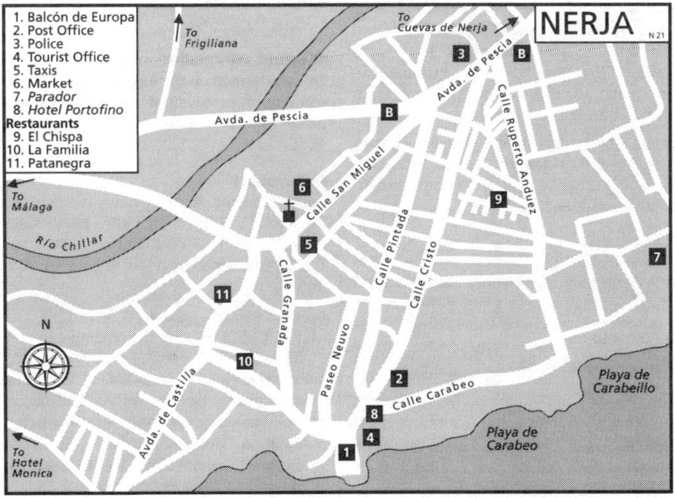

with parades and singing. Easter week processions as part of *Semana Santa*; 15 May *Romería de San Isidro*; 24 Jun *Fiesta de San Juan*; last fortnight of Aug ballet displays in the Cuevas; 8 Sep, *Fiesta de la Virgen de las Maravillas*; 9-12 Oct fiestas of *San Miguel* and *Nuestra Señora de las Angustias*.

Local information

● Accommodation

It is best to book in advance during the height of the summer. **A** *Parador de Nerja*, Calle Almuñécar 8, T 2520050, F 2521917, 73 rm, pool, tennis, a/c, TV, set on the cliff top amongst attractive gardens, lift to the beach, all that one would expect from a *parador*; **A** *Monica Playa de Torrecilla*, T 2521100, modern beach hotel with everything on tap for the package tourist; **A** *Balcón de Europa*, Paseo Balcón de España, T 2520800, 106 rm, TV, sauna, private beach, situation also convenient for shops.

B *Perla Marina*, Calle Mérida 7, T2523350, new, located on sea front on the W side of town.

C *Portofino*, Puerta del Mar 4, T 2520150, central location, restaurant, closed Oct-Mar.

● Pensiones

D *Don Peque* on Calle Diputación 13, T 2521318, small, comfortable, central position; **D** *Miguel*, Calle Cristo 31, T 2521523, bed and breakfast, close to the Balcón; **D** *Fonteinbleau*, Calle Alejandro Bueno 5, T 2520939, NE side of town, British run, 22 rm, bath, patio, laundry, friendly; **D** *Mena*, Calle Alemania 15, T 2520541, 10 rm.

Those looking for an out-of-town location could try **C** *Al Andaluz*, Ladera del Aguila, Maro, T 2521022, small, quiet hotel close to the caves and the village.

● Camping

Almayate-Costa, Ctra Málaga-Almería Km 267, near Maro, top category, bar, restaurant, beach. Booking necessary in high season.

● Places to eat

There is a wide selection of restaurants to suit all pockets and tastes in Nerja, although those along the Balcón tend to have inflated prices and be directed at the foreign community. ♦♦♦ *Pepe Rico*, Calle Cristo 26, T 2520247, international cuisine, good quality; *Casa Luque*, Plaza Cavana 2, T 2521004, Spanish and international cuisine, good value for money; *Rey Alfonso*, Paseo Balcón de Europa, T 2520195, good views, international cuisine. ♦♦ *El Chispa*, Calle San Pedro 12, T 2523697, fish; *Marisquería La Familia*, Calle Diputación 17, T 2520046, seafood; *La Noria*, Ctra de Frigiliana 1.5 Km, Spanish style mesón in an old farm building, good fish and game dishes, moderate prices; ♦♦ *Meson Patanegra*, Plaza la Marina, T 2520222, good Spanish cooking at moderate prices. ♦Those on a budget could try the lunch time offerings of fish and seafood in the *chiringuitos* on Burriana Beach or *Pizzería Jímenez*, Avda de Pescia 17, T 2521998.

● Chemists

M Acosta, Calle Carlos Millón 4 and *L Molina*, Calle Diputación 18.

● Hospital

Clinic, Calle Bronce 8, T 2520358, open 24 hrs. **First aid**: on T 2520935.

● Post Office

Correos is located near the junction of Puerta del Mar and Calle Carabeo.

● Telephones

Local code: 95(2). Cabins are available around the town, including on the Balcón de Europa.

● Travel agent

Jaime Tours, Calle Pintada 79, T 2522790; *Benamar*, Calle Carmen 18, Balcón de Europa, T 2520554.

● Tourist information

Office is located on the Balcón de Europa and has very cooperative staff who will provide a useful town plan. Open 1000-1400 Mon-Fri, 1000-1300 Sat. T 2521531.

● Transport

Local **Car hire** Autos Unidos-Hertz, Calle Diputación 7, T 2524250; **Autos Nerja**, Calle Cruz 22, T 2520694; **Costasol**, Calle Jaén, T 2522796. **Taxis** Plaza Ermita on the old N-340.

Road Daily bus departures from Calle San Miguel 3 are as follows: 12 to **Málaga** and the coastal towns to the W; 8 to **Motril** and **Almuñécar**; 2 connect directly to **Granada**, which can also be reached by changing at **Motril**. There are daily long distance coaches to **Córdoba**, **Cádiz** and **Sevilla** plus local buses to the inland villages of the Axanquía such as **Frigiliana**, **Torrox** and the hospital at **Velez**.

Excursions from Nerja

The most popular excursion is to the **Cuevas de Nerja**. These caves were discovered accidently in 1959 by local schoolboys and are now a national monument. In addition to all the usual features of limestone caves, such as caverns, stalactites, stalagmites and pillars – all imaginatively lit – there is evidence that the caves were occupied by Cro-magnon man and the archaeological finds are displayed near the entrance. There are also a number of prehistoric wall paintings, mainly of animals, but these are not open to the public. The caves are located 4 km E of Nerja near to the village of **Maro**. There is a regular bus service to and from Nerja. Open all year 1030-1800, entrance fee 400 Ptas, children 200 Ptas. During the summer season, the main chamber of the caves is used as an auditorium for a festival of music and dance. For the programme, contact the Tourist Office in Nerja.

The small village of **Maro** is located on the cliff top 4 km E of Nerja, close to the caves. The original community was Roman, but 3 16th century monuments are worth a visit; the small village church Iglesia Maravillas de Maro; the old sugar factory and best of all the **Puente de Aguila**, a magnificent tiered aqueduct which carried water across a valley to the sugar factory.

La Axarquía is defined as the area inland to the E of Málaga and consists largely of small villages, of which Nerja has in recent years developed as the main coastal town. The local authorities have been actively encouraging independent excursions into the La Axarquía region. **Frigiliana**, steeped in Muslim atmosphere, was the site of one of the last battles between the Christians and the Moors in 1569 and ceramic plaques record the event on the walls of houses in the old part of the town. Most of the Moorish castles which were once common in the area have been completely destroyed, although in the capital of the area, **Vélez-Málaga**, a restored tower remains. In the villages of **Salares** and **Archez**, minarets remain attached to Christian churches. **Competa** and **Macharaviaya** were famous for grape cultivation. Throughout the area, the street patterns remain from Moorish times and *mudéjar* architecture is common.

Five routes have been designated for visiting La Axarquía, each colour-coded and way-marked. The **Sun and Avocado Route** starts at Rincón de la Victoria and visits the agricultural villages of the Vélez valley. The **Sun and Wine Route** includes the main wine producing villages such as Competa and Frigiliana. The **Mudéjar Route** concentrates on architecture, looking at villages such as Archez, Salares and Sedilla. The **Route of the Pass** looks at the more mountainous villages in the NW of the area. The **Route of the Oil and the Mountains** examines the olive growing villages such as Periana and Alcaucín in the N of the area. Unfortunately, owing to the terrain, most of the routes are not 'round tours' and involve re-tracing one's steps in places, but they are, nevertheless, highly recommended. A detailed brochure can be obtained from the Nerja Tourist Office.

Nerja to Málaga

W of Nerja there is almost continuous ribbon development to Málaga, with a string of undistinguished holiday resorts largely used by *malagueños* at the weekends. The largest are **Torrox Costa, Torre del Mar** and **Rincón de la Victoria**. The latter is now bypassed by the extension of the Málaga ring road.

MALAGA TO MARBELLA

Málaga

Pop 500,000 *Alt* Sea level.

Málaga is located at the mouth of the Rio Guadalmedina, its suburbs stretching to the foot of the surrounding mountains. Climatically, Málaga is located in one of the most favoured parts of Spain, with the mountains to the N cutting out cold winter winds so that average Jan temperatures are around 15°C, while in the summer, sea breezes usually make the heat bearable. Rainfall figures for Málaga itself are low, but plentiful rain in the sierras inland, along with a plethora of reservoirs, ensure that water supply is not a problem. Málaga has a long history dating back to Phoenician times, deriving its name from the word *malac*, meaning to salt fish. Today it is a busy regional, administrative and industrial centre and although the port does not handle its former volume of shipping, it is a regular stopping point for cruise liners.

ACCESS Air Málaga's busy airport (4.9 million passengers in 1993) is located at San Julián, some 7 km W of the city centre. A new international terminal was completed in Nov 1991 and the former international terminal is now the national terminal. *Transport to town:* the cheapest and most convenient link to the city is by the Fuengirola-Málaga electric railway which runs half-hourly, between 0714 and 0014, from the airport, 130 Ptas, takes 15 mins. There is also a bus service available running to the Cathedral every 20 mins between 0640 and 2230. The taxi fare to the centre is currently about 1,200 Ptas.

Train Train travellers arrive at the station on Calle Cuarteles, while the new bus station has recently opened conveniently close to the RENFE on Paseo de los Tilos, a 20 min walk from the centre. Local buses run from here to the centre. Both bus and train stations have Tourist Offices.

Things to see

Fortunately most of the places of interest in Málaga are contained within a small area N of the main E-W thoroughfare and can be covered on foot. This thoroughfare starts in the E at the Plaza de Toros and passes first through the Paseo del Parque, a tree-lined promenade, past the Plaza de la Marina, along the Alameda Principal, a 19th century boulevard, over the dried-up bed of the Rio Guadalmedina, ending at the area around *El Corte Inglés*, the post office and the Fuengirola line railway station.

WARNING As in any large city, watch out for pickpockets and be sure to leave no valuables accessible in cars, even when driving through the town.

Moorish past In Moorish times, Málaga was the main port of the province of Granada and a busy trading centre. When the Catholic Kings drove the Moors out of Spain, Málaga was under seige for over 3 months during 1487. Centuries of decline followed and it is only in quite recent history that Málaga's fortunes have revived.

The **Alcazaba**, this former fortress and palace was built by the Moors in the mid-11th century on a site originally oc-

CLIMATE: MALAGA

	Jan	Feb	Mar	Apr	May	Jun	Jul	Aug	Sep	Oct	Nov	Dec	Av/Tot
Max (°C)	17	17	18	21	23	27	29	30	27	23	20	17	22
Min (°C)	8	9	11	13	15	19	21	22	20	16	12	10	15
Rain (mm)	61	51	62	46	26	5	1	3	29	64	64	62	474

cupied by the Phoenicians and the Romans. It suffered badly during the Catholic Reconquista, but was carefully restored in 1933. Today it consists of a series of terraced, fortified walls and fine Moorish gateways laid out with gardens and running water. There are fine views over the port and city. Open 1000-1300 and 1700-2000, Sun 1000-1400. Admission 20 Ptas.

The **Castillo Gibralfaro** 'Lighthouse Hill' is a ruined Moorish castle built in the early 14th century. It is linked to the Alcazaba below by parallel walls. A path leads up to it from the side of the Alcazaba, but this is a stiff walk and in the summer heat it might be prudent to approach it by road from the *Parador* side

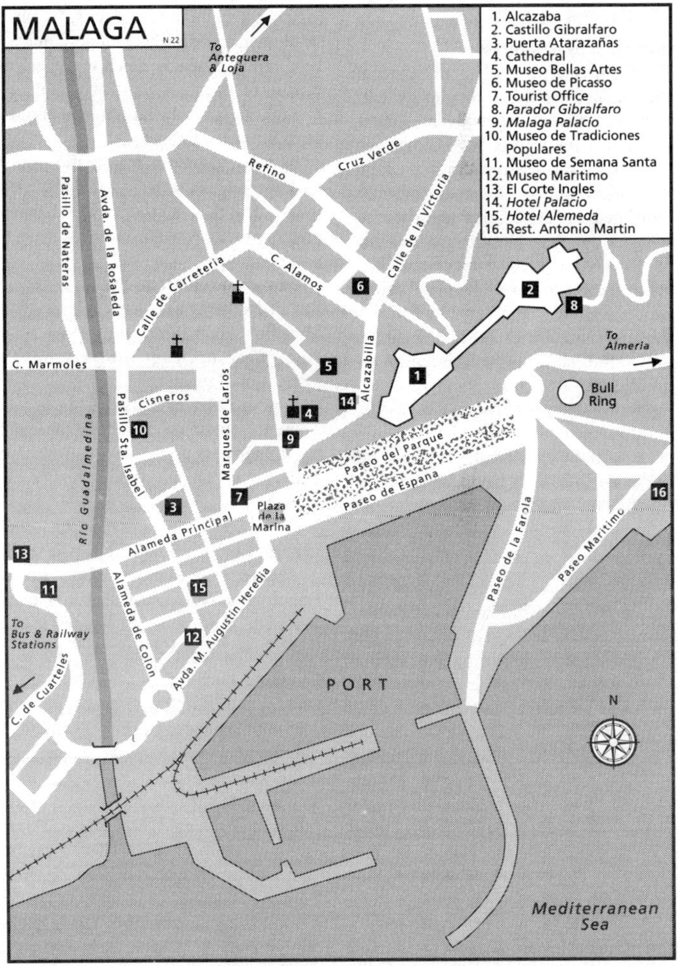

of the hill. Open 1000-1300 and 1700-2000.

There are 2 other Moorish curiosities in Málaga. In the underground car park at the W end of the Parque de Paseo are the remains of the **Moorish City Walls**, while further W at the entrance to the city market is the **Puerta de Atarazañas**. This was originally the gateway into the Moorish dockyard and it displays a crest of the Nasrid Dynasty.

Other places of interest

The Cathedral was built on the site of an Arab mosque in the 16th century, with numerous modifications at later dates. One of its 2 towers was never completed, giving it a lop-sided appearance, leading to the nickname of *la Manquita* variously translated as 'the cripple' or 'the one-armed lady'. An ugly, gloomy building, its one saving grace is the choir, where behind the stalls are some 40 superb carvings of saints produced by Pedro de Mana in 1662. Open 1000-1300 and 1600-1730. 'Tourists' will be charged an entrance fee of 100 Ptas.

Immediately N of the Alcazaba is the **Teatro Romano** which has recently been partially excavated. More of it lies under the **Casa de la Cultura**, which will shortly be demolished.

Museums

Museo de Bellas Artes in Calle San Augustín 8 is in a restored 16th century palace. It displays work mainly by Spanish artists such as Belgrano, Murillo and Cano. There are interesting seascapes by Ocon y Rivas and some more modern pieces by Villa and Oliva. In an upstairs room are early ink and wash sketches by Picasso, who lived in Málaga until he was 14. Also exhibited is work by Muñoz Degrain, who was Picasso's first tutor. Open 1000-1330 and 1700-2000, closed Mon and Sun afternoon in winter. Entrance fee 250 Ptas. Pensioners and students under 21 from EU countries free.

Museo de Picasso His birthplace in the Plaza de la Merced has been restored as a museum of his life and work.

Museo de Tradiciones Populares, Pasillo de Santa Isabel 10. Look for the inn sign outside labelled Mesón de Victoria, as this museum is housed in an old 17th century inn overlooking the dried up river bed. This is a visit which should not be missed. The museum consists of a somewhat haphazard collection of items from everyday life, including fishing boats, an olive press, guns, farming implements and a whole range of household relics. There is much to appeal to visitors of all ages. Open 1000-1300 and 1700-2000, closed Sat afternoon and Sun. Entrance free.

Museo Arqueológico in the upper part of the Alcazaba is small but contains ceramics, statues and Moorish plasterwork. Closed Mon and Sun afternoon.

Museo de Semana Santa, Plaza de San Pedro (near El Corte Inglés). Open Mon-Fri 1030-1230 and 1900-2100. Holy Week museum with exhibits of processional regalia.

Acuario Museo Aula del Mar, Avda Manuel Agustin de la Heredia (near the port). Marine museum with aquaria and underwater caves containing turtles, octopuses and coral, T 2229287. Open Tues-Fri 1700-1900, Sat and Sun 1100-1330 and 1715-1900. Entrance 400 Ptas.

Museo Diocesano de Arte Sacro, Palacio del Obispo (near Cathedral). Museum of religious art housed in the recently restored Episcopal Palace.

Festivals

Málaga is noted for its *fiestas*, starting with the *Carneval* in late Feb. Then comes the Easter *Semana Santa* when local brotherhoods mount processions each day, arguably the best in Spain, and a prisoner is released. *San Juan*, 23 Jun, sees huge bonfires on which satirical images are burned. On 16 Jul, the *Virgen del Carmen* is taken in procession to the sea by local fishermen. In Aug Málaga has its annual *Feria de Málaga*, with bullfights, flamenco, processions and fireworks. In Dec, *Verdiales*, folk song competitions, take place in the mountains N of Málaga.

Local information

Accommodation

Price guide:			
AL	US$90+	D	US$20-40
A	US$75-90	E	US$10-20
B	US$60-75	F	under US$10
C	US$40-60		

Despite its size and importance, Málaga has a surprisingly poor choice of accommodation. Nearby Torremolinos, however, can rectify this, providing that the visitor can tolerate the distractions! **AL** ***Málaga Palacio***, Calle Cortina del Muelle 1, T 2215185, 223 rm, imposing, traditional, centrally placed, rooftop pool, a/c, TV.

A ***Don Curro***, Calle Sancha de Lara 7, T 2227200, F 2224889, central location, close to cathedral, usual city noises are accentuated by the hotel's bingo hall; **A** ***Las Vegas*** Paseo de Sancha 22, T 2217712, large, traditional establishment, located near bull ring, convenient for city attractions, tropical gardens; **A** ***Parador de Gibralfaro***, Paseo García del Olmo, T 2221902, F 2221904, a small, regional style hotel on the hill next to the Moorish castle, marvellous views, TV, parking, restaurant, only 12 rm, rec, booking essential.

C ***Carlos V***, Calle Cister 6, T 2215120, in shadow of Cathedral, garage.

Pensiones

There are a numerous *pensiones* but these need to be chosen with care, as some can be rather squalid. Insist on seeing the room first! **C** ***Derby***, Calle San Juan de Dios 1, n°4, T 2211301, clean, some good views.

D ***Avenida***, Alameda Principal 5, T 2217729, centrally placed; **D** ***Pensión Chinitas***, Pasaje Chinitas 2, T 2214683, simple but clean.

Torremolinos

Visitors prepared to put up with the frenzy of nearby Torremolinos might consider the following which are convenient for beach, town and access to Málaga: **A** ***Melía Torremolinos***, Avda C. Alessandri 109, T 2380500 with all the expected luxury and facilities.

B ***Don Pablo***, Paseo Marítimo, T 2383888, on beach, good facilities.

C ***Miami***, Calle Aladino 14, T 2385255, comfortable, traditional Andalusian atmosphere.

Youth hostel

Plaza de Pio XII 6, T 2308500, 100 beds, suitable for wheelchairs, meals provided, reservations recommended, near Carranque multisports facilities.

Camping

The nearest is ***Balneario del Carmen***, Avda Pintor Sorolla on the coast road E of Málaga, T 2290021, bar, restaurant, beach, tennis. There are other sites at Torre del Mar and Torremolinos.

Places to eat

Price guide:
♦♦♦Expensive; ♦♦average; ♦cheap.

Despite the nearby tourist areas and the obvious attraction of Málaga to visitors, the restaurants in the city are designed to cater primarily for malagueñas. The emphasis, therefore, is on regional cooking, especially seafood. For *tapas* and snacks, the pedestrianized Calle Marín García between the Cathedral and the market has scores of small bars including ***La Tasca*** and ***La Manchega***. For more substantial meals, go to the area known as La Malagueta, S of the Plaza de Toros. ♦♦♦***Antonio Martín***, Paseo Marítimo, T 2222113, long established, popular, specializes in seafood; ***La Taberna del Pintor***, Calle Maestranza 6, T 2225315, probably the best meat restaurant in Málaga; ***Casa Pedro***, Playa de El Palo, typical malagueño food. ♦♦***El Corte Inglés*** department store's top floor buffet libre and grill is a popular stop for shoppers; ***Restaurante Tormes***, Calle San José 6, good food; ***La Manchega***, Calle Marín García 4, regional cuisine. ♦a small number of Chinese restaurants and pizzerías have recently begun to appear in Málaga and the former, particularly, might appeal to those on a budget. Try ***Chino Hong Kong***, Paseo Las Farolas 25; ***La Tarantella***, Calle Granada 61, fast food.

Banks

All the main Spanish banks and savings banks have branches in Málaga, mainly concentrated at the W end of the Alameda Principal.

Consulates

Canada, Plaza de la Malagueta, T 2223346; **France**, Duquesa de Parcent 8, T 2226590; **Germany**, Paseo del Limonar 28, T 2227866; **Italy**, Palestina 3, T 2306150; **Netherlands**, Alameda de Colón, Pasaje Linaje 3, T 2379954; **UK**, Duquesa Parcent 8, T 2217571.

● Garages/petrol

Citroën: Ctra Cádiz 239, T 2315400; **Renault**: Ctra Cádiz 178, T 2315000; **Seat-Volkswagen**: Ctra Cádiz, T 2315300; **Ford**: Ctra Cádiz 239, T 2355511.

● Post Office

The main ***Correos*** can be found in the Avda de Andalucía, almost opposite *El Corte Inglés*, T 2359008.

● Shopping

The main shopping area is W of the Cathedral and N of the Alameda Principal and in the streets around the Plaza de la Constitución. Further W in the Avda de Andalucía is ***El Corte Inglés***, the comprehensive department store. It has a popular restaurant and convenient parking. Open all day, Mon-Sat. Between the store and the river are numerous street stalls, with bargain jewellery and souvenirs, which is good value as their trade is aimed largely at locals rather than tourists.

● Sport

Aeronautics at Aeroclub de Málaga, Ctra de Cádiz, T 2230595.

Equestrian Centre, Apartado 94, Alaurin de la Torre, T 2412818.

Marina has berths for 235 pleasure craft.

● Telephones

Locutorio at Calle Molina Larios 11. Open Mon-Sat 0900-2100, Sun 1000-1300. **NB**: as with much of the province of Málaga, a 2 prefix has been added to many telephone numbers, in which case the code is 95.

● Travel agents

There are over 30 travel agents' offices in Málaga, so the following are but a small selection: ***Benamar***, Avda Aurora 2, T 2349800; Larios Travel, Aeropuerto, T 2352463; ***Melia***, Alameda Principal 1, T 2211071; ***Wagon-Lits Cook***, Calle Strachen 20, T 2212664.

● Tourist information

The main Regional Tourist Office is at Pasaje Chinitas 4, T 2213445. Open Mon-Fri 0900-1400, Sat 0900-1300. Additional Municipal offices at the international airport terminal and the train and bus stations are more likely to be open in the afternoon.

● Transport

Local Car hire This is most conveniently done at the airport, where all the international firms have offices. Local Spanish firms are equally reliable and may offer better deals. Firms have offices either in the arrival lounge or on the airport approach road to which they will transport customers by minibus. The following firms have offices in the city: **Hertz**, Alameda de Colón 17, T 2225597; **Avis**, Calle de Cortina del Muelle, T 2216627.

Taxi There are taxi ranks at the bus and train stations and in the Alameda Principal; **Radio Taxi**, Plaza de Toros Vieja, T 2327950 and T 2328062.

Air Málaga has a busy airport from which Iberia and its subsidiary run internal flights to **Madrid**, **Valencia**, **Almería**, **Sevilla**, **Melilla**, **Tanger** and **Palma de Mallorca**, while there are charter and scheduled flights to many North European cities. Information T 2136166. **NB**: taking the train out to the airport there are 2 stops called aeropuerto – avoid the first one which is marked 'cargos'. Trains leave every 30 mins between 0600 and 2230.

Train The RENFE station is on Calle Cuarteles, but there is an office in the city in Calle Strachen, T 2312500. There is a twice daily *Talgo* to **Madrid** which will take you 5 hrs, departs Málaga 0940 and 1620, while the 4 other daily trains might take you as much as 2-4 hrs longer. The same trains stop at **Córdoba**, while there is also a direct link with **Sevilla**. Other Andalusian destinations involve a change at **Bobadilla** junction. The Fuengirola-Málaga local electric line has an additional station almost opposite *El Corte Inglés* department store, while another branch line runs N to **Alora**. The electric railway has new air-conditioned rolling stock introduced in 1992, playing classical music over the public address system. Strains of Vivaldi are particularly welcome travelling through the rather seedy suburbs of Málaga!

Road Bus The station is on Paseo Tilos, T 2350061. A number of bus companies use the station, with Portillo covering the area W of Málaga and Alsina Graells running services to the E. Local connections are generally at half-hourly intervals, links with other cities every 2 hrs. Printed timetables are, as usual, difficult to obtain and travellers may have to rely on the information on the wall.

Sea Ferry To **Melilla**, Trasmediterránea, Calle Juan Díaz 4, T 2224393.

Excursions from Málaga

The larger travel organizations run a full programme of excursions, including day trips to Granada, Ronda and Gibraltar,

2-day trips to Córdoba and Sevilla, plus visits of varying length to Morocco. *Autos Lara* run Jeep safaris to the mountains N of Málaga, Calle Cruz 52, Torremolinos, T 2383140.

El Chorro and the Guadalhorce Reservoirs

Leave Málaga on the C-357 which follows the valley of the Rio Guadalhorce (visitors staying in Fuengirola can join this route via Mijas, Alhaurín el Grande and Cártama). After 38 km, branch off W to **Alora**, an ancient hill town with a distinct Moorish flavour. Its 17th century church is the largest in Málaga province after the city's cathedral. There are the remains of a Moorish fortress on the hill top. Continue N into the **El Chorro Gorge**, a 400m deep cleft eroded by the Rio Guadalhorce and utilized for a hydro-electric scheme. The Málaga-Antequera railway uses this gorge, twisting through a series of tunnels. Along the side of the gorge it is possible to see **El Camino del Rey** (the King's Path), constructed when the hydro-electric scheme was opened by King Alfonso VIII in 1921. It is now in an *extremely dangerous state* and should be avoided at all costs. The road continues N into the **Bobastro** valley where there is a small 9th century church, said to contain the tomb of Ibn-Hafsun, who set up a rebel kingdom in the area around 880.

Further N are the reservoirs of the **Guadalhorce** comprising Andalucía's 'Lake District'. With their blue water, pine-clad sides and perfect swimming, they are an obvious tourist attraction. Camping sites, picnic spots and restaurants are slowly appearing, but the area sees few visitors except on summer weekends. Birdwatchers will appreciate the birds of prey, especially golden eagles and ospreys on passage (see page 36). The return journey to Málaga is by the same route.

Costa del Sol

The Costa del Sol is the name given to the coast W of Málaga which consists of a rather dreadful, continuous strip of resorts, urbanizations, concrete and leisure complexes which have totally obliterated the original fishing villages. Driving along the N-340 it is often hard to tell where one resort ends and the next begins. To make matters worse, this extremely dangerous road intersects many of the towns, which means that tourists have to cross it in order to reach the beach. Immediately W of Málaga is **Torremolinos** which, with its slightly less frenetic neighbour **Benalmádena**, has little to interest the serious traveller, apart perhaps from a wide selection of accommodation.

Fuengirola

At first glance this resort might be a carbon copy of its neighbours to the E, but in fact it has much to recommend it, especially the fishermen's quarter of Santa Fé which has somehow retained its original whitewashed cottages. Fuengirola is located at sea level at the mouth of the Fuengirola river which forms a broad valley extending inland. It has a similar climate to Málaga but, being further W, it is more open to Atlantic influences and has slightly cooler summers.

ACCESS Air Fuengirola, in the Province of Málaga, is now only a 25 min drive from Málaga airport since the new motorway was opened running from the Fuengirola bypass to the outskirts of Málaga. **Train** The train station is in Avda Santos Rein. **Road** The bus station is 100m from the train station on the corner of Avda Ramón y Cajal and Calle Alphonso XIII. Much of the life of the town revolves around the Plaza de la Constitución, where the main church is located.

Things to see

Moorish past Fuengirola has a long and fascinating history, but relatively few sites to visit. Roman remains are currently being excavated at **Torreblanca**, while at **Los Boliches** a Roman arch has been erected from remains recovered from the sea bed by divers.

It was the Romans, too, who probably

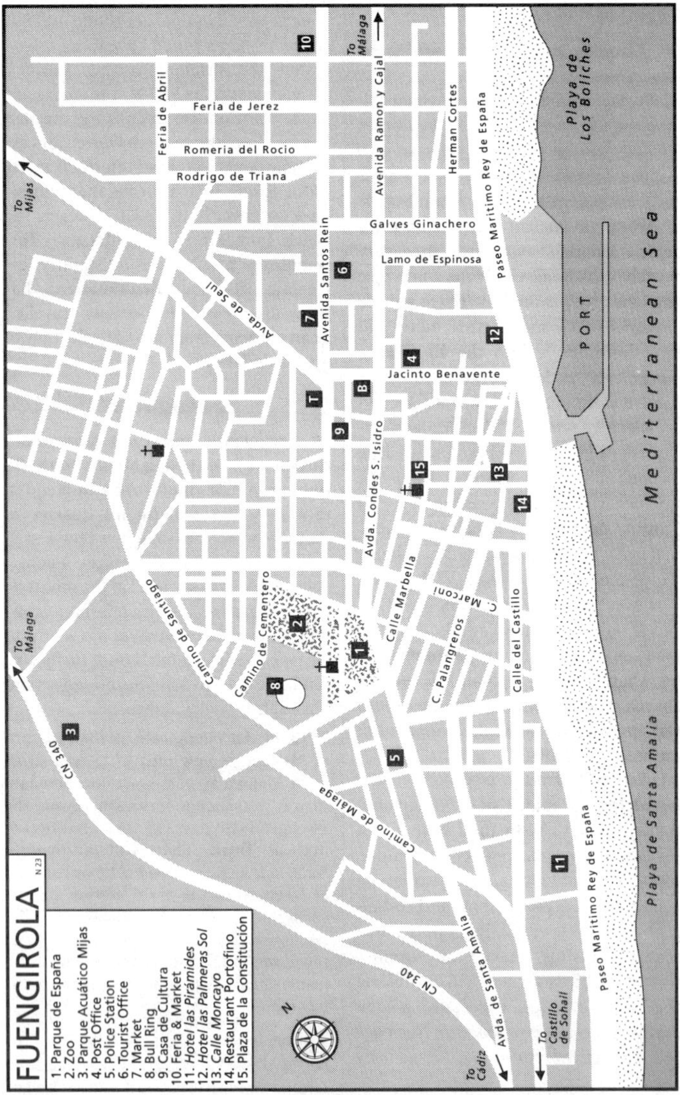

built the first structure at the site of the **Castillo de Sohail** located by the river at the W end of the town. In the 8th century it was extensively re-built by Caliph Abd Al-Rahman III after which much of the history of the town was linked with the castle. Its protection attracted farmers and fishermen and led to the beginnings of the present town. The castle was destroyed in 1485 in the Christian Reconquista of the area, the Moors surrendering on the day of San Cayetano, the patron saint of Fuengirola today. In 1730 the castle was re-built to defend the coast against the British who had taken over Gibraltar in 1704 (see page 137). During the Peninsular War in 1810, a British expedition of 800 men under General Blayney landed at the Castle and advanced on Mijas, but later they retreated to the castle where, humiliatingly, they were obliged to surrender to 150 Polish mercenaries. It is interesting to note that at this time the population of Fuengirola was a mere 60 people! The town became independent of Mijas in 1841, but the big expansion was not to come until the tourist boom of the 1960s and 1970s.

The Castillo de Sohail is undergoing renovation. There are plans to turn it into a cultural centre and outdoor auditorium. Meanwhile, the exterior can be viewed by taking the track from the coast road along to the river mouth and then proceeding along the beach to the W of the castle.

Other places of interest

Travellers with younger visitors to entertain might find the following venues helpful:

Parquesam Zoo, Calle Camilo José Cela, small and certainly not the best example of its kind, with a reptile house, children's playground, mini-train and boats. Open daily 1100, closure according to season. Adults 300 Ptas, pensioners 175 Ptas, children 150 Ptas.

Aquaparks on both the Torremolinos and Fuengirola bypasses with similar hours, attractions and admission fees. **Parque Aquático Mijas**, for example, has a variety of pools, watershoots, slides and rapids, open Apr-Oct, daily at 1000, closure according to season. Adults 1,450 Ptas, children 1,100 Ptas (no charge for 2nd child), pensioners 600 Ptas.

Piccolo Park, Paseo Marítimo, Fuengirola. Play park with slides, climbing mazes, remote controlled cars and lazer games. Open daily 1900-0100 (times which certainly reflect the hours Spanish children keep!).

Tivoli World Large amusement park at Benalmádena with gardens, computerized fountains, rides, restaurants, flamenco shows and a large outdoor theatre featuring internationally- known stars. The admission price includes all the entertainment. The nearest railway station is Arroyo de la Miel, T 2441896. Entrance 1,400 Ptas.

Coin Film City The site of the ill-fated BBC soap opera *Eldorado*. It is now being used for the production of Spanish TV films and will soon have a cinema school for some 60 students. A tour of the site costs 1,500 Ptas (3,000 Ptas with buffet lunch), 1,000 Ptas for children.

Adults might be more interested in: **Casino Torrequebradna**, Ctra de Cádiz Km 226, Benalmádena-Costa, T 2442545, Games room, Fortuna night club with cabaret, piano bar and restaurant. Open Fri and Sat from 2230.

Festivals

There are the usual Semana Santa processions during Holy Week. On July 16th, the *Fiesta de la Virgen del Carmen* is one of the best of its type along the coast. The statue of the virgin is carried from the church in Los Boliches in a 2 hr procession to the beach and into the sea. An amazing spectacle, with half the inhabitants on the beach and the other half in the sea, either swimming or in boats. The *Feria del Rosario* is celebrated in early Oct on the permanent showground between Los Boliches and Fuengirola where there are *casetas* for the various societies and brotherhoods. All this is accompanied by bullfights and flamenco.

Local information

● Accommodation

A ***Las Palmeras Sol***, Paseo Marítimo, T 2472700, 537 rm, used extensively by package companies, wide range of facilities, can be noisy at night, a/c, pool, tennis, disco, gym; **A** ***Las Pirámides***, Paseo Marítimo, T 2470600, at the quieter end of the Paseo, 320 rm, restaurant, usually live entertainment in the evening, pool, tennis, parking, convenient for the beach.

B ***Sol Puerto***, Paseo Marítimo 32, T 2470100, lively location close to beach and fishing port, well used by package companies, rooftop pool and terrace.

C ***Florida***, Paseo Marítimo, T 2476100, another popular package venue, but good value, 116 rm, restaurant, pool, gardens, close to beach.

● Pensiones

D ***Santa Fé***, Avda de los Boliches 66, T 2474181, probably the best of the *pensiones*; **D** ***Agur***, Calle Tostón 4, T 2476662, conveniently situated for town and beach; **D** ***El Amigo***, Avda Los Boliches 114, low cost accommodation on the main street; **D** ***Las Islas***, Urb Torreblanca del Sol, pool, T 2475598.

● Youth hostels

The nearest are in Málaga and Marbella.

● Camping

La Rosaleda, Ctra Nacional 340 Km 211, Camino la Salina, Loma Baja, T 2460191, bar, pool, tennis, beach; ***Fuengirola***, Ctra Nacional 340 Km 207, T 2474108, bar, restaurant, beach, games area; ***Calazul***, Ctra Nacional 340 Km 200, Mijas-Costa T 2493219, bar, restaurant, beach, watersports.

● Places to eat

There is a vast, cosmopolitan range of choice in Fuengirola, varying from simple Spanish fish food, through to Indian, Chinese and exotic Indonesian. Street musicians often entertain diners to add to the ambience, although they will generally be after a tip! ♦♦♦***Portofino***, Paseo Marítimo 29, T 2470643, Italian and international menú, quite expensive, booking rec; ***La Langosta***, Calle Lopa de Vega, T 2475049, shellfish specialities; ***Los Marinos***, Paseo Marítimo, T 2476291, closed Mon, excellent fish and seafood on the beach. ♦♦***Bali Mas***, Calle Martínez Catena, T 2471994, authentic Indonesian *rijstafel*; ***Bélgica Antiqua***, Avda Condes San Isidro 67, T 2471596, Danish and Belgian cuisine and fish dishes. ♦ for those who enjoy simple Spanish food, especially fish, the pedestrianized Calle Moncayo can be recommended. There are numerous restaurants here, such as ***La Gondala***, ***Sal y Pimiento*** and ***Romy*** where an excellent *menú del día* can be had for under 1,000 Ptas. There are also small fish bars for *raciones* around the sport harbour. Cheaper still are the *buffet libre* restaurants, where for a set price the diner can eat his fill. The following (prices in brackets) are all located along the Paseo Marítimo, ***Buffet Pyr*** (895 Ptas); ***Las Palmeras*** (630 Ptas, children 345 Ptas); ***Buffet Saturno*** (630 Ptas); and ***Buffet Versalles*** (625 Ptas). In the summer, locals and long-term residents head for the *ventas* on the Mijas Golf Rd, including ***Venta Perea*** and ***Venta La Marena***. At the Mijas-Alhaurin crossroads, the ***Venta Los Morenos*** is as good as any. All offer good basic Spanish country cooking at reasonable prices, but they can be crowded at weekends.

● Banks

All the main Spanish banks and *cajas de ahorro* have branches in Fuengirola, mainly close to the Plaza de la Constitución. Some English and other foreign banks are also represented.

● Consulates

Most of the nearest consulates are located in Málaga, except **USA**, Centro Comercial las Ramblas, T 2474891 and **Ireland**, Avda Los Boliches, T 2475108.

● Post Office

The ***Correos*** on Avda Bailén, close to the railway station, is to be relocated at the former indoor market site on Calle España.

● Shopping

There is a daily indoor **market** located in a modern building at the junction of Avda Suel and Avda Santos Rein. The weekly outdoor Flea Market held on Tue is at a new site at the fairground on Avda Santos Rein. The so-called **leather market** next to *Hotel Las Palmeras Sol* sells a variety of goods, for which those with North African experience can take part in active bargaining!

● **Telephones**
Local code: 95. **Fire**: T 2473157. **First Aid/emergency service**: T 2472929. **Police**: T 2473157. A *locutorio* cabin containing several booths and accepting credit cards is located in the Plaza de la Constitución. Others, found on Paseo Maritimo, are open Apr-Oct.

● **Travel agents**
Rusadir, Calle Marbella 37, T 2474885; *Perla Travel*, Paseo Marítimo, T 2463076; *Centro*, Las Rampsas 10, T 2470208; *Benamar*, Paseo Marítimo, Edificio El Yate, T 2473762.

● **Tourist information**
The office is at the old railway station, Avda Santos Rein, T 2467457, very cooperative staff. The office also acts as an organizational centre for foreign residents' organizations and clubs.

● **Transport**
Local Car hire is probably best arranged at the airport, but local firms include **Helle Hollis** T 2479800 and **Marinsa** T 2382180. **Taxis** The main taxi rank is opposite the bus station in Calle Alphonso XIII; also **Radio Taxis**, T 2471000.

Train The electric railway runs half-hourly to **Málaga** via the airport. The RENFE station is in Avda Santos Rein, T 2360202.

Road Bus The bus station is on the corner of Avda Ramón y Cajal and Calle Alphonso X111, T 2475066. Portillo buses run half-hourly along the coast road and to **Mijas** while there are a number of long distance coaches – 4 daily to **Granada**, **Ronda**, **Coín** and **La Linea**; 11 daily to **Algeciras**, with 3 proceeding to **Cádiz**; 1 daily to **Jerez** and **Almería** and 5 daily to **Madrid**. These buses are cheap and reliable and therefore crowded, so booking is advisable well in advance, especially in the summer.

Excursions from Fuengirola

Mijas An excursion to Mijas is on the itinerary of most visitors to the Costa del Sol. It is described in the brochures as a 'typical Spanish hill village'. Nothing could be further from the truth. Over half its inhabitants are foreign residents and the whole place is geared to catering for the tourist, from donkey rides to garish souvenirs and English-run restaurants. Despite all this, Mijas has a certain charm and is well worth a visit. The village itself is located 425m above sea level at the foot of the mountains, and the *vista panorámica* in gardens above cliffs gives superb views along the coast. The nearby **Iglesia de la Concepción Inmaculada** was built in the 17th century on the site of Moorish remains. Some ancient wall paintings have recently been uncovered. Next to the church is a small **Plaza de Toros** with an attached **Museo Taurino**. Entrance an expensive 400 Ptas. To the W of this is a modern outdoor **Auditorium**.

● **Accommodation** Mijas has some high class hotels, including: **AL** ***Byblos Andaluz***, Mijas Golf, T 2473050, F 2476783, one of the top hotels in Spain, with excellent sports and leisure facilities. **A** ***Hotel Mijas***, Urbanización Tamisa, T 2485800, F 2485825, a well appointed establishment in a quieter part of the village. Try also **A** ***Club Puerta del Sol***, Ctra. de Fuengirola, T 2486400, large, new hotel in Andalusian style, fitness centre. **D** ***El Mirío Blanco***, Plaza de la Constitución 13, small, cosy, on main square. At the other end of the scale is the **Youth hostel** at *Urbanización 'El Chaparral'*, Km 209, Ctra Nacional 340, Mijas-Costa, 140 beds, 7 km from Fuengirola, temporarily closed.

● **Camping** See Fuengirola section.

● **Places to eat** ♦For a meal under 1,000 Ptas try *La Malagueña*, Plaza de la Paz, T 2485128.

MARBELLA TO GIBRALTAR

Marbella

Pop 80,000 *Alt* Sea level *Best seasons* Spring, summer, autumn.

Located 27 km W of Fuengirola is the town of Marbella, the most up-market resort on the Costa del Sol. It has a long history, having been populated at various times by Phoenicians, Visigoths and Romans, as well as once being a well-fortified Arab town. In the early years of this century, it was little more than a large village struggling to earn a living from agriculture and iron mining.

The changes began in the mid-1950s when a Spanish nobleman named Ricardo Soriano introduced his friends to the area. His nephew, Prince Alfonso von Hohenlohe, built the Marbella Club, attracting a wealthy international set to the area.

Marbella's inhabitants include Arab kings, arms dealers, stars of the media, famous sportsmen and notorious criminals. A visitor to Marbella might be surprised at its reputation as life seems entirely normal on the surface, but the social life goes on behind closed doors in the luxury yachts and palatial villas. Marbella was in danger of becoming rather seedy by the late 1980s, but the mayor has given the town a facelift and it continues to thrive.

ACCESS Air Nearest airports are at Málaga and Gibraltar, the latter confined to connections with Britain. **Train** The nearest railway stations are at Málaga to the E and Algeciras to the W. **Road** Marbella can only be reached by road from the N-340, one of the most dangerous in Europe. The bypass opened in July 1993 has significantly reduced traffic in town and the journey time along the coast. The bus station is located at the junction of Avda Ricardo Soriano and Calle Calvario.

Things to see

Moorish past Marbella's **Old Town** is a compact area located to the N of Avda Ricardo Soriano. In its centre is the Plaza de Naranjos (Orange Tree Square) with numerous extremely expensive open air cafés facing the Town Hall. Leading from the square is a maze of alleyways retaining the original Moorish street pattern. The square itself was opened up by Christian town planners on the site of the Moorish medina. In the NE of the old town, particularly in Calle Trinidad, are good stretches of the old Moorish walls, and at the W end of this street stands one of the towers of the original **Castillo** built by the Moors in the 9th century. The old walls continue into Calle Carmen and Calle Salinas. A tour of the old town could probably be completed in half a day. There are no admission fees.

Other places of interest

In the SW corner of the square is the **Fuente de la Plaza**, a fountain built in 1604, while in the opposite corner is the **Ermita de Nuestro Señor Santiago**, Marbella's first Christian church built at the end of the 15th century. Also here is the **Casa del Corregidor** with a 16th century stone façade, now a café, and the **Casa Consistorial**, dating back to 1572 with a mudéjar entrance and coat-of-arms. To the E, is the Plaza de la Iglesia and the white **Santa María de la Encarnación** church, work on which began in 1618. Also in the E of the town are 2 'hospitals', the Renaissance **Palacio de Bazán** and **San Juan de Dios**, founded by the Catholic kings.

Museums

Museo Arqueológico, Plaza Naranjos 1. Open Mon-Fri afternoons only. Contains Visigothic, early Christian and Roman artefacts.

Museo de Bonsai, Arroyo de la Represa, Marbella, T 2862926. Open daily 1700-2000; Sat, Sun and holidays 1200-1400 and 1700-2000.

Festivals

Middle of Jun *Feria y Fiesta de San Bernabé* is marked by concerts and firework displays.

Local information

● Accommodation

AL *Meliá Don Pepe*, Finca las Merinas, T 2770300, F 2770300, 218 rm, faces the sea, with a sports and leisure complex which includes an 18-hole golf course, indoor and outdoor pools, television, parking, garage, restaurant, squash and tennis courts; **AL** *Don Carlos*, Ctra de Cádiz Km 192, T 2831140, F 2833429, 10 km E of Marbella, the ultimate beach hotel, 232 rm, with sub-tropical gardens leading down to a beach club, pool, TV, restaurant and the Women's World tennis centre.

B *Artola*, Ctra de Cádiz 194, T 2831390, F 2830450, 12 km E of Marbella, traditional hotel with modern extension and small 9-hole golf course, restaurant, pool, parking; **B** *Re-*

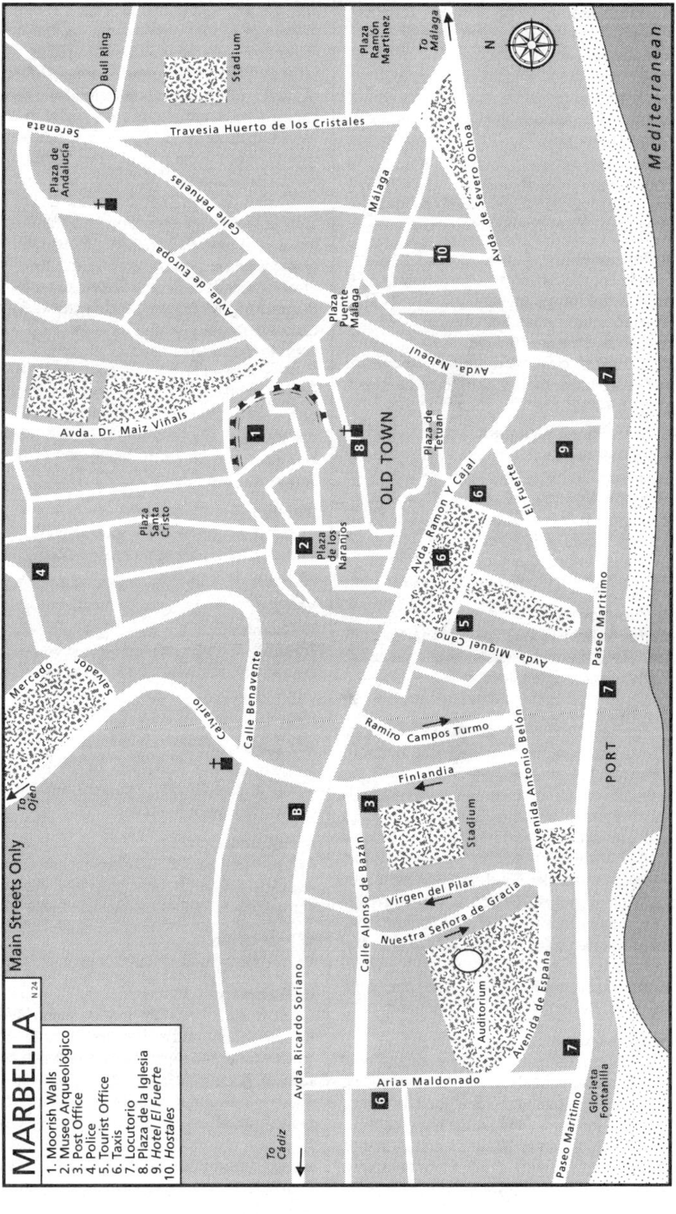
MARBELLA
N 24
Main Streets Only
1. Moorish Walls
2. Museo Arqueológico
3. Post Office
4. Police
5. Tourist Office
6. Taxis
7. Locutorio
8. Plaza de la Iglesia
9. *Hotel El Fuerte*
10. *Hostales*
Bull Ring
Stadium
Plaza Ramón Martínez
To Málaga
N
Mediterranean
Serenata
Travesia Huerto de los Cristales
Plaza de Andalucía
Calle Peñuelas
Málaga
Avda. de Severo Ochoa
Avda. de Europa
Plaza Puente Málaga
Avda. Nabeul
Avda. Dr. Maiz Viñals
OLD TOWN
Plaza de Tetuán
Avda. Ramon Y Cajal
El Fuerte
Plaza Santa Cristo
Plaza de los Naranjos
Avda. Miguel Cano
Paseo Maritimo
Mercado
Salvador
Calvario
Calle Benavente
Ramiro Campos Turmo
Finlandia
Avenida Antonio Belón
PORT
To Ojén
Stadium
Virgen del Pilar
Nuestra Señora de Gracia
Calle Alonso de Bazán
Avda. Ricardo Soriano
Auditorium
Avenida de España
Arias Maldonado
Glorieta Fontanilla
Paseo Maritimo
To Cádiz

fugio de Juanar, Sierra Blanca, T 2881000, formerly a hunting lodge and parador, now a management-run cooperative, peaceful mountain location with ibex and eagles, functional but comfortable, cosy fires in winter, tennis, pool, no dogs allowed; **B** ***Guadalpin***, Ctra de Cádiz Km 179, T 2771100, situated on coast road between Marbella and Puerto Banus, good value; **B** ***Pinomar***, Ctra de Cádiz Km 189, T 2831345, F 2833948, ideal for beach holiday, watersports facilities.

● **Pensiones**

The cheaper accommodation is mainly located around the fringes of the old town. Try **D** ***El Castillo***, Plaza de San Bernabé 2, T 2771739, simple and clean; **D** ***Juan***, Calle Luna 7, T 2779475, clean and simple; ***Isabel de Pacheco***, Luna 24, T 2771978 or ***La Luna***, Luna 7, T 2825778.

San Pedro de Alcantara Visitors requiring easy access to Marbella without wishing to pay inflated prices might consider the town of San Pedro de Alcantara just 10 km W for accommodation. **B** ***El Cortijo Blanco***, Ctra de Cádiz Km 172, T 2780900, Andalusian style with pleasant gardens; **D** ***El Cid***, Calle Extremadura 11, T 2780639, simple but good value.

● **Youth hostel**

Calle Trapiche 2, T 2771491, 113 beds, suitable for wheelchair users, meals provided, kitchen, pool, central location.

● **Camping**

There are 3 excellent camp sites in the vicinity of Marbella, all on the main coast road, but close to a beach. All are open throughout the year and winter use by recreational vehicles is high. Booking advisable during the height of the summer. ***La Bouganvilla***, Ctra Nacional 340, Km 188, T 2831973, top category, bar, restaurant, laundry, beach, pool, watersports, golf, riding, tennis; ***Marbella 191***, Ctra Nacional 340 Km 181, T 2778391, bar, laundry, beach, watersports; ***Marbella Playa***, Ctra Nacional 340 Km 128, T 2833998, located 12 km E of town despite its name, close to one of the best beaches in the area, bar, restaurant, pool.

● **Places to eat**

It is no surprise to find that there are plenty of eating places in Marbella and the surrounding area, but with careful choice a good meal need not cost the earth. ◆◆◆ at the top end of the range is ***La Hacienda***, Urbanización Las Chapas, T 2821267, run by Paul Schiff, the famous Swiss chef, unique *menú*, very expensive; ***La Meridiana***, Camino de la Cruz-Las Lomas, T 2776190, modern restaurant with inventive international cooking, one of Marbella's top eating spots, very expensive; ***Gran Marisquería Santiago***, Paseo Marítimo, T 2770078, good seafood and other dishes, favoured by locals. ◆◆ ***El Mesón del Pasaje***, Calle Pasaje 5, T 2771261, traditional restaurant in the old part of town; ***Rama***, Urbanización Marbesa, T 2832438, family restaurant which has risen from beach bar origins to number cabinet ministers among its clientele (is this a recommendation?!). For those seeking average prices and American fast food at *mañana* pace Avda Ricardo Soriano can provide ***Burger King***, ***McDonald's*** and ***Kentucky Fried Chicken***. ◆Locals looking for cheap food outdoors in the summer head for the collection of 3 *ventas* located on the mountain road 3 km S of Ojén on the C-337, which specialize in game dishes, especially rabbit and partridge. In town opt for *tapas* at one of the bars such as ***Bar Taurino***, Calle Lobatas 46 or a pizza at ***Pizzería Sanermo***, Paseo Marítimo, T 2774333.

● **Banks**

Branches of all the main Spanish banks and savings banks, plus some foreign banks, may be found in Marbella, mainly along Avda Ricardo Soriano.

● **Chemists**

These are open on Sat morning and weekdays 0900-1400 and 1700-2030. The name of the duty night chemist is shown in the window of each shop.

● **Garages/petrol**

Showrooms and workshops of all the main European car firms are located along the N-340 on the E fringe of the town.

● **Hospitals**

Marbella Clinic, T 2774282, is located on the Avda de Severo. A new hospital is nearing completion 5 km E of Marbella on the N-340.

● **Post Office**

Correos is located in Calle Alvaro de Bazán.

● **Shopping**

Good quality shops are located along Avda Ricardo Soriano and in the alleyways of the old town. Many of these specialize in jewellery and fashion goods and can be very expensive. There are also a number of art galleries and craft shops. The large street market, held on Mon near the football stadium, is well worth a visit. The San Pedro outdoor market is held Thur. There is also an indoor market in Marbella located in Calle Benavente selling fresh fruit, vegetables and fish. Open daily.

● Sport

Riding at Club Hípico Elvira, T 835272; Club Hípico Los Monteros, T 770675; Centro de Equitacíon, lakeview, T 786934. **Golf**, **tennis** and **watersports** at all major hotels.

● Telephones

Local code: 95. *Locutorios* are located at intervals along the seafront, Avda Duque de Ahumada. Payment can be made by credit card.

● Travel agents

Benamar, Ctra de Cádiz, Hiper Marbella, T 2781962; ***Marbella Travel***, Avda Ansol, Edificio Platero, T 2772270; ***Viajes Meliá***, Avda Ricardo Soriano, T 2773548.

● Tourist information

Avda Miguel Cano 1, T 2771442. An additional tourist office is now located under the 'triumphal arch' at the E entrance to Marbella.

● Transport

Local Car hire Both international and national companies have their headquarters at Málaga Airport (see Málaga, **page 126**).

Taxi ranks are located at Calle Arias Maldonado (close to the outdoor Auditorium); at the Alameda, and next to the bus station, both in Avda Ricardo Soriano; **Radio Taxi**, T 2770053. For the San Pedro area, T 2783838.

Air The nearest airport is at Málaga, 56 km N. There is an Iberia office on Paseo Marítimo, Complejo Marbella 2000, T 2770284, reservations T 2773082.

Road Bus station, T 2772193. Local buses operate half hourly along the coast road to the E and W. Five buses a day link **Ojén**, **Monda** and **Coín** inland to the N. Coaches run to **Algeciras** 8 times a day, **Ronda** and **La Linea** 4 times a day. **Cádiz**, **Sevilla** and **Jerez** are also served and there are 5 coaches daily to **Madrid**.

Excursions from Marbella

There are a number of villages located in the hills inland from Marbella. **Istán**, described by developers as the 'village on the lake', is, in fact, some distance from a recently built reservoir and has little to commend it. The village of **Benhavis**, on the other hand, has an attractive setting just N of a picturesque gorge. It is the home of a number of artists and has one or two good restaurants.

Just 8 km N of Marbella is the expanding village of **Ojén**, which was Moorish until 1570 and still retains much of the flavour of that time. The road through the olive groves both above and below Ojén is winding and dangerous, particularly at the present with a continual passage of construction lorries carrying stone from the nearby quarry. A new road due to open soon should ease the problem. Continue through Ojén and over the pass, after 4 km turn left through the pine forests to the **Refugio de Juanar** (see Hotels, page 134). From this former parador a rough track leads for 3 km to a *mirador* at 1,000m, from which there are stupendous views over Marbella and the coast. Allow 1½ hrs for this walk. Birds of prey, including booted and Bonelli's eagles, may be seen here particularly on migrations. Small family groups of ibex are not uncommon. A return route to Marbella could be made via **Monda**, **Coín**, a bustling market town of some 22,000 people, **Mijas** and **Fuengirola**.

Submarino Amarillo, Puerto Banus (the up-market development and marina W of Marbella). Underwater submarine trips twice daily at 1300 and 1600. T 2818500.

Casino Nueva Andalucía, *Hotel Andalucía Plaza*, Nueva Andalucía, Marbella, T 2810919. Games room with American and French Roulette, Black Jack, Punto y Banca and fruit machines, restaurant.

West to Gibraltar

About 10 km W along the coast, one comes to **San Pedro de Alcantara**, part of the Marbella administrative district, but largely undeveloped and retaining some of the charm it possessed as a fishing village. There are 3 interesting archaeological items in the San Pedro area, a 2nd century **Roman Villa** at Rio Verde,

3rd century **Roman thermal baths** at Las Bovedas and the 4th century **Paleolithic-Christian basilica** at Vega del Mar.

San Pedro is the first location in Spain for a **Cable Ski**, whereby water skiers are towed by cable for distances up to 20 km. Situated on the landward side of the coast road, cable-ski provides full equipment and charges vary from 1,000 Ptas for 4 rounds to 10,000 Ptas for 100 rounds. Instruction is also available. **Ronda** is an easy excursion from here, see page 101. Then follows a ribbon development of coastal urbanizations until **Estepona** is reached. Despite a new marina, Estepona remains an essentially 'Spanish' resort. The new bypass opened July 1993 has removed the traffic congestion.

Five km W of Estepona, a winding road leads inland to **Casares**, which claims to be the 'most photographed village in Spain'. Its whitewashed houses clothe the side of a hill which is capped by the ruins of a Moorish fortress, which shares its position with the local cemetery. The 17th century Church of San Sebastián can be visited on the way to the fortress. There is a good quality restaurant and craft shop at the entrance to the village, giving fine panoramic views. The alternative route back to the coast at Manilva passes through attractive vineyards but the road surface is poor.

GIBRALTAR

Gibraltar, 127 km SW of Málaga, is a peninsula some 6.5 km in length with an altitude rising to 430m , joined by a low isthmus to Spain. It is separated from North Africa by the 13 km wide Straits of Gibraltar. It has a population of 30,000, of which 20,000 are native Gibraltarians, 6,000 expatriate Britons and the remainder guestworkers from Morocco or EU countries. However, since the border was reopened in 1985, many Gibraltarians now live in Spain and commute back over the border daily to their work. The Moroccans, who were brought over to work in the dockyards when the border with Spain was closed, now find that they have little work or employment protection. They have mounted a permanent protest outside Government House. The British forces withdrew from Gibraltar in 1991, leaving the Rock in the hands of the locally-recruited Gibraltar Regiment. Gibraltar remains a European problem, but the colony is developing its own identity through tourism and financial services, and the impression is growing that Gibraltarians are more than capable of sorting out their future.

The **climate** of Gibraltar is milder and windier than the Costa del Sol. Midday temperatures average 14°C in January and 22°C in July. The *levante*, an E wind, forces cloud onto the summit of the Rock, ensuring higher rainfall figures than in neighbouring Spain.

ACCESS Air Gibraltar airport was built during WWII on reclaimed land and a feature of the road into town is that it passes over the runway, which is shared with the RAF, and traffic is stopped as each plane lands and takes off. **Train** The nearest train stations are at San Roque and Algeciras, with connections to Málaga and other Andalusian cities. **Road** The town itself is accessible by taxi or a 70 pence/35 Ptas bus ride from outside the airport terminal which is also just beyond the border control. On the Spanish side, the La Linea bus station is a short walk from the border crossing. **NB**: visitors by car should seriously consider parking at La Linea and walking over the border as there can be very long delays in each direction. Ignore rough-looking characters on the La Linea side of the border who wish to park and guard your car, as they have no authority whatsoever. A pay and display car park, 100 Ptas an hour, is on the E side of the entrance gates. In Gibraltar there are usually spaces available in the car park next to the Cable Car entrance at the N end of Main Street or beside the War Memorial sports ground on the W side of the town. Approach both of these car parks via Queensway NOT through Main Street, which is largely pedestrianized. To circumnavigate the Rock via the E side, turn left at the first roundabout after crossing the runway.

Things to see

Moorish past Gibraltar has a long and interesting history. It was known to the Phoenicians and also the Greeks, who gave it the name *calpe*. Together with Abyla, the high mountain in Morocco, it was one of the 2 Pillars of Hercules. It was the Arabs who gave Gibraltar its name. They invaded Spain in the 8th century using Gibraltar as a staging post led by Tarik ibn-Zeyad. It became known as *Jebel Tarik* (Tarik's Mountain) and was under Moorish rule for the next 6 centuries, although it was not until 1160 that a permanent settlement was built. Gibraltar was captured by the Christians in 1492, and remained in Spanish hands until it was taken by the British under Admiral Rooke in 1704.

The most obvious, but not the best, Moorish location is the **Moorish Castle**. It was built in 1333, probably on the site of an earlier fortress, as an old wall reaches from it S along the side of the

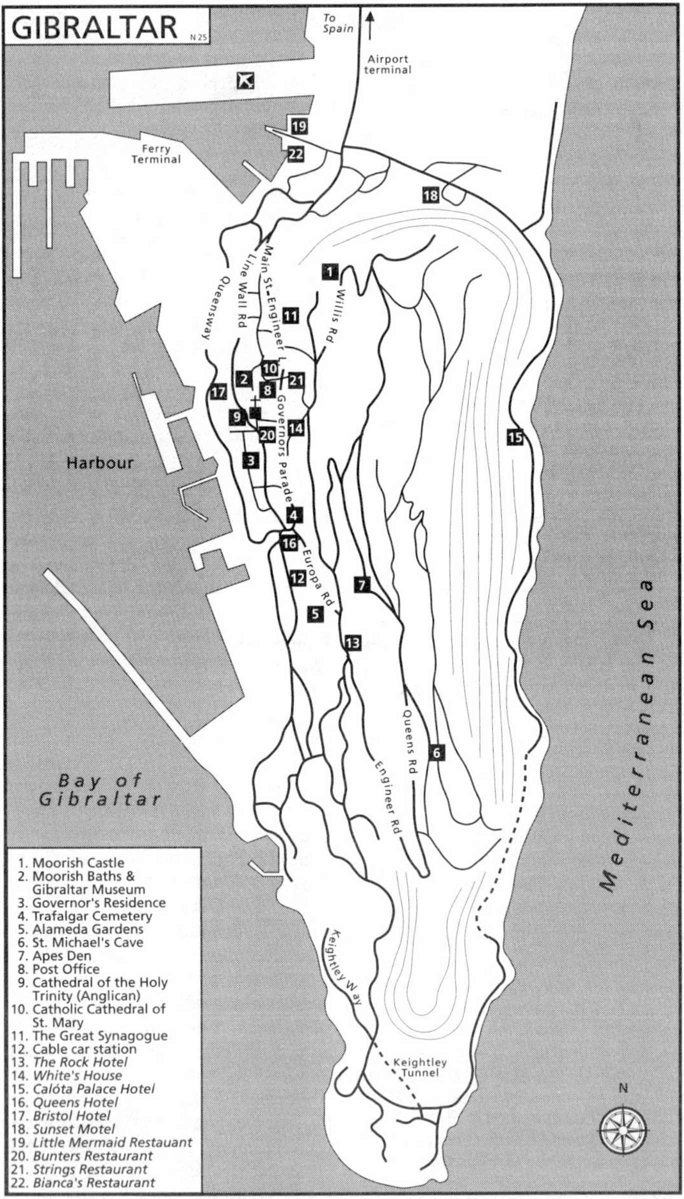
GIBRALTAR
N 25
To Spain
Airport terminal
Ferry Terminal
Harbour
Bay of Gibraltar
Mediterranean Sea
Main St.
Line Wall Rd
Queensway
Engineer L.
Willis Rd
Governors Parade
Europa Rd
Queens Rd
Engineer Rd
Keightley Way
Keightley Tunnel
N
1. Moorish Castle
2. Moorish Baths & Gibraltar Museum
3. Governor's Residence
4. Trafalgar Cemetery
5. Alameda Gardens
6. St. Michael's Cave
7. Apes Den
8. Post Office
9. Cathedral of the Holy Trinity (Anglican)
10. Catholic Cathedral of St. Mary
11. The Great Synagogue
12. Cable car station
13. *The Rock Hotel*
14. *White's House*
15. *Calóta Palace Hotel*
16. *Queens Hotel*
17. *Bristol Hotel*
18. *Sunset Motel*
19. *Little Mermaid Restauant*
20. *Bunters Restaurant*
21. *Strings Restaurant*
22. *Bianca's Restaurant*

Rock. Originally, the castle's defences stretched down to the edge of the town where Casemates gate now stands, but they were destroyed in the various seiges. The main part of the castle remaining is the **Tower of Homage**. The castle can be viewed from the road above it, the route of which is included in the Official Tour of the Rock (see Excursions). Unfortunately the castle is hemmed in by recently-built blocks of flats and entry is not permitted as it is currently used as Gibraltar's prison. The exterior actually looks much more impressive at night when it is cleverly floodlit.

The **Moorish Baths** are an essential visit for any student of Moorish history in Spain. They are located in the **Gibraltar Museum**, 18 Bomb House Lane, T 74289, a building which was converted from 2 officers' quarters in 1930. The tour of the baths is best started at their entrance, where part of the main flue or hypocaust has been uncovered. The Main Hall has a central dome over a series of arches, the columns of which are of particular interest, 4 being Moorish, 1 Roman and the other 3 Visigothic, a mixed bag. The hall originally contained private cubicles. Next is a Cold Room, with higher ceilings to retain the cooler temperature. The Hot Room is entered through a large, rounded arch. A sunken structure would have contained the steam bath and hot plunge bath. Some of the original lead piping may be seen and the whole area is in a good state of preservation (see Museums below). Open Mon-Fri 1000-1800, Sat 1000-1400. Last entry ½hr before closure. Entrance £1.50.

Other places of interest

The **Governor's Residence** is still known as 'The Convent' as it was originally in the 16th century a Franciscan convent. The ceremony of the Changing of the Guard takes place here outside in Convent Place. Next to the Southport gate at the top of Main St is the **Trafalgar Cemetery**, where the tombstones tell a bloody story. Nearby, and less gloomy, are the sub-tropical **Alameda Gardens**. The varied background of the Gibraltarians is reflected in their places of worship. The Catholic **Cathedral of Santa María** in Main St stands on the site of an old mosque, while the Anglican **Cathedral of the Holy Trinity** is located in Cathedral Square (see map). Gibraltar's 750 Jews worship in the **Great Synagogue** in Engineers Lane.

To view the features of the upper part of the Rock, it is best to take the **Cable Car**, the bottom station being located in Rosia Rd close to the Alameda Gardens and the *Bristol Hotel*. The service is open 0930-1715, weather conditions permitting, closed Sun. Admission: adults £4, children under 10, £2. A £9 ticket includes a luncheon voucher for the restaurant at the top but this is not a good bargain if the view is poor. The ticket includes the entry fee for **St Michael's Cave** and the **Apes' Den**. The view from the top of the Rock can be superb, providing conditions are right, with vistas of the Costa del Sol, Algeciras Bay and the mountains of Morocco. There is a mid-way stop on the cable car at the Apes' Den. The so-called Barbary Apes are in fact a species of monkey – the only ones on the mainland of Europe, which is something to be grateful for! There is a saying that as long as the apes survive the British will never leave, which ensures their well-being! Visitors are warned, however, not to feed the apes or make sudden movements, as they are not nearly as loveable as they look.

It is possible to walk from here to **St Michael's Cave**, which is basically a huge cavern containing all the usual stalactites, stalagmites and pillars which one expects in a limestone area. This cave is just one of a whole maze of natural and man-made caves which honeycomb the Rock. St Michael's Cave was used as a hospital during the war and is now frequently the venue for concerts. The Moorish Castle can be viewed by walking down from the Apes' Den. Note that all of these features are visited in the Official Tour of the Rock by taxi or minibus.

Independent travellers may be tempted to drive up to the well-advertised **Upper Rock Nature Reserve**. If you expect to find way-marked nature trails, hides and displays you will be disappointed! Narrow roads lead to a kiosk from which there is no escape from a charge of £3. High stone walls and speeding taxis and minibuses shut out any wildlife. Your ticket entitles you to free entry to the Cave and the Apes' den, but if you have already visited them, the term 'rip-off' readily springs to mind. All is not lost for naturalists, however, for the top of the Rock is an excellent place for observing the migration of eagles, vultures and storks during spring and autumn. In addition, **Dolphin Safaris** run from Shepherds Marina. Ring Mike Lawrence, T 71914.

Museums

In addition to the Moorish Baths, the **Gibraltar Museum**, which is actually larger than it appears from the outside, also has sections on archaeology, geology, natural history and local history. A large scale model of the Rock as it was in the 19th century shows the extent of the Moorish Castle before the area was cluttered with housing. Another room shows details of the military history of Gibraltar and includes a variety of paintings. The Museum is open Mon-Sat 1000-1800, Sat 1000-1400. Entrance £1.50. The Museum is also acting as a Tourist Information Office since the main one in Cathedral Square closed.

OFFICIAL TOURS of the rock can be made by taxi or minibus with informative drivers. They visit all the main sites and take about 90 minutes, although serious visitors might wish to take longer under their own steam. Taxis cost £16 for 4 people, minibuses £5 per person. Information from Bland Travel, T 79200.

Local information

● Accommodation

in Gibraltar are generally far more expensive than comparable hotels in Spain, so budget travellers should consider *pensiones* in La Linea. A number of hotels claim to be in the 'luxury' grade but travellers used to this category will almost certainly be disappointed. **A** *The Rock Hotel*, Europa Rd, T 73000, F 73513, 146 rm, TV, garage, pool, restaurant, located on the side of the Rock in a landscaped garden in the best colonial tradition; **A** *Whites* (formerly the *Holiday Inn*), Governors Parade, T 70500, F 70243, 123 rm, recently refurbished but still with the usual international sterility, pool, jacuzzi, sauna, TV, restaurant; **A** *Caleta Palace*, Catalan Bay Rd, T 76501, F 71050, modern hotel on the E of the Rock, 167 rm, some package tours, sandy beach, pool, restaurant, garage.

There are more modest hotels in the town centre, including: **C** *Queens*, 1 Boyd St, T 74000, F 40030, comfortable, conveniently located for the cable car and shopping; **C** *Bristol Hotel*, 10 Cathedral Square, T 76800, F 77613, 60 rm, centrally situated, pool, gardens, sauna, TV, restaurant; **C** *Sunset Motel*, 60 Devils Tower Rd, T 41265, F 41245, located beneath the N cliff of the Rock and convenient for the airport, built 1991, 36 well-fitted rm, but few other facilities; **C** *Montarik Hotel*, 1 Bedlam Court, T 77065, central location, good value; **C** *Continental*, 1 Engineer Lane, T 76900, F 41702, just off the main street.

D *Gibraltar Beach Hotel*, self catering aparthotel.

F *Toc H Hostel*, at the very end of Line Wall Rd, T 73431, try here if you really must stay in Gibraltar on a budget, but at £6 a night they are almost certainly fully booked, rm generally let on a weekly basis! This list covers just about all the accommodation in Gibraltar – except the prison.

● Camping

There is literally no room for a camp site in Gibraltar. The nearest sites in Spain are at Algeciras to the NW and Manilva to the NE.

● Places to eat

Unlike accommodation, budget travellers will find no problem in Gibraltar when it comes to cheap food. There are numerous pubs, most of which serve some sort of food, usually with an English flavour. The pubs in the Main St, such as ***The Angry Friar***, ***The Royal Calpe*** and ***The Gibraltar Arms*** are invariably a magnet for both shoppers and tourists, but ***The Clipper*** in Irishtown and ***Sir Winston's Tavern*** in Cornwalls Parade are equally good. Passable restaurants have to be searched out. ♦♦♦***Bunters***, 1 College Lane, T 70482, sophisticated international *menú* plus traditional English desserts, fairly expensive, evenings only; ***Strings***, 44 Cornwalls Lane, international *menú* including Moroccan dishes, closed Mon, booking advisable, fairly expensive. ♦♦***Gallo Negro***, Convent Place, T 75654, friendly Italian bistro; ***Bianca's***, Marina Bay, T 73379, specializes in pizzas, appeals to a youthful clientele; ***Little Mermaid***, Marina Bay, recently opened Danish restaurant with typical Scandinavian specialities, cheap to average prices. ♦ for cheap fish and chips try ***Casements Fishery*** on the 2nd floor of the International Commercial Centre, open 0930-2130, take away or eat in; ***Mac's Kitchen***, 245 Main St, T 71155, very cheap, acceptable fast food.

● Banks
There are branches of all the main British and Spanish banks, mainly located around the Main St/Line Wall Rd area.

● Casino
International Casino Club, 7 Europa Rd, T 76666. Apart from the gaming tables, there is a restaurant and fine views.

● Consulates
Belgium, 47 Irish Town, T 78553; **Denmark**, Cloister Building, Market Lane, T 72735; **France**, 2nd Floor, 209 Main St, T 78830; **Israel**, 3 City Mill Lane, T 75955; **Italy**, 12 College Lane, T 78123; **Netherlands**, 2-6 Main St, T 79220; **Norway**, 315 Main St, T 79520; **Sweden**, Cloister Building, Market Lane, T 78456.

● Currency
The official currency is the Gibraltar pound and the colony issues its own notes and coins, but in reality British, Spanish and even US currency is widely accepted in all commercial establishments. Gibraltar also issues its own stamps, which are widely collected and the only valid stamps for mail posted on the Rock. Contact the Philatelic Bureau, P.O. Box 5662, Gibraltar.

● Hospitals
UK residents are entitled to free medical treatment provided they have a temporary address in Gibraltar. Other EU nationals must provide Form E 111. ***St Bernards Hospital***, T 73941. There is also a *Health Centre* in Casemates Square, T 78337.

● Post Office
The main branch is located at 104 Main St. Open 0900-1300 and 1400-1700, Sat 1000-1300.

● Shopping
Gibraltar is sales tax-free and therefore has considerable attractions not only to expatriates on the Costa del Sol, but also to Spaniards living over the border who flock in for their petrol and cigarettes. Be warned that there are limits on the goods you are permitted to import into Spain. For those who can brave the narrow, crowded pavements and busy traffic of the main street, there are branches of well-known firms such as ***Safeway***, ***Marks & Spencer*** and ***Mothercare***. The larger branch of Safeways opposite the airport terminal is well patronized by the Spanish. Particularly worth buying can be electrical goods, jewellery, watches and perfume, but don't assume you are getting a bargain just because you are buying in Gibraltar. Shopping hours tend to resemble those of UK rather than Spain.

● Telephones
When telephoning out of Gibraltar, the international prefix is 00 (except for Spain). To call Gibraltar from Spain dial first 9567 (except in Cádiz province where the code is 7). Telegrams, telexes and faxes can be sent from the offices of Cable and Wireless, 25 South Barracks Rd. Telephone cabins in Gibraltar are the traditional red British version.

● Tourist information
Is available at offices just inside the border, another at the airport and a third at the museum. In contrast to Spanish offices, most of the more useful items have to be paid for. Some of the offices are staffed by students during the summer. They do their best!

● Transport
Local Bus Frequent departures from the border and the town centre (70 pence/35 Ptas). There are no formal bus services, but as there are 3 minibus firms and nearly 150 taxis, this is not a problem.

Car hire A car is a dubious advantage in Gibraltar and many Gibraltarians keep their vehicles on the Spanish side of the border. Congestion and parking problems are normal and vehicles are enthusiastically wheel-clamped. Many international companies have their desks in the airport terminal arrival hall, including **Avis**, **Budget**, **Europcar** and **Hertz**, in addition to several local companies. Costs about £15 per day.

Taxi Readily available at the border or in the town centre, reasonable rates.

Air GB Air (at airport, T 75984) run twice daily to **London** (Gatwick) and daily to **London** (Heathrow); twice a week to **Manchester** on Sun and Tue at 1310; to **Tanger** on Fri and Sun 2130 and Tue 1310; to **Casablanca** on Mon, Tue, Wed, Thur and Sat at 2140; to **Marrakech** on Sat at 1515. T 79300 for information. Price to London return £189/38,000 Ptas; Tanger return £58-90/12,200-15,840 Ptas; Marrakech return £103-147/20,000-30,000 Ptas; Casablanca £84-110/17,000-22,000 Ptas.

Road Bus Portillo buses from the Spanish side of the border link with resorts on the Costa del Sol and **Málaga**.

Sea Tourafrica International provide a ferry link with **Tanger** sailing on Sun, Mon, Wed and Fri. Return fare for adults is £28. Day excursion with sightseeing tour and lunch for £35, T 77666.

NB: a passport is required for entry into Gibraltar. The Spanish Customs are usually awkward in view of the widespread smuggling of cigarettes and drugs which goes on in the area, so delays of half an hour for re-entering Spain are not uncommon and Fri evenings can be very slow.

THE GUADALQUIVIR VALLEY

CONTENTS

MAPS

From its source at 1,600m in the Sierra de Caz Cozorla, part of the Sierra Nevada in the province of Jaén, the Río Guadalquivir (the Great River) flows 657 km down to the Atlantic at Sanlúcar de Barradmeda on the Gulf of Cádiz. This major water course with over 800 tributaries drains an area of 57,390 sq km. It is noted for the rich and varied animal and plant life. On the mountain sides are pine, oak and brushwood which provide cover for wild boar, deer, wild goat, chamois and partridge. The areas irrigated by this mighty river produce the world famous vines for sherry, the olives which cover over 30% of the basin and make Spain a major olive oil exporter, citrus fruit and cereals (another 30% of the basin). The major towns of Jaén, Córdoba and Sevilla, from which the river is navigable to the coast, are found in its valley.

Jaén

Pop 105,000 *Alt* 574m.

Jaén, 105 km E of Córdoba and 94 km N of Granada, is the capital of the inland Jaén Province in the N of Andalucía. Historically the crossroads between Castilla and Andalucía, the town still claims the title of 'gateway to Andalucía' with mountains to the NE and S and the plains of the Guadalquivir to the NW. The river Guadalbullón just to the E of Jaén is a tributary of the Guadalquivir. The area now plays a key role in Spain's olive production.

ACCESS Train The train station is at the N edge of town at the bottom of the hill. Paseo de la Estación leads up to the centre. **Road** Castillo buses run a service from the station. A short walk downhill from the town centre, the bus station is in Plaza Coca de la Piñera. The nearest airport is in Granada.

Things to see

Moorish past During its period as capital of a Moorish state, the town was known to its inhabitants as *Geen*, referring to its role as a caravan route. The Moorish armies under Muhammad II al-Nasir stopped in Jaén in 1212 en route for the disastrous **Battle of Navas de Tolosa** in which they lost much of their territory to Alfonso VIII. Jaén itself was ceded to Fernando III by Muhammad Ibn Nasr in 1246, after which time it played a key role as a Christian frontier town during the final stages of the Reconquista. In 1368 it was sacked by the Moors during an attempt to recapture it. The displaced Moorish ruler moved to Granada to found the Nasrid Dynasty. Jaén was also used by the Catholic kings as a meeting point for their army prior to the final expulsion of the Moors from Granada in 1492 (see page 85).

King Alí's Baths are underground

Arab baths, *hammam*, discovered in 1914 and dating from the 11th century. According to local tradition, Alí was murdered here by his Moorish enemies. Covering 470 sq m , these baths have been well restored and are amongst the most significant in Spain. Their lack of expected decoration is explained by the fact they were intended for public rather than private use. Access is via the **Palacio de Villadompardo** which also houses 2 museums. Open Tue-Fri 1000-1400 and 1700-2000 and Sat-Sun 1000-1400. Admission free.

The original section of the **Castillo de Santa Catalina** standing on the hill overlooking the town 5 km from the centre was once an Arab palace built by Ibn Nasr. Almost entirely re-built after its capture from the Moorish King Alhamar and now restored, it has been converted into a *parador*. The *barrio* of la Magdalena at the base of the Castillo still retains the narrow winding streets established during the Moorish occupation. The interior is presently closed for archaeological excavations but coffee in the adjacent *parador*, which occupies the restored section of the Castillo, provides an opportunity to walk along the path to the white cross and admire the spectacular view.

The **Iglesia de la Magdalena**, the oldest of Jaén's many churches, was built on the site of an even older mosque and retains the Moorish patio, arches and ablutions pool. Open 1800-2000. Admission free.

Other places of interest

While much of the city is modern, resembling a smaller version of Madrid, it is still very pleasant. The city's outsize Renaissance **Cathedral**, also built on the site of a mosque, was designed by Vandaelvira and is most noted for its W façade and a holy relic, a cloth with which St Veronica is reputed to have wiped Christ's face. Open 0830-1300 and 1630-1900. The gothic-mudéjar style **Arco de San Lorenzo** slightly N of the **Cathedral** is a National Monument and all that remains of a parish church in which King Fernando IV's body is said to have lain when he died in Jaén in 1312.

Museums

The Palacio de Villadompardo contains the **Museo de Artes y Costumbres Populares** and the **Museo de Arte Naif** contains a collection of international naive art. Open Tue-Fri 1000-1400 and 1700-2000, Sat-Sun 1000-1400. Admission free. The **Cathedral Museum** contains some interesting sculptures and canvasses by Cano and ought not to be missed. Open Sat-Sun 1100-1300. Admission 50 Ptas. The **Museo Provincial** on Paseo de la Estación contains a fine collection of archaeological exhibits, sculpture and paintings. Open summer Tue-Sat 0900-1400, Sun 1000-1400. Winter Tue-Sat 1000-1400 and 1600-1900, Sun 1000-1400. Admission 250 Ptas, EU citizens free.

Festivals

Night of 16 Jan *Fiesta de las Lumbres* (Fires) *de San Antón*; nationally recognised *Semana Santa* celebrations; pilgrimage of *Cristo del Arroz* second Sun in May; in Jun Corpus Christi is marked by a procession; 11 Jun *Fiesta de Nuestra Señora de la Capilla*, Jaén's patron saint,

CLIMATE: JAEN

	Jan	Feb	Mar	Apr	May	Jun	Jul	Aug	Sep	Oct	Nov	Dec	Av/Tot
Max (°C)	12	14	17	20	24	30	35	34	29	22	16	12	22
Min (°C)	5	6	8	10	13	17	21	21	18	13	9	6	12
Rain (mm)	70	77	99	66	49	14	5	4	29	51	57	73	594

marked by flowers, a fair, procession, etc; 12-20 Oct *Feria de San Lucas* dates back to the 15th century and is Jaén's major festival, with bullfights and sports; 25 Nov **pilgrimage** to the Castillo de Santa Catalina.

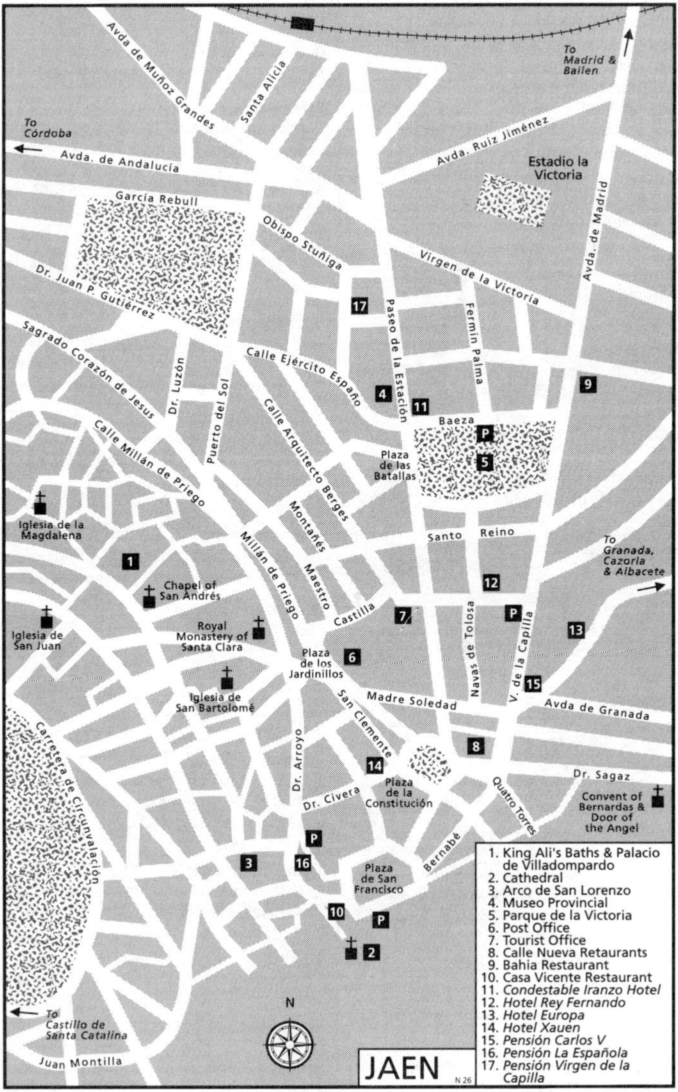

Local information

● Accommodation

Considering its importance as a regional centre the amount of accommodation is surprisingly small. **A** *Parador Nacional*, Castillo de Santa Catalina, T 264411, F 223930, 43 rm, a/c, heavily restored section of the Castillo, quiet with excellent views, restaurant, parking; **A** *Condestable Iranzo*, Paseo de la Estación 32, T 222800, F 263807, 147 rm, restaurant, central location, a/c, modern, exterior rooms rather noisy, garage, disco.

B *Xauen*, Plaza Deán Mazas 3, T 264011, 35 rm, old building, no restaurant, a/c, garage; **B** *Rey Fernando*, Plaza Coca de la Piñera 7, T 251840, no restaurant, noisy by bus station.

C *Europa*, Plaza Belén 1, T 222700; **C** *Reyes Católicos*, Avda de Granada 1, T 222250, 28 rm, no restaurant, out of town.

● Pensiones

D *Martín*, Calle Cuatro Torres 5, T 220633; **D** *Carlos V*, Avda de Madrid 4, T 222091, no rooms with bath, noisy main road; **D** *La Española*, Calle Bernardo López 9, T 258434, with restaurant, quiet pedestrian area near Cathedral; **D** *Virgen de la Capilla*, Calle Cristo Rey 2, T 220024, restaurant, cheapest rooms with bath in town, near Museo Provincial.

● Camping

There is none near Jaén.

● Places to eat

Local dishes include *gazpacho* with grapes and apples and *ensalada de pimientos asados* (salad made with roasted peppers).

Prices tend to be slightly above average in Jaén's restaurants and bars. ♦♦♦*Montemar*, Calle Roldán y Marín 7, T 234262, fish and seafood; *Casa Vicente*, Arco del Consuelo 1, T 262816 local cuisine; *Jockey Club*, Paseo de la Estación 20, T 251018. ♦♦*Bahía*, Plaza San Roque 1, T 251450; *Zeluan*, Plaza San Francisco 3, T 271860; *Batavia*, Paseo Estación 31, T 266032, traditional cuisine. ♦reasonable *platos combinados* and *raciones* in Calle Nueva: *La Gamba del Oro*, n°3, T 261613; *Los Mariscos*, n°2, T 253206; *Mesón Río Chico*, n°12, T 228502.

● Banks

These are concentrated mainly around Plaza de la Constitución.

● Entertainment, cuisine and crafts

Bullfights are held at the Plaza de Toros.

Handicrafts from surrounding towns include glazed ceramics, rugs and wickerwork while **Marmolejo** produces ironwork and guitars. The **flea market** is held on Thur. Student nightlife is centred around the Paseo de la Estación.

● Garages/petrol

Avda de Granada; Santa María del Valle.

● Hospitals

Centro Hospitalario Princesa de España, Ctra de Madrid, T 222650; *Cruz Roja*, Carmelo Torres 1, T 251540; *Hospital Ciudad de Jaén*, Avda del Ejército Español, T 258404 and T 250459.

● Post Office

Plaza de los Jardinillos. Open Mon-Sat 0900-1400.

● Telephones

Local code: 953. No *locutorio*, but cabins in most of the squares including Plaza de la Constitución and Plaza de San Francisco.

● Travel agents

Ecomar, Navas de Tolosa 14, T 256650; *Halcon*, Plaza Coca de la Piñera s/n, T 259600; *Sacromonte*, Pasaje Mazas s/n, T 222212.

● Tourist information

Arquitecto Berges 1, T 222737. Open Mon-Fri 1800-1430 all year and Sat 0900-1300 except Jul and Aug.

● Transport in Jaén

Local Bus Castillo run regular services around the town from Plaza de La Constitución. **Car hire**: **Autos del Pino**, La Luna 6, T 250901; **Avis**, Avda de Granada 7, T 223137; **Hertz**, Viajes Sacromonte, Pasaje Maza, T 222212.

Taxi Plaza de las Batallas, T 251036; Plaza Coca de la Piñera, T 251026; Plaza de la Constitución, T 265017; Plaza de San Francisco, T 265019. Parking in Jaén is very difficult especially on weekdays. Use underground parking if possible.

Train The huge RENFE station, T 255607, is visited by very few trains since the line S of **Jaén** was abandoned. There are 2 daily to **Madrid**, 2 to **Cádiz** and a bus at 1730 to nearby **Espeluy** station for connections to other towns in Andalucía, including **Córdoba** and **Sevilla**.

Road Bus From the bus station on Plaza Coca de Piñera, T 250106, frequent buses to **Granada**, **Córdoba** and **Sevilla** and all local towns.

East of Jaén

About 50 km E of Jaén are the hilltop towns of **Baeza** and **Ubeda**, justifiably described as architectural gems. It has often been claimed that little of architectural significance in Andalucía came after the Moors, but these remarkable towns are surely the exception, and anyone seeking the Renaissance style should head in this direction. Aided by wealth created by the 16th century wool trade, Ubeda and Baeza were developed by 2 men – the architect Andes de Vandelvira and the nobleman Francisco de los Cobos, secretary to Charles V. Together they provided a number of civic and public buildings ranging from churches and universities to granaries and abbatoirs, which form classic Andalusian Renaissance masterpieces.

Baeza

Pop 14,799 *Alt* 790m *Best seasons* Spring and Autumn.

Baeza is located on a hilltop some 50 km E of Jaén.

History

Baeza was an important Moorish settlement, but was one of the first Andalusian towns to be captured in the Reconquest. It saw its main development in the 16th and 17th centuries, so that today it gives

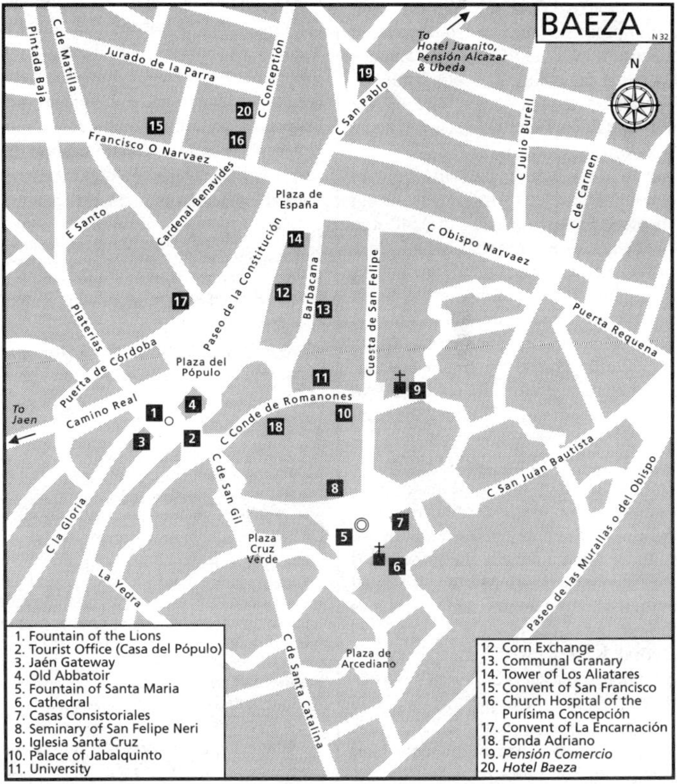

an overwhelming impression of sleepy Renaissance charm, set off by the honey-coloured sandstone of its buildings.

ACCESS Road Recommended by road. **Train** There is a railway station, officially named Linares-Baeza, but this is over 20 km away and bus connections are scanty, particularly at weekends. The bus service connecting Ubeda with Jaén passes through Baeza.

Things to see

Fortunately, most of the worthwhile buildings in Baeza are concentrated within a small area, so that it is possible to see the best features within half a day if necessary, although a longer stay would certainly be more rewarding. Most visitors will arrive from the Jaén direction and approaching the main square should turn right into the **Plaza de los Leones** (1). Here the charmingly old fashioned **Tourist Office** (2) is located in the **Casa del Pópulo**, the former law courts. On the W side of the square is the **Jaén Gate** (3), part of the original walls and built in honour of Charles V. Opposite is the **old abbatoir** (4) dating back to 1540 and displaying a huge imperial coat-of-arms. In the centre of the Plaza de los Leones is a small fountain from whose badly eroded lions the square takes its name. From here take the back streets SE to **Plaza Santa María**. The square is dominated by the 13th century **Cathedral** (6) built on the site of a mosque, but comprehensively updated by Vandelvira 300 years later. The oldest part of the cathedral is the Door of the Moon in 13th century Gothic-Mudéjar style, with a delightful 14th century rose window above it. In the square outside the cathedral is the **Fuente de Santa María** (5), a small fountain with a triumphal arch, which is the symbol of the town. Next to the cathedral is perhaps the most beautiful building in Baeza, the **Casas Consistoriales** (7), once the upper town hall and now a national monument. The walls display the coat of arms of Juana the Mad and her husband Philip the Fair. On the N side of the square is the **Seminary of San Felipe Neri** (8). The walls here show the traditional grafitti of successful students. Heading NE the Cuesta de San Felipe leads on the right to the early mediaeval **Iglesia Santa Cruz** (9) and on the left to the 15th century **Palacio de Jabalquinto** (10). The palace has a richly ornamental Gothic façade, an impressive Renaissance courtyard and a majestic Baroque staircase. A 16th century **University** (11) is adjacent to the palace. It is now a high school, but visitors are admitted to see the Mudéjar ceiling in the main hall and the superb patio. There are countless other sites of interest in Baeza, including the **Corn Exchange** (12), the nearby **Granary** (13) and the **Tower of Los Alitares** (14). Further away from the main sites, but worth the walk, is the partially ruined **Convent of San Francisco** (15), also attributed to Vandelvira. It is still impressive despite the ravages of an earthquake and the attentions of French troops in the 19th century.

Local information

● Accommodation

B *Hotel Baeza*, Calle Concepción 3, T 744361, F 742519, modern and comfortable, central location.

C *Hotel Juanito*, Avda Arca del Agua, T 740040, small, garage, out-of-town location.

● Pensiones

D *Comercio*, Calle San Pablo 21, T 740100, central location, somewhat gloomy, but friendly and popular with the locals; **D** *Fonda Adriano*, Conde Romanones 17, T 740200, large house in back street, plenty of atmosphere, despite the grumpy manager.

● Camping

None in the vicinity, but plenty in the Cazorla National Park to the SW.

● Where to eat

The main hotels and pensiones, particularly the *Juanito*, provide the best possibilities. Try also the ◆◆◆*Restaurante Andrés de Vandelvira*, Calle San Francisco 14, regional dishes.

Ubeda

Pop 28,718 *Alt* 757m.

After the charm of Baeza, the traveller might expect its larger neighbour Ubeda to be something of an anticlimax, but this is not the case.

History

It was known to the Romans as Betis, on whose foundations Abd al-Rahman built the Moorish town of Ubbadat al-Arab. It was finally conquered by Ferdinand III in 1234 and became an important staging post in the remainder of the Reconquista. Its heyday, however, was in the 16th century during the times of Charles I and Philip II, when much of the older part of the town was constructed.

ACCESS Entirely by road. The nearest international airport is at Málaga.

Things to see

Ubeda is neatly divided into old and new sections, the latter being of little interest. Start in the old sector at the **Plaza Vásquez de Molina**, a beautiful square flanked by a collection of honey-coloured Renaissance buildings. The 2 churches are Vandelvira's **Sacra Capilla del Salvador** (1), built for Cobos who is buried there, and **Santa María de los Reales Alcázares** (2) with its Renaissance façade and Gothic cloisters. The **Condestable Dávalos Palace**, a large 16th century mansion, is now a *parador* (3). The **Casa de las Cadenas** (4), a 16th century palace designed by Vandelvira is named from the chains around its courtyard. Its N side is the town hall and tourist office (5). Completing the Plaza Vásquez de Molina are the **Cárcel del Obispo** (the Bishop's Prison) (6) and the **Antiguo Pósito** (old granary) (7). Leading E from the Plaza is the Calle Baja del Salvador in which is the **Hospital de los Honrados Viejos del Salvador** (8), a unique setting for an old folks' home! At the end of the street is the **Redonda de Miradores** (9), a paseo giving superb views of the rolling, olive-treed landscape and the Cazorla mountains beyond. Elsewhere in the old quarter, among the narrow roads and alleyways, are many other Renaissance treasures. The **Plaza Primero de Mayo**, for example, has the 14th century Rosebush Gate and the **Church of San Pablo** (10), also showing the handiwork of Vandelvira. Other churches and convents include **San Pedro** (11), with its Romanesque apse, the **Real Monasterio de Santa Clara** (12) dating from 1290, the **Oratorio de San Juan de la Cruz** (13), and the **Iglesia de la Trinidad** (14), with an exuberant Baroque frontage. On the outskirts of the town is Vandelvira's most extraordinary building, the **Hospital de Santiago** (15), which has been described as an 'Andalusian Escorial', with a magnificent arcaded patio and large quadrangle. It is now a cultural centre. On the border of the old and new areas, in the Plaza de Andalucía, is a modern feature which brings a smile. It is a statue of a fascist civil war general, which after the war was riddled with bullets. It remains today with its self-evident message!

Local information

● Accommodation

The *Parador*, located in the centre of the Renaissance area, is undoubtedly the place to stay in Ubeda. **A** ***Parador Nacional Condestable Dávalos***, Plaza Vasques de Molina 1, T 750345, luxury and atmosphere. For those with fewer pesetas to spend, there are several more modest hotels and *pensiones* in the newer part of the town, mainly in the Avda de Ramón y Cajal.

C ***Hotel Consuelo***, Avda Ramón y Cajal 12, T 750840, garage, suitable for wheelchair users; **C** ***Hotel La Paz***, Calle Andalucía 1, T 750848, garage, change facilities.

D ***Pensión Sevilla***, Avda Ramón y Cajal 9, T 750612, garage; **D** *Pensión San Miguel*, Avda Libertad 69, T 752049, the smallest and cheapest accommodation in Ubeda, out of town.

● Camping

None in the vicinity, but plenty in the nearby Cazorla National Park.

● Places to eat

The best restaurant in Ubeda is undoubtedly at the ◆◆◆*Parador*. The bars of the two hotels mentioned provide tapas, but their restaurants are uninspiring. Visitors staying in the Avda Ramón y Cajal area could try ◆◆*Restaurant Gallo Rojo*, Tr Torrenueva 16, T 752038, pleasing ambience, moderate prices and regional dishes.

● Banks

Some branches of Spanish banks located in the newer part of town, mainly in the roads leading off the Plaza de Andalucía.

● Garages/repairs

Mercedes, **Opal**, **Peugeot** and **Renault** all

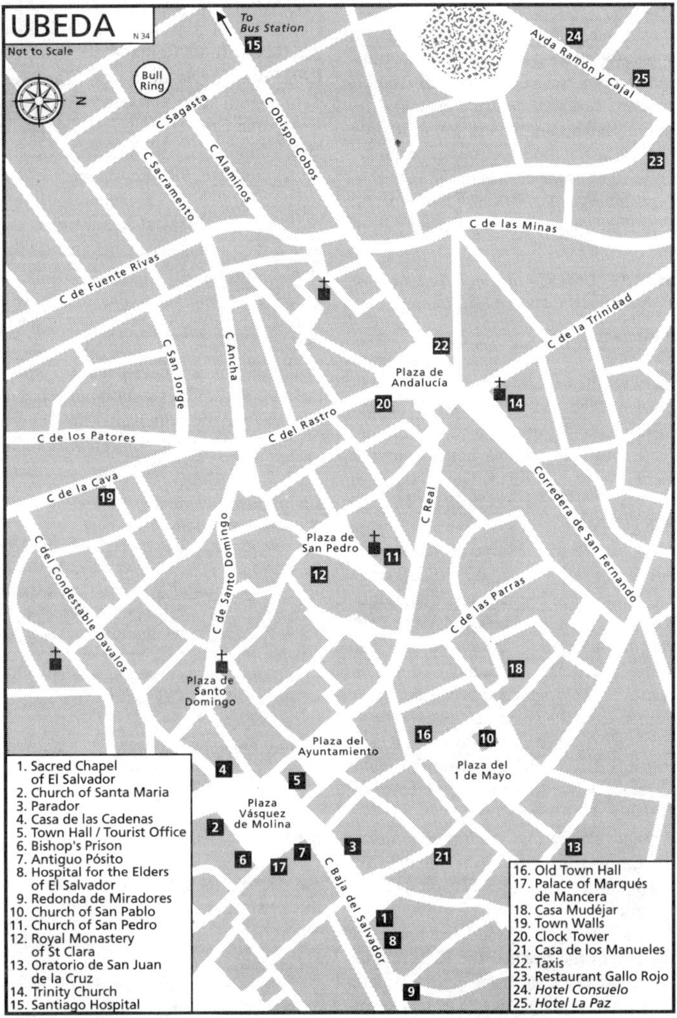

have workshops on the Ctra de Circumvalación.

● Hospitals
General Hospital, Ctra de Linares, T 797100. *Red Cross*, Calle Santiago, T 755640.

● Post Office
Correos, Calle Trinidad 4, T 750031.

● Shopping
The main shopping area is in the newer section of the town in the roads leading off the Plaza de Andalucía. Local craft specialities include ceramics, mats and baskets (established in Moorish times), ironwork, carving and gilding.

● Telephones
Local code: 953.

● Tourist Information
Town Hall, Plaza del Ayuntamiento, open 0800-1445. The tourist office in Hospital de Santiago cultural centre arranges guided tours of the town.

● Transport
Local Bus The Alsina Graells company operates 9 buses a day to Jaén and Granada and 5 buses a day to Linares. There are daily direct coaches to Granada, Almería, Málaga and Madrid, while local buses serve surrounding villages. **Taxis** available in the Plaza de Andalucía. The bus station is in Calle San José.

Excursions from Ubeda/Baeza

Parque Natural de Cazorla

The Sierras of Cazorla and Segura form the largest of the Spanish nature parks, covering a surface area of 214,336 sq km. This mountainous region closes in the Guadalquivir basin in the E and connects the Sierra Morena with the mountain ranges of Andalucía. As well as mountain scenery, there are pine forests, lakes, gorges and stretches of bare limestone. The whole area is a naturalist's paradise. It is outstanding for flowers and alpine plants, including the unique Cazorla violet. Birds are also well-represented, including a wide variety of raptors.

CAZORLA NATIONAL PARK

Mammals include wild boar, ibex and Red, Roe and Fallow Deer. For maximum bird and flower species, May and Jun are ideal months. Summer weekends are best avoided. A number of round tours can be made by car from Ubeda. The best route follows the N322 NE through Villacarillo. After a further 9 km turn right just before Villanueva del Arzobispo on the road to Tranco reservoir along a superb gorge. The road then follows the edge of the reservoir SW over the Doves Pass and down to La Iruela and Cazorla. The return to Ubeda can be made via the C323, but visitors with more time at their disposal should follow the C328 calling at Quesada and the Tiscar Pass. The true magic of the Cazorla is best appreciated by getting off the roads and on to the footpaths which are well marked. Walking maps are available from ICONA or from the tourist office in Ubeda.

• **Accommodation** **A** *Parador Nacional El*

Olive Oil

From an aircraft window at 10,000m, across the Mediterranean region from Jaén province of Andalucía to the Tunisian Sahel, the traveller will notice the chequerboard pattern created by the ubiquitous olive trees. At ground level the impression is confirmed by the rolling landscape of endless hectares of olive groves.

The olive tree (*Olea europaea*), which is very fire- and drought- resistant, is a long-liver. Many pueblos in Andalucía are proud of their 1,000-year-old tree. Methods of harvesting and processing have barely changed since Roman times. The ripe olives are shaken or struck from the trees, washed and taken to local mills where they are ground under large rotating stones which in many rural areas are still driven by donkeys or mules. The pulp is pressed under mats of esparto grass and the resulting oil filtered into a series of settling tanks, where the oil and water separate, the oil being drawn off for purification. The result is pure virgin olive oil.

Olive trees were first introduced to Andalucía by the Romans, who transshipped the product back to Rome. (The best Spanish olive oil is still exported to Italy and often re-exported as an Italian product!). The Moors extended the cultivation and called the oil *az-zait* meaning 'juice of the olive' giving rise to the Spanish word *aceite*. Today, Spain is the world's largest producer of olive oil and Andalucía accounts for 20% of this amount.

Selecting a bottle of olive oil from the supermarket shelf, however, is not so simple. The label needs to be studied carefully and the percentage of *acidez* noted. The best oil, *virgin extra*, comes from olives which are picked ripe and milled immediately and which can contain a maximum 1% acidity. *Fino* is allowed 1.5% and *corriente* 3.3%. The higher the acidity, the stronger the flavour and the lower the price. Another kind of oil is *aceite de orujo* made from the 'cheese' left from the first pressing, which is largely used for industrial purposes. To encourage production of high quality oil, a control board, as with wine, issues some *denominación de origen* labels. Of the 4 already issued, 2 are in Andalucía, at Sierra de Segura (Jaén) and Baena (Córdoba). In some parts of the S of Spain, oil tasting takes place in the same way that wine is sampled.

Folklore has always claimed that olive oil was beneficial to health, contributing to good complexions, efficient digestion and strong hearts. Modern nutrition, with its emphasis on the 'Mediterranean diet' seems to be confirming this belief. Olive oil contains no cholesterol!

Adelantado, Sierra de Cazorla, T 721075, F 721075, small, beautiful setting, resembles a hunting lodge, pool, good restaurant. Cheaper accommodation can be found at the *pensión* **D** *Mari-Mer*, La Vega, Quesada, T 733125. **Youth hostel** *Mauricio Martínez 6*, 23470 Cazorla, Jaén, T 720329, 76 beds, meals available. **Camping** There are 3 sites in the Sierra de Segura and 6 in the Sierra de Cazorla. Most are well-equipped and in unspoilt surroundings. The only 1st category site is *Fuente de la Canalica*, Ctra las Acebeas, Siles, T 491004.

From Ubeda to Córdoba

The N322 and later the E25 largely follow the Rio Guadalquivir. The towns of Linares, Bailén and Andúcar are industrial and of little distinction, although Linares is the birthplace of the guitarist Andrés Segóvia. Fortunately all 3 are now bypassed, but the time saved must certainly be used by the discerning traveller to make the 10 km detour N from Bailén to the small hill village of **Baños de la Encina** with a wonderful Moorish castle built in 967 by Al-Hakam II. The castle, composed of golden sandy conglomerate, is in an excellent state of preservation, despite the fact that it was won and lost again 6 times by the Christians. It has no fewer than 14 towers, a huge courtyard (used for village dancing at fiesta time) and an impressive Tower of Homage giving spectacular views of the village and surrounding countryside. Viewing hours are informal and depend entirely on the ancient guardian and his equally ancient key. His surprising agility around the rickety steps usually earns him a tip. The village of Baños de la Encina itself is well worth a stroll. Take a look at the pretty Plaza de la Constitución and the imposing Iglesia Parroquial de San Mateo with its Gothic 15th century nave and its octagonal Renaissance tower.

JAEN TO CORDOBA

To continue by car along the Guadalquivir valley, travel N on the minor road direct to **Andújar** on the banks of the river. Although it played an important strategic role on the route to Castilla and developed under the Moors until it was captured by Ferdinand III in 1225, nothing remains of its Moorish castle. A further 20 km W, the minor road C-327 leads to **Lopera**, 10 km S of the main road, which has a fully restored but privately-owned Moorish castle in the centre. Although it can be admired from the outside, it is closed to the public. Back on the main road, **Villa del Río** lies 4 km further W towards Córdoba. Its small Moorish castle now houses the police station and civic office.

Córdoba

Pop 300,000 *Alt* 124m.

Córdoba, one of Spain's oldest cities, situated 176 km N of the Mediterranean coast and 140 km NE of Sevilla, was once the capital of the influential Caliphate of Córdoba but is now simply the capital of Córdoba Province. The Sierra Morena mountain range runs to the N while the town itself, like Sevilla, is in the fertile plains of the **Vega del Guadalquivir**.

ACCESS Air Nearest airport is in Sevilla. **Train** The train station is on Avda de América on the N edge of town, a 20 min walk from the old town via the commercial centre. Taxis are available and a local bus service runs around the town. **Road** The Ureña bus depot on Avda de Cervantes, and Alsina Graells on Avda de Medina Azahara are in the same area as the train station.

Things to see

Moorish past In 711, with the aid of its disillusioned Jewish inhabitants, the Moors captured Córdoba along with much of the rest of Iberia. In 758, Abd Al-Rahman I of the Ommayyad dynasty arrived from Damascus and established an independent Emirate, although the settlement had been established by the Romans in 3 BC. Much of the Iberian Peninsula was then ruled from the city which was the capital of the western Caliphate from 929 to 1031 following Independence from Baghdad. Córdoba grew in importance and influence under Abd Al-Rahman's successors, especially Abd Al-Rahman III and Hakkam II, until internal disputes and a revolt by the Berbers began to weaken the Ommayyads, leading to the abdication of Hisham II in 1031. The Caliphate of Córdoba then split up into a number of minor *taifas* (kingdoms) while the city itself came into the hands of first the Almoravides in 1094 and subsequently the Almohades in 1149. Having been taken by the Christians under Fernando III in 1236, Córdoba began to decline.

The **Mezquita** (mosque) is Córdoba's most famous example of Arab architecture. Although not quite as fabulous as Granada's Alhambra, in its own way the Mezquita is an equally significant remnant of Spain's Moorish heritage and is a must for any visitor to Andalucía.

Construction was begun in 785 by Abd Al-Rahman I on the site of a Visigothic church and a Roman temple. His intention was to build Islam's most grandiose mosque. Abd Al-Rahman II, Mohammed I and Hakkam II later made significant extensions to the building and the final addition under Hisham II's minister Almanzor was completed by 990. The constant need for expansion reflects the progressive growth in Córdoba's population during the peak of its influence and the ease with which extensions could be made by adding extra rows of columns and arches without interfering with the overall design. The importance of this mosque is indicated by the extent to which it served as a model for later constructions throughout the Islamic world, with innovations produced by the Mezquita's architects being incorporated into other new buildings.

The Mezquita began to take its present form only after the Reconquista when, in 1384, the Christians began to convert the mosque into a church, the Iglesia de la Asunción, by adding the **Capilla Real** (Royal Chapel) and a pulpit. The most drastic alteration occurred in 1523 under Charles V (also renowned for his interference with the Alhambra in Granada) who had a cathedral built in the very centre of the mosque. The result is a curious juxtaposition of Islamic and Renaissance style in a massive rectangle 174m long and 137m wide with a huge fortified wall surrounding it, and the Guadalquivir to the S. At the front is the **Patio de los Naranjos**, the oldest existing example of its kind. It is planted with orange trees and palms interspersed with fountains and was originally used for purification rituals before prayer. You will notice that many of the columns in this courtyard are in different styles, this is due to the practice of reusing remnants of older constructions; in this case some of the columns are thought to have come from other countries within Europe.

The main entrance below the belfrey is the **Puerta del Perdón** (Door of Forgiveness), built after the Christians re-

CLIMATE: CORDOBA

	Jan	Feb	Mar	Apr	May	Jun	Jul	Aug	Sep	Oct	Nov	Dec	Av/Tot
Max (°C)	13	16	19	23	26	32	37	36	31	25	19	14	24
Min (°C)	5	6	8	10	13	17	20	20	17	13	9	5	12
Rain (mm)	86	72	101	65	56	11	2	3	21	82	72	93	664

captured the city but in Arab style. The *mihrab* was added at the end of the 10th century and is an octagonal room richly decorated with mosaics. Its most unusual feature is that, instead of facing towards Mecca, it is directed towards the city of Damascus from which the Ommayyads had fled before settling in Cór-

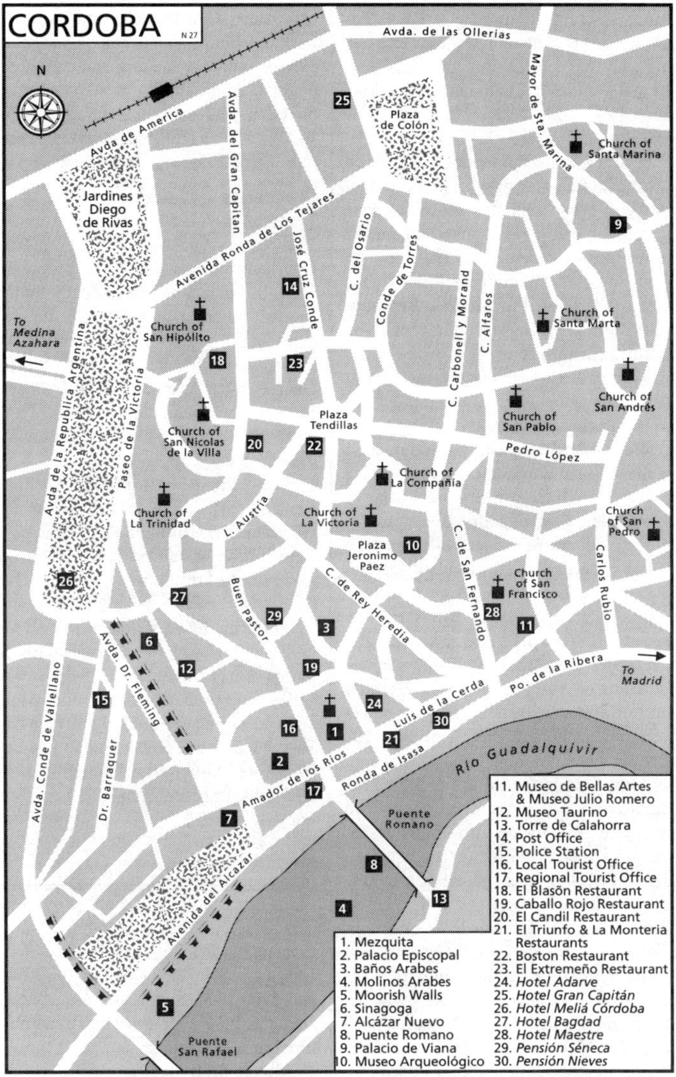

doba. The most incongruous aspect of the Mezquita is the cathedral tower, built in the 16th century at the orders of Charles V. It rises awkwardly out of the middle of the Islamic symmetry in a futile attempt to impose a Christian identity on the intrinsically Moorish nature of this building. Open Apr-Sep 1030-1330 and 1600-1900, Oct-Mar 1030-1330 and 1530-1730. Admission 600 Ptas, children 300 Ptas.

The **Palacio Episcopal** beside the Mezquita was originally constructed by the Visigoths, then became an alcázar which the resident Caliphs had linked to the mosque by means of a bridge. The Omayyad court abandoned this alcázar when they moved to **Medina Azahara**. However the oldest surviving part of the building is 15th century. It is due to the existence of this Moorish fortress that the nearby Christian building is known as the **Alcázar Nuevo**.

Baños Arabes In a private house in Calle Velázquez Bosco in the **Judería** there is a 10th century *hammam* or sauna. The owner claims these are the oldest baths in Andalucía, adjacent to a small open patio surrounded by arches and they certainly have plenty of atmosphere. There was once a passage between the baths and the nearby Mezquita. The opening hours are dependent on the presence of a friendly and informative owner who will expect you to take photographs. Admission 100 Ptas.

Other reminders of the Moorish occupation are the churches with Arab minarets transformed into belfries, for example the 9th century minaret on the **Iglesia de San Juan** in Calle Barroso N of the Mezquita, and the 10th century minaret on the **Iglesia de Santiago** in Calle Agustín Moreno. There are also some remnants of the original walls along Avda del Alcázar and Avda del Corregidor and 3 ruined **Molinos Arabes** (Moorish Flour Mills) in the river Guadalquivir near the **Puente Romano**.

The **Judería** (Jewish Quarter), in which both the Mezquita and the Alcázar are located, stretches from the Plaza de las Tendillas S to the Guadalquivir. It has survived since the expulsion of the Jewish community by Fernando and Isabel in 1492. Even more extraordinary is the survival of the **Sinagoga**, Andalucía's oldest synagogue, on Calle Judíos. Open Tue-Sat 1000-1400 and 1530-1730, Sun 1000-1330. Admission 50 Ptas.

Other places of interest

The **Alcázar Nuevo** was begun in the 13th century for Alfonso X and was later enlarged and used as a palace by the Catholic kings, becoming a centre for the Inquisition from 1490 to 1821. Its gardens, which are illuminated during the summer months, are also worth seeing. Open Tue-Sat, May-Sep 0930-1330 and 1700-2000, Oct-Apr 0930-1330 and 1600-1900. Sun 0930-1330. Admission 200 Ptas, free Tue.

The **Puente Romano** (Roman Bridge) with its 16 arches across the Guadalquivir is built on Roman foundations which were first restored by the Moors in the 8th century, although it has been restored many times since.

The **Palacio de Viana** in Plaza Don Gome is an opulent mansion with 14 patios, a magnificent art collection, and a library devoted to hunting. Open Mon-Tue and Thur-Sat Jan-May and Oct-Dec 1000-1300 and 1600-1800, Jun-Sep 0900-1400. Sun 1000-1400. Admission: adults 200 Ptas, children 100 Ptas. (Temporarily closed.)

Museums

Museo Arqueológico Provincial in Plaza Paez contains a display of coins, ceramics, tools etc inside a Renaissance mansion. Open Tue-Sat, May-Sep 1000-1400 and 1800-2000, Oct-Apr 1000-1400 and 1700-1900. Sun 1000-1330. Admission 250 Ptas. Free to EU citizens with proof of identity.

Museo de Bellas Artes in Plaza del

Potro, once the Catholic Kings' Hospital of Charity, contains a small collection including some Goyas. T 473345. Open Tue-Sat, May-Sep 1000-1400 and 1800-2000, Oct-Apr 1000-1400 and 1700-1900. Sun 1000-1330. Admission 250 Ptas.

Museo Julio Romero de Torres, also in Plaza del Potro, adjacent to the 14th century inn immortalized in 'Don Quixote', is dedicated to the work of this local exponent of Modernism and Symbolism. Open Tue-Sat, May-Sep 0930-1330 and 1700-2000, Oct-Apr 0930-1330 and 1600-1900. Sun 0930-1330. Admission free.

Museo Taurino y de Arte Cordobés in Plaza de Maimonides contains ceramics and crafts and a section devoted to *tauromaquía* (the art of bullfighting) with special attention devoted to Manolete, a local matador killed by the bull Islero in 1947. A statue to Manolete is to be found in Plaza Lagunilla. Open Tue-Sat, May-Sep 0930-1330 and 1700-2000, Oct-Apr 0930-1330 and 1600-1900. Sun 0930-1330. Admission 200 Ptas, free Tue. EU students free.

The **Torre de Calahorra** on the S side of the Puente Romano gives an audio-visual history of Moorish Spain in addition to displaying some armour which once belonged to *El Gran Capitán* – Gonzalo Fernández de Córdoba, and items connected with the local 16th century poet Luis de Góngora. Open May-Sep 1000-400 and 1730-2030, Apr-Oct 1030-1800. Admission 350 Ptas plus 500 Ptas for full audio-visual programme.

Festivals

Carneval in Feb; traditional Easter processions take place for *Semana Santa*; 5-12 May *Fiesta de los Patios* is marked by concerts and *flamenco* in addition to a competition for the best decorated patio; 25-28 May *Feria de Nuestra Señora de la Salud* for which the city's women dress in traditional garb; Córdoba's patron saint is celebrated during the *Fiesta de Nuestra Señora de la Fuensanta* in Sep; 24 Oct fiesta of *San Rafael Arcángel*.

Local information

● Accommodation

AL *Adarve*, Calle Magistral Glez Francés 15, T 481102, F 474677, 103 rm, modern, a/c, TV, garage, cafetería, no restaurant, opposite Mezquita; **AL** ***Meliá Córdoba***, Jardines de la Victoria, T 298066, F 298147, 106 rm, a/c, garden, pool, TV, restaurant (but best to eat out), views of Judería and Mezquita; **AL** ***Parador Nacional Arruzafa***, Avda Arruzafa 33, T 275900, F 280409, out of the town in the hills in what was once Abd Al-Rahman I's palace, 83 rm, a/c, garden, pool, tennis, garage, parking.

A *El Califa*, Calle Lope de Hoces 14, T 299400, F 295716, 46 rm, a/c, garage, central, quiet; **A** *Los Gallos Sol*, Avda de Medina Azahara 7, T 235500, F 231636, 105 rm, a/c, TV, pool, modern facilities, originally constructed by the bullfighter El Cordobés; **A** *Husa Gran Capitán*, Avda de América 5, T 470250, F 474643, 100 rm, a/c, garage, restaurant, city centre.

B *Marisa*, Cardenal Herrero 6, T 473142, F 474144, no restaurant, opposite Mezquita.

● Pensiones

C *Baghdad*, Calle Fernández Ruano 11, T 202854, new, N edge of Judería; **C** ***El Triunfo***, Corregidor Luis de la Cerda 79, clean, efficient, a/c, near Mezquita; **C** ***Maestre***, Calle Romero, Barrios 4, T 475395, small, spotless, garage, highly recommended.

D *Séneca*, Calle Conde y Luque 7, T 473234, near Mezquita, slightly basic, beautiful courtyard; **D** ***Ronda***, Avda de las Ollerías 45, T 480250, rather remote; **D** ***El Portillo***, Calle Cabezas 2, T 472091, in the Judería, communal bath; **D** ***Rey Heredía***, Calle Rey Heredía 26, T 474182, near Mezquita, communal bath; **D** *Perales*, Avda de los Mozárabes 13, T 230325, clean and basic, near station; **D** *Mari*, Calle Pimentera 6, off Calle Calderos, T 479575, clean and basic.

E *Nieves*, Calle Cara, T 475139, near river off main road.

● Youth hostel

Plaza Judás Leví, T 290166 impressive new building, 88 beds, 2 beds per rm, meals. Max stay 3 days.

● Camping

Campamento Municipal, Ctra de Córdoba-Villaviciosa, Km 2, T 472000, top grade site, pool, 10 km N of town but frequent buses run to city; ***Carlos III***, Ctra Nacional IV, Km 429.5, La Carlota, T 300697, pool, tennis, 30 km S.

● Places to eat

♦♦♦*El Blasón*, Calle José Zorilla 11, T 480625, very expensive, set in an old house; ***Almudaina***, Campo Santo de los Mártires 1, T 474342; ***El Caballo Rojo***, Calle Cardenal Herrero 28, T 475375, Andalusian and old Arab recipes. ♦♦ ***El Candil***, San Felipe 15, T 475305, good food; ***El Triunfo***, Calle Luis de la Cerda 79, T 475500, clean and efficient, meal of the day 1,100 Ptas; ***La Montería***, Calle Corregidor Luis de la Cerda 77; ***Boston***, Plaza de las Tendillas, T 485989, Andalusian cuisine, *platos combinados*, *menú* includes wine; ***Siena***, Plaza de las Tendillas 5, T 473005, *menú* and *platos combinados*. ♦***Cafetería Monaco***, Ronda de los Tejares 3, reasonable *platos combinados*; ***El Extremeño***, Plaza Benavente 1, T 478314, local and Extremaduran cuisine; ***El Tablón***, Calle Luis de la Cerda 75, T 476061, patio, friendly service; ***Mesón de Luna*** and ***Mesón la Muralla*** are adjacent restaurants in ramparts of the Judería, their proximity ensures value for money.

● Banks

Avda Del Gran Capitán, Ronda de los Tejares.

● Crafts and cuisine

The tourist shops are full of leatherwork, a legacy of the Moors, and silver filigree. Local specialities include the rather dry *pastel cordobés* (flaky pastry with a candied centre), which is said to have its origins in Moorish cuisine. *Salmorejo* (*gazpacho* with eggs) and *gazpacho* itself are frequently on the *menú*. Notable local beverages are **sherry** from Montilla and Moriles and **anis** from Rute.

● Consulates

France, Calle Manuel de Sandóval 4, T 472314; **Monaco**, Calle Gran Capitán 32, T 474391.

● Entertainment

Bullfights take place throughout the season at the *Plaza de Toros de los Califas*.

Concerts take place on Sun in the Alcázar and there are open air shows in the *Teatro Municipal*, including the International Guitar Festival. Check with the tourist office for details. The bullring is in the modern town to W of historic quarter.

Flamenco Córdoba is famed for its *flamenco* and bullfighting traditions. A national *flamenco* competition takes place every 3 years and there are numerous festivals during the summer months. ***Tablao Cardenal***, Calle Cardenal Herrero 15 is one of the best displays. Open Tue-Sat 2230. Admission 1700 Ptas including a drink.

● Garages/petrol

Avda de la República Argentina, Plaza de Colón, Plaza Santa Teresa.

● Hospitals

Casa de Socorro, Avda República Argentina 4, T 234646; ***Cruz Roja***, Paseo de la Victoria, T 293411; **Ambulances**: T 295570; **Emergencies**: T 291133.

● Post Office

Correos, Calle Cruz Conde 15. Open Mon-Fri 0800-2100, Sat 0900-1400. Telegrams T 472009 or T 470345. Open Mon-Fri 0800-2100, Sat 0900-1900.

● Sport

Riding at Cortijo la Ventilla, Hacienda El Cordobes, Gran Capitán, 14001 Córdoba, T 474794.

● Telephones

Locutorio **Local code**: 957. Plaza Tendillas 7. Open Mon-Fri 0930-1400 and 1700-2300, Sat 0930-1400.

● Travel agents

Viajes Vincit, Avda Burgos 1, T 472316; ***Viajes Intercontinental***, Avda del Gran Capitán 16, T 470694.

● Tourist information

Calle Torrijos 10, in the Palacio de Congresos, T 471235. Open summer Mon-Fri 0930-1400 and 1700-1900, Sat 1000-1300. Winter Mon-Fri 0930-1400 and 1530-1730, Sat 1000-1300. Also Plaza Judas Levi, T 472000. Open Mon-Fri 0900-1400 all year.

● Transport

Bus *Bonobús* tickets for 10 journeys available from kiosks for 475 Ptas. Most local buses pass through Plaza de las Tendillas.

Car hire **Avis**, Plaza Colón 35, T 476862; **Europcar**, Avda Medina Azahara 7, T 233460; **Hertz**, Ctra de Guadalhorce, T 477243. **Coche Caballo**: based beside the Mezquita, agree the price before setting off.

Taxi T 470291, T 415153.

Air There is a minor national airport in **Córdoba**, but any international flights must be made via **Sevilla** or **Málaga**. The Iberia office is in Ronda de los Tejares 3, sales T 471227, reservations T 472695.

Train The station is on Avda de América, an additional RENFE office for information and tickets is on Avda Ronda de los Tejares 10, T 475884. Information T 479302. The Madrid-Cádiz and Madrid-Málaga train lines meet at Córdoba resulting in frequent trains to many destinations. 12 run to **Sevilla** daily, 2 to **Algeciras** and 6 to **Málaga**.

Road Bus Transportes Ureña on Avda de Cervantes 22, T 472352, run 5 buses daily to **Jaén**, and 3 to **Sevilla**; Alsina Graells on Avda Medina Azahara 29, T 236474, run 2 to **Málaga**, 4 to **Granada**.

Excursions from Córdoba

Medina Azahara (City of Flowers) is 10 km W of Córdoba off a minor road from the C-431. Hitchhiking is the best means of reaching the ruins if you are without a car, otherwise check current bus services with the tourist office since days, times and departure points vary. Construction on the site began in 936 for the Caliph, Abd Al-Rahman III, in honour of his favourite wife, Azahara. The resulting palace and gardens were spectacular, immense (housing 20,000 people and covering 2½ sq km) and short lived since Medina Azahara was destroyed by invading Berbers in 1013, subsequently sinking into obscurity until its rediscovery in the 1940s. Parts of the site have been incorporated into other buildings over the centuries. Controversial reconstruction work has been carried out since that time, most notably on the Salón de Abd Al-Rahman III, T 234025. Open Tue-Sat 1000-1400. Admission 250 Ptas (free to residents of EU).

CORDOBA TO SEVILLA

Almodóvar del Río is 17 km further W along the C-431, following the Guadalquivir with the Sierra Morena to the right. This heavily restored 8th century castle, fortified by Abd Al-Rahman III, sits on a steep hill beside the Guadalquivir castle. Visits are possible if the guardian can be located. From here the C-431 can be followed along beside the river to **Lora del Río**, from where it is worth making a detour away from the Guadalquivir to **Carmona** on a hill above the plains 27 km SW on the C-432.

Ecija, 52 km from Córdoba, is known as the town of the sun and towers. The main road bypasses to the S while the town nestling on the W bank of the Rio Genil boasts 11 towers, a rich heritage of Renaissance and Baroque architecture. Visit Iglesia San Juan Bautista for the best tower, the Palace of Condes de Valdehermoso for Renaissance and Las Descalzas for the Baroque. St Paul is said to have visited here – but not in summer when the place sizzles in temperatures at times above 45°C.

• **Accommodation & food** C *Hotel Plateria*, T/F 4835010, to E of Playa Mayor, best hotel in town tucked into small quiet side road, 18 rms with bath, a/c, TV, telephone, good restaurant.

Carmona

Situated 33 km E of Sevilla at an altitude of 248m, Carmona is a beautiful and genuine town in the centre of Sevilla province in the Guadalquivir basin to the S of the river itself. With a population of only 22,000, surrounded by an area primarily dedicated to olive and cereal crops, Carmona has remained largely unaffected by its proximity to, and easy communications with Andalucía's capital city. The old town with its maze of narrow streets and enclosing walls, gives a strong flavour of its Moorish past.

ACCESS **Train** There is no train service to Carmona, the nearest station is in Sevilla, as is the nearest airport. **Road** Road communications are good, however, especially via the NIV motorway. The Casal company runs a frequent bus service from Sevilla along this route, stopping outside the dingy *La Parada* bar on the main street of Carmona's new town.

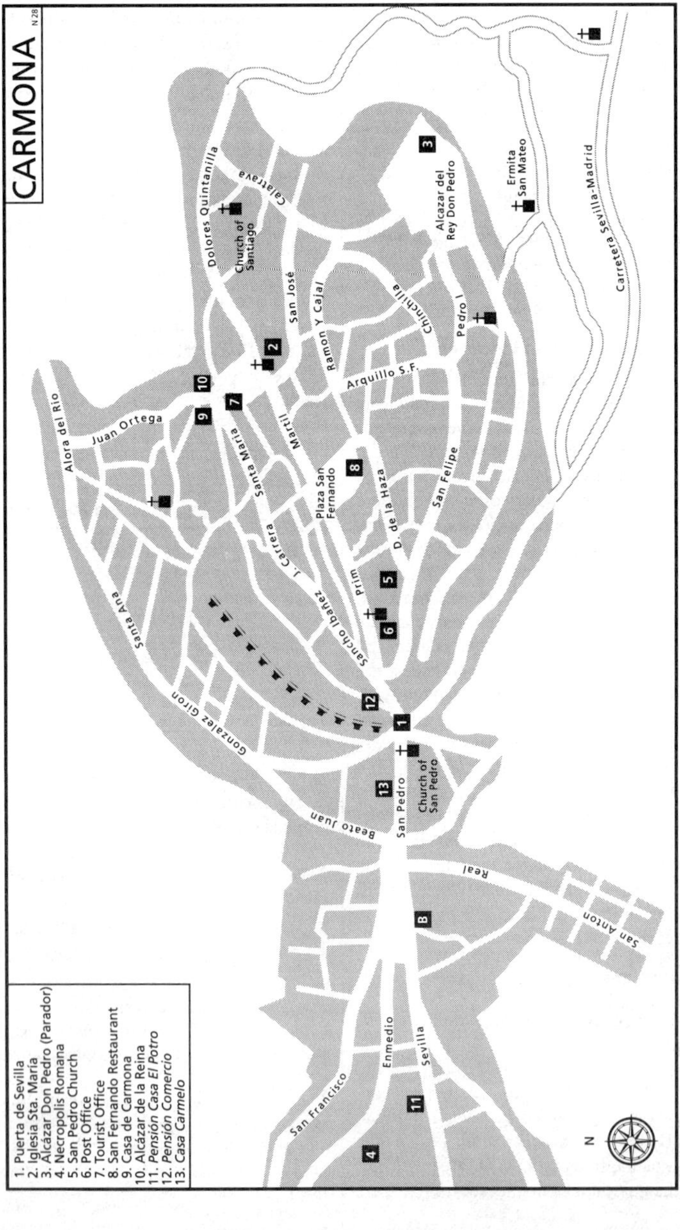
CARMONA
N 28
1. Puerta de Sevilla
2. Iglesia Sta. María
3. Alcázar Don Pedro (Parador)
4. Necropolis Romana
5. San Pedro Church
6. Post Office
7. Tourist Office
8. San Fernando Restaurant
9. Casa de Carmona
10. Alcázar de la Reina
11. Pensión Casa El Potro
12. Pensión Comercio
13. Casa Carmelo
Dolores Quintanilla
Calatrava
Church of Santiago
San José
Ramon Y Cajal
Chinchilla
Alcazar del Rey Don Pedro
Ermita San Mateo
Carretera Sevilla-Madrid
Pedro I
Arquillo S.F.
Juan Ortega
Alora del Rio
Martil
Santa Maria
Plaza San Fernando
D. de la Haza
San Felipe
J. Carrera
Prim
Sancho Ibáñez
Santa Ana
Gonzalez Giron
Church of San Pedro
San Pedro
Beato Juan
Real
San Anton
Enmedio
Sevilla
San Francisco
N

Things to see

Moorish past Although there is evidence that the town was occupied from Paleolithic times, it also played a significant role during Moorish occupation. Following Tarik's defeat of the Visigoths, Carmona was besieged by Muza Ben Nosair, finally falling into Moorish hands after negotiations which preserved the town and meant that the only a few Jewish occupants were taken prisoner. Jewish occupation in Carmona (it is believed there was a synagogue at the time of the Visigoths' defeat) continued until the 16th century. After the Caliphate of Córdoba collapsed, Carmona was the capital of a *taifa* (small kingdom) until its capture by Fernando III in 1247.

The **Alcázar de la Puerta de Sevilla** at the entrance to the old part of the town, contains some Moorish elements although various sections were constructed prior to and after the Moorish occupation. Due to staff constraints, this is only open on Fri and Sat morning. Admission 175 Ptas.

Running to the left as you enter the Puerta de Sevilla are some remains of the original walls. In addition to the Moorish contribution, parts of these were built by the Romans and, after the Reconquista, by Christian occupants of the town.

The gothic 15th century **Iglesia de Santa María la Mayor** on Calle Santa María de Gracia at the corner with Calle San José is constructed on the site of an earlier Almohad mosque and retains evidence of this in its traditional ablutions patio just inside the main gate, where the atmosphere is more Moorish than Christian.

Clear evidence of Carmona's Moorish past is provided in the form of the Almohad **Alcázar**, on the far edge of the old town, with its complex defence system and excellent views over the surrounding countryside. This has now been restored and converted into the *parador*. If you are not keen to pay for 4 star accommodation, this monument is best appreciated via the bar, although prices there are not in the budget range either!

Other places of interest

The **Necropolis Romana** on Avda Jorge Bonsor, up a turning to the right (coming from the Puerta de Sevilla) at the W edge of the new town, is a major site. It dates from the 1st century AD, was excavated at the end of the 19th century and consists of underground burial chambers, 1,000 of which have been discovered. Open Tue-Sat 1000-1400 and 1600-1800, Sun 1100-1400.

Festivals

Late Feb to early Mar the *Carneval*, which dates back to the 18th century, is celebrated with children parading in fancy dress, dances and competitions. *Semana Santa* is along the lines of that in Sevilla with 8 *cofradías* (brotherhoods) involved in the processions; the *Feria de Mayo* takes place in mid-May and lasts 4 days, again along the lines of Sevilla's own *Feria*. The *Romería de la Virgen de Gracia*, a pilgrimage to the shrine, takes place on the first Sun in Sep. Another pilgrimage, that of *San Mateo* takes place around the *Ermita San Mateo* to mark the reconquest of Carmona by Fernando II on 21 Sep 1247.

Local information

● Accommodation

There are only 6 *pensiones* and 4 hotels in Carmona, providing a clear choice between basic or luxury accommodation. **AL** *Parador Alcázar del Rey Don Pedro*, Calle Los Alcázares, T 4141010, 63 rm, restaurant, bar, a/c, exchange facilities, good views, parking, pool, garden, TV; **AL** *Casa de Carmona*, Plazuela de Lasso 1, T 4143300, quiet, in the old town.

A *Alcázar de la Reina*, Plaza de Lasso 2, T 4190064, based on a 16th century palace, in the old town, good view, quiet, parking.

● Pensiones

D *Pensión Comercio*, Calle Torre del Oro 56, T 4140018, restaurant, clean, noisy cockerel next door, eccentric landlord, just by the Puerta de Sevilla; **D** *Pensión Casa Carmelo*, Calle San Pedro 15, T 4140572, restaurant, in new town, slightly noisy, formerly a casino.

E ***Casa Huéspedes El Potro***, Calle Sevilla 78, T 4141465, capacity 10, basic, in new town, restaurant, some noise from road.

● Places to eat

♦♦♦ All the hotels listed above have good international restaurants. Also worth trying is ***San Fernando***, Calle Sacramento 3, T 4141223. ♦ As with accommodation, restaurant prices polarize around luxury and budget levels. Any of the *pensión* restaurants is worth a try, although they are generally patronized primarily by their residents.

● Banks

On Calle San Pedro in the new town.

● Garages/petrol

Repsol garage on the road out W to Sevilla.

● Hospital

Cruz Roja, Ctra de Madrid, T 4140751; **Emergencies**: ***Paseo de la Feria***, T 4140997, T 4140761.

● Post Office

Calle Prim 29. Open 0900-1400. Telegraphs 0900-1500.

● Telephones

No *locutorio* but cabins may be found on Plaza San Fernando in the old town and Calle San Fernando in the new.

● Travel agents

Triana Viajes, Paseo del Estatuto 6, T 4190745.

● Tourist information

Inside the Casa de Cultura. Open Mon-Fri 0800-1500 and Sat 0800-1300. The Casa de Cultura itself is open in the afternoon so you might be able to get some information even when the Tourist Office is closed.

● Transport

Local Bus Casal buses run virtually every hour on the hour to **Sevilla** and back for only 240 Ptas until 2200. The direct buses are rather more rapid. Check times at 'La Parada' or, during summer, the attendant at the nearby icecream kiosk will probably have a timetable too. Connections to any other towns will have to be made via **Sevilla**.

Taxis: Paseo del Estatuto, T 4141359.

Sevilla

Pop 710,000 *Alt* 9m *Highest temperature recorded* 46°C, *lowest* -3°C.

Sevilla stands 115 km up the Rio Guadalquivir (*Wadi el Kebir* – the Great Water) from the Atlantic Ocean. Sevilla's geographical position has been responsible for its importance since it was a Phoenician settlement. For example in the 16th century during the conquest of the New World, all goods entering Spain were required to come via the port of Sevilla. Today it is Spain's fourth largest city, the capital of Andalucía's largest province and the capital city of Andalucía as a whole.

The fertile plains around the Guadalquivir are vital to Sevilla's agriculture. However the gradual silting up of the river which began in the 18th century was reflected in the town's progressive decline in importance until the advent of industrialization. Port activities continue today, but only thanks to constant dredging. To the SW of Sevilla, towards **Cádiz**, the plains give way to a huge delta and the marshland which houses the **Coto de Doñana** nature reserve before reaching the Atlantic Ocean.

Sevilla is situated between 2 mountain ranges: the Sierra Morena follows the boundary of Andalucía to the N while the Sistema Bético range separates it from the Mediterranean Sea to the SE.

ACCESS The city's facilities and communications underwent many improvements for Expo '92, some of which continue to benefit the city.

Air A new airport has been built beside the old one at San Pablo 12 km E of the city for both national and international flights. An hourly bus (route EA) links the airport to the city centre at Puerta de Jerez, via the train station. Price 200 Ptas. Taxis are also available. **NB**: watch out for fiddled fares from airport. You should be charged approx 1,500 Ptas depending on baggage.

Train From the new train station, Santa Justa, catch bus No 70 to the bus station at Prado de San Sebastián near Plaza de España, or a taxi to Plaza Nueva, the central square, approx 500 Ptas.

Road If arriving by car, parking can be difficult although parking areas have been increased. Theft of, or from, cars is widespread, so no possessions should be left visible inside the car. The **bus** station at Prado de San Sebastián is within walking distance of the centre. Cross Calle Menéndez Pelayo and at Plaza Don Juan de Austria turn down Calle San Fernando to Puerta de Jerez where a right turn takes you down Avda de la Constitución past the tourist office and Cathedral.

Things to see

Moorish past In 712, only a year after the Moors first landed in Spain, Sevilla was captured by the Moors under Musa (see Algeciras, page 107). The town later became subject to the Caliphate of Córdoba, despite its own great wealth and status. In 1023, following the disintegration of the Caliphate, Sevilla took the opportunity to declare its independence. The town was successively ruled by the Abbasids, the Almoravides and the Almohades. It was under the Almohad Emirs that the city achieved great prosperity especially from 1068-95 under Al-Mutamid. However in 1248 the city was reconquered by the Christian King Ferdinand III.

Reales Alcázares Work on the Moorish fortress in Plaza del Triunfo originally began in 712 following the capture of Sevilla. In the 9th century it was transformed into a palace for Abd-Al-Rahman II. The wall which still runs between the Plaza del Triunfo and the Barrio de Santa Cruz dates from this period. During the prosperous rule of the Almohads, the palace was extended further. The Patio del Crucero and Patio del Yeso are remnants of this 11th century expansion. However much of the existing Alcázar was built in the 14th century for Pedro the Cruel who employed Moorish architects to undertake the work, some of them from the neighbouring Moorish Kingdom of **Granada** under Yusuf I. Many fragments from earlier Moorish buildings such as the **Medina Azahara** near **Córdoba** (see page 159) were incorporated during its construction. Successive centuries saw various additions to both the building and the cool gardens followed by attempts at restoration, some of which are out of keeping with its Moorish character. However it is significant that it should be this Moorish palace rather than any other which should have remained popular with Spanish royalty for so many centuries. Open Tue-Sat 1030-1730, Sun 1000-1400. Admission 600 Ptas.

The **Casa de Moneda** (Coin House) located in Calle Santander was originally the palace of Abbu Hafs, an Almohad Sultan. Following the Reconquista it was used as a prison for the upper classes until precious metals from the New World began to flow into the city in the 16th century. The palace then acquired its present name since the metal was brought there to be turned into coins. The 18th century saw another change of hands when it was taken over

CLIMATE: SEVILLA

	Jan	Feb	Mar	Apr	May	Jun	Jul	Aug	Sep	Oct	Nov	Dec	Av/Tot
Max (°C)	15	17	20	24	27	32	36	36	32	26	20	16	25
Min (°C)	6	7	9	11	13	17	20	20	18	14	10	7	13
Rain (mm)	66	61	90	57	41	8	1	5	19	70	67	79	564

by rich Spaniards who had returned from the colonies. It is now due for restoration work prior to being opened to the public.

La Giralda in the Plaza del Triunfo was built in the 12th century, a few decades before the Almohads lost control of the city, to be the main minaret on Sevilla's mosque, Islam's second largest mosque at that time. The Emir who ordered its construction in 1184 (12 years after work had begun on the mosque itself) instructed the Maghribian architect, Ahmad Ibn Baso, that it should be more beautiful than any other minaret in existence. It is 100m high and built on a Visigothic base. Renaissance additions under Christian rule are the belfry containing 24 bells, the upper tower and the *giraldilla* (weathervane) representing Faith, from which the tower's name has been derived. Un-

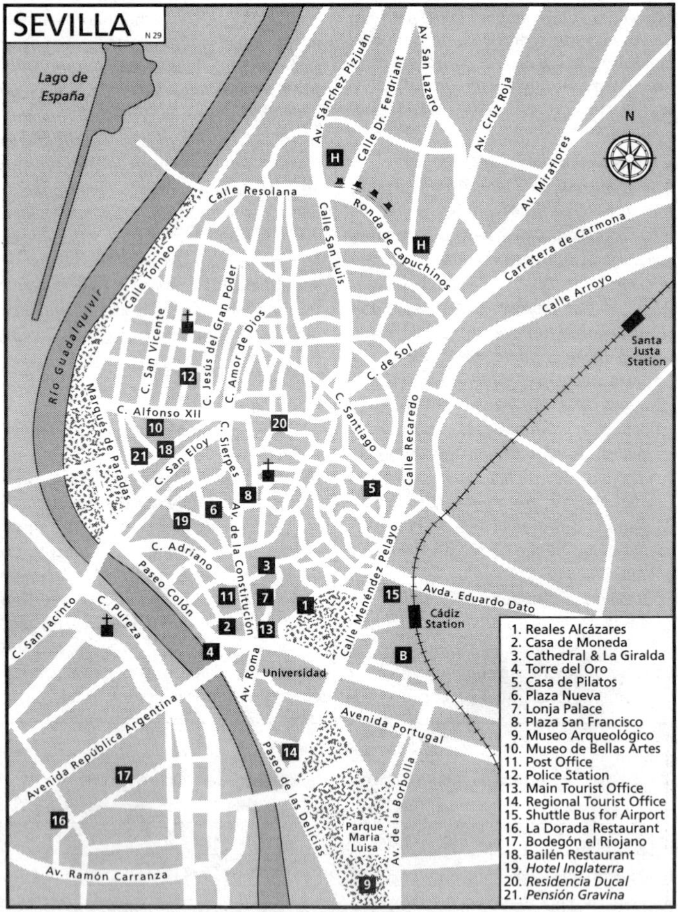

usually, access to the summit is via a ramp, rather than steps, apparently designed to be sufficiently wide to allow 2 horsemen to pass simultaneously!

The most ancient surviving part of the mosque is the **Patio de los Naranjos** (Orange Tree Court), in the centre of which is a Visigothic fountain which was used by the Moors for their ablution rites. Unfortunately the remainder of the mosque was destroyed in the 15th century to make way for the **Cathedral** (see below). Open daily 0930-2000. Entrance fee around 400 Ptas.

The **Torre del Oro** (Golden Tower) in the Paseo de Cristóbal Colón is so named for the golden tiles which originally decorated it. Together with a twin on the other side of the river which no longer exists, the tower was part of the city's fortifications (which once included 166 towers and 12 gates). The Torre del Oro was completed by the Almohads under Yusuf II in 1220 to protect the city from the Christians when the latter had become a threat following their victory at the Battle of Las Navas de Tolosa in 1212. Now houses the **Museo Marítimo**. Open Tue-Fri 1000-1400, Sat-Sun 1000-1300. Admission 25 Ptas. River cruises depart from here (see Transport in Sevilla).

Other places of interest

There are numerous historic monuments and churches in the city, including the 15th century gothic **Cathedral** in Plaza del Triunfo, built on the site of a mosque and designed to be so enormous that people would think its architects were madmen. It is still the world's third largest church after St Peter's Rome and St Paul's London. See **La Giralda** for admission details.

Despite its resemblance to the Alcázar and extravagant Mudéjar architecture, the **Casa de Pilatos** in Plaza de Pilatos is not a Moorish palace. It was built in 1540 for the Marquis of Tarifa and was thought to be modelled on Pontius Pilate's home in Jerusalem, hence its name. Open daily 0900-1800. Admission 1000 Ptas. Ring the bell if gate is closed during opening hours.

Originally notable only for its old monastery which is now undergoing restoration, a 215 ha site on **La Isla de la Cartuja** on the W bank of the Guadalquivir was developed as the location for the 1992 World Expo. As a result of massive investment it has remained a notable area of the city.

Following the closure of Expo, the Isla de la Cartuja has been developed as a theme park, **El Parque de los Descubrimientos** (The Park of Discoveries), T 4461616, closed Mon. It includes 4 theme pavilions (Navigation, Discovery, Nature and Future), a digital planetarium and Omnimax space theatre. The Spanish and regional pavilions have been retained. The park also features a cable car, Banesto panoramic tower, fairground, restaurants, picnic area and entertainments. Entry 500 Ptas just to walk around, 1,000-2,000 Ptas to visit the pavilions.

Parque de María Luisa donated by the sister of Queen Isabel II is well worth a visit, a most refreshing site. There are extensive formal gardens, lakes, exotic trees and within this setting are some of the pavilions built for the 1929 Ibero-América Exhibition. Visit here the Plaza de España with tile pictures representing scenes from all the Spanish provinces and others depicting scenes from the Reconquista (reflecting Primo de Rivera's methods of solving the Moorish problems of the 1920s).

Numerous palaces grace Sevilla. The **Lonja** on Avda de la Constitución was designed for Felipe II by Juan de Herrera and completed in 1598. However it is most notable for its contents, the 4 million documents of the **Archivo de las Indias** relating to Spain's New World conquests. Open Mon-Fri 1000-1300, Sat 0900-1200. Admission free.

The **Universidad de Sevilla** on Calle

San Fernando is Spain's second largest building. Completed in 1771 as a tobacco factory it is famed as the workplace of the fascinating Carmen, immortalized in a novel by Merimée and later in Bizet's opera.

Museums

NB: entrance to public museums is free for EU citizens with proof of identity.

Museo Arqueológico, Plaza de América, Parque de María Luisa, notable Phoenician items and Roman artefacts discovered locally, especially in the ruins of Italica. Open Tue-Sun 1000-1400. Admission 250 Ptas. T 4232401.

Museo de Arte y Costumbres Populares, Plaza de América, Parque de María Luisa provides a fascinating insight into traditional crafts and customs. Open Tue-Sun 1000-1400. Admission 250 Ptas. T 4232576.

Museo de Bellas Artes, Plaza del Museo 9, is second only to the Prado Museum in Madrid for its collection of fine art. Painters from the 'Sevilla School' on display include Murillo, Zurbarán and Valdés Leal. Open Tue-Fri 1000-1400 and 1600-1900, Sat-Sun 1000-1400. Admission 250 Ptas. T 4221829.

Museo Marítimo in the Torre del Oro, presents the naval history of Sevilla. Open Tue-Fri 1000-1400, Sat-Sun 1000-1300. Admission 25 Ptas.

Festivals

The *Labalyata de los Reyes* (Cavalcade of the Magi) takes place early in Jan with the 'kings' throwing sweets from their floats; *Semana Santa* celebrations in the week leading up to Easter are the most famous in Spain with effigies of Christ and the Virgin Mary being paraded through the streets accompanied by the sinister hooded *cofradías* (brotherhoods) of penitents; *Feria de Abril*, held about 2 weeks after Easter (usually starting 18 Apr), is marked by bullfights, fireworks and dancing lasting for a week; *Corpus Christi* is also celebrated by a procession through streets decorated with petals and herbs, while choirboys dance according to a 14th century tradition. Triana holds its own smaller version of the event, the *Corpus Chico*, the following day; *Virgen de los Reyes* on 15 Aug celebrates the patron saint; the *Bienal de Flamenco* takes place in Sep in even years; International Jazz Festival is in Nov.

Local information

● **Accommodation**

Price guide:			
AL	US$90+	**D**	US$20-40
A	US$75-90	**E**	US$10-20
B	US$60-75	**F**	under US$10
C	US$40-60		

The price of accommodation in Sevilla and the surrounding area still remains ridiculously high in the aftermath of Expo, particularly with the glut of available rooms. Hopefully, prices will eventually fall to more reasonable levels. **AL** *Alfonso XIII*, Calle San Fernando 2, T 4222850, F 4216033, 149 rm, 5 star, extremely luxurious, built 1920s, a/c, parking, restaurant, garage, pool, TV, central; **AL** *Hotel Inglaterra*, Plaza Nueva 7, T 4224970, F 4561336, 120 rm, 4 star, central, a/c, garage, parking, restaurant, TV; **AL** *Doña María*, Calle Don Remondo 19, T 4224990, F 4219546, 61 rm, 4 star, near Giralda, no restaurant, TV, garden, pool; **AL** *Hotel Macarena*, Calle Juan de Rivera 2, T 375700, F 4381803, 305 rm on the W edge of town, a/c, pool, parking.

A *Monte Carmelo*, Calle Turia 9, T 4279000, F 4271004, 68 rm, quiet, near the grounds used for the Feria de Abril just S of the river; **A** *Fernando III*, Calle San José 21, T 4217307, F 4220246, 156 rm, some with balconies, a/c, pool, relatively quiet area, convenient for monuments, garage, garden.

B *Hotel Italica*, Edificio Empresa Casal, Calle Antonio de la Peña 5-9, T 4515922, F 4511518, near the station and airport; **B** *Residencia Murillo*, Calle Lope de Rueda 7, T 4216095, F 4219616, by the Reales Alcázares, an old part of town, rather noisy.

C *Residencia Ducal*, Plaza Encarnación 19, T 4215107, 51 rm, fairly central, public parking and bus routes nearby, no restaurant; **C** *Hotel Simón*, Calle García Vinuesa 19, T 4226660, F 4562241, noisy street.

● Pensiones

Accommodation queries by telephone on T 4237474, Mon-Sat 1000-2200. The **Barrio Santa Cruz area**, known for basic (but no longer very cheap) rms, is central, try **C** ***San Pancracio***, Plaza de los Cruces 9, T 4413104, clean, popular, shared shower.

D ***Florida***, Menendez Pelayo 27, clean; **C** ***Pensión Fabiola***, Calle Fabiola 16, T 4218346, by the Iglesia de Sta Cruz, simple but clean. **D** ***Goya***, Calle Mateos Gago 31, T 4211170, right by the cathedral, comfortable; **D** ***Nevada***, Calle Gamazo 28, T 4225340, near Plaza Nueva; **D** ***Gravina***, Calle Gravina 46, off Calle Alfonso XII, basic, no private bath; there are 3 other hostels on Calle Gravina **C** ***Gala***, n° 52, T 4214503, **C** *Granadina*, n°82, T 4213122 and **D** ***Romero*** n°21, T 4211353, any of which is worth a try; **D** ***Pensión Archeros***, Calle Archeros 23, T 4418465, decent rooms.

● Youth hostel

Fernando el Santo, Calle Isaac Peral 2, T 4613150, off Avda de la Palmera away from centre but accessible from Plaza Nueva on Bus No 34. Crowded, 198 beds with shared bathrooms, TV lounge, meals available, suitable for wheelchair users, airport 14 km, train 7 km.

● Camping

Warning: camping in high summer can be uncomfortably hot. ***Sevilla***, Ctra Madrid-Cádiz Km 534, T 4514379, 12 km from city near airport, hot showers, pool, restaurant, bar; ***Villsom***, Ctra Sevilla-Cádiz Km 554.8, Dos Hermanas, T 4720828, 14 km from city, pool, hot showers, open Feb-Nov only; ***Club de Campo***, Avda de la Libertad 13, Dos Hermanas, T 4720250, 12 km city, swimming pool, restaurant. A Los Amarillos bus runs to Dos Hermanas every 45 mins.

● Places to eat

Price guide:
♦♦♦Expensive; ♦♦average; ♦cheap.

♦♦♦***La Dorada***, Calle Virgen de Aguasanta 6, T 4450220, luxury fish and seafood; ***Bodegón el Riojano***, Virgen de las Montañas 12, T 4450682, good regional cuisine; ***El Burladero***, Calle Canalejas 1, T 4222900, Sevilla's only 4 fork restaurant, international and local cuisine, rather expensive; ***Bailén***, Calle Bailén 34, T 4225281, Andalusian home cooking. ♦♦ ***VIPS***, Calle República Argentina 25, young people's cafetería with a late night music and grocery shop, slightly over-priced; ***Las Meninas***, Calle Santo Tomás 3, T 4223355, Andalusian cuisine and fish; ***Victoria Eugenia***, Plaza Villasis, T 4227459, off Calle Martín Villa, local dishes. ♦***El 3 de Oro***, Santa María la Blanca 34, T 4422759, self service Andalusian cuisine in Puerta de la Carne; ***El Baratillo***, Calle Pavia 12, off Calle Dos de Mayo, T 4229651, good value, near Cathedral; ***Casa Diego***, Plaza Curtidores 7, T 4415883, off Calle Menéndez Pelayo, cheap regional dishes; ***Casa Cabo***, Menendez Pelayo 5, near *Barrio Santa Cruz*, good *menú del día* (lunch and dinner).

● Banks

Open Mon-Fri 0830-1400, Sat 0830-1300. Closed Sat May-Oct. Numerous banks in Avda de la Constitución, Plaza Nueva, Calle Tetuán. Several hotels and Santa Justa station have exchange facilities outside banking hours: *Hotel Alfonso XIII*, Calle San Fernando 2; *Hotel Macarena*, Calle San Juan de Rivera 2; *Hotel Los Lebreros*, Calle Luis de Morales 2.

● Consulates

Austria, Calle Marqués de Paradas 26, T 4222162; **Belgium**, Avda San Francisco Javier 20, 3A, T 4647061; **Canada**, Avda de la Constitución, T 4229413; **Denmark**, Avda Reina Mercedes 25, 1B, T 461489; **Finland**, Calle Adriano 45, 2B, T 4225079; **France**, Plaza Santa Cruz 1, T 4222896; **Germany**, Avda Ramón de Carranza 22, T 4457811, T 4457976; **Greece**, Ctra de Carmona 30, T 4419000; **Italy**, Calle Luis Montoto 107, T 4577102; **Netherlands**, Calle Gravina 55, T 4228750; **Portugal**, Pabellón de Portugal, Avda del Cid, T 4231150; **Sweden**, Avda Reina Mercedes 25, 1B, T 4611489; **Switzerland**, Calle Luis Montoto 112, A, T 4575355; **UK**, Plaza Nueva 8, T 4228874/5; **USA**, Pabellón de los EEUU, Paseo de las Delicias 7, T 4231883.

● Entertainment, crafts & cuisine

Bullfights are held in the Plaza de Toros de la Real Maestranza, Paseo de Cristóbal Colón from Mar-Oct. Tickets are cheaper bought direct from bullring.

Concerts Various concerts take place throughout the year ranging from pop concerts to recitals in the Cathedral, check in *El Giraldillo*, the free monthly tourist office magazine for details.

Cuisine The most innovative local **cuisine** can be found in *tapas* bars. Specialities include *huevos a la flamenca* (baked eggs), *riñones a* *la Jerezana* (kidneys in sherry sauce), *rabo de toro* (ox tail), *pescaíto frito* (fried fish) and *gazpacho andaluz* (cold tomato and garlic soup).

Flamenco Good flamenco shows at ***El Arenal***, Calle Rodó 7, T 4216492, 2200-0130; ***Los Gallos***, Plaza de Santa Cruz 11, T 4216981, 2130-0130, reputedly the best in town; ***Patio Sevillano***, Paseo de Colón 11, T 4214120, 2130-0200. Admission approx 2,000 Ptas including a drink.

Handicafts: pedestrianized Calle Sierpes is the main shopping street. Local handicrafts include leatherwear, flamenco costumes, ceramics, fans and silver and gold jewellery. Local markets are held on Thur in Calle Feria, on Sun morning in Alameda de Hercules, Plaza Alfalfa (pets) and Plaza Cabildo (stamps).

● Garages/repairs

Citroën, Polígono Industrial, Ctra Amarilla, T 4554500; **Ford**, Avda de Andalucía 1, T 4576880; **Renault**, Autopista San Pablo, T 4360100; **Seat/Volkswagen**, Ctra de su Eminencia 2, T 4644766.

● Hospitals

Cruz Roja, T 4350135, emergencies T 4369750; ***Casa de Socorro***, T 4411712; ***Hospital Universitario***, Avda Dr Fedriani, T 4378400; ***General Hospital***, Avda Manuel Siurot, T 4558100, emergencies T 4558195.

● Post Office

Correos, Avda de la Constitución 32, Mon-Fri 0900-2000, Sat 0900-1400. Telegrams by telephone 24 hr service within Spain T 4222000, outside Spain T 4226860.

● Telephones

Local code: 95. *Locutorio* in Plaza de la Gavidia. Open 1000-1400 and 1730-2200.

● Travel agents

Viajes Barceló, Calle Reyes Católicos 4, T 4227103; ***Viajes Iberia***, Calle Tetuán 24, T 4224095; ***Viajes Meliá***, Avda de la Constitución 13, T 4220251.

● Tourist information

Regional Office: Avda de la Constitución 21B, T 4221404, open Mon-Fri 0930-1930, Sat 0930-2000, Sun 1000-1400; Municipal Office: Paseo de las Delicias 9, Costurero de la Reina, T 4234465, open Mon-Fri 0900-1315 and 1630-1845; Aeropuerto de San Pablo terminal building, T 4255046; Santa Justa station, daily 0830-2330.

● Water

Serious water shortages are encountered each summer and water is 'rationed' by turning it off.

● Transport

Local Bike hire From Bici Rent Sevilla at Paseo de Colón, Plaza de España and Calle del Torneo Bajo, T 4219474, T 4616311. Bikes must be returned to the pick-up point. One hour costs 400 Ptas, half day 1,700 Ptas, full day 2,500 Ptas, not including deposit.

Bus A map of TUSSAM's bus routes is usually available from tourist offices or the special kiosk on Plaza Nueva near Avda de la Constitución, 50 Ptas. Also available are special tourist tickets, *tarjeta turística,* 800 Ptas for 3 days, 1,200 Ptas for 7 days gives cheap access to frequent users of Sevilla's good public transport system. A *bonobús* for 10 bus trips from kiosks and tobacconists costs 525 Ptas with transfers, 500 Ptas no transfers. Useful buses are C1, C2, C3, C4 which go round inner ring road. **Boat hire**: rowing boats for rental by the hour in the centre of Parque María Luisa.

Car hire **Atesa**, Calle Almirante Lobo, Edificio Cristina, T 4226449; **Avis**, Avda de la Constitución 15, T 4216549; **Hertz**, Avda de la República Argentina 3, T 4278887; **Regente**, Paseo de las Delicias 1, T 4211858; **Rentalauto**, Calle Fernando IV 3, T 4278184. (According to El Pais there are about 2,000 unofficial 'car minders' in Sevilla – all to be avoided!) **Coche caballo** carrying up to 4 people can be found at the Cathedral, Torre del Oro, Plaza de España and Jardines de Murillo. Agree price before setting out, usually approx 3,000 Ptas per hour.

Hitchhiking Arrangements at Compartecoche SA, Calle Amparo 22, 2° D, T 4215494 which is a hitchhikers association.

Moped hire Alkimoto, Calle Recaredo 28, T 4411115, 3,000-5,000 Ptas per day excluding insurance and 5,000-10,000 Ptas deposit.

River cruises In summer 9 Cruceros Panorámicos depart from Torre del Oro daily, 1130-2215. Price 500 Ptas, children free.

Taxis RadioTaxi, T 4580000; TeleTaxi, T 4622222; Radio Teléfono Taxi, T 4359835.

Air National and international flight tickets and information from Iberia Calle Almirante Lobo 3, T 4228901 and T 4218800.

Train The new Santa Justa train station (with exchange facilities) is on Avda de Kansas City, T 4414111 (information), T 4421562 (reservations). The RENFE office is at Calle Zaragoza 29.

Cádiz and **Jerez** 13 departures daily, 2 hrs, 850 Ptas; **Córdoba** and **Huelva** 6 daily, **Málaga** and **Granada** 3 daily. The new TAV high-speed trains now get to **Madrid** in under 3 hrs – a journey which previously took 10 hrs!

Road The main bus station is by Prado de San Sebastián in Calle Manuel Vázquez Sagastizábal, T 4417111. Several companies operate from here including Alsina Graells, T 4418811, with frequent services to **Granada, Córdoba** and **Málaga**; Comes SA, T 4416858, to **Jerez de la Frontera, Cádiz** and **Algeciras**; Los Amarillos, T 4415201, to **Ronda** and **Arcos de la Frontera**. Nearby, on the corner of Calle Carlos de Borbón and Calle Diego de Raño, the Casal service to **Carmona** leaves approx every hour on the hour. Bus to **Cadiz** 1,000 Ptas takes 2¼ hrs (1hr 40 mins on autopista).

Excursions from Sevilla

Local travel agents have information on fairly expensive organized tours, such as those of *Pullmantur* and *Trapsatur*, including a 3 hr tour of Sevilla, night cruises, flamenco evenings and excursions to nearby towns. Information and tour departures from Calle Almirante Lobo 13. *Sevirama*, Calle General Sanjurjo 2, T 4560693, run a multilingual city tour in open-topped buses lasting 1 hr. Departures from Torre del Oro. Tours start 0900 summer, 1100 winter. Adults 1,000 Ptas, children 500 Ptas.

Alcalá de Guadaira, 10 km SE of Sevilla on the N-334, is worth a visit. The spectacular fortress for which the town is named was built by the Almohads on the river Guadaira as part of the defence system for Sevilla itself. It is one of the best remaining examples of Almohad military architecture and the largest of their fortresses which has survived. Following its capture in 1246 by Fernando III, it was modified for use as a prison by Pedro the Cruel. Also of interest is the **Iglesia de San Miguel** which was originally built as a mosque. As in Sevilla, cars and their contents are vulnerable.

WEST FROM SEVILLA

West from Sevilla the N431 and the A49 run parallel with each other over gently rolling, prosperous farmland with little to tempt the traveller until 27 km from Huelva, the town of **Niebla** is reached. This small town was important in both Roman and Moorish times. A well-preserved Roman bridge crosses the Rio Tinto, while the Arabs built the impressive red sandstone walls, in places 15m wide, which are fortified with towers and gates. The castle dates from the 12th century, but was modified after the town was recaptured by the Christians in 1257.

Also worth a diversion is the small settlement of **Moguer**, 7 km from the mouth of the Rio Tinto. It has some fine Gothic and Baroque architecture, including the Convent of Santa Clara with its defensive walls, the Church of Nuestra Señora de la Granada and the Neoclassical Town Hall.

Moguer was the birthplace of the poet Juan Ramón Jímeniz, winner of the 1956 Nobel prize for literature. There is a novel statue in his memory, while his house in Calle Nueva is now a museum.

Huelva

Pop 139,000 *Alt* Sea level to 50m.

Huelva is the most westerly of the regional capitals of Andalucía and its Atlantic location ensures a maritime climate. It is a port of some antiquity, founded by Phoenician traders over 3,000 years ago, when it was known as *Onuba*. The Romans used it as a mining port, as did the Arabs who knew it as *Guelbah*. Alphonso X *el Sabio* (the wise) recaptured it from the Moors in 1257. Unfortunately, little of this rich historical past is evident today, largely due to the 1755 earthquake (the same one which destroyed Lisbon). The nearby Rio Tinto mines and 20th century industry have resulted in a dreary town, with little to commend it.

ACCESS Air The nearest airport is at Sevilla. **Train** The train station, T 246666, is in Avenida de Italia, to the E of the town. There are daily express trains to Madrid and Sevilla, and numerous slower trains to Sevilla, where connections can be made to other regional centres. There is also a route W to Ayamonte on the Portuguese border. **Road** The main bus company serving Huelva is Damus SA, Avda de Portugal 9, T 256900, with links to Algeciras, Cádiz and Sevilla, plus services to local villages.

Things to see

Cathedral de la Merced Once a convent, it was designated a cathedral in 1953, but is notable only for its elegant façade. **Iglesia de San Pedro**, built over a mosque, it is the oldest church in the city and is mainly 16th century Baroque. **Museo Provincial**, Alemada Sundheim 13, open daily (except Mon) 1000-1400 and 1600-1900, T 259300. It has a comprehensive archaeological section and a fine arts section with a special hall devoted to Vásquez Dias. An architectural curiosity in Huelva is the **Barrio Reina Victoria**, which is a neighbourhood of company housing built by the Rio Tinto mining organization on the lines of those built by the industrial philanthropists in England. The area is now decaying badly, despite its designation as being of 'historico-artistic interest'. Frankly, there is little else of interest in modern-day Huelva, which gives the overall impression of dreary industrial boredom. Fortunately, the surrounding area has much to commend it.

Local information

● Accommodation

The best hotel in Huelva is the **A** ***Luz Huelva***, Alameda Sundheim 26, T 250011, garage, 18 hole golf course.

Also recommended is the **B** *Tattessos*, Calle Martín Alonso Pinzón 13, T 282711. At the other end of the scale there are a number of cheap, but adequate *pensiones* in Calle Rascón, including the ***Calvo***, ***Las Delicias*** and ***Nuestra Señora de la Cinta***. Many visitors, however, including businessmen, prefer out-of-town hotels in more attractive locations. The nearest parador is at Ayamonte, close to the Portuguese border.

● Youth hostels

Albergue de Huelva, Calle Marchena Colombo 14, 21004 Huelva, T 253793, 130 beds, meals available, suitable for disabled, city centre location; ***Mazagon***, Cuesta de la Barca s/n, 21130 Mazagon, Huelva, T 536262, 100 beds, meals available, free kitchen, suitable for wheelchair users, 25 km SE from Huelva on coast; ***Punta Umbria***, Avenida Océano 13, Punta Umbria, 21100 Huelva, T 311650, 84 beds, meals available, suitable for wheelchair users, directly S of Huelva but across the river.

● Camping

There are 11 camp sites within 30 km of Huelva, mainly at coastal locations. The only 1st category site is ***Camping Doñana Playa***, Ctra Huelva-Matalascañas Km 29, T 376281, beach, pool and restaurant.

● Places to eat

As Huelva is a fishing port, it is no surprise that some good seafood is available. Try ◆◆***Doñana***, Gran Via 13, T 242773 where local seafood specialities include sardines with peppers, skate in paprika and clams in saffron sauce.

● Banks

Most Spanish banks are represented and are mainly located in the streets leading off the Plaza de las Monjas.

● Garage/repairs

Citroën, Ctra de Sevilla Km 637, T 229609; **Ford**, Pol San Diego, T 228512; **Peugeot**, Ctra de Sevilla Km 638, T 221988; **Renault**, Legión Española 2, T 254964; **Seat/Volkswagen**, Ctra N431 Km 637, T 234051.

● Post Office

Correos, Avda Tomás Domínguez 1, T 249184.

● Telephones

No *locutorios*, but plenty of cabins. Local code: 955.

● Tourist Information

The Provincial tourist office is located at Avda de Alemania 14, T 257403. Normal office hours.

● Transport

Local Car hire Hertz, Alameda Sundheim 16, T 258211; **Avis**, *Hotel Luz*, Alameda Sundheim 4.

Excursions from Huelva

The area immediately E of Huelva has rich connections with **Christopher Columbus** (known in Spain as Cristóbal Colón) and his quest to find the New World. At the narrow tip of land between the mouths of the Rio Tinto and the Rio Odiel, the **Punta del Sebo**, is the imposing monument to Columbus, known as the *Spirit of Exploration*, completed by the American sculptress, Gertrude Whitney, in 1929. Facing the monument on a small hill is the monastery of **La Rábida**. This Franciscan building was dedicated in the 13th century soon after the Reconquista. Columbus came here in 1491, after failing to gain royal approval of his plans. He met 2 friars, Antonio de Marchena and Juan Pérez (the latter having been formerly the Queen's confessor) and they took his case to the court and gained permission for his venture. The monastery today receives visitors from all over the world who see it as an important symbol of the Hispanic World. La Rábida was probably built on the site of a Moorish structure and is centred around a Moorish-style courtyard, with cloisters. These were re-built after the 1755 earthquake. A feature today are the murals painted by Huelva artist Vásquez Diaz in 1930, based on the theme of the 'Discovery of America'. Nearby is the 15th century church in Gothic-Mudéjar style, with frescoes from the same period. In the upper part of the monastery is the Flag Room, with standards from all the South American countries along with caskets of their soil. The friars give guided tours at regular intervals. There is no charge, but a donation is expected. Just 5 km N of La Rábida is the small town of **Palos de la Frontera**, the port from where Columbus set out in 1492 on his first voyage and which was the home of many of his sailors such as the Pinzón brothers. It is worth seeking out the 14th century Mudéjar Iglesia San Jorge (where Cortez, 35 years later, prayed before leaving to conquer Mexico). There is also the Roman fountain, now dry, from where Columbus is said to have taken on water for his 3 caravels. The port of Palos today is silted up and the town makes its living from agriculture, specializing in strawberry growing.

Between Huelva and the mouth of the Rio Guadalquivir, the Atlantic coastline consists of wide sands backed by high dunes, behind which are pine forests, marshes and farmland. Resorts include **Mazagón** (with the Cristobal Colón Parador), **Torre de la Higuera** and the newly developed **Matalascañas**, a featureless urbanization which has been carved out of the dunes. It does, however, have some reasonable beach front hotels which can provide suitable accommodation for visitors to El Rocío and the Coto Doñana nature reserve.

• **Accommodation** **A** *La Gaviota*, Sector H, Parcela 72, T 430552, F 430564, pool and restaurant. **B** *Tierramar*, Sector M, T 440300, pool, change facilities, good restaurant. The best of the *pensiones* is **C** *Los Taramindos*, Avda Las Adelfas 31, T 430119.

• **Places to eat** Decent restaurants are hard to find in Matalascañas – it is advisable to use the hotels.

The road inland from Matalascañas leads, after 15 km, to **El Rocío** which with its sand covered streets and houses with verandas, looks like a set from a Wild West film. It would have little of interest were it not for the annual *Romería* or pilgrimage at Whitsun. Hundreds of thousands of *rocieros* from all over Andalucía and beyond make their way here on foot, horseback or in flower-strewn covered wagons to pay their respects to the Virgin of the Marshes. On Whit Sunday, the statue of the virgin is carried in procession around the town. The colourful costumes, flamenco dancing, camp fires and general merry-making create a remarkable atmosphere and make the *Romería* a unique event.

El Rocío is also the centre of the

Parque Nacional de la Coto Doñana, one of Europe's best wetland reserves. See Wildlife, **page 36**). It gets its name from Doña Ana, wife of the 7th Duke of Medina Sidonia, of Armada fame, who once owned the whole area. It was for centuries the hunting ground of nobility, but in 1969 it was given the protected status of a National Park and was later classified by UNESCO as 'Biosphere Reserve'. The Coto Doñana consists of 4 distinct habitats: **the beach-tidal sands**, supporting a variety of gulls and waders; **high mobile dunes**, with marram grass; **older, stabilized dunes** covered with scrub vegetation (*mator-rales*) and woodlands of pine, juniper or oak; **the Marismas**, marshland which is inundated each winter and spring by the flood waters of the Rio Guadalquivir. More than 250 species of bird have been recorded, including winter wildfowl from N Europe, spring and autumn passage migrants and breeding birds in the spring and early summer. Flamingoes have recently become established as breeders, while other water birds include egrets, herons, bitterns, spoonbills and white storks. Among the rarities are Imperial Eagle, Crested Coot, Purple Gallinule and Black Winged Kite.

Access to large areas of the Coto Doñana is restricted, but there are a number of official locations around the fringe of the reserve which will satisfy all but the most fanatic of birders. **The bridge and promenade at El Rocío**, which give excellent views of a range of water birds; **La Rocina sub-centre**, T 955 406140, 1 km from El Rocío on the main road to Almonte, which has an information centre and an excellent hide overlooking a lake and the marsh; **Acebron Palace**, located 7 km along a minor road from the Rocina centre, with exhibition centre and woodland walks; **El Acebuche Centre**, T 955 430432 the park headquarters where there are educational displays, an audio-visual presentation, a shop, restaurant, and a string of excellent hides overlooking lakes. It is also possible to book Landrover tours from the Acebuche Centre, leaving twice a day and lasting 4 hours. Whilst these tours give a good indication of the various habitats, they are usually crowded with noisy tourists who have little interest in wildlife and could prove frustrating to the serious naturalist.

• **Accommodation** There are a couple of small *pensiones* in El Rocío, but it is probably better to stay in the beach hotels of Matalascañas, where the nearest camp sites can also be found.

• **When to visit Coto Doñana** The period between Feb and mid-May is the most rewarding for the maximum number of species. In summer, the *marismas* dry out, the heat is intense and the mosquitoes are irritating. Avoid the Whitsun *Romería*.

SEVILLA TO JEREZ DE LA FRONTERA

Utrera, 35 km SSE of Sevilla on the SE-424 (or 14 km E from the A4/E5 toll motorway), has a ruined Moorish alcázar which, together with 4 other fortified villages to the E of the city (**Carmona**, **Ecija**, **Marchena** and **Osuna**), was originally part of Sevilla's outer defences under the Moorish occupation.

Lebrija, 63 km S of Sevilla on the C-441, can be reached via the A4/E5 toll motorway or the N-IV. Known to the Moors as *Nebrishah*, the town is notable for the **Iglesia de Santa María de la Oliva** which is a converted 12th century Almohad mosque with a strong resemblance to Córdoba's Mezquita, while the 18th century bell-tower is modelled on the Giralda.

Jerez de la Frontera

Pop 187,000 *Alt* 55m *Best seasons* Spring, summer, autumn.

Jerez de la Frontera lies 83 km S of Sevilla and 3 km N of Cádiz, in the agricultural plains S of the river

Guadalquivir. The white, chalky soil in the area has proved ideal for cultivating vines which produce the *fino* sherry for which Jerez has been famed for centuries. Many of the powerful sherry families were originally English, some having been involved in sherry production since the time of England's Henry VII. The city was known as *Ceret* in Roman times, but renamed *Scherish* by the Moors. This later changed to *Xeres* and finally Jerez. The 'de la Frontera' element of the city's name, as with many other towns in the area, dates from around 1380 when it marked a Moorish frontier and also reflects the fact that Jerez changed hands numerous times during the course of the Reconquista.

ACCESS Air There is an airport 10 km N of the town for internal flights. There is no bus available, taxi is approx 1,000 Ptas. **Train and road** The bus station on Calle Cartuja and train station in Plaza de la Estación at the end of Calle Cartuja

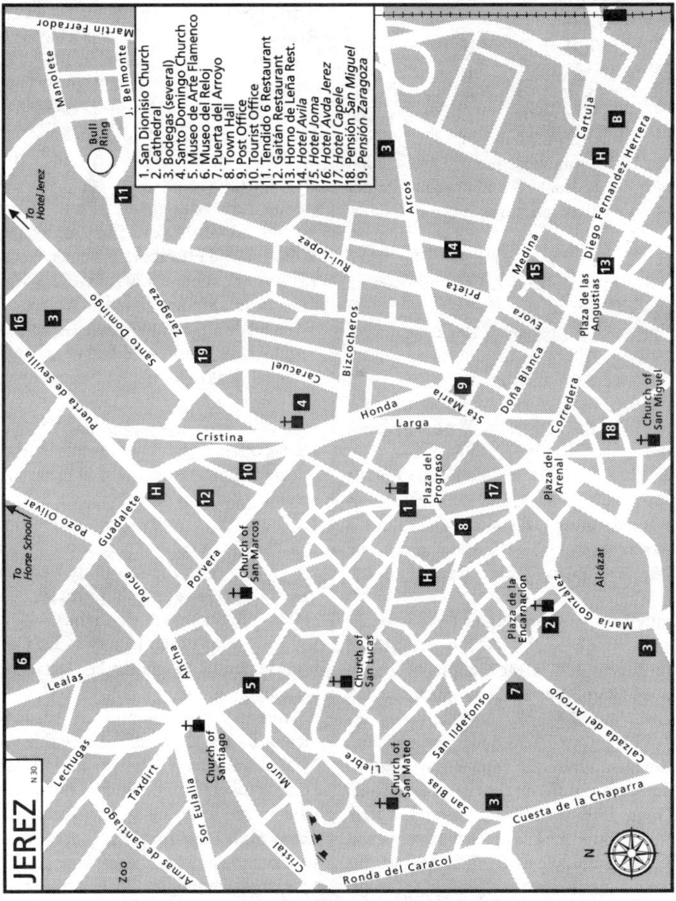

are close together within walking distance of the central Calle Larga and Plaza del Arenal. There are normally taxis at the station.

NB: the one-way system in Jerez is extremely confusing, while street parking is difficult. Car crime is rife, but fortunately there is fairly secure underground parking in the Alameda Cristina, in Calle Madre de Dios and in Plaza Monti. Visitors should also take sensible precautions against petty street crime.

Things to see

Moorish past Despite being outnumbered almost 10 to 1, the Moors under Tariq first captured Jerez in 711 following a battle against its Visigothic residents on the plains to the E of the town. The town was reconquered in 1251 by Fernando III, but subsequently lost in 1264 by his son Alfonso X and the commander of the Christian forces, Garcí Gómez Carillo, who so impressed the Moorish victors that they captured rather than killed him! **Lebrija**, **Arcos** and **Medina Sidonia** fell to the Moors at the same time. After a major siege lasting 5 months, Alfonso was able to recapture the town permanently.

Just off Plaza del Arenal is what remains of the 11th century **Alcázar**, once the residence of the Caliphs of Sevilla. It has been heavily restored and consists mainly of walls and the 12th century octagonal tower. The interior contains a mosque which was transformed into the **Iglesia de Santa María la Real** by Alfonso X when he recaptured the town. On the same hill are the **Baños Arabes** (*hammam*) which date back to the period when Jerez was part of the Caliphate of Córdoba. Open Mon-Sat 1100-1330 and 1700-2000, Sun 1100-1330. Admission is free.

Nearby on Plaza de la Encarnación, the town's baroque 18th century **Cathedral** is also built on the site of a mosque. Open daily at 1800. Admission is free. In the same area, a further reminder of Jerez's past role as a defensive outpost can be seen in the fragments of the original city walls from the Almohad-Almoravid period which still remain, such as the **Puerta del Arroyo** at the junction of Calle Calzada del Arroyo and Puerta de Rota.

Other places of interest

Bodegas Most visitors to Jerez will want to visit one of the famous sherry cellars, most of which welcome visitors and offer guided tours and free tasting. It is best to phone beforehand as the larger bodegas may be fully booked with organized tours. The largest bodegas are **González Byass**, Calle Manuel María González, T 340000, whose tours feature a famous drunken mouse, visits 1000, 1045, 1130, 1215, 1300, and 1345 by prior reservation; **Pedro Domecq**, San Ildefonso 3, T 331900, visits at 1000, 1100 and 1200, by prior reservation. The smaller bodegas include, **Sandeman**, Pizarro 10, T 301100, visits 1030 and 1330, highly rec; **Williams and Humbert**, Nuno de Canas 1, T 331300, visits at 1200 and 1330; **Wisdom and Walker**, Calle Pizarro 7, T 184306, visits at 1230 and 1345, except Thur at 1100 and 1400; **Harveys**, Calle Arcos 53, T 151030, visits 1200. Note that the bodegas may be closed in late Aug/early Sep when the grape harvest or *vendimia* takes place, but muthis in itself is a marvellous festival, so that the visitor should not feel deprived!

There are numerous interesting churches in Jerez, such as those in the old quarter of town: **San Juan**, **San Lucas**, **San Marcos** and **San Mateo**. Several km SE outside town on the C-440 is the 15th century monastery of **La Cartuja de Santa María de la Defensión** which is inhabited by a closed order but notable for its magnificent baroque façade, its historical role in breeding the local thoroughbred horses and its archaic refusal to allow women to participate in the evening visits. **Municipal Town Hall** built in 1575 combines the styles of Plasteresque and Mudéjar.

Parque Zoológico in Calle Taxdirt

has botanical gardens and a park in addition to the zoo. Open Tue-Sun all year, summer 1030-2000, winter 1030-1800. Admission 500 Ptas.

Real Escuela de Arte Equestre (Royal Andalusian School of Equestrian Art), Avda Duque de Abrantes s/n, T 311111, located in the palace of the Cadenas, a 19th century mansion built by Garnier, the architect of the Paris Opera. The training sessions can be watched, plus a tour of the stables, on 4 days a week, 1100-1300, entrance 400 Ptas. On Thur an 'equestrian ballet' is performed by the Dancing Horses of Andalucía at 1200, entrance 1400 Ptas. Many tour companies combine the horse show with a bodega visit. Jerez's equestrian tradition is further demonstrated at the **Horse Fair** (*Feria del Caballo*), see **local festivals** below.

Museums

Museo de Arte Flamenco, Palacio de Pemartín at Plaza San Juan 1 has a collection of musical instruments and the history of the art, which Jerezanos claim began in their town. Audiovisual presentations every hour on the hour. Open Mon-Fri 0930-1330 and 1800-2100, Sat

Sherry – Amber Nectar Spanish Style

The three main sherry producing centres are in Andalucía, in Jerez de la Frontera, Puerto de Santa Maria on the Bay of Cádiz and Sanlúcar de Barrameda which is on the mouth of the Rio Guadalquivir.

Around 90% of the vines are Palomino which can yield up to 80 hectolitres per hectare, the rest being Pedro Ximénez and a little Muscatel. The long days of sunshine and low rainfall produce a uniform wine – the soil type causing only minimum variations. The quality of the wine depends on ageing for at least 3 years and skillful blending. The *solera* system of blending entails gradually mixing young wines with wines from earlier years, the end result being a uniform product.

Wines of Jerez are initially stored in uncovered casks and over the best wines a thick layer of white yeast (*flor*) develops protecting it from oxidation. This is the fino sherry. Oloroso produces less *flor* and the poorest wine produces none at all. The quality of sherry is strictly controlled by the *Consejo Regulador de la Denominacion de Origin*.

Fino – a very dry, very delicate sherry
Oloroso – slightly more robust with a higher alcohol content
Amontillada – matured in the barrel. The best is kept for 50 years
Manzanilla – comes from the coastal *bodegas* of Sanlúcar de Barrameda where the higher humidity, lower temperatures and salt laden air affect the flavour. Recommended to drink with seafood.
Cream sherry – smooth, sweetened by blending in wine made from the sugary sundried Muscatel grapes and 'arrope' (a wine reduced by cooking).

Visit a *bodega* and admire the dexterity of the vintner who dips his *venencia* (a silver cup on the end of a long pole) into the barrel and pours the amber liquid in the 4 glasses in his left hand without spilling a drop. Visits are welcome on weekday mornings. With some it is necessary to book. The cost for admission is around 400 pesetas. Check with the local tourist offices in Jerez (**see page 177**), Sanlúcar at Calzada de Ejército, T 366110 and Puerto de Santa Maria, Guadalete, T 863145.

Surprisingly sherry is not a favourite drink in Spain. The leading market is the UK, followed by the Netherlands and Germany.

1000-1300. Admission free.

The **Museo del Reloj** (Clock Museum) has a fascinating collection of more than 300 clocks from the 16th to 19th centuries on show at La Atalaya Palace on Calle Lealas. Open 1000-1300. Admission 200 Ptas.

The **Museo del Vino** in the Casa del Vino on Avda Domecq traces the history of sherry making. Open Sun-Fri 1000-1300.

Festivals

Traditional Easter processions take place during *Semana Santa*. The impressive *Feria del Caballo* is held in May, marked by races, shows and competitions featuring the locally bred Cartuja horses and 17th century traditions. In the week prior to 24 Aug the *Fiesta de la Vendimia* takes place, celebrating and blessing the grape harvest. The *Circuito de Jerez* race track hosts the Spanish Grand Prix in Sep. Also in Sep during the first fortnight is the *Fiesta de la Bulería*.

Local information

● Accommodation

NB: high season rates are charged in Jerez during the *Feria*, not in high summer. **AL** *Jerez*, Avda Alvaro Domecq 35, T 300600, F 305001, 121 rm, a/c, garden, pool, TV, tennis, parking.

A *Royal Sherry Park*, Avda Alvaro Domecq 11 bis, T 303011, F 311300, recently built, 173 rm, a/c, garden, pool, TV, parking, gym, sauna; **A** *Avenida Jerez*, Avda Alvaro Domecq 10, T 347411, F337296, 95 rm, a/c, TV, video, parking, cafetería, functional.

B *Hotel Joma*, Calle Medina 22, T 349689; **B** *Hotel Serit*, Calle Higueras 7, T 340700, F 340716; **B** *Avila*, Calle Avila 3, T 334808, cafetería.

C *Hotel Capele*, Plaza de las Angustias, T 346400, F 346242, 30 rm, central, a/c, garage, TV, rather functional; **C** *Hotel Nova*, Calle Arcos 13, T 341459, clean, colourful rm, telephone, bath.

● Pensiones

There is no very cheap accommodation in Jerez. **B** *Hotel Virt*, Calle Higueras 20, T 322811; **C** *Trujillo*, Calle Medina 36, T 342438, new, TV, garage.

D *Nuevo Pensión*, Calle Caballeros 23, T 331600, TV, 45 rm, central; **D** *San Miguel*, Plaza San Miguel 4, T 348562, telephone, pets allowed, 38 rm, near the Alcázar; **D** *Sanvi*, Calle Morenos 10, T 345624, 25 rm; **D** *Las Palomas*, Calle Higueras 17, T 343773, off Calle Medina, 53 rm; **D** *Zaragoza*, Calle Zaragoza 2, T 334427, small, 14 rm, near the Plaza de Toros; **D** *San Andrés*, Calle Morenos 12, T 340983, 71 rm, one of the cheapest.

● Youth hostel

Avda Carrero Blanco 30, 11408 Cádiz, T 342890, S edge of town, 128 beds, shared rm, meals available, suitable for wheelchair users, sports facilities. Take your IYHF card.

● Camping

There are no camp sites in Jerez itself. The nearest are approx 25 km W on the Atlantic coast between **Rota** and **El Puerto de Santa María**. *El Pinar de Chipiona*, Ctra Chipiona-Rota, Km 3, Chipiona, T 372321, restaurant, bar, beach; *Punta Candor*, Ctra Chipiona-Rota, Km 13, Rota, T 813303, top grade, restaurant, bar, beach, fishing; *Guadalete*, Ctra Madrid-Cádiz, N-IV, Km 658, El Puerto de Santa María, T 561749, top grade, restaurant, bar, beach, pool, launderette; *Playa las Dunas de San Antón*, Paseo Marítimo, Playa de la Puntilla, El Puerto de Santa María, T 870112, top grade, restaurant, bar, launderette, beach, tennis, fishing.

● Places to eat

♦♦♦*La Mesa Redonda*, Calle Manuel de la Quintana, T 340069, good home cooking; *El Bosque*, Avda de Alvaro Domecq, T 303333, local cuisine; *Tendido 6*, Calle Circo 10, T 344835, good fresh fish. ♦♦*Gaitán*, Calle Gaitán 3, T 345859, modern and traditional cuisine, closed Sun; *Mesón El Patio*, Calle San Francisco de Paula, T 340736. ♦*Cafetería San Francisco*, Plaza Esteve 2, T 344914, reasonable and cheap; *Restaurante Económico*, Calle Fontana 4, T 334000, good value; *Horno de Leña*, Plaza de las Angustias, good quality, T 346400.

● Banks

Several in Calle Porvera and Calle Larga.

● Garages/repairs

Most of the main car firms are clustered along the Ctra Madrid-Cádiz; **Citroën**, T 344401; **Ford**, T 305200; **Renault**, T 306900; **Seat/Volkswagen**, T 306300; **Peugeot**, Ronda Muleros 12, T 344663.

● Hospitals
First Aid from ***Casa de Socorro***, Calle Diego Fernández Herrera 5, T 341331; ***Cruz Roja***, Avda de la Cruz Roja, T 345474.

● Entertainment
Flamenco can be seen at the ***Bar Rociero Camino del Rocío***, Calle Velázquez; ***Tablao Flamenco Los Jereles***, Plaza Cocheras; ***Sala Rociera los Varales***, Calle Divina Pastora; ***Reuelo***, Calle Lealas.

Sherry The *fino de Jerez* and brandy for which the town is principally famous can be bought direct from the *bodegas* (**see page 174**) or sampled in the many *tapas* bars around Plaza Arenal, Calle Divina Pastora and Calle José Cádiz Salvatierra.

● Post Office
Correos, Calle Veracruz, off Calle Santa María. Open Mon-Fri 0800-2100, Sat 0900-1400 (0900-1900 for telegrams).

● Telephones
Local code: 956. Cabins at Plaza Banco and Calle José Primo de Rivera 4.

● Travel agents
Ecuador, Calle Consistorio 8, T 341301; ***Marsans***, Calle Larga 53, T 341010; ***Sherrytours***, Plaza de la Yerba 4, T 343912.

● Tourist information
Calle Alameda Cristina 7, T 331150. Open 0800-1400 and 1700-2000.

● Transport
Local Bike hire From Casa de la Juventud, Calle Rosario 14, T 344314, 250 Ptas per day with 1,500 Ptas deposit.

Bus There are 12 local bus lines, most departing from Plaza Arenal, Plaza Esteve or Plaza Angustias. Lines 8 and 9 are circular.

Car hire Avis, Calle Sevilla 25, T 344311, **Europcar**, Calle Honda 18, T 303466, **Hertz**, Calle Sevilla 29, T 335520.

Taxi: **Teletaxi**, T 344860.

Air: national flight tickets and information from *Iberia*, Plaza del Arenal 2, T 339908. Daily flights to **Madrid**, less frequent to other cities and the **Canary Islands**. Airport information T 334300.

Excursions from Jerez

Arcos la Frontera (population 28,000), reputed to have been founded by one of Noah's sons, is the best of the Andalusian *pueblos blancos* and has been made a national monument. Only 24 km E of the toll motorway or 30 km from the N-IV near Jerez, Arcos is perched on a narrow plateau above the river Guadalete. The view from the terrace of the *Parador* is spectacular, if you can find a parking space in the square outside. The well-preserved 11th century castle established by the Ben Jazrum Dynasty was captured from its Moorish residents in 1264 by the Spanish King Alfonso X (now privately owned). Other Moorish legacies are the internal patios and the layout of the *barrio antiguo* (old town) near the *Parador* which consists of a maze of narrow streets which should be explored on foot, so leave your car in the Plaza de España or come by bus from Jerez. Indeed the streets are so difficult to navigate that the floats used in the impressive *Semana Santa* processions have been specially customized. The whole town is subject to a one-way system. The **Iglesia de San Pedro** on Plaza Blasinas is believed to have been built on the site of an Arab fortress, incorporating part of the Moorish fortifications while at the far E end of the town the **Puerta Matrera** has an 11th century wall and tower.

CADIZ

Pop 157,000 *Alt* 4m.

Cádiz is a seaport located at the end of an isthmus protruding into the Atlantic. The provincial capital but not the largest town, Cádiz has a long and fascinating history and claims to be the oldest continuously occupied urban settlement in Western Europe. In Phoenician times, it was known as *Gadir*, the port exporting minerals from the interior. Its strategic position also attracted the Romans, who called it *Gades*. Julius Caesar was given his first public office here. The Moors, whilst occupying the area, were not great seafarers, so there followed a period of decline until the 16th century when Spain became an important maritime power and with the colonization of the

Americas, Cádiz became a major seaport again. This importance, inevitably, attracted the attention of rival seafaring nations such as England, Holland and France, who regularly came to sack and pillage. Cádiz survived and is well worth a visit. Do not expect, though, another Córdoba or Granada. Cádiz has a unique atmosphere. Its people are more cosmopolitan than those in the rest of the province and have more varied features and colouring. Even the motorists in Cádiz seem more courteous than those elsewhere in Andalucía!

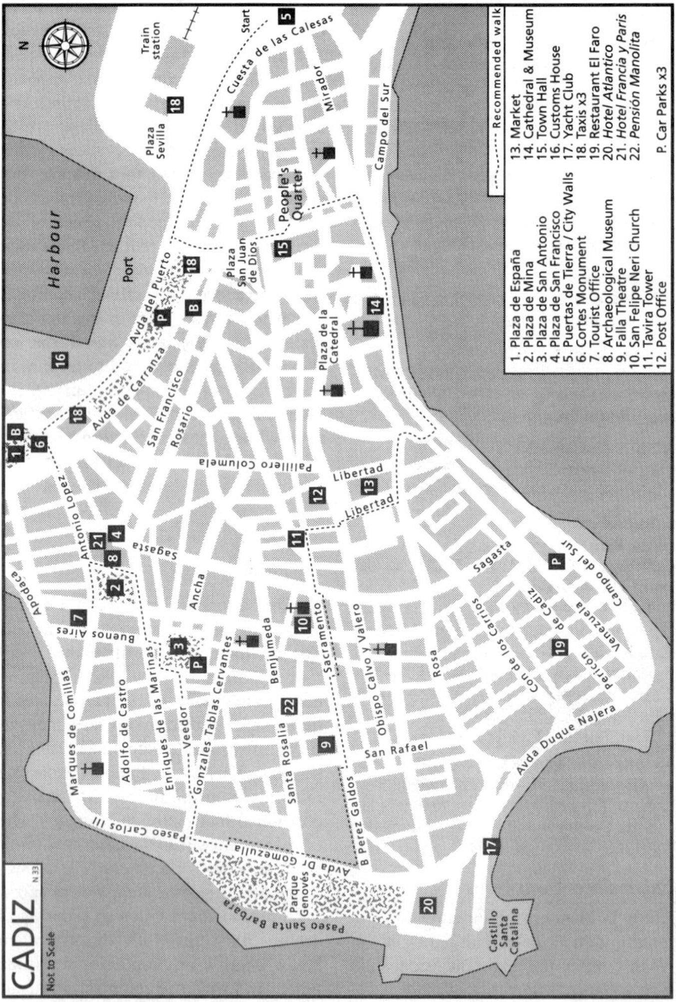

ACCESS Air The nearest airport is at Jerez. **Train** Trains run daily from Jerez and Sevilla to the station close to the entrance of the old town. **Road** The approach to Cádiz by road is somewhat dreary, the causeway being flanked by endless marsh and saltpans of interest only to bird watchers. Once in the old city located at the end of the isthmus, street parking is inevitably difficult, but fortunately there are 3 large underground car parks (see map), which, because of the Spaniards' in-built resistance to paying for parking, usually have plenty of spaces. **Buses** from the N arrive at Avda Ramón de Carranza close to the port, from the S and E at Plaza de España. Ferries arrive at the NE side of the isthmus convenient for the centre of town.

Things to see

Fortunately, all the worthwhile features of Cádiz are contained within a very small area of the old part of the city and can easily be covered in half a day, although if time is to be spent in museums then longer should be allocated. Many visitors will be quite content to wander at will around the narrow streets, but the following itinerary will cover all the recommended places. The start of the older area is marked by the old **City walls** dating back to 1757 and the **Puertas de Tierra** (5) which was the former entrance to Cádiz. Proceed by the port (and the first of the underground car parks in Cuesta de las Calesas) to the **Plaza de España**. Here, in the middle of the square, stands the **Monument to the Cortes** (6) (parliament), built for the centenary of the short-lived liberal constitution of 1812. From the plaza it is a short stroll along Calle Antonio López to the **Plaza Mina**, on the corner of which is located the **Tourist Office** (7). Helpful and cooperative, they will provide an excellent town plan to assist the tour. The Plaza Mina is a beautiful tree-clad square, encircled by fine buildings including the **Museo de Bellas Artes y Arqueológico** (8). Its ground floor contains an excellent collection of archaeological remains from Paleolithic, Phoenician, Moorish and Roman times. The first floor houses the fine art collection, with rooms devoted to Zurbaran, Murillo and 16th century painters. The second floor has an 'ethnographic' display, including a remarkable selection of marionettes. Visitors from EU countries will be delighted to find that entrance is free and that they will be given a comprehensive guide in their own language. Open Tues-Sat 0930-1400. Closed Mon and festivals.

From the Plaza Mina, proceed to the nearby **Plaza de San Antonio**. This equally attractive square has been stripped of its trees and cobbled over to form the roof of another underground car park. From here it is a short walk W to **Parque Genovés** and the shore of Cádiz Bay. Return towards the city along Calle Sacramento, passing on the left the brick-built **Falla Theatre** (9) in the university quarter. Further along Calle Sacramento is the little church of **San Felipe Neri** (10) where the 1812 Declaration of Independence was made by a group of refugees from Napoleon's occupation of the rest of Spain. The Baroque, oval-shaped building has a fascinating façade covered with plaques sent from other countries. Inside is a painting of the *Immaculate Conception* by Murillo. Official opening times are 0830-1000 and 1930-2200, which are the usual times for services. At other hours, be prepared for locked doors and disappointment. At the other end of the same block is the **Museo Histórico Municipal**. Its most noteworthy exhibit is a scale model of Cádiz as it was in 1779. Entrance free. Open Mon-Fri 0900-1300 and 1700-2000. Sat and Sun 0900-1300. After passing the **Tavira Tower** (11), the old watch tower, fork right into **Plaza Topete**, the site of a Phoenician temple where first-born babies were sacrificed. It is now the home of the open and covered **Market** (13), where appetizing displays of fruit, vegetable and fish can be seen.

From the Plaza Topete it is a short walk to the shore and to one of the best photo opportunities in Cádiz – the view of the gold-domed **Cathedral** (14), flanked by colour-washed houses. There are actually 2 cathedrals, the oldest, the Church of Santa Cruz, was largely destroyed by fire in 1596, the newer built in Baroque style in the 18th century. The composer, Manuel de Falla, is buried in the cathedral crypt. Most of the valuable possessions of the church are kept in the **Cathedral Museum** and include paintings by Zurbaran and sculptures by Roldana and Montanes. Open Mon-Sat 1000-1300 (tours every half hour), Sun and festivals closed. Entrance adults 250 Ptas, children 150 ptas. In front of the cathedral is a small square with numerous bars and restaurants. The route continues from the cathedral along the shore, striking inland along Calle San Juan de Dios and into the **Barrio del Pópulo** (People's Quarter), a labyrinth of narrow streets dating from the 18th century, having survived the attention of Drake and others. Nearby is the **Plaza de la Merced** flanked by the **Ayuntamiento** (Town Hall) (15), an impressive building in Elizabethan Neoclassical style. Immediately W of this square are the main pedestrianized shopping streets and the underground car park where the walk began.

Festivals

The usual religious celebrations take place at Semana Santa and Corpus Christi, but Cádiz is more famous for *Carnaval* in Feb. Dating from the 19th century, even Franco was unable to suppress it. The carnival is a riot of eating, drinking, dancing, singing and masquerades with a distinctly South American flavour.

Local information

● Accommodation

The top hotel in Cádiz is **A** ***Atlántico***, Avda Duque de Nájera 9, T 226905, F 214582, state-run hotel, located at the point of isthmus, good views over the Atlantic and the bay, outdoor pool. **B** ***Francia y Paris***, Plaza San Francisco 2, T 222348, F 222431, central location; **B** ***San Remo***, Paseo Marítimo 3, T 252202, F 252203, small, beach location, in the newer part of town.

At the cheaper end of the range, **D** ***Pensión Manolita***, Calle Benjumeda 2, T 211577, clean and adequate; ***Casa de Huespede***, 4 Naciones, Placio 3, near Plaza Juan de Dios, basic, clean no bath. For even cheaper accommodation look for the *camas* signs in windows. In carnival week book well in advance.

● Youth hostels

None in Cádiz. The nearest are in Jerez and Algeciras.

● Camping

Nearest at Puerto de Santa María and Puerto Real. ***Las Dunas de San Anton***, Las Dunas de la Puntilla, T 870112, 1st category, pool and restaurant; ***Guadalete***, Ctra Nac, Km 655, Puerta de Santa María, T 561749; ***El Pinar***, Ctra Nac 1V, Km 666, Puerto Real, T 830897.

● Places to eat

Not surprisingly, seafood comes top of the menu in Cádiz. The best (and most expensive) seafood restaurant in town is ♦♦♦***El Faro***, Calle San Felix 15, T 211068. More reasonable is ♦♦*Achuri*, Calle Plocia 15. Even cheaper are the *freidurias*, the Cádiz version of the fish and chip shop. For *tapa* bars, try Calle Zorilla, next to the tourist office. In the newer part of town, ♦***Chino Marco Polo***, Paseo Marítimo, *menú del dia* 900 Ptas.

● Banks

The main Spanish banks and regional savings banks have their branches close to the Plaza de San Juan de Dios/Calle Nueva area.

● Consulates

Denmark, Alameda Apodaca 21, T 221364; **Holland**, Plaza Tres Carabelas 5, T 224500; **Italy**, Calle Ancha 8, T 211715; **France**, Ctra Madrid-Cádiz, Km 634, T 302354.

● Garages/repairs

Citroën, Calle Algeciras, T 281438; **Ford**, Calle Algeciras, T 271054; **Peugeot**, Autocenter Jimena de la Frontera, T 2255445; **Renault**, Ronda del Puente, T 280300; **Rover**, Calle Gibraltar, T 264308; **Seat/Volkswagen**, Automoviles Bahía, Calle Algeciras, T 250207.

● Post Office

The main *Correos* is in Plaza Topete.

● Shopping

The chief shopping streets are Calles San Francisco, Nueva, Columela and San José. The more gaudy tourist items are happily rarely in sight.

● Tourist Information

Regional Government Tourist Office, Calle Calderón de la Barca 1 (corner of Plaza de Mina), T 211313; **Municipal Tourist Office**, Calle Marqués de Valdenigo 4, T 253254. There is a further temporary municipal office in the summer months at the entrance to Victoria beach.

● Transport

Car hire Atesa, Plaza de San Juan de Dios 16, T 258207; **Avis**, Avda Cayetano de Toro 16, T 258250; **Hertz**, Calle Condesa Villafuente Bermeja, T 271895.

Taxis There are taxi ranks in the Plaza de San Juan de Dios and near the Plaza de España. Radio Taxi is T 221006; Tele Taxi T 286969.

Train Daily trains go N to Jerez and Sevilla via San Fernando. Information T 234301.

Road Bus 2 bus companies serve Cádiz, Los Amarillos covers the area N to Rota and Sanlúcar with their buses leaving from Avda Ramón de Carranza close to the port. The Comes company serves the area S and E of Cádiz to Medina Sidonia, Tarifa and Algeciras, their station is located by the Plaza de España. Bus to Vejer de la Frontera 500 Ptas.

Sea Ferries to Puerto de Santa María across the bay take 45 mins and leave at 1100, returning at 1400. Seagoing ferries leave Cádiz weekly for Almería, Genoa and the Canary Islands. Contact the Transmediterrania office in Avda Ramón de Carranza 26, T 284162.

North from Cádiz

The area N of Cádiz as far as the estuary of the Rio Guadalquivir consists of rolling farmland given over largely to the production of grapes. The attractive coastline is a series of fishing ports and small resorts. The first of these is **El Puerto de Santa María**, a multi-purpose town, fishing and commercial port, resort and sherry producer with an interesting history. The Mudéjar Castle of San Marcos dates from the 13th century and has been carefully restored. Other old buildings include the Baroque Church of San Francisco and the monastery of Nuestra Señora de la Victoria built in the 12th century. The bull ring, just over 100 years old, is one of the most important in Andalucía. El Puerto is one of the 3 towns making up the 'sherry triangle' and it is possible to visit the following *bodegas* by private arrangement: **Osborne**, Calle Fernan Cabellero 3, T 855211; **Terry**, Calle Gilos s/n, T 483000. A recommended way of eating in El Puerto is to visit the harbour-side *marisquerías*, collect bags of fresh fish and shellfish and take them to the nearest bar to eat them with a drink.

Just outside El Puerto is a new British-built luxury development around a marina known inevitably as **Puerto Sherry**. A minor road now leads along the coast, heading briefly inland to avoid the US naval base at **Rota** and re-joining the shore at the town itself, which is a minor resort. It does, however, have some medieval walls still intact and the remains of the 13th century Luna Castle. The coast road now runs N to a headland on which the town of **Chipiona** is located. Although there is evidence of Roman occupation, it is today a quiet family resort with excellent beaches.

The road, with its accompanying railway line, now runs along the estuary of the Rio Guadalquivir to the town of **Sanlúcar de Barrameda**, the third part of the 'sherry triangle'. Sanlúcar was the port from where Columbus left on his 2nd Atlantic crossing and Magellan's last port-of-call before his attempt to circumnavigate the world. The old part of the town has an attractive atmosphere. There are numerous churches worth a visit, particularly the Nuestra Señora de la O in the Plaza de la Paz, with a 16th century Mudéjar doorway. Sanlúcar is famous for its *manzanilla* sherry, produced by the local Barbadillo family who make 5 varieties. The Dukes of Medina Sidonia played an important role in the history of Sanlúcar, but their *palacio* functions today as a small, exclusive guest house. The rather ordinary Castle of Santiago gives fine views across the estuary to the Coto Doñana nature reserve and foot passengers can cross the river by motor boat from the fishing quarter of Bajo de Guia. To get there by car, however, requires a 150 km, 3 hr round trip via Sevilla, which is the lowest bridging point of the river!

The return journey to Cádiz can be made inland by following the C440 to Jerez and then using the E25.

• **Accommodation** Top of the range in every respect is the exclusive **AL** ***Puerto Sherry-Yacht Club***, Avda de la Libertad s/n, T 562541, F 562712, every possible facility and prices to match. Also recommended in the El Puerto area is **AL** ***Meliá Caballo Blanco***, Avda de Madrid 1, T 562541, F 562712 with all the usual features one associates with the Meliá chain. For more affordable prices in El Puerto, try the **D** ***Pensión Tiburón***, Avda Valencia 1, T 875334. The coastal resorts of Rota, Chipiona and Sanlúcar all have a wide range of accommodation available, although nothing in the luxury range. Apartments are readily available at cheap rates in the off season.

South from Cádiz

This part of the Costa de la Luz remains mercifully under-developed, containing fine beaches, flower-strewn meadows, salt flats, rolling farmland, mountains and a number of small, but fascinating, towns.

Leaving behind the salt marshes S of Cádiz, the first town of note is **Chiclana de la Frontera**, a growing settlement of some 50,000 inhabitants, which is increasingly becoming a dormitory of Cádiz. It is well-known for its traditional dolls. The main development is to the W of the town in the Barrosa beach area. Off-shore stands the island of Sancti-Pectri, with the remains of a Temple of Hercules, a 13th century castle and a more modern lighthouse. Novo Sanctri-Petri is a new tourist complex with golf courses, apartments and 3 large hotels.

About 20 km E of Chiclana, along the C346 is the hill town of **Medina Sidonia**. Here a dukedom was created in the 15th century to defend the area around Cádiz which provided the name of the Spanish Armada's admiral. The town is dominated by the 15th century Church of Santa María, built on the site of an old castle, parts of which still survive. The church tower can be climbed and the exertion is rewarded by impressive views N over the cliff edge and across the plains towards Arcos. Other places of interest include 3 surviving Moorish arches, the churches of San Augustin and Santiago, the 18th century *ayuntimiento* and the ducal palace.

Returning towards the coast, the N340, known here as La Ruta de las Dos Mares, runs S past the luxury development of **Roche**, through a prosperous market gardening area, to **Conil de la Frontera**. This small fishing village is now making rapid progress as a holiday resort, based on its broad sandy beaches. Visitors are advised, however, to avoid the polluted river mouth.

The coast road continues S through open undulating countryside growing grain and sunflowers to the town of **Vejer de la Frontera**, population 13,000, located on a cliff above a gorge eroded by the Rio Barbate. Vejer has a distinct Moorish atmosphere, with its ruined alcazar, narrow streets and whitewashed patios. The 13th century Church of El Salvador was built on the site of a mosque and is notable for its reredos containing statues and tilework. It is still possible to see the women of Vejer wearing the *cobija*, a dark cloak which probably originated in North Africa.

Nine km S of Vejer is the busy fishing port of **Barbate de Franco**, with a cannery and fish auction. To the W of the town, the wooded cliffs lead to **Cape Trafalgar**, where Nelson defeated the combined French and Spanish fleets in 1805. There are fine beaches to the S of Barbate, but access is restricted by the military. **Zahara de los Atunes** (literally translated as 'Flower of the Tuna Fish') has, for most of the year, totally deserted beaches. The village, along with Barbate, has an important tuna industry, and twice a year the migrating tuna are herded into nets and slaughtered.

One further diversion from the coast road is to **Bolonia**, through fields which are noted for their wild flowers, attracting botanists from throughout Europe. In Jan the paper white Narcissus are in full display and the colours and varieties increase during Spring. By late Apr the fields, which have never experienced weedkiller or plough, are a riot of colour with squills, clover, lupins, iris and vetch. Reaching Bolonia itself, the major attraction (apart from the magnificent beach) is the remains of the old Roman town of **Baelo Claudia**. Thought to have been founded in 171 BC the remains have been partially excavated from the sand revealing a main street, a temple of Jupiter, a theatre and market place. Large stone vats have also been discovered, which apparently contained *garum*, a type of soupy fish paste, highly regarded and exported widely through the Roman Empire. Guided tours of Baelo Claudia are available Mon-Sat at 1000, 1100, 1200, 1300, 1800 and 2000, Sun afternoon only. A notice informs that entrance for Spaniards is free on production of their DNI while 'Foreigners' are obliged to pay 250 Ptas. There is a small reception area nearby. If there is no sign of life, ask for Isidoro at the nearest bar.

• **Accommodation** The luxury class of accommodation is limited to the 3 golf hotels at Nuevo Sancti Petri: **AL** *Costa Golf*, T 494535, F 494626; **AL** *Playa La Barrosa*, T 494824, F 494860; and **AL** *Royal Andaluz Golf*, T 494109, F 494490. **A** *Hospedería del Convento de San Francisco*, La Plazuela s/n, Vejer, T 451001, F 451004, quite unique; **A** *Flamenco*, Calle Fuente de Gallo s/n, Conil, T 440711, F 440542, cliff top location, closed Nov-Mar. **C** *Tres Jotas*, Calle San Sebastián 27, Conil, T/F 440450, clean and comfortable, **C** *Gran Sol*, Calle Sánchez Rodríguez s/n, Zahara, T 439301, F 439197, beach location, spotless, excellent restaurant, recommended; **C** *Pensión La Janda*, Calle Cerro Clarinas s/n, Vejer, T 450142.

• **Camping** There is an abundance of camp sites in the area, including 6 at Conil, 2 at Chiclana, 3 at Vejer and 3 at Barbate. Most are located either on the coast or near to the N340. The following are 1st category sites: ***Caños de Meca***, Ctra Vejer-Caños de Meca Km 10, T 450405; ***Camping Pinar Tula***, Ctra Nac 340 Km 20, Conil, T 445500; ***La Rana Verde***, Pago de la Rana Verde, Chiclana, T 495061; ***Camping Vejer***, Ctra Nac 340 Km 39, Vejer, T 450098.

Tarifa

Tarifa, 21 km W of Algeciras and only 14 km N of Morocco in the Province of Cádiz, is the southernmost town on the Iberian peninsula. The town's exposed position between the Atlantic Ocean and the Mediterranean Sea at the entrance to the Straits of Gibraltar has recently brought it new prosperity as a windsurfers' paradise, causing its population of 16,000 to double during the summer. Nevertheless Tarifa still retains its Moorish character. The **Campo de Gibraltar**, as the S tip of Spain is known, has historically been largely in the hands of the military which, together with the exfoliating wind which is reputed to blow 45% of the year, explains why the magnificent beaches around Tarifa, especially the 8 km **Playa de los Lances**, remain largely unspoilt. Wind farms are spreading across the hill slopes taking advantage of the winds – but certainly spoiling the area.

ACCESS Air The nearest airport is in Gibraltar, which is accessible by international flights only. For internal Spanish flights, Jerez airport (120 km) can be reached via the daily Comes bus to Jerez or in 2 hrs by car. Málaga airport is 164 km E along the coast road. **Train** The nearest station is in Algeciras at the end of the line from Madrid. **Road** There are frequent buses from Algeciras to Tarifa. Turn off the N-340, part of the Ruta de las Dos Mares, which bypasses the town.

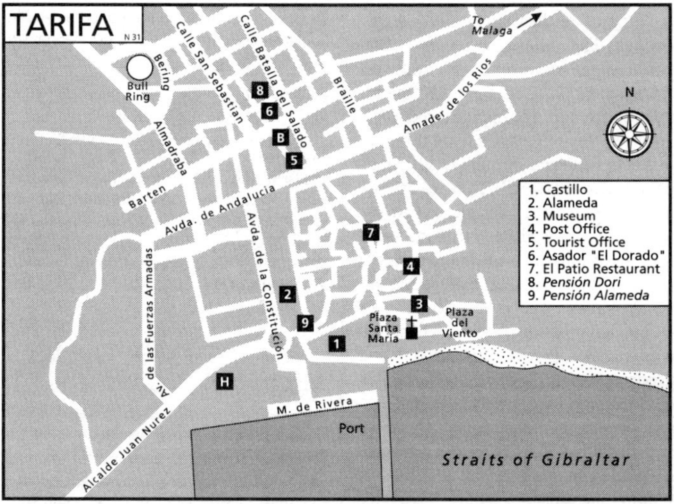

Things to see

Moorish past When the Moors first crossed the Straits of Gibraltar to assess the possibilities of the Iberian Peninsula, they landed in this area. Local legend has it that the Commander Tarif Ben Malik gave the site where they landed on Andalusian soil the name of *Al-Yazirat Tarif*. The town was recaptured from the Moors in 1292 by Sancho IV, although their attempt to regain it 2 years later is more memorable. The Moors threatened to murder the young son of the Christian commander, Alonso de Guzmán, unless Tarifa surrendered. Guzmán's response was to throw down his own dagger preferring 'honour without a son to a son without honour'. His son was duly murdered while Guzmán acquired the title of *el Bueno* (the Good) and the lands which later formed the dukedom of Medina Sidonia under his descendants. Fifty years later Tarifa was again threatened by Moors led by Yusuf I of Granada. However King Alfonso XI defeated them in the decisive **Batalla del Salado** in 1340.

The **Castillo de Guzmán el Bueno** was built between 950 and 960 when the Caliph of Córdoba, Abd Al-Rahman III decided the area needed defending against any invasion from North Africa. A small town grew up around the castle, in the quarter now known as the Barrio de Jesús. The tower known as the **Torre de Guzmán** is more modern. The whole site is still controlled by the Spanish army and you can climb up to the ramparts although the castle itself is closed to the public. The **Alameda** joins the castle to the mainland. The church of **Santa María**, adjacent to the castle, is built on the site of a mosque, as is **San Mateo**.

The *Al-Medina Bar* in Calle Almedina off Plaza Santa María is worth a visit for a quick drink since it has an entrance arch which was originally a point of access to the castle.

Museums

The only one in town is the **Museo Municipal**, Plaza de Santa María. Admission is free.

Festivals

6 Jan procession for the *Día de los Reyes*; Feb *Carneval* marked by dancing, cos-

tumes, masquerades etc; traditional processions mark *Semana Santa*; May 15 *Romería del Conejo*, pilgrimage in honour of San Isidro; 24 Jun the fiesta of *San Juan* is celebrated with bonfires in nearby **Facinas**; first fortnight of Jul, *Feria de Tahivilla*; 16 Jul *Fiesta del Carmen*, the statue of the *Virgen del Carmen* is taken out in a fishing boat to bless the waters; first fortnight in Aug, *National Folk Music Festival*; early Sep a fair, fiesta and pilgrimage in honour of *Nuestra Señora de la Luz*, patron saint of Tarifa.

Local information

● Accommodation

NB: hotels in the area tend to be relatively expensive due to Tarifa's resort status. Beach hotels are generally closed in winter. **A** ***Balcón de España***, Ctra Nacional 340, Km 76, T 684326, F 684326, 40 rm, garden, pool, riding, tennis, parking; **A** ***Hurricane***, Ctra Nacional 340, Km 77, T 684919, garden, pool, squash, horse riding, wind surfing, health club, beach, parking; **A** ***Hotel Dos Mares***, Ctra Nacional 340, Km 79.5, T 680090, F 681078, pool, tennis, bike hire, restaurant, windsurfing school, parking.

● Pensiones

It is very difficult to find cheap accommodation in Tarifa, owners of even the most basic *pensión* ask and get inflated prices due to the town's massive influx of tourists during the season. The following hostels all have rm with bath. **C** ***Tarik***, Calle San Sebastián 36, T 685240.

D ***Pensión Dori***, Calle Batalla Salado 55, T 685317, slightly noisy road; **D** ***Pensión Medina***, Calle Algeciras, T 684904; **D** ***Alameda***, Paseo Alameda 4, T 680264, good, central position; **D** ***Pensión Correo***, opposite post office, popular, clean; **D** ***La Calzada***, in old town.

E ***Fonda Villanueva***, Avda Andalucía, near tourist kiosk, some rm with bath, clean, pleasant, secure, modern, recommended.

● Youth hostel

The nearest is in Algeciras in the ***Parque Natural 'Los Canutos'***, T 956 679060, 10 km from Tarifa, 108 beds, meals, parking, sailing.

● Camping

Paloma, Ctra Nacional 340, Km 72.6, T 684203, beach, restaurant, bar, riding; ***Río Jara***, Ctra Nacional Km 80, T 680570, beach, bar, riding; ***Tarifa***, Ctra Nacional Km 78.7, T 684778, restaurant, bar, launderette, beach; ***Torre de la Peña I***, Ctra Nacional Km 78, T 684903, restaurant, bar, beach, launderette; ***Torre de la Peña II***, Ctra Nacional Km 75, T 684174, restaurant, bar, beach.

● Places to eat

♦♦♦***El Rincón de Manolo***, Ctra Nacional 340, Km 76.6, is the most expensive restaurant in Tarifa, with good fish and seafood; ***Alameda***, Paseo de la Alameda, good position but rather over-priced; ***Hostería Tarifa***, Calle Amador de los Ríos, T 684076, steak; ***Mesón de Sancho***, Ctra Nacional 340 Km 94, T 684900, those with transport should drive the few km E to this excellent roadside restaurant flanked by 2 petrol stations, popular at all times of the day, the accommodation here is reasonable too (**B** category). ♦♦ ***El Patio***, Calle de la Luz 20, T 684085, good food, fast service but very N European atmosphere; ***Avenida***, Calle Batalla del Salado, reasonable *platos combinados*. ♦ The cheaper food and accommodation is around Calle Batalla del Salado, the main road out of Tarifa. ***Asador de Pollos "El Dorado"***, Calle Batalla del Salado 37, chicken and chips to take away; ***El Pato Rojo***, Batalla del Salado 47, cheap *menú*; ***Bar-Freiduría Parame***, Calle Huerta del Rey, T 681435, fresh fish; ***Freiduría Sevilla***, Calle Sancho IV el Bravo.

● Banks

There are 2 on Calle Sancho IV el Bravo, 2 on Calle Nuestra Señora de la Luz, 1 on Avda de Andalucía and 1 on Calle Batalla del Salado.

● Entertainment & shopping

Bullfights: check locally for the next bullfight in the Plaza de Toros in Calle Bering.

Handicrafts: the ***Bazar Hispano Arabe*** in Avda de Andalucía contains leather goods more reminiscent of Morocco than Spain. Indeed some local women can be seen wearing Moorish dress.

● Garages/petrol

On Calle Batalla del Salado towards the N-IV.

● Hospitals

Cruz Roja, Calle Juan Nuñez 5, T 684896; ***Servicio de Urgencia*** (emergencies), Calle Calzadilla Téllez, T 680779.

● Post Office

Correos, Calle Colonel Moscardó 9. Open Mon-Fri 0900-1400, Sat 0900-1200.

● **Sport**

Horse riding: enquire at *Hotel Dos Mares* (T 684035), or *Hotel Balcón de España*.

Windsurfing: 21 recognised 'spots' requiring varying degrees of expertise. Several shops are devoted to windsurfing gear.

● **Telephones**

Local code: 956. There are numerous private *locutorios*, including **Estudio 21**, Calle Batalla del Salado, 35; **Baelo International**, Sancho IV El Bravo, 19.

● **Travel agents**

Marruecotur, Calle Batalla del Salado 57, T 680256; ***Tourafrica***, Estación Marítima, T 684751.

● **Tourist information**

Cabin on Avda de Andalucía. Opening hours variable.

● **Transport**

Local Bike hire Enquire at *Hotel Dos Mares*, T 684035. **Car hire Citroën-Dal Auto**, Avda Andalucía 18, T 643726; **El Estrecho**, Batalla del Salado 20, T 684147; **Marruecotur**, Batalla del Salado 57, T 684001. **Taxis** Avda de Andalucía, T 684241.

Train train travellers should go to Algeciras or Cádiz.

Road Bus Comes SA have a frequent service to **Algeciras**, 200 Ptas (½ hr), 12 daily; 8 to **Cádiz**, 4 to **Sevilla**, 3 to **Málaga**, 2 to **La Linea**, 400 Ptas (1¼ hrs), 1 to **Jerez**. The bus station is at Calle Batalla del Salado 19. Open 0900-1100 and 1600-1900 for booking and advance tickets. Long-distance buses can be caught in Algeciras. T 684038.

Sea Ferry to **Morocco** departs Tarifa 1000 daily except Sun, return departs **Tanger** 1530. Takes approx 1 hr. T 684751.

Excursions from Tarifa

Many birds migrating from Africa cross the Straits of Gibraltar near Tarifa (see Wildlife, page 36). The best point from which to see Morocco on a clear day is the viewpoint at **El Cabrito** a few steep, winding km along the N-340 towards Algeciras. Don't stop on the road, turn off into the *mirador* on the right at the top of the pass.

Tanger Tour departs 1000, returns 1900, cost 6,500 Ptas including lunch and guide. Essential to book in advance at tourist kiosk.

INFORMATION FOR VISITORS

Contents

Before you go

General note

Travellers will have no difficulty getting to Andalucía. As a major tourist destination, it is served by frequent flights from other European countries and recently improved motorways from other Spanish regions. Tourism is the primary source of income and visitors are made welcome.

Entry requirements

● Visas

American and Japanese citizens require a passport and EU citizens a passport or national identity card to enter Spain for a stay of up to 90 days. No visas are required. Visitors from North Africa will require visas and should check current requirements when planning their journey. For document requirements if you wish to visit Morocco, **see page 355**.

All foreign drivers need an **International Driving Licence** (or ordinary EU driving licence), while those in their own cars also require insurance and vehicle documentation. Non-EU citizens will also require a Green Card and it is advisable to obtain a **Bail Bond** in order to avoid imprisonment in the event of a serious accident. You should carry the required documentation whenever you are in the car.

● Vaccinations

No innoculations are required for Spain, but visitors should ensure that their tetanus injections are up-to-date. The usual precautions should be taken against AIDS.

● Representation overseas

Canada, 350 Sparks St, 802 Ottawa, T 613 2372192; **Egypt**, 41 Sharia Ismail Muhammad, Zamalek, Cairo, T 202 3406397; **France**, 22 Ave Marceau, 75381 Paris, T 1 44431800; **Libya**, 36 Sh Abdel Kader El Yazain, Tripoli, T 332752; **Morocco**, 105 Allal Ben Abdellah, Rabat, T 212 770 7600; **Tunisia**, 22 Ave Dr Ernest Conseil, Garden City, 2001 Tunis, T 2161280613; **UK**, 39 Chesham Place, London SW1, T 071 235 5555; **USA**, 2700 15th St, Washington DC 20009, T 202 265 0191.

● Spanish tourist offices abroad

Australia, 203 Castlereagh St, Suite 21, Sydney NSW 2000, T 02 264 7966; **Canada** 102 Bloor St W, Toronto, Ontario M5S 1MB, T 416 9614079; **France**, Ave Pierre 1 de Serbie, 75381 Paris, T 14 4723 3775; **Italy**, Piazzo di Spagna 55, Roma 00187, T 396 8272; **UK** 57-18 St James St, London SW1A 1LD, T 071 4990901; **USA** 665 Fifth Ave, New York NY 10022, T 212 7598822.

● Tourist information

Every town and city in Andalucía has a **Tourist Office** either regional or municipal. Some also have a **Municipal Tourist Office** operated by the *Ayuntamiento*. The former is generally more useful and should be the first stop for travellers arriving at a town. The staff are usually good linguists and sometimes outstandingly pleasant and helpful, although some are ill-informed and a few make it very clear they have been asked the same question a thousand times before. Do not be put off as many of the free brochures available are informative, (although they would benefit from proof reading) particularly the town plans, while lists of accommodation and monument prices can usually be produced. **Tourist office hours** vary considerably from town to town and even from year to year. The primary consideration appears to be the convenience of the staff, rather than that of the tourists. However accommodation and other information is often displayed in the window.

● Specialist tour companies

Abercrombie and Kent (UK), Andalusian Safari around Ronda with mules, 8 days £980, T 071 7309600; ***Ace Study Tours*** (UK), historical/cultural tours, T 0223 835055; ***Andalucía Trails***, horse trekking, English, Centro de Equitación, *Hotel Salobreña*, 18680 Salobreña, Granada, T 958 610261; ***Benamorda***, rambling, horse riding, mountain biking, nature tours, Spanish, Sociedad Cooperativa Andaluza de Actividades Turístico-Culturales, Postigo 66, 29492 Jubrique, Málaga, F 95 2152336; ***Burro-Aventura***, donkey treks in the Alpujarras, Spanish, Camping de Pitres, 18414 Pitres, Granada, T 958 766112; ***Explore*** (UK), walking tours, 15 days from £445, T 0252 3444161; ***Exodus*** (UK), walking in the Sierra Nevada, 8 days from £400, T 081 6735550, highly recommended; ***Peng*** (UK), offer naturist holidays 3 miles from Estapona, T 04024 71832; ***Rancho Los Lobas***, horse trekking, English/German, Estación de Jimena de la Frontera, Cádiz, T 956 640429; ***Taste of Spain***, specialized tours of Andalucía by jeep, horse or on foot, English, Apartado 349, 29680 Estepona, Málaga, T 95 2886590.

When to go

● Best time to visit

Although sunseekers arrive in Jul and Aug, serious sightseers are better advised to visit Andalucía during the cooler and less overcrowded periods of spring and autumn. Ecija, between Córdoba and Sevilla, is not known as Spain's frying pan for nothing! Spring and autumn are also times of climatic transition, with the former being particularly attractive as the countryside is green and there are wild flowers in profusion. There are attractions for visitors in all seasons, therefore, depending on the purpose of the visit.

● Climate

There are probably more hours of sunshine in southern Spain than anywhere else in Europe. Winters are agreeably mild on the coast, averaging 15-17°C, although much colder inland, especially in the Sierra Nevada. Summers are hot, particularly inland, but the coasts have the benefit of sea breezes. Midday temperatures in Jul are usually 25-30°C and many areas receive no rain at all from May to the end of Oct, although thunderstorms are always possible in late summer. The area from Gibraltar to Cádiz often experiences the windsurfer's delight, the strong *levante* wind from the E, which can last for days on end.

Health

● Staying healthy

Citizens of EU countries are entitled to health care from the Spanish health service, providing they can show Form E111, which should be completed before arriving in Spain. Travellers are advised, however, that this is ineffective in practice for short stays and they should obtain a comprehensive travel insurance to cover every medical eventuality. Those requiring special treatments or diets are advised to carry a letter from their doctor translated into Spanish, indicating the nature of the condition and the requirements.

● Medical services

Doctors If you need the services of a doctor (there are often multilingual ones in the tourist areas) expect to pay a consultation fee of between 3,000 and 4,000 Ptas – keep the receipt for insurance claims.

Farmacías (chemists), identifiable by a green cross, will provide most medicines, often without a prescription. They are used to dealing with people who do not wish to pay a doctors' fee. Local duty chemists will be listed in the window.

Health problems tend to be caused by unaccustomed food, an excess of alcohol, overexposure to sun or polluted drinking water. It is probably prudent to drink bottled water in rural areas.

Helicópteros Sanitarios Any visitor staying on the Costa del Sol for some time and regularly using the dangerous N-340, might consider joining *Helicópteros Sanitarios*, who fly injured motorists speedily to the nearest hospital, probably safer than some of the erratically driven private ambulances, T 2826119.

● Further health information
See main health section on page 19.

Money

● Currency
The local currency is the Peseta. **See page 9** for table of exchange rates at Jun 1994. Notes in circulation are: 1,000, 2,000, 5,000, 10,000. Coin values range from 1 to 500 Ptas. You should have no difficulty exchanging travellers' cheques or foreign notes in any bank (look out for the *Cambio* sign), and commissions will be lower here than in specialized exchange offices or hotel receptions. Spaniards generally pay for goods in cash and often carry large amounts with them, although this is not recommended. Keep a separate note of any travellers' cheque or credit card details and telephone numbers.

● Credit cards
Major credit and charge cards, especially Master Card, Visa and American Express are widely accepted, although smaller shops and restaurants may only accept cash. They can also be used to withdraw cash from many cashpoint machines, although you should check how much commission your bank/card company will charge you for this service. **NB**: be warned that at times of fluctuating exchange rates, credit card companies usually contrive to make the situation as unfavourable as possible for you.

● Taxes
Variable rates of VAT (sales tax – IVA in Spanish) are applicable, from a basic 6% to 12% or 33% for luxury goods. Major department stores such as *El Corte Inglés* (Málaga) and *Galerías Preciados* (Granada) operate VAT exemption schemes for non-residents. If you make any large purchases, consult the multilingual staff for details.

Getting there

● Air
From Europe There are frequent air services from all the main European countries to Sevilla or Málaga. Additional services via Madrid involve transferring to Aviaco, the national service, to reach the smaller national airports. During the summer, charter flights to Málaga make it possible to find very cheap flights, especially through bargain bucket shops. Travellers from England and North Africa have the option of flying to Gibraltar.

From USA There are numerous charter flights during the season. Although these are cheaper, they not always reliable. Waiting for a standby seat on a flight is also worth considering if funds are short. If you prefer more comfort and fewer delays, American and European companies operate scheduled services to Spain, although you may find it cheaper to fly to another European capital before changing for a flight to Andalucía.

From North Africa Gibraltar Airways advertise connections with Tanger Fri and Sun; Casablanca Mon, Tue, Wed and Thur; Marrakech Sat. Airfares: cheapest return fares to Tanger 12,250 Ptas; Casablanca 21,000 Ptas; Marrakech 25,750 Ptas. Connections to Málaga are available from Cairo, Casablanca and Tunis (via Barcelona). Connections via Madrid widen the choice.

Airfares vary greatly depending on the route chosen, whether you are booked on a charter or scheduled flight, and whether you are travelling in or out of high season. Cheapest scheduled flights from UK to Málaga in 1994 were in the region of £110 return, and to Jerez £99 return.

● Train
There is easy access to Spain's rail network from the rest of Europe via France (through Hendaye/Irun or Port Bou/Cerbère) or Portugal (Valencia de Alcantara/Marvao). To reach Andalucía you will generally need to go via Madrid and possibly cross town to a different station. Make sure you know whether your connection leaves from Atocha or Chamartín! Use the Metro if you need to change stations, or a taxi if time is short. If you are not travelling on an InterRail or Eurail ticket, you will find Spanish fares on ordinary trains very reasonable. On long overnight journeys it is worth investing in a *litera* (bunk).

● Road
There are numerous good road connections from France and Portugal. From France it is best to choose a route near either the W or E coast in order to avoid the Pyrenées. From North Africa, cars can be brought across on the many ferry services.

Automobile Club RACE (Real Automobil Club de España) runs a 24 hr breakdown service. This is centred in Madrid, T 91 4412222 and has some English speaking staff. However you are unlikely to find yourself near a telephone once outside town and are more likely to be helped by a passing Guardía Civil –

take a book to read while you wait!

● Sea

Fares on the many ferry services depend on the length of the crossing and can be rather expensive, particularly if you are taking a car. You should enquire before departure about prices on the specific crossing you will be using.

Ferries to North Africa There are numerous services to North Africa, the Canary Islands and the Balearics, most of them run by Transmediterránea who will have an office in the departure port. Crossings include Cádiz-Tenerife, Algeciras-Ceuta (**see page 355**), Gibraltar-Tanger (**see page 356**), Málaga-Melilla (**see page 355**) and Málaga-Palma. Travelling by boat from England, Brittany Ferries run Portsmouth to Santander Nov-mid Mar and Plymouth to Santander the rest of the year. The voyage takes 23 hrs and reduces the driving distance to Málaga via Calais by half. Fares from £244 return (low season), increasing to £531 (high season) for 2 adults plus car. £71/£118 per person return without car. In addition there is a new P&O line Portsmouth-Bilbao which runs twice weekly. You will arrive on the N coast and need to travel down to Andalucía by train or road. Options range from beds to chairs, depending on your budget.

● Customs

Duty free goods You may import up to 200 cigarettes or 50 cigars from European countries (double from outside Europe), a camera and a video camera with film, 2 litres of wine and one of spirits (2 litres if under 22%). In practice, customs controls are very slack in tourist areas, but you should abide by these restrictions. You are most likely to encounter difficulties at the crossing from Gibraltar into Spain where clearance can be very slow on the days when they decide to examine everything! It is also important that you bring with you receipts for any valuables you are bringing into the country, to avoid any problems when you leave. There are no restrictions on EU citizens taking home wine or tobacco, providing they are for personal consumption. There are duty free stops at Sevilla and Malaga airports.

Most Spanish wines, spirits and tobacco are cheaper in supermarkets where there is also a better selection so buy your 'duty free' with care at the airports. There are duty free shops at Sevilla and Málaga airports.

Import/export bans Travellers are advised not to take any risks by carrying drugs, since this can lead to prison sentences. Any prescription drugs should be clearly labelled.

When you arrive

● Clothing

Over the past decade Spanish dressing has become much more relaxed, with shorts a common sight in the streets. Generally there are no restrictions, although it is advisable to dress decently if you are planning to visit churches. In general, the Spanish dress up very smartly during the evening or when taking the traditional pre-dinner *paseo* (stroll) through the park or streets. While topless sunbathing is almost universal, you should check you are on a *playa de nudistas* before removing any more clothes!

● Electricity

Modern sockets are 220v and can be used with 240v appliances. American travellers will require adaptors, but British and other visitors should also bear in mind that Spanish sockets are for 2 pin plugs and an adaptor will be needed for appliances with 3 pins. Although you will often find sockets in bathrooms in Spain, do bear in mind that this can be extremely dangerous. Ideally you should try to find one elsewhere in your room. Lighting in hotel rooms is generally very poor – Spaniards do not read in bed – so you may need to do any reading in a communal lounge.

● Hours of business

These are generally 0900-1400 and 1700-2000, although these are variable – tourist shops stay open very late while large department stores do not close for lunch. Businesses are more likely to operate according to standard 0900-1800 timetables, although they may start and end earlier in summer. Banks are open Mon-Thur 0830-1630, Fri 0830-1400, Sat 0830-1300. They operate *horario de verano* from mid-May to mid-Oct. This is usually 0800-1400 with no Sat morning service.

● Metal detectors

May not be used unless an import licence for the detector has been obtained. For details contact the Spanish Commercial Office – in UK T 071 486 0101.

● Official time

GMT + 1hr (GMT + 2 hr from last Sun of March to last Sun of Sep).

● **Photography**
There are very few limitations on photography. One point to bear in mind is that new films and film developing are relatively expensive.

● **Plane spotting**
This is prohibited in Spanish airports.

● **Police**
Should you be robbed, it will be necessary to report the theft to the police, who can issue a certificate for any insurance claim. You should go to the **Policía Nacional**, who wear a brown military-style uniform and normally deal with crime investigation. The **Policía Municipal**, who have limited powers, mostly direct traffic, while the **Guardía Civil** wear green uniforms and are responsible for highway patrols. As few policemen speak anything but Spanish, volunteer linguists are sometimes around in police stations to help tourist victims.

● **Religion**
Spaniards are predominantly Roman Catholic, although for an increasing number of the population adherence to the Catholic Church is largely nominal. Most sizeable towns will have a small evangelical church for Protestants. In tourist areas this may even be English speaking while on the Costa del Sol there is an Anglican community. Unfortunately tourist offices are generally unable to inform you about any non-Catholic or non-Christian services, so it is a question of enquiring locally or looking in the telephone directory.

● **Shopping**
Best buys Leather goods range from basic to luxury quality and are popular with tourists. However they are not particularly cheap. Rough pottery vases and plates, often painted in a traditional blue and white indicative of their Moorish heritage, are still relatively cheap although sometimes bulky to transport. Items such as bowls and spoons made out of olive wood, and silver filigree jewellery can be attractive and not too expensive if you shop around. Traditional rugs are also worth looking at, although they may be expensive.

● **Safety**
Security Crime in Andalucía is largely an urban phenomenon fuelled by unemployment, drug dependence and tourism. Both Málaga and Sevilla have particularly bad reputations for street crime. The most common forms likely to affect the tourist are pickpocketing, mugging and theft from cars. Sevilla is known for its *semáforos* who smash car windows at traffic lights, steal whatever is available and make off down side streets on mopeds. Some simple precautions will reduce the risk of becoming a victim. Try to choose an hotel which has a lock up garage for cars, but in any case remove all luggage and valuables from your car at night. Do not have cameras etc on display in a car when travelling through a city. Leave valuables in hotel safety deposit boxes. Don't carry handbags unless absolutely necessary or keep wallets in rear pockets. Avoid poorly lit and less salubrious areas of cities, especially late at night.

● **Tipping**
A service charge is included in restaurant and hotel bills, but an additional tip of 5-10% will be appreciated by the ill-paid waiters. Everyone from cinema ushers to porters and monument guides will expect a small tip.

● **Weights and measures**
The metric system is used. See conversion table on **page 17**.

Where to stay

In Andalucía, this is state-registered and there is sufficient variety to satisfy any requirements. All establishments are shown by blue plaques with letters – Hotels (H), Residential Hotels (HR), *Pensión*(P), *Casas de Huéspedes* (CH). Accommodation is graded by stars, up to 5 for hotels and up to 3 for *pensiones*. This system depends entirely on facilities provided and does not consider atmosphere. The term *hostal* has been phased out and all *hostales* have to decide whether to describe themselves as a hotel or a *pensión*. **Youth hostels**, 147 to choose from, are located in most large towns. Minimum age 13 for unaccompanied children, those under 26 years have priority, overnight fee for members 1,300-1,700 Ptas, breakfast 125 Ptas, lunch/dinner 700 Ptas, open 0800-2230 winter, 0800-2330 summer.

The Andalusian tourist office produce booklets annually giving comprehensive details of both hotels and *pensiones*. Be warned that safety regulations relating to fire exits etc are often not complied with. Many of the largest and most highly-rated hotels are located in the coastal resorts, but these may suffer from noise at night from discos, while not everyone would wish to share their hotel with package tour parties. On the Costa del Sol 'residential tourism' is more important than 'hotel tourism' and consequently

Hotel Classifications

AL US$90+. International class luxury hotel. All facilities for business and leisure travellers are of the highest international standard.

A US$75-90. International hotel with air conditioned rooms with WC, bath/shower, TV, phone, mini-bar, daily clean linen. Choice of restaurants, coffee shop, shops, bank, travel agent, swimming pool, some sport and business facilities.

B US$60-75. As **A** but without the luxury, reduced number of restaurants, smaller rooms, limited range of shops and sport.

C US$40-60. Best rooms have air conditioning, own bath/shower and WC. Usually comfortable, bank, shop, pool.

D US$20-40. Best rooms may have own WC and bath/shower. Depending on management will have room service and choice of cuisine in restaurant.

E US$10-20. Simple provision. Perhaps fan cooler. May not have restaurant. Shared WC and showers with hot water (when available).

F under US$10. Very basic, shared toilet facilities, variable in cleanliness, noise, often in dubious locations.

there are literally thousands of apartments and villas available for hire. Out of the season, reduced rate bargains can be negotiated, but make sure exactly what is included in the rental agreement.

● *Paradores*

These state-run hotels are often located in historic buildings. They tend to be furnished with appropriate antiques, while their restaurants concentrate on local specialities. Some modern *paradores* have been built in resort areas, but maintain the usual high standards. Prices are high and booking essential, although there is a rumour that rooms are held for government officials until 1800, after which time fortunate visitors may be able to take them without booking. They can be booked in advance from the Madrid head office at Requena 3, 28013 Madrid, T 559069, F 5593233 and in UK through ***Keytel International***, 402 Edgeware Rd, London W2N 1ED, T 071 402 8182. Do not be deterred if you arrive at your pre-booked *parador* and they try to persuade you they have no record of your reservation. Polite, firm insistance should secure you your room.

● Camping

There are some excellent camp sites in Andalucía, particularly on the coast. They are rated in categories 1 to 3 depending on their facilities and many sites have swimming pools, restaurants, sports and supermarkets. The more popular sites may need to be booked in advance at the peak of the summer season, while during the winter months, the coastal camp sites attract large numbers of caravans and recreational vehicles. Official camp sites are listed in the regional government's accommodation booklet *Guía de Camping*, available from tourist offices. Reservations may be made through the ***Federación Española de Empresarios de Camping***, General Oraa 52-2°D, 28006 Madrid, T 5629994, F 5637094. **NB**: inland camp sites can be few and far between. The province of Córdoba, for example, has only 3 listed sites, Jaén only 6.

Food and drink

● Food

Eating out in Spain is no longer a cheap option, so you may prefer to stock up at a *hipermercado* or local shop. Budget travellers who do go to restaurants are advised to find one with a range of fixed price *menús* to choose from. There is generally a range to suit any taste, including some Spanish specialities such as the iced soup *gazpacho andaluz* and the ubiquitous *paella*, often served as a starter or ordered in advance as a main course. Seafood and fish can be excellent, especially near the coast. Desserts are generally disappointing, usually a choice between fruit, *flan* (caramel custard) and mass-produced ice cream. Despite the prolific output of excellent fruit from areas such as Almería, much of that available for sale is Andalucía is of poor quality. Check whether IVA (sales tax) is included in *menús* and if it is not, make sure you are only charged 6%.

As an alternative to a full meal in the evening, you can ask for *raciones* (portions) of *tapas* such as whitebait, omelette, mussels,

Restaurant Classifications

Given the variations in price of food on any menu our restaurants are divided where possible into three simple grades: ♦♦♦ expensive, ♦♦ average and ♦ cheap.

cheese and ham in bars. Although a single portion may be only 600 Ptas, by the time you have sampled several delicacies and the local beverage this is not a cheap alternative to a full meal. Be particularly careful if asking for ham, since portions of speciality hams can cost thousands of Ptas per serving!

Bear in mind that, for Spaniards, lunch is the main meal and usually begins around 1400 and dinner at 2300 or later. However be warned that restaurants aimed specifically at tourists and hotel dining rooms may close as early as 2230 – before Spaniards even start thinking about dinner!

● Drink

In Andalucía you will find a full range of local and international wines and spirits at reasonable prices. In the area around Jerez you can sample the *fino* at the various *bodegas* and any restaurant can provide Spanish wine from the Rioja region. Cold draught beer is available from any bar, ask for *una caña* or a bottled variety such as San Miguel.

A good thirst quencher on a hot day is *horchata*, a non alcoholic drink made from ground almonds and barley. **NB**: remember in bars that your drinks and *tapas* will often double in price if you choose to enjoy them outside rather than at the bar.

● Water

Contrary to popular opinion, Spanish **tap water** is perfectly safe to drink, although its flavour may be rather chemical. Mineral water, either *sin gas* (still) or *con gas* (carbonated), is also widely available in plastic bottles, useful on journeys.

Water shortages are becoming more pronounced. During the summer, parts of the coastal region experience restrictions and up to 12 hrs per day without supply.

Getting around

● Air

The main factor to be considered regarding air connections within Andalucía is that there are no services between Spain and Gibraltar. *Iberia* and *Aviaco* run a good service between national airports for around 14,000 Ptas depending on distance. Special rates are available for unlimited travel within Spain, information from *Iberia*, although this is probably not worthwhile if you are only visiting Andalucía.

● Train

Train buffs recognize that RENFE is Europe's most eccentric railway. It has improved its timetabling and rolling stock considerably over the last decade, but suffers from having an incomplete rail network and a huge length of single-track line, leading to much frustrating time spent in stations and sidings waiting for another train to pass. There are, in fact, over a dozen types of train service varying from the **TAV high speed train** connecting Madrid to Sevilla down to **'regional trains'** which stop at every hamlet. In between there is the **TALGO** which is fast and costly and the **TER** which is much the same. Then there are the ***expreso*** and the ***rápido***, which are neither quick nor fast. If travelling from Madrid or further, you might be advised to book an inexpensive ***litera*** (bed) on an overnight train rather than losing a whole day travelling. There is a good, cheap ***Motorail service***. There is a vast range of discounts and supplements, such as the 25% reduction on 'blue days'. RENFE offers a tourist card which allows travellers to use all lines and all scheduled trains in Spain for periods of 8, 15 or 22 days. The card is also valid on international trains, except the Madrid-Paris Talgo. The card is available only to travellers who normally live outside Spain. Details from RENFE's General Agency for Europe in Paris, T 47 235201. As lengthy negotiations about these arrangements can go on at ticket office windows, early booking (up to 60 days in advance) is recommended. There is a separate RENFE office in the centre of all the Andalusian cities. Students might consider the feasibility of a **EURAIL** pass or a **Tarjeta Joven**.

Try to take food and drink with you on the train, since anything you might be able to purchase en route will be expensive.

● Road

Bus The main cities of Andalucía are all linked by long distance coach services and this is a cheap form of travel. However the services are run by a number of private bus companies, whose offices may not be at the main bus station, while the bus station itself is often remote from town centre. *Horarios* (timetables) are rarely printed, but each separate company will usually display theirs on the wall of the bus station. It is worth getting an overall picture of the bus services from the local tourist office, who will also advise you of any cheap period tickets. Buses generally run on time and are clean, cheap and popular. **Long distance**

coaches have air conditioning in summer and often show videos. Book your ticket well before departure, as ticket offices have erratic hours and those who turn up at departure time are likely to encounter a full bus, especially in summer or at weekends.

Car (See also Documents above.) Vehicles drive on the right. Andalusian roads have improved beyond all recognition in the last decade, with the help of EU grants and money to improve the infrastructure for EXPO '92 at Sevilla. Most cities are now linked by motorways or dual carriageway roads. Some motorways, such as the A-4 from Sevilla, have tolls although there is a free, slower alternative running in parallel. Safety on the notorious N-340 between Málaga and Marbella is much improved, despite the volumes of confused tourists. However the standard of Spanish driving still leaves much to be desired; tailgating and dangerous overtaking are national sports. The worst times to be on the road are Jun and Jul when the tired Moroccan workers drive homeward in crowded, overladen vehicles from Europe towards the ferry, and the first and last weekends in Aug, when nearly every Spaniard is on the move. When turning left on main roads you should look out for a loop to the right, marked *cambio de sentido* as turning directly left is often illegal. Speed limits are 60 kph in built up areas, 100 kph on main roads and 120 kph on motorways.

Petrol is expensive in Spain. Self-service filling stations are rare, as are those accepting credit cards. Petrol comes in 3 types – Normal (92 octane), Super (96 octane) and diesel. The type of petrol required will generally be indicated on a hired car. *Sin plomo* (lead free) is beginning to appear in the tourist areas.

Spanish **parking** habits are appalling and most towns have now introduced parking meters, wardens and wheel clamping. Do not leave your car in the path of a procession or it will be towed away: getting it back will be expensive and stressful! Seat belts are now mandatory. In large cities it is worth paying the price for underground supervised parking (generally marked on tourist maps) rather than risking having your car broken into or stolen. This will cost between 1,000 and 2,000 Ptas per day. Check the parking area will be open if you plan to leave on Sun or a fiesta (see Security, **page 191**).

Radar speed traps are becoming increasingly common and on the spot payment of fines (compulsory for non-residents) will cost upwards of 15,000 Ptas. Discounts of 20% may be available. **NB**: being foreign is no defence and if you cannot pay, your car (or the hire car) will be impounded by the Guardía Civil until you do so. Cars flashing their lights coming from the opposite direction are probably warning you of a speed trap ahead.

Car hire The big international companies are based at the airports and tend to be fairly expensive. ATESA, a government-owned Spanish firm is cheaper and reliable. Small local firms will be even cheaper, but may not have efficient back-up services. Prices are currently in the region of 7,000 Ptas per day if hiring for a week with unlimited mileage. More reasonable rates may be obtained via home travel agents in advance.

Cycling Mopeds and bicycles can be hired, particularly on the coast. Cycling is a major sport in Spain and racing cyclists are common on the roads of Andalucía, mainly at weekends. Leisure cyclists are less obvious and mountain bikes have not penetrated the Spanish market to any great extent despite the suitable terrain. Motorists are obliged by law to give cyclists 2m clearance when overtaking, a manoeuvre which many Spaniards take seriously, often to the detriment of other road users. Bicycle helmets are almost unheard of although in some towns helmets are becoming compulsory for moped and motorbike users. Unfortunately, Spaniards generally prefer to carry these over their arm, so any visitors who value their heads are advised to make their own safety arrangements and take out insurance.

Hitchhiking Away from the tourist areas, hitchhiking will involve some long, hot waits. Spanish drivers are reluctant to pick up strangers, especially backpackers, and are likely to regard women hitchhikers without backpacks as prostitutes. This is not a recommended way of travelling and is frowned on by police.

Taxis are reasonably cheap, but not always metered. Since there are supplements (eg at night, from airports, for baggage) it is best to clarify the price in advance. Official rates should be displayed inside any licensed taxi. There are usually taxi ranks in city centres and it is possible to hail a cab in the street; look for the *libre* notice on the windscreen or the green light on the roof at night. Tourist information material will usually quote a local radio taxi number. Tipping should be approximately 10%. Nervous passengers will often need to keep their eyes shut!

● Walking

Andalucía has some marvellous walking country, but this is not a popular Spanish pastime and there are few marked footpaths with the exception of the National Parks. In some agricultural areas, walkers are likely to be attacked by farm dogs. A stout walking stick is advisable, particularly as rabies is not uncommon in Spain.

Communications

● Language

Andalusians use standard *castellano* (Castilian Spanish), although those familiar with accents in the centre and N of Spain may find this difficult to believe! The local intonation leaves words without endings and takes some time to become accustomed to. Those familiar with South American Spanish may have less difficulty. While locals will generally respond favourably to your efforts in their language, people in contact with tourists in bars, restaurants or shops are likely to speak English and possibly French or Italian.

● Postal services

The *Correos* is famous (or infamous) for its unreliability and slow service. Many letters still fail to reach their destinations at busy times, while a letter can take months to travel between neighbouring towns! The service within large cities is usually the least unsatisfactory. Look out for a yellow *buzón* (post box) or use those at post offices which are open standard hours. Urgent mail will cost you more and should be posted in a red *buzón*. Postage within Europe is currently 55 Ptas. Stamps are also available at tobacconists. Postcards are more likely to arrive before you return home if enclosed in an envelope.

● Telephone services

The most expensive place from which to make a call is your hotel room. The best means is an official Telefónica ***locutorio*** where you are assigned a cubicle and pay afterwards. The latter is particularly recommended for international calls as you will quickly run out of 100 Ptas pieces if you use a cabin on the street. Credit cards are often accepted. Disabled travellers are advised that some special lower level cabins are available in most towns.

To call abroad dial 07 and wait for the constant high pitched tone, then continue with the country code and the rest of the number. If calling Spain from abroad, the country code is 34 and the initial 9 of the regional code should be dropped.

The cheapest times to call are Mon-Fri 0000-0800 and 2200-2400, Sat 0000-0800 and 1400-2400 and all day Sun. Normal rate applies Mon-Fri 1700-2200 and other times are peak rate.

Holidays and festivals

The National Holidays affecting Andalucía are as follows:

1 Jan: New Years Day.
Jan 6: *Reyes.*
Mar/Apr: *Semana Santa*, Holy Week lasts a week climaxing on Good Friday.
1 May: Labour Day.
Jun: *Corpus Christi* (moveable date).
25 Jul: Santiago Day.
15 Aug: Assumption of the Virgin.
12 Oct: Columbus Day.
1 Nov: All Saints Day.
6 Dec: Constitution Day.
8 Dec: *Immaculate Conception.*
25 Dec: Christmas Day.

Nearly every province, city and even small village have local festivals – see town-by-town under **Festivals** for full details.

Entertainment

● Media

Newspapers; foreign language newspapers and sometimes magazines are readily available in cities and tourist areas and are usually only a day or two old. In smaller towns check on the vintage before you buy. In Gibraltar, British newspapers are available by the afternoon of the day they are printed. Informative publications such as *Sur* and *The Entertainer* are available in English along the Costa del Sol while most towns will have their own *What's On?* guide, usually only in Spanish.

Television: given the standard of Spanish television, a hotel room without one is probably an advantage. Besides you will doubtless have it inflicted on you in most restaurants and bars, usually at the same time as music!

● Sport

The streets are virtually empty when a major football match is taking place as every Spaniard is glued to his TV. More traditional sports include bullfighting, which is also televised, and hunting which takes the form of shooting anything that moves, down to the smallest bird. It would be hard to find a sport that is not practised somewhere along the coast. Even the smallest town boasts a modern sports centre. Golf is increasingly popular amongst the middle classes as are skiing and watersports.

Further reading

● Books

Background on the Moorish perspective can be obtained from Burchkardt, T (1972) *Moorish Culture in Spain*, London; Melville with Ubaydli (1992) *Christians and Moors in Spain, Vol III*, Warminster; Montgomery Watt (1965) *A History of Islamic Spain*, Edinburgh; and Wishaw, B (1986) *Arabic Spain*, London; *Hiking* by the Andalusian Tourist Board, 600 Ptas, gives sketch maps and descriptions of 200 walks in the region; Fletcher R, *Moorish Spain*, a good general history, (pub) Weidenfeld and Nicholas 1992, now Phoenix paperback (1994) price £12.99.

● Maps

Andalucía is covered by ***Michelin 446***, scale 1/400,000. ***Firestone T-29*** also covers the area, scale 1/200,000. **Walkers** will require the military maps, scale 1/50,000 published by ***Servicio Geográfico del Ejército***. The **Costa del Sol and Gibraltar** are covered by a Leisure Map, which is available in most bookshops. There is also a map of the **Sierra Nevada**, scale 1/50,000, published by the ***Federación Española de Montanismo***.

MOROCCO

Contents

Map

Introduction

An African country, so close that it is visible from the European side of the Mediterranean, Morocco contains in its 703,000 sq km, long sandy beaches, snow capped mountain peaks, barren desert, Roman ruins, colourful weekly markets and mud-built *ksour.* Avoid the places where tourists throng, ignore or refuse politely the attentions of 'guides' and discover the spirit of traditional Morocco.

Basics

OFFICIAL NAME al-Mamlakah al-Maghribiyah (Kingdom of Morocco)

NATIONAL FLAG Red background with a green pentacle in the centre

OFFICIAL LANGUAGE Arabic

OFFICIAL RELIGION Islam

INDICATORS *Population* 26.2 million. *Urban population* 49%. *Religion* Muslim (mainly Sunni) 98.7%, Christian 1.1%. *Birth rate* 32 per 1,000, *Death rate* 8 per 1,000, *Life expectancy* 62 men, 65 women. *GNP per Capita* US$1,030.

Environment

Land

Morocco at 458,730 sq km is only a fifth the surface area of Algeria or Libya and is slightly smaller than Spain. Morocco has 703,000 sq km if the Moroccan controlled territory of Western Sahara is included.

Borders

Morocco has a 1,835 km coastline from Saidia on the Algerian frontier to La Gouera on the border with Mauritania, of which only a fifth lies on the Mediterranean and the rest facing the Atlantic. Border problems affect both the Western Sahara where Moroccan occupation is challenged by the Saharois and the SE where the line with Algeria in the region of Tindouf is not firmly settled. Morocco itself has long-standing claims to the Spanish enclaves of Melilla and Ceuta. The border disputes periodically affect freedom of transit for travellers, through military action in the Western Sahara and occasional but temporary frictions elsewhere.

Main regions

Morocco is a country of great variety of topography in which huge mountain

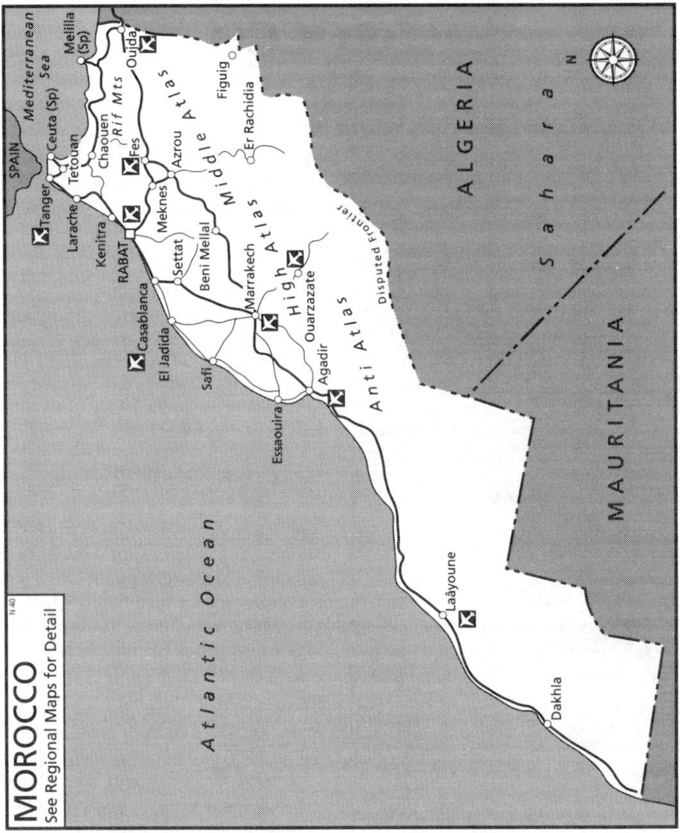

chains lying SW to NE dominate the relief (see map, **page 198**). The Rif rises sheer from the Mediterranean, few areas lying below 1,500m and the limestone peaks rising to 2,458m in Mount Tidiguin. Together with its outlier, the Jebala, these mountains all but seal off the rest of Morocco from coastal North Africa. To the S lie the Atlas Mountains in 3 great chains – the Middle Atlas, the High Atlas and, in the S, the Anti-Atlas.

The Middle Atlas attains heights of 3,290m and in parts is well wooded and fertile. The great mass of the High Atlas begins in a series of well watered hills on the Atlantic coast but rapidly achieves altitudes of 2,000m and peaks in the Jbel Toubkal at 4,165m high to the S of Marrakech. The country's richest agricultural area is in the plain of the Gharb and the inland basins around Fes and Oujda. The coastal region aligned along the Atlantic between Rabat and Essaouira and limited to the E by the High and Middle Atlas forms a broken plateau of 210m average height. To the E of the High Atlas and S of the Middle Atlas is the W fringe of the High Plateau which run in fuller form through Algeria. To the S of the Anti-Atlas is the Sahara desert.

The chains of the Atlas Mountains both by scale and height tend to present problems for communications. Travellers should plan their journeys through the limited number of passes such as those at Tizi-n-Test and Tizi-n-Tichka in daylight to maximize enjoyment of the scenery. Heavy snows and landslides can disrupt transport through these passes from time to time in the winter and early spring. In most years mountain snows melt away by June.

Traditional regional loyalties are influenced largely by the topographic divisions of the country and comprise (1) The Rif mountains in the N, (2) the agriculturally rich Rharb plain with Meknes and Fes, (3) the Haouz (region) of Marrakech, (4) the Sous which takes in the valley of the Oued Sous and the adjacent lands of the Anti-Atlas and (5) the Tafilalt desertic areas of E Morocco. Racial, tribal, linguistic and historical elements give these regions distinctive flavours among which there is as both rivalry and co-operation.

The average height for the country as a whole is 800m above sea level, making Morocco the most mountainous in North Africa.

There is a complex set of river systems, the majority running to the sea from the high mountain zone. In the NE the Moulouya takes its origins in the Middle Atlas and collects the streams of the E Rif before reaching the Mediterranean at Saidia. The Rif proper is drained by a series of fast flowing streams to the Mediterranean such as the Oued Bou Frah and the Oued M'Ter but to the S, surface water runs to the Sebou and its tributary the Ouerrha and thence to the Atlantic near Kenitra. The Jebala is drained by the Loukkos and its tributaries to the Atlantic coast at Larache. The Oum Er Rbia drains the vast areas of the Middle Atlas around Beni Mellal and the coastal plateau with the Oued Tensift taking flows from the area immediately to the S from the Marrakech basin. In the S of the country 2 important rivers, the Sous and the Draa run from sources in the High Atlas towards the Atlantic. On the E side of the High Atlas, streams such as the Rhéris and the Guir run S to inland drainage basins.

There are considerable variations in flows of streams in Morocco depending on the level of rain and snow fall in winter. The larger streams drawing their sources in the higher mountain areas flow for most of the year with snow melt persisting through as late as July but many oueds elsewhere are short-lived.

Climate

As is to be expected with a country as large as Morocco, there is a wide range of climatic types. The N coast falls into the Mediterranean climatic zone, though the usual régime of mild wet winters and warm dry summers is affected by the proximity of the Atlantic from which depressions move across N Morocco, bringing heavier and more reliable rainfall than in much of the rest of the Mediterranean basin. The Atlantic coast in the S feels the moderating influence of the ocean even in summer thanks to the cold Canaries current which drifts S along the littoral.

Away from the coasts, high altitudes and the influence of the Sahara make for a complex set of microclimates. In general, movement S and E brings the effect of the Sahara nearer, including higher daytime and lower night temperatures together with greater aridity. Increasing altitude in the Atlas reduces temperatures and also means very cold nights in exposed areas and higher risks of rain and snow in the months of Nov-Mar. Winters can be bitterly cold and wet throughout the Middle and High Atlas. Marrakech averages only 16°C in Jan but 33°C in June. Rabat on the coast has temperatures in Jan of 19°C against 25°C in June. Rainfall has great importance since the majority of people still rely on agriculture for a living. The rains in recent years have been above average and agriculture has thriven but periods of extreme drought are frequent and mean disaster for rural peoples. Rabat on the Atlantic coast receives an average of 530 mm of rain while Marrakech, further S and in the foothills of the High Atlas, receives only 230 mm. In the SE arid desertic conditions prevail. Rain is often in the form of heavy showers, some with intense thunder and lightening which can occur in the N at any season of the year. In July 1992, for example, there was an entire week in the Rif punctuated by thunder storms. During storms there is a high risk of flash floods, with oued beds carrying violent spates for short periods.

The prevailing winds in Morocco are from the Atlantic Ocean and variably W. Occasional S winds from the desert known as the *shergui* bring high temperatures, very low relative humidity and dust storm conditions, a miserable combination for the traveller. In the Tanger area and the Straits of Gibraltar a 'levanter' wind from the E can bring misty and cold conditions throughout the year.

Flora and fauna

Morocco has a wide variety of environments, so offering an interesting range of flora and fauna. Semi desert scrub is widespread, and vivid desert flowers appear after rain in contrast to the heavily wooded mountain areas and scented Mediterranean *maquis*. Migratory birds crossing the narrow Gibraltar Straits include huge storks and vultures and smaller (in comparison) buzzards and eagles. Distinctive coloured flamingoes, bee-eaters and hoopoes are found in many areas. Snakes and lizards are common and scorpions too on the drier areas. Larger mammals such as antelopes and gazelle are delightful sightings, the wild boars of the Rif and the Barbary Apes of the Middle Atlas perhaps less so.

Agriculture

Land use

Morocco, excluding Western Sahara, has proportionately more economically useable land than any other country of North Africa. Land use in 1989 was given as:

Land Use	**(%)**
Arable and orchard	20.7
Meadow and pasture	46.8
Forest and woodland	17.8
Other uses	14.5
Total	100.0

Source: *Encyclopaedia Britannica*

The 15,500,000 ha of land under cultivation carry crops of cereals, including wheat, barley and maize, sugar beet, citrus fruits, potatoes, tomatoes, olives and beans. Hill areas of the interior are intricately terraced for agricultural purposes, otherwise the main areas of cultivation are the plains and river valleys.

Land tenure

Moroccan land tenure conditions are dominated by large landlords, communal lands and religiously endowed land known in Morocco as *habous*. The landlord class is well entrenched politically and largely coopted by the régime with support and favour. No reform of tenure conditions has been attempted and large estates farmed by landlords using daily-paid labour or share croppers are the norm except for pockets of small landlords in the Sous and other limited areas. The land is very densely populated, forms of tenure apart, and more than 60% of people still live off farming either directly or indirectly. The country has experienced a steady drift of people from the land for some years, especially from the Rif and Atlas mountain zones where farming is made difficult by the hostile environment and limited material rewards. The above average rainfall of recent years has eased some of the strains in these communities but the respite will not be permanent.

Potential

Morocco has a number of important advantages over other countries of North Africa. It is comparatively well-watered over large areas. It has a vigorous and innovating agricultural community. The climate is generally kind, with potential for growing a wide range of crops such as citrus and early vegetables in demand in nearby Western Europe. The climate, varied terrain and rich heritage also open up possibilities for tourism for the same market. The endowment of raw materials is generous, giving Morocco a substantial role as a producer of phosphates, semi-precious stones and non-ferrous minerals. All these resources offer the basis for industrial processing. In many ways Morocco is currently in the throes of urbanization and modernization and seeking to make the best of its natural advantages to accommodate a 26 million population rapidly increasing at 2.4% each year and support a US$21,200 million foreign debt.

People

The population of Morocco was estimated in 1992 at 26.2 million, of which half was male. Although the crude birth rate has fallen sharply in recent years to 33 per 1000 population, potential fertility is high, as improved medical facilities enable improvements in the child survival rate. At the same time, death rates are also down to 8 per 1000 and life expectancy, now 63 years on average, will improve to swell the total population.

Morocco, unlike other Arab states, is an intermixture of Arab and Berber peoples. The two sections have intermarried over many centuries so that there are few pure residual groups. Differentiation at the present day is more linguistic that ethnic. The principal Berber-speaking areas are clustered in the mountainous areas of the country, reflecting the retreat of the Berbers to regions of refuge during the Arab invasions. For convenience there are 3 main Berber areas where somewhat different forms of Berber are spoken – *Rifian* in the N mountain zone, *Amazigh* among the communities in the Middle Atlas and *Chleuh* in the Sous and adjacent areas of the High Atlas Mountains. The Arab inhabitants came in waves of adventurers and conquerors in the long period of invasions, including those of the Beni Hillal and Beni Sulaim between the 7th and 12th centuries. Small numbers of other racial strains came into the population including an important Jewish community, some locally based among rural Berbers but reinforced from Iberia during the flight of Jews after the *reconquista* (see page 80) by highly educated and talented urban groups. Many Jews left Morocco after the foundation of the Jewish state of Israel in 1948. Trade with trans-Saharan Africa in goods and slaves introduced Negro blood, while Morocco's Mediterranean connection brought in traders from as far away as Malta and, in the late 19th century and 20th century, settlers from France and Spain during the colonial period.

The population is concentrated in the coastal cities and plains. Approximately half the population now lives in cities, the great concentrations being in Casablanca with 2.2 million, Rabat with 520,000, Fes with 450,000 and Marrakech with 440,000 (1988 figures). Areas of heavily settled land with 60-95 people per sq km are found round the Mediterranean and N Atlantic shores, notably in the Rif, Jebala, the Rharb plain and the coastal plateaux and valleys as far S as the Sous. Densities decline rapidly inland. Other than the great cities of Marrakech, Meknes and Fes, the inland area carries low population densities, averaging between 20-60 per sq km. The E and S of the country is sparsely settled with less than 20 people per sq km.

The population is fairly young on average. More than 40% of people are under the age of 15 and a mere 6% over 60. Educational progress has increased adult literacy rates to 50%. Some 37% of Moroccans enjoy the benefits of secondary and 1% tertiary education. Morocco is the poorest of the Maghreb states with average personal incomes estimated at US$1,030 in 1991. National income is maldistributed. The income of rural people is very low – less than US$250 per year in many cases and the urban poor, crowded in shanty areas, are little better off. Nutrition levels are improving, however, and aided by continued good rainfall there is a fragile air of prosperity to the country at the present time continued.

History since Independence

Morocco became independent on March 3, 1956 through the efforts of Sultan Mohammed V, who was determined that the Sultanate should be the supreme political power within independent Morocco. The only competitor for control of the newly independent country was the Istiqlal party. Although Istiqlal formed the first government of independent Morocco, the monarchy sought to widen political representation to balance its influence. The Royal Palace favoured the Mouvement Populaire, a rural-based, pro-Berber and royalist movement but continued to collaborate with Istiqlal until, in 1959, the party itself split, with a new, more radical wing becoming a separate political party, the Union Nationale des Forces Populaires, under Mehdi Ben Barka. This provided the monarchy with the opportunity to dominate the political process by arbitrating between the different political parties.

The government had to contend with a series of rural rebellions. The most serious of these which occurred in the Rif was crushed by Morocco's new army. Central government distrust of the Rif as a result of the rebellion still persists today.

King Mohammed V died unexpectedly in 1961 and was succeeded by his eldest son, Crown Prince Hassan. The new king had long been groomed for government, with an education both in Arabic in Morocco and in French at Bordeaux and with experience of government, both as an army commander and as premier in the period just before his father's death. Although the Sultanate has been traditionally powerful because of the religious legitimization of its occupant as Amir Al-Muminin (Commander of the Faithful), King Hassan II, like all new Sultans, faced immediate threats to his survival on the grounds of his personal competence. The new monarch sought to introduce limited parliamentary democracy within a constitutional monarchy. The experiment was not very successful and came to an end in Nov 1963, only a few months after it had been begun.

For the next 7 years King Hassan ruled without parliament, and Morocco was placed under a 5 year state of emergency. A new constitution, designed to increase the role of pro-Royalist parties, was promulgated in 1970 but the parliament elected in the subsequent elections was dissolved. A coup attempt against the king took place on the king's birthday on 10 July, 1971, involving an army-backed attack against him and his guests at his summer palace of Skhirat, just outside Rabat, and a simultaneous military attempt to take over the government. Both prongs of the plan failed, in the case of the attack on the king, largely because of his personal courage. The ringleaders were killed or later executed and widescale purges of army and government took place.

The coup highlighted the serious problems of growing corruption and ostentatious amassing of wealth within the administration. Economic conditions inside Morocco had also worsened. The government attempted to respond to both types of complaint, but on 26

Aug, 1972, units of the airforce attempted unsuccessfully to shoot down the king's aircraft. Once again, King Hassan survived largely because of his personal bravery. On this occasion it was established that the person responsible for both this attack and the coup attempt the preceding year was the minister of defence, General Mohammed Oufkir.

The Western Sahara issue

King Hassan tried to rally support throughout Morocco for the monarchy by reviving Morocco's claim to the Western Sahara. In 1974 Morocco began a diplomatic campaign to force Spain to evacuate the region. Inside the Western Sahara, a national movement, the **Polisario Front**, founded in 1973, had widespread support. Morocco persuaded the UN to place the competing claims for the Western Sahara before the International Court of Justice in The Hague. The Court determined in 1975 that Morocco did not have a sustainable claim of full territorial sovereignty. Morocco none the less assumed that the Court had backed its claim and, in a massive display of popular support, organized the **Green March**, a demonstration involving 350,000 Moroccans, to the border of the Western Sahara. Spain acquiesced in a secret deal and created a temporary tripartite administration in the Western Sahara between Morocco, Mauritania and Spain itself. The Polisario Front with Algerian and Libyan support was not prepared to accept Moroccan occupation and moved around 30,000 Sahrawi into refugee camps in Algeria and undertook a guerrilla war to liberate the Western Sahara. Although the Polisario Front succeeded in forcing Mauritania to abandon its occupation in 1978 (Morocco simply moved forces in instead) and in forcing Moroccan forces back into the major towns, it was not able to end Morocco's hold on the region. Starting in 1980, Morocco slowly won back control over virtually all the territory.

By the end of the decade, the UN had stepped in, with a proposal for a referendum over self-determination which was formally accepted by both sides. Morocco, however, made it clear that it would not abandon control of the Western Sahara.

Modern Morocco

Government

Morocco remains officially a constitutional monarchy. The system in use is one chamber, a House of Representatives, which is summoned and dissolved by the king at will. In theory, the House of Representatives can bring forward its own legislative programme but this can effectively be vetoed by the king who can also issue laws for endorsement through popular referendum. The king is commander of the armed forces. Four main political parties exist but those which fail to accept the central role of the monarchy are suppressed. The palace has attempted to recruit more support among the previously alienated intellectual classes and universities aided by improvements in living standards and promises of political liberalization.

The autocracy of the centre has been somewhat modified recently by the grant of limited autonomy to local administrations – city, town and region – and to the regional offices of the ministries so that decision-making can genuinely reflect local sentiments. Governors are appointed by the king. Administration in the Western Sahara is in the hands of the military.

Despite successes in foreign policy, King Hassan has not yet been able to democratize the political system without endangering the position of the monarchy. It remains to be seen to what degree he will be prepared to relinquish power after the forthcoming elections, in the face of considerable domestic political pressure to do so. The king's position has been rendered more malleable by the misjudgement of the popular mood his government had made during the war against Iraq in 1991. Moroccans generally had opposed the US-led Multinational Coalition, although the Moroccan government had initially supported it. Nonetheless, King Hassan has proved to be a consummately skilful political operator in the past and will, no doubt, show an equal sureness of touch in dealing with this current problem.

Economy

Traditional agriculture

Almost 40% of the labour force in Morocco is engaged in agriculture, by far the majority in traditional farming. In the traditional sector there are many peasant proprietors with smallholdings but most are tenant farmers. It is estimated that 33% of farmland is owned by 3% of the farmers. Much of the area of private land is under traditional tenancies with holdings of less than 10 ha. Forms of nomadism persist but there is an increasing tendency for livestock to be herded by shepherds rather than entire families on the move and for former nomadic groups to become settled. Similarly, the traditional valley cultivation areas of the high mountains are being deserted as the low returns and high demands on manual labour are rejected by people seeking easier living in the towns. Despite these changes, traditional farming remains the backbone of the economy, heavily involved with cereal growing and vegetable production in which the country, unusual for North Africa, is mainly self-sufficient. Peasant farmers and herders also own the bulk of the country's 17.5 million sheep, 6.1 million goats and 3.4 million cattle and a heavy concentration of fodder production results from this.

Modern agriculture

Modern farming is limited to the fertile plains of the Rharb, Marrakech and other smaller areas, much originally developed as medium-to-large scale enterprises by French settlers. The French have now been replaced by Moroccan owners, some of whom have also invested in reclaiming land elsewhere to take advantage of new irrigation water or modern farming methods. Most large scale farms produce export crops with concentration on citrus, where Morocco has been successful in breaking into Western European markets, sugar beet and specialist early vegetables such as potatoes and soft fruits. The modern farms have taken the largest share of newly provided irrigation water and state credits to the detriment of the small traditional units. There are some 8 million ha under cultivation with approximately 800,000 ha under irrigation. Farm output has expanded in recent years, helped by good rainfall:

Agricultural Output

('000 tonnes)	1989	1990
Wheat	3,927	3,711
Barley	2,990	2,138
Oranges	994	...
Potatoes	800	880

Source: *FAO*

Morocco has a major **fishing** industry, the 1989 catch being 520,354 tonnes and efforts are being made to develop the industry with foreign aid. Morocco is the world's largest producer of sardines. The over-exploited **forests** yield 2,136,000 tonnes per year of timber though a great deal of indiscriminate cutting is used to produce firewood.

Energy/petroleum

Morocco has very poor domestic sources of fuel. Its small reserves of oil in the Rharb are being run down very rapidly and, despite intensive exploration, few discoveries have been made. Oil production was 114,000 billion barrels in 1990 with natural gas at 50,741,000 cu m. There is some generally low grade coal available, 1990 output being 526,000 tonnes. Other than natural gas, internal output is inadequate to satisfy demand of 1,762,000 tonnes of coal and 41,544,000 billion barrels of oil, the balance of which is imported. Morocco is favoured by Saudi Arabia and the UAE and was given 50,000 barrels per day of oil to offset its energy problems. Increasing use is being made of hydroelectric power to support a total electricity consumption of 9,628,000,000 kwh. Much hydroelectric potential remains to be developed. The Meskala gas fields remain under-exploited as a result of cash shortages and technical difficulties.

Economic policies and plans

Morocco has put little reliance on economic planning and its experiences have been generally negative. In the 1960s there was an attempt in the national plan to foster rapid industrialization, mainly using state monopoly agencies. Other plans have tended at various times to be sectoral, providing for agriculture, industry or energy as separate entities but rarely extending, as was claimed, to an integrated national economic plan on the French model on which they were supposedly based. The indicative 1988-92 development plan forecast economic growth at 4% per year in real terms (see also Trends in the Economy, page 205). Current policies are designed to cultivate private investment in modern industry, transport and communications. Special incentives apply to investment by foreign interests in Morocco for which tax holidays and preferential treatment are offered.

A key element in Moroccan economic policy is alignment towards the EU. This arose originally from the close relationship between Morocco and France but has since been widened to include Germany, Spain and UK and the EU as an entity. Morocco has sought special terms of association with the EU to gain access for its products and labour. The anti-North Africa sentiment in France and elsewhere has not deterred the Moroccan government from continuing to look for closer commercial links with the EU.

Industry

Is now as important a contributor to national income as agriculture, being valued at MD39,000 million in 1990. It provides only a modest proportion of employment, however, with 15.5% against 39.2% in agriculture. A large segment of industry is still French-owned despite an accelerated programme of Moroccanization. Processing of agricultural products is a major activity, including olive pressing, flour milling, vegetable and fruit canning and milk treatment. There has been increasing success with using phosphates and other minerals as raw materials for domestic industrial use rather than simply for export. Phosphates in particular are the basis for a set of industrial developments related to phosphoric acid and other chemicals. Construction materials, above all cement, form another area of rapidly growing industrial activity. There is a strong traditional craft manufacturing industry located in the major cities, especially Marrakech, Meknes, Fes and Tanger. World famous for design and quality are leather goods, hand-woven rugs and textiles, pottery and metalwork.

Industrial Production 1989

	(tonnes)
Cement	4,641,000
Wheat products	2,592,000*
Carpets (sq m)	1,642,900
Tyres (units)	1,002,500*
Refined sugar	751,979

Source: *Encyclopaedia Britannica*
* 1988 figure

Trends in the economy

The war in the Western Sahara contributed towards Morocco's growing economic crisis. The government had, in 1976, decided to make an accelerated push for development in the hope of diffusing the growing social tensions which had contributed so much to the domestic political unrest of the early 1970s. Morocco pushed ahead with ambitious development plans using borrowed funds. However, by 1983, the costs of development, together with those of the war, had created an impossible situation.

Economic Structure 1990

	(%)
Agriculture	15.5
Mining	2.7
Manufacturing	18.7
Utilities	7.2
Other services	50.4
Construction	5.5
Total	100.0

In Sept 1983, Morocco had to reschedule its debt in the face of a worsening economic crisis and, despite the likelihood of the need to impose severe austerity measures, turned to the IMF for help. It had already had to face growing domestic discontent and there was every sign that this would recur. Indeed, the IMF economic restructuring plans, which insisted on the removal of consumer price subsidies on staples, such as sugar, flour and cooking oil, produced precisely that effect in Jan 1984. Riots swept the country and the government was forced to rein in its planned austerity measures. Since then the Moroccan government has plotted a very careful economic course, balancing off the need to satisfy its foreign creditors against domestic tensions. Its foreign debt rose from US$11 billion in 1983 to around US$23 billion in 1992. Morocco has also benefited from aid from the World Bank and from official aid donors, mainly in Europe. The result has been that the economy has been liberalized, the state sector is being dismantled and many observers now expect Morocco to begin slightly more rapid economic growth.

Symbolic of Morocco's desire for modernization has been a privatization programme, in which $2 bn of state companies will be handed over to private enterprise by 1995. Convertibility of the dihram for international transactions began in 1994, with full convertibility scheduled for later. In April 1994 the GATT (General Agreement on Tariffs and Trade) annual meeting was held in Marrakesh when Morocco officially joined the organization. Despite some criticism that membership of GATT will impede domestic economic growth, accession to membership was seen as endorsing Morocco's growing maturity as a developing economy.

Main economic indicators

Despite a brief surge in the value of national output in the late 1980s, the Moroccan economy is now growing only modestly at 2.4% per year, which, with population increasing at the same rate, means stagnation of personal incomes. Unemployment is officially put at 11% but, with seasonal unemployment and underemployment taken into account, a much larger number is less than gainfully employed. Inflation rose sharply in 1990-92 to close on 10% per year. Morocco's trade performance has been dismal, with a large deficit on current account.

ECONOMIC INDICATORS

	1988	1989	1990	1991
GDP (MD billion)	167	140	106	...
Imports (MD billion)	39	48	57	56
Exports (MD billion)	30	35	35	38
Balance of Trade (MD billion)	-9	-14	-16	-13
Inflation (1985=100)	114.3	117.9	126.0	138.1
Foreign Debt (US$ billion)	18.6	19.9	22.0	21.2

Source: IMF, *Encyclopaedia Britannica*

RABAT AND ENVIRONS

Contents

Maps

Rabat and Sale may lack for travellers the exotic appeal of Fes, Marrakech or Tanger, but these two cities have an impressive architectural legacy which reflects their long and turbulent histories. The massive but incomplete HassanTower, the Kasbah des Oudaias overlooking the river and sea, the ruins of the Merinid necropoli of Chellah, and the Abul Hassan Medersa with its intricate carving, are some of the most important and rewarding sites in Morocco. The medinas of Rabat and Sale are small and easy to explore, with beautiful houses and public buildings, and interesting markets and shops. The French built *ville nouvelle* (new town) retains much of the ambience of the colonial capital city, and has a surprisingly relaxed atmosphere. It is a comfortable and convenient place to stay, and perhaps a better first-stop than Casablanca.

RABAT

Pop 518,816 (1982). *Alt* 65m. *Best season* Fine all year round, as the humid summer, with high Jul and Aug peak temperatures, is relieved by sea breezes.

History

City of Old and New

The name 'Rabat', a shortened and corrupted form of 'Ribat al-Fath', literally a 'monastery of conquest', indicates an initial role as a religious retreat and fortification. The city, located on the bank of the Oued Bou Regreg, with the kasbah on a promontory overlooking both the Atlantic Ocean and the estuary, lies opposite its historic rival, Sale. Rabat, capital since 1912, is Morocco's second largest city. The ambitiously extensive city walls laid out by the third Almohad Sultan Abu Yusuf Ya'qub al-Mansur now enclose, with the river and the sea on the remaining sides, the kasbah, the old medina, and the core of the *ville nouvelle*, the old and new directly alongside each other unlike the more common French pattern found in Fes, Marrakech and Meknes, where the new town was built some distance from the medina.

Early origins

Sala Colonia and the Ribat The first settlement of this area was probably outside the present city walls, on the site of the later Merinid mausoleum of **Chellah**. There is conjecture of prior Phoenician and Carthaginian settlement, but it is with the Roman **Sala Colonia** that Rabat's proven urban history began. Ac-

Climate: Rabat

	Jan	Feb	Mar	Apr	May	Jun	Jul	Aug	Sep	Oct	Nov	Dec	Av/Tot
Max (°C)	17	18	20	22	23	25	28	28	27	25	21	18	23
Min (°C)	8	8	10	11	14	16	18	18	17	15	12	9	13
Rain (mm)	86	65	67	49	21	7	0	2	9	35	91	103	525

corded municipal privileges, Sala Colonia was the most southwesterly town of the Roman Empire for the 2 centuries they ruled it, a trading post on the Oued Bou Regreg (which has since changed course), and a defensive settlement, located close to the line of frontier outposts, running through the modern-day suburbs to the S of the city.

Sala Colonia was then occupied by Berbers from the 8th to the 10th century, but their heretic Kharajite beliefs represented a challenge to the orthodoxy of the inland Muslims. In the 10th century the Zenata tribe built a fortified monastery, or *ribat*, on the site of the current **Kasbah des Oudaias**, as a base from which to challenge the heretics on both sides of the river, and their supporters, the powerful Berghouata tribe. This led

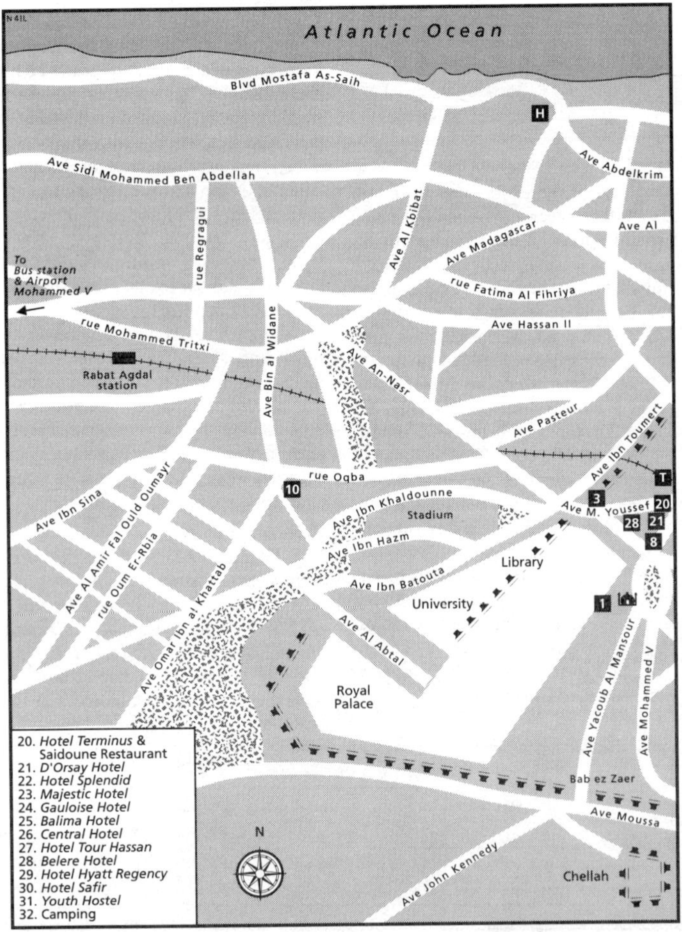

eventually to the abandonment of Sala Colonia.

Rabat under the Almohads
The *ribat* was used by the Almoravid Dynasty, but it was the Almohad Sultan Abd al-Mumin who redeveloped the settlement in 1150, transforming it into a permanent fortress town with palaces, the main mosque which still stands, reservoirs, and houses for followers, and using it as an assembly point for the large Almohad army. However, it was his grandson, Ya'qub al-Mansur, who from 1184 carried out the most ambitious programme of development, with his dream of Rabat as one of the great imperial capitals. He ordered an enormous city to be built, surrounded by extensive walls. These walls were probably completed by 1197, and ran along 2 sides of the city,

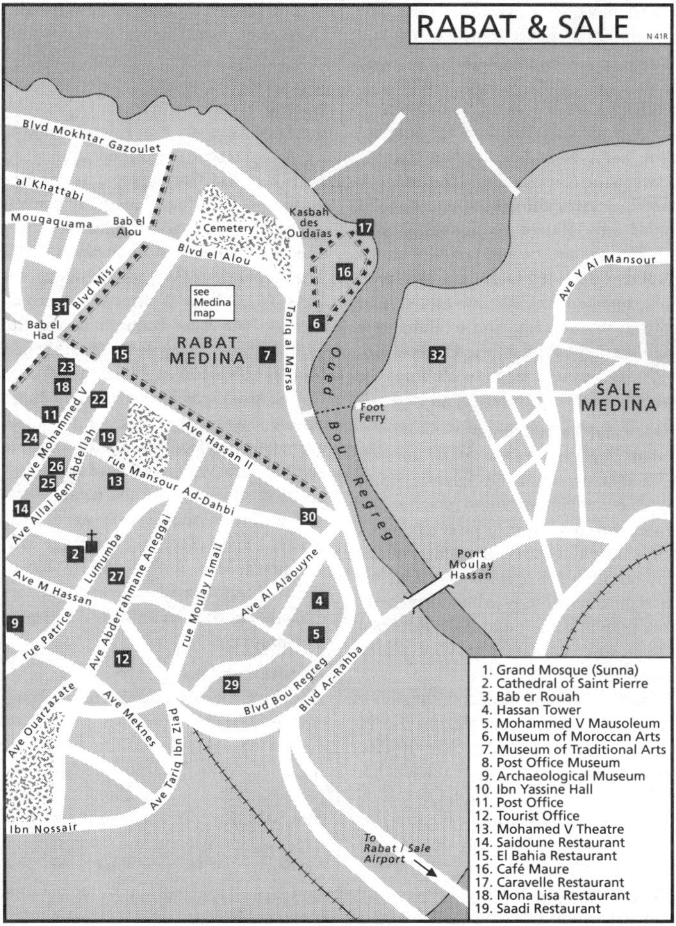

broken by 4 gates, most notably the **Bab er Rouah**. A grid of broad streets, residential quarters, a covered market, public baths, hotels, workshops and fountains were built, along with a new gateway to the medina. A bridge to Sale, and its **Grand Mosque**, were also constructed.

Yet the most impressive monument from this period, the Hassan Mosque, was never completed. Projected to be the largest mosque in western Islam, the vast minaret never reached its full height, and little more than pillars remain of the rest. Ya'qub al-Mansur's death in 1199 led to the abandonment of the project. Rabat then fell into decline, some of it destroyed in fighting between the Almohads and Merinids, so that Leo Africanus, visiting in 1500, found only 100 or so houses, 2 or 3 inhabited quarters, and very few shops. As Rabat declined under the Merinids, Sale prospered. The dynasty's most noteworthy contribution to Rabat was the funeral quarter on the **Chellah** site, with its impressive mausoleums, but even that was eventually neglected.

Piracy and Andalusians

Rabat's fortunes did not revive until the 17th century, when the Atlantic Ocean became more important to international trade, and corsairing, or piracy, boomed. For a time Rabat was the centre of this piracy, with 'the Sallee Rovers' of historical repute more likely to have been based here than in present-day Sale. Robinson Crusoe was a fictional captive of 'a Turkish rover of Salle'.

Rabat also benefited from the flow of Muslims leaving Spain during the Inquisition. First rejected by Sale, the Hornacheros settled in the Rabat kasbah in 1609, and the other Andalusians in the Rabat medina in 1610. The medina they settled in was considerably smaller than the city Ya'qub al-Mansur had envisaged, as indicated by the 17th century rampart, which, when built, demarcated the extent of the settlement, and now runs between the medina and the *ville nouvelle*. The area beyond this rampart was used for agricultural purposes, and most of it remained undeveloped until the arrival of the French. The Andalusian influence can be observed in the medina, in the regularity of the street plan, in the motifs on doors, and in the past and present styles of decorative arts and crafts.

A fierce rivalry existed between the Hornacheros and the Andalusians, both of which had set up autonomous city-states, and the period 1610 to 1666 was marked by intermittent strife between the 3 towns of the Bou Regreg estuary. By 1627 these were united under the control of the Hornacheros as the Republic of the Bou Regreg, a control against which the Andalusians frequently rebelled, most notably in 1636. The Republic lost its independence in 1638. In 1641 the 3 cities were united, and in 1666 were brought under the authority of the Alawite Sultanate, when Moulay al-Rachid captured the estuary.

The principal background to these conflicts was the struggle for control over the gains from piracy, a profitable activity. Piracy was a form of trade, but also fed off trade, and the legal, illegal and governmental aspects were often closely linked. Rabat was popular with corsairs, many of whom originated in the Mediterranean, because, unlike several other ports, it had not been occupied by Europeans.

Alawite Capital

Under the Alawites, Rabat changed considerably. Trade and piracy were taken over as official functions, the profits going to the state. The port declined, replaced initially by Mogador (Essaouira). Moulay al-Rachid took over the kasbah, expelling its residents and strengthening the walls, and built the **Qishla** fortification to overlook and control the medina. However Sultan Moulay Ismail, most closely associated with Meknes, ignored Rabat, and broke the power of the corsairs.

From 1768, Mohammed Ibn Abdellah had a palace built in Rabat, and since then the Alawite Sultans have maintained a palace there, making the city one of their capitals. Increased trade with Europe in the 19th century temporarily revitalized Rabat's role as a port, but it was gradually supplanted, perhaps because of the shallow mouth of the Bou Regreg and the poor harbour facilities which were inadequate for larger boats, but also because newer towns and cities, notably Casablanca, were more easily controlled by Europeans. In 1832 the rebellious Oudaia tribe were settled in the abandoned kasbah, giving it its current name, whilst the kasbah continued to be administered separately from the medina until the 20th century.

Rabat in the Twentieth Century

The French landed in Rabat in 1907, and occupied it until 1912, when the Protectorate was officially declared. Fes was initially chosen as the capital, but as it remained a centre of dissidence and rebellion, and the inland areas remained insecure, Rabat was its replacement, formally confirmed in 1913. The first Resident-General, Lyautey, with his architect Henri Prost, planned and built the majority of the new capital, the *ville nouvelle*, both within and outside Ya'qub al-Mansur's walls, leaving the medina much as they found it. Rabat's economy today is primarily based on its role as Morocco's capital, with massive numbers on the government pay-roll. The economic growth of the city has continued to attract migrants from the countryside, with population growth outstripping the supply of housing. Thus Rabat today is a city of extremes, with streets of ostentatious and luxurious villas not far from crowded, decrepit and insanitary tin-shack slums, or *bidonvilles*.

ACCESS Air Regular buses from **Airport Mohammed V** to Rabat, taking 90 mins, cost MD50. Tickets are sold at the booth outside the front entrance of the airport, from where the buses depart, to both Casablanca and Rabat. The buses arrive in Rabat outside the *Hotel Terminus*, Ave Mohammed V, beside the station. Grand-taxis, which also leave just outside the airport, are expensive as they cannot be shared. The local **Rabat-Sale airport**, T 727393, off the P1 Sale to Meknes road, has flights from Casablanca, Oujda, Tetouan and Paris. For the town centre follow the signs to Sale, cross the river and continue up Ave Hassan II. There is a train service into town from the new station.

Train The main railway station, **Rabat Ville**, T 767353, is on Ave Mohammed V, in the city centre, close to the main hotels. There are luggage lockers, but they are often all occupied. There is another station, **Rabat Agdal**, T 772385, in rue Abderrahman El Ghafiki, closer to the university, the newer ministry buildings and residential areas, but otherwise not convenient. All trains from Marrakech, Oued Zem, El Jadida and Casablanca stop at both stations, as do some of those from Tanger, Meknes, Fes and Oujda.

Road From Tanger and N the P2 brings the traveller through Sale, as does the P1 from Meknes, Fes and E. To get to Rabat, from the roundabout near the Bab Mrisa, cross the Pont Moulay Hassan and turn right, up to Ave Hassan II. From Casablanca and the S on the P36, turn right along Ave An-Nasr, and into the walled city via Bab er Rouah. **Bus** The principal bus terminal, for both CTM buses and those of the private lines, is inconveniently located at Place Zerktouni, 3 km out from the centre. Catch a No 30 bus to Ave Hassan II, or a petit-taxi for about MD10.

Things to see

Routes through the city

The Kasbah des Oudaias, the medina and the Chellah have to be explored on foot.

Start at the kasbah, carry along Tarik al Marsa to the **Hassan Tower** and the **Mohammed V Mausoleum**. From there follow Blvd Abi Regreg, Ave Tariq Ibn Ziad and Ave Moussa Ibn Nossair to the **Chellah**. Enter the *ville nouvelle* by **Bab ez Zaer** to the **Sunna Mosque**. Turn along Ave Moulay Hassan and through **Bab er Rouah** to view it from the outside. Pass down Ave Ibn Toumert, past **Bab el Had** to **Bab el Alou**, and right into the medina. Turn right down Blvd Mohammed V and carry on through the medina to Ave Hassan II. Those with transport must park here and explore the medina and the *ville nouvelle*. Blvd Mohammed V is the only drivable road in the medina, Ave Mohammed V in the *ville nouvelle* is one way S from Ave Hassan II to the post office.

The Walls and Gates

Rabat has 3 sets of walls: the **Almohad** wall around the kasbah, the 5 km of **Almoravid** wall around much of the city centre dating from the 12th century, and the wall now separating the **medina** and the *ville nouvelle* built by the Andalusians in the early 17th century. The walls are mainly built of *pisé* or *pisé*-cement and, whilst they have inevitably been considerably repaired, strengthened and adapted, they are much as they were originally. There are 4 gates still standing in the Almoravid wall: **Bab el Alou**, **Bab el Had**, **Bab er Rouah** and **Bab ez Zaer**. **Bab er Rouah** is the most important and impressive of these, but **Bab el Had** is worth seeing. Located at the intersection of Ave Hassan II and Ave Ibn Toumert, the substantially remodelled **Bab el Had** has a blind arch and is flanked by two 5-sided stone towers. Currently you pass through 2 chambers, at different levels. A number of traditional scribes work in this area.

Bab er Rouah, at Place An-Nasr, can best be approached along Ave An-Nasr from outside the walled city, when its scale and beauty is most obvious. The gate is now used as a gallery, and is only open when exhibitions are being held, so it is well worth taking any opportunity to see inside it. The arch of the gate is framed by a rectangular band of Kufic inscription. Between the arch and the frame there is a floral motif, with the scallop symbol on either side. The arch itself, with an entrance restored by the Alawites with small stones, is made up of 3 different patterns, of great simplicity, producing the overall effect of a sunburst confined within a rectangle. The entrance passage inside follows a complex double elbow. This, combined with the 2 flanking bastions outside, indicate that the gate was defensive as well as ceremonial.

Kasbah des Oudaias

The Kasbah des Oudaias, originally a fortified *ribat*, later settled by Andalusians, is both beautiful and peaceful, and well worth a visit. It can be reached along rue de Consuls through the medina, Blvd el Alou along the N of the medina, or by Tarik al Marsa along beside the Oued Bou Regreg. There is a number of entrances to the kasbah, but the best is by the imposing **Bab al-Kasbah** gateway at the top of the hill. At this point avoid the unofficial guides as the kasbah is very small and quiet and easily explored without assistance.

Bab al-Kasbah was located close to the **Souq el-Ghezel**, the main mediaeval market, whilst the original palace was just inside. The gateway was built by Ya'qub al-Mansur in about 1195, inserting it into the earlier kasbah wall built by Abd al-Mumin, and it did not have the same defensive role as the **Bab er Rouah**. The gate has a pointed *outrepassé* arch surrounded by a cusped, blind arch. Around this there is a wide band of geometric carving, the common *darj w ktaf*. The 2 corner areas between this band and the rectangular frame are composed of floral decoration, with, as in the **Bab er Rouah**, a scallop or palmette in each. Above this are more palmettes, a band of Koranic lettering, and on top a wide band of geometric motifs. There would originally have been a porch roof. The entrance to the kasbah is via stairs and through two rooms, a third room being closed to the public. The inside of the gate is also decorated, though more simply.

Inside the gate, the main street, rue al-Jama, runs past the **Kasbah Mosque**, dating from 1150, the oldest in Rabat. It leads to the semaphore platform, where there is a carpet factory. This gives an excellent view over the sea, the Oued Bou Regreg with its natural sand-bar defence, and Sale. Steps down from the platform lead to the *Caravelle Restaurant*, in a small fort built by an English renegade, and the popular, but not too clean, kasbah beach.

Coming back from the platform take the second on the left, rue Bazzo. This narrow and cobbled street with steps winds down through the whitewashed Andalusian-style houses to the bottom of the kasbah, directly into the *Café Maure* alongside which is a small but beautiful Andalusian style garden, developed by the French, which is also a pleasant place for a rest. On the other side of the garden is a section of the **Museum of Moroccan Arts** exhibiting traditional dress from many regions of Morocco. In the building of a 17th century palace, where Moulay Ismail once lived, is the main **Museum of Moroccan Art** (0830-1200, 1500-1830, except Tue) entrance fee MD10, with arms, instruments, jewels and carpets. This is worth seeing just for the interior, and the decoration of the building. There are a number of reception rooms around a central courtyard, in particular seek out the palace baths, the *hammam*.

The Medina

Most of the buildings in the medina date at the earliest from the arrival of the Andalusian Muslims in the 17th century. The Andalusian character of the buildings and decoration sets the medina apart from those such as Marrakech. Whilst Rabat medina is smaller and more limited in the range of markets, shops and buildings than Fes, Marrakech and Meknes, and less distinct in its way of life, its accessability, size and the simplicity of its grid-like street pattern make it a good first experience of Moroccan medinas. Physically close to the *ville nouvelle*, the medina is very different in the design of buildings and open space, and the nature of commerce and socialization. It as an interesting and safe place to wander, with little risk of getting lost or hassled. Blvd Mohammed V is one of the major arteries of the medina, but the second right, **rue Souika**, and its continuation **Souq es Sebbat**, are the main shopping streets, with an unusually wide range of shops for such a small area. The **Grand Mosque**, on rue Souika, is much restored Merinid. Just opposite the **Grand Mosque**, on a side turning, is the interesting stone façade of a fountain, now a bookshop, but dating from the 14th century reign of the Merinid Sultan Abu Faris Abd al-Aziz.

Souq es Sebbat leads down to the river, past the *mellah* on the right. The *mellah* is the former Jewish area, still the poorest area of the medina, with small cramped houses and shops, and narrow streets. It is a triangular zone, bound by rue Ouqasson (the continuation of rue des Consuls), the medina wall, and the river. As in many Islamic cities, Jews were kept in one area, for both protection and control, and so that they would be easily accessible to the seat of power to carry out tasks Muslims could not perform. There are few Jews left in the *mellah*, most having emigrated to Israel. The streets around here now support an interesting *joutia*, or flea market.

Turning left off **Souq es Sebbat** one can follow the rue des Consuls to the kasbah. This road was where many European consuls and important merchants once lived. Rue des Consuls is

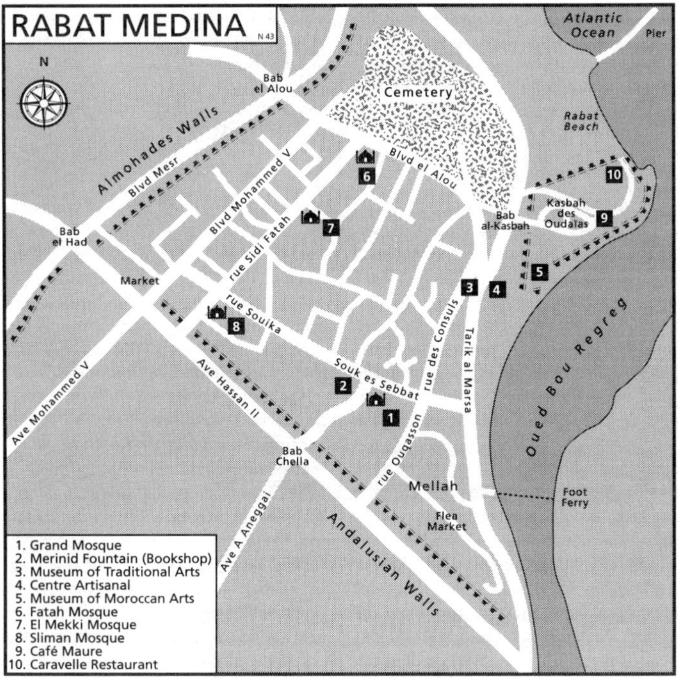

now lined with the more expensive shops selling leather work and carpets. There is a carpet market on the street on Tue and Thur mornings. Turn right at the end of rue des Consuls and you are in Tarik al Marsa. On the left is the **Museum of Traditional Arts**, with crafts and arts. Opposite is the **Centre Artisanal**, with fixed prices for looking at, or buying, craft products. Open 0830-1200, 1500-1830, entrance fee MD10.

The Hassan Tower and Mohammed V Mausoleum

The Almohad **Hassan Tower** dominates the skyline of Rabat, and even unfinished it is an impressive building, testimony to Ya'qub al-Mansur's unfulfilled vision of his imperial capital. It overlooks the Oued Bou Regreg and Sale, and can be reached most easily by Blvd Bou Regreg, or by turning right at the end of Ave Hassan II.

The building of the mosque was abandoned on Ya'qub al-Mansur's death in 1199, leaving most of the minaret, but just part of the columns and walls. All the portable parts, tiles, bricks and the roofing material, have been taken for use in other buildings. The remains of the mosque were excavated and reconstructed by the French and Moroccans. The mosque would have followed a T-shape, with the main green-tile roof section between the minaret and the modern mausoleum. The *mihrab* (prayer niche) would have been in the S *qibla* wall, where the mausoleum is, and therefore was not properly orientated towards Mecca. It is also unusual to find the minaret opposite the *qibla* wall.

The minaret of the Hassan Mosque, when completed, would have been 4 times as high as it was wide, with the lantern making it 5 times as high. This is in keeping with the classic North African minaret style, as with the **Koutoubia** in Marrakech (page 299 and the **Giralda** in Sevilla (page 164). The incomplete minaret is 45m high, and would have been 64m high when completed, 80m when including the lantern. This compares to 57m for the Koutoubia and 74m for the Giralda. It is decorated with geometric designs, there being no inscription or floral decoration, but their scale and clarity of execution makes them clearly discernible from a distance. Each of the faces has a different composition, interweaving designs, arches and windows. The common Moroccan motif of *darj w ktaf*, resembling a tulip or a truncated *fleur de lys*, and formed by intersecting arcs with superimposed rectangles, is present, notably on the N and S upper registers.

Adjacent to the **Hassan Tower** is the **Mohammed V Mausoleum**, dedicated to the first king of independent Morocco and father of the current king, and dating from 1971. The tomb chamber, but not the mausoleum's mosque, is open to non-Muslims, and shows a number of traditional Moroccan motifs and techniques of religious architecture, with a carved and painted ceiling, the carved marble tomb, and the *zellij* tiles (mosaic) on the walls. Open 0800-1830 daily, entrance free.

The Chellah

The Chellah is reached by going past the main **Sunna Mosque** in the *ville nouvelle*, and carrying on S down Ave Yacoub al Mansour and through the **Bab ez Zaer**. This walled Merinid necropolis was built between 1310 and 1334, approximately on the site of the Roman town of **Sala Colonia**. The second Merinid Sultan, Abu Yusuf Ya'qub built a mosque and Abul Hassan then built the enclosure wall and the gate. The Roman ruins at the bottom of the **Chellah** enclosure have been excavated, and include a forum, baths, shops and a temple.

The gate is smaller and less impressive than the Almohad **Bab er Rouah**. It is decorated with carving, and coloured marble and tiles, with an octagonal tower on either side. The entrance is on the elbow pattern and you turn right through 3 chambers, before walking out into a wild and lush garden. To get to the mausoleum take the wide path to the bottom, where it is on the right, the Roman ruins on the left. On the far right are the tombs of local saints, surrounding a pool.

The door into the Merinid mausoleum, facing the Roman ruins, opens into the mosque of Abu Yusuf Yaqub, which consists of a small courtyard, followed by a 3-aisled sanctuary. The arched doorway on the left has the remains of floral and geometric *zellij* in 5 colours. Entering the sanctuary the *mihrab*, is straight ahead. A door to the right leads to an area including the remains of the mosque's minaret, and a pool. From this one enters the area of tombs, including those of Abul Hassan and his wife Shams al-Dawha. The remaining area of the mausoleum is taken up with the *zawia*, or mosque-monastery, of Abul Hassan. This includes a minaret, and a ruined funerary chapel, with very intricate carving, notably on the exterior of the S wall. The main part of the *zawia* is a rectangular courtyard with a small mosque at one end, and surrounded by small cells. It had a pool surrounded by a columned arcade, the bases of the columns still discernible. The *mihrab* has some intricate stucco carving. The tiles on the upper portion of the minaret are perhaps recent, but the original effect would have been a bright tiled structure.

The Ville Nouvelle

This contains some fine examples of

French colonial architecture, which in Morocco incorporated an element of local design tradition, and is called *Mauresque*. Note particularly the main post office (PTT Centrale) and the Bank al-Maghrib, both on Ave Mohammed V. This main boulevard is wide and particularly impressive in the evening, when it is crowded with people out for a stroll. Off to the left, opposite the railway station, is the **Catholic Cathedral of Saint Pierre**. Below the station is the Parliament building. Just past the *Hotel Terminus* is a small postal museum exhibiting stamps. The 18th century but much restored **Sunna Mosque** dominates the view up Ave Mohammed V. To the left of the mosque is the **Archaeological Museum** (open 0830-1200, 1430-1800, closed Tue), which has a small but impressive collection, particularly of Roman bronzes, mainly from Volubilis. To the right of the **Sunna Mosque** is the vast palace complex, where King Hassan II spends part of the year. It is not possible to go beyond this point up the central avenue of the complex.

Festivals

Rabat is the best place for the state festivals, the Coronation on 3 Mar, the Green March on 6 Nov and Independence Day on 18 Nov.

Local information

● Accommodation

Price guide:			
AL	US$90+	D	US$20-40
A	US$75-90	E	US$10-20
B	US$60-75	F	under US$10
C	US$40-60		

In summer hotels can fill up early. There are not many good, cheap hotels in Rabat. The budget hotels in the medina, for which prices can be very flexible, are in general best avoided. The centre of the *ville nouvelle* provides a wide range of good hotels. **AL** *Hotel Hyatt Regency*, Souissi, T 771234, F 773039, 192 rms, former Hilton, luxurious, set in an extensive park on the road out past the **Chellah**, rather far from the city centre, but it has almost everything, including a business centre, mini golf-course, art gallery, pool and *hammam*; **AL** *Hotel de la Tour Hassan*, 26 Ave de Chellah, T 733815, Tx 32788, 158 rms, convenient location, perhaps the most atmospheric of the top class hotels, dating from the Protectorate, excellent restaurant, popular nightclub and bar, no pool; **AL** *Hotel Safir*, Place Sidi Makhlouf, T 731091, F 725408, convenient, at end of Ave Hassan II overlooking the river and Sale, built around a courtyard in an approximation of a Moroccan palace, quite luxurious, pool, most other facilities and services.

C *Hotel Belere*, 33 Ave Moulay Youssef, T/F 769901, 763749, Tx 31793, conveniently located near the station.

D *Hotel Balima*, 173 Ave Mohammed V, BP 173, across from the station, T 707755, 708625, Tx 31738M, popular café-bar, restaurant, snack bar, salon de thé, nightclub, formerly top hotel in Rabat, a faded grandeur, reasonably priced; **D** *Hotel d'Orsay*, 11 Ave Moulay Youssef, near station, T 761319, convenient, less interesting than *Balima*.

E *Hotel Splendid*, 24 rue Ghazza, T 723283, good rooms, friendly staff, pleasant courtyard with meals from restaurant opposite; **E** *Hotel de la Paix*, 2 rue Ghazza, T 722926, 732031, not very friendly, some rooms no bath, no communal shower; **E** *Hotel des Oudaias*, 132 Blvd el Alou, near the kasbah, T 732371, convenient for sightseeing, and well-fitted, one of the few respectable hotels in the medina; **E** *Hotel Central*, 2 rue Al Basra, T 767356, beside the *Balima*, well-run hotel, very good and crazily decorated double rooms, singles not so good, one of the best cheap options for sharers; **E** *Hotel Gauloise*, 1 rue Hims, off Ave Mohammed V, T 723022, 59 tatty rooms; **E** *Hotel Majestic*, 121 Ave Hassan II, T 722997, cheap and recommended.

F *Hotel Berlin*, 261 Ave Mohammed V, T 703435, cheapest in the *ville nouvelle*. There are a number of small, cheap hotels in the medina; **F** *Hotel des Voyageurs*, best of these 3, *Hotel du Marché* and *Hotel Alger*, are all on rue Souq Semara, second left off Ave Mohammed V, tatty; **F** *Maghreb al Jedid*, *Hotel El Alam*, best of these 3, and *Hotel Marrakech*, all on rue Sebbahi, right off Ave Mohammed V, tatty and cheap.

● Youth hostel

43 rue Marassa, Bab el Had, T 25769, 60 beds,

MD25 bed/breakfast for IYHA members, kitchen, basic and friendly, you can make an identity card here, with a photograph and your passport. Train 1.2 km and bus 150m.

Camping

Is an inconvenient option in Rabat, the two nearest sites being Sale and Temara (**see pages 222** and **222**).

Places to eat

Price guide:
♦♦♦Expensive; ♦♦average; ♦cheap.

Most higher quality restaurants are located within the walled *ville nouvelle*. A range of fairly cheap restaurants are to be found throughout the city, but the budget options, small Moroccan canteens and café-restaurants, are located in the medina, along Ave Mohammed V, rue Souika, rue Sidi Fatah and adjacent streets. This is also a good area to wander and sample juices, pâtisseries, snacks and sandwiches, particularly from the *laiteries* that make sandwiches to order. ♦♦♦***Justine's***, in *Hotel Hyatt Regency*, Souissi, T 771234, reservations required, very expensive, prestigious, with a large range of European dishes; ***El Andalous***, in *Hotel Hyatt Regency*, Souissi, T 771234, reservations required, vast selection of Moroccan dishes, live music; ***La Couronne*** in *Hotel de la Tour Hassan*, 26 Ave de Chellah, T 721402, reservations recommended, high standard international cuisine, good value and very good service, music in the evening; ***El Mansur***, in *Hotel de la Tour Hassan*, 26 Ave de Chellah, T 721402, reservations recommended, very good Moroccan food, particularly the *pastilla* and the *tagines*, with the option of eating at low tables, Moroccan music accompanies the meal; ***Kanoun Grill***, in *Hotel Chellah*, 2 rue d'Ifni, T 764052, reservations recommended, a big menu of good Moroccan food, particularly grilled.

♦♦***Le Relais du Père Louis***, Zankat Ibn Haoqual, behind the *Hotel Balima*, T 769629, good Moroccan and French food, licensed; ***Les Fouquets***, 285 Ave Mohammed V, T 708007, good Moroccan food and service, specializes in fish, licensed; ***Hotel Balima***, 173 Ave Mohammed V, continental cuisine on the terrace or inside, but better for drinks; ***La Mamma***, 1 Zankat Tanto, Italian food; ***Café Restaurant Saadi***, 81 bis Ave Allal Ben Abdellah, T 769903, good Moroccan meals, licensed; ***Hong Kong***, 261 Ave Mohammed V, Vietnamese/Chinese food.

♦***Café Anaouil***, Ave Moulay Abdellah, good *tagines*, salads and juices, European food also; ***Mona Lisa***, Passage Derby, 258 Ave Mohammed V, reasonable *tagines*, Moroccan food, salads; ***Restaurant Saidoune***, mall off Ave Mohammed V, opposite *Hotel Terminus*, very good value Lebanese restaurant, friendly, and with some tasty dishes; ***Restaurant El Bahia***, Ave Hassan II, in the wall near junction with Ave Mohammed V, Moroccan food in a courtyard, good value, erratic service; ***Restaurant de l'Union***, 260 Ave Mohammed V, medina, cheap but unexciting meals; ***Restaurant de la Jeunesse***, Ave Mohammed V, medina, cheap snacks and meals; ***Elfarah Restaurant***, 10 Zankat Sidi Mohammed El Ghazi, 3rd right off Ave Mohammed V, medina, Moroccan canteen: cheap, basic, clean and good, set lunch, *harira* and *brochettes* in the evening; ***Café Taghzout***, rue Sebbahi, similar as above in nearby street.

Bars

Piccadilly Piano Bar, in *Hotel Hyatt Regency* popular for those who can afford it, nightly jazz band; ***Hassan Bar***, in *Hotel de la Tour Hassan*, 22 Ave de Chellah, similarly expensive, with dated charm; ***Hotel Balima***, 173 Ave Mohammed V, one of the most popular places to drink a beer or coffee, particularly during the evening promenade; ***Baghdad Bar***, Zankat Tanto, belly-dancing awaits you.

Cafés, Pâtisseries and Glaceries

There are many good cafés, pâtisseries and glaceries on or near Ave Mohammed V, two of the best being ***Lina*** (a smoke-free café with excellent pâtisseries), at the top of Ave Allal Ben Abdellah, and ***Le Petit Poucet***, on Ave Mohammed V. The ***Café Maure*** in the Kasbah des Oudaias serves mint tea and pastries, good views, waiters in traditional dress, a pleasant place to while away the time. There are excellent stand-up juice bars in the medina.

Banks

ABM, 19 Ave Allal Ben Abdellah, T 724907; **Banque al Maghrib**, Ave Mohammed V, T 763009; **Banque Marocaine de Commerce Exterieur (BMCE)**, 241 Ave Mohammed V, T 721798, the best for change (cash, travellers' cheques and VISA/Mastercard) for which it has a separate door (open 0800-2000 weekdays, 1000-1200 and 1600-2000 weekends); **Banque Populaire**, 64 Ave Allal Ben Abdellah; **BMAO**, Ave Allal Ben Abdellah, T 769980; **Credit du Maroc**, Ave Allal Ben

Abdellah, T 721961; **Wafabank**, Ave Mohammed V, T 721181/82.

● Chemists

Pharmacie du Chellah, Place de Melilla, T 724723, and another on rue Moulay Slimane, if not, look in a newspaper or T 726150 for the name of the night chemist.

● Embassies & consulates

Algeria, 46 rue Tarik Ibn Ziad, T 765591; **Austria**, 2 rue Tiddas, T 764003; **Belgium**, 6 Ave de Marrakech, T 764746; **Canada**, 13 bis rue Jaafar Assadik, T 771375/7; **Denmark**, 4 rue de Khemisset, T 767986; **Egypt**, 31 Ave d'Alger, T 731833; **France**, rue Sahnoun, T 777822; **Germany**, 7 rue Madnine, T 765474; **Greece**, 23 rue d'Oujda, T 723839; **Italy**, 2 rue Idriss El Azhar, T 766598; **Libya**, Zankat Chouaib Doukally, T 766863; **Mauritania**, 6 rue Thami Lamdour, off Ave John Kennedy, T 770912, 756817; **Netherlands**, 40 rue de Tunis, T 733512/3; **Norway**, 4 Zankat Jaafar As-Sadik, Agdal, T 773871/2; **Portugal**, 5 rue Thami Lamdouar, T 756446; **Senegal**, rue Cadi Ben Hammadi Senhadji, T 754171; **Spain**, 3 rue Madnine, T 768988; **Sweden**, 159 Ave John Kennedy, T 759303/759308; **Switzerland**, Square Berkane, T 766974; **Sudan**, 9 rue de Tedders, T 761368; **Tunisia**, 6 Ave de Fes, T 730636/37; **UK** (also used by **Australia, Ireland** and **New Zealand**), 17 Blvd de la Tour Hassan, T 720905/06; **USA**, 2 Ave de Marrakech, T 762265.

● Emergency

Ambulance: T 15. **Fire**: T 15. **Police**: rue Soekarno, behind the PTT Centrale, T 19.

● Entertainment

Rabat has little of the entertainments one might expect in a capital city, particularly late at night.

Art galleries: *Galerie Arcanes*, 130 Blvd el Alou, T 735890; *Galerie L'Atelier*, 16 rue Annaba; *Galerie Le Mamoir*, 7 rue Baitlahm; *Galerie Marsam*, 6 rue Oskofiah.

Cinemas: the 4 biggest cinemas are easily found, 3 in Ave Mohammed V, and 1 at the junction of Ave Allal Ben Abdellah and rue al-Mansur ad-Dahbi which has perhaps the best range of films. Most films are in French.

Discos and nightclubs: the most recommended is *Queen's Club, Hotel de la Tour Hassan*, 22 Ave de Chellah, very popular, open from 2230, entrance MD50; otherwise try *Biba* or *Jefferson* in Ave Patrice Lumumba, or the *Balima* in Ave Mohammed V.

Theatres and concert halls: *Theatre Mohammed V*, rue Al Kahira, has a range of plays and concerts. The various national cultural centres, such as the Russian Cultural Centre in Ave Moulay Abdellah and the British Council in rue Tanger, advertise and promote events. Check *Al Bayane*, *L'Opinion* or *Le Matin* newspapers for other listings.

● Garages

Concorde, 6 Ave Allal Ben Abdellah; *Garage Citroen* (SIMA), at the junction of rue de Congo and rue de Senegal.

● Hammams (Public baths)

On Ave Hassan II, beside the *Rex*, or for residents at the *Hyatt Regency*.

● Hospital

Hôpital Avicenne, Ave Ibn Sina, T 773194, 774411.

● Language centres

American Language Center, rue Tanger, it may also be possible to arrange Arabic lessons here; *British Council*, 36 rue Tanger, BP427, T 760836.

● Laundry

Most hotels will do your laundry for you for an arranged price. Otherwise try *Rabat Pressing*, 67 Ave Hassan II.

● Libraries

British Council, 36 rue Tanger, BP427, T 760836, free entry, reference books, novels, some books on Morocco, magazines and newspapers, Sky News on the TV, small café; *George Washington Library*, 35 Ave el Fahs, also has some newspapers.

● Motoring Club

45 Ave Patrice Lumumba.

● Post, telephone and telegrams

PTT Centrale, Ave Mohammed V, 0800-1200, 1400-1830. Rue al-Mansur ad-Dahbi, just off Ave Mohammed V, opposite the post office has a permanent facility for telephoning and collecting letters. Check with staff that previous call is cleared before using cabin.

● Religious services

Catholic: Cathedrale Saint Pierre, rue Abou Inan, T 722301. **Jewish**: Synagogue Talmuch Torah, 9 Ave Moulay Ismail, information, T 724504. **Protestant**: Temple, 44 Ave Moulay Abdellah, service: 0945.

Shopping

Books and maps: The ***American Bookshop*** at the American Language Center in rue Tanger has a very useful selection of novels, guide-books and books on Islam and Morocco, all in English. There is an English language bookshop at 7 Zankat Alyamama, behind the railway station, which sells a large selection of second-hand paperbacks. For books in French there are a number of well-stocked bookshops in Ave Mohammed V, such as ***Kahla wa Dimna***, and Ave Allal Ben Abdellah. Bookshops in Ave Mohammed V stock simple maps of Rabat or Morocco. For hiking maps go to the **Division de la Cartographie**, 31 Ave Moulay al Hassan, which sells official maps if it is not being too bureaucratic.

Markets: local markets are on Thur at Sale, Fri at Bouznika, Sat at Temara, Sun at Bouknadel and Skhirat. In Rabat medina the vegetable market is best on Sun, and carpets in rue des Consuls on Tue and Thur morning. In the *ville nouvelle* there is an underground vegetable and fruit market at Place Moulay al Hassan, with excellent flower sellers above ground outside.

Modern shops: there are a range of large shops on Ave Mohammed V and Ave Allal Ben Abdellah. It should be possible to get most things you need here.

Moroccan shops: use the **Centre Artisanal (Coopartim)** in Tarik al Marsa to get an idea of the range, then go out and bargain in the small boutiques in the medina, on or just off Ave Mohammed V, rue Souika, **Souq es Sebbat** and rue des Consuls. There are a number of larger shops, in the *ville nouvelle*, on Ave Mohammed V, or in the malls just off, where the high prices may be negotiable.

Newspapers and magazines: there are 3 or 4 boutiques on the pavements of Ave Mohammed V stocking a full range of British, American, French and international newspapers and magazines. However the best is perhaps inside the main railway station. The international edition of *The Guardian* arrives in Rabat about 1800.

Sport

Flying: *Aéro-Club Royal Aerodrome*, T 751335.

Golf: *Royal Golf Dar Es Salam*, 12 km from Rabat on rue de Zaers, T 754692, is the largest and most famous course in Morocco, with 45 holes, Red course 6,825m par 73, Blue course 6,205m par 72, Green course (9 holes) 2,150m par 32, fees approx MD500 per day; there is also the smaller Golf Club du Souissi, T 750359. For information: *Moroccan Royal Federation of Golf*, 2 rue Moulay Slimane, T 731693.

Horse-riding and polo: the *Royal Polo Equestrian Club* is at the Royal Golf Dar Es Salam, rue de Zaers, T 754692.

Swimming: the main beach in Rabat is that below the kasbah, which is popular but not too clean. That at Sale is similar, and both have dangerous currents from the river. It may be worth going further afield, to the Plage des Nations, Temara or Skhirat (**see page 222** and **page 222**). Try the pools at Royal Golf Dar Es Salam, the *Hotel Hyatt Regency* or the *Hotel Safir*.

Tennis courts: *Club des Cheminots*, Agdal, T 770048; *Club El Wifak*, rue de Zaers, T 754539; *Olympique Marocain*, 2 rue Ibn Khaldoun, T 771872, 7 courts; *Riad Club*, rue Abdelaziz Boutaleb, Agdal, T 722776, 6 courts; *Stade Marocain*, Ave Haroun Rachid, T 771903, 7 courts.

Walking and climbing: information from Alpine Club 19, Blvd de la Resistance, T 727220.

Water sports: Yacht Club de Rabat, Quai de la Tour Hassan, T 720254; Fath Union Sport, Port de Rabat, T 733679; Olympique Marocain, Quai Léon Petit, T 725123; information from Yachting Federation, Ave Ibn Yassine Bellevue, Agdal, BP332, T 771782.

Tourist Information

Office du Tourisme, 22 Ave d'Alger, T 730562; **Syndicat d'Initiative**, Ave Patrice Lumumba, T 723272, not very useful.

Travel agents & airline offices

Afric Voyages, 28 bis Ave Allal Ben Abdellah, T 709646/47, 706833; ***First International Tours***, 32 Ave Ben Khattab, T 775060; ***Gharb Voyages***, 289 Ave Mohammed V, T 767311; ***La Royale***, Immeuble Montfavet, Place Mohammed V, T 707031; ***North Africa Tours***, Residence El Minzah, rue Kadira, T 769747, F 762298; ***Rainbow Travel***, 1 rue Derna, Place Pietri, T 762563, 762568; ***Wagons-Lit Tourisme***, 1 Ave Moulay Abdellah, T 769625; ***Welcome Voyages***, 29 Ave d'Alger, T 702871/72, F 702873. ***Air France***, 281 Ave Mohammed V, T 767066; ***Iberia*** 104 Ave Mohammed V; ***Royal Air Maroc*** Ave Mohammed V, T 709766, 9 rue Abou Faris Almarini, T 709700, reservations: T 708076, 709710.

● Transport

Local Buses run all over the city, many originating from Ave Hassan II, near **Bab el Had**, or just past Parc du Triangle de Vue. 6 and 12 go to Sale, 17 to Temara, 1, 2 and 4 for the **Chellah**, get off at **Bab Zaer**. **Petit-taxis**: in Rabat are blue. They are some of the best in Morocco, nearly always metered, and often shared. They can be picked up anywhere, most easily at the stand on Ave Hassan II, close to the junction with Ave Mohammed V. Alternatively, T 720518, 730311. A Rabat petit-taxi cannot take you to Sale, which has its own taxis.

Car hire **Avis**, 7 Zankat Abou Faris El Marini, T 767503, 769759, Tx 31029, also at Rabat-Sale Airport; **Budget**, Rabat-Ville Railway Station, T 767689; **Hertz**, 467 Ave Mohammed V, T 709227, 707366, Tx: 31977, also at Rabat-Sale Airport; **Holiday Car**, 1 bis Ave Ibn Sina, T 771684, 771351; **Inter Rent-Europcar**, 25 bis rue Patrice Lumumba; **La Royale**, Immueble Montfavet, Place Mohammed V, T 763031.

Air buses to Airport Mohammed V run from in front of *Hotel Terminus*, Ave Mohammed V. Tickets can be bought at the kiosk for MD50. Departures: 0500, 0630, 0830, 1000, 1230, 1530 and 1830, journey time 90 mins. For Rabat-Sale airport, T 727393, 730316, follow the P1 Sale-Meknes road. 9 flights a week to Casablanca, 1 a week to Algiers (Thur), Rome, Oujda and Tetouan, 4 a day to Paris.

Train **Rabat Ville** station, T 767353, Ave Mohammed V, departures – Casablanca: 35 daily between 0429 and 2345; **Marrakech**: 8 daily between 0429 and 2345; **El Jadida**: 1936, **Oued Zem**: 1905; **Meknes and Fes**: 9 daily between 0723 and 2323, **Meknes, Fes** and **Oujda**: 1035, 1515, 2141, 2323; **Tanger**: 0027, 0813, 1948; **Aeroport Mohammed V**: 0510, 0625, 0750, 1020, 1500. **Rabat Agdal** station, T 772385, rue Abderrahman El Ghafiki, departures – Casablanca, Marrakech, El Jadida and Oued Zem: as above, 4-6 mins later, Meknes, Fes, Oujda and Tanger: as above 6-8 mins earlier.

Road **Bus** The main bus terminal for all buses is at Place Zerktouni, 3 km from the centre. Catch a petit-taxi there, or a No 30 bus from Ave Hassan II. Current buses – Casablanca: 10 a day (1½ hr), Tanger: 2 a day (5 hrs), Meknes: 3 a day (4 hrs), Fes: 6 a day (5½ hrs).

Grand-taxi Shared between 6 passengers, run from the bus station for distant locations, and for local locations, such as Temara, Skhirat, Sale and Bouknadel, from the stand on Ave Hassan II, just past the Parc du Triangle de Vue.

Sale

History

Sale, pronounced and often written as Salé, is Sala or Sla in Arabic, after the Roman Sala Colonia. Sale was founded in the 11th century, and its Great Mosque dates from 1163-1184. The town was embellished and fortified by the Merinids in the 13th century, becoming an important commercial centre. Great rivalry, even armed conflict, has existed between Rabat and Sale, although they were united in the Republic of the Bou Regreg. Up until the 17th century Sale had enjoyed long periods as the more important of the two cities, being known for religious learning and piety. In the 20th century Rabat has outstripped Sale, the latter becoming more and more a dormitory settlement for the former, with little of its own economic activities. Sale is worth a day-trip from Rabat to visit the beautiful **Abul Hassan Medersa** and explore the medina and the *souqs*, which are far more traditional than those of Rabat, and less visited by tourists than Fes or Meknes.

Things to see

Bab Mrisa means 'Gate of the Little Harbour'. This was originally the sea gate of the medina, as there was once a channel running to it from the river. The gate is easily found, dominating the approach to Sale from Rabat, on the left side. This gate is very large, its *outrepassé* arch opening of 11m in height sufficient to allow access to the sailing boats of the day. Bab Mrisa was built by the Merinid Sultan Abu Yusuf in the 1270s. However in style it is closer to the Almohad gates, with the triangular space between the arch and the frame covered with floral decoration centred on the palmette, with the use of the *darj w ktaf* motif down the sides. Originally it had a porch. Alongside the tower there are 2 tall defensive towers. It may be possible to get access to the top of the gate. A custodian guards a small door on the left, inside the gate, which gives access to a small garden leading to a round tower. From this tower walk back along the top of the rampart to the gate. There is another similar sea gate, the next gate around the wall to the left.

Abul Hassan Medersa This *medersa*, or religious school (open 0800-1200, 1430-1800), is the most important building to visit in Sale, being the only *medersa* in this region. It was built by the Merinid Sultan Abul Hassan and finished in 1342. To reach it follow the city walls around to the left from Bab Mrisa to a small square at Bab Bou Hajar, alongside a park. Just beyond this there is an area where cars should be parked. Take the small lane off to the far right at the end of this area. Take the first left, then the first right. 200m later, just after the lane passes under a house, turn left. The particularly large **Grand Mosque** in front was built by the Almohad Sultan Abu Yusuf Ya'qub in the late 12th century, although the minaret and door are both modern. Just beyond the mosque is the tomb of Sale's patron saint, Sidi Abdellah bin Hassun. The *medersa* is to the left of the mosque.

Note at the entrance the intricate decorations, with complex designs of inscription around a cusped, interlaced arch, below a green tiled roof resting on cedar. The *medersa* is quite small, with a courtyard surrounded by a gallery, its columns decorated with *zellij* mosaic tiling. The walls above the columns are decorated with geometric and floral motifs, whilst the ceilings of the ground floor have panelled wood in geometric patterns. There has been restoration to both wood carving and stucco, but much is original, and in good condition. The decoration which covers almost all the *medersa*, is finely executed. To reach the upper floors, return to the entrance and climb the stairs. These are the students' cells, which seem tiny and ill-lit, but give an insight into the nature of *medersa* life. From the roof is a view of Sale, and beyond it, Rabat.

The Medina Sale medina is small and easy to explore. Walking in any direction you are likely to arrive at the *souqs*, the **Grand Mosque** and **Abul Hassan Medersa**, or the city walls. The **Mausoleum of Sidi Bin Ashir at-Tabib** is located close to the W wall of the cemetery that lies between the medina and the sea. This 14th century Muslim saint was famous for curing people, and the sick still visit his tomb for its curative powers. The building is comparatively tall, and in stark white.

The **Fondouk al Askour** is worth seeing for its decorated portal. From **Bab Bou Hajar** follow rue Bab al-Khabbaz, and take the fourth lane on the left past the park, which is obstructed by 3 concrete posts. This leads to a textile *souq*. After 120m the **souq** passes under an arch. On the right is the *fondouk*. It was originally built in about 1350 as a *medersa* by Abu Inan, son of Abul Hassan. It was later a merchants' hostel. The door is surrounded by a partially restored *zellij* mosaic of the *darj w ktaf* pattern. Above this is a panel of *zellij* with the traditional 8 pointed star motif, and above that a row of 9 niches carved into a plaster panel. Inside there is a courtyard with 2 storeys of arcades around it.

In this area there are some interesting *souqs*, which are perhaps more traditional than those of Rabat, and worth exploring. This textile market is **Souq el-Merzouk**, while **Souq el-Ghezel** is the wool market. There are stone-masons and carpenters in rue Kechachine, and blacksmiths and brassworkers in rue Haddadine. The **Sidi Marzouq Souq** is noted for its jewellery and embroidery. The medina of Sale is also noted for a procession of candles, or thick poles bearing various representations, which occurs every year on the afternoon before the Prophet's birthday, Moulid an-Nabi. This proceeds through the town, culminating at the **Tomb of Sidi Abdellah bin Hassun**. The seafaring past of the city is particularly visible in this event, with the men in pirate costumes.

Local information

● Accommodation and places to eat

Very few travellers stay in Sale, as there are few hotels, and the city is easily accessible from Rabat. There is the cheap **E** ***Hotel des Saadiens***, by the bus station. *Camping de la Plage* is by the river and the sea, with toilets, showers and a shop. There are a number of small and cheap café-restaurants just inside both main gates, and along rue Kechachin. *Café Marhaba* near the SGMB bank is also recommended.

● Transport

Local Bus To get to Sale take a bus No 6 or 12 from Ave Hassan II in Rabat, a grand-taxi from the stop on the same street, or walk down to the quay below the kasbah and take a rowing boat across the river, from where you can walk up to **Bab Bou Hajar**. Rabat petit-taxis are not allowed to cross the river. Once in Sale it should be possible to explore most of the centre on foot, but if not, the city has its own petit-taxis. If you have your own transport, go along Tarik al Marsa, Ave Hassan II or Blvd du Bou Regreg and cross the bridge below the **Hassan Tower**. It is possible to walk this route in about half an hour.

EXCURSIONS FROM RABAT

Northwards

The **Mamora Forest** is a peaceful area of cork and eucalyptus trees, a pleasant change after Rabat. It lies off the road to Meknes. Turn off left at Sidi Allal Bahroui. Return via the P2 and P29.

The **Jardins Exotiques** are about 20 km from Rabat, on the P2, and the 28 bus route. They are the work of a French horticulturalist, François, in the 1950s. There are many species of plants from Morocco and all over the world, laid out with pools, bridges and summerhouses, often in the manner of one particular area. They are well-worth a visit and are open from 0900-1830.

The **Plage des Nations** is at Sidi Bouknadel, about 30 km of Rabat. It is very popular with the affluent, and more a family beach than those of Rabat-Sale, but the currents can be dangerous. Take the bus No 28 from Sale, and walk the 1 km from the turning, or share a grand-taxi, also from Sale. The C *Hotel Firdaous*, T 780407, has a bar, restaurant, pool and is recommended. Further on Mehdia and Kenitra can be visited as an excursion from Rabat, by train, bus or car (see page 252).

Southwards

Temara is 16 km from Rabat, off the P36. Bus 17 from Ave Hassan II goes to the town and the ruins of a kasbah. The beach is a 4 km walk to the W. There are two hotels, D *Hotel La Feloque*, T 744388, 23 rms, restaurant, bar, pool, tennis, and E *Hotel Casino*, as well as *Camping de Temara*, the first from Rabat on the coastal road. There are also a number of popular discos. Temara Zoo is open from 1000 to sunset.

Skhirat is 31 km from Rabat and is clearly signposted off the P36, P1 and RP36. There are 2 trains from Rabat-Ville each day, at 0730 and 1855, taking 17 mins. Skhirat town has little of interest itself beyond a Sunday *souq*. The palace near the beach was the scene of a bloody but unsuccessful *coup* attempt in July 1971. Skhirat beach is upmarket, as are the restaurants and hotels nearby, including C *La Kasbah*, Rose Marie Plage, T 749133, F 749116, 42 rms, pool, tennis, restaurant, bar, parking, and the recommended D *Amphitrite* hotel, Km 28, route de Rabat, T 742317, 36 rms, restaurant, bar, pool, tennis.

TANGER, MEDITERRANEAN COAST & THE RIF

Contents

Maps

Tanger (Tangier) is a city which reflects its position at the crossroads of Africa and Europe, the Mediterranean Sea and the Atlantic Ocean, as well as its historical experience as an international zone. It is a shabby and bustling city, full of character. Ceuta and Melilla are Spanish enclaves, other towns such as Chaouen, Ouezzane and Tetouan reflect the Andalusian input into the area, whilst Al Hoceima is a more recent Spanish input, that of the 20th century protectorate. The Mediterranean Sea coast is a succession of large, characterless resort complexes and small, isolated, idyllic fishing villages. The Rif, inland, is a wild mountain range with a history of rebellion and a controversial role in hashish production.

TANGER

Pop 266,346 *Alt* 75m.

Tanger has a highly individual character, a product of its location at the gate to the Mediterranean Sea and at the meeting point of Africa and Europe, and of its recent historical past, notably as an international city from 1923 to 1956, when its tax-free status and reputation attracted many writers, artists and other famous Westerners, as well as a sizeable banking industry. Tanger also had fame as a gay resort. It remains today a lively city, popular with travellers, including those arriving or just visiting from Spain, interesting to explore, and with a wide range of restaurants and entertainments. The beach is popular. The city is now an important passenger port and tourist resort. Tanger is well worth a visit, particularly for the **Kasbah**, former residence of Sultans, and the **Medina**, a small and complex maze of houses, shops and narrow, steep streets.

In Tanger it is almost impossible not to recall the numerous celebrated figures that once visited the city. They are part of the official and unofficial hard-sell, and are closely bound up in the history and the buildings. Visitors include English diarist Samuel Pepys, film stars Marlene Dietrich and Errol Flynn, writers Oscar Wilde, Brion Gysin, Allen Ginsberg, Joe Orton (*Entertaining Mr Sloane*), Paul Bowles (author of *The Sheltering Sky* and numerous short stories set in North Africa), Ian Fleming, Jack Kerouac, William Burroughs, Richard

Climate: Tanger

	Jan	Feb	Mar	Apr	May	Jun	Jul	Aug	Sep	Oct	Nov	Dec	Av/Tot
Max (°C)	15	16	17	19	21	24	26	26	25	22	19	16	21
Min (°C)	10	10	12	13	15	17	19	19	18	16	14	12	15
Rain (mm)	148	119	127	60	39	9	0	2	20	57	126	153	860

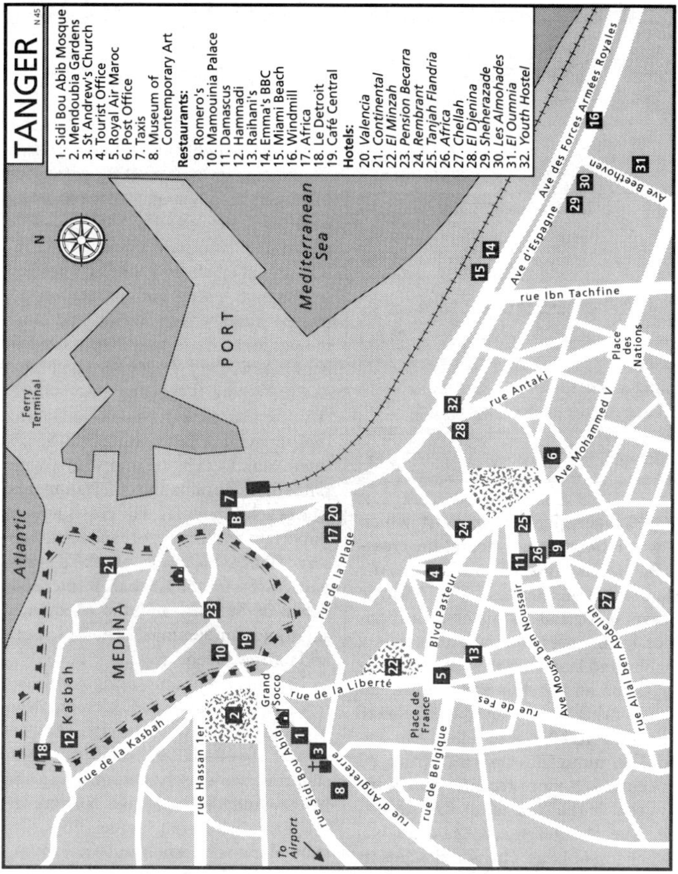

Hughes (*High Wind in Jamaica*), James Leo Herlihy (*Midnight Cowboy*), Tennessee Williams, painter Francis Bacon, and French composer Camille Saint-Saën, as well as the Woolworth heiress Barbara Hutton, Truman Capote, Winston Churchill, Ronnie Kray, Gertrude Stein and the photographer Cecil Beaton. The French painter Eugène Delacroix visited in 1832, and Henri Matisse in 1912, both completing many paintings of Tanger. This expatriate population has since declined, and Tanger can now seem to be resting on its former glories and notoriety.

Early History

Perhaps the oldest city in Morocco, Tanger was active as early as 1600 BC. There was a Phoenician settlement here. Roman mythology ascribes its founding to the Greek giant Anteus, son of Poseidon, god of the earth, and Gaia, goddess of the earth. Anteus challenged Hercules, Hercules killing the giant and having a child by the widow, Tingis. Hercules pulled apart Spain and Africa to give this son, Sophix, a city protected by the sea. King Sophix named his city Tingis. Tanger was known to the Phoenicians, Romans, Vandals and Byzantines and has always been important in view of its strategic location commanding the Straits of Gibraltar. The Romans made it at one point capital of their N African provinces, and controlled it until 429 AD. Later, the Vandals and Byzantines struggled to control the city. Arabs took the city in 706 AD. Tanger remained at the centre of conflict between the major Arab and Berber Dynasties.

Mediaeval History

Tanger achieved commercial importance in the Mediterranean sphere during the 1300s. It was conquered by the Portuguese in 1471, became Spanish in 1578 and Portuguese in 1640. The city was part of English King Charles II's dowry when marrying the Portuguese Catherine of Braganza in 1661, but the English departed in 1684, destroying the kasbah as they left. Sultan Moulay Ismail rebuilt the town after the English left.

Modern History

In the 19th century Tanger became a popular base for European merchants and housed a large European colony, as well as the focus of political competition between expansionist European powers. In 1923 the city became a tax-free International Zone controlled by a 30 member international committee. The city was reunited with Morocco in Oct 1956 but its tax-free status was maintained until 1960. Since independence, Tanger has declined in international economic importance, but has also rapidly developed its tourist industry. In the 1960s the Moroccan government initiated a 'clean-up' of the city, closing down a number of gay bars.

NB: Hassle and guides

A major drawback of Tanger is that the hassling of tourists for business can be heavy duty, constant and very skilled. If you need a guide, it is better to wait until you can get to the Tourist Office or one of the larger hotels to arrange an official guide. This should keep away the unofficial guides who will otherwise approach at any opportunity. However if you are accompanied by an official guide (or indeed an unofficial guide) you will pay an undeclared commission every time you purchase something. There is also considerable pressure to buy hashish, grown in the nearby Rif mountains. It is unadvisable to succumb to this pressure, in view of the often close links between the dealers and the police. Deterring the attentions of unofficial guides, drug dealers or others will take incredible patience, politeness and firmness. A much more minor problem is that a number of streets have 2 names: the original and still widely used French name and the newer Arabic name found on the street signs. A few have a third Spanish name.

ACCESS Air Tanger's Boukhalef airport is 15 km SW of the city, T 935129, 934717, on the P2 road to Rabat. Catch bus 17 or 70 from the terminal to the Grand Socco (Place de 19 Avril 1947), or take a grand-taxi MD70 by day MD100 after 2100.

Train Arriving by train from Marrakech, Casablanca, Rabat, Meknes and Fes the traveller stops first at Tanger Ville, and then at Tanger Port. The former is convenient for the city and its main hotels.

Road The P2 from Rabat brings the driver into Tanger along rue de Fes. The S704 from Ceuta twists along the coast and feeds into Ave Mohammed V, as does the P38 from Tetouan. **Bus** CTM buses arrive at the terminal in Ave des Forces Armées Royales, adjacent to the port gates and Tanger Ville railway station. Private lines arrive at the terminal at the end of rue de Fes.

Sea Transmediterranea and Limadet jointly run the car/passenger ferry service from Algeciras, Spain. Hopefully passports will have been stamped on the boat. In the terminal there is a *bureau de change* for cash and travellers' cheques, as well as a ticket office for trains. Hydrofoils from Algeciras and catamarans from Gibraltar dock close by. Just outside the terminal is Tanger Port railway station for immediate departure to Asilah, Meknes, Fes, Oujda, Rabat, Casablanca and Marrakech, as well as a rank for both kinds of taxis. Negotiation over prices will be necessary but hard.

Things to see

The Kasbah is constructed on the highest point of the medina. Follow rue d'Italie and rue de la Kasbah and enter by Porte de la Kasbah. From the medina, follow rue des Chrétiens from the Petit Socco, and then rue Sidi Ben Rassouli to Bab el Assa.

There has been a similar construction on the site of the kasbah since Roman days, and it was the traditional residence in Tanger of the Sultan and his harem. It was burnt to the ground by the English as they left in 1685. More recently, during the hey-day of Tanger as an international city, the kasbah was considered a fashionable address for people such as the novelist Richard Hughes (who lived at 'Numéro Zero, Le Kasbah, Tanger').

The **Musée de la Kasbah**, T 932097, open 0930-1300, 1500-1800, closed Tue, is in the former palace of the kasbah, the **Dar al-Makhzen**, and includes Moroccan arts and antiquities. The palace was built by the Sultan Moulay Ismail in the 18th century, and was used as the Sultan's palace up until 1912, when Sultan Mawlay Hafid, exiled to Tanger, lived there, alongside his extensive harem. The museum has a wide range of carved and painted woods, carpets and textiles. The palace is itself worth seeing, with an impressive central courtyard, whilst the rooms off it have intricate wall and ceiling carving, particularly in the Fes room, which has ceramics from Fes and Meknes. The garden of the palace is worth exploring, a beautiful mature Andalusian arrangement, with fragrant plants. As you leave the palace stop at *Le Detroit* for a drink and pastries, and an impressive view of the city and sea.

To the left of the palace is the **Museum of Ethnography and Archaeology**. In front of the palace is the Place de la Kasbah, where criminals were once punished or executed. Note the **Grand Mosque** adjacent to the port. In the sea wall a gate leads out onto a belvedere with excellent views of the seascape. On the other side of the Place de la Kasbah, just outside the kasbah gate on rue Sidi Hassani, is the **Musée International d'Art Contemporain**. Also nearby is **Villa Sidi Hosni**, former residence of Barbara Hutton, the American heiress whose Tanger life is famous.

The Medina Lying below the kasbah, and running from the Grand Socco (Place de 19 Avril, 1947) down to the port, the medina is focused on the Petit Socco, and is full of narrow, twisting streets and old houses, many of which are now shops, hotels or restaurants catering for tourists. It is a quarter which has captured the imagination of numerous European and American writers, with the stories of Paul Bowles amongst the most evocative. It is easy to get lost here, so it might be advisable for the visitor with limited time to take an official guide. Unaccompanied, unofficial guides will hawk for business continuously.

The Grand Socco is where the medina begins. Nowadays it is a busy place, but no longer a thriving market square with street entertainers and food stalls. It now has a few fruit shops, cheap restaurants, and several cafés. Note the tiled minaret of the **Sidi Bou Abid Mosque** on the corner of the Grand Socco and rue Sidi Bou Abid. On Thur and Sun Rifi Berber women sell all sorts of wares in rue de la Plage (rue Salah Eddine El Ayoubi). Along rue d'Angleterre they also sell woven blankets. On the rue Bourrakia side of the Grand

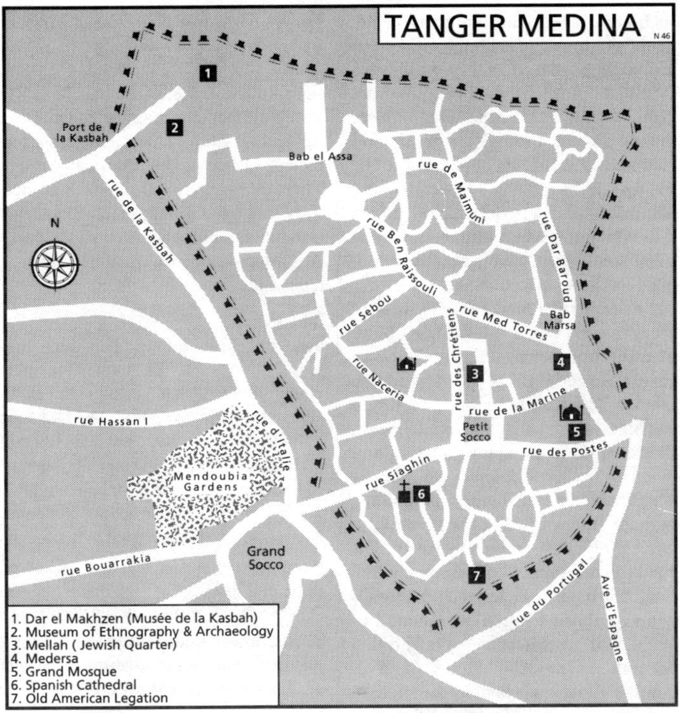

Socco, the arch with Arabic on it leads in to the **Mendoubia Gardens**, quiet but unimpressive, and normally closed. The **Mendoubia Palace** is the former residence of the Sultan's representatives.

Rue Siaghin, the old silversmiths' street, running from the Grand Socco to the Petit Socco, is still an important commercial area of the medina, and the easiest route by which to enter the main area of the medina. To the right of rue Siaghin, is the *mellah*, the Jewish quarter. One also passes the **Spanish Cathedral**, now boarded up. Rue Siaghin leads into the Petit Socco, which lies at the heart of the medina. This market square was once bigger, but now seems strangely cramped. It is surrounded by a number of famous but primitive *pensións*, and the *Café Central*, formerly a café-bar attracting the likes of William Burroughs, Allen Ginsberg and Jack Kerouac, but now with no alcohol sold in the medina it is just a fairly ordinary café with a pleasant terrace to watch life pass by.

Below the Petit Socco, the **Grand Mosque** lies in between rue de la Marine and rue des Postes. This is built on the site of a Portuguese cathedral, although that had been predated by a mosque and, probably, a Roman temple. Opposite is a 14th century *medersa*. Also on rue des Postes (rue Mokhtar Ahardan) is the *Pensión Palace*, where Bertolucci filmed *The Sheltering Sky*, based on the Paul Bowles novel.

The **Old American Legation**, 8 Zankat d'Amerique, T 935904, open 0930-1200,

1600-1830, is the oldest American diplomatic property, given to the US by the Moroccan Sultan in 1821 and used as a Consulate until 1961. From rue des Postes turn right after the *Hotel Mamora* into rue Ikiredj, through a confusing region at the heart of the medina, into rue de Four, right into rue Haybender, and left into rue d'Amerique. It is now a museum and study centre, with a good collection of prints. Note also the building's classic architecture.

Tanger's ***ville nouvelle*** has little of great interest but it is a pleasant place to explore. Place de France (Place de Faro) has a good view of the bay, with the famous *Café de France* alongside, where wartime agents met and made deals. Blvd Pasteur is the main shopping and business street of the new town. Rue de la Liberté is also worth wandering along, perhaps stopping off at the *Centre Culturel Français*'s Galerie Delacroix if it has an exhibition.

At 50 rue d'Angleterre, **St Andrew's** is an Anglican Church consecrated in 1905, with architecture and internal decoration modelled on Moorish Granada. The key is kept by the friendly and helpful groundsman, Mustapha, who will unlock the church and give you a guided tour. Note the Arabic inscriptions of the Lord's Prayer and Gloria at the altar end. Memorials and graves, both inside and outside, feature a number of important former residents of Morocco, including 19th century British consul Sir John Drummond Hay, early 20th century *Times* correspondent Walter Harris, Caid Sir Harry McLean, Scottish adviser to Sultan Mawlay Abd al-Aziz, and Emily Keane, 19th century wife of the Sherif of Ouezzane.

Nearby, the **Musée d'Art Contemporain de la Ville de Tanger**, 52 rue d'Angleterre, T 938436, has a wide selection of the more important painters of Morocco, but is not very impressive on the whole, entrance MD10. Originally this was the English consulate.

Forbes Magazine Museum of Military Miniatures, Palais Mendoub, rue Shakespeare, just W of the stadium, T 939606, open 1000-1700, closed Thur. Malcolm Forbes, American magazine owner, set up this museum of toy soldiers in a former residence of the Moroccan Sultan. There is a vast collection of miniatures, some arranged in historical reconstructions of famous battles, with a number of Arab figures. Essential for the enthusiast, a pleasant change for others.

The Beach
and the clubs alongside it were previously known as an expatriate zone where anything was permissable and a good time easily available. The clubs are a shadow of what they once were but still offer a range of drinking, eating and dancing opportunities. Try *Emma's BBC*, *The Windmill* or *Miami Beach*. The beach is popular, particularly with Moroccans in Jul and Aug. There is no shortage of more relaxing, less crowded and cleaner beaches either way along the coast.

Tanger is a splendid place for watching the birds which migrate across the Straits of Gibraltar - the easiest crossing place between Europe and Africa. Literally hundreds of species make use of the thermals to cross N in spring and S in autumn, the flocks of huge storks and vultures being the most impressive sight.

Local information

● Accommodation

AL *Hotel El Minzah*, 85 rue de la Liberté (Zankat el Houria), T 935885, Tx 33775, F 934546, 100 rms with bath, pricey but central, dates from the 1930s, beautiful gardens set around an Andalusian courtyard, convenient for exploring the medina, 2 restaurants, wine bar, coffee bar, tea room, mini-golf, tennis, pool; **AL** *Hotel Les Almohades*, Ave des Forces Armées Royales, T 940431, F 946317, near the beach, most with sea views, luxurious, 4 restaurants, bar, nightclub 'Up 2000', pool, sauna.

B *Hotel Rembrandt*, Ave Mohammed V, T 937870/2, Tx 33040, centre of the new town, luxurious and prestigious, restaurant and popular bar, garden, pool.

C ***Tanjah Flandria Hotel***, 6 Ave Mohammed V, T 931231/936285, Tx 33692, F 934347, centre of the new town, 170 rms, comfortable, 2 restaurants, piano bar, disco (2100-0300), sauna (men: 1200-1400, 1900-2100, women: 1000-1200), art gallery, bank, pool; **C** ***Africa Hotel***, 17 rue Moussa Ben Noussair, T 935511, 86 rms, comfortable and lively, bar, pool, restaurant, nightclub; **C** ***Hotel El Oumnia***, Ave Beethoven, T 940366, in the new town, pool; **C** ***Hotel Sheheradze***, Ave des Forces Armées Royales, T 940500, 140 rms, close to the sea, pool, private beach bar and terrace.

D ***Chellah Hotel***, 47-49 rue Allal Ben Abdellah, T 943389, 180 rms not all with a/c, good value, disco, tea room; **D** ***Hotel Marco Polo***, Ave d'Espagne, T 938213, 9 rms, German run, restaurant and bar, overlooking the sea.

E ***Valencia***, 72 Ave d'Espagne, junction with rue de la Plage (Zankat Salah Eddine el Ayoubi), T 930770, 45 rms, clean but basic, no restaurant; **E** ***Mansora Hotel***, 19 rue des Postes, T 934105, only good hotel in the centre of the medina; **E** ***Continental Hotel***, 36 rue Dar Baroud, in the medina, T 931024, 931143, Tx 33086, by far the best cheap option, has fallen on hard times but is being renovated, convenient, with a sea view, historic decoration, restaurant; **E** ***Hotel El Djenina***, 8 rue El Antaki (rue Grotius), just off Ave d'Espagne, T 936075, 21 rms, recommended; **E** ***Hotel El Muniria***, rue Magellan, includes the *Tanger Inn Bar*, both popular, numbering William Burroughs, Kerouac and Ginsberg among former residents; opposite is the **E** ***Hotel Ibn Batouta***, 8 rue Magellan, T 937170, with restaurant; nearby is the crumbling **E** ***Hotel Panoramic Massilia***, 11 rue Targa, T 935015, tatty but friendly and with a good view from some rooms; **E** ***Hotel Celil*** and ***Hotel Biarritz***, Ave d'Espagne; **E** ***Hotel Olid***, 12 rue des Postes, T 931310; **E** ***Hotel Mendez***, Ave d'Espagne, reasonable prices, separate shower.

F ***Hotel Grand Socco***, rue Imam Layti, behind the Grand Socco, is cheap, dirty and noisy, but convenient; **Petit Socco** (Place Souq Dakhil) is the heart of the medina and its *pensións* have a history, but they may be poorly equipped, try **F** ***Pensión Mauritania***, T 934671, which has a cold shower; or ***Pensión Beccara***, which has no shower; just off, on rue des Postes (Ave Mokhtar Ahardan) **F** ***Pensión Palace*** is good; in the *ville nouvelle* there are cheap and basic *pensións* in rue de la Plage, where prices do not seem to be fixed, but many do not have showers, including **F** ***Royal***, ***Madrid***, ***Le Detroit***, ***Miami***, ***Familia Talavera***, ***Playa*** and ***Atou***, the last being particularly cheap, whilst the ***Miama*** and ***Le Detroit*** are recommended.

● **Youth hostel**

T 46127, 8 rue El Antaki, Ave d'Espagne, 60 beds, overnight fee, MD20, advanced booking essential, station 800m, bus 100m.

● **Camping**

Camping sites are not much cheaper than a budget hotel and rather far from the city. ***Camping Miramonte***, T 937138, is 3 km W from the city, on bus routes 1, 2 and 21. ***Camping-Caravaning Tingis***, T 940191, is 6 km E, well-equipped but 2 km from the beach. ***Robinson Plage Camping***, 8 km E by Caves of Hercules, good but far, take the ***Boughaz*** minibus.

● **Places to eat**

♦♦♦ ***El Erz***, *Hotel El Minzah*, 85 rue de la Liberté, T 935885, reservations recommended, popular restaurant with a wide range of European dishes, often with music; ***El Korsan***, *Hotel El Minzah*, 85 rue de la Liberté, T 935885, reservations recommended, Moroccan food amid traditional decor and music.

♦♦ ***Romero's***, 12 Ave du Prince Moulay Abdellah, T 932277, highly recommended Spanish cuisine, fair prices but not cheap; ***Restaurant Mamounia Palace***, 6 rue Semmarin, Petit Socco, T 935099, set menus of Moroccan food with authentic decor and folklore/music; ***Dar Tajine***, rue du Commerce, high-class Moroccan meals, some tour parties; ***Damascus***, 2 bis Ave du Prince Moulay Abdellah, T 934730, Moroccan food, bar and tea room; ***Restaurant Chez Bernard***, off Blvd Pasteur near the *Hotel Rembrandt*, Spanish menu dominated by fish; ***L'Ibis***, rue Khalid Ibn Oualid, near Place de France (Place de Faro), moderately priced but unexciting French restaurant/bar; ***Restaurant Hammadi***, 2 rue de la Kasbah, opposite junction with Paseo del Docteur Cenarro, T 934514, Moroccan meals in 'authentic' surroundings; ***Restaurant El Mabrouk***, rue Ahmed Chaouki, off Place de France, has very reasonably-priced set menus with good Moroccan food; further up the same road ***Raihani's***, T 934866, also has reasonable menus with excellent Moroccan cuisine, ***Restaurant le Detroit***, Ave du Prince Moulay

Abdellah, Spanish food, cheaper than nearby Romero's; ***Negresso***, rue Mexique, a bar, snack-bar and restaurant, offers French, English and Moroccan drinks and food; ***Brenda's***, Ave du Prince Moulay Abdellah, is a cheap English restaurant; try also ***La Presse Salon de Thé/Restaurant***, Blvd Pasteur; ***Emma's BBC***, Ave d'Espagne, famous and cheap beachside bar-restaurant, open summer only; ***Miami Beach***, Ave des Forces Armées Royales, T 943401, 1000-1800, beachside bar-restaurant, gay bar and disco at night; ***Windmill***, Ave des Forces Armées Royales, T 940907, oldest beachside restaurant patronized by writer Joe Orton, fish, Moroccan and Spanish food.

♦ ***Restaurant Africa***, 83 rue de la Plage (rue Salah Eddine El Ayoubi), T 935436, a good cheap option; ***Restaurant Hassi Baida*** and ***Restaurant Cleopatre*** are in the same road and similar; ***Dallas*** is a cheap fish restaurant in rue El Moutanabi; the Grand Socco has several cheap places to eat and the ***Café-Restaurant Ataif***; in the medina, there are a number of cheap, basic restaurants, such as ***Mauritania*** and ***Assalam*** in rue de la Marine, and ***Aladin***, ***Grece*** and ***Andaluz*** in rue du Commerce. The latter, at No 7, is particularly good.

● Bars

Patio Wine Bar, *Hotel El Minzah*, 85 rue de la Liberté, T 935885, a wine bar in which to explore the wines of Morocco and overseas, a little pricey; ***The Pub***, 4 rue Sorolla, T 934789, food, beer and other drinks in a pub atmosphere; ***Caid's Bar***, *Hotel El Minzah*, 85 rue de la Liberté, T 935885, Moroccan decoration and expensive drinks in an atmospheric and celebrated bar; ***Tanger Inn***, 1 rue Magellan, T 935337, small bar popular with expatriates; ***Emma's BBC***, Ave d'Espagne, beachside bar; ***Number One***, 1 Ave Mohammed V, T 931817, popular with gays.

● Cafés

As you leave the palace in the kasbah, stop at the ***Salon de Thé/Restaurant le Detroit***, T 938080, which is pricey for food, but good for tea, coffee, pastries and a view of the palace, kasbah and the sea, established by the writer Brion Gysin. ***Café de France***, 1 Place de France, has a history as a meeting place of the important and famous, popular with Francis Bacon, William Burroughs, Tennessee Williams and Truman Capote. The ***Café Central***, in the Petit Socco, has a similar history, but is now just a nice place to watch the hustle and bustle of the medina.

● American Express

c/o **Voyages Schwartz**, 54 Blvd Pasteur, T 933459, 0900-1230 and 1500-1900 Mon-Fri, 0900-1230 Sat.

● Banks

BMCE, Blvd Pasteur, with a *bureau de change*. **BMCI** 8 Place de France, T 935553. **Banque du Maroc**, 78 Ave Mohammed V, T 935553. **Credit du Maroc**, Agence Grand Socco, rue de l'Italie. Banks are open 0830-1130 and 1430-1630.

● Chemists

Pharmacie de Fes, 22 rue de Fes, T 932619, 24 hrs a day; ***Pharmacie Pasteur***, Place de France, T 932422.

● Consulates

Belgium, 5A Immeuble Jawara, Place Al Medina, T 943234; **Denmark**, 3 rue Ibn Rochd, T 938183; **France**, Place de France, T 932039, 932040; **Germany**, 47 Ave Hassan II, T 938700; **Italy**, 35 rue Assad Ibn Forrat, T 937647; **Netherlands**, 47 Ave Hassan II, T 931245; **Norway**, 3 rue Henri Regnault, T 931245; **Portugal**, 9 Place des Nations, T 931708; **Spain**, rue Sidi Bouabid, T 937000, 935625; **Sweden**, 31 Ave Prince Heritier, T 938730; **Switzerland**, rue Henri Regnault, T 934721; **UK**, 9 rue d'Amerique du Sud, T 935895; **USA**, 29 rue El Achouak, T 935904.

● Cultural & language centres

American Language Center, 1 rue M'Sallah; Centre Culturel Français, rue de la Liberté.

● Dentist

Dr Ibrahim Filali, 53 Ave du Prince Moulay Abdellah, T 931268, speaks English.

● Doctor

Dr Joseph Hirt, 8 rue Sorolla, T 935729, speaks English, and will pay calls to hotels.

● Emergency

Ambulance: T 15; **Fire**: T 15; **Police**: rue Ibn Toumert, T 19.

● Entertainment

Art galleries: ***Galerie Delacroix***, rue de la Liberté; ***Tanjah Flandria Art Gallery***, rue Ibn Rochd, behind the *Hotel Flandria*, T 933000.

Cinemas: ***Ciné Alcazar***, junction of rue de l'Italie and rue Ibn Al Abbar (Paseo del Doctor Cenarro); ***Cinema Rif***, Grand Socco, not very good looking. Preferably look around Blvd Pasteur.

Discos and nightclubs: the continuation of

rue Mexique, rue Sanlucar (Zankat El Moutanabi), has a number of clubs/discos including ***Churchill's***, ***Scott's*** and ***Koutoubia Dancing***. Also try the more upmarket ***Up 2000*** in *Hotel les Almohades*, Ave des Forces Armées Royales, T 940431, built on the roof of a hotel; or ***Ali Baba*** at *Chellah Hotel*, 47-49 rue Allal Ben Abdellah. ***Morocco Palace***, 11 Ave du Prince Moulay Abdellah, T 938614, has belly-dancing until 0100, when it becomes a disco.

● Garage
Tanjah Auto, 2 Ave de Rabat.

● Hospital
Emergencies: T 934242; Hôpital Al Kortobi, rue Garibaldi, T 931073; Hôpital Español, T 931018.

● Library
Tanger Book Club, the Old American Legation, 8 rue d'Amerique, the medina, T 935317 (0930-1200, Tue-Sat).

● Post & telephone
The main post office (PTT) is at 33 Ave Mohammed V, T 935657 (0830-1215, 1430-1745, Mon-Fri). Also telephone from the PTT at the junction of rue El Msala and rue Belgique. Local telephone code 9. All numbers are 6 figs in most cases beginning with the area code.

● Religious services
Anglican St Andrew's Episcopal Church, 50 rue d'Angleterre, T 934633, services on Sun 0830 and 1100 and Wed. **Interdenominational Protestant** American Church, 34 rue Hassan Ibn Ouezzane (rue Léon l'Africain), T 932755, service on Sun 1100.

● Shopping
Food: there is a food market between rue d'Angleterre and rue Sidi Bou Abid. The stalls along rue d'Angleterre are not very impressive. There are numerous fruit sellers along rue de la Plage and its side streets. Just off, on rue El Oualili, is another food market.

Handicrafts and antiques: Tanger is not the best place to buy handicrafts, for although it has a large selection, Marrakech and Fes have better access to the different producing regions, and prices will be lower. The pressure to buy in Tanger is intense, with bazaarists and hawkers used to gullible day-trippers and weekend visitors from Spain. The cheapest shops and stalls, with the most flexible prices, will be found in the medina. Shops in the *ville nouvelle* may claim fixed prices but in most this is just another ploy. ***Coopartim, Ensemble Artisanal***, rue de Belgique, T 932580, is a good place to start, a government controlled fixed price shop with a vast range of goods from all over the country, where one can get an idea of prices. Also try ***Sahara***, 30 rue des Almouahidine; ***Bazaar Chaouen***, 116 rue de la Plage; and in the medina, ***Marrakech la Rouge***, 50 rue es Siaghin. For crafts and antiques see the amazing ***Galerie Tindouf***, 64 rue de la Liberté, T 931525.

Newspapers and books: foreign newspapers can be brought from shops in rue de la Liberté or outside the post office in Ave Mohammed V. For books in French, and a few in other languages, go to ***Librarie des Colonnes***, 54 Blvd Pasteur, T 936955.

● Sport
Flying: *Royal Flying Club*, Boukhalef Airport, T 935720.

Golf: *Royal Club de Golf*, Boubana, T 938925, 18 hole, 5,529m par 72, fees MD450 per day.

Riding: *Country L'Etrier*, Boubana.

Tennis: *M'Sallah Garden Tennis Courts*, rue de Belgique, T 935203; ***Municipale***, Ave de la Paix, T 943324.

Yachting: *Tanger Yacht Club*, the Port, T 938575.

● Tourist Information
Office du Tourisme, 29 Blvd Pasteur, T 938239/40 open 0800-1400, Mon-Sat; **Syndicat d'Initiative**, 11 rue Khalid Ibn El Oualid, T 935486.

● Travel agents & airline offices
Holiday Service, 84 Ave Mohammed V, T 933362; ***Wagons-Lit Tourisme***, rue de la Liberté. ***Air France***, 20 Blvd Pasteur; ***GB Airways***, 83 rue de la Liberté, T 935877; ***Iberia***, 35 Blvd Pasteur, T 936177; ***Royal Air Maroc***, Place de France, T 934722.

● Transport
Local Bus Tanger is fairly small and thus it is unlikely that you will want to use local buses. If you do they can be picked up in the Grand Socco or in Ave des Forces Armées Royales outside the port gates. Boughaz minibuses, from just outside the port gate, may be useful to get to the private bus station, or on excursions from Tanger westwards.

Bicycle & motorcycle hire Mesbahi, 7 rue Ibn Tachfine, just off Ave des Forces Armées Royales, T 940974, renting bicycles, 50cc and 125cc motorbikes, deposit required for 3 days or more.

Car hire Avis, 54 Blvd Pasteur, T 938960, 933031, and at the airport; **Budget**, 7 Ave du Prince Moulay Abdellah, T 937994, and at the airport; **Europcar**, 87 Ave Mohammed V, T 938271; **Hertz**, 36 Ave Mohammed V, T 933322, 934179, and at the airport; **Leasing Cars**, 24 rue Henri Regnault, and at the airport, a little cheaper.

Grand-taxis can be picked up from the Grand Socco or in front of **Tanger Ville** railway station, to destinations within or outside of the city. You will need to set a fare with the driver. Tanger's turquoise **petit-taxis** may be cheaper, although that will depend on your skill as the meters are not always operated. For a taxi T 935517.

Air Tanger's Boukhalef airport is 15 km from the city along the P2, T 935129, 934717. Catch bus 17 or 70 from Grand Socco or a grand-taxi. Arrive 1½-2 hrs early. There are flights to Agadir, Al Hoceima, Casablanca, Laayoune and Marrakech and direct international flights to European cities including Amsterdam, Barcelona, Brussels, Gibraltar, London, Madrid and Paris.

Train There are 2 stations in Tanger, very close together. All trains go from **Tanger Ville**, T 931201, on Ave des Forces Armées Royales in the town centre, some leave just before from **Tanger Port**, beside the ferry terminal. Departures – **Rabat and Casablanca**: 0715, 1128, 1625; **Rabat, Casablanca and Marrakech**: 0810, 2340; **Meknes, Fes and Oujda**: 0055, 0945. All trains stop at Asilah.

Road Bus Information: T 932415. CTM buses depart from the ticket office near the entrance to the port in Ave des Forces Armées Royales. Current departure times – **Kenitra, Rabat and Casablanca**: 1100, 2230, 2330, 2400; **Souq El Arba du Gharb, Ksar el Kebir, Larache, Asilah**: 1100, 1630, 1800, 2230, 2330, 2400; **Sidi Kacem, Meknes, Fes**: 1800; **Agadir, Tiznit**: 1630; **Paris**: 0500. Private buses, running from the terminal at the end of rue de Fes, go to most destinations and are generally cheaper. Departures: **Tetouan** every 15 mins (1 hr); **Asilah** 0915, 0945, 1100 (30 mins; Larache every hour (90 mins); **Meknes** 0700, 1000, 1300, 1600 (5 hrs); **Fes** 1000, 1600; (6 hrs); **Chaouen** 0545, 0800, 1045, 1300, 1330, 1815 (2½ hrs); **Ceuta** 0730, 0945, 1245 (2 hrs); **Ouezzane** 0900, 1400 (4 hrs). To get to the terminal take a petit-taxi or a Boughaz minibus.

Taxi to many destinations take a shared grand-taxi from the bus terminal at the end of rue de Fes. To Tetouan and Ceuta this is a quick, practical and not too expensive option. For excursions from Tanger to the Caves of Hercules or Cap Malabata negotiate for a grand-taxi in rue de Hollande.

Sea Ferry tickets to **Algeciras** can be bought at the Limadet Agents in Ave du Prince Moulay Abdellah, just off Blvd Pasteur, at travel agents in Blvd Pasteur, or at the ferry terminal. Transmediterranea and Limadet jointly operate this car and passenger service 3 or 4 times a day in the summer and 2 in the winter. Passengers from MD196, cars from MD8500. Check in at least 1 hour early, to allow time to collect an embarkation card, complete a departure card, and have your passport stamped. For tickets for the Bland's Line ferry to **Gibraltar** go to Med Travel, 22 Ave Mohammed V, T 935872/3, or to the port. Departures Mon 0930, Wed, Thur and Fri 1430, Mon and Fri 1830 and Sun 1630, single: MD220 (£18), return: MD440 (£30) Day trip £26 Journey takes 75 mins. **NB**: holding a return ticket for a specific sailing is no guarantee you will be allowed on the boat – Bland's excursion customers come first. Tickets to **Sete** can be bought from Voyages Comanov, 43 Ave Abou El Alaâ El Maâri, T 932649, Tx 33009, F 932320. There is a ferry every 3-4 days. Passenger tickets from MD2720. Car and 2 passengers from MD3740. **NB**: at the port avoid all touts selling embarkation cards which are free from the officals.

Atlantic beach, the Caves of Hercules and ancient Cotta

The excursion W is a rewarding experience, with a dramatic drive en route. The options are to negotiate a round-trip price with a grand-taxi driver in rue d'Angleterre, take a Boughaz minibus from the port gates, or in your own transport, follow rue Sidi Bou Abid and rue Sidi Amar on to the S701. This goes past Montagne, an exclusive suburb of royal palaces and villas. 11 km from Tanger is **Cap Spartel**, the extreme NW corner of Africa, with a notable lighthouse, and the *Café-Bar Sol*. This is followed by the long and wild Atlantic (or Robinson) Beach. This is a dramatic place, and swimmers

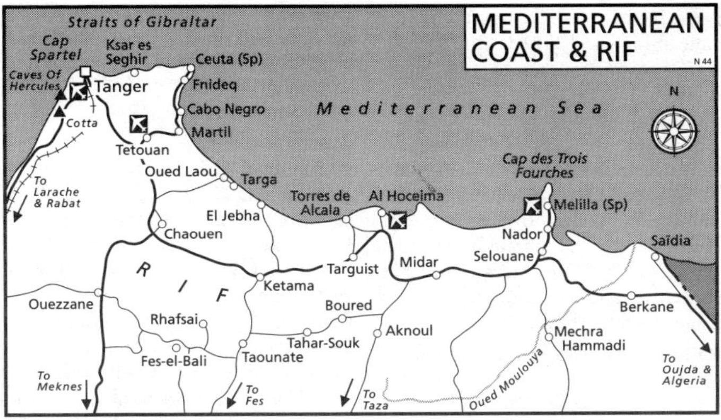

should exercise caution. Nearby is the C *Hotel Les Grottes d'Hercules*, T 938765; and the E *Hotel Robinson*; as well as *Camp Robinson* and the *Robinson Café-Restaurant*.

The **Caves of Hercules** are natural formations which have been extended by quarries for millstones up to the 1920s. Later prostitutes worked here, and a number of Tanger's rich and famous held parties. The natural rock chambers are open from 1000 to sunset, for a nominal charge. From a window shaped like Africa which overlooks the sea there is an impressive view.

After the Caves of Hercules take a rough farm track off the road to the **Ancient Cotta**. This is a small site, less impressive than Volubilis, centred around a factory for *garum*, or anchovy paste. Also note remains of the temple.

Cap Malabata, Ksar Es Seghir

From Tanger, E along the S704 road around **Cap Malabata**, are a number of large tourist developments, including the Club *Mediterranée* complex, as well as some excellent beaches. By the Oued Melaleh estuary is an old Portuguese settlement. Further on the **Chateau Malabata** is a Gothic folly, inhabited by a Moroccan family.

Ksar es Seghir is a small seaside town 37 km E of Tanger, dominated by the ruined Portuguese castle. The town was named Ksar Masmuda under the Almohads, and Ksar al Majaz under the Merinids, who added walls and gates in 1287. The Portuguese took the town in 1458. The floor of the *hammam* and mosque should be noted, as well as the intact sea gate arch. The F *Café Restaurant Hotel Kassar al Majaz Tarik Ibn Ziad*, is basic. There are a number of other cafés and restaurants, including the recommended *Restaurant Caribou*, possibilities for camping, and a nice beach. Onwards, between Ksar es Seghir and Ceuta, there is a string of beautiful and often deserted beaches.

Gibraltar/Algeciras

Catamaran/ferry excursions take only 75 mins. Day trips cost MD200 to Gibraltar, MD196 to Algeciras. See transport details, page 232. See section in Andalucía, page 142.

CEUTA

Ceuta is a Spanish enclave within Morocco, administered not as a colony but as an integral part of Spain, with a mixed population of Spaniards, Spanish Moroccans and Moroccan immigrant workers. Ceuta was a strategic site for the Phoenicians, Romans, Vandals and

Byzantines. It was taken by the Portuguese in 1415, and passed to the Spanish in 1580, who have occupied it ever since. Morocco makes periodic claims for Ceuta and the other enclave, Melilla, pointing out the parallel with Spanish claims for Gibraltar. Its contemporary role is as a military base, a passenger and car port and a duty free zone. Ceuta, which straddles the isthmus between Mt Hacho and mainland, is a convenient alternative arrival point in Africa to Tanger, with less hassle.

ACCESS **Road** From Ceuta follow the signposts to Morocco. The frontier post is on the S side of the peninsula, a little way out. Petrol is cheaper in Ceuta than Morocco. For those without transport, pick up a Spanish taxi or take bus 7 from Plaza de la Constitución. There are some long distance Spanish buses, from the bus station on the S coast road in Ceuta, to Casablanca, Al Hoceima and Nador. Tetouan is a better option for finding bus services. Arriving from Morocco, drive through Fnideq to the frontier. There are bus and grand-taxi services between Fnideq and Tetouan, and between Fnideq and Tanger. Between the frontier and Fnideq there is a grand-taxi, currently costing MD2. **The Frontier**: passports have to be checked and stamped by Moroccan officials both ways, and there are often lengthy queues. Travellers with their own transport have to have their vehicles registered and their papers, including insurance, registration and licence, checked. This can take some time. Cash can be exchanged on the Moroccan side of the frontier at the Banque Populaire booth.

Sea The Algeciras-Ceuta ferries are cheaper and quicker than those between Algeciras and Tanger, with passengers from MD130 and cars from MD645, taking 80 mins. There are normally 6 services a day Mon-Sat, 5 each Sun generally with refreshments available. Tickets can be bought from Transmediterranea in Cañonero Dato, T 509496, F 509530; from Isleña de Navegación, in the port building, T 509139/40; or from the numerous travel agents around the town centre. The port is in the centre of the town and the main destinations are clearly signposted. The hydrofoil service to Algeciras should be booked in advance at 6 Muelle Cañonero Dato, T 516041.

Things to see

Our Lady of Africa is the 18th century town cathedral in Plaza de Africa on the site of a former mosque, large but not very interesting, with a small museum. Wander around the older quarters of town centre, around Paseo del Revellin and Calle Real. The **Museo Municipal**, Paseo del Revellin, has a collection of archaeological exhibits and maps closed Sun. The **Museo de la Legión**, Paseo de Colón, open 1100-1400 and 1600-1800, Sat and Sun, entry free, includes a large collection of exhibits relating to the Spanish Foreign Legion.

The town leads on to a tree-covered hill, at the end of the peninsula, the Monte Hacho, a pleasant place for a stroll. At the far E edge is an old Portuguese fort. Stop off at the **Ermida de San Antonio**, a convent rebuilt in the 1960s. In the fort there is a small military museum, 5 rms, the **Museo Militar del Castillo del Desnarigado** includes such attractions as Franco's cape. Absolutely fascinating if you can read Spanish and have a knowledge of Spanish history. Open 1100-1400 and 1600-1800, Sat and Sun. Fortifications and walls separating isthmus from mainland on way to port.

Local information

● Accommodation

The best and most expensive hotel is the parador **AL** *Gran Hotel la Muralla*, 15 Plaza Virgen de Africa, opposite the Cathedral, T 514940, 106 rms, pool, bar, nightclub. Similarly expensive is the **AL** *Hotel Ulises*, 5 Calle Cameons, 124 rms, T 514540, with pool. The main area to try for cheaper hotels is Paseo del Revellin, Calle Cameons and Calle Real.

In Calle Real, try **C** *Pensión Real*, 11 rms, or **C** *Pensión La Perla*, 7 rms, or the very good **D** *C.H Rociera*. At the foot of Paseo del Revellin, opposite the Banco Popular Español, is the **D** *Pensión Revellin*, 16 rms, No 2, T 516267. Also try the **C** *Atlante*, 1 Paseo de las Palmeras, T 513548 and **D** ***Bohemia*** in Calle Cameons, clean, rec.

● Youth hostel
27 Plaza Viejo, T 515148, only open in Jul and Aug. Often crowded but the cheapest place in summer.

● Camping
Camping Marguerita, T 523706, is located 3 km W of the town. Take the Benzu road and then turn left, at the signs, just after a bar. We have received comments regarding poor facilities and high charges here and have been recommended another site closer to the town.

● Places to eat
♦♦♦Try the expensive and recommended ***La Torre***, 15 Plaza de Africa; ***Casa Silva***, 3 Almirante Lobo, T 513715, expensive array of Spanish fish and seafood dishes, as well as good wine; ***El Sombrero de Copa***, 4 Padilla, T 518284, seafood specialists; or ***Casa Fernando***, at the Benitez Beach, T 514082, good for seafood. ♦For a cheaper option, sample some of the *tapas* in a number of the bars.

● Banks
Banco de España, Plaza de España; **Banco Popular Español**, 1 Paseo del Revellin.

● Beaches
Either avoid the rubbish on the town beaches, or head out W to the more pleasant beach at Benzu.

● Discos
Bogoteca, Calle Real; ***Coconut***, Carretara del Jaral; ***San Antonio***, Monte Hacho.

● Festivals
Fiesta de Nuestra Patrona, La Virgen d'Africa, 5 Aug; **Carnival** in Feb.

● Post & telephone
Plaza de España, T 509275.

● Shopping
There are numerous shops selling duty-free goods, but the savings are not enormous but shop around for bargains, especially spirits. Fuel is cheaper here than in Morocco. For travellers heading on to Morocco, stock up on Spanish cheese and wine from the local supermarkets. Excellent fresh fish and shell fish.

● Tourist information
Oficina de Información de Turismo, Muelle Cañonero Dato, by the port, T 509275.

● Transport
Local Taxis In Ceuta T 505406, 505407, 505408.

TETOUAN AND ENVIRONS

Tetouan is the first major centre along the P28 from the border with Ceuta. There is a number of appealing resorts between Ceuta and Tetouan and also further round the coast which can be visited en route, or as an excursion from Tetouan.

Tetouan

Tetouan with a population of 200,000 has a striking location, between the Rif and the Mediterranean Sea. The city is dramatically beautiful with the white buildings of the medina heavily influenced by Andalusian Islamic architecture, often with balconies and tiled lintels. Some impressive colonial architecture is found in the more recent Spanish town. The city is an interesting place to explore, albeit with more noise and hassle than Chaouen and Ouezzane to the S. Although Tetouan is perhaps not the best place to visit first in Morocco, it should not be missed.

Tetouan was founded in the 3rd century BC as Tamuda, but destroyed by the Romans in 42 AD. The Merinids built a kasbah at Tetouan in the 14th century. Sacked by Henry III of Castille in 1399, Tetouan was neglected until it was taken over by Muslims from Granada in 1484, bringing with them the distinctive forms and traditions of Andalusian Islamic architecture, still observable in the medinas of Granada and Cordoba. Many of the Andalusians worked as corsairs. In 1913 Tetouan was chosen as the capital of the Spanish Protectorate in N Morocco which influenced its character and has remained an important regional centre in independent Morocco.

WARNING Tourists to Tetouan must be

careful as hashish dealers, pickpockets, and unofficial guides are out in force. It is advisable to pay great attention to one's personal belongings and preferably to avoid having any dealings with people operating in this manner. The tourist office and the larger hotels can arrange official guides.

ACCESS Air Tetouan's airport, used for internal flights from Rabat, Al Hoceima and Casablanca, is Aéroport Saniat R'Mel, T 971233, 5 km from the city. It is currently being redeveloped. Take a grand-taxi into the city. **Road** The P38 from Tanger, and the P28 from Ceuta to the N and Chaouen, Meknes and Fes to

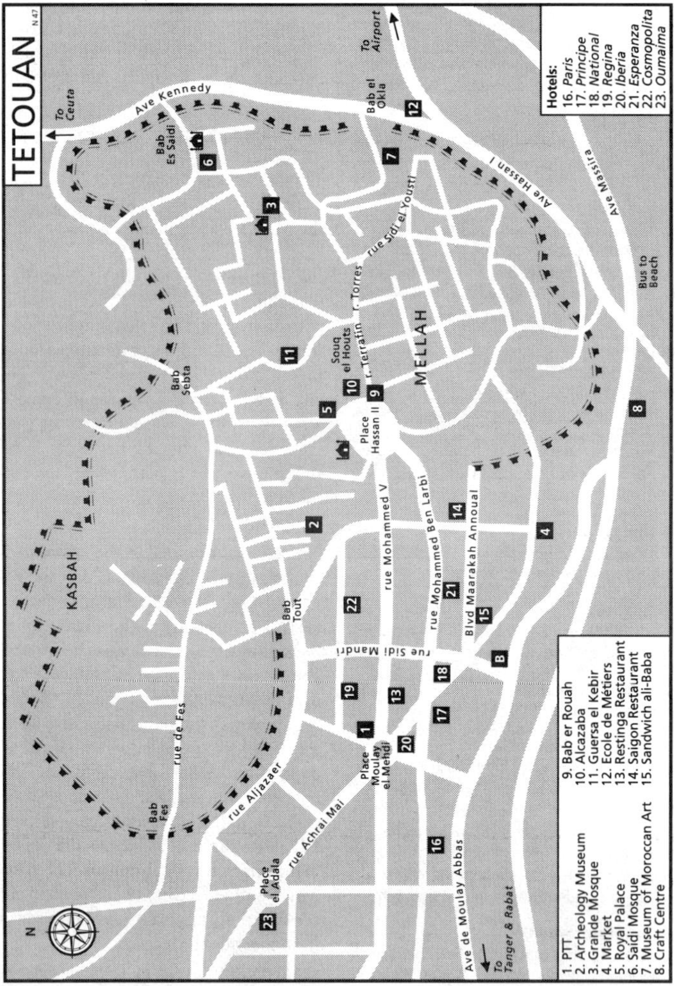

the S, both feed into Ave Hassan I, from where the medina and the centre of the *ville nouvelle* are clearly signposted. **Bus** CTM and most private line bus services arrive at the bus station at the corner of Ave Hassan I and rue Sidi Mandri, close to both Place Moulay el Mehdi and Place Hassan II. The ONCF coach service, for passengers leaving the rail network at Tnine Sidi Lyamani, arrives at Place el Adala. Local buses from the beaches normally drop passengers on Ave Massira or outside the main bus station.

Things to see

A good point to start is **Place Hassan II**, the focal point of the city and former market, and the best place to stroll or sit in a café terrace in the evening. It is dominated by the gleaming Royal Palace, originally from the 17th century but much added to recently, as the place has been redeveloped. Unfortunately parts have been cordoned off and it has lost some of its atmosphere. The other major centre in the *ville nouvelle* is Place Moulay el Mehdi, along Blvd Mohammed V from Place Hassan II dominated by an impressive golden-yellow cathedral.

Bab er Rouah, in the corner of Place Hassan II, leads into the medina. The **medina** of Tetouan is a confusing maze of streets and *souqs*, well worth exploring, although perhaps with the assistance of an official guide. In the *souqs* look out for artifacts with Tetouan's favoured red colouration. Rue Terrafin is a good route through the medina, leading into rue Torres and rue Sidi el Yousti, and out at Bab el Okla. N of rue Sidi el Yousti is an area with some of the larger and more impressive houses.

Souq el Houts, with pottery, meat and fish is to the left of rue Terrafin behind the palace. Behind the *souq* is a small 15th century fortress, the **Alcazaba**, now taken over by a cooperative. Take the left-hand of the 2 N-bound lanes from the Souq el Houts and on the right is Guersa el Kebir, a textile *souq*, selling in particular the type of woven blanket worn by Rifi women. Further on from this *souq*, leading up to Bab Sebta, is a number of specialist craft *souqs* and shops. Running between Bab Sebta and Bab Fes is rue de Fes, a more general commercial area, although with a number of *souqs* around. From Bab Sebta the road out of the city passes through a large cemetery. Above the medina is the crumbling kasbah, closed to visitors, and nearby a vantage point providing stunning views over the city.

On Place Hassan II, the first alleyway S of Bab er Rouah leads on to the main street of the *mellah*, the 19th century Jewish quarter, where there is a number of abandoned synagogues but few of the original inhabitants. The previous *mellah* is near the Grand Mosque.

The Archaeological Museum, Blvd Aljazaer, near Place Hassan II (0900-1200 and 1400-1800, except Tue), contains a small archaeological collection from the Phoenician, Roman and Muslim periods, notably exhibits from Lixus, near Larache. Note particularly the Roman coins and mosaics. There is also an extensive Spanish library.

The Musée d'Art Marocain/Musée Ethnographique (open 0830-1200 and 1430-1730 Mon-Fri, 0830-1200 Sat), Bab el Okla, contains traditional domestic exhibits and local costume, weapons and Andalusian musical instruments, with an Andalusian garden. Nearby, the **Ecole de Métiers** (Artisan School) (open 0900-1200, 1430-1730, except Tue and Sat), has craftsmen and students at work on *zelij* tiles, leatherwork, carpentry and pottery.

Local information

● Accommodation

Tetouan is not very well provided with hotels at the more expensive end of the market, whilst the budget hotels or *pensiones*, in and near the medina and Place Hassan II, are often primitive and unhygienic. **C** ***Hotel Safir Tetouan***, Ave Kennedy, T 970144, a little far from the centre, but Tetouan's best hotel, frequented by package tours, garden, pool, tennis, restaurant, nightclub (2300-0300).

E ***Hotel Oumaima***, rue Achra Mai, T 963473, central, convenient and respectable; **E** ***Paris Hotel***, 11 rue Chakib Arsalane, T 966750, similar, with garage; **E** ***Hotel Principe***, 20 Ave de la Resistance, T 962795, large, clean, not all rms have hot water; **E** ***Hotel National***, 8 rue Mohammed Torres, T 963290, recommended and not too expensive, with a café; **E** ***Hotel Regina***, 8 rue Sidi Mandri, T 962113, a cheaper hotel in the *ville nouvelle*, all 58 rms with bath, no hot water.

F ***Pensión Iberia***, above BMCE, Place Moulay el Mehdi, small and cheap with hot water; also good are **F** ***Pensión Esperanza***, Ave Mohammed V; and **F** ***Pensión Cosmopolita***, 5 Blvd General Franco.

● Camping

A number of camping sites at a little distance from Tetouan along the coast, the nearest by the river and beach at Martil.

● Places to eat

Tetouan does not have any exceptional restaurants. The city is known for its sweets. ♦♦♦ ***Hotel Safir Tetouan***, Ave Kennedy, T 967044, well-recommended and reliable. ♦♦***Zarhoun***, 7 Ave Mohammed Torres, near the bus station, Moroccan decor and music, and set Moroccan meals, bar; ***Restaurant Marrakech de Tetouan***, in the medina, has good Moroccan food and music, busy at lunch time; ***La Restinga***, 21 rue Mohammed V, good well-priced Moroccan food with good *tagines*; ***Restaurant Saigon***, rue Mourakah Anual, Moroccan and Spanish food. ♦***Café-Restaurant Moderne***, 1 Pasaje Achaach, near the bus station, cheap Moroccan food; ***Sandwich Ali Baba***, rue Mourakah Anual, is a popular place for cheap local food; also try the places around rue Luneta and Bab er Rouah.

● Banks

Banque Marocaine, Place Moulay el Mehdi; **BMCE**, 11 Ave Mohammed Ibn Aboud (0800-2000 Mon-Fri, 0900-1300 and 1500-2000 Sat-Sun); **BMCI**, 18 rue Sidi Mandri.

● Police

Blvd General Franco, T 19.

● Post & telephone

Place Moulay el Mehdi, T 966798.

● Shopping

Try the *souqs*, or the ***Ensemble Artisanal***, the government fixed-price shop on Ave Hassan I.

● Tourist information

Office du Tourisme (ONMT), 30 rue Mohammed V, T 967009.

● Transport

Local Much of Tetouan can be reached on foot. A petit-taxi is a cheap alternative.

Air Aéroport de Saniat R'Mel, 5 km away, T 971233, services to Rabat, Al Hoceima and Casablanca; Royal Air Maroc, 5 Ave Mohammed V, T 966610.

Road Bus The bus station, at the corner of Ave Hassan I and rue Sidi Mandri, T 966263, has both CTM and private line services to most major destinations. Services to **Fnideq** (for Ceuta, ½ hr), **Chaouen** (1½ hrs), **Tanger** (1½ hrs), **Meknes** (8 hrs) and **Fes** (9 hrs). ONCF also operates a coach service to link up with the rail network at Tnine Sidi Lyamani. Through tickets can be bought from the office at Place el Adala, where the coach also departs from each day at 0650 and 1555. Buses to Martil, Cabo Negro and Mdiq leave from near the old railway station on Ave Massira, those for Oued Laou from the main bus station. **Taxi** Much of Tetouan is quite manageable on foot, but a cheap and reasonable alternative is a petit-taxi. Grand-taxis to Tanger, Fnideq (for Ceuta), Chaouen, the beaches and other places, leave from Blvd Maarakah Annoual or nearby.

Around Tetouan: the beaches

From Fnideq to Tetouan, the P28 passes through a flat strip of beaches and marshes, and a number of tourist developments. **Restinga Smir** has a long beach, a *Club Mediterranée* and the *Marina Smir* tourist complex. Travellers can stay at the C *Hotel Golden Beach*, T 975096 or D *Hotel Carabo*, T 977070, 24 rms, bar, restaurant, pool, tennis, disco, or the *Al Fraia* campsite. After Restinga Smir the road passes through **Kabila**, another beach and marina, with the highly recommended B *Kabila Hotel*, T 975190, 96 rms.

Further on, **Mdiq** is more of a genuine settlement, albeit still with a number of large tourist complexes. For those breaking their journeys here there is the E *Hotel Playa*, T 975166, and a campsite, as well as the *Restaurant du Port*. After Mdiq turn off the P28 for **Cabo Negro**.

At Cabo Negro is another large *Club Mediterranée*; as well as D *Hotel Petit Merou*, T 978115/6, 23 rms, restaurant, bar, disco; and the *Restaurant La Ferme*, with French food.

From Tetouan, Restinga Smir, Kabila, Mdiq and Capo Negro are all practical excursions. **Martil** is another excursion, although on its own road out of the city. Tetouan's former port, and a pirate base, it is now another resort, with a popular beach. Stay at the E *Hotel Etoile de la Mer*, Ave Mawlay al Hassan, T 6776; E *Hotel Nuzha*, rue Miramar; or *Camping Martil*, by the river. Buses from Tetouan to Martil, Cabo Negro and Mdiq leave from Ave Massira, near the old railway station.

Oued Laou is 44 km from Tetouan, along the spectacular coastal road, the S608. It is a relaxed fishing village with an excellent beach but only basic facilities. Stay at **F** *Hotel-Café Oued Laou*; **F** *Hotel-Restaurant Laayoune*; or *Camping Laayoune*. Eat at the hotels or food stalls. Note the tiled octagonal mosque. An option from Oued Laou is to drive inland or take a bus to Chaouen.

The road continues along the coast through the villages of **Targa**, **Steha**, **Bou Hamed**, and **Dar M'Ter**. Possibly a more convenient place to stop is the final settlement, **El Jebha**, built by the Spanish. It is another fishing village and beach, with a *souq* on Tue morning. Stay at the **F** *Grand Hotel* or the **F** *Petit Hotel*, neither very good. It is also served by buses from Tetouan, as well as from Chaouen. A tortuous mountain road, the 8500, takes the intrepid traveller to meet the P39 W of Ketama.

CHAOUEN AND THE NORTHERN RIF

Chaouen

Pop 23,563 (1982) *Alt* 600m.

Chaouen, also called Chefchaouen, is a beautiful blue and whitewashed Andalusian town in the Rif, set above the Oued Laou valley. Chaouen lies below the twin peaks, Jbel ech-Chaouen, that have given it its name 'the horns'. Just nearby is the P28, N to Tetouan and S to Ouezzane, and the P39 E through the Rif to Al Hoceima. Lying within easy reach of ar-

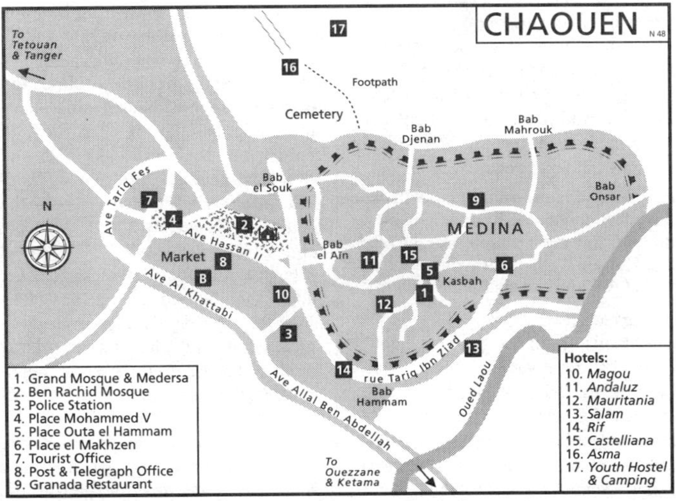

rival at Ceuta or Tanger, it is an excellent and peaceful introduction to Morocco. The selling of hashish is a big business here, but persistent refusal should rid travellers of unwanted attentions.

Chaouen was founded in 1471 by Sherif Moulay Ali Ben Rachid, a follower of Moulay Abd es-Salam Ben Mchich, the patron saint of the local Djeballa area whose tomb is nearby, in order to halt expansion further S of the Spanish and Portuguese. The city's population was later supplemented by Muslims and Jews expelled from Spain, particularly from Granada, and for a time the rulers of Chaouen controlled much of N Morocco, whilst the town also grew in importance as a pilgrimage centre.

From 1576 Chaouen was in conflict with, and isolated from, the surrounding area, with the gates locked each night. Prior to 1920 only 3 Christians had braved its forbidding walls, the Frenchman de Foucauld disguised as a *rabbi* in 1883, Walter Harris, Times correspondent and author of *Morocco that Was*, in 1889, and the American William Summers, poisoned in Chaouen in 1892. In 1920 Chaouen was taken over by the Spanish as part of their protectorate, when they found Jews still speaking 15th century Andalusian Spanish. The Spanish were thrown out from 1924 to 1926, by Abd al-Karim's Rifian resistance movement, but then returned to stay until independence in 1956.

ACCESS Buses and grand-taxis will drop travellers on Ave Al Khattabi. Walk up through the market alongside to reach Ave Hassan II, then turn right to reach Bab el Aïn and the medina.

Things to see

The Spanish-built new town of Chaouen is small and not very spectacular, but a pleasant and relaxing place. The centre is Place Mohammed V, with its small Andalusian garden. Ave Hassan II leads to Bab el Aïn and the medina. The market is down some steps from Ave Hassan II, on Ave Al Khattabi. Normally a food market, there is a local *souq* on Mon and Thur.

The Medina of Chaouen is one of the most rewarding to explore, sufficiently small not to get lost, but with intricate Andalusian architecture, arches, arcades and porches, white or blue-washed houses and clean, quiet cobbled streets. By car, park in Place el Makhzen and explore the rest on foot. Approaching the medina on foot, enter by Bab el Aïn. From Bab el Aïn a small road leads through to Place Uta el Hammam. This is the main square, lively at night, and surrounded by a number of stalls and café-restaurants, popular with *kif* (hashish) smokers.

The square is dominated by the 15th century kasbah, now the **Musée de Chefchaouen** (including the **Centre d'Etudes et de Recherches Andaluses**) (open 1000-1200 and 1400-1900, 0900-1700 in Ramadan). As a prison it housed the Rifi leader Abd al-Karim from 1926. The museum has an unremarkable exhibition of local costume, tools and instruments, but it is an interesting building, worth climbing to the top for a good view of the town from the roof, and exploring the dungeons and prison cells below. There is a quiet garden to relax in. Note the beautiful **Grand Mosque**, with its octagonal minaret, beside the kasbah, dating from the 15th century, but restored in the 17th and 18th. Next door is a 16th century **medersa**, unfortunately closed. Opposite the *Restaurant Kasbah*, at No 34, is an old *caravanserai*.

Further on, Place el Makhzen, the picturesque second square, has stalls along the top side, the **Ensemble Artisanal** at the end. Chaouen has a large number of artisans employed in metalwork, leatherwork, pottery and woodwork, amongst other crafts, and is particularly known for weaving the striped Rifi blankets, as seen on country women. It is well worth exploring the *souqs*, many of which are in the alleys S of Place Outa el Hammam.

For swimming there are several popular pools down in the Oued Laou, either walk or get a taxi. A pleasant pool to visit, and rest in a nearby café, is Ras el Ma, above the medina. Leave Place el Makhzen and head out above Bab Onsar.

Chaouen is a good base for **mountain walks**, with some spectacular scenery and plentiful animal and bird-life. Either take a guide or buy a map in Rabat. Expect suspicious questioning, and be prepared for a long and strenuous day.

Local information

● Accommodation

B ***Hotel Parador***, Place el Makhzen, T 986324, 35 rms, bar, restaurant, pool, the best in Chaouen, this hotel has a wonderful location at the centre of the town, and is comfortable and well-equipped, reservations needed.

C ***Hotel Asma***, T 986002, 94 rms, is an ugly hotel, both inside and out, placed insensitively on a hill above the town, but with an excellent view of the medina and the valley beyond, pool, bar, 2 tearooms, restaurant.

D ***Hotel Magou***, 23 rue Moulay Idriss, outside Bab el Aïn, T 986257, 986275, 32 rms with bath, clean and recommended.

E ***Hotel Salam***, 38 rue Tarik Ibn Ziad, T 986239, just below the medina, clean rooms with hot water, breakfast; **E** ***Hotel Rif***, 29 rue Tarik Ibn Ziad, T 986207, bar and restaurant, a friendly hotel with a restaurant and a good view from higher rms; **E** ***Hotel Ibiza***, rue Sidi Mandri, T 986323, on the entry to the town from Tetouan, a small hotel which is highly recommended.

The cheap hotels and *pensións* in Chaouen are often very good, basic but clean and very reasonably priced. The **F** ***Andaluz*** is clean and friendly with hot water, a few minutes walk from Place Outa el Hammam, follow signs; the **F** ***Pensión Castilliana***, signposted just off the main square; and **F** ***Auberge Granada***, up rue Targhi from Place Uta El Hammam, are also cheap; **F** ***Pensión Mauritania***, 20 Kadi Alami, below the square, is a friendly place with music and a café; **F** ***Pensión Ibn Batouta***, clean and quiet, just off the road between Bab el Aïn and Place Outa el Hammam.

● Youth hostel

With 30 beds, meals available, kitchen, overnight fee MD10 and **Camping Municipal** are together, 2 km above the town near the *Hotel Asma*. Follow the signs from the road in from Tetouan, or walk (diplomatically) through the cemetery above the medina. there is a small café, a shop, simple toilets and showers, tents amongst the trees, good view of the valley.

● Places to eat

♦♦ ***Restaurant de l'Hotel Magou***, 23 rue Moulay Idriss, recommended Moroccan food. More upmarket are the ***Hotel Asma*** and the ***Hotel Parador***, the latter with an extensive French-Moroccan menu. ♦There are several cafés and restaurants on the main square, Place Uta el Hammam such as ***Restaurant Kasbah***; also try ***Restaurant Tissemlal***, 22 rue Targhi, with excellent Moroccan food; ***Restaurant Zouar***, rue Moulay Ali Ben Rachid, near the main square, wide range of cheap Spanish dishes including fish; ***Restaurant Azhar***, rue Moulay Idris, friendly restaurant near the *Hotel Magou*; ***Restaurant La Plaza Grande Kazba***, rue Targhi, cheap Moroccan food near the main Place Uta el Hammam. For a modestly priced licensed restaurant go to ***Restaurant-Bar Omo Rabi***, on rue Tarik Ibn Ziad. ***Pâtisserie Magou***, Ave Hassan II, is good for bread and cakes; the *Hotel Parador* and *Hotel Asma* are good for a drink and view.

● Banks

Banque Populaire, Ave Hassan II; **BMCE**, Ave Hassan II.

● Chemists

Beside the *Hotel Magou*.

● Post Office

PTT, Ave Hassan II.

● Telephone

Local code 09.

● Tourist Information

Syndicat d'Initiative, Place Mohammed V, open mornings.

● Transport

Road Bus: CTM is just down from Bab el Aïn. Private line buses run from the station next to the market, on Ave Al Khattabi. Buses are often through services and can thus be full. There are several buses a day for **Ouezzane**, 2 daily for **Meknes** (5 hrs), 1 per day for **Fes** (7 hrs), several a day for **Tetouan**, 2 daily for **Al Hoceima** (8 hrs), 2 a week for **El Jebha** (7 hrs). **Grand-**

taxis: leave from the bus station on Ave Al Khattabi to most destinations.

The Northern Rif

The P39 from Chaouen to Al Hoceima is one of Morocco's most dramatic journeys, a route through a succession of small villages with stunning views over the remote valleys and towards the snow-capped Rif Mountains. Care must be taken on this narrow, hill-top road which may be closed by snow in winter. Traditionally this was an area of unrest against central authorities, notably in the Rif rebellion of Abd el-Krim against the Spanish from 1921 to 1926, whilst more recently bandits have preyed on travellers. Today the situation has improved, and the main dilemma is how to replace the production of *kif* (hashish) as the principal economic activity. Despite government programmes and pressures from Europe, production continues. Along this road it will be assumed that all travellers are there for the sole purpose of buying *kif* (hashish), and the numerous vendors are unlikely to believe anything else, and can be aggressive, so do not stop. There is often close cooperation between the police and the vendors, and sentences can be stiff.

Ketama is the centre of hashish growing and selling, although it had a previous importance as a walking resort. Although it has little else of interest and can be a stressful place to stay, it is perhaps thc most comfortable along this road, with the C *Hotel Tidighine* in the town centre, 67 rms, an old Spanish hotel with tennis, pool, bar and restaurant. Cheaper options are the F *Café-Hotel Saada* and F *California*.

The S302 runs S from Ketama to Taounate, Aïn Aicha and Fes. This road, the *Route de l'Unité*, was built just after Independence by voluntary labour battalions, to link the Spanish Protectorate of the N with the French Protectorate to the S.

E of Ketama, along the P39, the Rif becomes increasingly barren. After 12 km 8500 branches off to the left, a 61 km drive to the small coastal resort of El Jebha (see page 239). 30 km further there is another road, the 8501 to Torres de Alcala, a tiny fishing village, with some basic café-hotels. Just E of Torres de Alcala is the site of the port of Badis, destroyed in 1564, and offshore, the small island of Penon de Velez de la Gomera, still owned by the Spanish. 4 km W of Torres de Alcala is a campsite near Kalah Iris one of the most beautiful Mediterranean beaches.

Back on the P39 the next stop is Targuist by the Oued Rhis, a more peaceful alternative to Ketama, and a safer place from which to explore the mountains. There are many walks and rides in the cedar forests here. This is where Abd al-Karim finally surrendered. Stop at the F *Hotel Chaab* or F *Hotel Café-Restaurant El Mostakbel* by the square where the buses stop. Visit the small handicraft centre. There are fairly regular buses and grand-taxis to Al Hoceima.

THE MEDITERRANEAN COAST

Al Hoceima

Pop 41,662, Tanger 300 km, Melilla 170 km, Algerian border 250 km.

Al Hoceima (previously Alhucemas), is a beautiful though not overly developed resort. The *Club Mediterranée* lies about 10 mins E of the town, and the Maroc-Touriste complex is down from the centre by the beach. The beauty of its location, above a clear blue bay, makes a visit well worthwhile though the difficulty of approach by road reduces the flow of casual visitors. The character of the centre is distinctly Spanish, reflecting input in the protectorate years. Established by the Spanish in 1926 as Villa Sanjurjo, it was built as a garrison to control the Beni

Ouriaghel tribe, of which Abd al-Karim was the chief, immediately after the Rif rebellion. To the E of Al Hoceima is the long and less busy beach of the Alhumecas bay, offshore is Peñon de Alhumecas, a remarkable idiosyncrasy of history. This small rocky island, topped by a few buildings and a church, is owned and occupied by Spain and apparently used as a prison. It is completely dependent on Melilla for supplies and even water, and has no contact with the Moroccan mainland, off which it sits like a ship at anchor.

Things to see

View the vibrant Place du Rif, from the crazily decorated *Florido Café*. The souq, busiest on Tues, is unremarkable. The new town of Al Hoceima is dominated by Ave Mohammed V (banks and cafés) which leads down to the rather characterless Place du Marche Verte. Rue Tarik Ibn Ziad to the left has some crumbling Spanish colonial buildings while to the right a road curves down to the main beach (note on the left the intricate and colourful old Spanish school) and the port. The beach is dominated by the *Hotel Quemado* complex, open to non-residents, busy in the summer. There is no shortage of good beaches nearby. Visit the port area, which includes a fishing port (some good fish restaurants) as well as a naval port closed to visitors. A relaxed place to wander.

Local information

● Accommodation

D ***Hotel Quemado***, reservations by Maroc Tourist in Rabat T 763915, an ugly complex but with an ideal beach location, comfortable rms, bungalows and villas, restaurant, bar, night club, tennis; **D** ***Hotel Maghreb El Jadid***, Ave Mohammed V, T 982504, 40 good rms, restaurant, the best option in the town.

E ***Hotel Karim***, 25 Ave Hassan II, T 982184, clean and reasonable establishment, bar and restaurant; **E** ***Hotel National***, 23 Rue Tetouan, T 982141, 16 a/c rms with bath, telephone, breakfast room and TV room.

F ***Hotel Florido***, 40 Place du Rif (Sahat Rif), T 982235, a stylish pink and white Spanish building dominating the main square, once the town's casino, friendly, clean, best rms overlook the square, cold showers, restaurant, café; or as a fall-back the **F** ***Hotel de Station***, Place du Rif, basic, cold showers, friendly, convenient for buses; **F** ***Rif Hotel***, rue Sultan Moulay Youssef, also recommended; or at the camping sites, ***El Jamil***, T 982009, 2 km E; ***Kalah Iris***, nearby and cheaper.

● Places to eat

There are few top eating options in Al Hoceima but try ♦♦♦ ***Hotel Maghreb El Jadid***, Ave Mohammed V, T 982504, with a mixed French, Spanish and Moroccan menu, or ***Hotel Karim***, 25 Ave Hassan II, T 982184, French and Spanish cuisine, good for fish. At the port there are several good **fish restaurants** including ♦♦ ***Restaurant Karim***, T 982310, licensed; ***Restaurant Scorpio Sahara***, T 4410, ***Restaurant Chez Mimoune***, and the rougher, licensed ♦ ***Bar-Restaurant des Poissons***, most do not speak French. Other economic options in town are ***Restaurant Mabrouk*** or ***Restaurant Al Hoceima*** in rue Izzemounen just off Place du Rif, both serving *tagines*.

● Banks

Mainly on Ave Mohammed V, including **Banque Populaire** (at No 47), **BMCE**, **BMC** and **SGMB**.

● Hospital and pharmacists

Hôpital Mohammed V, Ave Hassan II, nearby to a number of pharmacists.

● Markets

Souq is on Tue, fish market each morning.

● Tourist Information

Délégation Regionale du Tourisme, Immeuble Cabalo, rue Tarik Ibn Ziad off Place Marche Verte, T 982830 (0830-1200 and 1400-1800), small but friendly.

● Transport in Al Hoceima

The town is small enough to explore on foot but for the port or beaches hail one of the blue and beige petit-taxis.

● Transport

Air The airport, Aéroport Côte du Rif is at Charif al Idrissi, 17 km from Al Hoceima, T 982063, with flights to **Amsterdam** and **Brussels** (1 a week), **Tanger** and **Casablanca** (2 a week) and **Tetouan** (1 a week). **By bus**: all buses leave from Place du Rif, which has ticket booths for the different companies.

Most buses leave early in the morning. CTM (T 982273) services to **Casablanca** (2000: 10 hrs), **Nador** (0500, 1230: 7 hrs), **Tetouan** (3 per day), **Targuist** (3 per day); private line services to **Tetouan** (0700, 0800, 1900, 10 hrs), **Nador** (0600, 0955, 1315, 1400, 1530, 1745), **Targuist** (0315, 0700, 0815, 0945, 1900), **Tanger** (0800), **Oujda** (1100, 5 hrs), **Fes** (0315, 0945, 12 hrs), **Ketama** (0315, 0945). **By taxi**: Grand-taxis leave from just off Place du Rif, to **Nador**, **Taza** and **Targuist**, amongst other destinations.

Nador

Between Al Hoceima and Nador the P39 winds inland through the foothills of the Rif, which are fairly deserted. One can stop at two roadside towns, **Drouiche** with the basic **F** *Hotel Es-Salam*, and **Mont Aroui**, with the similar **F** *Hotel Hassan*. At **Selouane**, a small mining and industrial settlement, the P39 continues inland to Nador and Melilla, whilst the P27 leads off to Berkane, Ahfir, Oujda and Algeria.

Nador, population 62,040, is a relaxed settlement with the atmosphere, commerce and transport of a border town, and it is most likely that travellers will pass through only en route or from Melilla. This modern city is now a major port and industrial centre and has a university. It is not a typical Moroccan town. There is a pleasant walk by the lagoon on Blvd Zerktoun, the cafés and evening promenade are on Ave Mohammed V, where the banks and travel agents are located.

20 km round the lagoon to the E is a good beach at Qariat Arkmane, where there are also some good fish restaurants, the *Karia Plage* camping site and birdwatching opportunities. Some continue to Ras el Ma for birdwatching.

Local information

● Accommodation

C *Hotel Rif*, 1 Ave Youssef Ben Tachfine, T 603635, at seaside, restaurant, nightclub, pool and tennis, large and well-equipped; **C** *Hotel Ryad*, Ave Mohammed V, BP60, T 607715, F 607719, 41 rms, 18 suites, lavish decor, restaurant with Moroccan and international cuisine, 2 bars, café, 24 hr rms service.

D ***Hotel Mediterranée***, 2-4 rue Youssef Ben Tachfine, opposite *Rif*, T 602611, restaurant.

E ***Hotel Annoual***, pleasant but over-priced; **E** ***Hotel le Marche Verte*** also called ***Hotel al Massira Khadra***, 106 rue Ibn Rochd, T 606721, an excellent option in the lower-price bracket. The cheap hotels are in and around Ave Youssef Ben Tachfine.

● Places to eat

♦♦♦ ***Hotel Rif***, T 606535, and ***Hotel Ryad***, T 607715, both have international and Moroccan cuisine. ♦♦ Slightly less expensive, with good fish dishes, is ***Restaurant Romero***, on the corner of Ave Hassan II and Ave Yacoub El Mansour. ♦There are cheap reasonable restaurants serving Moroccan food in Ave Hassan II, try ***Restaurant Centrale*** or ***Restaurant Kanaria***. The best cafés are on Ave Mohammed V.

● Tourist Information

80 Blvd Ibn Rochd, T 606518.

● Transport

Road The bus station, a noisy, busy, dirty place is at the end of Ave Hassan II, near the junction with Ave des Forces Armées Royales. CTM buses run to **Tetouan** (0930, 1800), **Al Hoceima** (0900, 1645), **Oujda** (0600, 0800, 0900, 1500) and **Casablanca** (2000); private lines run to **Ras El Ma** (1130, 1400), **Kariat Arekmane** (0900, 1230, 1730), **Guercif** (1220), **Oujda** (14 from 0600-1830), **Tanger** (0415, 1600, 1700, 2130), **Tetouan** (0415, 0530, 0800, 1700, 1800, 1900), **Ceuta** (1900), **Chaouen** (0415, 1900), **Targuist** (0415, 1115, 1700), **Al Hoceima** (10 between 0415-1700), **Casablanca** (1600, 1700, 1800, 2000, 2030), **Rabat** (1900, 2000), **Meknes** (0500, 1030, 1730), **Fes** (0000, 0500, 0630, 0800, 1200, 1730), Taza (1300, 1340), **Taourirt** (1345, 1500, 1515), **Berkane** (1130, 1330), and to **Ketama** and **Bab Taza**. ONCF, the railway company, run a bus at 2015 to **Taourirt** to connect with the trains to **Fes**, **Meknes**, **Rabat** and **Casablanca**. **By taxi**: grand-taxis from beside the bus station, with numerous destinations including **Ahfir** (over 1 hr) and from there to **Saïdia**, to the border with **Spanish Melilla** (MD 4), to **Al Hoceima** (MD 50), **Meknes** and **Fes**. **By boat**: there is a Comanov car and passenger ferry service from Nador to Séte in France, every 4 days from June to Sept, tickets and information from Comanov Passages, Immeuble Lazaar Beni Enzar, BP 89, T 06608538, or from the same company in Casablanca, 43 Ave des Forces Armées Royales, T 03310015/6.

Melilla

Melilla, just beyond Nador, has been a Spanish enclave since 1497. As with the larger Ceuta, although it has N African influences, it is clearly European, and a change for those on a long visit to Morocco, but is a declining and unexciting town.

The old quarter of **Medina Sidonia**, separated from the new town by the garden of the Plaza de España, and on an outcrop beside the ferry terminal, is an interesting quarter to explore, with a mixture of Moroccan and Spanish architectural influences and narrow winding streets, contained within the 16th century citadel walls. Enter by **Puerta de Santiago** on Paseo General Macias or **Fosa de Hornabeque** by the port. Whilst in the citadel find time to visit the **Iglesia de la Concepción**, a church, and the **Museo Municipal** (open 0900-1300 and 1500-1800), with coins, maps and historical archives, and Roman pottery.

Construction of the new town began in the 19th century, with many buildings designed by the modernist architect Enrique Nieto, but like Ceuta it is an uninspiring town. Ave de Juan Carlos I is the most popular street in the evening. There is a bull-ring at the Plaza de Toros.

Local information

● Accommodation

A *Parador Don Pedro de Estopina*, T 684940, with 27 rms.

B *Hôtel Nacional*, T 684540, 10 Avenida Primo de Rivera.

C *Hostal Residencia Miramar*, Paseo General Macias.

D *Hostal España*, T 684645, Avenida de Juan Carlos I, homely and reasonable; **D** *Pensión Numéro 7*, Ave de Generalisimo. There is also a camping site.

● Places to eat

For those missing Moroccan food already, or impatient to try it, go to ***Le Marrakech***, near the port. For reasonably-priced Spanish food try ***Bar El Rincón***, rue Lopez Moreno; or ***El Mesón de Comidas***, at 9 Calle Castelon, a good street for bars and restaurants, including also ***Bodegas Madrid***. A selection of *tapas* in some of the bars is a good option. Food can turn out quite a lot more expensive than in Morocco. After the disappointing ice-creams of Morocco, **Heladeria Alaska**, Ave du Generalisimo, may come as a welcome relief.

● Services

Banks are on Avenida de Juan Carlos I.

Duty free As with Ceuta there is a range of duty-free shops, with unimpressive prices, and Moroccan *bazaars*, best wait for the genuine thing.

Tourist Office 20 Calle del General Aizpura (open 0900-1400 and 1600-1800, Mon-Fri, 1000-1200, Sat).

● Transport

Air There are several flights a day for Málaga.

Road Buses to near the **border** with Morocco run from Plaza de España. From the other side take a grand-taxi, or one of the regular buses, into Nador. **NB:** the border into Morocco will take time and patience to cross. Hire cars cannot be taken across.

Sea Ferry services connect Melilla with Almería (Mon-Sat in the summer, 3 per week in the winter, 8 hrs) and Málaga (daily Mon-Sat, 10 hrs). Buy tickets from the RENFE office on Calle Gen O'Donnel, Transmediterranea on Calle Gen Marina or from the ferry terminal.

Eastwards towards Algeria

From just S of Nador, at Selouane, the P27 branches off the P39, leading to the Algerian border at Ahfir, 91 km to the E a pleasant if undramatic journey through the Rif foothills. From Berkane, 79 km from Nador, an interesting diversion to the S takes travellers through the **Zegzel Gorges**, dramatic both in the rock formations and the vegetation on the slopes and terraces. It is an exhilarating place for a walk, and quite trouble-free after the hashish producing areas. Those without their own transport can also visit the area by taking a grand-taxi to Taforalt and another from there through the gorges. Stop off at the unlit **Grotte du Chameau cave**, just before the gorges, for the stalactites and hot stream, but be careful not to get lost in the tunnels. Back on the P27 the next town after Berkane is Ahfir, a quiet border town. From here there are 3 options, N to the nearby resort of Saïdia about 20 km, E into Algeria or S through the Col de Guerbouss with good views, and the flat Plains des Angads into Oujda.

Saïdia

The road to Saïdia runs parallel to the Algerian border, at one point through a narrow gorge when all that separates the traveller from Algeria is the narrow but ironically named Oued Kiss. Saïdia is a pleasant resort popular with Moroccans, which has not been overly developed, and perhaps lacks some comforts. It is packed in the summer, with no shortage of places to eat, but limited and expensive hotels, some of which are closed in winter, when the place is fairly deserted. There is a long attractive beach, views of the Spanish held Islas Chafarinas and of Algeria, and a still occupied 19th century kasbah. It is an easy place to walk around, with a grid of brightly coloured houses, restaurants and hotels parallel to the beach.

• **Accommodation** Hotel options are limited, particularly as many are closed out of season, but try **C** ***Hotel Hannour***, rue Sidi Mohammed, T 615115, a large, ugly place, good for a meal or drink. **D** ***Hotel Select***, rue Sidi Mohammed, similar to *Hannour*, T 615110. **E** ***Hotel Al Kalaa***, rue Laayoune, by the beach, T 615123, 33 rms, also with a small restaurant and bar; and **E** ***Hotel Mediterannée***, rue Laayoune, cold showers, best of basic hotels. There are also several camp sites: ***Camping du Sit*** for families, ***Camping Caravaning Al Mansur***, and ***Camping Tours***. Saïdia is well-connected with Oujda by bus and grand-taxi.

• **Places to eat** Several standard restaurants on rue Sidi Mohammed, open all year round, including ♦***Café Restaurant Plus***. Try ♦***Café Bleu*** in rue Laayoune, relaxed and friendly atmosphere.

• **Transport** Grand-taxis leave from rue Laayoune or from the tree-lined road behind and parallel to rue Sidi Mohammed, to **Ahfir** (20 mins), and on to **Oujda**, **Berkane** and **Nador**.

OUEZZANE AND THE SOUTHERN RIF

An alternative route follows the P28 from Chaouen to Ouezzane, and the P26 and S304 from Ouezzane to Aknoul. However, whilst Ouezzane is a memorable town imbued with the atmosphere of an historic pilgrimage centre, and the scenery E is impressive, the opportunities for visitors are sparse.

Ouezzane

Ouezzane with a population of 41,000 is 60 km S of Chaouen along the P28, and like the latter has a dramatic hillside location, with impressive views of the rugged Rif Mountains and the verdant valleys between. It is worth visiting en route from Chaouen to Meknes or Fes.

The town was founded in 1727 by Moulay Abdellah Sherif founder of the Tabiya Islamic order. This brotherhood achieved great national prominence from the 18th century when the *zaouia*, or monastery, they had founded in Ouezzane, became the focus of extensive pilgrimage activity. Ouezzane had close links with the Sultan's court, which was often dependent on the *zaouia* and its followers for support.

Ironically, in view of the veneration Muslims accorded the *sherifs*, the then *Sherif* of Ouezzane married the Englishwoman Emily Keane in 1877 in an Anglican service, after they had met at the house of the American Consul where Keane was governess, although she later separated from him to live out her dotage in Tanger, where she is now buried in the Anglican Church. The *zaouia's* importance was destroyed by the *sherif's* growing connection with the French.

Ouezzane has importance today in the production of olive oil, and because of its *souq* on Thur, drawing in local farmers and tradesmen.

ACCESS **Road** The P28 to the N leads to Chaouen and Tetouan, S to Meknes. The P26 is to Fes and the P23 to Rabat and Casablanca. These roads meet at Place de l'Indépendence, the main square. There are numerous grand-taxis to Chaouen, and others to Souq El Arba du Gharb and Meknes. Buses to Chaouen (80 mins), Meknes (4 hrs) and Fes (5½ hrs) pass through Ouezzane, calling at Place de l'Indépendence.

Things to see

The **medina** of Ouezzane has some of the most interesting architecture in the Rif, with the picturesque tiled roof houses along winding cobbled streets. The focus of the town is the 18th century ***zaouia***, on rue de la Zaouia, a distinctive green-tiled building with an octagonal minaret. Non-Muslims should not approach too close. Nearby are old lodgings for the pilgrims and the decaying Sherifian palace.

Place de l'Indépendence, the centre of the medina, is busiest during the town *souq* on Thur. To get to the permanent craft *souqs*, centred around Place Bir Inzarane, follow rue Abdellah Ibn Lamlih up from Place de l'Indépendence. Ouezzane is particularly known for woollen carpets woven in the weavers' *souq* at the top of the town. The smiths' *souq* is along rue Haddadine. There is a **Centre Artisanale** on Place de l'Indépendence, and another on Ave Hassan II, open 0800-1900.

Local information

● Accommodation and places to eat

Ouezzane is very limited for hotels, and is perhaps best visited in passing or as an excursion from Chaouen. Choose between **F** *Marhaba*; **F** *Horloge*; and **F** *El Elam*, on Place de l'Indépendence; or the basic **F** *Grand Hotel* on Ave Mohammed V, although none of these is an attractive option. Eat at the basic café-restaurants on Place de l'Indépendence.

East of Ouezzane

From Ouezzane, the P26 goes E as far as Fes-el-Bali. This Rifian village is on the site of the ruined Almoravid 11th century city, the walls of which can still be seen, along with the *hammam*. From here the P26 continues S, 84 km to Fes. The S304 weaves E through the Rif, with a daily bus from Ouezzane to Fes-el-Bali. From Ourtzargh, 17 km further on, a side road takes intrepid drivers to the village of Rafsai (Ghafsai), an olive market, from where a track leads to Jbel Lalla Outka, a 1595m mountain from which there are extensive views over much of the Rif.

The next stopping point is Taounate, an uninteresting town with a large *souq* on Fri. From here it is possible to continue N to Ketama and S to Fes on the S302 (the **Route de l'Unité**). It is a long and tortuous drive to Aknoul from which there is a 39 km drive N to the P39 between Al Hoceima and Nador, and 53 km S to Taza on P1, with grand-taxis.

NORTHERN AND CENTRAL ATLANTIC COAST

CONTENTS

MAPS

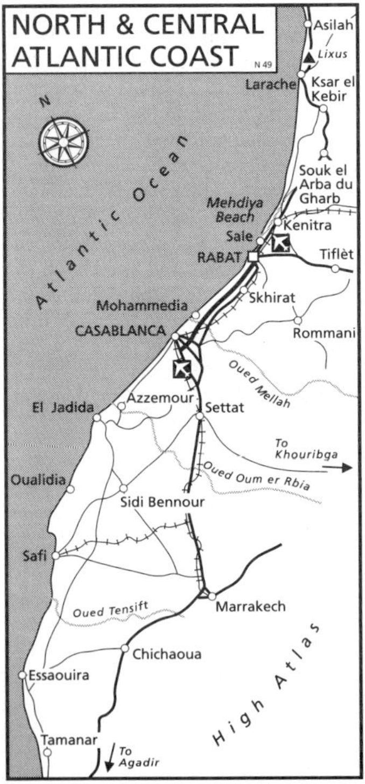

The Atlantic Coast has a wide variety of environments, reflecting its great length. At its centre is the immense axis of cities which dominate the country demographically, industrially, economically and politically, from Kenitra in the N, through Sale, Rabat, Mohammedia, to Casablanca in the S. This massive city, the second largest in Africa, has many of the facilities and problems of cities elsewhere in the Third World and is just as typical of modern Morocco as Fes or Marrakech. Elsewhere are a series of walled cities, initially built by the Portuguese, and now often relaxed beach resorts, including Asilah, El Jadida, Safi and Essaouira.

THE NORTHERN COAST

Asilah

With a population of 19,000 (1982), Asilah is a striking fishing port and coastal town of white and blue houses, surrounded by ramparts and lying alongside an extensive beach. As the first stopping point S of Tanger by road or rail, it provides an excellent introduction to Morocco, in spite of the extent to which tourism dominates. If it is possible, visit in Aug for the cultural festival, the International Festival of Asilah.

History

The site of Asilah was occupied by the Phoenicians, who called it **Silis**, and later by the Carthaginians, Byzantines and Romans. After destruction by the Romans, the town was rebuilt in 966 by El Hakim II, ruler of Cordoba. It was the last stronghold of the Idrissid Dynasty. The Portuguese occupied Asilah from 1471, and built the town's impressive fortifications, and in 1578 King Sebastian landed there on his way to defeat in the **Battle of the Three Kings**. This defeat led to the Spanish absorption of Portugal, and thus of Asilah, but the Portuguese influence on the town is still quite discernible.

The Moroccans recovered Asilah in 1691, under Moulay Ismail. In 1826 Austria bombarded Asilah, then a base of piracy, as did the Spanish in 1860. In the late 19th and early 20th century Ahmed al-Rasouli, the bandit chief who terrorized much of the NW of Morocco, was based in the town, as described by his one time hostage and later friend, Walter Harris, in *Morocco That Was*. Al-Rasouli built his palace in the medina, and from it exercised power over much of the region, being for a time its governor. The Spanish took Asilah in 1911, as part of their protectorate of N Morocco.

ACCESS Train The train station is just to the N of the town, a distance which can be walked, or if heavily laden, travelled in a taxi or local bus. There are frequent trains from Tanger, so this is a practical day excursion. **Road** Just off the P2 from Tanger to Rabat. Buses arrive in the town centre, 5 mins walk from the medina. Grand-taxis take an hour from Tanger, and drop passengers a short walk from the medina, near the bus station.

Things to see

The **medina** is the main interest of Asilah, a quarter of predominately white and blue buildings, reflecting in their design the influences of Portuguese and Spanish occupation. Note the modern murals on some of the houses in the medina, painted by artists during the festival. The ramparts were built by the Portuguese in the 15th century, and are broken by a number of important gates, including **Bab el Kasbah**, **Bab el Bahar**, 'the sea gate', **Bab el Hamar** 'the land gate', an impressive structure topped with the eroded Portuguese coat of arms, as well as **Bab el Jbel**, 'the mountain gate', and **Bab Ihoumer**. At points it is possible to climb the fortifications for impressive views of the town and along the coast. Within the medina, **Le Palais de la Culture** is a cultural centre converted from the former residence of the brigand Ahmed al-Rasouli, built in 1909 right beside the sea. It is difficult to gain access except during the festival, but it is quite possible to visualize those who incurred al-Rasouli's wrath being made to walk the plank from the palace windows over the cliff front.

The Souq The Thursday market attracts farmers from the surrounding area. In addition to the sale of the usual fruit, spices and vegetables, handicrafts distinctive of the Rif region are also on display.

The International Festival of Asilah, a cultural festival which has taken place in Asilah since 1978, involves performers from all over the world. Events throughout the town each Aug attract many spectators.

The Beach

The beach is often windy, frequented by bathers, men touting camel rides, and fishermen, but at times can be quite perfect. The beach stretches beyond the building works to the N of the city, and to the S.

Local information

● Accommodation

C *Hotel Al Khaima*, Route de Tanger, BP 101, T 917230, F 917566, 113 rms with bath, on edge of town with restaurant, disco, bar, pool, tennis.

D *Hotel Ouad El Makhazine*, Ave Melilla, T 917090, 917500, 29 rms with a/c, no showers, best hotel in the town centre, restaurant, bar and café, but with unexciting atmosphere and decor; **D** *Hotel Mansur*, 49 Ave Mohammed V, T 917390, 8 rms with bath, is a reliable choice.

E *Hotel l'Oasis*, 8 Place des Nations Unies, T 917186, 12 rms, an old palace with restaurant and bar.

F *Hotel Asilah*, 79 Ave Hassan II, T 917286, 11 rms, reasonable, friendly and central; **F** *Hotel Sahara*, 9 rue Tarfaya, T 917185, 24 rms, not very exciting; **F** *Hotel Marhaba*, 9 rue Zallakah, T 917144, near the medina, adequate and cheap, rms poorly sound-proofed but with colourful decor; **F** ***Hotel Nasr***, Place Zallakah, cheap and basic.

● Camping

There are several camping sites just N of the town along the road to Asilah, including ***Camping International***, with full facilities; ***Camping Ocean***; ***Camping Atlas***; and ***Camping Echrigui***, T 917182, with a shop and restaurant.

● Places to eat

♦♦***La Alcazaba***, 2 Place Zallakah outside the ramparts, T 917012, an excellent Italian/Spanish restaurant concentrating on fish and seafood dishes; ***Casa Garcia***, rue Ya'qub al-Mansur, is also recommended for similar food. ♦***El Espignon*** and ***El Oceano*** are both on Place Zallach just outside the ramparts. Several places here sell excellent and very fresh fish dishes.

● Banks

Banque Hispano-Marocaine, Place Mohammed V, T 917321.

● Chemist

Pharmacie Loukili, Ave de la Liberté, T 917278.

● Police

Ave de la Liberté, T 19 or 917089.

● Hospital

Ave du 2 Mars, T 917318.

● Post & telephone

PTT, Place des Nations Unies.

● Transport

Train: Asilah railway station is just outside the town alongside the P2 to Tanger, T 987320, and can be reached by local bus, by either petite or grand-taxi from Place Mohammed V. There are 6 trains daily to **Tanger**; 4 daily to **Meknes**, **Fes** and **Oujda** and 2 daily to **Rabat** and **Casablanca**.

Road Bus The bus station is on Ave de la Liberté, T 987354. There are regular bus links with Tanger, Ouezzane, Tetouan, Meknes, Rabat and Casablanca. **Taxi** Grand-taxis which are particularly convenient for Tanger, leave from Place Mohammed V.

Larache

Although with less appeal than Asilah, Larache is a relaxed, faded seaside town, with a good beach and not too many tourists, a halfway house between Spanish and Moroccan urban life. The town is easily reached by the P2 from either Tanger or Rabat. The bus station is just off Ave Hassan II.

Larache is called El Araish in Arabic, a name which refers to the vine arbours of the Beni Arous, a local tribe. The occupation of the area dates back to the Phoenician, Carthaginian and Roman settlement of nearby Lixus. Larache was occupied by the Spanish from 1610 to 1689, and as part of their protectorate, from 1911. They then added the harbour and the new town, using it as the principal port of their N Morocco zone. Larache has fruit processing and exporting activities, as well as fishing, but has lost its status as a major port. Amongst a small foreign population a former resident of Larache was Jean Genet, French playwright, now buried in the Spanish graveyard.

Things to see

On the way into Larache from Rabat, travellers pass **La Cigogne** (also called Castillo de las Ciguenas or Al Fath), a large fort built either by Moulay Ahmed al-Mansur and his Christian slaves in 1578, or during the subsequent Spanish occupation. The 16th century **Kebibat Fortress** is near the port, seeming to rise out of the sea, and now used as a hospital. Ave Mohammed V is the main street of the new town, with gardens on either side as well as a castle on the right and the **Iglesia de Nuestra Señora del Pilar** on the left (as heading to the centre). The circular Place de la Liberation with a fountain, is the heart of the town, lying between the medina and the new town.

Bab el Khemis leads off Place de la Liberation to the medina, a poor quarter but with some architectural appeal. Just inside is the Spanish built market square. There is a number of *souqs* in the medina, notably **Socco de la Alcaiceria**, the cloth market, a picturesque sight, in an otherwise unexciting old town. At the edge of the medina is the **Moroccan National Academy of Music**, built by the Spanish in 1915, near to an **Archaeological Museum**, open 0900-1200 and 1500-1730, Wed-Sun, which includes some items from Lixus. The medina is surrounded by a thick rampart. Through this **Bab el Kasbah** leads through to the ruined mediaeval kasbah.

For the main beach take town bus No 4, or a boat across the estuary. This is an extensive strip of fine beach, with a number of cafés nearby.

Local information

● Accommodation

D *Hotel Riad*, Ave Moulay Mohammed Ben Abdellah, T 912626/29, Tx 33803, a converted former residence of the Duchess of Guise, large well-maintained gardens, good restaurant and bar, tennis and pool, 24 rms, half-board required.

E *Gran Hotel España*, 6 Ave Hassan II/Place de la Liberation, T 913195, is the best cheap option.

F *Hotel Cervantes*, Place de la Liberation, a rather dismal place; the *pensións* just off Ave Moulay Mohammed Ben Abdellah, **F** *Pensión Es-Saada*; **F** *Pensión Amal*, T 912788; and **F** *Pensión Palmera*; and *Pensión Atlas* in the medina.

● Places to eat

Restaurant Al Khozama, 114 Ave Mohammed V, T 914454; ♦Cheaper eating options are *La Grotte de Pêche*, 7 rue Tarik Ibn Ziad, a fish restaurant; *Le Medina*, a small Moroccan place in the medina; *Restaurant Oscar*, just off Ave Mohammed V; and *Restaurant Larache*, on Ave Moulay Mohammed Ben Abdellah.

● Services

Shopping: the *Ensemble Artisanal* is on the road out to Rabat.

Tourist office: there is a **Syndicat d'Initiative** on Ave Mohammed V, T 913532.

Excursion to ancient Lixus

Lixus is perhaps the second most important Roman site in Morocco after Volubilis, and lies just N of Larache on the right bank of the Loukkos Oued. Some writers located at Lixus the Garden of Hesperides, with the golden apples harvested by Hercules to gain his place on Mount Olympus more likely to have been oranges. There was a Phoenician and Carthaginian settlement here, and the Romans made it a colony, with particular importance under the Emperor Claudius, when it exported salt, olives and fish. Lixus had a strategic position on the road from Tingis (Tanger) to Sala Colonia (Rabat) and was occupied until the 5th century AD.

To reach the site follow the Tanger road out of the town, take a bus across from the town, or bus No 4. The site is open during daylight hours. The lower town includes several salt factories. The upper town includes an acropolis complex, with temples dating back as far as the 7th century BC, and a Christian basilica. Between the 2 parts of the site are a bath house, an amphitheatre and theatre.

Ksar el Kebir, Souq el Arba du Gharb and Moulay Bousselham

Ksar el Kebir means the 'Great Fortress'. An 11th century settlement here was expanded and fortified by Ya'qub al-Mansur in the late 12th century. Near the town in 1578 was fought the famous Battle of Three Kings, where King Sebastian of Portugal, Saadian Sultan Abd al-Malek, and a claimant to the throne, former Sultan El Mutawakkil, all died. Moulay Ismail destroyed much of the town in the 17th century. The Spanish occupied Ksar el Kebir in 1911, rebuilding it and calling it Alcazarquivir, and developing it as a military centre. There is a large regional market (Sun) outside the station, as well as permanent *souqs* throughout the town, and a tannery. The town has an Almohad **Grand Mosque**, near to a Merinid *medressa*. Accommodation: F *Café-Hotel Andaluz*, very basic. Getting there: there are 6 trains a day to Tanger, 4 a day to Fes, Meknes and Oujda, 4 a day to Rabat and

Casablanca, and 2 a day to Marrakech.

Souq el Arba du Gharb is an important market town, with a *souq* each Wed, at the centre of the rich agricultural region of the Gharb, which extends as far N as Larache, and as far S as Kenitra. This region has been important for cereal, and then citrus and vegetable, production.

• **Accommodation** **E** *Hotel Gharb*, Route de Rabat-Tanger, T 902203, 902441, with a restaurant and bar; also a number of basic hotels and restaurants, but little else. **Transport**: there are regular trains to Tanger, Meknes, Fes, Oujda, Rabat, Casablanca and to Marrakech, as well as regular buses and grand taxis to Ouezzane and Moulay Bousselham.

Moulay Bousselham is a small beach resort with a relaxed atmosphere and rough swimming conditions. Although easily reached from Souq el Arba du Gharb, Moulay Bousselham is bypassed by most tourists. The place is named after a 10th century saint, who is commemorated in a nearby *koubba*, and a festival, or *moussem*, in July. The beach is spectacular but dangerous for swimming, although not bad for fishing. The lagoon, Merja Zerja, is safer for swimming, and attracts a number of species of birds, notably flamingos. Boats can be hired by those who want to bird watch from local fishermen. Bargain firmly.

• **Accommodation** **D** *Hotel le Lagon*, T 902603, with restaurant, bar, nightclub and pool; at the cafés; or at the basic *Camping Moulay Bousselham*. Eat at *L'Ocean*.

Kenitra

Kenitra, population 188,194 (1982) is an industrial and military centre of importance within Morocco, but perhaps of little attraction to the traveller. Kenitra was a small Moroccan military fort until 1913 when the French built a new town, as well as an artificial harbour used as a military port and to export citrus fruit and other products from the rich agricultural areas of the surrounding Gharb region. The port was developed to replace Larache, in the Spanish zone, and Tanger, in the International Zone. In 1933 the French renamed Kenitra Port Lyautey, after their first Resident-General of the Moroccan Protectorate. US troops landed here in Nov 1942 as part of Operation Torch, and experienced heavy casualties under fire from the port at Mehdiya, but from 1947 the USA returned to establish an important naval base, which they used until 1977. After Independence Port Lyautey was renamed Kenitra. Kenitra is still important as military centre and port. It lies on the P2 from Rabat to Tanger, close to the beach at Mehdiya.

• **Accommodation** **C** *Hotel Safir*, Place Administrative, T 365600, Tx 91995, good but unexciting, from an established chain with restaurant, bar, nightclub and pool. **D** *Hotel Mamora*, Ave Hassan II, T 363007, 365006, with a good restaurant and bar, nightclub and pool. **E** *Hotel la Rotonde*, 50 Ave Mohammed Diouri, T 363343/4, with a restaurant and bar; as well as cheaper hotels along Ave Mohammed V.

• **Camping** *Camping la Chenaie*, T 363373, with a restaurant and shop.

• **Places to eat** There is no shortage of restaurants on Ave Hassan II and Ave Mohammed V. *Hotel Mamora* and *Hotel la Rotonde* are recommended as places to eat and drink.

• **Post Office** Ave Mohammed V.

• **Sports** **Horse riding**: at *Club Equestre de la Mamora*, the Hippodrome; **Tennis**: at the *Tennis Club de Kenitra*, Ave des Sports, BP 131, T 363160, which has 6 courts; **Watersports**: wind surfing and yachting organized through *Union Athlétique de Kenitra*, Clos Dublin Kenitra, T 362012.

• **Tourist information** **Syndicat d'Initiative** on Ave Mohammed V, T (07) 162277.

• **Transport** **Train** From the railway station, T 365095, 363402, trains leave regularly to Asilah, Tanger, Meknes, Fes, Oujda and Marrakech, and there are 21 services to Rabat and Casablanca between 0353 and 2304. **Road** the bus station is on Ave Mohammed V.

Mehdiya

This is the beach for Kenitra, noted for windsurfing but more interesting to visit for its kasbah, and the nearby nature reserve around Lac de Sidi Bourhaba. Mehdiya is 11 km from Kenitra, with plentiful grand-taxis.

The **kasbah** was built by the Portuguese, and changed greatly by Moulay Ismail. In the 17th century it was used as a governor's palace, but was damaged by the US troops during their 1942 landing. The nature reserve is an extensive area focused on the **Lac de Sidi Bourhaba**, popular for birdwatching, and in the summer, for picnicking. The *koubba* has a festival in Aug.

• **Accommodation** **D** *Hotel Atlantique*, 21 rms, with a popular nightclub featuring live music; **F** *Auberge de la Forêt*; and *Camping Mehdia*, T 4849, open in the summer with pool, restaurant and shop.

• **Places to eat** There are cafés near the beach. *Restaurant-Café Dauphine* is recommended for fish meals.

CASABLANCA AND ENVIRONS

Mohammedia

Just to the N of Casablanca, stands Mohammedia, population 105,120 (1982), one of Morocco's major ports since the opening of an oil refinery in 1961. Industrial activities are centred around a rock salt factory. It is also a popular recreational area for the people of Casablanca.

• **Accommodation** **A** *Hotel Miramar*, rue de Fes, T 322021, F 324613, 188 rms, a luxurious place with restaurant, bar, nightclub, tennis and pool. **C** *Hotel Samir*, Blvd Moulay Youssef, T 310770/4, F 323330, 154 rms, good value with all facilities. **F** *Hotel Castel* and **F** *Hotel Voyageurs* are much more basic. There is a camping site, the *Camping International Loran*, T 322957, with pool, restaurant and shop.

• **Places to eat** ♦♦♦The restaurant in *Hotel Samir* is good, but expensive; *Le Frégate*, rue Oued Zem, particularly good for fish; *Auberge des Grands Zenata*, T 352102, midway between Casablanca and Mohammedia, sea food specialities, pricey.

• **Sport** Mohammedia is very well equipped for sports. **Golf**: the course, T 322052, with 18 holes is one of the best in Morocco, despite the high winds, 5,909m, par 73, fees MD450. **Horse riding**: *Club Equestre* on Blvd Moulay Youssef. **Tennis**: *Tennis Club de Mohammedia*, 9 courts, T 322037. **Watersports**: a number of yachting regattas between Oct and May through the *Yacht Club de Mohammedia*, Port de Mohammedia, T 322331, well-equipped club-house. A water sports centre at the *Ibn Batouta Nautic Base de Mohammedia*. Water skiing is popular here. The beach is good, despite its proximity to Casablanca.

• **Tourist information** at 14 rue Al Jahid, T 324299.

• **Transport** **Train** There are regular trains from Mohammedia to Rabat between 0625 and 2342, to Casablanca Port between 0728 and 2256, and to Casablanca Voyageurs between 0517 and 0025, as well as to all other major destinations. **Road** **Bus/taxi** There are frequent bus and grand-taxi services into Casablanca.

Casablanca

Pop 2,150,000 (1982) *Alt* 50m *Best Season* Any time of year except Jul-Aug which can be humid.

Casablanca is also known as El-Dar-el-Beida, both names meaning 'the white house'. The city is the economic capital of Morocco, the centre for trade, industry and finance, a major port handling a wide range of commodities including phosphates, and by far the largest city in the country, the 2nd largest in Africa after Cairo. Travelling through the city its immense size is impressive, less so the sprawling *bidonvilles*, tin-shack slums, which house much of the city's rapidly expanding population. Casablanca is a city where extreme poverty and wealth co-exist uncomfortably, where crime, prostitution and unrest are more evident than elsewhere in the country. The city does not have the historic monuments of

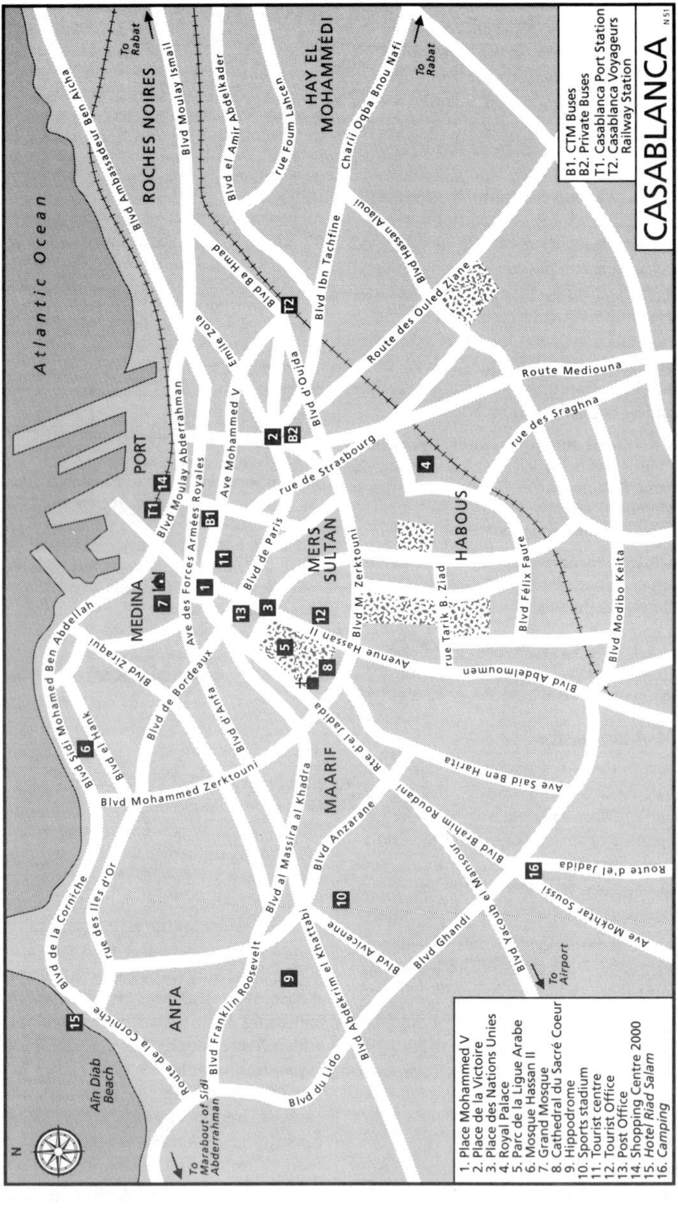
CASABLANCA
N51
B1. CTM Buses
B2. Private Buses
T1. Casablanca Port Station
T2. Casablanca Voyageurs Railway Station
1. Place Mohammed V
2. Place de la Victoire
3. Place des Nations Unies
4. Royal Palace
5. Parc de la Ligue Arabe
6. Mosque Hassan II
7. Grand Mosque
8. Cathedral du Sacré Coeur
9. Hippodrome
10. Sports stadium
11. Tourist centre
12. Tourist Office
13. Post Office
14. Shopping Centre 2000
15. Hotel Riad Salam
16. Camping
Atlantic Ocean
To Rabat
To Rabat
To Airport
To Marabout of Sidi Abderrahman
Aïn Diab Beach
ROCHES NOIRES
HAY EL MOHAMMEDI
PORT
MEDINA
MERS SULTAN
HABOUS
MAARIF
ANFA
Blvd Ambassadeur Ben Aicha
Blvd Moulay Ismail
Blvd el Amir Abdelkader
rue Foum Lahcen
Charii Oqba Bnou Nafi
Blvd Ba Hmad
Blvd Ibn Tachfine
Blvd Hassan Alaoui
Route des Ouled Ziane
Route Mediouna
rue des Sraghna
Emile Zola
Ave Mohammed V
Blvd d'Oujda
Blvd Moulay Abderrahman
Ave des Forces Armées Royales
rue de Strasbourg
Blvd de Paris
Blvd M. Zerktouni
rue Tarik B. Ziad
Blvd Félix Faure
Blvd Modibo Keita
Avenue Hassan II
Blvd Abdelmoumen
Blvd Sidi Mohamed Ben Abdellah
Blvd Ziraoui
Blvd de Bordeaux
Blvd d'Anfa
Blvd el Hank
Blvd Mohammed Zerktouni
Rte d'el Jadida
Ave Said Ben Harita
Blvd Brahim Roudani
Blvd al Massira al Khadra
Blvd Anzarane
Route d'el Jadida
Ave Mokhtar Soussi
Blvd Yacoub el Mansour
Blvd Ghandi
Blvd Avicenne
Blvd Abdekrim el Khattabi
Blvd Franklin Roosevelt
Blvd de la Corniche
rue des Iles d'Or
Route de la Corniche
Blvd du Lido
N

Rabat, Fes and Marrakech, and has a noisy westernized air that is unlikely to appeal to many travellers. However, as Morocco's largest city it is an interesting place to see, and is as representative as any of contemporary society.

History

There is believed to have been a Phoenician settlement at Casablanca, and a later Berber town. It was conquered by the Almohads in 1188, and developed by Sultan Abd el-Moumen as a port. In the 14th century the Portuguese established a settlement here on the site of the village of Anfa, but when it became a pirates' base in 1468, they destroyed it, repeating this act in 1515. The Portuguese reestablished themselves in the late 16th century, renaming the town Casa Blanca, staying until 1755, when an earthquake destroyed the settlement. The town was rebuilt at the end of the 18th century by Sultan Mohammed Ibn Abdellah, including the construction of the **Grand Mosque**, but it declined in the early 19th century.

In the 19th century, European traders settled at Casablanca, and at the beginning of the 20th century the French obtained permission from Sultan Abd al-Aziz to construct an artificial harbour, which marked the beginning of Casablanca's rapid expansion. The French occupied Casablanca in 1907, and expanded and developed the medina, which from 1918 until the establishment of Israel, became a largely Jewish quarter. In 1915 the French resident-general, Lyautey, and his chief architect, Henri Prost, planned the new city centre which bears a heavy imprint of French planning, with a grid of wide boulevards, large white commercial and residential constructions, and key state buildings designed in a style amalgamating European and Moroccan traditions, known as *Mauresque*. The city has subsequently sprawled far beyond this core, with vast planned projects and unplanned *bidonvilles*. Anfa was the site of the Casablanca Conference of Allied leaders in Jan 1943. Moroccan trade unions developed in Casablanca during the French protectorate, and were important in the nationalist struggle, notably in the riots of 1952 and insurrection from 1953-5.

ACCESS Air: Aéroport Mohammed V, T 339100, for most international flight arrivals and the centre of Royal Air Maroc's national network is 30 km to the S of the city at Nouasseur, and there are regular buses price MD25 to the city centre, arriving at the CTM terminal on rue Leon l'Africain. There are also expensive **grand-taxis** costing MD150 and taking 1 hr. The airport has a BMCE bureau de change, open most hours, car hire agencies, and desks for the major hotel chains, as well as a bar, restaurant and post office. An express train direct to Casablanca Ville or Casablanca Port takes 20 mins and costs MD30 economy class.

Train: the city has 2 main stations: Casablanca Port, at the end of Blvd Houphouet Boigny, which is most convenient for the city centre; Casablanca Voyageurs, at the end of Ave Mohammed V, which has more services; and the small suburban station of Aïn Sebaa, to the E of the city.

Road: Casablanca is well connected by road, with the P36 from Rabat and the N

CLIMATE: CASABLANCA

	Jan	Feb	Mar	Apr	May	Jun	Jul	Aug	Sep	Oct	Nov	Dec	Av/Tot
Max (°C)	17	18	20	21	22	24	26	26	26	24	21	18	22
Min (°C)	8	9	11	12	15	18	19	20	18	15	12	10	14
Rain (mm)	78	61	54	37	20	3	0	1	6	28	58	94	440

entering the city centre via Blvd Emile Zola, which leads into Ave Mohammed V; the P8 from Agadir and El Jadida enters via Blvd Brahim Roudani; the P7 from Marrakech via Ave Hassan II. **Bus**: CTM buses arrive at the terminal on rue Leon l'Africain, off Ave des Forces Armées Royales, private line services at the square near Place de le Victoire, from here it will be necessary to get a petit-taxi.

Things to see

The City Centre of Casablanca is a bustling place full of life, an example of the diversity of Moroccan society. The buildings are large, dirty, white constructions with balconies and shutters, revealing the predominate French influence on the design, and indeed it has the feel of a European Mediterranean city. The centre piece is the Place des Nations Unies, surrounded by major state buildings designed by the French in the *Mauresque* style, an amalgam of European and Moroccan architecture. This has a square and fountain popularized by western and Moroccan tourists, with crazily-dressed water-sellers wandering through the crowd. There is a lights display, 3 nights a week, which brings the city centre to life. Near the square is the pleasant Parc de la Ligue Arabe, and adjacent to that is the exuberant design of **Cathedral de Sacré Coeur**, built in 1930 and now used as a school.

The Medina the site of the old city, is a ramshackle, tatty quarter, dating primarily from the 19th century, and occupied for a while by a Jewish population. It can easily be explored in a couple of hours, entering from Place Mohammed V. The **Grand Mosque** was built by Sultan Sidi Mohammed Ibn Abdellah at the end of the 19th century. The medina is a good place to shop, although real bargains or high quality handicrafts are difficult to find.

The Port was constructed at the beginning of the 20th century, and is now a massive complex used for fishing, phosphates, commerce and industry, pleasure boats and cruise ships. There is a shopping centre, Centre 2000, and a number of fish restaurants, beside the port.

Grand Mosque Hassan II was inaugurated Aug 1993, the culmination of 5 years of intensive labour by over 30,000 workers and craftsmen. Apart from 50 chandeliers, all the materials and labour is Moroccan. This exceptionally beautiful new mosque has a highly decorative minaret, a landmark in the city. It is huge, in terms of covered area the largest in the world, and has space for 80,000 worshippers as well as a library and a museum. It is built out over the sea, the water washing against the windows of the ablutions room, the bay windows of the prayer hall (which has a mobile roof allowing it to be opened to the sky) looking over the Atlantic Ocean. The costly operation has been paid for by public subscription. Now support is required for the maintenance and day to day running costs. Non-Muslims may not enter. The easiest way to get there is by petit-taxi.

Aïn Diab is the beach quarter, along which the Corniche sweeps. To get to it take Bus 9 from the centre. The beach is not clean, but there are some interesting beach clubs along the Corniche, with cafés, restaurants and bars, most of which charge an entrance fee. The **Marabout of Sidi Abderrahman**, 3 km further W, still visited by Muslims, dedicated to an ascetic from Baghdad, is on a rock off the coast.

The New Medina, an area also called the **Quartier Habous**, was built in the 1930s. It was an interesting attempt by the French to solve a housing problem and incorporate features of traditional Moroccan house design and community layout with modern streets and utilities. Perhaps they failed, but it is an appealing area nevertheless. Take Bus 4 or 40 from the bus station at the junction of Blvd de Paris and Ave des Forces Armées Royales. Incidentally, the Quartier Habous sells excellent pickles and olives.

Local information

● Accommodation

Price guide:

AL	US$90+	D	US$20-40
A	US$75-90	E	US$10-20
B	US$60-75	F	under US$10
C	US$40-60		

Hotels in Casablanca are often booked up early in the day. The lower range hotels are often more expensive than elsewhere in Morocco and unusually can often be of a lower standard of cleanliness. **AL** *Hotel Hyatt Regency*, Place Mohammed V, T 261234, F 220180, 300 rms, one of the centre-pieces of the town, very modern and luxurious, 5 restaurants, bar, nightclub, hairdresser, health club, sauna, art gallery, squash courts and pool; **AL** *Hotel Sheraton*, 100 Ave des Forces Armées Royales, T 317878, F 315136, 306 rms, well-equipped and luxurious hotel with 5 restaurants, 3 bars, business centre, hairdresser, sauna, health club, *hammam* and nightclub; **AL** *Hotel El Mansur*, 27 Ave des Forces Armées Royales, T 313011/2, F 314818, 170 rms, very comfortable place with 2 restaurants, coffee bar, bar, hairdresser, health club, sauna and pool.

A *Hotel Riad Salam Meridien*, Blvd de la Corniche, T 363535, Tx 24692, 140 rms, the best place by the beach, with health facilities, restaurant, bar, nightclub, tennis and pool; **A** *Hotel Safir*, 160 Ave des Forces Armées Royales, T 311212, Tx 24896/7, 310 pleasantly decorated and well-equipped rooms, 4 restaurants, 2 bars, nightclub and heated pool; **C** *Hotel Transatlantique*, 79 rue Colbert, T 220764, Tx 24955, 60 rooms, a large old hotel with a restaurant and popular bar.

D *Hotel Plaza*, 18 Blvd Houphouet Boigny, T 221262, 27 rooms, satisfactory place with restaurant and bar; *Hotel Excelsior*, 2 rue Nolly, T 200048, 54 rms, 32 with bath, central, with a more illustrious past; **D** *Hotel Windsor*, 93 Place Oued El Makhazin, T 278274, 32 good rms, no restaurant, bar; **D** *Hotel George V*, 1 rue Sidi Belyout, T 312448, fair prices and convenient; **E** *Grand Hotel de Paris*, 2 rue Branly, T 273871, 34 rms, reasonable for Casablanca; **E** *Hotel Guynemer*, 2 rue Pegoud, T 275764, a friendly, good and clean hotel in a quiet but central location; **E** *Hotel Rialto*, 9 rue Claude, T 275122, fine; **E** *Hotel de Foucauld*, is to be avoided; **E** *Hotel Touring*, 87 rue Allal Ben Abdellah, T 310216, very good large rooms often with balconies, fills up early.

F *Hotel du Perigord*, 56 rue de Foucauld, not very clean but could be worse; **F** *Hotel Kon Tiki*, 89 rue Allal Ben Abdellah, unfriendly but often has rms, convenient; **F** *Hotel Les Négociants*, rue Allal Ben Abdellah, good and cheap; **F** *Hotel Bon Reve*, rue Allal Ben Abdellah, similar; **F** *Hotel Genève*, 44 rue du Marché aux Grains, in the medina, is clean and basic; **F** *Hotel Soussi*, rue de Fes, nearby, is also good value.

● Youth hostel

6 Place Amiral Philbert, T 220551, a square in the medina off Blvd des Almohades, 80 beds, meals available, overnight fee MD30 includes breakfast, bus and train 350m, renovated and friendly.

● Camping

Camping de l'Oasis, Ave Mermoz, T 253367, this is the nearest, in the direction of El Jadida, take Bus 31; in the same direction are *Camping Tamaris*; and *Camping Desserte des Plages*, both at rue Azemmour, Km 16.

● Places to eat

Price guide:
♦♦♦Expensive; ♦♦average; ♦cheap.

♦♦♦*Ma Bretagne*, Sidi Abderrahman beyond Aïn Diab, T 362111, excellent fish and good wine cellar, sea view; *Oriental Restaurant*, *Hotel El Mansur*, 27 Ave des Forces Armées Royales, T 313011, excellent Moroccan specialities; *Andalus Restaurant*, *Hotel Sheraton*,

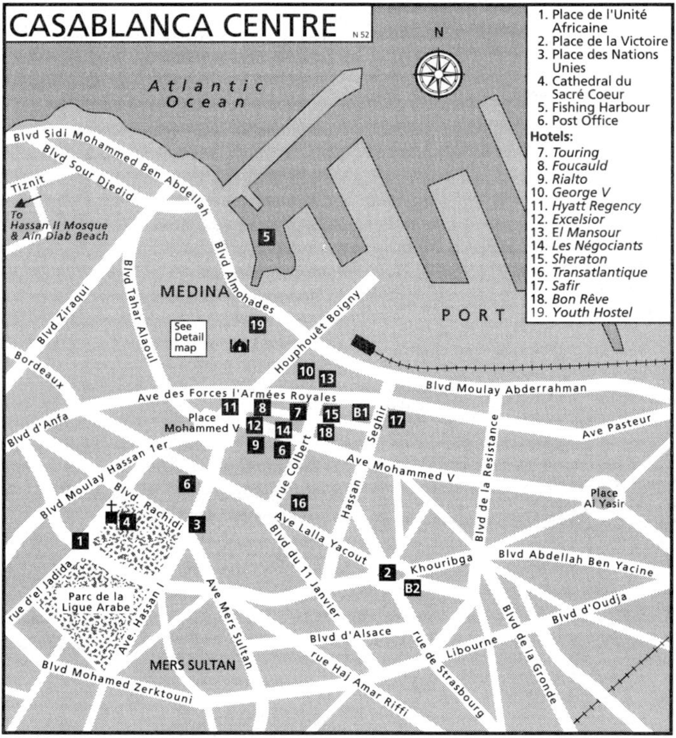

100 Ave des Forces Armées Royales, T 311194, is also good for local food; ***Dar Beida***, *Hotel Hyatt Regency*, Place Mohammed V, T 261234, reservations needed, sumptuous restaurant with all Moroccan specialities and music; ***Restaurant Wong Kung***, *Hotel Hyatt Regency*, T 261234, the best Chinese restaurant in Morocco, including on its extensive menu excellent seafood dishes; ***La Cambuse*** at Aïn Diab, T 367105, noted for fish dishes; ***Al Mounia***, 95 rue du Prince Moulay Abdullah, T 222669, Moroccan food.

♦♦ ***Maharaja Restaurant***, 46 rue Mohammed El Qorri, T 273780, a very good and reasonably priced Indian restaurant with alcohol; ***La Tajine***, Centre 2000, by the port, good Moroccan food; ***La Marignan***, 63 rue Mohammed Smiha, excellent Japanese food; ***Las Delicias***, 18 Ave Mohammed V, good Spanish restaurant; ***Le Petit Poucet***, 8 Ave Mohammed V, licensed French restaurant, very reasonable; ***Taverne du Dauphin***, Blvd Houphouet Boigny, T 221200, good for seafood; ***Restaurant Saigon***, 40 rue Colbert, T 286007, good Asian food.

♦A cheap area for eating is around rue Colbert and rue Allal Ben Abdellah, try ***Café Restaurant Anwal***, 116 rue Allal Ben Abdellah, T 319630, standard Moroccan fare but clean; ***Café Intissar***, rue Allal Ben Abdellah, cheap and reliable; another cheap area is in the medina, with the ***Restaurant Widad*** a good choice.

● Bars

Rick's Bar, in the *Hotel Hyatt Regency* on Place Mohammed V, is not the original, but has marginal curiosity value; ***Le Sphinx***, Ave Mohammed V, is a cheaper option; the ***Churchill Club***, rue Pessac, Aïn Diab is an expatriate club for English speakers.

Cafés and pâtisseries
Casablanca's reputation for ice-cream is quite without foundation, but for exotic combinations try ***Olivier's***, Ave Hassan II. There are some good cafés along Ave Mohammed V, and a popular scene around Place Mohammed V.

American Express
Voyages Schwartz, Ave Moulay Abdellah.

Airline Offices
Air Afrique, Tour des Habous, Ave des Forces Armées Royales, T 312866; **Air France**, 15 Ave des Forces Armées Royales, T 294040; **British Airways** and **GBAir** (Tour Atlas), 57 Place Zellaqa, T 307607; **Iberia**, 17 Ave des Forces Armées Royales, T 294003, 294008, Aéroport Mohammed V, T 339260; **KLM**, 6 Blvd Mohammed El Hansali, T 203232; **Lufthansa**, Tour des Habous, Ave des Forces Armées Royales, T 312371; **Libyan Airlines**, Tour des Habous, Ave des Forces Armées Royales, T 311500; **Royal Air Maroc**, Airport T 912000, 44 Ave des Forces Armées Royales, T 311122, 90 Ave Mers Sultan, T 268712, 44 Place Mohammed V, T 203270, reservations, T 314141; **Swissair**, Tour des Habous, Ave des Forces Armées Royales, T 313280; **Tunis Air**, Direction 10, Ave des Forces Armées Royales, T 273914.

Banks
ABM, Place du 16 Novembre, T 221275, 279 Blvd Brahim Roudani, T 258625; **Banque du Maroc**, Blvd de Paris, T 224110; **Banque Populaire**, 101 Blvd Mohammed Zerktouni, T 270540, 224111; **BMAO**, 115 Blvd d'Anfa, T 278828, 323 Ave du 2 Mars, T 220409, Place Zellaqa, T 301429; **Credit du Maroc**, 48-58 Ave Mohammed V; **GMB**, 55 Blvd Abd el-Moumen, T 224134, 2 Ave des Forces Armées Royales, T 222351; **SMDC**, 79 Ave Hassan II, T 224114, 27 Blvd Moulay Youssef, T 261171, 81 rue Colbert, T 224143.

Chamber of Commerce
Chambre Brittanique, 185 Blvd Zerktouni, T 256920.

Chemists
Pharmacie de Nuit, Place des Nations Unies, T 269491.

Consulates
Algeria, 159 Blvd Moulay Idriss I, T 288435; **Austria**, 45 Ave Hassan II, T 266904; **Belgium**, 13 Blvd Rachidi, T 222904; **Denmark**, 30 rue Sidi Belyout, T 316656; **France**, rue Prince Moulay Abdellah, T 265355; **Germany**, 42 Ave des Forces Armées Royales, T 314872; **Greece**, 48 Blvd Rachidi, T 277142; **Italy**, 21 Ave Hassan Souktani, T 277558; **Japan**, 22 rue Charam Achaykh, T 253264; **Netherlands**, 26 rue Nationale, T 221820; **Norway**, 44 rue Mohamed Smiha, T 305961; **Portugal**, 104 Blvd de Paris, T 220214; **Spain**, 29 rue d'Alger, T 276379, 220752; **Sweden**, 88 Blvd Lalla Yacout, T 319003; **Switzerland** (Visa Office), 43 Blvd d'Anfa, T 205856; **UK**, 60 Blvd d'Anfa, T 221653, 223185; **USA**, 8 Blvd Moulay Youssef, T 264550, 224149.

Discos & nightclubs
La Fontaine, Blvd Houphouet Boigny, has belly dancing and music; ***La Cage***, by the port, popular with the youth; ***Le Balcon***, Aïn Diab, a good disco; also try ***Caesar's*** in the *Hotel Sheraton*, 100 Ave des Forces Armées Royales, T 311194.

Doctors
Dr A El Kouhen, 24 rue Nolly, T 275343, speaks English; alternatively contact the *Croissant Rouge*, T 340914.

Emergency
Ambulance: T 15; **Fire**: rue Poggi, T 15; **Police**: Blvd Brahim Rodani, T 19.

Garage
Renault-Maroc, Place de Bandoeng.

Laundry
Pressing Mers Sultan, 116 Ave Mers Sultan, T 264194.

Motoring Club
Touring Club de Maroc, 3 Ave des Forces Armées Royales (0900-1200 and 1500-1830, Mon-Fri).

Post & telephone
The main PTT is on Place des Nations Unies, for collecting *poste restante* and good for telephoning, there is another PTT on Ave Mohammed V.

Religious services
Catholic: Eglise Notre-Dame de Lourdes, Rond Point d'Europe, T 220852; Eglise Saint-François d'Assise, 2 rue de l'Eglise, T 300930; Eglise d'Anfa, 13 Ave Jeanne d'Arc, T 361913. **Jewish**: Temple Beth-El 67, rue Verlet-Hanus; Synagogue Téhila Le David, Blvd du 11 Janvier; Synagogue Benarrosh, rue de Lusitania. **Protestant** Temple, 33 rue d'Azilal, T 301922; **Anglican** Church, 24 rue Guedj, T 365104 (1030, Sun).

● Shopping

Books: *English Forum*, 27 rue Clemenceau; *American Language Center Bookshop*, Blvd Moulay Youssef.

Handicrafts: the best fixed price shop, and a friendly place just to look, is the government-run *Coopartim* in the Grande Arcade Complexe Commerciale, just off Place des Nations Unies, T 269444. There are smaller shops in the medina and along Blvd Houphouet Boigny.

Food: there is a large covered market on Ave Mohammed V which has some excellent and cheap foodstuffs for sale.

Newspapers: there are newspaper stalls, some selling European papers, on Place Mohammed V and along Ave Mohammed V.

● Sport

Archery: *Archery Les Compagnons de l'Arc*, 25 rue des Flamants, T 277981.

Bowls: *La Boule Fédérale*, Parc de la Ligue Arabe, T 272868.

Boules: *La Boule Fédérale*, Parc de la Ligue Arabe, T 272868.

Golf: *Royal Golf d'Anfa*, 9 holes, T 251026, 10 mins from the centre of the city, a prestigious course with a luxurious club-house and a restaurant.

Horse Riding: *L'Etrier*, Quartier des Stades, Route d'El Jadida; *Club Equestre Bayard*, rue Schuman; CAFC, Quartier des Stades, Route d'El Jadida, T 259779, 255005.

Hunting: *Club La Gazelte de la Chaouia*, 21 rue d'Oudin le Romon, T 252911.

Rowing: *RUC*, Jetée Moulay Youssef.

Swimming: the beach is an unadvisable option, there are, however, pools in the Aïn Diab area, try the *Miami* beach club.

Tennis: *Cercle Athlétique de Casablanca*, Ave Jean Mermoz, T 254342, 18 courts; *Cercle Municipal de Casablanca*, Parc de la Ligue Arabe, T 279621, 6 courts; *Racing Universitaire de Casablanca*, Clos d'Aviation, Route d'El Jadida, T 254572; *Stade Olympic* Casablancais, Route d'El Jadida, T 254023, 8 courts; *Union Sportive Marocaine/Tennis Club de Casablanca*, Parc de la Ligue Arabe, T 275429, 8 courts.

Watersports: *Water Skiing Federation*, Port de Casablanca, T 227775.

Yachting: *Société Nautique de Casablanca*, Jetée de Delure, T 225721; Centre National de Voile, Royal Naval Club.

● Travel agents and airline offices

Comanov Voyages, 7 Blvd de la Resistance, T 303012, 302006; ***Discover Morocco***, 62 rue de Foucauld, T 273519; ***Gibmar Travel***, 8 rue Nolly; ***Menara Tours***, 57 Place Zellaqa, T 307607, 307629; ***Olive Branch Tours***, 35 rue de Foucauld, T 223919; ***Sun Tours and Travel***, 75 rue Driss Lahrizi, T 200196; ***Transalpino***, 98 Ave Mers Sultan, T 270096; ***Wagons-Lit Tourisme***, 60 rue de Foucauld, T 203051.

● Tourist information

Office du Tourisme, 55 rue Omar Slaoui, T 271177, F 205929; **Syndicat d'Initiative**, 98 Ave Mohammed V, T 221524, 274904.

● Transport

Local Bus The local bus station is at the junction of Blvd de Paris and Ave des Forces Armées Royales, take No 9 for Aïn Diab, No 4 and No 40 for the Habous quarter, No 31 for *Camping Oasis*.

Car hire **Avis**, 19 Ave des Forces Armées Royales, T 312424, 311135, and at Aéroport Mohammed V, T 339072; **Euro Rent**, 3 rue Assaâd Ibnou Zarara, T 254033; **Hertz**, 25 rue de Foucauld, T 312223, 294413; **Inter-Rent Europcar**, Tour des Habous, Ave des Forces Armées Royales, T 313737; **Inter-Voyages**, 4 Ave des Forces Armées Royales; **Leasing Cars**, 110 Blvd Zerktouni, Y 265331, a cheap option.

Taxi Casablanca's red petit-taxis are numerous, efficient and usually metered, although they are more expensive than their Rabat counterparts, hail them anywhere or T 255030.

Air Aéroport Mohammed V, T 339100 S of the city at Nouasseur connected by trains from Casablanca Voyageurs and Casablanca Port and by buses from inside the CTM terminal on rue Leon l'Africain and grand-taxis outside. There are flights to/from Casablanca to **Agadir** (at least 2 daily), **Al Hoceima** (2 weekly), **Dakhla** (2 weekly), **Fes** (daily), **Laayoune** (daily), **Marrakech** (2 daily), **Ouarzazate** (5 weekly), **Oujda** (daily), **Rabat** (daily), **Tanger** (2 daily), **Tan-Tan** (2 weekly) and **Tetouan** (weekly), as well as to most major cities around the world.

Train Departures from **Casablanca Port**, T 223011, 271837, to **Rabat** 18 a day between 0650 and 2035; **Meknes** and **Fes**: 0850; **Meknes**, **Fes** and **Oujda**: 2035. Departures from **Casablanca Voyageurs**, T 243818, 240800 to **Rabat** 16 a day between 0605 and 2320; **Marrakech**: 0130, 0623,

0740, 0948, 1211, 1405, 1506, 1755, 1928; **El Jadida**: 0850, 2038; **Oued Zem** 1012, 1710, 2007; **Meknes** and **Fes**: 0603, 1052, 1230, 1720; **Meknes, Fes** and **Oujda**: 0932, 1355, 2217; **Tanger**: 1850, 2320; **Aeroport Mohammed V** 11 a day between 0600 and 2055.

Road Bus The CTM terminal is at 23 rue Léon l'Africain, off rue Colbert and Ave des Forces Armées Royales, T 268061-7; daily services to Essaouira (5 hrs), El Jadida, Agadir, Tiznit, Beni Mellal, Marrakech, Fes, Tanger and Rabat. Private line buses leave from the terminal on rue Strasbourg, near Place de le Victoire. The following destinations are served daily: **Rabat** (51), **El Jadida** (32), **Mohammedia** (22), **Agadir, Fes** (11), **Meknes** (10), **Essaouira** (9), **Marrakech** (6), **Tafraoute** (5), **Ouarzazate** (4), **Azzemour, Inezgane, Tiznit** (3), **Khenifra, Khouribga, Oued Zem, Kasbah Tadla, Safi, Taza Tetouan, Sefrou** (2), **Nador, Taroudant, Oujda, imine, Kenitra, Larache** (1). **Taxi** Grand-taxi to Mohammedia and Rabat from by the CTM terminal.

Sea By boat Marinasmir, has 7 km of quay, and places for 454 private boats with draught up to 65m, T 306066.

EL JADIDA AND ENVIRONS

Azzemour

With a population of 24,774 (1982), Azzemour, is located at the mouth of the Oued Oum er Rbia, 15 km N of El Jadida. The white medina built alongside the river is striking, and the beach one of the best, but the town attracts few visitors. There is a train from here to Casablanca and Rabat at 0827, and buses and grand-taxis to and from El Jadida, and is best visited as an excursion, although there is the F *Hotel de la Victoire*, 308 Ave Mohammed V.

There was a trading post here called Azama in the Carthaginian period. In the 15th century Azzemour was an important trading port on the routes between Portugal and West Africa. The Portuguese occupied Azzemour in 1513 as a base from which to attack Marrakech, but under opposition from the Saadians had to withdraw in 1541. The town assumed regional importance under the Saadians, but soon lost ground to the growth of its near neighbour, El Jadida. Azzemour is known for embroidery. The town is sometimes referred to as Moulay Bou Chaib, after its patron saint, who has a *zaouia* above the town.

The walls of the old medina can be explored by the rampart walk, with excellent views of the town. Enter the medina, with its clear Portuguese architectural influences and impressive wooden doors, by **Bab es-Souq** and visit the *kissaria*, or covered market, the **Sanctuary of Moulay Abdellah Ben Ahmed**, and the **kasbah**, which also had a role as a *mellah*, or Jewish quarter. In the kasbah, visit the **Dar el Baroud** building. Climb its tower for a view of the town. Outside the town is the popular beach of Haouzia, a walk away, with the usual cafés.

El Jadida

El Jadida, population 81,500 (1982), is a popular beach resort, particularly for Moroccans, and has a faded elegance rather like some English seaside towns. The main historic site of walled citadel is, however, distinctly Portuguese in character.

El Jadida is a contraction of '*Al Brija al Jadida*', meaning 'the new little port', but before Independence was known as Mazagao, or Mazagan. The town was the site of an Almohad *ribat*, or fortress, later abandoned. The Portuguese founded a town at Mazagan in 1515, and it became one of their most important bases, holding it after the fall of their other enclaves. Sultan Mohammed Ibn Abdellah retook the town in 1769, and it expanded beyond the walls of the Portuguese city. There was a significant influx of Jews from Azzemour in the 19th century, and the town was further developed by the French, as the chief town of the Douk-

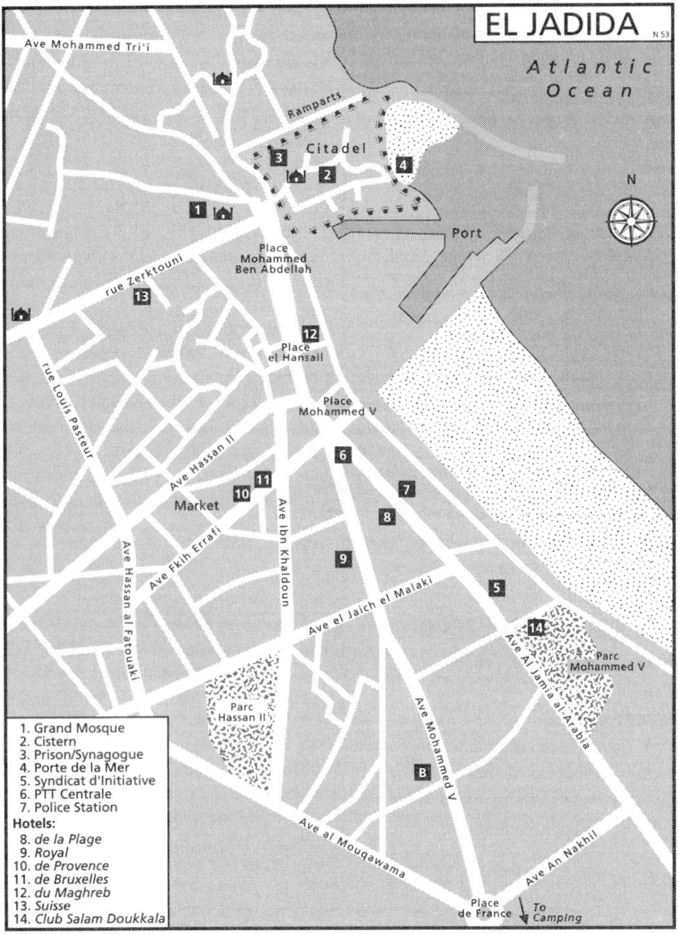

kala region. The town has an important port, with involvement in sardine fishing. The major deep-water port is just to the S of the town, at Jorf Lasfar. Each summer there is an influx of Moroccan tourists, particularly from Marrakech.

ACCESS Train The train station lies to the NW of El Jadida, and trains are met by a local bus to carry people in the town. **Road** The bus station is S of the centre, along Ave Mohammed V. From here it is a 5-10 mins walk to Place Mohammed V, the focus of the town.

Things to see

The Citadel was built by the Portuguese from 1513, and its distinctive character was maintained after their departure in 1769 by European and Jewish merchants who settled here from 1815. The quarter is small and relaxed, and very easily explored. The ramparts, access from the right of the main gates, which are surmounted by the escutcheons of the Portuguese kings, were completed in 1541. The gates are broken on the coastal side by the **Porte de la Mer**, from where the Portuguese finally left. The old walled city includes a chapel, hospital, prison and Governor's palace, a lighthouse converted into the **Grand Mosque**. The **Church of Our Lady of the Assumption**, a Portuguese construction, was restored by the French in 1921, and later converted into a mosque. The citadel's prison was converted into a synagogue.

The Cistern, a most distinctive feature of the citadel, underground on Praça do Terreiro (open 0800-1200 and 1400-1800), dates from the 16th century and was designed originally to store munitions. It served as a fencing school before being used as a tank to store water for times of shortage. The symmetrical construction has a vaulted roof supported by 25 pillars, with just one window. The floor is covered with water, which produces a remarkable effect of the shimmering reflection of the roof in the half-light of the cistern. Orson Welles used it in his film of Othello.

The Beach of El Jadida has a long elegant corniche, flanked by cafés, restaurants and beach clubs but the beach itself is not always clean.

Local information

● Accommodation

Hotels are often heavily booked in the summer, so ring ahead if possible, particularly if arriving late at night. The best are **C** ***Hotel Club Salam Doukkala***, Ave Al Jamia al-Arabi, T 343737, Tx 78014, 85 rms, a modern, well-equipped, unexciting hotel, restaurant, bar, nightclub, tennis, pool, and a sea view.

D ***Hotel le Palais Andalous***, Ave de la Nouie, T 343745, Tx 78001, charming hotel from the Protectorate period, a good restaurant and excellent bar.

E ***Hotel de Bruxelles***, 40 Ave Ibn Khaldoun, T 342072, clean and reasonable doubles with bath; **E** ***Hotel Royal***, 108 Ave Mohammed V, T 342839, Tx 78968, a comfortable establishment with restaurant and bar; **E** ***Hotel Suisse***, 145 rue Zerktouni, T 342816, reasonable value and quiet.

F ***Hotel de Provence***, 42 Ave Fkih Errafi, T 342347, a good value and friendly place with restaurant and bar; **F** ***Hotel de la Plage***, Ave Al Jamia al-Arabi, T 342648, cheap and reliable; **F** ***Hotel du Maghreb***, rue Lescoul, just off Place Mohammed V, basic and convenient.

● Camping

Camping International, Ave des Nations Unies, T 342547, with a restaurant, shop and pool.

● Places to eat

◆◆ *Restaurant du Port*, near the *Provence*, 42 Ave Fkih Errafi, T 342347, French meals. ◆ *Restaurant Chahrazad*, 38 Place el Hansali, off rue Zerktouni, reasonable Moroccan food; *Café des Amis*, Place el Hansali; *Chez Chiquito*, fish by the port.

● Bars

One of the best is at *Hotel le Palais Andalous*, Ave de la Nouie, T 343904, 343745; also try *Hotel de la Plage*, Ave Al Jamia al-Arabi.

● Post & telephone

PTT Centrale, Place Mohammed V.

● Shopping

The main traditional shops and stalls are around Ave Zerktouni. A *souq* is held near the lighthouse on Weds.

● Sport

Horse Riding: *Real Club Equestre S/C de Tribunal Regional*. **Tennis**: *Tennis Club Jedidi*, Parc Hassan II, T 342775, 5 courts. **Yachting**: *Association Nautique d'El Jadida*, Port d'El Jadida, T 342718.

● Tourist information

Office du Tourisme, Immeuble Chambre du Commerce, Ave Ibn Khaldoun, T 332724; **Syndicat d'Initiative**, Ave Al Jamia al-Arabi, T 342080.

● Transport

Local Train Trains leave to Casablanca and Rabat at 0810 and 0816. The train station is far out of the town, and will entail a trip in a petit-taxi, or in the bus which leaves from in front of the citadel ramparts. **Road** The bus station is in Ave Mohammed V, with regular services to Azzemour, Casablanca, Safi, Settat, Essaouira and Agadir.

Excursion to the beaches and Moulay Abdellah (Tit)

The beaches S of El Jadida on the S121 are reached by bus No 2 and grand-taxis. First is Sidi Ouafi and after the more developed Sidi Bouzid, with a bar, café-restaurants and a camp site. **Moulay Abdellah (Tit)** is a fishing village with an attached site of religious importance, lying 10 km from El Jadida. Tit, meaning 'the source', was founded by Ismail Amghar, an ascetic from Arabia, who settled here in the 11th century. The minaret of Ismail Amghar dates from the Almoravid period, and is almost intact. The place was renamed Moulay Abdellah, after a son of Ismail Amghar who founded a *zaouia* and another mosque here, and built the fortifications. The Almohad *zaouia* attracts many pilgrims to its annual *moussem*, or festival, in Aug.

CENTRAL ATLANTIC COAST

Oualidia

The coastal road from El Jadida to Safi with its 40 km long chain of lagoons is popular with bird watchers during the spring and autumn migrations, particularly at Sidi Moussa and Cap Beddouza. The main reason, however, to take this road, is Oualidia, an attractive port village, with a beach and kasbah, 78 km S of El Jadida, 64 km N of Safi. The town has a market (Sat), and good opportunities for sailing, surfing and fishing.

• **Accommodation** **D** *Hotel Hippocampe*, T 346499, small, very relaxed, good restaurant, bar, tennis and pool, beautiful setting above lagoon. **E** *Hotel Auberge de la Lagune*, T 346477, even smaller, has town's best restaurant and bar. **Camping** *Camping Municipal* and *Camping International de Oualidia* sites.

Safi

With a population of 197,309 (1982), Safi is a port and an important industrial centre. While not the most attractive of the coastal resorts, there is a **medina** worth visiting, and it is a convenient stopping point on the way down the coast. Its harbour has been important since pre-Roman times and it was one of the first areas of Morocco to receive Islam. Later it was the site of a *ribat*, or holy fortress. The Almohads surrounded the city with ramparts and built the **Zaouia of Sheikh Mohammed Saleh**. During their reign, Safi had an active intellectual and religious life. The Portuguese occupied the city in 1508, built a citadel and repaired the Moroccan kasbah, before leaving in 1541. The Saadians developed the city's trading role, notably in sugar, and built the **Grand Mosque** in the medina. The Alawites added further buildings and restored the medina. In the 17th century, European countries had a significant trading presence in Safi, and Moulay Ismail was instrumental in developing the city in the early 18th century. Safi had importance as the base of a large sardine fishing fleet, which continues to this day.

The French developed it as a port for exporting phosphate rock, connecting it by rail to the mines around Youssoufia, and from 1964 a new processing complex enabled the export of phosphate fertilizers, as well as unprocessed phosphates, and established Safi as one of the largest ports. The city also has important fish processing industries, and a reputation for producing some of the best pottery of the country.

ACCESS Both the railway station, on rue de R'bat, and the bus terminal, on Ave du President Kennedy, are to the S of the town centre, which is easily reached by local bus or petit-taxi. Trains run from Benguerir, which is on the line from Marrakech to Settat. The town is on the S121 coastal road from El Jadida and the P12 from Marrakech. Approaching on the main P8 from Casablanca and El Jadida to Essaouira and Marrakech turn along the P12 from Tleta de Sidi Bougedra.

Things to see

The Medina with its ramparts and large towers, can be entered by the main gate, **Bab Chaaba**. The main thoroughfare is rue du Socco, around which are located the main *souqs*. Just off this street is the **Grand Mosque** with a notable minaret, and behind it a ruined Gothic church built by the Portuguese, and originally intended as part of a larger cathedral. There is also an interesting old *medressa*. On the E flank of the medina is the **Kachla** (open 0900-1200 and 1500-1900), a large kasbah built by the Saadians, clearly identifiable with its towers and green-tiled roofs. On the right of its entrance is a large round tower built by the Portuguese, and within the **Kachla** is the **Bahia Palace**, an 18th century governor's residence surrounded by gardens. There are good views from the fortress.

Dar el Bahar Just outside the medina ramparts, overlooking the sea, is the Dar el Bahar fort and prison (open 0900-1200 and 1400-1600, Mon-Fri), built by the Portuguese in 1523, and used by them as the governor's residence. It is worth entering the building, if only for the view. There are also some 17th century cannons.

The Potters' Quarter at **Bab Chaaba** is worth a visit to watch the craftsmen at work, using traditional processes and materials. The predominate Safi colours are blue and white. Safi also produces the green tiles which are found on many major buildings throughout Morocco.

Beaches

The best local beach is Sidi Bouzid, just N of the town and on the No 15 bus route, with cafés and the very good *Le Refuge* seafood restaurant. Further afield is the Lalla Fatma beach, just past Cap Safi.

Local information

● Accommodation

C ***Hotel Safir***, Ave Zerktouni, T 464299, Tx 71071, 90 rms, a modern place from an established chain with restaurant, bar, nightclub, tennis and pool; **C** ***Hotel Atlantide***, 50 rms, rue Chaouki, T 462160/1, Tx 71724, restaurant, bar.

D ***Hotel les Mimosas***, rue Ibn Zeidoune, T 463208, Tx 71765, restaurant, bar.

E ***Hotel Assif***, Ave de la Liberté, T 462311, friendly place with restaurant.

F ***Hotel Majestic***, Ave Moulay Youssef, friendly and clean; there are other cheap places around the medina.

● Camping

Camping de Sidi Bouzid, 3 km N of Safi at Sidi Bouzid, T 462871, shop.

● Places to eat

Restaurant in *Hotel les Mimosas*, rue Chaouki, T 462160, is recommended; as is ***Restaurant Calypso***, near Place de l'Indépendence; and ***Restaurant de Safi***, 3 rue de la Maraine; cheaper places are around the medina.

● Bank

BMCE, Place Ibnou Sina.

● Post & telephone

PTT, Place de l'Indépendence.

● Shopping

The best bargain in Safi is pottery, for which the town is celebrated.

● Sport

The beach at Sidi Bouzid is known for surfing. There is horse riding at *Club Equestre*, Route de Sidi Ouassel.

● Tourist information

Rue Imam Malek, T 464553.

● Transport

Car hire Europcar, Place Ibnou Sina, T 462935.

Train The railway station is to the S of the town, on rue de R'bat, T 463375, 462176, there are trains to Benguerir at 0600 and 1700 connecting with trains to Marrakech and Casablanca.

Road There are regular buses to Marrakech, El Jadida and to Essaouira, the latter takes 3 hrs. The bus terminal is on Ave du President Kennedy.

Essaouira

Essaouira, population 42,000 (1982), is one of the most relaxed of the coastal resorts, with little of the large scale tourist infrastructure found elsewhere, but is understandably popular with independent travellers and surfers. It has a friendly, peaceful atmosphere and an interesting medina.

There was a small Phoenician settlement at Essaouira, previously called Magdoura or Mogador, a corruption of the Berber word *Amegdul*, meaning 'well-protected'. The Romans were interested in the purple dye produced from shellfish, which they used to colour the robes of the rich. Mogador was occupied by the Portuguese in the 15th century who built the fortifications around the harbour. The town was one of their 3 most important bases, but was abandoned in 1541, from when it went into decline. Visited by Sir Francis Drake, Christmas 1577. In 1765, the Alawite Sultan Sidi Mohammed Ibn Abdellah transformed Mogador into an open city, enticing overseas businessmen in with trade concessions, and it soon became a major commercial port, with a large foreign and Jewish population establishing the town as a major centre of trade. The Sultan employed the French architect Cornut to design the city and its fortifications. Mogador was shelled by the French in 1844.

Orson Welles stayed here for some time, filming part of Othello at the **Skala**. From Independence the town was called Essaouira, a local name meaning 'little fortress'. In the 1960s Essaouira had a brief reputation as a 'happening place', which attracted hippies, notably the rock star Jimi Hendrix. Essaouira now seems to be emerging from several decades of decline, for on top of fishing, fish processing, a small market and handicraft industries, particularly woodwork, the town is attracting greater numbers of tourists, notably surfers.

ACCESS Essaouira is connected to Marrakech via the P10, and lies just to the W of the P8 from Casablanca to Agadir. The new bus station is to the N of **Bab Doukkala**, and it is worth taking a *calèche* or petit-taxi as far as the gate to the medina or Ave Mohammed V.

Things to see

The Medina is Essaouira's major attraction. Entering from **Bab Doukkala** the main thoroughfare is rue Mohammed Zerktouni, which leads into Ave de l'Istiqlal, where there is the **Grand Mosque**, and just off, on Darb Laalouj, the **Museum of Sidi Mohammed Ibn Abdellah** (open 0830-1200 and 1430-1800, except Tues), which has an interesting collection of weapons, as well as handicrafts such as woodwork and carpets, and the **Ensemble Artisanal**. Ave de l'Istiqlal leads into Ave Okba Ibn Nafi, on which is located the small **Galerie des Arts Frederic**, at the end of the street a gate on the right leads into Place Moulay Hassan, the heart of the town's social life and although recently repaved and modernized, still with character. The town's *souqs*, are mainly located around the junction between rue Mohammed Zerktouni and rue Mohammed El Gorry, although there is an area of woodworkers inside the **Skala** walls to the N of Place Moulay Hassan, where some fine pieces can be picked up with some good-natured bargaining.

The Harbour and Skala Off Place Moulay Hassan is the small but vibrant harbour, which principally supports a fishing fleet, and is worth a visit. Adjacent to the harbour and continuing along the coastal side of the medina is the **Skala**, an old Portuguese sea defence and battery, with cannons still in position. Just to the N of Place Moulay Hassan it is possible to go on to walls, from where there is an impressive view along the coast and other to the islands. This part is separated from that by the port, which can also be visited.

Cemeteries Outside the walls is the Consul's cemetery for British officials who died there converting Mogador into a trading post with strong UK links. Across the road in the Jewish cemetery

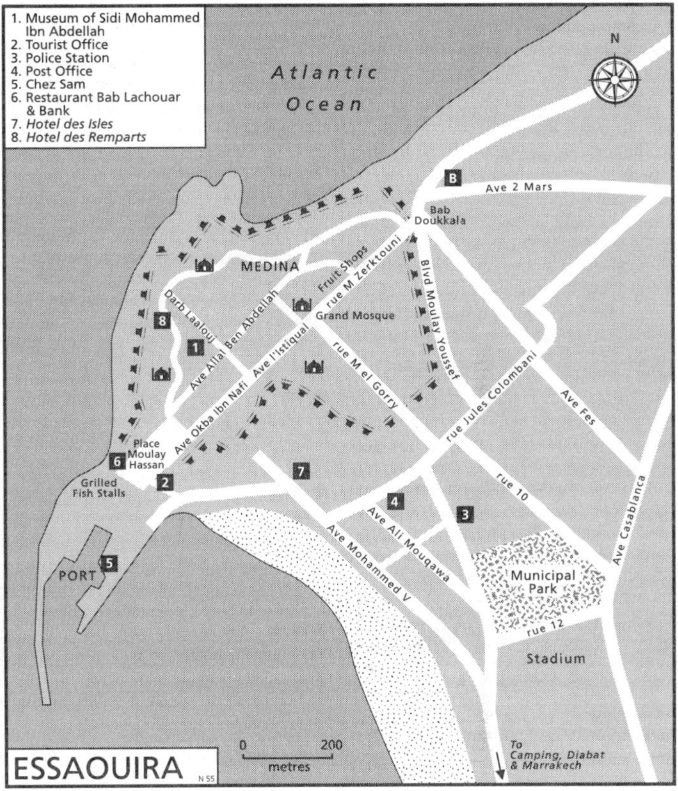

– if you can find the man with the key – is the resting place of Leslie Hore-Belisha who invented the first pedestrian crossing light.

The Beach at Essaouira is very beautiful, isolated but fiercely windy. The wind, known as the *alizee*, stirs up a lot of sand, and it is cold for swimming, but ideal for surfing. When walking far along the beach it should be noticed that the incoming tide makes the small stream below Diabat into an impassable river.

Diabat The ruined palace/pavillion below Diabat is worth a detour from a beach walk, just after the stream which crosses it, but the village of Diabat is dreadfully miserable.

Isles des Purpuraires These islands are a bird sanctuary, particularly for White Falcons. It is possible to visit the main island and the ruins of a prison, by contacting the Tourist Information Office on Place Moulay Hassan. They will direct the visitor to the Province office off Ave Mohammed V where a permit can be obtained for MD50, and will arrange a boat for transport, for a negotiable price.

Local information

● Accommodation

For hotels in Essaouira it is important to get a well ventilated room with windows, and preferably a view of the sea, for the others can be dark, claustrophobic and damp. **C *Hotel des Iles***, Ave Mohammed V, T 472329/74, Tx 71042, 65 rms, an historic hotel with tasteful period decoration, restaurant, bar, nightclub and pool.

D *Hotel Tafoukt*, 98 Ave Mohammed V, BP 38, T 472504/5, Tx 71022, 40 rms, a reasonable hotel, with tearooms, bar and restaurant, try and get a sea view.

E *Hotel Sahara*, Ave Okba Ibn Nafi in the medina, T 472292, 70 rms, comfortable and central; **E *Hotel Mechouar***, Ave Okba Ibn Nafi, T 472018, 24 rms, a bit cheaper.

F *Hotel Smara*, just inside the ramparts N from Place Moulay Hassan, is by far the best cheap option, clean and friendly, although make sure the room is one of those with a stunning sea view, the others are damp, good roof terrace; **F *Hotel des Remparts***, 18 rue Ibn Rochd, a popular place with friendly staff and a spectacular view from the roof terrace, but damp and with poor utilities; **F *Hotel Beau Rivage***, on Place Moulay Hassan, central, overlooking main square and friendly, double rms with bath, very damp; **F *Hotel du Tourisme***, rue Mohammed Ben Messaoud is cheap but poorly-equipped and very damp.

● Camping

Camping Municipal d'Essaouira, along Ave Mohammed V from the medina.

● Places to eat

♦♦♦***Chalet de la Plage***, 1 Ave Mohammed V, T 472158, good fish dishes but a wide range of other fishes; ***Chez Sam***, in the harbour, a fish and seafood restaurant and bar, with good food and drink and a distinctive atmosphere, particularly good lobster; ***Restaurant Riad***, Ave Allal Ben Abdellah, a wide range of Moroccan dishes. ♦♦ ***Restaurant El Khaima***, Place Moulay Hassan, a good licensed restaurant with Moroccan specialities; also try ***Restaurant Bab Lachouar***, on Place Moulay Hassan. ♦By far the best cheap eating option is to sample the freshly caught fish grilled at open air restaurants between Place Moulay Hassan and the port; accompanied by a tomato salad this makes a delicious meal at a reasonable, negotiated price. There are also a series of so-called Berber Cafés off to the left of rue Mohammed Zerktouni as walking towards Bab Doukkala. Other good cheap options include ***Café-Restaurant Essalam***, Place Moulay Hassan; and ***Mustafa's***, on Ave Allal Mohammed Ben Abdellah. The latter street has a number of cheap places.

● Bars

Try ***Chez Sam***, in the harbour; or *Hotel des Isles*; and *Hotel Tafoukt*, both on Ave Mohammed V.

● Cafés

The best cafés are on Place Moulay Hassan, particularly ***Chez Driss***, a good place to have breakfast, or watch the evening social life pass by. There are several beachside cafés, ideal for a rest from the wind.

● Bank

Place Moulay Hassan.

● Post & Telephone

The PTT is on Ave Lalla Aicha, back from the seafront and Ave Mohammed V.

● Tourist Information

Place Moulay Hassan.

● Transport

Local Bus CTM and private line bus services operate from the terminal N of Bab Doukkala, with connections to Casablanca, Safi, Marrakech and Agadir. **Taxi** Grand-taxis operate from a parking lot beside the bus terminal.

FES, MEKNES AND CENTRAL MOROCCO

Contents

Maps

The region of Central Morocco is the pivotal strategic region of the country, through which military and trade routes have always passed, as well as a productive agricultural area. It is thus a region in which power has often been concentrated, and some of the greatest urban settlements have evolved.

Under the Romans power was, for a time, concentrated at the site of **Volubilis**, still the best preserved and most informative site of the period. Nearby, Moulay Idriss, the father of the Moroccan state is honoured in the pilgrimage town of the same name, a memorable settlement, with houses cascading down hills on either side of a large sanctuary. Moulay Idriss founded **Fes** which went on to become an imperial capital, and the undisputed intellectual, spiritual and cultural centre of the country. Today it is full of stunning examples of different periods of Islamic architecture, as well as *souqs*, each with its own speciality, still functioning at the heart of the city. **Meknes**, just to the W, is associated above all with Sultan Moulay Ismail, who built a huge capital, much of it now in ruins. To the E of Fes, towards Algeria, Taza and Oujda are regional centres which have held vital strategic roles. To the S of Fes and Meknes lie the Middle Atlas mountains, with peaceful small towns amidst attractive wooded valleys.

MEKNES AND ENVIRONS

From Rabat to Meknes the P1 passes through the Mamora Forest and a belt of fertile, relatively prosperous and unexciting countryside. The only major town en route is Khemisset, with a *souq* on Tues, and a reputation for the best *brochettes* in the small restaurants along the main street. The former imperial capital

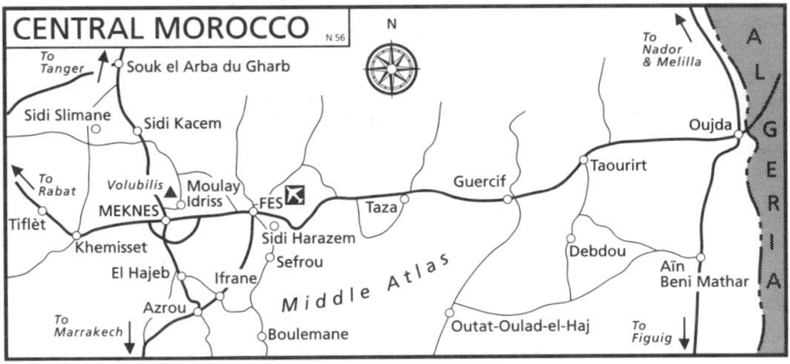

of Meknes lies between the Middle Atlas and the Cheraga hills. It is an essential stop en route to Fes, with a traditional medina and the ruins of Moulay Ismail's vast imperial city on either side of the huge and brightly tiled **Bab Mansur**. The shrine town of Moulay Idriss and the ruins of the Roman capital of Volubilis, the best ancient site in Morocco, are easy excursions from Meknes.

Meknes

History

Meknes is one of the great historic cities of Morocco, pre-eminent during the reign of Moulay Ismail when its vast, and now mostly ruined, imperial city was built. Meknes also has an historic medina quarter which includes the intricately decorated **Bou Inania Medersa**, the traditional but vibrant *souqs*, and numerous minarets. The *ville nouvelle* was built by the French on the opposite bank of the Oued Boufekrane, a calm place to drink a coffee or tea and watch the evening *promenade* pass by.

Early origins Meknes was originally a kasbah from the 8th century, used by the Kharajite Berbers against the Arabs. The town itself was founded by the Zenata Berber tribe in the 10th century and then destroyed by the Almoravids in 1069. A later kasbah was destroyed by the Almohad Sultan Abd el-Moumen in order to build a new grid-patterned medina, some features of which still remain. This city was ruined during the conflict between the Almohads and the Merinids, but was partially rebuilt and repopulated in 1276 under Sultan Moulay Youssef. The Merinids also built the *medersa*.

The Reign of Moulay Ismail The reign of the Alawite Sultan, Moulay Ismail (1672-1727) witnessed the peak of Meknes' glory, as the dynamic Sultan used his immense power as *pasha* to develop the city before his succession to the imperial throne. Meknes was chosen as his capital rather than the rebellious and self-important rivals of Fes and Marrakech. Moulay Ismail is renowned for his ruthless violence, but many of the stories recounted by the guides may be apocryphal. What is certain is that he made a great impression on the visitors to the court from Europe, and Meknes became a kind of Moroccan Versailles, indeed, some suggest that the Sultan was trying to rival Louis XIV, who was building his French palace at the same time. Moulay Ismail conquered and then controlled Morocco and left his mark all over the country, particularly with the kasbahs built by his troops as they pacified the numerous rebellious tribes, but also with an array of mosques, public buildings and medinas.

Moulay Ismail's vision of Meknes was vast, and although much of the *pisé-cement* city is in ruins, those walls still standing are testimony to its original scale. The city was built by a massive army of slaves, both Moroccan and Christian, and the Sultan was in particular famed for his barbaric treatment of these people, supposedly interring them in the walls. He built several palaces to accommodate his wives, concubines, children and court, as well as quarters for his army of Abids, black slaves, which was the instrument of his power. The city contained within it all that was necessary for such a large population and military machine, with store houses, stables, armouries, exercise areas, gardens and ponds.

After Moulay Ismail After Moulay Ismail's death Meknes gradually declined. His huge court and army could not be held together without his authority, and his successors Moulay Abdellah and Sidi Mohammed returned the emphasis to Fes and Marrakech. Furthermore the earthquake of 1755 destroyed many of Moulay Ismail's creations. The French revitalized Meknes, appreciating its strategic position in the corridor linking E Morocco and Algeria with the coastal belt around Rabat and Casablanca. They built their *ville nouvelle* apart from the medina and the Imperial City, on the E bank of the Oued Boufekrane, as part of their policy of separate development of Moroccan and European quarters. Meknes was an important army base for the French, and was not neglected in the way that Fes or Marrakech were.

Although Meknes is perhaps overshadowed by its near neighbour Fes, with a population of 319,783 (1982) it is today the 5th largest city in Morocco with both tourism and industrial activities, and the centre of a highly productive agricultural region, noted particularly for its wines which are the best in the country.

ACCESS Train: the main railway station is at Ave de la Basse, T 520017, 520689, but most trains also call at the Al Amir Abdelkader station, E of Ave Mohammed V, both in the *ville nouvelle*. **Road**: coming in from the E from Rabat along the P1, the principal route skirts the medina, crossing the Oued Boufekrane and reaching the *ville nouvelle* at the junction of Ave Moulay Ismail and Ave des Forces Armées Royales. Another route continues into the medina via Bab Khemis. From Fes and the E the P1 leads into Ave de Fes in the *ville nouvelle*. The P6 from Tanger and the N brings the traveller into the *ville nouvelle* along rue de Yougoslavie (Ave Al Moutahadia). **Bus**: CTM buses arrive at the terminal at 47 Ave Mohammed V, T 522583. Private line buses call at the large open space below Bab Mansur.

Things to see

The Medina: Place el Hedim and the Dar Jamai It is best to start exploring the medina from Place el Hedim ('the square of destruction'), opposite **Bab Mansur**. This main square has been considerably altered in recent years but still retains something of a focal role. It is also the area most frequented by the unofficial guides and pickpockets who are some of the most skilled and persistent in Morocco. To the left of the square is a crowded, covered food market with vast displays of vegetables and pickles. On the right-hand corner of the square is **Dar Jamai**, a 19th century palace, owned by officials at the court of Sultan Moulay Hassan, now a museum open 0900-1200 and 1500-1800, entrance MD10. Exploring the house gives one an insight into the houses and life of the 19th century Muslim élite, with an interesting exhibition of craftwork and antique household items, mixing Berber and Andalusian influences, including pottery from Meknes and Fes, and carpets from the Middle Atlas. Note also the wall tiles and jewellery. The upstairs includes a furnished reception room.

The souqs and the mellah Meknes has a number of traditional *souqs*, which whilst not quite of the order of those in Marrakech or Fes, are worth exploring. The lane behind the **Dar Jamai** leads to the main medina thoroughfare, to the right **Souq Sebbat**, including sellers of *baboushes*, and tourist shops, to the left **Souq Nejjarin**, the carpenters' *souq*, following a textiles *souq*. After the carpenters and the Almoravid **Nejjarin Mosque**, an entrance on the left leads to the parallel **Souq Joutia az-Zerabi**, selling rugs, and a good place to buy for the patient. Souq en Nejjarin leads into rue des Seraria, with the **Souq Bezzarin**. This is a long *souq* containing areas of different craftsmen and tradesmen.

To the left of the *souq*, the *mellah* leads downhill around Ave du Mellah, a quarter built by Moulay Ismail in 1682 for his large Jewish community, walled off from the Muslim medina. The **Bab Berima Mosque** dates from the 18th century when the *mellah* was becoming increasingly Muslim, as the Jews were moved further downhill into the medina.

Follow the outside of the medina along **Souq Bekkani** to the 12th century Almohad **Bab Jedid** gate. Continue beyond this to **Bab Siba**. A road on the right leads to the 18th century tomb of

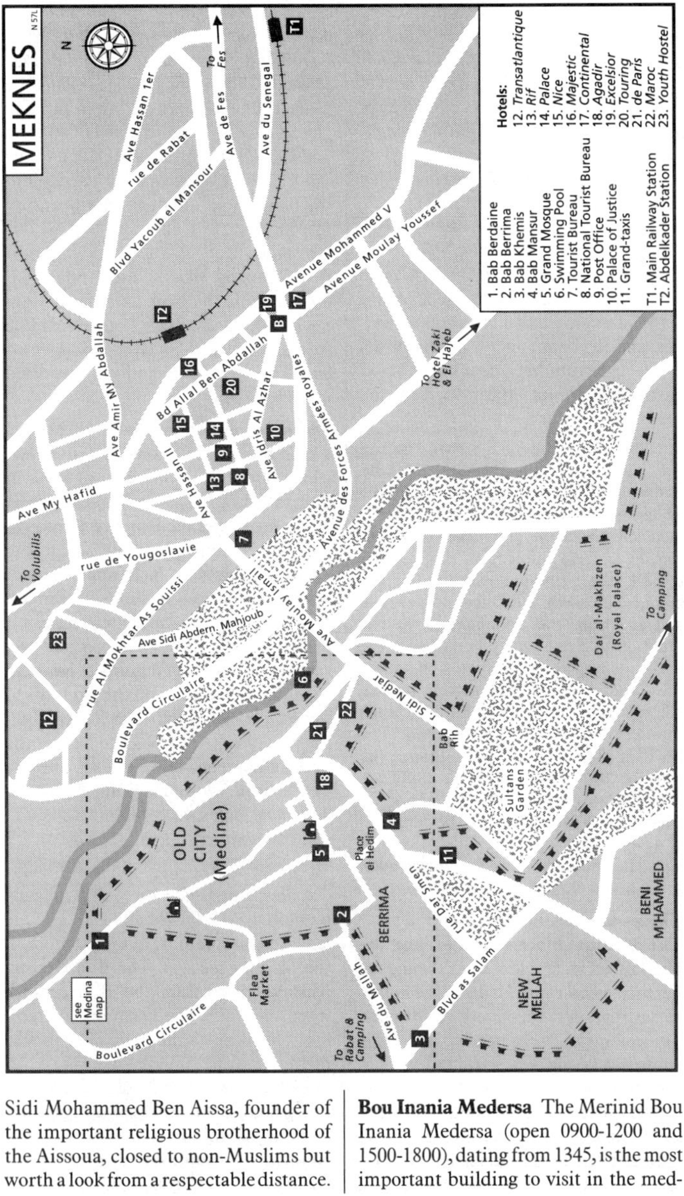

Sidi Mohammed Ben Aissa, founder of the important religious brotherhood of the Aissoua, closed to non-Muslims but worth a look from a respectable distance.

Bou Inania Medersa The Merinid Bou Inania Medersa (open 0900-1200 and 1500-1800), dating from 1345, is the most important building to visit in the med-

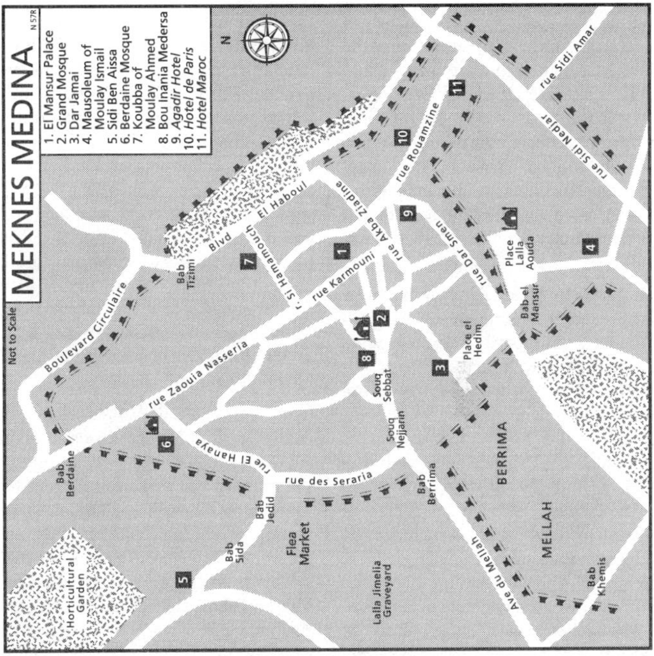

ina. From Place el Hedim, leave at the small gate on the right hand side of the square. Follow a street to the 13th century Merinid **Grand Mosque**. Turn left and cross the main street of the *souq*. The door to the *medersa*, part of a cedar screen, is just past a dome, notable for its ribbed design.

This religious school has 40 cells for its students, on both floors, around an oblong courtyard including a pool, with arcades surrounded by a screened passageway. As with many of the *medressa* there is a good range of decoration, the *zellij* tiling catching the eye, whilst the carving on the beams and screens are also skilfully and beautifully executed. There is a plentiful display of intricate Koranic inscription executed in a range of materials around the walls and pillars.

Turn right to the green and yellow tiled prayer hall. The door is ornamented with *zellij* tiling, as well as the customary and perhaps a little over-the-top stalactite style plasterwork. Note the inscriptions by the *mihrab*. Climb up onto the roof for a view of the medina, including the domed roof of the Great Mosque, the minaret of the Nejjarin Mosque, and other minarets.

Bab Berdaine The N medina is less frequented by tourists. Either weave through the medina from the *medersa* or the *souqs*, or more easily, leave via Place el Hedim, go E along rue Dar Smen and follow the walls around to the N, along by the Oued Boufekrane. Bab Berdaine, the second gate around, dates from the 17th century, a decorated building flanked by two immense towers. Inside, on Place el Berdaine, is the **Berdaine Mosque**. Travelling S the streets continue through an area of the traditional medina, less spoilt by the demands of tourism, and indicating the nature of the Islamic City. In such a city private and public space are clearly differentiated, commercial areas zoned by function, with each quarter having its own mosque, *hammam* and *four* (bakers), the 3 most important facilities in the neighbourhood. Eventually one will pass the **El Mansur Palace**, another 19th century house.

Bab Mansur Meknes is dominated by the monumental gate at the top of the hill in the medina, opposite Place el Hedim. Bab Mansur dates from the reign of Sultan Moulay Ismail, completed by his son Moulay Abdellah, and marks the entrance to the huge grounds of his Imperial City. The gate is named after one of the Sultan's Christian slaves, Mansur the Infidel. The huge size is more of a testimony to its Sultan than a reflection of defensive strength, as design is more ceremonial, for example the decorated flanking towers do not have firing posts.

The *outrepassé* arch is surrounded by a blind arch including the *darj w ktaf* motif and colourful *zellij* tiling. The frame is a band of *darj w ktaf* and *zellij* surmounted by inscription, and between the arch and the band is a black tiled area with floral patterns. The overall effect of the main gate is an exuberant and powerful display of the architecture of Moulay Ismail's reign.

The Imperial City of Moulay Ismail is a massive area of crumbling walls and ruins well worth taking a day to explore at leisure. Immediately through Bab Mansur from Place el Hedim there is Place Lalla Aouda, a relaxing and pleasant area to rest. In the far corner is the **Lalla Aouda Mosque**, the story being that it was built by Princess Aouda as penance for eating a peach during the Ramadan fast.

Straight ahead from Bab Mansur is **Bab Filala**. Through this, another square leads to **Bab Moulay Ismail**. To the right note the domed **Koubat al-Khayyatin**. In the 18th century this was used to receive ambassadors, and later to make uniforms. In front of this building steps lead down to an underground space, variously explained as a prison or a storehouse. Looking back at Bab Moulay Ismail, turn right along the road until an opening in the wall leads to a golf course. This was originally to have been a lake, but was converted into its present usage by the present king. Behind the golf course is a later palace of Moulay Ismail, the **Royal Palace** or **Dar al-Makhzen**, still in use and now heavily restored, closed to visitors.

Going through Bab Moulay Ismail, the **Mausoleum of Moulay Ismail** is on the left. Non-Muslims can enter an annex to the mosque and look around from that vantage point. With splendid *zellij* and plaster stucco, the chambers and courts are worth a brief look. Just past the mausoleum is an entrance to **Dar al-Kebira**, Moulay Ismail's late 17th century palace. The palace is in ruins, and occupied by squatters in an ironic statement on Morocco's housing situation, but the nature and vast scale of the original basic structure of the building can be easily discerned. Back out on the road pass under the passage of the **Bab ar-Rih**, a long, arched structure. Follow the walled road, running between the Dar al-Kebira and the Dar al-Makhzen and turn right at the end. Carry straight ahead until the large **Heri as-Souni** building is reached.

Heri as-Souni is a large, impressive structure dating from the reign of Moulay Ismail, used variously as a granary, warehouse and water point, to provide for the court, army and followers in either the normal run of events or in case of conflict or drought, and indicating the scale of the imperial city which Moulay Ismail built. The first, long room exhibits typical furniture, decoration and woodwork from the richer Meknes houses. The second room is surrounded by large storerooms and wells, the latter were used with a donkey- powered system of chain-buckets. Behind this is a vast space originally used as a granary. From the roof there is a good view of the palaces. Beside is a basin storing water for irrigation purposes.

From Heri as-Souni pass through the arches, turn right and then take the 2nd left. On the left is the **Dar al-Baida** built by Sultan Mohammed Ibn Abdellah in the 1790s, now a military academy closed to visitors. He also built the **Djemaa Rouah** in 1790, down to the first right, with columns from the **Badia Palace** in Marrakech. To the left is a small *medersa* used as a Koranic school. Nearby is a long canal alongside of which were the stables, the Rouah, heavily ruined, but revealing much about the size of the Sultan's retinue. To the right is the **Heri al-Mansur**, a large storehouse, above which is another palace of Moulay Ismail.

Local information

● Accommodation

B ***Hotel Transatlantique***, rue El Meriniyine, T 525050, F 520057, 120 rms, 2 restaurants and a bar, tennis, good pool, an elegant and well-equipped hotel with excellent view of the medina, dating from the 1930s.

C ***Hotel Rif***, rue d'Accra, T 522591/4, Tx 41039, 120 rms, new, comfortable, Moroccan decor, lively nightclub, sometimes putting on folklore (2230-0230), restaurant, good bar, pool; **C** ***Hotel Zaki***, Blvd Al Massira, T 520063, Tx 41079, 2 restaurants, 2 bars, nightclub and pool, recommended.

D ***Hotel Bab Mansur***, 38 rue Emir Abdelkader, T 525239/40, restaurant, bar, nightclub, new, in *ville nouvelle*; **D** ***Grand Hotel Volubilis***, 45 Ave des Forces Armées Royales, T 520102, restaurant, bar, nightclub (the *Oriental Cabaret*), quite old, conveniently located; **D** ***Hotel de Nice***, 10 rue d'Accra, T 520318, restaurant, (the *New York Bar*), centre of *ville nouvelle*, good rms; **D** ***Hotel Palace***, 11 rue Ghana, T 525777, restaurant, bar, a bit basic but central.

E ***Hotel Majestic***, 14 Ave Mohammed V, T 522033, good but with some noisy rms; **E** ***Hotel Continental***, 92 Ave des Forces Armées Royales, T 520200, similar; **E** ***Hotel Excelsior***, 57 Ave des Forces Armées Royales, T 521900, clean but a bit noisy; **E** ***Hotel Touring***, 34 Ave Allal Ben Abdellah, T 522351, cheap, respectable.

F ***Hotel Maroc***, rue Rouamzine, the best of a bunch of hotels in the medina, clean and peaceful; **F** ***Hotel de Paris***, rue Rouamzine, good rms but no showers; also try **F** ***Hotel Agadir***, rue Dar Smen.

● Youth hostel

T 24698, Ave Okba Ibn Nafi, 1000-1200, 1600-1700, near the municipal stadium and *Hotel Transatlantique*, 60 beds, MD20 per night, kitchen, meals available, bus 25m, train 1.2 km. This is the YHA headquarters in Morocco and is one of the best and most friendly hostels with dormitories around a garden.

● Camping

Camping Agdal, 2 km from Meknes centre on the road to Rabat, take buses 2 or 3, there is a shop, café and hot showers, and it is clean and well organized.

● Places to eat

♦♦♦***Restaurant Bellevue*** in *Hotel Transatlantique*, rue El Meriniyine, T 520002, an atmospheric restaurant with a mixture of excellent French and Moroccan dishes, ask the waiter for a recommended local speciality; ***Restaurant Ismailia***, in *Hotel Transatlantique*, rue El Meriniyine, T 520002, reservations recommended, selection of Moroccan specialities such as *tagines*, Moroccan music; ***La Hacienda***, Route de Fes, T 521092, outside Meknes, excellent French and international food in a farm atmosphere, particularly grilled food, nightclub below, highly recommended. ♦♦***Pizzeria Le Four***, 1 rue Atlas, T 520857, friendly and efficient place with good Italian food; ***Bar Restaurant La Coupole***, Ave Hassan II, T 522438, mixed French/Moroccan menu, good quality at reasonable prices; ***Restaurant Zitouna***, 44 Jamaa Zitouna, T 530281, near Bab Tizimi, 'authentic' Moroccan door, excellent Moroccan food, a bit pricey; ***Le Dauphin***, 5 Ave Mohammed V, T 523423, licensed Moroccan restaurant strong on seafood; ***Rôtisserie Karam***, 2 Ave Ghana, good chicken, chips, etc. ♦***Novelty***, Ave de Paris, T 522156, cheaper Moroccan food, licensed; other cheap options are on rue Dar Smen, such as ***Restaurant Economique***.

● Bars

Hotel Transatlantique, rue El Meriniyine, is an

excellent place for a relaxing drink, not least because of the view over the medina; also try the *Hotel de Nice*, 10 rue d'Accra; ***La Caravelle***, 6 rue de Marseille; ***Bar Continental***, Ave Hassan II; and ***Jour et Nuit***, Ave Mohammed V.

● Cafés
The aromatic mint tea of Meknes is recommended. Try one of the cafés on rue Dar Smen, or one of the classy hotels.

● Banks
ABM, Angle Blvd Nehru and rue Ali Ben Rahal, T 520015; **Banque du Maroc**, 33 Ave Mohammed V; **BMAO**, 15 Place 2 Septembre; **BMCE**, 98 Ave des Forces Armées Royales, T 520352, and at 66 rue Rouamazine; **Credit du Maroc**, 33 Ave Mohammed V; **SGMB**, Place Al Wahda Al Ifriquia, T 527896; **Wafabank**, 11 Ave Mohammed V, T 521151.

● Chemists
Pharmacie d'Urgence, Place Administrative, T 523375, 0830-2030; also the night chemist in Place Administrative, T 523375 (2030-0830).

● Cultural Centre
Centre Culturel Français, Zankat Farhat Hachad, Ave Hassan II, cultural and social programme.

● Discos & nightclubs
Bahia, *Rif Hotel*, rue d'Accra (2230-0030); ***Cabaret Oriental***, *Grand-Hotel Volubilis*, 45 Ave des Forces Armées Royales.

● Emergency
Ambulance, T 15; **Fire**, T 15; **Police**, T 19.

● Hammam
4 rue Patrice Lumumba.

● Hospitals
Hôpital Mohammed V, T 521134; Hôpital Moulay Ismail, Ave des Forces Armées Royales, T 522805, 522806.

● Post & telephone
PTT Centrale, Place Administrative, 0800-1400, T 0800-2100; also the PTT on rue Dar Smen, in the medina.

● Religious services
Catholic Church: Notre Dame des Oliviers, Place Poereiam, services Sat 1800, Sun 1030.

● Shopping
Handicrafts Centre, Charii Riad, T 530784.

● Sports
Golf: *Royal Golf Club*, El Mhancha, T 530753; **Riding**: *L'Etrier* (Haras Régional); **Swimming**: *Lahboul Park*, Rond-Point Bou Amer, BP 45, T 520415; **Tennis**: *Club de Meknes*, Lahboul Park, Rond-Point Bou Amer, BP 45, T 520415.

● Tourist information
Office du Tourisme (ONMT), 27 Place Batha-l'Istiqlal, T 521286; **Syndicat d'Initiative**, Palais de la Foire, T 520191.

● Travel agents and airline offices
Wagons-Lit Tourisme, 1 rue de Ghana, T 521995; ***Wasteels Voyages***, Ave Mohammed V, T 523062. ***Royal Air Maroc***, 7 Ave Mohammed V, T 520963.

● Transport
Bus buses No 5, 7 and 9 run between the *ville nouvelle* and the medina.

Car hire **Stop Car**, 3 rue Essaouira, T 525061; **Zeit**, 4 rue Antsirebe, T 525918.

Taxi Use the silver and black petit-taxis.

Train The main station is at Ave de la Basse, T 520017, 520689. Departures for Rabat and Casablanca: 0240, 0408, 0810, 1037, 1233, 1521, 1632, 1927, 2035; for Tanger: 0500, 0810, 1408; for Fes: 11 a day between 0545 and 0212; for Oujda: 0212, 0545, 1341, 1451, 1825, 0028. Some trains also stop at Meknes El Amir Abdelkader station, just below Ave Mohammed V, and closer to the centre of the *ville nouvelle*.

Road Bus CTM buses to Rabat, Casablanca and Fes (7 a day), Tanger, Ifrane, Azrou, Ouezzane and Er Rachidia (daily) leave from 47 Ave Mohammed V, T 522583. Private line services go from the open terminal below Bab Mansur. **Taxi** Grand-taxis which are a particularly good option to both Fes and Azrou, leave from the car park below Place el Hedim, opposite the private line buses. Ask the drivers hanging around for the destination. Grand-taxis for Moulay Idriss (and then a short walk to Volubilis) leave from rue Yougoslavie.

Excursion to Moulay Idriss and Volubilis

The shrine town of Moulay Idriss is 30 km to the N of Meknes. Leave Meknes by rue de Yougoslavie in the *ville nouvelle*, and follow the P6 as far as Aïn el-Kerna, and from there the P28 to Moulay Idriss. Take a grand-taxi from rue de Yougoslavie, or from the square below Place el Hedim, to Moulay Idriss. There are also regular buses from below Bab Mansur. The last bus back is at 1900. Volubilis is a clearly signposted 5 km drive from Moulay Idriss, a pleasant walk on a nice day, or a short taxi ride. Alternatively, bargain in Meknes for a grand-taxi all the way.

Moulay Idriss

Coming round the last bend from Meknes, Moulay Idriss is a dramatic sight, houses and mosques piled up around two rock outcrops, with the *zaouia*, or sanctuary, in between. The centre of the Jbel Zerhoun region, Moulay Idriss is a pilgrimage centre, including as it does the tomb of its namesake, the great-grandson of the prophet, the town a Mecca in Morocco for those unable to do the ultimate pilgrimage. Moulay Idriss came to Morocco from Arabia, after defeat at the Battle of Fakh in 786. In 788 he was accepted as *Imam* by the Berber Aurora tribe at Volubilis, and went on in his short life in Morocco, before he was poisoned in 791, to win over the loyalty of the tribes to the Idrissid Dynasty he established, and to spread further Islam. This town and Fes were 2 of his major legacies.

However, the town of Moulay Idriss was mainly developed in the 18th century by Sultan Moulay Ismail, in part using materials lifted from nearby Volubilis, which the Sultan plundered without restraint. Moulay Idriss was closed to non-Muslims until 1912, and even today is primarily a Muslim sanctuary, best visited during the day as an excursion, and although not unfriendly, certainly a place to be treated with cautious respect. A religious festival, or *moussem* is held here in Sept, when the town is transformed by an influx of pilgrims and a sea of tents.

From the bus and taxi park the *souqs* are above, followed by the **Moulay Idriss Zaouia**. Many of the *souqs* are taken up with items associated with pigrimage, such as rosaries, scarves and candles. The sanctuary itself, with its green-tiled roofs, a succession of prayer halls, ablution areas and tombs, is closed to non-Muslims. From higher up either of the 2 hills, with the Tasga quarter on the right and the Khiber quarter on the left, it is possible to get a good view from above the sanctuary, showing the courtyards and roofs, with the royal guesthouse beside. Below and around, the medina, whilst not as remarkable architecturally as Chaouen, Fes or Marrakech, is a dramatic place to explore, with houses stacked up the hills, along steep alleyways. The road through the town, keeping right, leads to a Roman bath just above the stream. Further on, beyond the road, there is a ruined 18th century palace with a good view of the town.

There are no hotels in Moulay Idriss, but there is a camp-site, *Zermoune Belle Vue*, en route to Meknes, whilst opposite the turning to Volubilis the proprietor of the café allows people to camp. For lunch ***Baraka de Zerhoun***, 22 Aïn Smen-Khiber, T 44184, with good Moroccan food at average prices, is recommended.

Volubilis

Volubilis is the most impressive Roman site in Morocco, and whilst much has been removed to adorn other cities over the centuries, or taken to museums such as that in Rabat, the structure of the town, the nature of its society and economy, and the design of the buildings is clearly discernible from the ruins, whilst there are also a number of floor mosaics still intact. Lying just below the Jbel Zerhoun and 5 km from Moulay Idriss along the P28, the site has a café and ticket office but little else, and is best viewed in a day trip from Meknes. In summer start early to avoid the heat. Admission is MD 20, and the site is open from 0800 to sunset. On the way in, note the collection of mosaics and sculptures.

Archaeological evidence points to the

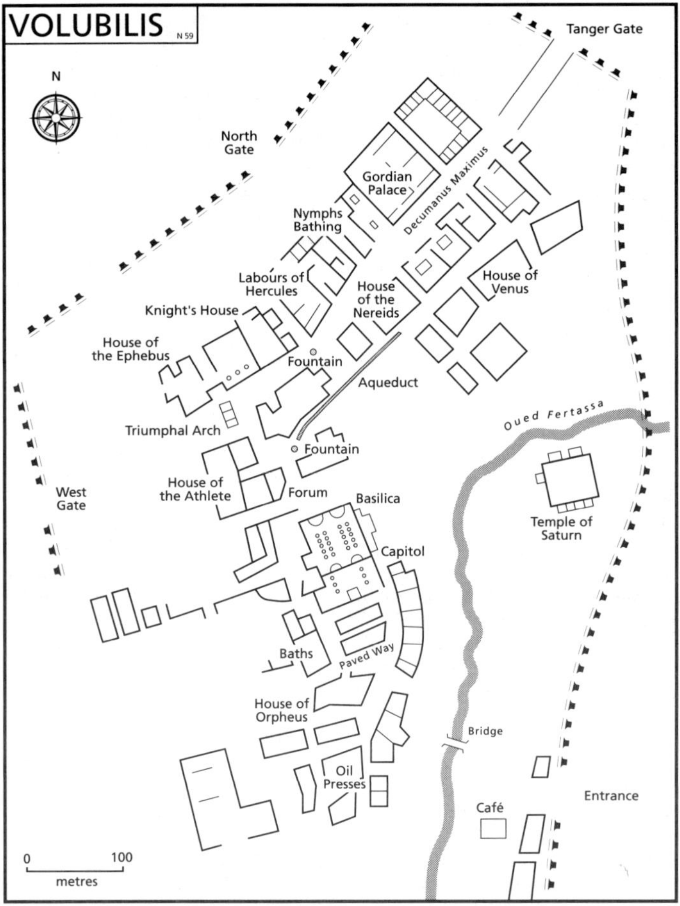

possibility of a Neolithic settlement at Volubilis, whilst tablets found show there was a 3rd century BC Phoenician settlement. In AD 24 it was the Western capital of the Roman kingdom of Mauritania, and from AD 45 to 285 the capital of the Roman province of Mauretania Tingitania. Under the Romans the immediate region was rich agriculturally, with significant production of olive oil, and contained scattered villas. However Volubilis was at the SE extremity of the province, connected to Rome through the Atlantic ports, its weak position necessitating the extensive city walls.

Under the Emperor Diocletian, Rome withdrew to the coastal areas, leaving Volubilis at the mercy of neighbouring tribes, but the city survived with diminished importance, notably with Christian and Jewish inhabitants, and later as the Christian enclave

Oualila during the 8th century. Moulay Idriss was proclaimed as Sultan in Volubilis but during his reign he gave greater emphasis to Fes, so the city of Volubilis became totally deserted by the 11th century. Volubilis suffered when Moulay Ismail ransacked it to build Meknes, and further in the earthquake of 1755. French excavations and reconstruction began in 1915. The metal tracks on the site date from this work.

From the ticket office the entrance to the city is by the SE gate. A path, with sculptures and tombstones alongside it, leads down to a bridge across the Oued Fetassa. Up on the other side the first important remains in an area of small houses and industrial units is of an **olive press** complex. The mill stones, for crushing the olive stones, and the tanks for collecting and separating the oil, can be seen. Olive presses can be found through much of the city, as olive oil production was an essential element in its economy, as it is in the area today, where many of the same techniques are still used.

Right of the olive press is the **House of Orpheus**, a large mansion. In this building, as in most, some areas will be clearly roped off, and it is advisable to respect this, to avoid the whistle and wrath of the otherwise very friendly guardian. The first entrance gives access to a room with an intricate dolphin mosaic, to a kitchen with a niche for religious figures, and to a paved bathroom and boiler room. Note the complex heating system. The second entrance leads to an open court with a mosaic of the goddess Amphitrite, with living rooms around, including a dining room with an Orpheus mosaic, showing the hero playing his harp.

Heading further down and then to the right lie the **Baths of Gallienus**, public baths in the manner of a Moroccan *hammam*. Beyond this the large public square in front of the **Basilica** is the **Forum**. In this area are a number of monuments to leading Roman figures. The **Basilica** is one of the most impressive ruins, with a number of columns intact. This 3rd century building was the court house for the city.

Beside the Basilica is the **Capitol**, also with columns. In the court in front there is an altar, and steps leading up to the temple. This temple is dedicated to Juno, Minerva and Jupiter Optimus Maximus. This building had great state importance, being the place where the council would assemble on great occasions.

Adjacent to the Forum is the **House of the Athlete**, named after the mosaic of an athlete winning a cup. The **Triumphal Arch** dominates the skyline, as well as the **Decumanus Maximus**, the roadway leading to the Tanger Gate. This was built in 217 AD to honour Emperor Caracalla and his mother Julia Domna. Originally topped by nymph fountains, and with medallions honouring its dedication, the arch was heavily reconstructed by the French. **Decumanus Maximus** was lined with a columned arcade with small shops, in front of a series of large houses, some containing interesting mosaics.

Starting on the left, from just beside the **Triumphal Arch**, the **House of the Ephebus** was built around a courtyard with a pool. Note in one of the surrounding public rooms a mosaic of Bacchus in a chariot. Two houses up, the **Knight's House** has an interesting mosaic of Bacchus, Eros, Ariadne and Theseus. The **House of the Labours of Hercules** has a mosaic with individual pictures of Hercules' life, and another of Jupiter. Further up the **House of the Bath of the Nymphs** has a mosaic showing nymphs undressing in front of Pegasus and Acteon. The largest house on this side, the **Gordian Palace**, is fronted by columns but the remains are quite plain. This may have been the governor's residence from the time of Gordian III, with both domestic quarters and offices.

On the right hand side of Decumanus Maximus from the Triumphal Arch there is a large public bath and fountains, fed by an aqueduct. Three houses up is the **House of Nereids** with a pool mosaic. Behind this and one up is the **House of Venus** has one of the best array of mosaics. The central courtyard pool has a mosaic of chariots. There are also mosaics of Bacchus, on the left, and Hylos and 2 nymphs, on the right. Nearby is a mosaic of Diana and the horned Acteon. From the House of Venus cross back over the Oued Fetassa to the remains of the **Temple of Saturn**, a Phoenician temple before the Romans took it over. From here, follow the path back to the entrance, perhaps for refreshments in the café after the labours in Volubilis.

FES AND ENVIRONS

Fes (also called Fez, and derived from the Arabic word for the pickaxe used in its construction) is a city which will take several days to come to terms with, several days to take in the atmosphere, and several days to explore, but is worth giving the time. Spread out over 3 sites, the 2 most historic areas are full of memorable buildings, centred around the **Qarawiyin Mosque**. Fes is also a base from which to explore nearby regions, Bhalil and Sefrou to the S and the springs of Sidi Harazem to the SE, as well as sites further afield, the Middle Atlas resorts of Azrou and Ifrane, and the historic sites near Meknes, Volubilis and Moulay Idriss.

Fes

Pop 448,823 (1982). *Alt* 415m.

History of a city at the heart of Morocco The historic city of Fes lies in the Oued Sebou basin, astride the traditional trade route from the Sahara to the Mediterranean, as well as on the path from Algeria and the Islamic heartland beyond into Morocco. For centuries the dominant axis within Morocco was of Fes and Marrakech, 2 cities linked by their immense power as well as by their rivalry. Even today, when the coastal belt centred on Rabat and Casablanca dominates the country in demographic, political and economic terms, Fes is still seen as the spiritual and cultural capital, and holds an enduring fascination for visitors, as one of the largest historic medina, full of monuments reflecting the different periods of Morocco's imperial and architectural development. Fes has for long supplied the mercantile and intellectual élite of the country, and the *Fassi* (the people of Fes) are to be found in most towns and cities. The *Fassi* are rightly proud of their city and history, and often have a self-confidence quite beyond that of most Moroccans. Perhaps it does not have the immediate friendliness of the villages and towns of the mountains or the desert, but it is a city well worth giving time.

The Three Cities The city is composed of 3 distinct parts. On either side of the Oued Fes, a tributary of the Oued Sebou, lies Fes El Bali, the oldest part of the city, a medina divided by the river into Adwa al Andalusiyin (on the E bank) and Adwa al Qarawiyin (on the W bank). On a

CLIMATE: FES

	Jan	Feb	Mar	Apr	May	Jun	Jul	Aug	Sep	Oct	Nov	Dec	Av/Tot
Max (°C)	15	18	20	22	26	31	36	36	32	26	20	16	25
Min (°C)	5	5	8	9	12	15	18	18	16	12	9	6	11
Rain (mm)	80	72	71	64	37	12	1	3	15	36	61	85	537

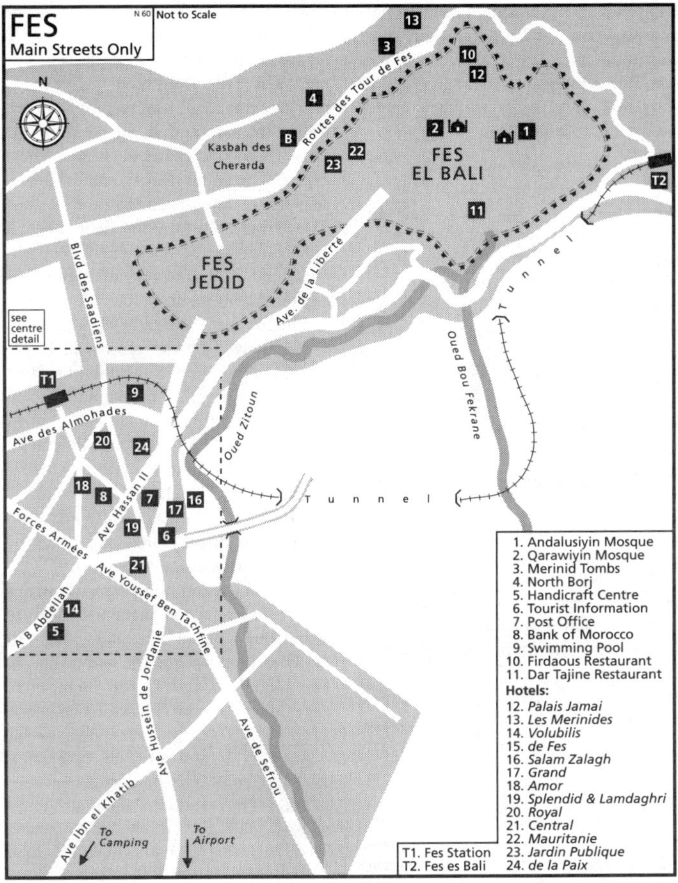

plateau just to the W lies Fes El Jedid, containing the royal palace and the *mellah*, which could be described as the new historic city. To the SW, on another raised area, lies the *ville nouvelle*, the modern city built by the French which has taken over many of the political, administrative and commercial functions of Fes.

Andalusiyin and Qarawiyin The first settlement here was the village Medinat Fes founded in 789/90 by Moulay Idriss, the Sultan and saint commemorated in the shrine town bearing his name near Meknes. However the town proper was founded by his son Idriss II as Al-Aliya in 808/9. 8,000 families of refugees from Cordoba and surrounding areas of Andalucía soon took up residence in the Adwa al Andalusiyin quarter. Later 3,000 from Kairouan in modern-day Tunisia settled on the opposite bank, forming Adwa al Qarawiyin. The **Qarawiyin Mosque**, perhaps the religious centre of Morocco, is the centre of a university founded in 859, including several important *medressa*, and one of the most prestigious of the Arab World. The **Andalusiyin Mosque** was also founded in this period. The minarets of both major mosques date from 955/6.

Almoravids and Almohads The 2 parts of Fes El Bali were united by the Almoravids in the 11th century, and as the focus of independent Morocco, became one of the major cities of Islam. In the 12th century the Qarawiyin mosque was enlarged to its present form, when it was one of the largest in N Africa and can take up to 22,000 worshippers. The Almohads strengthened the fortifications of the great city. Under both dynasties Fes was in competition with the S capital of Marrakech.

The Growth of Fes under the Merinids Fes reached its peak in the Merinid period, when the dynasty built the new capital of Fes El Jedid reflecting its power, containing the green-roofed **Royal Palace** still occupied by the monarch, the **Grand Mosque** with its distinctive polychrome minaret dating from 1279, and the Jewish *mellah*, to which the Jews of Fes El Bali were moved in 1438. The Merinid Sultans Abu Said Uthman and Abu Inan left a particularly notable legacy of public buildings. Among the achievements of the period are the **Bou Inania Medersa** and other *medressa*, several mosques and the **Merinid Tombs**. The **Zaouia of Moulay Idriss**, which holds the tomb of Idriss II was rebuilt in 1437. In the 15th century Fes consolidated its position as a major centre for artisanery and trade.

Saadian and Alawite Fes Under the Saadians Fes declined, with a degree of antagonism between the authorities and the people. Their main act was to refortify the city, adding the **South Borj** and **North Borj** fortresses.

Under the Alawites Fes declined further, with in 1889 the French writer Pierre Loti describing it as a dead city. However the dynasty had added a number of new *medressa* and mosques, and reconstructed other important buildings. The French entered Fes in 1911, but were unable at first to gain full control of the city and its hinterland and thus abandoned plans to make it their capital, choosing Rabat instead. The *ville nouvelle* was founded in 1916, but dates principally from the 1920s. French policies left the historic quarters intact, preserved in their traditional but perhaps stagnant form.

During the 20th century Fes has been overshadowed by the growth of Rabat and Casablanca, and the medina faces critical conservation problems, which a current programme by UNESCO aims to address. The large and beautiful houses of the historic city are being abandoned by the élite who move to the *ville nouvelle*, or to Casablanca and elsewhere, and often being taken over by poor migrants from the country. With rapidly increasing population densities the houses and the infrastructure are crumbling. There are, however, still many impressive houses, and a walk in Fes El Bali is one of the memorable experiences of a visit to Morocco.

ACCESS Air: Aéroport Fes Saiss is 15 km to the S of the city, off the P24, T 624712. Take Bus 16 to the railway station.

Train The railway station is at the end of Blvd Chenguit, in the *ville nouvelle*, T 622501, 625132. Head down this road and slightly to the left into Ave de la Liberté. This joins Ave Hassan II, the main street of the new town, at Place de Florence.

Road Fes lies at a crossroads in Morocco, and is an excellent base from which to plan and carry out the next stage of travels. The P1 W from Meknes, Rabat and Casablanca arrives in the city at the corner of the walls of the royal palace, continue straight ahead for the medina (Fes El Bali), or right into Blvd des Saadiens for the *ville nouvelle*, the P26 N to Chaouen, Tetouan and Tanger and the P1 W to Taza, Oujda and Algeria arrive to the N of Fes El Bali, from where gates enter the old quarter, or the Route du Tour de Fes circumnavigates the city, either way, leading to Fes El Jedid and the *ville nouvelle*. The P24 S to Azrou and Marrakech and the P20 S to Sefrou lead into Place de l'Atlas. Turn left into Ave Allal ben Abdellah, and then right into Ave Hassan II. **Warning**: on the routes into the city men on motorbikes often drive alongside motorists to tout for unofficial guide work – it is advisable to ignore them. **Bus** CTM and most other buses arrive on Place Baghdadi, for the CTM terminal T 622041.

Things to see
In Fes there are lots of sites to see. If time is short, try at least to see the Merinid Tombs, with their view over the medina, the Qarawiyin and Andalusiyin Mosques, Bou Inania Medersa and souqs in Fes El Bali, and the palace in Fes El Jedid. Other sites can be fitted in at the convenience of the visitor, depending on the amount of time to be spent in Fes. It is worth noting that Fes El Bali can only be explored on foot. It has a complex layout, and it may save time to engage the services of an official guide, as long as the balance between sites of interest and expensive shops is agreed to the visitor's preference. Avoid the numerous unofficial guides and 'students' who will profer their services. The Route du Tour de Fes circles Fes El Bali and is a good introductory tour of the ramparts.

The Merinid Tombs, whilst not the most important site in Fes, are a good place to start because of the panoramic view of the city they afford from their hilltop site to its N. The tombs are near the *Hotel des Merinides*, beside the Route du Tour de Fes, best approached from Fes El Jedid by car or petit-taxi. These 14th century tombs are badly damaged. Much of the ornamentation documented by visitors in the past has not survived. On the way back down notice the **North Borj**, a fortress built the Saadian Sultan Ahmed al-Mansur in 1582. The building contains an **Arms Museum** (closed Tues). Open 0900-1200 and 1500-1800, entrance fee MD10. The building, whilst small, is an interesting example of the fortress architecture of the period, with a good view of parts of Fes El Bali from the roof. The exhibition is a diverse display of weapons and military paraphernalia from all periods, including an array of European cannons. At the bottom of the road, near Fes El Jedid, is the square **Kasbah des Cherarda** (after the Cherarda tribe who occupied it in the early 20th century), also called the **Kasbah el-Khemis** (after the nearby Thur *souq*). This was built in 1670 by the Alawite Sultan Moulay al-Rachid, and is now occupied by a hospital and 2 schools.

The Bab Boujeloud Area Perhaps the best approach to Fes El Bali, the oldest part of Fes, is along Ave des Français from Fes El Jedid. On the left is an Alawite wall, on the right are the **Boujeloud Gardens** or **Jardins de la Marche Verte**. Open 0900-1800 daily, entry free. A pleasant place to wander before braving the medina. Rue de l'UNESCO on the right leads to **Dar al-Baida**, a late 19th century palace. As Fes El Bali approaches the Almohad **Boujeloud Mosque** is passed on the right. Behind the mosque a small road leads to the **Dar Batha**, a 19th century palace, and now a **Museum of Moroccan Arts and Handicrafts** (open 0900-1130 and 1500-1800 except Tue), with an excellent display of local handicrafts, including particularly fine tapestries, pottery and carved wood, as well as craftsmen at work. Have a walk in the palace's beautiful garden.

Continuing on from the mosque, however, one reaches the **Bab Boujeloud**. This large blue-tiled structure may look historic but is in fact from 1913-1916, an earlier version lying just to the left. The area around the gate is busy with buses, fruit stalls and people. Pass through the gate and into Fes El Bali, the historic city. Just inside the gate is a square with small cafés, beyond which is the **Sidi Lazzaz Mosque**. Immediately after the mosque, on the right, a turning leads to Place de l'Istiqlal, and off that turning to the left is rue Talaa Seghira, one of the 2 major thoroughfares of the medina. The other major thoroughfare, Talaa Kebira, leads directly on past the Sidi Lazzaz Mosque, and the next major building, the Bou Inania Medersa.

Bou Inania Medersa, open 0900-1800 every day, entrance fee MD10, and one of the most important sites to visit in Fes,

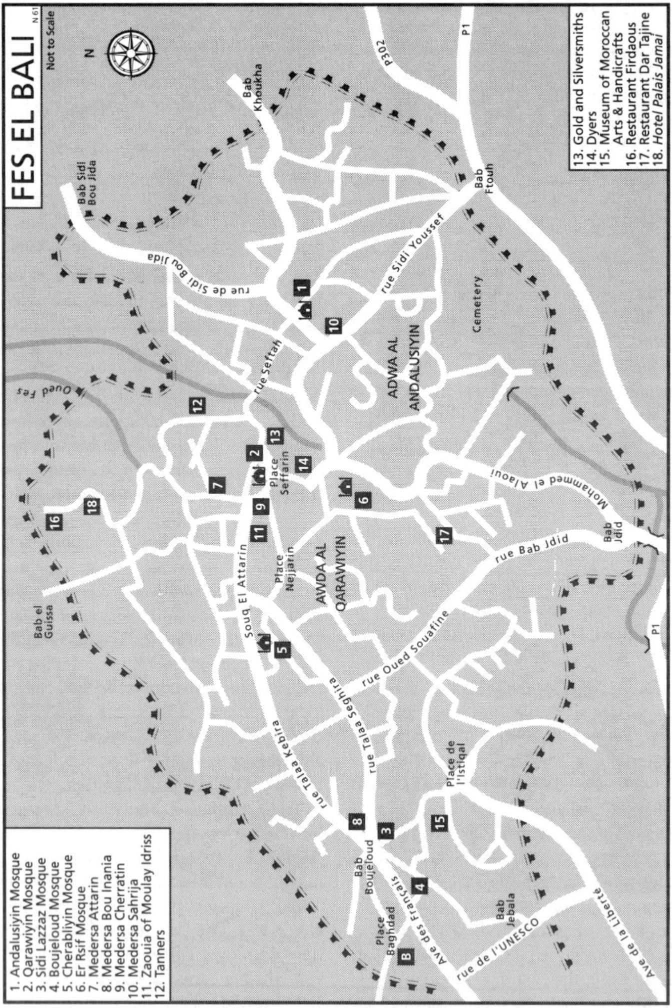

was built by the Merinid Sultan Abu Inan. It is a large and particularly impressive example of the architecture of the period, dating from 1350-5, and would have been used to accommodate students studying at the university, as well as providing some lessons itself. Enter through a highly decorated vestibule roofed by a stalactite dome. Inside the building a channel of water separates the prayer hall from the courtyard. The channel marks the limit for non-Muslims, as the prayer hall is closed, still being used as a mosque. The mosque area has a highly decorated minaret, indicating that it was far more important than most *medressa*, which normally do not have minarets, or even pulpits for the Friday prayer. Indeed, the *medersa* has the status of a Friday mosque, and for a time rivalled the great Qarawiyin Mosque.

The courtyard is decorated with *zellij* tiling, Koranic inscriptions, and some fine carved woodwork, well worth close inspection. Around the courtyard are a number of students' cells, with decorated ceilings, which give an indication of the life led by the students here, studying zealously in often cramped conditions. There are similar cells on the 2nd floor. Take the next flight of stairs up to the roof for a view of the surrounding area and of the minaret.

Leaving the *medersa* note the complex clock built into the wall opposite, dating from 1317. This clock was important, as the *medersa* was visible to both the Qarawiyin Mosque and the Grand Mosque of Fes El Jedid, and signalled the time for prayer to them both. Nearby is a Merinid ablutions hall.

Rue Cherabliyin Talaa Kebira, one of the main commercial thoroughfares of the city, continues past a series of shops and workshops, and just before a fork, a *fondouk*, or tradesmen's rest-house. The right hand fork leads into rue Cherabliyin, the best place to pick up a pair of *baboushes*, the type of leather slipper worn outdoors, and most famous in Fes. Note on the left a traditional *hammam*. Past this, on the right, is the **Cherabliyin Mosque** (Slippermakers' Mosque), dating from 1342, and the reign of Sultan Abul Hassan. Observe the tiled and carved minaret, with a series of designs including the *darj w ktaf* motif.

Souq El Attarin at the bottom of rue Cherabliyin, was originally just the spice sellers' *souq*, but is now one of the major *souqs* of the city, with a wide range of goods, and the focus of the commercial area of Fes El Bali. On the *souq* is the *Dar Saada*, a recommended restaurant for lunch. To the right is the **Souq al Henna**, where the powder used to the colour the feet and hands of women is sold, as well as other beauty products, although there are now a large number of pottery stalls. To the left of the Souq El Attarin is a number of small *souqs*, including **Souq Tellis**, **Souq el-Haik**, **Souq Selham** and **Souq El Bali**. Souq El Attarin leads into the **Kissaria**, a covered area selling textiles and other goods, rebuilt after the original structure was destroyed by fire.

To the right of Souq El Attarin is the **Moulay Idriss Zaouia**. Non-Muslims may not enter the *zaouia*, but can enter the precinct through a wooden screen and circulate around the building. The building contains the remains of Idriss II but was rebuilt most recently in the 18th century. The Sultan is considered a saint, and numbers amongst his devotees women, who can be seen in one of the rooms opening on to the precinct. On the way round note that the exterior of the sanctuary includes a circular porthole through which offerings are passed.

Head W along Bab Moulay Idriss to the **Place Nejjarin** (Carpenters' Square). On this square is a fountain decorated with tiling, and the 18th century **Nejjarin Fondouk**, much of which is still preserved. Nearby is the carpenters' *souq*, where craftsmen still work on ornately carved furniture and other items. Adjacent is a metalworkers' *souq*.

The **Qarawiyin Mosque** dominates Fes and is the centre of a complex of *medressa*, added mainly by the Merinids. It is however a frustrating building for the non-Muslim, as it is impossible to get a clear view of the structure, surrounded as it is by the city. Walk around the mosque taking diplomatic glances in where possible, but no photographs. The mosque was the main building of the Qarawiyin quarter of the city, and owes its original construction to the generosity of a rich emigrant family in 857. It was enlarged in 956 and most importantly under the Almoravids between 1135 and 1144. The Almohads built a large ablution hall, whilst the Merinids built a time-keeper's room and redecorated the courtyard and minaret. The original minaret dates from 956, the oldest in Morocco. There is also the **Borj an-Naffara** tower, used during *Ramadan*. On the SW side is an Almoravid funeral chapel.

The Attarin Medersa On the N side of the Qarawiyin Mosque is the Merinid Attarin Medersa (open 0900-1200 and 1400-1800), a remarkably decorated Islamic school dating from 1323, built by Sultan Abu Said, used to accommodate students from the NW of Morocco, and functioning as a constituent college of the Qarawiyin University, which instructed students in religious and related subjects.

The courtyard is one of the most elaborately decorated in Morocco, with carved stucco, cedar wood carving, and *zellij* tiling, surrounded by the arches of the overhanging gallery. The prayer hall has a chandelier bearing the name of the *medersa*'s founder. The niche is on the right, flanked by 2 pilasters in marble.

As with most *medressa*, the 2nd floor has a succession of student's cells which are interesting to see. From the roof of the *medersa* is one of the best views of the minaret and interior of the Qarawiyin Mosque. To the left of the Attarin Medersa is the closed and partially ruined Merinid Misbahiya Medersa.

Seffarin Place and Seffarin Medersa From the Attarin and Misbahiya *medressa* continue around the Qarawiyin Mosque, past the 14th century Titouani Fondouk, originally for merchants from Tetouan and now a carpet shop, and the *Palais de Fes* restaurant, with its good view of the mosque. At the S extremity of the mosque lies Place Seffarin (Brassworkers' Square). On the right is the **Qarawiyin Library**, founded in 1349, and closed to non-Muslims. On the left is the **Seffarin Medersa**, the earliest *medersa*, from the 13th century, a partly ruined building in the style of a *fassi* house, but with some interesting carving and a small minaret.

Further around the Qarawiyin Mosque to the W is the Alawite **Cherratin Medersa**, built in 1670 by Sultan Moulay al-Rachid. This is a more modern *medersa*, and unlike the Merinid structures, is on 3 storeys, in order to house a greater number of students. The design of the *medersa* is different from the others, notably with the 3 arches leading from the prayer hall to the courtyard.

The Dyers' and Tanners' Souqs Turn left at the end of Place Seffarin and right in to the dyers' *souq*, **As-Sabbaghin**, still in use to dye huge amounts of wool and other materials in an array of bright colours. It is a highly photogenic area, but those who work there are well aware of the possibilities. The *souq* lies beside the Bou Khrareb Oued, or Oued Fes.

To get to the tanneries return to Place Seffarin and turn right in to Derb Mechattine. This alleyway leads to the tanneries, or **dabbaghin**, where leather is tanned and dyed in ancient pits, as in time immemorial. This is somewhat of a dirty quarter with strong smells.

The Andalusian Quarter Cross the Oued Bou Khrareb and follow rue Seftah to the **Andalusiyin Mosque** dating from

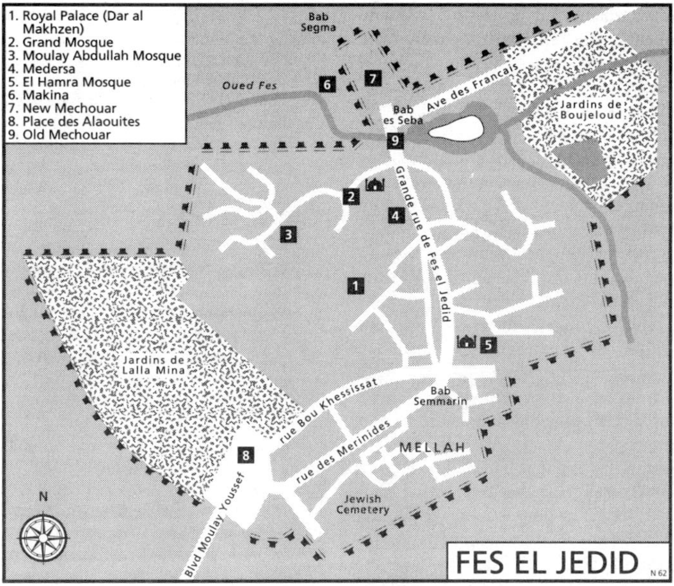

the same period as the Qarawiyin Mosque but smaller and less important. The minaret dates from the 10th century, and the mosque was enlarged in the 13th century, with an architect from Toledo designing the impressive doorway, surmounted by carved wood.

Adjacent is the **Sahrija Medersa** from 1321-3, built for students studying at the mosque. It is a heavily restored building but there is still some memorable *zellij* tiling and wood carving. Note the scallop motif, much in evidence. The white marble basin from the courtyard has been removed. The view from the roof of the *medersa* is recommended. From here, return to the Qarawiyin quarter by rue Sidi Youssef and the El Aouad bridge, noting the potters at work in the area. Alternatively take the No.18 bus from the **Mosque er Rsif** to Place de la Resistance.

Fes El Jedid Enter the Merinid capital of Fes El Jedid via **Bab Segma**, a gate with 2 towers built in 1315 by Sultan Abu Said. Turn right from here through **Bab Kribat as-Smen**, from 1886. This opens into the New Mechouar, a wide street often full with entertainers and the *Fassi* people milling around. Alongside this is the **Makina** (machine), a former arms factory from the late 19th century, run under Italian supervision. This now contains a rug factory, sometimes open to visitors.

The large 3 arched gate at the end of the New Mechouar is **Bab es Seba**, originally built in 1276. This opens onto the Old Mechouar, another busy space, particularly vibrant in the evening. At its end is the normally closed entrance to the **Dar al-Makhzen** and Royal Palace, just to the left of this an arch leads into Grande rue de Fes El Jedid. To the right of the Old Mechouar is the quarter of Moulay Abdellah, which had a previous reputation as a red-light district, but whose main attractions are now the water wheel, and beyond, the **Grand Mosque of Fes El Jedid**, dating from 1287 and the reign of Sultan Abu Yusuf Yaqub.

The Grande rue de Fes El Jedid is the main market street of this area of the city. Note the **El Hamra Mosque**, dating from 1339, with a memorable decorated minaret. The gate at the end is the 20th century **Bab Semmarin**. Rue Bou Khessissat leads to the right towards the *ville nouvelle*, past the 16th century Merinid gates to the Royal Palace, a vast complex extended under King Hassan II. The quarter on the left-hand side of rue Bou Khessissat is the *mellah*. This includes a number of old synagogues and Jewish public buildings, although the area is now predominantly Muslim. See the **Serfati Synagogue** and the **Fassiin Synagogue**, both used for other purposes now. The houses are quite distinct in architectural style to those of the surrounding city.

Local information

● Accommodation

AL ***Hotel Palais Jamai***, Bab El Guissa, T 634331/3, F 635096, 99 rms, 2 excellent restaurants, bar, popular nightclub, *hammam*, tennis and a pool, a former palace with excellent views of the medina, and a beautiful garden, reservations advisable; **AL** ***Hotel Les Merinides***, Borj Nord, T 645225/6, F 645225, pool, restaurant, bar, nightclub, pool, modern, overlooking the medina with 4 restaurants, 2 bars, the *Nightclub Les Merinides*; **AL** ***Hotel Jnan Palace Fes***, Ave Ahmed Chaouki, T 653965, 193 rms.

A ***Hotel de Fes***, Ave des Forces Armées Royales, T 623006, Tx 51988, F 620486, 280 rms, modern, comfortable, in *ville nouvelle*, extensive gardens, 2 restaurants, coffee shop, bar, tennis and pool.

C ***Hotel Salam Zalagh***, 6 rue Mohammed Diouri, T 622810, 622531, good atmosphere, rms moderate, restaurant, bar, nightclub and pool; **C** ***Hotel Sofia***, 3 rue de Pakistan, BP 2098, T 624265/7, F 644244, restaurant, bar, nightclub, pool; **C** ***Hotel Volubilis***, Ave Allal Ben Abdellah, T 621125, F 621125, restaurant, bar, pool, good hotel from the PLM chain with a pleasant garden; **C** ***Hotel Batha***, rue de l'Unesco, T 636437/9.

D ***Hotel de la Paix***, 44 Ave Hassan II, T 626880, Tx 51636, stylish, in *ville nouvelle* from the Protectorate period with bar and restaurant; **D** ***Le Grand Hotel***, Blvd Chefchaouni, T 625511-2, Tx 51631, a 1930s building in centre of *ville nouvelle* with style and atmosphere, a restaurant, bar, and nightclub; **D** ***Hotel Mounia***, 60 rue Asilah, T 624838, Tx 51801, this is a mock kasbah with modern, comfortable rms, *hammam*, restaurant and a bar; **D** ***Moussafir Hotel***, Ave des Almohades, T 651902, part of the chain attached to the railway company, efficiently run and comfortable, near the railway station; **D** ***Splendid Hotel***, 9 rue Abdelkrim El Khattabi, T 622148, 626770, Tx 51763, good pool; **D** ***Hotel Olympic***, Ave Mohammed V, T 624529, central location, restaurant, reasonable and comfortable.

E ***Hotel Amor***, 31 rue de Pakistan, T 623304, restaurant; **E** ***Hotel Lamdaghri***, 10 Kabbour El Mangad, T 620310, small and highly rec, around a courtyard, with a restaurant and bar; **E** ***Hotel Royal***, 36 rue d'Espagne, T 624656; **E** ***Hotel Kairouan***, 84 rue du Soudan, T 623590, reasonable, near railway station; **E** ***Hotel Central***, 50 rue du Nador, T 622333, big and clean rms, very cheap; **F** ***Hotel Mauritanie***, by the **Bab Boujeloud** gate, one of best in medina, clean and with efficient and friendly management; nearby is the almost as good **F** ***Hotel Erraha***, near the bus station; ***Hotel Jardin Publique***, near the Boujeloud Mosque is a safe bet; in the *ville nouvelle* cheap options are ***Hotel Rex***, Place de l'Atlas; ***Hotel Regina*** and ***Hotel Maghrib***, Ave Mohammed es Slaoui.

● Youth hostel

18 rue Abdestam Serghini in the *ville nouvelle*, T 624085, 60 beds, kitchen, bus 300m, train 350m, overnight fee MD15, cheap option for those with a YHA card. Unfavourable reports have been received about a manager here.

● Camping

Camping du Diamant Vert, near Aïn Chkeff, right off the P24, expensive but well-equipped site with shop and restaurant.

● Places to eat

◆◆◆ ***Al Fassia***, in *Hotel Palais Jamai*, Bab El Guissa, T 634331, reservations advisable, this is one of the best Moroccan theme restaurants, with an array of extravagant dishes, including *tagine* of quail, and traditional Moroccan mu-

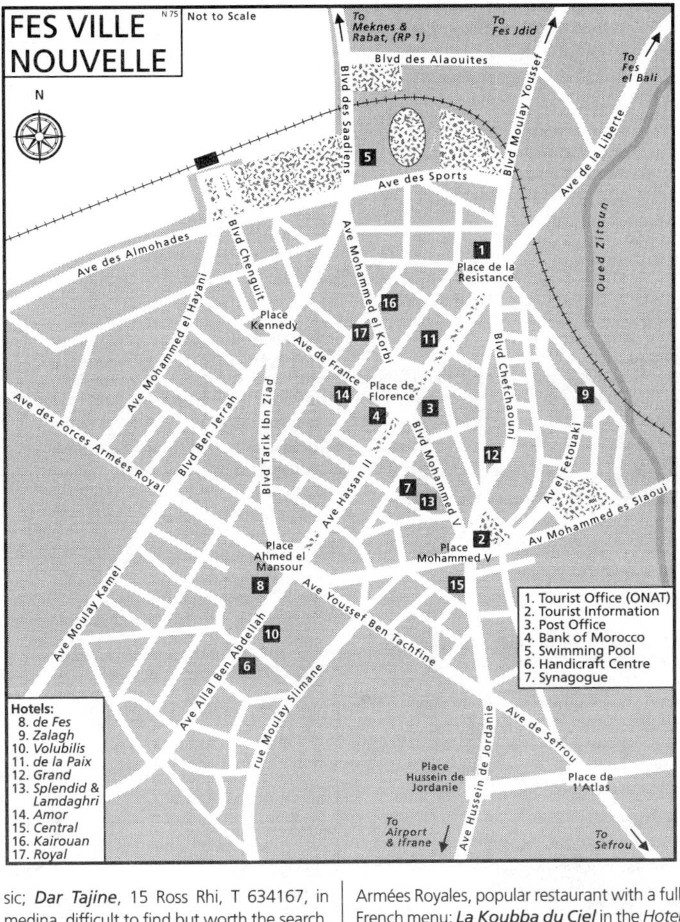

sic; ***Dar Tajine***, 15 Ross Rhi, T 634167, in medina, difficult to find but worth the search, with fixed Moroccan menus in a 19th century palace with exquisite decor, try the speciality dish of *pastilla*, as well as the excellent salads; ***Restaurant Al Firdaous***, reservations advisable, 10 rue Jenjfour, Bab Guissa, T 634343, good Moroccan food around a courtyard with evening entertainment; ***Restaurant Dar Saada***, 21 Souq Attarin, T 633343, in centre of medina, a good choice for a refreshment stop or for a relaxing and delicious lunch during a tour, closed in the evening; ***Restaurant El Minzah***, in the *Hotel de Fes*, Ave des Forces Armées Royales, popular restaurant with a full French menu; ***La Koubba du Ciel*** in the *Hotel les Merinides*, Borj Nord, the usual range of the best in Moroccan cuisine, but with the added advantage of an excellent view of the medina and entertainment from musicians and dancers; ***Pizzeria La Four***, 1 rue Atlas, a well-recommended change from local cuisine.

♦♦ ***La Coupole***, Ave Hassan II, T 622483, mixed Moroccan and European cuisine; ***L'Adour Restaurant***, 9 rue Abdelkrim El Khattabi, T 622148, a mixed French and Moroccan menu at a competitive price; ***Palais Mnebhi***, 15 Souq Ben Safi Talaa Sghira, T 633893, in the medina with good Moroccan food; ***Restaurant Zitouna***, 44 Jamaa Zitouna near Bab Tizimi, T 630281, good Moroccan dishes and ambiance.

♦A wide range of cheap restaurants can be found around much of the city, particularly near **Bab Boujeloud** and **Bab Ftouh**, including ***Restaurant Bouayoud***. In the *ville nouvelle* try ***Restaurant Novelty***, 12 rue de Paris, good Moroccan food, licensed; or ***Marhaba***, 23 Ave Mohammed V, closes at 1900, very good *tagines* and salads. ***Restaurant du Centre*** on 105 Ave Mohammed V is very good and cheap; whilst ***Chawarma Sandwich*** at 42 rue Normandie is also reasonable and clean.

● Bars

A drink in the *Hotel Palais Jamai* is a good break in the medina, the *Hotel des Merinides* has a good view of the city. In the *ville nouvelle* try ***Es Saada***, on Ave Slaoui.

● Cafés

The best cafés are in the *ville nouvelle*, but the best for watching *fassi* life are in the medina. In the *ville nouvelle* try ***L'Elysée***, 4 rue de Paris; or *Café l'Opéra*.

● Banks

ABM, Ave Hassan II, T 651515; **BMAO**, Immeuble Mamda, Place de Florence, T 650785; **Banque al Maghrib**, Ave de France, T 625596-8; **BMCE**, Place Mohammed V; **Banque Populaire**, Ave Mohammed V; **Credit du Maroc**, Ave Mohammed V; **SGMB**, Ave Lalla Yacout, T 625011; **SMDC**, 3 Blvd Bir Anzarane, T 642611; **Wafabank**, Ave Mohammed V, T 622591.

● Cultural Centre

Centre Culturel Français, rue el-Bahrein, T 623921, library and films.

● Chemists

There is an all night chemist at the Municipalité de Fes, Blvd Moulay Youssef, T 623380 (2000-0800); during the day try ***Bahja***, Ave Mohammed V, T 622441; or ***Bab Ftouh*** at Bab Ftouh, T 649135.

● Disco & nightclubs

Nightclub Les Merinides, in the *Hotel Les Merinides*, Borj Nord, T 645225 (2130-0300), a fashionable but expensive place, with drinks from MD50; also try ***Nightclub*** in the *Hotel Palais Jamai*, Bab El Guissa, T 634331 (2200-0300), similarly expensive but popular with those that can afford it.

● Emergency

Fire: T 15; **Police**: Ave Mohammed V, T 19.

● Garages

Fiat, Ave Mohammed V, T 623435; Renault, rue d'Espagne, T 622232.

● Hospital

Hôpital Ghassani, Quartier Dhar Mehraz, T 622776.

● Post & telephone

The PTT Centrale is at the junction of Ave Hassan II and Ave Mohammed V. Telephone facilities are open 0800-2100. There is another post office in the medina, at Place Batha.

● Shopping

Books and Newspapers: try the ***English Bookshop*** of Fes, 68 Ave Hassan II, near Place de la Résistance. Newspapers from the stalls in Ave Mohammed V.

Handicrafts and Moroccan goods: the *souqs* in Fes have a fascinating display of products from all over Morocco, but bargaining a half-way reasonable price can prove to be a difficult and at times aggressive experience. Try in the shops on Talaa Kebira and in ***Souq El Attarin***, as well as near Place Nejjarin. Fes El Jedid is perhaps less traumatic but more expensive, the *ville nouvelle* more so in both ways. Prices are fixed but the selection still good at the ***Coopartim Centre Artisanale***, Blvd Allal Ben Abdellah, T 625654 (0900-1400 and 1600-1900). In Fes look out for the blue and white pottery, as well as the metalwork.

● Sport

Riding: at *Club Equestre Moulay Idriss*, Hippodrome Moulay Kamel.

Swimming: in the large hotels, mainly *Hotel Salam Zalagh*, rue Mohammed Diouri, or at the municipal pool, Ave des Sports.

Tennis: at *Sporting Club Fassi*, Clos de la Renaissance, 10 rue Moulay Slimane, T 641512, with 5 courts or *Tennis Club Fassi*, Ave Mohammed El Kori, T 624272, with 7 courts.

● Tourist Information

Office du Tourisme, Place de la Résistance, T 623460, F 623146; **Syndicat d'Initiative**, Ave Mohammed V, T 625301.

● Travel agents and airline offices

Azur Voyage, 3 Ave de Mauritanie, T 625115; ***Fes Voyages***, 9 rue de Turquie, T 626063; ***Number One***, 41 Ave Slaoui, T 621234; ***Tak Voyages***, 41 Ave Mohammed V, T 624550, 622455, Tx 51967, F 652736; ***Wagons-Lits***

Tourisme, *Immeuble Grand Hotel*, T 622958. *Royal Air Maroc*, 54 Ave Hassan II, T 625516-7, reservations T 620456-7.

● Transport

Road Bus These can be a convenient option in Fes. No 1 runs from Place des Alawites to Dar Batha, No 3 from Place des Alawites to Place de la Résistance, No 9 from Place de la Résistance to Dar Batha, No 10 from Bab Guissa to Place des Alaouites and No 18 from Place de la Résistance to Bab Ftouh.

Car hire Avis, 50 Blvd Chefchaouni, T 626746; **Budget**, at the *Grand Hotel*, Blvd Chefchaouni, T 620919; **Europcar-Inter-Rent**, 41 Ave Hassan II, T 626545; **Hertz**, at the *Hotel de Fes*, Ave des Forces Armées Royales, T 622812; **Holiday Car**, 41 Ave Mohammed V, T 624550, 622455, Tx 51967, F 652736; **Zeit**, 35 Ave Mohammed Slaoui, T 625510.

Taxis are a cheap and quick way to get around Fes, can be found around much of the city, and sometimes have meters. Parking can be a major problem approaching the medina, so it is better not to use one's own car.

Air Aéroport Fes Saiss is 15 km from the city, off the P24, T 624712. Day flights to Casablanca with connections to internal and international destinations (**see page 255**), one a week to Agadir, Er Rachidia and Marrakech, as well as direct flights to Marseille (Sun) and Paris (Mon). To get to the airport take Bus 16 from the railway station.

Train The railway station is at the end of Blvd Chenguit, T 622501, 625132. Departures to **Oujda**: 0634, 1430, 1541, 1921, 0115; **Meknes**: 11 a day between 0750 and 1943; **Rabat** and **Casablanca**: 0150, 0318, 0720, 0940, 1137, 1435, 1545, 1838, 1943; **Tanger**: 1310, 0150, 0415.

Road Bus CTM buses leave from the station at Place Baghdadi, T 622041, for Beni Mellal at 2300, Marrakech at 0630 and 2100, Tetouan at 0730, Tanger at 0730 and 1800, and Oujda at 1230. Buses for the Middle Atlas leave from the Laghzaoui terminal, rue Ksar el Kebir. Some buses for the E (Taza and Oujda) leave from Bab Ftouh. **Taxi** Grand-taxis leave from Place Baghdadi, except for Sefrou and Azrou which leave from rue de Normandes.

Excursions to Sidi Harazem, Bhalil and Sefrou

Sidi Harazem In restaurants all over Morocco the mineral water is almost exclusively from Sidi Ali or Sidi Harazem. Sidi Harazem was originally buried in Marrakech. The source and spa centre of that name is an easy day excursion from Fes, with buses from the CTM bus station and Bab Boujeloud, and grand-taxis from Bab Ftouh. Visit the thermal baths for a relaxing swim, or the stream, for a more public display. There is a 17th century *koubba*, and an expensive hotel, the C *Hotel Sidi Harazem*, T 645522/30, 64 a/c rms, with health facilities, restaurant and bar.

Bhalil En route to Sefrou, 5 km before the town off the P20, is Bhalil. This village may have had a Christian population before the coming of Islam. Behind the picturesque village are several troglodyte dwellings, with people still inhabiting the caves.

Sefrou

Sefrou is 32 km S of Fes along the P20. It is unlikely to be reached en route, as the P24/P21, via Ifrane and Azrou, is a better route from Fes to Er Rachidia and the S, but is certainly worth visiting as an excursion from Fes or to stay for a few days, as this is one of the most appealing towns in Morocco, an unspoilt historic walled town lying in a beautiful wooded valley, with a calm and genuinely friendly atmosphere. Both buses and taxis arrive and leave from Place Moulay Hassan, by Bab Taksebt and Bab M'Kam, where the road from Fes meets the old town.

Although now bypassed by new roads, Sefrou once lay astride the major caravan routes from Fes and the N, to the S and the Sahara beyond, and is an important market-place for the surrounding agricultural region. Sefrou always had a distinctive character due to its Jewish roots, which predated Moroccan Islam, and although converted to

Islam by Moulay Ismail, it returned to its status with the migration of Jews from Tafilalt and Algeria in the 13th century. This characteristic lasted until the emigration of Jews to the large cities, Europe and Israel after WWII and the 1967 Arab-Israeli War. More than any other equivalent small town it has fascinated Western academics, with the anthropologists Geertz, Rosen and Rabinow carrying out reseach here. Recently Sefrou was created a province in its own right, and received new and badly-needed investment, as it was a town declining into shabby anonymity.

The market place below Ave Mohammed V is a relaxed place to wander, best during the Thur **souq**. The town, which is known for olive and cherry production, has a large **Fête des Cerises** in June, and other smaller *fêtes* during the year. There is a *moussem*, or religious gathering, for Sidi Lahcen Lyoussi. Adjacent to Place Moulay Hassan is a Centre Artisanal (0800-1200 and 1400-1900, Mon-Sat).

The *mellah*, on the S side of the river, and the *mellah*, on the N, are small, maze-like quarters, but it is difficult to get seriously lost. Entering the *mellah* from the market place, beside a mosque built into the wall, bend right and down the main street, beside small restaurants, butchers, shops and craftsmen, and then left to reach one of several small bridges over the Oued Aggaï. Alternatively, take one of the small side turnings to discover the cramped design of the *mellah*, now mainly occupied by poorer Muslims, with small houses often built over the narrow streets.

Over the river in the medina, the **Grand Mosque of El Jamaa Kebir**, restored in the 19th century, lies beside the river, and the *souqs* just upstream. In the *souqs*, where bargaining will be less fierce than in Fes, note the silversmiths and the woodworkers. Past the *souqs* is the **Zaouia of Sidi Lahcen ben Ahmed**. In the medina there is a clearly discernible difference in the design of the quarter, reflecting the strict regulations and conditions under which Jews in the *mellah* lived. Sefrou is quite remarkable, however, in that the *mellah* is as large as the medina. The medina can also be entered from **Bab M'Kam**.

Ave Moulay Hassan runs from here over the Oued Aggaï, where there is a **Syndicat d'Initiative**, T 660380, past the Jardin Publique, which has a swimming pool. Ave Moulay Hassan continues around into Ave Mohammed V, the main street of the unexciting new town, with the Post Office, and a few shops and simple café-restaurants, the *rôtisseries*, for grilled chicken, being one of the places. The medina and *mellah* lie below this, on either side of the Oued Aggaï.

• **Accommodation** The 2 best places to stay are the **D** *Hotel Sidi Lahcen Lyoussi*, off Ave Moulay Hassan, T 660497, 24 rms, a dated but comfortable place with a restaurant, bar and pool; and **F** *Hotel les Cerises*, Ave Mohammed V, T 661528, a large, impersonal but cheap hotel; there is also the **F** *Hotel Lafrenie*, Route de Fes, T 662030, a small *pensión*. Follow rue Ziad, by the post office on Ave Mohammed V, to a campsite, *Camping de Sefrou*, 2 km from the town, and on a fork off that road, the **F** *Hotel-Café Boualserhim*, by the green-roofed **Koubba of Sidi Bouserghine**, Sefrou's patron saint.

TAZA AND ENVIRONS

Taza

The town is divided into three quite separate parts, the area around the railway and bus station, the *ville nouvelle* around Place de l'Indépendence, and the quiet medina on the hill. Unfortunately its most impressive historic buildings are closed to non-Muslims.

History

Taza, population 77,216, is a modest market town which has in the past achieved considerable regional importance under successive dynasties. The town has been settled since Neolithic times, and has gained importance with its highly strategic location in the Taza Gap, between the Rif and the Middle Atlas. The town was developed by the Meknassa tribe of Berbers, and was an important but finally unsuccessful fortification against the advance of the Fatimids from the E. The Almohads under Sultan Abd el-Moumen captured the city in 1141-1142, making it their second capital, and used it to attack the Almoravids. The Almohads built a mosque and provided much of the city's fortifications.

Taza was the first city taken by the Merinids, who added considerably to the Almohad city. Its important defensive role continued under the Merinids and the Saadians, and was again pivotal in the rise to power of the Alawites, who further extended and fortified the city, later using it as a defence against the French threat from the E.

The eccentric pretender, Bou Hamra, proclaimed himself as Sultan here in 1902, and controlled much of E Morocco until 1912, when he was caught and killed. He was known as a wandering miracle-maker, travelling Morocco on a donkey. Taza was occupied by the French in 1914, and became an important military centre.

ACCESS Taza is well connected by road and rail. The railway station, private bus station and grand-taxi rank are N from the centre of the *ville nouvelle*, Place de l'Indépendence, beyond walking distance. Buses, taxis and car parking in Place Moulay Hassan in the medina.

Things to see

The *ville nouvelle* for hotels, restaurants, banks and other services is a quiet place centred around the old French buildings on Place de l'Indépendence.

The older buildings are in the small, attractive medina reached from Ave de la Gare. The focus of the medina is the **Mechouar** which runs parallel to Place Moulay Hassan with its cafés and transport and the souqs which stretch in a line between the 2 principal mosques. The souqs, refreshingly, are not aimed at tourists, and refreshing to wander in, and include an interesting second-hand section. One can perhaps gain a brief passing glance of the **Zaouia of Sidi Azouz** and note the beautiful wall-basin beside the door. The **Grand Mosque** at the end of the souq is difficult to gain a good view of. The mosque, including the existing minaret, was built by the Almohads in the second half of the 12th century, with further elaboration by the Merinids in the late 13th century and the Alawites in the late 17th century. The minaret follows the classic proportions of 1:5, as does the **Koutoubia** mosque in Marrakech (see page 302). Turning left along the Mechouar the street broadens. On the right note the carved woodwork lintel of the 14th century Merinid **Medersa of Abul Hassan**. The Andalusian mosque, with a small 12th century minaret, requires some neck stretching to see. Behind it, to the right, is the ruined house of Bou Hamra, the early 20th century pretender, and if one can find the doorkeeper it may be possible to get access.

A tour of the ramparts of Taza is recommended. These walls were originally laid out by the Almohads, and repeatedly improved since. Note the Almohad **Bab er Rih** gate facing NNW, and the circular **El Sarasine** tower, also Almohad. There is a large weekly market outside the walls.

Turning left along the Mechouar head towards the 12th century minaret of the Andalusian mosque. Before reaching the mosque note on the right the 14th century **Medersa of Abul Hassan**, named after a Merinid Sultan. This is closed but the exterior shows a carved lintel in cedar wood, and a porch roof overhanging the road. At the end of the Mechouar, in a lane to the right of the mosque, Zankat Dar al-Makhzen, there is the former house of Bou Hamra the pretender.

With its commanding location, a tour

of the ramparts of Taza is recommended. These walls were originally laid out by the Almohads, and repeatedly improved since. Note the Almohad **Bab er Rih** gate facing NNW, and the circular **El Sarasine** tower, also Almohad.

Local information

● Accommodation

D *Hotel Salam Friouato*, Ave de la Gare, T 672593, 58 rms, top hotel in town, bar, restaurant, tennis and pool, but inconveniently located between the medina and the *ville nouvelle*.

E *Grand Hotel du Dauphine*, at the centre of the town on junction of Ave de la Gare and Place de l'Indépendence, T 673567, 26 rms, some with shower but no communal shower for those without, comfortable, recommended bar and restaurant, dating very obviously from the Protectorate period with style and charm.

Cheaper and more basic options include **F** *Hotel de la Poste*, Place de l'Indépendence, T 672589; and *Hotel Guillaume Tell* on Place de l'Indépendence, basic and not very clean.

● Camping

At *Zeitoun*, off Ave de la Gare en route to the medina.

● Places to eat

♦♦♦The *Hotel Salam Friouato*, T 672593, has reasonable, unexciting meals. A better option is the ♦♦*Grand Hotel du Dauphine*, junction of Place de l'Indépendence and Ave de la Gare, T 673567. ♦ *Café Restaurant Majestic*, Ave Mohammed V, Moroccan food, and on same street *Restaurant Azzam* and *Restaurant des Gouts*. Try also Ave de Tetouan.

● Banks

Wafabank, Place Moulay Hassan; **BMCE**, Ave Mohammed V.

● Post & telephone

Rue Moussa Ibn Noussair, near Place de l'Indépendence.

● Tourist Office

Ave Hassan II, T 672737.

● Travel agents

Taza Voyages, Ave Mohammed V.

● Transport

Taxi It is advisable to take one of Taza's light blue petit-taxis between Place de l'Indépendence and the railway station (MD 3-5), or the medina (MD 5). There are also town buses.

Train At 0337, 0607, 0855, 1700, 1819 and 2207 to **Oujda** (3½ hrs), at 0147, 1051 and 2308 to **Tanger** (8 hrs) and regularly to **Fes** (2 hrs), **Meknes** (3 hrs), **Rabat** (6 hrs), **Casablanca** (7 hrs). **By bus**: CTM buses leave from their office on Place de l'Indépendence to **Oujda** at 1500 and **Fes** at 0700 and 1500. Other companies operate from near the railway station, turn right at the end of Ave de la Gare. Regular services to **Oujda** at 0600, 0700, 0900, 1000, 1100, 1200, 1300, 1530, 1600 (4 hrs), **Fes** between 0500 and 1800 (2 hrs), **Nador** at 0700, 0800, 1100, 1300, 1400 (4 hrs), other services to **Al Hoceima** (4 hrs), **Aknoul** (1 hr). **By Taxi**: grand-taxis leave from the bus station to **Oujda** (2½ hrs), **Fes** (1½ hrs), **Al Hoceima**, **Nador**, amongst other places.

Excursion on the Tazzeka Road

To the S of Taza and the P1 lies the **Jbel Tazzeka National Park** in an area of outstanding mountain scenery. The S311 winds its way through this area from S of Taza, rejoining the P1 31 km further W. This is an excursion primarily for those with their own transport, but it may be possible to bargain for a grand-taxi part of the way, from the rank by the railway station. En route travellers should stop at the waterfalls, the **Cascades de Ras El Oued**, and further on, the **Dayat Chiker**. Nearby is the **Gouffre du Friouato**, an immense series of caves, dominated by a 180m deep underground bowl, worth exploring with a torch. After the caves, continue on to the Bab Taza pass from which a rough and challenging track goes N up to the Jbel Tazzeka, where there are incredible views of the surrounding mountains. After, or avoiding, the Jbel Tazzeka the road continues through the narrow gorge by the Oued Zireg and back to the P1.

OUJDA AND ON TO ALGERIA

Oujda

History

Oujda, with a present population of 260,000, is the most significant city in the E of Morocco, its essential character determined by its location close to the Algerian border. Indeed the city has many Algerians involved in cross-border commerce. There are few visitors enjoying the fairly peaceful, comparatively modern medina or taking a day trip to the Sidi Yahia oasis. It is a convenient stopping point for those crossing the border into Algeria or Spanish Melilla, or planning to journey down S to Figuig, in the Sahara. It is a well-equipped city which can be a useful last stop in relative comfort for the determined Saharan traveller.

Although Roman ruins have been found at Marnia, in 944 Zenata Berbers founded Oujda, strategically located on the main route from Rabat and Meknes to Algeria. It has traditionally been contested by the rulers of Fes, in Morocco, and Tlemcen, in Algeria. Captured by Sultan Youssef Ben Tachfine in 1206, it was a major centre for the Almohads. Later the Ottoman Regency of Algiers gained control of the city, but Moulay Ismail regained it in 1687. Oujda was acknowledged as part of Morocco by treaties with Morocco, but was occupied by French forces in 1844 and 1859. In 1903 Oujda was the centre of the insurgency by Bou Hamra, and was again taken by French forces from Algeria in 1907. The city was a centre of nationalist activity prior to Independence.

ACCESS Air Aéroport Oujda-Les Angad is 15 km from the city, off the P27, T 683261. Take a grand-taxi into town. **Train** Oujda is at the E end of the Moroccan rail network. The railway station is on Place de l'Unité Africaine, at the end of rue Zerktouni not far from the town centre. **Road** Oujda is a long haul over the P1 from Rabat, Fes and Taza to the W, which brings motorists over the Oued Nachaf into Blvd Mohammed ben Lakhdar, along with the P19 from Figuig, a hard drive across the Sahara. The P27 from Melilla, Nador and Ahfir enters Oujda along Blvd Abdellah Chefchaouni. From Ahfir continue to Saïdia and the Mediterranean. E to Algeria along the P1 follow Ave Mohammed V. **Bus**: CTM and other buses run into the Oued Nachef terminal, across the river from the town centre, take a petit-taxi to the town centre. Some CTM buses terminate in Place du 16 Août in the town centre. **Grand-taxis** from Nador, Berkane, Ahfir and the border terminate near Place du Maroc in the town centre, those for Figuig, Bouarfa and Taza stop at the bus station.

Things to see

Oujda is not a city to visit for sightseeing. Its small medina is surrounded by the *ville nouvelle*, and is not particularly distinct from it, being a primarily 20th century quarter, with no notable buildings, but is pleasant to wander in. At night the streets are deserted and not very inviting. The area is partly surrounded by Merinid ramparts. Place du Maroc and Ave des Marchés are busy commercial areas with stalls, and with *souqs* alongside. From rue de Marrakech **Bab Ouled Amrane** leads into the *mellah*, Oujda's Jewish quarter.

Along Ave des Marchés, **Bab Abd el-Ouahab** is the main gate to the medina, above which the heads of criminals used to be placed on poles. Just inside and outside the gate is an area where people gather, particularly in the evening, to watch and listen to the entertainers, including acrobats, musicians and storytellers, and sample the wares at the food stalls. Inside the gate is a large *kissaria*, or covered market, and a small area of *souqs*, a relaxing place in which to browse and bargain, best on Wed and Sun. The first of these is the busy **Souq el Ma**, or irrigation market, alongside the **Sidi Oqba Mosque**, with a striking minaret. Turn left from the rue des Marchés, past vegetable stalls, into Place Al-Attarine, with the *koubba* of Sidi Abd el-Ouahab, as well as the Merinid **Grand Mosque** and **medressa**, built by Sultan Abu Yaqub. Adjacent to the Place is the kasbah, former residence of government officials. On rue el Ouahda is the **French Cathedral**.

The **Lalla Aisha** gardens are small, pleasant to wander in or relax, but nothing remarkable. They contain the **Lalla Aisha ethnographic museum**, open 0900-1200 and 1430-1730. The city also has the **Lalla Meryem museum**.

Following Blvd de Sidi Yahia 6 km from the medina takes one eventually to the **Shrine of Sidi Yahia**. This is thought to be the tomb of St John the Baptist, and has been revered by Jews, Christians and Muslims. It is a pleasant area of trees around a stream, popular with pilgrims and visitors, with stalls, a few areas reserved for Muslims, and has 2 *moussems* (religious festivals) in honour of Sidi Yahia, in August and September. Take a town bus from Bab El Ouahab, they run every 10 mins and take 20 mins, or a petit-taxi to here from the city centre, perhaps with food for a picnic.

Local information

● Accommodation

C ***Hotel Terminus***, Place de l'Unité Africaine, T 683211-2, F 686378, 106 rms, comfortable with a good and popular bar, restaurant, tennis and pool, convenient for the railway station, the best top choice; **C** ***Hotel al-Massira Salam***, Blvd Maghreb al-Arabi, T 685300-3, Tx 61617, 108 rms, pool, tennis, bar, restaurant, nightclub from 2230, reliable, in the **Salam** chain.

Also **D** ***Hotel Oujda***, Ave Mohammed V, T 685600/2, Tx 61062, conveniently situated and comfortable with restaurant, bar and pool; **D** ***Grand Hotel***, rue Beni Marine, T 680508, this a good, modern hotel; **D** ***Hotel la Concorde***, 57 Ave Mohammed V, T 682328, 70 a/c rms, bar, restaurant, disco; **D** ***Hotel Moussafir***, Blvd Abdallah Chefchaouni/Place de la Gare, T 688202, F 688208, 72 rms or suites each with a/c, TV, shower, telephone, restaurant, bar, pool, exchange.

E ***Hotel Simon***, Blvd Tarik Ibn Ziad, T 686304, 43 rms, bar and restaurant, changes money; **E** ***Hotel Lutetia***, 44 Blvd Hassan Loukili, T 683365, 40 rms, convenient and adequate, with a bar; **E** ***Hotel Royal***, 13 Blvd Zerktouni, T 682284, 60 good rms, clean and friendly, an efficient management.

The best cheap hotel is the **F** ***Hotel Zeglel***, near the bus station, very friendly; whilst **F** ***Hotel Majestic***, Ave Hassan II, T 682948, is a basic hotel but without hot water; **F** ***Hotel Afrique*** in the medina, near Bab el Ouahab, is another good cheap option; as is **F** ***Hotel du 16 Août***, rue de Marrakech, 23 clean rms, cold showers, mainly used by Algerian traders; **F** ***Hotel Ziri***, Ave Mohammed V, T 684540, good view, 30 basic rms with bath (cold water); ***Hotel Victoria***, 74 Ave Mohammed V, T 685020, 10 rms, clean.

● Youth hostel

11 Ave Allal ben Abdellah, T 0788, 45 beds, kitchen, meals available, bus 100m. train 500m, overnight fee MD15.

● Places to eat

♦♦♦The ***Brasserie-Nightclub de France***, 87-89 Ave Mohammed V, T 685981, serves good Spanish, Moroccan and continental food and has an excellent bar; also try the restaurant in ***Hotel Terminus***, Place de l'Unité Africaine. ♦♦ ***Le Dauphin***, near Blvd Ahfir, is a good Moroccan restaurant known for fish; ***La Chaumière***, rue de Marrakech, is good for French cooking. ♦Try ***Restaurant Bab el-Garbi***, near the gate of that name, for cheap Moroccan food; or ***Sandwich Taroudant***, Blvd ben Abdellah, with a good range of dishes. Perhaps the best cheap meals can be had at the stalls near **Bab el Ouahab**.

● Banks

BMCE, 93 Ave Mohammed V; **Credit du Maroc** and **Wafabank** on Place du 16 Août.

● Car hire

Avis, 110 Ave Allal ben Abdellah, T 683993, 684618, and at the airport; **Hertz**, 2 Immeuble El Baraka, Ave Mohammed V, T 683802, Tx 61639, and at the airport.

● Chemist

All night on rue de Marrakech, T 683490.

● Consulates

Algeria, 11 Blvd de Taza, T 683740-1; **France**, 16 rue Imam Lechaf, T 682705.

Post Office

PTT, Ave Mohammed V/Place du Jeddah.

Shopping

More expensive places than the *souqs* in which to shop, but good to sample the range of goods, are the official ***Ensemble Artisanat***, Place Dar al-Makhzen; and the ***Maison de l'Artisanat***, Blvd Allal ben Abdellah.

Sport

Sporting Tennis Club, T 682545, and **Riding Club**, T 682499.

Tourist information

Delegation Regionale du Tourisme, Place du 16 Août, BP 424, T 684329 (open 0800-1200 and 1430-1830).

Transport

Taxis Petit-taxis are red. Watch out for unofficial red vehicles without signs. Taxi from Ave Mohammed V to Oued Nachaf bus station MD5.

Air There are flights to Casablanca (6 a week), Rabat (1 a week), as well as to Amsterdam, Bastia in Corsica, Brussels, Dusseldorf, Frankfurt, Marseille and Paris. Take a grand-taxi from Place du Maroc. **Royal Air Maroc** has an office at the *Hotel Oujda*, Ave Mohammed V, T 683963-4, as does **Air France**.

Train The train station is in Place de l'Unité Africain, T 683133. There are 3 trains per day to **Tanger** (12 hrs), 5 a day to **Fes** (6½ hrs), **Meknes** (7½ hrs), **Rabat** (9½ hrs) and **Casablanca** (10½ hrs). There is also a once weekly train down the E flank of the country into the Sahara. This train leaves on Sat at 2242, calling at **Aïn Beni Mathar** (4 hrs) and **Bouarfa** (8½ hrs), and is useful for **Figuig**, 109 km to the SE of the latter station and connected by buses. Trains do run to Algiers and Tunis, leaving at 0830, but it is worth checking up on this at the station in advance.

Road CTM buses leave from 12 rue Sidi Brahim, just off Place du 16 Août, T 682047, to **Fes** (1100), **Nador** (0500, 1000, 1300, 1530) and **Casablanca** (2000, 2030), and from the Oued Nachaf bus station at Place du 3 Mars to Fes (0500, 1100) and **Nador** (0700, 1000, 1300, 1530). Private line buses leave from the Oued Nachaf bus station, T 682262, to **Casablanca** (0430, 0630, 1600, 1700, 1800, 1930, 2030), **Fes** (0500, 0830, 1100), **Meknes** (1430), **Taza** (0400, 0730, 0930, 1200, 1300), **Taourirt** (1400, 1500, 1600, 1700, 1730), **Midelt** (0600), **Figuig** (0600, 1000, 1500 – the earlier the better to avoid the heat), **Bouarfa** (0700, 1700), **Nador** (10 between 0200 and 1315: 2 hrs), **Al Hoceima** (1400), **Berkane** (9 between 0740 and 1315), **Saïdia** (0800, 0900, 1330, 1420, 1610), **Ahfir** (regularly from 0635 to 1740).

Taxi Grand-taxis to Berkane, Ahfir (40 mins) and the border leave from just off Place du Maroc. For Saïdia change at Berkane or, preferably, Ahfir. Grand-taxis to Taza, Figuig and Bouarfa leave from by the bus station.

The Algerian Border

The border with Algeria, so long problematic, is now open, however it can take several hours to cross, and is closed from 1100-1500. There are grand-taxis over the 13 km to the border, leaving from rue de Marrakech, and some local buses. Hitching with other travellers is also an option. It is wise to check in Oujda with the Tourist Office, or the Algerian Consulate, that the border is open, particularly for travellers on foot.

Travellers from most European, N American and Commonwealth countries need visas for Algeria. These can be obtained from the Algerian Consulate in Oujda, but expect considerable delays. A much quicker option is to obtain a visa in Rabat. It will be necessary to change at least AD1000 (see page 218), so a visit to Algeria cannot really be an economic weekend option for the budget traveller.

MARRAKECH, THE HIGH AND MIDDLE ATLAS

CONTENTS

MAPS

An ideal tourist location, Marrakech lies within reach of beautiful High Atlas valleys and arid pre-Saharan plains. The city itself is one of the great Islamic cities of North Africa, with the KoutoubiaMosque a memorable building which dominates the city, and the DjemaaElFna square, a place of continual activity and entertainment. Around these the medina stretches, its narrow streets and flat-roofed red houses accommodating a way of life which has retained many characteristics from over the centuries. Within easy reach of Marrakech, the Ourikavalley and the ToubkalNational Park are some of the most popular areas of the High Atlas, and there is excellent skiing at Oukaimeden N of Marrakech, where the Middle Atlas mountain range runs up towards Meknes and Fes, with the relaxed Alpine-style resorts of Azrou and Ifrane.

MARRAKECH

Pop 439,728 (1982). *Alt* 470m.

Along with Fes, Marrakech is the most important historic city in Morocco, with the **Koutoubia Mosque** and **Ben Youssef Medersa** among its most distinctive buildings. Marrakech has a memorable beauty, with its palm-lined streets and red earth walls, surrounding a huge medina of flat-roofed, red houses. The High Atlas mountains, snow-capped until Apr, loom above the city, a venue for numerous excursions. Above all Marrakech is worth visiting because of the vibrant mass of people that mill around in the unique **Djemaa El Fna** square, with its grill-stalls, traders and entertainers, and the vast network of *souqs*, people that come from all over the surrounding plains, the High Atlas and the Sahara. The character of the city owes much to its continuing role as a trading centre and capital for the S of the country. Tourist hassle which deterred some visitors in the past is now much reduced and the predominant atmosphere is very relaxed, best appreciated from a café terrace beside Djemaa El Fna.

The city of Marrakech, or Marrakesh, takes the Arabic form of 'Marrakch', whilst in some early European maps it appears as 'Morocco City'. The location of the city is particularly impressive. It is situated in the Tensift valley, in the rich agricultural Haouz plain, normally called the 'Haouz of Marrakech'. The city is surrounded by extensive palmer-

CLIMATE: MARRAKECH

	Jan	Feb	Mar	Apr	May	Jun	Jul	Aug	Sep	Oct	Nov	Dec	Av/Tot
Max (°C)	18	20	23	25	29	33	38	27	33	28	23	19	27
Min (°C)	5	7	9	12	14	17	20	20	18	15	10	7	13
Rain (mm)	29	31	31	33	20	8	2	3	10	17	27	34	245

ies, into which areas of villas and hotels are gradually spreading. Yet there are also sandy, arid areas near, and even within, the city, which give it a semi-Saharan character. The other dominant landform is the mountains. Arriving from Fes or Meknes one crosses the end of the Middle Atlas range, and from Casablanca or Rabat the dry, sparsely populated Bahira Jbilet. But from most points in Marrakech it is the High Atlas which is the visible mountain range, its often snow-covered peaks appearing to rise from just behind the city. Indeed the popular mountain destinations of the Ourika Valley, Oukaimeden, Asni and the Toubkal Park are easily accessible from Marrakech. Marrakech is also an important crossroads, the focal point of the S, linking roads from Fes/Meknes, Rabat/Casablanca, Safi, El Jadida, Essaouira, Agadir, Taroudant and Ouarzazate/the Sahara, whilst it also has an airport and is the S terminus of the railway network.

Marrakech covers a large area, with distinct zones separated by less populated areas. For the visitor this will entail long walks between the main points of interest and utility in the medina, the French built *ville nouvelle*, and the 2 gardens of Agdal and Menara, or more probably reliance on taxis, *calèches*, buses or their own transport. The long, wide tree-lined boulevards of the *ville nouvelle*, a number of which are focused on the beautiful **Koutoubia Mosque**, give the city an impressive feeling of spaciousness, which contrasts with the equally impressive density of the medina.

Marrakech is Morocco's 4th largest city, with a population including Arab, Berber and mixed elements, whilst many of its residents are immigrants from surrounding rural regions, and further S. The economy of the city includes administrative activities and modern shops and services, whilst it has for many centuries been an important regional market for trade in agricultural produce and other goods. There is still a wide range of handicraft production and small-scale industry, particularly in the medina. There are a number of factories and industrial units, notably in agro-processing. However the city's economy and employment are heavily dependent on tourism, Marrakech being one of the major tourist attractions of Morocco. Furthermore many of the city's large unemployed or under-employed labour force supplement their incomes by casual work with tourists, their unwanted attentions having in the past given Marrakech a bad name.

History

Almoravid origins Although Marrakech has probably been occupied since Neolithic times, it was first founded properly in 1062 by the Almoravids, as a base from which to control the High Atlas mountains. A kasbah, **Dar al-Hajar**, was built close to the site of the Koutoubia Mosque. Under Youssef Ben Tachfine Marrakech was an important capital and marketing centre, with the building of several mosques, palaces and the city's famous walls, as well as the development of extensive gardens and an irrigation system. The city attracted leading mediaeval thinkers from outside Marrakech.

Marrakech under the Almohads Marrakech was taken by the Almohads in 1147, who almost totally destroyed and then rebuilt the city, making it the capital of their extensive empire. Under the Almohad Sultan Abd el-Moumen the **Koutoubia Mosque** was built on the site of Almoravid buildings, with the minaret added by Ya'qub al Mansur. Under the latter Marrakech gained palaces, gardens and irrigation works, and again became a famous centre for musicians, writers and academics, but on his death it declined and fell into disarray.

Merinid neglect and Saadian revival Whilst the Merinids added several *medressa* to Marrakech, Fes received much

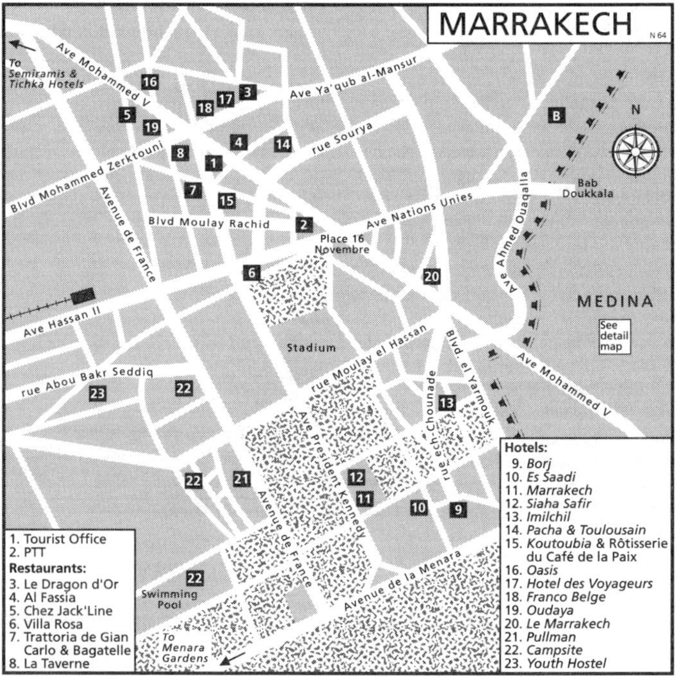

of their attention, and was preferred as capital, although from 1374 to 1386 Marrakech was the centre of a separate principality. Marrakech was revitalized by the Saadians from 1524 with the rebuilding of the **Ben Youssef Mosque**, and the construction by Ahmed al-Mansur Ad-Dahbi of the **El Badi Palace** and the **Saadian Tombs**. Marrakech also became an important trading post, due to its location between the Sahara and the Atlantic.

Alawite Marrakech The Alawites took control of Marrakech in 1668. In the early 18th century the city suffered from Moulay Ismail's love of Meknes, with many of the major buildings, notably the **El Badi Palace**, stripped to glorify the new capital, and a significant shift in power and wealth. The destructive effects of this period were compounded by the civil strife following his death. However, under the Alawite Sultan Moulay Hassan I, from 1873, and his son, Marrakech gained a number of important buildings and reestablished its prestige. From 1898 Thami el-Glaoui and his family controlled the city as a powerful *pasha* with considerable autonomy from central control. A number of leading merchants built palaces in the city.

The French took control of Marrakech and its region in 1912, crushing an insurrection by a claimant to the Sultanate. The French built the *ville nouvelle*, Gueliz, in the 20th century, but Marrakech stagnated in comparison to the coastal cities of Casablanca and Rabat. In recent decades the city has grown enormously, with the authorities developing its tourist appeal and capacity, as well as its role as a conference centre.

ACCESS Air Aéroport Marrakech-Menara, T 430939 and 447903, is 5 km to the SW of the city near the Menara Gardens. It has a *bureau de change* open until 1800. Road 6010 leads to the city, the routes are clearly signposted. There are taxis from the airport, MD50 by day, MD90 after 2100 as well as bus No 11.

Train The railway station is in Gueliz, on Ave Hassan II, T 447768, 447947. There is usually no shortage of taxis waiting for the arrival of trains, although fixing a reasonable rate may be difficult for the new arrival. Most hotels in the *ville nouvelle* or the medina should be reached for MD5-10, and MD8-15 at night. Alternatively take bus No 3 or 8 from outside the station along Ave Hassan II and Ave Mohammed V, to the medina.

Road The P10 from Essaouira and Agadir enters the city along Ave d'Essaouira and Ave Hassan II, into Gueliz, and at Place 16 Novembre turn right along Ave Mohammed V for the medina. On the approach along the P9 from Safi (via the P12) and El Jadida cross the roundabout for the medina, and turn right along Ave Mohammed Abdelkrim Al Khattabi for Gueliz. From the P7 from Rabat and Casablanca turn right along Ave Allal Al Fassi for the medina, for Gueliz continue ahead. The P24 from Fes and Meknes skirts the N ramparts, from Bab Doukkala follow the outside of the walls to reach Djemaa El Fna and the centre of the medina, turn along Ave des Nations Unies for Gueliz. From the P31 from Ouarzazate follow the ramparts round to Bab Doukkala. Route 501 from Taroudant reaches Marrakech at a roundabout near Bab Rob, pass through the gate for the medina, turn left for Gueliz. **Bus** All long-distance buses arrive at the Gare Routière at Bab Doukkala, T 433933, from where taxis and bus No 3 or 8 can easily be taken. CTM services for Agadir and Casablanca also call at the office in Gueliz, in Blvd Mohammed Zerktouni. ONCF buses from Laayoune and Agadir arrive at the railway station in Ave Hassan II.

Things to see

Main areas of interest Marrakech is clearly divided into the large historic city, the medina, and the *ville nouvelle*, Gueliz. The focal point of the medina, and indeed of the whole city, is the **Djemaa el Fna**, an open place full of street entertainers and food sellers, adjacent to which are the most important markets, as well as numerous hotels, restaurants, cafés and shops. This is a good base from which to explore the historic sites of the medina. The gates in the city walls are also important centres, notably **Bab Rob**, **Bab Doukkala** and **Bab el Khemis**. The major thoroughfare of the Gueliz is Ave Mohammed V, and the evening promenade along its length is very popular. There is little to see in the Gueliz but it is a pleasant place to wander or rest in a café. The **Menara Gardens** are to the S of Gueliz, the **Agdal Gardens** directly to the S of the medina. On the E side of Marrakech, across the Oued Issil, is the **Palmery**.

It is worth attempting to coincide a visit to Marrakech with the **National Festival of Popular Art**, an extravagant mixture of music, dance and folklore displays. The exact date in the summer for this varies annually so check with a tourist office.

Djemaa El Fna The Djemaa El Fna is unique in Morocco, perhaps the greatest pull for tourists, yet still a genuine social area for the Marrakchi people, and those flooding in from the surrounding regions, with much aimed solely at Moroccans. It is a large irregular space full of people hawking their goods or talents and others watching, walking, talking and arguing. Its activity never seems to finish, and at each point of the day has a distinctive character. It is particularly memorable during Ramadan when the day's fast ends. Whatever the time of the day or year, Djemaa El Fna is somewhere that the visitor will return to again and again, responding to the magnetic pull that affects locals as much as tourists, to mingle with the crowd or watch from the terrace of the *Café de France* or *Café-Restaurant Argana*.

Djemaa El Fna means 'assembly of the dead', and may refer to the traditional display of the heads of criminals, executed here until the 19th century. In 1956 the government attempted to close down the square by converting it into a corn market and car park, but soon reverted it to its traditional role. Visit it during the day to explore the stalls and collections of goods spread out on the floor: fruit, herbs and spices, clothes, shoes, electrical goods and handicrafts, as well as the snake charmers and monkey tamers, who pose for photographs. Return in the evening to watch and listen to the folk-healers, dancers, musicians, boxers, acrobats and storytellers that crowd the square, each with a throng of people gathered around. Those with courage may sample the food from the stalls, but it is wise to eat only what is cooked on request. Try the excellent freshly-squeezed orange juice from one of the stalls surrounding the square.

WARNING It is wise to take extreme caution with pickpockets, and to deal patiently with the numerous unofficial guides, 'students', or 'friends' that will seek business.

The Koutoubia Mosque, currently clad in scaffolding, dominates the whole of Marrakech, a landmark throughout much of the medina, and around which the French laid out their road network. It is clearly visible as, unlike the Qarawiyin Mosque in Fes, it is set apart from the dense areas of historic building, and has a tall minaret, of over 60m. According to legend as this structure overlooked the harem, only a blind muezzen was allowed to climb it to call the faithful to prayer. However it is a memorable structure with both elegance and simplicity in the design. The name, meaning the 'Bookseller's Mosque', reflects the trade which used to go on in the immediate surrounds.

The Koutoubia Mosque is at the end of Ave Mohammed V, close to the Djemaa El Fna. In viewing the site it is wise to be extremely careful, as the mosque is closed to non-Muslims and, as the most important in Marrakech, does not welcome close inspection. However it is possible to walk around and through the surrounding areas, where there are some interesting points from which to take photographs.

The site of the mosque is itself historic, with its prior occupation by a late 11th century kasbah, the **Almoravid Fortress**, or **Dar al-Hajar**. This was built by either Youssef Ben Tachfine or Abu Bakr, and formed the focus of the town. The configuration of the walls of this fortress can be seen between the mosque and Ave Mohammed V. The walls consist of 2m wide parts, with a gap down the centre. It is an impressive structure indicating a highly developed indigenous building capability. At the W extremity of the walls are the sites of a S facing gate and a fountain. These were decorated with painted panels from the Almoravid period which are now in the **El Badi Palace**. The fortress ruins are the oldest Almoravid site in the country, and one of the few remaining in Marrakech.

On the corner of the 2 sections of the wall is **Bab Ali**, named after the son of Youssef Ben Tachfine. This is the ruins of a tower and entry arch, an entrance into the kasbah. It is suggested that it may have been the place where the Almohads finally defeated the Almoravids.

The successful Almohads destroyed much of the Almoravid city, and in 1147 built a large mosque, located between the kasbah and the later Koutoubia Mosque. The *mihrab* of this mosque was located on its S wall, bordering the existing building, and it is suggested that its location was wrong and led to the mosque's destruction. The 2 mosques existed for some time together, the bricked-up spaces on the N wall of the Koutoubia Mosque indicating the doors which connected them. However the complex was excessive in size and the older structure fell into disrepair and eventual ruin. The site was excavated from 1948. These excavations also revealed a *maqsura* or screen, in front of the *mihrab*, which could be wound up through the floor to protect the Sultan, and a *minbar*, or pulpit, which was moved into position on wooden rollers. The 2 cisterns in the centre are probably from a previous Almoravid structure. On the E flank of this mosque was an arcade of which a niche and the remains of one arch remain. Along this arcade runs a paved street where the booksellers worked.

The existing Koutoubia Mosque was built by Abd el-Moumen in 1162, soon after the building of the first mosque. The minaret is 12.5m wide by 67.5m high, and is the mosque's principal feature, rightly ranked along with the later Almohad structures of the **Hassan Tower** in Rabat (see page 214) and the **Giralda Tower** in Sevilla (see page 164). The minaret, with its 1:5 proportions, had great influence on subsequent buildings in Morocco.

The minaret is composed of 6 rooms, one on top of the other. The cupola on top of the minaret is a symmetrical, square structure surmounted by a ribbed dome and 3 golden orbs. These are alleged to have been made from the melted down jewellery of Ya'qub al-Mansur's wife, in penance for having eaten 3 grapes during Ramadan. The cupola has 2 windows on each side, above which is a panel of stone-carved *darj w ktaf*. The main tower has a band of hexagonal and square tiles at the top, below which is a different series of arches and windows on each side, including a representation of many Almohad design motifs. The main building itself is fairly plain. Behind the mosque, on rue Sidi Mimoun, is a small tomb to the Almoravid Sultan Youssef Ben Tachfine, the founder of Marrakech.

The Souqs of Marrakech, many of which retain their original function, and the presence of both craftsmen and traders, are worth at least a morning to explore. It is, however, far from a relaxing experience, with traders continually besieging tourists with pleas of 'just for looking' or similar. It is worth getting an idea of prices before choosing a reasonable trader and getting down to serious bargaining. An unofficial guide is likely to be more trouble and expense than he is worth, and certainly one should not believe the 'Berber market, only open today' line, which is used everyday. **NB**: it is important to inspect goods closely, especially anything involving gold, silver or gems, as these are often fakes. The increasing business in antiques often involves new products which have been treated.

The main *souqs* lie to the N of Djemaa

Neatly Shod

The traditional footwear, *barbouches*, soft leather slippers worn with the heel turned in, vary in design. Men's slippers lined with sheepskin and having stronger, goatskin soles are normally dyed yellow but grey slippers are becoming more common. Women's outdoor slippers are most often black or red leather while the indoor slippers or those for special occasions are of brighter colours, lighter material and heavily decorated in gold or silver thread with stylised designs of leaves, flowers and geometric shapes. When purchasing, look for the craftsman's seal on the heel.

El Fna. The entrance is to the left of the mosque. Follow this round to the left and then turn right in the main thoroughfare of the *souqs*, **Souq Semmarin**. Alternatively enter through the small touristic pottery market, further round to the left on Djemaa El Fna. Souq Semmarin is a busy place, originally the textiles market, and although there are a number of large, expensive tourist shops, there are still some cloth sellers. To the left is a covered *kissaria* selling clothes. The first turning on the right leads past **Souq Larzal**, a wool market, and **Souq Btana**, a sheepskin market, to **Rahba Kedima**, the old corn market, now selling a range of goods including traditional cures and cosmetics, spices, vegetables and cheap jewellery, and with some good carpet shops. Walk back onto the main *souq* via a short alley with wood-carved goods. Here the *souq* forks, into **Souq el Attarin** on the left and **Souq el Kebir** on the right.

To the right of Souq el Kebir is the **Criée Berbère**, where carpets and *jallabahs* are sold. This was where slaves, mainly from across the Sahara, were auctioned until 1912. Further on is the **Souq des Bijoutiers**, with jewellery. To the left of Souq el Kebir is a network of small alleys, the ***kissarias***, selling Western goods. Beyond the *kissarias* is the **Souq Cherratin**, with leather goods, somewhere to bargain for camel or cow hide bags, purses and belts.

Continuing back on the other side of the *kissarias* is the **Souq des Baboushes**, a far better place to buy slippers than in the tourist shops. This feeds into **Souq el Attarin**, the spice and perfume *souq*, which itself leads back into Souq Semmarin. West of the Souq el Attarin is the **Souq Chouari**, with carpenters. From here walk on to a Saadian fountain and the 16th century **Mouassin Mosque**. South of Souq Chouari is the **Souq des Teinturiers**, or dyers' market, where wool recently dyed is festooned over the walkways, the most picturesque area of the medina. Nearby are the blacksmiths' and coppersmiths' *souqs*.

The Almoravid Koubba and Ben Youssef Medersa These buildings are close to each other, to the N of the Djemaa El Fna, see map page 303.

The **Almoravid Koubba** (**Koubba el-Baroudiyin**) dates from the 11th century, and is a rare example of the architecture of this period, the only complete Almoravid building surviving. It dates from the reign of Ali bin Youssef (1107-43), and perhaps formed part of the toilet and ablutions facilities of the mosque which at the time existed nearby.

At first glance it is a simple building, with a dome surmounting a square structure. The dome is quite decorated, however, with a design of interlocking arches, and a star and chevron motif on top. The arches leading into the *koubba* are different on each side. Climb down the stairs to look at the structure close-up. Inside, the ceiling below the dome is intricately carved. It includes an octagon within an 8 pointed star, and the use of a range of Almoravid motifs, including the palmette, pine cone and acanthus. Around the corniche is a dedicatory inscription in cursive script.

Close by the *koubba* is the large 12th century **Ben Youssef Mosque**, rebuilt in the 19th century. On a side street just to the E of the mosque is the Saadian **Ben Youssef Medersa** (open 0900-1200 and 1430-1800, closed Fri), an impressive example of religious architecture of the period, with strong influences from Andalucía. A boarding school for religious students, it was founded in 1564-5 by Sultan Moulay Abdellah, on the site of a previous Merinid *medersa*. The *medersa* is centred around a courtyard containing a pool, and with arcades on 2 sides. The arcades and walls are comprehensively decorated with a variety of different designs and scripts, with use of *zellij* tiling on the arcade floor, walls and

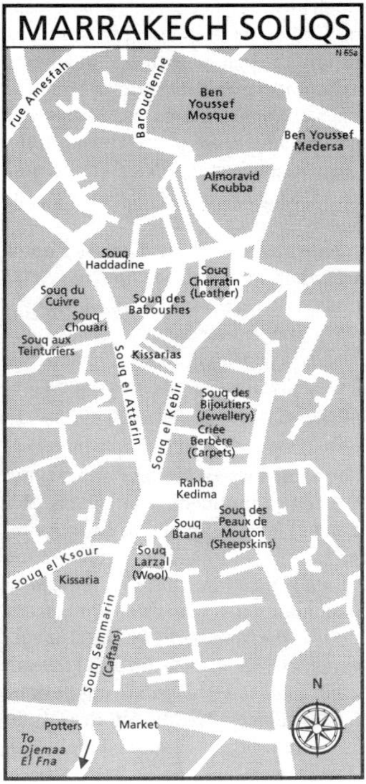

pillars. Inscriptions are in Kufic and cursive lettering, interwoven with floral patterns.

At the far end is the *mihrab*, or prayer hall. Note the stalactite ceiling of the *mihrab*, and the carved stucco walls, in which the pine cone motif is prominent. There are small students' cells on both levels of the building, around separate courtyards. On the 2nd level they often have a tiny sleeping room above, entered by bars on the wall.

On the way out of the *medersa*, the smelly toilets on the right of the vestibule have an elaborate stalactite design on the ceiling. There is also a 10th century Andalusian ablution basin in the vestibule, decorated with eagles and Cordoban floral designs.

To the N of the Ben Youssef Medersa is an area of the medina which is worth exploring for an indication of the structure and working of the traditional Islamic city, unspoiled by the demands of the tourist industry which have so influenced areas closer to Djemaa El Fna. This area includes the **Shrine of Sidi bel-Abbes**, one of the 7 saints of Marrakech. He was born in Ceuta in 1145 and during his life in Marrakech was patronized by Ya'qub al-Mansur. The shrine, recently restored, is strictly closed to non-Muslims. Nearby is the **Zaouia of Sidi Ben Slimane el-Jazuli**, a 14th century *sufi*.

Bab Agnaou, Saadian Tombs and El Badi Palace Bab Agnaou marks the entrance to the kasbah quarter. To get to it, follow rue Bab Agnaou from Djemaa El Fna, or enter the medina at Bab Rob. The kasbah quarter dates from the late 12th century and the reign of the Almohad Sultan Ya'qub al-Mansur. Bab Agnaou is also Almohad. The gateway itself is surrounded by a series of arches within a rectangle of floral designs and a further band of Kufic inscription.

The road from the gate leads to rue de la Kasbah, turn right along this and then along the first left. On this road is the much restored **Kasbah Mosque**, dating from 1190. The minaret has the *darj w ktaf* (*fleur de lis*) and *shabka* (net) motifs on alternate sides, with a background of green tiles, above which is a band of coloured tiles. The minaret is not as impressive as that of the Koutoubia Mosque but is worth noting en route to the Saadian Tombs.

The entrance to these lies directly to the right of the mosque. The late 16th century **Saadian Tombs** (open 0800-1200 and 1400-1800) are the mausoleums for the dynasty's Sultans and their families, and were discovered in 1917, having been sealed off by Moulay Ismail. There is a series of chambers and tombs off a small garden, with carved cedarwood and plasterwork which is in a remarkably good condition. The design is influenced strongly by the Andalusian tradition. The *mihrab* of the first main mausoleum is particularly impressive, and in this room is the tomb of Moulay Yazd. The second room contains the tomb of Ahmed al-Mansur, with finely carved columns. The 2nd and older mausoleum was built for the tombs of Ahmed al-Mansur's mother, Lalla Messaouda, and Mohammed es-Sheikh, founder of the Saadians. In the garden and courtyard are the tombs of numerous princes and household members. As a small site the Saadian Tombs can become crowded with tour groups.

The **El Badi Palace** (open 0900-1200 and 1430-1730) was built by the Saadian Sultan Ahmed al Mansur Ad-Dahbi between 1578 and 1593, following his accession after the Battle of the Three Kings at Ksar el Kebir. To get to it, return to the Bab Agnaou and head right inside the ramparts, and then take the 2nd right. This road leads more or less directly to Place des Ferblantiers. Pass through Bab Berima, the gate on the S side. The entrance to the palace is on the right.

The El Badi Palace was a lavish display of the best craftsmanship of the period, using the most expensive materials, including gold, but was largely destroyed in the 17th century by Moulay Ismail, who stripped it of its decorations and fittings and carried them off to Meknes. Little now remains except the palace's *pisé*-cement walls. The palace probably had a largely ceremonial purpose, being used for receptions. Past the mosque is the central courtyard, built above water channels connecting a number of pools. The largest of these even has an island. The ruins on either side of the courtyard were probably summer houses, that at the far end called the **Koubba el Hamsiniya** after the 50 pillars in its construction. The complex contains a small museum which includes the movable *minbar* from the Koutoubia Mosque. The scattered ruins of the palace, with odd fragments of decoration amidst the debris, include also stables and dungeons. To the S of the El Badi Palace is the **Dar al-Makhzen**, the modern-day Royal Palace, now one of King Hassan II's favourite residences.

Nearby, the **Musée Dar Al Funun Ashaabia**, 154 Derb Sahrige, rue Arste Moussa Riad Zitoune Kedim, T 426632, has audio-visual displays on various themes of Moroccan arts including dance, theatre and the marriage ceremony, each lasting between 20 and 45 mins.

The Southeastern Medina To get to the SE area of the medina follow rue des Banques from just past *Café de France* on the Djemaa El Fna. This leads into rue Zitoun Jedid. Off to the left is the **Dar Si Said** museum (open 0900-1200, 1600-2100 in the summer, 1430-1800 in the winter, closed Tues) is on Riad Zitoun Jedid, T 442464. This palace was built by Si Said, *Visir* under Moulay El Hassan, and half-brother of Ba Ahmed Ben Moussa, who built the El Bahia Palace. The museum includes pottery, jewellery, leatherwork from Marrakech and carpets from Chichaoua. It is particularly strong on Berber artifacts, notably jewellery and arms. The palace itself is small but with a cool and pleasant courtyard.

At 8 rue de la Bahia, between the El Bahia Palace and Dar Si Said, is ***Maison Tiskiwin***, T 443335. This includes a shop, a café and a museum, the latter concerned with Moroccan rural culture and society, a collection put together by the art historian Bert Flint. There is an exhibition of craftsmen's materials and techniques from regions as far apart as the Rif, High Atlas and the Sahara, including jewellery and costume. Note the nomad's tent from the Middle Atlas. The building itself, around a courtyard, is an authentic and well-maintained ex-

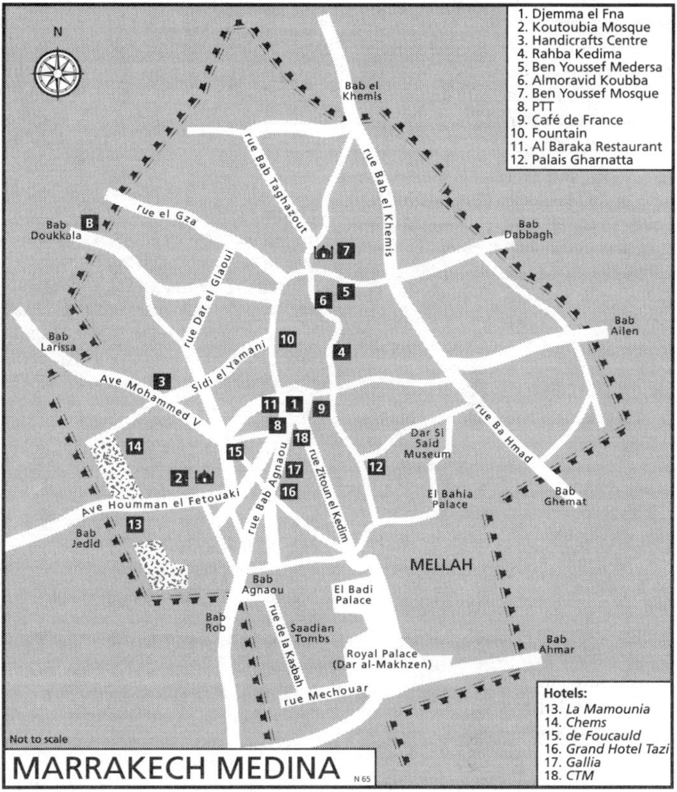

ample of traditional domestic architecture.

Further to the S, the **El Bahia Palace** (open 0800-1200 and 1430-1800) was built in the 19th century by the *Visir* Ba Ahmed Ben Moussa, or Bou Ahmed, a former slave who exercised considerable power under Moulay Hassan and Abd al-Aziz. The palace has the Andalusian-inspired decor of the period, although executed in a garish fashion which does not do justice to the craftsmanship of the city. Bou Ahmed was so hated that, on his death in 1900, his palace was looted and his possessions stolen by slaves, servants and members of his *harem*. The building is centred around a marble courtyard. There is a colourful garden of fruit-trees and flowers.

The ***mellah***, the Jewish quarter, was created in 1558. This lies S of the El Bahia Palace and to the W of the El Badi Palace. This is an extensive quarter reflecting the community's historic importance to the city, when they were involved in the sugar trade and banking, as well as providing most of the jewellers, metalworkers and tailors. There were several synagogues, and under the control of their *rabbis*, the area had considerable autonomy. There are now few Jews left, but the quarter is still distinct in the cramped houses and narrow streets. Conditions here remain worse than in much of the medina, with unpaved roads and insanitary drainage. It is worth asking around to be let into one of the synagogues.

The Walls and Gates The extensive ramparts of Marrakech (20 gates and 200 towers stretching for 16 km) are predominantly Almoravid, excepting those around the Agdal Gardens, although extensively restored since. The reconstruction is a continual process as the *pisé*-cement walls, made of the distinctive earth of the Haouz plains, gradually crumble. The ramparts and gates are one of the distinctive sights of Morocco, and a tour in a horse-drawn *calèche* is recommended. All the gates are clearly named.

Bab Rob, near the buses and grand-taxis on the SW side of the medina, is Almohad, and is named after the grape juice which could only be brought through this gate. **Bab Dabbagh** (the Tanners' gate) on the E side, is an intricate defensive gate with a twisted entrance route and wooden gates which could shut off the various parts of the building for security. From the top of the gate there is a good view of the tanneries. It is possible to look around the tanneries. Note that hides are often laid out to dry on the banks of the nearby *oued*. **Bab el Khemis**, on the NE side, opens into the **Souq el Khemis** (Thurs market) and an important area of mechanics and craftsmen. There is a small saint's tomb inside the gate building. **Bab Doukkala**, on the NW side by the bus station is a large gate with an *outrepassé* arch and 2 towers. The medina side has an *outrepassé* arch and a cusped, blind arch, with a variation on the *darj w ktaf* motif along the top.

The Gardens The **Agdal Gardens**, stretching S of the medina, were established in the 12th century under Abd el-Moumen, and expanded by the Saadians. The vast expanse includes several pools, and extensive areas of olive, orange and pomegranate trees. They are in the main closed when the king is in residence, but are worth visiting at other times. Of the pavilions, the **Dar al-Baida** was used by Sultan Moulay Hassan to house his *harem*. The largest pool, **Sahraj el Hana** receives its coach-loads of tourists, but in between times is a pleasant place to relax, although not to swim.

From the medina and the Agdal Gardens, Ave de la Menara leads past the **Oliveraie de Bab Jedid** to the **Menara Gardens**. This is an olive grove, itself not very interesting but a good place for a picnic. At the centre is a rectangular pool with a good view of the Atlas Mountains, a picture on numerous postcards and brochures. The green-tiled pavilion alongside was built in 1866. Inside, above the small display of carpets and other Berber artifacts, is an impressive painted cedarwood ceiling.

The Jardin Majorelle, also called the **Bou Saf-Saf** (open 0800-1200 and 1400-1700 in the winter, 0800-1200 and 1500-1900 in the summer), is off Ave Ya'qub al-Mansur. This is a small tropical garden laid out by a French artist, Louis Majorelle. The buildings are a vivid blue, but the overall effect is worth seeing. There is also a small **Musée d'Art Islamique** in the grounds.

The Palmery includes around 180,000 trees used mainly for wood. It is a good place for a drive or a *calèche* tour, but is gradually being expropriated by large villa and hotel developments. Take the Route de Palmeraie off the P24 to Fes to explore it.

Local information

● Accommodation

Price guide:

AL	US$90+	**D**	US$20-40
A	US$75-90	**E**	US$10-20
B	US$60-75	**F**	under US$10
C	US$40-60		

AL *La Mamounia*, Ave Bab Jedid, T 448981,

F 444940, historic hotel, patronized by the rich and famous for decades, formerly a royal palace, recently renovated with lavish decoration, perhaps the most luxurious establishment in Morocco, 171 double rms start at MD1500, 57 suites decorated on themes including Churchill, a former patron, and 3 bedroom villas set in 7 ha of relaxing gardens, tennis, one of the best hotel pools in the country, 4 bars, 4 restaurants, a brasserie, nightclub, casino, business centre, ballroom, beauty centre, jacuzzis, sauna, *hammam*, squash court and gym; **AL** ***Hotel Es Saadi***, Ave Kadissia, Hivernage, T 448811, similarly luxurious hotel set in large gardens, with a recommended restaurant, bar, casino, nightclub, tennis and pool; **AL** ***Sheraton***, Ave de la Menara, T 448998, F 448972; **AL** ***Palmerie Golf Palace***, T 301010, F 305050, in Les Jardins de la Palmerie, 77 ha site, 314 rms, 5 pools, 18 hole golf course, 7 restaurants.

A ***Hotel Semiramis Le Meridien***, Route de Casablanca, BP 525, T 431377, F 447127, restaurant, bar, nightclub, tennis, and an excellent pool; **A** ***Hotel Safir Marrakech***, Ave President Kennedy, T 447400, 448126, Tx 72026, F 448730, a fully equipped hotel with a disco, 2 tennis courts, bar, restaurant, shops, *hammam* and a pool surrounded with palm trees; **A** ***Hotel Pullman Mansur Eddahbi***, Ave de France, T 448222; **A** ***Imperial Borj***, 5 Ave Echouhada, T 447322, modern, conference centre, restaurant, bar and popular nightclub.

C ***Hotel Siaha Safir***, Ave President Kennedy, T 448952, F 448730, 243 rms, pool and *hammam*; **C** ***Hotel le Tafilalet***, Ave Mohammed Abdelkrim El Khattabi, T 434518, Tx 72955, pleasant rms, a good garden; **C** ***Hotel Tichka***, Route de Casablanca, Semlalia, T 448710, Tx 74855, 138 rms, beautifully designed and decorated, restaurant, bar, nightclub, tennis, and very good pool; **C** ***Hotel Chems***, Ave Houmane El Fetouaki, BP 594, T 444813, Tx 72008, small and reasonable hotel with restaurant, bar and nightclub.

D ***Hotel Koutoubia***, 51 Blvd Mansur Eddahbi, T 430921, very good *ville nouvelle* hotel with restaurant, in the central courtyard there is an excellent (when in use) pool; **D** ***Hotel Oudaya***, 147 rue Mohammed El Baqal, T 448512, F 435400, 15 suites, 77 rms, modern hotel with pool, restaurant and bar; **D** ***Grand Hotel Imilchil***, Ave Echouhada, T 447653, Tx 74073, modern hotel with pool, restaurant and bar; **D** ***Hotel Pacha***, 33 rue de la Liberté, T 431626/7, highly recommended small hotel with dated charm, bar and restaurant, on a quiet street; **D** ***Grand Hotel Tazi***, rue Bab Agnaou, T 442152, Tx 74021, memorable rms with extravagantly painted ceilings and furniture, one of the few bars in the medina, a very good Moroccan restaurant at average prices, and a pleasant pool, strongly recommended and very convenient for the sights; **D** ***Hotel de Foucauld***, Ave El Mouahidine, T 445499, 33 rms, a good hotel with restaurant and bar, same management as the *Tazi*; **D** ***Hotel Ali***, 10 rue Moulay Ismail, T 444979, an efficient and friendly hotel with small, clean rms and a rooftop view of the Djemaa El Fna; **D** ***Hotel Gallia***, 30 rue de la Recette, T 445913, conveniently located just off the Djemaa El Fna (via rue Bab Agnaou), in an old building and some good rms.

E ***Hotel Toulousain***, 44 rue Tarik Ibn Ziad, Gueliz, T 430033, perhaps the best cheap option in the *ville nouvelle*, quiet location around a courtyard; in this area also try ***Hotel Oasis***, 50 Ave Mohammed V, T 447179, good but noisy, with restaurant and bar; ***Hotel des Voyageurs***, 40 Blvd Mohammed Zerktouni, T 447218, reasonable and central; ***Hotel Franco Belge***, 62 Blvd Mohammed Zerktouni, T 448472, similar; ***Hotel CTM***, on the Djemaa El Fna, T 442325, good and clean rms, some with a view of the square, often full; **E** ***Hotel Souria***, 17 rue de la Recette, in the medina, not very friendly but with satisfactory rooms.

There are a large number of cheap hotels in the medina, on the small alleys between rue Bab Agnaou and rue Zitoun el Kedim, to the S of Djemaa El Fna, of very variable quality, it is best to see a room before taking it. Try **F** ***Hotel Oukaimeden***, a basic place on the Djemaa El Fna; **F** ***Hotel de France***, 197 rue Zitoun el Kedim, T 443067; **F** ***Hotel Central***, **F** ***Hotel Afriquia*** with a good patio and roof terrace, and **F** ***Hotel Nouazah*** on the first left off rue Bab Agnaou; and **F** ***Hotel El Atlas***, a friendly, efficient place on rue de la Recette.

● Youth Hostel

Rue El Jahed, Quartier Industriel, T 432831, 80 beds, kitchen, meals available, bus 200m, train 700m, overnight fee MD15.

● Camping

Camping Municipal is off Ave de France, S of the railway station, T 431707, with shop, showers and café.

Places to eat in Gueliz

Price guide:
♦♦♦Expensive; ♦♦average; ♦cheap.

♦♦♦ ***Al Fassia***, 232 Ave Mohammed V, T 434060, reservations recommended, an excellent Moroccan restaurant on the main street, delicious desserts; ***Le Jacaranda***, 32 Blvd Mohammed Zerktouni, T 447215, French food, strong on fish, closed Tues and Wed lunch time, bar; ***La Trattoria du Gian Carlo***, 179 rue Mohammed El Bequal, T 432641, a very good Italian restaurant with an excellent selection of wines, in an art deco villa; ***Villa Rosa***, 64 Ave Hassan II, T 430832, a small Italian restaurant with terrace specializing in pasta and fish; ***Le Dragon d'Or***, 10 bis Blvd Mohammed Zerktouni, T 433341, Chinese food.

♦♦ ***Rotisserie du Café de la Paix***, 68 rue Yougoslavie, Gueliz, T 433118, there is a garden in the summer, and reasonable grilled food all the year round; just opposite is ***Restaurant Bagatelle***, 101 rue Yougoslavie, T 430274, good French food served in the restaurant and vine shaded courtyard open 1200-1400 and 1900-2300; ***Chez Jack'Line***, 63 Ave Mohammed V, T 447547, Italian, French and Moroccan dishes, good for pizzas; ***Restaurant La Taverne***, 23 Blvd Mohammed Zerktouni, T 446126, fixed standard menus and a bar.

♦Top of the cheap range in the *ville nouvelle* is ***Brasserie du Regent***, 34 Ave Mohammed V, T 448749; also try ***Le Petit Poucet***, Ave Mohammed V, T 448238, bar and restaurant with basic but good French dishes; or ***Café Agdal***, 86 Ave Mohammed V, T 448707, good for chicken, no alcohol.

Places to eat in the Medina

♦♦♦***Restaurant Marocain du Mamounia***, in the *Hotel Mamounia*, Ave Bab Jedid, T 448991, reservations recommended, lavishly decorated restaurant with one of the best introductions to élite Moroccan cuisine, an excellent *pastilla* (pigeon dish), music/folklore in the evening; ***Restaurant La Calèche***, in the *Hotel Mamounia*, Ave Bab Jedid, T 448991, top-notch French food with a view over the hotel's famous gardens; ***La Maison Arabe***, 5 Derb Ferrane, near Bab Doukkala, T 422604, with a reputation for the best food in Morocco, expensive, reservations necessary; ***Restaurant Riad***, rue Arset El Maach, T 425430, in the medina, with expensive but excellent Moroccan meals accompanied by folklore entertainment; ***Restaurant Relais Al Baraka***, Djemaa el Fna, near the police station, T 442341, Moroccan meals around a courtyard with fountain, convenient after sightseeing, reservations recommended; ***Restaurant Palais Gharnatta***, 56 Derb el Arsa, Riad Zitoun Jedid, T 445216, near the El Bahia Palace, this restaurant offers Moroccan dishes at high prices, clients pay for the supposedly 16th century palace surroundings, reservations recommended; ***El Bahia***, 1 Riad Zitoun Jedid, similar arrangement with evening entertainment; ***Restaurant Stylia***, 34 rue Ksour, T 443587, reservations recommended, a 15th century palace, with variations on Moroccan traditional dishes.

♦♦ ***Restaurant de Foucauld***, in the *Hotel Foucauld*, Ave El Mouahidine, good *couscous* and *tagines* near the Djemaa El Fna; ***Restaurant Tazi***, in the *Grand Hotel Tazi*, rue Bab Agnaou, similar restaurant run by the same management, the cheapest licensed establishment in the medina; Buffet dinner in *Hotel Ali*, rue Moulay Ismail, near the Djemaa El Fna massive choice and very reasonably priced; ***Café-Restaurant Argana***, Djemaa El Fna, food with a view; ***Restaurant Etoile de Marrakech***, rue Bab Agnaou, very good value set meals with view of Djemaa El Fna from the roof.

♦ In the medina, the most popular option is to eat at the open-air restaurants in the **Djemaa El Fna**. Each of these has a different variety of cooked food, some of which tastes very good. The conditions are, however, far from sanitary, and so it is best to go for the food cooked to order whilst waiting, as other dishes may have been around for some time. For a safer meal try the excellent value ***Chez Chekrouni***, on Djemaa El Fna, left of the *Café de France*; the somewhat smelly ***Café de Fath*** which has very good *tagines*; or ***Restaurant Toubkal***, in the opposite corner. There are a series of cheap restaurants along Bani Marine, in between rue Moulay Ismail and rue Bab Agnaou, such as ***Casse-Croûte des Amis***.

Bars

Piano Bar, at the *Hotel Mamounia*, Ave Bab Jedid, T 448981, 1800-0100, drinks are not cheap but the Western atmosphere and music a pleasant change; ***La Renaissance***, Ave Mohammed V, go up the lift to the rooftop bar with the best view of the Gueliz; ***Le Petit Poucet***, 56 Ave Mohammed V, no view but fairly cheap drinks; also try ***Ambassadeurs***, 6 Ave Mohammed V; or ***Haouz***, Ave Hassan II.

Cafés

One of the best places for a drink is beside the **Djemaa El Fna**: ***Café-Restaurant Argana*** has a good terrace view; even better is the ***Café de France***, with several levels and an excellent panorama over the square, and the medina beyond, scattered with minarets. In Gueliz Ave Mohammed V and Blvd Mohammed Zerktouni meet at a roundabout with popular cafés on each side, including the ***Brasserie des Négociants*** and ***Café Renaissance; Boule de Neige***, on rue de Yougoslavie just off Ave Mohammed V, is a trendy place for pricey but excellent drinks, ice cream and breakfasts; next door is ***Pâtisserie Hilton***, with a full range of Moroccan sweets and cakes; the best is perhaps ***Pâtisserie Zohor***, rue de la Liberté. For late night coffees or ice creams (most places close by 2130), try ***Café-Glacerie Siroua***. Locals swear by ***Café Zohor***, rue de la Liberté; ***Café Firdaous***, Ave Mohammed V, also has an authentic local clientele.

Casinos

Grand Casino de la Mamounia, at the *Mamounia Hotel*, Ave Bab Jedid, T 444570, open from 2000 or 2100; ***Hotel Es Saadi***, Ave Kadissia, T 448811.

Activities & entertainment

Cinemas

The major cinemas showing films in French, are the ***Colisée***, Blvd Mohammed Zerktouni; the ***Regent***, Ave Mohammed V; try also the ***Centre Culturel Français***, Route de Targa, Gueliz, T 447063, 446930.

Discos & nightclubs

Disco Paradise, at the *Hotel Pullman Mansur Eddahbi*, Ave de France, T 448222, admission MD80, 2200-0700, a large disco with the latest equipment; ***Cotton Club***, at the *Hotel Tropicana*, Semlalia, T 433913, admission MD60, 2100-0500; also try ***L'Atlas*** and ***Le Flash*** on Ave Mohammed V; ***Le Diamant Noir*** at the *Hotel Marrakech*, Ave Mohammed V; or ***Temple de Musique*** at the *Hotel PLM N'Fis*, Ave de France.

Folklore & fantasia

The ***Cappa Club*** at the *Hotel Issil*, the ***Hotel le Marrakech***, Ave Mohammed V, and the ***Club Mediterranée*** all have large folklore displays but can be difficult to get into. The best bet is the ***Restaurant Riad***. For fantasia, drive or take a taxi to ***Chez Ali***, in the **Palmery** after the Tensift bridge, T 448187; ***El Borj***, after the Tensift bridge, T 446376, ***Zagora*** Route de Casablanca, T 445237; ***Ancien Casino de Marrakech***, Ave el Kadissia, T 448811, food and extravagant displays from 2100, admission MD100; ***Restaurant Chaouia***, near the airport, T 442915, displays of horsemanship, sword play, dance and music.

Hammams

Try one of those on rue Zitoun el Kedim; or *Hammam Dar El Bacha*, rue Fatima Zohra, with amazing decor.

Shopping

The ***souqs***, N of the Djemaa El Fna, are the best place to search for bargains in carpets and handicrafts, but a visit can be a tiresome experience as the tourist is besieged by traders and misled by absurd prices. Bargaining is a long activity requiring patience, and should be carried out without assistance from guides, whose commission will be added on to any price. ***Souq Semmarin*** is the main area with the largest boutiques, some with supposedly fixed prices, and can be more expensive. ***Rahba Kedima***, off to the right, has some interesting small shops. Leather goods should be bought in ***Souq Cherratin***, Moroccan slippers from the ***Souq des Baboushes***, where they are often made as well as sold.

Coopartim Ensemble Artisanale, Ave Mohammed V, 5 mins walk from the Koutoubia Mosque, T 443664, can be treated as an exhibition, a massive selection of locally-made handicrafts, even some craftsmen working on the premises, but one can also buy at fixed prices.

Souqs which can be reached by excursion from Marrakech include Ourika (Mon), Amizmiz (Tue), Tahanaoute (Tue), Ouirgane (Thur), Setti Fatma (Thur), Asni (Sat) and Chichaoua (Sun).

Foreign newspapers can be bought from the stands along Ave Mohammed V, and in the large hotels. They normally arrive a day late. Books in French from Ave Mohammed V, particularly ***Librarie Chatr Ahmed***, No. 19, T 447997.

Spectator sport

The *Kawkab* football club of Marrakech, one of the best in Morocco, can be seen at the **Stade al Harti**, rue Moulay El Hassan, Hivernage.

Sport

Ballooning: take off behind *Oasis Restaurant*, MD2,000 for 1 hr.

Flying: ***Royal Flying Club***, Aéroport Marrakech Menara, T 431769.

Go-Karting at *Kart Hotel*, Sud Quad.

Golf: the ***Royal Golf Club***, 6 km S off the Ouarzazate road (P31), T 443441, is a large 18 hole course set in orchards, 4,805m, par 71, fee MD400. ***Palmeraie Golf Palace***, 18 hole, par 71, fee MD350, 15 km S of town.

Riding: at ***Club de l'Atlas*** (Haras Régional), Quartier de la Menara, T 431301; or there is another 4 km along the road to Asni, T 448529.

Skiing: call at ***Skiing Club***, Ave Mohammed V, T 434026, the best site is 76 km from Marrakech at Oukaimeden.

Swimming: at the municipal pool in the ***Moulay Abd es-Salam Garden***, rue Abou el Abbes, near the Koutoubia Mosque. The large hotels have pools, the cheapest and most convenient for the medina is the ***Grand Hotel Tazi***, on rue Bab Agnaou.

Tennis: ***Royal Tennis Club de Marrakech***, 8 courts, Jnane El Harti, rue Oued El Makhazine, T 431902. 30 tennis courts in hotels.

Other Services

● American Express

Voyages Schwartz, Immeuble Moutaouskil, rue Mauritania, T 433321.

● Banks

ABM, 55 Blvd Zerktouni, T 448912; **Banque Al Maghrib**, Djemaa El Fna, T 442037; **Banque Populaire**, 69 Ave Mohammed V, T 434851; **BCM**, Blvd Zerktouni, T 434805; **BMAO**, 75 rue Bab Agnaou, T 425600; **BMCE**, 144 Ave Mohammed V, T 431948/9; **BMCI**, Blvd Mohammed Zerktouni; **Credit du Maroc**, Ave Mohammed V, T 434851; **SGMB** 59 rue de Yougoslavie, T 448702; **Uniban**, rue Moulay Ismail, T 425285; **Wafabank**, 213 Ave Mohammed V, T 433840.

● Cultural & language centres

American Language Center, 3 Impasse Moulin du Gueliz, weekly film, small library and bookshop; **Centre Culturel Français**, (open 0830-1200 and 1430-1830, except Mon), Route de la Targa, Gueliz, with a café, library and pleasant garden, has films, exhibitions and other cultural events.

● Chemists

Pharmacie Centrale, 166 Ave Mohammed V, T 430151; ***Pharmacie de Paris***, 120 Ave Mohammed V; ***Pharmacie Bab Ftouh***, Djemaa El Fna, T 422678. There is an all night chemist, ***Pharmacie de Nuit***, at rue Khalid Ben Oualid, T 430415.

● Dentists

Dr Hamid Laraqui, 203 Ave Mohammed V, T 433216; and Dr E Gailleres, 112 Ave Mohammed V, both speak English.

● Doctors

Dr Ahmed Mansouri, rue de Sebou, T 430754; and Dr Perez, 169 Ave Mohammed V, T 431030, both speak English.

● Emergency

Ambulance: T 15 (private ambulance service: 10 rue Fatima Zohra, T 443724); **Fire**: rue Khalid Ben Oualid, T 16; **Police**: rue Ibn Hanbal, T 19.

● Garages

Peugeot: Toniel S.A., rue Tarik Ibn Ziad; **Renault**: CRA, 55-61 Ave Mohammed V, T 432015; others are **Auto Hall**, rue de Yougoslavie; and **Garage Ourika**, 66 Ave Mohammed V, T 430155.

● Hospitals

Hôpital Ibn Tofail, rue Abdel Ouahab Derraq, T 448011; *Hôpital Avenzoar*, rue Sidi Mimoun, T 422793.

● Post & telephone

The Central PTT for post, telegrams, poste restante and telephones is on Place 16 Novembre, Gueliz, the telephone service being particularly inefficient, slow and expensive, open till 2100. There is also a reasonable post/telephone office on the Djemaa El Fna.

● Religious services

Catholic: *Eglise des Saints-Martyrs*, rue El Imam Ali, Hivernage, for information T 430585. **Jewish**: *Synagogue Bet-el-Gueliz*, Arset El Maash, for information T 447832, 447976. **Protestant**: *Protestant Church*, 89 Blvd Moulay Rachid, T 431479.

● Travel agents and airline offices

Menara Tours, 41 rue Yougoslavie, T 446654, handles **GB Air** and **British Airways**, has English speaking staff; also try ***Atlas Tours***, 40 Ave al-Mansur Ad-Dahbi, T 433858; ***Sahara Tours***, 182 Ave Abdelkrim El Khattabi, T 430062; ***Comanov Voyages***, 149 Ave Mohammed V, T 430265; ***Atlas Voyages***, 131 Ave Mohammed V, T 430333; ***Safir Voyages***, at the *Hotel Safir*, T 434626; ***Wagons Lits Tourisme***, 122 Ave Mohammed V, T 431687. **Royal Air Maroc**, at the *Hotel Asni*, Ave de France, T 430939.

● Tourist information

Office du Tourisme, Place Abd el-Moumen

Ben Ali, T 448889; **Syndicat d'Initiative**, 176 Ave Mohammed V, T 432097, 434797.

● Transport

Local: Buses can be caught from rue Moulay Ismail, just off the Djemaa El Fna, and elsewhere along Ave Mohammed V and Ave Hassan II. No 1 is the most useful, running from Djemaa El Fna along Ave Mohammed V, No 3 and 8 run from the railway station to the bus station, via Djemaa El Fna, No 10 from Djemaa El Fna to the bus station, No 11 from the Djemaa El Fna to the Menara Gardens.

Bicycle/motorcycle hire *Hotel de Foucauld*, Ave El Mouahidine, T 445499; **Peugeot**, 225 Ave Mohammed V; several cheaper places in Bani Marine, the road in between rue Moulay Ismail and rue Bab Agnaou.

Calèches: these green-painted horse-drawn carriages can be hailed along Ave Mohammed V, or from the stands at Djemaa El Fna and Place de la Liberté. There are fixed prices for tours around the ramparts, other routes are up for negotiation, but they are not normally prohibitively expensive, and this is a pleasant way to see the city.

Car hire **Avis**, 137 Ave Mohammed V, T 433727; **Europcar Inter-Rent**, 63 Blvd Mohammed Zerktouni, T 431228 and at the airport; **Euro Rent**, 9 Ave al-Mansur Ad-Dahbi, T 433184; **Hertz**, 154 Ave Mohammed V, T 434680; **La Royale**, 17 rue Mauritanie, T 447548; a less known firm with more competitive rates is **Concorde Cars**, 154 Ave Mohammed V.

Taxi: **Petit-taxis** are easy to find around the city, beware as many do not operate meters, and inflate their prices dramatically for tourists. From the medina to Gueliz should cost MD5-10 during the day, and MD8-15 during the late evening and night. Few journeys should cost much more than this. Major ranks are to be found in Djemaa El Fna, at the Gare Routiere by Bab Doukkala, and outside the *marché municipal*, Gueliz. **Grand-taxis**: are normally more expensive, can be found at the railway station and the major hotels. They also run over fixed routes, mainly to outlying suburbs, from Djemaa El Fna and Bab Doukkala.

Air Aéroport Marrakech Menara, T 447862, is to the W of the city, by the Menara Gardens, and clearly signposted from the centre. There are flights from Marrakech to Casablanca (several a day), Ouarzazate (4 a week), Agadir (3 a week) Fes (2 a week), as well as to Brussels, Geneva, Las Palmas, London, Lyon, Madrid, Rome and Paris.

Train The railway station is in Gueliz, on Ave Hassan II, T 447868, 447947. Although there are long-term plans for an extension of the line S to Agadir and Laayoune, at present ONCF operates only bus services to the S, connecting with the arrival of the express trains. Express trains for **Casablanca** (3 hrs) and **Rabat** (4hrs) leave at 0910, 1400 and 1820, and non-express services at 0100, 0720, 1155, 1550 and 1945.

Road Buses run from the Gare Routière at Bab Doukkala, T 433933, which is easily reached by taxis and local buses. There is often a choice between a number of different companies, including CTM, with different prices and times. CTM departures are currently: **Ouarzazate** 0445, 0730, 1300 and 1700; **Er Rachidia** 0445; **M'Hamid** 0730; **Beni Mellal** 0630, 1900 and 2100; **Agadir** 0800 and 1830; **Laayoune** 1900; and **Casablanca** 0630, 1230, 1630 and 1800. There are also private line services to **Beni Mellal** (19 a day), **El Kelaa des Srarhna** (17 a day), **Rabat** (13 a day), **El Jadida** (9 a day), **Essaouira** (6 a day), **Ouarzazate and Skoura** (5 a day), **Agadir** (4 a day), Safi (3 a day), **Taroudant** (2 a day), **Fes, Tiznit, Tafraoute, Ouarzazate** and **Essaouira** (all 1 a day), as well as to Asni, **Oualidia, Khouribga, Ifni** and **Demnate**. It is wise to call at the station the previous day as some services, notably across the High Atlas to **Taroudant** and **Ouarzazate**, leave early in the morning. There are CTM services to Paris every day except Fri and Sun at 1700, cost MD1150. The private line alternative leaves at 1200. CTM services for **Agadir** and **Casablanca** can also be taken from Gueliz, in Blvd Mohammed Zerktouni, but places should be reserved a day in advance. Buses to the **Ourika Valley, Asni** and **Moulay Brahim** run from Bab Rob.

Taxi Grand-taxis running over fixed routes, with fixed prices, leave from a variety of places around the city. For Ourika, Asni and Ouirgane leave from Bab Rob. For most other destination, including Chichaoua, Essaouira and Agadir, go to Bab Doukkala.

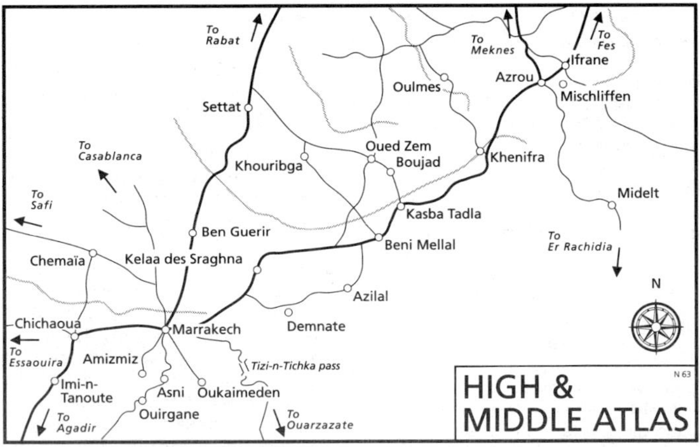

THE HIGH ATLAS

Marrakech is an ideal base from which to make excursions to the High Atlas, which provide welcome relief both from the hassle and the heat of the city, as well as having a distinct interest of their own. Transport for most of these is by bus or grand-taxi from the rough ground outside Bab Rob.

Chichaoua and Amizmiz

Chichaoua is a small town, 100 km from Essaouira, at the intersection with the road to Agadir. There are garages, café-restaurants and a small Sunday *souq* near the crossroads, and a *Centre Cooperative Artisanal* (closed Sun) where the carpets for which the town is well known are exhibited and sold. There are regular buses (MD13) and grand-taxis (MD15) to and from Marrakech. The road from Marrakech is over flat plains and in through the western residential and industrial quarters of the city.

Amizmiz, 55 km from Marrakech at the end of the S507, is known for its acrobatic school which has existed since mediaeval times, and now trains the acrobats which appear in Marrakech and in Europe. It was founded by a *marabout*, Sidi Ahmed. There is also a semi-ruined kasbah, a former *mellah*, and an important Tues morning *souq*, specializing in carpets and pottery. The *F Hotel de France*, with attached bar, is adequate. There are regular buses (2½ hrs), and much quicker grand-taxis, to and from Bab Rob in Marrakech.

Asni, the Toubkal National Park and Ouirgane

Asni There are regular grand-taxis from Bab Rob to Asni, as well as the Taroudant buses which leave from the *gare routière* at Bab Doukkala and call at Bab Rob. En route from Marrakech to Asni the S501 passes through the large village of **Tahanaoute** with a good *souq* on Tues and a *zaouia* to Moulay Brahim, who brings luck to childless women.

Asni itself has a *souq* on Sat, and is a busy village with houses in dark earth stacked in clusters around the green valley. It is a pleasant place to stop en route to Ouirgane, Tin Mal or Taroudant, or on to the Toubkal National Park, if one avoids the attentions of the jewellery sellers.

• **Accommodation** The main option is the **D** *Grand Hotel de Toubkal*, T Asni 3, a converted kasbah, 19 comfortable rms, celebrated restaurant with local specialities, bar, pool and a delightful garden with fruit trees and rose bushes. **Youth hostel**, T 47713, on Route d'Amlil, through the market and to the left, 40 beds, kitchen, overnight fee MD15.

• **Places to eat** Limited choice available. Eat expensively at ***Grand Hotel de Toubkal*** or in the centre of the village at the number of stalls and cafés cooking *harira* soup and *tagines*. This is the last place to stock up on basic supplies for a visit to the Toubkal region.

Toubkal National Park is reached by a track which leads off left in Asni, through the market. For those without transport either hike or negotiate a grand-taxi. It is possible to walk from Asni to **Imlil**, or to **Tachedirt**, which has a *Refuge Club Alpin Français*. In Imlil one can stay and eat at F *Café du Soleil*, a tiny and basic place; the F *Etoile de Toubkal*; or at the *Refuge Club Alpin Français*, which provides clean but minimal facilities. Mules and guides can be hired in Imlil, most easily in the *Refuge* or at *Ribat Tours*.

• **Walking** options include the **Aremd circuit**, a refreshing hike through remote villages and past breathtaking views, and a hike to the **Lac d'Ifni**. Another is to walk to **Setti Fatma**, in the Ourika Valley. Much more challenging is to climb **Jbel Toubkal**, the highest mountain in North Africa at 4167m. It is necessary to break the walk at the ***Refuge Club Alpin Français*** at Neltner, a simple dormitory place with no meals. In winter this is a difficult trek and full equipment is essential. A wise plan is to purchase specialist hiking books, such as Robin Collomb's *Atlas Mountains*, and maps, for the region, before arriving.

Ouirgane is a beautiful village about 1 hr drive from Marrakech in a dramatic valley location, on the S501. It can be reached by bus from Marrakech (the Taroudant service), or by grand-taxi from Asni. The 2 hotels in Ouirgane offer wonderful food and the opportunity to explore the valley in easy rambles. The C *Le Val de La Roseraie*, BP 769, T 432094, F 432095, 23 a/c rms, is a beautiful and peaceful hotel set in extensive and profusely flowering grounds, with 2 fine restaurants, bar, disco, nightclub, *hammam*, hydrotherapy centre, tennis, horse riding and pool; whilst the D *L'Hostellerie au Pont d'Ouirgane 'Auberge Au Sanglier Qui Fume'*, T Ouirgane 9, is an *auberge* run by a Frenchwoman, with 14 old style chalets amidst the gardens, a restaurant serving excellent French country food, a bar, tennis and a pool in the summer, as well as camping for those who have a meal in the restaurant.

Tin Mal

Tin Mal is a ruined settlement high in the Atlas mountains, off the S501 from Marrakech to Taroudant. It was the holy city of the Almohad Dynasty, and it enables the non-Muslim to see the interior of a major mosque, with examples of 12th century Almohad decor intact amidst the ruins.

Tin Mal is 100 km from Marrakech, just past the village of Ijoujak. From Marrakech drive, or take a Taroudant bus as far as Ijoujak, where there are several basic cafés with rooms. Just after the village, on the right, is the **Talat n-Yacoub Kasbah**, the home of the Goundafis, who formerly ruled the area, and a ruined summer pavilion with a ribbed dome, and further along, on the left, another kasbah of the Goundafi family. Carry on walking, and across the river to the right can be seen the square structure of the **Tin Mal Mosque**. Cross the river on the next bridge (often impassable by car), and walk up past Tin Mal village to the mosque.

The town, the base of the Almohad revolt against the Almoravids, became a necropolis for its rulers, with the burial there of Ibn Tumart, Abd el-Moumen, Abu Ya'qub and Abu Youssef. The tombs and the mosque became venerated as a pilgrimage centre, even after the Merinid destruction of 1275-6. The mosque dates from 1153-4, during the reign of Sultan Abd el-Moumen, and was built by the tomb of Ibn Tumart.

The mosque has a rectangular shape, with thick *pisé*-cement and stone and a

HANDMADE CARPETS

The visitor will be surprised at the number of carpets on display in the *souqs* of North Africa. There is a great variety of designs, materials and unusual colours. A carpet is a splendid memento of a holiday in North Africa and a better choice will be made with a little knowledge and by taking your time in making your selection. North African carpets, unlike Persian carpets, are best not considered as investments.

There are two main types of handmade carpet, the flat woven *kilims* and knotted carpets usually of wool on a cotton base.

Kilims are flat woven rugs and include tapestries with woven scenes. They have the great virtue of being cheap, light in weight and easily packed. Very decorative are the thin Bedouin rugs in bright reds and golds, while there are also coarse rag rugs made from scraps of material common in Egypt. Most valuable are the *kilims* made entirely of wool and dyed in natural colours or mixed fibres, some in very bright hues.

Handknotted carpets and rugs are more expensive than *kilims*. The number of knots per square centimetre determines the quality of a handknotted carpet, as does the materials of which it is constructed. The backing (the warp) may be of cotton, wool or silk and the knots of wool or silk. Coarse woollen material is used when knot densities are low, on average about 25 per centimetre, while the fine wools and silks require higher densities of up to 69 knots per centimetre, take longer to make and therefore cost more.

Designs for the handknotted carpets are very varied, though the best usually take their patterns from tile designs from the walls of the famous mosques. Often however designs are adapted from traditional patterns made popular elsewhere in the Middle East – Persian, Turkish and Caucasian being most widespread. Pleasing designs on small rugs follow the classical patterns of the tree of life, formal hunting scenes, the Persian garden, bird carpets and central medallions.

low minaret of brick, unusually located behind the *mihrab*. The *mihrab* niche, with its stalactite dome, is built into the minaret, in between the door used by the *Imam*, and a room used to store the pulpit. Below the courtyard is a cistern fed by 2 conduits. The mosque is decorated with plaster applied to the brick facing, and is simple as befits the conservative tastes of the period. The *mihrab* niche has a distinctive shape, accentuated by the configuration of 2 arches and rectangular frame surrounding it, with rosettes in the spaces between the arch and frame. Around this is a geometric pattern of interlacing 8-pointed stars and rectangles. The 3 windows above the niche are surmounted by a band of interlacing 6-pointed stars. The stalactite dome above once included plaques of Almohad floral decor, 2 of which remain in this dome. The remainder of the mosque includes a large number of arches and several areas of stalactite plaster work. Examples of the *darj w ktaf* and palmette motifs can be found, but little inscription. Stairs up lead to an impressive view over the valley.

The Tizi-n-Test and the road to Taroudant

The S501 from Marrakech to Taroudant, is one of the most spectacular routes in Morocco, winding its way up and then down through the High Atlas mountains, above the beautiful valleys of this region and past isolated villages, eventually reaching the Tizi-n-Test pass, with its

Most small rugs were and to an extent are still produced as prayer mats and incorporate a triangular top portion to act as the indicator of the direction to Mecca copied from the *mihrab* in the wall of the mosque.

The most prolific producers of fine carpets and rugs are Egypt, Tunisia and Morocco, all of which have their own favourite colours and designs. It is best to buy a local speciality. The fact that carpets are slightly misshapen is not a sign of poor quality. Handlooms are all different and little credit is given in the traditional as opposed to tourist orientated weaving areas to mathematical accuracy. Indeed, in Morocco some Berber carpets are made deliberately out of square by women who make a portion of their carpet to reflect each separate month of their pregnancy. The nine-strip carpets bulge interestingly towards the central area !

Machine made carpets, normally to be avoided, can be distinguished by the fringe which will often have been sewn on later, or by the sides which are much neater and flatter than handmade rugs, and by the back which does not show the pattern very clearly and is quite smooth. Fold back the carpet for a close examination of the knots and pattern on the rear of the carpet to check the mathematical precision of weaving which gives away the fact that it is factory made.

Each carpet will have to be bargained for with patience and humour. The following pointers will help during this process. In Morocco carpets ought to carry a government seal indicating the price. In official handicraft shops fixed prices are generally the rule, though this might not make them cheaper than the souq for the avid bargainer. In Tunisia and particularly Morocco tourist guides will lead you to carpet shops which will give him a commission on your purchase. This is already included in the price. There is no need to be rushed in your purchase – the tale that the 'shop is closed tomorrow' is often a ploy used to clinch a sale. If possible take your carpet with you rather than let the shop arrange delivery to your hotel or your home address.

breathtaking views across the Sous valley to the Anti Atlas mountains. There are buses between the 2 cities, although check that they are *par Tizi-n-Test*. Driving has been feasible since the road, a traditional trading route, was formerly opened in 1928, following the work of French engineers. Some of its sections are a bit scary, but it is a highly recommended experience, particularly when tied in with visits to Asni, Ouirgane and Tin Mal. Signs on the exit to Marrakech will indicate if the pass is open. The S501 joins the P32 from Taroudant to Ouarzazate.

Oukaimeden

Oukaimeden, the meeting place of the 4 winds, is Morocco's major ski resort, open Dec-Mar, with an extremely high ski lift up the 3,273m Jbel Oukaimeden. The skiing is reputedly good, with a range of standards, although the slopes often become wet by the afternoon. There are instructors working in the resort, and a skiing shop is located beside the *Hotel de l'Angour*. It is also possible to climb the Jbel Oukaimeden in a day. Another option is to walk the piste which leaves the road S of Oukaimeden, and cross the hills to the S501 to S of Asni. In summer visitors can walk, climb and parasail while in spring the drive through the blossoming walnut and almond trees is breathtaking.

To get to Oukaimeden, follow the S513 from Marrakech, branching off the Ourika valley just before Arhbalou. For accommodation the choice is between the D *Hotel Imlil*, T 459132, a comfortable place with restaurant, bar, and *après-ski* nightclub; E *Hotel de l'Angour* (also called *Auberge Chez Juju Oukaimeden*), T 459005, with a good restaurant, bar, half-pension required, but reasonably priced; and the *Refuge de Club Alpin Français* which often has beds for non-members, a restaurant and bar; *Camping Oukaimeden* is open only to caravans.

The Ourika Valley

The Ourika Valley is a beautiful area of green, terraced fields above the winding Oued Ourika, the most popular excursion for Marrakechis, particularly the young who can court here without police harassment. Buses and grand-taxis to Ourika leave from Bab Rob, Marrakech. It is worth going all the way to Setti Fatma, at the head of the valley. Once in Ourika, a good means of transport is a lift in the open top vans and lorries which speed along the valley. **NB**: the valley has a problem with flooding, which campers should bear in mind.

Dar Caid Ourika is the first major settlement, with a Mon *souq* often crowded with tourists. Don't be confused by the field of donkeys which are local transport and not for sale. It also has a *zaouia* and a ruined kasbah. Some buses terminate here. The next big village is Arhbalou, which has one of the best hotels of the valley, the C *Hotel Ourika*, T 433993, 27 a/c rms, with good food, a pleasant atmosphere, nightclub and pool; also try the E *Auberge Ramuntcho*, T 446312, with a good restaurant, bar and pool. Three other good places to eat in Arbalou are *Hotel Restaurant Bar le Lion de l'Ourika*; *Bar Restaurant Amnougour*; and *Bar Restaurant Kasbah de l'Ourika*, all patronized by coach parties. There is also a shop selling antiques, carpets and ceramics, the *Musée d'Aghbalou*, just beyond the village.

The road ends at **Setti Fatma**, where there is a small market and a number of basic hotels, including F *Hotel Café Atlas*, good rms; also F *Hotel Azrou* and F *Hotel Asgaoua*. However the main part of Setti Fatma is further on, entailing a climb along the right hand side of the river. At the main village, cross over to the grassy area where the youth of Marrakech picnic and relax. There are a number of café-restaurants along the bank, F *Hotel Café Bouche de la Source*, provides basic rms and cheap *tagines*; alongside, and marginally better, is F *Auberge des Routards/Restaurant les 7 Cascades*; beyond is the *Restaurant des Cascades*. The 7 cascades are 30 mins scramble up from Setti Fatma, following the path up behind the first café. There is a café perched up where the path ends, beside the first waterfall. Setti Fatma is also another good point to start a walking tour, with guides who will accompany tourists the 10 km to Tachedirt, where there is a *Refuge Club Alpin Français*.

Tizi-n-Tichka, Kasbah Telouet and the road to Ouarzazate

The P31 from Marrakech to Ouarzazate, and its Tizi-n-Tichka pass, is a larger road and safer option than the route over the Tizi-n-Test, but is still an exhilarating experience with similarly stunning views, passing through the range of environments, from the Haouz plains, through the verdant foothills, to the barren peaks and the arid regions around Ouarzazate. The route is often lined with mineral and fossil sellers, and there are a number of café stops en route. Before the pass is the village of Taddert, with the French-run E *Le Noyer auberge*, (inn).

Just past the pass is a turning on the left leading to the **Kasbah Telouet**. This was the base of the el-Glaoui family, who from the late 19th century, under the brothers Madani and Thami controlled much of S Morocco, a dominance which continued under the French, who used them to establish control over the region. Thami el-Glaoui was a ruthless and powerful *pasha* of Marrakech as late as 1956. The kasbah itself is a vast, labyrinthine, decaying place, built by Thami el-Glaoui. A guardian will appear to unlock the door and show groups round part of the building. There are grand-taxis from the village of Irherm to Telouet. From the pass the road sweeps down to Ouarzazate. The kasbah of Aït Benhaddou can be visited en route, or the next day as an excursion, see page 338.

BENI MELLAL AND ENVIRONS

Beni Mellal

This is one of the major centres of central Morocco, with a population of 95,003 (1982), and an important *souq* on Tues. The town is scruffy but relaxed, and with adequate facilities for a pleasant stay. At the entrance to the town is the **Kasbah Bel Kush**, built in the 17th century by Moulay Ismail, but heavily restored in the 19th century. The main thing to do in Beni Mellal is to walk up from the town to the small and quiet gardens, which lie below the ruined **Kasbah de Ras el Aïn**, perched precariously on the cliffside. There is a nice café in the gardens.

• **Accommodation** **B** *Bassatine*, Route de Ben Salah, T 482227, 61 a/c rms, pool, restaurant. Both **C** *Hotel Ouzoud*, Route de Marrakech, T 483752/3, with restaurant, bar, tennis and pool; and **C** *Chems*, Route de Marrakech, BP 68, T 483460, Tx 24891, 77 rms, with restaurant, bar, nightclub, tennis and pool, are a bit far out from the centre.

The more central options include **E** *Hotel Gharnata*, Ave Mohammed V, T 483482, 14 comfortable rms, restaurant with European food, and a bar; **E** *Hotel de Paris*, Nouvelle Medina, T 482245, with a restaurant and bar; **E** *Auberge du Vieux Moulin*, Ave Mohammed V, T 482788, 9 rms, good restaurant and a bar. Much cheaper options are the **F** *Hotel des Voyageurs*, Ave Mohammed V, basic but satisfactory; the **F** *Hotel El Amria*, Ave des Forces Armées Royales, T 483531, simple; and the **F** *Hotel de l'Aïn-Asserdoun*, Ave des Forces Armées Royales, T 483493, a modern place with restaurant.

• **Places to eat** There are several cheap restaurants in the town centre, but one of the best places to eat is *Auberge du Vieux Moulin*, Ave Mohammed V; another on the same street is in *Hotel Gharnata*. A good place to drink a tea or coffee, or eat a delicious pastry, is the *Salon de Thé Azouhour*, 241 Ave Mohammed V; similarly good is *Salon de Thé El Afrah*, Place Afrique; there are several other good *laiteries* and *cafés* along the main street.

• **Tourist information** A tourist office is located on the first floor of Immeuble Chichaoui, Ave Hassan II, T 483981.

• **Transport Road** ONCF buses for Casablanca, which connect with the trains at Khouribga, leave from Beni Mellal at 0636 (3 hrs 20 mins). CTM buses leave from the terminal on the Route de Marrakech. There are regular connections with Marrakech and 3 a day for Fes. From the bus station it is a 10 mins walk up Ave des Forces Armées Royales to the town centre.

Excursion to Bin El Ouidane, Azilal and the Cascades d'Ouzoud

This region around Azilal, to the S of Beni Mellal, is predominantly Berber, a forested, mountainous area popular with walkers. The villages clustering around its slopes have adobe houses with added stone and woodwork. Skiing is popular from Feb to Apr, and there is good hiking in the Mgoun mountains. The Taghia ravine is a popular climbing site. There are a number of high altitude refuges.

The **Bin El Ouidane dam** and lake, 38 km S of the P24, is good for fishing, swimming, sailing and wind-surfing. Stay at the E *Auberge du Lac*, a clean and reasonable place with a restaurant serving Moroccan and European food, and which hires out boats for use on the lake.

28 km further on is **Azilal**, a small town with a Thur *souq*. Accommodation is available at the E *Hotel Tanout*, T 488281, 12 rms, restaurant. Azilal has a tourist

office on Ave Hassan II, T 488334, and is connected by buses with Beni Mellal and Marrakech. The **Cascades d'Ouzoud** are 41 km from Azilal, along a turning off the S508. For those without a car hire a grand-taxi from Azilal. The Cascades d'Ouzoud is a picturesque Middle Atlas site which has become very popular, particularly with young Moroccans camping in the summer. Camping is possible at various small sites, whilst there are also rooms at *Hotel Dar es Salam*, which has a reasonable restaurant.

Kasbah Tadla

Kasbah Tadla was built in 1687 by the Alaouite Sultan Moulay Ismail. The town is a military garrison with a relaxed air but little to see. There is the kasbah, now crumbling and squatted by families of soldiers, as well as an old bridge with 10 arches over the Oum er Rbia, also built by Moulay Ismail. The **Jamia Mosque** on the main market square is from the same period. Nearby is a covered market and a small medina. The *souq* is on Mon.

• **Accommodation** The town has one reasonable hotel, the **D** ***Hotel Bellevue***, just outside the town off the P24 from Fes to Beni Mellal, T 418731/2/3. There are 3 basic hotels in the centre: **F** ***Hotel des Allies***, Ave Mohammed V, T 418171, is perhaps the best; the others are **F** ***Hotel El Atlas***, rue el Majati Obad, T 418046; and **F** ***Hotel Oum Rbia***, 26 Blvd Mohammed Zerktouni, with no shower. There are a few basic restaurants in the town centre.

• **Transport Road** CTM buses leave at 1035 for Fes, 1145 for Marrakech, 1335 for Casablanca and 1705 for Beni Mellal, and private line buses from *Agence SLAC* for Beni Mellal at 1300, Boujad and Oued Zem at 1700, and Rabat at 0430, 0730 and 1300. These can all be caught from the agencies on the main street, Blvd Mohammed Zerktouni.

Detour to Boujad, Oued Zem and Khouribga

Boujad has a beautiful and historic medina, with cobbled streets and white houses, and had importance as a pilgrimage centre up to the 19th century, dating from the 16th century establishment of a *zaouia*, although much of the town was destroyed in 1785. The medina is dotted with shrines and mosques, most notably the **Shrine of Sidi Othman** and the **Mosque of Sidi Mohammed Bu'abid ech Cherki**, the town's founder. There is one hotel on the main square, Place du Marché, the F *Café-Hotel Essalyn*, and several cheap restaurants nearby. This is also from where regular buses and grand-taxis leave to Kasbah Tadla and Oued Zem.

Oued Zem, population 58,744 (1982), is an uninteresting phosphates town with useful railway connections and a busy market in the centre. The F *Hotel El Salam*, is very cheap and central; the other option is the F *Hotel des Cooperatives*, on rue Rachid II. There are cheap restaurants in the centre. Trains to Casablanca leave at 0640, 0810 and 1500 and take between 2 hrs 15 mins and 3 hrs.

Khounbga is an important and prosperous city with a population of 127,181 (1982), owed much to its central role in the phosphates industry, but is singularly lacking in any charm or appeal. There is one luxury hotel, the A *Hotel Safir*, T 492013, 493013, with restaurant, bar, tennis and pool; the best cheap hotel is the excellent value, clean and comfortable F *Hotel de Paris*, 18 Ave Mohammed V, T 492716; the only other is F *Hotel des Hotes*, 1 rue Moulay Ismail, T 493030, a basic and unfriendly place. Around the market, just off the main street, are a number of basic restaurants. Trains to Casablanca, with connections to Marrakech, El Jadida, Safi, Rabat, Fes and Tanger, leave at 0713, 0855, 1543 and to Oued Zem at 1223, 1936 and 2155.

THE MIDDLE ATLAS

Khenifra and environs

El Ksiba Continuing on from Kasbah Tadla, the P24 passes El Ksiba, just off to the S of the road. This is a pleasant place to stay (E *Hotel Henri IV*, excellent food, good rms; or at *Camping Taghbalout*).

Khenifra is a relaxed Middle Atlas resort with a population of 38,840 (1982). It has a large Wed and Sun *souq*, and a reputation amongst Moroccans as a centre of prostitution. The town was the site of a large defeat for the French in 1914, at the hands of a local *caid*. The top place to stay is C *Hotel Hamou Azzayani Salam*, in the new town, T 586020, Tx 41932, 60 a/c rms, with restaurant, bar, nightclub, tennis and pool; a much cheaper option is the basic but clean F *Hotel-Restaurant de France*, Quartier Forces Armées Royales, T 586114; or the F *Hotel Voyageurs*, nearby. There is a tourist office at Immeuble Lefraoui, Hay Hamou-Hassan.

A popular excursion from Khenifra is to the tree-lined lake of **Aguelmane Azigza**, 24 km along the 3485. The road continues to the source of the Oued Oum er Rbia and Aïn Leuh, and then back onto the P24 just SW of Azrou. 96 km N of Khenifra, just off the 2516 to Rabat, is **Oulmes-Tarmilate**, a spa from where *Oulmes* sparkling mineral water originates. There is a hotel here, the D *Hotel les Thermes*, T 552355, 42 rms, restaurant, bar, and there are waterfalls just below at Lalla Haya. Back on the P24, in between Khenifra and Azrou, is **Mrirt**, with a large and fascinating Thur *souq*.

Azrou

Azrou is a small Berber market town and hill resort named after the rock around which it is built. The town has a relaxed air and good hiking in the wooded vicinity. The ruined kasbah was built by Moulay Ismail. The French built the **Collège Berbère**, which trained many of the civil and military staff of the Protectorate, as part of a divide and rule policy.

All buses, except those of CTM, arrive at a rough patch of land surrounded by food and fruit stalls, in front of the town's distinctive rock. The heart of the town, Place Mohammed V, is to the right on leaving the bus stop. There is a covered market near Place Mohammed V, whilst the *Ensemble Artisanal* (open 0830-1200 and 1430-1800), is situated off Ave Mohammed V, with a fixed price shop and a number of craftsmen working on the premises, look out for the Middle Atlas carpets. There is a large Berber *souq* (market) held just above the town on Tue, with vegetables, textiles and some interesting Middle Atlas car-

BOTTLED UP

Travellers can be easily identified by how quickly they take to the bottle.....of water. There are three main brands. *Oulmès*, SW of Meknes gives its name to a spring of naturally gaseous water, with health-promoting trace elements including calcium, magnesium, sodium and iron. *Oulmès* sold in small glass bottles has been on the market for over half a century. From the same area comes the non-gaseous *Sidi Ali*, commonly used as table water and recommended for salt-free diets. It is sold in the ubiquitous semi-transparent blue plastic bottles. This is more recent, first marketed in 1977, and now selling more than 500,000 hectolitres annually. The third source, known since Roman times, is the spring at *Sidi Harazem* just 10 km from Fes. This is also non-gaseous but contains sodium which can be noted in the taste. This too is sold as table water though in less quantities than *Sidi Ali*.

pets, as well as traditional entertainment from musicians and others. The town also has a small pool for summer use.

• **Accommodation** A pleasant hotel with a good view is the **D** ***Hotel Panorama***, T 562010, 39 rms, recommended restaurant and bar, good view. **E** ***Hotel Azrou***, Route de Khenifra, T 562116, reasonable place with 9 rms, restaurant and noisy bar. The best economic hotel is the **F** ***Hotel des Cèdres***, Place Mohammed V, T 562326, a clean establishment with hot water, communal showers and a good restaurant; also try **F** ***Hotel Salam***, on a square off Place Mohammed V opposite the *Hotel des Cèdres*; alongside the less recommended **F** *Hotel Ziz* and **F** *Hotel Beau Séjour*. **Youth hostel** T 2496, Route de Midelt, Azrou, BP147, to get to it follow the signs from Place Mohammed V, and turn left off the road to Midelt, clean and friendly, 60 beds, kitchen, overnight fee MD15.

• **Places to eat** The best meals are in the restaurant of ***Hotel Panorama***; at the ***Café Restaurant Relais Forestier***; or the restaurant of ***Hotel des Cèdres***, both on Place Mohammed V, or at the cheaper places along the road to Marrakech and around the bus stop.

• **Banks** The **Banque Populaire** is on Place Mohammed V.

• **Transport Road** CTM buses depart from near Place Mohammed V, at 0730 for Casablanca, 0800 for Midelt, and at 0730 and 0800 for Meknes. There are other CTM or private line services from Azrou to Rissani, Er Rachidia, Marrakech, Khenifra and Fes, and numerous grand-taxis to Khenifra, Ifrane, Immouzer du Kandar, Meknes and Fes.

Aïn Leuh, the waterfalls and Aguelmane Azigza

At 19 km S of Azrou, a turning off the P24 leads to **Aïn Leuh**, a Berber village with a Wed *souq* important to the semi-nomadic Beni M'Guid tribe, a ruined kasbah from the reign of Moulay Ismail, and nearby **waterfalls**. 20 km S of this is the source of the Oued Oum er Rbia, with a footpath leading from the road to the numerous and impressive waterfalls, falling from a cliff into a dangerous pool. Further on again is **Aguelmane Azigza**, a crater lake ideal for swimming. The tree-lined spot has its devoted followers amongst Moroccan campers and is an ideal location. There is also accommodation in a café. The road continues to rejoin the P24 at Khenifra.

Detour to Midelt and on to Er Rachidia

Midelt lies in the Atlas mountains, a convenient stopping point en route from Fes, Meknes or Azrou to Er Rachidia and the Sahara, a town with little to recommend except a calm, friendly atmosphere and a large *souq* on Sun. In the town, the minerals and fossils of the region are energetically sold by the young and in shops. Also look out for the town's **excellent carpets**, which have the distinctive vegetable-dyed geometric patterns of the region. These can be found in the permanent market opposite the bus station. They can also be bought at a weaving school, the **Atelier de Tissage**, run by Franciscan sisters in a convent off the road to Tattiouine.

• **Accommodation D** *Hotel Ayachi*, rue d'Agadir, T 582161, 28 rms, a quiet hotel with restaurant, nightclub and garden; there are several more basic hotels, the best perhaps ***Hotel Minlal***, on the N entrance to the town and with a good restaurant; also try ***Hotel Toulouse*** in the centre; and ***Hotel Roi de la Bière***, near the S exit. The ***Camping Municipal*** is on the road to Er Rachidia.

• **Places to eat** *Restaurant de Fes*, 2 Ave Mohammed V, which has very good *couscous* and other dishes; ***Excelsior***, also in the town centre; or ***Brasserie Chez Aziz***, by the Er Rachidia exit.

A possible excursion is to **Er Rachidia** on the rough pistes of the Cirque Jaffar, to the W of Midelt, signposted from the town, and only possible for part of the year. The P21 continues to Er Rachidia and into the Sahara, past the military fort at Aït Messaoud and the uninteresting village of Rich, before entering the spectacular **Ziz Gorge** and then Er Rachidia.

Ifrane, Mischliffen and an excursion to the Lakes

Ifrane is a mountain resort developed by the French, which now has numerous large villas and chalets, as well as a royal palace and hunting lodge. When this is occupied by the king, the town becomes busy with staff and politicians. From the town there are good walks in the cedar forests, and a drivable excursion round the *dayats* (crater lakes). There is skiing at the nearby resort of Mischliffen.

• **Accommodation** The most luxurious hotel is the **A** *Hotel Michlifen*, BP 18, T 566416/18, Tx 41972, 106 rms, with restaurant, bar, night-club and pool; more reasonable options are the **D** *Grand Hotel*, Ave de la Marche Verte, T 566407, 33 rms, has dated style, and is comfortable and calm; and the **D** *Hotel Perce Neige*, rue des Asphodelles, T 566404, 566210, a friendly place with restaurant and bar; the budget alternative is the **F** *Hotel Tilleuls*. The **Youth hostel** on Route de Vittel not always open.

• **Camping** *Camping International* is very busy in the summer but open all the year round, signposted from the town centre.

• **Places to eat** Good places to eat are *Café-Restaurant de la Rose*, 7 rue des Erables, T 566215; and *Au Rendez-Vous des Skieurs*, on the main street.

• **Services** There is a **Syndicat d'Initiative** information centre and a municipal swimming pool in the town, and regular buses from Ifrane to both Azrou and Fes.

Skiing at Mischliffen near Ifrane is from Jan to Mar with good but short slopes, sometimes with patchy snow cover. Hire equipment from the *Chamonix* restaurant in Ifrane and take a taxi to the resort. This is a small area with cafés and ski lifts but little else.

Aoua, Afourgan and Ifrah Dayats N of Ifrane, leave the P24 to the right for a tour of the *dayats*, lakes formed from craters. There are 3 lying between the P24 and the P20: Aoua, Afourgan and Ifrah. Dayat Aoua is a scenic place to picnic, or for those with more time, to stay, in the D *Hotel Chalet du Lac*, Route de Fes, T Ifrane 0, an atmospheric hotel with French restaurant and bar, which rents out boats. The lake itself is freshwater, and attracts a diverse selection of birdlife.

Immouzer de Kandar

This is a small mountain resort, a lively place during the **Fête des Pommes** in July, and with *souq*, Mon, in its ruined kasbah. It is a popular excursion from Fes, from where there are regular buses and grand-taxis. One of the main activities is swimming in the municipal pool with its spa water, near the town centre, which is open in the summer.

• **Accommodation** **D** *Hotel Royal*, Ave Mohammed V, T 663080, 663186, with restaurant and bar; the better value **D** *Hotel des Truites*, Ave Mohammed V, T 663002, a small and friendly place with a good restaurant and bar; and the basic **F** *Hotel du Centre*, near the bus stop. **Camping** at *Camping d'Immouzer*.

• **Places to eat** One of the best restaurants is *La Chaumière*, near the Marrakech and Azrou exit of the town, with moderately-priced European food; another reputed one is the *Auberge de Chamotte*.

SOUTHERN MOROCCO

Contents

Maps

The S of Morocco is quite different from the centre and N, with the arid areas of the Sahara a great attraction to travellers. Morocco has its dunes, near Zagora and Erfoud, but the most beautiful features of the desert are the oases and fertile valleys, with the distinctive earth-built *ksour* and kasbahs, areas of housing clustered together behind impressive but crumbling fortifications. The Draa, Dades and Ziz valleys are memorable areas in which to explore the date palmeries and small villages, whilst the Dades and Todra gorges are striking natural formations, where the rivers descend from the High Atlas. The Sous valley has the historic town of Taroudant at its centre: at its mouth lies the modern city of Agadir, the most popular tourist destination in Morocco noted for its beach and fine weather conditions. To the S of Agadir there are more remote towns, where travelling becomes harder. The Western Sahara has been incorporated within Morocco, but resistance from the Independence movement Polisario continues around its borders with Algeria and Mauritania. At the moment it is still relatively undeveloped for tourists.

AGADIR AND ENVIRONS

Agadir

Pop 110,479 (1982). *Alt* 20m.

The city of Agadir, lying on the Atlantic coast at the mouth of the Sous valley, takes the largest number of tourists in Morocco, and has perhaps the best facilities for them, with a vast number of

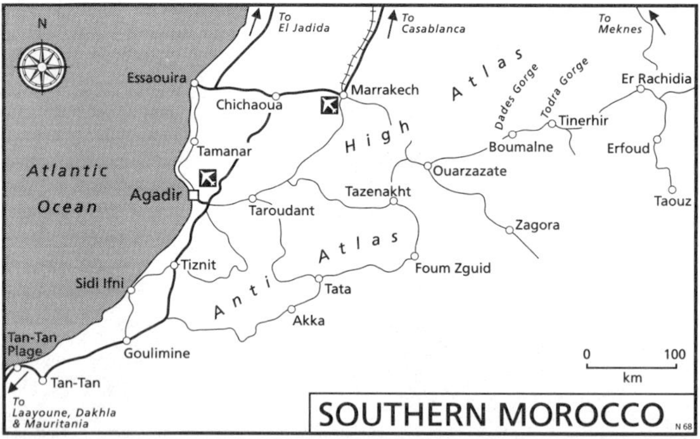

hotels. This popularity and infrastructure is for one reason: the beach. Agadir has a vast strip of sand stretching around the bay, and excellent weather conditions which enable tourists to swim and sunbathe for almost all of the year. Many of these tourists are on package holidays, based in whole or part in one of the larger hotels. Agadir is also an excellent entry point to Morocco, with regular flights arriving at its new airport, and can serve as a good base for exploring nearby regions, the Sous valley, the Sahara, the Atlantic coast, the Anti Atlas and High Atlas mountain ranges. Whilst the city has the relaxed air of beach resort, it has perhaps little which is distinctively 'Moroccan', as the old settlement was almost totally destroyed in the earthquake of 1960, and has been rebuilt and developed around its tourist potential, in the image of a European resort. There are not many places to visit in the city, nor is it a good place to shop, but the onward connections are good, particularly by bus from Agadir or nearby Inezgane.

History

Agadir under the Portuguese and Saadians The name Agadir, a shortened form in this case of Agadir n Irir, refers to the Berber word meaning 'a fortified granary'. Agadir was occupied by the Portuguese who built a fort on the site in 1503 which was known as Santa Cruz de Aguer. The Berber tribes of the Sous valley carried out a *jihad*, or holy war, against the colony, and the Saadian Emir of the Sous, Mohammed Echeikh El Mehdi, captured it in 1541, pre-empting the Portuguese departure from most of their Atlantic strongholds. His son, Moulay Abdellah El Ahalib, built the kasbah on the hill overlooking the city, the ruins of which still stand. With the development by the Saadians of the agricultural potential of the Sous valley, Agadir became an important trading centre in the 17th and 18th centuries, exporting goods such as sugar cane, olive oil, gold and spices, both from the immediate hinterland of the Sous valley, and further afield from the Sahara. However Agadir declined during the reign of Sidi Mohammed Ibn Abdellah, who preferred to develop Essaouira, to the N, and closed down Agadir's port.

Agadir in the 20th century In 1911 an incident occurred offshore, when a German gunboat appeared 'to protect German interests', in spite of the 1906 Algeciras treaty. This crisis was settled by negotiations between the French and Germans, recognizing France's rights in Morocco, in exchange for territorial concessions in the Congo. The French occupied Agadir in 1913. They constructed the port in 1914, and enlarged it in 1930 and 1953. The town was destroyed by the earthquake of February 29 1960. The town had to be totally rebuilt to the S, planned on a Western influenced layout as a major tourist resort, with distinct functional zones separated by green swathes, with the large hotels kept well apart from the local population. Much of the architecture of the city has the characteristic functional blocks of the period, with little influence of Moroccan design, except in the token embellishment of more recent constructions. The port escaped total destruction and was soon brought back into use. It has been further developed as the base for a large fishing

CLIMATE: AGADIR

	Jan	Feb	Mar	Apr	May	Jun	Jul	Aug	Sep	Oct	Nov	Dec	Av/Tot
Max (°C)	20	21	23	23	24	25	27	27	27	26	24	21	23
Min (°C)	7	9	11	13	15	17	18	18	17	15	12	9	13
Rain (mm)	55	33	22	17	7	0	0	1	8	14	35	47	239

fleet and as the centre of an industrial zone. The city has grown rapidly in size, population and prosperity.

ACCESS Air Agadir Al Massira Aéroport, T 839002, is 28 km from the city. Take a grand-taxi or a bus which will drop you off at Place Salam where a petit-taxi can be hired.

Road From Rabat, Casablanca, El Jadida and Essaouira entrance to Agadir is via the P8, leading into Ave Mohammed V; from Marrakech and the P40 turn left along Blvd Mohammed Cheikh Saadi into the town centre; from the airport and Inezgane, and beyond along the P32 to Taroudant or the P30 to Tiznit and the S, one enters along either Ave Hassan II or Ave Mohammed V. **Bus** There are ONCF buses from Marrakech, connecting with the trains from Rabat and Casablanca, which arrive on rue Ya'qub al-Mansur just off Place Lahcen Tamri, as do CTM and private line services. Some buses, however, go to Inezgane, connected to Agadir by Bus No 5, Bus No 6 or a grand-taxi.

Things to see

The beach is Agadir's main asset, an excellent strip of sand and enjoyable swimming, as well as an impressive array of people besporting themselves in a most un-Moroccan manner. It is clean and relatively free of hassle, and well provided with cafés. From the city centre walk down Ave du Prince Heritier Sidi Mohammed, turn right along Ave Mohammed V, and then left down to Blvd du 20 Août, which runs parallel to the beach.

The Port To get to the port take a petit-taxi for MD5, or Bus No 1 or walk along from the beach. The main reason for visiting, beyond any curiosity in Moroccan industry, is to sample the wares on offer at the small and excellent fish restaurants to the right of the port's entrance.

The Kasbah was built in 1540 to launch an attack on the Portuguese city, and was retained after the victory as a fortification against local insurrection. Whilst ruined by the 1960 earthquake, the ramparts and entrance way have been maintained in a reasonable condition, as Agadir's one historic site. The kasbah, which has a good view over Agadir, used to be a densely populated area, but was not resettled after 1960. It is reached by a winding road to the N of the centre, off Ave Mohammed V.

Architecturally the city is far from memorable, except for the marginal appeal of the modern **Grand Mosque**, on Ave des Forces Armées Royales, and the particularly ugly post office and shopping centre on either side of Ave du Prince Heritier Sidi Mohammed. Off Ave du Prince Moulay Abdellah is the dull **Jardin Ibn Zaidoun**. **The Folk Museum** (open 0930-1300 and 1430-1800), opposite the *Hotel Salam*, has a small but interesting display of local handicrafts from S Morocco, as well as occasional visiting displays. **La Vallée des Oiseaux**, lying between Ave Mohammed V and Blvd du 20 Août is a pleasant place to wander and listen to bird song.

Local information

● Accommodation

AL *Europa Hotel Safir*, Blvd du 20 Août, T 821212, F 823435, 221 rms, luxurious hotel with Moroccan-influenced design and decor, 3 restaurants, 2 bars, laundry, business centre, art gallery, tennis, pool; **AL** *Sheraton Hotel*, Ave Mohammed V, T 843232, F 844379; **A** *Club PLM Dunes d'Or*, on beach, T 840150, Tx 81827, 450 rms, price includes all activities, famous tennis courts which host professional events, sauna, *hammam*, gym, horse riding, volleyball and basketball, 2 pools, 5 restaurants, 6 bars and a nightclub, constant activity, not the place for a rest; **A** *Hotel Sahara Agadir*, Ave Mohammed V, T 840660, F 840738, popular and luxuriously equipped with 234 pleasant rms, 2 restaurants, 2 bars, nightclub, hairdresser, sauna, *hammam*, tennis and volleyball, children's and adult's pools; **AL** *Hotel Atlas-Amadil*, Route de l'Oued Sous, T 840620, F 823663, 322 rms, beside the beach but further from the town centre, a reliable place 3 restaurants, a wine bar, 2 bars, a coffee shop, nightclub, hairdresser, laundry, library, pool, tennis; **A** *Hotel Tamlelt-Agador*, Quartier des Dunes d'Or, T 841525, 659 rms, this complex links 2 hotels, the *Tamlelt* inspired by Moroccan medinas, the *Agador* by the kasbahs, luxurious establishment, large gardens, numerous fountains, 4 restaurants, a nightclub, hairdresser, several bars, 4 pools. Not suitable for disabled.

B *Agadir Beach Club*, near the beach, T 840791, F 825763, 374 rms, another extravagant Moroccan-influenced hotel, although do not trust their view of Moroccan architecture, luxurious rms, nightclub, 2 bars, nightclub, laundry, hairdresser, tennis, magnificent pool; **B** *Hotel Oasis*, just off Ave Mohammed V, T 843313-6, F 842260, excellent view, 132 rms, 2 restaurants, 2 bars, pool, sauna, *hammam*, nightclub, tennis and golf; **C** *Hotel Atlas*, Ave Mohammed V, T 843232, F 844379, 156 rms, and bungalows amidst the gardens, a recommended and reasonably priced option, 2 restaurants, tennis, pool, nightclub; **C** *Hotel Oumnia*, Quartier des Dunes, T 823351, close to the beach, well-equipped and friendly; **C** *Hotel Sud Bahia*, rue des Administrations Publiques, T 840741, F 840863, 246 rms, comfortable, central, pool, restaurant, bar and nightclub.

D *Hotel Mabrouk*, Blvd du 20 Août, T 840606, 40 rms, nearer town centre, reasonable place, pool and bar; **D** *Hotel Royal*, Ave Mohammed V, T 840675, 73 rms/bungalows amidst pleasant gardens, with bar, restaurant and pool; **D** *Hotel Miramar*, Ave Mohammed V, T 840770, a pleasant, quiet place near the port, reasonable restaurant; **D** *Hotel les Palmiers*, Ave du Prince Heritier Sidi Mohammed, T 843719, a friendly and relaxed place with a restaurant and bar; **D** *Hotel Sindibad*, Place Lahcen Tamri, T 823477, small and popular place on a busy square with bar and adjoining restaurant; **D** *Hotel Ayour*, 4 rue de l'Entraide, T 824976, modern and comfortable, with a pool.

E *Hotel Petite Suede*, Ave Hassan II, T 840779, 840057, a friendly place with reasonably priced and comfortable rms; **E *Hotel El Bahia***, rue El Mehdi Ibn Toumert, T 822724, 823954, breakfast available, the traveller hang-out, very friendly, recently renovated with spotless, well-equipped rms; **E *Hotel Moderne***, rue El Mehdi Ibn Toumert, T 823373, quite good and quiet; **E *Hotel Excelsior***, rue Ya'qub El Mansur, T 821028, near the bus station but otherwise not brilliant and rather noisy; **E *Hotel De La Baie***, rue Allal Ben Abdellah, T 823014, reasonable and convenient; **E *Hotel Paris***, Ave Kennedy, T 822694, clean, quiet, recently redecorated, the best value place around; **E *Hotel Diaf***, rue Allal Ben Abdellah, T 825852, adequate establishment at a reasonable price.

F *Hotel Select*, behind *Restaurant Salam*, rue Allal Ben Abdellah, shower outside, reasonable and convenient; **F *Hotel Tour Eiffel***, rue Allal Ben Abdellah, small and simple; ***Hotel Amenou***, 1 rue Ya'qub al Manour, T 823026, clean and welcoming; ***Hotel Tifawt***, rue Ya'qub al-Mansur, T 824375, quite basic.

● Camping

Camping Caravaning International d'Agadir, T 840374, 840921, a well-equipped and reasonably priced place near the centre, with showers, shops.

● Places to eat

♦♦♦*La Tour de Paris*, Ave Hassan II, T 840906, closed Sat, reservations advised, an elegant restaurant in the town centre with *nouvelle cuisine* and traditional French dishes; the ***Golden Gate***, Blvd du 20 Août, T 840820, 2 restaurants with excellent fish dishes, a bar.

♦♦ ***Restaurant Daffy***, rue des Oranges, set menus, including good value *mechoui*, *pastilla* and *tangia* specialities; ***Restaurant Copenhagen***, Prince Moulay Abdellah, Danish food in Agadir may be bizarre but this is the place for it; ***Restaurant Marine Heim***, Ave Mohammed V, T 840731, excellent German food and drink centred around fish, friendly and efficient; ***Via Veneto***, Ave Hassan II, T 841467, high quality European food and a very popular place, reservations advised; ***Restaurant la Tonkinoise***, Ave du Prince Heritier Sidi Mohammed, reasonable Chinese food; the ***Miramar***, Italian food; ***Le Jardin d'Eau***, Blvd du 20 Août, T 840195, very good French food and Moroccan dishes, particularly the lamb *mechoui*, reasonable prices; ***Darkhoum Restaurant Marocain***, Ave du General Kettani, T 840622, reservations advised, below the *Hotel Sud Bahia*, Moroccan decor, food and music; ***Restaurant du Port***, T 843708, a seafood restaurant by the port with mixed reports; ***Pizzeria Annamunda***, Ave du Prince Heritier Sidi Mohammed, music and Italian food.

♦The ***Resto Poissons*** restaurants by the port have cheap and excellent fresh fish, open 1230-2030, standards and reasonable prices maintained through hectic competition. Take a petit-taxi there for MD5, or Bus No 1; in another good area try ***Restaurant Sindibad***; ***Restaurant Mille et Une Nuits***, which has good Moroccan main courses and salads; ***Restaurant Chabib***, recommended for a cheap *tagine*; or ***Restaurant Coq d'Or***, all on Place Lahcen Tamri; nearby there are 2 good fish restaurants on rue du 29 Février; and the satisfactory ***Café-Restaurant Select***, in *Hotel Select* on rue Allal Ben Abdellah; ***Chez Redy***, Ave du Prince Heritier Sidi Mohammed, has standard fare, lots of alcohol and a lively atmosphere.

● Cafés

Oufella's, rue Allal Ben Abdellah adjacent to *Hotel Select*, is a *pâtisserie* with a good selection of cakes, sweets and drinks.

● Bars

Try ***Corniche Restaurant Bar***, by the beach, with bands each night.

Activities & entertainments

● Discos & nightclubs

Are plentiful in the large hotels but they are of variable quality, try the ***Tan Tan***, at the *Hotel Almohades*, Blvd 20 Août, T 840233, 840096; the ***Byblos***, at the *Club PLM Dunes d'Or*, on the beach front, T 820150 (open 2130-0500), admission: MD60, popular and the drinks are reasonable; ***Black Jack Disco***, at the *Hotel Agador*, T 841525 (open 2130-0500), admission MD60.

● Excursions

Sahara Tours, Ave General Kettani, T 840634, 840421, organize a range of excursions outside Agadir starting at MD130, including visits to Taroudant, Marrakech, Tafraoute and Essaouira, usually including at least one meal. Other agents in the same building also organize trips to Immouzer des Ida Outanane, Tata and Akka, and imine.

● Folklore

Sahara Tours, Ave du General Kettani, T 840421, 840634, organize evening meal and folklore excursions out of Agadir, better than the tame displays at the Agadir hotels.

● Shopping

Handicrafts Agadir has no shortage of handicrafts for sale, notably from the traders displaying their wares along the paths and roads leading from the big hotels to the beach. The quality of these goods is, however, questionable, and the prices often exorbitant. Similarly, the fixed price shops, around the shopping centre located between Ave du Prince Moulay Abdellah and Ave Hassan II, and along Ave Sidi Mohammed, are expensive, although their prices are often in fact negotiable. The best display and most reliable, although inflexible, prices, are to be found as with most Moroccan cities, at the ***Centre Artisanal Cooperative*** in rue du 29 Février.

General For more general shopping try the Moroccan quarter rather than the expensive tourist quarter. Perhaps the best stock is held by the supermarket ***Uniprix***, Ave Hassan II, (open 0830-1230 and 1430-1930), which also does handicrafts. There is a number of good beer and wine shops on Ave Mohammed V, right from Ave du General Kettani. European newspapers can be bought from stalls outside the major hotels and on Ave Hassan II. There is a bookshop, the ***Crown English Bookshop***, in the shopping centre off Ave du Prince Moulay Abdellah.

Souq The best days for Agadir's ***souq*** are Sat and Sun. It is located on rue Chaïr el Hamra Mohammed ben Brahim, which is left turn off Ave Mohammed V on the S edge of the city. Agadir's souq is not very impressive in comparison with places such as Taroudant.

● Sports

Golf: at ***Royal Club de Golf***, 12 km from Agadir, between Inezgane and Aït Melloul, 9 holes; ***Club Les Dunes***, 27 holes, fees MD550, MD2,500 for 6 days.

Horse riding: at ***L'Etrier***, BP 20, Route d'Inezgane, MD150 for 1½ hrs, bring your own hard hat.

Swimming: apart from the sea, a pool by the beach front, turn off Ave Mohammed V by the **Syndicat d'Initiative**.

Tennis: 120 clay courts at ***Royal Tennis Club d'Agadir***, Ave Hassan II, T 23395, 23738, 7 courts.

Yachting: ***Yacht Motor Club***, Port d'Agadir.

● Other services

American Express Voyages Schwartz, Ave Hassan II, T 822894.

● Banks

ABM, Ave Prince Heritier Sidi Mohammed, T 841567; **Banque du Maroc**, Ave du General Kettani, T 840172; **BCM**, rue des Administrations Publiques, T 840808; **BMAO**, Ave Hassan II, T 820425; **SGMB**, Ave du General Kettani, T 840281; **SMDC**, Ave Al Mouquaouma, T 821676; **Wafabank**, 43 Ave du General Kettani, T 840496.

● Chemists

Pharmacie, Municipalité d'Agadir, T 820349, open all night.

● Consulates

France, Blvd Mohammed Saadi, T 840826; **Spain**, rue Ibn Batouta, T 822126; **UK**, rue des Administrations Publiques, T 827741.

● Emergency

Ambulance: T 15; **Fire**: T 15; **Police**: rue 18 Novembre, T 19.

● Hospital

Hôpital Hassan II, Route de Marrakech, T 841477.

● Post Office

The PTT is located on the corner of Ave Prince Heritier Sidi Mohammed and Ave du Prince Moulay Abdellah.

● Religious services

Catholic: *Eglise Saint Anne*, rue de Marrakech, T 822251. **Jewish**: *Synagogue Beth-El*, rue Afghanistan. **Protestant**: *Temple*, 2 rue Chouhada.

● Travel agents and airline offices

Atlas Voyages, rue de l'Hotel de Ville, T 821284; ***Comanov Voyages***, 5 bis Ave Mohammed V, T 840669; ***Menara Tours***, 341 Ave Hassan II, T 821108; ***Wagons-Lits Tourisme***, 26 Ave des Forces Armées Royales, T 823528. **Air France**, 287 Ave Hassan II, T 842546, 825037; **Royal Air Maroc**, Ave du General Kettani, T 840808, 840145, 840045, reservations, T 840793.

● Tourist information

Office du Tourisme, Immeuble A, Place Prince Heritier Sidi Mohammed, T 822894, 841367 (open Mon-Fri 0800-1500 (June-Sept), 0800-1200 and 1430-1830 (Sept-June); **Syndicat d'Initiative**, Ave Mohammed V, T 822695.

● Transport

Local Bus No 5 and 6 go to Inezgane, Bus No 1 goes to the port. Place Salam is a good place to pick up services.

Bicycle/motorcycle hire There are several individuals hiring bicycles, mopeds and motorbikes from Blvd du 20 Août, but they can often be rather expensive.

Car hire **Afric Car**, Ave Mohammed V, T 840750; **Agadir Voitures**, Immeuble Baraka, rue de Paris, T 22426; **Avis**, Ave Hassan II, T 841755, and at the airport, T 840345; **Budget**, Ave Mohammed V, T 840762; **Hertz**, Bungalow Marhaba, Ave Mohammed V, T 840939, and at the airport; **Inter-Rent Europcar**, Ave Mohammed V, T 840367; **Lotus Cars**, Ave Mohammed V, T 840588; **Tiznit Cars**, Ave Hassan II, T 20998; **Tourist Cars**, Ave Mohammed V; **Week-End Cars**, Ave Mohammed V, T 20567.

Taxis Agadir is quite a wide spread city and therefore its plentiful petit-taxis, painted orange, can be useful, particularly to get to the kasbah or the port.

Air Agadir Al Massira Aéroport is 28 km from the city, T 839002. Take a grand-taxi, or as bus from Place Salam. There are several flights a day to Casablanca, and a week to Tanger, 2 a week to Dakhla, Ouarzazate and Laayoune, 1 a week to Tan-Tan, 2 a week to Las Palmas, as well as regularly to European cities. The loudspeakers at the airport are impossible to understand. Watch the departure boards with care.

Road Bus ONCF buses, T 841207, leave from rue Ya'qub al Mansur, connecting with the trains at **Marrakech**, departures 0450, 0940, 1400, 2000. CTM and private line services leave from the same place. There are private line services to **Marrakech** (5 a day), **Casablanca** and **Taroudant** (4 a day), **Essaouira** and **Tiznit** (3 a day), **Safi, Tata, Tan-Tan** and **imine** (2 a day), **Akka, Tafraoute, Rabat, Meknes, Fes, Oujda, Taza** and **Tanger**. CTM services also leave from here. Local buses to the airport, **Inezgane** (5 and 6) and **Tarhazoute** (12 and 14) leave from Place Salam. **Taxi** Grand-taxis leave for various destinations, particularly Inezgane and Taroudant, from Place Salam.

Excursion north to Tarhazoute and Immouzer des Ida Outanane

The coast to the N offers the potential for rewarding excursions, and some limited opportunities for staying out of the city. Although this potential is gradually being realized by developers, the area remains idyllic and tranquil, with the **Paradise Beach** and others stretching 30 km to the N of Agadir. To the E the **Paradise Valley** is a beautiful gorge and river basin, dotted with palm trees and waterfalls, leading up into the mountains.

Tarhazoute is the main settlement on this area of the coast, 19 km N of Agadir. The village is being developed with the construction of many homes, but remains a relaxing place to enjoy the superb beach. To get here, catch Bus 12 or 14 from Place Salam in Agadir. It is possible to rent cheap rms in private houses, normally for a week minimum. The official camp site is to the S, with a café and basic facilities, an official site is nearby. Near the camp site is the best restaurant, *Taoui-Fik*, other cafés are around the village. 6 km to the S of Tarhazoute is Tamrakht, in a banana grove, and a good place to buy them.

Immouzer des Ida Outanane 12 km N of Agadir, just before Tamrakht, a road turns off to the right. This leads through Paradise Valley for part of the way, through a beautiful gorge with possibilities of camping, although beware of flooding. Stop on the way at *Café-Restaurant Tafrite*, a good restaurant. At the end of this valley, 61 km from Agadir, at an altitude of over 1,000m, is the small market town of Immouzer des Ida Outanane, named after the confederation of Berber tribes in this area. There is a daily bus from Place Lahcen Tamri in Agadir (1400). Camping is possible near the *Café de Miel*, but the best option is the D *Auberge des Cascades*, T 16, a wonderful hotel with 18 rms, terrace or balcony, with bath, excellent food in the restaurant, bar, tennis, pool and a garden of fruit and olive trees located above the waterfalls. The village, which has a *souq* on Thur, is known for honey production, with a honey festival in July. The celebrated waterfalls lie below the village, and although they have been reduced in volume in recent years, are popular for both sightseeing and bathing. The village is also a good place for bird watching and walking, be it rambles in the immediate surrounds, or more strenuous walks further afield.

Inezgane and Oued Massa

Inezgane, population 17,592 (1982), lies 13 km S of Agadir and is almost a suburb of it now. It is primarily a transport hub, with taxis, local buses and coaches to Casablanca, Rabat, Marrakech, Taroudant (1 hr), Ouarzazate, Tiznit and Laayoune, amongst other places, with far more services than Agadir. This is likely to be the main reason for staying overnight, for there is little of interest in the town, and the buses make it extremely noisy. All long-distance buses and grand-taxis stop along the wide, busy main street lined by bus agents, including CTM, small shops and cheap restaurants. At the end of this is the main square, with the local bus stands. Off to the right of the square is a relaxed and mildly interesting covered market, with the main market day on Tues. 42 km S of Agadir the Oued Massa lagoon provides a splendid spot for bird watching. The estuary is home to flamingoes, bald ibis, spoonbills and rare herons. A week's visit can be organized for MD1,300.

• **Accommodation and Places to eat** The best hotel lies just outside Inezgane, the **C** *Hotel Club Hacienda*, Route de l'Oued Sous, T 830176, with bar, restaurant, nightclub, tennis, pool and horse riding; also recommended is the **D** *Hotel-Restaurant les Pergolas*, T 830841, along the road to Agadir, with 23 rms, a bar and a highly-recommended restaurant serving French food; **D** *Hotel Provencal*, nearby, T 831208, 44 rms, bar, restaurant and pool; **D** *Hotel les Pyramides*, Route de l'Oued Sous, T 834705, a quiet place with 20 rms, a pool, restaurant, bar and horse riding; and **D** *Hotel Hagounia*, 9 Ave Mokhtar Sousi, T 830783, with 48 rms, located on the road just before the town centre. Grouped around the main square are 9 cheap hotels, preferably choose the **F** *Hotel El Merjane*.

• **Places to eat** There are no shortage of restaurants, but a good inexpensive one is the ♦ *Café-Restaurant Bateau de Marrakech*, on the main square.

• **Transport Road** Between Inezgane and Agadir take Bus 5 or 6, or a grand-taxi.

TAROUDANT AND ENVIRONS

Taroudant

Taroudant, population 36,000, is nicknamed by the locals 'grandmother of Marrakech', and indeed it has some of the character of the more famous city, although on a smaller scale and with a far more relaxed air. The small medina is enclosed by impressive red earth walls and is focused on 2 intimate and friendly squares, in between which lie a range of interesting *souqs* selling handicrafts for which Taroudant is famous. Although without any distinctive monuments, the town is well worth a visit, and after Agadir, feels far more 'Moroccan'. Taroudant is also a good base, with Agadir and the coast to the W, the High Atlas and the Tizi-n-Test pass to the N (see page 316), the Saharan oases of Tata and Akka to the S (page 335), and the routes to Ouarzazate and the Draa, Dades and Ziz valleys to the E (see page 335). It is also well provided with good hotels and restaurants, and has a handicrafts and folklore fair in Apr.

Taroudant has always been a major population and marketing centre of the fertile Sous valley and has played a strategic role, although rarely achieving any national prominence. The town was conquered by the Almoravids in 1056, but under the Almohads had greater independence. From 1510 the Saadians gave greater prominence to Taroudant, when their first leader, Mohammed al Quaim, was based here as Emir of the Sous. Even after the Saadians gained control of Morocco, Taroudant remained for a while their capital. Taroudant supported Moulay Ismail's

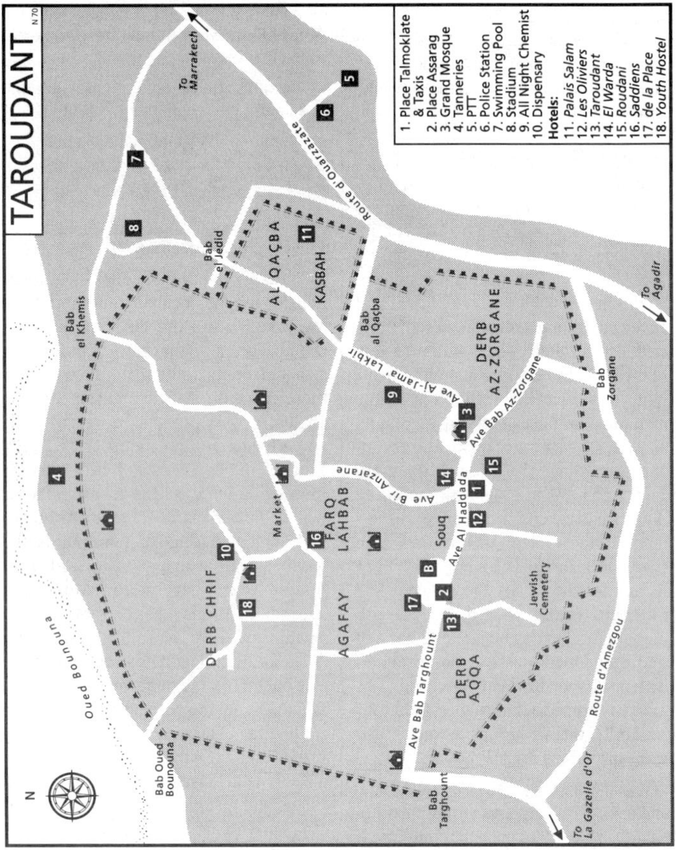

nephew in his rebellion, and when the Sultan overcame the town in 1687 he extracted his revenge by slaughtering the population and destroying much of the town. Decline set in, which continued into the 18th and 19th centuries. In the early years of the French protectorate Taroudant harboured the rebel Sultan El Hiba and was consequently sacked by the colonial forces. The French neglected Taroudant after this, and the town now remains little more than a regional market.

ACCESS Buses from Inezgane, Agadir, Marrakech and Ouarzazate deposit their passengers either at Place Talmoklate or Place Assarag. The town is small enough to walk around, although there are petit-taxis, painted light brown, and horse-drawn *calèches*, around the town.

Things to see

The Souqs in Taroudant are excellent and this is likely to be an easier place to shop or appreciate handicrafts than the central and northern cities, whilst offering more variety than elsewhere S of

The Argane Tree – The Tree Of The Flying Goats

Visitors to this particular area of Morocco might be forgiven in thinking that the trees are full of flying creatures. The creatures are goats but though they are perched on the extended boughs of the argane tree they climb, they do not fly.

The argane tree is found today only in this small region of Morocco between Agadir and Essaouira and eastwards along the Souss valley beyond Taroudant and in parts of Mexico.

At first glance one could mistakenly think that the area was under olive cultivation. The trees are well spaced and the average height is the same, around 4m, although some specimens reach 20m. The short trunk, however, is thicker, perhaps 8m in girth. In fact it is not one trunk but a fusion of stems and the canopy of clumps of argane can spread to 40m. The trees grow very slowly but live a long time, with an estimated average lifespan of 125 years.

The wood from the tree is extremely hard and makes excellent charcoal and the small pale green leaves set among vicious spines make nutritious fodder. The small greenish flowers are produced in spring and sometimes in autumn and the resulting fruit, something like a wrinkled yellow plum, appears between May and Sept. Don't be tempted to try one.

The fruit is much prized. The fleshy cover makes a rich, longlasting cattle cake, while being particularly rich in sugar the juice can be fermented to produce an alcoholic drink.

The oil from the kernels within the hard shell is used by the local population who have acquired the taste. It is honey coloured with a nutty flavour. It is used in cooking, in the preparation of sweets and mixed with almond paste and honey it makes a delicious 'butter'. A bowl of argane oil into which hot bread is dipped is served at most meals.

The goat herders collect the fruits from the ground. Officially they are forbidden to beat the trees to make the fruits fall. Some fruits are dislodged by the feeding goats, in other cases the stones which are spat out by the goats who have eaten the pulp and the stones which have travelled through the animal's system are collected. The nuts can be stored for years, providing food in times of scarcity. The women produce the oil in small quantities because it cannot be stored. They break the shell, roast the kernel often using the shell casing, grind the kernels into a paste which is mixed with tepid water and from this squeeze the oil. The work is tedious and the yield is very low, estimated at about 2 kg of oil for every 100 kg of kernels. The oil's reputation as an aphrodisiac is widespread.

Marrakech. The busiest days are Thur and Sun, the *souq* days, bringing in people from the villages, but much of it operates during the week. The *souqs* lead off from Place Assarag, beside the bank, and weave across to Place Talmoklate. Notable specialities of Taroudant amongst its excellent handicrafts are jewellery, some of it antique or mock antique, limestone sculptures, and the excellent carpets of the region. There are numerous small stalls to shop at, as well as bigger tourist shops, of these *Ali Baba*, 95 Joutia, T 852435, is friendly. Off the other side of Place Talmoklate is an area of small stalls, notably selling spices, herbs, medicines and pottery.

The Walls and Kasbah The Saadian *pisé* walls interspersed with towers are still intact and are worth following around the town, preferably by *calèche*. They are broken by 5 gates, at least one of which can be mounted for a view over gardens and olive groves. En route they pass the kasbah, now looking like a more densely-populated and poor area of the town, but in fact it was once a fortress for Moulay Ismail. Outside the walls are the tanneries, left from **Bab el Khemis**, a smelly area understandably located beyond the medina, where skins of a variety of animals are still cured by traditional methods.

Local information

● Accommodation

AL ***Hotel la Gazelle d'Or***, Route d'Amezgou, T 852039/48, F 852537, 2 km outside the town, one of the 2 most luxurious, exclusive and expensive hotels in Morocco, with 30 individual bungalows set amidst beautiful gardens and orange groves, as well as 2 restaurants, bar, tennis and pool,

C ***Hotel Palais Salam***, Route d'Ouarzazate, T 852312, F 852654, 144 rms in a beautiful 18th century palace and bungalows amidst gardens, 3 restaurants, bar, tennis, pools, car and bicycle hire.

D ***Hotel Saadiens***, Borj Oumansour/Annasim, T 852589, small and friendly, in the medina with 57 rms, restaurant, bar, tearoom, pool, parking.

E ***Hotel Taroudant***, Place Assarag, T 852416, old, French run, friendly atmosphere, 37 good rms around a verdant courtyard, with roof-terrace, excellent bar, and a very good restaurant selling reasonably priced and large meals.

F ***Hotel Roudani***, Place Assarag, reasonable, hot water; **F** ***Hotel El Warda***, Place Talmoklate, noisy but cheap; **F** ***Hotel de la Place***, Place Talmoklate, cheap, cold water only; **F** ***Hotel les Oliviers***, just off Place Talmoklate, clean, only cold water.

● Camping

There is an unofficial area of camping in front of the police station, Route d'Ouarzazate.

● Places to eat

♦♦♦ ***La Gazelle d'Or***, Route d'Amezgou, T 852039, reservations necessary, one of the best Moroccan restaurants, with a diverse menu including an excellent pigeon *pastilla* and desserts; ***Hotel Palais Salam***, Route d'Ouarzazate, T 852312, reservations recommended, for lavish Moroccan cuisine, specialities should be ordered in advance. ♦♦***Hotel Taroudant***, Place Assarag, T 852416, big portions of good French-Moroccan cuisine; ***Hotel Roudani***, good Moroccan food; ***Hotel Saadiens***, a recommended place for reliable Moroccan cuisine. ♦***Restaurant Tout Va Bien***, Place Talmoklate, with good prices and food, particularly *couscous*; ***Café-Restaurant Dallas***, Place Assarag, is fine and cheap but with dodgy *couscous*; ***Restaurant Sindibad***, Place Assarag, is also good; other cheap places are located between the 2 main squares.

● Bars

In *Hotel Taroudant*, Place Assarag, T 852416, a small friendly bar with a good atmosphere and low prices; of another class is the cocktail bar at the *Hotel Palais Salam*, Route d'Ouarzazate, T 852312.

● Cafés

In Place Assarag there is a large café with seating on the square, a pleasant place to relax; and several on Place Talmoklate, including the excellent ***Pâtisserie El Ouarda***.

● Bank

Banque Populaire, Place Assarag.

● Doctor

Dr Ahmed Iben Jdid, T 852032 (clinic), T 853626 (home).

● Hammams

There is a *hammam*, near the *Hotel Taroudant*, another is off Place Assarag opposite.

● Sport

Tennis: *Tennis Roudani*, near the *Hotel Palais Salam*. **Cycle hire** MD13 per hour.

● Tourist information

Syndicat d'Initiative, Maison de Jeune de Téromo.

● Transport

Road Bus Bus agencies are located on Place Assarag and Place Talmoklate, although some of the services leave early in the morning. There are regular buses to **Inezgane** (1 hr), and other services to **Ouarzazate** (5 a day, 3 hrs), **Tata** (3 a week), **Casablanca** and **Agadir** (4 a day). A bus leaves for **Marrakech** via the spectacular Tizi-n-Test pass at 0400, taking 9 hrs. There is another service to **Marrakech** via the less impressive route through Agadir. **Taxi** Grand-taxis are a practical option to Inezgane and Agadir, entailing a change at Ouled Teima.

Tioute 33 km from Taroudant on the road S to Tata has a splendid palmery and a newly restored 16th century kasbah overlooking the 7 small villages. *Restaurant Kasbah Tioute*, T 851048, is highly recommended for lunch, ask for the chicken tajine served in traditional style.

Detour southwards to Tata and beyond

Just 7 km E of Taroudant, a road leaves the P32, and follows a 171 km route across the Anti Atlas mountains and down into the Sahara at Tata. This is a spectacular journey, rarely travelled by tourists, but worth it for devotees of wilderness, and now passable by car. From Tata, the options are to travel E to Foum-Zguid and Zagora, along the Jbel Bani mountain range, or W along the P30 through a series of oases to Bou Izakarn, and connect with the Agadir-Tiznit-Laayoune road. There are 4 buses a week between Taroudant and Tata, and daily buses between Tiznit, Bou Izakarn and Tata. The roads are passable by car, although spare parts and petrol are less plentiful in this region. 93 km from Taroudant the road reaches **Irherm**, which has a Wed *souq*, a petrol station, and the *Café de la Jeunesse*, with basic accommodation.

Tata is the principal town of the region, a pink settlement built around an oasis. The oasis, with its scattered housing and several *ksour*, is cultivated by the Berber-speaking population who wear distinctly Saharan clothing. At the centre of the town is a garden square, and nearby are all the facilities, the bank, the post office and basic café-restaurants. The best place to stay is at the E *Hotel de la Renaissance*, 96 Ave des Forces Armées Royales, T 802042, 45 rms, with the town's top restaurant; the other options are the F *Hotel Sahara*; and the F *Hotel Salam*, both basic.

East from Tata There are police checks along this route, and it may be necessary to get a permit: check with the police in Tata. Transport is by 4 wheel drive vehicle, or by hitching a lift on a lorry. 70 km E from Tata, **Tissint** has 5 *ksour* and is known for its excellent dates. **Foum-Zguid** has a Thur *souq*, basic accommodation, and buses to Ouarzazate. There is a rough road from Foum-Zguid to Zagora.

West from Tata **Akka** lies 70 km W of Tata, a village with an interesting old quarter, with a history as a trading post, and with basic accommodation at the F *Hotel-Café Tamdoult*. Further on, **Foum El Hassan** is another oasis, with rock carvings in the town centre. 4 km from the town, up the track into the mountains, are some remarkable carvings of animals.

From the village of **Timoulay Izder**, a road leads 10 km to **Ifrane de l'Anti Atlas**, an historic settlement surrounded by a number of *ksour*, spaced around the slopes of the mountain bowl. Ifrane had a large Jewish population, who still revisit the necropolis just to the N. The village has an interesting *souq* on Sun morning. There are 3 places to stay, marginally the best is the F *Hotel Anti-Atlas*; the others are the F *Café-Restaurant de la Poste*; and the F *Café du Paix*. Back on the main route, **Bou Izakarn** lies on the junction with the Agadir to Laayoune road, with regular transport to Goulimine and Tiznit, and a Fri *souq*. The E *Hotel Anti-Atlas*, T 874134, 10 rms, on the road to Goulimine, has a restaurant, pool and garden, and is a pleasant place to stay. From here there are buses and grand-taxis to Ifrane de l'Anti Atlas.

OUARZAZATE AND THE DRAA VALLEY

The road from Taroudant to Ouarzazate incorporates all ranges of scenery – intensive oasis agriculture, dry farming, argane culture, expanses of gravel desert grazed by goats and camels and extensive views from the winding road through the Anti Atlas. Stop at **Talioune** as *Hotel Ibn*

Touret or *Café Renaissance*. Town also has pharmacy, mechanics and taxis.

Ouarzazate

Pop 19,000. *Alt* 1,135m.

Ouarzazate's primary attraction is not in the settlement itself, an unexciting town and military garrison with a crumbling *ksar*, but as a base for exploring the Saharan regions, and as a transit point en route to the desert. For this, it is well-equipped and a pleasant enough place to stay.

Located at the confluence of 3 rivers, Ouarzazate is in a strategic location, and has been garrisoned since the Almohad period. A tribal war in the late 19th century left Ouarzazate in the hands of the el-Glaoui family, and the kasbah became the power base from which they expanded control over the S. The town was the chosen by the French in 1928 as a military garrison and administrative centre – the buildings from this period struggle along the main street. Around and above them are the large hotels, which have been built in recent years, giving Ouarzazate a prosperity unusual in this region. This is compounded by the role of the town and its immediate vicinity as a film location. From the point that *Lawrence of Arabia* was filmed at Aït Benhaddou, this area has become a popular director's choice, and there is now a permanent studio nearby. Ouarzazate hosts a handicrafts fair in May and a *moussem* in Sept.

ACCESS Air The airport is at Taorirt, NE of Ouarzazate, T 882345. **Road** Road access is by the P31 NW from Marrakech; and by the P32 W from Taroudant; E to Boumalne, Tinerhir and Er Rachidia on the P32; and SE on the P31 to Zagora. **Bus** The CTM bus terminal is on a square on the main street, Ave Mohammed V, private line buses arrive at Place 3 Mars, and grand-taxis on Place Mouahidine. Most of the important buildings are located on or near Ave Mohammed V.

Things to see

The main days for the town market are Sun and Tue, but beyond this the main point of interest in Ouarzazate is the **Kasbah Taorirt**, located E of the town centre along Ave Mohammed V. This was an el-Glaoui kasbah, built in the 19th century, reaching its height of importance in the 1930s. The kasbah would have housed the extended family of the chief, his servants and followers, as well as a community of tradesmen, artisans and cultivators, gathered together in a continuous area of building for common security. The kasbah is heavily ruined, but is still in part occupied, on its rear side, by some of the poorest people in Ouarzazate in a maze of narrow passageways, small houses and shops. The area of the kasbah adjacent to the road has been maintained and is open to public view (open 0830-1200 and 1500-1800 Mon-Fri, 0830-1200 Sat). This would have been the quarters of the family and immediate associates, and includes a courtyard and several reception rms. Upstairs are a small dining room and salon.

Opposite the kasbah in the *Ensemble Artisanal* (open 0800-1200 and 1300-1800 Mon-Fri, 0830-1200 Sat), which has a number of sculptors working on the premises, as well as a selection of local handicrafts. The local woollen carpets of the Ouzgita Berbers are worth

CLIMATE: OUARZAZATE

	Jan	Feb	Mar	Apr	May	Jun	Jul	Aug	Sep	Oct	Nov	Dec	Av/Tot
Max (°C)	17	19	23	26	30	35	39	40	35	27	21	17	27
Min (°C)	2	3	7	10	14	17	21	21	17	12	7	3	11
Rain (mm)	8	5	15	7	6	5	2	10	21	20	17	19	135

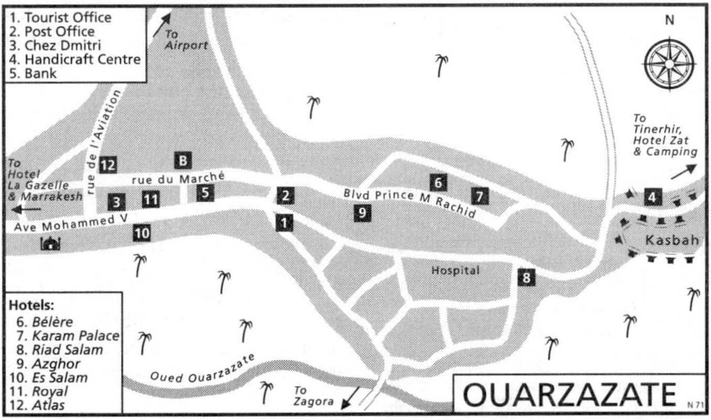

looking out for. In the town centre there is also a *Coopérative Artisanale des Tissages de Tapis*, another fixed price shop. *Atlas Studios*, where film work is regularly in process, is open to public view (0800-2000), and is located 3 km from the centre, along the road to Marrakech. Outside Ouarzazate, to the E, the Barrage al-Mansur, is a large man-made lake with the partly ruined **Tamdaght Kasbah**. To the S, off the P31, lies the **Kasbah Tifoultoutte**, now used as a hotel, with good food, T 882813.

Local information

● Accommodation

A ***Hotel Bélère***, Ave Moulay Rachid, T 882803, F 883145, cool, spacious, excellent facilities, helpful manager, second best hotel in town; **A** ***Hotel Karam Palace***, Blvd Prince Moulay Rachid, T 882225, luxurious, 150 rms, restaurant, bar and pool; **A** ***Hotel Riad Salam***, Ave Mohammed V, T 882206, 2 converted kasbahs, luxuriously equipped, 14 suites, 63 rms, restaurant, bar, spectacular pool with waterfall, as well as a sauna, massage, horse riding and tennis.

C ***Hotel Azghor***, Blvd Prince Moulay Rachid, T 882612, above the town, a good place with 150 rms, a restaurant, bar, nightclub and pleasant pool; **C** ***PLM Hotel Zat***, Aït Gief, T 882521, 60 rms, a quieter hotel on the outskirts, with an excellent restaurant, a bar and pool.

D ***Hotel Tichka Salam***, to be avoided until manager is changed and standard of rms and cooking improved; **D** ***Hotel la Gazelle***, Ave Mohammed V, T 882151, a good option with 30 rms, an excellent bar-restaurant, small pool, a little out of town on the Marrakech road.

E ***Hotel Es Salam***, Ave Mohammed V, T 882512, a well-run hotel, some of the 50 rms are poorly lit; **E** ***Hotel Royal***, 24 Ave Mohammed V, T 882258, a friendly place with good rms with bath, and fair prices.

F ***Hotel Atlas***, 13 rue du Marché, T 882307, behind the main street, cheap and satisfactory.

● Camping

Camping Municipal, T 882578, is on the Tinerhir exit of the town, a friendly place with running water, café and simple restaurant, a bit expensive.

● Places to eat

◆◆◆***PLM Hotel Zat***, Aït Gief, T 882521, a very good restaurant; ***Le Palais Vert***, Aït Kdif, opposite the *PLM Hotel Zat*, T 882428, with Moroccan decor, specializes in local food. ◆◆***Le Mimosa***, Ave El Moukaouama, T 883115, an excellent selection of dishes at reasonable prices; ***Chez Dmitri***, on Ave Mohammed V, in the town centre, is an excellent bar-restaurant, once the focus of Ouarzazate, serving excellent European/Italian food, with a good *lasagne*; further out from the centre is the recommended restaurant of the *Hotel la Gazelle*, Ave Mohammed V, T 882151. ◆The cheapest places are along rue du Marché and nearby streets, ***Restaurant Es-Salam***, Ave du Prince Heritier Sidi Mohammed, is a reasonable cheap option for Moroccan food; ***Restaurant El-Helah***, 6 rue du Marché, is a good 2nd choice.

● Bar

The best place for a drink is *Chez Dmitri*, Ave Mohammed V.

● Banks

Banque Populaire, Ave Mohammed V; **BMCE**, Ave Mohammed V.

● Chemist

Pharmacie de Nuit, Ave Mohammed V, T 882708.

● Police

Ave Mohammed V, T 19.

● Post & telephone

The PTT is on Ave Mohammed V.

● Sport

Sporting Club, *Hotel Karam*, T 882225; **Riding Club** to E of town beyond kasbah; **Swimming** at major hotels and municipal pool.

● Travel agent

Ksour Voyages, Place du 3 Mars, T 882997; *Palmiers Voyages*, Place de la Poste, T 882617; *Top Voyages*, *Hotel Karam*, T 883645, for excursions in the region.

● Tourist office

Ave Mohammed V, opposite the CTM bus terminal, T 882485 (open 0900-1200 and 1430-1830 Mon-Fri). Syndicate d'Initiatives et du Tourisme, Kasbah de Taourirt.

● Transport

Car hire: **Budget**, Ave Mohammed V, on the road to Marrakech, T 882892; **Hertz**, Ave Mohammed V, T 882048; **Inter-Rent**, Place du 3 Mars, T 882035; other agencies around Place du 3 Mars.

Air There are flights from the Taorirt airport, NE of the city, T 882348, to Casablanca and **Marrakech** (4 a week), Agadir (2 a week) and Fes (1 a week). International flights to Europe (mainly Paris) in season.

Road **Buses** to Marrakech cross the High Atlas by the impressive Tizi-n-Tichka pass. There are also several services a day to **Zagora**, E to **Boumalne**, **Tinerhir**, **Er Rachidia**, and W to **Taroudant** and **Inezgane**. CTM buses leave from the terminal on Ave Mohammed V, private line buses from the nearby Place du 3 Mars. **Taxi** Taxis from Place Mouahidine go to Skoura, Boumalne and Zagora amongst other destinations.

Excursion to Aït Benhaddou

Aït Benhaddou is a spectacular village with kasbahs scattered around a dramatic hillside location, their red towers on splendid vantage points. This was a strategic location on the old route from Marrakech to Ouarzazate since the 16th century, but with few people living there now. The village, however, attracts day-trippers from Ouarzazate, because of both its intrinsic appeal and its role in the film industry, with *Lawrence of Arabia* and *Jewel of the Nile* filmed here, as well as *Jesus of Nazareth*, for which part of the settlement was rebuilt. Guides will show tourists around the kasbahs, which are intricately decorated, and well preserved. The village also includes a large *agadir*, or storehouse, on the hill top. Getting there: to get to Aït Benhaddou leave Ouarzazate on the Marrakech road, the P32 and then the P31, and turn right after 22 km.

• Accommodation and Places to eat

F *Café-Restaurant la Kasbah*, above the village, with 8 dormitory rms and a bar-restaurant; or **F** *Auberge-Restaurant Al Baraka*, below the village, a small place with a restaurant and 5 rms, or sleeping possibilities on the roof or in the tent in front; there is a camping site nearby. These 2 places are fine for lunch and adequate for dinner.

Detour to Zagora and the Draa Valley

The Draa Valley The road to Zagora is spectacular, first winding its way across the Jbel Anaouar mountains, and then down along the Draa valley, a strip of intense cultivation of settlement, a band of vivid colour weaving through the desert. The P31 is a good road, with frequent villages en route, but it is worth allowing adequate time and taking sufficient water. There are regular buses and grand-taxis connecting Ouarzazate, Agdz and Zagora, but one's own transport will enable visits to the numerous smaller and less spoilt oases and villages that are passed.

Agdz is the first major settlement of the

valley, with a Thur *souq*. The buses, often full, pass through here, and there are grand-taxis. It is possible to stay at the F *Hotel-Café-Restaurant de Draa*, with 17 rms, breakfast provided, a friendly place; or F *Kissane*, Ave Mohammed V, 29 rms. *Camping la Palmeraie*, clean, with showers and a simple restaurant. The village has carpet and pottery shops, and the palmery nearby is a pleasant place to wander.

Zagora

Zagora is the main town of the valley, an administrative centre, the best place to stay and the destination of most tour groups. The influx of tourists has encouraged some inhabitants to be over enthusiastic in their attempts to make sales. It dates from the 13th century when it was founded by an Arab tribe. Although Zagora is itself an unexciting settlement it is an excellent location to explore the nearby areas of the valley, with paths through the date palmeries and to the various *ksour*. Particularly pleasant is the **Amazrou date palm oasis** across the river, where there is also some accommodation. In Amazrou there is a former Jewish kasbah, where their traditions of silverwork are still carried on. Above Zagora and within walking distance are 2 hills, from where there is an excellent view over the valley and towards the dunes. Nearby are the ruins of an 11th century Almoravid fortress.

During the *mouloud*, there is a major religious festival held in Zagora, the *Moussem of Moulay Abdelkader Jilala*. The town's market days are on Wed and Sun. Look out for the blue cloth worn by the men of the desert tribes, called in the tourist literature 'blue men'. The *souq* is an important place for the exchange of produce and livestock for the surrounding region. Camel excursions can be organized, try *La Fibule du Draa*, 1 km to the S in Amazrou.

Local information

Accommodation

For a small town, Zagora has a reasonable selection of hotels. Among the more expensive places, choose between the modern **B** ***Pullman Hotel Reda***, T 847079, F 847012, 155 rms, restaurant, bar, tennis and 2 pools.

D ***Grand Hotel Tinsouline***, T 847252, 90 reasonable rms, beautiful gardens, a good restaurant, bar and pool; and the **D** ***Hotel-Restaurant Kasbah Asma***, T 113, along the M'Hamid road towards Amazrou; **D** ***La Fibule du Draa***, T 847318, 26 rms, 1 km to the S in Amazrou, an idyllic and relaxing little place with pool and recommended restaurant-bar.

The cheaper places include the **E** ***Hotel de la Palmeraie***, Ave Mohammed V, T 847008, friendly with 16 rms, restaurant, popular bar; **F** ***Hotel Vallée du Draa***, Ave Mohammed V, basic but adequate, with restaurant; **F** ***Hotel-Café-Restaurant des Amis***, Ave Mohammed V, friendly, clean and with a reasonable restaurant, cold water; **F** ***Hotel Oued Draa***, Ave Mohammed V, T 10, clean hotel with restaurant-bar.

Camping

At ***Camping d'Amezrou***, 1 km to the S in Amazrou, basic and friendly; ***Camping la Montagne***, further to the S, friendly and with a pool; ***Camping Sindibad***, beside the *Grand Hotel Tinsouline*, in a small palmery with a small restaurant and pool.

Places to eat

Include ***Grand Hotel Tinsouline***, T 22; and the cheaper ***Hotel de la Palmeraie***, Ave Mohammed V, T 08; ***Restaurant Timbuctou***; ***Café-Restaurant Essahara***; or ***Restaurant l'Afrique***. The best place is a 1 km walk away in Amazrou: ***La Fibule du Draa***, reasonably priced and not to be missed. Drink at the ***Hotel de la Palmeraie***.

Services

Ave Mohammed V has most of the town's facilities, including the grand-taxi park, the bus station, post office, the **Banque Populaire**, ***Pharmacie Zagora*** and the ***souq***. Bicycles can be hired in Ave Hassan II.

Tamegroute lies 20 km SE from Zagora on the left bank of the Oued Draa and is visited mainly because of the ***zaouia*, or monastery**, founded in the 17th century, headquarters of the influential Naciri Islamic brotherhood, which had great importance in the Draa region until recently, and is visited by scholars from the Islamic world. The outer sanctuary and library are open to public view (closed 1200-1500), the latter containing a number of impressively old *korans*. Whilst there, the village is interesting to explore, a close-knit area of old housing typical of the region, with potters at work, and a *souq*, main day Sat. It is possible to stay in Tamegroute, at the F *Hotel Said Naciri*, a welcoming place; or the F *Hotel-Restaurant Riad Dar Nousri*, a reasonable establishment with 18 rms, restaurant, pool and garden. There is a daily bus, and grand-taxis, to Tamegroute. S of Tamegroute are the **Tinfou dunes**, popular with tourists seeking the stereotypical desert view. There is a small inn, the F *Auberge du Repos des Sables*, which is popular amongst independent travellers, and boasts an impressive collection of art for sale.

M'Hamid can be reached by bus or by a negotiated grand-taxi from Zagora. It is a 90 km drive S along a reasonable road through the desert, the main reason for the excursion, an impressive view of stony desert interspersed with verdant oases. M'Hamid has basic facilities, cafés and accommodation, a Mon *souq*, and dunes nearby. M'Hamid is a good place from which to arrange short camel rides. There is very poor accommodation and food at F *Hotel Sahara*, T 9, 10 rms, separate shower or camping 2 km from the town. A second small hotel is being built. Hire of camel MD275 and Land Rover MD1,200 per day available.

From Zagora to Rissani and Foum-Zguid

Rough tracks exist E from Zagora to Rissani, just S of Erfoud, and W to Foum-Zguid (and then to Tata). **NB**: these are difficult journeys only to be undertaken in a 4 wheel drive vehicle. Ask at the hotels for details of the vans and lorries covering the routes. There is a better route to Rissani which is generally passable with a sturdy car, but 4 wheel drive vehicles are recommended (**see page 42**). Drive 60 km N from Zagora and turn E across the Oued Draa through the small oases of Nkob (42 km from junction) and Mellal towards Tazarine (75 km from junction) a small settlement which offers petrol, shop, camping and F *Hotel Bougafer*, T 10, 40 rms, restaurant, very basic. Here the black top ends and although there are signs that the old road is being upgraded and in places a new road is under construction there are 31 bumpy, dusty km of *piste* to cross. Back on the smoother surface pass through the tiny oasis settlement of Tiguerna (128 km from junction), the airstrip where anti-locust spray planes are parked before reaching the more major oasis settlement of Alnif with 2 hotels, F *Hotel Restaurant Bougafer*, very basic, fairly clean, well meaning staff and opposite the similar F *Gazelle du Sud*. Meals provided at both places. Mechanics, petrol and shop available. With just 90 km to go to Rissani, small villages such as Achbarou with shops and a café and after a further 30 km Maoisis with school, petrol and café *Levée de Solei* are passed, before crossing the dry river bed and turning S the last 3 km into Rissani.

The Dades Valley

The Dades valley has a similar if less dramatic appeal than the Draa valley: a belt of productive agricultural land beside the river, and a series of earth-built and crumbling *ksour* stretching from Skoura to Boumalne, flanked by arid mountains on either side. Skoura and El Kelaa des M'Gouna are practical excursions from Ouarzazate, or can be visited en route to Boumalne and the Gorges du Dades.

The Skoura oasis is more interesting than the village at its centre: a large palmery surrounded by kasbahs and *ksour*. Before the village, to the left of the road, is **Kasbah Amerhidl**, the largest of Skoura's kasbahs, with a particularly decorative design. The village also includes 2 kasbahs formerly occupied by the el-Glaoui family, **Dar Toundout** and **Dar Lahsoune**. Skoura village has a *souq* on Mon and Thur, a few basic restaurants, and the F *Hotel Nakhil*, a somewhat primitive establishment.

El Kelaa des M'Gouna Beyond Skoura, this is another area of *ksour* along the valley, including another el-Glaoui kasbah. The village, which has a Wed *souq*, is known for the production of rose water, with a rose water factory, and a rose festival in late May/early June. It is possible to stay at the C *Hotel des Roses du Dades*, T 18, 102 rms, above the town, the cool interior gives welcome relief from the heat, reasonable restaurant, bar, tennis, horse riding and a good pool; or the much more basic but friendly F *Hotel du Grand Atlas*, Ave Mohammed V, T 37, 12 rms, communal showers.

THE GORGES

Oued Dades and Oued Todra both descend from the High Atlas mountains through narrow and spectacular gorges that are attractive excursions from Boumalne and Tinerhir. Both gorges offer options for walking up into the hills beyond, but most people choose just to walk in the gorge and enjoy the scenery from the pleasant vantage point of the restaurants located nearby.

Boumalne

Boumalne is a small town, with a market on Wed, and a reasonable selection of hotels. The town has grown from a very basic settlement to its current size mainly in the 2nd half of the 20th century. In the Muslim cemetery there is a *koubba* to Sidi Daoud, who is commemorated in an annual festival, when bread is baked from flour left at the grave, and fed to husbands to ensure their fertility.

• **Accommodation** C *Hotel Madayeq*, T 04 834031, 100 rms, comfortable, good restaurant, bar and rooftop pool; **E** ***Auberge de Soleil Bleu***, off to the right before the *PLM Hotel Madayeq*, T 153, 12 rms with bath, good restaurant; **E** ***Hotel-Restaurant Vallée des Oiseaux***, T 04 834138, a new place with 12 comfortable rms and a restaurant; **F** ***Hotel-Restaurant Salam***, opposite the *PLM Hotel Madayeq*, a friendly and helpful place which provides free transport to Aït Oudinar in the gorge, 15 rms, communal showers, heating, rooftop terrace and restaurant with local food; **F** ***Hotel Adrar***, opposite the *souq*, T 04 830355, 27 rms around a courtyard, with restaurant.

• **Places to eat** The best restaurant in town is at the ♦♦♦***PLM Hotel Madayeq***, T 31, 32; cheaper options are the ♦♦ ***Hotel-Restaurant Salam***, recommended for regional specialities; and the ♦***Café Atlas***, in the centre, good for for food or just a tea or coffee; just outside Boumalne, on the Er Rachidia road, ***Restaurant Chems*** is highly recommended, with reasonable prices and a pleasant terrace.

• **Transport Road** There are grand-taxis from Boumalne to Tinerhir or Ouarzazate. There is a variety of vehicles available for the journey up into the gorges, including grand-taxis, vans, Land Rovers and lorries. Msemrir, beyond the gorges, is also possible by local transport.

Excursion to the Gorges du Dades

The 6901 leaves the P31 at Boumalne and follows the Oued Dades through limestone cliffs which form the striking Gorges du Dades. The principal destination is the section of the gorges following Aït Oudinar, but the track continues up into the High Atlas, with public transport as far as Msemrir. There are very basic *pistes* into the mountains, and around into the Gorges du Todra.

Just beyond Boumalne is **Aït Arbi**, where there are a series of striking *ksour* above the road. The road continues past areas of unusual rock formations, through Tamnalt and Aït Oudinar, where there is basic accommodation. The valley narrows after Aït Oudinar, creating the most striking area of the gorges, where the cliffs are in vivid shades of red. From Aït Hammou the road continues in theory, linking with the 6902 through the Gorges du Todra, and up into the High Atlas.

• **Accommodation** In Tamnalt accommodation and food are available at the **E** ***Hotel-Restaurant Kasbah***. But the best place in the gorges is the **E** ***Auberge des Gorges Dades 'Aït Oudinar'***, with a restaurant; there is camping nearby. Further on is the **F** ***Café des Peupliers***, with 3 rms and camping and the **E** ***Kasbah de la Vallée de Dades***, with 6 rms and a restaurant. At Aït Hammou there is the **F** *Café-Hotel Taghea*, with several rms but no electricity. Basic accommodation is available at Msemrir.

Tinerhir

Tinerhir is a modern administrative centre alongside a large oasis and older settlement, ideal for visiting the Gorges du Todra, but in itself a pleasant and interesting place to stay. The oasis settlement is a walk away behind the town, and a visit here is recommended. Hire a guide for MD35. The main part of the settlement was previously the Jewish quarter and has olive and fruit trees intercropped with grains and vegetables, and is interspersed with *ksour*. The main population is the Aït Atta tribe, often divided into small clans. Above the town and oasis is the massive ruined **el-Glaoui kasbah**, officially closed but normally possible to enter. There is a Tue *souq*, behind the *Hotel Todgha*. PTT is on Place Principale and the Banque Populaire on Ave Mohammed V.

• **Accommodation B** *Hotel Bougafer*, Blvd Mohammed V, T (04) 833200/80, F 833282, 2 km W of town, new, comfortable, clean, good pool, but footsteps and door slamming echo through building; **C** ***Hotel Sargho***, T (04) 834181, on the Ouarzazate road, with the appearance of a *ksar*, 62 comfortable rms, a restaurant, bar and pool; **E** ***Hotel Todgha***, 32 Ave Hassan II, T (04) 834249, 30 rms, restaurant, over-priced; **F** ***Hotel Oasis***, Place Principal, cheap, clean, central, welcoming, upstairs restaurant with good food and views over town; **F** ***Hotel El Salam Saada***, Place Principal, basic.

• **Camping** There are 3 camping sites 8 km along the road leading to the gorges, recommended are ***Camping Atlas***, small and friendly with a restaurant; ***Camping du Lac***, bar, restaurant, more expensive. ***Camping Almo*** is in centre of town.

• **Places to eat** *Hotel Sargho* has the best restaurant; ***Hotel Todgha***, 32 Ave Hassan II; and ***Hotel Oasis***, Place Principal are cheaper; ***La Gazelle d'Or***, in the town centre is also good; ***La Kasbah***, Ave Mohammed V, T 13, a friendly place with delicious food. A good café is ***Chez Habib***.

• **Transport Road** Buses and grand-taxis to all locations, including Ouarzazate, Boumalne and Er Rachidia, leave from Place Principal. *Grand-taxis* and vans run from Place Principal to the gorge. Hotels organize trips to the gorge for MD55.

Excursion to the Gorges du Todra

The Gorges du Todra are more spectacular than the Gorges du Dades, particularly popular in the evening when the rocks are coloured in bands of bright sunlight and dark shadow. There are places to stay near the narrowest part of the gorge, a highly recommended break from the activity of the major towns.

8 km from Tinerhir are the 3 camping sites already mentioned, in an idyllic location beside a pool and palmery. 6 km further on is the most visited section of the gorge, where the high cliffs leave just enough space for the road and river. It is a particularly photogenic sight at sunset, and is also excellent for birdwatching. Just before the gorge are the 3 hotels: the F *Hotel Restaurant El Mansur* is very basic with shared rms but is the cheapest option, it also has a restaurant; further on the E *Hotel des Roches* has 10 good rms and a restaurant in a ceremonial tent; the E *Hotel Yasmina*, T (04) 833013, newly extended with 12 'Moroccan' rms, and a large and recommended restaurant in a traditional black tent, often used by tour groups. Camping here by arrangement.

It is possible to continue along the pistes from the gorges, either across to the Gorges du Dades, or up into the High Atlas towards Imilchil. **NB:** passable only in 4 wheel drive vehicle. Alternatively, try to get a lift from a lorry.

From Tinerhir to Er Rachidia

Buses run from Tinerhir to Er Rachidia, or from Tinejdad, en route, across to Erfoud. There are grand-taxis from Tinerhir to Tinejdad, Tinejdad to mima, and mima to Er Rachidia. **Tinejdad** is a Berber and Haratin town in a large oasis, with some significant kasbahs, notably the **Ksar Asrir**; and the F *Hotel-Restaurant Tizgui*, with basic accommodation and food. **mima** is similar, a large number of *ksour* around a palmery, with a basic town at the centre, a camp site, and the F *Hotel Gheriz*, with reasonable rms and good food.

ER RACHIDIA AND THE ZIZ VALLEY

Er Rachidia

ACCESS Buses from **Aéroport Er Rachidia**, T 572350, stop at the bus station off Ave Mohammed V, the main street, and the grand-taxi park opposite.

Er Rachidia, population 27,040, previously known as Ksar Es Souq, was established by the French, initially by the Foreign Legion, as a military and administrative centre, a role it retains today. The town has little of interest for the visitor, beyond a **19th century *ksar*** near the Erfoud exit. However Er Rachidia is a convenient stopping point at the meeting of routes to Ouarzazate, Erfoud, Figuig and Fes, and is such is reasonably well equipped and with a relaxed atmosphere. The town, an important local *souq*, has its biggest market days on Sun, Tue and Thur.

• **Accommodation** C *Hotel Rissani*, Ave de la Marche Verte (direction Erfoud), T 572186, F 572585, pleasant location on the town's outskirts, 60 rms, restaurant, bar, disco, tennis and pool; **D** ***Hotel Oasis***, 4 rue Abou Abdellah, T 572519, a modern place with 46 rms, restaurant and bar; **E** ***Hotel Meski***, Ave Mohammed V, T 572065, 25 comfortable rms with restaurant, café and pool; **F** ***Hotel-Café la Renaissance***, 19 rue Moulay Youssef, T 572633, 20 clean rms, people are helpful and friendly, good restaurant; **F** ***Hotel des Oliviers***, 25 Place Hassan II, T 572449, satisfactory.

• **Camping** 2 km along the Erfoud road there is a basic camp site with a pool.

• **Places to eat** ♦♦***Hotel Oasis***, 4 rue Abou Abdellah, T 572519, 572526, has a good and clean licensed restaurant serving Moroccan food; ***Restaurant Lipton***, Ave Mohammed V, good food throughout the day and night; ***Restaurant Imilchil***, Ave Mohammed V, T 572123, good traditional Moroccan food in a licensed establishment. ♦The most economic place is ***Restaurant Sijilmassa***, Ave Mohammed V, with a simple but good menu; ***Hotel-Café la Renaissance***, 19 rue Moulay Youssef, T 572633, is reliable, with excellent *couscous*. There are other cheap places along Ave Mohammed V.

• **Bank** **Banque Populaire**, Ave Mohammed V.

• **Post Office** PTT, just off Ave Mohammed V near the *Banque Populaire*.

• **Shopping** The ***Complexe Artisanal***, near the bridge, has a selection of fixed-price goods.

• **Tourist office** Ave Moulay Ali Cherif, T 572733 (open 0830-1200 and 1400-1800).

• **Transport to & from Er Rachidia** **By air**: there is a weekly flight to Fes, and from there to other destinations, from Aéroport Er Rachidia, T 572350. **By bus**: buses leave from the bus station off Ave Mohammed V, with a several a day for Erfoud and Rissani (2 hrs), Midelt (3 hrs), Tinerhir (3½ hrs), Fes (9 hrs), and Meknes (8 hrs), and one each morning to Figuig (8 hrs). **By taxi**: there are frequent grand-taxis to Erfoud, Meski and Tinejdad, the park is opposite the bus station.

Excursion to Meski

Meski, also known as Source Bleu, was developed by the French Foreign Legion. It is a springwater pool surrounded by palms, with the ruined **Meski Ksar** and a popular camp site, the *Camping de la*

Source Bleu, T 249, which in the summer has a lively atmosphere but can become overcrowded: its restaurant is not recommended. Lying to the W of the Erfoud road 18 km S of Er Rachidia, **the *source*** is well worth a visit, and there is frequent transport to and from Er Rachidia.

Detour along the Ziz Valley

The Tafilalt From Meski, the P21 follows the Ziz valley S. This is another of the memorable valleys of the S, a succession of *ksour* alongside a heavily cultivated riverside area, with on either side the vast stony expanses of the Sahara. Many of the settlements of the valley were destroyed in the flood of 1965. The S stretches of the Ziz valley, a region known as the Tafilalt, are particularly fertile, and historically of considerable importance. This was due in part to its location on the trans-Saharan trade routes, with the town of Sijilmassa a major mediaeval population centre, whose rapid decline has not yet been fully explained. In the 8th and 9th centuries the region was a separate kingdom, and became known as a centre of religious unorthodoxy – of the Kharajite Berber heresy and later of Shi'ism. The present Alawite dynasty of Moroccan Sultans originated in Rissani. From 1916 to 1931 French control of the region was challenged and effectively thwarted by local forces. Nowadays it is a poor date-producing region with a small flow of tourists.

Erfoud is the administrative centre of the Tafilalt, built in the 1930s, and an excellent base for exploring the valley and nearby desert areas. On the other side of the river from the town is the **Borj Est**, a military fort with impressive views. There is a *souq* on Sun in the town centre, and a Date Festival in Oct. A visit to the interesting **Marmar Marble Factory**, near the *Hotel Salam*, is worthwhile.

• **Accommodation** C *Hotel Salam*, Route de Rissani, T 576424, F 576426, modern, well-equipped in traditional style, 100 rms, 45 deluxe suites, bar, a good restaurant, pool (not always!), gardens, vehicle and driver hire; **C** ***Hotel Sijilmassa***, T 576522, modern, fully-equipped. **D** ***Hotel Tafilalt***, Ave Moulay Ismail, T 576036, F 576036, 64 a/c rms, bar, restaurant, pool and garden; **D** ***Hotel la Gazelle***, Ave Mohammed V, good apart from noisy rms at the front, a reasonable restaurant. **E** *Hotel Farah Zouar*, Ave Moulay Ismail, T/F 576230, 30 a/c rms, restaurant serving typical Moroccan food. **F** ***Hotel-Bar Ziz***, 1 Ave Mohammed V, T 576154, 20 rms some with showers, good licensed restaurant; **F** ***Hotel des Palmiers***, 36 Ave Mohammed V, 15 rms, communal shower, cheap restaurant; **F** ***Hotel-Restaurant de la Jeunesse***, Ave Mohammed V, basic, with restaurant; there is also **camping** near the *Hotel Salam*, with basic facilities and a pool, not recommended.

• **Places to eat** ♦♦*Hotel Salam*, Route de Rissani, T 576426 offers the best meals. ♦ There are cheaper meals at the excellent ***Hotel-Restaurant de la Jeunesse***; and the recommended ***Café-Restaurant les Fleurs***; as well as at the ***Restaurant-Café du Sud***; ***Restaurant Merzouga***; and ***Hotel-Bar Ziz***, all in Ave Mohammed V.

• **Services** The post office, a branch of the **Banque Populaire**, and the bus station are located in the town centre on Ave Mohammed V.

• **Telephone** Local code 05.

• **Transport** There is a bus each day to Er Rachidia. Transport onwards to Rissani is by bus, or by a hired Land Rover.

Rissani, 22 km S of Erfoud, birthplace of the Alaouite dynasty is a modern village close to the site of the ruined town of Sijilmassa. It includes a 17th century *ksar*, housing most of the population, and a street with a bank and cafés. It is possible to stay at the E *Hotel-Café-Restaurant Sijilmassa*, Place Massira Khadra, T 5042, 8 rms, modern and clean, nearest to the ruins and the mechanics, over-priced; or the F *Hotel El Filala*, good size rms but often dirty. The village has an interesting *souq* on Sun, Tue and Thur, and there are several handicraft shops.

Sijilmassa was once the Berber capital of the Tafilalt region, and a major trading centre. It was founded in 707 by the Arab leader Musa ben Nasser, and its location on the major Sahel to Europe trade route, from Niger to Tanger, gave it considerable importance and prosperity. The ruins, little of which remain, are between the town and the river. The kasbah was kept up by Moulay Ismail, but the Aït Atta tribe destroyed the town in 1818. The current Alawite dynasty settled in the surrounding region in the 13th century before gaining the Moroccan Sultanate in the 17th century. The ruins are of historical interest only and the 'guides' are ill informed. The fanciful tales of earthquake destruction must be discounted.

To the SE of Rissani is the **Zaouia of Moulay Ali Sherif**, closed to non-Muslims, where the founder of the Alawites is buried. Adjacent to this is the **Ksar d'Akbar**, a ruined Alawite palace from the 19th century, whilst 2 km to the S is the **Ksar Ouled Abd el-Helim**, a striking structure dating from 1900. Getting there: there is a daily bus to Er Rachidia, and a Land Rover taxi each Thur along the rough piste to Zagora. There are lorries and Land Rover taxis from the village centre to Merzouga.

Merzouga, 61 km from Erfoud, has one attraction, the huge dunes called **Erg Chebbi**, a vast pile of sand stretching into the Sahara. There is little else, beside the other tourists and a small village with a Sat *souq*, but then the calm and wilderness is part of the appeal. A short walk across the dunes is a must once there. There are also camel excursions organized by the *Auberge La Grand Dune*, and some good bird watching particularly the pink flamingo in Feb by the adjacent lake. The *piste* continues S to Taouz.

• **Accommodation** It is possible to stay at Merzouga, although accommodation is often taken early in the day. The options include the **D** *Auberge-Kasbah Derkaoua*, near the dunes at Erg Chebbi, BP 64, full board, very good French-Moroccan licensed restaurant, pool. **F** *Hotel Merzouga*, a friendly place with good food; **F** *Café des Amis*; **F** *Auberge la Grand Dune*; and **F** *Café-Restaurant de Palmeraie*, all basic places with dormitory accommodation.

THE EASTERN SAHARA

Bouarfa

The road from Er Rachidia to Figuig, the P32 as far as Bouarfa, and the P19 from then on, is a long and impressive journey through the relative wilderness of the E Sahara – red mountains and stony desertscapes, broken only by small villages which are unlikely to detain the traveller for long. At the junction with the P19 from Oujda to Figuig is **Bouarfa**, a small administrative and military town. The town makes some interesting carpets from cloth scraps.

• **Accommodation** **F** *Hotel Tamlatte*; and the **F** *Hotel Hauts Plakas*, on the main street, basic.

• **Transport** **Train** There is a weekly train from Oujda to Bouarfa, leaving at 2240 on Sat and arriving at 0635 on Sun, and making the return journey to Oujda from 0920 on Sun, arriving at 1701 the same day, this is a useful service for visitors to Figuig. **Road** buses from Oujda to Figuig pass through Bouarfa. There are 2 buses a day to Er Rachidia.

Figuig

Figuig is a large palm oasis lying on the border with Algeria. This has given it a strategic position, and it has often been fought over between the Moroccan Sultanate and the powers to the E, most recently in 1963 and 1975 between Algerian and Moroccan forces. Nowadays the border is open (see below), and this is a popular place to cross.

ACCESS In Figuig buses stop in front of the *Hotel Sahara* on Ave Hassan II, the ticket office is nearby. There are 4 buses a day to Oujda, and a daily morning service to Er Rachidia.

Things to see

The *ksour* of Figuig are distinctly separate, and were more so in the past, when bitter disputes existed, particularly over water. The construction of the *ksour* is thus highly defensive. It is worth visiting one or 2 of the **ksour**, built with a maze-like system of alleys and houses. **Ksar El Ouadarhir** is to the left of the main street, **Ksar El Maiz** is an attractive area to the right of the street, **Ksar El Hammam el Foukanni**, with a hot spring, beyond that. **Ksar Zenaga** is perhaps the best to visit, a large area with a mosque, and above it a platform from which there is a good view over the oasis.

The oasis has 7 distinct *ksour*, with the main street, Ave Hassan II, running through the centre, along which most of the town's facilities are located: the *Banque Populaire*, shops and basic café-restaurants. There is some attractive leatherwork and silverware for sale in Figuig. The oasis, with its clearly discernible community structure and strongly religious nature, is an interesting place to stop for a few days en route to or from Algeria.

Local information

● Accommodation

F *Hotel Camping*, best place, pool, restaurant, satisfactory rms and a camping area; **F** *Hotel Meliasse*, a basic place at the entrance to the town; **F** *Auberge de la Palmeraie*, a good place with a restaurant, at Ksar Zenaga; or the **F** *Hotel Sahara*, Ave Hassan II, cheap and adequate.

● Places to eat

Café El Fath and *Café Oasis* both on Ave Hassan II, both reasonable.

Algerian Border To go into Algeria it is necessary to get one's passport stamped at the police station (0800-1500) on the main street. From here walk, hitch or drive to the border, where one passes through Moroccan and Algerian checkpoints, and the Algerian customs, before arriving at the small Algerian town of Beni Ounif (see page 464).

THE DEEP SOUTH

Tiznit

To the S of Agadir, is Tiznit, an important garrison and market town, with pinkish brown houses surrounded by large *pisé* walls, well worth a wander after an overnight stop. The town was founded in 1882 by Moulay Hassan, enclosing a number of separate *ksour* within the walls, and was the first base for El Hiba's insurrection against the French from 1912, following the example of his father Ma el Ainin in 1910.

Things to see

The town *souq* is on the Tafraoute exit, with its main days on Thur and Fri. There is an interesting jewellery *souq*, on the right between Place du Mechouar and the town walls. Along rue de l'Hôpital from the square is the **Grand Mosque** with a minaret reminiscent of the Sahelian style, with protruding perches. Adjacent to this is the **Source Bleu de Lalla Tiznit**, a spring named after the town's saint, a reformed prostitute. From **Bab Targua**, on the N side of the town, it is possible to get onto the walls. There are 2 religious festivals in Tiznit in Aug, the Moussem of Sidi Abderrahman, and the acrobat's Moussem of Sidi Ahmed ou Moussa.

Local information

● Accommodation

The top 2 hotels in Tiznit are the **D** *Hotel de Tiznit*, rue Bir Inzaran, on the edge of the town, T 862411, 862119, 40 rms, with the *Anzli Club* nightclub, restaurant, bar and good pool.

E *Hotel de Paris*, Ave Mohammed V, T 862865, 20 rms, fine restaurant.

F *Hotel du Bon Acceuil*, Place du Mechouar, clean and basic; **F** *Hotel Atlas*, Place du Mechouar, clean and reasonable, good restaurant; **F** *Hotel des Amis*, Place du Mechouar, satisfactory; **F** *CTM Hotel*, near the bus terminal, friendly with bar and restaurant.

● Places to eat

There is good food at the ♦♦*Hotel de Tiznit*, rue Bir Inzaran; and cheaper but still tasty meals at the ♦*Hotel Atlas*, Place du Mechouar; and the *Hotel du Bon Acceuil*, on the same square.

● **Services**
Around the square are a tourist information office, the **Syndicat d'Initiative**, T 869199, a bank and post office, as well as hotels and cafés.

● **Transport**
Road Most buses and grand-taxis arrive at Place du Mechouar, the focal point of the town. There are private line buses from Place du Mechouar, including several services a day to Tafraoute, Tata, Goulimine, Sidi Ifni and Agadir, and CTM services to Agadir and Laayoune from the nearby **Bab Ouled Jarrar**. Grand-taxis leave from Place du Mechouar, with Land Rover taxis from the Tafraoute road.

West of Tiznit is the beach of **Sidi Moussa d'Aglou**, with a long sand strip, dangerous swimming and a small troglodyte village of fishermen's families. There is good accommodation at the **F** *Motel d'Aglou*; and a camp site; as well as good food at the *Café-Restaurant Ouazize*. Grand-taxis from Tiznit leave from near Place du Mechouar.

Detour to Tafraoute and the Ameln Valley

Tafraoute is the most rewarding town of this area of the Anti Atlas mountains, located in the attractive Ameln Valley, with its unusual granite rock formations and beautiful villages. There are 2 approaches to Tafraoute, along the 7074 from Tiznit or the S509 from Agadir. The road from Tiznit passes through a series of oases, several with basic accommodation, and the impressive **Col du Kerdous**, at 1,100m. The road from Agadir and Inezgane is also scenic, through a mountain landscape, and including the Wed *souq* of Aït Baha.

Tafraoute is the modern administrative centre of the valley and the best base for exploration. There is a large almond festival here, the Fête des Amandes, in Jan-Feb, and a *souq* on Wed. The town has a post office and a **Banque Populaire**, both on Place Hassan II, as well as a branch of the **BMCE**. Tafraoute market is an excellent place to pick up handicraft bargains. Visitors should on no account omit a visit to La Maison Touareg, Ave Mohammed V, T 800210, which behind its unprepossessing exterior has an amazing range of carpets and other goods, and very friendly staff. It is also the only place to change money in the evening and at weekends. friendly staff.

● **Accommodation C** *Hotel Les Amandiers* is the most luxurious here, but offers little for the price, located on a rock above the town, T 800088, with 62 rms, a restaurant, bar and pool; **E** *Hotel Tafraoute* in the town centre is the best bargain, with hot water, clean rooms and friendly staff; the nearby **F** *Hotel Redouane* and **F** *Hotel Tanger* are basic places with minimal facilities and hygiene standards, but friendly staff. **Camping** the site along the Tiznit road, is reasonably equipped and has a café.

● **Places to eat** *Hotel les Amandiers* has the best restaurant and the only bar, *Restaurant Etoile du Sud* which caters for large groups, is cheaper and often good; cheaper still are the *Hotel Tanger*; and the *Café Atlas*, the latter with excellent value meals of local specialities. *Snack Sportive* is excellent value in the cheaper range.

● **Transport Road** Most buses from Inezgane and the N pass through Tiznit and along the 7074. There are several buses a day from Inezgane and Tiznit, and even one from Casablanca. Grand taxis, often Land Rovers, connect Tafraoute with Tiznit. Transport out to the villages is difficult. There are 2 buses a day, other options will be hitching, or bargaining with grand taxi drivers.

The Ameln Valley, or Valley of Almonds, is scattered with villages in between areas of irrigated agriculture, producing argane oil (see page 333) and almonds. Many of the men work elsewhere, returning for holidays or retirement, and are known for their participation in the grocery trade. Across the river, reached by bus or taxi, is the village of **Oumesnate**, a large community with some bizarre house designs, notably a number on

Blooming Trees

Snow drifts are common in the Atlas massifs but the drifts of blossom in early spring which clothe the slopes for a second time are much more attractive. There are over 12 million almond trees to delight with their pale pink and fragile white blooms in Jan and Feb. Both roads from Marrakech to Agadir, the road from Agadir to Tafraoute and the whole region fed by the Oued Draa are breathtakingly beautiful at this season. These groves of self-seeded almonds have adapted to the environment, are resistant to drought and cold and provide, despite their low yields, an important source of income. While the early almond blossom here is in sharp contrast to the barren earth the blossom on trees in the oasis gardens has a green backcloth. In addition there are almond plantations especially in the Haouz of Marrakech which are equally beautiful and show greater profits. The almond is Morocco's second most important tree crop and Morocco is the world's fifth largest producer of almonds.

stilts. To the W of this are a series of villages, an enjoyable day's exploration. To the S of Tafraoute is **Agard Oudad**, built below a rock named after Napoleon's horse. From here you should get a guide to show you the '*les Pierres Bleus*'. These are rocks and mountain sides painted in various colours by the Belgian landscape artist Jean Verame, known for performing art projects on a massive scale. This is an impressive and vast piece, one of the truly memorable sights of Morocco, even if it has faded a little since 1984.

Goulimine

Goulimine has become a major stop on the tourist network, a regular excursion from Agadir. This is because of its camel *souq*, on Sat morning, which is, however, nowadays geared almost totally towards the demands of the tourist industry, with the nomadic tribesmen distinguished by their blue clothing, the 'blue men', in dutiful attendance. The market is along the road to Tan-Tan. More genuine, however, are the religious festivals, or *moussems*, held in Jun (at Asrir) and Aug, when Touareg nomads are in plentiful supply. From the 8th century Goulimine was an important trading post on a route swapping Saharan salt and West African gold. From the 12th century the town declined, but still retained some importance, with a large camel market. The town is located in an area of calm wilderness, but it is likely that the traveller will move on fairly quickly. There is a **kasbah** above the market.

• **Accommodation** **E** *Hotel Salam*, Route de Tan-Tan, T 872057, friendly, 20 rms, bar and restaurant; **F** *L'Ere Nouvelle*, Ave Mohammed V, basic, reasonable restaurant; **F** *Hotel Bir Nazarene*, cheap, cold water only. **Camping** signposted from Place Hassan II, is not recommended.

• **Services** In the village there is a bank and post office. Tourist office, 3 Residence Sahara, Blvd d'Agadir, T 872545. The grand-taxi stop is on Place Bir Nazarene, and the café-restaurants on Place Hassan II; nearby is the bus stop.

Detour to Sidi Ifni

Sidi Ifni is one of the strangest towns in Morocco, a crumbling port town with a distinctive Spanish feel, and some unusual architecture. It was occupied by the Spanish from 1476 to 1524, and again from 1860, as a consequence of the Treaty of Tetouan. Sidi Ifni was always an enclave, surrounded by Morocco from 1860-1912 and from 1956-1969, and between 1912 and 1956 by the French Protectorate. The town had a port and an airstrip, and a role as a duty free zone. The economic survival of the town was based on the fact that the border was open to trade. In the 1960s Morocco grew tired of the continuing Spanish presence, and forced Spain into negotiations from 1966. The enclave was returned in 1969. Sidi Ifni is a wonderfully relaxing place to stay and wander for a few days, but after that its ghost town feel can get oppressive.

The **Plaza de España**, renamed Place Hassan II, is the centre of the colonial town, a pleasant garden and fountain surrounded by bizarre Art Deco buildings: the church, which is now the tribunal, the town hall, the Spanish consulate which opens 1 day a month, the *Hotel Belle Vue*, and several others. From there a promenade winds down the cliff to the beach. This is a long and often deserted strip with excellent swimming. To the S is the defunct Spanish port, an odd offshore construction on a concrete island linked to the mainland by a cable car. The Moroccans have built a new port nearby. The main *souq* on Sun is very disappointing. There is a large *moussem* in June.

• **Accommodation** **E** *Hotel Belle Vue*, 9 Place Hassan II, T 875072, an old building, 14 rms in need of decoration, restaurant and bar; **E** *Hotel Aït Ba Hamran*, rue de Plage, T 875267, 20 rms, restaurant and bar, a sad, dead place; **E** *Hotel Suerta Loca*, T 875350, is by far the best in town, friendly, clean, excellent food, with some lovely new rooms overlooking the sea, a popular hang-out in the evening, downhill from Place Hassan II; **F** *Hotel Beau Rivage*, modern, popular bar and restaurant. **Youth hostel**, Complex Sportif, T (10) 3402, 40 beds, kitchen, overnight fee MD15. **Camping** site, signposted from the town centre, is basic.

• **Places to eat** Excellent food at the *Hotel Suerta Loca*, order 2 hrs in advance, otherwise try *Hotel Belle Vue*, *Hotel Beau Rivage*, *Hotel Aït Ba Hamran*, or near the market, the cheap and basic **Café-Restaurant de la Marine**.

• **Bars** The 2 bars are at the *Hotel Belle Vue* and the depressing *Hotel Aît Ba Hamran*.

• **Transport** There are regular grand-taxis between Sidi Ifni and either Tiznit or Goulimine, as well as daily buses to Agadir, Tiznit and Goulimine.

Tan-Tan was the starting point for the Green March into the Spanish Sahara, now incorporated into Morocco as the Western Sahara, albeit with an ongoing conflict with the local Independence movement, the Polisario. The town is a dull administrative centre, with duty-free shops and a fishing port. The blue cloth worn by the formerly nomadic inhabitants of this area is sold in the *souq*. There is a beach 25 km away, with some good fish cafés.

• **Accommodation** Travellers who decide to stay have the choice of the **E** *Hotel Amgala*, Ave de la Jeunesse, T 877308, 29 rms, restaurant; the **E** *Hotel Etoile du Sahara*, 17 rue El Fida, T 877085, clean, 34 rms, restaurant; or the **E** *Hotel Dakhla*, Place Tan-Tan, a satisfactory hotel. Camping possible on beach.

• **Places to eat** *Restaurant le Jardin*, Ave Mohammed V, the most popular place in town.

• **Bank** BMCE, Ave Hassan II, T 877277.

• **Transport** **Air**: there are flights from Aéroport Tan-Tan, Place Blanche, 9 km out of the town, T 877143, 877164, to Laayoune and Casablanca (3 a week), and Agadir (1 a week). The *Royal Air Maroc* office is on Ave de la Ligue Arabe, T 877259. From Tan-Tan the onward options are to Laayoune, or inland to Smara. **Road** There are buses, grand-taxis and Land Rover taxis on from Tan-Tan.

Tarfaya lies SW of Tan-Tan, just off the road to Laayoune. A grand-taxi from Laayoune to Tarfaya takes 90 mins and costs MD40. On the way into the town several wrecked ships are passed. The town is an oppressively quiet place with a few old sand blown Spanish colonial buildings. Spanish from 1916 as Villa Bens, capital of the S zone of their protectorate of Morocco from 1920 to 1956, and prior to that, between 1878 and 1895, it was a British trading post known as Port Victoria. The post office is the prominent building in the centre. The market is near the mosque. The **Dar Mar** is a square structure just off the beach, supposedly British. There is also an abandoned church and colonial buildings. There is not much in the way of facilities in Tarfaya, although there are basic cafés, which do snacks and *harira*, and a few shops. **F** *Hotel-Café Tarfaya* is at the end of the main street near the port.

Laayoune

Laayoune, with a population of 93,875 in 1982 and known before as El Aioun, was the capital of Spanish Sahara, and is the provincial capital under the Moroccans. The Moroccan government, to underline their claim to the region, have carried out an extensive programme of development, establishing facilities and constructing buildings unrivalled S of Agadir, and settling a large population from Morocco in the town, in addition to the big military garrison. Beyond the political curiosity of seeing the effect of post-colonialism, there is little to do in the town. It is, however, a strangely calm place, and not unpleasant to stay in.

ACCESS Hassan I Aéroport is 2 km outside the town, T 893346/7. There are taxis into the town, although it may be necessary to wait a while. For the energetic, it is a manageable walk. The CTM buses arrive on Ave de la Mecque, in the centre, the ONCF buses at the stadium a little further out.

Things to see

The Place du Mechouar is interesting architecturally, a square with large canopies, with an exhibition space commemorating the Green March in 1975, and the modern **Grand Mosque** alongside. There is also a bird sanctuary, the **Colline des Oiseaux**, a calm place with some interesting species, on rue Okba Ibn Nafi, opposite the *Hotel Parador*. The Malhfa, on Blvd Kairouan, off Ave de la Mecque opposite the *Hotel Massira*, is the main market area. Below the town is the lagoon, a beautiful spot, but not for swimming in. See **Travel agents** below for excursions.

Local information

● Accommodation

A *Hotel Al Massira*, 12 Ave de la Mecque, BP 12, T 894225, Tx 28801, comfortable, 72 rms, restaurants, bar, nightclub, tennis and pool, often taken by tour groups; **A** *Hotel Parador*, rue Okba Ibn Nafih, BP 189, T 894500, Tx 28800, 31 rms, small, luxurious, restaurant, popular bar, tennis, good pool.

C *Hotel Nagjir*, Place Nagjir, a fork on Ave de la Mecque, T 894168/9, Tx 28019, with a bar, restaurant, nightclub.

D *Hotel El Alya*, 193 rue Kadi Ghallaoui, T 893133, Tx 20087, 32 comfortable rms, restaurant; **D** *Hotel Lakouara*, Ave Hassan II, near the market, T 893378/9, 40 rms in a sleepy faded establishment.

F *Hotel Rif*, in a square opposite rue Cheikh Maalaouine, T 894369; **F** *Hotel Marhaba*, 36 rms, not very friendly but the best cheap option, clean rms, hot communal showers, roof-terrace, above a café.

● Youth hostel

Complexe Sportif, Sakiat Alhamra, T 3402, 40 beds, kitchen, overnight fee MD15.

● Places to eat

Hotel Parador, rue Okba Ibn Nafih; and the *Hotel Al Massira*, Ave de la Mecque have good restaurants and there are several cheap restaurants on Ave Mohammed V; *Snak Fes* on Ave Hassan II, with reasonable and nourishing food.

● Banks

Banque Populaire, Ave Mohammed V; **BMCE**, rue Mohammed Zerktouni; **Wafabank**, 5 Ave Mohammed V, T 893598.

● Hammam

An experience not to be missed, MD10, spotlessly clean.

● Travel agents and airline offices

Agence Massira Tours International, 20 Ave de la Mecque, BP 85, T 894229, who organize excursions to Tarfaya for fishing, to Laayoune Plas International, 20 Ave de la Mecque, BP 85, T 894229, who organize excursions to Tarfaya for fishing, to Laayoune Plage and to Oasis Lamsaid, and hire out Land Rovers and drivers; *Bureau du Tourisme du Sahara*, Oum Saad, T 894224; *Agence de Voyages Sahara*, rue Kadi Ghellaoui, T 894144. **Royal Air Maroc**, 7 Place Bir Anzarane, T 894071/77.

● Tourist information
Ave de l'Islam, BP 471, T 892233/75.

● Transport
Car hire: **Comptoir Sakia Al Hamra**, Quartier Industriel, Sahat Dchira, T 893345; **Ouled Abdellah**, Assurance Ouled Abdellah, T 893911; **BTS**, T 894224.

Air Hassan I Aéroport is 2 km outside Laayoune, T 893346/7, with flights to Casablanca (1 a day), Tan-Tan and Las Palmas (2 a week), Agadir and Smara (2 a week), Dakhla (1 a week).

Road CTM buses leave from Ave de la Mecque, by *Agence Massira Tours International*, services to Boujdour/Dakhla, Smara/Tan-Tan and Agadir/Marrakech. ONCF services to Agadir and Marrakech, from near the stadium. **Taxi** Grand-taxi from the roundabout at the end of Ave Hassan II, by the market, go to Agadir (MD150) and Marrakech (MD220). For grand-taxis to Tarfaya and Tan-Tan go by petit-taxi across the river to the *police controle* on the road out to the N, and pick one up there.

Around the Western Sahara

Laayoune Plage and Port To get to Laayoune Plage, it will probably be necessary to hire a whole grand-taxi, as the regular services go to the port, which is a distance from the beach. However the beach itself is not very clean. It is possible to stay at the F *Maison des Pêcheurs*. Laayoune Port, which no longer has ferries to the Canary Islands, is a phosphates port located 25 km from Laayoune, MD6 by grand-taxi. It is a sand-swept settlement with a few semi-operational café-restaurants, but little else.

Smara There is little to draw the traveller along this route, apart from a long desert journey, and one is likely to incur considerable police and army suspicion. Smara is a garrison with 2 basic hotels, the F *Hotel Erraha*; and the F *Hotel Sakia El Houria*, and 2 flights a week to Laayoune.

Dakhla For those who wish to continue along the coastal road, there are lorries making the journey to Dakhla, and an ONCF bus service leaving Laayoune at 0745. **Boujdour** has a fishing port and beach. Dakhla is in a beautiful location with impressive beaches and cliffs. It was formerly called Villa Cisneros and was built on a spit protruding from the coast. Today it is a minor military and administrative centre with fishing and surfing.

● Accommodation There is only basic accommodation, including the **F *Hotel Imlil***, near the *souq*; also try the ***Pensión Atlas*** or the ***Hotel Bahia***; there are a basic restaurants around the town. Free camping possible on beach opposite city entrance, secure. Camping also reported 7 km N of town at hot springs.

● Services There is a tourist office at 1 rue Tiris, T 898228, and a travel agent, ***Dakhla Tours***, on Ave Mohammed V, T 141. **Bank**: **BMCE**, Ave Mohammed V. The **Royal Air Maroc** office is on Ave des PTT, BP 191, T 897050.

● Transport Air From Aéroport Dakhla, 5 km from the town, T 897049; flights to Casablanca and Agadir (2 a week) and Laayoune (1 a week). **Road** bus from Laayoune.

Mauritanian border There is a road S of Dakhla to the border with Mauritania. All formalities in Dakhla, allow whole day to cross border, camping at border, customs minimal, convoys to border once/twice a week.

INFORMATION FOR VISITORS

Contents

Before you go

Entry requirements

● Visas

No visas are required for full passport holders of the UK, USA, Canada, Australia, NZ, Canada, Ireland and most EC countries. Obtain a separate passport if the current one has an Israeli or South African stamp in it. On the aeroplane or boat, or at the border, travellers will be required to fill a form with standard personal and passport details, an exercise to be repeated in almost all hotels throughout the country. From the point of entry travellers can stay in Morocco for 3 months.

Visa Extensions will require a visit to the **Immigration** or **Bureau des Etrangers** department at the police station in a larger town, as well as considerable patience. An easier option is to leave Morocco for a few days, preferably to Spain, if not to Ceuta or Melilla.

● Vaccinations

None required unless travelling from a country where yellow fever and/or cholera frequently occurs. It is advised to be up to date with polio, tetanus, typhoid and hepatitis protection. See Health, **page 19**.

● Representation overseas

Algeria, 8 rue des Cèdres, El Mouradia, Algiers; **Australia**, 2 Phillis Lane, North Curl, Sydney, NSW, T 6496019; **Belgium**, Blvd Saint-Michel, 29 Brussels 1040, T 02 7361100; **Canada**, 38 Range Rd, Ottawa, T 2367391; **Denmark**, Oregarrds Allé 19, 2900 Hellerup, Copenhagen, T 624511; **France**, 5 rue le Tasse, 75016, Paris, T 4050 6879; **Germany**, Gotenstrasse 7-9, Badgodesberg 5300, Bonn, T 228 355044; **Netherlands**, Oranje Nassaulaan 1-1075, Amsterdam, T 736215; **Spain**, Serrano 179, Madrid, T 4580950; **Sudan**, PO Box 2042 Amarat, St No 1, Khartoum; **Sweden**, Kungsholmstorg 16, Stockholm, T 544383; **Switzerland**, 22 Chemin François-Lehmann, Grand Saconnex, Geneva, T 981535; **UK**, 49 Queens Gate Gardens, London SW7, T 071 5815001/4627979; **USA**, 1601 21st Street NW, Washington DC 20009, T 202 4627979. **Consulates Spain**, Ave de Francisco 4, Algeciras, T 56673698 and Ave de Andalucía 63, Málaga, T 52329962; **USA**, 437 Fifth Ave, New York, 10016, T 212 7582625.

● Information offices

Many towns have an **Office du Tourisme** (Tourist Office) and a **Syndicat d'Initiative** (Information Office). These are rarely of much use, and will normally only have the fairly general official brochures, and addresses for hotels and restaurants. They may be of most use in arranging excursions and getting the services of an official guide. The national tourist organization, **ONMT**, has offices in **Australia**, 11 West Street, Sydney, NSW 2060, T 9576711; **Belgium**, 66 rue du Marché-aux-Herbes, Brussels 1040, T 027361100; **Canada**, 2 Carlton Street, Suite 1803, Toronto, Ontario M5B 1K2, T 4165982208; **France**, 161 rue Saint-Honoré, Place du Théâtre-Français, 75001 Paris, T 42604724; **Spain**, Calle Quintana 2 (2°e), Madrid, T 5427431; **Sweden**, Sturegaten 16, Stockholm 11436, T 66099; **Switzerland**, Schifflande, 5, 8001

Zurich, T 2527752; **UK**, 205 Regent Street, London, T 071 4370073; **USA**, 20 East 46th Street, Suite 1201, New York NY 10017, T 2125572520.

Specialist tour companies

Alpinschule of Innsbruck, In der Stille 1, A-6161 Natters, Innsbruck, Austria, organize walking tours based on Taroudant. The walks are not too strenuous and participants are taken to and from the walk by Landrover. ***Exodus Walking Explorer***, 9 Weir Road, London SW12 0LT, T 081 675550. 7-23 day treks supported by guides and mules in the High Atlas. Winter treks in the Jbel Sahro. ***Creative Leisure Management***, 4a William St, London SW1 9HL, T 071 2350123 provide a reliable 'Morocco Made to Measure' service and will arrange whatever is required. ***The Best of Morocco***, Seend Park, Seend, Wiltshire, SN12 0NZ, UK, T 380 828533 offer unlimited flexibility using quality hotels. ***Nature Trek***, Chautara, Bighton, Hampshire, offer natural history and bird watching tours in S Morocco. Tutored ***Artscape Painting*** courses in Marrakech and El Kelaa available, contact 18 Hamlet Court Rd, Westcliffe on Sea, Essex.

When to go

Best time to visit

This will depend on requirements. Sun seekers congregate in the N between Apr-Oct and move S in the winter to places like Agadir. For sightseeing, from Marrakech S the heat can be oppressive during the day from June to Sept. Routes from Tanger are busy in summer with returning migrant workers from Europe in overloaded cars and are best avoided as is Tanger itself with day-trippers from Spain. Worst on Wed.

Climate

In general Morocco is pleasant all the year round. Some of the coastal towns can be humid, particularly near rivers. Desert and pre-desert areas are obviously dry and hot, but from Dec to Feb can get cold at night. Equally, whilst the mountain areas are cold at night and during the winter, they can get quite hot during the summer days. Occasional but heavy showers occur turning the dry river beds into dangerous flash floods and snow blocks the high passes in winter. See Climate, **page 199**.

Health

Staying healthy

Morocco is well provided with fairly reliable chemists, dentists, doctors and hospitals, although none are free. Addresses are to be found in this guide book, or via larger hotels, the **Syndicat d'Initiative** or the **Office du Tourisme**. For ambulances T 15. Most standard medicines can be obtained in medium and large-sized towns. In general Morocco is a clean and fairly low risk country – the worst experience being diarrhoea. Tap water is generally good, but the short-term visitor may wish to play safe by buying the very cheap bottled mineral water. Some rivers and oases have bilharzia, making drinking or bathing hazardous. Travel insurance, including coverage for health risks, is advised. Tampons can be bought at general stores in towns and cities.

Further health information

Read the section on Health, **see page 19** and be prepared for some stomach upsets due to heat and a change of diet.

Money

Banking hours

Are 0830-1130 and 1500-1630. In the summer and during the fast month of Ramadan they are 0830-1400. There are also separate *bureaux de change* in the major cities, mainly of **BMCE**, often open for longer hours (0800-2000), which give the same rates of exchange. There are several different banks in Morocco, with **BMCE, Credit du Maroc, Wafabank** and **Banque Populaire** all widespread. The latter is often the only bank in southern towns. Banking in Morocco is a slow, tortuous process, with several different desks for different purposes.

Cost of living

It is possible to live in Morocco for US$20-25 a day. Accommodation, food and transport are all cheap, and there is a lot to see and do for free. Imported goods, notably cosmetics, toiletries and electrical goods, are expensive. Top quality hotels, restaurants, nightclubs and bars are similar to Europe. Rabat, Casablanca and Agadir are the most expensive places while goods in remote rural areas cost more. There are plenty of things to buy in Morocco, and the prices, if you bargain, can be quite reasonable. Sample prices: bottled water MD8, beer MD8, tea/coffee MD4.

Credit cards
These are widely accepted at banks, top hotels, restaurants and shops, but it is wise to check first. *American Express* are represented by *Voyages Schwartz* in Morocco, with limited services.

Currency
The major unit of currency in Morocco is the **dirham** (in this Handbook: MD). 1 **dirham**=100 **centimes**. There are coins for 1 (very rare), 5, 10, 20 and 50 **centimes**, and for 1 and 5 **dirhams**, as well as notes for 5 (quite rare), 10, 50, 100 and 200 **dirhams**. Currency is labelled in Arabic and French. Most transactions are in cash. To the complete confusion of travellers, many Moroccans refer to **francs**, which equal 1 centime, and **reals**, which equal 5 centimes, but these only exist in speech. For exchange rates for June 1994 **see page 9**.

Currency regulations
Foreign currency may be imported freely.

Eurocheques
These are accepted in Morocco, and can be a good way to make sure one will not run out of money. Try at banks with the *Eurocheque* sticker.

Travellers' cheques
These are usable in Morocco, although the traveller may be sent from bank to bank before the appropriate one is found. Use traveller's cheques from a bank/company that will be familiar to the cashiers, and preferably with UK, US, French or German currency, although this is not an absolute rule. Some hotels and shops will exchange travellers' cheques.

Getting there

Air
There are numerous scheduled and charter flights to Morocco, and reasonably convenient and quite cheap flights on from Spain or Gibraltar. A number of airlines fly to Morocco, and flights are fairly cheap, but only when bought outside Morocco. The state airline, **Royal Air Maroc**, is a reliable and not overpriced company which has large international and national networks. Its main services go through **Casablanca**.

From Europe Most of the major European airlines fly to Morocco, including **Air France**, **Iberia** and **British Airways**. The most competitive from UK are normally **KLM**, **GBAir** (75 Regent Street, London W1, T 071 4399584) and **Royal Air Maroc** (205 Regent Street, London W1, T 071 4394361). The latter also has flights from Amsterdam, Athens, Barcelona, Bastia, Bordeaux, Brussels, Copenhagen, Dusseldorf, Frankfurt, Geneva, Lisbon, Lyon, Madrid, Málaga, Marseille, Milan, Munich, Nice, Paris, Rome, Stockholm, Strasbourg, Toulouse, Vienna and Zurich. **Air France** and **Royal Air Maroc** offer cheap flights from Paris. Charter flights or package holidays bought in Europe can be a cheap alternative, particularly to Tanger or Agadir.

Fly-boat It is possible to get a cheap flight to Gibraltar, Almería or Málaga, and then continue by boat to Melilla, Ceuta or Tanger. **GBAir** have London-Gibraltar-Morocco flights. **GBAir** flights can be booked in Morocco at their Tanger office, 83 rue de la Liberté, T 935211, or via **Menara Tours** in either Casablanca or Marrakech. Flights to Málaga are particularly cheap if one shops around and takes a standby.

From the Americas **Royal Air Maroc** flies between Casablanca, and Montreal, New York and Rio de Janeiro.

From Africa and the Middle East In North Africa all the national carriers fly to Casablanca. **Royal Air Maroc** runs regular services between Casablanca and major cities in the other countries, including 14 a week from **Algiers**, 8 a week from **Tunis** and **Tripoli**, 2 a week for **Benghazi** and **Cairo**, and a weekly service for **Oran**. From the Canary Isles (Las Palmas) there are services to and from Agadir, Casablanca, Marrakech and Laayoune. There are 3 flights a week between Casablanca and **Nouakchott**. Elsewhere in Africa there are flights from Casablanca to Abidjan, Bamako, Conakry, Dakar and Libreville, and in the Middle East to Abu Dhabi, Istanbul, Jeddah, and Riyadh.

Train
Train travel to Morocco is a relatively cheap option for those under 26, and a convenient way to tie in a visit to Morocco with a short stay in Europe. An **InterRail** ticket bought in any participating European country includes the Moroccan train network, and a reduction on the Algeciras-Tanger ferry. Travelling through Spain often entails extra cost, as there are supplements to be paid on a number of trains. **British Rail International**, London Victoria Railway Station, T 071 8342345, and

Eurotrain, T 071 7303402, sell tickets from London Victoria to Tanger, including both ferry crossings. These are very reasonably priced, and enable the traveller to stop off at any point on the fixed route for any length of time within the 2 month validity of the ticket. Rail entry from Europe is only through Tanger. Rail entry from Algeria in more settled times is at Oujda.

● Road

Car See below for car ferries. It is compulsory to have full and valid Green Card Insurance, and this will be inspected at the border, along with the vehicle registration document and International Driving Licence (or national licences). The car will be entered in the drivers' passport, and checked on leaving the country, to ensure that it has not been sold without full taxes being paid. It should be noted that some car hire companies do not allow customers to take cars into Morocco from Europe. The minimum age of driving is 21. Car entry is not possible from Mauritania. From Algeria the crossing points are Oujda and Figuig.

Bus There are regular coach services to Morocco from Paris and other French cities. From London Victoria there is **Eurolines/Iberbus** to Algeciras, which takes 2 days, T 071 7300202. Coach services use the Algeciras-Tanger ferry.

● Sea

The many sea routes from Europe to Morocco provide relatively cheap travel. The principal passenger arrival point is Tanger. Other scheduled passenger services run to the Spanish enclaves of Ceuta and Melilla, as well as to the Moroccan towns of Mdiq, near Ceuta, and Nador, near Melilla. There is a commercial port at Casablanca, and some cruises stop here but there are no scheduled services.

Between Algeciras and Tanger The main ferry route between Spain and Morocco is the Algeciras/Tanger passenger and car service, operated jointly by **Transmediterranea** and **Isleña de Navegación**. This is very convenient for onward rail or bus transport from Tanger. Algeciras has regular bus services from Gibraltar and Málaga, both towns having cheap flights from UK. Algeciras has a train service from Madrid, and tickets can be bought from London to Algeciras or Tanger. The ferry terminal, near the town centre, has a ticket office and money changing facilities. There are similar facilities in the Tanger terminal. The ferry takes 2-3 hrs, and there are normally between 6 and 10 services a day, either way, with some seasonal variation. **Note** that although services usually leave late one should allow at least an hour to clear the police and customs, particularly in Tanger. Be cautious about scheduling onward journeys on the same day, in view of the delays. The passenger fare is currently around MD196/2700 Ptas (MD98/1350 Ptas for children), with cars from MD618/8500 Ptas and motorbikes and bicycles from MD75/2400 Ptas. Dependent on exchange rates, it is likely to be cheaper to buy a return in Tanger than two singles, if applicable. Tickets can be bought at either terminal or at numerous agents in both towns.

The ferries are often dirty and crowded with the usual bars, restaurants, cafés and lounges, as well as a *bureau de change*. When travelling from Algeciras to Tanger all passengers must have their passports stamped by Moroccan border police whilst on the boat. **NB** This ferry service is booked solid in summer.

The **hydrofoil service** runs Mon-Sat and takes 1 hr. Contact **Transtour**, T 956 665200.

Between Algeciras and Ceuta The connection between Algeciras and the Spanish enclave of Ceuta, which lies E of Tanger and N of Tetouan, is cheaper and quicker, but onward travel from Ceuta is more difficult than from Tanger, and accommodation is more expensive. Ferries are run by the same companies from the same terminal in Algeciras. There are between 6 and 9 services every day except Sun, when there are 5, the journey taking 1½ hrs. Passenger fares are from MD130/1,650 Ptas, children 4-12 half price, car fares from MD516/7,500 Ptas, bicycles and motorbikes from MD128/1,700 Ptas. It is possible to buy tickets at either terminal or from numerous agents. Ceuta is a comfortable if unexciting place to stay, but more expensive than Morocco, except for some duty free goods. There is a reasonable number of transport options from the scruffy town of Fnideq, just in Morocco, and there is a *bureau de change* at the border. It can take a while to pass through the border. There is also a faster (½ hr) but more expensive and slightly less frequent **hydrofoil**, 6 Mon-Sat, 4 on Sun, between Algeciras and Ceuta. Contact T 956 509139.

Between Málaga or Almería and Melilla A long distance service from Málaga and Almería, leaving at 1300, plies to the Spanish enclave of Melilla. Fares are from 2,530 Ptas for passengers, 7,300 Ptas for cars, and 2,900 Ptas for bicycles and motorbikes.

Between Sète and Nador or Tanger **Comanov** run car and passenger ferry services from Sète in the S of France to Nador, adjacent to Melilla. Passenger fares are from MD1,390 (Nador) and MD1,200 (Tanger), car fares from MD1,700 (Nador) and MD1,340 (Tanger), bicycles and motorbikes from MD620 (Nador) and MD490 (Tanger). These are relatively luxurious services, running every 4 days between Nador and Sète from June to Oct, and daily between Tanger (leaving 1800) and Sète (leaving 1900). **Comanov** are at 7 Blvd de la Résistance, Casablanca, T 302412, F 308455; 43 Ave Abou El Alaâ El Maâri, Tanger, T 932649, F 932320; Immeuble Lazaar Beni Enzar, BP 89, Nador, T 608538, F 608667; **SNCM Ferryterranee**, 4 Quai d'Alger, BP 81,34 202 Sète Cedex, France, T 67747055, F 490545; **Compagnie Charles Leborgne**, 6 Quai François Maillol, 34 202 Sète Cedex, France, T 67745055, F 67743304. Bookings also through **Continental Shipping and Travel**, London, T 071 4914968.

Between Gibraltar and Tanger Direct services from Gibraltar run daily and take 2½ hrs. 1994 fares were MD280 single. Tickets can be purchased in Tanger from **Med Travel**, Ave Mohammed V, T 935872/3, and in Gibraltar from **Seagle**, 9B George's Lane, T 76763. Bland's day tour travellers take precedence over booked return tickets – be warned.

Between Gibraltar and Mdiq There is a weekly (Thur) catamaran service in summer between Gibraltar and Mdiq, a small town S of Ceuta, with regular transport to Tetouan. Contact **Seagle**, 9B George's Lane, Gibraltar, T 76763.

Between Faro and Tanger There are 3 car and passenger ferries a week from Faro, in Portugal, to Tanger, taking 9-10 hrs. Contact **ACP Viages**, 49A Rua Rosa Araugo, Lisbon, T 01 560382, or **Comanov**, 43 Ave Abou El Alaâ El Maâri, Tanger, T 932649, F 932320.

● Customs

Visitors may take in, free of duty, 400 grammes of tobacco, 200 cigarettes or 50 cigars and such personal items as a camera, binoculars, a portable radio receiver, computer or typewriter.

Prohibited items There are severe penalties for possession of or trade in narcotic drugs: 3 months to 5 years imprisonment and/or fines up to MD 240,000.

When you arrive

● Airport taxes

There are no airport taxes. On entry into Morocco vehicles and larger electronic equipment will be entered in the passport, to prevent re-sale without paying taxes which can be as high as 100%.

● Airport information

The principal destination is the much improved **Aéroport Mohammed V**, which is at **Nouasseur**, 30 km SE of Casablanca, T 339100. From here there are trains to Casablanca and regular bus services to both Casablanca (40 mins) and Rabat (90 mins). They drop and collect passengers at the CTM terminal in Casablanca, off Ave des Forces Armées Royales, and in Rabat in front of the *Hotel Terminus*, on Ave Mohammed V. There are also more expensive grand-taxi services. The airport terminal includes a restaurant, bar, post office, a **BMCE** *bureau de change* and agencies for the larger hotels, tour companies and car hire companies.

Agadir is the next major destination as large numbers of tourists fly there direct. **Aéroport Agadir Al Massira**, is a modern construction 28 km from the city, T 839002, with connections by bus and grand-taxis.

Other important international airports are: **Aéroport Marrakech Menara**, 6 km from Marrakech, undergoing improvements; **Aéroport Les Angads**, 15 km from Oujda; and **Aéroport Boukhalef**, 15 km from Tanger. There are also some international flights to **Aéroport Charif Al Idrissi**, Al Hoceima; **Aéroport Fes Saiss**, Fes; **Aéroport Hassan I**, Laayoune; **Aéroport Taorirt**, Ouarzazate; and **Aéroport Rabat-Sale**, 10 km from Rabat. All airports are well-connected by buses or grand-taxis.

● Conduct

Morocco is more relaxed than many Muslim countries and therefore it is possible to wear clothing that exposes arms and legs in coastal resorts. However, to minimize hassle, women are advised to cover themselves away from the hotel compounds at social occasions and visits in traditional rural areas. Full coverage of limbs and head is recommended when travelling in the heat. Winter temperatures can be low and night temperatures in the desert and at altitude are low all the year round so carry extra garments.

● Electricity
Most of the country runs at 220V, although some areas are on 110V. International adaptors are a good investment.

● Hammam
These are public baths where most Moroccans wash, relax and gossip and are worth a visit. The **hammam** is a succession of hot steamy rooms with plentiful water, and masseurs and assistants on hand. Men and women will either have separate premises or hours. Foreigners may be less welcome in some hammams than others – it is worth asking at the hotel, youth hostel or campsite for a recommendation.

● Hours of business
Working hours are normally 0900-1200 and 1400-1800. There are different working hours for summer and during Ramadan. On Fridays the midday break is normally longer to allow for prayers.

● Laundry
Laundries and dry-cleaners are available everywhere, cheapest in the medina, where they are speedy but of varying quality. Hotels are expensive but reliable.

● Monuments – entry
Entrance fee to government run sites is always MD10 – except at Volubilis.

● Official time
Morocco follows GMT all year round, 1 hr behind the UK and a surprising 2 hr behind Spain in summer.

● Photography
Many people, including Moroccans, dislike being a subject for a photograph, and it is very unwise to photograph women. People like water-sellers, musicians, animal tamers and camel owners expect to be paid for posing while small children will get in the way and then demand remuneration. Take great care near military or sensitive installations. Protect your camera from the dust and heat. Films are available for purchase in Morocco, but can be of variable quality. If possible purchase where the film has been properly stored or only recently imported. In selecting films and the camera to take remember that the sunlight is bright and the main subjects are likely to be buildings and scenery.

● Safety
Security Morocco is neither the most dangerous nor the safest country in the world. If reasonable precautions are taken the risk can be minimized. It is advisable never to carry valuables or large amounts of cash and to carry money and documents securely, ie. in a money belt. Camp-sites are notoriously insecure places while hotels are normally much better. Never leave valuables in the car, and preferably entrust the car to a **gardien** for a small fee. Most importantly travellers should trust their personal instincts, and not go anywhere with anyone who seems suspicious or overly keen.

Airports and ports can be chaotic due to complicated bureaucracy and lack of order. Baggage is normally hastily checked. All papers should be correct otherwise even greater delays will occur. The traveller often arrives confused and insecure, particularly at the bustling port of Tanger, and this a favourite time for pickpockets and con-artists to strike. Do not believe a word the latter say, but go immediately to the hotel, railway or coach station already chosen.

Guides Travellers are likely to be hassled by guides often posing as 'students' or 'friends', and extreme caution should be taken in accepting help from these people, as it will lead to considerable expense (whatever the initial fee) and possible personal danger. The worst places are Tanger, Fes, Meknes and Marrakech. These people are often extremely skilled at the job, and have considerable linguistic abilities. Travellers will be well advised to use an official guide from the tourist office or manage without. The only medinas where guides may be necessary are Fes, Meknes and Marrakech. A much less threatening variation on the ***faux guides*** is the children in S villages who ask for money or presents, or who offer their help in exchange for a small remuneration.

Hashish Throughout Morocco, although particularly in the Rif, travellers will be offered hashish. It should be borne in mind that hashish dealers often tip off the police, and that there are considerable risks involved, despite the attraction of the cheap prices. The charity **Prisoners Abroad** supports a number of travellers who succombed to the temptation – be warned.

Police Throughout the country the police are normally helpful to tourists, and there is no problem approaching them for directions. The traveller will have more dealings with the grey-uniformed **Sûreté** than the khaki-uniformed **Gendarmerie**.

Women should be careful when travelling in

Morocco, and preferably should not travel alone. Hassle from Moroccan men can be quite heavy-duty.

Shopping

Many of the main tourist towns now have fixed price shops, although some of these can be negotiated despite the label. The best is the ***Ensemble Artisanal***, run by the government, which is normally a good guide to the range of products available, although it is a bit expensive. The best bargains, and the more authentic experience, are to be had in the ***souqs***, the areas of traditional shops found in most historic cities. Similarly cheap and interesting are the markets which are held on a daily or weekly basis in large villages and towns throughout the countryside, as well as specialist markets in larger urban centres.

Best buys include leather goods, pottery. metalwork and woodwork. Essaouira has excellent carved cedarwood products. Pottery is best in Safi and Fes. In leather, belts and ***baboushes*** (slippers) are cheap. Jewellery was traditionally the preserve of Jews, but despite their emigration good pieces can still be bought. Carpets are excellent and come in a variety of forms, from basic rugs, to vast silk carpets, and reflect regional traditions. It is worth inspecting the weave closely. Chichaoua and Taroudant are good places to buy.

Tipping

It is normal to tip waiters in cafés, restaurants and bars, who often receive a very low basic pay. In some more expensive restaurants service is included in the bill. Tipping is also advisable for porters on buses and trains and in hotels. It is optional with taxi-drivers, but recommended (10%) when the meter is being used.

Do not tip for taxi journeys where the meter is not being used, as the negotiated price will be generous anyway. For handling baggage in hotels tip around MD2-3, MD3-5 on buses and MD5 on trains and in airports.

Weights & measures

Morocco uses the metric system. See conversion table on **page 17**.

Where to stay

Hotels

Rooms are normally easy to find except in some popular places in peak seasons. The most difficult place all year round is Casablanca, where cheap rooms go early in the day. It is wise to reserve rooms in the top hotels in most cities. In almost all hotels, the night's accommodation ends at 1200, although some will be flexible in view of travel plans, and most will look after bags between 1200 and a later departure. On arrival at the hotel it will be necessary to fill a form giving name, occupation, address, date of arrival in Morocco, passport details, etc. Hotels in Morocco cover a wide range from the super luxurious like the *Mamounia* in Marrakech and the *Gazelle d'Or* in Taroudant, to absurdly cheap and small establishments that have little more than a bed and ceiling. At the cheapest end the hotels (also called *auberges* and *pensións* in some places) are basic rather than miserable. Moroccan hotels are classified

Caveat Emptor – The Art Of Bargaining

Most artisanal goods in Morocco are bought by haggling. This is a great skill in Morocco, and quite entertaining to witness, although less entertaining when the purchase price is considered later. There is the potential to be heavily ripped-off. Most dealers recognise the wealth and gullibility of travellers and start at exorbitant prices, so although the final price may seem to have involved the dealer coming down greatly, in fact it is the purchaser who will have paid way above the real price. It is better to be relaxed and get in a conversation with the dealer, taking time and inspecting the good closely. Do not be pressurised, and do not believe anything that the dealer says, such as the price he bought it at, etc. Do not feel guilty about ripping the dealer off, for one can be sure that he will not sell without making a profit. It is wise to compare prices and quality in a number of shops before buying. Walking away from the dealer normally brings the price down rapidly. It may be possible to exchange Western electronic goods or clothing for Moroccan goods and make a good deal.

HOTEL CLASSIFICATIONS

AL US$90+. International class luxury hotel. All facilities for business and leisure travellers are of the highest international standard.

A US$75-90. International hotel with air conditioned rooms with WC, bath/shower, TV, phone, mini-bar, daily clean linen. Choice of restaurants, coffee shop, shops, bank, travel agent, swimming pool, some sport and business facilities.

B US$60-75. As **A** but without the luxury, reduced number of restaurants, smaller rooms, limited range of shops and sport.

C US$40-60. Best rooms have air conditioning, own bath/shower and WC. Usually comfortable, bank, shop, pool.

D US$20-40. Best rooms may have own WC and bath/shower. Depending on management will have room service and choice of cuisine in restaurant.

E US$10-20. Simple provision. Perhaps fan cooler. May not have restaurant. Shared WC and showers with hot water (when available).

F under US$10. Very basic, shared toilet facilities, variable in cleanliness, noise, often in dubious locations.

in a number of starred bands from 5 down to 1B, with the remainder, the cheapest places, unclassified. It is advisable to see the room before agreeing to stay in all but the 5 and 4 star hotels. Unclassified hotels are often found in the old part of town, the medina, where there is often a problem with water. The more expensive hotels are normally in the new town.

● Youth Hostels (auberges de jeunesse)

11 in total affiliated to the IYHA, and a cheap option for anyone with a YHA card, are found in the largest cities: Casablanca, Rabat, Fes, Meknes and Marrakech, as well as at Azrou in the Middle Atlas and Asni in the Grand Atlas. The headquarters is in Meknes, in Ave Oqba Ibn Nafi. Overnight charge MD10-25, use of kitchen MD2, maximum stay 3 nights, priority given to people under 30 years of age. Opening hours: summer 0800-1000, 1200-1600 and 1830-2400; winter 0800-1000, 1200-1500 and 1800-2230.

● Refuges

In the High Atlas there are a number of refuges run by *Club Alpin Français* which have basic sleeping and cooking facilities.

● Camping

Sites are found all over Morocco. Security can be a problem, as can the climate. Sites are often poorly equipped, and far from the town centre, whilst they are often not much cheaper than basic hotels.

Food and drink

● Food

Most Moroccan towns have cafés, some of which offer *croissants*, *petit-pain* and cake, occasionally soup and basic snacks. Restaurants will be divided into **medina** and **ville nouvelle** establishments, the former cheap, basic but not terribly unhygienic, the latter normally more expensive. Restaurants may be limited to larger settlements, those with a tourist appeal, or on major roads. Fast food joints are beginning to appear in larger cities. **Laiteries** and snack bars will make up sandwiches to order. Beyond these options there are food stalls and open air restaurants in every village, town and city serving various types of soup (normally the standard broth, *harira*), snacks and grilled meat. The best place for the adventurous open air eater is the Djemaa El Fna square in Marrakech, which is full of stalls in the evening. Another good place is near the port in Essaouira, where fresh fish are grilled. Obviously there is a greater risk of food poisoning with this type of food, so it is better to go for dishes that are cooked as one waits, or that are on the boil.

Moroccan food in restaurants can often be simple, centred around meat, and somewhat dull for vegetarians. Real Moroccan cuisine, in top restaurants, or in houses, is excellent, and worth seeking out. The following are the main specialities:

Harira: a staple soup, the exact composition varying according to availability of ingredients, normally involves vegetables, meat and chick peas. This is a filling and tasty snack available for a few dirhams in most restaurants

RESTAURANT CLASSIFICATIONS

Given the variations in price of food on any menu our restaurants are divided where possible into three simple grades: ♦♦♦ expensive, ♦♦ average and ♦ cheap.

and at many stalls or cafés.

Kebab and Kefta: the main meat in cheaper restaurants are *kebabs*, made of beef, mutton or lamb, which are also called *brochettes*. Minced meat, called *kefta*, is also common. These are often served with chips (*frites*).

Couscous is Morocco's most famous speciality, steamed granules of semolina cooked with various combinations of meat and vegetables. In some houses and restaurants this is reserved for Fri, the holy day, a very approximate equivalent of Sun lunch.

With ***tagines***, meat, fish or vegetables are stewed in a conical ceramic utensil, with combinations of potatoes, olives, lemon, prunes and spices. This very tasty dish is found in the top restaurants and roadside cafés, and will often involve local ingredients.

Pastilla is most famous in Fes. This sweet layered pastry dish usually made with pigeon, saffron and almonds often has to be ordered in advance.

Mechoui involves mutton roasted on a spit, and is often eaten at festivals. In restaurants order in advance.

The speciality of Marrakech is ***Tangia***, a tall ceramic pot in which meat is baked in butter, spices and olives for hours, normally in the embers of the local *hammam*.

Salads are good, although risky, (see Health, **page 22**) in cheaper establishments. The local combination is called, unsurprisingly, *salade marocaine*, there is also *salade verte*, *salade des tomates* and *salade nicoise*. Finely chopped tomato and onion are a popular accompaniment to *kebab* or *kefta*.

Sweets Morocco has good pastries, although the quality varies from *pâtisserie* to *pâtisserie*. Distinctive are the coiled sticky sweets eaten at the daily breaking of the Ramadan fast. Try the yoghourt made in the local *laiterie*. Fresh ***fruit*** is excellent, and cheap, in season. Oranges are particularly cheap, as are prickly pears, sold off barrows.

● Drink

All over Morocco the main drink apart from water is **mint tea** (*thé à la menthe* or *thé marocain*) a cheap, refreshing drink which is made with green tea, fresh mint and masses of white sugar. The latter two ingredients predominate in the taste. **Coffee** is most commonly drunk black and strong, although the preferred strength can be requested. *Café au lait* (with milk) is common. For a half-way version ask for *demi-demi* or *nus-nus*. Prices in cafés are fixed by the government according to the quality. **Fruit juices** are excellent, notably the freshly squeezed orange juice (*jus d'orange*) available in most cafés. Similar, although less common, is grapefruit juice (*jus de pamplemousse*), and lemon juice (*jus de citron*), the latter to be taken with sugar. Altogether different are banana juice (*jus de banane*) and apple juice (*jus de pomme*), as these are in fact a sort of milk shake. Similar, delicious, although a bit less common are almond juice (*jus d'amand*) and avocado juice (*jus d'avocat*). Very good cafés may have strawberry juice (*jus de fraise*), pineapple juice (*jus d'ananas*), raspberry juice (*jus de framboise*), and a mixed cocktail (*panaché* or *mélange*).

Soft drinks are also common and popular, often called collectively *limonades*. There are many varieties, including *Coca-Cola* and *Pepsi-Cola*, both of which seem to taste different in Morocco, and lemonade, such as *7-Up*, *Sprite* and the local *Cigogne*. Still mineral water (*eau naturel*) is almost always *Sidi Harazem* or *Sidi Ali*. There is also fizzy mineral water (*eau gazeuse*).

Despite its Islamic status, Morocco is fairly relaxed about **alcohol** which officially is only for sale to non-Muslims. Imported lager, wine and spirits are readily available. Morocco also makes its own wine and beer, which are of course cheaper. The wine, in red, rosé and white, can often be quite good, particularly *Guerrouane* from Meknes, Morocco's main producing area. There are also some very poor wines. Moroccan beers, *Stork*, *Flag Pils* or *Flag Special* are all inoffensive lagers.

Getting around

● Air

Royal Air Maroc and its subsidiary **Royal Air Inter** serves the country's major cities. The head office is at Aéroport Casa-Anfa, Casablanca, T 02 912000, Tx Marocair 21880 M, F 02 912397. The network includes Agadir, Al Hoceima, Casablanca, Dakhla, Er-Rachidia, Fes, Laayoune, Marrakech, Ouarzazate, Oujda, Rabat, Smara, Tanger, Tan-Tan and Tetouan.

● Train

The **ONCF** rail service is limited by the physical geography and recent development of Morocco. At present the track is single except between Kenitra and Casablanca and delays occur, but in general the service is speedy and reliable, particularly if the traveller picks the special rapid services. Between Casablanca,

	Agadir	Al Hoceima	Beni Mellal	Casablanca	El Jadida	Er Rachidia	Essaouira	Fes	Laayoune	Marrakech	Meknes	Nador	Ouarzazate	Oujda	Rabat	Safi	Tanger
Al Hoceima	1019																
Beni Mellal	467	564															
Casablanca	511	536	210														
El Jadida	419	632	271	99													
Er Rachidia	681	616	375	545	506												
Essaouira	173	887	370	351	252	745											
Fes	756	275	291	289	388	364	640										
Laayoune	649	1740	1116	1160	1066	1330	822	1396									
Marrakech	273	758	196	238	197	510	176	485	922								
Meknes	740	335	278	231	328	346	580	60	1389	467							
Nador	1095	175	628	628	727	510	979	339	1736	822	399						
Ouarzazate	375	992	398	442	399	306	380	687	1024	204	652	816					
Oujda	1099	293	632	635	731	514	983	343	1748	826	403	104	820				
Rabat	602	445	260	93	190	482	442	198	1251	321	138	535	528	541			
Safi	294	792	351	256	157	683	129	545	943	157	486	884	361	888	347		
Tanger	880	323	538	369	468	608	720	303	1529	598	287	1086	811	609	278	625	
Tetouan	892	278	536	385	484	602	736	281	1541	675	258	437	820	555	294	641	57

Morocco: distances by road between major cities (Km)

Kenitra and Rabat there are regular **Trains Navettes Rapides**. For Rabat the train is more convenient than the bus.

The network has 3 branches from Sidi Kacem; S through Kenitra, Sale, Rabat, Mohammedia, Casablanca, Settat and Marrakech; E through Meknes, Fes, Taza and Oujda; N to Asilah and Tanger. A weekly service uses freight lines from Oujda to Bouarfa, on the E flank of the country, N of the Figuig crossing into Algeria. In addition, **ONCF** buses connect with its trains, from Tnine Sidi Lyamani (just S of Asilah) to Tetouan, from Taourirt (in between Taza and Oujda) to Nador, from Khouribga to Beni Mellal, and from Marrakech to Agadir, Laayoune and Dakhla. Most train stations have *consigne* (left luggage depots) but normally only for locked baggage.

1st class compartments are spacious and generally quieter than 2nd class. 2nd class train fares are little more expensive than the Compagnie de Transporte Marocaine, CTM buses, and compartments are very comfortable. 'Economic' compartments are very basic and crowded, but quite feasible for the budget traveller. The trains normally have a drinks and snacks trolley.

● Road

Bus Morocco has a highly competitive bus service. The government company, **Compagnie de Transporte Marocaine (CTM)**, is by far the most reliable and comprehensive. It runs to a fixed timetable. Its buses leave on time and do not dawdle en route. Except for a few so-called 'rapid' services with videos, the private companies are normally cheaper and less comfortable, and far slower. The private companies do however reach some small places which CTM ignores, and will follow more difficult routes, such as the spectacular road over the High Atlas mountains and the famous Tizi-n-Test pass, between Taroudant and Marrakech.

Bus travel is confusing. Some towns have

one terminal for all buses while others have separate terminals for CTM and private companies. Others have different terminals for different lines and destinations. Where tickets do not specify seats it is worth being early to avoid competition for the best places. Luggage will be stowed in the boot or on top of the bus, it is normal to tip the man for this job. For early morning buses it is worth buying tickets in advance.

Most larger towns have local urban buses which are very crowded, when pick-pocketing is a great danger. The buses are cheap, but then so are petit-taxis. The buses are perhaps only necessary for getting around Fes, Marrakech, Rabat and Casablanca, and for visiting outlying sites of interest, beaches and airports.

Bicycles/motorcycles can be hired in the larger towns. Cycling is a tough but rewarding option in Morocco, with 4 mountain ranges to confront, where mountain bicycles are particularly suitable on the pistes. There is no shortage of mechanics for either bicycles or motorbikes, as both are popular with Moroccans. Security will be more of a problem. City centres have **gardiens** who wear blue coats and tin badges and guard cars, motorbikes, mopeds and bicycles, for a small fee (bicycles normally MD1-2). Trains, buses, grand-taxis and trucks will take travellers' bikes for a small fee.

Car hire is relatively easy in Morocco. There are international agencies and smaller and local firms, in most large towns. It is possible to arrange one-way hire. Before leaving the agency check that the car is fully equipped with all the necessary spares. Prices begin at MD400 per day plus MD2 per km or MD900 per day unlimited distance. The cheapest car is almost always the *Renault 4*, which is quite suitable for rough Moroccan roads. See Car hire details town by town.

Grand-taxis run over fixed routes within cities, between different towns and cities, or from urban centres to outlying settlements. There is a fixed price for each route, and passengers pay for a place, with 6 in a Mercedes and 9 in a Peugeot. The taxis wait until they are full, but each passenger has the right to pay for the remaining places in order to leave sooner or have more space.

Between towns, grand-taxis are quicker than trains and buses and normally only a little more expensive. Each town has a taxi rank, where someone will point travellers to the first car leaving for the appropriate destination.

Hitch-hiking is possible, although it usually involves some payment. This is one of the main ways to get around the more isolated mountain and desert areas. Vans and lorries will pick up passengers for a bargained price. **NB:** hitch-hiking is unadvisable for women on their own.

Petit-taxis are used within a town, have a limited range, are normally small or medium sized saloons, and colour coded, blue in Rabat, red in Casablanca and buff in Marrakech. Officially they are metered, with an initial fare (MD1 in Rabat, MD5 in Casablanca) followed by increments for time and distance, and a 50% surcharge in the late evening and during the night. Petit-taxis may pick up to 3 passengers which makes fare calculation confusing. For taxis that are not metered, it will be necessary to estimate one's own fare. As a general rule most city centre journeys should not be more than MD5. Tipping is welcomed. Taxi drivers have very variable standards of French.

Roads Morocco has a good road network, and plentiful petrol stations and mechanics, except in mountainous and desert areas. A 4 wheel drive vehicle is advisable for more adventurous exploration off the major roads in the Sahara and the mountains. Mountain roads are narrow and winding and should be approached with caution. The only fast, wide route is the toll road (cars: MD10) between Rabat and Casablanca. Roads are not heavily congested, there are few private cars, but numerous taxis, buses and lorries that thunder down the roads at dangerous speeds. Driving and parking in town is relatively easy, although some roads within the old medinas are extremely narrow. Employ a **gardien** to guard the car when parking in cities. The only cities with traffic problems similar to western conurbations are Rabat and Casablanca. The overall speed limit is 100 km per hr. Night driving is more dangerous. Always drive with a good spare tyre.

Communications

● Language

The official and predominate language is Arabic. A large minority, particularly in rural regions speak Berber, which has 3 distinct dialects, based in the Rif, the High Atlas and the Sous valley. Many Arabs and Berbers also speak Spanish and French, the latter being the language in which much business and politics is carried out, and the main vehicle for tourists. Street signs are in Arabic and French, and occasionally in tourist towns in English. English is becoming increasingly popular as a foreign language.

● Postal services

Letters to or from Europe can take up to a week. Posting letters is relatively easy, with the *PTT Centrale* of each town selling the appropriate stamps. It is best to post the letter in the box inside or just outside this building as these are emptied more frequently than those elsewhere. For those without a contact address to receive letters, instruct that they should be addressed clearly, with the surname underlined, to: Poste Restante, PTT Centrale, the town, Morocco. Each ***PTT Centrale*** will have a **post restante** section, where letters are kept for a number of weeks. There is a small charge on collection. Post offices are open 0800-1200 and 1500-1800 Mon-Fri in the winter, 0800-1500 in the summer. Some travellers use ***American Express*** offices to collect mail, in Morocco this is c/o *Voyages Schwartz*. Postage costs to Europe are MD3.5 for a letter and MD3.2 for a post card.

● Telephone services

Telephone call boxes are plentiful, they are often very busy, and sometimes out of order. For internal calls put in several MD1 coins and dial the region code , followed by a 6 figure number. For overseas calls, put in at least 3 MD5 coins, dial 00 and wait for a musical sequence before proceeding. Most call boxes only accept the 'silver all over' coins. Calls can also be made at the **PTT Centrale**, or the ***permanence telephonique*** cabins where generally the number is given to the telephonist who dials it and then calls out a cabin number where the call is waiting. This is more expensive than the call boxes and can be a lengthy and frustrating process, particularly when dialling overseas. It is simpler but more expensive to phone from a hotel.

Calling Morocco from abroad the code is **212**.

Regional codes:
02 – Casablanca
04 – Marrakech and Safi
05 – Meknes
06 – Fes and Sefrou
07 – Rabat/Sale and Kenitra
08 – Agadir and the south
09 – Tanger

Fax and telex facilities are available from luxury hotels and the main PTT offices.

Entertainment

● Media

Newspapers Moroccan newspapers are produced in Arabic, French and Spanish. Although some represent opposition parties criticism of the monarchy is rare, as there is strict government control. In French ***Le Matin du Sahara*** and ***Maroc Soir*** are most pro-government, whilst ***L'Opinion***, ***Liberation*** and ***Al Bayane*** are more independent. These newspapers are cheap and give an insight into Morocco and its politics, but will have limited interest for the traveller. Coverage of overseas news is limited. Foreign newspapers are available in larger towns and cities. ***The Guardian*** (International edition) and ***Le Monde*** reach Rabat and Casablanca in the evening, ***Le Figaro***, which is printed in Casablanca, the same morning.

Radio *BBC World Service Radio* broadcasts on short wave (**see page 17** for frequencies), although reception can be difficult in the night and morning. The commercial radio station *MIDI-1* gives news and music in Arabic and French. The state radio service is predominantly in Arabic and French, but has an afternoon slot in English. Northern areas can pick up broadcasts from Gibraltar, Spain and Portugal.

Television Satellite TV in some hotels provides Sky and other overseas channels. The few houses with TVs receive the state run channel, with programmes in Arabic and French. Others who have a decoder can get the commercial TV station.

● Sport

Golf is the favoured sport of the King, and boasts international tournaments. There are excellent courses at Agadir, Rabat, Mohammedia, Marrakech and Tanger.

Hiking There are considerable opportunities for climbing and hiking, and in areas such as the Toubkal National Park in the High Atlas, guides are available. Specialist maps and guides will be useful to hikers.

Hunting and Fishing Wild boar in the countryside around Asni and Amizmiz; partridge and quail in the Ourika valley; pike, perch, roach, carp and trout in lakes and rivers.

Riding is a good way to explore the High Atlas. Riding centres are listed for most towns.

Skiing and mountain sports are being developed in Morocco at a number of sites in the Middle and High Atlas mountain ranges. The best places are the Mischliffen resort near

Ifrane, in the Middle Atlas just S of Fes, and the skiing centre of Oukaimeden, S of Marrakech in the High Atlas. Both have ski lifts and good slopes, as well as equipment for hire and instruction. Mountain Information Centre of Ministry of Tourism, 1 rue Oujda, Rabat, T 7701280, has details of escorted and individual cross-Atlas treks.

Swimming Large towns have municipal pools but these can be crowded. In the summer the luxury hotels are very tempting, with their pools. There are occasional cheaper establishments with facilities. There is some good sea swimming, but beware of currents.

Tennis Morocco has an international tournament in Agadir, and excellent tennis facilities at larger hotels and tennis clubs.

Water sports centres are found in Agadir and Mohammedia. Essaouira is excellent for surfing. Equipment can normally be hired. Salt and fresh water fishing is popular.

● Spectator sports

The major cities have arenas with Basketball, Handball, Athletics and Football. Check the local press for details. Football is seriously popular, with kick-arounds in the most remote locations, and an excellent standard on beaches and in town pitches. The national team qualified for the 1994 World Cup. The national league is strong, with particularly strong teams at Casablanca (WIDAD and RAJA) and Marrakech (KACM).

Holidays and festivals

1 Jan:	New Year's Day
3 Mar:	Coronation of King Hassan II – celebrated with processions/ dancing
1 May:	Labour Day
23 May:	National Day
9 July:	King's Birthday and Youth Day
14 Aug:	Allegiance Day
6 Nov:	Anniversary of Green March
18 Nov:	Independence Day

The dates of the Islamic holidays and the fast, Ramadan, vary each year, as they are calculated according to the moon. Ramadan is strictly observed by most Moroccans, and it is advisable not to eat or drink in public during this period in the daytime. The breaking of the fast each evening is a very sociable and entertaining time, particularly when invited to a house.

Approximate dates in 1995:

1 Feb:	Beginning of Ramadan
4/5 Mar:	Aïd es Seghir (end of Ramadan)
10/11 May:	Aïd el Kebir
31 May:	Islamic New Year
9 Aug:	Prophet's Birthday

There are a number of large **moussems**, or religious festivals, each year throughout the country. The following are worth seeing:

Tafraoute	Feb – almonds
Immouzer des Ida Outanane	Apr – honey
Moulay Bousselham	May
Goulimine	Jun
Sefrou	Jun – cherries
Setti Fatma (Ourika)	Jul
Moulay Abdellah (El Jadida)	Aug
Moulay Idriss	Sept
Imilchil	Sept – Berber marriages

Further reading

● Books

Anthropology and society Crapanzano, V (1980) *Tuhami: Portrait of a Moroccan*, University of Chicago Press; Deshen, S (1980) *The Mellah Society*, University of Chicago Press; Dwyer, K (1982) *Moroccan Dialogues: Anthropology in Question*, John Hopkins University Press: Baltimore; Gellner, E (1969) *Saints of the Atlas*, Weidenfeld & Nicolson: London; Mernissi, F *Beyond the Veil*, London, Al-Saqi; Warnock, E *A Street in Marrakech*, Doubleday; Westermarck, E (1926) *Ritual and Belief in Morocco*, MacMillan: London, 1926.

Archaeology and monuments Landau, R (1969) *The Kasbahs of Morocco*, Faber and Faber: London; Burckhardt, T (1992) *Fez: City of Islam*, Islamic Texts Society: Cambridge; Paccard, A, *Traditional Islamic Craft in Moroccan Architecture*, Editions Atelier; Parker, R (1981) *A Practical Handbook to Islamic Monuments in Morocco*, Baraka Press: Virginia.

Food Wolfert, P *Good Food from Morocco*, John Murray.

Historical travelogues Cunninghame-Graham, R.B. (1898) *Maghreb el Acksa: A Journey in Morocco*; Harris, W (1921) *Morocco That Was*, Eland Books; Ibn Khaldoun (1967) *The Muqaddimah: An Introduction to History*, Routledge, translated from the Arabic, London; Lewis, W (1983) *Journey into Barbary*, Black Sparrow Press: Santa Barbara; Maxwell, G (1983) *Lords of the Atlas* Century; Meakin, B (1901) *The Land of the Moors*, London; Wharton, E (1920) *In Morocco*, MacMillan: London.

History Abun-Nasr, J.M. (1971) *A History of*

the Maghreb in the Islamic Period, Cambridge University Press; Barbour, N (1965) *Morocco*, Thames and Hudson.

Politics Amnesty International (1989) *Morocco File*, Amnesty International: London; Hodges, A (1983) *Western Sahara: the Roots of a Desert War*, Croom Helm; Rogers, P.D. (Reprinted 1989) *A History of Anglo-Moroccan Relations*, London.

Short stories and novels Bowles, P (1982) *Points in Time*, Arena; Bowles, P *Sheltering Sky*, Granada; Bowles, P *Their Heads are Green and Their Hands Are Blue*, Abacus; Bowles, P *The Spider's House*, Arena; Bowles, P *Two Years Beside the Strait: A Tangier Journal, 1988-89*, Peter Owen; Bowles, P *Without Stopping*, Papermac; Burgess, A *Earthly Powers*, Penguin; Charhadi, D *A Life Full of Holes*, Grove Pres; Chraibi, D (1972) *Heirs to the Past*, Heinemann: London; Choukri, M (1987) *For Bread Alone*, Grafton: London; Gysin, B *The Process*, Paladin; Hughes, R (1979) *In the Lap of the Atlas*, Chatto & Windus: London; Jallounn, Tahar Ben (1988) *The Sand Child*, 1988, Quartet.

Travel and hiking Brown, H *Great Walking Adventure*, Oxford Illustrated Press; Collomb, R.G. (1987) *Atlas Mountains*, Goring: West Col.; Peyron, M *Grand Atlas Traverse*, Goring: West Col.; Smith, K *Atlas Mountains: A Walker's Guide*, Cicerone Press; Winter, Bert and Mabel (1989) *The Rogues' Guide to Tangier*, Tanger.

Travel accounts Canetti, E (1978) *The Voices of Marrakech*, Marion Boyars; Mayne, P *A Year in Marrakech*, Eland Books.

● Maps and town plans

Simple town plans are printed in the brochures available from tourist offices, others are available from street kiosks in Tanger, Rabat, Casablanca, Fes, Meknes, Marrakech and Agadir. Maps of Morocco as a whole are best bought before reaching the country, notably from *Stanfords* in Long Acre, London, T 071 8361321. Try the *Michelin* or the *Hildebrand* road maps. Topographic maps suitable for hiking are sometimes available from the **Division de Cartographie**, Ave Moulay Al Hassan, Rabat. Others are sold in the hiking base, Imlil.

MAURITANIA

CONTENTS

MAPS

INTRODUCTION

Most of Mauritania is arid sand desert and most of its small population were until recently nomadic. Today the settled majority live in the two main coastal towns of Nouakchott and Nouadhibou, in scattered desert towns, or in villages in the wetter southern region near the Senegal river. Culturally it is a transitional region being partly Arab and partly African. There is very little physical provision made for the traveller but those who are adventurous enough to place Mauritania on their itinerary will be rewarded with a dramatic travel experience.

Basics

OFFICIAL NAME al-Jumhuriyah al-Islamiyah al-Muritaniyah (Islamic Republic of Mauritania)

NATIONAL FLAG Green field with large crescent and star both yellow, placed centrally.

OFFICIAL LANGUAGE Arabic

OFFICIAL RELIGION Islam

INDICATORS *Population* 2.1 million; *Urban* 48%; *Religion* Muslim 99.4% (mainly Malekite), Christian 0.6%; *Birth rate* 49 per 1000, *Death rate* 19 per 1000, *Life expectancy* 43/48; *GNP per capita* US$510.

Environment

Land

Mauritania has a surface area of 1,030,700 sq km, more than twice the size of neighbouring Morocco but half the size of Algeria. It spreads 1,287 km from N to S and 1,255 km from W to E. Its coastline on the Atlantic runs for 666 km from the delta of the Senegal River to Cap Blanc in the N.

Borders

Mauritania has lived uneasily in its national borders, surrounded by more powerful neighbours. Morocco is a key influence in the N through its occupation of the Western Sahara and until recent years also had territorial claims on Mauritanian territory. Mauritania gave up all claims to, and withdrew from, the Western Sahara in 1979. Mauritania has no border disputes with Algeria in the NE, though Morocco has frequently claimed that Saharoui forces have operated from Algerian territory through Mauritania in their guerrilla war. There is a long international border with Mali which is geometric and permeable. In the S, Mauritania's uneasy

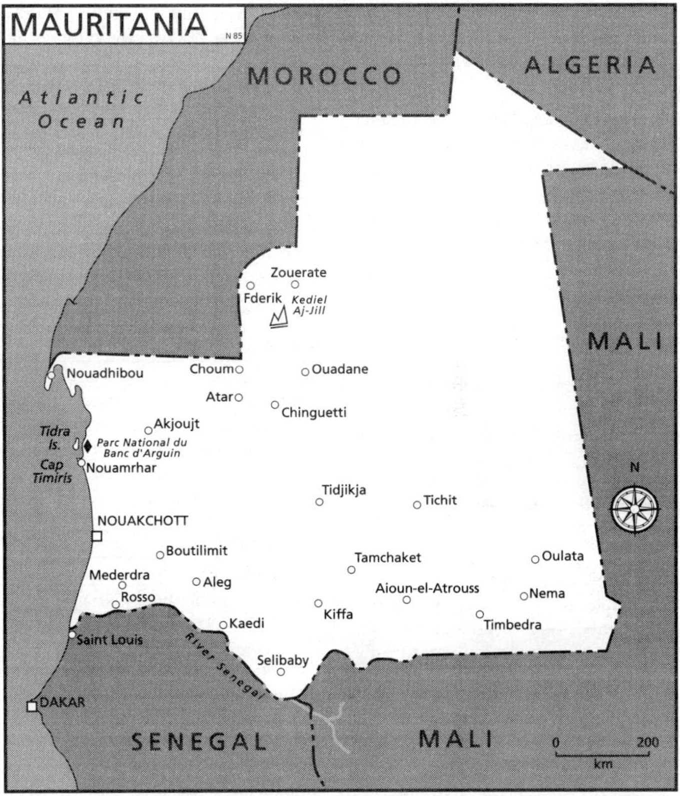

border with Senegal runs along the N bank of the Senegal River. The country's position as a residual Saharan territory between North Africa and black Africa is reflected in the uncertain border situation, its poor allocation of resources and the many claims by foreign interests upon its territory.

Major regions

The landscape in Mauritania is unspectacular in respect of altitudes, especially in comparison with Morocco and Algeria. It is formed by 3 large regions of rather uniform relief. In the N is a vast territory of low altitude, broken only by the occasional rocky ridge and sand covered areas where dune series are aligned roughly NE-SW. The highest point in the region is the peak of **Kediel Aj-Jill** at 915m. In the central zone, extending E to the border with Mali, is a vast basin where the rock series form scarp slopes facing towards the centre separated by gravel plains. Sand dune cover, in places highly ridged and attaining heights of 90m, is general in this area, with low points where salt lakes are found. The interior is at altitudes of little more than 220m with the coastal plains below 45m. The Mauritanian S is a narrow strip made up of the basin of the Senegal River, with richer sedimentary soils. Overall the topography is constrained, with the bulk of the country lying well below 100m.

Rivers

The arid centre and N carry few streams other than temporary *wadis* in spate after storms. Most drainage is internal to salt lakes or indeterminate seepage areas. Very little water reaches the sea. The exception to this is the S where the Senegal River drains the better-watered Mauritanian side of the basin in streams such as the Gorgol Al-Abiad and the Wadi Guélaour. The Senegal River is entirely within Senegalese territory and cannot be counted as a Mauritanian river but is considered as an international resource shared by member states of the OMVS (l'Organisation pour la mise en valeur du fleuve Sénégal), Guinea, Mauritania, Mali and Senegal.

Climate

Other than the region of the Senegal River valley, Mauritania receives negligible rainfall and is profoundly arid. Rainfall at Nouakchott comes erratically but principally between July and Sept and is less than 150 mm on average. Further N rainfall is even less, an average of less than 125 mm at Atar and 35 mm at Nouadhibou. In the S, the N rim of the Senegal valley at sites such as Kiffa, receive 365 mm on average and the immediate river banks such as Selibaby approximately 390 mm. Most rain in the S falls in summer between July and Sept.

Temperatures in Mauritania are extreme. The coast benefits to a small extent from proximity to the sea as at Nouakchott, though temperatures of 45°C have been recorded there. In the centre and E, Saharan conditions prevail with very hot daytime temperatures but cold nights. The S has more tropical thermal conditions of the savanna type with less extremes both season to season and between day and night temperatures. Maxima run at 25°C in Dec against 30°C in June and minima at 18°C in Dec against 23°C in June at Rosso, for example.

The prevailing winds are the NE trades, which are dry. In summer a shift in wind belts brings South Westerlies to the area and rainfall principally for the S region. Travellers should be ready to cope with the hot dry wind from the E, the **harmattan** in Dec, Jan and Feb, which pushes up temperatures and leads to rapidly diminishing relative humidity.

Flora and Fauna

Animal life is, of course, sparse in the desert but look out for leopards, jackals, antelopes, gazelles and ostriches. The most interesting areas are the coast, and for birdlife particularly visit Parc National du Banc d'Arguin.

Agriculture

Mauritania was a country of nomads. Until recent years and the terrible effects of the Sahelian droughts, it is estimated that 85% of the population was traditionally nomads, semi-nomads and seasonally migrating herdsmen. Thus land use is registered in forms of pasture. The S is savanna grasslands with occasional trees, merging gently into the Sahel, or 'rim' of the Sahara, where thin grasslands and drought resistant shrubs survive eventually fading out N into patchy scrub in areas where annual rainfall averages less than 150 mm per year. Here in the large regions of the centre, N and NE pasture is scant and confined to temporary pastures receiving erratic rainfall or to *wadi* basins. In recent years of drought all the pastures have been depleted by lack of rain and overgrazing.

Land use	(%)
Arable and orchards	0.2
Forests and woodlands	4.3
Pastures and meadows	38.3
Waste and other uses	57.2

Source: *Encyclopaedia Britannica*

Only a tiny proportion of the country is under permanent forms of cultivation – less than one quarter of 1%. The cultivated area is almost entirely in the S region of the Senegal except for pockets of oasis cultivation in the deserts of the centre and N.

Land tenure

In the past the complex land tenure system strongly reflected the hierarchical nature of Mauritanian society. In the case of the nomadic Moors, if pasture was not owned as such, access was determined by the position a given group occupied in the social hierarchy. The dominant warrior tribes collectively controlled most of the nomadic zones, while the few wells that existed were dug and owned by tribes of religious scholars known as *zawaya* who were obliged to provide water for the warriors. A third group, who were mainly herders, paid tribute to the warriors in return for access to water and pasture. The numerous palmeries situated in the oases of Adrar and Tagant were owned by *Zawaya* individuals and families, as were the main zones of cultivation under Moorish control in the S. The oases and fields were tended by slaves and ex-slaves (*haratin*), as the Moors disdained physical labour associated with agricultural work. In the S, in the areas where African groups predominated, elite African lineages owned most of the land.

During the colonial period the tenure system was slightly modified. The French encouraged free access to pasture, and built a large number of wells. The colonial administration did little, however, to change the land ownership system, which persisted into the independence period. Eventually, in 1983, after the devastating droughts of the previous decade, the government introduced sweeping land reforms. These reforms, which were designed to resolve the problems caused by increasing competition over land and water, became the source of considerable inter-ethnic tension.

Potential

Mauritania started its national life at Independence with a very poor and basic economy. However, the raw material resources are promising. In particular iron ore near Zouerate and copper deposits in Akjoujt, could provide the basis for a large scale extractive industrialization programme once political security and management of the economy is improved.

Despite setbacks caused by the drought, and economic mismanagement, the existence of natural resources suggests that the potential for dramatic improvement is considerable. Aside from the resources already mentioned, offshore the fish resources of the Atlantic within the country's economic zone are enormous. At the same time, provision of more reliable water supplies for arable farming offer prospects for the country being able to feed itself. The small population at some 2 million is a constraint on national economies of scale but also means that the state is not yet faced with an insurmountable problem of population growth and numbers.

People

Total population

The population of Mauritania was estimated at 2.1 million in 1992 against 1.86 million in the 1988 census. Growth is averaging about 3.2% per year but tending to rise slightly towards 2.7% as the fertility rate goes up. The crude birth rate is rising and the crude death rate is much improved but life expectancy at 44 years for males and 50 years for females remains poor.

Racial origins

The country's position on the interface between the Wet Equatorial and Arid Sahara zones is matched by its parallel situation as the meeting point for two worlds: one Arabo-Berber, the other African. Today, the Arabo-Berber Moors—who call themselves *bidan* (the whites)—constitute with the *haratin* (ex-slaves mainly of African origin) the majority of the population. They speak *hassaniyya*, an Arabic dialect, and until recently shared a nomadic way of life.

All Moors belong to a particular tribe in a ranked hierarchy. In the pre-colonial period warrior and raider tribes of Arab descent were supreme and tribute and taxes were paid to them by other social groups in return for protection, access to pasture and passage through territory under warrior control. Another powerful social category, known as *zawaya* (marabouts), was comprised of tribes of religious specialists (Islamic scholars, judges, mystics, saints, healers) of Arab and Berber descent. In addition to religious activities, these tribes owned most of the herds and slaves, organized agricultural enterprises, the caravan trade and were responsible for digging many of the wells. A lower rung in the hierarchy was occupied by tribes of *zenaga*, herding specialists.

The French occupation modified the social hierarchy. From the 1950's, tributary payments ceased and many of the *hassan* became involved in herding or commerce. On the other hand, *zawaya* tribes, with a background in religious learning and trade were the first to take advantage of the colonial education system and the commercial opportunities offered by the introduction of the market economy. Although some warrior tribes have considerable power in Mauritania today, all religious leaders, and most politicians and entrepreneurs come from a *zawaya* background.

Apart from a very small minority of Lebanese traders and professionals, of whom some are Christian, the remainder of Mauritania's present day population is composed of several Muslim African minorities—the Halpulaar, Soninke, Wolof, Peul and Bambara. With the exception of the Peul, who are cattle nomads, all the other African groups are by tradition agriculturalists living mainly in the S of the country, along the Senegal River valley, in Gudimaka and in the regions bordering Mali.

The precise demographic breakdown of the different ethnic groups is hard to establish due to the politically sensitive nature of this question in Mauritania. At Independence the *bidan* and *haratin* together made up about 75% of the population. This proportion has increased in recent years with the expulsion of African Mauritanians, and the return of Moors from Senegal during 1989.

Beyond their cultural and linguistic differences each ethnic group shares an adherence to Sunni Islam and follows the Maliki legal school. This common religious tradition and shared religious identity is emphasized in the naming of Mauritania as an Islamic Republic, and is frequently held up as the one key factor uniting the diverse population within the state. Indeed, although the Arabization policies of the Moor elite have become a source of increasing inter-ethnic tension, inter-ethnic religious alliances have remained important.

Distribution & density of the population

A sign of the effects of the drought and modernization is the growing urbanization of the country, with 48% of the population now living in towns and cities in contrast to a mere 25% some ten years ago. The main towns are Nouakchott, the capital, with 393,325 people in 1988, Nouadhibou (formerly called Port Etienne) with 59,198, Kaedi 30,515, Kiffa 29,292 and Rosso 27,783.

A second feature of population distribution is the concentration of more than 90% of people in the S zone where rainfall runs at more than 100 mm per year – roughly S of the Nouakchott-Nema road. Here densities are comparatively high at 5 people per km sq but the national average is a mere 2 people per km sq. There is a slight seasonal bias to population distribution with the semi-nomads gathering in their millet and fruit growing lands of the S for the period of rainfall and agricultural activity but spreading N in search of pasture later in the year. In the N the two plateau areas of Adrar, N of Atar, and Zouerate are centres of small, relatively densely settled, districts.

Age groups

Mauritania, in common with most developing nations, has a youthful population. No less than 44% of Mauritanians is under 15 years of age, 50% in the principal working age group between 15-59 and only 6% 60 years and over.

Literacy

Literacy among adults, probably exaggerated by official statistics, is 34%, with a far greater proportion of men (47%) than women (21%) having had schooling. School participation rates are very low with a mere 10% of children attending at primary level.

Income per head

Mauritania is among the poorest (about 32nd in UN rank) countries of the world with income per head put at US$510 in 1991. While Mauritania seems to have avoided the very worst effects of maldistribution of income, there is a skew that benefits the new urban elite and those of the traditional leadership who also control land and water ownership.

History since Independence

Mauritania became independent in 1960. In many respects, the new state was a French colonial artefact in which different and potentially antagonistic ethnic groups had been thrown together. At the time of Independence the majority Moorish population were divided among themselves: some supported the pre-Moroccan Nahda party, founded in 1958, while others, including the future President Mokhtar Ould Daddah, opposed Moroccan claims on the region and favoured Mauritanian independence. Although a considerable proportion of the African minorities supported Ould Daddah's party, the AJM (l'Association de la Jeunesse Mauritanienne), others pursued an African nationalist line, and looked to the S for their political inspiration.

The Ould Daddah government

Mokhtar Ould Daddah, elected premier in 1959, became president of Mauritania in 1960. He replaced the long standing multiparty system with the PPM (le Parti du Peuple Mauritanienne) which remained the sole legal party until the coup d'état of 1978. Ould Daddah, from a prestigious maraboutic family, was an astute diplomat who, at least initially, attempted to steer a middle course between the demands of Arab and African nationalists. He placed great emphasis on Mauritania as the the link between Arab and African worlds. The first in a series of inter-ethnic conflicts erupted in Nouakchott in 1966 and in subsequent years Ould Daddah also faced protests from Moorish students and trade unionists who demanded reforms including nationalization of the mining industry and the creation of a national currency. After serious unrest in 1968, 1969 and 1971, Ould Daddah introduced a series of reforms, which met the demand of the protesters, many of whom then joined the PPM.

In foreign affairs, the Ould Daddah régime attempted to pursue a non-aligned stance, and enjoyed good relations with most African states. This position was partly imposed by the refusal of virtually every Arab state, except

Tunisia, to recognize Mauritania in 1960. By the end of the decade, however, most Arab régimes, including Morocco, had recognized Mauritania, thus paving the way for the latter's entry into the Arab League in 1973. During the 1970s Ould Daddah, who had enjoyed close relations with Algeria, switched alliances to support Moroccan claims to the former Spanish Sahara. Indeed, Mauritania was persuaded to make its own claim on the S part of the colony – the Rio de Oro or the Tiris Al-Gharbia – and, when Spain withdrew in 1976, Mauritania, after a short period of tripartite administration with Spain and Morocco, took over the Tiris Al-Gharbia.

The Polisario Front, the Western Saharan national liberation movement which, with Algerian backing, was fighting for the right of the Western Saharans to self-determination, decided to direct its major military effort against Mauritania, by far the weaker of the two occupying powers. By 1978, after attacks on Zouerate and even Nouakchott, the Mauritanian government accepted a ceasefire in return for withdrawal from the Tiris Al-Gharbia. The presence of 9,000 Moroccan troops added to the considerable domestic unrest and, in July 1978, Ould Daddah was overthrown by a military coup led by Lieutenant-Colonel Mustafa Ould Saleck. A succession of governments followed, until Colonel Mohammed Khouna Ould Haidallah took power, initially as Prime Minister in 1979, then as President in 1980.

In mid-1979, after a nine month truce, the Polisario Front attacked Mauritania again, forcing the Haidallah government to negotiate a peace agreement – the Algiers Agreement – with the Polisario Front's government-in-exile, the Saharan Arab Democratic Republic, renouncing all claims to the Western Sahara. Mauritania did not actually recognize the Republic until 1984, largely because of Moroccan pressure. Morocco, in response, occupied the region itself and began to support Mauritanian exile groups.

Tensions between the two countries arose intermittently as Morocco extended its control over the Western Sahara during the 1980s, particularly when Morocco's defensive wall system abutted against the railway line from Zouerate to Nouadhibou after 1987. Morocco also regularly accused Mauritania of allowing the Polisario Front's guerrillas to use Mauritanian territory in organizing attacks on Moroccan forces. Relations between the two countries were eventually normalized when both joined the Maghreb Arab Union (UMA), a regional unity agreement signed in Marrakech by Morocco, Mauritania, Algeria, Tunisia and Libya in early February 1989. Earlier, in 1983, Mauritania had joined a mutual support treaty arrangement with Algeria and Tunisia.

Internally the Haidallah régime continued to have constant problems. In spite of introducing a number of reforms including the abolition of slavery, the introduction of the Sharia in 1980, land reform in 1983, by 1984 Ould Haidallah had alienated most Mauritanians. In Dec 1984, the chief-of-staff of the armed forces Colonel Maaouiya Ould Sid'Ahmed Taya took power.

Although initially welcomed by Mauritanians, the Ould Taya régime rapidly ran into problems. Several of Ould Taya's plans, the Arabization programme, closer integration into the Maghreb and wider Arab world, permitting Moor entrepreneurs to buy land in the Senegal River valley, were viewed with great disquiet by African Mauritanians. In 1987, a failed coup attempt on the part of Halpulaar army officers led to 3 executions and life imprisonment for many others. Another alleged coup attempt in 1988 by pro-Iraqi Ba'ath elements in the army was met with further oppression by the régime.

During Ramadan 1989, anti-Moor riots and looting erupted in Senegal. As reports of these reached Mauritania, massacres of Senegalese and other West African nationals took place in Nouakchott and Nouadibou. These in turn led to massacres of Moors and *haratin* in Dakar. The subsequent international airlift repatriated over 200,000 Moors and *haratin* to Mauritania and over 60,000 Senegalese. In the backlash more than 50,000 African Mauritanians, mainly Halpulaar and Peul, took refuge in Senegal. Mauritania and Senegal broke off diplomatic relations, and by early 1990 were on the brink of war. The crisis strengthened the alliance between Mauritania and Iraq, the sole Arab state to lend their unequivocal support to Mauritania during the conflict. In return the Mauritanian government lent its tacit support for Saddam Hussain in the Gulf crisis, a position that led to serious problems with the allies, notably Saudi Arabia and Kuwait who were hitherto principal donors of aid to Mauritania.

In April 1991 Ould Taya, in a bid to shore up his credibility, announced, possibly under pressure from France, his decision to implement a series of democratic reforms.

Modern Mauritania

Government

Mauritania is an Islamic republic. A new constitution was adopted following a referendum in July 1991 which provided for a two chamber national assembly to replace the military rulers in 1992. The new constitution, which aside from references to Islam was largely inspired by the constitution of the French Republic, was approved overwhelmingly in the referendum, although black and Islamist politicians, who had recommended a boycott, accused the government of falsifying the figures. Nonetheless, political parties were allowed to form and elections were promised for the following year. A general amnesty was announced after the referendum for all political dissidents who had opposed the military régime. In subsequent months more than 10 political parties formed, all of whom, except the Islamist party (Umma), who had opposed the referendum, were granted official recognition. The first open presidential elections were held in 1992, in which Ould Taya, the incumbent, defeated Ould Daddah, the younger brother of the former president. The results were contested by the main opposition parties who boycotted the legislative and senatorial elections, allowing Ould Taya's party to dominate the 2-chamber National Assembly. In spite of continuing to question Ould Taya's legitimacy, the main opposition groups agreed to participate in local municipal elections in Jan 1993.

Economy

Traditional agriculture

As many as 90% of the Moors were engaged in various forms of pastoral nomadism until the early 1970s. During the droughts of the 1970s, many herds, particularly camels, were sold at rock bottom prices to urban based entrepreneurs who hired the former nomads as salaried herders. A fair proportion of the country's 4.2 million sheep, 3.3 million goats, 1.4 million cattle and 920,000 camels remains, however, in the hands of nomads. Camel nomads are nowadays mainly found in the N and E, while cattle nomads, mainly Peul, are found in the Assaba and Gorgol regions. The Sahelian drought reduced animal numbers by an estimated 45% but there has since been a recovery. The nomadic herdsmen retain as many animals as they can and dispose of them only when they need money or when the pastures will no longer support the herds. The animal trade can be seen at Kaedi, Kiffa, Timbedra and Nema where the dealers and exporters are centred. In recent years the government has attempted to rehabilitate and modernize the pastoral sector and the World Bank has funded a project for pastoralist associations.

The country is not self-sufficient in grain and the loss of farmers from the land during the drought and the fighting by Polisario in the N made the situation worse. In the S, sedentary rainfed or flood based agriculture is undertaken by *haratin* or African farmers in the Senegal River belt, where the main crops are millet, vegetables and pulses. In the Adrar and Tagant date palm oases continue to produce important harvests. The palmeries are owned by Moors but tended by *haratin* who keep a share of the produce and are nowadays often paid a salary. Farming in the N is possible only with irrigation water withdrawn from cistern water-stores or from wells dug into the beds of *wadis*.

Modern Agriculture

Some attempts have been made to improve the quality of pastoralism. The French colonial administration set up wells and fodder points in the N zone to help ensure fewer disputes over land and water. A veterinary service was also set up which brought about significant improvements in the quality of animals. Some small scale development works were attempted in the oases and a rational system of marketing and taxation was established. Some of this structure was lost as a result of Independence and the drought. The new government of Mauritania attempted to pursue food self-sufficiency as a goal and concentrated its efforts on the Senegal River area. Rice became the main crop on the 300,000 ha Golgol project which used water drawn from the Senegal River at Kaedi. The construction of a series of dams in the early 1980s made irrigated agriculture possible on a wide scale and attracted the interest of Moor entrepreneurs. Tensions between the latter and black farmers have been a major source of ethnic unrest in recent years. In spite of the introduction of irrigated agriculture Mauritania still spends over 30% of its available foreign exchange on imported foodstuffs.

Agricultural production 1991

	(tonnes)
Millet and sorghum	63,000
Rice	52,000
Pulses	21,000
Dates	14,000
Vegetables	8,000
Maize	1,000

Source: *FAO*

Energy/petroleum

Mauritania produces neither coal nor petroleum and its electricity output of 123 million kwh is produced with imported fuels. A refinery produces 730,000 tonnes per year of petroleum products, inadequate to fulfil domestic demand. Imports of crude oil and products account for 7% of the country's total import bill.

Economic plans

A series of economic development plans has been adopted by independent Mauritania, beginning in 1963 with the first 4-year plan. Funds for the plan came from revenues earned from mining operations and from foreign aid, notably from Spain and China. The plan went far from smoothly and by 1966 it became inoperative. In practice, the various plans involved taking on foreign debt and the need for state management of large scale ventures which eventually overwhelmed the abilities of the government. The problems were exacerbated in 1972 by nationalizations of most trade activities. The impact of the Sahelian drought after 1973 brought the economy into an increasingly depressed state. This was worsened by the war in the Western Sahara. Aid from the EU and Arab countries did little other than enable the country to survive. Mauritania is presently in the midst of an extensive World Bank/IMF Structural Adjustment programme and in late 1992, the Ougiya was devalued 28%.

Industry

The principal industry in Mauritania is mining. The iron ore extracting industry is based on the Kediel Aj-Jill deposits which are limited and reaching exhaustion. Other low grade ore occurs E of Zouerate but require large investments in new plant at a time of low profitability for iron ore exports. The iron industry is controlled by SNIM (Société Nationale d'Industrialization Minier). The Akjoujt copper mine began output in 1973 based on modest reserves of 28 million tonnes. Copper concentrate is carried to Nouakchott by a specially constructed road from a mining town at Akjoujt. The company, Somima, was less than successful as a result of internal difficulties and falling prices for copper on the world market. It was also nationalized and amalgamated in the state-owned SNIM. A shut-down occurred in 1978 and, despite a project for re-opening it in 1989, problems continue. The mining industry produced 11.3 million tonnes of iron ore and 6,000 tonnes of gypsum in 1989. Other small scale industry relies on processing animal and food products.

Trends in the Economy

Growth in the economy has been feeble at about 1.4% per year in the last decade, obviously hindered badly by war, the Sahelian drought and internal mismanagement of the economy. National income was worth only US$1,030 million in 1991 and is still growing inadequately to outstrip the increase in population. Agriculture dominates the economy despite mining and the expansion of government services in recent years.

Structure of GDP	(%)
Agriculture	29.0
Mining	6.9
Manufacturing	11.7
Public Utilities/Construction	5.6
Other Services	46.8

Source: *Encyclopaedia Britannica*

Economic Indicators

Most economic indicators are adverse, including inflation at 4% and foreign debt at US$1 billion, far exceeding the annual value of total GDP.

ECONOMIC INDICATORS

	1988	**1989**	**1990**	**1991**
GDP (UM million)	72.63	118.0	125.0	135.6
Inflation (1985=100)	117.7	133.0	141.7	
Exports (UM million)	33.63	37.45		
Imports (UM million)	27.19	29.17		
Balance of Trade (UM million)	+4.58	+8.28		
Foreign Debt (US$ billion)	1.83	1.86	0.99	

US$1 = 85.09 Mauritanian Ouguiya

Source: IMF, EIU, *Encyclopaedia Britannica*

NOUAKCHOTT AND ENVIRONS

Nouakchott, capital since 1958, is located on the Atlantic coast and offers the best access both to the desert and to the sahel. It struggles against the encroaching Sahara, is the government and administrative centre and has the best hotel, hospital and educational facilities.

Pop 393,325 (1988), a 1984 estimate was 500,000. *Alt* 1m.

History

Construction of Nouakchott began in 1958 as an extension of an old **ksar**, or fortified town, and a French military post. It was made capital of the newly independent Mauritania in 1960. Before this the French colony had been governed from St. Louis in Senegal. Nouakchott was chosen as capital because it was in a neutral zone situated outside the areas associated with the most powerful Moorish tribes. At that time Nouakchott was some distance from the Sahara, but desertification has brought arid, sandy conditions to the edge of the city. Indeed the ever present wind from the desert blows sand around the city streets. It is lying in drifts everywhere. The general impression is of a yellow haze/fog hanging over the town, particularly to the E. For the traveller arriving from overseas, Nouakchott is shockingly primitive, with very few of the facilities and services normally associated with a capital city. Like the rest of the country, Nouakchott has a somewhat sleepy air, a city waiting for something to happen to it. Do not rely on the few traffic lights being obeyed. Traffic discipline is poor. The city is relaxed, the people are shy but not unfriendly, but has little to occupy the traveller after 2 or 3 days.

Originally designed for 12,000, Nouakchott's population has swollen as drought has forced people to migrate to the capital to escape from the difficult economic conditions prevailing in the interior. As a consequence there are vast areas of shacks on all sides of the city, some made only from waste packaging materials and containers. Many recent migrants use tents. Nouakchott has one of the worst cases of over-urbanization in Africa, with high unemployment and great shortages of basic services and utilities, as well as the housing dilemma. The problem is that Nouakchott has a very shallow economic base, with few vigorous economic concerns, perhaps a consequence of its hasty planning and construction.

The city of Nouakchott is located in a flat, sandy area close to the sea, and is centred around an older Moorish town, the ksar, and the modern town centre which has wide streets but few impressive buildings. Most of the larger public buildings are little more than functional. The city is, however, the location of most of the country's important commercial and industrial corporations.

The city does have a large and interesting market area, as well as a long and pleasant beach, where travellers can take an invigorating swim or watch local

CLIMATE: NOUAKCHOTT

	Jan	Feb	Mar	Apr	May	Jun	Jul	Aug	Sep	Oct	Nov	Dec	Av/Tot
Max (°C)	29	31	33	34	34	34	32	33	35	36	34	29	33
Min (°C)	13	15	16	18	19	22	24	25	25	23	18	14	19
Rain (mm)	1	2	0	0	0	1	15	61	47	10	4	10	151

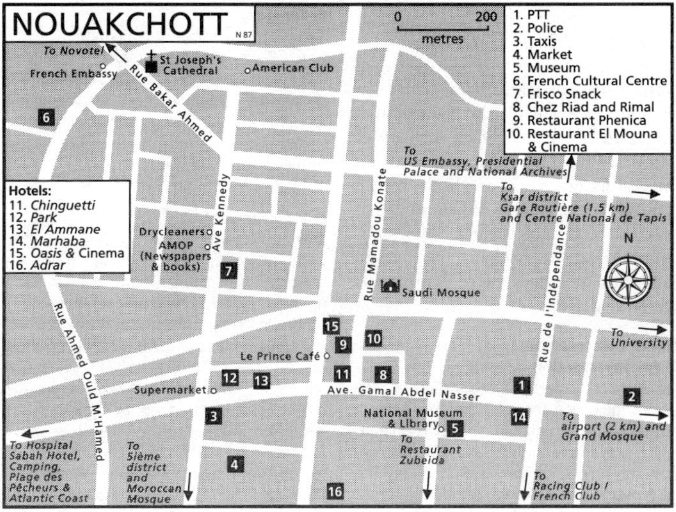

fishermen at work. The construction of a wharf has made Nouakchott the country's second most important port, but in an economic backwater like Mauritania that is not saying much.

ACCESS Air The airport, 3 km to the the E, has minimal facilities, a drinks counter, a small shop, and a *bureau de change* which is occasionally open. There is no airport bus service. Travellers must rely on a taxi to the centre, 10 mins away, which may cost as much as UM300, after hard bargaining.

Road Taxi from Rosso, the SE or the Adrar terminate at the *Gare Routière* in the Ksar area of the city, not far from the airport. Either take a taxi, or ask directions to where the yellow and green minivans labelled *Transports Urbaines* will stop.

LAYOUT The airport and *Gare Routière* are in the Ksar district of the city. Ave Gamal Abdel Nasser is the main thoroughfare running into the centre and on to the sea. The intersection with Ave Kennedy marks the city centre, or what there is of it. Ave Kennedy runs from the government and diplomatic quarters to the market and residential areas in 5ième district to the S.

Things to see

The City Centre Just off Ave Kennedy is the large covered **Central Market**, where a large variety of goods are sold. It is best to visit here early in the day. There is a women's centre behind the market. Along Ave Général de Gaulle is the **Maison du Parti et de la Culture**, containing the **National Museum** (1000-1200 Tues-Sat and 1430-1745 Tues-Sun), with ceramic and historical exhibits. There are few architecturally impressive buildings in Nouakchott. Perhaps one should see the two main mosques, one donated by Saudi Arabia and the other by Morocco.

The Cinquième District The most interesting area of Nouakchott is the 5ième district, an area of economic housing and popular commerce. A 5 min minibus ride away from the city centre, it is an enjoyable place to wander. The main target will be the market, a rambling area full of stalls selling everything from fruit and vegetables to handicrafts.

The Ksar is the old Moorish town of

the Nouakchott area which was destroyed by a 1950 flood and rebuilt. It is a run-down area, with some traders, notably sellers of rugs. There is also a women's rug school, the **Centre National du Tapis**, rue Ghary, perhaps an expensive place to buy carpets but an interesting place to visit. On the road S to Rosso is the **Centre Artisanal**. It is a good place to look at and buy handicrafts. Along this road and the route to the Adrar are large areas of shanty town accommodation.

Local information

● Accommodation

Nouakchott's hotels are very expensive, the grades indicating the price and facilities but not the general rundown, shabby conditions which prevail everywhere, and give little opportunity for economizing without misery. The **AL** ***Novotel Dar el Barka***, behind the French Embassy, BP 1366, T 53526, is perhaps the best of this limited choice, with pool, bar, restaurant and a/c rms.

B ***Hotel Marhaba***, BP 2391, T 51838, 51686, Marba, a/c rms with TV, also suites, lunch/dinner at UM1500 and breakfast at UM500-800 in the restaurant, as well as a bar, snack bar, *bureau de change*, a small handicrafts stall and a pool.

C ***Hotel El Ammane***, Ave Nasser, BP 13, T 52178, F 53765, reasonable rms, adequate restaurant with breakfast for UM300 and meals for UM1500; **C** ***Park Hotel***, BP 150, T 51444/6, a/c rms with balconies, a bar selling non-alcoholic drinks, reasonable restaurant with breakfast for UM300; **C** ***Sabah Hotel***, BP 452, T 51552, 51564, Tx 821, is located 100m from the beach and 6 km from the town, with 40 reasonable a/c rms and suites, a covered pool, a poor restaurant, bar, disco, free transport to/from airport (ask at the *Sabah* café), and transport to/from town.

D ***Hotel Oasis***, Ave Général de Gaulle, BP 4, T 52011, restaurant and reasonable but overpriced a/c rms; **D** ***Hotel Chinguitti*** next to *Restaurant Phenica*, T 53537.

E ***Hotel Adrar***, is a dirty, smelly, shabby place doubling as a brothel, which although it is comparatively cheap and quite friendly, is only for the hardened traveller with a streak of madness.

● Camping

Camping is possible and permitted on the beach, 6 kms W of the city, which is comparatively secure and safe. Camping costs UM500 per person. Huts which sleep 5 or 6 available for UM3,000. Common rms available for lounging in but be very careful as the tea and coffee so readily served is very expensive and causes unpleasant situations.

● Places to eat

♦♦♦ Restaurants in the hotels include ***Novotel***, said to serve the best food in the city but is commensurately expensive and certainly not busy; ***Hotel El Ammane*** serves excellent continental food and is one of the most popular establishments in town; ***Le Dragon d'Or***, opposite Saudi Mosque, T 53211, serves Chinese food; ***Park Hotel*** also has a reasonable conventional menu at slightly cheaper prices. ♦♦ ***Frisco Snack*** serves Western food and a few Lebanese dishes, a bit pricey, but clean and friendly with reasonable food; ***Restaurant Phenica***, T 525-75, standard European/Middle Eastern food, reasonably good and popular; ***El Mouna*** situated opposite the *Phenica* is slightly cheaper and less recommended; ***Rimal***, Ave Gamal Abdel Nasser, serves Lebanese food, has pleasant terrace; ***Sindibad***, across from the downtown market, has a wide range of cheap dishes; ***Chez Riad*** serves reasonable Lebanese food at good prices; ***Zubeida*** is a good Moroccan restaurant on Ave Gamal Abdel Nasser, although it is not very cheap. ♦ there are few cheap places to eat, but try along Ave Kennedy; ***Le Palmier***, near the market is economical; ***Le Prince*** near *Park Hotel* serves good food, popular with locals.

● Bars

Are only found at the ***Novotel***, the ***Hotel Marhaba*** and the ***American Club***.

● Airline offices

Air Afrique, BP 51, T 252084; **Air Algérie**, Ave Gamal Abdel Nasser, T 252059; **Air Mauritanie**, Direction Commerciale, Ave Gamal Abdel Nasser, BP 41, T 52211/2, Tx 573 AIRRIM, F 53815; **Iberia**, Ave Gamal Abdel Nasser, BP 727, T 252654; **Royal Air Maroc**, Ave Gamal Abdel Nasser, T 253564; **UTA**, Ave Gamal Abdel Nasser, BP 662, T 253916.

● Cinemas

There are three choices for films, normally in French or Arabic, the *Cinéma Oasis*, the *Cinéma El Mouna* opposite, and the *SNC Theatre*, near the post office.

● Banks

Banque Arabe Africaine en Mauritanie (BAAM), Imm. Afarco, Ave Gamal Abdel Nasser, BP 622, T 52826; **Banque Al Baraka Mauritanienne Islamique (BAMIS)**, Ave du Roi Fayçal, BP 650, 4944, T 51424, F 51621; **Banque Arabe Libyenne Mauritanienne (BALM)**, Ave Gamal Abdel Nasser, BP 626, T 52142, F 53382; **Banque Internationale pour la Mauritanie (BIMA)**, Ave des Dunes, BP 210, T 52363; **Société Mauritanienne de Banque (SMB)**, Ave Gamal Abdel Nasser, BP 614, T 52602.

● Car hire

Avis, T 51713; **Cotema**, T 52352; **Europcar** T 51136; **Lacombe**, T 52221.

● Car repair

This is most likely to be in the Ksar district of the town. Try ***Peyrissac***, on Ave Gamal Abdel Nasser, T 252213.

● Embassies

The few embassies in Nouakchott include **Algeria**, T 52182; **Egypt**, BP 176, T 52192; **France**, BP 231, rue Ahmed Ould M'Hamed, T 51740; **Germany**, BP 372, T 51394; **Libya**, T 52552; **Morocco**, BP 621, T 52304; **Senegal**, BP 611, T 52106; **Spain**, BP 232, T 52080; **Tunisia**, T 52124; **USA**, BP 609, T 52068.

The nearest embassies for other countries are in Dakar, Senegal: **Canada**, BP 3373, T 210290; **Italy**, BP 348, T 220076; **Japan**, BP 3140; and the **UK**, BP 6025, T 217392, Tx 548.

● Emergency

Police, T 17; **Hospital**, T 252135.

● Post & telephone

PTT, Ave Gamal Abdel Nasser (0800-1230 and 1400-1830) for post, poste restante and telex. For telephones use the *Novotel*, the *Hotel Marhaba* or the cheaper *cabine telephonique* found throughout the city. Fax can be sent/received at *Novotel* and many *cabine telephonique*.

● Shopping

Books and newspapers Try *Gralicoma* or SLIM near the market for books, or the boutique in the *Novotel*, or the AMDP situated in Immeuble el Mamy on Ave Kennedy for a wide range of press. The AMDP also sells French language books, although prices can be high. The French Cultural Centre sells French books on Mauritania at very reasonable rates, and also has an excellent specialist library on Mauritania. Another useful library collection is located at the Catholic Church.

Food There are 2 supermarkets near the *Hotel El Ammane* in Ave Gamal Abdel Nasser, which sell imported foreign foodstuffs at inflated prices.

Handicrafts The best place to get bargains is the open market in the 5ième district. Look for engraved silverware, dyed leather cushions, carpets, wood carvings, hand-crafted leather tobacco pouches and local-style pipes. The various markets are also good for buying cloth such as the colourful locally dyed *melafhas* worn by Moorish women and the richly dyed and embroidered *bazin* cottons used to make up the *boubous* worn by Moorish men and African Mauritanians. Buying cloth can also provide an interesting opportunity for meeting Moorish women who run the stalls. Higher quality items can be bought in the ***Centre Artisanal***, such as copper and silver jewellery, daggers, carpets, wooden boxes and chests; or from the dealers in front of the ***Hotel El Ammane***. ***L'Artisanat Feminin*** (0800-1100 and 1600-1800 Sat-Thurs), opposite the central market, is a women's cooperative selling clothes, purses, pillows, leather cushions and tents. ***Le Grand Marché*** and ***Le Souk***, off Ave Gamal Abdel Nasser, sell leather goods. The ***Centre National du Tapis*** in rue Ghary has an expensive selection of carpets.

Laundry and Dry Cleaners Available at *Novotel* and *Hotel Marhaba* are very expensive. Better value from the various *blanchisserie* around the market and the dry cleaner in Immeuble el Mamy on Ave Kennedy.

● Sports

Fishing The area is good for fishing, but equipment is difficult to find. **Softball** Fri at 0900, ask at the American Embassy. **Swimming** There are pools at the *Novotel*, the *Marhaba* and the *Sabah*, as well as the sea at the Plage des Pêcheurs.

● Tourist Office

Direction à l'Artisanat et au Tourisme, off Ave General Nasser, BP 246, T 53337, ext'n: 368, 322, 374; **Société Mauritanienne du Tourisme et de l'Hôtellerie (SMTH)**, BP 552, T 2353.

● Transport

Local: Taxis are generally green and yellow, though there are considerable variations, and some surprisingly decrepit vehicles. Green and yellow minivans, labelled **Transports Ur-**

baines, run over the city along fixed routes, and are very cheap, often overcrowded and subject to frequent stops by the police. There are no buses from the airport to the town centre, taxis are the only option and will entail serious bargaining.

Air Air Mauritanie has international flights to **Casablanca**, and domestic flights to towns throughout the country. Taxis leave from the *Gare Routière* near the Ksar and the airport.

Road Transport to **Nouadhibou** is difficult as there is no direct road. The most practical way is by aeroplane. A cheaper option is by truck, which can be picked up from the 5ième district of Nouakchott. Trucks and *bâches* (converted pick-up trucks) leave from this district to Nouadhibou, Atar and Kaedi.

Excursion

Plage des Pêcheurs and the Wharf The Wharf is a small, old port, now mainly used by small-scale fishermen and artisans, with deep sea fishing and facilities available for hire. The best time to visit is around 1600 when the fishing boats return. This is a good place to buy fish. It has recently been developed as a small modern port. The Chinese built port, S of the wharf, is also worth a visit although access can sometimes be difficult. Fishing also takes place at the Plage des Pêcheurs, which is also a pleasant place to wander or swim. After the little sightseeing that Nouakchott has to offer this is the main place to spend time, a long, unspoilt beach stretching into the distance. To get there follow the tarred road W from the Ave Kennedy/Ave Gamal Abdel Nasser intersection or get a green Renault taxi costing UM25.

THE NORTH

The coast N from Nouakchott to Nouadhibou, a distance of 525 km, contains some excellent beaches and some spectacular flora and fauna. It passes Cap Timirist and the Parc National du Banc d'Arguin, a huge reserve for migrating birds.

THE COAST FROM NOUAKCHOTT TO NOUADHIBOU

In this unusual country there is no black top road between the two main towns. Even the *piste* N from Noukchott to Nouadhibou is frequently undefined. Few vehicles (mainly lorries carrying water/fuel and trucks piled high with goods and passengers, few private cars) make this journey and most (perhaps 20-30 trucks a day) use partly *piste* and, depending on the tide, the 3m band of firm sand exposed on the shore. It is recommended to take a guide if aiming for Nouadhibou as particularly further N there are numerous vehicle tracks over a very wide area and the route to Bou Lanouar where one turns W for Nouadhibou is certainly not as clear as the maps indicate. Only 4 wheel drive drive vehicles stand a chance of completing the journey. It is possible, but quite unnecessary, to do this journey in 2 days. Allow 3 full days with 2 nights camping en route.

Officially one needs an authorization to take a vehicle out of the town and this may be asked for at the road check on the town's outskirts – but not of course if you drive up the beach from beside the *Sabah Hotel*.

Nouamghar, 155 km N of Nouakchott, a collection of about 200 shanties, is the major village of the Imraguen, a group of about 800 coastal dwellers who depend on fish for their livelihood, particularly mullet, the main season for which is Oct-Dec. The sea here is very shallow, the net is positioned into a semi-circle and the fish are driven into the net by hitting the water with large flat boards. The dolphins, frequent visitors to this coast, are always in evidence at this time. While it is romantic to assume that the dolphins are there to assist the fishermen, the more likely explanation is that they are only there for the food. Boats may be hired here but **Iwik** further N is a better place for bird watching.

The **Parc National du Banc d'Arguin** is a very significant site for aquatic birds migrating between Africa and Eurasia. They include broad-billed sandpipers, black terns, flamingoes, white pelicans, spoonbills, herons, white herons and cormorants. Some birds remain and breed here in this tranquil and food-rich environment. The birds often inhabit the offshore sand islands, and thus a boat is required for proper birdwatching. The main entrance to the park is at Nouamghar. The man who sells the tickets is in one of the smarter shacks. Entrance UM800 per day. Just say for how many days. Once in the park—

CLIMATE: NOUADHIBOU

	Jan	Feb	Mar	Apr	May	Jun	Jul	Aug	Sep	Oct	Nov	Dec	Av/Tot
Max (°C)	24	25	27	26	27	28	27	28	31	30	27	25	27
Min (°C)	13	14	15	15	16	17	19	20	20	19	17	15	17
Rain (mm)	2	2	2	1	0	0	1	4	8	7	6	2	35

which is really no more than a strip of coast, much of it quite swampy, backed by a huge area of desert—one is free to ride. We recommend you to take a guide who will navigate across the erg rather than the very poor quality *piste*.

Trips to sail round the islands are best arranged from **Iwik**, another small collection of shacks 60 km N of Nouamghar. The main island is **Tidra** but there are many smaller ones too. It is necessary to consider the weather. The sailing boats can only operate if there is a wind but the birds are only there if it is calm ... so try to book on a day with a light breeze. The boat which can take 4-6 passengers will cost, after some hard bargaining, about UM10,000 for 4-6 hrs. Be firm too about the time scale as the boat owner will return you sooner if he can. There is much to observe without landing. Special permits are required to land on the islands and to walk among the birds. These are only given to genuine ornithologists. Restrictions to protect the birds from visitors in the breeding season do not appear to operate. Permits may be granted at Iwik but make enquiries both at the tourist office in Nouakchott and at the park entrance in case the routine has changed – it is too far to go back. For specialist tours to this area see page 396.

There are some cabins for visitors near the manager's house in Iwik although the two main camping spots are both N of Iwik, at **Cap Tafarit**, noted also for fishing, though jackals can be a problem here and **Cap Tagarit**, only 8 km further N, which is much prettier and has fewer jackals.

Nouadhibou

Pop 59,198 (1988), *Alt* 8m.

History

Nouadhibou, formerly called Port Etienne, is Mauritania's 2nd city and the capital of the Dakhlet-Nouadhibou (Baie du Levrier) region. It is the most northerly settlement in Mauritania, on the coast, on the sheltered side of a peninsula shared with Moroccan Western Sahara but administered in the whole by Mauritania. This is a very barren area of coast. Nouadhibou is the country's main port, with economic activities centred around iron ore and fishing, for this is one of the richest fishing grounds in the world. It lies at the terminus of the iron ore railway line from Zouerate, which brings in vast amounts of this raw material, which is then exported in large ore carriers, from Port Minéralier which is S of the city centre. The state-controlled iron-ore company, *SNIM*, runs the railway line, the port and Cansado, an autonomous settlement for company employees, 6 km S of the town on the peninsula tip. There is a substantial W African immigrant population, who arrive in Nouadhibou as the last stop, before the border with Morocco. Many seek to stow away on boats to the Canary Islands or Europe.

ACCESS The train from Choum or Zouerate arrives at Port Minéralier, S of the city centre. Taxis or the police will take travellers from the train into town. Arriving at the rather tumbledown airport (aptly described as just a more level piece of erg between Nouadhibou and La Gouèra), the city centre is a short taxi ride away, taking 5-10 mins and costing UM30-50. Coming in by road there is a customs post about 16 km N of Nouadhibou. It is not always easy to get through here and travellers report that sometimes 'presents' are demanded in return for the car documents.

Things to see

The town, such as it is, has one main street running N-S with minor ones parallel and alleys connecting across. To the N is a large area of shanty dwellings. The town has no real centre except the point on the main road at the taxi stand where there are some 2-storey buildings, banks etc. There are half a dozen restaurants and the liveliest area is around the shops.

The town is unusual in Mauritania, because of its mix of ethnic communities, European and Far Eastern workers at the port, and W Africans looking for work or a passage to Europe. This is reflected in the shops and restaurants around Nouadhibou. The Paris to Dakar rally passes through each Jan. Near the airport are the ruins of Tcherka, formerly occupied by the Canary Islanders. South again are the ports for cargo and fishing while the harbour to the E is noted for its 150 or so rusting hulks out to sea. South again another 6 km is Cansado – perhaps slightly less run down than Nouadhibou. Further S again is Port Minéralier where the train line from Zouerate terminates and the iron ore is loaded on to boats.

There is no swimming in the bay to the E as it is polluted. Swim instead off the W coast. Monk seals can be seen off shore here but there are more on the W coast where they come out of the water. Between 50-100 such seals have been counted. Cap Blanc at the southern tip of the peninsula has a lighthouse, and good views.

It is possible to go on the W side of the peninsula where there is a very attractive beach with bays and headlands and a huge wrecked freighter. This attractive area which sometimes gets good surf, at other times provides good swimming. The bottom is very rocky. The Atlantic coast N along the peninsula has some spectacular cliffs. You will need a car to get there. It is not possible to go further N than **La Gouèra**, an old Spanish fishing village, as this is occupied by the Mauritanian army. **Take great care** on the W side of the peninsula. Although the beach itself is not mined do not venture on the dunes behind the beach or the land as far E of the central border.

There are no maps available of the area but the restaurant *Le Surf* has some amazingly detailed maps of Cap Blanc peninsula on the wall.

Local information

● Accommodation

Nouadhibou has several good hotels. Try the **B** *Sabah Hotel*, near the airport, BP 285, T 45317/77, F 45499, with pool, disco and bar.

D *Hotel du Maghreb*, Blvd Median, BP 160, with breakfast at UM200 and lunch/dinner at UM1200, and a bar; the more economic **D** *Hotel des Imraguens*, 1 km from the centre, BP 160, T 2272, with 21 rms, restaurant and nightclub; and the **D** *Hotel Niabina*, rue Sonney, BP 146, T 45983. Apparently the Catholic Mission also has accommodation.

In Cansado, the iron ore company runs a good hotel, the **C** *Hotel Oasian*, Cansado, BP 42, T 2700, on coast, views of bay, 36 rms, 3 suites, TV, phone, frig, with a restaurant, bar and pool.

● Places to eat

Seafood is a popular speciality. Try ♦♦♦*Le Surf* in *Hotel Oasian* for shellfish. ♦♦*Le Marin* is good for fresh fish. *Le Cabana*, in the Port de Pêche, near the town centre, is a good bet for fish and other food. There are a number of bars selling alcohol in Nouadhibou.

● Banks

Banque Al Baraka Mauritanienne Islamique (BAMIS), BP 205, T 45663/4, Tx 4450, F 45665; **Banque Arabe Libyenne Mauritanienne** (BALM), T 45132, F 45133.

● Sport

Fishing Nouadhibou has good fishing all year, particularly of sea bass, sea bream, ray, umbrine and trout. Surf casting is very popular and there are fishermen in the port that will take enthusiasts out for a negotiated price. However, serious fishers will want to go to the *Centre de Pêche Sportive*, in the Baie de l'Étoile, 15 km N of Nouadhibou. This is a residential centre, with excellent opportunities for fishing, mainly surf casting, for an immense variety of species. The centre has 8 double rooms, a restaurant, vehicles, staff and guides. *Air Afrique* organizes package tours to the centre, including the air ticket, lodging, meals and fishing gear, from Nouakchott or Paris, and varying in length from a few days to weeks. Contact: Service Tourism, **Air Afrique**, 29 rue du Colisée, F-75008, Paris, T 42257169. **Swimming**. There are good beaches on the peninsula.

● Transport

The easiest way to get to Nouakchott is by aeroplane, a cheaper way is by truck. However, as there is no road this is a problematic route.

Local: Nouadhibou has taxis to the airport, as well as to Cansado and Port Minéralier.

Air Air services from Nouadhibou include **Air Mauritanie** to Atar, Zouerate, Nouakchott (2 flights daily by airbus 300, takes 35 mins, costs UM550 single) or Las Palmas, and **Iberia** to Las Palmas. There may also be *Aeroflot* flights.

Train The trains to Choum or Zouerate leave from Port Minéralier.

THE ADRAR REGION

If there is only time for one tour, then perhaps the Adrar should be the destination, as it offers some of the most dramatic scenery and two historic towns.

The Adrar region is a large massif of mountains, plateaux, dunes and canyons in the N of Mauritania, with some breathtaking desert scenery. It is one of the most interesting areas of the country, an historic area of settlement, and a region where nomads have traditionally lived. Indeed, the Adrar has been occupied since Neolithic times, as stone tools and other remains testify. Its warriors were known throughout the area, and it was the base of an Emirate until French colonization. More recently, the Adrar was known as a centre of opposition to the rule of the republic's first president, Ould Daddah. There is a number of oases, several associated with historic sites and towns. In the oases and gorges a

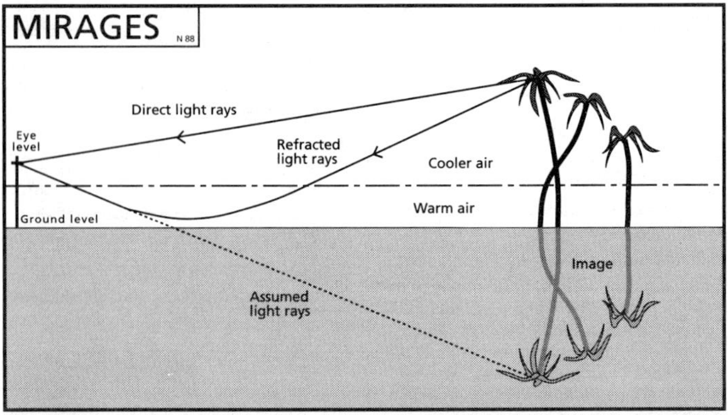

MIRAGES – ILLUSIONS IN THE DESERT

A mirage is a type of optical illusion caused by the refraction (bending) of rays of light as they pass through air layers of varying temperatures and densities. The most common mirage occurs in the desert where what appears to be a distant pool of water, perhaps surrounded by palm trees turns out, to the disappointment of the thirsty traveller, to be only another area of dry sand.

The rays of light that come directly to the eye show the palm trees in their correct position. The rays of light that travel through the warmer, less dense air travel faster as they meet less resistance and change their direction. They bend nearer to the ground but are assumed to have come directly to the eye so the brain records the trees and the blue sky as reflections in a pool of water.

The rays are real, just misinterpreted, thus a mirage can be photographed but that does not, alas, make the shimmering 'water' available to quench the thirst.

number of crops are cultivated for local consumption, including millet, sorghum, barley, tomatoes and green vegetables, but dates dominate. However, as in much of Mauritania, the towns and cultivated areas are often threatened by encroaching sand. Cut into the plateaux are some impressive canyons, and there are some interesting ancient rock paintings. Travel to the Adrar can be by aeroplane to Atar (from Nouakchott or Nouadhibou), by taxi or private vehicle from Nouakchott. The only other possibilities, for the adventurous, are the train to Choum and then a taxi to Atar, or across the deep desert from Tidjikja, Nema or Ouadane, in a camel or 4 wheel drive vehicle convoy.

Akjoujt, although not actually in the Adrar, is the first town en route from Nouakchott to Atar, and stands at the end of the black top road. The 250 km black top road itself is of a poor quality, but will be passable by most vehicles in about 6-9 hrs. This town, which is the administrative centre of the Inchiri region, is based around the mines for the copper resources discovered in 1941, notably at Guelb Moghrein, which have since closed down. There are shops, tea houses and fuel at Akjoujt. The track from Akjoujt to Atar is not black top, but there are taxis.

Terjit and **Oujeft** could be visited enroute to Adrar, or as an excursion from Atar. Terjit, signposted to the right of the piste before Atar, is worth visiting, with its tree-lined hot and cold springs, where swimming is pleasant. A further 35 km S of Terjit is Oujeft, a scenic oasis with verdant palmeries and interesting archaeological relics.

Atar

Pop 16,326 (1976), *Alt* 226m.

This is the capital of the Adrar region, an old oasis settlement lying on the route of the historic salt caravans, and an important marketing centre for the nomads of the region, with an historic core, the ksar. The town has had a considerable colonial influence, and in fact there are still French there, at the Inter-Arab Ecole Militaire, for Atar is also a military base. Atar is a pleasant, relaxed town and a good base for exploring the surrounding region. There is a petrol station and basic provisions shops. Walk along the dike that separates the town from the rural area, and from the beautiful date palm groves that surround the town.

Things to see

Atar is divided into an interesting **ksar** area with narrow streets, and a modern area of wider streets and bigger buildings. The **market** between the two has a small selection of things to buy, including leatherware, jewellery and rugs. There are also workshops for leather, jewellery and metal work in the surrounding areas of the town. Near the hotel is a **French fort** dating from WWII, as well as a contemporary military school. Exploration of the date palmery is interesting because of the use of traditional systems of irrigation. The locals enjoy the walk along the dike at sunset. This can be reached from either the town or the palmeries, or from the grounds of the hotel.

CLIMATE: ATAR

	Jan	Feb	Mar	Apr	May	Jun	Jul	Aug	Sep	Oct	Nov	Dec	Av/Tot
Max (°C)	28	30	33	35	39	42	42	41	40	37	33	27	36
Min (°C)	13	14	16	19	23	26	27	27	26	23	18	13	20
Rain (mm)	4	4	1	0	0	2	8	31	36	20	7	6	119

Local information

● Accommodation

Atar has a good hotel, the **D** ***Hotel des Almoravides***, which has a/c rms with bath, restaurant and non-alcoholic drinks bar, with a set meal at UM800 and breakfast at UM200. Ask directions from the town centre. There is also a basic and run down rest house near the centre. Apparently it is also possible to stay at the Catholic Mission.

● Places to eat

Apart from the hotel, basic meals can be had at establishments in the old part of town. The situation there changes quickly in these cheap places so be selective.

● Transport

Air Atar is connected by air with Nouakchott and Nouadhibou. Taxis to/from the airstrip cost UM500.

Road A place in a taxi to Nouakchott costs UM2500, with driving time approximately 8 hrs. There are also taxis to Choum to meet the Zouerate-Nouadhibou trains, along a rough but just passable track. Land Rovers make the run to Chinguetti, these cost UM700 outside and UM1000 in the cab. They wait till they are full and therefore do not leave every day, but one can take a Land Rover alone and immediately for UM9000. The journey takes 1 hr. Places are also available on the twice-weekly food lorry to Chinguetti. The track to Chinguetti and on to Ouadane is not an easy one. A car and driver can be hired for 1 day, with the itinerary fixed by the client, for UM15,000. Travellers with their own 4 wheel drive vehicle will probably need a guide to get to Amogjar, Chinguetti or Ouadane. For those with less time, there are some feasible short excursions from Atar. As well as Terjit, Oujeft and Amogjar which can mainly be reached only by personal transport, there are the ruins at **Azougui**, which can be reached by taxi costing UM50/100.

Excursions

Azougui lies along a scenic route, 15 km to the NW of Atar. This oasis has the ruins of a citadel, dating from the Almoravid period of the 11th and 12th century, when it was capital of the Adrar. This was the base for conquests of the Empire of Ghana, notably Aoudaghost, and the establishment of the powerful Moroccan Dynasty that toppled the Idrissids. Close to the citadel is the Almoravid Imam Hadrami's necropolis.

Amorgar (or Amogjar) is a mountain pass 70 km along the track from Atar to Chinguetti, the summit of the Adrar plateau which has impressive views. A day excursion from Atar is a spectacular experience, passing through dramatic mountain scenery. En route there are fortifications marking Mauritania's period of involvement in the W Sahara war. Near the pass itself, to the left of the track are rock paintings of suns, giraffes, cows and hunters. These are of great antiquity but still discernable. The verdant landscape depicted in the paintings indicates how the environment of the region has changed. 6 km further on, on the right, are some more curious rock paintings. From the rock paintings, return to Atar or continue along the rough piste to Chinguetti.

Chinguetti

Mauritania's most famous historic city, Chinguetti dates from the 13th century. Named 'Shinqit' in Arabic, a name also used for the whole country before the French colonization. It is located on the salt caravan route. It was both a Moorish capital and a religious centre famous around the Islamic World, and reckoned to be Islam's 7th city. It was the point where the pilgrims from the region gathered for the caravan across Africa to Mecca. Chinguetti was known for its poets and Islamic scholars, and still has an important mosque and libraries. The town is now declining both in status and in physical terms with erosion, being literally worn away by the sand. The visitor arrives first in the newer area of the town. The fort in Chinguetti, originally occupied by the Foreign Legion, was used in *Fort Saganne*, a French film from the early 1980s. Near the fort there is also a curious non-functional solar demonstration pump, and the police station, where travellers are required to register.

Across the *wadi* is the old town, with its impressive stone buildings. It is still owned today mainly by members of the Idaw'ali and Laghlal *zawaya* tribes. The 16th century mosque is famous and quite striking, but closed to non-Muslims, although views of it from around the town should satisfy the curiosity. Its minaret has 5 pinnacles, each surmounted by the *oeufs d'autruche* (ostrich eggs). The principal Koranic library has some 1300 ancient manuscripts, some as old as the 3rd century. The market displays some interesting items to buy, including ancient tools and arrow heads.

• **Accommodation** Accommodation is in the basic **E** *Maison du Bien Etre*, or with local people. There is nowhere to eat, but food can be bought at the market stalls or shops.

• **Transport** Travel on to Ouadane is over a rough desert piste that leaves the piste from Atar just before the town. Follow either the 120 km Piste du Dhar Chinguetti, or the Piste du Batha over sand dunes. Both require a 4 wheel drive vehicle, the latter a guide too. There are few vehicles making the journey.

Ouadane

In a country of ruins Ouadane is one of the most impressive, a hillside of stone buildings in a dramatic landscape of stones above a beautiful palmery. It is rewarding at the end of the long journey from Atar via Chinguetti, but only the dedicated travellers will make it. The town of Ouadane dates from either the 9th or the 12th century, according to different accounts. Some of its earliest inhabitants were the Berber Idawalhaj tribe. Today Ouadane is still home to Idawalhaj families as well as members of the Kunta and Amgarish tribes. Ouadane soon became an important and prosperous camel caravan centre, located as it was between the W African states and the trade routes to the N. These caravans were mainly taken up with salt, dates and gold. Even the Portuguese recognized its economic importance, setting up a significant trading post in the 15th century. However, Ouadane's location in the N of Mauritania meant that it suffered more than most places from the conquests of the powerful Moroccan Dynasties, the Saadians and the Alawites.

There are beautiful views from Ouadane's hill location, over the oasis, palm groves and surrounding desert areas. The ruins include a mosque and the Ksar el Klali. Other than basic rest house accommodation in Ouadane, which may be available, travellers will be dependent on the hospitality of the locals.

Tinlabbé

Whilst in Ouadane travellers should not miss the opportunity to visit the cave dwellings and rock paintings of Tinlabbé, 7 km NW of the town. Ask directions in Ouadane. It's a long, hot walk but worth it.

THE FAR NORTH

Mauritania reaches a considerable distance N, its joint border with Algeria and Morocco is parallel with Laayoune in Morocco and In Salah in Algeria. In this immense area of generally low-lying land the massif of Kediel Aj-Jill at 915m is conspicuous. The towns associated with the exploitation of the iron ore in this massif are the only settlements in the region.

Choum can be reached by a rough, bumpy, but often spectacular taxi journey of 120 km from Atar. The only reason to go to Choum is because of the Zouerate to Nouadhibou train line. Choum has basic tea tents/houses where travellers wait for the train.

Zouerate, 190 km N from Choum, with the associated settlement of Fderik, and formerly Fort Gouraud, used to be on the western caravan route across the Sahara. It has grown to a population of 17,500 (1976), as a town devoted to iron ore mining, the centre of that activity in Mauritania, and at the end of the long iron ore railway to Nouadhibou. There is little of interest in the town, but for those visiting, the mining company runs a hotel and restaurant. Transport runs as far as the town, but onward travel is impossible because of problems in the Western Sahara.

Camels – Ships Of The Desert

There are two kinds of camel, *Camelus Dromedarius,* the Arabian camel with one hump and *Camelus Bactrianus*, the Bactrian which has two. Arabian camels, found in North Africa, though only as domestic animals, are about 3m long and about 2m high at the shoulder. They range in colour from white to black.

They are not the most attractive of creatures, looking particularly ragged and scruffy at the spring moult. Large bare leathery areas on legs and chest look like some serious skin complaint but are normal and act as cushions when the animal kneels down.

Interesting physical characteristics which allow these animals to survive in the desert include hairs inside the ear opening as well as the ability to close the nostrils between breaths, both preventing sand penetration; thick eyebrows to shade the eyes from the sun's glare; a pad of skin between the two large toes on each foot forming a broad, tough 'slipper' which spreads the animal's weight over a larger area and prevents sinking in the loose sand; the ability to store a reserve of fat in the hump and to go for days without water. Each eye has three eyelids, the upper and lower lids have very long eyelashes to protect the eyes from sand whipped up by desert winds, while a third, thinner lid blinks away dust from the eyeball. The skin inside a camel's mouth is so tough that cactus thorns do not penetrate, hence a camel can eat anything, 'even its owner's tent'.

Camels can go for many days without food as the hump can store up to 35 kilos of fat as emergency rations. They can go without water for even longer, depending on the weather and the kind of food available. As camels do not sweat but instead function at a higher body temperature without brain damage, their demands of fluid are less. At a water hole they drink only enough to balance their body moisture content.

Less pleasant characteristics include a most unpredictable nature, especially in the mating season, which includes nasty habits like using its long sharp teeth to bite people and other camels, viciously kicking with the back legs, spitting and being generally awkward. When a camel stands up it moves in a series of violent jerks as it straightens first its hind legs then its front legs. When a camel walks, it moves both the legs at one side at the same time, giving a very rolling motion which can give the rider travel sickness.

Camels are unwilling beasts of burden, grunting and groaning as they are loaded and generally complaining at being made to lie down or stand up. Once underway though, they move without further protest.

These large, strong beasts are used to pull ploughs, turn water wheels and carry large loads for long distances across difficult terrain. They can carry up to 400 kg but usually the load is nearer 200 kg. Despite moving at a mere 5 or 6 km an hour, camels can travel 100 km in a day. They also provide their owners with hair for cloth, rich milk and cheese, dried dung fuel and eventually meat, bones for utensils and hides for shoes, bags and tenting.

The Arabian dromedary, bred for riding and racing, is of a slighter build but can cover 160 km in a day and reach speeds of up to 15 km per hour.

Bir-Moghrein, formerly called Fort Trinquet, used to be a caravan post. It has a rest house and rock paintings which ought not to be missed if you have got so far. Located 400 km N from Zouerate, one needs **permission from the police** in Nouakchott to go this far.

Zouerate, Choum and Nouadhibou

The state iron ore company has a railway line between the iron ore mines at Zouerate and the port at Nouadhibou. It runs 2 daily trains each way. These trains are, at 2.5 km, the longest in the world. The train consists mainly of open wagons of iron ore. However there is often, but not always, a passenger wagon attached, tickets being reasonably priced, about UM300. Many Mauritanians choose to travel for free on top of the iron ore rubble. Indeed this is the only means when a passenger wagon is not laid on. This is a most dramatic way to travel, perhaps one of the world's memorable journeys, if not just for the serious discomfort of the swirling invasive dust, and at night, the biting cold. Take warm clothes and preferably a blanket or sleeping bag, a plastic sheet to lie on, a scarf to wrap tightly round the mouth and eyes, and food and water. The train also stops at Choum, with one of the services leaving at about 1800 for Nouadhibou. The taxi will take its passengers to the train. The train journey from Choum to Nouadhibou takes about 12 hrs.

THE SOUTH

Southern Mauritania which experiences winter rains in varied proportions encompasses very diverse regions, dunes and sandstone plateaux with villagers dependent on livestock rearing, small areas of cereal cultivation and bare rock outcrops. In the extreme S the Senegal River valley contains areas of sedentary agriculture, even irrigation.

THE ROUTE DE L'ESPOIR

The Route de l'Espoir, the Road of Hope, was built by the Brazilians. It connects the S and SE of the country to Nouakchott. The building of this road means that it is now significantly quicker for the people of these regions to reach the capital. As a consequence, migration from the rural areas, where livelihoods are difficult to maintain, has rapidly increased to the capital where there is the dream of gainful employment, but the reality of great hardship. Along the road lie a succession of towns, of varying interest, but with the advantage of comparatively frequent transport. It is possible to complete the Route de l'Espoir to Nema in 2 days, but why go so fast? Off the road there are interesting detours to the Tagant region, the Koumbi Saleh archaeological site, and the desert religious centre of Oualata with its beautiful houses.

Boutilimit is the first town along the road, 265 km and 2 hrs from Nouakchott. It was founded in the 19th century by a religious scholar and mystic, and remains today one of the most renowned centres for religious learning in the region with several *medressa* still functioning. This century it had fame as the birthplace of the country's first president, Mokhtar Ould Daddah. The town is now also known as the location of an Institute for High Islamic Studies, an important centre in West Africa. Boutilimit has a large **market**, which is worth seeing as the town is known for its craftwork, particularly silverware and rugs.

After **Aleg**, the centre of the Brakna region but an unexciting place where taxis often stop for tea breaks, the next major settlement is **Kiffa**, population: 29,292 (1988), the main town, administrative centre and market of the Assaba region. The town is connected by an air service with Nouakchott. It has little to see except a reasonably interesting market, with some local handicrafts for sale. However the town does have accommodation, at the D *Hotel de l'Amitié et du Tourisme à Kiffa*, BP 46, T 233, meals UM200-500, a well-run place with electricity but no air-conditioning, and clean, basic rooms with just a mattress, and a separate shower room. The alternative is to stay with local people.

From Kiffa 2 routes lead off to the N. It is not a great problem to find transport along the 120 km deviation NE to **Tamchaket** but **Tagdawst**, the archaeological site of the Sanhadja Berber capital of Aoudaghost, 40 km further, is only reachable by those with their own transport. This was a very important trading city, through which passed large caravans of horses and bullocks from Morocco from at least 500 BC, and which attained greater prosperity with the arrival of the camel as a transport animal from the 3rd century AD. The city retained its importance until 1050, when it was captured by the Empire of Ghana, and by the Almoravids under Yahya Ibn 'Omar, in 1054. Archaeological excavations have revealed that the town had been rebuilt on successive levels as the sand covered it, notably in the 16th and 17th centuries, but was then abandoned. The site is not very rewarding to the visitor.

The second route N from Kiffa is to Tidjikja – a rough route not to be undertaken lightly. See Tidjikja, page 392.

Aioun-El-Atrouss 210 km E of Kiffa along the main road is a well established town, the administrative centre of the western Hodh area, with a hotel, bank, post office and shops, and some attractive sandstone houses. There are flights from the town's airstrip to Nouakchott, contact Air Mauritanie in Nouakchott, or the distance can be covered by public transport in 2 days. There is accommodation at the D *Aïoun Hotel*, BP 41, T 90079, 90060, a quiet friendly place, simple rms with bath, supposed to have electricity and a/c, but both are unreliable.

A wander amongst the houses is pleasant, whilst there are good views from the rocks that ring the town. A very scenic area with some strange rock formations. There is an interesting market with a good line in beads.

The *piste* S from Aioun-El-Atrouss goes to Mali, about 180 km. There is a customs post on the border. Problems are reported of 'fines' of up to $40 per person for not spending a minimum of UM10,000 per day while in Mauritania. Appeals to the chief of police might save you.

Timbedra, which has an important animal market, lies 170 km E of Aioun-El-Atrouss and it may be possible to get a lift from vehicles en route to Mali. **Koumbi Saleh** is 70 km SE of Timbedra along a quite reasonable track. This is Mauritania's most important archaeological site. Koumbi Saleh was once one of the most populous cities of the world, as capital of the Empire of Ghana from the 3rd century. It included two distinctive settlements, a royal town and a large area of residential districts and mosques, the two connected by further houses. It is the main residential district that is the archaeological site to be seen, revealing impressive stone houses and one of the large mosques.

Nema, 106 km beyond Timbedra, is the capital of the E Hodh region, an area of the Kunta people, and known for its use as a place of exile for political prisoners. The town marks the end of the Route de l'Espoir, although there are plans to continue this to Mali. Nema has many houses built from stone and clad with clay, in a similar but less decorative style than Oulata (see below). The town has a petrol station, police, a bank, a post office, shops, a market, and an airstrip with weekly flights to Nouakchott. Camel convoys still leave for the Saharan regions to the N, and it is a good place to arrange transport and vehicles. The long taxi journey to Nouakchott will probably have to be taken in sections, perhaps changing vehicles in Aioun-El-Atrouss and Kiffa. There is an occasional and very slow bus which makes the journey to Nouakchott. There is no hotel, but accommodation with the family of Sass Ould Moulay Abdelmalek, Commerçant, BP 27 is recommended, which will probably cost UM550 plus meals, as arranged, ask in the town for 'Maison Sass' or 'Commerçant Sass'. All passport formalities must be carried out at the police station in Nema for entry into Mali or Senegal. At Adel Bagrou there are customs but no problems are encountered there.

Oualata, 95 kms N of Nema, is a mediaeval fortified settlement which has had great importance as a Saharan caravan post and Islamic centre, with a famous **Koranic school** that is still running, and includes an important library. The **Muslim cemetery** at Tirzet is nearby. Oualata is built on a high terrace, an impressive location. Most striking in Oualata are the houses, which were traditionally heavily ornamented, with intricate decorations executed in gypsum and different colours of clay. Many of these older houses have been abandoned, and the art has declined. However the interiors and studded wooden doors are impressive. Sensitivity over photography should be borne in mind, as this town is also used for internal exile, and indeed the police must be visited on arrival. There is no accommodation in Oualata other than with families. There are some vehicles which make the journey from Nema, particularly after the flights from Nouakchott arrive.

THE TAGANT REGION

The Tagant Region is a dramatic area of stony plateaux with impressive views, prehistoric rock painting, archaeological remains, and some interesting old forts and towns which are now being over-run by sand. The name itself means 'forest' in the Zenaga language, implying the environment was more verdant in the past. Although very appealing, the Tagant is a difficult region to visit. Travellers will find it easiest to use the weekly flight from Nouakchott to Tidjikja (despite uncertainties about day or time of departure). Public land transport is difficult, the best option being a *taxi-brousse* from Nouakchott, or closer at hand from Aleg or Magta-Lahjar. For those with their own 4 wheel drive vehicles, turn off the Route de l'Espoir at Sangarafa, 20 km E after Magta-Lahjar. From Sangarafa there is a rough sandy track to Tidjikja. The fuel supply is unreliable in the region.

Tidjikja

The capital of Tagant, this is a small town, with a busy market but few facilities for tourists except the airstrip. There is a **French colonial fort** built by Xavier Coppolani, assassinated here in May 1905, and near the town there are remains from the Neolithic period, including arrowheads and pottery. Tidjikja was founded in 1680 by Idaw'ali exiles from the Adrar. The historic area lies on the NE bank of the *wadi*, with an old mosque, housing and Tidjikja's celebrated palm groves dating from the original settlement. Although some of the houses are vacant or ruined, the Tagant region's impressive architecture is highly evident in Tidjikja. The houses are built from stone with clay added. The buildings have flat roofs, palm-trunk waterspouts, narrow rooms and elevated latrines carved into stone. The distinctive features are the decorative niches with carved geometrical designs, and gargoyles on the roofs. The historic quarter is threatened by sand.

To the SW of the *wadi* is the modern area, with a bank, post office, shops, a hospital and a petrol station. Tidjikja has a lake but we do not recommend swimming. 4 wheel drive vehicles can be hired in Tidjikja, for a 40 km drive to Rachid, or for the 200 km, more expensive, journey to Tichit. This is the starting point of the 470 km to Atar, only negotiable by high clearance 4 wheel drive vehicles in convoy with guides. There is a basic rest house in Tidjikja, otherwise accommodation must be with locals.

Rachid lies 40 km to the N of Tidjikja, an impressive fort settlement with rock engravings, ruined buildings and a delightful palmery. It was a bedouin citadel built by Kunta in the 18th century, a refuge for those who would rob caravans. Access is mainly by private 4 wheel drive vehicle.

Tichit

200 km to the E of Tidjikja, Tichit is very difficult to get to, but fascinating in architectural and social terms, and worth visiting whilst it struggles on as a functioning settlement, a ghost of its impressive past. Tichit is a fortified caravan town founded around 1150 AD, from when it was a stopping point on the route between West Africa and the Sahel, and Morocco and the Mediterranean, and a large city. It has declined rapidly, with encroaching sand, changing economic circumstances and rapid emigration.

Now only a handful of families remains. These families reflect the traditional complex ethnic diversity of Tichit and its position as a transit point for Moor tribes nomadizing in the region. They include the Masena, blacks who speak Aser; Abid, former slaves often still working in similar situations and Haratin Moors, slaves liberated much earlier.

The old houses are impressive structures built from local rock, often using colouration and carvings, of a similar style but more elaborate than in Tidjikja. Green, white and red stone is used, and the ornamental niches are quite beautiful. There are also distinctive wooden doors. However, many of the houses are partly ruined and poorly maintained. The town mosque is worth seeing, although much of its fabric dates from frequent repairs. The surrounding area has other ruins and ancient rock paintings. There is an archaeological site nearby at Akreijt. Palm groves stretch S from Tichit, with a date harvest in July.

• **Transport** From Tidjikja, this is very difficult, with lifts only possible after the arrival of flights at the airstrip. A chartered flight continuation from Tidjikja is an expensive option. For motorists a 4 wheel drive vehicle, plentiful petrol (there is none in Tichit) and a guide are essential. The route is straightforward to Leckcheb, and then much more difficult over a bad piste and dunes to Tichit. From Tichit those with time and petrol could follow a 400 km long piste to Oulata, along an old caravan route.

THE SENEGAL VALLEY

South of the Route de l'Espoir is a more fertile area, firstly dry savanna and bush, and nearer the River Senegal irrigated crop lands, producing rice and millet. The region is mainly populated by black people speaking languages other than Arabic although in recent years the Moor and Haratin populations have increased.

Rosso, with a population of 27,783 (1988), is the administrative centre of the Trarza region, an area of mixed ethnic groups reflecting a diverse environment in which agriculture and cattle-rearing are dominant. It is an uninteresting town, only normally visited for travel to, or from, Senegal. There is a basic rest house/restaurant, the E *Hotel Trarza*, with 9 rms, and a Catholic mission. There is a black top road to Nouakchott, which was rebuilt after the floods of 1950, a dull journey, although look out for encampments of nomads. Taxis take approximately 3 hrs to Nouakchott, and can be found at the *Gare Routière*, 500m N out of the town. Horse-drawn *calèches* carry people from the town centre. The airstrip has no scheduled service.

From Rosso there is a ferry to the Senegal bank of the river, every 20 mins from 0700-1230 and 1500-1700, taking 3 mins, with frequent waits due to heavy traffic. There is a black top road from the river to Dakar, with frequent taxis. As relations between Mauritania and Senegal have been strained the border has on occasion been closed.

Mderdra is 20 km from Rosso, reachable for those with 4 wheel drive vehicles. Traditionally a gum arabic centre, it is now famous for inlaid wooden chests made for nomads, and silverware.

Keur Massène, W of Rosso, located in the River Senegal delta, close to the ocean. Keur Massène is a village with an 8 bungalow *campement de chasse*, or hunting centre, run by **Air Afrique**. This offers surf-casting on the ocean as well as shooting of a wide variety of wildfowl. Contact: Service Tourisme, **Air Afrique**, 29 rue du Colisée, F-75008 Paris, T 42257169, or the Nouakchott office, BP 51, T 52084.

Bogué is an unremarkable town on the River Senegal. However, it is well connected, with a recently constructed paved road covering the 60 km distance S from Aleg on the Route de l'Espoir. A *pirogue*, an open boat, takes foot passengers across the river to the Senegalese Isle à Marfil. There may be a car ferry operating.

Kaedi, population: 30,515 (1988), is the largest town in the Valley region and the economic centre of the E, linked by 100 km of piste to Bogué. It has an airstrip with a regular link to Nouakchott, and a rest house. The town is best known for its large market, one of the most interesting in the country and with good handicrafts. Kaedi is the capital of the Gorgol region, an economically diverse area with strong agriculture, fishing and cattle-rearing sectors.

Selibaby is the capital of the Guidimakha region, where the Soninke people live. It is an area of savanna and subtropical forest, a wide variety of crops and produces. The town has an airstrip, with a service to Nouakchott.

INFORMATION FOR VISITORS

Contents

Before you go

Entry requirements

● Visas

Visas are required for most visitors. Exceptions include France, Italy and some African countries. The difficulty may be finding an embassy. Visas require 2 forms, 2 passport photographs and a return air ticket as evidence of intention to limit stay. A letter from your Travel Agent will not do but a letter from a Mauritanian may be useful. In Paris the cost is FF122, one is asked to go in person but postal requests are accepted. Time to process the visa here varies from immediate to 24 hrs, or, alas, a refusal and a suggestion to try in Rabat. There is a problem for overland travellers who may have to buy an air ticket to get the visa then return to the travel agency for a refund. Available also in Bonn, Brussels, Madrid and Rabat (reported to be cheaper than in Paris). For visa renewals go to the Commisariat Centrale, on Ave Gamal Abdel Nasser, in Nouakchott.

Entry into Senegal and other African countries Visas for Senegal are not available in Nouakchott or at the river crossing, but are available on arrival at the airport in Dakar. The French embassy in Nouakchott provides visas for a number of Francophone African countries, takes 24 hr usually with no fuss.

Departure Provided you retain all receipts for financial transactions and are in no great hurry, leaving is no problem.

● Vaccinations

Travellers no longer require certificates of immunization against Yellow Fever and Cholera, but protection against these is advisable on health grounds anyway (**see Health page 20**). There are mosquitoes and anti-malarial medication is also recommended.

● Representation overseas

Algeria, BP 276, El-Mouradia, Algiers; **Belgium**, Ave Colombie 6, Bruxelles, T 322 6724747; **Egypt**, c/o the Senegal Embassy, 46 Abdel Moneim Riad Street; **France**, 69 rue du Cherche Midi, 75006 Paris, T 45482388; **Libya**, BP 4664, Tripoli; **Mali**, BP 135, Bamako; **Morocco**, 30 Ave d'Alger, Rabat; **Senegal**, BP 12019, Dakar; **Spain**, Calle Velázquez 90, Madrid, T 3415757007; **Tunisia**, Route du Hilton, Notre Dame, Tunis; **UK**, nearest is the embassy in Paris; **USA**, 2129 Leroy Place NW, Washington DC 20008, T 2441491. There are also embassies in China, Gabon, Germany, the Ivory Coast, Nigeria, Russia and Zaire. Some travellers have obtained visas at the border, but this a very unreliable option. It is possible to get visas in neighbouring countries such as the Canary Islands and Morocco, but one will need a letter of introduction from one's own embassy. French embassies are often helpful in African countries without a Mauritanian embassy. Mali, for example, does not have a Mauritanian embassy.

● Tourist information

That little information that there is can be had from either the **Direction à l'Artisanat et au Tourisme**, off Ave Gamal Abdel Nasser, BP 246, Nouakchott, T 53337, ext'n: 368, 322, 374; or the **Société Mauritanienne du Tourisme et de l'Hôtellerie (SMTH)**, BP 552,

Nouakchott, T 2353. It is probably better to go to one of the travel agents below.

Specialist tour companies

These include **Agence-Dayna Voyages et Tourisme**, Ave Gamal Abdel Nasser, and **Inter Tour**, Ave Gamal Abdel Nasser, BP 708, T 53217. One of the most helpful is **Adrar Voyages**, BP 926, Nouakchott, T 51717, F 53210 (0800-1230 and 1500-1830 Sat-Wed, 0800-1230 and 1500-1700 Thur). This company offers pre-arranged tours, and tours designed for the customer, primarily centred around desert safaris and water sports, with guides, vehicles, food and accommodation laid on. On a daily basis desert safari costs are approximately: vehicle, driver, food and fuel – UM45,000. A sample week-long tour takes in Nouakchott, Akjoujt, Atar, Chinguetti, Azougui and Terjit. **Adrar Voyages** in conjunction with Sodetour also runs safaris and fishing holidays along the coast, through the Parc National du Banc d'Arguin to Nouadhibou. The company works with a number of travel agents in France, Italy, Switzerland and South America. Staff speak French, Arabic and English.

Encounter Overland, 267 Old Brompton Rd, London SW5, T 071 3706845; Backerstr 52, Postfach CH8026, Zurich, T 01 2971112; Schipholweg 101, PO Box 360, 2300 Leiden, Netherlands cover Mauritania and the W Desert in their itineraries. **Explorator**, 16 Place de la Madeleine, 75008 Paris, T 42666624 organizes birdwatching in the Parc National du Banc d'Arguin. **Dragoman Overland Expeditions**, T 0728 861133, include Mauritania in their trans African trips.

When to go

Best time to visit

The heat is most manageable between Nov and Feb, but even then it can be uncomfortable. Avoid July to Oct for visiting the Senegal Valley.

Climate

Mauritania has a Saharan climate in the N and centre, hot and very dry with hardly any rain. The rain that does fall comes between July and Oct, although it is rarely above 30 mm. The hottest season is May to Sept, with peak temperatures between 40 and 45°C. Night temperatures in the desert can be as low as 13°C in Nouakchott. These cool night temperatures occur mainly in Dec to Feb. The coast is a little, but not much, cooler. The S, near the Senegal River, has a more humid climate.

Clothing

The most appropriate clothing is light cotton, covering the whole body, with a scarf to wrap around the face as protection from blowing sand and sun on journeys, sunglasses and headwear. Women should avoid exposing arms and shoulders in respect of religious sensibilities.

Health

Staying healthy

Visitors must be immunized against Yellow Fever and Cholera to enter the country. They should also be immunized against polio, typhoid, meningitis, hepatitis B, and take appropriate anti-malarial pills, particularly in the S. Water should be boiled or sterilized. Mineral water is a fairly cheap alternative. On long journeys it is essential to drink sufficient water. Protection from the sun is essential throughout the year. Travel insurance is of course recommended. There is a reasonable hospital in Nouakchott, with French doctors.

Further health information

Visitors are recommended to read the section on Health, **see page 19**.

Money

Banks

There are no Western banks, but a number of Mauritanian banks: the **Banque Centrale de Mauritanie** (BCM), **Banque Arabe Africaine Mauritanienne** (BAAM), **Société Mauritanienne de Banque** (SMB), **Banque Internationale pour la Mauritanie** (BIMA), **Banque Mauritanienne pour le Développement et le Commerce** (BMDC) and **Banque Arabe Libyenne-Mauritanienne pour le Commerce Extérieur et le Développement** (BALM). Banks are easy to find in Nouakchott and Nouadhibou, but very rare elsewhere except in Atar, Aioun-El-Atrouss, Kaedi, Kiffa, Nema and Rosso. Banks are open 0800-1300 every day except Fri and Sat.

Credit cards

These are not normally accepted outside the few large hotels, or airlines. American Express has no representation in Mauritania.

Cost of living

In comparison with Morocco, Egypt or Tunisia, Mauritania is an extremely expensive country. Distances to be covered are long and prices high, with travellers often having to resort to air travel. A day's travel can be upwards of UM2,800. There is little choice in hotels, which are also highly priced, often above UM1,500 for quite basic accommodation. Meals in Nouakchott or Nouadhibou restaurants are similarly exorbitant. Local meals are cheaper.

● Currency

A **currency declaration**, of cash and travellers' cheques, must be made at the place of entry. Fill in all financial transactions and keep it safe. It is unwise to be economical with the truth as the fines are steep. Mauritanian currency cannot be taken out of the county. There is no restriction on foreign currency, in fact officially one should have sufficient funds for the duration of the stay and a return journey (or air ticket).

The Mauritanian currency is the Ouguiya (UM), pronounced 'oogeeya', which equals 5 khoums. It is unlikely that visitors will come across anything other than 5, 10 and 20 UM coins, and 100, 200 and 1000 UM notes.

Regulations and money changing There is no limit, within reason, on bringing foreign currency into the country. Both currency and travellers' cheques have to be declared fully on arrival by filling out a form. The receipts from money changing should be kept in case they are needed on departure. As it is difficult to find banks outside the main towns plan well ahead. There are limited possibilities for informal transactions, but not at greatly preferential rates. Most Western currencies are acceptable but it is safest to stick to US, UK, German or, preferably, French, currency as you get 10% more for changing cash than changing travellers' cheques. For exchange rates for July 1994 **see page 9**.

● Eurocheques and Travellers' cheques

It is unlikely that these will be usable in Mauritania, so cash is the best option.

Getting there

● General note

It is both difficult and expensive to get to Mauritania. European flights are mainly restricted to services from Paris and Las Palmas. There are limited flights from nearby African countries. Overland travel is straightforward from Senegal, difficult from Mali and almost impossible from Morocco or Algeria. There are no scheduled shipping routes.

● Air

Mauritania has only two international airports, at Nouakchott and Nouadhibou. Travellers will find the facilities quite primitive. Taxis wait outside both airports for the short trip into the centre – they tend to charge exorbitant prices. There are connecting flights from both these airports to regional airports.

International services To Mauritania are limited, with no direct flights from the Americas. From New York **Air Afrique** flights are via Dakar. There is a service 4 times a week between Paris and Nouakchott run by **Air Afrique/Air France**, which takes 5 hrs. **Aeroflot** runs an occasional service from Moscow or Budapest to Nouadhibou. **Air Afrique** runs a weekly service between Nouakchott and Jeddah.

Within Africa There are services between Nouakchott and Algiers (**Air Algérie**), Banjul and Casablanca (**Royal Air Maroc** and **Air Mauritanie**), Conakry (**UTA**), Niamey and Ndjamena (**Air Afrique**), daily to Dakar (**Air Afrique**, **Air Mauritanie** and **Air Sénégal**, although the last is unreliable) and 3 times a week to Las Palmas in the Canary Islands (**Air Mauritanie** and **Iberia**). From Nouadhibou there are links with Bissau (**Aeroflot**), Conakry (**UTA**) and twice weekly with Las Palmas (**Air Mauritanie**).

● Road

The main road approach is from Dakar in Senegal, across the River Senegal ferry at Rosso. There is a black top road from Dakar to the river. There is a ferry every 20 mins from 0700-1230 and 1500-1700. The crossing takes 3 mins but there can be quite a wait due to heavy traffic. There is also a reasonable black top road from Rosso to Nouakchott. Relations between Mauritania and Senegal are somewhat strained, and the border has on occasion been closed. Along the Senegal riverbank there is a black top road, on the Mauritanian side an unmade track. It is possible to cross at other points up the river, notably between Matam and Sive.

Entry from Mali into Mauritania is quite possible although the roads are of a poor quality. Many travel from Aioun-El-Atrouss, across the border to Nioro. Another route is from Nema to Nara in Mali. Travellers should get their passports stamped in the last Mauritanian town.

Due to the Western Saharan conflict it is difficult to enter from Algeria, via Tindouf, the

Polisario stronghold, but it is worth checking the current situation at the time of travel.

From Dakhla in Morocco there are 1 or 2 convoys a week to the border where all formalities must be concluded. Camping is available at the border and while the customs are more interested in vehicles than people and are happy to accept 'gifts', no serious problems have been reported. It is advised to hire a guide if driving S to Nouakchott as there is no defined road.

Motoring Drivers will need to have an **autorisation d'importation** to bring a car into the country. For information contact the Direction des Douanes, BP 183, Nouakchott.

Taxi and bus By taxi the route from Dakar to Nouakchott, via Rosso, will take about 11 hrs, changing at the border. There are both car and minivan taxis, as well as lorries, running from Rosso to Nouakchott which terminate at the *Gare Routière*. There are also taxis which make the journey from the Malian border.

● Sea

There are no regular ferry services to or from Mauritania, but from the major port of Nouadhibou it is occasionally possible to arrange passage on cargo vessels to Las Palmas in the Canary Islands, and further afield to Casablanca and Dakar (Senegal). Contact the Port Autonome de Nouadhibou, BP 236, Nouadhibou, T 2134. Similarly, ask around in Las Palmas, Casablanca or Dakar.

● Customs

There are no taxes. Importation of alcohol is strictly banned.

When you arrive

● Hours of business

Banks are open 0800-1300 Sun-Thurs, Government offices 0800-1500 Sat-Weds and 0800-1400 Thurs, Private offices 0800-1230 and 1500-1700 Sat-Thurs, and shops 0800-1230 and 1500-1700 Sat-Thurs.

● Official time

Mauritania is in the same time band as Morocco and the UK.

● Photography

This is allowed without a permit, but there is sensitivity about official and military buildings and installations. Be discrete when taking photographs in Nouakchott and along the Sengal River. The largest hotels in Nouakchott will sell film but its age must be checked. Better to bring your own supplies.

● Shopping

For handicrafts and many other items, purchase is by haggling, which is usually good natured and less exploitative than in Morocco. Trading in Western goods can get the traveller a good deal. A few shops and cooperatives are listed for Nouakchott. Otherwise the best place to shop is in the markets, which in different areas will reflect the local handicraft and other industries.

Best buys At the upper end of the market are carpets and wooden chests, but prices are much above the usual range in N Africa. Try for jewellery and the colourful cloths that Mauritanian women wear. In some areas interesting Neolithic artifacts, such as tools and arrow heads, are sold.

● Safety

Crime in Nouakchott and the rest of the country is relatively scarce. There are frequent roadblocks in Mauritania, when the police attempt to read passports and ask irrelevant questions. There is normally a checkpoint at the entry to each town, and the police will often accompany travellers to the central police station for registration. Some police like to write in one's passport, which can be annoying after several towns. Vehicle searches do occur. Women will find in Mauritania less hassle than in Morocco, although there may be a lot of curiosity. It is perhaps unadvisable to travel alone. Hints: cover hair to minimize unwanted attention, don't offer to shake hands with a man unless he does so first and avoid lying on the back or stomach in public.

● Tipping

Tipping is rarely demanded and it is up to the client in restaurants and hotels. 10% is reasonable.

● Weights and measures

Mauritania uses the metric system. See conversion table on **page 17**.

Where to stay

Hotels
There are few hotels in Mauritania, particularly outside Nouakchott and Nouadhibou. Few are anything to write home about, and most are over-priced.

Hotel Classifications

AL US$90+. International class luxury hotel. All facilities for business and leisure travellers are of the highest international standard.

A US$75-90. International hotel with air conditioned rooms with WC, bath/shower, TV, phone, mini-bar, daily clean linen. Choice of restaurants, coffee shop, shops, bank, travel agent, swimming pool, some sport and business facilities.

B US$60-75. As **A** but without the luxury, reduced number of restaurants, smaller rooms, limited range of shops and sport.

C US$40-60. Best rooms have air conditioning, own bath/shower and WC. Usually comfortable, bank, shop, pool.

D US$20-40. Best rooms may have own WC and bath/shower. Depending on management will have room service and choice of cuisine in restaurant.

E US$10-20. Simple provision. Perhaps fan cooler. May not have restaurant. Shared WC and showers with hot water (when available).

F under US$10. Very basic, shared toilet facilities, variable in cleanliness, noise, often in dubious locations.

Camping
This is legal in most places, but there are no organized sites.

General
There are no **Youth hostels** in Mauritania. The Peace Corps is mentioned in some guides as a possible source of accommodation. Please note this is NOT the case. Some trainees/volunteers may put people up if they meet them, but this is not a reliable source. The ***Maison du Passage*** just outside Kiffa does not have accommodation, and that in Chinguetti is closed. Accommodation is occasionally possible at **Catholic Missions**. In many towns the main source of accommodation is often **local hospitality**. Gifts such as biros, lighters, or small Western items are the usual means of recompense.

Food and drink

Food
Travellers should not go to Mauritania expecting a taste sensation. The food, much of which is imported, is often dull. It is often difficult to get fruit and vegetables outside Nouakchott and Nouadhibou, indeed food supplies are difficult in the interior and travellers should be prepared with their own back-up. Mauritanian food is dominated by lamb, beef, camel, chicken and fish, with rice, *couscous* and pasta. Dates are easy to find. The fruit in the S is varied and good. Travellers can purchase plenty of expensive imported tinned food in both Nouakchott and Nouadhibou.

Restaurant Classifications

Given the variations in price of food on any menu our restaurants are divided where possible into three simple grades:
♦♦♦ expensive, ♦♦ average and ♦ cheap.

Drink
Mauritanians drink a lot of tea, served bitter in small glasses, which should be drunk quickly so the glass can be passed on for the next person to use, as well as *zrig*, milk mixed with water and sugar. Canned and bottled soft drinks, and mineral water, can be bought in most towns. **Alcohol** is officially banned in Mauritania, but is available in a few large hotels in Nouakchott and Nouadhibou, and at the American and French clubs in Nouakchott.

Where to eat and drink
In Nouakchott and Nouadhibou there are a number of restaurants, in the hotels and outside, primarily serving European food. Prices can be as expensive as in Europe. Elsewhere there are tents serving basic food, although hygiene is often inadequate.

Getting around

Air
This is one of the best means of getting around the country, with fares only 2 or 3 times that of the taxis, whilst the services are, of course, far quicker. **Air Mauritanie** runs a reasonably good network, although services can be cancelled or delayed at short notice. There are daily or twice daily services between Nouakchott and Nouadhibou. There is a weekly service connecting Nouadhibou with Atar, and an-

other with Zouerate. There are 3 services a week between Atar and Nouakchott, 2 a week between Zouerate and Nouakchott, 2 a week connecting Nouakchott with Tidjikja and Kiffa, and another 2 with Selibaby and Kaedi, and a weekly service between Nouakchott, Aioun-El-Atrouss and Nema. The airline's offices are at Ave Gamal Abdel Nasser, BP 41, Nouakchott, T 52211, and BP 10, Nouadhibou, T 45022.

● Train

Mauritania has only one railway line, which runs from the NE iron ore town of Zouerate to the port of Nouadhibou. The train is primarily for transporting iron ore, it is slow and very long. The operating company normally attaches a basic passenger compartment, but many Mauritanians travel for free in the open trucks on top of the piles of iron ore. This is a very cold and extremely dusty way of travelling, so take warm clothing and a scarf to cover the mouth and eyes. There are two trains a day either way. These can be taken from Zouerate or Nouadhibou, or either way from Choum, mid-way along the line, between the Moroccan border and the town of Atar. See also **page 385**.

● Road

The main road in the country is the Route de l'Espoir, from Nouakchott through Kiffa and Aioun-El-Atrouss to Nema, although even this is narrow and pot-holed in parts. There are also adequate roads from Rosso to Nouakchott, Nouakchott to Akjoujt and Aleg to Bogué. There is, incredibly, no black top road from Nouakchott to Nouadhibou, nor for that matter, anywhere else in the country. Consequently public transport is limited, infrequent, very slow and expensive, and driving in one's own vehicle is difficult.

Bicycles/motorcycles These are totally impractical in Mauritania.

Bus These run along the Route de l'Espoir, between Nouakchott and Nema. They are very slow, uncomfortable and infrequent, but much cheaper than the shared taxis. Buses leave from the *Gare Routière* in Nouakchott.

Car hire Car hire in Mauritania is expensive and limited to Nouakchott and Nouadhibou. There is a **Europcar** at Nouakchott airport. In some places, such as Atar, Land Rovers can be hired, with or without a driver.

City minibuses In Nouakchott the best means of transport, and a fairly cheap one at that, is the green and yellow *transports urbaines* minibuses that hurtle around the city. Travellers will need to ask locals where to wait. Each minibus has a boy hanging out the back door, who takes the money and knows the route.

City taxis In Nouakchott and Nouadhibou are not as standard in appearance as in many cities, but are usually fairly recognizable. There is a base price, but prices are in general negotiable as there are no meters.

Hitch-hiking Most transport in Mauritania will require payment.

Motoring It is important to bear in mind that there are very few black top roads in Mauritania. Those in the desert can become hazardous and difficult to follow because of drifting sand, those in the S can become waterlogged because of rain. Coastal routes are dangerous because of sandbanks and tides. Thus a 4 wheel drive vehicle, careful planning, and all necessary equipment, are essential prerequisites of a journey. Stock up on petrol, oil, water and food, and carry a first aid kit and shelter at all times, as well as a repair kit with all essential spare parts, shovels, ropes and sand ladders. When one is stuck in sand, let out air from the tyres. In a breakdown, stay near the vehicle. Inform the authorities in each settlement of the route to be followed, and in the deep desert it is preferable to travel in convoy and to hire a guide. Take into account that there is little help on hand for motorists with problems. See main introduction, **page 42**.

Nouakchott to Atar (8 hrs) is fairly straightforward, as is Nouakchott to Kiffa, Aioun-El-Atrouss and Nema, and Nouakchott to Rosso. The track from Atar to Choum is rough but possible, that from Atar to Chinguetti and Ouadane is very difficult. Nouakchott to Nouadhibou is not black top, indeed it runs along the beach for part of the distance. This route is not advised for the independent motorist.

Taxis brousses These are normally large Peugeot 504 estates, which take 9 passengers. They will leave when 9 passengers are assembled. There are standard fares, about which the drivers are normally honest. If in doubt, check with the police. Journeys will be interrupted by frequent tea stops, in addition to the prayer stops. The taxi driver will normally pay for the tea. Drivers and passengers are quite casual about deciding to stop for the night under a tent, and equally casual about transferring passengers from one car to another. It is relatively straightforward to get taxis between Nouakchott and Rosso, Nouakchott and Atar, and along the Route de l'Espoir, between Nouakchott, Kiffa, Aioun-El-Atrouss and Nema. There are also services in the Senegal Valley area.

Trucks and Land Rovers Off the black top roads, trucks and Land Rovers act as taxis, notably between Nouakchott and Nouadhibou. Trucks and minivans also follow the same routes as the *taxis brousses*, but are less comfortable and slower.

Communications

● Language

Arabic is the main language, and has the status of official language. The form of Arabic spoken in Mauritania is Hassaniya. In the S a number of African languages are spoken by a substantial minority, including Wolof, Fula, Pulaar and Soninke. Other languages are spoken by migrants from Mali, Senegal and other W African states. Due to the linguistic diversity of the state French is often used as a language of communication between the different linguistic groups. English is very rarely spoken.

● Postal services

There are large *PTTs* (post offices) in Nouakchott and Nouadhibou, and smaller offices in regional centres such as Nema, Aioun-El-Atrouss, Kiffa, Kaedi, Rosso and Atar. Post from and to Mauritania is very slow. Letters can be received *poste restante*, although it is perhaps best to use just Nouakchott *PTT Centrale* for this. DHL have an office next to *Hotel Marhaba* in Nouakchott.

● Telephone services

The Mauritanian telephone system is connected by satellite with the international system, but it is not cheap to call overseas. It is easiest to call from the large hotels or *cabine telephonique*.

Entertainment

● Media

Daily papers, and some aged international newspapers, are available in Nouakchott. There is an extremely lively local press published in French. The best are 'Mauritanie Novelles' and 'Le Calame'. The state owned radio service, run 0by the *Office de Radiodiffusion et Télévision de Mauritanie*, broadcasts in French, Arabic, Wolof, Toucouleur and Sarakolé. The BBC World Service (Africa) can be picked up for part of the day on long wave frequency. There is a basic TV service broadcast in colour which began in 1984. Finding a TV set may be difficult, with little reward when found.

● Sports

There are almost no sporting facilities in Mauritania. The most likely activities are swimming and fishing. The latter is a popular activity because of Mauritania's rich fishing grounds and a great variety of fish is caught by enthusiasts. **Air Afrique** and **Adrar Voyages** organize a number of packages, at, for example, Keur Massène (**see page 393**), Baie de l'Étoile (**see page 383**) and Banc d'Arguin (**see page 381**).

Holidays and festivals

1 Jan: New Year's Day
26 Feb: National Reunification Day
8 Mar: Women's Day
1 May: Labour Day
25 May: Organization of African Unity Day
10 July: Armed Forces Day
28 Nov: Independence Day
12 Dec: Restructuration Day

The dates of the Islamic religious holidays and the fast, Ramadan, are celebrated on different dates each year as they are calculated according to the moon (**see page 30**). Approximate dates for 1995:

1 Feb: Beginning of Ramadan
4 Mar: End of Ramadan
10 May: Festival of Sacrifice
31 May: Islamic New Year (Anno Hegira 1416)
9 Aug: Prophet's Birthday

Further reading

● Books

Abeille, Barbara (1979) *A Study of Female Life in Mauritania*, USAID: Washington DC – study for American aid organization; Calderini, Simonetta; Cortese, Delia; Webb, James, L.A jnr (1992) *Mauritania* (World Bibliographical Series Vol.141), Clio Press: Oxford – a comprehensive bibliography of sources in European languages; de Chassey, Claude (1984) *Mauritania 1900-1975*, L'Harmattan: Paris – introduction to the country; Gerteiny, Alfred G. (1981) *Historical Dictionary of Mauritania* (African Historical Dictionaries No 31), Scarecrow

Press: Metuchen (NJ) – basic historical facts, people and places; Gerteiny, Alfred G. (1967) *Mauritania*, Pall Mall: London – useful summary of Mauritania, its geography, history and people; Handoff, Robert E (ed) (1990) *Mauritania: A Country Study*, US Government Printing Office: Washington D.C. – official study in this comprehensive series, covers most aspects of the country in some detail; Hudson, Peter (1990) *Travels in Mauritania*, Virgin Books: London – a very readable account of a recent visit to Mauritania; Moorhouse, Geoffrey (1986) *The Fearful Void*, Penguin: Harmondsworth – aborted trans-Saharan journey; Norris, H.T. (1986) *The Arab conquest of the western Sahara*, Longman: Harlow – draws on local sources to describe the process of Arabization, and the structure of society in the past; Ould Daddah, Mokhtar (1973) *Mauritania: A Land of People*, Centre d'Information et de Formation: Nouakchott – dated and superficial propaganda from the then president; Stewart, C.C. (1973) *Islam and Social Order in Mauritania: a case study from the nineteenth century*, Clarendon Press: Oxford – a biography of a 19th century sheikh who founded Boutilimit; Stone, Diana, 'The Moors of Mauritania' in Carmichael, P. (1991) *Nomads*, Collins and Brown: London – focussing on a group of contemporary camel nomads; Toupet, C., 'Nouadhibou (Port Etienne) and the Economic Development of Mauritania', in Hoyle, B.S./Hilling, D. (eds) (1970) *Seaports and Development in Tropical Africa*, London – for those with a fascination for ports; Westebbe, Richard M. (1971) *The Economy of Mauritania*, Praeger: New York – comprehensive but dated guide to the depressed economics of the country.

● Maps and town plans

There are no useful town plans of Nouakchott or Nouadhibou. Other towns are easy to explore in a few minutes. For maps of Mauritania the choice is limited to a few undetailed large-scale sheets available at well-stocked map specialists. Michelin 953 gives an overall view. The French (IGN) map costing £7.50 (must be ordered from Stanfords bookshop in London) has also been recommended.

ALGERIA

Contents

Maps

Introduction

Tourism, until recently, has been Algeria's greatest potential earner of foreign exchange yet those who travelled there did not find the crowds of foreigners so common in Tunisia or Morocco. The country offers a succession of contrasts, an Algiers bursting at the seams and an unpopulated desert; roads made impassable by snow and roads lost under drifting sands; mountain chains reaching over 2,500m and salt lakes below sea-level. To appreciate these, one had to overcome the problems of access and the lack of suitable accommodation. At present more serious problems prevail. **It is a source of great regret that currently the political unrest makes it impossible to recommend travel here**. (See Political Risks page 28 and Safety page 433.)

Basics

OFFICIAL NAME al-Jumhuriyah al-Jaza'iriyah ad-Dimuqratiyah ash-Shabiyah (Democratic and Popular Republic of Algeria).

NATIONAL FLAG Rectangular, with equal green and white fields vertically separated at the centre; a red crescent and star in central position overlapping the 2 coloured fields.

OFFICIAL LANGUAGE Arabic.

OFFICIAL RELIGION Islam.

INDICATORS *Population* 26.4mn. *Urban* 51.7%. *Religion* Sunni Muslim 99.1%, Christian 0.5%. *Birth rate* 34 per 1000, *Death rate* 7 per 1000, *Life expectancy* 66/66. *GNP per capita* US$1,980.

Environment

Land

The Democratic Republic of Algeria takes its name from Barr Al-Jazair meaning 'lands of the islands'. At 2,381,741 sq km, Algeria is the largest of the 3 Maghreb countries and the second largest country in Africa. By surface area it is the tenth largest in the world and is the equivalent in size of Western Europe, thus being 5 times the size of Spain and 10 times the size of the United Kingdom.

The northern frontier runs 1,200 km along the Mediterranean Sea. Land borders straggle for 6,000 km along the eastern border with Libya and Tunisia. Morocco lies to the W and Mali, Niger and Mauritania run along the southern frontier. There are 3 main physical regions.

The Coastal Hills and Plains

In the N of the country is a fertile, narrow and discontinuous coastal strip where the majority of the population is found. The coast is hilly except for limited

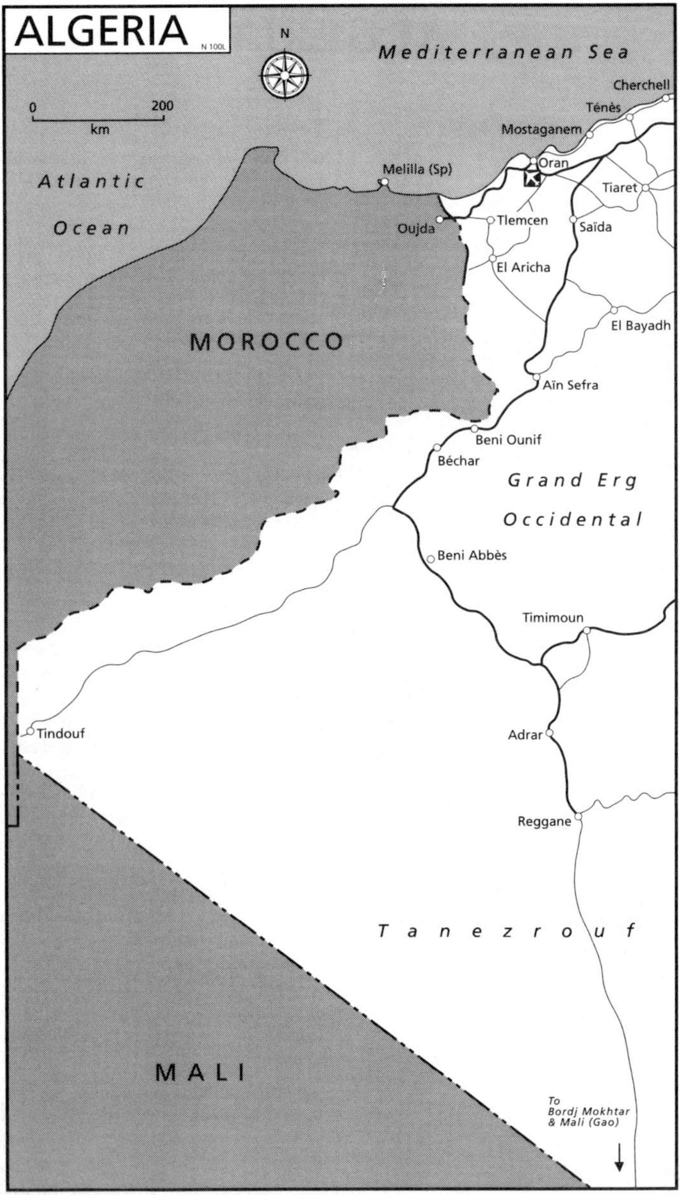
ALGERIA
N 100L
N
0
200
km
Mediterranean Sea
Atlantic
Ocean
Cherchell
Ténès
Mostaganem
Oran
Melilla (Sp)
Tiaret
Oujda
Tlemcen
Saïda
El Aricha
El Bayadh
MOROCCO
Aïn Sefra
Beni Ounif
Béchar
Grand Erg
Occidental
Beni Abbès
Timimoun
Tindouf
Adrar
Reggane
Tanezrouf
MALI
To
Bordj Mokhtar
& Mali (Gao)

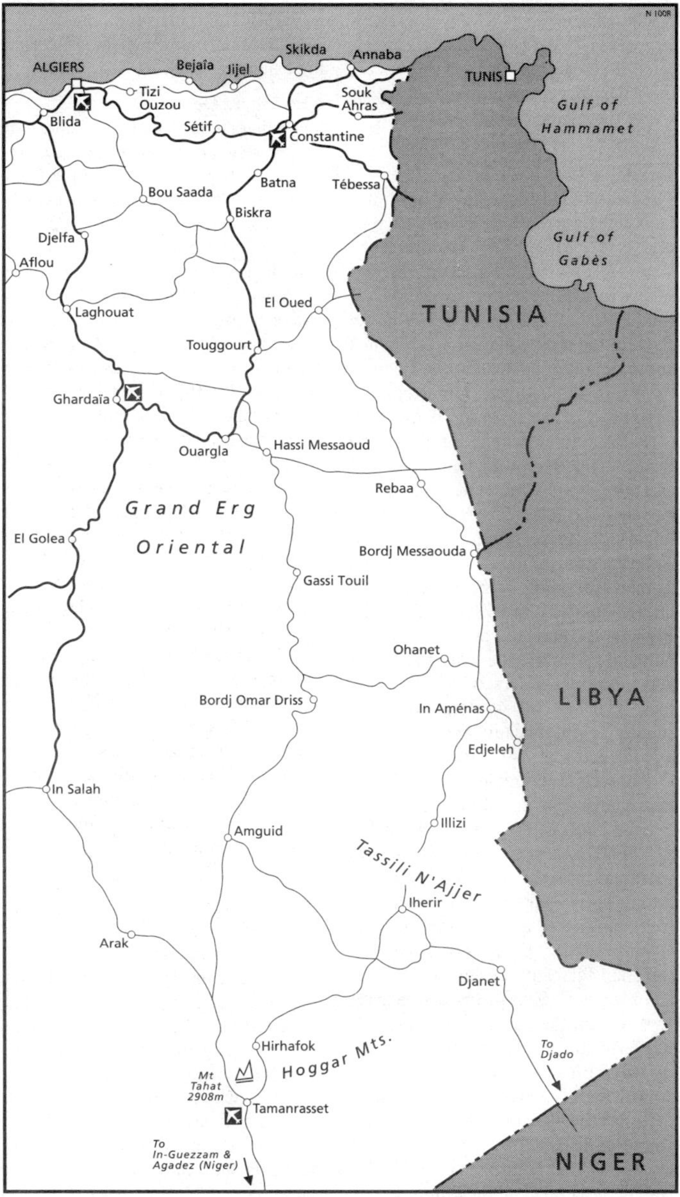
N 100R
ALGIERS
Bejaïa
Jijel
Skikda
Annaba
TUNIS
Tizi
Ouzou
Souk
Ahras
Gulf of
Hammamet
Blida
Sétif
Constantine
Batna
Tébessa
Bou Saada
Biskra
Djelfa
Gulf of
Gabès
Aflou
El Oued
Laghouat
TUNISIA
Touggourt
Ghardaïa
Ouargla
Hassi Messaoud
Rebaa
Grand Erg
Oriental
El Golea
Bordj Messaouda
Gassi Touil
Ohanet
Bordj Omar Driss
In Aménas
LIBYA
Edjeleh
In Salah
Illizi
Amguid
Tassili N'Ajjer
Iherir
Arak
Djanet
Hirhafok
Hoggar Mts.
To
Djado
Mt
Tahat
2908m
Tamanrasset
To
In-Guezzam &
Agadez (Niger)
NIGER

reaches of plain on which Algeria's main cities, Algiers, Annaba and Oran, are located. To the immediate S of the coast is the Atlas range, a mountainous region where the main ridges run from SW to NE, more or less parallel to the coast.

The Atlas

The great eroded folds of the Atlas Mountains date from the Tertiary age and comprise 3 sub-regions. First, the **Tell Atlas** made up of hills, internal basins and valleys runs in the W from the Moroccan frontier to Cap Carbon at Bejaïa in the E. Here the most productive farmlands are to be found in the Mitidja Plain to the S and W of Algiers. Unfortunately, large areas of the plain are being built over as Algiers city expands rapidly. The Bejaïa Plain is another zone of intense agricultural development. Most other basins in the Tell are more arid, lacking reliable irrigation water supplies and suffering from extremes of temperature. The highest points of the Tell are in the Djebel Ouarsenis at 1,985m and the Kef Righa at 1,714m, both now conserved as national parks, together with the Titteri and Djurdjura ranges, which attain almost 3,000m. This is a region of outstanding natural beauty and well worth a prolonged visit.

The second sub-region, the **High Plateaux**, runs from the Moroccan frontier E of the Chott Ech-Chergui on a roughly SW to NE axis to Chott El-Hodna and terminating in the detached basin E of Batna. The area is undulating with altitudes ranging from 1,300m in the W to 400m in the E. The western districts of the High Plateaux are famous for their abundance of esparto grass (see page 554) though the area in general is austere, arid and relatively featureless.

The third sub-region is the **Saharan Atlas** which is a high rim to the immediate S of the plateaux. There are 3 main chains in the system, the Djebel Amour in the SW, the mountains of the Oulad Nail in the centre and the Monts du Zab in the NE. Rainfall on the Saharan Atlas is higher than on the plateaux and there are extensive ranching pastures.

The Sahara Desert

The Sahara in the S makes up more than 80 per cent of the surface area of the country. It begins as a low flat plain and rises gradually over great distances to the S to become the volcanic Hoggar Massif, 800 km across and 3,000m in altitude. The Hoggar is the geographical centre of the Sahara, its highest peak, Mount Tahat, standing 2,918m. Sand seas and dunes make up a quarter of the region, mainly in the eastern quadrant. The W is characterized by arid gravel and pebble deserts. The deserts contain small pockets of settlement in oases where date production and small scale farming can be carried on using irrigation from shallow wells. In the N is the M'Zab Plateau where esparto grass is the main natural product (see page 554). The M'Zab Plateau is the effective division between the Grand Erg Oriental and the higher Grand Erg Occidental.

NE Algeria differs strongly from the rest of the country. Here the parallel ridges and plateaux are absent and in their place is a set of massifs between the Mediterranean coast and a southern line set by the Hodna and Aurés Mountain blocks. The area includes Lesser Kabylia, Constantine and Annaba in a region of tremendous variety of landscape and culture.

Rivers

Most surface streams in Algeria are seasonal. The main rivers are the Chelif, which drains the Tell Atlas over 200 km, and the Soummam, which flows from a source in Grande Kabylia. Other river valleys, notable for providing routeways from N to S, include the Rhumel and the Seybouse, which drain the high plains of Sétif and Constantine. In the E, the streams are short in length with steep gradients and they are harnessed in places to provide hydroelectric power while the longer river systems have dams to provide irrigation. In the height of summer most rivers are no more than a string of pools joined by small trickles of water. In winter however, stream flow can be violent and it is wise never to camp in a dry river valley. The streams of the High Plateaux are unpredictable while those of the Saharan Tell are seasonal. Many of the streams from these areas drain into the temporary salt lakes and marsh lands such as the Chotts of the High Plateaux and the areas S of the Aurés Mountains. Many of the dry water courses have a subterranean water flow.

Climate

Climate, more so even than terrain, is the important factor for agriculture and settlement. Rainfall diminishes from N to S with as much as 1,000 mm per year on exposed northern mountain slopes, reducing to 130 mm in the sheltered regions and to virtually nil in the deep S. Most rainfall comes in the winter, with little in the summer months. The further S and the more arid the conditions, the less reliable and significant the precipitation becomes. The narrow coastal strip enjoys a Mediterranean climate with warm westerly winds in winter and hot dry summers as does, to a more limited extent, the N-facing slopes of the Tell Atlas. Here the rain falls generally in the 3-4 winter months in many cases as snow in the higher hill ranges. In summer the shade temperature can reach 40°C but averages are 12°C in the winter and 25°C in the summer. High relative humidity can make temperatures feel very high.

The climate in the Tell Atlas is much the same but is slightly modified by the higher altitudes which moderate temperatures and increase the amount of rain as well as the length of the rainy period. The High Plateaux are semi-arid with longer rainless summers and overall very erratic precipitation. Annual average rainfall is generally around 400 mm but can be as low as 200 mm. Temperatures are slightly lower than the High Plateaux. The Saharan S is arid, with precipitation less than 130 mm. Many years are entirely rainless. The average daily range of temperature can be 32°C and maximum recorded shade temperatures have reached 55°C. Travellers should remember that in the Hoggar Mountains, altitude reduces temperatures. Beware of winter snows in the Kabylia Mountains, which can block roads and make travel hazardous or at times impossible.

Westerly winds in winter are pleasantly associated with rainfall but the hot dry winds from the S, known as the *Sirocco* or *Ghibli*, are less welcome. Such winds are common on the High Plateaux where they can occur for as many as 50 days a year though they occur less in the coastal areas of the country where their incidence is down to some 20 days a year. Nevertheless, the fall in relative humidity and increase in temperature and dust in the atmosphere associated with the *Sirocco* can cause distress. In the summer the sea breeze on the coast helps to temper the heat of the day.

Sunshine is experienced in most months of the year and Algeria is among the least cloudy regions of the world even in winter.

Flora and Fauna

Wildlife resembles that of other Mediterranean countries (see page 36) but the fauna of the desert region is very specialized. There are still a few leopard and panther, but the animals most commonly found in the desert are the gazelles, antelopes and hyenas. In the mountains to the N, wild boars and red deer are common. The Sahara has scorpions and reptiles such as snakes, vipers, and Monitor lizards.

There is a wide variety of birds, many of them staying only during the winter months. These include bustard, plover, snipe, heron, pelican, stork, eagles, vultures, hawks and ostriches.

Agriculture

Climate, especially the level of rainfall, is the dominant factor governing agricultural output. In the northern zone a wide range of Mediterranean crops is produced, often with the aid of irrigation. Dry farming is also practised and there are large areas given over to livestock herding. Some forestry and natural product gathering is possible in the cork oak forests.

Land use in 1990 is given as agricultural land 3.2%, meadows and pastures 13.1%, forests 2.0% and desert and other 81.7%. Only 7.5 million ha are suitable for agriculture, and these are of variable quality, approximately 1 million ha concentrated in the narrow fertile coastal strip, 1 million ha in the High Tell and the remaining, often poor lands of 5.5 million ha, situated in the High Plateaux.

Land tenure

Agricultural land holding has been reformed under state direction since the repatriation of most of the French colonists. Approximately one third of all farmed land, including the best agricultural areas, was under French control but was sequestrated after Independence. Until recent years one fifth of the land was held by large and often absentee Algerian landlords and an unsuccessful attempt was recently made to distribute this to peasant farmers. On the remaining farming land, about 47% of the total, small private farmers have a mass of tiny and fragmented holdings. Many plots were assimilated into "socialist villages" in the 1970s and 1980s. Remarkably, the private sector produces the bulk of cereals, vegetables and meat. Since 1985 the government has tried to develop the private sector to compensate for the virtual failure of the state and co-operative farms. So far, however, little of a serious nature has been done to improve the situation in agriculture and to reduce dependency on imported foodstuffs.

Development potential

The potential for development in Algeria is considerable. Improved provision of irrigation water, better use of existing resources and a positive attitude towards farming from the government would all give the country a better level of farm output. Rapid urbanization and growth of the total population has probably already outstripped the capacity of domestic farmers to feed all Algerians. However the diversity of food available could be much developed despite climate constraints on farming as a whole.

People

Total population

The distribution of population is directly related to the amount of rainfall and soil fertility. The majority of people live in the richer, well-watered northern region of the country adjacent to the Mediterranean coast. The population in 1992 was 26,401,000 and is projected to be 33,000,000 by the year 2000. This implies a doubling of the population within 28 years, posing immense problems for the future.

Racial composition

The ethnic composition in 1983 was Arabs 83% and Berbers 17%, although there are large overlaps between the 2 populations where inter-marriage has taken place over many years.

It is estimated that about 82% of the population speak Arabic and the others speak forms of Berber with Arabic as a second language. Many Algerians speak French, but very few speak English. Forms of Berber include Taqbaylit (spoken by the Kabilis in the northern mountains of that name) and Tamashak, spoken by the Touareg nomads of the S. There is still speculation as to the origins of the Touareg tribes. It is suggested that they came from SW Asia in about 3000 BC. According to Ibn Khaldoun they were only converted to Islam in the 9th century and rejected the faith 14 times. They call themselves Imaghzen, '*the free ones*' and still pursue their independent ways of life. The role of the women is important, and in contrast to the Arab population, the women are unveiled and the men wrapped in long blue scarves, covering all but their eyes. The Kabyles are also an important group of Berber origin. They are thought to have come from Yemen, but again this is only speculation.

Location of population

With 53% of the people living in towns, Algeria is becoming a highly urbanized country. The main concentration of population is in the large towns of the N, with something like 94% of the population living in the northern part of the country, covering only 14% of the total area. Greater Algiers, the capital and chief industrial centre, has a population of 3 million and towns like Oran, the second port and an equally important industrial centre has 1 million. Other important northern towns include Constantine, an administrative and commercial centre with a population of 750,000, Annaba 450,000, Tizi Ouzou 350,000, Sétif 200,000, Tlemcen 200,000, and Batna 182,000.

Population densities

The average population density for the country as a whole is given as 11.1 people per sq km (1992). In the northern region it does not fall below 30 people per sq km with some *wilayat* (provinces) reaching 1100 people per sq km (Tizi Ouzou). The density of population in parts of the Sahara is given in sq km per person rather than people per sq km.

Age groups

The demographic boom has caused a severe imbalance in age structure. In 1990, 75% of the population was under 20 years of age. On the other hand the male-female ratio is stable and was almost at an equal balance in 1990, with 49.86% females. The age breakdown for 1990 was 43.6% under 15, 28.7% between 15 and 29, 22.3% between 30 and 59 and 5.4% over the age of 60.

Literacy

Education remains a big problem with such a large proportion of the population under 25. According to government figures, 85% of children between the age of 6 and 13 attend school. The literacy rate in 1991 was 52.0% for the population over 15 years of age, with male literacy being 60.0% and female 45.0%. In 1989, 38% of the population over 15 had no formal education. Due to lack of infrastructure, some schools operate on an alternate morning and afternoon basis, in order to cater for all the children. Although far from perfect, the system is nevertheless giving a minimum of education to a majority of the children. Universities and technical colleges are found in Oran, Constantine, Annaba, Batna, Tizi-Ouzou, Tlemcen and Algiers.

Income per head

Income per head in Algeria was estimated at US$1,980 in 1991.

Crude birth rates

Algeria's most demanding problem is the huge rate of increase in population. The population which was only 5 million in 1930 is today over 26 million. The high birth rate and the low death rate give a natural increase of 25.0% against a world average of 17.3%. Life expectancy at 66 years is low compared to European standards.

The number of unemployed stands at 21% of the work force whilst under-employment, though impossible to measure, is estimated to be still greater. Unemployment hits the young particularly hard, the under-25s making up a high proportion of the jobless. Women are also affected but they do not make

Fundamentalism

Islam has been marked over the course of history by the emergence of rigorous revivalist movements. Most have sought a return of the faithful to the fundamentals of Islam – the basic doctrines of the Prophet Mohammad – uncluttered by the interpretations of later Islamic jurists and commentators. Behind the movements was generally the idea that Muslims should go back to the simple basics of their religion. Some, like the Wahhabi movement in Saudi Arabia were puritan in concept, demanding plain lives and an adherence to the tenets of Islam in all daily aspects of life. Others, imposed a rigorous schedule of ritual in prayer and avoidance of the 'unclean' in public life. A good example of this type of reformist tendency was the Senusi Movement in Libya which in the period from the close of the 19th century to 1969 created an educational, commercial and religious society throughout eastern Libya and northern Chad.

Until recent times the fundamentalist movements inside Islam arose from a desire to cleanse the religion of unnecessary ideology and to make all Muslims observe the basic pillars of the Islamic religion – prayer, belief and actions on a consistent and demonstrable basis. In the last 100 years there has been a growing tendency in the Islamic world for revivalist movements to be reactions to political, military and cultural setbacks experienced at the hands of the Western industrialized world. The aim of the reformers has been to make good the disadvantage and backwardness of the Muslim states in contrast with the powerful countries of Europe, America and the Far East. The matter is varied and complex, depending on the particular cases involved, but the clear linkage between an increasingly dominant Western culture and economy and the growth of reactive Islamic movements is inescapable. In North Africa, the power of the Muslim Brotherhood in Egypt was an early form of revivalist movement of this kind. Founded by an

up an important proportion of the work force. Long term unemployment, of over 2 years, is quite frequent and many qualified workers and university graduates are finding it very difficult to find work. An additional problem is the 400,000 young people each year ending school without any kind of diplomas or skills. These high unemployment figures, particularly within the young population, add to social problems and create a fertile ground for political unrest as well as fuelling the black economy.

History since Independence

For the history of this region before Algeria gained Independence see The History of North Africa (see page 57).

After Independence there was a brief struggle for power which ended with **Colonel Boumedienne**, backed by the FLN, in control. **Ahmed Ben Bella** was elected premier to run Algeria as a revolutionary Arab-Islamic state based on principles of socialism and collective leadership. Co-operative farms were set up on what had been French-owned land and handed over to landless peasants. Yet socialism did not extend so far as to redistribute the lands of wealthy and influential Algerians. The marriage of socialism and Islam was not easy; for example the socialist view of equality for women in the new state conflicted with Islamic principles.

Following the bloodless coup of 1965, Colonel Boumedienne attempted to sort out the problems of under-employment, unemployment and lack of expertise in public administration. Many Algerians

Egyptian school teacher, Hassan al-Banna in 1928, it initially tried to take Islam back to its roots and therefore to its perceived strengths but was later taken over by extremists who used its organization for political ends. The development of the Muslim Brotherhood as a clandestine political group and the harnessing of religious fervour to political objectives, including the assassination of political enemies, set the pattern for most later movements of the kind.

The Iranian revolution of 1979, taken over by fundamentalist religious leaders after the overthrow of the Shah, gave a great boost to revivalist Islamic groups by demonstrating that Islam could be used as a means of changing the political system, defying the West and bringing about radical social reform.

In North Africa there was a rapid spread of fundamentalism in the 1980s and early 1990s. In Egypt the Muslim Brotherhood remained the main organization though other smaller sects were also founded. The Iranian model of Islamic revolution was adopted in Algeria where the Fundamentalist Islamic Salvation Front has become a serious contender to take over the established but politically isolated National Liberation Front government. Fundamentalism in Sudan has been adopted as a system of government and many of the attributes of the Iranian revolution have been copied, some with Iranian assistance. Libya has not been threatened by Islamic fundamentalism on the scale experienced elsewhere in the region. The régime in Libya has some Islamic credentials with which to protect itself though a Wahhabi movement did emerge among university students on a small scale in the 1980s. Morocco, although deeply Islamic, has always had its own form of Muslim rule through the royal family, itself of descent from the Prophet Mohammed. Islam in Morocco is also something of a law unto itself with a heavy bias towards vernacular mystical forms, which makes the appeal of puritanical and fundamental Islam less appealing than elsewhere.

found their only source of employment was as guest workers in France despite the racial tensions there. Concentration on industrial development and the loss of French farmers caused agricultural production to fall below pre-revolutionary levels. Attempts were made to distribute more land and to reduce illiteracy. After his death in 1978, Boumedienne was replaced by **Colonel Chadli Benjedid**, who was the head of state until Jan 1992. The 1980s saw the agricultural sector still in poor health, despite its enormous labour force. The **FLN** remained the only political party while the problems of a cumbersome centralized bureaucracy grew acute. Positive attempts were made to reduce dependence on imported goods but the Algerians faced increasing economic hardship, for which they blamed the government. The 1980s also saw the rise of Islamic fundamentalism, leading to riots in 1985 when the government was called a *'band of atheists'* by its Islamic opponents.

In 1985 Chadli's new charter removed most of Boumedienne's appointees and reinstated many who had been previously disgraced. Legislation was passed to encourage private sector involvement as government controls and central planning were reduced. But President Chadli moved slowly so as to preserve a political balance. Following the riots of Oct 1988, a new constitution was approved. Under this, the role of the ruling FLN was reduced, political opposition groups were allowed but with some controls, the role of the army was limited to defence and public sector workers were given the right to strike.

In July 1989, a new law permitted opposition groups to form political parties but with many restrictions, effectively preventing the FLN from losing its dominant role, although in practice many of these restrictions seem to have been later ignored.

In Dec 1991, a **general election** was held, but the second round of the elections was never held due to the resignation of President Chadli. He was pressurized into resignation by the imminent victory of the **Islamic Salvation Front** whose political agenda was the creation of an Islamic state. The country is now led by a transitional government the core of which is military men.

Algerian foreign policy is anti-imperialist and supports struggles for liberation. Algeria has been noted for its conciliatory efforts in the Iran-Iraq war and in various border disputes between neighbouring states. The country gives support to the Polisario guerrillas in their conflict with Morocco in former Spanish Sahara, though it is phasing out its role in that arena. The Algerian-Morocco border reopened in 1988, but entry points are limited and a full political rapprochement is awaited despite both sides' adherence to the UMA (Maghreb Arab Union).

Modern Algeria

Government

The republic Algeria is a multiparty republic with one legislative house known as the National People's Assembly which contains 295 members elected by universal adult suffrage. The political system is presidential, the head of state appointing the prime minister and other ministers who meet weekly. In Feb 1989, a new Constitution guaranteeing multiparty democracy was approved by referendum, giving rise to the Dec 1991 parliamentary elections. The Head of State and government was, until Jan 1992, Chadli Benjedid, elected by popular suffrage in 1979 for a period of 5 years and reelected in 1984 and 1989.

Until the Dec 1991 elections, the largest Party was the **National Liberation Front (FLN)** of which the president was secretary-general. The results of the election's first round gave the newly formed Islamic Salvation Front (FIS) some 188 seats and the FLN only 15. The second round of the elections was never held due to the resignation of President Chadli. A group of army officers stepped into power and established the **Higher Council of State (HCS).** This amounted to a military takeover to prevent the FIS from gaining power as they were certain of victory in the second round of the elections. On Feb 9, a state of emergency was declared and the FIS was banned. In early 1994 a new president was appointed to lead a transitional régime. The new president, Liamine Zeroual, a former senior army officer and minister of defence, is determined to open dialogue with the banned FIS. The most likely outcome of the transitional presidency will be a coalition régime leading to new elections under much stricter electoral laws..

Provincial administration is executed through 48 ***wilayat*** (provinces) headed by a wali, an elected member of the central government who runs the province with the assistance of an elected executive council. The *wilayat* are also divided into *dairate*, which are smaller municipal areas. Each town has its municipal council, the Assemblée Populaire Communale, which is elected. Since 1989, the government has been trying to give more independence to the provinces and the push towards decentralization has been welcome.

Economy

The Algerian economy has shifted dramatically from the dominance of agriculture at the time of Independence to dependency on urban services and industry. The confidence and security needed for industrial development were provided by exploitation of oil and natural gas reserves. The economy grew rapidly, with investments in large industrial projects, as well as the extensive development of the hydrocarbon sector.

The 1980s were less successful, falling oil revenues and rising debts reducing the industrial growth. The 1989 loan package from the IMF of US$1 billion indicates the size of the problem at that time. By the late 1980s, Algeria was oil-dependent with large shares of GDP arising in state-funded oil, construction and services. Much economic activity was undertaken in the informal so-called 'black economy' and not necessarily included in official GDP.

Structure of the Economy 1987	(%)
Agriculture	14.9
Construction	17.3
Hydrocarbons	17.7
Transport/Communications	5.1
Other mining	0.4
Trade	14.2
Manufacturing	13.6
Other services	15.4
Public utilities	1.4
Total	100.0

Source: *Encyclopaedia Britannica.*

Agricultural production

Agricultural production from what was once termed '*the bread basket of the Roman Empire*' has fallen dramatically since Independence, from 93% self sufficiency to an import dependency of more than 60% of requirements of cereals. Agriculture's contribution to GDP in 1987 was only 15% and a mere 14% of the work force were in farming against twice those proportions 20 years earlier.

The major livestock holdings in 1991 were sheep (13,350,000) with smaller numbers of goats (3,800,000) and cattle (1,443,000). Asses (see box, p 431) are used rather than mules, donkeys or camels and there are 24,000,000 chickens. The supply of red meat has remained constant whereas the rearing of white meat from battery chickens has increased substantially.

Traditional crops

The main crops are **cereals**, such as soft wheat, hard wheat, barley, oats, maize, sorghum and rice, **vegetables**, including beans, peas, lentils, chick peas, fresh vegetables like potatoes, cucumbers, tomatoes, onions, French beans, carrots, melons and water melons and artichokes, as well as tobacco, sunflower, sugar beet, tomatoes for tinning and sunflower as industrial crops. **Vines** are also grown for grapes and wine. Large numbers of **citrus fruits** are cultivated such as oranges, mandarins, clementines, lemons, and grapefruit.

Most production is for local consumption and the main agricultural exports are olives, figs, the famous *deglet nur dates*, wine and tobacco. Wine has been an increasing problem as freedom of access to the French market has declined and the area under the vine has drastically reduced.

Due to climatic constraints, most products are grown in the northern areas. Citrus fruit comes mainly from the coastal districts where water is available. Olives are grown in the western coastal belt and the Kabylia region and dates are a speciality of the southern oases.

Agriculture is in a poor state as the farmers need more encouragement from the government to improve production. Without more irrigation, water and easier availability of credit to purchase fertilisers and machinery, it is hard to see how they can succeed. Improved storage facilities for crops, as well as better roads and electricity supply are also badly needed. The government has never been seriously interested in agriculture and promises of land reform, privatization and development funds have never been fulfilled. The 5-year plan of 1985, for example, aimed to channel 40% of state investment into agriculture, principally for the purchase of farm equipment and fertilisers, but this had little effect due particularly to the decrease in state resources caused by falling oil prices.

The forested area has been much reduced by clearance but the Tell Atlas still has suitable conditions for pines and cork oak. A programme for reafforestation has begun, concentrating on the more drought resistant pines in areas of the High Plateaux.

Fishing
Algeria makes only modest use of its sea coast for fishing. The fish catch in 1990 was 91,093 tonnes.

Primary industry
Primary industries make up 17% of GDP (1988). The main products mined are mercury, iron ore, phosphates, gypsum, barite, zinc and silver. Current output is moderate:

Production of minerals 1990

	(tonnes)
Iron ore	2,700,000
Barite	42,800
Phosphates	1,224,000
Zinc	10,000
Gypsum	275,000
Silver (troy ounces)	96,500

Source: *Encyclopaedia Britannica*

Manufacturing industry
Other than petrochemicals, produces mainly for internal consumption and represents 14% of GDP (1988). The main items are for construction such as cement, bricks, structural steel and basic materials for other industries like ferro-alloys and crude steel. There is a growing automobile assembly industry with other light consumer goods and food processing industry in the main towns of the N.

Service industry
This sector represents 36% of GDP (1988). Investment continues in domestic water supply, sewerage, telecommunications and transport infrastructure, all of which are tremendous tasks in so large a country. Unfortunately much of the boom in services has been funded by the central government in non-commercial areas and very large proportions of national wealth are absorbed unproductively in defence and the civil service.

Tourism
Is a trade that is still in its infancy in Algeria. There are no large tourist towns on the coast as in Morocco and Tunisia, adding to the charm of the country. The government intends to develop tourism as a source of foreign currency. In 1990, receipts from tourism were US$149 million. Institutional changes needed to promote tourism such as the loosening of currency restrictions and easier provision of visas are still awaited.

Energy
Hydrocarbons earned 87% of foreign currency in 1992, generated 17.7% of GDP and provided 38.1% of government income and this despite a fall in the international price for crude oil in recent years. Proven reserves for petroleum are only 9,200 million barrels, good for only 21 years at present rates of output. Deteriorating crude reserves has led to an effort to concentrate on exploitation of the more abundant natural gas. Published proven reserves of natural gas in 1991 stood at 3,600 million cubic metres enough to last for 70 years at current levels of output. Algeria is a member of Opec and, through it, is pressing for an improved international oil price. Oil and gas are looked on as a source of industrial raw materials and fuel in Algeria rather than simply as primary product exports. A large petrochemical and refining industry has been set up at sites such as Arzew, Bejaïa and Skikda to which natural gas and crude are carried by pipelines from the southern fields. Unfortunately these efforts at industrialization using hydrocarbons have been dogged by inefficiencies and have starved the rest of the economy of resources.

Trends in the economy
Exports are mainly in the form of mineral fuels and lubricants (98% of GDP)

mainly sold to the EU (74%) and the USA (19%). Imports in 1991 were high including raw materials for industry at 6.0%, machinery and equipment at 62.4%, food and beverages at 26.0% and consumer products at 4.6%. These came mainly from EU countries (64%), USA (11.5%) and Japan (5%). Foreign exchange and imports are controlled by the government, so only Algerian goods are available in shops. Since 1991, the government has clamped down on non-essential imports and the total import bill was cut by 20.5%, to the bare minimum needed to keep the economy functioning.

Exposure to **modern communication systems** such as television and telephones remains quite low. In 1990, there was 1 telephone per 23 inhabitants and 1 television per 16 inhabitants.

The main trends in the economy have been adverse since 1985/86 and markedly so since 1987 after which **GDP** per head at US$2,752 fell steadily to US$1,980 in 1991. The economic crisis, caused by the sustained fall in oil prices, severe foreign indebtedness and economic mismanagement is having serious effects. Industrial production is down by 5.5%, with industry only working at 57% of capacity. This is due to shortage of spare parts, working capital and trained personnel. **Inflation** stands at approximately 17% and is worsening as price liberalisation proceeds and the Dinar loses value against foreign currencies. **Foreign debt**, excluding trade related debt, was estimated at US$24,316 million in 1990. Repayments put great pressure on the country. There is now a new IMF loan of US$1 billion and debt rescheduling will take place soon. Meanwhile, Algerian workers are finding it difficult to find jobs in Western Europe, reducing the US$274 million per year remittances formerly coming from this source. There are no simple economic solutions for Algeria for as long as the oil price remains low and domestic output so depressed. The government's economic plan calls for growth through increasing the productivity of existing industrial capacity. Tax collection are also being reformed and attempts made to bring the black market under control.

Economic Indicators

	1988	1989	1990	1991
GDP (US$ billion)	51.9	53.1	51.6	
Imports (US$ billion)	7.4	9.2	10.4	9.1
Exports (US$ billion)	7.7	10.4	15.2	
Balance of Trade (AD billion)	+4.5	+2.3	+13.6	
Foreign Debt (US$ billion)	23.2	24.0	24.3	28.6
Inflation % (1985=100)	127.9	139.8	163.0	

Sources: IMF, EIU, *Encyclopaedia Britannica*

ALGIERS AND ENVIRONS

Contents

Maps

Because of the immense size of Algeria, many tours do not begin in the capital but fly into a more convenient starting point. However, the region around Algiers in 'just a few short steps' encompasses the essence of Rome's domination (evidenced in the coastal residences of Tipasa), the prosperity of the Ottomans when the large kasbah was constructed, the magnificence of Islam with its variety of mosques and minarets and the more recent French cathedral. Beyond these lie the golden beaches of the Sidi-Fredj complex and, behind, the ski resorts nestling under the 1,510m peak of Chréa. Algiers makes an excellent first stop and the transport network allows easy and speedy departure in any desired direction.

ALGIERS

Pop 2,500,000 *Alt* 50m.

History

Algiers, originally known as **Icosium** during the pre-Christian era, was, according to legend, founded by 20 of Hercules' companions who abandoned him during his Mediterranean tour. During the Phoenician and Carthaginian periods, Icosium remained relatively unimportant, not developing until the Arab invasion. In the 10th century, **Bologhine Ibn Ziri** founded the new town named **El Djezaïr**, which rapidly developed into an important commercial centre. The prosperity of the new town was subjected to foreign domination over the following years. In 1235 it fell to the Hafsid King **Abou Zakarya** and in the 14th century for a short period to the Merinids. By the start of the 15th century, the Hafsids had retaken the city and at the beginning of the 16th century the **Spanish**, seeking to consolidate their presence in North Africa, seized control of El Djezaïr. In 1516, threatened by the Spanish presence, the inhabitants called on the pirate **Barbarossa** for assistance. The ensuing struggle between Barbarossa and the Spanish lasted 13 years, El Djezaïr eventually falling into the pirates' hands in 1529. Stones from the partially destroyed fort were used to build the harbour's protective walls, and the town was transformed into a pirates' lair. Many unsuccessful attempts were made by the Spanish and the British to dislodge them.

Climate: Algiers

	Jan	Feb	Mar	Apr	May	Jun	Jul	Aug	Sep	Oct	Nov	Dec	Av/Tot
Max (°C)	16	17	19	21	24	27	28	30	28	25	21	17	23
Min (° C)	10	10	12	14	16	19	22	23	21	18	14	11	16
Rain (mm)	115	85	59	61	27	13	3	7	22	89	108	140	729

On June 14 1830, a **French** attack on the town, now called Algiers, succeeded and a planned short military action resulted in a full occupation until 1962. During those 132 years, the French made many changes to the town. The walls of the kasbah were razed and large boulevards were built. The town expanded rapidly, and for the first time developed outside its original walls. During WWII, Algiers was an important strategic asset. Charles de Gaulle set up his headquarters of the Free French army there in 1943, and the town kept its military importance until the liberation of France. From early Jan 1957, Algiers was in the forefront of the struggle for Independence and when it was granted in 1962, was the scene of great jubilation. As capital of independent Algeria, Algiers has been faced with the endemic problems of overpopulation, shortage of housing and traffic congestion. Nevertheless, Algiers has gained an important place within the international community, organizing important conferences, involving the OAU, Opec and the Non-Aligned movement. In 1980, Algiers hosted a conference on the Iraq-Iran war.

Location

Algiers has an idyllic coastal location, overlooking a beautiful bay with a backdrop of steep wooded mountains. The town, once known as White Algiers due to the whitewashed walls, faces E and is at its most beautiful in the morning sun. The present skyline has 2 important landmarks; to the SE of the centre, the Martyrs' Monument reaching 90m into the sky, and more central, the square shape of the up-market *Hotel Aurassi*. The town is divided into 2 parts. The old town, known as the kasbah lies on the hill, behind the place des Martyrs. The new town, mostly French built, starts by the waterfront at the S of the kasbah and continues S round the bay. One of the main commercial streets is rue Larbi Ben M'Hidi with the central Post Office at its S end. By the sea front between the kasbah and the post office are the train station, the ferry terminal and the Air Algérie air terminal.

Climate

The climate is typically Mediterranean, but with a cooler light wind from the sea. The hottest months are June, July and Aug while the season from Nov to Feb is mild, sometimes rainy and generally humid.

ACCESS Air The airport is situated 22 km outside the city. The easiest and cheapest way to the city centre is the bus that leaves opposite the terminal building. The trip takes about 40 mins and costs AD10. Buses run from 0530 until about 2300 every 20 to 30 mins and stop at the Air Algérie air terminal, by the *Hotel Aletti* close to the sea-front. Otherwise, take a taxi, but agree on a price before departure if it does not have a meter. It should cost no more than AD100.

Trains from the W stop at Agha station which is S along the sea-front. The main bus station is also on the sea front near the train station. The ferry terminal and main train station are on the quayside, in front of the place Port Saïd, below the street level. There is a lift to the street for a minimal fee. There is also a cheap, no time limit, left-luggage deposit at the station. For information, T 647380. It is an easy 4 min walk to the town centre from here.

Road The long distance bus station *Gare Routière* is on route de l'Armée de Libération Nationale near where this approaches the Bassin de l'Agha on the quayside, 10 mins walk at most from place du 1er Mai and 15 mins walk SE from the Grande Poste. Buses No 5, 77 and 72 from here go to place des Martyrs. Between the long distance bus station and the Grande Poste is the bus station for local buses that serve the suburbs of Algiers and the local area.

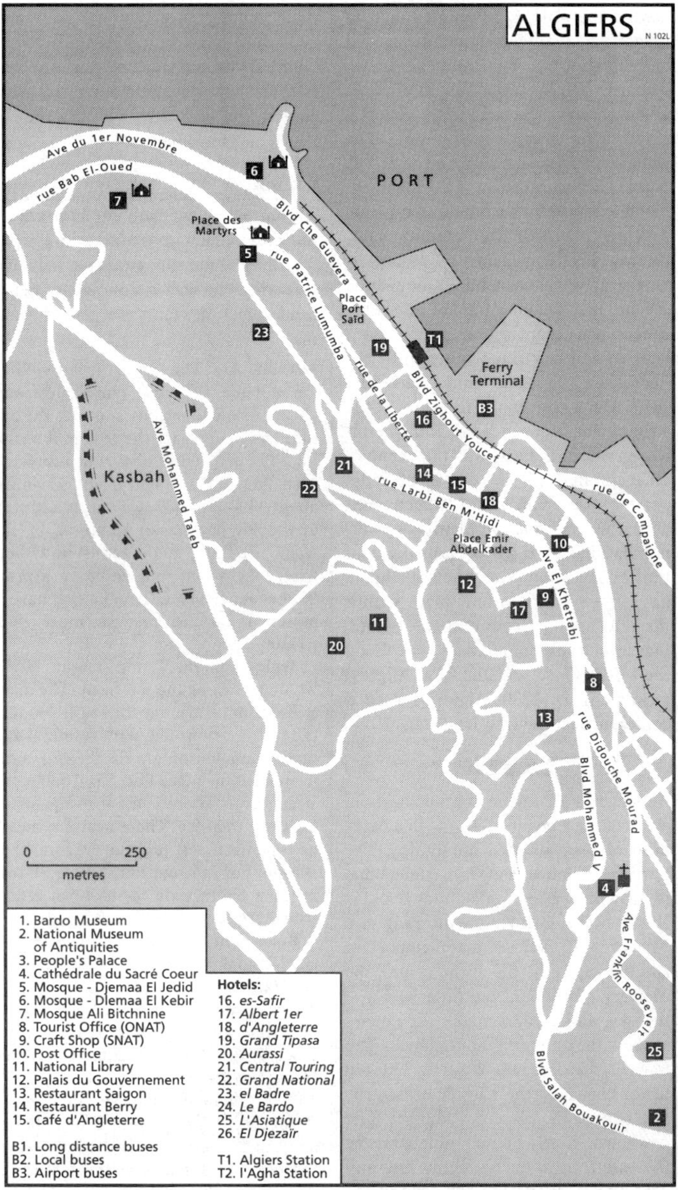
ALGIERS
N 102L
PORT
Ave du 1er Novembre
rue Bab El-Oued
Place des Martyrs
Blvd Che Guevera
rue Patrice Lumumba
Place Port Saïd
T1
Ferry Terminal
B3
rue de la Liberté
Blvd Zighout Youcef
Kasbah
Ave Mohammed Taleb
rue Larbi Ben M'Hidi
rue de Campaigne
Place Emir Abdelkader
Ave El Khettabi
rue Didouche Mourad
Blvd Mohammed V
Ave Franklin Roosevelt
Blvd Salah Bouakouir
0 250
metres
1. Bardo Museum
2. National Museum of Antiquities
3. People's Palace
4. Cathédrale du Sacré Coeur
5. Mosque - Djemaa El Jedid
6. Mosque - Djemaa El Kebir
7. Mosque Ali Bitchnine
8. Tourist Office (ONAT)
9. Craft Shop (SNAT)
10. Post Office
11. National Library
12. Palais du Gouvernement
13. Restaurant Saigon
14. Restaurant Berry
15. Café d'Angleterre
B1. Long distance buses
B2. Local buses
B3. Airport buses
Hotels:
16. es-Safir
17. Albert 1er
18. d'Angleterre
19. Grand Tipasa
20. Aurassi
21. Central Touring
22. Grand National
23. el Badre
24. Le Bardo
25. L'Asiatique
26. El Djezaïr
T1. Algiers Station
T2. l'Agha Station

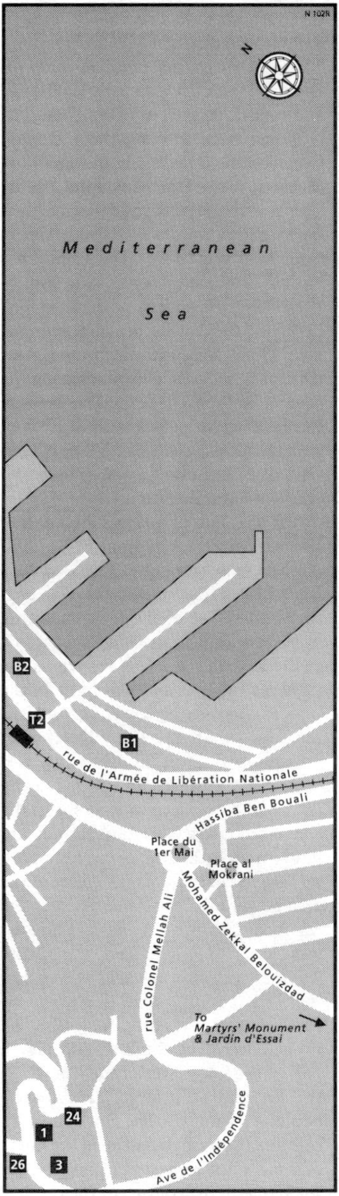

Things to see

Around the city

The *centre ville* is the modern part of the city that stretches more or less from the place Port Saïd to the rue Didouche Mourad. The **rue Larbi Ben M'Hidi** is the main commercial street in Algiers and is now a crowded pedestrian zone. There are a great number of shops, including the *Gallerie Algériennes*, of neo-Moorish style, that should not be missed. A third of the way down is the elegant **place Emir Abdelkader**, with an enormous statue of Abdelkader, the famous resistance fighter. Continuing down the rue Larbi Ben M'Hidi brings you to the **Grande Poste**, a large neo-Moorish building, that is worth a look, even if you do not need to post anything. Opposite the Grande Poste, the Ave El Khettabi leads to the rue Didouche Mourad, another important commercial street, lined with large French style buildings. This street continues up a hill, twisting a little, to the **Cathedral du Sacré Coeur** and to the **Bardo** and **National Antiquity museums.**

The sea front, along the Blvd Che Guevara to the N of the corniche is lined by French buildings with arcades. Behind the sea front, by the Djemaa El Jedid Mosque, is the **place des Martyrs**. This square is the centre of life in the lower part of the kasbah and is extremely lively at all times. Close by, on a square off the rue Amar El-Kama, is the colourful **Chaat market**, selling everything from clothes to fresh fruit and spices.

Most of the mosques and many of the monuments cannot be visited. The hours and days open will be indicated when appropriate. It is important to dress correctly when visiting a mosque. If time is limited, there are a few places that should not be missed. By the sea front, next to the place des Martyrs is the **Djemaa El Jedid mosque**, also known as the Mosquée de la Pêcherie. Built in 1660 by the Turks of the Hanefite sect, it is surprisingly built in the shape of a cross. Legend has it that the mosque was built by a Christian slave, who paid with his life for his sacrilegious efforts. Two streets away, along the sea front is the **Djemaa El Kebir mosque.** The date of its construction is not clear, but it was built in the place of one of the Christian basilicas and is the oldest mosque in Algiers. The main building was probably erected in the 11th century by Youcef Ben Tachfin, and the minaret in 1324. The main courtyard, with its 2 fountains gives an overall impression of great simplicity. Originally the mosque had no ornaments on the outside walls, but in 1837, the French took a marble portico from a demolished mosque and added it to the rue Al Mourabitine side of the mosque. Unfortunately neither mosque can be visited by non-Muslims. Going back towards the NW corner of place des Martyrs you can take the rue Bab El Oued, which leads to the **Ali Bitchnine mosque.** Built in 1623 by Piccini, a rich Italian pirate working for the Turks, the mosque follows the plans of Byzantine churches, with a great octagonal dome over a square room. On 3 sides of this room are galleries, each covered in a small dome. During the French occupation the mosque was converted into a Christian church.

The street on the right side of the Mosque leads to the **Museum of Popular Arts and Traditions**, situated in an old traditional palace built in 1570 by the Turks. In 1830 the palace became the first French town hall and has since been converted into a very interesting museum. The building is as interesting as the exhibits, with beautiful rooms and the ceiling of the main first floor room is particularly attractive. The items displayed include a large variety of regional carpets, highlighting thcir regional differences, together with jewels, pottery and furniture. On the first floor, rooms have been arranged and decorated in the traditional manner. The museum is situated off the rue Hadj Omar, on the left. Open daily 1000-1200 and 1400-1700, except Fri and Sat.

Going back S along the rue Hadj Omar, on the right, along the small rue Mechtri, is the **Dar Mustapha Pacha**. This was the private residence of Mustapha Pacha, who was Bey of Algiers from 1798 until 1805. The palace was built in 1799. Now it serves as an administrative office, so it is possible to look in during the day. Return along the rue Hadj Omar which leads into the place Cheikh Ben Badis. Before reaching the square, on the right is the **Dar Hassan Pacha**, a winter palace built in 1790, of typical Moorish style. The inside may be visited, as the building now houses government administration.

On the left of place Cheikh Ben Badis is the Dar Aziz Bent El Bey, and the Ketchaoua mosque. The **Dar Aziz Bent El Bey** was built in the 17th century and is one of the few remaining important buildings in the lower part of the kasbah. It is also known as the Princess's palace and was built in the typical Moorish style. The courtyard can be visited. The **Ketchaoua mosque** was built in 1794, but was completely restored in 1845. During the French occupation it was initially converted into a Christian church and later into a cathedral. From here walk up into the kasbah, which starts in the area beyond the rue Amar Ali and the rue Abderrahmane Arbadji. **The kasbah** used to encompass the entire town. It was only towards the end of the 19th century that the town expanded outside its original walls. The French destroyed the walls and a large part of the lower area of the kasbah by the sea, and built large, French-style boulevards and houses. Until the 19th century, the kasbah had been the home of some of the richest families in Algeria, but with the coming of the French,

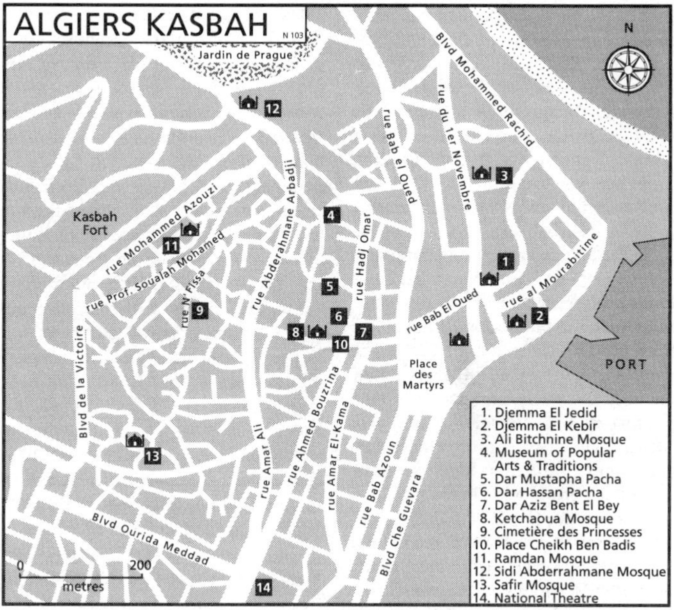

the kasbah became poorer and more decrepit and the wealthy moved out to new, more comfortable, houses. In the 1950s, the colonial government moved half the inhabitants out of the old town, but the kasbah soon refilled with people from the country in search of work. The result was overcrowding, poor living conditions and poorly maintained buildings. For many years the government ignored the problem and it took an important demonstration by the kasbah's inhabitants in 1985 before an organization for the restoration of the kasbah was set up in collaboration with UNESCO. The kasbah has not had a total facelift and problems of overpopulation still exist, but walking around it is still a very interesting experience. The little narrow streets wind up the hill, through arches and short tunnels. The houses are built tightly together and inter-communicate by their roof terraces. If the opportunity arises, visit a house and from the roof admire the superb view over the other white terraces and the bay. In the kasbah few streets are named and it is quite easy to get lost, but people will willingly give you directions, and in any case, all roads downhill lead to the harbour.

Do not miss the **Cimetiére des Princess**, off the rue N'fissa, a quiet spot where one can sit in the shade surrounded by Muslim tombstones. The **Kasbah Fort** built in 1592 and once the Bey's palace dominates the town and the bay. It is here the incident later used by the French as a pretext for the 1830 invasion took place (see page 68). Unfortunately, the fort cannot be visited. From the Kasbah Fort take the Blvd de la Victoire, and then the rue Mohammed Azouzi and on the right, down a small street is the **Sidi Ramadan mosque**. Built in the 16th century before the arrival of the Turks, it is one of the oldest mosques in Algiers but cannot be visited. Take the rue Mohammed Azouzi down some stairs to the **Sidi Abderrahmane Mosque** built between 1696 and 1730. By the entrance is the tomb of a highly venerated 15th century saint. From here you can walk back down the rue Abderrahmane Arbadji to the lower part of the kasbah and the town centre.

To the S there are a number of places of interest. **The Bardo Museum**, 3 Ave Franklin Roosevelt, is at the top of the rue Didouche Mourad: take bus no 15 from in front of the Grande Poste. The museum, set in a beautiful Moorish style mansion has a very large section on the pre-history and ethnography of North Africa. The display of costumes and crafts from the different Algerian ethnic groups is very good. There is also an impressive display of jewellery, especially from Kabylia. On the second floor are displayed objects from the Sahara, in particular from the Hoggar. These include leather goods, camel saddles, clothing and weapons. Open daily except Fri morning and Sat 0900-1200 and 1400-1700.

Further up the hill, in the Parc de la Liberté, is the **National Museum of Antiquities** which has a collection of items including antique mosaics, Roman glass and sculptures and some Islamic art. Open daily except Fri morning and Sat 0900-1200 and 1400-1700. Entry is free on Fri afternoons. The **People's Palace**, is 400m further up the road from the Museum of Antiquities, just off the Ave Franklin Roosevelt. It was the President's residence but in 1987 he gave it to the town of Algiers. It contains a History Museum, with a good display of swords and jewellery dating from the Turkish period, and a Natural History Museum with a great variety of plants, trees and stuffed animals from around the world. The surrounding park is open daily 0900 to 2100 except Mon. The museums are open 0900-1200 and 1400-1800, and closed on Fri.

To go S of Algiers take buses No 7 or 90 and change at place du 1er Mai onto buses No 32 or 65 to reach the **Martyrs Monument** which was built in 1982 and commemorates all those who died in the struggle for Independence. The 3 stylized palm fronds reach a height of 95m and make the monument hard to miss. On the large esplanade in front of the monument is the massive Riad el-Feth commercial centre. Its 3 storeys with fountains and patios, include many restaurants and an open-air theatre. Under the Martyrs monument is the **Jihad Museum**, which covers the entire struggle for Independence since 1830. Unfortunately, the period from 1954 to 1962 is covered rather superficially, and most material is in Arabic. Open daily 0900-1700, except Sat and Sun mornings.

On the other side of the esplanade, the **War Museum** is set in a splendid marble-floored building. This museum is to a certain extent the continuation of the Jihad Museum, covering the same period, but without a clear link between the displays. It nevertheless has some interesting displays, such as a plan of Algiers in the 1830s, showing the defensive logic of the architecture, as well as a real guillotine, and various rooms with displays on the struggle for Independence.

The **Museum of Fine Arts**, is opposite the Jardin d'Essai, at the bottom of the hill, under the Martyrs monument. The bus No 9 from Place des Martyrs stops at the Martyrs monument. The collection has some interesting paintings from well known European painters, and some from contemporary Algerian artists. Open 0930-1200 and 1430-1700 daily except Fri and Sat.

Opposite the museum is the **Jardin d'Essai**, the National Nature Museum, once a very impressive botanical garden which today suffers from neglect. Open 1000-1800, closed Sat.

Parks

Parc de la Liberté is S of the town, at the S end of the rue Didouche Mourad (from the place de La Grande Poste, take bus No 35). This is an attractive park set out in terraces. **Jardin de Prague** situated to the N of the kasbah, behind the Sidi Abderrahmane mosque is a small garden, wonderfully fresh during the warm days. The **War Cemetery** is 500m before Déli-Ibrahim, 10 km to the SW of the city on the N side of the N36. A second area has been dedicated for war graves at the El Alia civil cemetery on the road to El Harrach. It lies to the S side of the W118 from El Harrach.

Local information

CURFEW At time of going to press 2230-0400.

● Accommodation

Price guide:			
L	US$90+	D	US$20-40
A	US$75-90	E	US$10-20
B	US$60-75	F	under US$10
C	US$40-60		

Warning It can be difficult to find a hotel in Algiers, as the town is over-crowded and many Algerians live in hotels. Start searching early as, after midday, finding a room can be very difficult. Ignore the '*complet*' sign which is often on constant display, as they may well have rooms. Also, do not hesitate to ask for directions, as hotels often only have a sign in Arabic, or even none at all.

A *Hotel El Djezaïr*, 24 Ave Souidani Boudjemma, T 601010, F 606408, formerly the *Hotel St George* and traditionally the most fashionable hotel in Algiers, delightful Moorish architecture, attractive bars and terrace, large and well appointed restaurant, 155 elegant rms, fine views over city and bay and (limited) parking space, payment by foreign guests in hard currency only, booking essential; **A** ***Hotel El Aurassi***, Ave Frantz Fanon, T 748252, F 632292, 400 rms with excellent views, pool, tennis, good restaurant, booking essential.

B *Hotel Es-Safir*, 14 Blvd Zighout Youcef on sea-front, T 635040, 150 rm with bath, a/c, some with sea view, good restaurant, payments by foreign guests in hard currency only.

C *Hotel Mouflon d'Or*, BP165, Hydra, T 568225, 60 rms, spacious hotel in very pleasant situation on heights above Algiers, restaurant, bar, shop, pool, garden terrace, car park; **C** ***Hotel Albert 1er***, 5 Ave Pasteur, one block up Blvd Mohammed Khémisti from the Grande Poste, T 630020-2, F 637368, 69 rms, 116 beds, pleasant bar and restaurant, mainly business visitors, payment by foreign guests in hard currency only.

D *Hotel d'Angleterre*, 11 Blvd Ben Boulaïd Mustapha, T 636540, a block to E of place Emir Abdelkader; **D** ***Hotel Samir***, 74 rue Didouche Mourad, T 643064; **D** ***Central Touring Hotel***, 9 rue Abane Ramdane, T 635440, 300m to the S of place Port Saïd, all rm with bath.

E *Grand Hotel Tipaza*, 4 rue Rachid Kessentini, T 630040; **E** ***Grand Hotel Modern***, 7 rue de la Liberté, T 636374; **E** ***Grand Hotel National***, 1 rue Patrice Lumumba, T 634173, close to place Port Saïd at the intersection with the rue Larbi Ben M'Hidi; **E** ***Hotel El Badre***, 31 rue Amar el-Kama, in lower part of kasbah, a small street off place Port Saïd, T 620812, clean, well-kept hotel, over 80 rm, rarely full, communal pay shower (hot), in a noisy area.

● Youth hostels

There are 2 youth hostels: ***213 rue Hassiba-Ben-Bouali***, T 675430, open 0800-1200 and 1400-2200, 74 beds, kitchen, laundry, 4 km from bus station and ferry terminus, train 1 km.

● Camping

Nearest camping site is at **Zeralda**, 40 km W of Algiers by the sea, well connected to Algiers, any bus going to Cherchell or Tipasa stops there. The journey takes 1 hr, and the campsite is 2-3 km further on.

● Places to eat

Price guide:
♦♦♦Expensive; ♦♦average; ♦cheap.

♦♦♦ *Le Bardo*, upper end of rue Didouche Mourad, just below the Musée du Bardo and roughly opposite the Ministry of Public Works (Ministère des Travaux Publics), T 607343, currently fashionable with reputation for good expensive food; ***L'Asiatique***, 2 rue François Garnier, off N side (left side going up) of the upper end of rue Didouche Mourad, near Ministry of Information and opposite Parc de la Liberté, Chinese and Vietnamese cuisine provided by kitchen staff formerly of the celebrated (but now closed) *Saigon*, good food, good service, pleasant ambiance, chic clientèle, seats 60-70, booking advisable.

♦♦ ***Restaurant le Berry***, 8 Blvd Mustapha Ben Boulaïd, behind *Hotel Es Safir*, T 633414/633424, range of interesting dishes including seafood, at reasonable prices served in quiet and rather sober surroundings; ***Restaurant Café d'Angleterre***, 11 Blvd Mustapha Ben Boulaïd, moderate food, moderate service and tolerably priced.

♦For cheap food, the area E of the kasbah is the best place to go. Around the place des Martyrs, and between the place Emir Abdelkader and the place Port Saïd, there are many food stalls and small restaurants selling brochettes, chicken and *merguez* (spicy sausages). In front of the Djemaa El Jedid mosque a small ramp leads to a number of small fish restaurants. **NB:** before ordering any fish, be sure of the price, as this depends on the pre-cooked weight. ***Le Simbad***, on the ramp in front of the El Jedid mosque, expensive, one of the best fish restaurants in Algiers; ***Restaurant La Porte de la Mer***, first restaurant on the right, going down the ramp in front of the Djemaa El Jedid mosque, simple but good local food at very cheap prices; ***Restaurant Bassora***, Blvd Che Guevara, towards the place Port Saïd, good and filling food, Moorish decor, restaurant closes at 2200.

● Airline offices

See Information for Visitors, **p 481**.

● Banks

Banque Central d'Algérie, 8 Blvd Zighout Youcef; **Banque National d'Algérie**, 47 rue Didouche Mourad, Hall Air Algérie, 1 place Audin (open daily 0800-1800 except Fri) and Air terminal, rue Colonel Ben Abderrazak (open daily 0800-1230 and 1330-1900).

● Chemists

All night chemists can be found at 19, rue Abane Ramdane, T 633631 and 2 rue Didouche Mourad, T 634743.

● Discotheques/ night clubs

These are found at the beach resort hotels. Try *El Djazaïr Hotel* and *Hotel Aurassi*.

● Embassies & consulates

See also Information for Visitors, **p 479** for Representation overseas. **Australia**, 12 Ave Emile Marquis, Djenane El-Malik, Hydra, T 601965/602846; **Canada**, 27 bis, rue des Frères Benhafid, Hydra, T 606611; **France**, 6 Ave Larbi Alik, Hydra, T 604488; **UK**, 7 chemin Capt Hocine Slimane, T 605038/605411; **USA**, 4 chemin Cheikh Bachir El Ibrahimi, El Biar, T 601186/601425.

● Emergency numbers

Ambulance T 623333; **Police** T 17.

● Hospitals

Hôpital Mustapha, close to the place du 1er Mai, T 663333.

● Post office

The main Post office is on the Place Grande Poste at the S end of the rue Larbi Ben M'Hidi. Open 0800-1900 and Thur 0800-1300, closed Fri.

● Shopping

Bookshops Most bookshops are along the rue Didouche Mourad and rue Larbi Ben M'Hidi, with a couple in the rue Hamani which joins the bottom of rue Didouche Mourad. There is a shop selling mainly books on Berber culture on the Blvd Zighout Youcef as it approaches Square Port Saïd. Most shops tend to sell only books in French and Arabic. Bookshops are also the place to buy town plans of Algiers.

General The main shopping area with many large stores is in the rue Larbi Ben M'Hidi, and across the place de la Grande Poste, along the rue Didouche Mourad. Crafts can be found in the 3 SNAT (Societé National d'Art et Tradition) stores specializing in local traditional crafts: 2 Blvd Mohammed Khémisti, 1 rue Didouche Mourad and 3 rue Maitre Ali Boumendjel.

● Sport

Golf There is an 18 hole course on Route de Chérage, near the Olympic Stadium.

Skiing For information about the adjacent skiing resorts, contact Fédération Algérienne de Ski, 30 Blvd Zighout Youcef, Algiers.

Tennis Fédération Algérienne de Tennis, 60 rue Larbi Ben M'Hidi.

Sailing is available at Moretti and Sidi Fredj.

Swimming Numerous pools including Olympic pool on Route de Chérage and many good beaches.

● Telephones

Local code 02. The telephone exchange is by Place Grande Poste on the corner of rue Asselah. Open 24 hours.

● Tourist information & travel agents

ONAT (Office National Algerian de Tourisme): Central Office 5 Blvd Ben Boulaïd, T 641550 and at 2 rue Didouche Mourad, T 631066 and 4 rue Elisée Reclus, T 663583. There are also branches in the *Hotel Aurassi*, T 640148 and at the airport, T 753367. All *ONAT* agencies have a travel agency service and sell tickets for all major airlines. They organize interesting half-day tours of the town for which you register the day before.

● Transport

Local: Bus for short distances you will probably need only 1 or 2 routes during your stay in Algiers. For information, go to the bus station either on the Place Grande Poste or on the Place des Martyrs. Bus No 35 or 40 goes from Place Grande Poste to the Bardo Museum. Bus No 5, 72 or 77 from Place des Martyrs to the main bus station, by the sea front. Bus No 32 from place Audin for the Martyrs' monument.

Car hire ONAT, 4 rue Elisée Reclus, T 663583; **Avis**, 109 rue Didouche Mourad, T 668427; **Algérie Auto Tourism**, 120 rue Didouche Mourad, T 616456; **Europacar**, 32 Blvd Mohammed V, T 647793; **Central Auto Location**, 54 Blvd Mohammed V, T 636087; **Algiers Location Auto**, 14 rue Dr Saadane Cherif, T 636905.

Taxi These are plentiful but there are no taxis stations, so flag them down. Each taxi has a meter, but make sure it is used or else negotiate the price beforehand. It may be difficult to find a taxi in the rush hour.

Air To get to the airport either take a taxi or the bus in front of the *Hotel Es-Safir*, on the Blvd Zighout Youcef. The buses run every 30 mins from 0600 to 2300 and the journey takes 45 mins.

For **international flights** see Information for Visitors, **page 481**. In summer, seats are scarce so book well in advance. In Algiers, you will most probably have to pay with Algerian Dinars changed at the official rate, and proved by a document (*Attestation de Cessation de Devises).*

Internal flights: Annaba, Constantine and **Oran** 3 or 4 flights daily; **Béchar** Mon 0715, Tue, Sat 0815, Wed, Fri 0645, Thur 1400, Sun 0800; **Djanet** Mon, Tue, Thur, Sat 0815, Sat 0630; **El-Golea** Tue 0630; **El-Oued** Mon 1015, Wed 0705, Fri 0705, 0800, Sat 0945, Sun 1245; **Ghardaïa** Mon, Wed, Sat 0600, Tue, Thur 0800, 1045, Wed 1600, Fri 1900, Sat 1730, Sun 0930, 1700; **In-Salah** Mon, Wed, Sat 0630. Sun 0900; **Tamanrasset** 2 or 3 flights daily beginning 0600; **Timimoun** Tue 0745.

Train The station is on the quayside by place Port Saïd. Take the lift from the street. For information, T 647380. **Bejaïa** 0530, 0830, 1445, 1545. **Constantine** 0830, 1900, 2100. **Annaba, Souk Ahras, Tunis** 1900. **Tizi-Ouzou** 0550, 1740. All other destinations to the W of Algiers including **Oran** and **Tlemcen** leave from the Agha station, which is S along the sea-front, after the Place du Pérou. For information, T 611510.

Road Bus There are 3 bus stations in Algiers. The main station for direct buses for the Algerian main towns, including Béchar, Ghardaïa, El Oued, Oran and Bejaïa, is after the Agha train station, by the water front. From the place des Martyrs the buses no 5, 72 and 77 go to this bus station. For buses to the W coast to Zeralda, Tipasa, Cherchell and Ténès, the bus station is situated on the sea front, by the Customs House, opposite the place du Pérou. For buses to the E coast the bus station is at the lower level in front of the *Hotel Es-Safir*. **NB:** the main station is well organized with all prices and time displayed. Tickets can be bought in advance, and in summer it is recommended to book at least a day in advance.

Taxi These leave from the ramp by the main train station, in front of the place Port Saïd to all major cities.

AROUND ALGIERS

The N11 coast road W from Algiers goes through a built up area for the first 30 km with only occasional glimpses of the sea. Beyond Aïn Benian, the road swings inland leaving the coastal strip for tourist development and intensive market gardening.

The coast to the west

Moretti and Sidi Fredj

These are both important seaside resorts, mostly frequented by people from Algiers. Their beautiful beaches make these typical resort towns very pleasant for a day trip out of the capital. Unfortunately there are very few hotels and they all tend to be expensive. **NB:** Sidi Fredj is named Sidi-Ferruch on the Michelin map.

Moretti which is only 25 km away

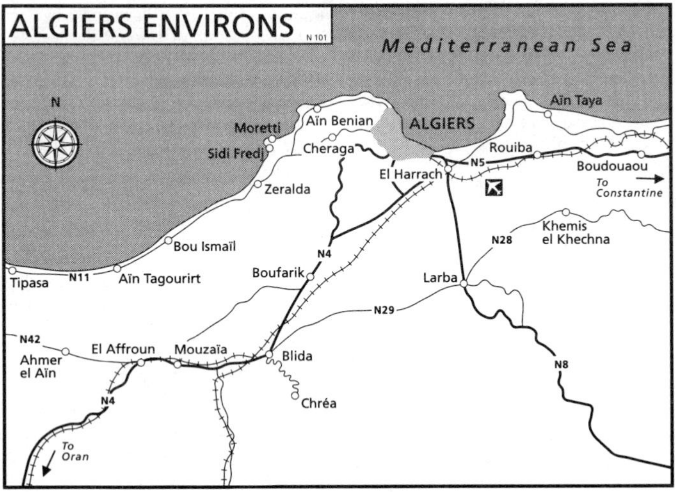

from Algiers via Cheraga along the shorter N41 is particularly accessible for a day trip. **Accommodation** C *Hotel El Minzah*, T 391435, 95 rm, the only hotel in Moretti.

Sidi Fredj

Has a longer history, is strategically placed and has a much larger infrastructure. This is the place where the French landed in 1830 and where the Allied troops sent to liberate North Africa in WWII began their campaign. Today Sidi Fredj is above all an important and highly successful seaside resort. A very ambitious project has transformed this town into a well-planned, modern tourist complex. There is an excellent yacht harbour, an activity centre and an open air theatre in the old fortress. The beaches, part of the 'Turquoise coast,' are really beautiful and live up to expectations.

• **Accommodation** **C** *El Riadh*, T 814402, 125 rm, pool; **C** *El Manar*, T 783816, 400 rm, pool; **D** *El Marsa*, T 801315, 100 rm, pool. **Youth hostel**, T 814682, open July, Aug and Sep only, 24 beds, meals available, 1 km from bus.

• **Transport** There are buses to the airport and Algiers, provided for hotel visitors, but can be used by anyone.

Zeralda

30 km from Algiers Zeralda is another seaside resort noted for its beach of fine sand and for its peaceful natural park within the neighbouring pine forest. Many facilities are available and this little town makes a nice day trip.

• **Accommodation** **C** *Les Sables d'Or*, T 396924, Tx 63112, tourist Complex with 258 rm, pool and tennis. **D** *Mazafran*, T 812614, 200 rm, pool and tennis; **D** *La Résidence*, T 782922. **Youth hostel** on beach adjacent to Tourist Complex, T 396981, open Jul 1 to Sep 15 only, 30 beds, kitchen, laundry. **Camping** permitted in grounds.

Further along the N11 coast road, 84 km from Algiers, beyond **Aïn Tagourirt** the W40 leads up to the hill top site of the **Mausoleum of the Mauritanian Royal Family**, confusingly called the Tomb of the Christian Girl. The huge monument, perhaps dating back to 100BC, cylindrical in shape, and decorated with 60 columns, had 4 fake doors. The actual entrance leads by a devious route into an

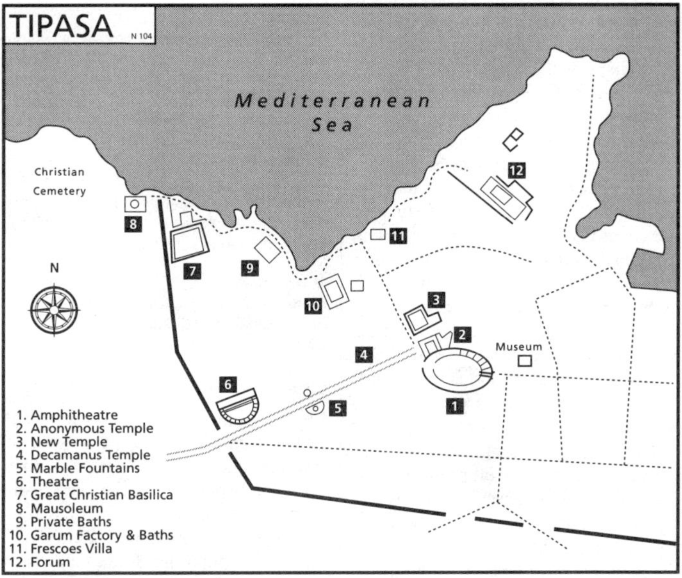

empty chamber. When 'discovered' in 1865 this was empty. There is a splendid view from here.

Tipasa

71 km from Algiers, Tipasa is both an important archaeological site and a seaside resort. The town has 2 separate parts, **Tipasa-plage** the tourist complex, and **Tipasa-ville**, where the ruins are situated. The village in itself is quite charming, but the real interest is the ruins.

History

Originally a Phoenician trading post, it became a Roman colony in the 2nd century AD and one of the most important Christian settlements in this area of North Africa. In 430 AD, the Vandals took control of Tipasa and tried to convert the inhabitants to the heretical belief in Arianism. A large proportion of the population fled to Spain, and those who remained were persecuted. Myth has it that their tongues were cut out, but that they still continued to speak. This was hailed as a miracle throughout the Christian world. In 534 AD, the Byzantines retook the town which was already declining in prosperity and falling into ruin. By the time the Arabs invaded, there was little left. They named it Tefassed, which in Arabic means 'the damaged'.

The site

The site by the sea is magnificent, and still relatively free of tourists. By the entrance are the imposing remains of an amphitheatre. Further along are the **Anonymous Temple** and the **New Temple**, later converted into a Christian Basilica. Between these 2 temples, lies a well preserved 200m long section of the **Decamanus Maximus**, the ancient road that linked Cherchell to Algiers, at the far end of which stands the **Nyphaeum**, a marble fountain. A little further on are the remains of a **theatre**. By the sea, stands the 4th century AD **Great Christian Basilica**. It is 52m long, 40m wide and has 9 naves with mosaic-covered floors. Around the main building are other remains including a **chapel with mosaics**, and a **baptistery**. To the W lies a **large Christian cemetery**. One of the most interesting monuments here is a large round 5th **century mausoleum** containing 14 places for sarcophagi and inscriptions indicating the date of construction. Return to the Great Christian Basilica and follow the path to the E which passes some small well-preserved private baths. Further on is the *garum* factory (producing a spicy fish-based sauce) and some smaller baths. By the sea is the **Frescoes Villa**, clearly once owned by a rich inhabitant. Most of the frescoes from here are in the museum.

Continuing E along the coast, the road leads to a very well preserved **Forum**, the oldest area within Tipasa. Open 0900-1200 and 1400-1700 closed Sat. At end of the tour of the site, visit the small, very interesting **museum**. It contains some superb mosaics dating back to the 1st century AD which were found in the Basilica. It is on the left of the road as you leave the site. Entrance AD1. Open 0900-1700.

Local information

CURFEW At time of going to press 2330-0400.

● **Accommodation**

C *Hotel Simbad*, is the only hotel in the village.

B *Hotel de la Baie* at Tipasa-plage (1½ km W of the village), T 461822, 111 rm, tennis, pool.

C *Hotel de la Résidence* at Tipasa-Plage, T 461824, 352 rm, 4 pools, all sports facilities, garden; **C** *Hotel les Pavilions*, 2-3 km E along the Algiers road, T 461761, 500+ bungalows.

● **Youth hostel**

T 463513, open Jul, Aug and Sept, 30 beds, meals available, 700m from bus route.

● **Camping**

At Chenoua-plage which lies W of Tipasa. Beyond Tipasa, turn right onto the W109 and Chenoua is reached after about 3 km. Tents for hire or take your own. Has a good beach, but the facilities are far from perfect.

● **Places to eat**

The restaurants near the entrance to the site are best described as up-market. ♦♦ *Le Progrès* is recommended as average. ♦Those nearer the port are cheaper.

● **Transport**

Road There are regular buses from and to Algiers and Cherchell. **NB:** out of season check when the last buses leave.

Chréa and Blida

Chréa, 20 km on the N37 from Blida and 70 km from Algiers via the N1, is a ski resort that lies at 1,500m. In the summer it is equally popular for the many walks around the mountains. The view from the road up to Chréa, back towards Algiers is breathtaking. **Blida** today is an important regional and agricultural centre dealing mainly in olives and citrus fruits. The town was founded by Andalusian immigrants in the 16th century who introduced irrigation in order to grow oranges.

CURFEW At time of going to press 2330-0400.

● **Accommodation** **E** *Hotel Royal*, in Blida, place du 1er Novembre (main square), T 03 492801; **E** *Hotel El Kebir*, 74 Blvd Laichi Abdellah, in Blida, T 634952; **E** *Hotel des Cédres*, in Chréa, T 03 14, 30 rms, 1,000m up in the forest. **Youth hostel**, Kritli Mokhtar, Blida, T 499601, 40 beds, kitchen, bus 500m, train 1 km.

● **Transport** There are regular buses to/from Algiers. Local buses for Chréa leave from the main street in Blida. Blida train station, directly W of the centre, is on the main line from Algiers and Oran.

THE EAST

Contents

Maps

This region, stretching E from Algiers to the border of Tunisia, includes the important towns of Constantine, Annaba, Bejaïa and Sétif, starting point for visits to the ruins of Roman Djemila. Tourists are attracted to the forested Grand and Petit Kabylie ranges, the Djurdjura National Park, a region of outstanding beauty, and the awesome gorges in the Aurés Massif between Batna and Biskra. The forested hills and the intensively cultivated patches of fertile ground, the tiny villages clinging to the mountain sides and the breathtaking views from the tortuously winding roads, make any journey here memorable.

Kabylia

This region extends from Algiers E to Bejaïa. It is often subdivided into the Grande and Petite Kabylies. Grande Kabylie is the region around the Djurdjura massif with summits reaching 2,000m. The Petite Kabylie is the Bejaïa hinterland also with high mountains, the Babors, which reach 1,200m. These mountain ranges, well wooded and cut with deep gorges, rise straight from the coast making access difficult.

The landscape, and the inaccessibility of many villages has ensured that the Kabyles have kept a strong and individ-

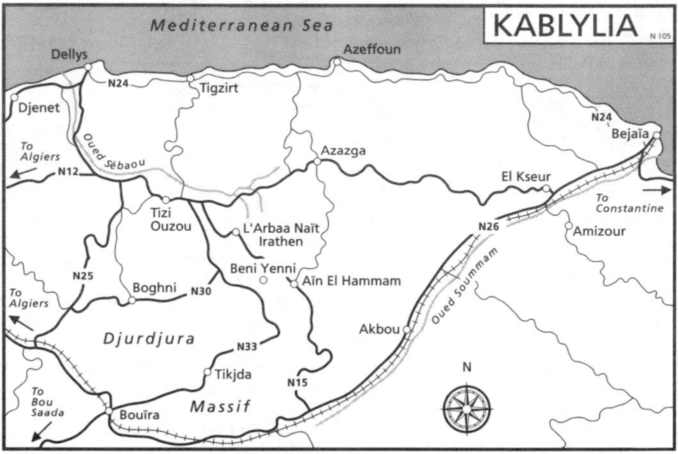

ual identity, the physical isolation encouraging an independent streak amongst the people of the area. They speak Kabyle, a Berber dialect, and it is said that they speak French as a second language and Arabic as a third. Family units are very strong, and women enjoy a greater freedom, unveiled and colourfully clothed.

The landscape of Kabylia is intriguing in the way that remote villages appear to cling to the mountain side. Life here in winter can be very harsh, and many roads are blocked or dangerous to use due to snow.

ALGIERS TO BEJAIA VIA THE N12

The 300 km route crosses the low-lying plain behind Algiers as a dual carriageway, the quickest way to cut through the straggling suburbs. The road makes use of the valleys of the Isser and Oued Sébaou as far as Azazga. Sit on the S side of the coach for the best views of the Djurdjursas. It then twists and winds its way up through the northern ranges of the Grand Kabylie through passes at almost 1,000m before its descent to El Kseur on the Oued Soummam and thence to Bejaïa.

Tizi Ouzou

On the main N5/N12 road from Algiers, Tizi Ouzou is the administrative capital of the *wilaya* of Greater Kabylia. With its population approaching 400,000 and growing fast, it is situated 100 km E of Algiers and mid way between Algiers and Bejaïa. It is better as a departure point for those wishing to explore the region than as a place to stay. Being the only town in a remote area, Tizi Ouzou offers both commercial and administrative facilities. It is known for its large market, every Thur.

Local information

● Accommodation

C *Hotel Lalla Khedidja*, at the S exit of the town, on the road to Mechtras, 10 mins from station, T 402901, 60 rm; **C** ***Hotel Amraoua***, T 408546, opened 1982, situated at foot of Beloua mountain near Tala Allam, on NW outskirts of town, most expensive and well appointed hotel in Tizi Ouzou, attractive bar, good restaurant, 154 comfortable (if somewhat gloomy) rms, tennis, pool, splendid terrace, magnificent views.

D *Beloua*, 16 rue Larbi Ben M'Hidi, T 401990, more convenient (if less dramatic) central location a short walk from the bus station, 60 rms; **D** *Hotel les Andalouses* by the mosque and the police station.

E *Hotel Olympia* rue Larbi Ben M'Hidi, central, 10 mins from station.

● Youth hostel

Is on rue Boulila Amar, B P 456, Tizi Ouzou, T 201212, 50 beds, kitchen, bus 1 km, train 2 km.

● Places to eat

♦♦♦Restaurant at ***Hotel Amraoua*** serves a choice of expensive European and Algerian cuisine in spacious restaurant or on the splendid terrace which can seat 200 and has magnificent views over the town and the mountains of Kabylia to the S. ♦There are 2 small restaurants at the ***Olympic Pool*** for cheaper food. **Rue Larbi Ben M'Hidi** has cheap eating places too.

● Telephone

Local code 03.

● Tourist information

ONAT, 3 rue Larbi Ben M'Hidi, T 402711.

● Travel agent

Air Algérie, 1 rue Larbi Ben M'Hidi, T 406992.

● Transport

Road Bus The bus station, a large blue building on the rue Larbi Ben M'Hidi, the road on the W from Algiers, provides a helpful information desk. Buses run frequently to Algiers (usually 6 daily) and to various points in Kabylia such as Aïn El Hammam, Azazga, Beni Yenni, Dellys, Tigzirt and Tikjda. Local buses also leave from the main bus station or from the streets immediately N of the large roundabout at the E end of rue Larbi Ben M'Hidi.

Taxi To the W, these leave from opposite the bus station on rue Larbi Ben M'Hidi. Those

Asses, Donkeys and Mules

There is a certain amount of confusion when naming the normally overladen and generally undernourished beasts of burden found in the countries of North Africa and Spain. While there can be no confusion as to what is a **horse**, *Equus caballus*, or even an **ass**, *Equus asinus*, despite the fact that it is most commonly called a **donkey**, except in Spain where it is a **burro**, a **mule** requires some definition.

The term **mule** can refer to any hybrid but as a beast of burden it is the offspring of a male donkey (jack) and a female horse (mare), while the offspring of a male horse (stallion) and a female donkey (jenny) is correctly termed a **hinny**.

A mule is a horse in the middle with a donkey at either end. It has longer ears, and a thinner mane and tail than its mother and carries the typical 'cross' markings on the shoulders and back. The hinny is less popular, being nearer the size of a donkey and has the shorter ears and thicker mane and tail of its father.

A mule is stronger than a horse, has a much longer working life under the right circumstances, can withstand extremes of temperature without long-term ill effects, is less vulnerable to sickness and can survive on a very limited diet. Mules are noted for being surefooted and for being fast and accurate kickers. Mules are generally considered to be infertile though instances of offspring are recorded.

The Algerian wild ass originally roamed the Atlas Ranges. The Romans carefully preserved them on mosaics but are held responsible for their demise. The Nubian wild ass, of a distinctive reddish hue, roamed the semi-desert areas between the River Nile and the Red Sea shores. It survived into the 20th century.

The Egyptians used asses. Illustrations from 2500BC show us that even then these domesticated beasts were carrying loads and passengers out of all proportion to their size. They also had mules which are thought to have first been bred around 1750BC. Models of this hybrid were found in the pyramids and a mule drawing a chariot is depicted on a vase found in Thebes.

The Romans placed heavy reliance on the mule, for riding, to draw carts and farm implements and to carry equipment. To assist copulation they devised a wooden cage with a ramp to enable the shorter jack ass reach the taller mare.

Facts The Food and Agriculture Organization's (FOA) latest figures place Morocco (470,000) and Algeria (160,000) second and third for mule populations in Africa and Spain (129,000) first in Europe.

to the N, S and SW in Kabylia leave from the other side of the main roundabout and the nearby main square half way down rue Abane Ramdane. Taxis to the E and SE (Aïn El Hammam, Tassaft etc) leave from the E edge of town.

Excursions from Tizi Ouzou

The steep, winding mountain road N from Tizi Ouzou to **Tigzirt**, 39 km (see page 433), has amazing views over the sea. The Shrine of Sidi Beloua, Tizi Ouzou's patron saint, on the summit of the Beloua mountain immediately N of town provides a magnificent panorama of the region for the energetic.

L'Arbaa-Naït-Irathen is on the scenic N15 and has a huge fort, built in the 1850s by the French when controlling the area, which provides commanding views over the valleys on both sides. Currently it is a craft centre. From here it is only 20 km of scenic road to Aïn El Hammam (see below).

Tala Guilef which in Berber means 'the fountain of the wild boar' at 1,500m is a splendid spot on the N side of the **Djurdjura Range** towards their W end. From

Tizi-Ouzou take the N12 to the E, after 6 km take the N30 S and at 53 km from Tizi-Ouzou, after some very winding roads and very beautiful scenery, you arrive at Boghni. From here there are 19 km of narrow road but Tala Guilef is well worth visiting for the walks and scrambles in the surrounding forests, plus rock climbing and skiing in season.

• **Accommodation** C *Hotel El Arz*, T 422476-8, built in mid 1970s but still has good reputation, 200 beds in 80 rms with bath and balcony, restaurant with 165 places, bar/café, pool, tennis. **Youth hostel**, T 402821, 80 beds, kitchen.

Beni Yenni Kabylia's most famous tribe inhabit a group of 7 very interesting mountain villages from which there are amazing panoramic views over the surrounding mountains, particularly beautiful at sunset. Two of the villages, **Aït Larbaa** at 760m and **Taourirt Mimoun** are well known for their traditional jewellery and silverwork, and there are a few shops with fixed prices. Take the N12 E from Tizi Ouzou, after 6 km take the N30/N33 S and at about 38 km from Tizi Ouzou look out for the minor road signed to Aïn El Hammam on the left. Take this but don't miss the spectacular views at this junction, and shortly turn left again to Beni Yenni which is a further 2 km. Complicated but worth it. Buses run from Tizi Ouzou which save all the effort but they don't stop for photographs. Accommodation D *Hotel Le Bracelet d'Argent*, T 59, 24 clean rm.

Aïn El Hammam is along a very winding road from Beni Yenni. At 1,080m it offers more gorges, peaks and breathtaking views of the Grande Kabylie and for the more energetic a starting point for mountain walks. Another 16 km S beyond Aïn El Hammam, is the Col de Tirourda (1,780m) beyond which the road snakes down to the Oued Sahel. The road is steep and liable to be closed for 3 or 4 months in winter. Accommodation D *Hotel Djurdjura*, T 409325, small, clean and very pleasant.

Tikjda

With an altitude of 1,600m on the N33, Tikjda is an idyllic spot in the **Djurdjura National Park**, in the very heart of the Djurdjura mountains, in sight of the highest peak, Tamgout n'Lalla Khedidja, 2,308m. It is a popular winter skiing resort for the nearby Akouder and Tigounatine *pistes*, and in summer attracts rock climbers and walkers in the surrounding cedar forests. The road from the pass of Tizi-N'Kouilal to Tikjda is both steep and winding. Just 2 km beyond Tizi-N'Kouilal is **Point de vue du Djurdjura** which speaks for itself and in another 5 km before Tikjda, stop at the **Gouffre de l'Akouker**, for the incredible view. The entire Kabylia lies below and on clear days, the sea can be seen on the horizon. The road from Tikjda to Tizi Ouzou is often closed in winter due to snow and in summer because of landslides. Be sure to check before a journey. If you only want to visit Tikjda it is straighter and quicker to reach it by bus or taxi from Bouïra via the N5. Numerous buses stop at Bouïra en route from Algiers.

• **Accommodation** C *Hotel Djurdjura*, on N 15 in Aïn El Hammam, T 03 527270, pool, 80 rm, 171 beds, restaurant with 160 places and bar, pool; **F** *Chalet refuge des Cheminots,* in an older chalet style building at foot of the *Hotel Djurdjura*, T 03 527201, originally established for workmen, it is basic but clean with plain, good meals, cheapest place.

Excursions from Tikjda

It is possible to visit the **Takouatz Guerrisséne glacier**, which is on the S flank of the Ras Timedouine mountain. It is about 3-4 km along a track to the N.

The extraordinary **Goulmin lake** cradled high in the mountains to the W is very beautiful, but further away. Follow the Bouïra road for 5 km until you see the DNC Chalet. Walk from here up the mountain path on the right, allow 4 hrs for the complete walk. The N12 continues E to **Azazga**, noted mainly as a cross roads, to Yakouren and on to El Kseur, a busy town worth stopping at to look at the craft goods in the market. **Yakouren** is a small and pleasantly quiet town, on the N12, 11 km E of Azazga, the best jumping off point for exploring the E districts of the Grande Kabylia and the Soummam valley, especially the vast forest of Akfadou which straddles the two.

• **Accommodation** D *Hotel Tamgout*, T 0315414, friendly atmosphere, 128 beds in 49 rms, restaurant with 80 places, 2 bars, volley ball, table tennis and children's playground. **Youth hostel** open July-Sept, 80 beds, meals available, bus 1 km.

ALGIERS TO BEJAIA VIA N24 COAST ROAD

This is an option for those with more time and offers splendid ocean views at Cap Blanc (44 km) and Cap Djenet (78 km). Beyond Delly the road surface deteriorates and at Azeffoun it is best to return to the N12 via the W158, as the last 93 km to Bejaïa are really rough.

The first recommended beach E of Algiers is 21 km away at **Aïn Taya**. There are huge quantities of sand and huge crowds from Algiers. **Dellys**, 106 km, is a recommended lunch stop. The cafés on the harbour offer fresh fish meals.

Tigzirt

This is a small coastal town on a sheltered bay protected by a small rocky island. Although advertised as relatively untouched by tourism this is quickly changing. It originates from Roman times when it was known as *Iomnium* and was an important harbour. Today the remains of a **Christian basilica** (5th-6th century) can be seen in the centre of town.

• **Accommodation** C *Hotel le Mizrana*, T 03 046, pool, tennis, 30 rm, sea views. **Youth hostel** Camp des Jeunes open Jul-Sept inc, 20 beds, meals available, bus 1500m.

Around Tigzirt

The coast road E leads to many small deserted beaches. The virtually untouched village of **Azzefoun**, clinging to the mountain side, 38 km from Tigzirt along the coast once was an important port for exporting charcoal. Beyond Azzefoun the road towards Bejaïa, 77 km, affords splendid views and passes yet more secluded beaches. The road is only partially surfaced and is not recommended in bad weather. An alternative is to take a minor road, the W43, S up through the hills, and join the main road to Bejaïa.

Bejaïa

Population 150,000. This is an important regional town with recently developed petrochemical industries. Pipelines carry oil from Hassi Messaoud, 660 km away in the S. The town is situated by the sea, on the side of the Gouraya mountain and protected by Cap Carbon. The town centre and its maze of narrow streets which climb up the hillside are the main points of interest for the visitor. The view over the Gulf of Bejaïa is worth a visit in its own right.

History

The town was established as a trading post by the Phoenicians and then the Romans but today few remains exist. In the 11th century, the Hammamid chief developed it into an important town, En Nassria, and in 1090, his son, El Mancour, made it the capital of his Kingdom, and built many impressive monuments. The town prospered during his reign with an important boat-building industry and a population reported at about 100,000. The town fell into the hands of the Almohad leader, Abd El Moumin in 1151 and later into Hafsid hands where its prosperity declined. In the 16th century, the inhabitants turned to piracy. Because of this, the town was attacked and then occupied by the Spanish for 50 years. Next it was taken by the Turks. The

French who captured it in 1833 renamed it Bougie (after its importance in candle wax manufacture). By the end of the 19th century the population was reduced to 2,000, and the city had lost all evidence of its glorious past.

Things to see

The place du 1er Novembre is the lively centre of the town. It is lined by houses with arcades and a magnificent view over the sea. Under the place du 1er Novembre, there is the **Archaeological Museum** with exhibits from the Roman and Hafsid periods. The **Emile Aubry Museum**, rue Youcef Bouchebah, (between the place Abane Ramdane and the kasbah) displays contemporary Algerian paintings. Open 0900-1200 and 1400-1700.

La Réunion **War Cemetery** with 200 graves, mainly British, lies 14 km to the SW along the N12.

Excursion

Cap Carbon, 5 km N of town is definitely worth a visit. From the car park it is another 30 minute walk to the top for a splendid view over the bay and coast. The **Spanish fort**, at an altitude of 660m provides yet another impressive view over the bay. To get there, leave by the Porte du Ravin, pass by the **Pic des Singes** which also provides good views, and continue on to the fort.

ACCESS **Air** The airport is 4 km S of the town. **Road** Long distance buses stop at the bottom of the town so there is a long uphill walk to the centre. Local buses are available. Ask for place Cherif Medjahed.

Local information

● Accommodation

D *Hotel de l'Etoile*, place du 1er Novembre, T 920350; **D** *Hotel de l'Orient*, 7 rue Si-Lahoues, T 921131.

E *Hotel Terminus*, 22 Ave Ben Boulaïd, T 921049.

● Youth hostel

A.J. Mohammed-Issiakhem, Citédes Frères Chabati, Bejaïa 06000, T 924865, open 0800-1200 and 1400-2200, 50 beds, kitchen, train 3 km, bus 500m.

● Places to eat

♦♦ ***Le Seville*** on rue Cheikh Amar Amah, recommended for European food; ***La Brise de Mer*** on Baie de Sidi Yahia for seafood of course, and ♦the fish restaurants on rue Si El Haoues.

● Banks

Main bank on place du 1er Novembre.

● Post office

On place Chérif Medjahed. The **telephone office** is in the same building.

● Telephone

Local code 05.

● Travel agents

Air Algérie, rue de la Liberté, T 225731.

● Tourist office

ONAT, place Chérif Medjahed, T 928001.

● Transport

Air To Algiers Mon, Tue and Sat 0920 and Fri at 1400. The airport is 4 km S of the town.

Road Bus The bus station is to the S of the town, at the bottom of the hill. There are regular buses to Algiers, Constantine, Jijel and Sétif. The bus station is reasonably organized, with a booking office. **Taxi** For out of town, these leave from the intersection of the Algiers and Jijel road.

BEJAIA TO JIJEL

The Corniche Kabylia from Bejaïa to Jijel, also known as 'the Sapphire Coast', is a scenic road which winds along the coast, clinging on to, and in places cutting into the mountains which drop steeply into the sea. This part of the coast is one of the most beautiful in Algeria. The road starts at Souk et Tnine, about 30 km E of Bejaïa where the N43 continues to follow the coast and the N9 goes inland S through the Kherrata gorges. On the coast, E of Ziama Mansouria, visit an amazing rock cavern, the **Grotte Merveilleuse**. Unfortunately, a new road tunnel cuts out the most impressive views, but it is nevertheless still a grand sight.

Tichi

This small town 17 km E of Bejaïa has been transformed into a tourist complex which is, perhaps, a little too near the petrochemicals of Bejaïa for comfort. It has a beautiful soft sandy beach. A convenient day trip, it is very busy in summer.

• **Accommodation** **C** *Les Hammadites*, T 575859, by sea, 140 rm, tennis, water sports. **E** *Hotel la Grande Terrace* is in the village, 30 rooms.

The turning inland on the N9/N43 junction at Souk Et Tnine takes you through the 8 km long **Kherrata gorges**, one of the deepest cuttings in the Atlas Mountains. Its name *Chabet El Akra* means 'Death Ravine'.

Back on the Corniche Kabylia at the fishing village of Zama Mansouria 50 km from Bejaïa, turn right to the Barrage de Merdj-Ez-Erraguene (30 km) along a winding minor road. Turnings to the right and left along forest roads make pleasant detours through the woodlands: a track to the left has a good viewing point at 846m. It is possible, vehicle, weather and road conditions permitting, to return to the Corniche Kabylia down the W137.

Jijel

Is a small, quiet town at the E end of the Corniche Kabylia. Its main attraction is a large sandy beach. It is a convenient and pleasant overnight stop.

• **Accommodation** **D** *Hotel du Littoral*, modern, Ave du 1er Novembre, T 96507; **D** *Hotel le Beau Rivage*, Blvd Zighout Youcef, T 964158; **E** *Hotel Tindouf*, 14 rue Larbi Ben M'Hidi, T 962071. **Youth hostels** There are 2: **A.J. Jijel**, rue de Frères Khecha, T 460980, 50 beds, open 0800-1200 and 1700-2200, kitchen, bus 2 km; and **A.J. Taher**, rue de 1er Novembre, T 960427 open 0800-1200 and 1400-2200, 70 beds, kitchen, laundry facilities, bus 500m, reservations required.

• **Places to eat** ♦♦restaurants in the hotels and along Blvd Zighout Youcef near *Hotel le Beau Rivage*.

• **Banks** In the main street, Ave du 1er Novembre.

• **Post office** Ave du 1er Novembre.

• **Telephone** Local code 05.

• **Travel agent** *Air Algérie*, Ave du 1er Novembre, T 964636.

• **Transport Road** The bus station is about 100m from place de la République. There are regular departures for all the main towns. There are frequent buses to Bejaïa.

AROUND CONSTANTINE

This region extends from Kabylia to the Tunisian border and from the coast to the Aurés mountains with extremely attractive and varied landscape which should not be missed. The main city, Constantine, has a rich historical heritage and an impressive situation by the **Rhumel gorges** while the second city, Annaba, is an important commercial centre with excellent communications. There are Roman sites to visit, the most interesting being **Djemila** one of the most perfectly preserved cities, and **Hippo Regius**.

Sétif

Sétif, situated at an altitude of 1,100m which makes it pleasant even in the summer heat, and with a population of 200,000, became important following the French occupation in 1838. The town had existed since the Roman times, but had largely fallen into decay. The French transformed Sétif into a major military garrison, and rebuilt the town in a geometric grid pattern. In 1945, Sétif was drawn to world attention as the scene of a horrible massacre, the result of a nationalistic outburst, in which 84 Europeans were massacred, and over 2,000 Algerians were killed in retaliation by the French army. Today the town is a medium-sized typical colonial town, with a distinct French atmosphere. The main street, Ave du 8 Mai 1945, lined with arcades housing the main shops and

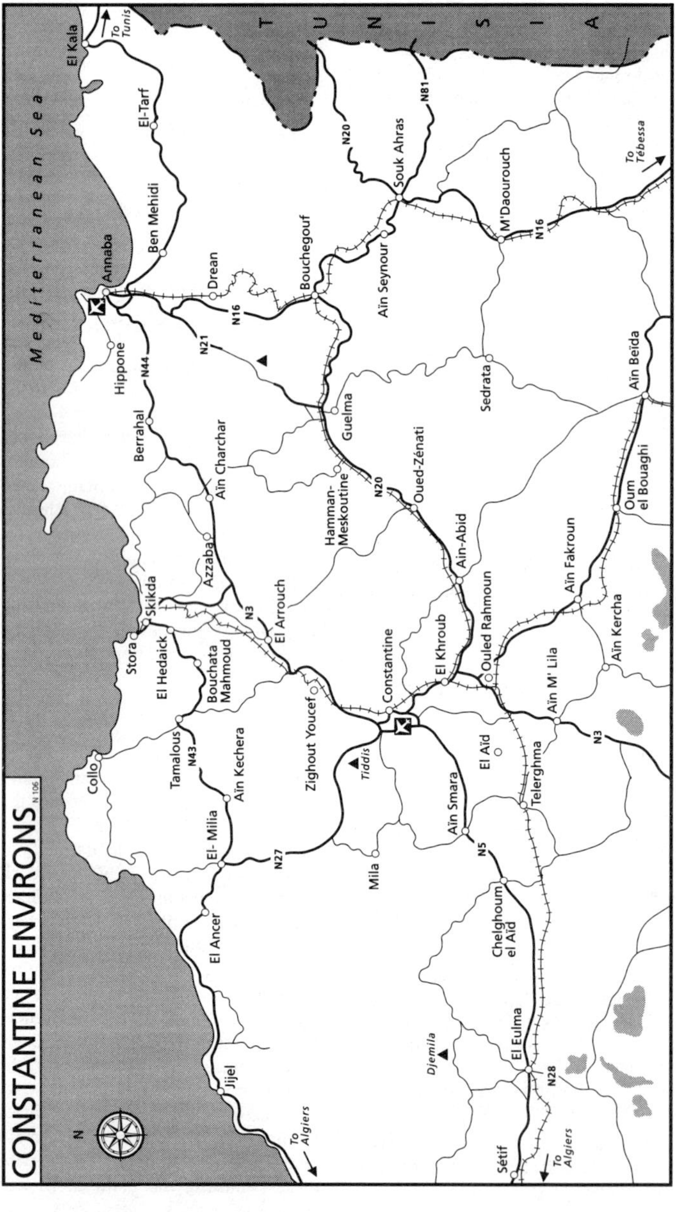
CONSTANTINE ENVIRONS
N 106
Mediterranean Sea
TUNISIA
To Tunis
El Kala
El-Tarf
Ben Mehidi
Annaba
Hippone
Drean
Bouchegouf
Souk Ahras
Aïn Seynour
M'Daourouch
To Tébessa
N20
N81
N16
N21
N44
Berrahal
Aïn Charchar
Guelma
Sedrata
Aïn Beïda
Hamman-Meskoutine
Oued-Zénati
Oum el Bouaghi
Azzaba
Aïn-Abid
Aïn Fakroun
Skikda
Stora
El Hedaick
Bouchata Mahmoud
El Arrouch
N3
Constantine
El Khroub
Ouled Rahmoun
Aïn Kercha
Aïn M' Lila
Zighout Youcef
Tiddis
El Aïd
Telerghma
Collo
Tamalous
N43
Aïn Kechera
El- Milia
N27
Mila
Aïn Smara
N5
Chelghoum el Aïd
El Ancer
Djemila
El Eulma
N28
Jijel
Sétif
To Algiers
To Algiers
N

banks, is the most lively in the town. Sétif is recommended as a base from which to visit Djemila which has virtually no accommodation. (See Djemila Access, page 437.)

Things to see

The **museum** on rue de la Palestine, has a collection ranging from pre-historic local finds, to Roman, Christian and Muslim remains. The most interesting exhibits are the **Roman mosaics** including the 4th century '*Venus upon a dolphin*', and '*Bacchus' Indian Triumph*'. The museum is open 0900-1200 and 1400-1800, closed Fri morning and Sat. To the N of the place de l'Indépendence on the square Rafaoui is a restored **Roman water tank** and further N are the remains of the **Byzantine walls** and 2 **basilicas**.

ACCESS Both the bus and the train station are to the SE of the town, no great distance to walk from the centre. Sétif has a bypass to the S so hitch-hikers may have a longer walk to the centre.

Local information

● Accommodation

C ***Hotel El Hidab***, Blvd Cheikh Laif, T 904043, 130 rm, central, pool, restaurant.

D ***Hotel Mountazeh***, 12 Ave Ben Boulaïd, 2nd street on the right, off Ave du 8 Mai 1945, after the place de l'Indépendence, 72 rm, T 904828.

E ***Hotel Port Said***, 6 Ave Ben Boulaïd, T 907183; **E** ***Hotel El Riadh***, 2 rue Frères Meslem, T 907847, 60 rm.

● Places to eat

♦♦♦ ***Hotel El Hadab*** on Blvd Cheikh Laif; ♦♦ ***Hotel Riadh*** on 2 rue Frères Meslem and adjacent to *Hotel Port Said* on Ave Ben Boulaïd.

● Bank

In the Ave du 8 Mai 1945.

● Post office

Is on Ave du 1er Novembre, a continuation E from the Ave du 8 Mai 1945.

● Telephone

Local code 05.

● Tourist office

ONAT, 13 Ave du 8 Mai 1945, T 902502.

● Travel agents

Air Algérie, 13 Ave du 8 Mai 1945, T 851818; *Air France*, 14 Ave du 8 Mai 1945, T 903572.

● Transport

Train Connections to **Algiers** and **Constantine**. Take the third street right off Ave du 1er November after the post office, and the station is at the end.

Road The bus station is on the first street right off Ave du 1er Novembre, just after the post office. Regular buses to **Algiers, Batna, Bejaïa, Constantine** and **Ghardaïa**. The buses for **Djemila** leave from in front of the train station.

Djemila

The little village of Djemila, 50 km from Sétif, is particularly noted for the remains of **Cuicul**, an important Roman town, one of the most remarkable and well preserved in Algeria.

ACCESS There are a few, unreliable, direct buses that leave from Sétif, information possibly available from the bus station in Sétif. It is easier to take a bus to Constantine from in front of the train station in Sétif and get off at El Eulma where taxis are readily available to do the remaining 20 km.

History

The town, known as Cuicul, was founded in the 1st century AD by the Roman emperor Nerva. It was at first a military garrison, but influenced by the surrounding fertile lands, agriculture became an important activity. By the 2nd century the population had grown to 10,000 and was organized with a central elected administration. By the 3rd century, the town had outgrown the original walls, and the southern ramparts were pulled down to make way for the new forum, which was surrounded with grand monuments. This period was the height of Cuicul's prosperity. By the 4th century, the introduction of Christianity gave a new lease of life to Cuicul with the erection of new monuments, including a church and a baptistery. After the 5th century, Cuicul fell into disuse, and it was

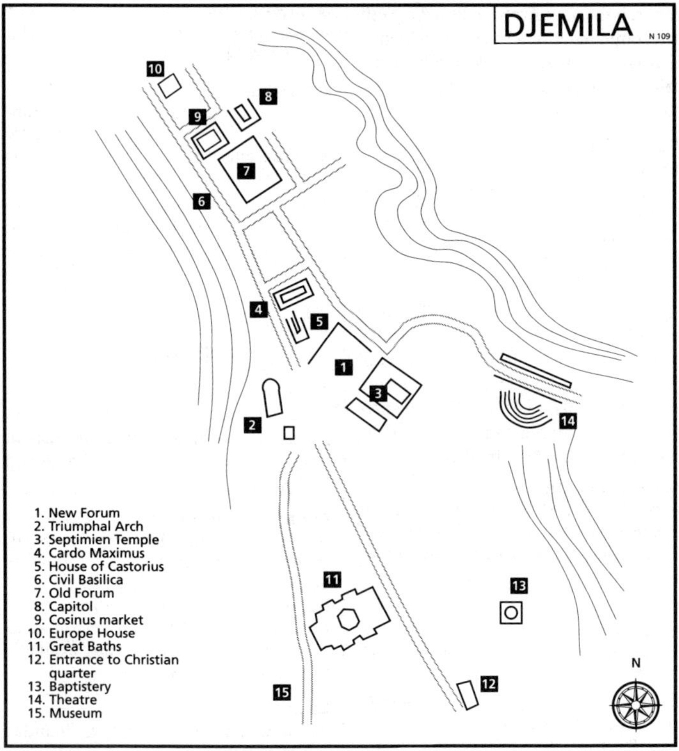

not until the French arrived in 1839 that the site was again occupied. Excavations began in 1909.

The site

From the entrance near the museum, the tree-lined path leads past the Grand Baths to the **New Forum**. To the W of the Forum stands the **Triumphal Arch**, dedicated to the Emperor Caracalla, built in AD 216. The road through the arch went originally to Sétif. On the S side of the Forum is the **Septimien Temple**, dedicated to Septimus Severus and built in 229. From the Forum take the Cardo Maximus, or main street that leads N from the corner in front of the Arch. On the right stands the **House of Castorius**, noted for its private baths. Further on the left, stands the **civil basilica**, originally used as a Tribunal and trade centre. Up the road, on the right, is the **Old Forum** with its well-preserved original paving stones. To the N stands the **Capitol**, a temple dedicated to the triple cult of Jupiter, Juno and Minerva. To the left of the Capitol is the **Cosinus Market**, named after its donator, Cosinus Primus. The market, entered through an arch on the Cardo Maximus, is one of the most remarkable monuments in Cuicul. The merchants' tables, organized around a central courtyard, are still in place and well preserved.

After the market, to the N, stands the **Europe House**, named after a mosaic found inside. The house is large and luxurious, with 18 rooms arranged around a central courtyard lined with Ionic columns. The Cardo Maximus leads to the N gate, where the road for Jijel started. To the S of the New Forum lies the Christian part of the town, built in the 4th century. From the New Forum, take the path directly opposite the Cardo Maximus, leading towards the **Great Baths**. The baths, to the SW of the path are in a very good condition and in some rooms it is still possible to see the pipes and double panels where the hot water circulated. To the N of the baths, is a large courtyard, where a good view over the ruins can be enjoyed. The entrance to the Christian quarter is delimited by a great door, at the end of the path coming from the New Forum. Follow the path up the hill to the large circular **Baptistery** which still contains all the original mosaics and is today covered by a restored dome. The **theatre**, built outside the boundaries of the town is situated to the E of the New Forum. It is thought that the theatre was not built within the walls due to the great expansion of the city in the 3rd century and its capacity of 3,000 seats indicates the size of the population at that time. From the theatre there is a wonderful view over the surrounding landscape. Open daily 0700-1800 in summer, 0700-1700 in winter.

The Museum Situated by the entrance to the ruins, it has an impressive collection of mosaics. The 3 main rooms are covered in mosaics, to an almost overpowering extent. There are also some marble statues as well as small but interesting everyday objects, such as oil lamps and cooking implements. Open 0900-1200 and 1400-1700, closed Sat.

WARNING On arrival at the site, and even long before, you may be offered many 'original' items such as coins or oil lamps. Some of these may be genuine, but be very careful before buying anything. Similarly, on entering the ruins, you will undoubtedly be offered the services of a guide. Most guides are unofficial. If you are interested, it is best to agree on a price beforehand.

Constantine

Constantine is an amazing town of 500,000 inhabitants perched at 694m on the summit of a rock. To the E, the town is built along the rim of the precipitous Rhumel Gorges, some 200m below. The situation is made more dramatic by the 4 bridges that cross the gorges.

ACCESS Air The airport is 9 km out of town. There are at least 3 daily flights from **Algiers**, 3 a week from **Oran**, and 1 a week from **Tamanrasset**. There are daily flights from **Lyon, Paris** and **Marseille**. A bus runs into town. **Train** There are daily trains from **Algiers, Skikda** and **Touggourt**. There is also a daily train from **Tunis** leaving at 1255. **Road** The main bus station is by the river 3-4 km S of the town, so it is possible to walk rather than catch the bus. Constantine is well connected to all the major towns in Algeria.

History

Founded by the Phoenicians and called **Cirta**, it was taken over by Massinissa in 203 BC and made the capital of Numidia. During Massinissa's reign, agriculture developed and a strong centralized state system was established and aligned with Rome. In about 154 BC Jugurtha, Massinissa's grandson, tried to rid himself of the Roman tutelage but failed. During the first years of the Christian era, Cirta was part of a confederation of cities in the region, and by the end of the 2nd century it became a colony of Cuicul (Djemila). At this time, the town really prospered, becoming one of the richest cities in North Africa. In AD 311, the town was destroyed by Maxence following an insurrection, but Constantine rebuilt the town and gave it his name, Constantina. In the 8th century, the town was taken by Abou El Mouhajer, coming from Kai-

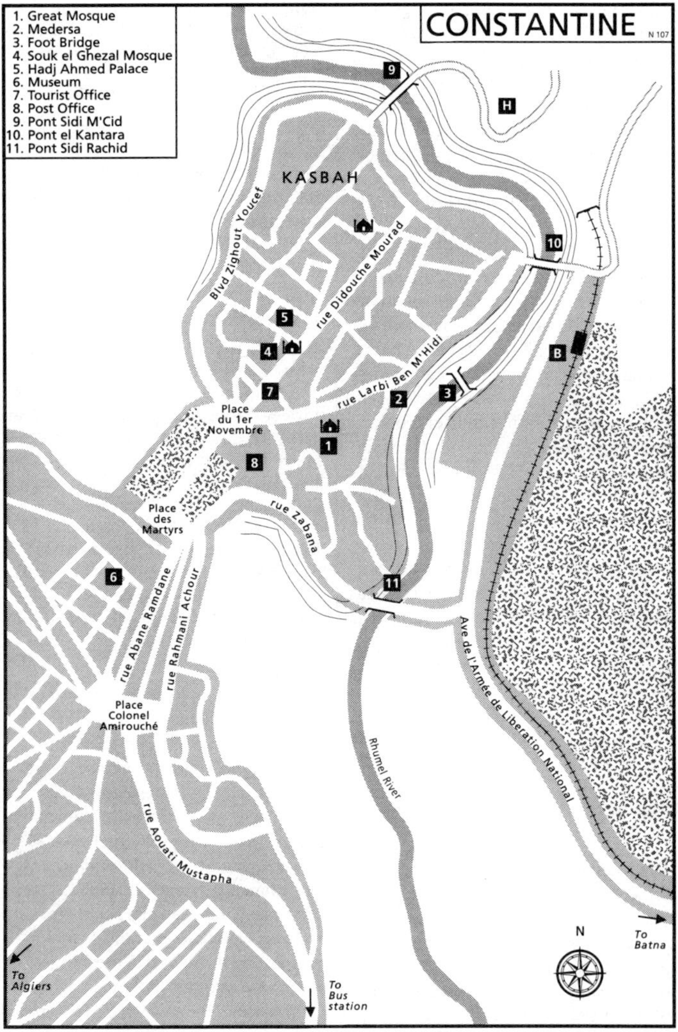

rouan in present day Tunisia and fell in turn into the hands of the Zirids, Hammadids, Almohads and the Hafsids. In the 16th century, the Turks from Algiers took control of the town. From 1830, the town was effectively independent from Algiers and not taken by the French until 1837, after many unsuccessful attempts. Today, Constantine is a strongly Islamic city where traditions are still important.

Things to see

The place du 1er Novembre is the centre of town, with a great number of cafés. It extends W into a large esplanade where an amazing view over the gorges can be enjoyed. From here, the rue Larbi Ben M'Hidi, leads into the old town. On the right is the **Great Mosque**, or Djemaa El Kebir. It has a modern façade, was constructed from 'recycled' Roman columns and capitals and was built on the remains of an ancient Temple: 11th century inscriptions have been discovered. The rue Larbi Ben M'Hidi, opens out on to the place Mohammed Tahar Ladjabi, where stands an interesting **neo-Moorish medersa**. There is also a footbridge leading directly to the station on the other side of the gorges. To get to the bridge, there is an elevator on the square that leads directly down to the bridge. At the end of the rue Larbi Ben M'Hidi, the El Kantara bridge spans a distance of 128m at a height of 125m over the Rhumel gorges and there is an excellent view from the bridge.

In the rue Didouche Mourad, the main commercial street in Constantine, is the **Souk El Ghezal mosque**. The mosque was built in 1730 by a Moroccan architect and in 1838 was transformed into a catholic church by the French. The **Hadj Ahmed palace** is situated on the place du Commandant Si El Haoues, off the rue Didouche Mourad. The palace was built in 1835 by the last of the Beys and is luxuriously decorated with marbled columns, painted Italian tiles and frescoes. The rue Didouche Mourad leads to the gorges and on the right, to the impressive **Sid M'Cid suspension bridge**. The bridge was built in 1912 and is 168m long with a most impressive view from the centre of the bridge, towering over the Rhumel, 175m below. The Blvd Zighout Youcef, hugging the side of the cliff leads from the bridge to the place du 1er Novembre. The view from the boulevard, over the cliff, is amazing. The **museum** is behind the place des Martyrs to the S. The most interesting items are the Numidian exhibits and the Roman displays, though these are of less importance. Open 0800-1200 and 1400-1700 except Fri mornings and Sat.

Local information

● **Accommodation**

C *Hotel Panoramic*, 59 rue Aouati Mustapha, T 942477, 35 rm, fine views; **C** *Hotel Cirta*, rue Rahmani Achour, T 9440331, 126 rm.

E *Grand Hotel*, 2 rue Larbi Ben M'Hidi, T 933047; **E** *Hotel de Paris* 1 rue Larbi Ben M'Hidi.

● **Youth hostel**

Cité Filali, Constantine, T 695461, 25 beds, bus 500m, train 2 km.

● **Places to eat**

♦♦*Hotel Cirta* on rue Rachmani Achour. Continue along this avenue for a selection of cheaper eating places – choose with care.

● **Banks**

Banque Central d'Algérie, Blvd Zighout Youcef; **Banque National d'Algérie**, place du 1er Novembre.

● **Post office**

Place du 1er Novembre. Telephone office next to it, open 24 hours.

● **Telephone**

Local code 04.

● **Travel agent**

ONAT, 6 rue Zabana, T 943954; *Air Algérie* 1 place des Martyrs, T 937070; *Air France*, 8 rue Abane Ramdane, T 935987.

● **Tourist information**

ONAT, 16 rue Didouche Mourad, T 941403. There is also a local office at 32 rue Abane Ramdane, T 932661.

● **Transport**

Air The airport is 9 km out of town. For information contact, T 936962. **Algiers** at least 3 flights daily, **Oran** Mon 1410, Tue, Sat 1230, Fri 1030 and 2000, **Tamanrasset** Thur at 1230. **International flights** daily to **Lyon, Marseille** and **Paris**.

Train The station is on the E side of the gorge. The quickest way is to take the foot bridge. Trains go to **Algiers, Skikda** and **Touggourt**. There is a daily train to **Tunis** at 1255.

Road Bus There are 2 bus stations. The first for towns close to Constantine is opposite the railway station. The second, and main one, for long distance is situated a few 3-4 km to the S of the town, by the river. There are buses to virtually everywhere in Algeria and a bus every 2 days to Tunis. For long journeys, particularly in summer, places should be booked in advance. **Taxis** leave from the main bus station, by the river.

EXCURSIONS FROM CONSTANTINE

Tiddis

Take the N2 NW from Constantine for 23 km then turn left at the crossroads, clearly signed. Be prepared to walk from the main road. Amidst the wild flowers on the S facing hillside are the ruins of **Castellum Tidditanorum** with its steep winding mainstreet. The water systems both hot and cold are worth examination. Up the hill beyond the water storage tanks admire the view across the steep Rhumel gorge.

Annaba

The town of Annaba, population 450,000 is situated at sea level on one of the few coastal planes in the E of Algeria. It is a thriving city, with important industries such as the El Hadjar steel works 12 km S and a large busy port. Today, Annaba is the third biggest city in Algeria. The city is of little interest apart from the ruins of Hippo Regius but is nevertheless pleasant enough for a stopover.

History

Annaba, ancient **Hippo Regius** (also known as Hippone, see page 444) was founded by the Phoenicians and allied, until its destruction, to Carthage. For a century Hippo Regius was independent and was one of the favourite residences of the Numidian kings. Due to the war between Caesar and Pompeii, and the subsequent annexation of Numidia by Caesar, Hippo Regius became a Roman colony in 46 BC. For the following 4 centuries the town prospered until the invasion by the Vandals. At the end of the 4th century, the town was a centre for Christianity, Augustine the Bishop having a great influence throughout the Christian world. He died in 430 during the siege by the Vandals, the town remaining under their control for a century before being taken by the Byzantines who initiated large reconstruction projects, the city having suffered heavily during the Vandal's rule.

In the 7th century, the invading Arabs took little interest in the town and after having pillaged it, decided to build a new town, 2 km away, on the site of the present Annaba. Over the centuries, Annaba, like many other coastal towns was involved in piracy. In 1522 it was occupied briefly by Barbarossa, and then by the Spanish. In 1830 the French attacked the city, but were obliged to retreat, only successfully gaining control of the town 2 years later. During WW1 the town was bombarded by the Germans and in WWII served as an operation base for the Allied Forces in North Africa. The town was again heavily bombed during the winter of 1942-43.

ACCESS Air The airport is 12 km out of town. For information, T 828302. There are 3 daily flights from Algiers, **El-Oued** Wed and Fri 0845, **Ghardaïa** Tue 1015, Sat 1030, **Oran** Tue 1520, Thur 1805. International flights from **Lyon** Wed and Sat 1850, **Marseille** Thur, Fri, Sat, Sun at 1720 and **Paris** Fri and Sun 1520. **Train** Daily trains from **Algiers, Constantine** and **Tunis** leaving at 1255. The train station is across the square at the S end of the Cours de la Révolution. **Road** The bus station (see map), is just 500m from the train station on Ave de l'Armée. There are frequent buses from all the major Algerian towns and a daily connection with **Tunis** leaving from the Tunis-South bus station at 0500. **Sea** The port is at the S end of the Cours de la Révolution and the ferry terminal just 100m away – very central.

Things to see

The best thing to do in Annaba is to stroll

along the tree-lined Cours de la Révolution, the main N-S artery, and the main area of social activity with its numerous cafés. The **old town** is to the E of the Cours de la Révolution, with at its centre the place du 19 Août 1956. The square is pleasant, with many cafés and the **Salah Bey mosque** (built in 1790) to the S. To the SE, and dominating the old town and the harbour is the much older **Sidi Bou Mérouane mosque**, built in the 11th century. The new (1900) **Basilica of St Augustine** is on a small hill S of the town. The **war cemetery** with 870 graves adjoins the leisure park. About 5 km W of Annaba on the N44 take the road to Saraidi.

Local information

● Accommodation

A *Seybouse International*, rue du 24 Février 1956, T 822125, all rm a/c, good restaurant, splendid views.

D *Grand Hotel d'Orient*, Cours de la Révolution, T 822051; **D** *Hotel Regina*, 6 rue Bakhli Mokhtar, T 823461.

● Youth hostel

On rue Abdaoui Mouloud, 23000 Wilaya d'Annaba, T 844983, 38 beds, kitchen, bus 3 km, trains 2 km, ferry 4 km, airport 13 km.

● Places to eat

♦♦♦restaurant in *Seybouse International Hotel*; ♦♦ Try ***Le Bosphorus*** on Cours de la Révolution and ♦select from the cafés in the same street.

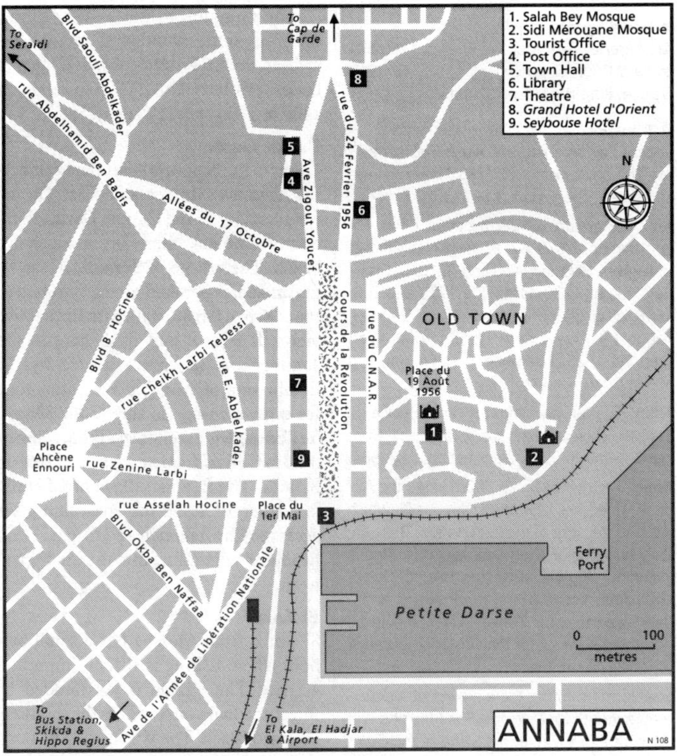

● **Banks**

Banque Centrale d'Algérie, 7 Cours de la Révolution; **Banque National d'Algérie**, 17 Cours de la Révolution.

● **Crafts**

There is a state run craft shop, the ***SNAT***, at 2 Cours de la Révolution.

● **Ferry tickets**

At the **CNAN**, 2 Cours de la Révolution, T 822230.

● **Post office**

Rue Zighout Youcef.

● **Telephone**

Local code 08.

● **Tourist information**

ONAT, 1 rue Tarik Ibn Zaid, T 825886.

● **Travel agents**

Air Algérie, Carrefour Sidi Brahim, T 837474 and at 2 Cours de la Révolution, T 820020; ***Air France***, 8 bis rue Prosper Dubourg.

● **Transport**

Local: Car hire Algérie Auto Tourisme, 3 Ave Zighout Youcef, T 827288. They also have an office at the airport, T 822330.

Air The airport is 12 km out of town. For information, T 828302. At least 3 daily flights to **Algiers, El Oued** Wed and Fri 1015, **Ghardaïa** Tue at 1230, **Oran** Tue 1720 and Thur 1605, **Ouargla** Sat at 1245. There are international flights to **Paris** Fri Sun 1000, **Lyon** Wed Sat 1525, **Marseille** Thur, Fri, Sat, and Sun at 0940.

Train The railway station is on the place du 1er Mai. There are daily trains to Algiers, Constantine and Tunis. For information, T 824904.

Road The bus station is 700m along the Ave de l'Armée de Libération Nationale, which starts to the right of the train station. There are daily buses to all the major towns in Algeria including **Algiers, Constantine, El-Oued, Ghardaïa, Tebessa** and **Souk Ahras** and a daily departure for **Tunis**. Tickets should be bought in advance for long distance journeys, especially in summer.

Sea In the summer there are about 4 departures a month for Marseille. The ferry port is at the centre of town, at the S end of the Cours de la Révolution.

Around Annaba

Hippo Regius

The ruins of Hippo Regius (see also p 442) are just 1½-2 km out of town. To get there, take the Ave de l'Armée de Libération National, which starts on the right of the station, and the site is further on the left. In the ruins, the mosaic floor of the **Great Christian Basilica** where St Augustine was bishop is particularly interesting. The **Great Baths** to the N are well preserved, the heating systems visible in the walls. To the SW of the Baths is the imposing **Forum**, built in the 1st century. Open only at 0830, 1030, 1230 and 1430 Wed, Thur and Fri. Be punctual. No photography allowed.

The **museum**, to the S of the ruins, contains some wonderful mosaics as well as everyday objects found during the excavations. Open 0800 to 1100 and 1400 to 1700 except Fri and Sat.

Cap de Garde

12 km to the N of Annaba, offers wonderful views over the sea and coast. On the road leading to the Cap de Garde, 4 km out of Annaba, there is an extensive beach. The village of **Seraidi**, 10 km W of Annaba, is perched at nearly 900m, in the cork oak forest, again with impressive views. It is cool and fresh here in the summer and much frequented by the inhabitants of Annaba. Recommended for birdwatching. To the W the **Massif de l'Edough** is excellent walking country. Stay in C *Hotel El Montazah*, T 822699 in Seraidi. The fishing village of **Chetaïbi** is further W along the coast and gives access to Cap Takouch and Cap de Fer, 2 headlands extending into the Mediterranean.

El Kala

87 km E from Annaba has a small harbour where fishing is still an important activity. The village is surrounded by forest and looks out towards the sea: there is a good beach. The W166 leads W along the coast to the remains of Vieux El Kala

while further inland the W109 beside Lac Oubaïra branches to **Cap Rosa**, takes in a view point towards Annaba, and returns to the main coast road. El Kala is also a good point for getting into Tunisia. The frontier is 36 km away and Tabarka only 45 km.

• **Accommodation** There is one good hotel, **C** *El-Morjane*, T 820242, 100 rm, own beach. **Youth hostel** A.J. El Kala, Cité du 19 Juin, Wilaya de Tarf 36100, T 650534, 20 beds, free kitchen, bus 2 km, train 2 km.

Souk Ahras on the N16 SE of Annabas is on the best route into Tunisia. There is a choice of the N 20 to the frontier at Ghardimaou on the way to Jendouba, or the minor road W30 to the frontier at Sakiet Sidi Tousssef on the way to Le Kef. There is no direct transport into Tunisia but you can take a bus or a taxi to the border and walk across. There is also a daily train for Tunis at about 1230, the railway line following the Oued Medjerda.

The Aurés Mountains

The Aurés mountains are part of the Saharan Atlas range, running from the SW to NE across Algeria. The N, around Batna, is climatically cool whilst the S, near Biskra is virtually Saharan. The landscape varies dramatically and is most impressive. The people of the Aurés mountains, like the Kabyles, have a strong identity. They speak a Berber dialect, are of Berber origin, and are known as the Chaouia. One of the interesting local crafts is the weaving of goats' hair carpets. The result is a hard-wearing, though somewhat coarse, material.

There are 2 main N-S routes from Batna to Biskra. The N3, the quickest, lies to the W of the mountains, leading through some spectacular scenery, particularly at the Défilé, close to the village of El Kantara. This is the main road used by the bus. The other road,the N31, E of the range is the quieter scenic route following the Oued El-Abiod. No direct

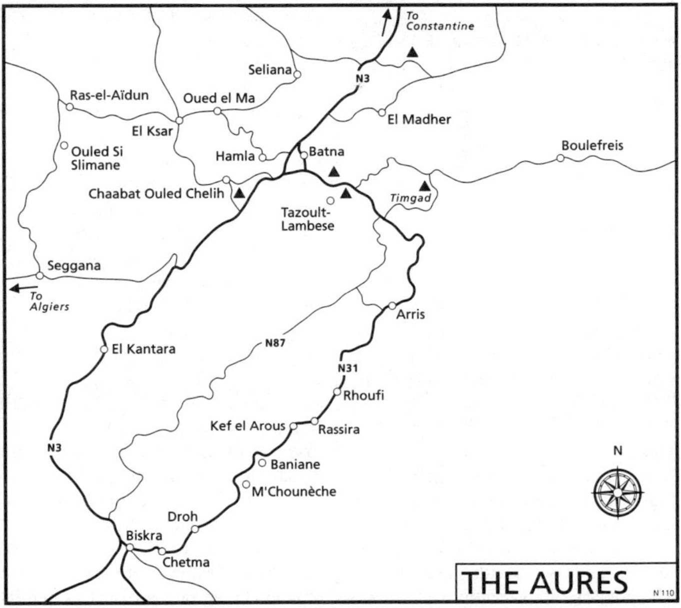

buses from Batna to Biskra go this way.

Batna

The town, altitude 1,038m, was built in 1844 by the French as a military camp for the protection of the road to the Sahara. Today, the town is prosperous and is an important educational and industrial centre. Batna is a good base for reaching the ruins of Timgad or exploring the surrounding area.

• **Accommodation B** *Hotel le Chélia*, 2 allée Ben Boulaïd, T 873362. **C** *Hotel Laverdure*, 3 Ave de l'Indépendence, T 551163. **D** *Hotel Amin*, rue Mohammed Khémisti, T 873404; **D** *Hotel Hyatt*. **Youth hostel** rue des Abattoirs, T 553807 open 0800-1200, 1400-2200, 30 beds, bus 300m, self catering.

• **Telephone** Local code 04.

• **Travel agent** *Air Algérie*, rue des Frères Maazouzi, T 552665.

• **Tourist information** ONAT and **Car hire,** allée Ben Boulaïd, T 559345.

• **Transport Road** The bus station is in the town centre. There are daily buses to **Algiers, Annaba, Biskra** and **Constantine**. There are normally 5 buses a day to Timgad from here, but the times tend to vary. **Taxi**: the taxi rank is 500m from the bus station.

Timgad

15 km E of Batna, Timgad is famous for the remarkable remains of the ancient Roman town of **Thamugadi**. Being very well preserved by the Sahara sands, the old town gives a very good idea of everyday life virtually 2,000 years ago.

ACCESS There are up to 5 buses a day to and from Batna, but the timetable varies. Check when the last bus leaves if you don't want to stay overnight. The taxis congregate around the site entrance.

History

The Roman colony of Thamugadi was founded by Trajan in the year 100 AD, and was mainly built by Roman soldiers. The purpose of the town was to provide retired legionnaires with a place to live, where culture and leisure were important. The town was destroyed in the 6th century by the Berbers but soon rebuilt by the Byzantines. It was destroyed and abandoned during the Arab invasion in the 7th century. In 1795 an English traveller rediscovered the site but excavation work only began in 1880.

The site

The town was built in a geometric pattern, with the main axes cutting through from N-S and E-W. From the gate, take the Cardo Nord leading to the **Forum**. The paving stones are still in good condition and wheel ruts are clearly visible. There is evidence of a sophisticated drainage system under the paving stones. On the left, along the Cardo Nord are the remains of the public library. The Cardo Nord meets the Cardo Maximus at right angles. The Cardo Maximus is lined with small arcades, once shops. The Forum, entered by stairs at the S end of the Cardo Nord, is a large rectangular square surrounded by arcades. To the E stands the **Civile Basilica**, where judgments and conferences took place.

To the S of the Forum is the **Theatre**, large enough to seat over 3,000. The **Great Southern Baths** are S, slightly outside the town's perimeter. They were built in the 2nd century and are much smaller than the **Great Northern Baths**. A Byzantine fort built in 539, stands 300m to the S of the site. The **Capitol** is at the SW corner of the town, curiously beyond the town's perimeter. The Capitol must have been enormous, with a large flight of 28 steps leading to it. The columns at the front, originally 6, were 14m high with beautiful capitals. For a good view over the entire site, climb up the hill directly S of the Capitol. Marking the entrance to the town, stands one of the main monuments, **Trajan's Arch**, built in the early 3rd century. At the W end of Cardo Maximus is the **Sertius Market**, also 3rd century. **Mescula Gate** stands at the E end of Cardo Maximus. The Market was arranged around the central courtyard, each merchant having his own stand. The slates for displaying food are visible today. To the N outside the perimeter are the **Great Northern Baths**. This enormous building, with over 30 rooms, houses many pools, hotrooms and gymnasiums. Open daily 0700 to sunset.

The Museum
To the left of the main gates holds a collection of very beautiful mosaics, and a number of interesting objects which give a good idea of the sophistication of everyday life. Open 0800-1200 and 1400-800, closed Sat.

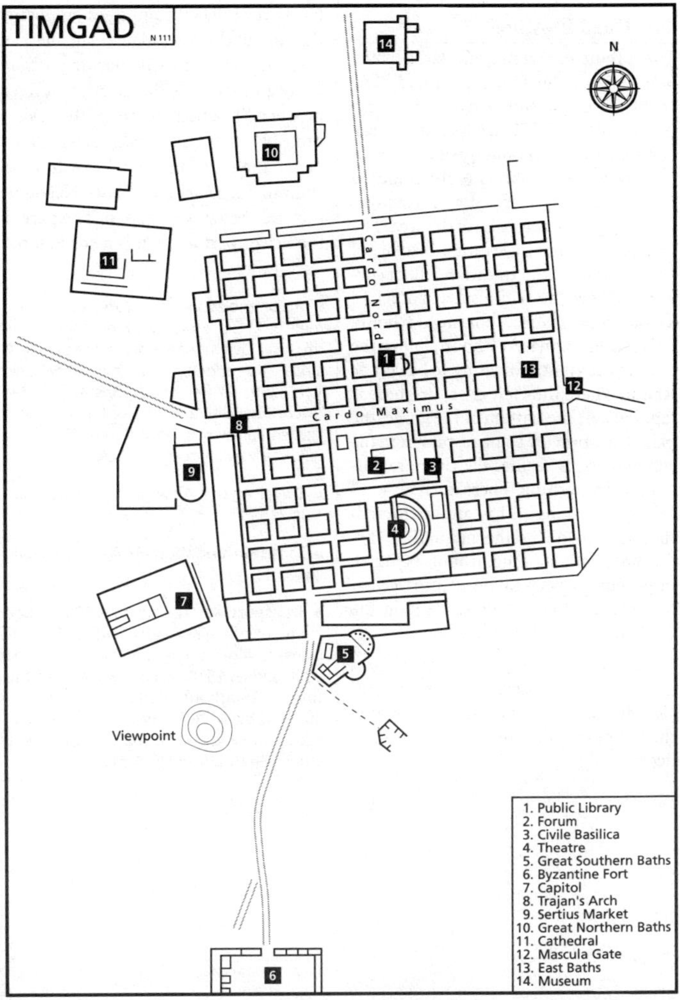

Local information

● **Accommodation**

The best thing to do is to stay in Batna and come for a day trip. **D** *Hotel El Kahina*, most rooms have a/c, far from perfect. **E** *Hotel Timgad*, 70 rooms, quiet.

● **Places to eat**

The only places recommended are the hotels.

The Oued El-Abiod

The E route to Biskra from Batna by the N31 follows the Oued El-Abiod. The landscape is beautiful. **Arris**, 56 km from Batna, altitude 1,171m, is a *dechra* village clinging to the mountainside. *Dechras* have been described as earth coloured 'terraced hamlets topped by fortress silos' and are characteristic of the area. The **Museum of Aurés** in Arris has displays of silver jewellery and traditional floor coverings. View the white-sided gorges of Tighanimine before stopping at **Rhoufi**, 90 km from Batna. At Rhoufi, follow the road to the right indicating **le balcon de Rhoufi** where the view over the gorge is fabulous. At the bottom of the gorge, the palm trees provide some respite from the sun and walks besides the river are particularly refreshing. There is a river walk to Baniane taking 2-3 hrs, and on through the gorges to M'Chounèche another 3 hrs for those with stamina. Rhoufi being an important carpet weaving centre for goat hair carpets has hopeful sellers on the road on either side of the village.

El Kantara, is on the N28, the main road from Batna to Biskra. The **Défilé** at El Kantara is really spectacular, dividing the 2 regions, for S of El Kantara is the desert.

• **Youth Hostel** T 718532, 50 beds, kitchen, bus and train 1 km.

Biskra

This is the first real oasis town when arriving from the N. It is not as interesting as others further S but is nevertheless an agreeable town. The large oasis contains over 150,000 palm trees producing the famous *deglet nur* dates. The market, best visited in the early morning, is very lively and sells a wide selection of fresh products. The best way to see the oasis is probably by taking a *calèche*, which are better than average and leave from in front of the *Hotel Les Zibans*. Negotiate the price before you step in. The park in the newer part of town is a shaded, colourful walk.

• **Accommodation C** *Hotel Les Zibans*, route de M'Cid, T 04 713067, pool, tennis, 100 rms, used by tour operators so can be full. **E** *Hotel Guendouz*, Blvd Emir Abdelkader, T 715769, 60 rm. **Youth hostel**, 12 Hadi Tayeb, Vieux Biskra, 1 km S of town, 50 beds, kitchen, family rms, open 0800-1200, 1700-2200, railway 2 km, airport bus.

• **Travel Agent** *Air Algérie*, Ave Benbadis, T 04 715804.

• **Tourist information** 37 Ave de la République.

• **Transport Air** The airport is 10 km out of town. For information, T 04 714052. There are planes to **Algiers**, Tue 0900, Wed 1145, Thur 0900 and Fri 1515. **Train** Daily to **Constantine** and **Touggourt**. **Road** The bus station is 400m to the N of the main street. Daily connections to **Algiers, Batna, Constantine, El Oued, Ghardaïa** and **In Aménas**.

NORTHWEST ALGERIA

CONTENTS

MAPS

The fertile plain that extends from Algiers W to the Moroccan border offers pleasant and refreshing landscapes. The coast has many attractive beaches and secluded bays but there is a shortage of accommodation. The best itinerary is to follow the coast as far as Oran and then cut inland towards Tlemcen, leaving out the less interesting inland towns. Oran is an important industrial and commercial centre with some remains of French architectural influence but is not an essential visit, whereas Tlemcen should not be missed.

ALGIERS TO ORAN

Cherchell

30 km W from Algiers, Cherchell is a small seaside town, with a population of 100,000 and is famous historically, with monuments visible in and around the modern town.

History

Founded in the 4th century BC by the Phoenicians it was later named Caesarea by Juba II, a Numidian prince. The town was made capital of Mauritania, but by 40 BC was made a Roman colony. Caesarea became the capital of a large province, stretching as far E as Sétif. It was fortified and prospered greatly accumulating rich monuments and works of art. An aqueduct, over 28 km long, brought water from near Menaceur. In 372 the town was ruined by the Vandals but regained a certain importance under the Byzantines. The Arabs occupied the town in the 10th century. In the 15th century, a great number of Andalusians sought refuge in Cherchell, and in 1518 Barbarossa occupied the town. A number of unsuccessful attempts were made by the French to take the city until in the 1830s, France gradually occupied Algeria and Cherchell finally fell into their hands in 1840.

ACCESS There are frequent buses from Algiers, Blida and Mostaganem which will drop you off at the bus station which is at the W entrance to the town, close to the Roman baths on the road in from Algiers.

Things to see

There have been very few excavations at Cherchell, partly because the new town is built over the ancient city. Some monuments are still visible. The best pieces are in the archaeological **Museum** on the E side of the place des Martyrs, the town's central square. Of note are the copies of Greek statues which are incredibly well executed. These statues were probably made in Cherchell and demonstrate the great skills of the local artisans. Of the statues, that of Apollo is a perfect copy of one of Phidias' creations. Also worth a look is the gigantic statue of Hercules and another of Venus. The mosaics depicting agricultural scenes are recommended too. The museum is open 1000-1200 and 1430-1700. Closed Fri mornings and Sat. Photography not allowed.

To the S of the place des Martyrs is the area where remains of the Forum and Civile Basilica have recently been discovered. Further to the S is the Roman Theatre, built in the 1st century but transformed into an amphitheatre in the 3rd century. At the W entrance to Cherchell, stand the **Baths** which have only been partially excavated. Many of the statues in the museum were found here. A 1 km walk to the E of the town in a magnificent setting on the coast stands a 17th century shrine (koubba) containing the tomb of **Sidi Brahim el Ghobrini**, a noted religious teacher.

The road directly S of the town crosses the river and climbs up to give a good view over the settlement.

Local information

● Accommodation

C *Hotel Césarée*, place des Martyrs, T 051/467161, 31 rm.

● Tourist information

On rue Abdelhak (off place des Martyrs), T 67460.

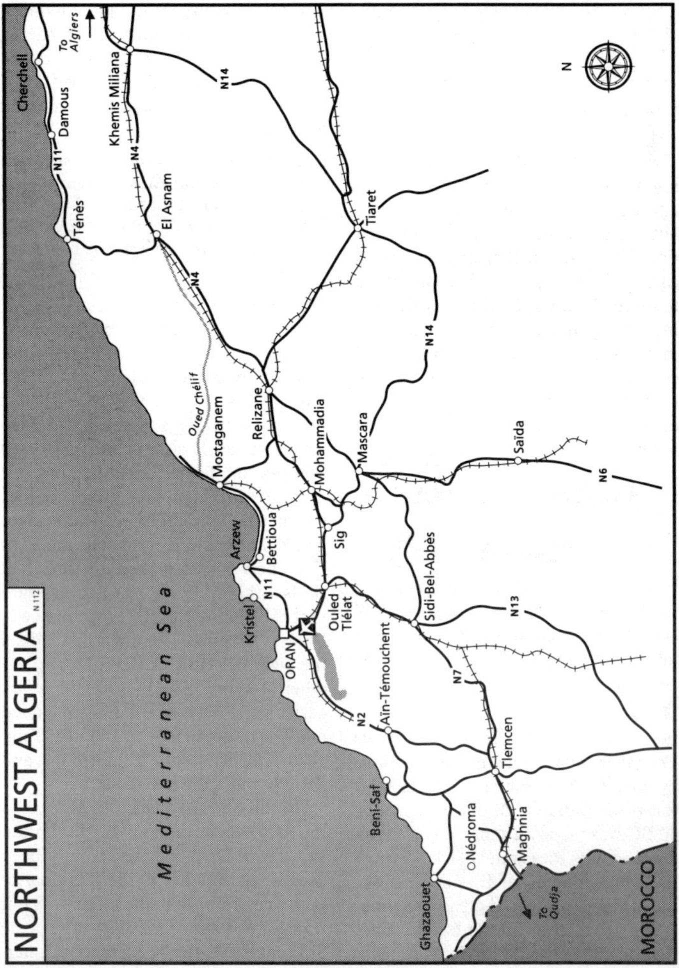

- **Travel agent**
Air Algérie 2 rue Abdelhak, T 445800.

From Cherchell to Ténès

The N11 coast road, the Corniche Dahra from Cherchell to Ténès is 108 km long. It is particularly beautiful, the best part undoubtedly being the 41 km between the river crossing at Damous and Ténès.

Ténès

ACCESS Buses from Algiers, El Asnam and Mostaganem. The nearest airport is at El Asnam, 53 km.

The new town built in a geometric pattern is of very little interest to the traveller but the old town founded in 875 which is 2 km SE out of town along the road to El Asnam, is well worth a visit. Remains of the walls and a door can be seen as well as an interesting mosque constructed from parts taken from older buildings.

- **Accommodation** **C** *Hotel Cartenna*, route du Phare, T 457510. **D** *Hotel des Arts*, rue de la Révolution.

Mostaganem

ACCESS Buses from Algiers, Ghardaïa, Mascara and Oran stop in the town centre. The station, trains from Oran and Algiers via Mohammadia lies to the E of the town, too far to walk.

This important fishing port with a certain charm is a pleasant stop-over. Arriving from either E or W, you will end up in the centre of the new town on Ave Benaied Bendehiba and the place du 1er Novembre. The place du 1er Novembre is bordered with arcades and cafés with a good view to the W towards the sea and to the N the old Turkish quarter. From the other end of the Ave Benaied Bendehiba, a bridge links the old town.

- **Accommodation** **B** *Hotel Royal*, 53 Ave A. Cherif, T 262372. **D** *Hotel Es Sahel*, rue Benguedda Tayeb, T 262433.**E** *Hotel Albert 1er*, rue Khelifa Mohammed, T 262923, dated, 40 rm some with bath.
- **Telephone** Local code 06.
- **Travel agent** *Air Algérie*, Ave Benaied Bendehiba, T 212427.
- **Tourist information** ONAT, 2 Blvd Khémisti, T 266221.

The first 48 km between Mostaganem and Oran are along the N11, a low-lying coast road through agricultural land. The obtrusive oil town of Arzew is best avoided by turning off at Bettioua. The detour to Kristel on the W27 offers a winding, picturesque ride through a narrow gorge and then vineyards to the coast, a view across the bay and access to Oran at the harbour.

Oran

Pop 700,000 *Alt* 90m.

Oran, the second biggest city in Algeria, offers the visitor a lively atmosphere. The town is thriving and renowned for its liberalism and Western outlook.

History

Oran is one of the few Algerian towns which does not seem to have been settled by the Romans, though there are signs of prehistoric life in caves throughout the surrounding area. The town was founded in 937 by Andalusian sailors, prospered under the Zianids and developed good trading relations with the Spanish. It was occupied by the Spanish from 1509 until

CLIMATE: ORAN

	Jan	Feb	Mar	Apr	May	Jun	Jul	Aug	Sep	Oct	Nov	Dec	Av/Tot
Max (°C)	16	17	19	21	24	27	30	31	29	25	21	17	23
Min (°C)	7	8	10	11	14	18	20	21	19	15	11	8	13
Rain (mm)	63	54	40	40	22	10	2	1	10	33	44	82	401

1708 when it was taken by the Turks. 24 years later the Spanish retook Oran but left 2 years after the massive 1790 earthquake that destroyed most of the town. At the time the French entered the city in 1831, the population was estimated at 4,000. The town's development suffered in 1849 in a major cholera epidemic. In the second half of the 19th century, French and Spanish settlers introduced

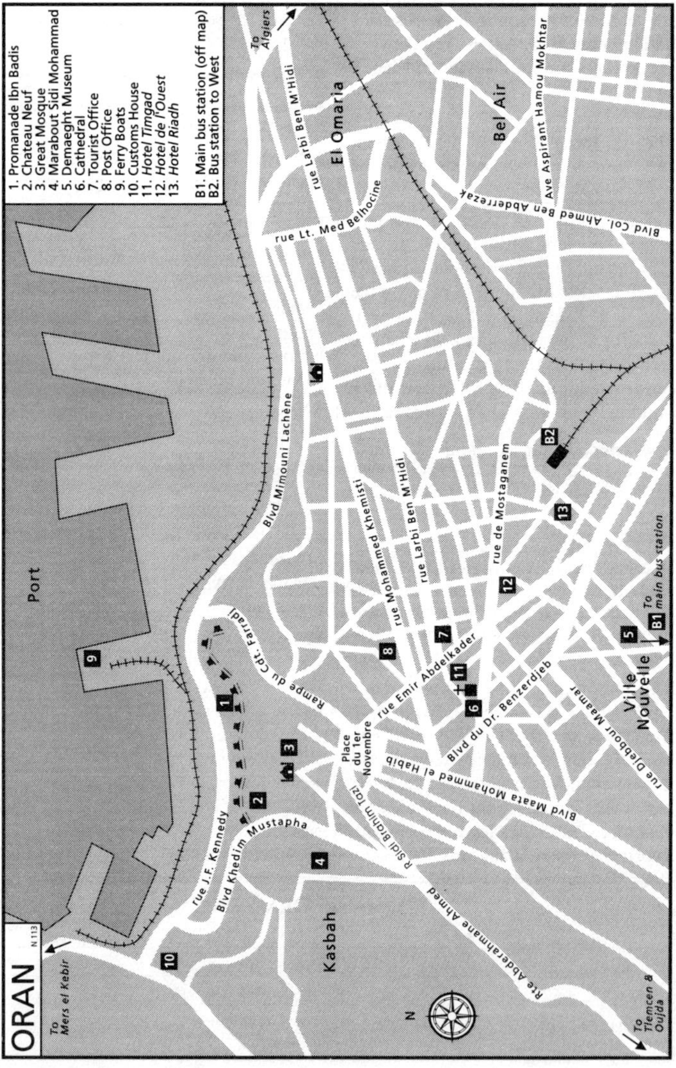

a certain European aspect to the town. After Independence, 200,000 Europeans left the city, reducing it to a virtual ghost town. It took some time for Oran to regain its previous vitality, but today it is the second major town in Algeria and an important industrial, cultural and educational centre.

The Nobel prize-winning French writer Albert Camus was born in Oran, the town being the setting for 2 of his most famous books *The Plague* and *The Stranger*. Fashion designer Yves Saint Laurent was also born here.

ACCESS Air The airport is 22 km away along the motorway at Tafraoui. Buses will take you to place 1er Novembre. There are 5 flights daily from Algiers and flights at least once a week from Adrar, Annaba, Béchar, Constantine, Tamanrasset and Tindouf. There are buses to the central square, place 1er November 1954. For information, T 418500. **International Flights** to Oran from: Geneva Thur 1550. Lyon Thur and Sat 1300. Marseille daily except Wed and Sat 1210. Paris daily 1825 and Wed, Sat and Sun 1355. Toulouse Wed and Sat 1805. Zürich Thur 1430.

Train The train station is at the top of the Blvd Mellah Ali, to the E of the town, a 1 km downhill walk to the central square with trains from Algiers, Mohammadia and Tlemcen.

Road Buses from Tlemcen and places W terminate near the railway station while all other buses terminate S of the town.

Sea Ferries from France and Spain dock in the centre of the port, which is about 1 km walk up to the central square. Sailings from: Marseille in summer (Jul, Aug, Sep) there are 4 return journeys a month, otherwise there are 2 a month. Alicante in summer 8 return journeys a month, otherwise 4 a month. Sète in summer 3 return journeys a month.

Things to see

The centre of the town is place du 1er Novembre from which the town's main 4 arteries spring. The **Promenade Ibn Badis** which starts on the left of the Rampe du Commandant Farradj, downhill from the place du 1er Novembre is a garden created by the General Létang in 1847. It contains a collection of exotic trees and plants and has a commanding view over the harbour. On top of the hill behind the Promenade stands the **Chateau Neuf**, a fortress built by the Spanish and subsequently used as a residence by the Spanish governors and Beys. Today it is being transformed into a luxury hotel and cannot be visited. Directly to the S of the Chateau Neuf is the **Great Mosque**, Djemaa el Kebir, built in 1796 to commemorate the departure of the Spanish. Particularly interesting is the **octagonal minaret** which can be climbed, with permission, for a splendid view. The Mosque is open 0800-1200 except Fri.

To the W, the **Marabout Sidi Mohammed El Haouri** built in 1793 has an attractive minaret and is clearly influenced by Andalusian architecture. To the S along the rue Sidi El Haouri, stands the Porte d'Espagne. The **Demaeght Museum** on the Blvd Zabana has 3 interesting sections. The prehistoric section displays finds from throughout the Maghreb during Palaeolithic and Neolithic times. The ethnographic display on the first floor covers the tribes in the Maghreb and Asia, with a room devoted just to Oran. A natural history display of animals from the Maghreb is situated on the lower ground floor. The museum is open 0900-1200 and 1500-1900 in summer, 0830-1200 and 1430-1800 in winter, closed Fri afternoon and all day Sat.

The present library with stained glass windows and mosaics which depict religious scenes over the doors, was the **Cathedral of Sacré Coeur**. Worth seeing, entrance free.

Le Petit Lac Military Cemetery lies 4 km SE of Oran on the approach road to the airport on the S side of Ave Di Sidi Chami.

Beaches

It is necessary to get right out of Oran to find a decent beach. Go W to Mers El Kebir and beyond along the W84 to **Les Andalouses** 32 km. Here is a lively summer resort with accommodation and water sports.

Local information

● Accommodation

C ***Hotel Timgad***, 22 Ave Emir Abdelkader, T 394797, 200 rm, restaurant.

D ***Hotel Murdjadjo***, 3 rue Ampère, T 334568, 68 rm.

E ***Hotel de l'Ouest***, 6 Blvd Mellah Ali, T 364698, 43 rm; **E** ***Hotel Riadh***, 46 Blvd Mellah Ali, T 363846.

● Youth hostels

There are 2 youth hostels: 3 rue Benadjila, Lahouari, Seddikia, T 350245, 40 beds, kitchen, 200m from bus and 2 km from train station; and 19 rue Maoued Ahmed, T 398026, 40 beds, 500m from bus and 1 km from train station.

● Banks

Banque Centrale d'Algérie, 13 Blvd de la Soummam; **Banque Nationale d'Algérie**, 4 Blvd de la Soummam.

● Crafts

SNAT, 3 Blvd de la Soummam. Large number of local goods and crafts for sale.

● Hospital

76 Blvd Ben Zerdeb, T 344311.

● Post office

Blvd Mohammed Khémisti.

● Telephone

Local code 06.

● Travel agents

Air Algérie, 2 Blvd Emir Abdelkader, T 391555; *Air France*, 5 place Abdelmalek Ramdane, T 336965; ***CNAN***, 13 Blvd Abane Ramdane, T 332767, for ferry tickets.

● Tourist information

ONAT, 10 Blvd Emir Abdelkader, T 391611. They issue air tickets and have a car hire service. For **local information**, 4 rue Mohammed Khémisti, T 335130.

● Transport

Air The airport is at Tefraoui, 22 km. Buses to the airport leave from the place du 1er Novembre. For information, T 418500. **Internal Flights** from Oran to **Algiers** 4 daily; **Adrar** Mon 1450, Tue 1505, Wed 1620, Sun 1510. **Annaba** Tue 1520 and Thur 1805. **Béchar** Mon and Fri 0750 and Thur, Sat and Sun 1500. **Constantine** Tue 0735 and 1430. Fri 1230 and Sat 1430. **Tamanrasset** Fri 1135. **Tindouf** Tue, Thur, Sat and Sun 0900. **International Flights** to **Geneva** Thur and Sat 0915. **Lyon** Thur and Sat 0915. **Marseille** daily except Wed and Sat 0635. **Paris** daily 1400 and Wed, Sat and Sun 0930. **Toulouse** Wed and Sat 1440. **Zürich** Thur 1000.

Train There are departures to Algiers, Mohammadia (for Béchar) and Tlemcen. A night train for Algiers leaves at 2200. Be there at least 1 hour before if you want a seat. For information, T 340621.

Road There are 2 bus stations in Oran. The bus station for the W and Tlemcen is by the train station. Buses to all other main towns leave the main bus station 1½ km beyond the museum on Blvd Zabana.

Sea Ferries leave from directly below the Ramp de Commandant Ferradj. For frequency see Access above.

Excursions

Most visitors aiming for Tlemcen, 138 km away, take the direct N2. This road skirts the huge salt sea for 30 km, climbs easily through a rich agricultural landscape to **Aïn-Témouchent** and then winds and turns up to Tlemcen nestling at the foot of the Monts de Tlemcen. Travellers with their own transport are recommended to take instead the N2 W, the corniche to **Mers el Kebir**, with fine sea views and one or 2 good beaches, in particular Les Andalouses (15 km from Oran) which is just beyond the lighthouse perched on **Cap Falcon**. Aim back to the N2 at Bou-Tlélis or El Amria. Further roads to the W lead down to pleasant beaches and the N35 and Aïn-Témouchent before cutting through the wooded Traras mountain range to **Beni-Saf**, a thriving port. The N22 S goes on to Tlemcen.

INLAND TO TLEMCEN

Tlemcen

Tlemcen, altitude 830m, population 200,000, lies 170 km from Oran and is one of the finest cities in Algeria, noted for its unique cultural and architectural heritage. Despite modern additions on the outskirts it remains a truly beautiful city situated in an equally beautiful region which one must take time to explore and appreciate.

History

The area was inhabited by cave dwellers during prehistoric times, and was also the site of a Roman legionnaire's camp of which very little remains. In the 8th century, the Arab town, established by Idris I, was named Agadir meaning fortress. The actual town of Tlemcen was founded in the 11th century by the Almoravid Youcef Ben Tachfin, who made it his capital and built the Great Mosque. It reached its peak under the Zianids, or Abd El Ouadites whose leader was the Berber Yaghmoracen, and became the capital of the central Maghreb prospering in trans-Saharan trade. Bitter rivalry between the Zianids in Tlemcen and the Merinids from Fes prompted a struggle for the control of Tlemcen. The first siege was in 1299, when Abou Yacoub, the Merinid leader, built the city of Mansourah, just outside Tlemcen. In 1307, Abou Yakoub was assassinated and Mansourah evacuated. Two subsequent sieges, in 1337 and 1359, took place before the Merinids finally controlled Tlemcen. They established their capital in Mansourah.

During the early 15th century, the Zianid's power decreased and control of the town oscillated between the Merinids and the Hafsids of Tunis. In 1511, the Zianids finally succumbed to Spanish influence from Oran, and in 1555 the Turks ended all Zianid power and took the town which declined during their rule. At this time a new and important ethnic group was formed, the Kouloughlis, descendants of Turkish men and local women. With the French occupation of Algiers in 1830, Tlemcen was divided,

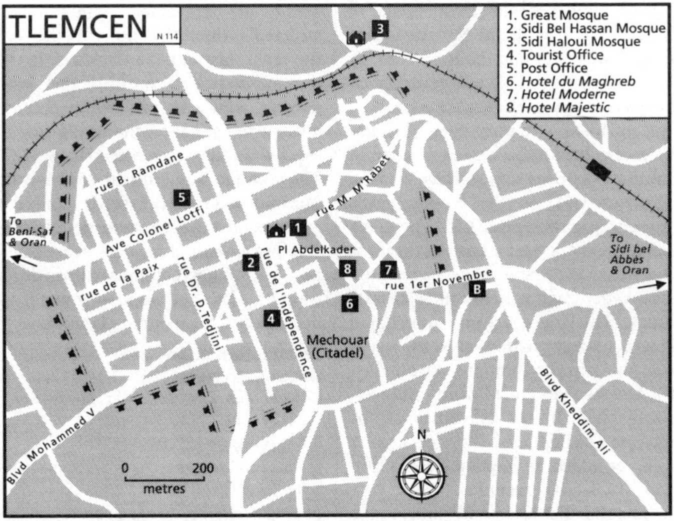

the Kouloughlis siding with the French and the Moors and Berbers supporting Emir Abdelkader. The French finally took Tlemcen in 1842 but the seeds of Algerian nationalism were already in place. Ahmed Messali Hadj, born in Tlemcen, founded the first Independence movement in 1924. By 1946, he was head of the MTLD (Mouvement pour le Triomphe des Libertés Démocratiques). Many leaders who came to prominence in the struggle for independence came from this movement.

ACCESS Air The airport is at Zénata, 24 km N. There are buses to the centre of town. For information, T 220314. **Train** From Oran and the Moroccan border trains stop at the station to the E of the town about 15 mins walk. The bus station is on the corner of rue du 1er Novembre and Blvd Gaouar Hocine. The station is well organized. **Road** There are buses from Algiers, Béchar, Oran, Sebdou, Tiaret and the Moroccan border.

Things to see

The centre of town is the place Emir Abdelkader. This is a lively square, with a great number of cafés, most popular in the early evening. To the N of the square is the **Great Mosque**, built in 1082 by Youcef Ben Tachfin. It was embellished by the Almoravid Ali Ben Youcef in 1135 and enlarged a century later by Yaghmoracen. It is styled on the mosque in Córdoba (see page 154) and has 13 naves. The entrance, on the E side, leads straight into the prayer hall. The dome above the *mihrab* is remarkable, the intricate decoration simulating stalactites. The *mihrab* itself is richly and elegantly ornate. The large courtyard, over 20m in length, once covered in onyx, has a central fountain for ablutions, surrounded by benches decorated with multicoloured tiles. In the N corner of the mosque, stands the 35m rectangular minaret added by Yaghmoracen. Open daily 0800-1100 except Fri.

The **Sidi Bel Hassan Mosque**, to the W of the place Emir Abdelkader, has been deconsecrated and transformed into a museum. This mosque was built in honour of Yaghmoracen, in 1296. It is thought that the mosque was named after the famous theologian Abou El Hassan, who started teaching before Yaghmoracen's death. Inside, the mosque is separated into 3 naves supported by 8 onyx columns. The carved plasterwork is noteworthy. The museum's exhibits are displayed in the prayer hall and an adjoining room mainly consisting of intricate mosaics, 12th century carved woodwork, funerary steles, minerals, fossils and pottery. Open daily 0900-1200 and 1400-1800, closed Fri afternoon and Sat all day. Entrance free.

The Hadars, the old Andalusian quarter, starts from the NE of the place Emir Abdelkader. The main street in this area, rue Mohammed M'Rabet, has been turned into a highly commercial pedestrian zone. This quarter, in the morning or late afternoon is incredibly lively and full of atmosphere. One block S of place Emir Abdelkader is the Mechouar, or citadel, mainly reconstructed in the 19th century. To the N of the town, just outside the walls, is the **mosque** dedicated to Sidi Haloui who gave up being a law professor to become a sweet seller, got on the wrong side of the Sultan and was executed in 1337. The mosque was built in 1353 by the Merinid Abou Inane Farés. It stands out white against the surrounding greenery. The prayer hall is divided into 5 naves held up by 8 onyx columns with intricate capitals. The rectangular minaret is decorated with coloured glazed tiles.

Local information

● Accommodation

B *Hotel Les Zianides*, Blvd Kheddim Ali, T 201821, best hotel in town, 10 mins from town centre, garden, pool, tennis.

D *Hotel du Maghreb*, place du Commandant Ferradj, T 203571, 78 rm.

E *Hotel Moderne*, 20 rue du 1er Novembre,

T 208796; ***Hotel Majestic***, place Cheikh Bahir Ibrahimi, T 200786, no showers.

● Youth hostel
Sidi Chaker, Tlemcen 13000, T 263226, open 0800-1200 and 1400-2200, 50 beds, laundry facilities, bus 500m.

● Camping
Municipal camp site 2 km to W of town in olive groves, sounds idyllic, actually very basic.

● Banks
Banque Centrale d'Algérie, Ave Colonel Lotfi (next to post office).

● Bargains
Fine embroidery, local and imported carpets, leather work and woodwork especially cabinets and inlaid boxes.

● Hammam
On rue 1er November, separate opening times for men and women so check! AD10 includes soap and towel.

● Music
Tlemcen is noted for its music making; classical Andalusian music is studied.

● Post office
Ave Colonel Lotfi, open 0800-1830 Sat-Wed, 0800-1600 Thur. Parcel department on left, telephones at rear.

● Telephone
Local code 07.

● Travel agents
CNAN, T 200071, rue 1er November for shipping; ***Air Algérie*** rue Dr Damerdji Tedjini, T 266762; ***Air France***, rue de La Paix, T 203901.

● Tourist information
Local place du Commandant Ferradj, T 203456. Open 0900-1200 and 1430-1900. Very helpful with good free map. **ONAT**, 15 rue de l'Indépendence, near mechouar entrance, T 208801. Travel agency and car hire available.

Around Tlemcen

Visit **Mansourah** about 2 km W of Tlemcen. The town was built in 1302 by the Merinid Abou Yacoub, while holding Tlemcen's first siege. By the end of the 14th century, the town was abandoned

THE FRENCH FOREIGN LEGION

The Légion Etrangère was set up in 1831 for service outside France, at that time principally in Algeria. The **Beau Geste** image of the Legion is deserved not simply because of the desert terrain and the colonial wars in which it fought but because conditions of service were and remain extremely tough. The Foreign Legion was deployed in Algeria and Morocco and its buildings, including forts and garrison towns, remain a characteristic symbol of the French occupation of the region. The group's headquarters were at Sidi Bel Abbès in Algeria until 1962 when the French gave Independence to Algeria. The Legion saw bloody but heroic service in Mexico, Spain and Crimea before being sent to Indochina in 1885 where it was a major military element of the French colonial presence. The Legion took part in the splendid but ultimately unsuccessful battle at Dien Bien Phu, after which the French administration ended.

The Legion's officers are French, with few exceptions. The ranks are made up of other mainly European nationalities who have joined the Legion because of its unique record of professionalism and its almost constant involvement in warfare in distant places. The backbone of the Legion has always been made up of an élite often originally trained in national armies and there is little truth in the belief that it was made up of untrained thieves, murderers and n'er do wells.

In recent years the Legion served with distinction not only in Indochina but in the great world wars. France deployed the Foreign Legion in Corsica after the withdrawal from Algeria and it is thus not far away from the North African territories where its legend was created.

and used as a source of building stone for Tlemcen, which accounts for the few remains. Still standing are parts of the walls which were originally 4 km long, reaching a height of 12m and 1½m in thickness, complemented by 80 towers. The best pieces remaining stand to the N and W of the site. The only other ruins include the **mosque** which has virtually disappeared and the minaret, still almost intact, apart from the S side. The **minaret** has been acknowledged as one of the finest examples of Hispano-Moorish architecture and ranks with the Koutoubia in Marrakech (see page 302) and the Giralda in Sevilla (see page 164).

At **El Eubbab**, 2 km to the E of the town, is the **Sidi Bou Medine mosque** and tomb. Sidi Bou Medine, was born in Sevilla in 1126. He was highly revered throughout the Maghreb and taught in Sevilla, Fes and Bejaïa after having been to Mecca. He died in Tlemcen on a journey to Marrakech in 1197 and was buried here. The shrine, reached through a splendid columned courtyard, has been frequently added to and restored. The mosque built in 1339 by Merinid Sultan Abou El Hassan Ali, is one of the finest examples of the Hispano-Moorish style, with spectacular arches and carved decorative plasterwork in floral and geometric designs, similar to the Palace of the Alhambra in Granada, and is unique in Algeria. The minaret which was built at the same time has beautiful designs in brick and tiles. It is possible to climb up to the top where there is a very good view. Next to the mosque, is a once beautiful **medersa**, which unfortunately has suffered neglect over the years. The famous historian and geographer Ibn Khaldoun frequently came here. The *koubba*, mosque and *medersa* are open 0800-1100 every day except Fri.

Beni Bahdel lake 32 km SW along the N22 and W54 over the Col d'Hafrir is surrounded by dense forest.

Cascades d'El Ourit 7 km E along the N7, a 7-layer waterfall from the dam outlet tumbles into the irrigated valley below.

Maghnia, 50 km W of Tlemcen through expanses of vineyards and orchards, is the last town before the border with Morocco, another 13 km on. Be prepared for tedious checking procedures as you cross. Make sure your financial documents are in order.

Nédroma, altitude 395m, is a quiet town 37 km N of Maghnia on the W46, which winds through areas of olives and vines before crossing the forested ridge of the Traras range. The Taza pass offers spectacular views. The Great Mosque built by the Almoravids and the remains of battlements recall the town's historic past. Today Nédroma is better known for its pottery and the woven and embroidered garments it produces.

The circuit back to Oran can be completed by taking the eastern route via **Sidi-Bel-Abbès**, a booming town, proud of its new university. For the first 40 km the N7 and the railway keep company, taking turns to cross first under then over as they cut through some pleasant, prosperous farming land with the wooded hills to the S. Sidi-Bel-Abbès was famous as the home of the French Foreign Legion (see box). **Accommodation** C *El Djazaïr* is recommended for an overnight stay. The road then follows the (dry) river bed N to Oued Tlélat and the busy motorway into Oran.

THE SOUTH

CONTENTS

MAPS

The Sahara Desert takes up a massive 85 per cent of the S of Algeria. No wonder 95 per cent of the population lives in the N of the country! The road network is good though many of the roads are not black top and traffic uses the N-S routes through the Grand Ergs Oriental and Occidental to the oases of Djanet, Regganne and In Salah, then on to Tamanrasset. This vast empty space sprawls under clear blue skies and has as its focal point the Hoggar range of mountains reaching 3,000m. It contains the chaotic landscapes of Tassili N'Ajjer, shelters one of the world's richest prehistoric art museums and reveals surprisingly luxuriant oases.

GRAND ERG ORIENTAL

The Grand Erg Oriental is the immense stretch of sand in the E of Algeria, going right up to the Tunisian and Libyan borders. It is considerably larger than the Grand Erg Occidental.

The Souf

The region in the N of the Grand Erg is known as the Souf and has its own traditions and way of life. First inhabited during the Neolithic period, the region was later settled by Berbers and Arabs, mostly from the Yemen. Today, the Souafas speak a very pure Arabic, only a few Berber words remaining. Despite recent efforts towards settling these people, nomadism still exists and a number of families still spend half the year with their animals, only returning to the oasis for date picking. Traditional activities such as carpet and *burnous* weaving continue wherever the women are. A remarkable aspect of life in the Souf is the ingenious cultivation system. Instead of making the water rise to the ground, the cultivation is done as close to the water table as possible. The 'gardens' are dug in the sands, reaching depth of 3 to 20m. The use of the *bour* circumvents the need for complex irrigation systems as the roots of the palm trees draw water directly from the underground water supply. Nevertheless, the work involved is not any less than in the maintenance of an irrigation system. The sand incessantly fills in the holes and it is a continuous effort to keep it at bay. The architecture of the region illustrates both the need to use any available materials in the building, and the rigours of the environment. All the houses are built to minimize the effect of the heat, with domes to deflect the sun and with few windows, while the thick walls reduce the heat inside.

El Oued

Known as the town of the Thousand Domes, El Oued is in the centre of the Souf region. In summer, temperatures of 45°C are not uncommon and even 50°C is reached. The town itself is very pleasant, with beautiful architecture and fits perfectly into the surroundings, with its rounded shapes and white walls. El Oued is a good place from which to enter Tunisia. There are taxis to the border and buses from there to Tozeur in Tunisia.

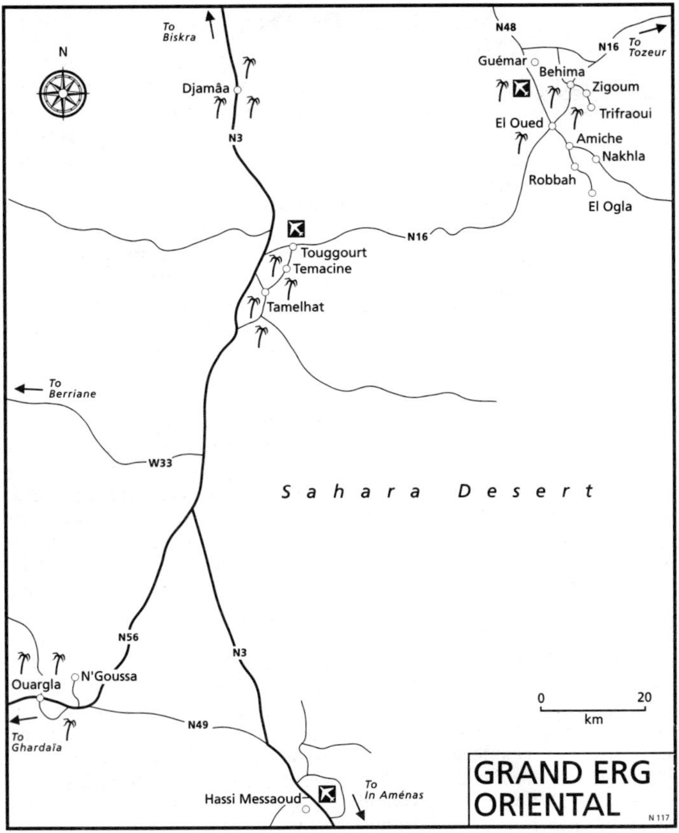

There is also a bank on the Algerian side of the border for converting Dinars.

ACCESS Air The airport is 18 km away on the road to Biskra, at Guémar. There are 6 flights from Algiers and 2 from Annaba. **Road** Buses from Annaba, Algiers, Biskra, Constantine, Ghardaïa and Touggourt stop at the main bus station 3 km N of the town along Ave Mohammed Khémisti.

Things to see

The town centre and major point of interest is the **market place** in the old part of town. The market takes place every day, but is best in the morning or evenings, especially on Fri. It is a colourful and lively market selling fresh vegetables, fruit and local *burnouses* and carpets. Local carpets frequently have a brown cross in the design. Prices are a bit lower than in Ghardaïa. Also interesting are *Affanes*, a kind of woollen slipper used by the nomads as protection from cold and from the burning sands. By the side of the road going to Tunisia, there is a market with sheep, horses and camels. From the market, ask to see the **Sidi Salem mosque** from which there is an excellent view over the city. The **museum**, on the Ave Taleb Larbi, by the Tourist Office has only one room, but contains some interesting exhibits. There is a collection of desert animals and insects as well as some sand roses and an explanation of how they are formed. A display of interesting geological finds proves that the Sahara was once a sea. The museum is open 0900-1200 and from 1500-1800, closed Mon. Entry AD1.

Local information

● Accommodation

C *Hotel du Souf*, S of the town, T 728523, pool, a/c, and a tower with a good view.

D *Hotel de l'Or Noir*, T 728219, on the outskirts of El Oued on the road to Biskra, 40 rms, pool.

E *Hotel Si Moussa*, Ave Mohammed Khémisti, T 728381, slightly out of the centre, close to the bus station, sleep on roof; **E** *Hotel Central*, Ave Taleb Larbi, T 728825.

● Youth hostel

17 km S at Nakhla, 50 beds, kitchen, bus and train 17 km.

● Camping

About 10 km out of El Oued, on the road to Tunisia.

● Places to eat

♦♦♦ in *Hotel du Souf*. For cheaper meals Ave Mohammed Khémisti is the best bet.

● Banks

There a few banks in the Ave Taleb Larbi, but be careful as they usually close on Fri and Sat. Possible to change money at the *Hotel du Souf*.

● Post office

This is in a small street, virtually immediately behind the tourist office.

● Telephone

Local code 04.

● Travel agent

Air Algérie, Ave Mohammed Khémisti, T 728666.

● Tourist information

There are 2 offices close to each other. The **ONAT** is at 17 rue Talbi Larbi, T 79175. The **Syndicat d'Initiative**, next door is more helpful.

● Transport

Local: Bus There is a local bus station in the Ave Taleb Larbi, close to the taxi station. The buses go to the surrounding towns and there is also a minibus service to the main bus station.

Air From **Guémar airport** to **Algiers**: Mon 1200, Fri 1010, Sat 1130, Sun 1430. **Annaba**: Wed and Fri 0845.

Road Bus From Ave Mohammed Khémisti to Annaba, Algiers, Biskra, Constantine, Ghardaïa, Ouargla and Touggourt. **Taxis** leave from Ave Taleb Larbi to Touggourt and the Tunisian border.

Around El Oued

The road SE from El Oued to El Ogla (17 km) is very interesting, especially the village of **Robbah** at 12 km, and beyond where there is an impressive concentration of *bours* for palm tree cultivation and many large dunes. The same road out of El Oued, but forking to the left at Amiche towards El Ogla, leads to **Nakhla** also with some impressive *bours*, and from here a track continues across the Erg to Ghadames in Libya, 450 km away. To the NE from El Oued along the N16 road to Tunisia lies **Z'Goum**, one of the oldest villages in the Souf region. From here you may be able to push on to Trifraoui, but the sand often makes the trip difficult. **Guémar**, on the N48 N from El Oued, is also an important town and has strong local traditions. Visit the *zaouia* and walk around in the streets. Very beautiful, particularly at sunset. The N16 S from El Oued to Touggourt, 95 km, passes through a landscape of impressive dunes.

Touggourt

The town is an important administrative centre. There are a few things that should not be missed. The Mestaoua quarter, W of the place des Martyrs, is an impressive labyrinth of small winding and covered streets. Unfortunately, the area is not being well preserved and is being slowly pulled down, making place for new developments, but it is still worth a look. To the E of the place des Martyrs is the large central market on Fri, which is very lively and has a large choice of fresh fruit and vegetables.

• **Accommodation** C *Hotel de l'Oasis*, S of the town towards the oasis, T 09 726916, pool, tennis. **E** *Hotel de la Paix* in the centre by the Post Office, sleep on the roof in summer; **E** *Hotel des Bédouins* 5 km out of town on the road to El Oued, a few bungalows and sleeping under large bedouin tents. **Youth hostel** A.J. Kheir-Eddine, Touggourt 30200, T 674709, open Sept-Jun incl, 80 beds, kitchen, laundry, meals available, free kitchen, train 100m, bus 150m.

• **Travel agent** *Air Algérie*, rue du 1er Novembre, T 09 726096.

• **Transport Air** The airport is 5 km E of the town on the road to El Oued. For information, T 09 766018. Daily flights to Algiers except Tue and Thur at 1425. **Train**: these run daily to Biskra around midnight. **Road Bus** The bus station is by the train station. There are buses to Algiers, Biskra, Constantine, El Oued, Hassi Messaoud and Ouargla. Most of the buses are just passing through, so getting a seat can be difficult. Be there early. For local buses to Temacine and Tamelhat, the bus stop is further down the road. **Taxi**: the taxi rank is at the start of the El Oued road, slightly out of town. Main destinations are Biskra, El Oued and Ouargla.

Around Touggourt

The oasis to the S of the town is enormous with over 1,300,000 palm trees producing the excellent *deglet nur* dates. Further S, the village of **Temacine** can be reached either along the minor road by the *Hotel de l'Oasis*, but this can be difficult, or more easily by turning left off the N3 road to Ouargla after 12 km. Buses and taxis run there from Touggourt. The village of Temacine looks like a fortress. Inside the walls are beautiful small, winding, covered streets. There is a good view from the top of the mosque's minaret, built in 1431. **Tamelhat**, 2 km further S, is very similar but seems to have been abandoned or fallen asleep. Inside the village, there are a great number of finely decorated beautiful houses, as well as a few houses badly in need of attention. The tomb and mosque of **Sidi El Hadj Ali** should not be missed. Next to the mosque is the mausoleum, also built in 1284, which has an impressive finely sculpted and coloured plastered dome as well as walls covered in glazed tiles.

Ouargla

This was once an important transit place in the gold and slave trade, with caravans coming up from the Sudan. It was also an important Ibadite city until they were forced to leave by the Almoravids, and went to settle in the M'Zab. Today, the city is an important link in the black gold trade, oil. Hassi Messaoud 80 km S has large oil reserves. Ouargla is the closest large town and serves as a necessary link. The result is of little interest for the visitor except for the Saharan museum which has a splendid collection of crafts produced in various Saharan regions including Ouargla. Open 0800-1200 and 1500-800, closed Fri. The market has a good supply of fresh foods as well as a great number of sand roses, many of an impressive size.

• **Accommodation** C *Hotel el Mehri*, T 09 722066, 60 rms, pool, in the centre of town. **D** *Hotel de Tassili*, T 09 703004, slightly out of town to the SW; *Hotel Des Rhimmels*, situated close to Air Algérie. **Youth hostel** There are 2 youth hostels: **A.J. Mostefa-Ben-Boulaïd**, Quartier Emire-Abdel-Kader, Ouargla 3000, open Sept-Jun incl. 40 beds, meals available, laundry, free kitchen, bus 200m, airport bus; and **A.J. Rose des Sables**, Avenue de la Palestine, Route de Ghardaïa, Ouargla, T 703820, open Sept-Jun incl., 40 beds, laundry facilities, airport bus. **Camping** *Camping Tahost* has tents, grass huts and showers.

• **Travel agent** *Air Algérie*, rue Chemine Kaddour, T 09 702858.

• **Tourist information** Ave Emir Abdelkader, close to the market, T 09 705183.

• **Transport Air** The airport is 8 km out of town. For information, T 09 704529. **Algiers**: at least 2 daily flights. **Djanet**: daily except Fri and Sun. **In Aménas**: Tue, Thur, Sat, Sun. **In Salah**: Sun. **Tamanrasset**: daily except Mon and Sat. **Road** There are buses to Ghardaïa, Touggourt, Hassi-Messaoud and 2 buses a week to In Aménas.

THE GRAND ERG OCCIDENTAL

The Grand Erg Occidental is the huge sea of sand in the W of Algeria. Access to this area is easy, as the Erg has a good black top road on both its E and W extremities. This region with particularly impressive dunes and some extremely beautiful oases is a good place to experience the desert without going further S.

Aïn Sefra

430 km S of Oran at an altitude of 1000m, at the S end of the Saharan Atlas could be your first encounter with the real desert. The golden red sand dunes at the foot of the mountains are most impressive. The N6 actually passes N of the town which in itself is of little interest except for the view over the gorge and the Ksour mountains. There is limited accommodation, except for the *C El Mekter Hotel*, T 07 311771, 30 rm, tennis, pool.

ACCESS Train The single daily train from N and S stops at the station between the town and the N6. **Road** Buses from Algiers, Béchar, Oran and Tlemcen will drop you in the main square.

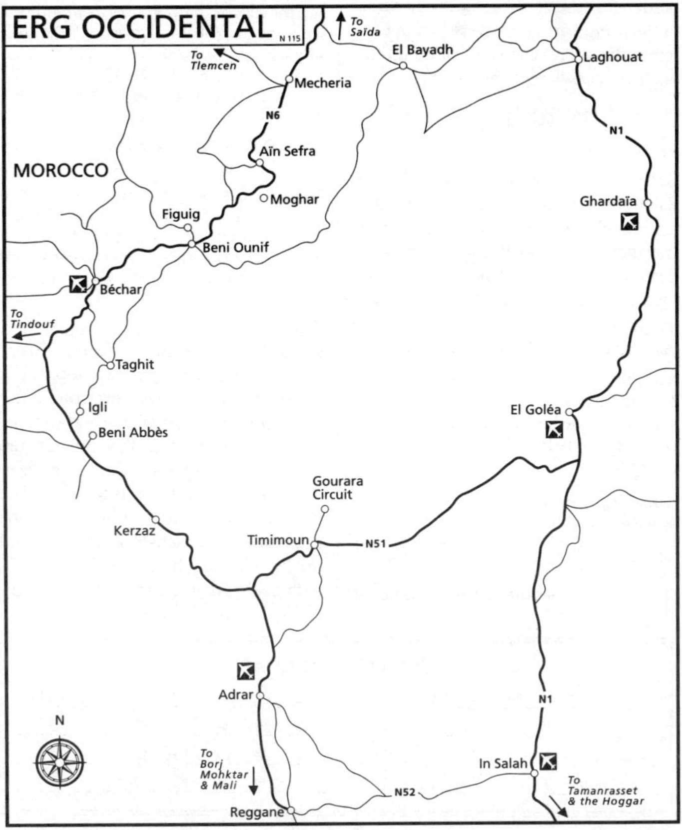

Towards Morocco

The N6 continues SW alongside the railway to Beni Ounif (153 km) on the way to Béchar, a further 114 km. Spare time to turn left off the road to the oasis of Moghrar-Tahtani or right at 85 km from Aïn-Sefra towards the Col de Founassa along a rough but picturesque road. The frontier post for Morocco is about 2 km N of Beni Ounif. There is a daily train from Mohammadia to Béchar and vice versa. Buses to Béchar from the N also go through Beni Ounif. The border crossing is to Figuig, and can take some time to cross on foot. Take a taxi from Beni Ounif to the border. It is then only a short walk across to the Moroccan side. The Algerian Customs officers are renowned for their thorough searches here, so be patient.

Béchar

Alt 772m.

Béchar, the largest town in the Western Sahara, is a modern administrative and commercial centre, of importance to the traveller as a stop on the way S, and a good place to stock up with petrol, water and food and change money. There are shops, a market near the mosque with fresh vegetables and fruit, and a few banks.

ACCESS Air The airport is about 5 km N of the town and a bus runs to the bus station in the town centre. **Train** The train terminus lies about 2 km to the W of the town.

Local information

● Accommodation

C *Hotel Antar* on Ave du 1er Novembre, T 237161, 100 rm.

D *Hotel de la Saoura*, 24 rue Belahreche, T 235404, 29 rm.

● Youth hostel

Cité Riadi, 0800 Béchar, T 810844, open 0800-1200 and 1400-2200, 50 beds, cooking facilities, laundry. 2 km from bus or train.

● Post office

This is on the main square, place de la République.

● Telephone

Local code 07.

● Travel agent

Air Algérie, rue Aspirant Djamel, T 836730, also does car hire.

● Tourist information

ONAT, 6 rue Aspirant Djamel, T 235537.

● Transport

Air The airport is 5 km N out of town and local buses go there. For information, T 235592. **Algiers** Mon 1400, Tue 1100, Wed 1300,1330, Thur 1700, Fri 1330, Sat 1700, Sun 1015. **Ghardaïa** Wed 1300. **Oran** Mon Fri 0950, Thur Sat 1615, Sun 1700.

Train Daily to **Mohammadia**. For information, T 235592.

Road The bus station is close to the market in the centre. For information, T 235388. It is very busy. There are buses to Algiers, Adrar, Beni Abbès, Ghardaïa, Oran, Taghit, Tlemcen and Timimoun. It is best to book a seat in advance.

Taghit

92 km S of Béchar, this is a beautiful oasis village, a wonderful place to stop. It has the most amazing views over the dunes of the Grand Erg, particularly at sunrise. The view from the top of the dunes to the E is superb, especially in comparison with the green of the oasis to the W. The houses of the village, built around the ksar, are constructed of brown mud bricks. The only hotel is C *Hotel Taghit*, with pool and 40 a/c rm, clean and simple. There are a few shops, a petrol station

CLIMATE: BECHAR

	Jan	Feb	Mar	Apr	May	Jun	Jul	Aug	Sep	Oct	Nov	Dec	Av/Tot
Max (°C)	16	19	22	26	30	36	40	39	34	27	21	16	27
Min (°C)	4	6	10	13	18	23	27	26	22	15	10	5	15
Rain (mm)	9	10	13	10	4	2	1	5	8	13	12	10	97

Corvo
Flores
São Jorge
Angra Do Heroismo
Terceira
Faiol
Pico
Açores (Azores) (Portugal)
São Miguel
Ponta Delgada
Formigas
Santa Maria
at the same scale
PORTUGAL
Beja
Faro
Huelva
Cádiz
Str. of Gibraltar
C. de S. Vincente
Madeira (Portugal)
Porto Santo
Funchal
Deserta Grande
Larache
Ksar-El-Kebir
Kenitra
Rabat
Casablanca (Dar-el-Beida)
El Jadida
Settat
Oued Zem
Safi
Beni Mellal
Essaouira
Marrakech
Haut Atlas
Toubkal 4165
Taroudannt
Ouarzazate
Agadir
Jbel Sarhro
Zagora
Ilhas Selvagens (Port.)
Islas Canarias (Canary Islands) (Spain)
Santa Cruz De La Palma
La Palma
Lanzarote
Arrecife
Santa Cruz De Tenerife
Tenerife
Gomera
Hierro
Las Palmas De Gran Canaria
Gran Canaria
Pto Del Rosario
Fuerteventura
C. Yubi
Tiznit
Tata
Anti Atlas
Bou Izakarn
Tan-Tan
Hamada du Dra
Tinfouchy
Jbel Ouarkziz
Tarfaya
Hagunia
Laâyoune
Tindouf
Hamada Tounassine
Saguia el Hamra
El Farsia
Smara
C. Bojador
Western Sahara
Guelta Zemmur
Bir Moghrein
Erg Iguidi
Chegga
Aïoun Abd el Malek
El Mzereb
Dakhla
B. de Rio de Oro
Tropic of Cancer
El Hank
Zouerate
F'dérik
El Mreiti
Tiris
Ausert
Aguenit
Tourine
Troudenni
Adrar Soutouf
Tichla
Bir Zreigat
Nouadhibou
Ras Nouadhibou
Azeffal
Akchar
Ouadane
Atar
Chinguetti
MAURITANIA
El Djouf
I. Tidra
Akjoujt
El Mreyyé
Nouakchott
Trarza
Tidjikja
Tichitt
Araouane
Aklé Aouana
Boutilimit
Brakna
Tagant
Aouker
Tamchaket
Hodh
Dhar Oualata
Aleg
Rosso
Aïoun El Atrouss
Affollé
L. Faguibine
Goundam
St-Louis
Dagana
Kaédi
Kiffa
Néma
Louga
Matam
Mbout
Timbédra
Niafounké
Linguère
Kébémer
Thiès
Touba
SEN
Bakel
Sénégal
Karakoro
Nioro
Nampala
L. Débo
40 N
30 W
20
30
10

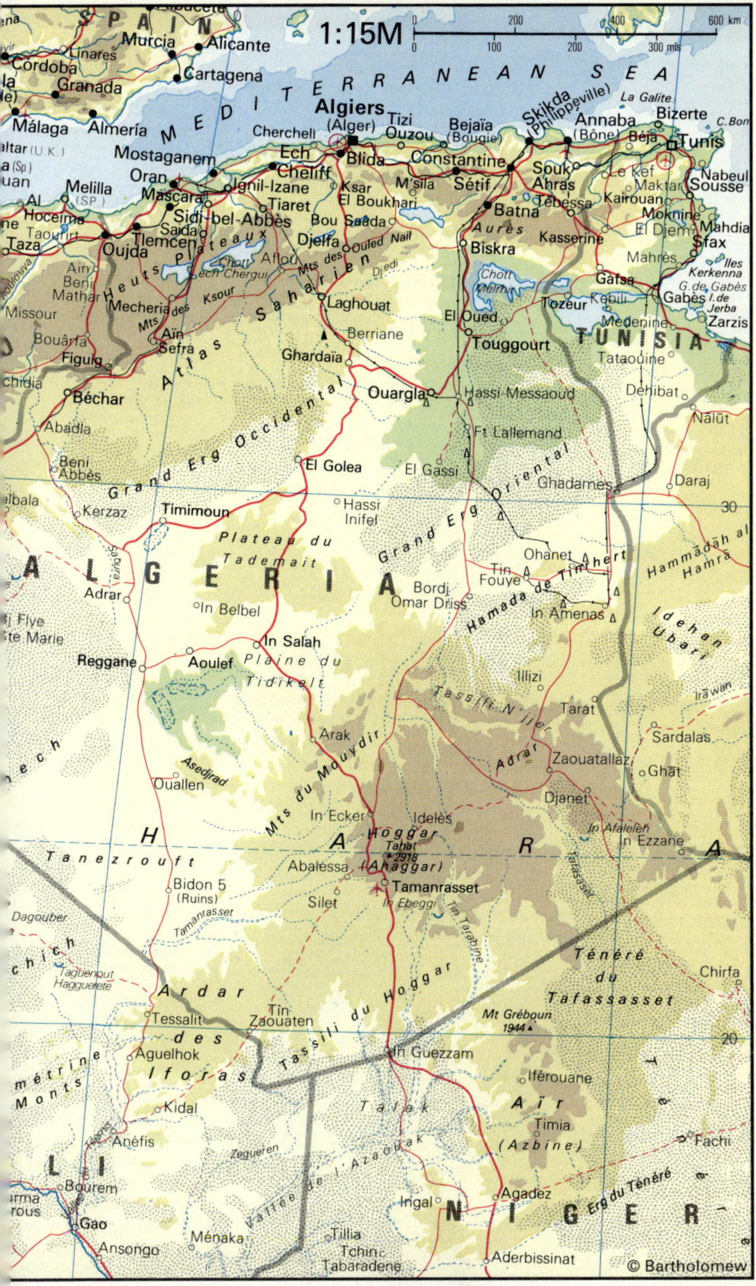
1:15M
0 200 400 600 km
0 100 200 300 mls
SPAIN
Murcia
Alicante
Linares
Córdoba
Granada
Cartagena
Málaga
Almería
MEDITERRANEAN SEA
Algiers
(Alger)
Tizi Ouzou
Bejaïa
(Bougie)
Skikda
(Philippeville)
La Galite
Annaba
(Bône)
Bizerte
C. Bon
Béja
Tunis
Cherchell
Ech Cheliff
Blida
Constantine
Mostaganem
Oran
Melilla
(SP.)
Mascara
Relizane
Tiaret
Ksar El Boukhari
M'sila
Sétif
Batna
Souk Ahras
Tébessa
Le Kef
Maktar
Kairouan
Nabeul
Sousse
Moknine
Mahdia
El Djem
Sfax
Al Hoceima
Taourirt
Taza
Oujda
Tlemcen
Saida
Sidi-bel-Abbès
Bou Saâda
Ouled Nail
Djelfa
Aurès
Biskra
Kasserine
Mahrès
Iles Kerkenna
G. de Gabès
Gafsa
Chott Melrhir
Tozeur
Kebili
Gabès
I. de Jerba
Zarzis
Medenine
Plateaux
Chott ech Chergui
Aflou
Mts des Ouled Nail
Djedi
Laghouat
Aïn Beni Mathar
Missour
Mecheria
Hauts
Mts des Ksour
Saharien
Atlas
El Oued
Touggourt
TUNISIA
Tataouine
Aïn Sefra
Bouârfa
Figuig
Berriane
Ghardaïa
Ouargla
Hassi Messaoud
Dehibat
Nalūt
Béchar
Abadla
Ft Lallemand
Grand Erg Occidental
El Golea
El Gassi
Grand Erg Oriental
Ghadames
Daraj
Beni Abbès
Kerzaz
Timimoun
Hassi Inifel
30
Plateau du Tademait
Ohanet
Hammādah al Hamrā
ALGERIA
Adrar
In Belbel
Bordj Omar Driss
Tin Fouye
Hamada de Tinrhert
In Amenas
Idehan Ubari
Reggane
Aoulef
In Salah
Plaine du Tidikelt
Illizi
Tassili N'Ajjer
Tarat
Irāwan
Sardalas
Ghāt
Arak
Mts du Mouydir
Adrar
Zaouatallaz
Djanet
Asedjrad
Oullen
In Ecker
Idelès
Hoggar
Tahat
2918
(Ahaggar)
In Afaleleh
In Ezzane
Tafassasset
Tanezrouft
Abalessa
Tamanrasset
In Ebeggi
Silet
Bidon 5
(Ruins)
Tamanrasset
Dagouber
Tin Tarabine
Taguenout Hagguerete
Ténéré du Tafassasset
Chirfa
Ardar des Iforas
Tin Zaouaten
Tessalit
Tassili du Hoggar
Mt Gréboun
1944
20
Aguelhok
In Guezzam
Iférouane
Kidal
Talak
Aïr
(Azbine)
Timia
Fachi
Anéfis
Zegueren
Vallée de l'Azaouak
Bourem
Ingal
Agadez
Erg du Ténéré
NIGER
Gao
Ménaka
Tillia
Ansongo
Tchin Tabaradene
Aderbissinat
© Bartholomew

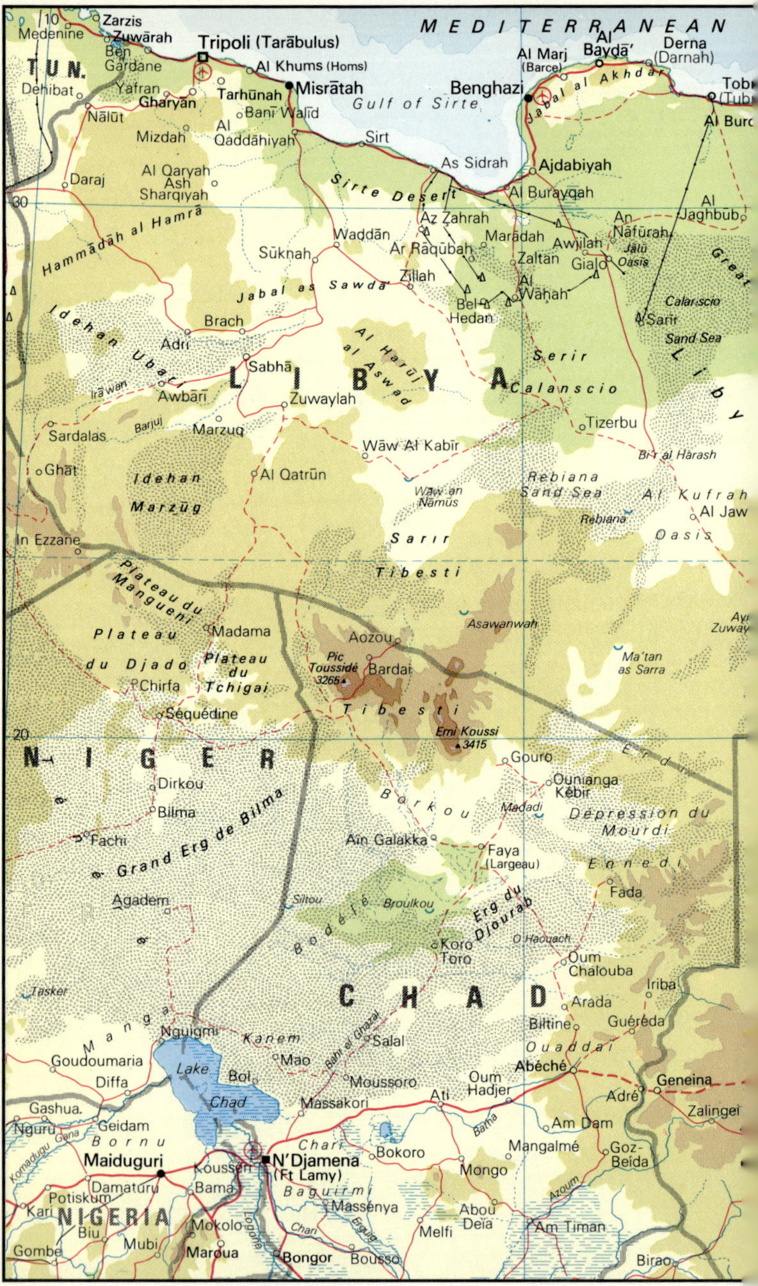

MEDITERRANEAN
10
Zarzis
Medenine
Zuwārah
Tripoli (Tarābulus)
Ben Gardane
TUN.
Al Khums (Homs)
Dehibat
Yafran
Tarhūnah
Misrātah
Gharyān
Benghazi
Gulf of Sirte
Al Marj (Barce)
Al Bayḍā'
Derna (Darnah)
Jabal al Akhdar
Tobruk (Tubruq)
Al Burdī
Nālūt
Banī Walīd
Mizdah
Al Qaddāhiyah
Sirt
Daraj
Al Qaryah Ash Sharqiyah
As Sidrah
Ajdabiyah
Sirte Desert
Al Burayqah
30
Hammādah al Hamrā
Az Zahrah
Waddān
Ar Rāqūbah
Marādah
An Nāfūrah
Al Jaghbūb
Awjilah
Jālū Oasis
Sūknah
Zaltan
Gialo
Great
Zillah
Jabal as Sawdā'
Al Wāḥah
Bel Hedan
Calanscio
Sarir
Sand Sea
Idehan Ubari
Brach
Adrı
Sabhā
Al Harūj al Aswad
LIBYA
Serir Calanscio
Libyan
Irawan
Awbārī
Zuwaylah
Tizerbu
Barjuj
Sardalas
Marzuq
Wāw Al Kabīr
Bi'r al Harash
Ghāt
Al Qatrūn
Idehan Marzūq
Wāw an Nāmūs
Rebiana Sand Sea
Al Kufrah Oasis
Al Jawf
Rebiana
In Ezzane
Sarır Tibesti
Plateau du Manguéni
Asawanwah
Aozou
Madama
Plateau du Djado
Plateau du Tchigai
Pic Toussidé 3265
Bardai
Ma'tan as Sarra
Zuwaylah
Chirfa
Tibesti
Séguédine
Emi Koussi 3415
20
NIGER
Gouro
Erdi
Dirkou
Ounianga Kébir
Borkou
Bilma
Madadi
Dépression du Mourdi
Fachi
Grand Erg de Bilma
Aïn Galakka
Faya (Largeau)
Ennedi
Agadem
Siltou
Bodélé
Broulkou
Erg du Djourab
Fada
Koro Toro
O Haouach
Oum Chalouba
Tasker
CHAD
Iriba
Arada
Manga
Nguigmi
Kanem
Bahr el Ghazal
Salal
Biltine
Guéréda
Ouaddai
Goudoumaria
Mao
Lake Chad
Bol
Abéché
Geneina
Diffa
Moussoro
Oum Hadjer
Ati
Adré
Massakori
Gashua
Nguru
Geidam
Am Dam
Zalingei
Komadugu Gana
Bornu
Chari
Batha
Mangalmé
Goz-Beida
Maiduguri
Kousseri
N'Djamena (Ft Lamy)
Bokoro
Mongo
Damaturu
Bama
Potiskum
Baguirmi
Azoum
Kari
NIGERIA
Massenya
Abou Deïa
Am Timan
Biu
Mokolo
Chari
Erguig
Melfi
Gombe
Mubi
Maroua
Logone
Bongor
Bousso
Birao

SEA
30
40
Haifa
ISRAEL
Tel Aviv
Yafo
Jerusalem
Jordan
Amman
Syrian
Desert
IRAQ
JORDAN
Dead Sea
Badanah
Marsa Matruh
Dumyat
Port Said
Suez Canal
Gaza
El 'Arîsh
Alexandria
El Mansûra
Damanhur
Tanta
Ismailia
Shibîn el Kôm
Zagazig
Ma'an
El Maghra
Qattâra Depression
-133
El Gîza
Cairo
(El Qâhira)
Suez
Nakhl
Al Jawf
An Nafud
Gebel el Tîh
Sinai
Aqaba
G. of Aqaba
El Fayoum
Beni Suef
Maghâgha
Beni Mazâr
G. of Suez
Bawiti
Bahariya Oasis
El Minya
Ras Gharib
Eastern Desert
Tabuk
Taymā'
Hā'il
Ras Muhammad
Hijaz
Ain Dalla
Mallawi
Farafra Oasis
Qasr Farâfra
Asyût
Hurghada
Akhmîm
2187
Shayib el Banat
Bur Safâga
EGYPT
Sohâg
Qena
Quseir
Al Wajh
Dakhla
El Balyana
Mut Oasis
El Khârga
Luxor
Khârga Oasis
Marsa Alam
Medina
(Al Madinah)
Idfu
Nile
Gilf Kebir Plateau
Aswân
1977
G. Hamâta
Aswân High Dam
Râs Banâs
Yanbu' Al Bahr
Lake Nasser
RED SEA
Bîr Tarfâwi
Allaqi
Bir Abu Husein
Bir Misâha
Halaib
Makkah
(Mecca)
2217
J. Asoteriba
Jiddah
Wadi Halfa
At Ta'if
Selima Oasis
Ras Abu Shagara
Dungunab
Nubian Desert
Abri
J. Oda
2260
Laqiya Arba'in
Port Sudan
Abu Hamed
Jebel Abyad
Dongola
Suakin
El 'Atrun Oasis
Sinkat
Karima
Tokar
Musmar
Merowe
Berber
Haiya
Ed Debba
Atbara
Karora
Ed Damer
Derudeb
Nak'fa
Eriba
W. el Milk
ERITREA
Shendi
Mits'iwa
(Massawa)
Goz Regeb
Abu 'Urug
Keren
Omdurman
Khartoum North
Sebderat
Asmera
Khartoum
Kassala
Adi Ugai
Malha
El Kamlin
Khashm el Girba
Barentu
Blue Nile
Om Hajer
Mareb
El Geteina
Wad Medani
Adwa
Takkaze
Adigrat
Sodiri
Ed Dueim
El Gezîra
Gedaref
Umm Bell
Bara
Sennar
Qala'en Nahl
Ras Dashan
4620
SUDAN
Singa
El Hawata
El Obeid
Kosti
Rahad
Gallabat
Dabat
Sek'ot'a
Umm Keddada
Khuwei
Dinder
3657
Umm Ruwaba
El Jebelein
Gonder
En Nahud
Er Rahad
Dunkur
Abu Zabad
Dilling
Tana
Debre Tabor
White Nile (Bahr el Abiad)
Bahr el Azraq
Nuba Mts
Rashad
Renk
Bahir Dar
4231
Guna
Ed Da'ein
El Fula
Er Roseires
Dangila
Choke Mts
El Lagowa
Kadugli
El Muglad
Burye
ETHIOPIA
Belfodiyo
Abbai
Kaka
Paloich
Asosa
Abbai (Blue Nile)
Debre Mark'os

CHAD
SUDAN
CENTRAL AFRICAN REPUBLIC
ZAIRE
ETHIOPIA
KENYA
Khartoum
Khartoum North
Omdurman
Shendi
Goz Regeb
Kassala
Khashm el Girba
Om Hājer
El Kamlin
Wad Medani
Gedaref
Qala'en Nahl
El Hawata
Gallabat
Sennar
Singa
Dinder
Rahad
Er Roseires
Dunkur
L. Tana
Dangila
Burye
Belfodiyo
Abbai (Blue Nile)
Asosa
Blue Nile
El Gezira
Ed Dueim
El Geteina
Bara
Sodiri
Umm Bell
El Fasher
Umm Keddada
Khuwei
El Obeid
En Nahud
Er Rahad
Umm Ruwaba
Kosti
El Jebelein
Renk
White Nile (Bahr el Abiad)
Abu Zabad
Dilling
Nuba Mts
Rashad
Kadugli
El Fula
El Lagowa
El Muglad
Taweisha
Ed Da'ein
Buram
W. Ibra
Nyala
Jebel Marra
3071
Zalingei
Geneina
Kutum
Malha
W. Howa
Abu 'Urug
Kaka
Paloich
Kodok
Malakal
Bahr el Ghazal
Bahr el Arab
Abyei
Bentiu
Nyamlell
Aweil
Pongo
Jur
Wau
Sudd
Fangak
Meshra'er Req
Abwong
Sobat
Nasir
Ayod
Akobo
Tor
Duk Faiwil
Pibor Post
Shambe
Rumbek
Yirol
Bor
Tali Post
Amadi
Mongalla
Juba
Torit
Kenamuke Swamp
Lotikipi Plain
Lokitaung
Lodwar
Jebel Kinyetti
3187
Nimule
Kitgum
Gulu
Moyo
Yei
Laylo
Aba
Arua
Albert Nile
Faradje
Watsa
Dungu
Uere
Niangara
Bambili
Bomokandi
Liénart
Doruma
Yambio
Maridi
Tambura
Sue
Numatinna
Tonj
Deim Zubeir
Raga
Boro
Obo
Djéma
Zemio
Gwane
Bomu
Chinko
Ouarra
Rafai
Haute Kotto
Yalinga
Bakouma
M'Bari
Bangassou
Oubangui
Mobaye
Mobayi
Yakoma
Monga
Bili
Bondo
Uele
Titule
Gemena
Zongo
Libenge
Bangui
Mbaïki
Nola
Boda
Boyali
Lobaye
Carnot
Berbérati
Bertoua
Yokadouma
Boumba
Mambéré
Bossembélé
Damara
Sibut
Ouaka
Kouango
Bambari
Bakala
Dekoa
Bria
Kotto
Bouca
Fafa
Batangafo
Bossangoa
Bocaranga
Bozoum
Bouar
Garoua Boulai
Meiganga
Ngaoundéré
Mbéré
Pendé
Baïbokoum
Goré
Tchollire
Bénoué
Garoua
Léré
Guider
Maroua
Mokolo
Bama
Logone
Pala
Moundou
Lai
Doba
Dik
Sarh
Maro
Ouham
Bamingui Bangoran Nat. Pk
Bamingui
Ndélé
Massif des Bongo
Ouadda
Ouanda Djallé
Dar Rounga
Bahr Aouk
Birao
Harazé
Salamat
Am Timan
Azoum
Abou Deïa
Melfi
Mongo
Mangalmé
Goz-Beïda
Am Dam
Adré
Abéché
Ouaddai
Oum Hadjer
Batha
Ati
Biltine
Guéréda
Iriba
Arada
Oum Chalouba
O. Haouach
Koro Toro
Salal
Bahr el Ghazal
Moussoro
Mao
Kanem
Bol
Lake Chad
Massakori
Ndjamena (Ft Lamy)
Chari
Kousseri
Baguirmi
Massenya
Erguig
Bokoro
Bousso
Bongor
Ethiopia
Jima
Abera
Mizan Teferi
Maji
Goré
Dembi Dolo
Sodo
Nek'emte
Nejo
Akobo
20
30
10

and a post office.

ACCESS There are buses from Béchar and Beni Abbès, but be sure to check return times if you wish to avoid a night in Taghit.

Things to see 15 km S of Taghit there is a cliff alongside the dry river bed with some Neolithic animal paintings. Worth a visit if you have no opportunity to see the other more famous Neolithic sites.

Beni Abbès

This is a small oasis town 250 km S of Béchar with the advantage of having 2 hotels and a few shops as well as a very pleasant municipal pool. There are 2 parts to the town. While the new town is the hub of activity, such as there is, the more interesting part is the old, typically Saharan, mud brick town, which unfortunately is slowly disintegrating. The dunes, rising steeply to the E, are well worth the climb for the amazing view over the seemingly endless sands. The panorama is especially memorable at sunset. The **municipal pool**, by the old town, is shaded by a few trees and is fed by spring water always at a constant 26°C. The **museum** in the new part of town, N of the main square, has a collection of desert fauna, prehistoric fossils and a section on Saharan traditional crafts. Open 0700-1200 and 1400-1700. Closed Fri. Next to the museum, a small zoo contains some of the more common Saharan birds and animals.

History

According to a myth, the town of Beni Abbès was founded in the 11th century by Sidi Othman. He and his companion were on their way to Egypt. While stopping in Beni Abbès, Sidi Othman pushed his stick into the sand and said that when he died, water would spring from the hole. Sidi Othman died that night, and the spring flowed, giving birth to the oasis. The village's development was hampered throughout the years by the feud with the rival Ghenanmas and the Doui Menia from Morocco, until in 1750 the inhabitants of Beni Abbès built a fortress and agreed a truce with their enemies. In 1901 the French troops came, and by 1957 the old town was almost abandoned in favour of the more modern houses in the new part of town.

Things to see

The **church** of Les Petites Soeurs de Jésus stands on a small rise to the S of the town. Mass is said daily. While the **museum** is worth visiting being surprisingly well organized and informative, the zoo in the adjacent botanical garden is not. The town has a post office, a bank, a market and a few shops.

Local information

● Accommodation

C *Hotel Rym*, T 07 233224, 40 rm, pool.
E *Hotel Grand Erg*, T 07 233439, 20 rm.

● Youth hostel

Open 0800-2400, 80 beds AD50, meals, family rms, laundry, watersports, bus 300m.

● Transport

Road Buses leave from the bus station in the town centre tom Béchar, Taghit, Timimoun and Adrar.

Kerzaz is situated 120 km S of Beni Abbès on the road to Timimoun. The old village is 2 km along the road on the left, just before the petrol station. The buildings are typical of Saharan architecture, walled with narrow, covered meandering streets. It is very attractive and well worth a stop if only to examine the system of lifting water from the deep wells, but it is not easy to get back on a bus as all those passing through are generally full. Buses go to Adrar, Béchar and Timimoun. There is no accommodation.

Timimoun

This little town is in one of the most beautiful oases in the Algerian Sahara. Built of red mud in a style similar to Sudanese architecture, it is a real delight. The old town has houses built virtually one on top of the other. The narrow winding streets are often covered and very unusual. The new town, built by the French, follows the traditional style very closely making the entire town very pleasant.

Things to see

The oasis itself is interesting as well as very refreshing. Timimoun has an ingenious system for supplying water by *foggaras*. These are underground tunnels, dug at a slight angle, transporting water from the spring. The tunnels were hand dug and reach distances of over 5 km in length. Vertical access tunnels are situated every 100m or less, to facilitate digging and maintenance. The system, widespread in Iran where they are known as *qanats*, limits the amount of water lost through evaporation and provides a steady and effortless water supply. Produce from the oasis includes a wide variety of vegetables and surprisingly, stoneless dates.

The Gourara circuit

This journey around the dried up lake, with incredible and unforgettable desert landscapes is not to be missed, having come so far. The circuit, about 80 km, does not necessitate a 4-wheel drive vehicle but it is wise to take a local with you to spot soft sand. Otherwise, the Tourist Office organizes daily trips. The circuit must be done in a clockwise direction to avoid getting stuck in the sand. Leaving Timimoun to the NE, and pass the village of Massine on the left which specializes in pottery. Shortly after Massine the road forks. Go right, following the edge of the lake to **El Kef Gabsa**. After this small village, the road starts climbing up to **Badriane**, a village which used to be an assembly point for the start of the pilgrimage to Mecca. The best view is from the small village of Tialet, 1 km further on. At **Izgzer**, there are large caverns where the inhabitants come to seek refuge from the sun and rest during the hot afternoons. From here the road continues with yet more breathtaking views along the ridge to Tindjillet and Semouta, a beautiful village from where the road leads down to the dry lake bed. At **Ouled Said** there is an important oasis with an intricate system of water rationing. The road then returns to Timimoun along the lake bed. About 6 km before Timimoun to the right of the road, sand roses can be dug up.

Local information

● **Accommodation**

C *Le Gourara*, T 234451, 60 rm, view the sunrise/sunset from the roof, tennis, pool; ***Hotel Rouge de l'Oasis***, T 234417; ***Hotel Ighzer***.

● **Places to eat**

The restaurant in *Le Gouara* is recommended.

● **Banks**

Banque National d'Algérie, along main street, close to the market.

● **Telephone**

Local code 07.

● **Travel agent**

Air Algérie on the main square, T 234555.

● **Tourist information**

In the municipality building.

● **Transport**

Air The airport is 8 km out of town. For information, T 932054. There is one flight a week from **Algiers** on Tue at 0745.

Road Bus station is on the main street. Most buses only pass through Timimoun and booking is not possible. There are a few that start in Timimoun going to **Adrar, Béchar, Ghardaïa** where booking may be possible.

Adrar

This regional centre is important for the traveller going to Mali as it is a good place to stock up with fuel and supplies and deal with customs formalities. If you do not have your own transport, it is probably best not to take the bus to Borj-Mokhtar, as it may be very difficult to get a lift from there on. Best to try and get a lift in Adrar.

• **Accommodation** **C** *Hotel Touat*, T 259933, 125 rm, pool. **E** ***Hotel Djemila***, 21 rm.

• **Youth hostel** *Maison de Jeunes de la*

Wilaya, 01000 Adrar, T 258284, open 0800-1200 and 1400-2200, 25 beds, cooking facilities, laundry, bus 200m.

- **Telephone** Local code 07.

- **Travel agent** *Air Algérie*, main square, T 259365.

- **Transport Air** The airport is 13 km out of town. For information, T 259020. Internal flights to **Algiers** Tue 1120, Fri 1100 and 1320, Thur, Sun 1100. **Borj-Mokhtar** Wed, Fri 1145. **Ghardaïa** Wed 0830 and Sat 0800. **Oran** Mon 1705, Tue 1720, Wed 1835, Sun 1725. **Tamanrasset** Tue, Thur, Sun 0700, Thur, Fri 0720. **Road** The bus station is N of the main square. Booking is available. Buses to **Aoulef, Béchar, Borj-Mokhtar, Ghardaïa** and **In Salah**.

El Goléa (El Meniaa)

About 450 km E from Timimoun, El Goléa is a large oasis, with 200,000 palm trees. It is an important stopover on the route S. The town is pleasant, dominated by the Ksar El Meniaa.

Things to see

The Ksar El Meniaa, situated on a rocky mound, overlooks the entire region. It is interesting to wander around the deserted ruins. 3 km to the N of the town, is the **tomb of Charles de Foucauld**, buried here in 1929. He set up the hermitage in the Hoggar, but his body was brought to El Goléa for burial. A church was built in these pleasant surroundings. The **museum** of local geological specimens is private but can be visited by specialists in this field. To the S is the Sebkha El Melah. To get there, take the road to In Salah, and 2 km after El Goléa, take a road on the left, after a large stone road sign. The lake is another 2 km further on. In El Goléa, the **market** on the main square has a large choice of fresh fruit and vegetables. The water here is very good, so if you are driving, stock up here.

Local information

● Accommodation

C *Hotel El Boustan*, by the oases, on the road to the Ksar, T 09 736142, pool, tennis.

D *Hotel Vieux Ksar* on the road to In Salah, T 09 733310, 30 rm.

● Travel agent

Air Algérie, rue de la Liberté, T 09 736100.

● Transport

Air The airport is 3 km out of town. For information, T 09 736101. Flights to **Algiers** Tue 1315. **Tamanrasset** Tue 0845.

Road The bus station is in the town centre. Buses go to **Adrar, Ghardaïa** and **Timimoun**. Unfortunately, all these buses only pass through El Goléa, and there is no certainty of getting a seat. There is also a bus to **In Salah** every 2 days.

Ghardaïa and the M'Zab

Ghardaïa is the name of the largest town in the centre of the valley known as the **M'Zab** which is one of the most beautiful and interesting areas in the Algerian Sahara and should certainly not be missed. The 5 towns in the pentapolis were all built by the Mozabites from the Ibadite sect, and are situated by an escarpment alongside the Oued M'Zab. Each is built around a central mosque on a rocky knoll. Ghardaïa, the main town and the centre for tourism with a number of hotels, is the most interesting town to visit, along with Melika (the Queen) and Beni Isquen (Sons of Those Who Keep Their Word). Bou Noura (Father of Light) and El Ateuf (the Turning) are less interesting.

History

The Mozabite sect goes back to the disappearance of the third Caliph in 656. This event created a schism within Islam and the rejection of the authority of Ali, the Prophet's son-in-law. The Kharejites formed their own sect with the belief that any Muslim could become Caliph, as long as he was an example of virtue and fidelity towards the Koran and the Sunna. The Kharejites broke away and soon split again, giving rise to the Ibadite sect, followers of Abdellah Ben Abad. Under the leadership of Ibn Rostem, the Ibadites came to North Africa and founded the prosperous town of Tahert (close to Tiaret in the NW of Algeria). In 911, the inhabitants of Tahert were defeated by the Fatimids and went to settle close to Ouargla. Once again, the prosperity of the town was to cause conflicts and by the 11th century the Ibadites moved to the M'Zab in the hope that nobody would come and find them in such an inhospitable environment. Between 1012 and 1048 they built the 5 towns, Ghardaïa being the last. The Mozabites today are mostly from Berber origin and speak a dialect very similar to Kabyle. The total population of the M'Zab now exceeds 100,000 people.

Architecture

In the building of the towns, the Mozabites have shown great simplicity, to a certain extent explained by the austere landscape and scarcity of building materials, but also due to the prevailing philosophy that no ornamentation was necessary. The result is absolute beauty and great harmony. The houses are built close together and painted only by white and blue (said to keep the flies away) and the ochre-coloured earth. The houses are softly curved with very few straight walls. The town is built around the central mosque, always situated at a certain height, expanding concentrically from the centre. Every house is near enough to hear the Muezzin. All the streets are built wide enough to enable the passing of a mule with side packs and each arch is high enough to permit a rider to pass mounted on his mule. The central market place was built slightly outside the main living area, in order to keep outsiders away from the real town. Houses were also built with great thought to privacy. The doors have a wall directly behind them, so hiding the life within the house from the passer-by. The houses are organized around a central room with no external windows, but a hole in the roof provides natural sunlight. The roof is reserved for the women. In the summer, when the heat gets excessive, the families move to the oasis, where they all have a 'summer house' near wells and under the shade of the palm trees.

Ghardaïa

Alt 441m.

Ghardaïa is the main town of the region with all the facilities and has greatly expanded beyond the old city and its walls. According to a myth, the town was founded by Sheikh Sidi Bou Gdemma who, passing by, saw some smoke coming from a cave. He stopped and saw a beautiful young woman known as Daia, who had been abandoned by all because she was pregnant. He was seduced by her beauty, asked for her hand in marriage and founded the town of Ghardaïa. The town's name in Arabic means Daia's cave (Ghar meaning cave).

ACCESS Air The airport is 18 km out of town on the road to El Goléa. For information, T 894062. There are flights from Algiers (daily), Adrar (2 a week), Annaba (1 a week), Béchar (1 a week), Djanet (4 a week), In Salah (1 a week) and Tamanrasset (3 a week). There is a bus from the airport to the town centre which stops in front of the Air Algérie Office. **Road** Buses from all main towns, including Adrar, Algiers, Biskra, Constantine, El Goléa and Timimoun stop at the main bus station on rue Ahmed Talbi just 2

CLIMATE: GHARDAIA

	Jan	Feb	Mar	Apr	May	Jun	Jul	Aug	Sep	Oct	Nov	Dec	Av/Tot
Max (°C)	16	19	22	25	31	37	40	39	34	27	21	16	27
Min (°C)	5	8	10	13	18	23	26	26	22	16	11	7	15
Rain (mm)	10	5	7	8	3	2	1	3	3	5	7	7	61

mins walk from the ONAT office. Local buses from the M'Zab area stop opposite the entrance to the old city.

Things to see

The town is divided into the old and new. The new town is centred around the Ave du 1er Novembre, rue Emir Abdelkader and the rue Ahmed Talbi. To reach the old town, take the rue Emir Abdelkader that leads to the rue Ibn Rostem which goes directly to the main market square. The square is lined with arcades, and there is a very colourful **daily market** selling everything from vegetables to carpets and silver trays. The best time is in the morning. On Wed and Sun a traditional **auction market** is held in the NE corner of the square in the Souk El Dellada, very similar to the one held in Beni Isquen. The **Great Mosque** is further up the hill after you go through the Souk El Dellada. The mosque has a very interesting pyramidal minaret and can be visited in the mornings, though you may have to be accompanied by a guide. Reach it from the market place by climbing the series of steps and ramps. To the S of the mosque, a covered street leads to the famous cave that according to the myth was at the origin of the town. It is still venerated by the Mozabite women.

The **Folk Museum** at the entrance to the old town, in the rue Emir Abdelkader, contains various interesting everyday items, but most interesting is the reconstruction of the interior of a traditional Mozabite house. Open daily 0830-1200 and 1500-1830. In winter open every evening 1930-2100.

Local information

● **Accommodation**

C ***El Djanoub***, T 894620/890630, 250 rms, pleasant situation, pool, restaurant.

F ***Hotel Atlantide***, Ave Ahmed Talbi, T 892536; **F** ***Hotel Napht***, in the first street on the left off Ave Ahmed Talbi, T 890009; **F** ***Hotel Es Saada***, place Andalouse, on the square behind *Hotel Napht*, T 891654; ***Hotel Carrefour***, on corner of rue Emir Abdelkader and rue Ahmed Talbi, T 893179; ***Hotel de la Palmeraie***, on the road to the oasis, 1½ km out of town, T 892312; ***Hotel le Rym***, Ave du 1er Novembre, T 893202.

● **Youth hostels**

There are 2 youth hostels: ***Maison de Jeunes Dahane Brahim à Metlili***, T 897668, 20 beds; and ***Maison de Jeunes Emir Abdelkader***, Ghardaïa Centre, T 894403, 38 beds, bus 500m.

● **Banks**

These are in the main street and money can be changed in the *Hotel Rostimedes*.

THE MOZABITES

The Mozabites are still very firmly attached to their traditions and live an austere and, for the women in particular, a secluded life. The austerity of the region forced the inhabitants to turn to trading as their main income, and this generally meant leaving the region for long periods. Trading however was greatly successful, many shops throughout Algeria still being owned by Mozabites. In order to preserve the traditions and shield themselves from outside influences, women were forbidden to leave the M'Zab and men to return with a 'foreign' woman. The women virtually never left their homes. Working on the principal that not to report a fault was as bad as doing it oneself, the society based itself on the two principals of delation (informing against each other) and surveillance. A group of women known as the *laveuses de mort* had the responsibility of washing bodies of the deceased people, but also and more importantly so, keeping an eye on the families whose husbands where absent. Another prevailing law is a kind of egalitarianism, where no external sign of wealth is to be shown, not even an indication that the pilgrimage to Mecca (the Hadj) has been completed, as this can be construed as a sign of wealth.

● **Post office**

Ave du 1er Novembre.

● **Telephone**

Local code 09.

● **Things to buy**

Ghardaïa is an important centre for carpets but quality can vary greatly. See advice in section on carpets, **p 316**. Burnouses, a type of wool jallabah, are very good quality but generally very expensive. There are also silver trays (of doubtful quality) and local jewellery. Beauty products such as khol or henna and spices are found in the central market and in the shops under the arcades.

● **Travel agent**

Air Algérie, Ave du 1er Novembre, T 894663.

● **Tourist information**

ONAT, rue Emir Abdelkader, T 891757.

● **Transport**

Local: **Bus** to other M'Zab towns leave from opposite the entrance to the Old City.

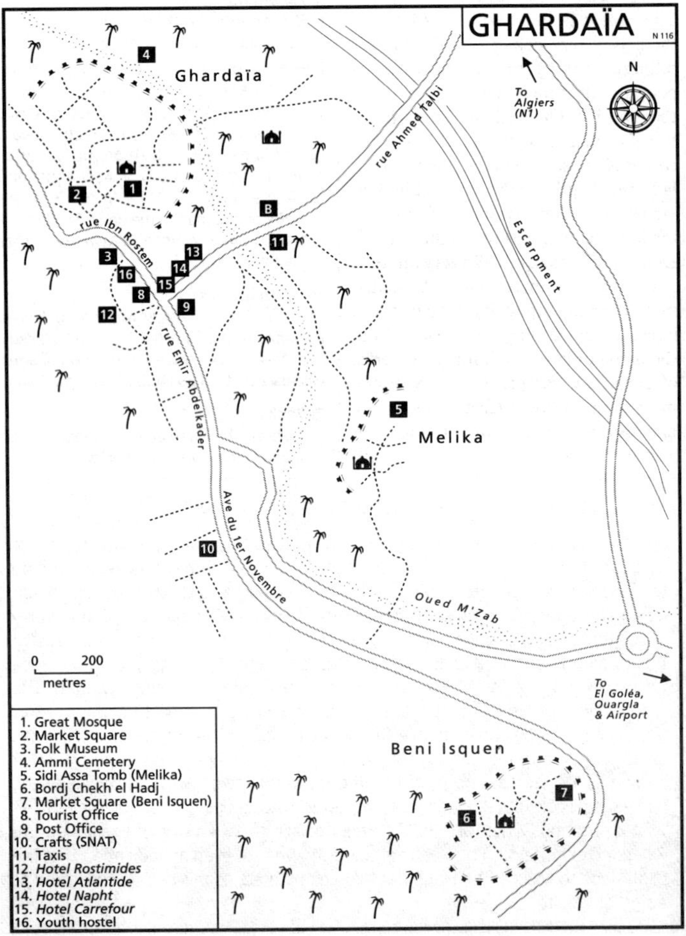

Air The airport is 18 km out of town on the road to El Goléa. There is a bus service that departs from in front of the Air Algérie office. Make sure you have reconfirmed your flight booking and to be on the safe side be there at least 2 hrs before the flight is due to leave. For information, T 894062. Flights to **Algiers** 2 or 3 daily. **Annaba** Tue, Sat. **Béchar** Wed. **Djanet** Mon, Wed, Fri, Sun. **In Salah** Tue, Thur. **Tamanrasset** Mon, Tue, Wed, Thur, Sat.

Road Bus The main bus station is along the rue Ahmed Talbi. There is a ticket office and it is possible to book. This can be important during busy periods. There are daily buses to all the main towns including Adrar, Algiers (3), Oran (3), Biskra, Constantine, El Goléa (3) and Timimoun. **Taxi** Long distance taxis leave from opposite the bus station and most go to **El Goléa** and **Algiers**.

Around Ghardaïa

From the bus station, follow the dry river bed to the NW. At about 500m there is the very large **Ammi Said cemetery**. According to tradition, the graves are not marked, and broken pots are left to aid recognition. In the centre of the cemetery there is an interesting mosque which has been dug into the ground. There is also an excellent view over the town of Ghardaïa. To visit the oasis which is 4 km to the NW, take a taxi or bus from the N side of the market. The old reservoir on the Oued M'Zab is very interesting. The river only ever has water once a year, but an ingenious system has been devised in order to distribute the water fairly throughout the oasis. The dam has many openings leading into lined underground tunnels all carrying the water to specific land plots within the oasis. Climb down an opening and take a look. The oasis itself which stretches further to the NW is very pleasant particularly in the late afternoon. In it there are over 200,000 palm trees which are underplanted with fruit and vegetables. There is a large number of houses here, which are used only in the summer to escape the intense heat.

Melika The closest town to Ghardaïa, 1 km to the SE is situated on the top of a rocky knoll. It was once the religious centre of the M'Zab and is a very attractive town. The 2 main points of interest are the cemetery and the view over the valley and Ghardaïa. The cemetery is to the N of the town. The tomb of Sidi Aissa and his family is particularly interesting, surrounded by a large prayer area, from which the view towards Ghardaïa is impressive. The other, again unmarked, tombs are covered in broken pottery to assist recognition.

Beni Isquen, situated 2½ km S of Ghardaïa, is the present religious centre of the M'Zab. It is strongly attached to local traditions and customs, trying to limit the outside influence to a minimum. At night the 3 gates are closed and visits are only permitted with a guide. The town is also closed off from 1200 to 1530 for prayer. The best time to visit is in the late afternoon when activity on the main square increases and the daily market with its auction takes place. To enter the town it is important to be correctly dressed and fulfil a number of other requirements, such as not smoking which are all listed at the entrance. Photographing people is forbidden. The only way to see anything is to take an official guide from by the main gates for a set tour. The tour goes to the **Bordj Cheikh El Hadj** in the E of the town, to admire the view and will probably end in the market place, where if you arrive before 1700 you will see the **auction**. There are also a number of shops selling carpets and other crafts.

Outside the town to the W, is the oasis which is smaller and more pleasant than the one in Ghardaïa. The open streams known as *saggias*, and the long and sinuous reservoir are all part of the important irrigation system.

El Ateuf situated 9 km E of Ghardaïa, was the first of the 5 towns to be built. When entering the town it may be difficult not to take a guide, so negotiate the price firmly. The town has an unusual

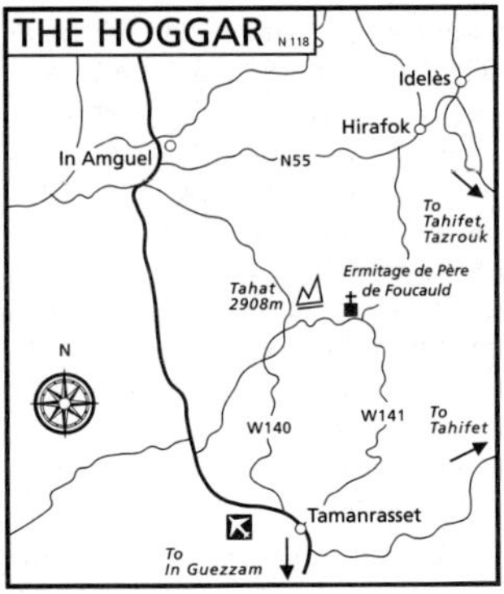

mosque. From outside, the **Sidi Brahim mosque** is unimpressive, but once inside it is a delight. The rooms are organized according to the time of day they were used. The coolest, below ground level, was used during the noonday heat. The room on the ground floor opens out with arcades on to a terrace and there is a large courtyard for important events. It is not in use so is open to anyone. The **cemetery** contains more of the strange tomb markers. Both well worth a visit.

The Hoggar

The **Hoggar mountains**, extending 800 km from E to W at the very centre of the Sahara, are one of Algeria's most stunning sights and at the same time, the most inhospitable region in Africa. The landscape is exceptional, with wind-eroded mountains rising to over 2,000m, erupting out of the sun-scorched arid desert plain. At the centre of the Hoggar is the Ermitage de Père de Foucauld at 3,800m. Sunrises and sunsets here are some of the most memorable you are ever likely to see.

The Touaregs, a Berber tribe, have, over centuries, remained the dominant population of the region. Local tradition alleges that the Touareg tribes all descend from the Touareg Queen Tin Hanan. She came from Tafilalet with her servant Takamat and settled in Abalessa. Here, according to the mythology, Tin Hanan and Takamat gave birth to 2 of the main Touareg tribes, the Kel Rela and the Dag Rali. Recently in Abalessa, a woman's skeleton and various jewels dating back to the 4th century were found and it is thought that this was the body of Tin Hanan.

The Touareg tribes developed a system of matrilineal inheritance, names and titles being passed from one generation to the next by the woman, whilst no male ancestors were recognized. This was at a time when the men were largely absent warriors. Traditionally, the Touareg society has been organized as a confederation of tribes with a strong hierarchy, noble tribes being at its centre. The noble tribes were mostly warriors, leaving on long expeditions while the other tribes looked after the lands. The lands were cultivated by slaves brought from the Sudan, as the Touaregs considered working the earth as a lesser task. With the abolition of slavery, the slaves became free men and established themselves as farmers in the oasis, but still working on lands owned by the Touaregs.

Today Touaregs are settling down in houses and working in farms, mines and administrative jobs. Nevertheless, centuries of customs and traditions have not been totally lost, and habits peculiar to the region are still obvious to the visitor, unveiled women still enjoying a large amount of freedom, whereas the men are almost fully veiled, only their eyes showing.

In Salah

This is the main stop on the way S to the Hoggar on the N1 road from El Goléa to Tamanrasset. It appears after 400 km of a flat and seemingly never-ending plateau, an attractive little town built in red bricks, surrounded by golden dunes and a large oasis. The inhabitants have to struggle against 3 fierce elements; the heat (in summer temperatures reach 60°C and rarely fall below 40°C); frequent sand storms (averaging one a week, the sand is slowly encroaching on the town); and the salty water (unpleasant to drink and making agriculture difficult – In Salah means 'salt spring'). The town was an important trading post, where European goods were exchanged for gold, ivory and slaves from the Sudan. Today the main activity is the production of dates from the 220,000 palm trees in the large oasis to the W of the town. Recently, natural gas was found in the vicinity and work is still being carried out to link this to the existing pipeline. As for the town itself, there is little to do or see here, but if you have brought your own water it is a pleasant place to stop.

There is an Air Algérie office (T 09 730239) and a bank in the main street. The market is just N of Air Algérie, but generally has little to offer. There are 2 hotels, but choose *Hotel Tidi-Kelt*, T 09 730393, 120 rm, just off the main road from El Goléa to Tamanrasset. In the centre, there is a camping site at the W end of the main street.

• **Transport Air** The airport is 10 km N of the town. For information, T 09 730093. **Adrar** Mon, Wed and Sat at 1000. **Algiers** Tue and Thur at 1140, Sun at 1140 and 1415. **Ghardaïa** Thur at 1250. **Tamanrasset** Mon, Tue, Wed and Sat at 1000. **Road** To Tamanrasset it is, in theory, black top all the way, but in reality due to the wear caused by the large numbers of trucks, in many places it is in an awful state. In many sections the piste on the side is often better than the bad road. Stock up with petrol, as you may not find any until Tamanrasset (700 km). Towards Reggane, the piste goes as far as Aoulef (90 km), and from then on it is black top. The piste is good and well signposted.The bus station is out of town on the main road from El Goléa to Tamanrasset. **Bus** There are buses to **Ghardaïa, Tamanrasset** and **Adrar**. The bus to Ghardaïa leaves around 1600 every second day and it is important to book your place the same day before 0900. Heading for Tamanrasset, the buses are a bit more unpredictable. The buses leave on Tue, Thur and Sun at 0400. Tickets have to be bought in advance. Seats are not numbered, so be there early to secure a comfortable place for the 20 hour journey. Buses to Adrar are advertised to leave twice a week, but they are often cancelled. Ask at the bus station. **Taxi** Main destination is **Aoulef**, from where you can take a bus to Adrar and further N.

Tamanrasset

Pop 30,000 *Alt* 1377m.

ACCESS Air The airport is at Aguemar, 12 km N of the town. For information, T 734276. **Road** The bus station is in the N of the town, on the road to In Salah.

Until recently this was a small village: now it is the place where all trans-Saharan travellers stop over and the centre for trips to the Hoggar mountains. Due to its altitude it is never unbearably hot, even in the middle of the summer and can be quite brisk in winter despite the sunshine. Trips into the Hoggar mountains, an opportunity that should not be missed, are organized around the mountains to Assekrem and the Père de Foucauld mountain top hermitage. Try any of the agencies on Ave Emir Abdelkader. As the rental of a 4 wheel drive vehicle is expensive, either try to form a group of 6-7 interested people, or ask around for a spare place. Finally, be care-

CLIMATE: TAMANRASSET

	Jan	Feb	Mar	Apr	May	Jun	Jul	Aug	Sep	Oct	Nov	Dec	Av/Tot
Max (°C)	20	23	26	29	32	35	35	34	32	29	25	21	23
Min (°C)	5	8	10	14	18	22	22	22	20	16	11	6	15
Rain (mm)	1	1	0	3	3	7	3	13	12	4	4	3	54

ful when changing money on the black market, as some changers have a tendency to denounce you to the police.

The buildings in Tamanrasset are constructed of brown mud bricks and the walls are plastered with brown mud. Fortunately in the sunshine it glows red and looks splendid. There is nothing specific to see, as this is essentially a modern settlement, apart from the defensive fort built by Foucauld and the market off the main street, Ave Emir Abdelkader, where food and Touareg crafts including beautiful jewellery can be bought. The museum on Ave Emir Abdelkader, displays Touareg items of leatherwork, weapons and jewellery.

A livestock market is held on the dry river bed which cuts through the town. Make an early start to visit this. The town is not unpleasant, and the mixture of people is in itself an attraction. The Touaregs are still present, sometimes seen riding their white camels. Dec is the busy month here when the fair takes place on the Assihar showground. Better to book in advance at that time.

All customs formalities for going on into Niger must be cleared here, including the currency form, but the passport control is done at the border in In Guezzam. If you are hitching, Tamanrasset is a good place to arrange for a lift right through to Niger.

Local information

● Accommodation

C *Hotel Tahat*, SE part of town, after the Customs office, T 734472, 120 a/c rm.

E *Hotel Ilamane*, rue de la Palestine, the road crossing the river, central position, 30 rm; **E** *Hotel Tin Hinane*, Ave Emir Abdelkader, T 734409, opposite the ONAT, parts a/c.

● Youth hostel

Is in Quartier Tahagart, T 734047, 100 beds, kitchen, bus 500m.

● Camping

Les Zéribas, S of the town, past the *Hotel Tahat*, on the right. Accommodation available in very small and basic local *zeribas* (small huts).

● Banks

Are in the Ave Emir Abdelkader. Money can also be changed in the *Hotel Tahat*.

● Consulates

Niger and Mali have consulates in Tamanrasset. They are situated next to each other, about 500m S of the town centre on the road to the *Hotel Tahat*.

● Customs

The customs office is situated to the S along the same road as the Consulates, before the *Hotel Tahat*.

● Post office

Ave Emir Abdelkader, close to Air Algérie.

● Telephone

Local code 09.

● Travel agent

Air Algérie, Ave Emir Abdelkader, T 734363.

● Tourist information

ONAT, Ave Emir Abdelkader, T 734117. They organize excursions into the Hoggar, camel treks and 4 wheel drive hire as do a number of private tour agents.

● Visas for Niger

It is necessary to produce 3 passport photos, have a cholera vaccination stamp and pay AD70. The issuing of the visas can take up to 3 days. For **Mali**, procedures are simple and visas are usually issued immediately.

● Transport

Air The airport is at Aguemar, 12 km N of the town. For information, T 734276. **Adrar** Mon 1215, Tue 1210, Wed 1215, Thur 1400, Fri 1020, Sat 1215. **Algiers** Mon 1015, 1750, Tue 0930, 1100, 1115, Wed 1015, 1045, 1240, Thur 0930, Fri 1045, 1750, Sat 1015, Sun 0920, 0930, 1745. **Constantine** Thur 1525. **El Goléa** Tue 1100. **Ghardaïa** Mon, Wed and Sat 1015. **In Guezzam** Thur at 1020. **In Salah** Tue, Thur and Sun 1930. **Oran** Fri 1445. **Ouargla** Tue 1115, Wed and Fri 1045, Sun 1745.

Road The road to In Guezzam is described as black top for first 50 km but it is in a poor state. After that it is piste which is quite good, but be very careful not to lose sight of the stageposts. There is no water between Tamanrasset and In Guezzam, and there may be no petrol in In Guezzam, so stock up. The border is 10 km further S after In Guezzam, and is closed from 1200 to 1600 and after 1800. The road to Djanet via Assekrem is virtually impassable, and certainly should not be ventured without

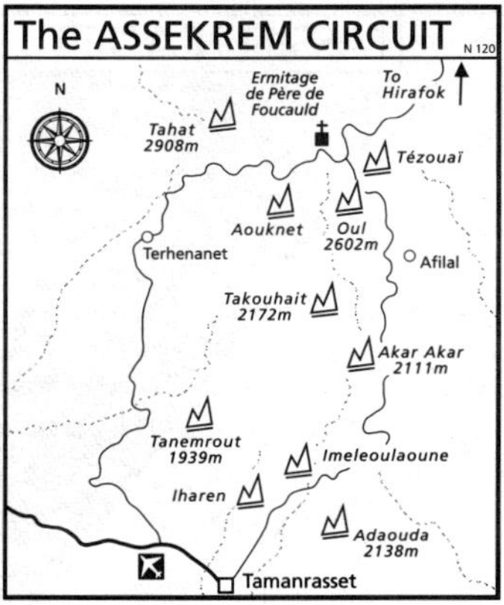

The ASSEKREM CIRCUIT

a 4 wheel drive vehicle. Go 100 km back up the road to In Salah, and follow the signs to Ideles.

Bus The main destination is In Salah with departures on Mon, Wed and Sat at 0400 and tickets have to be booked the evening before. Be there an hour before departure to get a good seat as the trip lasts 20 hours minimum. There is 1 departure a week to In Guezzam, but this is of little use as you will still have to hitch across the border.

Around Tamanrasset

Having travelled so far, do not miss **Assekrem** which is generally done as a circuit. The plateau is 80 km NE of Tamanrasset and will take about 3-4 hours by car. The road E goes between the volcanic peak of **Iharen** and by the **cascades of Imeleoulaouene**, such a panoramic landscape making progress slow as stops are made for photographs. A local guide will enable you to detour to see some ancient rock engravings. The Assekrem plateau summit can only be reached by foot and it is a 30 mins walk up to the top. The **Ermitage de Père de Foucauld** is on the plateau and the area has some of the most amazing scenery, particularly at sunrise. The Hermitage was built in 1910, at an altitude of 2,600m, by Père de Foucauld and is still run by Fathers. Limited accommodation is available (30 beds) in the refuge on the Assekrem pass, but food is not always provided. Returning by the W route gives views of Algeria's highest peak **Djebel Tahat** at 2,908m and majestic scenery. Access to the Assekrem plateau is only really possible in a 4 wheel drive vehicle which can be hired from the ONAT or any of the travel agencies in Tamanrasset. The hire rate is expensive (around AD1000 for 24 hours) but cars will seat 6-7 people. Otherwise, hitch a lift from Tamanrasset, or 'buy' a spare place. The travel agencies also organize the trip to Asskrem by camels. See ONAT or any travel agency.

The Hoggar circuit

The circuit of the Hoggar is more ambitious. Some 6 km before the refuge on the Assekrem pass, a winding track goes N to Hirafok. The volcanic material makes the track very rough and the scenery splendid. The Oued Zerzaoua emerges to the W of the track, its position marked by a thin line of vegetation. **Hirafok village**, where most of the dwellings are constructed of reeds, is surprisingly green. The irrigation water for the fruit and vegetables is lifted by solar energy. A local guide can take you to see more rock engravings about 6 km N of the village. The circuit continues NE to Idelès before turning SE towards **Tazrouk**. The road S crosses the Azrou pass and drops down to Tahifet which stands by a wide dry river bed. The water flowing over the falls at **Tamekrest**, a great improvement on those at Imeleoulaouene, supports beds of reeds and even trees.

Amsel This village is 30 km S of Tamanrasset on the road to In Guezzam, and has a reservoir where it is possible to swim. The village market has cheap fresh fruit and vegetables for sale. Stock up here if going to Niger.

Tassili N'Ajjer

The Tassili N'Ajjer is a huge high pla-

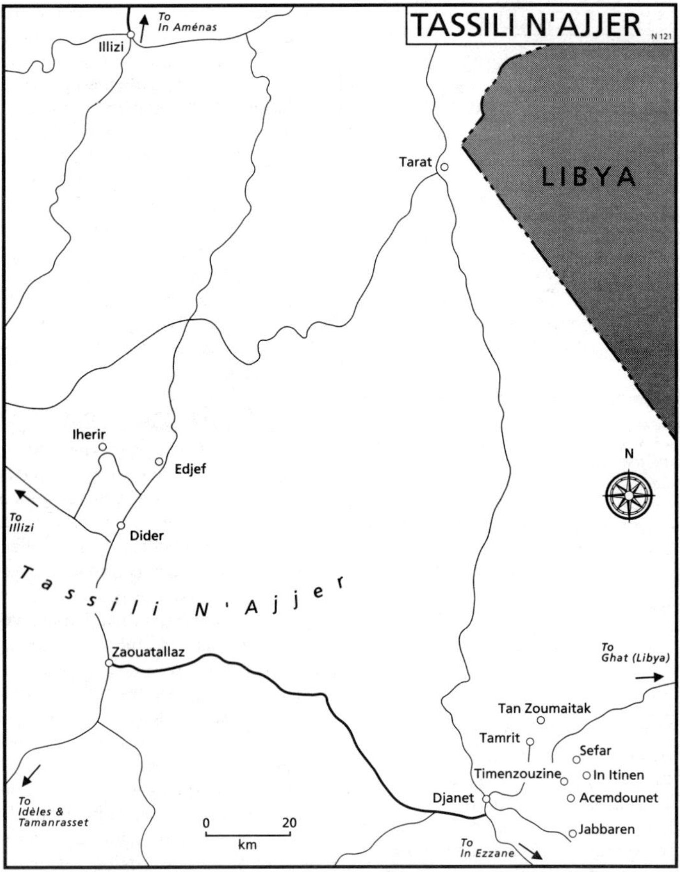

teau, about the size of England which runs along the NE of the Hoggar mountains. The area is particularly striking with unusual landscapes of deep chasms and steep cliffs, as the name implies. No vehicles can reach the centre. It contains a large number of rock paintings, some dating back 8,000 years.

The N3 road from Hassi Messaoud is black top until In Aménas. There is a bus to In Aménas, but nothing onwards to Illizi and Djanet. Without your own transport, the only way of getting there is by taxi, by hitching or by plane. Hitching is difficult from In Aménas down to Djanet, and there is no guarantee that you will find a ride. However the return journey down to Tamanrasset from Djanet is easier, either by hitching or by taxi.

In Aménas The town is modern and built purely for the oil industry. It is of no interest to the traveller, but a good point for stocking up with food, water and petrol. When arriving, it is compulsory to go to the municipal office and give them details of your trip to Djanet. There is only one hotel, the *Hotel Cash*. The airport is 14 km SE of the town. For information, T 09 739375. There are flights on Tue, Thur, Sat and Sun to Ouargla. There is one bus a week that goes to Biskra, but no buses going further S.

Illizi

This is a town of very little interest apart from being the main stop on the piste to Djanet. There are a few shops, petrol and a hotel. There is also an airport, 10 km N of the town. For information, T 09 731355. There are 4 flights to **Djanet**; 4 flights to **Ghardaïa**; and 6 flights to **Algiers** each week.

• **Youth hostel** *A.J.Tassili*, Illizi 33000, open 0800-1200 and 1400-2200, 50 beds, kitchen, airport 7 km, bus 1 km.

From Illizi to Djanet is about 380 km, the first 100 km of piste is difficult driving, but after Zaouatallaz the road is much better.

Djanet

ACCESS Air The airport is 15 km out of town, too far to walk and an expensive taxi ride. If you have contacted an agent for touring in the region get him to come and meet you.

This is really a cluster of villages rather than a small town, 700 km from Tamanrasset, situated at an altitude of 1,100m. It is the main settlement in the Tassili N'Ajjer and lies in pleasant surroundings beside an oasis (djanet means garden). It is dominated by a fortress from where there is a good view. It can get very hot here so take precautions.

The main interest of Djanet is in its proximity to the **Tassili National Park** with its large number of rock paintings and marvellous landscape. You can only enter the park if you are accompanied by a guide. The ONAT in Djanet organizes tours, but they are generally expensive and by foot, which entails covering distances of 15 to 20 km a day. If you require a permit to visit the National Park or permission to take photographs there, the office is on place du Marché. They have a small **museum** which exhibits Neolithic tools and has pictures of the wall engravings.

Djanet contains a mixture of people from the surrounding area, Senussi from Libya, Tibu from the Tibesti mountains and Touareg nomads. Water is drawn from deep wells, generally by animal power and the oasis produces cereals, vegetables and dates. There is a small souk just off the main road.

• **Accommodation** There is one hotel in Djanet, ***Hotel Les Zéribas***, where basic accommodation is provided in small huts.

• **Travel Agent** all at place du Marché.

• **Tourist information** ONAT, T 09 735024, place du Marché, on main square.

• **Transport Air** For information, T 09 735032. **Algiers** 5 flights. **Ghardaïa** 4 flights. **Illizi** 4 flights. **Ouargla** 7 flights each week. **Road** The road to Tamanrasset goes NW for the first 164 km before turning W. It is good until Idelès, but from here it is advisable to take the piste that continues W and joins the main N3 road from In Salah to Tamanrasset. The piste leading up through the Hoggar to Tahifet is very scenic, but should not be tackled without a 4 wheel drive vehicle. From Djanet it is also possible to go to Ghat in Libya. **NB:**there are no buses from Djanet, so you will have to hitch, take a plane or a taxi. The taxis run to Tamanrasset but a fair number of vehicles go this way and hitching should be relatively easy. If you want to go on to Ghat in **Libya**, there are expensive taxis that take you for the 300 km ride.

Excursions from Djanet

NB: it is not permitted to wander off into the wilderness of the Tassili on your own. For safety reasons it is necessary to obtain a pass – from L'Office du Parc National du Tassili (OPNT) – and for that you must go in person, taking your passport, a day-to-day itinerary with the precise places of overnight stay, name of your guide who must be a local and a valid reason for your visit – and you still won't get a pass unless you have the backing of a local agency. Better to join an organized group.

Be prepared for a deal of walking, and carrying your own provisions which you are advised to bring with you from the N. During the tourist season, Oct to Apr, a camp is set up permanently at **Tamrit**, giving a base from which to see the paintings at **Tan Zoumaitak** on the wall of a huge cave, the floor paintings of elephants at **Timenzouzine** and a visit to the greatest concentration of paintings, those at Séfar, calling in at In Itinen and In Etouham on the way. The paintings were discovered in 1933.

The paintings at **Jabbaren**, including the hunter, legions and warriors and herds of tended cattle can be reached via Alemdounet or by a very strenuous 3 hr climb over very rough terrain on a day trip from Djanet.

INFORMATION FOR VISITORS

Contents

Before you go

Entry requirements

● Visas

Obtaining a visa in advance from Algerian Embassies is easy. It is issued in 2-3 days, requires 3 passport photos and costs £20 for UK citizens. An invitation or reservation from a hotel in Algeria is required to be sent with the application form. All European nationals require visas. German and Dutch travellers may have to wait longer (up to 20 days). The visa is valid for 45 days from date of issue, but is renewable in Algeria. In UK, visas can be obtained at the Algerian Consulate, 6 Hyde Park Gate, London SW7, T 071 221 7800, open every day 0900-1130. US and Canadian visitors must obtain visas through the Embassies in Washington or Ottawa. Australians and New Zealanders can get their visas in the UK in 2-3 days. It may be possible to obtain a visa in Tunisia (Tunis) or Morocco (Rabat) but it is better to get it before. **NB:** at present, visas will be refused if the passport already contains stamps from Israel or South Africa.

Visas for other African countries In Algiers, most countries to the S have embassies, and it is easy to obtain any necessary visas from them. Both Mali and Niger have Consulates in Tamanrasset and it is easier and quicker to obtain them there. **Burkina Faso**, 23 rue Mouloud Belchouat, T 02 613897; **Cameroon**, 60 Blvd Colonel M'Hamaed Bougara, T 02 788195; **Central African Republic**, 6 Ave Larbi Alik, Hydra, T 02 604488; **Mali**, Cité DNC Villa 15, Chemin Ahmed Kara, Hydra, T 02 606118; **Niger**, 54 rue du Vercos, Bouzareah, T 02 788921; **Nigeria**, 27b rue Ali Boufelgued, T 02 606050.

● Vaccinations

Read the section on Health, **see page 20**. To enter Algeria no special vaccinations are required, except if arriving from a yellow fever zone. In this case a vaccination certificate is required. When entering from the S, make sure you have a valid International Health certificate, as a cholera vaccination is compulsory. Malaria is virtually non-existent in Algeria and the risk of catching it so small, that it does not justify taking tablets. However, if you are travelling further S it is recommended to have a cholera and yellow fever vaccination, as well as taking anti-malaria tablets. The **water** is safe to drink throughout the country and bottled water is available in most places.

● Representation overseas

Canada, 435 Ave Daly Kin 643 Ottawa, T 613 232 9453; **France**, 11 rue d'Argentine, Paris 75016, T 75016; **Morocco**, 8 rue d'Azrou, Rabat, T 65474; **Spain**, 12 Calle General Oraa, Madrid, T 4116065; **UK**, 54 Holland Park, London W11, T 071 221 7800; **USA**, 2118 Kalorama Rd NW, Washington, SCN 20008, T 202 3285300.

● Tourist information

Tourist Office (ONAT) Headquarters: 25-27 rue Khalifa Boukhaifa, Algiers, T 02 743376, F 02 743214; **Central Region**: 5 Blvd Ben Boulaïd, Algiers, T 02 631387, F 02 743214; **Western Region**: 6 Blvd Emir Abdelkader,

Oran, T 06 398210; **Eastern Region**: 1 rue Tarik Ibn Zaid, Annaba, T 08 825886; **Southern Region**: 2 Blvd Emir Abdelkader, Ghardaïa, T 09 891751; **Hoggar/Tassili Regions**: Blvd Emir Abdelkader, Tamanrasset, T 09 734117.

● Tours and travel agents

Africa Explored, Summerleaze, Magor, Newport NP6 3DE, T 0633 880224 advertise a 22 week Trans African (£1,250) and an 8 week Saharan Desert (£590) expeditions which include Algeria. ***Explore Worldwide***, 1 Frederick St, Aldershot, Hants GU11 1LQ, T 0252 319448 advertise a 13 day Tassili-Hoggar expedition.

When to go

● Best time to visit

The spring is the best season with autumn the second choice, due to the heat and the dust haze of the summer. The coast is pleasant to visit at any time of the year but humidity can be a problem. The best time to visit the Sahara is of course the winter.

● Clothing

Bear in mind the extreme daily range of temperature and take clothing to prevent feeling chilly in the evening, or freezing at high altitudes in the winter and in the clear Saharan night. Also essential are sunglasses, head covering against the sun and a scarf to keep out some of the sand which gets everywhere. Full coverage of limbs and head is always sensible when travelling in the heat. Algeria is a Muslim country and the suggestions in the introduction (**see page 27**) apply here.

Money

● Credit cards

Generally not accepted.

● Cost of living

The cost of living is cheaper than UK and has got cheaper with recent devaluations. Travel is particularly cheap. The AD1000 changed on entering Algeria should last about 5 days if staying at the cheapest hotels. Changing money on the black market alters the situation.

● Currency

The currency in Algeria is the Algerian Dinar (AD in this text), divided into notes of 5, 10, 20, 50, 100 and 200. The AD500 notes are no longer valid. The dinar is divided into 100 centimes. Coins in circulation are 5, 10, 20 and 50 centimes as well as 1, 5 and 10 dinars.

Currency regulations On arrival, all foreign currency (cash and travellers' cheques) must be noted down on the **Currency Declaration Form**. The Customs officials often demand to count the money. The form must be carried with you throughout your stay in Algeria, with all official transactions being recorded and it will have to be produced on leaving. The customs officials then check to see that the amount declared on entry adds up to the money left, minus the money spent during the stay. It is obviously very important not to lose this form, as its loss may require you to return to your point of entry and, at the very least face great hassle. If the sums do not balance on departure, you will probably be fined.

Officially, money has to be changed in a bank, or hotel, and the transaction noted down on the Currency Declaration Form. However, there is a thriving black market, and a great number of 'money changers' who will change at rates up to 3 times better than the official rate. It is generally easy to change money on the black market, but you should be careful of 'changers' coming up to you in the street. Using the black market involves smuggling money in that is not declared on the Currency Declaration Form. In most cases this is relatively easy, but in certain cases when leaving, checks by Customs can be quite thorough. In all cases, be careful to hide the non-declared money very well, or else you risk its confiscation. The best money to change on the black market is the French franc.

On entering, it is also compulsory to change the equivalent of AD1000 at the official rate. In most border posts you will have to change the money there and then, but there are certain places where no banks are available and money should in theory be changed in the closest bank. In this case it is possible not to change any money on the official market but you run the heavy risk of having to change it on departure and have the AD1000 confiscated by the Customs officials. Changing excess dinars back into another currency is in theory possible, but generally very difficult in practice. Be careful not to change too much money at a time.

For exchange rates for July 1994 **see page 9**.

● Travellers' cheques

The only bank that changes travellers' cheques is the **Banque National d'Algérie**, but a few hotels will change them as well.

Getting there

● Air

Algeria has 4 international airports, Algiers, Oran, Constantine and Annaba. Houari Boumedienne 20 km S of Algiers is the main airport, but the others also have international flights to Paris, Lyon and Marseille.

From Europe Flights to Algiers from London Heathrow: **Air Algérie** flies on Tue, Fri and Sun at 1630. Information contact Air Algérie in London, T 071 4875709; **Air France** (via Paris): every day at 1010 connecting for a flight for Paris-Orly at 1515, involving changing airport (T in London 081 7426600); **Swissair**: flies every Mon, Wed, Sat at 0800 via Geneva. Information contact, T 071 439 4144. **Iberia**: on Thur via Barcelona. Information contact, T 071 4375622; **Alitalia**: flies every day, but this involves an overnight stop in Rome. Information contact, T 071 602 7111.

Air Algérie also flies to other European destinations including Amsterdam, Barcelona, Brussels, Paris (3 flights daily), Rome (daily). Other Airlines that go to Algeria (but not direct from London) are Aeroflot, Egypt Air, Iberia and Royal Air Maroc.

From USA/Canada There are no direct flights to Algeria. The cheapest and most frequent flights are via Paris and London.

From African countries There are daily flights to and from Casablanca and Tunis as well as 3 flights a week to Tripoli. Air Algerie advertises flights from Cairo and Rabat too.

From Algiers there are good connections to West and Central Africa. Air Algérie flies to Bamako (3 times a week), Dakar, Niamey, Nouakchott and Ouagadougou (once a week).

Check in at least 2 hours before departure. Keep an eye on your luggage and try to see it is loaded on your plane!

● Train

There is a daily train between Tunis and Algiers crossing the border at Ghardimaou. The train leaves Algiers at 1350 and Tunis at 1255 and takes 24 hours. The train can be boarded at Constantine, Annaba and Souk Ahras.

● Road

Entering from **Tunisia** is easy as there are a number of border crossings. The most frequented is between Ghardimaou and Souk Ahras, but the border further N, at Oum-Teboul between Tabarka and El Kala is also good. In the S, the crossing at Bou Aroua between Nefta and El Oued is easy, and generally the customs officials are quite relaxed. **Bus** There is a daily bus from Tunis to Annaba. The bus leaves Tunis S station at 0700 and Annaba at 0500. Important to book.

To **Morocco**, there is a crossing between Tlemcen and Oujda. At this crossing it may sometimes not be possible to cross by foot, but is never a problem by car. The other crossing is further S, between Figuig and Beni Ounif and is far easier, but customs officials are known to be very thorough.

To **Niger**, the border is 10 km S of In Guezzam, but you still have to go to the custom office in Tamanrasset first. The border is closed to tourists at the time of going to press.

To **Mali**, the border is in Bordj Mokhtar, 600 km S of Reggane. Customs formalities may still have to be done in Reggane. Check before you set out on the 600 km trip, as the border crossing is closed at time of going to press.

To **Mauritania**, the border crossing S of Tindouf is effectively closed to all traffic.

● Sea

One of the nicest ways of arriving in Algeria is by ferry, but it is expensive, particularly with a car. In the summer, the boats run behind schedule and tend to be full. Booking early on is very important as well as being at the port of departure well in advance of the sailing time. There are ferries from France and Spain. Fares from Marseille range from £110/FF960 one way for a foot passenger and £200/FF1,750 return. Car return £500/FF4,400 including driver. Bicycles £12.50/FF112 one way. There are reductions for under 25s. Fares are cheaper to Tunisia and Morocco, so it may be worth while going via either of these, particularly if you have a car.

From Marseille (France) to Algiers and Oran: winter, every 3 days, summer daily. The crossing takes about 24 hours. Contact in London, T 071 4914968. Contact Algerian Ferries, 6 Blvd Khémisti, Algiers, T 632698/638279, Tx 67413.

From Alicante (Spain) to Oran and Algiers: 2 sailings a month in the summer but none in the winter. For information, T +34 6 208333.

From Palma (Majorca) to Algiers: 4 trips a month in the summer and one a month in winter. The boats go on to Marseille. For information, T +34 71 727141.

● **Customs**
On entering Algeria you can carry 200 cigarettes, 50 cigars or 400 gm of tobacco, one bottle of spirits and 2 bottles of wine. **Warning**: it is advisable to note down on the Currency Declaration Form (**see page 480**) any valuable personal effects such as cameras, skis, musical instruments, radios, etc, as some people having not done this, have had them confiscated on departure.

When you arrive

● **Banking hours**
These are 0900-1500, Mon-Thur, with some closing for lunch. In Ramadan the hours are shorter. The larger hotels will change money.

● **Electricity**
220 and in some places 120 volts. Be sure to check before connecting appliances. A continental adaptor plug is essential.

● **Hours of business**
Government offices, Sat-Wed 0800-1200 and 1400-1730, Thur open mornings only. Banks generally Sat-Thurs 0900-1500, but some have different hours. Shops tend to close 1200-1500 but there is no set rule on this.

● **Official time**
GMT plus one hour.

● **Photography**
Films and camera batteries are on sale everywhere, but check to make sure they are not beyond the sell by date. A good way of getting recent film is to buy it at a source that appears to have a good turnover.

As far as taking pictures there are little restrictions apart from aerodromes, military zones and installations and military personnel. When taking pictures of people, take the usual polite precautions, remembering that women in particular and most people in general object to being the subject of a photography without giving their permission.

People wishing to film on a professional level must have permission from the Ministry of Information or the Algerian Embassy in their home country.

● **Safety**
At present visitors are advised not to travel to Algeria in view of the current security situation. There have been a number of terrorist attacks in recent months and further attacks cannot be ruled out. Those who must make essential visits are advised to take all possible security precautions, limiting movements by road to a minimum and avoiding the densely populated poorer areas in and around Algiers. They should make their whereabouts known to their embassy (**see page 424**) who can provide further advice if necessary. Travel to the southern borders with Mali and Niger is not recommended at present.

● **Shopping**
Best buys are rugs and carpets if you have the space but be sure you know what you want before you start looking. Ghardaïa is a good centre for carpets. Touareg items, some genuine bargains but many made for tourists, can be found in Tamanrasset and El Oued. Bargaining is of course part of the fun and the only way to reduce the inflated asking price to something close to the real value of the article. Take some time to do this negotiation.

● **Tipping**
Tipping is not expected so don't be surprised that no-one rushes to help you carry a case! Service will be included in meal prices. Give the taxi driver 10%.

● **Weights and measures**
The metric system is used throughout Algeria. For conversion table, **see page 17**.

Where to stay

● **Hotels**
There tends to be a problem of under-capacity in Algeria, particularly in the large towns such as Algiers. Nevertheless if you start early enough, finding a room in large towns should not be a major problem, as there are a fair number of well run, clean, cheap hotels. When looking for a cheap hotel, do not be put off by the sign '*Complet*' as the hotel will often still have some rooms. Top end accommodation is rarer, but generally of a good quality, the only real inconvenience being that many require you to show your Currency Declaration Form if you are paying in foreign currency. In the S, many of these hotels have swimming pools (some may be empty!) which can be a real pleasure in the intense heat.

● **Youth hostels**
There are 41 youth hostels and associated youth centres which are usually open 1000-1200 and 1700-2200. The overnight fee is AD40. Some hostels have a free members' kitchen. Maximum stay 3 nights. Self catering

Hotel Classifications

AL US$90+. International class luxury hotel. All facilities for business and leisure travellers are of the highest international standard.

A US$75-90. International hotel with air conditioned rooms with WC, bath/shower, TV, phone, mini-bar, daily clean linen. Choice of restaurants, coffee shop, shops, bank, travel agent, swimming pool, some sport and business facilities.

B US$60-75. As **A** but without the luxury, reduced number of restaurants, smaller rooms, limited range of shops and sport.

C US$40-60. Best rooms have air conditioning, own bath/shower and WC. Usually comfortable, bank, shop, pool.

D US$20-40. Best rooms may have own WC and bath/shower. Depending on management will have room service and choice of cuisine in restaurant.

E US$10-20. Simple provision. Perhaps fan cooler. May not have restaurant. Shared WC and showers with hot water (when available).

F under US$10. Very basic, shared toilet facilities, variable in cleanliness, noise, often in dubious locations.

is available only in a limited number of hostels.

Camping

This is permitted at some youth hostels.

Food and drink

Food

Algerian cooking is very similar to Moroccan and Tunisian, but has a few regional specialities.

Chorba – soup served with onions, tomatoes, meat and carrots: it can be very spicy.

Bourek – is a speciality from Algiers. Mince meat, with onions, and fried eggs, rolled in a cigar shape and fried in batter.

Dolma – dishes with a mixture of tomatoes and peppers.

Couscous – chicken or mutton, served on steamed semolina, a traditional dish throughout North Africa.

Méchoui – roasted meat, generally lamb.

Merguez – spicy sausage.

Cakes are very good, generally made from semolina, almonds, dates and honey. Most cakes are served with fresh mint tea.

Restaurant Classifications

Given the variations in price of food on any menu our restaurants are divided where possible into three simple grades:
♦♦♦ expensive, ♦♦ average and ♦ cheap.

Drink

Algeria has some quite good wines, generally with a higher alcohol content than European wines. The ***Mascara*** is the best known, the ***Bordjia*** is a cooked wine best as an aperitif. Wines tend to be expensive and not always available. Beer is not bad, but by no means cheap whereas spirits are very expensive. Bottled water is found everywhere, but be sure to check that the seal has not been broken. The best and most refreshing drink is hot mint tea (*thé à la menthe*), but order it with fresh mint leaves, as it is sometimes made with mint syrup.

Getting around

Air

Internal flights are quite cheap, particularly when paid for in black market money, but this is generally very difficult as most Air Algérie offices ask for the Currency Form. 27 towns are listed as having airports. All major cities have regular air links and if going to the S, the plane can save you a lot of time. Flights are generally heavily booked, and re-confirming your booking is essential. Check-in time is a serious one hour before take-off. The paperwork always seems to take that long. It is rare for seat numbers to be allocated so be prepared to scramble.

Train

The train runs along the N coast, connecting the main towns of Oran, Algiers, Constantine and Annaba. There is also a line that runs S to Touggourt from Constantine, and a line from Oran to Béchar. The train is slow and a bit more expensive than the bus. It is nevertheless easier to get seats and some trains have couchettes.

Road

Bus The bus service is quite reliable and the best way of getting around. Almost all the towns in Algeria are on a bus route, including towns in the Sahara. Trips, however can be long and hot. On long distances, it is important to try and make a booking the day before as buses can get very crowded. In any case, be there an hour before the bus leaves.

Car hire It is very difficult to find cars to hire and if you intend to do so, try and arrange it from abroad. The prices are also very expensive, around AD250 a day and most companies **do not take credit cards**. Do not expect the car to be of a high standard or have a spare tyre. Minimum age for hire is 25.

Hitch hiking Relatively easy, particularly in the N. In the S, it is much more difficult, purely because of the large distances. The best is to try and hitch a ride with other tourists. To get a ride, go to a petrol station or restaurant and ask people directly rather than standing in the burning sun. Trucks, all run by the government SNTR are officially not permitted to take passengers, but they generally do. In the S, ask a driver who may then pick you up after the Police control. A small fee is sometimes required. Women hitch-hiking on their own should be careful: it is best to hitch with a male friend.

Motoring If you are bringing your own vehicle, a compulsory insurance has to be purchased at the point of entry. The prices are about AD60 for 10 days and 120 for 30 days. Fuel is quite cheap. When going to the S, always set out with a full tank of fuel and double-check where the next petrol station is.

Taxis Shared taxis are a cheap, popular and efficient means of travel. They are generally only marginally more expensive than the bus. Standard routes link and connect most of Algeria's towns and cities. In most towns the taxi station can be found beside the bus terminal.

Communications

● Language

Arabic is the official language throughout Algeria but French is still the language of business and administration. Some people do speak English, but this tends to be more the exception than the rule.

● Postal services

The postal system is very slow and it is well to expect letters to or from overseas to take from one to 3 weeks. Posting in a main town speeds the process. Letter Boxes – yellow – are widespread but Post Offices generally offer a more reliable and perhaps speedier collection.

Parcels are best sent if at all from the larger Post Offices. The parcels must be inspected before sealing. It is not possible to give an estimate of the transit time, but parcels sent by air take longer than letters and surface mail takes longer still!

● Telephone services

Telephones are not very good, particularly for overseas calls which can take a few hours to get connected. The connections from Algiers are much easier and considerably faster than from the other cities. For local calls, the problem is not the connection but the inevitable long queues. All the telephone exchanges are in, or by, the Post Office and some, as in Algiers are open 24 hours. Prices to Europe for a 3 minute call are around AD60, every additional minute costing AD20. The international code for Algeria is +213 plus the area code and number.

Entertainment

● Media

There are no newspapers in English. The major Arabic newspaper is *El Massaa*. The major French daily newspaper is *El Moudjahid*, which is reported to sell about 350,000 copies a day. The other French newspapers are *El Chaab* and *Horizons 2000* (which has one page in English). A French weekly paper is published in Algiers each Thur, *Algérie-Actualité*.

● Sport

In Algerian hotels, facilities are usually available for tennis and swimming. Coastal resorts offer the usual water sports with the added attraction of underwater fishing at Algiers, Oran, Annaba and Jiljil organized by the Algerian Federation for Subaquatic Activities. Wild boar hunting excursions into the regions of El Kala, Tlemcen and Kabylia take place in the winter months.

Holidays and festivals

Algeria is a Muslim country and observes all the main Islamic festivals as holidays (**see page 30**). The dates of the Islamic holidays and the fast, Ramadan, vary each year, as they are calculated according to the moon. Ramadan is strictly observed by most Algerians, and it is advisable not to eat or drink in public during this period in the daytime. In addition several national events are celebrated as holidays. Friday is the day of rest.

1 Jan: New Year's Day
1 May: Labour Day

19 Jun: Commemoration Day: Anniversary of the overthrow of Ben Bella
5 Jul: Independence Day
1 Nov: Anniversary of Revolution

Approximate dates for 1995:

1 Feb: Ramadan begins
4 & 5 Mar: Eïd al-Fitr
10/11 May: Eïd al-Adha
31 May: Islamic New Year (Anno Hegira 1416)
9 Aug: Prophet's Birthday

Further reading

● Books

Glen, Simon and Jan (1987) *Sahara Handbook*, Lascelles: London 1987; *Guide du Routard*, Hachette: Paris (French); *Polyglott* book (German); *Algérie*, Hachette Guides Bleus: Paris 1986.

Dickinson, Matt ed. (1991) *Long Distance Walks in North Africa*, Crowood Press; Dumas, Alexandre, *Adventures in Algeria (or Tangiers to Tunis (transl.) 1959);* Eberhardt, Isabelle (1987) *The Passionate Nomad*, Virago: London.

● Maps

Michelin 953 offers the best overall coverage, but it covers the whole of North and West Africa, and does not have quite enough detail. The best detailed map is the Michelin 172, covering the N as well as Tunisia, but leaving out an important part of the Sahara.

TUNISIA

Contents

Map

Introduction

Tunisia lying between 30°N and 38°N and 9°E and 12°E extends the furthest N of all the African countries. For the traveller it offers a gentle introduction to North Africa being very Western in character. It offers within a small area endless reliable sunshine, beautiful beaches, inspiring mountain ranges, palm-fringed oases and in the S, wide expanses of sandy desert. It contains spectacular Roman monuments, a wide range of Islamic architecture and unusual underground dwellings, all easily accessible.

Basics

OFFICIAL NAME al-Jumhuriyah at-Tunisiyah (Republic of Tunisia).

NATIONAL FLAG Red with a white circle in the centre, bearing a crescent moon and a 5 point star in red.

OFFICIAL LANGUAGE Arabic.

OFFICIAL RELIGION Islam.

INDICATORS *Population* 8.5 million; *Urban* 53%; *Religion* Sunni Muslim 99.4%, Christian 0.3%, Jewish 0.1%; *Birth rate* 25 per 1000, *Death rate* 6 per 1000, *Life expectancy* 66/69; *GNP per capita* US$1,420.

Environment

Land

The Republic of Tunisia has a surface area of 163,610 sq km, equal to that of England and Wales or half of Italy and is by far the smallest country in North Africa. It measures 750 km from N to S and averages 150 km from W to E. There are 1,600 km of coast, 330 km facing N and 1,270 km facing E to the central Mediterranean Sea. The Gulf of Tunis is included in the N zone while to the S, forming part of the E facing coast, are the Gulfs of Hammamet and Gabès, the latter lying between the islands of Djerba in the S and Kerkennah in the N.

Borders

Tunisia's borders have given some cause for conflict, though so far only in the offshore zone. A dispute with Libya arose in the late 1970s over the offshore zone in the region of the Gulf of Gabès. Arbitration at the International Court of Justice in 1982 favoured Libya, causing Tunisia to lose control of the important Bouri oilfield. Tunisia and Libya are contemplating joint development of other oilfields lying across the offshore bound-

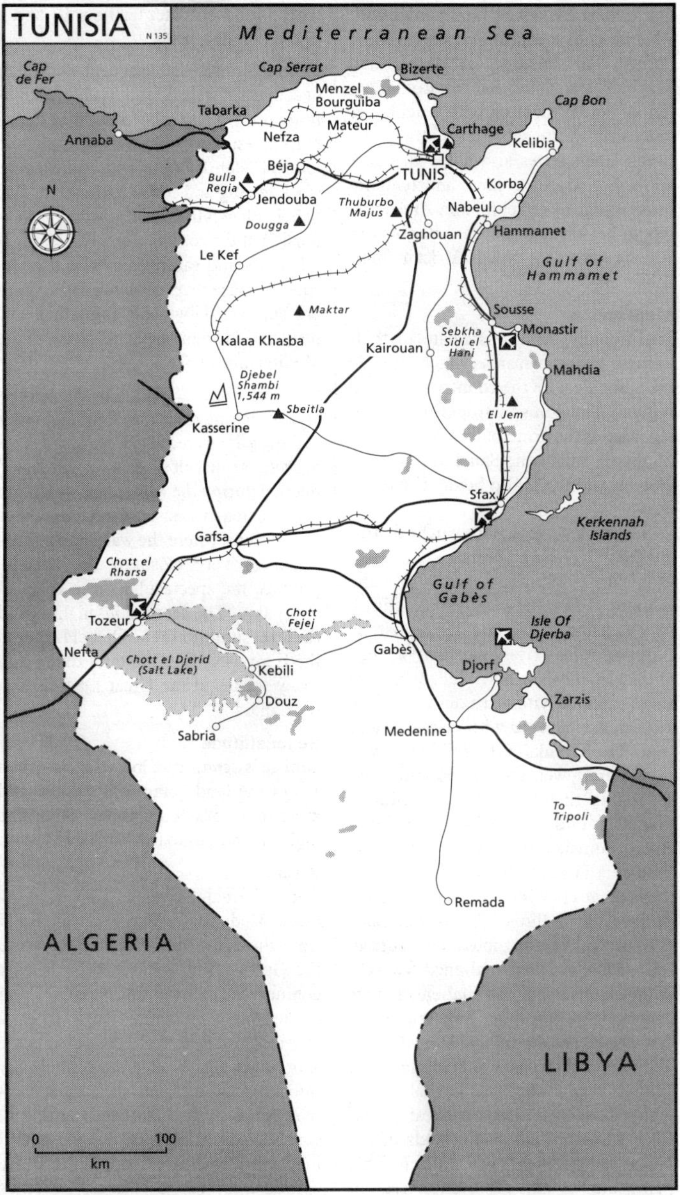
TUNISIA
N 135
Mediterranean Sea
Cap de Fer
Cap Serrat
Bizerte
Menzel Bourguiba
Cap Bon
Tabarka
Mateur
Annaba
Nefza
Carthage
Kelibia
Béja
TUNIS
Bulla Regia
Jendouba
Korba
N
Thuburbo Majus
Nabeul
Dougga
Zaghouan
Hammamet
Le Kef
Gulf of Hammamet
Maktar
Sousse
Monastir
Kalaa Khasba
Sebkha Sidi el Hani
Kairouan
Mahdia
Djebel Shambi 1,544 m
Sbeitla
El Jem
Kasserine
Sfax
Kerkennah Islands
Gafsa
Chott el Rharsa
Gulf of Gabès
Chott Fejej
Tozeur
Isle Of Djerba
Gabès
Nefta
Chott el Djerid (Salt Lake)
Djorf
Kebili
Zarzis
Douz
Medenine
Sabria
To Tripoli
Remada
ALGERIA
LIBYA
0
100
km

ary. Tunisia has a long land border with Algeria, with a multiplicity of crossing points. The creation of the United Maghreb Association has made other potential border disputes with neighbours less likely in the short term. Travel between UMA states also helps all UMA and other Arab travellers and tends to make it slightly easier for non-Arab tourists to get through border crossings in Tunisia and other North African countries.

Main regions

Traditionally, Tunisians relate to their tribal or hometown areas which often do not coincide with the country's physical regions. The Tunis metropolitan area is regarded as the principal region, with the Medjerda valley, the Sahel, the interior plateau and the S also being differentiated.

Three physical regions can be distinguished. **Northern Tunisia** is the economically dominant area. In the extreme N forming a rugged coastline – an extension of the mainly sandstone Algerian Atlas – rises a distinctive range known as the Northern Tell. In places these uplands with altitudes exceeding 1,000m are covered with cork oak and pine. The S flanks of the Tell in the Béja region are lower, more open and more fertile. To the E are the rich alluvial plains around Bizerte. The Medjerda River, Tunisia's only major perennial flow, cuts a wide fertile valley to the S of these ranges flowing NE to enter the sea in the Gulf of Tunis. This is the major agricultural region noted particularly for cereals. Further S, aligned SW-NE, is an extension of the higher, broader and mainly limestone Saharan Atlas. This forms the distinctive Dorsal/High Tell region with its harsher climate and sparser vegetation. The Dorsal range, which boasts Tunisia's highest point, Djebel Shambi at 1,544m, ends in the NE at the peninsula of Cap Bon. This peninsula is Tunisia's richest region, with a mild climate, fertile soils and a dense population.

Central Tunisia is a lower central plateau of semi-arid steppe land. Its harsh environment renders the area bleak and barren, especially in the W. Only the lower, E steppe offers opportunities for stock raising and cereal cultivation. The Sahel, a low-lying and flat westward extension of the coastal plain, has seasonal salt lakes and sandy soils with a widespread, dense cover of olive groves which are supported by light rainfall, heavy dews and the tempering influence of the Mediterranean Sea.

Southern Tunisia, lying S of the steppes and stretching from the Algerian border to the sea, is an area of low-lying salt lakes or *chotts*, some below sea level, which are flooded during the winter and which dry to give extensive seasonal salt flats. Other depressions, where the water table is exposed or very close to the surface, produce the spectacular green oases of date palms. The depressions in the N and the level summits of the Djebel Dahar to the E give way S to the sand dunes and rocky wastes of the Great Eastern Erg, the Sahara.

Relief/altitude

Tunisia is a country of low relief, less than 1% of the land being over 1,000m and more than 65% being under 350m. The highest land lies to the N and W.

Rivers

The only major river in Tunisia is the Oued Medjerda, which runs in the N from the Souk Ahras area in Algeria to the Gulf of Tunis. It has been heavily engineered for irrigation purposes and carries only a moderate flow in its easterly reaches. Elsewhere the streams are short *wadis* which often drain internally into seasonal salt lakes, the largest complex being in the Chott el Djerid, S of Gafsa. Wadis in spate are dangerous and in recent years heavy floods in the S have carried away whole villages. Travellers should not attempt to cross wadis in flood and should certainly not camp in stream beds.

Climate

The climate of the N region is archetypically Mediterranean in character with hot dry summers and warm, wet, westerly winds in winter. To the S the influences of the Sahara increase and the aridity of the landscape intensifies. Rainfall is irregular and decreases progressively to the S with annual averages ranging from 1,000 mm in N regions to 200-400 mm on the central plateau and less than 200 mm in the S. Rainfall, nowhere reliable, is most regular in the N. Humidity is generally low, especially away from the coast and further S. High temperatures and high relative humidity are an unpleasant combination, especially in Jun-Jul.

The prevailing wind is from the W, though in summer NE winds also occur. A fierce, hot sirocco-type wind from the Sahara, the *ghibli*, takes temperatures into the mid 40°C range, relative humidity to 10% and has serious effects on human and plant life. Temperatures are influenced by proximity to the coast. Average temperatures increase to the S and extremes of temperature between day and night occur in the desert. For the visitor, summers can be hot by day and over warm at night on the coast and unbearably hot (45°C) by day and surprisingly cool (10°C) by night inland. Winters are pleasantly mild in the N in the lowlands but temperatures fall quickly with altitude giving snow-blocked passes, while high daytime desert temperatures plummet at night making it 'too cold to sleep'.

The natural vegetation and farm crops are strongly influenced by the climate. The cork oak and pine forests of the wetter cooler N give way to thin pastures and esparto grass cover and eventually to desert in the S where the oases, supplied by natural springs, contrast sharply with the barren sands surrounding them.

Flora and fauna

The variety and quantity of vegetation is controlled by climatic conditions. Cork oaks clothe the mountain slopes in the N, esparto grass covers vast areas of the plains further S while the separate oases offer a wide selection. In spring the semi-desert in bloom is a sight to behold. The number of large wild mammals is declining but wild boar still roam in the cork forests of the N and gazelle bound across the scrub land in the S.

Lake Ichkeul and the surrounding reed beds in the N and the temporary lakes in the S provide resting places for migratory birds such as storks and flamingoes, bee eaters and hoopoes. There are many birds of prey at all times of the year. Other less attractive creatures such as snakes which are rarely seen, and scorpions, also to be treated with great respect, are natives of Tunisia. See page 36, section on wildlife of North Africa.

Agriculture

Land use

Is given as arable and orchards 31%, meadow and pasture 20%, forest and woodland 4% and non agricultural 45%. Yields are generally low as a consequence of the unreliable precipitation, small dispersed plots of land, outdated methods of farming and lack of investment by absentee landlords. Due to poor investment in vital water supplies, 75% of farm output comes from non-irrigated plots.

Land tenure

Currently nearly 65% of Tunisia's farms are under 10 ha, 31% are between 10 and 50 ha and only 5% are over 50 ha. Few farmers own their land, most is owned by absentee landlords. Tenants rarely have legal protection. The farms, already too small to be economically viable due to division for inheritance, are made up of geographically separate plots often some distance apart. A government move to consolidate plots through land reform was not popular. Some 220 co-operative farms exist, mainly in the N region and are mainly concerned with cereal growing.

Potential

The economic potential of Tunisia is considerable. There are large areas that could be brought under irrigation. Improved land tenure would also benefit farm output. Even in the Medjerda Valley the modern irrigation schemes are not fully and effectively used because of poor rural leadership and lack of incentives for farmers. Tunisia is rich in natural resources – phosphates, iron, zinc and

Scorpions – The Original Sting In The Tail

Scorpions really deserve a better press. They are fascinating creatures, provided they no not lurk in your shoe or shelter in your clothes.

Scorpions are not insects. They belong to the class Arachnida as do spiders and daddy longlegs. There are about 750 different kinds of scorpions. The average size is a cosy 6 cms but the largest, *Pandinus imperator*, the black Emperor scorpion of West Africa, is a terrifying 20 cm long. The good news is that only a few are really dangerous. The bad news is that some of these are found in North Africa.

They really are remarkable creatures with the ability to endure the hottest desert climates, revive after being frozen in ice, and survive for over a year without food or water. They have a remarkable resistance to nuclear radiation, a characteristic yet to be proved of great use.

Scorpions are nocturnal. They shelter during the heat of the day and to keep cool wave their legs in the air. They feed on insects and spiders, grasping their prey with their large claw-like pincers, tearing it apart and sucking the juices. Larger scorpions can devour lizards and small mammals.

Their shiny appearance is due to an impervious wax coating over their hard outer shell which protects them from any water loss. They have very small eyes and depend on their better developed senses of touch and smell. The sensitive bristles on the legs point in all directions and pick up vibrations of movements of potential prey or enemies. This sensitivity gives them ample warning to avoid being seen by heavy-footed humans.

The oft reported 'courtship dance' before mating is merely repeated instinctive actions. The grasping of claws and the jerky 'dance' movements from side to side are a prelude to copulation during which the male produces spermatozoa in a drop of sticky fluid to which the female is led so that they may enter her body. The male departs speedily after the 'dance' to avoid being attacked and devoured.

Scorpions bear live young. After hatching, the young crawl on to the female's back and are carried there for 2 or 3 weeks until their first moult. They gradually drop off after that time and have to fend for themselves.

Most scorpions retreat rather than attack. They sting in self-defence. The sting is a hard spine and the poison is made in the swelling at the base. The sole of the bare foot, not surprisingly, is most often the site of a sting, and the advice in the section on Health (**see page 24**) is not to be ignored. The African **fat-tailed scorpion** (we do not recommend measuring the size) is described as aggressive and quick-tempered. It is responsible for most of the reported stings to humans and most of the human fatalities in North Africa. The beautifully named *Buthus occitanus*, the small **Mediterranean yellow scorpion** and *Leirus quinquestriatus*, the **African golden scorpion**, also have neurotoxic stings that can be fatal.

lead – all of which offer the basis for further industrialization. The full extent of the country's petroleum resources is not yet known but good yields of both oil and natural gas are already contributing to foreign exchange earnings, while the country's position as a transit zone for an increasing volume of natural gas moving by pipeline from Algeria to Italy is an added bonus. Tourism has continuing potential for improvement, not just in the desert S where current efforts are concentrated, but in rehabilitation of the coastal areas of mass tourism, where age and poor management can be corrected to the advantage of the country's foreign exchange earnings. As with other states of North Africa, the potential will only be revealed if political stability can be maintained.

People

Ethnic origins

Tunisia is populated over the fertile plains and valleys by mainly Arab stock of the Beni Hillal and Beni Sulaim. As much as 98% of the population is Arab. The original Berber population and mixed Berber-Arab groups are found in the remoter inland areas and in the hills of the S. Pure Berber stock accounts for a mere 1% of the total population and are found in the Matmata region. There is a 3% residual element of the European colonists, of which more than half is French and the remainder Italian in origin. After Arabic, French is an important second language in the larger towns. Orthodox Islam is the main religion but revivalist Islam is increasingly prevalent among younger Tunisians.

Population density

Tunisia's estimated population in 1992 was 8.5 million, growing at a rate of slightly over 1.9% annually. The population distribution is biased heavily towards the N and the coasts. Greater Tunis now includes almost 2 million people. The capital, the Medjerda Valley and the coastal strip as far S as Sfax account for over 60% of the population. Kairouan province with 0.5 million and Gafsa with 0.25 million people are the only important population centres away from the N and E coasts. Migration from the land to the towns is increasing. Population densities in Tunis run at 2,000 per sq km against less than 10 in the deserts of the S. Tunisia has a youthful population with some 37% under 15 years of age.

Quality of life

Tunisia is attempting to improve the quality of its labour force and its educational system is struggling to lift standards. By 1990 approximately 63% of the population over 10 was literate (74% of males and 52% of females). Tunis has centres of academic excellence in its university institutes of higher studies.

Income per head is calculated at US$1,500. This is gradually improving but only erratically. Slumps in tourism, trade and remittance income from workers abroad have depressed levels in recent years. There is great variation in income levels between the better off people in Tunis and the poor semi-nomads of the deserts. The labour force is diversified including, among others, 23.0% in farming, 1.6% in mining, 17.9% in manufacturing industry and 12.5% in construction. Under-employment and unemployment remain a problem and many Tunisians emigrate to Libya or Europe for work.

History since Independence

For the history of this region before Tunisia gained Independence see The History of North Africa, page 57. For information on the Desert Campaign of WWII, see page 836.

Tunisia's Independence from the French Protectorate administration was achieved on 20 Mar, 1956. The transformation from self-government to Independence was managed by **Habib Bourguiba**, head of Tunisia's national liberation movement, the **Neo-Destour**, and later president. The new state had 3 basic, interconnected problems to resolve: its relations with France, the crucial issue of economic development, and its future political structures.

Relations with France began badly. In 1958 French aircraft bombed the Tunisian border village of Sakiet Sidi Youssef, apparently in retaliation for Tunisian support for Algerian Independence. In response, Tunisia demanded that French forces should abandon the naval base in Bizerte granted at NATO request. French refusal led to fighting and over a thousand Tunisians died before France withdrew.

In 1959 land belonging to European (mainly French) settlers in Tunisia was expropriated. The French left, taking their capital, a development which had an adverse effect on the Tunisian economy. Subsequently relations with France normalized and Tunisia became noted for its cautious, pro-Western attitudes in international diplomacy, President Bourguiba becoming a well-known independent voice in Arab affairs.

Economy After Independence the Tunisian Government concentrated on state-directed economic development, the collectivization of agriculture and government control of major industrial enterprises. By 1969, popular resistance and economic stagnation convinced the president of this policy's failure and a free market economy was instituted.

One consequence of this was a growing disparity between rich and poor which, by the 1980s, caused a rift between the governing **Destourian Socialist Party** on the one hand and the **UGTT** – formerly part of the Destourian Socialist Party – on the other. Severe riots during a general strike in Jan 1978 ushered in a period of social tension. Countrywide riots followed in Jan 1984 when the IMF, concerned over Tunisia's growing foreign debt, insisted the government remove food subsidies. A programme was introduced in 1987 to revive the economy, together with a wide-ranging programme of privatization. Tunisia, with Europe its major market, faces the negative implications of the new Single European Market.

Social and political affairs The need for economic development had social and political effects. Firstly, as part of the process of modernization and development, monogamy was introduced into the legal code. Then, in 1963, President Bourguiba attempted to abolish fasting during Ramadan in the interests of economic efficiency. Popular resistance undermined this initiative but, overall, Tunisia underwent a process of secularization and social modernization during the first 2 decades of Independence.

Secondly Bourguiba introduced a single-party system, in which his now renamed Destourian Socialist Party became the sole official party. The Communist Party was banned, re-emerging in the early 1980s, and leading members of the UGTT which, after the Jan 1978 'Black Thursday' riots found itself in opposition to government throughout the 1980s, were frequently imprisoned.

Islamic fundamentalism became a significant political movement in the early 1970s. By the 1980s its influence was widespread through Tunisian society. An organized Islamicist political movement, the **Mouvement de Tendence Islamique** (MTI), appeared. Though initially tolerated it was soon seen as a major threat and its leaders were imprisoned, while its frustrated supporters turned to urban violence in response.

The collapse of the Bourguiba régime The repression of the MTI was symbolic of events in Tunisia during the 1980s. As economic difficulties increased so, too, did the alienation of the Bourguiba régime from the population at large. The promise of political liberalization was replaced by repression and Tunisia acquired an unhappy reputation over human rights abuses. In foreign affairs Tunisia and Libya, but for a brief period in 1974, have not seen eye to eye. A friendship treaty with Algeria, conversely, worsened relations with both Libya and Morocco.

After 1984 President Bourguiba began increasingly to interfere with government, relying on a small group of advisers, particularly **Zine El-Abidine Ben Ali**, whom he appointed Interior Minister in 1986 and Premier in 1987. Within a week of being appointed, the new premier seized power in a 'legal' palace coup – legal because constitutional niceties were observed – and President Bourguiba, then in his eighties, was declared mentally incompetent to discharge his duties.

Tunisia today The removal of President Bourguiba reduced political and social tension, whereas the execution of the MTI leadership, which he had demanded and which had precipitated the coup, would have led to serious unrest. The new president proposed political liberalization with a multi-party system. Political prisoners were released, new political parties were permitted and political consensus was sought around a National Charter. Economic reform was pushed ahead and foreign confidence in Tunisia was restored. However the new régime could not bring itself to legalize the Islamicist movements, thus thwarting full political liberalization. In legislative elections in Apr 1989 all 141 seats were won by the old single political party, now renamed the **Rassemblement Constitutionnel Démocratique**, demonstrating its reluctance to abandon power.

President Ben Ali is being forced back on policies similar to those of his predecessor. The major domestic crisis, the relationship between government and the Islamicist movement, became increasingly bitter in the 1990s. Tunisia's future social and political scene will, however, depend largely on successful economic reforms and on improvements in its relationships with its North African and European neighbours. In Feb 1989 Tunisia joined neighbouring states in the **Maghreb Arab Union**. Within the wider Muslim world, Tunisia was increasingly isolated for its opposition to the UN-authorized war to force Iraq out of Kuwait in 1991.

Modern Tunisia

Government

The republic

Tunisia is a republic headed by a president with a 5-year term and considerable powers over the armed forces and the cabinet. The current president is Zine El-Abdine Ben Ali who constitutionally unseated Habib Bourguiba, Tunisia's president since Independence, in 1987. Ben Ali is a former army general and diplomat, chosen to change and protect the ruling party. There is an executive cabinet appointed by the president reporting to a single 141-member, 5-year elected legislative chamber. All Tunisians over 20 years of age are eligible to vote in elections. The socialist Democratic Constitutional Rally party has ruled since Independence (see History, page 491) under various names. Some secular, but generally innocuous, political opposition is permitted but radical Islamic groups are vigorously suppressed.

Domestic policy

Central government policies are concerned with maintaining political stability in a climate of growing Islamic revivalism. The cabinet's last major reshuffle in Oct 1991, leans towards the hard line in attitudes towards the fundamentalist Islamic groups. The government is also greatly concerned with keeping the economy developing to cope with a growing population and the pressures of worldwide recession.

Foreign policy

In foreign policy Tunisia has moved towards a slightly more Arab stance. Tunis was, until recently, the site of the PLO headquarters, and the Arab League has offices there. Tunisia is seeking better relations with its Maghreb allies but also needs US and European aid together with foreign visitors for its principal industry, tourism. Moderation thus tends to dominate foreign relations.

Regional government

This is through 23 *wilayat* (governorates) and sub-districts, while regional political representation is managed through delegations which have access to the higher levels of central government.

Economy

Tunisia has a more diversified economy than surrounding countries. Its modest endowment with oil has been an advantage in providing funding for non-oil development but has never been sufficient to encourage reliance on petroleum. There is, nevertheless, deep vulnerability to external economic pressures including the vagaries of international trade, foreign aid flows, variation in tourist numbers and access to the EU bloc for Tunisia's trade and labour. A youthful and fairly fast-growing population creates an added need for economic growth.

Agriculture

Is the basis of the economy, employs 23% of the labour force and produces about 15% by value of all national output. Chief crops are cereals, citrus fruit, olives, dates and grapes. Approximately 20% of the value of agricultural production comes from cereals. Olive oil is an important export crop accounting for 3% of the total but suffers heavy competition from Spain and Italy in the main European market. The Sahel is a monoculture of olives over much of its area. Irrigation is vital to ensure reliable cropping but large areas of the country with low rainfall lack provision of supplementary water supplies. Fishing and sponge gathering are important in the coastal ports, notably in the Gulf of Gabès. Fishing provides about 6% of the country's food supply with a catch of 95,000 tonnes per annum. Tuna fishing is declining as stocks in the Mediterranean dwindle. Esparto grass is collected to export for paper making and the oak forests of the N provide timber and cork.

Industry

Tunisia remains a large producer and exporter of phosphates with annual production running at some 7 million tonnes per annum from the Gafsa region. The main mines are at Djebel Mdilla, Redeyef, Metlaoui, and Phillippe Thomas. Phosphate and its products of phosphoric acid and fertilizer provide about 8% of all exports. Industrialization based on phosphates is developing slowly with plants to produce superphosphates and sulphuric acid. Other mineral resources being worked include lead and zinc at Laghouat and Djebel Hallouf and iron at Djerissa.

Manufacturing

Tunisia has made remarkable steps in effective industrialization, most of it small scale and private sector. Manufacturing now accounts for 18% of the work force and 15% of national production. The main products, principally from the N are cement, flour, steel, textiles, and beverages. The textile industry is most remarkable with piece-goods being made up in Tunisia for re-export back to manufacturers in Western Europe. In recent years this trade has provided 26% of Tunisia's total export earnings. There is a long established handicraft industry which has benefited through the tourist trade. Nabeul pottery, Kairouan carpets, decorative ironwork, leather goods, regional brass and hand-crafted textile wares are all world famous and find a steady market among tourists.

Energy

Tunisia's oil industry by no means compares with that of Libya or Algeria, with proved reserves of only 1,700 million barrels of crude oil (0.1% of the world total) and production of approximately 95,000 barrels per day with natural gas output of 304 million cubic metres per annum. Production comes from the El Borma field in the S, Sbeitla field in the S Atlas and the Itayem fields close to Sfax, all of which feed to a refinery and export complex at Sekhira. The Ashtart field offshore in the Gulf of Gabès is also productive and recent discoveries have been made both offshore and in the Cap Bon areas. It is hoped that oilfields lying across the offshore boundary line with Libya will eventually be exploited jointly. Crude and products sales account for 17% of exports.

Tourism

Is a major employer and foreign exchange earner. Considerable investment in new hotels has come partially from abroad. The number of tourists rose from a mere 56,000 in 1961 to 3 million in 1992. Receipts from tourism are estimated annually at US$1,000 million. The industry is developing from bases in Tunis/Sidi Bou Said along the E coast/Sahel to the S where desert tours are of increasing popularity and serve to spread the benefits of foreign tourists. Tunisians are aware of the negative social effects of tourism and deal fairly and sensibly with foreigners so that the country retains a good name and visitors return. Efforts are being made to provide high class hotels in the main coastal resorts to attract higher spending tourists, especially from Germany and France. Depression in Western Europe and political problems in Tunisia have tended in recent years to depress tourist numbers.

Trends

Economic trends have not favoured Tunisia recently. Rainfall has been irregular, falling for short periods unfavourable to farming but causing severe damage through flooding. The world depression has reduced the flow of foreign tourists and led to falling oil prices. The coming of the EU single market has adversely hit the Tunisian export trade, 70% of which has traditionally gone to Western European states. Fewer Tunisian workers, who annually sent back US$560 million in 1991 are now being accepted in Europe. The problem was clearly seen in the balance of merchandise trade where the deficit rose from TD690 million in 1985 to TD1,850 million in 1992. Membership of the United Maghreb Association (UMA), has so far failed to open up markets for Tunisia other than for migrant labour, though access to Libya has improved trade in recent years and encouraged Libyan tourism.

Gross National Domestic Product has run at about US$11,500 million per annum.

Tunisia has an increasing foreign debt, which stood at US$6,700 million by 1990 and has since worsened. Imports regularly outstrip exports in value and rising imports for defence and security

GROSS DOMESTIC PRODUCT 1990

	Value (TD000,000)	Share (%)
Agriculture	1,587.0	14.5
Mining	749.3	6.8
Manufacturing	1,644.6	15.0
Construction	540.0	4.9
Electricity/gas/utilities	163.8	1.5
Transport/communications	662.3	6.0
Trade	2,552.4	23.2
Other services	3,087.6	28.1
Total	10,987.0	100.0

Source: *Encyclopaedia Britannica*

are adding to the deficit. Inflation, officially put at 8% annually, is rather higher in Tunis and other urban centres. Expenditures in a roughly balanced state budget ran at TD2,746 million in 1990, of which the main areas were education, health, security, defence and agriculture.

Economic Indicators

	1989	**1990**	**1991**
Oil revenues (US$ mn)	399		543
Exports (TD mn)	2,782	3,086	3,785
Imports (TD mn)	4,150	4,852	4,998
Balance of trade (TD mn)	-1,090	-1,440	-1,038
Inflation index (1985=100)	129.5	138.3	149.7
Foreign debt (US$ mn)	6,085	6,716	8,296

Sources: IMF, EIU, *Encyclopaedia Britannica*

TUNIS

Contents

Maps

The history of the city, so close to Carthage, goes back to Punic times but it was not until the Arab invasion in the 7th century and the final destruction of Carthage that the city of Tunis flourished. The medina grew in importance with the Great Mosque Ez-Zitouna, the intellectual and religious centre, as its heart. The souks, commercial and crafts centres, developed around the Mosque. Tunis then became the second city in Afriqiya (a province of the Arab Empire) after Kairouan.

Pop 1,200,000 *Alt* 3m.

History

For a short time Tunis became the capital of the **Aghlabids** (894-905) but it was under the rule of the **Hafsid Dynasty** (1230-1574) that Tunis blossomed, with more than 100,000 inhabitants within its walls. The geographer and philosopher Ibn Khaldoun (1232-1406) was born during this period in Tunis when the intellectual and cultural importance of the city was at its peak.

Between 1534 and 1574 the town went through a period of turbulence. First attacked by Kherredine Pasha, better known as the pirate **Barbarossa**, from Turkey, then captured by the Algerians and subsequently by Don Juan of Austria. It was only with the Turkish invasion, in 1574, that a period of calm returned. The influx of 80,000 Moors from Spain at the start of the 17th century gave a renewed vitality to the city and its surroundings. Craftsmen trained in techniques unknown in Tunis made their appearance, including the makers of the important *chechias* (little red hats that were exported throughout the Mediterranean for over 3 centuries) (see page501).

The Husseinite Dynasty lasted until the French colonization in 1881, but not without internal rivalries and chronic clashes with the Algerians over supremacy in the Maghreb region. This period was highly prolific in terms of the construction of palaces, *medressa* and mosques and greatly contributed to the shaping of the old medina as we know it today. The Husseinite Dynasty, highly in debt, finally fell, giving way to French colonization. With the arrival of the French, large urban works were undertaken, giving rise to the new town built between the medina and the lake, with Ave de la Marine (today Ave Bourguiba)

Climate: Tunis

	Jan	Feb	Mar	Apr	May	Jun	Jul	Aug	Sep	Oct	Nov	Dec	Av/Tot
Max (°C)	15	16	18	21	25	29	32	32	30	25	21	16	23
Min (°C)	7	7	9	11	14	18	20	21	20	16	12	9	14
Rain (mm)	79	48	41	41	29	12	2	14	26	85	56	47	480

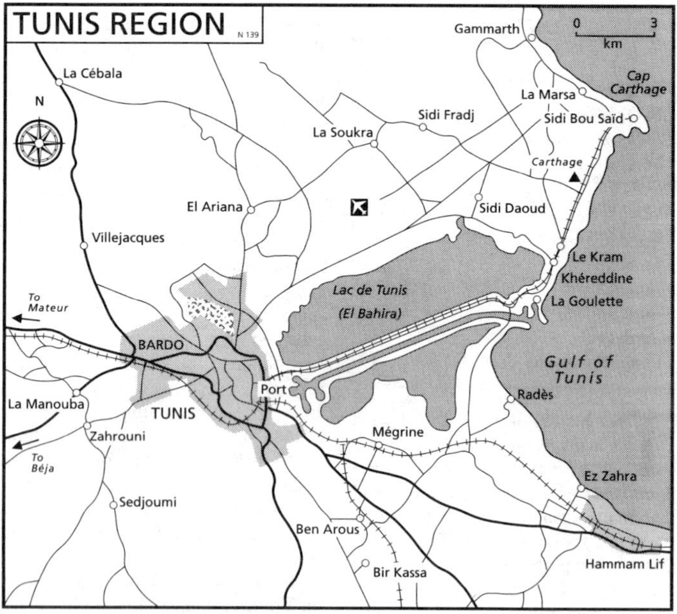

as its central point linking the city to the sea. The ville nouvelle became the centre of the modern town giving it a distinctly European air. (See History of North Africa, page 57.)

Tunis was occupied by the Germans for 6 months during WWII. Today it is a modern city and the centre of all the country's activities. Since Independence the population has increased dramatically from 400,000 to 1,200,000 resulting in overcrowding and the need for constant expansion. The city holds an interesting mixture of European and North African cultures, although in the ville nouvelle life has definitely been influenced by Europe, but enter the medina and you will be in another world. Indeed the medina is a good place to start your journey.ocation

The town is situated on the shores of a lake linked to the sea at La Goulette. The new city, with Ave Bourguiba as its centre, is laid out in a quasi-geometric fashion. The medina, in contrast, is full of small, confusing, winding streets. The medina is no longer walled, as the French replaced the old walls with large boulevards all around the old city. However no cars can penetrate into the medina, making a welcome change from the overcrowded and noisy streets of the new town. La Goulette, the link between the sea and the lake, is the first of the coastal resorts and is linked to Tunis by train (the TGM) and road, both of which cross the lake over a causeway. The train goes on to the other coastal resorts of Sidi Bou

Saïd, La Marsa and Gammarth, the smarter suburbs of Tunis full of luxurious villas. The first nice beaches are also situated here, and on summer weekends La Marsa is full of day-trippers from Tunis.

Climate

The climate is typically Mediterranean, but with a slight wind from the sea. The hottest season is obviously summer while the period from Nov to Feb is mild and sometimes rainy. The best seasons for a visit are late spring and autumn.

ACCESS Air The airport is situated 7 km outside the city. To reach the centre either take bus No 35 (cost TD0.75) that stops on Ave Bourguiba by Tunis Air. The airport bus links run day and night, but from 2400 to 0600 there is only one every hour. Otherwise take a taxi – this should not cost more than TD3, with baggage may be more. Beware of the unofficial taxis without meters. If you can't wait for an official one, be sure to agree on the price before getting in.

Train The main train station is very central, just 3 streets S of Ave Bourguiba, between Ave de Carthage and the medina. The suburban station TGM is 1 km away at the port end of Ave Bourguiba.

Bus There are 2 bus stations. Buses from Algeria and places S arrive at place Mongi Bali by the main train station. Buses from the N arrive at Bab Saadoun. Bus No 3 will take you to the town centre from here. The main louage terminus is 500m to the S of the train station but louages from Sousse, Medenine, Tozeur and Tataouine drop passengers by the medina walls 200m W of the train station and louages from Sfax at the station itself. From the port trains run every 10-15 mins to the TGM station and taxis are available to the town centre.

Things to see

Around the city

The **Ville Nouvelle** with few specific things to see, is the centre of the city's life. Walk in the late afternoon on Ave Bourguiba and the surrounding streets to see the city coming to life and the cafés filling up. Drink at the *Café de Paris* and watch people go by. Here you will find shops selling European newspapers (generally only a day late). The parks are pleasant all the year round (see Parks, page 505). Most of the monuments are in the old part of town.

Dar ben Abdallah Palace is off rue des Teinturiers along rue Sidi Kacem. The museum is located in a most beautiful traditional late 18th/early 19th century Tunisian mansion. The **Museum of Popular Arts and Traditions**, T 256195, is housed here. The building, with its sculptured and painted wood, its carved plaster work and marble tiles is as interesting as the collection it holds. The museum is organized around the central courtyard. The exhibits retrace traditional life throughout the 19th and 20th century in the medina showing everyday scenes covering everything from housekeeping skills to cooking implements, clothes and furniture. In the *hammam* (bath) there is an interesting map of the medina indicating the location of all the Moorish *hammam* throughout the old city. A very well kept and presented museum. Open daily 0930-1630 except Sun. Entrance TD1.

The Bardo National Museum, about 3 km W of the centre of Tunis, is set in a former 19th century Bey's palace whose many attractive features include its actual proportions, its decorated wooden and stucco ceilings and its walls covered with ornamental tiles. It contains very interesting archaeological collections from all the Punic and Roman sites throughout Tunisia, most notably a unique mosaic collection. The ground floor contains remains from the Punic sites, with mosaics from Thuburbo Majus (see page515), and Carthage (see page509) during the Christian period. Roman Carthage is on the 1st floor where, in the first room, mosaics, statues and sculptures from Carthage are displayed. In the Sousse room there is a magnificent mosaic of Neptune from the 2nd or 3rd century and, on the walls, a wonderful representation of Seigneur Julius found in Carthage. There are also mosaics from Tabarka and sculptures from Thuburbo Majus.

In the Dougga room (see page535) there is another magnificent mosaic of Neptune, jewellery and statues. The El Djem room (see page560) also holds some beautiful mosaics, particularly Bacchus's Triumph. Mosaics in the Althiburo room have the sea and fish as a central theme, which is strange considering this city was inland. The Virgil room also contains wonderful exhibits.

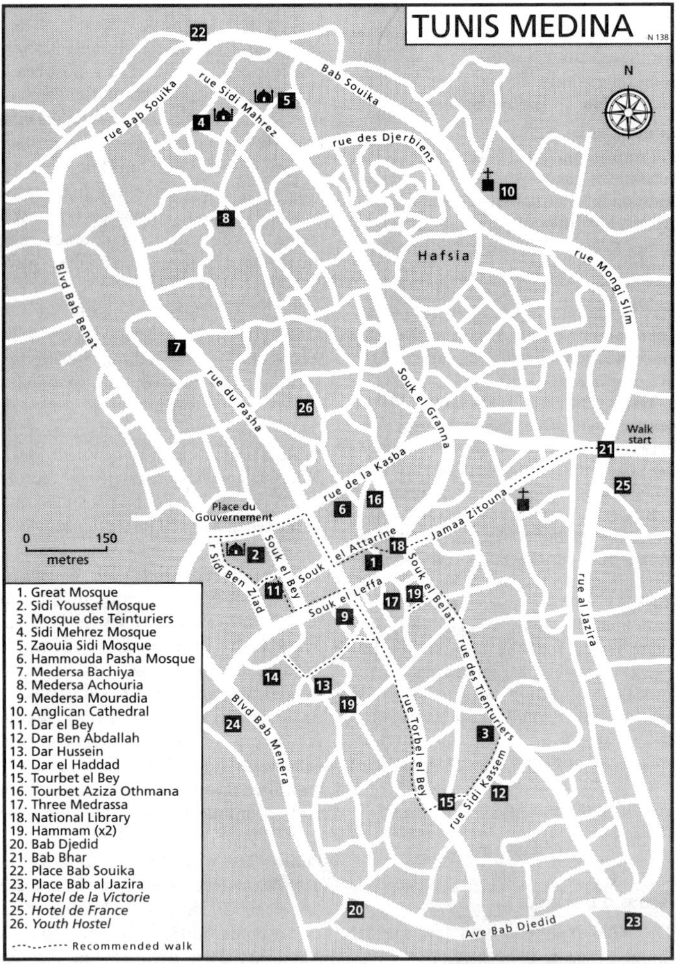

The Mahdia room (see page546) has exceptionally well preserved bronze and marble statues which were found on the sea bed off Mahdia at the beginning of the century by sponge divers. Apparently the boat transporting them from Greece sank in the early 2nd century. The museum, full of fascinating exhibits is open summer 0830-1730 and 0930-1630 winter, closed Mon, entrance TD3, photo fee TD2.

The **Medina** The mosque and many other monuments here are not open to the public. The admission times of those which are accessible are given in the text. **NB**: it is important to dress correctly when visiting a mosque. The following route visits the areas of interest within the medina.

Start from Place de la Victoire, inside Bab Bhar by the British Embassy. Walk up rue Jamaa Zitouna which is the centre for tourist shops selling a mixture of goods from all around Tunisia, but the best deals are not to be had here. Going up the street, the **Bibliothèque Nationale** is on the right and straight ahead is the **Great Mosque Ez-Zitouna**. Round the mosque to the right is the **Souk el Attarine**, which specializes in perfumes. Traditionally each perfume has a particular significance. For example, orange will be used for marriages. Although today the souk sells a wider range of goods it is still possible to buy concentrates of perfume essences very cheaply.

The **Tourbet Aziza Othmana** lies behind the souk up a small street. Follow the N side of the Great Mosque to its entrance by the minaret then turn right towards the **Hammouda Pasha Mosque** and rue de la Kasbah.

Turn W (left) up rue de la Kasbah through one of the oldest souks in the medina specializing in the round red felt *chechias*, the traditional men's headwear more likely associated with older Morocco (see page 497), to the **Sidi Youssef Mosque**, the place du Gouvernement, and another entrance to the medina. Continuing the tour turn back into the medina and take the narrow street to the right, rue Sidi Ben Ziad to the **Dar el Bey**. Keep this building on your right and walk ahead to the Souk el Leffa, a small covered street, specializing in carpets, though these can be bought more cheaply in Kairouan. Some of the carpet shops here have terraces with impressive views over the medina but walking through three storeys of carpets and not buying takes some nerve.

Continue down the Souk el Leffa to the back of the Great Mosque and go right between this and the **Medersa Mouradia** along the Souk des Femmes. A little street, the Souk des Orfèvres, on the right at the start of the Souk des Femmes sells lovely jewellery. A detour to the right at Souk el Kachachine leads first to the **Dar Hussein** and then the **Dar el Haddad**.

Souk des Femmes becomes rue Tourbet el Bey. Follow this until you come to **Torbet el Bey**. Turn left in front of the building and right down its E side and turn left into rue Sidi Kassem which has the **Dar Ben Abdallah** palace on the right and further down on the left on the corner of rue de Teinturiers is the **Mosque des Teinturiers**.

On either side along the rue des Teinturiers are small streets with dyers working using techniques that have hardly changed throughout the centuries. Go down one of these streets and take a close look. The dyers are accustomed to tourists 'peeping in' but it is better not to take too many pictures too conspicuously. Follow the rue des Teinturiers, which becomes the Souk el Belat, back towards the rue Jamma Zitouna, passing on the left, on the corner of rue du Trésor, a small mosque with a beautiful 14th century minaret.

At the street after this mosque turn left to the **Three Medrassa Complex** which includes **Medersa Slimania, Medersa Bachia** and **Medersa of the**

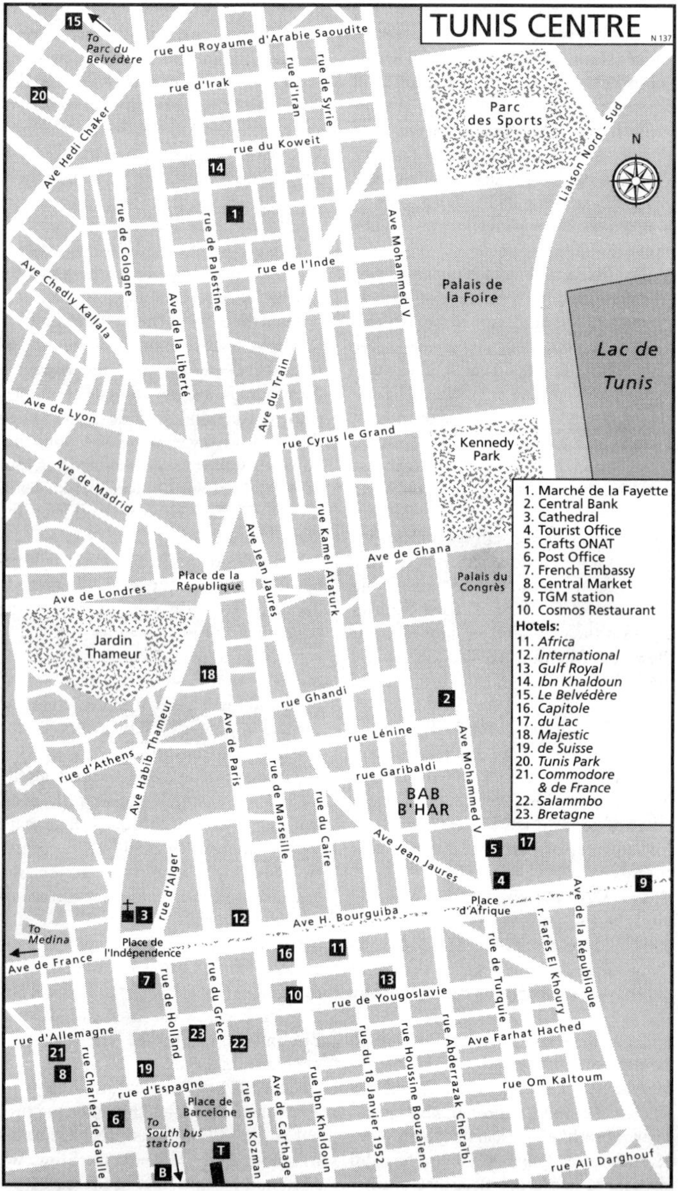
TUNIS CENTRE
N 137
Parc des Sports
Palais de la Foire
Lac de Tunis
Kennedy Park
Palais du Congrès
Jardin Thameur
BAB B'HAR
To Parc du Belvédère
To Medina
To South bus station
rue du Royaume d'Arabie Saoudite
rue d'Irak
rue d'Iran
rue de Syrie
rue du Koweit
Liaison Nord - Sud
Ave Hedi Chaker
rue de Cologne
rue de Palestine
rue de l'Inde
Ave Mohammed V
Ave Chedly Kallala
Ave de la Liberté
Ave du Train
Ave de Lyon
rue Cyrus le Grand
Ave de Madrid
rue Kamel Ataturk
Ave Jean Jaures
Ave de Ghana
Place de la République
Ave de Londres
rue Ghandi
rue Lénine
rue Garibaldi
Ave de Paris
rue de Marseille
rue du Caire
rue d'Athens
Ave Habib Thameur
rue d'Alger
Place d'Afrique
Ave H. Bourguiba
Place de l'Indépendence
Ave de France
r. Farès El Khoury
rue de Turquie
Ave de la République
rue de Yougoslavie
rue de Holland
rue du Grèce
rue d'Allemagne
Ave Farhat Hached
rue du 18 Janvier 1952
rue Houssine Bouzaiene
rue Abderrazak Cheraibi
rue Om Kaltoum
rue d'Espagne
Place de Barcelone
rue Charles de Gaulle
rue Ibn Kozman
Ave de Carthage
rue Ibn Khaldoun
rue Ali Darghouf
1. Marché de la Fayette
2. Central Bank
3. Cathedral
4. Tourist Office
5. Crafts ONAT
6. Post Office
7. French Embassy
8. Central Market
9. TGM station
10. Cosmos Restaurant
Hotels:
11. Africa
12. International
13. Gulf Royal
14. Ibn Khaldoun
15. Le Belvédère
16. Capitole
17. du Lac
18. Majestic
19. de Suisse
20. Tunis Park
21. Commodore & de France
22. Salammbo
23. Bretagne

Palm Tree.

Now you have seen the main sights it is time to wander in the small streets and perhaps find areas not frequented by tourists towards the Bab al Jazira, along the rue des Teinturiers, or towards Bab Souika to the N. It is interesting to look at the different houses and perhaps peep inside. The exterior of the houses are generally quite similar and do not give any idea of the hidden splendour. All the houses have large wooden doors, simply decorated with nails. The rooms are generally organized around a central courtyard with no external windows in order to ensure privacy. The houses are generally quite large as the entire family lives there, including married sons. Each house has its own well.

National monuments

The **Bibliothèque Nationale**, on rue Jamaa Zitouna is a very beautiful building with a spacious courtyard. It was originally built as a barracks in 1813 by Hammouda Husseinite and has now been converted into the National Library. Most books are in Arabic. Access is restricted to serious students.

Great Mosque Ez-Zitouna (The Olive Tree), rue Jamaa Zitouna is the largest and most venerable mosque in Tunis, built in 732 but some reports date it back to the foundation of the Islamic city in 698. The mosque is the centre of the medina and the old city expanded and developed around it, the most noble merchants being situated closer to the mosque (as for example the perfume sellers in the Souk el Attarine) whereas the less noble trades such as the dyers were relegated to the areas nearer the walls. All of the 184 columns surrounding the courtyard were brought from buildings in Carthage, giving an interesting architectural ensemble. The prayer room has antique columns and a finely sculpted stucco ceiling. Unfortunately, though, this part cannot be visited. Courtyard open to non-Muslims from 0930-1630 all year, closed Fri and Sun, entrance TD3.

Souk el Attarine Traditionally each perfume has a particular significance. For example, orange will be used at weddings. Although today this souk sells a wider range of goods, it is still possible to buy concentrates or perfume essences very cheaply. Other items for sale include candles and quilted baskets, traditional presents from the fiancé to his future bride.

Tourbet Aziza Othmana is at 9 Impasse Ech-Chammaia, off rue El Jelloud which leads towards the Great Mosque coming from rue de la Kasbah. Built c 1655, this is the tomb of the princess renowned for her generosity. Before dying she let her slaves go free and established a fund for a hospital, for poor girls who could not afford to marry and to provide fresh flowers for her tomb every day. Today the Tourbet is a private house and cannot be visited.

Tourbet and Mosque of Hammouda Pasha, rue Sidi Ben Arrous. The style of the mosque, built c 1655, shows a strong Italian influence, which is not surprising as Hammouda Pasha's father was Italian and converted to Islam in order to promote his career. The style is highly original and at the time was very innovative. This mosque influenced the style of the Bourguiba Mosque in Monastir.

Sidi Youssef Mosque is in Souk el Bey, just behind place du Gouvernement. An interesting mosque built in the 17th century by the Turks for the local Turkish merchants. It was architecturally innovative because it was the first mosque to have an octagonal minaret, setting the style for many future Turkish mosques.

Dar el Bey, place du Gouvernement. Built in 1795 this old royal guesthouse has been converted since Independence into the prime minister's office. It is an interesting building, particularly with regard to its Andalusian influences.

Medersa Mouradia College built in cloth market by Mourad II, son of Hammouda Pasha, in 1673. The huge studded door in a wide marble surround leads into a paved courtyard. Upstairs are the old narrow-doored students' rooms and prayer chamber. Young apprentices learn their crafts here today. Open 0930-1630 except Sun, entrance TD3.

Dar Hussein, place du Château. Built by Ismail Kahia (1758-1781) this is a beautiful mansion which was used by the French as their army headquarters while in Tunisia. With the coming of Independence it became the National Art and Archaeology Institute and houses beautiful manuscripts of the Koran, glassware from Kairouan and ceramics from Rakkada as well as valuable objects from other Islamic countries.

Dar el Haddad, Impasse de l'Artillerie. Built in the 16th century it is one of the oldest palaces in the medina and was once owned by a rich Andalusian, Said El Haddad El Andalousi. Over time it has been inhabited by many different families and left to fall into decay. It was bought by the city of Tunis in 1966 and declared a National Monument.

Tourbet el Bey, rue Tourbet el Bey. Built by Ali Pasha II (1758-1782), this mausoleum houses the tombs of the members of the royal family. Over the centuries, it has been extended many times with little regard to the overall harmony. The most prominent style is Italian and it is interesting to note the domes covered in green, scale shaped tiles. The previous leaders of the dynasty had been buried in the Tourbet Sidi Kacem, rue Sidi Kacem. An interesting building which can normally be visited 0930-1600 except Sun, entrance TD3.

Dar Ben Abdallah, built in 1796, houses the Centre of Popular Arts and Traditions where the collection of objects recreates bourgeois life in Tunis in the 19th century. There is a selection of gold embroidered/jewel encrusted costumes and unusually fine everyday objects. Open 0930-1630 except Sun, entrance TD3.

Mosque des Teinturiers (Dyers), rue des Teinturiers. Built by Hussein Ben Ali Tourki, the founder of the Husseinite dynasty, in 1716. No expenses seemed to have been spared, the ceramics coming from Turkey and the marble from Italy. Clearly influenced by the Sidi Youssef mosque with its octagonal minaret, it nevertheless has the novelty of sharing the central courtyard with a *medersa*.

Three Medressa These contain students' cells opening onto 3 sides of the courtyard with the mosque on the fourth side. The cloister round courtyard of **Medersa of the Palm Tree** (1714) is supported by horseshoe arches on stone columns with Turkish capitals. This surrounds a garden but the palm tree no longer exists. Black marble columns with white marble capitals support the arches in **Medersa Bachia** (1752). A stone fountain is incorporated in the design. The building is now a school for apprentice craftsmen. **Medersa Slimania** (1754) was built by Ali Pasha in memory of his son Suleimane who was poisoned by his brother. The entrance and courtyard are very beautiful and decorated with wonderful ceramics. It has now been converted into a cultural centre. Open 0930-1630 all year, closed Sun, entrance TD3.

Beaches

Tunis city has no beaches as it is on a highly polluted lake, but there are beaches nearby. The coast N from La Goulette is just one long beach. The preferred beaches tend to be further along at La Marsa and Gammarth. It is easy to reach them by taking the TGM to La Marsa which is probably better but gets crowded at weekends.

Parks

Belvédère Park is to the N of the city. To get there take the bus No 5 from place de l'Indépendence and get off at place Pasteur. It is then a short walk to this very large park which is pleasantly cool in summer. There is also a zoo and a museum of interesting contemporary Tunisian art. Tunis' other park, Jardin Thameur, in the centre of town, is attractive, well used and consequently crowded.

Local information

In town Around the ville nouvelle and Ave Bourguiba towards the medina you will find most of the cheap hotels, the shopping streets and the post office. On Ave Bourguiba are branches of most main banks and the large travel agencies and the tourist information office. To the S you will find the train station and the main bus and louages station for the S of the country.

● Accommodation

Price guide:

L	US$90+	D	US$20-40
A	US$75-90	E	US$10-20
B	US$60-75	F	under US$10
C	US$40-60		

Few of the cheaper hotels in the centre of Tunis have any character, and some prefer to cater for Tunisians rather than foreign travellers. Consider staying in pleasanter surroundings in Sidi Bou Saïd and visiting Tunis using the TGM. **AL** ***Africa Hotel***, 50 Ave Bourguiba, T 347477, 170 rm, a/c, 3 restaurants, 3 bars, movie theatre, pool, conference facilities; **A** ***Hotel des Ambassadeurs***, rue Hedi Chaker, T 288011, rooms facing the Belvédère Park, a/c, restaurant; **A** ***International Hotel***, 49 Ave Bourguiba, T 254855, 228 rm, central, good restaurants; **A** ***Mechtel Hotel***, T 783200, Ave Taieb Mehiri, Belvédère Park, 450 rm, pool.

B ***Hotel Gulf Royal***, Ave de la Yougoslavie, T 342422, expensive, poor value for money; **B** ***Hotel Ibn Khaldoun***, rue de Palestine, by the Marché Lafayette, T 783211, good, a/c, restaurant, organized entertainment; **B** ***Hotel Le Belvédère***, rue des Etats-Unis, T 783133, quiet, close to the Belvédère Park, a/c, restaurant; **B** ***Hotel Capitole***, 60 Ave Bourguiba, T 244997, clean, some rm with bath, bit expensive, noisy.

C ***Hotel Excel***, 35 Ave Bourguiba, T 355088, F 341929, central position, TV, no breakfast; **C** ***Hotel Tej***, 14 rue Lt. Aziz Tej, T 344899, clean, overpriced, a/c; **C** ***Hotel St. George***, 16 rue de Cologne, behind Ave de la Liberté, T 282937, 36 rm, 26 with bath, very good, clean hotel, a/c, restaurant, parking available; **C** ***Hotel du Lac***, Ave Bourguiba, central, T 258322, restaurant, 208 rm all a/c.

D ***Hotel de Suisse***, 5 rue de Suisse, T 243821, 23 rm, most with bath, clean, quiet, parking; **D** ***Hotel Majestic***, Ave de Paris, T 242848, old-fashioned, 100 rm, 40 with a/c, large terrace, central, restaurant; **D** ***Tunis Park Hotel***, 7 rue de Damas off Ave Taieb Mehiri by the Belvédère Park, T 286696, 28 rm, good, very quiet, restaurant; **D** ***Hotel Dar Masmoudi***, 18 rue du Maroc, off rue d'Algerie, T 342428, very close to medina, very quiet, most rm with bath; **D** ***Hotel Ritza***, 35 Ave Thameur, T 245428, close to the Thameur park, 30 rm, communal shower; **D** ***Hotel Transatlantique***, 106 Ave de Yougoslavie, T 240680, relatively quiet for a central hotel, most rm with bath, breakfast included; **D** ***Hotel Maison Dorée***, 6 rue de Hollande, just off Ave de la Yougoslavie behind the French Embassy, T 240632, has seen better days, good condition, spotlessly clean, good service, quite quiet, 54 rm with bath, breakfast included, restaurant; **D** ***Hotel Carlton***, 31 Ave Bourguiba, T 258167, clean, 40 rm with bath, a/c, slightly noisy position on main road, currently undergoing refurbishment.

E ***Hotel de France***, 8 rue Mustapha M'Barek, T 245876, very close to the *Hotel Commodore* and the medina, clean, 49 rm with bath, good value; **E** ***Hotel Commodore***, 17 rue d'Allemagne opposite the central market, T 244941, clean, quiet hotel just by the entrance to the medina, 48 rm, most have bath, no breakfast; **E** ***Hotel Salammbo***, 6 rue de Grèce, off Ave Bourguiba, T 337498, clean hotel, 52 rm, most with bath.

F ***Nouvelle Hotel***, T 243379, 3 place Mongi Bali, next to the station, could be cleaner, communal showers, noisy; **F** ***Hotel Cirta***, 42 Ave Charles de Gaulle, T 241582, communal pay showers, very cheap; **F** ***Hotel de l'Agriculture***, 25 Ave Charles de Gaulle, T 246394, opposite *Hotel Cirta*, very quiet situation, clean; **F** ***Hotel Crystal***, Ave de Carthage, quiet, clean, communal shower; **F** ***Hotel de Bretagne***, 7 Ave de Grèce, T 242146, 25 rm, quite clean and quiet; **F *Hotel Continental***, 5 rue de Marseille, T 259834, very quiet and cheap, communal shower; **F *Gare Hotel***, rue de Gare, recommended; **F *Hotel Rex***, 65 rue de Yougoslavie, T 257397, 29 rm, communal pay shower, rather depressing; **F *Hotel de la Victoire***, 7 Bab el Menara, T 26, 20 rm (those on front are noisy), communal shower, clean, best of this category.

● Youth hostels

1) Radès, 10 km SW of Tunis, T 483631, 120 beds, meals provided, take the train from the main station, a 10 minute walk from Radès station; 2) In the medina, 25 rue Saida Ajoula, T 567850, 70 beds, 500m from place du Gouvernement la kasbah, 1.5 km from central station; 3) *Centre d'hébergement Jelili ez Zahra*, Oued Meliane Ezzahara, BP1140, T 481547, 72 beds, kitchen, meals provided, take bus No 26A from place Barcelone; 4) Possibility of staying in the Bardo University campus in the summer, contact T 784241, rue du Mali, Tunis.

● Camping

Le Moulin Bleu, Hammam Plage, 20 km S of Tunis.

● Places to eat

Price guide: ♦♦♦Expensive; ♦♦average; ♦cheap.

NB: it is better not to eat fish on Mon as the fresh fish market is closed on Sun.

♦♦♦ ***Chez Slah***, 14 rue Pierre de Coubertin, T 258588, perhaps the best restaurant in Tunis, highly recommended but the bill will be large, good idea to book; ***Dar Jeld***, rue Dar Jeld in the medina, off place du Gouvernement, very good traditional Tunisian cooking set in an old house, a great night out with entertainment provided most evenings, closed Sun. ***L'Etable***, Ave Bourguiba, near place de l'Afrique, Tunisian specialities, alcohol; ***Bagdad***, Ave Bourguiba, very good Tunisian food, recommended; ***Chez Nous***, rue de Marseille, French cooking with some Tunisian specialities, alcohol; ***La Mama***, rue de Marseille, mixture of French and traditional Tunisian cooking, alcohol; ***Cosmos***, rue Ibn Khaldoun, very good food, especially the fish, service slow; ***Le Poisson Doré***, rue Ibn Khaldoun, specializes in seafood; ***La Trattoria***, 44 Ave Bourguiba, beside *Africa Hotel*.

♦♦ ***Cafè Zitouna***, Jamaa Zitouna in medina, Tunisian food served amid beautiful tiled decorations.

♦ ***Restaurant Novelty***, rue de Paris, self-service, very good, a warm welcome, cheap food, no alcohol, try the *coucha*; ***Midi Minuit***, Ave Bourguiba, Tunisian specialities including couscous and *tajine*; ***Le Carcassonne***, Ave de Carthage, very clean, cheap and good; ***Le Prince***, place de Barcelone, opposite the train station, self-service, clean, cheap, very good typical Tunisian food; ***Le Roi d'Espagne***, rue de Lénine, off rue de France, good food in a very simple setting, alcohol. ***Cafè Africa***, beside *Africa Hotel* for mint tea and an opportunity to watch the crowds.

● Banks

BIAT, Ave Bourguiba (American Express); **STB**, Ave Bourguiba, by the *Africa Hotel*, open daily 0700-1900 (Visa and Mastercard); **UBCI**, Ave Bourguiba (Visa and Mastercard); **BT**, (Visa and Mastercard); **American Express**, c/o Carthage Tour, 59 Ave Bourguiba, T 254820, open 0800-1900, Sun 0900-1200.

● Chemists

All night, 43 Ave Bourguiba, opposite *Africa Hotel*; 20 Ave de la Liberté, by Ave de Madrid; 44 Ave Bab Djedid.

● Discotheques/Night clubs

Most night clubs are outside Tunis centre along the N coast. However, most large 4 star hotels in town have night clubs. At Sidi Bou Said: *La Barraka*. At La Marsa: *Le Galaxy* by the *Hotel Tour Blanche*. This would appear to be the club most in fashion. In Tunis centre there are also a few cabarets: *Monseigneur*, 2 rue de Marseille; *La Potinière*, 11 rue de Hollande.

● Embassies & consulates

Algeria, 136 Ave de la Liberté, T 280082; **Canada** (and Australian affairs), 3 rue Didon, T 286577; **Egypt**, 16 rue Essayouti, T 230004; **France**, Place de l'Indépendence, T 245700; **Germany**, 18 Ave Challaye, T 281246; **Italy**, rue de Russie, T 361811 (open 0930-1130); **Ivory Coast**, 6 rue Ibn Charaf, T 283878; **Jordan**, 4 rue Didon, T 288401; **Libya**, 48 bis rue du 1 Juin, T 283936; **Morocco**, 39 rue du 1 Juin, T 288063; **Netherlands**, 6 rue Meycen, T 287455; **Norway**, 7 Ave Bourguiba, T 245933; **Senegal**, 122 Ave de la Liberté, T 282393; **Sweden**, 87 Ave Taieb Mehri, T 283433; **Switzerland**, 10 rue ech-Chenkiti, 1002 Belvédère, T 795957; **UK**, 5 place de la Victoire, T 245100; **USA**, 144 Ave de la Liberté, T 282566.

Hammams
Turkish baths, are an institution in Tunisia. Everybody goes there once a week. It is a revitalizing experience and well worth a visit. The morning is reserved for men and the afternoon (until 1800 after which the men can return) for women. Rue du Maroc, next to *Hotel Dar Masmoudi*, rue de Marseille, level with No 42, just off Ave Bourguiba. There are also many older ones in the medina (see map 501) and a few on rue du Pasha.

Hospitals
Hôpital Principal Aziza Othmana, place du Gouvernement, T 633655; Hôpital Charles Nicolle, T 663000.

Post office
Main PTT rue Charles de Gaulle, open Mon-Thur 0730-1230 and 1700-1900, Fri-Sat 0730-1330, Sun 0900-1100. A 24-hour telephone centre is off rue Gamal Abdul Nasser.

Shopping
Bookshops There are many **book shops** in rue de France, but most books are in Arabic or French. The only English books can be found in the *Africa Hotel* and they are generally not very good. If you read Arabic or French go to Librairie Clairefontaine, 4 rue d'Alger. There is also an interesting book shop, Librarie Alif, which often puts on small exhibitions at 3 rue de Hollande (behind the French Embassy).

Handicrafts Tunisian craftsmanship can be excellent and it is possible (after a bit of bargaining) to get a very good deal. Leather goods and brass objects are plentiful and of very good quality. The best place to go, at least to find out the official prices and have an overall idea of crafts produced, is the ***Office National de l'Artisanat (ONAT)*** on Ave Mohammed V, just beyond the Tourist Office, off place de l'Afrique has a showroom of local crafts and arts from around Tunisia. It is interesting to go there before leaving Tunis, as you will see the local diversities and specialities. It is also worth seeing the prices before entering the souks. They also have a list of the official prices for carpets according to the quality. You will find many of these, among lots of less interesting goods, in the medina in rue Jemaa Zitouna. Be selective.

By the Great Mosque, the ***Souk el Attarine*** specializes in perfumes and precious stones. Amber is generally well worked but watch out for plastic imitations (amber resists the heat of a match). **Jewellery** can be found in the ***Souk des Orfèvres***, and ***Souk el-Berka***. For **carpets and blankets** go to ***Souk el Leffa***, but carpets are generally cheaper in Kairouan. If you get a carpet be sure you have the receipt and that there is a quality stamp on the back. For **leather**, go to the ***Souk el-Sekkajine***, but be warned that the quality is sometimes mediocre.

Souvenirs If you are not looking for souvenirs, the best place to go is Ave Charles de Gaulle in the new city. You will find supermarkets (*Monoprix*), chemists, and camera shops.

Sport & recreation
Diving, the Centre Nautique International de Tunisie, 22 rue de Medine, T 282209, for information about diving and fishing; they also organize diving holidays on the island of Zembra (off the tip of Cap Bon).

Golf, there is an 18 hole course at La Soukra (close to the airport), T 765919.

Gliding, at the Federal Centre at Djebel Rassas near Tunis.

Swimming pools at El Menza (Cité Olympique) and the piscine municipale in Belvédère Park, by place Pasteur. You can also try the large 4 star hotels, *Hotel Africa* has a pool on the 3rd floor.

Tennis in the Belvédère Park and Park des Sports, Ave Mohammed V.

Telephone
Local code 01. Emergency numbers: **Police** and **Fire station** T 197, **Ambulance** T 491286, Doctor T 341250, T 346767.

Tourist information
Tunisian National Tourist Office, 1 Ave Mohammed V (place de l'Afrique), T 341077, F 350997, open 0730-1330 in summer, 0830-1200 and 1500-1800 in winter, closed Sun and public holidays; **ONTT**, branches at railway station and airport, also at 51 Ave de la Liberté; **Regional Tourist Office for Tunis**, 29 rue Hatem Ettai (corner of rue de la Palestine), T 289403/288720, Tx 15347.

Travel agents
La Maison du Voyage, Ave Gamal Abdul Nasser, beside the post office; ***Tourafrica***, Ave Bourguiba, next to *Africa Hotel*; ***Sedec*** Tour, rue de Marseille; ***Tunisian Travel Service***, 19 Ave Bourguiba, T 348100.

Transport
Local: Bus You will probably not need to use more than a few routes during your stay in Tunis. For more information go to the bus

station in front of the railway station on place de Barcelone. Bus No 3 leaves from Ave Bourguiba in front of Tunis Air, or from Ave de Paris in front of the *Hotel Majestic* and goes to the Bardo Museum and S bus station. Bus No 5 leaves from place de l'Indépendence and goes to place Pasteur by Belvédère Park. Bus No 35 leaves from Ave Bourguiba for a 30 min ride to the airport.

Car hire **Avis**, Ave Bourguiba, in the *Africa Hotel* lobby, Ave Bourguiba, T 341249; **Ben Jemaa**, Excelsior Garage, 53 Ave de Paris, T 240060; **Budget**, 14 Ave de Carthage, T 256806; **Carthage Tours**, 59 Ave Bourguiba, T 254605; **Chartago Rent**, 3 Ave Bourguiba, T 349168; **Europacar**, 17 Ave Bourguiba, T 340308; **Garage selection**, 65 Ave Hedi Chaker, T 284698; **Hertz**, 29 Ave Bourguiba, T 248559; **Topcar**, 23 Ave Bourguiba, T 344121.

Metro There is a brand new tramway system in Tunis which is rapidly expanding. At present there are 5 lines but many more are under construction. The tramway is the city's answer to severe congestion and has so far been successful. The central tram station is at the train station and another large station is on place de la République.

Taxis are quite cheap but can be difficult to find, particularly at rush hour. The maximum you should have to pay is about TD4-5 and that is for a long trip to La Marsa. All taxis have meters and use them, so make sure they have switched it on. The best place to find a taxi is in front of the main railway station. Most taxis are painted yellow, but this is a recent decision and some older taxis are different colours.

Train TGM: the TGM (Tunis-La Goulette-La Marsa) is the train linking Tunis to the coastal resorts and suburbs. The station is at the end of Ave Bourguiba, beyond place de l'Afrique. It is open 24 hours a day with trains every 10-15 mins during the day and every hour at night. The service goes to La Goulette, Carthage, Sidi Bou Said and La Marsa.

Air To get to the airport either take a taxi or bus No 35 from Ave Bourguiba, opposite *Africa Hotel*, 30 min.

Internal flights (Airport T 235000, 236000) to **Djerba**: Mon 1445 and 2100, Tue and Wed 2000, Thur 2000 and 2105, Fri 1900, 2100 and 2105, Sat and Sun 2100; **Tozeur** Thur 1400, Fri 1400 and 2105; **Monastir** Mon 1210; **Sfax** Thur 1310. Tunis Air subsidiary Tunisavia have introduced more flights using small 72 seater planes. This should increase the number of flights for Tozeur and Djerba. In summer it is important to book well in advance as places are hard to come by.

International flights, winter schedule (there are additional flights in summer): **London** Mon 1550, Thur 1535, Fri and Sun 1325; **Paris** daily at 1300 and 1750; **Brussels** Tue 1030, Wed 1450, Sat 0835, Sun 1450; **Casablanca** Mon 1200, Tue, Thur and Sun 0930, Wed 1730, Sat 1315; **Algiers** Mon and Sat 1145, Tue and Wed 1145 and 1640, Thur 0950 and 1145, Fri 1640 and 1810, Sun 1550; **Tripoli** Mon 0810, Thur 1700; **Cairo** Wed 1100, Sat 1610.

Airline information: Aeroflot, 24 Ave Thameur, T 340845; Air Algérie, 28 Ave de Paris, T 341590; Air France, 1 rue d'Athènes, T 341577; GB Air, 17 Ave Bourguiba, T 244261; Egypt Air, 49 Ave Bourguiba, T 341182 in the *International Hotel* ; KLM, 50 Ave Bourguiba; Lufthansa, Ave Ouled Haffouz, close to the Belvédère Park, in the *Mechtel Hotel*; Royal Air Maroc, 45 Ave Bourguiba T 249016, in the Le Colisée building, B stairs, 3rd floor; Tunis Air, 48 Ave Bourguiba, T 259189, central office 133 Ave de la Liberté, T 288100.

Train The main station is in the centre of the new city on place de Barcelone. Information on T 244440/427. **National departures**: **Bizerte** 0550, 1130, 1600, 1830; **Gabès** 0710, 2120; **Sousse** 0710, 1205, 1530 (to Monastir and Mahdia), 1305, 1410, 1730 (to El Djem and Sfax), 1840 (stops at Monastir), 2120 (to Metlaoui via El Djem, Sfax and Gafsa).

To **Algeria**: only one train goes on to Algiers, all the others stop at the border. **Algiers** 1255; **Ghardimaou** (border) 0635, 1200, 1425, 1620, 1750. All trains go via Béja and Djendouba (except the 1425).

Road Bus There are 2 bus stations in Tunis. The **N bus station** is situated at Bab Saadoun. To get there take the bus No 3 from Ave Bourguiba opposite *Hotel Africa*. Get off just after Bab Saadoun, the bus station is on the right. Buses from here go to the N coast. For information about buses to the N, T 562299/562532.

Departures: **Bizerte** from 0630-2000 every half hour, 10 a/c buses daily; **Raf-Raf** 1300, 1730 on Sun 0800; **Ras Jebel** 0730, 0830; **Aïn Draham** (via Béja) 0530, 0700, 1230, 1400; **Tabarka** (via Béja) 0630, 1330, 1630; **Tabarka** (via Mateur) 1000, 1130, 1230, 1430, 1530; **Béja** (via El Medjez) 0800,

0930, 1300, 1430, 1530, 1830; **Djendouba** (via Béja) 0900, 1000, 1100, 1600, 1700; **Le Kef** 0800, 0900, 1100, 1930; **Thala** (via Le Kef) 0700, 1400, 1500, 1600; **Teboursouk** 0830, 1630. Buses to **Le Kef** also stop here.

The **S bus station** is at Bab El Fellah and has buses to all other places including Algeria and Libya. To reach the station walk from the main train station, a distance of 800m. Take the rue de La Gare on the right of the station, at the end of the street the station is on the other side of the road. For information about buses to the S, T 495255/490391.

Departures: **Kairouan** 0930, 1030; (via Enfida) 1230, 1600, 1700 and (via El Fahs) 1500; **Kasserine** (most of these go via Kairouan) 0600, 0730, 1030, 1330, 1430, 1600; **Kebili** 1200, 1930; **Tataouine** 0930, 1900; **Ben Gardane** 1100, 2040; Djerba 0810, 2000; **Douz** 0800, 2100; **Tozeur** 1100, 1630; **Nefta** (and Tozeur) 1300, 2100; **Matmata** 2015; **Zarzis** 2030; **Medenine** 2115; **Gafsa** 0600, 1500; **Sousse** 0600, 0830, 1100, 1200, 1500. Hourly buses to **Hammamet** and **Nabeul** through which most buses going S pass. Also 7 buses a day to **Sfax** and **Gabès**. All buses going to Tataouine, Medenine, Ben Gardane and Matmata go via **Sfax** and **Sousse**. **El Djem** (via Sousse) 0710, 1410, 1730, 1805, 2120.

Buses to Algeria, Libya and Morocco: **Algeria** (Annaba) daily at 0700; **Libya** (Tripoli) Mon, Wed, Fri and Sun at 0700; **Morocco** (Casablanca) Sat at 0630.

NB: during the summer it can be difficult to get a seat on a bus. You may have to put up a bit of a fight at the ticket office. The best thing is to book. This service is available for most lines, but it is best to check.

Louages are large taxis that take 5 people and go from one city to another. The city names shown do not necessarily indicate where the car is going, but only where it is licensed. The louage stations are sited next to bus stations, at the front of the N station and to the left of the S station. If going S during the summer you will find that most louages go in the evening or at night, as it is cooler.

● Sea

Ferry information, see page 594.

AROUND TUNIS

The area to the NE of Tunis encompasses the important historical sites, the most expensive suburbs and the nearest beaches. Take the dual carriageway W from place de l'Afrique.

La Goulette

ACCESS from Tunis is very easy by the TGM or the road that runs alongside it on the causeway. There is a very practical, free ferry service between La Goulette and Radès which enables travellers going S to bypass Tunis. The service runs 24 hours a day. The harbour has berths for 60 yachts, min-max draft, 3-6m.

La Goulette (The Gullet) is at the narrow entrance to the Lake of Tunis and is the main harbour of Tunis. It is dominated by a fortress built by Charles V of Spain in 1535, when he assisted the Hafsids fight against Barbarossa. It functions as a harbour, an important naval base, a dormitory for Tunis and also as a highly industrialized area. Nevertheless in summer it is a very pleasant place to go for a meal of fresh fish or just to stroll. The main street, with restaurants and bars everywhere, comes to life in the evening.

From the **Fortress of Karraka** enjoy a splendid view over the harbour and the Gulf of Tunis. The fortress was a prison and has a gruesome history. Entrance TD1.

● **Places to eat** The best grilled fish restaurants are situated by the port. Try ***La Petite Etoile***, ***Café Vert*** and ***L'An 2000***. Cheaper restaurants can be found on the side roads.

Carthage

Carthage is now one of the smart suburbs of Tunis, well placed close to the sea. The remains of the old city of Carthage can be visited at various locations in the area, but there is little left of the grandeur. Nevertheless, the old Roman and Punic ruins are well worth seeing, to give an idea of past splendours.

History

According to Virgil, Carthage was founded in 814 BC by the Princess Dido (Didon). She was the one with the initiative and a sharp knife who wangled a piece of land large enough to build a new city – **Kart Hadascht**. It soon became a major power and trade centre, attempting to rival both the Greeks and the Romans by setting its sights, unsuccessfully, on Sicily. Everybody knows the extraordinary story of **Hannibal** (see box, page 512), who crossed the Alps with 40,000 men and 38 elephants to attack Rome. Unfortunately, the Romans eventually took revenge and Scipio's armies won a decisive battle in Zama in 202 BC. Carthage was subjected to a siege lasting 3 years and was eventually seized and razed to the ground in 146 BC to the delight of Cato who had had this in mind for some time.

However this was not to be the end of Carthage as the Romans, under Caesar in 44 BC, returned to make it the capital of the Roman Province of Afrique. At this time Carthage was known as Rome's bread basket due to its highly fertile hinterland. It later collapsed as a significant power after the successive invasions of the Vandals, Byzantines and Arabs. After the Arab invasion, Carthage was mainly used as a source of building material for Islamic monuments and the expanding city of Tunis. (See History of North Africa, **p** 57).

ACCESS From Tunis drive along the causeway and through La Goulette or take the TGM from the end of Ave Bourguiba. The stations are strategically situated for visiting the sites or, as an alternative, *calèches* are available at Carthage Hannibal station.

Things to see

All sites here open 0800-1900 summer, 0830-1730 winter, entrance TD4.

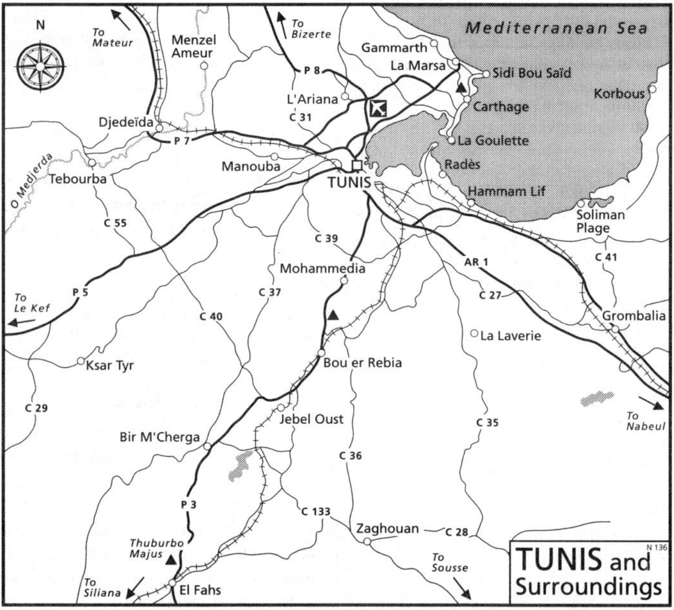

TUNIS and Surroundings

Local information

● Accommodation

A *Hotel Reine Didon*, on Byrsa Hill, T 275344, close to the museum, 22 rm, expensive, very quiet, overlooking the sea, excellent restaurant.

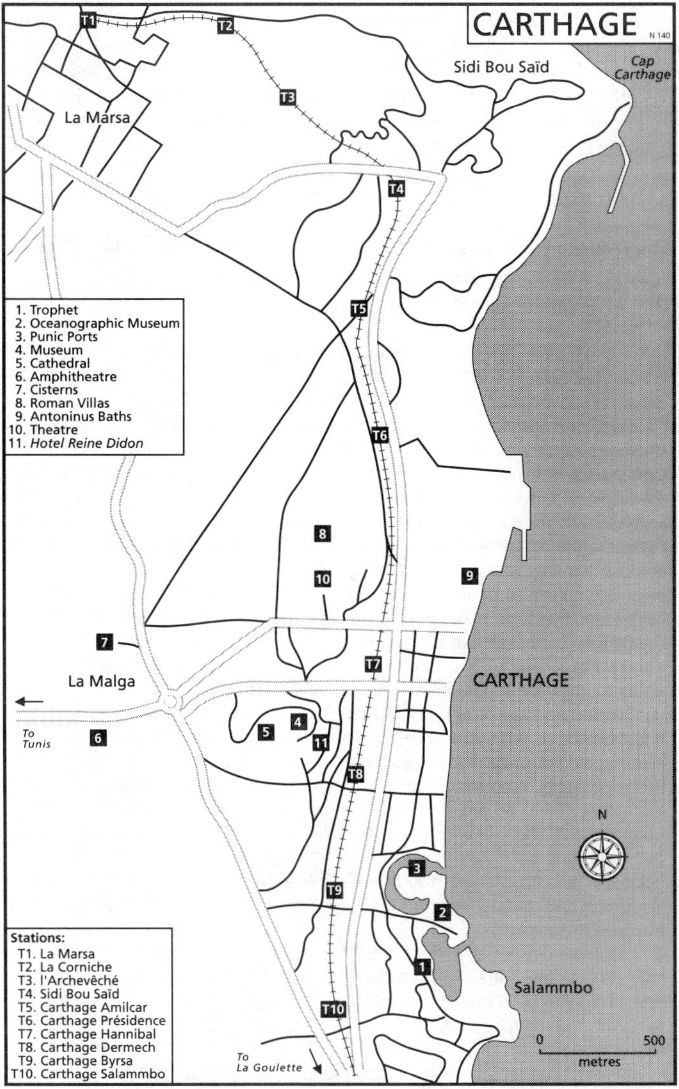

Tophet, Oceanographic Museum and the Punic Ports

Get off at the TGM station at Carthage Salammbo and walk down towards the sea. First is the Tophet (crematorium) and then along the road, on the right, the Oceanographic Museum and the Punic Ports. It is then only a short walk up to the TGM station Carthage Byrsa.

At **Tophet** are the remains of the sanctuary of the Carthaginian divinities Tanit and Baal. There is not much left to see. According to legend the Carthaginians brought their children here to be ritually sacrificed and urns containing ashes and remains of many children have in fact been found. Whether sacrifices actually occurred and how frequently is still unknown, but opinion tends to confirm that they did take place, along with a much more important form of animal sacrifice. The **Oceanographic Museum** is of most interest to those who are keen on fish and fishing.

The **Punic Ports** The main harbour used

Hannibal: Jumbos In The Passes And Carnage By Carthage

Hannibal, unfortunately recalled by many only as the man who crossed the Alps with a herd of elephants, deserves far greater acclaim.

He was one of the greatest army commanders of ancient times, recognized for his innovative military strategies and his charismatic leadership.

He was born in Carthage in 247 BC, the son of the military leader Hamilcar Barca. He spent much of his early life in regions of Spain then controlled by Carthage, fighting wayward Spanish tribes and consolidating Carthaginian power. He made such an impression that at the age of 26 he was promoted to Commander-in-Chief of the Carthaginian army. His expansionist policies upset the Romans and led to the Second Punic War with Hannibal commanding the Carthaginian side. In a bold manoeuvre he advanced on Roman Italy, crossing the Pyrenees, the Rhône in France and the Alps. He started this incredible military exercise leaving Spain with some 40,000 troops, numerous horses and 38 elephants to use as battering rams. He lost men by desertion, guerrilla warfare by the Gauls and natural causes, but gained supporters on the way. His arrival in the Po Basin, most probably via the Mt Cenis Pass, with 20,000 infantry, 6,000 cavalry and a handful of elephants showed conclusively Hannibal's considerable ability to organize and command. It was surely a glorious feat.

The first encounter between Hannibal's troops and Scipio's Roman forces sent N to meet them, was on the plains W of the Ticino river. Here Hannibal's numerically inadequate cavalry gained the upper hand. Their second meeting, known as the Battle of Trebia River, also went in Hannibal's favour. The Battle of Trasimene in the spring of 217 BC left thousands of Romans dead and Hannibal triumphant. Hannibal had one further impressive victory at Cannae where despite being far outnumbered, his troops encircled and trapped the Romans, and by attacking from the rear slaughtered about 50,000 enemy troops in one day. Hannibal's leadership and military tactics thus brought about the worst defeat ever suffered by the Roman army.

Hannibal did not take the opportunity to march on Rome but remained in Italy and, despite suffering from extended supply lines, a lack of naval support and allies who gave greater consideration to affairs of their own, continued to harass the Romans. His fighting strength gradually weakened and the Roman strategy of avoiding direct confrontation allowed him only minor victories.

Meanwhile the Carthaginians were forced out of Spain by Scipio, the Roman to be the very heart of Carthaginian prosperity. The N basin boasting safe anchorage for 220 vessels was the naval base and the S base was for merchant ships.

The museum, amphitheatre, theatre and Roman Villas Alight at TGM station Carthage Hannibal. Walk up Ave de la République to the museum on the left. Down the other side of the hill the amphitheatre is on one side of the road and a collection of cisterns on the other. Returning towards the sea down Ave Didon on the left is the theatre behind which lie the Roman Villas. If you visit the Basilicas of Damou and St Cyprien next then backtrack to the Baths of Antoninus you will have visited all the major sites and be back at the TGM station.

The **museum** is situated behind the cathedral and is divided into 3 sections, Punic, Roman and Christian. It is a worthwhile stop but is somewhat overshadowed by the magnificent collection in the Bardo museum.

In the **amphitheatre** early Christians were thrown to the lions and gladiators as entertainment for the audience. Unfortunately there is very little to see since only limited excavation work has been carried out.

The **cisterns** were the main reservoirs for the Carthage water supply. Today they are in a bad state.

The **theatre** has been completely restored and is currently used for the annual Carthage Festival. The building is not very interesting in itself as it is not very true to the original, but the festival receives great praise. The **Roman Villas** have also been restored badly.

The **Antoninus Baths** used to be the biggest baths in North Africa and were truly enormous. They are in a splendid position by the sea and are one of the best preserved sites in Carthage. Even though there are only a few pieces of building still standing they give a good idea of the grandeur that was.

general who went on to invade Africa in 204 BC. Hannibal at this point abandoned his campaign in Italy and rushed home to protect his country. Despite the peace proposals agreed between Scipio and the Carthaginian army, Hannibal broke the armistice and concentrated the remaining forces on present day Sousse. Details differ on the campaign which followed that culminated in the Battle of Zama, but in essence Hannibal's troops were defeated, over 20,000 men died and Hannibal fled. A treaty was signed between Rome and Carthage in 201 BC, a disappointing end for Hannibal to his military career.

Carthage was allowed a deal of self government by the Romans, with Hannibal a leading figure. While Carthage recovered rapidly under his hands he was not universally popular and it is understood that his speedy removal to Ephesus was to avoid arrest. He outstayed his welcome in Ephesus, his advice to King Antiochus on how to conduct his war against Rome was not heeded and when Syria lost the war in 190 BC, part of the price was Hannibal's surrender. Accounts vary on what followed but eventually by 183 BC, the Romans were in a position to demand his surrender. To avoid arrest, at the age of 64, Hannibal committed suicide.

Sidi Bou Saïd

Sidi Bou Said station is 10 min walk from the centre. The village is beautiful, a pleasant place to stay in contrast to Tunis. It is built on a cliff facing the Mediterranean, all the white painted houses having blue doors. The buildings go all the way down to the sea, ending by the small port. The narrow, winding streets follow the curves of the hill, and provide a most interesting walk. The architecture is superb and the houses have been very well preserved. There is an excellent view from the top of the hill where there is a small cemetery on the right.

For refreshments try the picturesque but expensive Moorish *Café des Nattes* in the cobbled square in the centre of the village. Another place to have a drink, particularly at sunset, is the *Café Sidi Chabaane*, situated at the end of the village. The view from here over the sea is quite exceptional. Follow the walk down to the harbour and along the path which continues back up the hill at the end of the Cap. Being on every tourist's itinerary Sidi Bou Saïd can get very crowded, especially in summer, but most people tend to congregate in the main streets and it is possible to find some peace in the small back streets.

• **Accommodation B** *Hotel Amilcar*, at the foot of Sidi Bou Saïd cliff, T 270788, all rm have a view over the Gulf looking towards the Cap Bon peninsula, private beach, pool. **D** *Sidi Bou Said*, on a hill slightly out of the village, T 740411, 34 rm, good standard, unfortunately no sea view. **E** *Hotel Boufares*, central, T 740091, a wonderful little hotel, 8 rm centred around a shaded patio in a typical house, very clean and cheap, very cold in winter months, excellent breakfast, it is vital to book in the summer season.

• **Places to eat** There is not much choice here. ♦♦♦ *Restaurant Pirates*, by the harbour at the bottom of the cliff specializes in fish and sea-food, expensive but worth it as the food is excellent. ♦ *Restaurant La Bagatelle*, at the bottom of the hill before the village, good setting, good, cheap food, very popular; *Restaurant Chergui* on the main street, on the right of the *Café des Nattes*, large terrace with a fantastic view, food is good value. There are lots of stalls selling nuts and sticky sweets.

• **Services Bank** UBCI, in the new town at the bottom of the hill, on the road to La Goulette. **Chemist** All night chemist next to the bank. **Hammam** near the bank, clean, recommended. **Harbour** has berths for 380 yachts, min-max draft 2-4m.

La Marsa

This town lies at the TGM terminus and is relaxed and quiet, full of luxurious villas. It has a beautiful beach lined with palm trees, far away from the bustle of Tunis and therefore popular at weekends, especially in summer. There is little to do apart from sit on the beach, in a restaurant or in a café. Accommodation is expensive along the coast, most of the hotels being three or four star. D *Hotel Plaza*, rue du Maroc, 5 mins from TGM station, beautiful surroundings. Have a drink at the *Café Safsaf*, and try some of their pastries or Tunisian cooking. In front of the café is an old well operated by an unfortunate camel walking round in circles.

Gammarth

Here, there is a long line of expensive villas, luxury hotels and restaurants strung along the coast. However it is possible to reach the beach to the N beyond the hotels (most of them are right on the beach). The beach is good, but crowded in summer, when it can be noisy and the litter builds up.

• **Accommodation B** *Abou Nawas*, T 271444, 80 bungalows with a/c, pool in summer, good beach, all sport activities are organized. **B** *Megara*, on Blvd Taieb Mehiri, T 270366, Moorish decor, 77 rm, large pool, lovely gardens. **C** *La Tour Blanche*, T 271697, is situated a little way up from the coast and therefore has a view, pool, *The Galaxy* – the trendiest night club in Tunis – is attached.

• **Places to eat** These are generally expensive. ♦♦♦ *Les Dunes hotel*, Baie des Singes, *Le Pêcheur*, beyond *Les Dunes*.

The road continues NW through the sand dunes and reaches Tunis via the P8.

Zaghouan

Lying 60 km S of Tunis, Zaghouan has a regular bus service from Tunis. A complex system of cisterns and aqueducts once carried fresh water over 132 km, following the contours to Carthage. Parts of the aqueduct can still be seen on the road from Tunis. Zaghouan is dominated by the towering 1,300m high Djebel Zaghouan. The spring and the beginning of the aqueduct can be visited, about 2 km out of town. A few reservoirs can still be seen, but the real interest is the beauty of the site.

• **Accommodation** C *Djebel el Oust*, T 79740, Complex Thermal, Djebel el Oust, bungalows, a/c in public rooms, views towards mountains; **C** ***Les Nymphes***, T 75094, Zaghouan 1100, PO Box 11, 1.5 km out of town towards Roman aqueduct. **Youth hostel** *Maison des Jeunes*, Zaghouan, 85 beds, meals available, T 75265.

• **Telephone** Local code 02.

Jebel Oust, 30 km from Tunis is one of Tunisia's three main health spas.

Thuburbo Majus

This is 55 km S down the P3 from Tunis. Access by bus or louage from Tunis. Get off at Fahs and walk or get a taxi. If coming from Tunis, ask the driver to stop at Thuburbo Majus (before you get to El Fahs) from which it is a short walk to the site. It is better not to follow the signposts, but to cut across between the 2 hills, just behind the signpost.

History

Thuburbo Majus was originally a Punic city, but when the Romans conquered Carthage they agreed to pay dues to Rome and so survived. In 27 BC the Emperor Augustus founded a colony of veterans in order to control the strategic situation of the city. Thuburbo Majus was placed in a central position, between the fertile lands of central Tunisia and the coast. The Punic heritage mixed well with the Roman presence and it was at this time that most of the major monuments were constructed, such as the Capitol and the Baths.

Things to see

The **Forum** and the **Capitol** dominate the ruins. The forum is well preserved and a statue of Jupiter from the Capitol has been taken to the Bardo. There is evidence that some of the buildings behind the Capitol were converted into olive oil presses. Olive oil was an important product exported from Thuburbo Majus. The **Temple of Mercury** is an example of the refined architecture of the

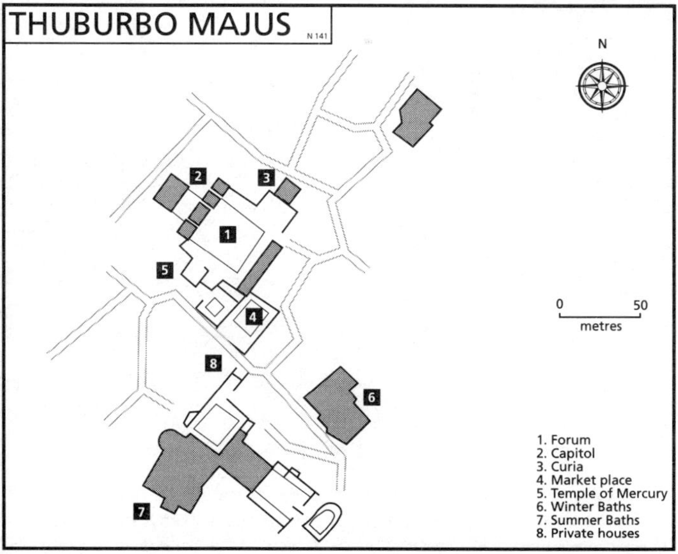

time, while the existence of baths and gymnasia shows that the town must have been wealthy. The site is interesting and the view over the surrounding area towards Djebel Zaghouan is impressive. Open 0800-1200 and 1500-1900 in summer and 0930-1630 in winter, closed Mon, entrance TD2.

Local information

● Accommodation

There is no accommodation at or near the site. Thuburbo Majus makes a good day trip from Tunis, returning via Zaghouan. The nearest **youth hostel** is in Zaghouan convenient for travellers going E to Enfida and Sousse.

To the E lies **Radès**. **Youth hostel**, Banlieu Sud, T 483631, 10 km from Tunis, 10 mins from Radès station, 56 beds, meals available, ring to book as it takes groups and can get full.

Further E, **Borj Cedria** has a good beach used by people from Tunis at weekends and in summer. Many of them come out by train. The German cemetery commemorating all who fell in the Tunisian campaign between Nov 1942 and May 1943 is down a small signposted road, opposite the station and to the left of the café.

● **Accommodation** **C** *Salwa*, T 290764, 116 rm, pool; **C** *Dar*, T 290188, 144 beach bungalows.

To the W lies **Massicault** with **Commonwealth World War II cemetery** at Borjel Amri (1,576 graves), 28 km SW of Tunis to the N side of the P5. Open 0730-1430 Sat-Thur.

CAP BON PENINSULA

Contents

Maps

This region, protruding like a thumb into the Mediterranean, was an essential part of the Roman Empire for food supplies. Today it is the source of fresh fruit and early vegetables for much of Europe and of Tunisian wine from its 33,000 ha of vineyards. Furthermore, with the growth of the all year holiday hotels built along the beautiful sandy beaches, it is the Tunisia of the package tourist.

TUNIS TO HAMMAMET

Hammamet

Hammamet, 65 km SE from Tunis, is probably one of the best known resorts in Tunisia. A once small, sleepy village adjoining a beautiful beach, it now has a population of 30,000 and welcomes tourists in their thousands. The change has been very carefully executed, with attention to the preservation of the site, no hotel permitted higher than a palm tree! The development of the town started in the 1920s, when Rumanian millionaire, **George Sebastian**, built a beautiful villa and invited many of his artistic friends such as Paul Klee, André Gide and Frank Lloyd Wright to visit. In 1959, George Sebastian's house was bought by the state and made into an International Cultural Centre. An open air theatre was built in the extensive grounds 4 years later. A very interesting **international festival** is held here annually in Jul/Aug, with dance, theatre and music (ranging from jazz to classical). During most of the year the house and gardens can be visited.

The town has kept some of its charm, even though a commercial centre (find the banks and a supermarket here) was recently constructed. Equally the medina, surrounded by its walls and lying adjacent to the sea, has kept its attraction. Escape from the tourist shops and walk around the small back streets. Ignore the museum in the kasbah but visit the small café at the top of the walls, with the view of the sea and the fishermen sorting nets near their colourful boats. The fishermen work at night, attracting the fish by means of powerful lamps.

ACCESS Frequent buses and trains come from Tunis and a train runs from Monastir airport. Buses and taxis stop near the medina. The station is a short walk away, or share a taxi.

Things to see

The **Medina** is the main landmark in Hammamet, built right on the beach. Originally constructed in 904, frequently damaged and restored, the walls protect the **Great Mosque**, the baths and the narrow, winding streets containing numerous stalls intent on attracting the tourists and the fresh food stalls of the daily market.

The **Kasbah** was originally built in the 12th century and has now been restored. It is more impressive as a setting than as a place to visit.

Local information

● Accommodation

As there are lots of expensive hotels along the coast to the N and to the S of the town, it is easy to find somewhere to stay. These same rooms, however, are much cheaper if booked as part of a package.

A *Hotel Manar*, route Touristique, T 81333,

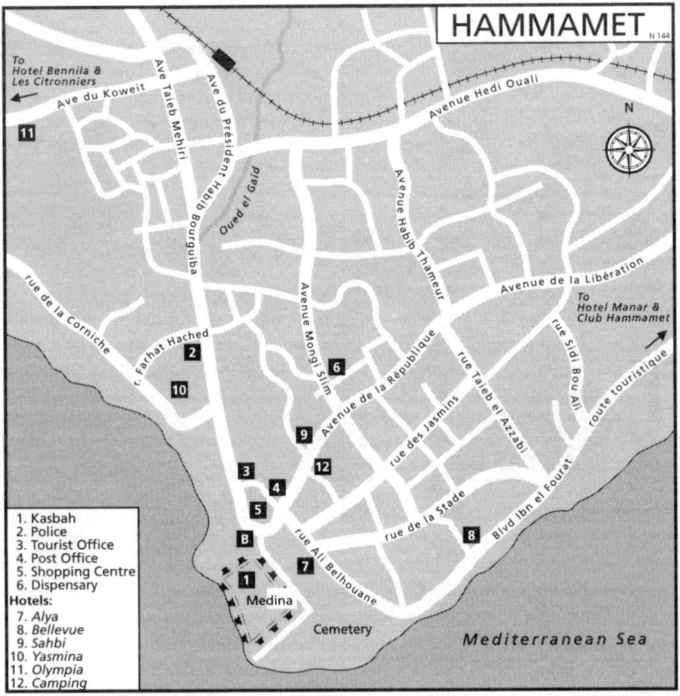

200 rm, 6 floors, a/c, 2 pools, tennis, golf; **A** ***Hotel Club-Hammamet***, route Touristique, T 81882, 337 rm on 2 floors, a/c, very good, beach, indoor pool complex, outdoor Olympic size pool, many activities, good food, large rm facing the sea.

D ***Les Citronniers***, route des Hotels, by *Hotel Bennila*, T 81650, modern, very close to beach, no views, barbecue, drinks, food on the beach; **D** ***Hotel Sahbi***, in town centre, T 80807, central, 200m from beach, pleasant large rm, some with views; **D** ***Hotel Alya***, rue Ali Belhouane, T 80218, central, very clean, half the rm look over the medina, the others over a street, roof terrace, bar, 300m from beach; **D** ***Hotel Bellevue***, Blvd Ibn el Fourat, T 81121, beach, central, clean rm, most with view.

E ***Hotel Bennila***, route des Hotels, from the centre take the road to Sousse and turn left by the UIB bank, T 80356, clean, pleasant rm, pool, quite cheap.

● Youth hostel
T 80440, 100 beds, meals, central location.

● Camping
Ideal Camping, Ave de la République, adequate, restaurant.

● Places to eat
♦♦♦ ***La Pergola***, T 80993, Shopping Centre, central; ***La Coupola***, T 81138, Ave du Koweit. ♦♦ ***Restaurant Achour***, T 80140, central, rue Ali Belhouane, reputedly the best fish restaurant in Hammamet, terrace; ***Restaurant Barberousse***, in the medina, wonderful terrace, pleasant decor, very touristy. ♦ ***Restaurant de la Poste***, central square, opposite the medina, terrace has a great view over the medina and the golf course, good food, quite

cheap; *Pizzeria* T 80825, Shopping Centre, central.

● **Banks**
Money can be changed in the big hotels or the banks in the centre of town. **STB**, Ave du Koweit; **BDS**, Ave du Koweit; **BT**, Ave Bourguiba; **UIB**, Ave des Nations Unies, an exension of Ave du Koweit.

● **Chemist**
Open nights, two on Ave de la République, T 80876 or T 80257.

● **Nightclubs**
Are mainly to the S of Hammamet, on the road to Sousse, in the direction of the route des Hotels. ***Ranch Club***, ***La Tortue***, ***Calypso***, and ***Mexico*** all in Hammamet Sud. ***Bedouina***, T 80095, Ave des Nations Unies, an extension of Ave du Koweit.

● **Post Office**
Ave de la République, Mon-Sat 0730-1230 and 1700-1900 in summer, winter 0800-1200 and 1500-1800. Sun always 0900-1100.

● **Sport**
All watersports are available, also horse (and camel!) riding, golf, tennis, and go-karting. Ask at any hotel. Hammamet Golf Course T 82722 has 18 holes, 6,114m and par 72, fees TD 28-30 per day. Hot air ballooning. **Leisure Centre**, T 80656, Ave Bourguiba.

● **Telephones**
Local code 02.

● **Theatre**
Centre Culturel, T 80656, Ave des Nations Unies.

● **Travel agents**
Hammamet Travel Service, rue Dag Hammarskjold, T 80193; ***Tourafrica***, rue Dag Hammarskjold, T 80446; ***Tunisian Travel Service***, Ave des Nations Unies, T 80040; ***Carthage Tours***, rue Dag Hammarskjold, T 80513.

● **Tourist information**
32 Ave Bourguiba, by the new shopping complex in town centre, T 80423.

● **Transport**
Car hire **Avis**, Ave du Koweit, T 80164; **Europacar**, Ave des Nations Unies, T 80146; **Intercar**, Ave des Nations Unies, T 80423; **Hertz**, Ave des Hotels, opposite *Hotel Miramar*, T 80187; **Topcar**, Ave des Nations Unies, T 81247. **Motorbike hire**: Locamob, Ave Dag Hammarskjold T 02 80339.

Taxis can be hired from in front of the medina. Some attempt is made at destination colour coding, but check.

Train The railway station is a bit outside the centre, on the road to Sousse. Information on T 80174. Departures **Sousse** and **Sfax** 0754 (goes on to **Gabès**), 1255, 1621 (terminates in Mahdia), 1817, 1915 (terminates in Mahdia). **Tunis** (TD3.50) 0553, 0644, 0754, 0857, 1255, 1621, 1915. All trains change at **Bir Bou Rekba**. In most cases the departure of the second train is immediate.

Road The bus station is front of the medina. Frequent departures for **Tunis, Sousse** and **Nabeul**.

NORTH TO CAP BON

Nabeul

Nabeul, 65 km SE from Tunis, with a population of 40,000, is really the capital of tourism in Tunisia, though it is difficult to know why. The town is by the sea, but the beach is much less attractive than in neighbouring Hammamet and the centre of the town is a collection of shops and services for tourists.

ACCESS The train station is in the town centre off Ave Bourguiba and the bus station on Ave Habib Thameur.

Things to see

Nabeul's speciality is **pottery**, its largest industry after tourism. The art of polychrome ceramics was introduced in the 15th century by the Andalusians. Try and visit a workshop to see how the various shapes are achieved. Other local crafts are **straw products**, **ironwork** and **sandstone** carved into intricate patterns (particularly in the village of **Dar Chaabane** 2 km N). In Dar Chaabane the mosque has an interesting, finely-sculpted doorway. Otherwise the town has little charm. On Fri a large market is held, but this is simply a tourist attraction. Busloads of tourists arrive and prices and quality respectively go up and down. Further S you can visit more authentic markets.

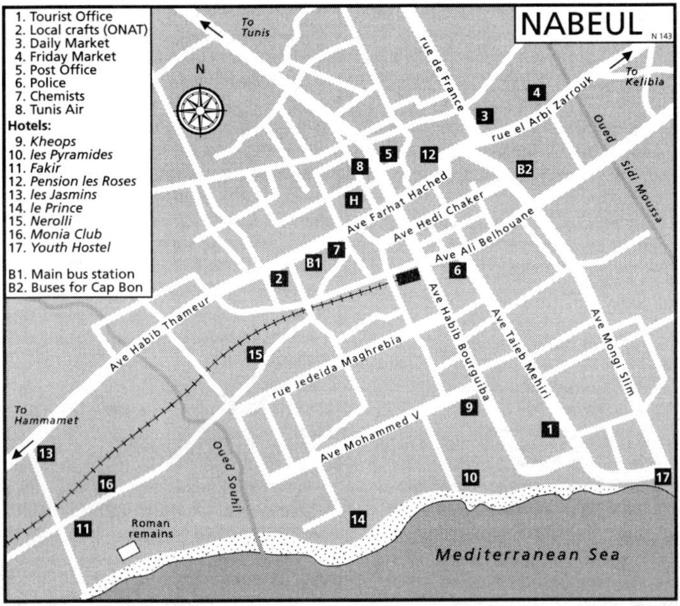

Local information

● Accommodation

A *Hotel Kheops*, outskirts of Nabeul, T 86555, beach, good restaurant, Olympic size pool, indoor pool, 300 rm, a/c, bath, TV, phone, terrace, watersports, tennis, disco.

B *Hotel Les Pyramides*, E end of Ave Bourguiba, T 85444, large hotel with accommodation in 350 bungalows, beach, pool, organized activities.

D *Hotel Fakir*, opposite the Roman remains of Neapolis, T 85477, brand new, small, pleasant rm, 200m from beach, very welcoming owner prefers individual travellers to groups.

F *Pension el Habib*, Ave Thameur, T 87190 outskirts of Nabeul coming from Hammamet, beach, very clean, communal bath/toilets, all rm with handbasin, roof terrace, main road is slightly noisy; **F** *Pension Les Roses*, rue Farhat Hached, T 85570, clean, well kept, central, communal bath/toilets.

● Youth hostels

2 km from town centre at the end of Ave Mongi Slim, by the beach, T 85547, 56 beds, closed all Feb. Also *Centre de Séjour et de Vacances 'La Gazelle'*, T 21366, 70 beds, meals available. Also *Maison des Jeunes*, T 86689, 80 beds, meals available.

● Camping

Hotel des Jasmin, on the road to Hammamet, 1 km out of town, hot/cold water, shop, restaurant, outdoor theatre in an extensive orange grove.

● Places to eat

Le Moderne, T 85709, 2 Ave Farhat Hached; *Les Oliviers*, T 86613, Ave Hedi Chaker; *La Rotonde*, T 85782, Ave Taieb Mehiri; *Karim* snack bar in central square. Also restaurants down by the beach.

● Banks

Most are on Ave Bourguiba and Ave Farhat Hached, in the town centre.

● Nightclub

Monia Club, T 85713, route de l'Hotel Neapolis.

● Post Office

Ave Bourguiba, open Mon-Sat 0800-1800.

● Shopping

Crafts are the best buys. Visit *ONAT* on Ave

Thameur to see the local products and check the prices without having to buy them. The traditional green/yellow pottery is a good buy. The wrought iron, like the stone carvings, are very weighty items to fit in your suitcase!

● **Telephone**
Local code 02.

● **Theatre**
Maison de la Culture, T 86817, Ave Farhat Hached.

● **Tourist information**
Ave Taieb Mehiri, T 86737. Towards the beach, from town centre. Bus and train times are normally posted outside the office.

● **Transport**
Car hire **Hertz**, Ave Thameur, T 85327; **Europacar**, Ave Farhat Hached, T 87085; **Rent a Car**, Ave Thameur, T 86679; **Matei**, Ave Bourguiba, T 85967.

Train Nabeul train station, off Ave Bourguiba, is the terminus. Information on T 85054. All trains go to **Hammamet** on a single track. Departures for **Tunis** 0535 (direct), 0625, 0737, 0840, 1230, 1604, 1858 (change at Bir Bou Rekba); **Sousse** and **Sfax** 0737 (goes to **Gabès**), 1236, 1604 (terminates in **Mahdia**), 1758, 1858 (terminates in **Mahdia**).

Road The bus station is on Ave Thameur. Information on T 85261. Frequent buses to Hammamet, Tunis (every half hour), Kelibia, Sousse and Kairouan.

Korba

14 km N of Nabeul, is a small village on Oued Bou Eddine used by *Club Mediterrané*. Its remains of a Roman aqueduct are worth a visit. A rough road inland leads up to a reservoir. **Youth hostel**, 100 beds, meals provided, family rms, T 89296.

Menzel Temime, 27 km N of Korba, has a **Youth hostel**, 40 beds, T 98116.

Kelibia

This is a small, pleasantly authentic, modern fishing village dominated by an impressive 7th century Byzantine fortress sitting on the hill. The village offers the visitor peace and quiet, particularly welcome if coming from Nabeul. The best beaches are situated 2-3 km N of Kelibia at the NE corner of Cap Bon.

Things to see

The Byzantine fort is much restored. Turn right off main road N of the village for a magnificent view. Entrance TD3, free for students. Alternate years in Jul an international amateur film festival is held here.

Local information

● **Accommodation**
D *Ennassim*, by the sea, T 296245, rm around a small courtyard currently being renovated and upgraded.

E *Florida*, by the sea, T 296248, small hotel next door to *Ennassim*, most rm with sea view, shaded terrace.

● **Youth hostel**
T 296105, 80 beds, on the road to Mansoura, by the sea, not very clean.

● **Places to eat**
The restaurants in both the hotels are good, as is ***Café Sidi el Bahri*** by the port where it is pleasant to have a drink in the afternoon and watch the fishing boats return. Try the fish, it should be fresh! ♦♦♦ ***El Mansoura***, T 296321, and ***Cluppea***, T 296296, both on the beach, in very good setting, fish dishes recommended. ♦♦ ***Le Relais***, T 296173, route de la Plage. Kelibia is noted for its dry wine. Try in particular the Muscat sec de Kelibia.

● **Sport**
Some watersports are available but the resort is not really set up for this. Harbour has berths for 20 yachts, min-max draft 2-5m.

● **Transport**
Road Buses leave every hour in the morning to El Haouaria and there are frequent departures to Nabeul.

Sea An interesting hydrofoil link with Trapani in Sicily is advertised during the summer, taking 4 hrs and carrying up to 180 passengers.

Kerkouane

About 12 km N from Kelibia and halfway between Kelibia and El Haouaria a small signposted road goes down towards the sea and the site. This remarkable Punic town, still well preserved, is thought to have been built in 5 BC and abandoned following the fall of Carthage to the Romans. It was never inhabited after that time, which accounts for its good state. The street layout and house foundations are clearly visible, with all the houses following the same pattern of a central courtyard with the rooms ranged around it. All the houses had baths, saying something about the sophistication of Punic civilization. The main economic activity seems to have been the manufacture of a purple dye from decomposed shell fish. Perhaps this explains the baths! Open 0830-1730 except Mon. Entrance TD3.

El Haouaria

12 km NE from Kerkouane, is El Haouaria, a small village famous for its falconry festival and its position at the end of the Cap Bon peninsula. The village itself is of little interest, but the surrounding countryside and beaches are delightful.

ACCESS The louages and bus station are on Ave Bourguiba in the town centre.

Things to see

The **Falconry Festival** is held every year in May. Three km from the village on the shore near the extremity of the Cap are the **Ghar el Kebirk Caves**. It is thought that the rock quarried from here was used to build parts of Carthage. You are advised to let the official guide show you round as he knows more than the unofficial ones! The mountains along the coast and behind the villages offer interesting walks.

Towards the end of the Cap Bon peninsula there is a beautiful little beach, **Ras Ed Drak**, which is quite secluded and still relatively unknown. It is 4 km from the village along a road leading to the end of the peninsula. The view from the end of **Cap Bon** is superb. It is said that on a clear night the lights of Sicily, 140 km away, can be seen.

Local information

● Accommodation

D *De l'Eperrier*, Ave Bourguiba, T 297017, F 297258, 10 rm, all with bath, very good restaurant.

● Places to eat

Restaurant in *De l'Eperrier* (English spoken) recommended. Try *Les Grottes*, T 97296, Grottes Romaines, and cheaper *Fruits de la Mer*, Ave Hedi Chaker, with fresh fish.

● Banks

BNA and **STB** on Ave Bourguiba near the post office.

● Post Office

At the start of Ave Bourguiba, by the louages and bus station.

● Sport

For hunting enquire at the Association de Chasseurs de Tunis for details of quail, woodcock, partridge and hare hunting.

● Transport

Road There is an irregular bus service, either via the N coast from Tunis (but this takes a while because the bus stops everywhere) or via Kelibia. Taking a **louage** is much faster.

CAP BON SOUTH TO TUNIS

Sidi Daoud

This small fishing village along the coast road to Korbous has a large and obtrusive fish canning plant. It hosts a traditional Fishing Festival in late May/early Jun each year. This festival, known as the *Matanza*, is quite violent, as the large tuna fish are caught in nets, dragged towards the shore and then harpooned, filling the sea with blood. Pacifists might prefer the splendid view from the village towards the island of Zembra.

Korbous

ACCESS From Sidi Daoud the road turns inland. Just beyond Sidi Aïssa at Bir Meroua you should turn right and go towards Korbous. This is a very scenic road which circles the hill and, on reaching the coast, follows the cliff with the sea literally below. The view towards La Goulette and Sidi Bou Saïd is very impressive. Worth the detour even if you have no intention of stopping at Korbous. The *Restaurant Dhrib* serves very good, cheap meals. There is only one café, down by the sea, with a large terrace.

A small thermal spa resort, overlooking the sea, Korbous was first discovered and used by the Romans. On the hilltop is a beautiful villa, previously used by Bourguiba as one of his summer resorts. The thermal institute and its baths which could be cleaner, can be visited and used. Strange atmosphere as many visitors have come for health reasons.

At **Aïn Atrous** the spring of heated sulphurous water (50°C) goes straight into the sea.

Local information

● Accommodation

Most of the hotels are expensive and used by the people undergoing treatment at the spa. **A** *Aïn Oktor*, T 94552, 4 km along the road to Soliman, 30 rm, overlooking the sea, no beach, thermal cures; **A** *Les Sources*, T 34533, large terrace overlooking the sea, 140 rm, thermal cures, pool; **A** *Chiraz*, T 93230.

● Places to eat

Chez Korbsi in town centre and *La Brise* at Sidi Rair.

Excursions

Grombalia and **Menzel Bou Zelfa**, about 40 km SE of Tunis are 2 interesting inland villages worth visiting. At Grombalia in September there is a Wine Festival, while Menzel Bou Zelfa has an Orange Festival in Apr-May. Menzel Bou Zelfa, 44 km from Tunis on the C43, can be reached via Soliman and Grombalia, 41 km from Tunis, is on the main P1 from Tunis to Hammamet and the main railway line from Tunis.

Zembra and Zembretta are small islands off the end of Cap Bon. They host the Centre Nautique International de Tunisie and have scuba diving equipment for hire and accommodation. Contact the centre in Tunis at 22 rue de Medine, T 01 282209 and they will provide information about organized diving holidays.

NORTHERN TUNISIA

CONTENTS

MAPS

The N of Tunisia has so far escaped the mass tourism of elsewhere in the country, but this may not be for long as there are many impressive Roman sites to visit and the landscape is exceedingly attractive. In summer the temperature is high but more bearable than in the S, with the mountains and wooded areas behind the coast being most welcoming. The coast between Bizerte and the Algerian border offers many secluded beaches, well off the main routes. The towns of Bizerte, Tabarka and Le Kef have much to interest the traveller and the Roman remains in Dougga are not to be missed.

TUNIS TO BIZERTE

Bizerte

Pop 400,000 *Alt* 5m.

History

Bizerte is the biggest town on the N coast and the fourth largest town in Tunisia. Its history goes back to Punic times when the natural harbour attracted the Phoenician sailors. The town was destroyed with the fall of Carthage, but later rebuilt by Caesar. Conquered by the Arabs in 661, Bizerte expanded during the Hafsid Dynasty. The arrival of the Moors from Spain in the 17th century, as in other cities in Tunisia, gave it a new lease of life and guaranteed its fortune. The opening of the Suez Canal in 1869, and the arrival, in 1882, of the French who appreciated its strategically important position (and thus were reluctant to leave in 1963) and turned the town into a naval arsenal, were other important factors in Bizerte's development.

Since Independence the industrial sector has expanded. There is an oil refinery and a large ironworks. Bizerte lies N of the bridge over the canal which joins the inland Lake of Bizerte (111 sq km) to the open sea. The road from the bridge leads into the regular grid pattern of streets, a legacy of the French, beyond which lies the medina and the old port. The town is currently undergoing an expansion of the tourist infrastructure. More hotels are planned and the marina will soon reach a capacity of 100 boats.

CLIMATE: BIZERTE

	Jan	Feb	Mar	Apr	May	Jun	Jul	Aug	Sep	Oct	Nov	Dec	Av/Tot
Max (°C)	15	15	17	19	23	27	31	31	29	24	20	16	22
Min (°C)	7	7	9	11	14	17	20	21	20	16	12	10	14
Rain (mm)	132	86	48	43	39	8	0	7	27	90	88	114	682

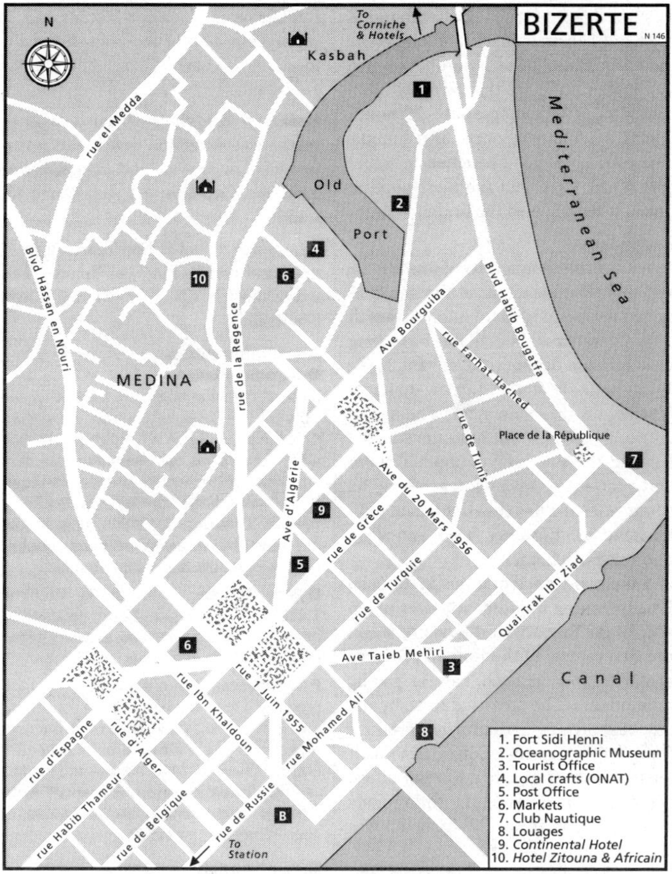

ACCESS Bizerte is 64 km from Tunis, 1 hr by taxi, a pleasant, slightly hilly, journey through fairly fertile farmland. Leave Tunis on the P8 heading NNW for Bizerte. The road crosses the wide flood plain of the River Medjerda, the only permanently flowing river in the country and the river responsible for the alluvial deposits which silted up the bay and reduced important trading ports to insignificance.

Things to see

The old harbour is charming with its blue and white houses overlooking the fishing boats and in the evening it has a different but equally pleasant atmosphere. From there you can penetrate into the **kasbah**, the old fortified town. The labyrinth of little streets with painted walls is fascinating to walk through and, leaving the old town, you can wander into the newer medina, peeping into doorways where craftsmen can be seen at work using techniques that are centuries old. The new city is of little interest except for the bustling life and cafés. **Local markets** are held. The main market is behind the old harbour and there is another on Ave Taieb Mehiri, before the town hall. Bizerte has an **Oceanographic Museum** which is not as impressive as it sounds. There are some good **beaches** on either side of the town, but the most popular one is at Remel, over the bridge to the S.

Excursions

Utica is an old Roman city of which little remains. The museum on the site contains a few small items of interest. Worth a visit if transport is available but a long walk on a hot day for little reward. It is a 1 km walk E from the new town of **Utique**, on the main road. The site is clearly signposted. The museum is on the left and the site itself is another 500m down the road. Open winter 0830-1730, summer 0900-1900, closed Sun and public holidays. Entrance TD3 and TD1 photography charge.

Like many ancient cities in Tunisia, Utica was first a Punic city, later taken over by the Romans. It was, at one stage, the first capital of the Roman province of Africa and, as such, rich in public monuments. The city used to be by the sea, exporting agricultural produce from its rich farm lands. Utica's collapse, like that of other Roman cities, came with the invasions by the Vandals and the Byzantines. The final fall was the Arab conquest.

The Roman site is not extensive and has only been partially excavated. The most visible monuments are the pool and wells in the **House of the Cascades**, centred around a patio. Some mosaics depicting fishing scenes are still well preserved under wooden covers. The Punic necropolis can be seen next to the pool.

The **Museum** is very small, divided into 2 rooms. The Punic room has some jewellery and small sarcophagi for the bones and ashes of children who, according to legend, were sacrificed here. The Roman room has a few statues and an interesting map of the area in the Roman times. There is no accommodation at Utica.

Kalaat el Andalous village stands on what was a headland before the sea retreated. The views S and E to **Sidi Bou Saïd** and **Cap Bon** are well worth the walk.

Also worth a visit is **Cap Blanc**, a rocky headland just 10 km N of Bizerte. This is the most N tip of Africa and is very beautiful.

Local information

● Accommodation

Most of the large hotels are situated on the Corniche which is about 3 km out of the town. **C** *Corniche*, route de la Corniche, T 431844, 4 km out of town, low season prices acceptable, beach, 87 rm with sea view, many organized activities, large nightclub, fully booked in summer; **C** *Nador*, T 431846, next to *Corniche* and very similar, 105 rm, beach, pool, no disco, tennis, fully booked in summer.

D *Petit Mousse*, route de la Corniche, T 432185, very pleasant, 12 rm, good atmosphere, beach across the road, excellent restaurant, eat outside in summer.

F *Continental*, rue d'Istambul, T 431436, probably one of the best deals if you want a cold shower and a clean, cheap bed, but don't expect much else; **F** *Zitouna*, place Slaheddine Bouchoucha, T 431447, edge of the medina, very noisy external rooms, no showers; **F** *Hotel Africain*, next to and similar to *Zitouna*, on edge of medina, T 434412.

● Youth hostels

1 km N of city centre up Blvd Hassan en Nouri, beyond the medina on route de la Corniche, kitchen, meals provided, 100 beds, T 431608. Also *Remel Plage*, 3 km from city centre, any bus going S of the canal will stop at the turn off, 50 beds, closed Feb, T 40804.

● Camping

Camping is permitted at Remel Plage hostel.

● Places to eat

♦♦ *L'Eden on Corniche*, T 439023 for seafood; *Le Petit Mousse*, in *Hotel Petit Mousse*, excellent food and fresh fish, not cheap but worth the price; ♦ *La Mamma*, T 433695, rue Ibn Khaldoun, sells pizzas and pancakes. *Res-*

taurant de la Liberté, next door to *Hotel Continental*, good, cheap food.

● Banks
The banks arrange a rota so one always stays open later. **BNT**, rue 1er Juin; **STB**, rue Farhat Hached, there is also another branch behind the ONAT, by the old harbour; **CFCT**, Ave Bourguiba which takes Eurocheque and Visa.

● Chemist
All night, 18 rue Ali Belhaoane, T 432461.

● Hospital
On rue du 3 Août, T 431422.

● Police station
T 431200, rue du 20 Mars 1956

● Post Office
Main office on Ave d'Algérie, takes parcels as well. Around the back of main building is the telecommunications office, also on rue el Medina and place Pasteur.

● Shopping
Visit the *ONAT* office just by the old harbour. They have a good selection of regional art. Bizerte specializes in ironwork, woodwork, pottery, carpets and embroidery.

● Sport
Club Nautique, on the right of the main beach in town, hires out surfboards and does various other watersports. Sub-aqua fishing is very popular. Otherwise try one of the hotels on the Corniche. The *Corniche* hotel organizes water skiing and rents surfboards. Horse riding is offered at some of the hotels. Some of the big hotels and small enterprises hire out bicycles, which is a cheap way of getting to the beach. Municipal swimming pool (heated) on Blvd Hassan en Nouri.

● Telephone
Local code 02.

● Travel agents
Tourafrica, Ave Bourguiba, T 432315; *Transtour*, rue d'Alger, T 432174; *Via Bizerte*, rue 1er Mai, T 432901.

● Tourist offices
National Tourist Office (ONTT), 1 rue d'Istambul, T 432703/432897. The office is hard to find. It is situated by the canal, about 100m before the bridge, towards the sea. Will provide a map of Tunisia, a map of Bizerte and information about places to stay in the region.

● Transport
Car hire **Avis**, 7 rue d'Alger, T 433076; **Budget**, 7 rue d'Alger, T 432174; **Europcar**, 52 Ave d'Algérie, T 439018; **Hertz**, Place des Martyrs, T 433679; **Inter Rent**, 19 rue Mohammed Rejiba, T 431455. **Shipping Co. Navitour**, 29 Ave d'Algérie, T 431440. **Bicycles & Motorbike hire**: **Ben Othman**, Ave Bourguiba; **Ben Kilani**, Ave Bourguiba, T 431622 and **Ben Aleya**, rue Sassi Bahri.

Air The nearest airport is Tunis. Information from Tunis Air, 76 Ave Bourguiba, T 432201.

Train The station is approx 15 mins walk SW along canal out of town. Information on T 431317. To Tunis 0540, 0810, 1350, 1835.

Road The main bus station is by the bridge over the canal. A short walk N up Ave d'Algérie to the town centre. Information on T 431222. Bus station for places W is on rue d'Alger. **Tunis (a/c)** 0545, 0700, 0800, 0830, 1000, 1200, 1300, 1400, 1500, 1600, 1645, 1710, 1810; **Tunis (normal)** every half hour from 0600-1830; **Ras Jebel** every half hour from 0600 until 1900; **Raf Raf** (via Ras Jebel) 1215; **Ghar El Melh** (via Ras Jebel) 0900, 1130, 1615; **Aïn Draham** (via Tabarka) 0600. **Louages**: leave by the canal under the bridge to all destinations, but some are harder to obtain if the demand is low. Louages terminate on the Quai Trak Ibn Ziad under the bridge or at the N end of Ave d'Algérie. Sometimes available at the station.

Ras Djebel

This is a small coastal town E of Bizerte on the road to the beaches of Raf Raf. The town has a café and a hotel but not much else of interest. By contrast the surrounding area is very beautiful. To the N, Cap Zebib offers magnificent views and the road from Bizerte to Ras Djebel is very scenic with a panoramic view over the coast by Bizerte. The beach at Ras Djebel is very crowded in the summer and as most people prefer to camp near the town, anywhere further W is better.

Raf Raf

ACCESS The buses from Bizerte, Ras Djebel and Tunis stop just by the beach.

The town of Raf Raf at the top of the hill which houses the well-to-do of Tunis in

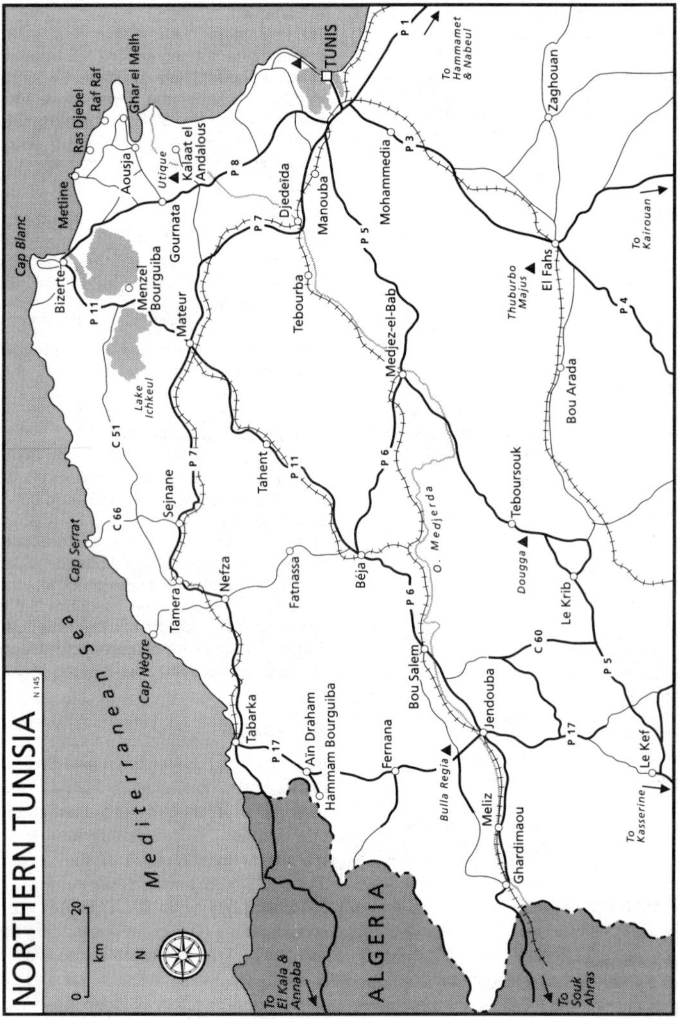

attractive villas is not particularly special, but Raf Raf plage is very beautiful. The white sand backed by dunes and the settlement extending virtually to the beach makes it a unique setting. Unfortunately there is little accommodation. It makes a pleasant day excursion from either Tunis or Bizerte. Consequently in the summer, especially at weekends, Raf Raf gets very crowded with trippers and the approach roads become jammed with cars.

Local information

● Accommodation

It is possible to stay in straw huts on the beaches which can be rented overnight for about TD10, but you will have to bring everything you need. **D** *Hotel Dalia*, small, only 22 rm, about half have sea view, very clean, close to beach.

● Places to eat

The restaurant in the ***Hotel Dalia*** is good and cheap. There are a few other restaurants along the beach, try ***Restaurant Andalous***, but they tend to be overpriced.

● Transport

Road: **Bus** Departures for Bizerte and Ras Djebel. Three daily to Tunis. **Louages** also available, but in summer towards the end of the day it can be quite crowded as everybody is leaving. Hitching may take time as most cars are already full.

Ghar el Melh

ACCESS Ghar el Melh is served by buses from Tunis and Bizerte. Return to Tunis 0545, 1700; to Bizerte 0600, 1000, 1330. There are no buses E to Sidi Ali el-Mekki.

This is a quiet, S facing fishing village by a salt lagoon with a notorious past of piracy and smuggling. The road continues past the village and on 6 km to the splendid beach of **Ras Sidi Ali el Mekki** with a small café/shop and a score of straw cubicles for camping, rented at TD5 per day. At the end of the peninsula, built partially into the cliff is the *marabout* of Sidi Ali el Mekki, a place of pilgrimage. This is an attractive and secluded spot.

Metline

This is a small town built into the hillside. **El Alia**, built on the crossroads, is a splendid example of the settlements built by returnees from Andalucía.

Menzel Bourguiba

A large provincial town on the W side of Lake Bizerte with nothing particular to attract visitors. Menzel Bourguiba does make a good base from which to visit Lake Ichkeul.

Lake Ichkeul

This animal sanctuary of 12,600 ha is 25 km away and is arguably the most interesting of Tunisia's 5 National Parks. Water birds and waders are among the thousands of over-wintering migrants found here and 75 species of mammal such as water buffalo, wild boars, porcupines, otters and jackals and around 500 species of reptile live in this protected marsh/lake/mountain habitat. Expeditions to watch the 180 species of bird (best Mar, Apr and Nov) are offered by some tour agents. The Tourist Office in Bizerte arranges visits to the reserve.

FROM BIZERTE TO TABARKA

The coast between Bizerte and Tabarka is quite wild, the sea hidden by thick forests, but the coastline is worth trying to reach, especially if you like deserted beaches, although access is difficult. By car from Bizerte to Tabarka take the road W towards Menzel Bourguiba and turn right 5 km after Bizerte on the C51, in the direction of **Sejnane**. This road, running in a valley for much of the way, is very beautiful. At Sejnane the route rejoins the main road to **Nefza** and **Tabarka**.

Sejnane

This is a good base from which to visit these attractive and very secluded N beaches, though you will need to have your own transport or be very lucky with lifts. Don't set off for any of these out of the way coastal spots without plenty of provisions.

On the C51, 11 km from Sejnane turn right at the cross roads (signposted) to **Cap Serrat**. This is a headland with a lighthouse and a good beach. It may be possible to buy food at the kiosk on the beach – but don't rely on it.

At Tamera, 10 km before Nefza on the Bizerte road, turn right and follow the winding track for about 10 km. At the end there is a small fishing village, **Sidi Mechrig**, and, of course, a beautiful beach. People set up camp here for the summer. There is a hotel. Leaving Tamera, branching from the Sidi Mechrig track, there is a scenic ride to the coast at **Cap Nègre**, an area once known for its coral fishing.

The closest beach to Tabarka is **Zouara** beach, only 20 km before the town. Turn right off the Bizerte road before Aïn Sebna (a sign indicates the way) and follow a fairly easy track for 5 km. This is a beautiful beach with fine sand, but again there is no infrastructure whatsoever.

Tabarka

A minor seaside resort, 175 km W from Tunis, situated where the Khroumirie mountains meet the sea. It is a magnificent setting, but unfortunately what used to be a small resort for Tunisians is just about to develop into a large one for foreigners. An airport is under construction and 2 new hotels are being built by the seafront in order to reach the target of 10,000 beds by the year 2000. Fortunately the projects are good quality. On the seafront, by the town, a project called Porto Corallo is under construction and appears very well designed. Eventually there will be a 280 berth marina here. The road system has been upgraded.

ACCESS The louage station is on the main street Ave Bourguiba. From the long distance bus station on rue du Peuple turn left down the hill to the central square. The local bus station is about 50m up the hill from the main square.

Things to see

Tabarka is the centre for diving on the N coast and the diving centre in the Yachting club on the seafront is open all year. The club also organizes other water sport activities including underwater photography. In autumn, hunting, especially of wild boars, is an expanding tourist industry. Archaeological museum open 0830-1730 winter, 0900-1300 and 1500-1900 summer, closed Mon, entrance TD1.

From the town walk along the coast past the old fort built by the Genoese to the impressive **Aiguilles** (needles), carved out of the rock by sea and wind. The view from the top of the old fort is impressive and worth the effort of walking up. An 18 hole golf course has recently been opened on the left of the road to Tunis after the town. The course overlooking the sea is in 100 ha of pine and oak forest. Coral jewellery is on sale and there is a **coral festival** in summer when the town is certainly more lively. There is a **World War II cemetery** with 500 graves 15 km E of town on the P7, open 0730-1430, Sat-Thur.

Local information

● Accommodation

It is difficult to find anywhere to stay here in the summer, other than room to camp on the beach, so booking is essential. Things will possibly ease as the new hotels are completed. **B** *Morjane*, on the road behind the sand dunes, T 644453, the first hotel built on the beach, very convenient.

C *Mimosas*, on the left as you enter the town, T 644376, on top of a hill overlooking the bay, pool, 70 rm with sea view.

E *De France*, Ave Bourguiba, T 644577, restaurant, old fashioned charm, probably the best of the cheap hotels but has certainly known better days; **E** *Hotel Novelty*, Ave Bourguiba, brand new, central, very clean; **E** *Hotel Corail*, Ave Bourguiba, cheap, but only recommended if funds are low or everything else is full.

● Places to eat

Hotel de France, good food at very decent prices; *Restaurant Les Agriculteurs*, Ave Bourguiba, good, cheap, very filling food.

● Banks

BNT and **UIB** on Ave Bourguiba.

● Hospital

On rue de Calle, T 644023.

● Police station

On rue du Peuple, T644021.

● **Post Office**
Ave Farhat Hached, 2nd road on the left after the central square.

● **Sport**
Golf at Montazah, T 644321, 6,400m, par 72, fees TD30-35 per day.

Deep sea diving at Tabarka yacht club, T 644478. The harbour has 60 yacht places, min-max draw is 2-4m.

Scuba diving on coral reef.

● **Telephones**
Local code 08.

● **Tourist Office**
32 Ave Bourguiba, T 644491, open 0900-1200 and 1600-1900, after the main square on the right.

● **Transport**
Road The long distance bus station is in rue du Peuple (1st street on the right going uphill from the central square). Information on T 44404. Departures **Tunis** (via Mateur) 0400, 0500, 0730, 0900, 1545; **Tunis** (via Béja) 0600, 1000, 1300. The local bus station is 50m uphill from the central square. Frequent departures to **Aïn Draham** and **Jendouba**. Two buses a day to **Bizerte**. Information on T 644097. **Louages**: the station is at the beginning of Ave Bourguiba. Departures for **Jendouba, Aïn Draham, Le Kef** and sometimes **Tunis**.

TABARKA TO AIN DRAHAM AND LE KEF

The road from Tabarka S to Aïn Draham is a typical mountain road and very scenic, with a wonderful view towards the coast. At Babouch there is a turning to Hammam Bourguiba, a thermal spa resort with a hotel and little else about 15 km from Aïn Draham. This road also leads to the Algerian border but the crossing in this area has about 10 km between control posts, a walk not to be undertaken lightly.

Aïn Draham

Aïn Draham lies 175 km W of Tunis and 26 km S of Tabarka. It is known as a spa town. It is a very picturesque village surrounded by thick cork-oak forests way up at 1000m in the mountains. The village is an ideal place in summer away from the unpleasant heat, but can be quite chilly in winter when snow is common. Aïn Draham is also the heart of the wild boar hunting region and it can be difficult to find places in hotels during the season from Oct to Mar. It is a quaint little town with one steep, central street, Ave Bourguiba (of course).

Things to see

The Association du Patrimoine Populaire et Historique Aïn Draham is found in a small office where products of the regional arts are displayed. It is interesting and the people are very welcoming.

Local information

● **Accommodation**
B ***Hammam Bourguiba***, in Hammam Bourguiba, T 647217.

D ***Les Chênes***, T 647211, 32 rm, slightly out of town, 7 km towards Jendouba, good, excellent food, rather secluded, set in the middle of the forest; **D** ***Rihana***, T 647391, at the end of the village on the road to Jendouba, 75 rm, comfortable hotel with a very memorable view overlooking the valley, within walking distance of the village, book in summer; **D** ***Beau Séjour***, Ave Bourguiba, T 647005, 30 rm, an old hunting lodge, restaurant, central, book in summer.

● **Youth hostel**
Is at the top of the hill, kitchen, 150 beds, T 647087.

● **Places to eat**
Grand Maghreb is good but expensive.

● **Banks**
Are all on Ave Bourguiba. **BNT, STB** are opposite Association du Patrimoine, and **BNA** is beyond the Tourist Office.

● **Hospital**
Is on route de l'Hôpital, T 647047.

● **Police**
Ave Bourguiba, T 647150.

● **Post Office**
Ave Bourguiba, further up the road after the Association du Patrimoine.

● **Sport**
Wild boar hunting is advertised for this region

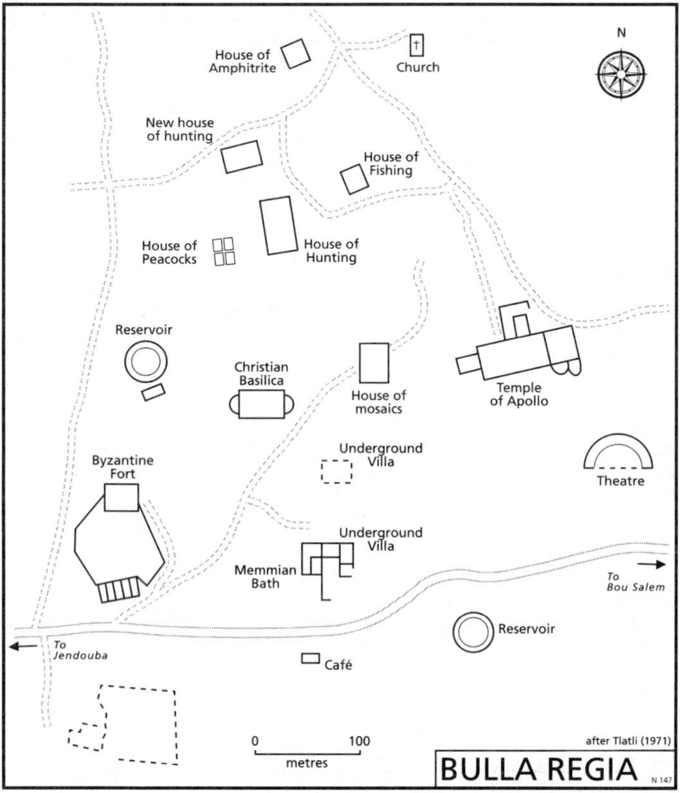

in winter.

● Telephones
Local code 08.

● Tourist office
Syndicat D'Initiative, Ave Bourguiba, towards the top, T 647115.

● Transport
Road The bus station is at the bottom of Ave Bourguiba, on the right, by the cemetery. Frequent buses to **Jendouba** and **Tabarka, Tunis** (via Béja) 0600, 1000,1300 and (via Mateur) 0400, 0500, 0730, 0900, 1545. **Louages**: the station is situated at the top of Ave Bourguiba, on the square. Main routes are to **Jendouba** and **Tabarka**.

Bulla Regia

ACCESS Bulla Regia lies 3 km E of the Aïn Draham-Jendouba road. Take a bus from Jendouba and ask to get off at Bulla Regia. The intersection is 6 km N of Jendouba so you will then either have to walk or hitch the remaining 3 km. There is no accommodation at the site. Open summer 0700-1900 and 0830-1730 winter, closed Mon, entrance TD2, photography fee TD2.

History In 2 BC, Bulla Regia was the capital of one of the 3 small Roman Kingdoms in Numidia, but prosperity came under the rule of Hadrian, when the town was annexed to the Empire.

Things to see The ruins are situated on a raised plateau by the side of a large plain, which is particularly hot in summer and cold in winter and there is no doubt that it was to escape the unpleasant extremes of this climate that the houses were built partly underground, as they are at Matmata (see page 578). These **underground villas** are the main attraction here. Despite earthquake damage to the surface features, due to the unusual architecture, many of the villas are well preserved. The general style was to have the eating and sleeping rooms centred around a large underground courtyard. Judging from the luxurious decoration, most of them belonged to rich inhabitants. Notice the ceilings are arched. Most of the better mosaics have been taken to the Bardo museum (see Tunis p 499), but in the **House of Fishing** and the **House of Amphitrite** some magnificent mosaics are still in place. Above ground structures which are still visible include the **Theatre** complete with stage, the **Memmian Baths** near the entrance, the **Forum** and the **Temple of Apollo**.

Jendouba

Jendouba, 44 km S of Tabarka and 154 km W of Tunis, is an important crossroads and administrative centre. This town is of very little interest, except that it provides easy access to Bulla Regia and the Algerian border. There are branches of all the main banks here.

• **Accommodation** **D** *Similthu*, on the right, by the roundabout when arriving from Bulla Regia, T 631695, new hotel, 26 rm, restaurant, on the main road, not very appealing. **E** *Atlas*, rue du 1er Juin 1955, T 630566, behind the police station, probably the only decent hotel in town. **Youth hostel** 60 beds, meals, T 631292.

• **Transport Train** The train station is off the main square, by the police station. Departures **Tunis** 0554, 1033, 1240, 1515, 1653; **Algeria** (Annaba/Algiers) 1539. **Road**: **Bus** The bus station is to W of town, past the railway lines. Information on T 630411. Frequent local buses to **Tunis**, **Le Kef**, **Tabarka** and **Aïn Draham**, also buses to the border at Ghardimaou. They do not cross the border so you will have to cross on foot. **Louages** For **Ghardimaou** they leave from the station on Blvd Sakiet Sidi Sousse. For Tunis they leave from rue 1 Juin 1955.

Excursions

Ghardimaou, 34 km W of Jendouba, is on the way out towards Algeria and is not worth a visit on its own account. There is the E *Hotel Thubernic* if you have to stay.

Before proceeding S to Le Kef, visitors are recommended to find time to make a journey NE to **Béja**, either by road or railway. For the first 22 km to Bou Salem, both are alongside the Oued Medjerda, the only river in Tunisia which flows all year round. The road, which never seems to be free of roadworks, crosses the 2 main tributaries, the Oued Mellègue and Oued Tessa which can be spectacular in flood and very disappointing at other times, while the railway line from Jendouba to Béja runs along the far side of the main valley. Bou Salem is a large successful market town dealing with the agricultural produce, mainly cereals but some grapes and some livestock, of this fertile valley. It is possible to see in this journey the area that the Romans used as their 'bread basket'. From Bou Salem the road climbs up the wooded slopes to Béja providing panoramic views back towards the route travelled, while the railway crosses and recrosses the main river before turning N to Béja.

Béja

Population 35,000 *Alt* 234m.

This town has had an eventful history, marked by various unfriendly visitors over the centuries razing it to the ground! Today, fortunately for the residents, there is less excitement but it is worth a wander round the medina and up the keep in the kasbah for a fine view. Béja has an attractive location, surrounded by excellent agricultural land with hills to the NW

CLIMATE: BEJA

	Jan	Feb	Mar	Apr	May	Jun	Jul	Aug	Sep	Oct	Nov	Dec	Av/Tot
Max (°C)	13	16	17	21	26	31	34	35	31	25	20	15	24
Min (°C)	5	5	6	9	11	16	18	19	16	13	8	7	11
Rain (mm)	123	74	61	55	33	11	5	9	27	81	63	103	645

and commands the junction of 6 important roads.

ACCESS The bus and train stations are at the bottom of the main street with frequent connections to/from Tunis and Jendouba.

Things to see

Trajan's Bridge, once part of the Roman E-W road network lies on the minor road C76 about 13 km SW of Béja. The road leaves Béja beside the station and crosses the railway before crossing the Oued Béja. This Roman bridge, which seemingly has nothing to do with Trajan at all, is still in splendid condition. Its 70m span is a monument to the workmanship from the time of Tiberius.

There are **World War II cemeteries** in the area. One is just outside the N limits of the town with 396 graves and another with 99 graves about 800m N of Thibar village which lies on the C75 between Béja and Teboursouk, adjacent to the agricultural college. Both open 0730-1430 Sat-Thur.

Local information

● Accommodation

There are 2 small hotels, **D** *Hotel Vaga*, T 450818, with 36 beds and **F** *Hotel Phoenix*, T 450188, with 30 beds.

● Youth hostel

T 450621, opposite the bus station, 80 beds, meals available.

Le Kef

Le Kef (The Rock) 58 km S of Jendouba is perched 750m up on a rocky hill. It is a very beautiful little town with a long history, mainly military in nature due to its important strategic position. It became a Roman colony in the 2nd century because of its situation. When the French entered Tunisia, they captured Le Kef in 1881 and made it an important military centre. During the WWII it became the provisional capital of the still free Tunisia. Today the town is an important economic and cultural regional centre. It is an interesting place to visit and remains authentic and relatively untouched by tourism. Also, due to its long history, it is rich in monuments.

Things to see

If you want to visit the town, it is a good idea to stop off at the **Association de Sauvegarde de la Medina**, on place de l'Indépendence. They have a charming little office and are very helpful. The best way to visit the medina is to walk around with no fixed itinerary. Some parts are as beautiful as Sidi Bou Saïd, with the advantage that here there are no crowds.

The **Regional Museum of Popular Arts and Traditions** is on the square at the top of the town. An interesting museum set in the old and very beautiful Zaraouia Sidi Ali Ben Aissa. There are 4 rooms, the most interesting presents elements of the everyday nomadic life, including a large tent. Open winter 0930-1630 and summer 0900-1300 and 1500-1900, closed Mon, entrance TD1.

The **kasbah** is an old fort built in 1601 with an impressive view. Entrance TD1. In summer the Bou Makhlouf festival takes place in the courtyard.

The **Mosque of Sidi Bou Makhlouf** is just behind the kasbah. This is a very beautiful mosque with interesting domes and an octagonal minaret. The inside is highly decorated with ceramics and stucco. Also worth a visit is **Dar el**

Kous behind Ave Bourguiba. This church is a 4th century basilica.

A minor road, the C72, climbs N to the side of the 1,500 ha lake held back by the Nebeur Dam. The lake is an impressive 18 km long. A better view is obtained from the dam on the Oued Mellègue by turning off the road to Jendouba after the steep winding road passes Nebeur.

Local information

● Accommodation

D *Hotel Sicca Veneria*, place de l'Indépendence, T 221561, ugly, 34 rm, 3 star, central, relatively cheap, restaurant.

E *Hotel Chez Venus*, Ave Bourguiba, T 224695, 20 rm with bath, good value, helpful owner.

F *La Source*, place de la Source, T 221397, 9 rm, central, set around a patio next to the Muezzin's loudspeaker, not very clean, slightly shabby; **F** *La Medina*, 18 rue Farhat Hached, T 220214, simple, new, fairly clean and welcoming.

● Places to eat

Restaurant Chez Venus, Ave Bourguiba, very pleasant atmosphere, probably the best food in town, a bit more expensive than the others; *Restaurant l'Auberge*, Ave Bourguiba, good, cheap Tunisian food; *Restaurant Ed Dyr*, Ave Hedi Chaker, good value.

● Banks

STB, place de l'Indépendence; **BT**, Ave Hedi Chaker.

● Post Office

Ave Hedi Chaker.

● Transport

Road The bus station is a 20 min walk downhill from Place de l'Indépendence. Information on T 20105. **Tunis** hourly from 0400-1700; **Sfax** 0400, 0530, 1230; **Kairouan** 0530, 1330; **Nabeul** 0530, 1245; **Gafsa** 0530, 1230; **Sousse** 0615, 1245; **Bizerte** 0700, 1245; **Djendouba** 0700, 0800, 1000, 1200, 1330, 1430, 1630. **Louage** The louages station is by the bus station.

Excursions

Hammam Mellègue, a thermal spa 4 km SW of Le Kef, turn right off P5. **Kalaat Es Senam** and **Table de Jugurtha**, turn right off P17 29 km S from Le Kef, before the railway and after 14 km bear left and S. Table de Jugurtha is 1,271 m and for the energetic there are views over to Algeria!

LE KEF TO TEBOURSOUK AND TUNIS

The P5 from Le Kef NW towards Tunis, passes through an interesting mixture of small present day Tunisian towns and ancient remains of Roman and Byzantine origin. This is a rich agricultural area of pasture, cereals and wooded hills.

Just N of the small town of Le Krib, on the left, are the ruins of the triumphal arch and several other remains of the Roman settlement of Musti. Just 10 km further along what remains of a Byzantine fort stands on a hill. This is the site of the ancient settlement of Agbia. Immediately beyond, on the left is the turn to **Dougga**.

On towards Tunis the older part of **Teboursouk**, on a hillside, overlooks the P5 while the modern part of town lies along the main road. **Aïn Tounga** immediately to the E of the road contains an imposing Byzantine fortress and remains of Roman Thignica, while **Testour** still reflects its Andalusian origins, home of the Moors driven from Spain in the 15th century.

Dougga

History

The Roman ruins of Dougga are 7 km S from the town of Teboursouk. It was originally a Punic town allied to Rome against Carthage. As a consequence, after the downfall of Carthage, the town was granted a certain degree of independence. Romanization only started towards 150 AD, after 2 centuries of coexistence. By the time Carthage had been rebuilt by the Romans, Dougga had become the economic and administrative centre of the whole region, enjoying

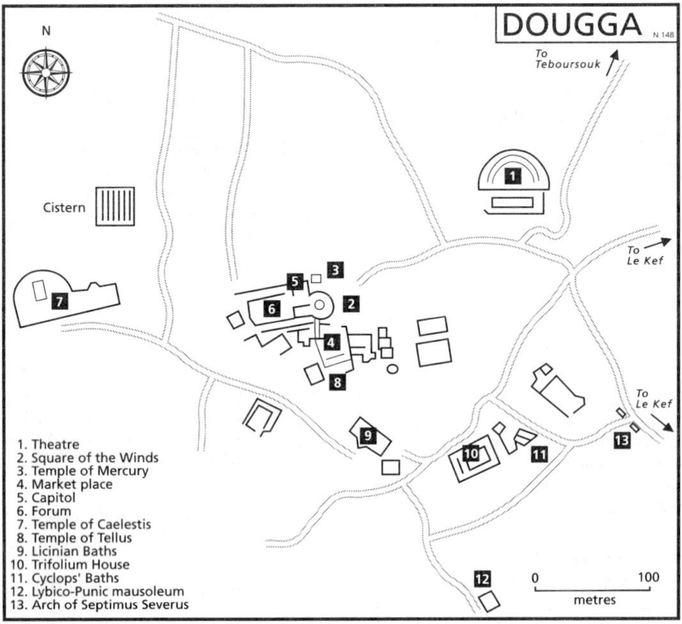

great prosperity. Having become a Roman colony by the end of the 2nd century, the town reached the height of its wealth under the rule of Septimus Severus. Its downfall in the 4th century was caused by the heavy dues paid to the Romans and religious quarrels. When the Vandals invaded, most of the population had moved to Teboursouk. Today the ruins of Dougga spreading over 25 ha still give a very good idea of the everyday life in the ancient city.

ACCESS Take a bus or louages to the new settlement of Dougga (set up to house the folk who were dwelling on the site) and walk up a track behind the village. The ruins are 3 km further on along a track. The easiest way is to go from Teboursouk and take a taxi or louages.

Things to see

Dougga is the largest of the Roman sites in Tunisia and is considered the most dramatic. This is the one site not to be missed. The ruins are on the slope of a small hill and the view and situation are beautiful. It is possible to do a superficial visit in an hour or so, but it is really worthwhile spending a great deal more time. On arrival, one of the 'guides' hanging round the entrance will no doubt want to show you around. Most of these guides are not official and do not hold a card issued by the Tourist Office. If you are in a hurry, it can be a good idea to take one, but be careful to agree on the price beforehand.

The Monuments are open 0830-1730 winter and 0700-1900 summer, closed Mon, entrance fee TD4, photography TD1. The **Theatre** is very well preserved. Built in 168 AD, it is quite modest in size but could nevertheless seat 3,500 people in its 19 tiers. Each summer there is a festival here at which theatre groups from around the world perform.

Down the track is the main section of the site including **The Capitol**, with its impressive steps and huge fluted columns which are in excellent condition. It was built in 166 AD and dedicated to the gods Jupiter, Juno and Minerva. The **Forum** and the nearby market place are in equally good condition. Note the compass-based inscription in the square Rose du Vents. The nearby **Licinian Baths** were built in the 3rd century and there is a good indication of how they must have been originally. The fireplace which heated the water and hot room are still visible, as are the pipes built into the walls.

The House of Trifolium, the brothel, named after the clover leaf shape of one of the rooms, dates from the 3rd century and is the best conserved and largest house yet discovered on the site. It is built on 2 levels with the entrance at street level and the rooms one floor lower. Interestingly, the houses in Dougga were built according to the more traditional African style that was to be used throughout the medinas. They have no external windows, but are constructed around an inner courtyard, with all rooms and windows looking in for privacy. **The Baths of the Cyclops**, associated with the House of Trifolium, are not in a very good state, except for the communal latrine!

The Libyo-Punic **Mausoleum**, dates back to the 2nd century BC. It was virtually destroyed by the British Consul in Tunis in the 1840s, because he wanted to take stones bearing bilingual inscriptions in Punic and Libyan back for the British Museum, where they are now kept.

The Temple of Caelestis, built in 222 AD, is surrounded by olive trees and has definite Greco-Roman influences. Continue past the temple to see part of the aqueduct bringing fresh water to the city. When walking around, notice the highly sophisticated drainage system under the marble stones.

Local information

● Accommodation

It is best to stay overnight in **Teboursouk**, although there is only one hotel there. **D** *Hotel Thugga*, on the main road to Tunis, T 465713, has obviously seen better days, rather poor quality.

● Youth hostel

In Teboursouk, T 465095, 40 beds.

● Transport

Road There is an hourly bus to **Le Kef** and **Tunis** and many links to **Béja** and **Jendouba**. Information on T 465016.

Medjez-el-Bab

This is a market town and an important crossing point of the Oued Medjerda. The British First and Eighth armies played an important part here in WWII (see The Desert War, p 836). It has 2 World War II cemeteries. One is 3 km SW of town on the P5 with 2,900 graves and a memorial to soldiers who died in Tunisia and Algeria and have no known grave. The other has 240 graves and is 17 km W of town on the P6 beside the church in the old town of Oued Zarga. Both open 0730-1430 Sat-Thur.

● Accommodation **E** *Hotel Membressa*, small, 14 rm, communal shower.

CENTRAL TUNISIA

CONTENTS

MAPS

Central Tunisia contains a diversity of interesting sights. It includes the Sahel bristling with olive trees; the busy coastal resort area accessed from Monastir airport; the holy city of Kairouan; Sbeitla and El Djem, the best preserved and most important Roman remains in the county; the busy city of Sfax and the peaceful Islands of Kerkennah. These are separated by long distances and the route we have devised takes in all these places and returns you, eventually, to the coast at Sousse.

The Sahel, or shoreland, is the low-lying E coastal plain of Tunisia extending from the Gulf of Hammamet to the Gulf of Gabès, and inland some 50 km, reaching a maximum altitude of around 275m. The region has a long history, going back to the Carthaginians and the Romans, with the amphitheatre in **El Djem** (Thysdrus) being one of the most important remains in North Africa. The cultivation of olive trees, introduced by the Romans, continues today with **olive oil** making an important contribution to the region's prosperity. The Sahel region was greatly influenced, both culturally and architecturally, by the Arab invasions and the founding of **Kairouan** which became the fourth holy city of Islam. The medinas in most of the coastal towns have been preserved as well as monuments dating back to the 7th and 8th centuries. The Sahel, because of its good beaches and pleasant climate which is tempered in summer by cool sea breezes, has become an important tourist area centred on Sousse and Monastir. Nevertheless, there are many areas where few tourists visit, such as the charming town of Mahdia and the quiet Kerkennah Islands.

THE GULF OF HAMMAMET

Sousse

Pop 300,000 *Alt* 6m.

Sousse is the third largest city in Tunisia. It is highly industrialized but the town centre is still very pleasant. It is a city of many facets making it an interesting place to visit. Situated by the sea on the Gulf of Hammamet, with the harbour right by the main square, it has long beaches and an elegant promenade. The walled medina, looking down towards the sea, contains narrow, winding streets.

History

Founded in the 9th century BC by the Phoenicians, Sousse is one of the oldest ports in the Mediterranean. In the 4th century BC, Carthage became the leading city, and Sousse entered into its sphere of influence. During the second Punic-Roman war, Hannibal used Sousse as his base, but was beaten in 202 BC. During the third Punic-Roman war, Sousse changed its allegiance to the Romans thereby avoiding destruction and

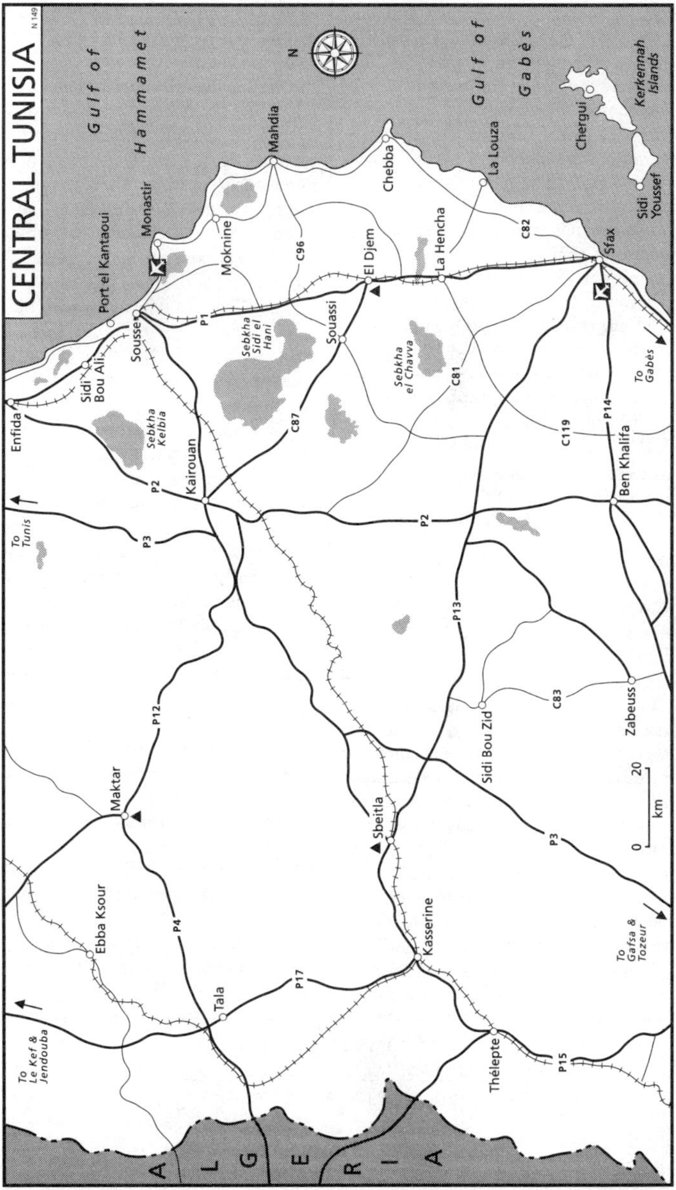
CENTRAL TUNISIA
N 149
Gulf of Hammamet
Gulf of Gabès
N
Kerkennah Islands
Chergui
Sidi Youssef
Mahdia
Monastir
Port el Kantaoui
Sousse
Moknine
Chebba
La Louza
El Djem
La Hencha
Sfax
Souassi
Sebkha Sidi el Hani
Sebkha el Chavva
Sidi Bou Ali
Enfida
Sebkha Kelbia
Kairouan
To Tunis
To Gabès
Ben Khalifa
Zabeuss
Sidi Bou Zid
Maktar
Sbeitla
Ebba Ksour
Kasserine
Tala
Thélepte
To Le Kef & Jendouba
To Gafsa & Tozeur
ALGERIA
P1
P2
P3
P4
P12
P13
P14
P15
P17
C81
C82
C83
C87
C96
C119
0
20
km

gaining the status of free town. Unfortunately, with the victory of Caesar over the armies of Pompeii in **Thapsus** (46 BC), Sousse was again in the position of having chosen the wrong side and Caesar imposed heavy taxation on the town. Nevertheless under the rule of **Trajan** (98-117 AD) the city became an important commercial centre.

Sousse managed to survive the many invasions that followed until the Arab invasion in the 7th century when it was destroyed. In the 9th century, with the coming of the **Aghlabite Dynasty** to Kairouan, it again prospered, as that inland city's port, but it was conquered again in the 12th century by the Normans and in the 16th century by Spain. During WWII it was again seriously damaged.

ACCESS Buses come here from all the major cities to one of the 2 bus stations, either on Bab el Djedid or by place Farhat Hached, the main square. The train station is very convenient, right in the middle of the town on Blvd Hassouna Ayachi. Taxis and louages arrive by Bab el Djedid on Ave Mohammed Ali. The nearest airport is Skanes/Monastir.

Things to see

The old **Medina** is still surrounded by the original walls, built in 859 and restored in 1205. The way to enter the medina is either via Bab el Djedid, or through the place des Martyrs beside the central square which leads to the Great Mosque. The breach in the walls was the result of bombardments during 1943.

The **Great Mosque** is by a large esplanade leading towards the ribat. Built in the 9th century by the Aghlabite Emir Abou Abbas Mohammed, it was probably a conversion of a kasbah built a few years earlier. Further renovations and restorations have since taken place. On 2 corners large, round towers dominate the marble floored courtyard and make it look like the fortress it may originally have been. Overall the monument is very simple, the courtyard being decorated solely by inscriptions around its sides. Only the courtyard can be visited. Open 0800-1300, closed Fri. Entrance tickets TD4 can be bought opposite the mosque and at the local ONTT.

The **Ribat** is a type of fortified monastery. It formed part of a chain of forts built by the Arab Aghlabids along the coast which functioned as religious centres and a means of protection for the Muslim population against potential invaders. They communicated by smoke signals, since they were all in sight of one another. The ribat at Sousse was built in 820, using some materials from older sites, as can be seen at the entrance where antique columns are placed on either side of the door. The interior is very plain. On the first floor a large prayer room takes up all the S side. Go to the top of the watch tower, up the narrow stairway, where the view over the city and the sea is fantastic. Open 0800-1900 in summer, 0930-1200 and 1400-1800 in winter, closed Mon. Entrance TD4, photo fee TD2.

The Zaouia Zakkak is a beautiful building dominated by a small Turkish octagonal minaret. You cannot visit the inside, but from the outside it is splendid.

The **museum** is set in the **kasbah**, at the SW end of the medina. The kasbah was built in the 11th century and ex-

Climate: Sousse

	Jan	Feb	Mar	Apr	May	Jun	Jul	Aug	Sep	Oct	Nov	Dec	Av/Tot
Max (°C)	16	17	19	20	23	28	30	31	29	25	21	18	23
Min (°C)	6	7	10	12	15	20	22	22	21	16	12	9	14
Rain (mm)	31	17	22	32	14	4	1	17	18	48	36	42	282

tended in the 16th, around an old signal tower (the Khalef) dating back to 859. The museum contains mainly mosaics which are well presented and well preserved. Though less numerous and interesting than the Bardo's collection in Tunis, Sousse has its share of masterpieces. The majority of the mosaics are

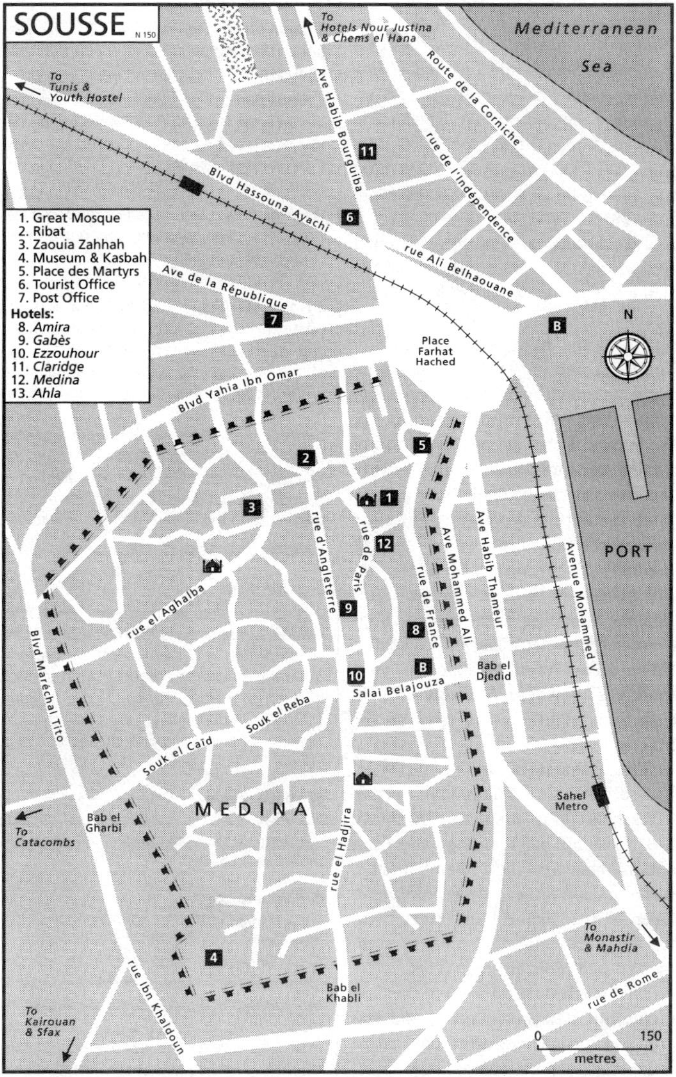

from the 3rd and 4th centuries, the central theme being the sea. Particularly worth seeing is the 3rd century '*Bacchus' Triumph*' in room 8. This mosaic, found in Sousse, illustrates the victory of a young god over the forces of evil. Another mosaic nearby portrays Zeus and Ganymède. See also the '*Lion and the Dog catching a Hare*' in room 14 dating from the end of the 2nd century. Entrance is via Blvd Maréchal Tito. Open 0800-1200 and 1500-1900 in summer, 0930-1200 and 1400-1800 in winter. Closed Mon, entrance fee TD4, photo fee TD2.

The **Souks** are mainly situated around the N end of the rue d'Angleterre. On the W is Souk el Reba, where material and perfume are sold. Again on the right is the Kalaout el Koubba, a building whose original function is unknown but which was probably built in the 19th century. Continue up the Souk el Reba and go out by Bab el Gharbi and turn left along the walls to come to the kasbah and the museum. After visiting the museum re-enter the medina by following the walls to the Bab el Khabli. Following the rue el Hadjira will bring you back to the rue d'Angleterre. Shopping in the tourist shops on rue d'Angleterre can be expensive. Either drive a hard bargain or buy your souvenirs elsewhere. **Markets** are held each Sun, slightly out of town on the Sfax road.

The Catacombs are to the W of Sousse, consisting of more than 250 galleries containing up to 15,000 tombs over a distance of 5 km. They were built and used between the 2nd and 4th centuries and are rather a disappointment. Open 0930-1200 and 1400-1800 in winter, 0800-1200 and 1500-1900 in summer. Closed Mon, entrance TD4.

The **beach** starts in front of the Corniche, but it is much nicer, and less crowded further N. Surfboards can be rented all along the beach.

Local information

● Accommodation

A *Hotel Chems el Hana*, T 228190/228192, elegant, adjacent to medina, 258 rm with bath, a/c, phone, TV, terrace, 2 restaurants, 2 pools, tennis, golf.

B *Nour Justina*, on Corniche, T 226382, seafront, food and service is reputedly not quite up to scratch.

C *Hotel Fares* , Blvd Hassouna Ayachi, just off place Farhat Hached, T 227800, central, private beach 200m away, a/c, high rm with view; **C** *Le Claridge*, Ave Bourguiba, T 224759, centre of new town, very noisy, very clean.

D *Hotel Ahla*, place de la Grande Mosquée, T 220570, clean, pleasant, very quiet, being refurbished and extended to 100 rm, owner says low prices will remain.

E *Hotel Medina*, behind the Great Mosque on rue de Paris, T 221722, very clean, some rm with bath, roof terrace, restaurant/bar, no phone bookings, so arrive early in summer; **E** *The Hotel Amira*, 52 rue de France, near Bab Djedid in the medina, T 226325, clean, half rm have bath, some with view, panoramic roof terrace; **E** *Hotel de Paris*, 15 rue des Rempart, by the walls close to place Farhat Hached, T 220564, very clean, some rm on the roof, close to the medina and the new town

F *Hotel Ezzouhour*, 48 rue de Paris, T 228729, in the medina, very simple, some rms with bath, otherwise communal shower, very cheap, pleasant manager; **F** *Hotel de Gabès*, 12 rue de Paris, T 226977, best of the cheap hotels, very clean, some rm on roof, good views from terrace, only 14 rm so book in summer; **F** *Hotel Perles*, 71 rue de Paris, T 224609, in the medina, very small, could be cleaner, communal shower, cheapest hotel in Sousse.

● Youth hostel

T 227548, 3 km out along Tunis road, at Plage Boujaafar, 2 km from station, kitchen, meals provided, 90 beds.

● Places to eat

There are plenty of places to choose from. Most restaurants cater for tourists with menus in many languages. Some cafés in the medina advertise only in Arabic. ♦♦♦ *Restaurant des Remparts*, T 226326, rue de l'Eglise, by medina walls close to place Farhat Hached, more expensive because it serves alcohol; *Restaurant Cherif*, by the harbour, specializes in fish and seafood; ***Le Bonheur***, T 225742, place Farhat Hached, good grilled meat and fish, large terrace on the street; ***Restaurant Mahlouf***, T 226508, place Farhat Hached, excellent food, particularly the fish, large terrace. ♦ ***Restaurant Hassoumi***, rue de Rabat, just off the Corniche, very cheap, good Tunisian food, clean; ***Restaurant Tunisien***, rue Ali Belhaouane, nice setting, some dishes a bit more expensive, very good fish; ***Restaurant Populaire***, rue de France, typical medina restaurant; ***Restaurant Ben Henda***, rue de Paris, in the medina, simple but tasty food.

● **Banks**

BDS and **STB** on Ave Bourguiba; **UIB**, Ave Habib Thameur; **BT**, rue Ali Belhaouane; **BNT**, rue de l'Indépendence. Money can also be changed in any of the large hotels along the Corniche.

● **Chemist**

Open nights, 38 Ave de la République, T 224725; 45 route de la Corniche; Ave H. Thameur.

● **Harbour**

The harbour has berths for 10 yachts, min-max draft 3-9m.

● **Hospital**

Ave Farhat Hached, rue Ibn el Jattar, T 221411.

● **Post Office**

Ave de la République, just off place Farhat Hached.

● **Telephones**

Local code 03.

● **Travel agents**

Carthage Tour, Ave Bourguiba, T 227954; *Tourafrica*, rue Khaled Ibn Walid, T 224277; *Tunisian Travel Service*, route de la Corniche, T 227599.

● **Tourist information**

Regional ONTT, 1 Ave Bourguiba, by place Farhat Hached, T 225157, Tx 230754, open 0730-1930 most days. The local office is opposite, T 220431.

● **Transport**

Car hire Avis, route de la Corniche, T 225901; **Budget**, 63 Ave Bourguiba, T 224041; **Europcar**, route de la Corniche, T 226252; **Hertz**, Ave Bourguiba, T 225428; **Inter Rent**, route de la Corniche, T 227562; **Top Car**, rue Ahmed Zaatir, T 226060.

Air Tunis Air, Ave Bourguiba, T 227955 for details of flights from Skanes/Monastir airport.

Train 'Sahel Metro' is one line which goes all the way to **Mahdia** along the coast stopping at all the resorts, small towns and Monastir international airport. Hourly from 0600-2000. The trip **Sousse-Mahdia** takes just under 2 hrs. The station is at the S end of Ave Mohammed V, 100m down from the Bab Djedid towards the harbour.

For Tunis: The station is on Blvd Hassouna Ayachi, up the road from place Farhat Hached. Information on T 221955. Departures to **Tunis** 0337, 0525, 0644, 0753, 1305, 1415, 1515, 1825, 2017; **Gabès** (via El Djem/Sfax) 0918, 1514, 1624, 1858, 2027, 2334; **Gafsa/Metlaoui** 2334.

Road There are 2 bus stations. The first is on place Sidi Yahya by the Bab Djedid, the second by place Farhat Hached, on the place du Port. Information on T 224202. Departures from Bab Djedid to **Kairouan** 0630, 0945, 1130, 1500; **Hammamet/Nabeul** 0430, 0515, 0815, 0930, 1520; Sfax 1730; **Gabès** and **Sfax** 0830, 0900, 1030, 1130, 1330; **Djerba** (via Zarzis) 1000, 2230; **Kebili/Douz** 1430, 2300; **Medenine** 0900, 1130, 1330, 2215, 2300; **Matmata** 2230; **Tataouine** 1130, 2130; **Port el Kantaoui** hourly from 0610 to 2110. Departures from place du Port Tunis 0700, 0800, 1045, 1430, 1500, 1700; **Bizerte** 1500. **Louages**: the louage station is by Bab Djedid, on rue Mohammed Ali.

EXCURSIONS FROM SOUSSE

Port el Kantaoui

10 km N of Sousse, Port el Kantaoui is a recently developed (1979) artificial tourist town. It has been created with a certain amount of good taste with many restaurants and cafés and lots of 4 star hotels. In addition, it boasts a 340 berth marina, yacht basin and golf courses. The overall impression is, fortunately, not too overpowering. Offering every imaginable facility, Port el Kantaoui is geared, unashamedly, towards mass charter tourism.

● **Accommodation AL** *Diar el Andalous* T 241855, luxurious, 300 rm, beach, a/c, indoor and outdoor pools, tennis, disco, free watersports; **AL** *Marhaba Palace* T 243633/240200, just like a palace, 250 splendid rm, indoor and outdoor pools, tennis, garden. **C** *Hotel Salem*, Ave Bourguiba, 261 rm, no a/c, pool, disco, no credit cards. **NB:** don't look for cheap hotels in this area.

• **Places to eat** are all expensive. All hotel restaurants provide good (pricey) meals as do *Le Beach Club*, T 241799, *Le Yacht Club*, T 241799 and *Le Club House*, T 241756. For cheap meals go into Sousse.

• **Sport Golf** El Kantaoui T 231755 has a 27 hole tournament golf course, par 108, 9,576m where green fees are TD30-TD40 per round and lessons are available. Monastir Golf course, shaded by olive trees, is 18 hole, par 72, 6,140m. **Sailing** Yachts and catamarans can be hired from the yacht basin or you can take a trip in an ancient sailing boat. Aquascope trips available to view underwater life. Harbour has berths for 300 yachts, min-max draft 2-4m. **Scuba diving** with tuition and equipment.

Enfida

43 km N of Sousse, Enfida is a large administrative centre of little touristic interest, situated where the P2 to Kairouan leaves the main P1 route from Tunis to Sousse.

Things to see The **Museum** in the old French church on the main street contains a mixture of old tombstones and mosaics. It is interesting as it demonstrates the diversity of Tunisia's cultural and religious past. Entrance TD1. Each Sun a highly colourful **market**, where all the farmers and bedouins from the surrounding areas meet, is held at the S end of town on the road to Sousse and Kairouan. Many things, including material and clothes, are much cheaper here than in Tunis.

A WWII cemetery lies to the W of town containing graves of 1,551 soldiers from Britain and the Commonwealth who died in 1943 during the Eighth Army's advance across North Africa.

Takrouna

A small Berber village perched 195m high on an outcrop, Takrouna has an amazing view. It is reached by leaving Enfida on the C133 to Zaghouan and taking the signposted 2nd turning on the left after 5 km. The village is noted for its honey.

S from Enfida the P1 cuts through the salt water marsh and lakes to Sousse. The road to **Hergla**, on the left 17 km from Enfida, offers an alternative, more scenic, route to Sousse and the opportunity to view the surrounding area.

Monastir

Lying on the coast about 25 km S of Sousse on a headland at the S point of the Gulf of Hammamet, Monastir is an attractive fishing port with an elegant promenade along the bay.

History

Habib Bourguiba was born here in 1903, and this has largely contributed to the development of the town. It is now part of a large tourist complex which continues N to Skanes and Sousse. Monastir's history goes back to Phoenician times, later becoming a major military base for Caesar. During the 7th century, with the construction of the ribat, it became part of the coastal defence system. Then, after the fall of Kairouan in the 11th century, Monastir became the religious capital. The Turks made it into a stronghold and it was not until 3 Aug 1903, when Bourguiba put in an appearance, that Monastir made it back onto the map.

ACCESS The 'Sahel Metro' runs from the airport, 9 km away, to town. The bus, train and louage stations are on Ave de la République just 5 min walk to the town centre.

Things to see

The **Ribat** was built in 796 by Harthama Ibnou Ayyoun, as part of the coastal look out system. One of the oldest and largest of the military structures built by the Arabs in North Africa, it was later re-fortified and surrounded by an additional wall in during the 9th and 11th centuries,

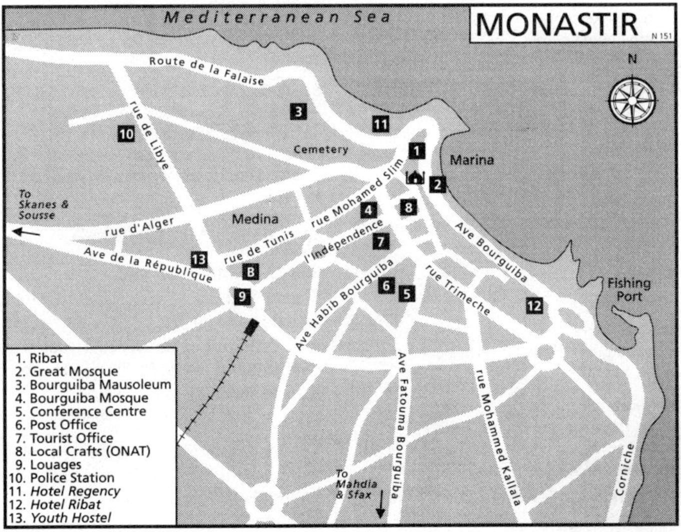

which gives the whole edifice an interesting mixture of contrasting styles and shapes. The view over the sea from the top of the Nador (watch tower) is recommended, especially at sunset. The ribat holds a small, interesting **Islamic Museum** mostly containing old manuscripts and miniatures and a unique Arab astrolabe (for measuring altitude) dating back to the 10th century. Open 0800-1900 in summer, 0900-1200 and 1400-1800 in winter. Closed Mon, entrance TD3, photo fee TD2.

The style of the **Great Mosque** is simple, in contrast with that of the ribat. Built in the 9th century, it was later extended in the 11th century. Notice that some of the pillars have capitals of an earlier date.

The **Bourguiba Mausoleum**, where ex-President Bourguiba is buried, was built in 1963 at the same time as the **Bourguiba Mosque**. The mosque is in the old town and was built following the richly decorated traditional style of architecture. The mosque cannot be visited.

The **medina** is over clean and sanitized and has been so extensively restored that it has lost its original character and much of its interest.

There is a weekly Sat **market** in Souk Essabt on place Guedir El Foul and the rue Salem B'Chir. Local **handicrafts** can be seen at the ONAT in quartier Chraga in the centre of Monastir.

Local information

● Accommodation

Most of the hotels are very expensive, and mainly uninspiring tower blocks. You are advised to go back to Sousse or on to Mahdia for the night. **E** *Hotel Yasmin*, route de la Falaise T 462511, very pleasant, 16 rm, cheap, welcoming, with a beach across road and a very good restaurant frequented by locals.

● Youth hostel

On rue de Libye, town centre, T 461216, 60 beds.

● Places to eat

Le Grill on marina, T 460923; *La Pizzeria*, T 460923, Port de Plaisance, on marina. Good snack bar at airport.

● Banks

STB and **UIB**, Ave Bourguiba; **BT**, place de

l'Indépendence. Money can also be changed in large hotels.

● Chemist
Charhine on Ave Bourguiba and Karoui on Ave de la République.

● Garage
There are 3 garages on Ave Bourguiba.

● Hospital
Hôpital Fattouma Bourguiba, Ave Fattouma Bourguiba, T 461141.

● Police
On rue de Libye, T 461432.

● Post Office
Ave Bourguiba, by the Palais des Congrès (conference centre).

● Sport
Golf There is a golf course, T 461120, 10 km out of town, on road to Sfax and Kairouan, 6,140m, par 72, green fees TD26-30.

Horse riding available, ask at any large hotel for details.

Watersports including scuba diving and sailing, at the Cap Monastir. Ask at *Hotel Marina* T 462066. Monastir Yacht club has 386 berths.

● Telephones
Local code 03.

● Tourist Information
ONTT, Quartier Chraga, in front of the Bourguiba Mosque, T 461960. Also in front of the airport, T 461205.

● Travel agents
Tourafrica, Ave Bourguiba, T 461381; *Carthage Tours*, in *Hotel Habib* on Corniche, T 461847.

● Transport
Car hire Avis, airport, T 461381; **Europcar**, airport, T 461314; **Hertz**, Ave Bourguiba, T 461404, and at airport, T 461088; **Inter rent**, airport, T 461314. **'Sahel Metro'** goes to the airport and to **Sousse** and **Mahdia** along the coast every hour from 0600-2000.

Air *Tunis Air* at airport, T 460300 and in Monastir close to *Hotel Ribat*, T 462550, ***Air Liberté***, airport, T 460300. Flight information Skanes/Monastir airport on T 461313. Departures to **Djerba** Tue 1620 and Fri 1635; **Tunis** Thur 0720. **Scheduled international flights, Rome** Mon 1505; **Frankfurt** Tue 0920; **Nice** Thur 0720; **Lyon** Fri 1055; **Paris** Sat 1530 and Sun 1530; **Brussels** Sun 0955.

Train Opposite the bus station. Information on T 460755. **Tunis** (via Sousse) 0610, 1238, 1758.

Road Bus: the bus station is at the S end of Ave de la République. Information on T 461059. Departures to **Tunis** 0445; **Sfax** 0500, 0600, 1100. There are also frequent buses to **Sousse. Louages: leave from in front of the bus station.**

Mahdia

South of Monastir and 60 km from Sousse, Mahdia is a charming little town which has so far escaped the tourist mania of the rest of the coast. Situated on the headland of Cap d'Afrique the town is surrounded by sea on 3 sides.

History

The history of Mahdia is closely linked with the Shi'ite branch of Islam. The Shi'ites believe that the Caliph must descend from Ali and Fatima (the prophet's daughter) and that the Sunnis are usurpers and heretics. After a 7 year war with the Aghlabids, **Obaid Allah**, known as **El Mehdi** (the Saviour), the founder of the Fatimid dynasty (followers of Fatima) finally secured victory and sought to establish his own capital. Mahdia was founded in 912 on an easily defended site and El Mehdi settled down in the still unfinished town in 921 in order to reinforce his power and protect himself. However his cruelty and his enemies' hatred made peace short-lived. In 944 the city was kept under siege for 8 months by the army of Abou Yazid. The siege was unsuccessful. The new dynasty moved to a city closer to Kairouan, Sabra el-Mansouriyya. The inhabitants of the abandoned capital concentrated on the sea for their welfare with the profits from fishing, commerce and piracy bringing a period of prosperity.

However reprisals followed, with first an unsuccessful Christian expedition to dislodge the pirates in 1088, then the occupation by Roger of Sicily in 1148. Later various other attempts were made to rid the town of the pirates, by a

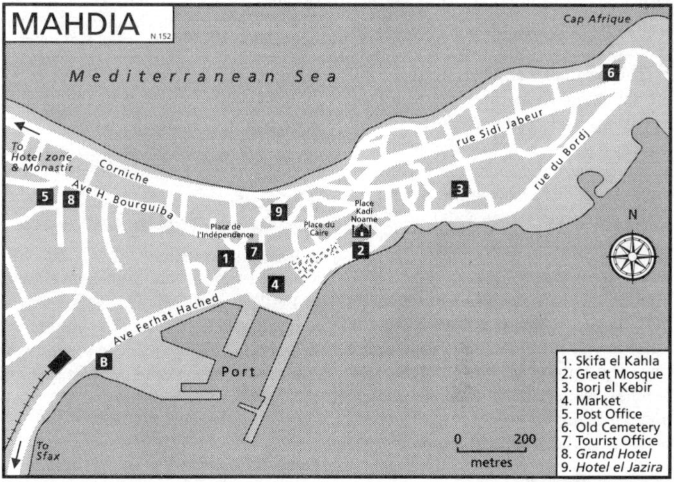

joint French-Genoan force in 1390 and in 1550 by Charles V of Spain. The Spanish were finally successful in 1554. As a result, the inhabitants were forced to revert to more traditional ways of life, such as olive cultivation and the production and weaving of silk. Today Mahdia is one of the largest fishing ports in Tunisia. The industry specializes in 'blue fish' such as mackerel and sardines, employing lamps at night to attract the fish.

ACCESS Bus station by the market and the harbour. The train station and louage station are nearby.

Things to see

The **Medina** is beautiful even though there are not many specific things to see. Stroll around on the marble paved streets and peep into the doorway of one of the numerous weaving workshops producing high quality silk and cotton material for wedding dresses. At night, go for a walk towards the main square in the medina, place du Caire, and have a drink in the café under the arcades. This is the local social centre and has a lot of atmosphere. There is a walk to the end of **Cap Afrique**, through the old cemetery to the lighthouse.

Skifa el Kahla (Obscure Gateway), is the main gate into the town. The tip of the Cap and the medina used to be behind a large wall and only 'safe' people were permitted to enter. At the time of El Mehdi only troops and a few, privileged people lived within the walls in order to minimize the risk of rebellion. The people lived outside, but within the walls were their shops and workshops. This meant that starting a rebellion during the day could jeopardize the life of their families outside, while to do so during the night would lead to the loss of their livelihood. The present gate was built in 1554, after El Mehdi's time, following the departure of the Spanish. There is an impressive view over the medina and the sea from the top. Entrance TD1.

The **Great Mosque** is on place Kadi Noamene, at the top of the main street. The mosque was totally rebuilt in 1963 following the original 10th century Fatmid plans. The work was done with great skill and faithfulness to the original. Unfortunately the mosque cannot be visited.

The **Bordj el Kebir** was built around the same period as the Skifa el Kahla. The Bordj is an impressive fortress built on the highest point of the headland overlooking the sea. The view from the top is good, but a visit to the Bordj is of limited interest. Open 0800-1200 and 1500-1900, closed Mon, entrance TD1.

Beaches

Mahdia has very beautiful beaches. By the village the shore is rocky, but the water is very clear. Further N along the Corniche, towards the hotels, the beaches are excellent. 'A Zone Touristique' is being built N of Mahdia which will reduce the area's attraction.

Local information

● Accommodation

B *Club Cap Mahdia*, along route Touristique, T 80300, 250 rm, beautiful, newly built, beach, quality service, pool, nightclub, tennis, horse-riding and all watersports, closed Nov and Dec, value for money.

D *Sables d'Or*, 3km N out of town, along the Corniche, T 681137, by the sea, beach, 68 rm are individual bungalows, sea view, most watersports; **D** *Grand Hotel (Panorama)*, Ave Bourguiba, by post office, T 680039, 1930s, charming, well placed for beach and medina, 35 rm, 10 with bath, some with balcony, roof terrace, new ownership.

F *Hotel el Jazira*, rue Ibn el Fourat, close to Skifa el Kahla, T 680274, only hotel in the medina, very simple, clean, communal bath/ toilet rather antiquated, uninviting, some rm with sea view.

● Youth hostel

In Mahdia, T 681559, 100 beds, meals available, family rms, signposted from railway station, about 5 min walk. Another at Chebba, T 683815, 37 km from Mahdia, 60 beds, convenient for those taking the coast road C82 S to Sfax.

● Places to eat

Restaurant le Lido, by harbour, very good fish; *Restaurant el Moez*, between main gate and market, very cheap, good food, typical local restaurant, no alcohol.

● Banks

BT and **STB** on Ave Bourguiba; **BNT** on place de l'Indépendence.

● Harbour

20 yacht berths, min-max draft 3-6m.

● Market

On E side of port sells fish daily and other fresh produce and general goods on Fri.

● Post Office

In the new part of town on Ave Bourguiba.

● Tourist information

Inside the medina's main gate, Skifa el Kahla, on the right, T 681098.

● Transport

Train 'Sahel metro' Train every hour 0600-2000 to **Monastir, Skanes/Monastir airport** and **Sousse. Train** station is down the street from the bus station, by the harbour. **Tunis** (via Sousse) 0500, 1130, 1645.

Road The bus station is by the harbour. Frequent buses to **Sousse** and **Monastir**. Less frequent buses to **Tunis, Sfax, Gabès** and **Kairouan**. **Louages** By the harbour, beyond the bus station, destinations **El Djem, Kairouan, Monastir, Sfax** and **Sousse**.

KAIROUAN

Pop 100,000 *Alt* 60m.

The recommended route goes inland now to Kairouan, situated 65 km SW from Sousse along the P12 in the middle of a large plain and visible for miles around. The spiritual and religious capital of Tunisia, the city was the first base for the conquering Arab, and Muslim armies from the E. Still surrounded by the original walls, the town has a particular charm. The early morning or evening light over its ochre buildings is especially beautiful. Kairouan is also the capital of traditional carpet manufacture and the market town for Tunisia's main fruit growing area. It has a healthy climate thanks to its altitude. It stands at the junction of roads to Tunis, Sousse and Gafsa.

History

The city was founded in 671 by Aqbar ibn Naffi as an outpost for the conquest of

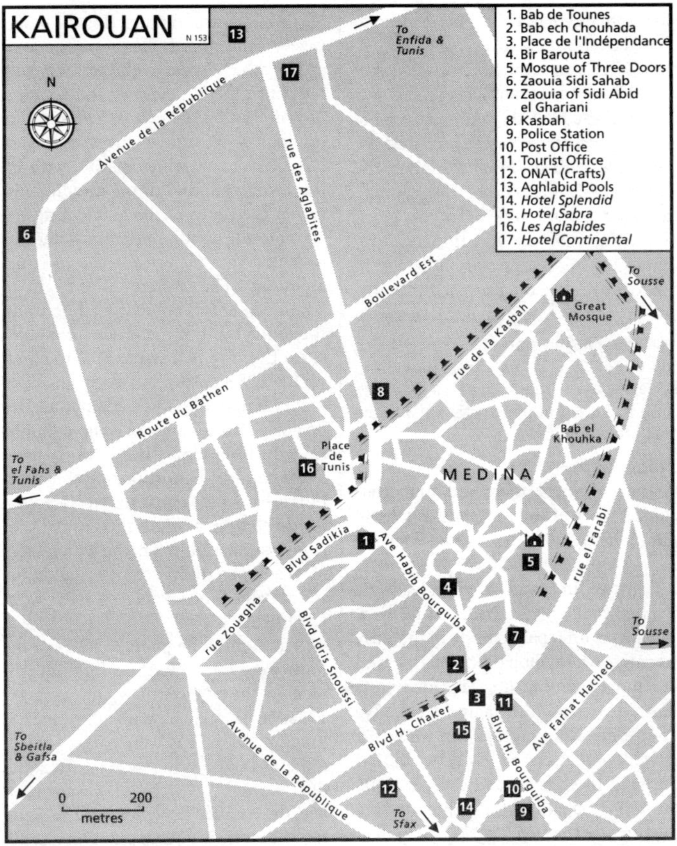

the Maghreb. He chose the site for its strategic value, being both far enough away from the coast where Byzantine fleets still threatened, and from the Berbers in the mountains who were strongly opposed to the new invaders. The town was attacked by the Berbers who won 2 significant victories, the more important in 688. The hostilities did not last long, however, with the Berbers soon converting to Islam. During the 9th century and the rule of the Aghlabids, the town found prosperity, and independence from Baghdad.

With the arrival of the Fatimids in North Africa in 909 a break occurred within Kairouan, an established centre for Sunnism, and the new Shi'ite leadership. As a result, El Medhi founded Madhia and moved his capital there. After the rebellion of Abou Yazid, in 953, the new Fatimid Caliph El-Mansor moved the capital back to a new city, Sabra el-Mansouriyya, just 2 km away from Kairouan. This meant the older settlement was bypassed commercially, most trade being done in the new city.

The real decline came with the invasion from Egypt in 1057, when Kairouan changed its allegiance from the Fatimids in Cairo to the Abbasids in Baghdad. The city was ransacked and it was not until the Hafsids were in control of Kairouan in the 13th century that the city redeveloped. Finally, under the Husseinite Dynasty in the 18th century, the city regained some of its past glory. Today Kairouan is a very important religious centre, the primary holy city in the Maghreb region, preceded in status only by Mecca, Medina and Jerusalem.

ACCESS The bus station is SE of Bab ech Chouhada, 15 mins walk from the centre. Louages from Tunis arrive at Bab ech Chouhada. All others arrive outside the post office.

Things to see

If time is short there are numerous guided tours of the town which take in the main sights. These leave from the Tourist Office.

The **Medina** is still surrounded by its original walls and is an interesting place to walk around, particularly in the early morning when shops are opening and the sun is coming up. The medina is centred around the main street, Ave Bourguiba. Walking up here from Bab ech Chouhada, on the right after the Bir Barouta, there is a small covered souk. Further up, again on the right following the signs for the *Hotel Marhala*, is a small busy market. The medina gets very lively in the morning towards the Bab de Tounes, at the N end of Ave Bourguiba.

The **Great Mosque**, built by Aqbar ibn Naffi, dates from the founding of the city in 671, and was built to be the centre of the new town. As such it is the oldest western mosque. It was severely damaged by the Berbers in 688, was virtually rebuilt in the 9th century and later enlarged, but nevertheless has kept its original style. The courtyard is very large, paved in white marble with an interesting sundial in the middle indicating the times of the 5 daily prayers. Close to the sundial the rain water was collected in a cistern for use in ritual ablutions. The minaret is thought to date from 836. The door leading up to the top is built of materials from older sites. Enquire if it is possible to climb up the 128 steps for a superb view. The prayer hall is filled with numerous imposing granite and marble columns brought from older sites in other parts of the country. Unfortunately non-Muslims are unable to view the woodcarving on the pulpit or the 9th century tiles from Baghdad in the niche which faces Mecca. Open daily except Fri and during prayers. Buy tickets TD4 at the Tourist Office.

The **Aghlabide pools** to the N of the town were built by Abou Ibrahim Ahmed in the 9th century. One is large, 128m in diameter, while the other is much smaller. They were part of a much more elaborate water system. An aqueduct carried water from a nearby river and the smaller pool was used to settle the silt carried in the water. Open 0830-1730 winter, 0800-1200 and 1500-1900 summer. Entrance TD4.

Zaouia Sidi Sahab (also known as the Barber's Mosque) is the burial place of one of the Prophet's companions, Abou Djama El Balaoui. The Zaouia is known as the Barber's Mosque because Abou El

CLIMATE: KAIROUAN

	Jan	Feb	Mar	Apr	May	Jun	Jul	Aug	Sep	Oct	Nov	Dec	Av/Tot
Max (°C)	16	19	21	24	28	33	37	36	32	26	22	18	26
Min (°C)	5	6	8	10	14	18	20	21	18	15	10	7	13
Rain (mm)	24	18	46	35	22	11	5	17	37	77	16	18	326

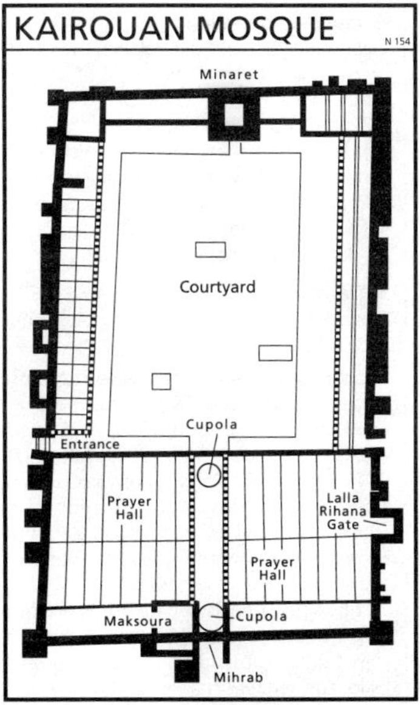

Balaoui carried about with him 3 hairs from the Prophet's beard, from which he would never be parted! The present building dates back to the 17th century. It is beautifully decorated with Andalusian style ceramics. To get to the mausoleum, you first enter into a small room and continue along an open air corridor, richly decorated in multi-coloured ceramics. The next small room with a finely worked plaster ceiling opens on to the main courtyard, with the mausoleum. Access is reserved to Muslims. Notice the painted wooden ceilings under the arcade surrounding the courtyard. On Fri when circumcision ceremonies take place and during the Mouled (the Prophet's birthday), there are numerous pilgrims.

Mosque of the Three Doors, on the E side of Bir Barouta, built in 866, is one of the oldest mosques in Kairouan which takes its name from the 3 large doors leading inside. There are interesting inscriptions above the doorway.

To reach the **Zaouia of Sidi Abid el Ghariani**, in the medina, take the 2nd road on the right after the main gate. This burial place of Sidi Abid, a 13th century saint, was constructed in the 14th century. Of particular interest is the room with the mausoleum. The ceiling is extremely finely worked wood, with fine plasterwork all around. The building in itself is very beautiful, based around 3 courtyards. Today it houses the office of the Association de Sauveguard de la Medina (an organisation dedicated to helping to preserve the medina) and the regional office of the National Art and Archaeology Institute. Open during office hours, entrance TD4.

Bir Barouta, in the centre of the medina, is an old well which functions by the movement of a camel going round in circles. Not an essential visit!!

Local information

● Accommodation

Don't worry about the address, all the hotels are all clearly signposted in English. **B** *Hotel Continental*, T 220607, to the N by the Aghlabides pool, 175 rm, a/c, large pool, garden.

C *Hotel les Aghlabites*, T 220855, rue de Fés, to the S of the town, 62 rm, a/c, pool; **D** *Le Splendid*, T 220522, rue du 9 Avril, 28 rm with bath, a/c, clean, basic, bar and busy restaurant, slightly over-priced.

E *Tunisia*, T 221855, Ave Farhat Hached, 11 rm, no restaurant, comfortable, very clean, no a/c but fans on ceiling.

F *Hotel Marhala*, T 220736, 35 Souk El Belaghjia in the medina, 30 rm, well run, small, view from top rm, roof terrace; **F** *Hotel Les Aglabides*, on the left of place de Tunis, T 220880, very simple hotel arranged round central courtyard, few rm have showers (cold), many pilgrims lodge here; **F** *Hotel Sabra*, T 220260, rue Ali Belhaouane, by the main gate, clean, pleasant, friendly staff, roof terrace, 56 beds, rm at back are quieter.

● Youth hostel

Ave de Fés, T 220309, in the new town, kitchen, 70 beds.

● Places to eat

Restaurant Faizour, signposted off Ave Bourguiba in the medina, good food, cheap; ***Restaurant El Karawan***, rue Soukeina Ben El-Houssein, behind *Tunisia Hotel*, typical Tunisian cooking, family run. ***Restaurant Sabra***, Ave Farhat Hached, an excellent, cheap place to eat typical Tunisian food; ***Roi du Couscous***, place du 7 Novembre, Tunisian food at cheap prices, closes in late afternoon, best for lunch or early dinner.

● Banks

BDS, UIB and **BT** on place de l'Indépendence.

● Bargains

Kairouan is one of the major centres for **carpets** in the country. Visit first the display of old and new carpets at the ONAT on Ave Ali Zouaoui, to get an idea of real prices even though carpets can be cheaper elsewhere. Be careful when walking around, the 'Musées de Tapis' (carpet museums) are really shops which have their own carpets on display.

● Hospital

By the Aghlabide pools, T 220036.

● Police

T 220577.

● Post Office

Place du 7 Novembre, rue Farhat Hached.

● Telephones

Local code 07.

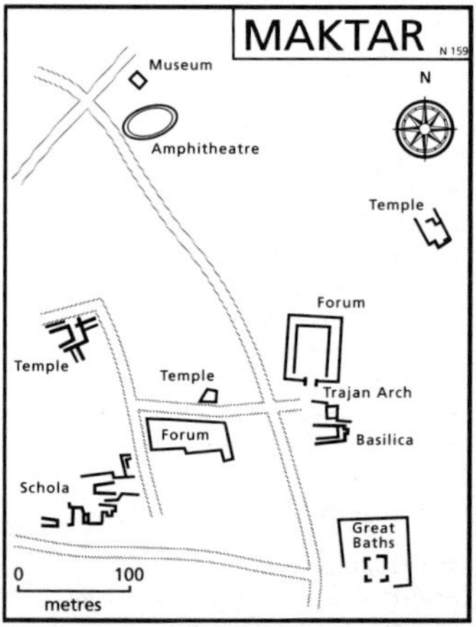

● Tourist information

Opposite gate to old city, Bab ech Chouhada, on the main square. There are 2 offices. The local Tourist Office (Syndicat d'Initiative), T 220452, open daily 0800-1700 is the place to buy tickets for the monuments. Welcoming, competent staff will organize you a tour or an official guide if requested. The National Office (ONTT) is next door, T 221797, closed Sun. Stocks of official maps often run out.

● Transport

Car hire Budget, Ave de la République, T 220528.

Road Bus: the station is on the road to Sousse. For information T 220125. Departures to **Tunis** 0530, 0600, 0700, 0900, 1000, 1130, 1215, 1300, 1345, 1515, 1545, 1730, 0200, 0230, 0315, 0330, 0430; **Kebili/Douz** (via Gafsa and Tozeur) 1030; **Gafsa** 0830; **Tozeur** 1330; **Djerba** (via Gabès and Djorf) 2200; **Zarzis** (via Medenine) 2230; **Medenine** 2330; **Nefta** (via Gafsa and Tozeur) 1551, 2330.

Louages Departures for **Tunis** are from Bab ech Chouahada. All other destinations leave from the post office. To **El Djem** possible by louage, requires changes and patience.

Around Kairouan

Kelbia Lake is halfway between Kairouan and Sousse. It lies to the SW of the P2, the main road from Nabeul to Kairouan just after the intersection with the MC48 road to Sousse. The best way to view the lake is to walk around the shore, but clear paths and viewing points are rare as the water level of the lake changes during the year. In summer it is dry. It is an important **Wildlife Reserve**, with a wide variety of birds. During the summer you may spot squacco herons, purple gallinules or the fantailed warbler. In the winter, migrating birds such as flamingoes pass through.

Maktar

Maktar, population 7,500, lies 114 km W of Kairouan along the scenic P 12. The Roman city of Mactaris which dates from around AD 200 was built on the site of an earlier Numidian defensive position. The ruins are entered by the museum through the Roman gate. The remains of the **amphitheatre** lie to the left and further left, across the Roman road are the remains of a **temple** dedicated to the Carthaginian god Hathor Miskar. The central section of the site contains the former forum and the remains of Trajan's Arch, looking less triumphal than in its heyday of 115 AD. Beyond are the foundations of the 5th century **Basilica of Hildeguns** and after another 100m are the **Baths** which are considered the best preserved thermal baths in Africa. Much of the splendour is in its mosaics.

To the W lies the **Schola Juvenum**, claimed as one of the prettiest ruins in Tunisia, once an educational establishment for young people and in the area around this is a temple dedicated to Bacchus, an open space that was the Forum, a cemetery and yet more baths.

Maktar town lies to the N of the site and at an altitude of over 900m is refreshingly cool. The town is built on the hillside and the buses stop at the lower end of the town while the louages stop higher up the main street.

- **Accommodation** C *Mactaris*, T 876014, 20 rms, reasonable standard.

Sbeitla

ACCESS The bus station is in the centre of the new town and the louages are next to it. Many buses come here from Kasserine, Gafsa, Tunis and Kairouan.

The 75 km journey S from Maktar to Sbeitla is along winding minor roads through the Dorsal region. Within 2 km of leaving Maktar, there is a magnificent view N to the mountains and as the P4 climbs through the Djebel Skarna (1076m), the Tunisia seen by the visitor here is in sharp contrast to the level plains of the Sahel. As the road descends, the ruins of the ancient settlement of Sufes at Sbiba lie to the left. 40 km beyond is Sbeitla.

The new city is of no special interest, but the old Roman ruins are really worth a visit, being considered one of the best preserved sites in Tunisia. Particularly interesting are the **Triumphal Arch** which forms part of the old walls to the S of the site and the **Forum**, a vast paved, square esplanade, which is entered through the Gate of Antoninus Pius and surrounded by a high wall. The 3 **temples** which stand opposite this gate are dedicated, it is assumed, to Juno, Jupiter and Minerva. They form an exceptional ensemble.

The central temple is larger and is more ornately decorated. The **Church of Servus the Priest** was built in the courtyard of an ancient pagan sanctuary. The **Basilica of Bellator** has 2 apses and a baptistery converted into a chapel dedicated to Bishop Juncundus (5th century) who is generally believed to have been martyred by the Vandals. The **Basilica Vitalis**, immediately adjacent, is larger, again with 2 apses.

The **Monumental fountain** is one of 3 public fountains dating from the 4th century. The **Theatre**, in rather a poor state of preservation, is still worth the detour if only for the magnificent view over the Oued Sbeitla. The tiers are in

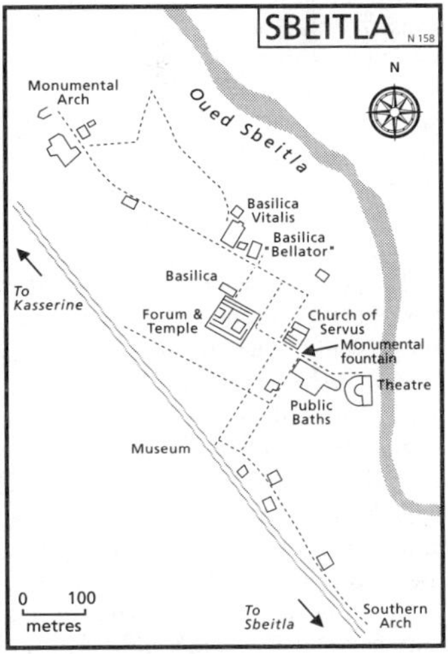

Esparto Grass – Paper In The Desert

Esparto grass, also called *Alfa* or *Halfa*, is a needlegrass (*Stipa tenacissima*) indigenous to northern Africa and southern Spain. It is very common on the infertile, dry, sandy soils of interior Tunisia and Algeria where nothing else will thrive. The plants grow in clumps maybe 2m across with the cylindrical stems reaching 1m in height. The young grass can be used as animal fodder but later becomes too tough even for camels to chew.

This grass has been used over the centuries to make ropes, mats, storage utensils, baskets and sandals. Today it is harvested for the manufacture of paper by a process developed in the UK in 1856. Esparto has a very high cellulose content. The fibres are strong and flexible, and standard in size and shape and make a better paper than either wood pulp or rags. The resulting paper is of high quality being uniform in texture, opaque and very smooth.

ruins but the orchestra pit is clearly visible as are the colonnades round the stage.

The Roman town, originally known as Sufetula, was probably built in the year 3 BC, but little is known about it until the period under the rule of Emperor Vespasian (69-79 AD). The town was very prosperous during the 2nd and 3rd centuries, judging by the remains of the public buildings. During the Byzantine period, the town was briefly made capital of the province then, in 646, the Governor Gregory declared himself independent from Constantinople called himself Emperor and moved his administration from Carthage to Sufetula, which he considered to be a better centre from which to defend the country against the Arabs. This proved not to be the case when Gregory was killed defending Sufetula in 647 and the town was taken by the Arabs.

The best time to visit this impressive ruined town is early in the morning or in the evening when the soft sunlight is particularly beautiful on the stones of the temples and one is less likely to have to share the experience with a bus-load of tourists. Open 0830-1730 winter and 0600-2000 in summer. Closed Mon, entrance TD2, photo fee TD2. Most of the site is accessible in a wheelchair.

Opposite the ruins (adjacent to the Coca-cola stall and coach park) is a museum containing artefacts and photographs of Sbeitla divided into 5 sections covering prehistory, Roman sculptures, ceramics, Christian/Byzantine and Muslim periods. A visit to the museum first may make the site visit more valuable. Open daily 0600-2000. Entry included in fee for ruins. There are toilets beside the museum.

Local information

● Accommodation

C *Hotel Sufetula*, just before the ruins en route from Kasserine, T 465074, pleasant, clean hotel, pool, a/c, it is the only good hotel in Sbeitla and charges accordingly.

● Youth hostels

In **Kasserine**, 67 km from Sbeitla, 3 km from Kasserine centre, T 07 470053, 70 beds, meals available; **Siliana**, 35 km N of Maktar, T 08870871, 70 beds.

Excursion to Kasserine

Kasserine lies 38 km SW of Sbeitla. Behind it to the W stands Djebel Shambi the highest peak in Tunisia providing an interesting dimension to the spectacular sunsets. Kasserine depends on esparto grass for its livelihood (see page24), and little else grows here. The town is dominated by the huge cellulose processing factory. The remains of the **Mausoleum of the Flavii** adjacent to the main road are more attractive. This is a 3 storey funeral tower of Roman origin and is the best preserved of its kind.

SFAX, THE KERKENNAH ISLANDS AND EL DJEM

Sfax

Pop 400,000 *Alt* 21m.

Sfax is the second largest city in Tunisia. It is highly industrialized, but the centre of the city has retained a lot of its charm. Sfax is a thriving city with 2 distinct parts: the new town, built to a geometric pattern, and the medina, still surrounded by its original walls. It is a delight for tired visitors for the site is absolutely flat.

History

Nothing remains of the ancient town of Taparura, but its commercial tradition is still well in place. In the 7th century the town was already a trade centre, exporting olive oil to Italy. By the 10th century, Sfax declared itself an independent state, only to be conquered by Roger of Sicily in 1148. It later put up a valiant resistance to the Venetians in 1785 and surrendered to the French in 1881 only after fierce attacks. Bombardment during WWII destroyed a large part of the town. Today, its main activity is centred around phosphate exports, but olive oil continues to be a major industry.

ACCESS The main bus station is at the E side of Ave Bourguiba, in front of the train station. There is another bus station at the other end of Ave Bourguiba at Ibn Chabat, beyond the market for services to Gabès and all destinations S. Louages stop on place de la République. The airport to the SW handles international package tours and internal flights.

Things to see

The **Archaeological Museum** is in place Hedi Chaker (in the new town), off Ave Bourguiba. This small museum displays Islamic, early Christian and Roman exhibits, mostly mosaics, manuscripts and pottery. There is a 3rd century Roman painted funeral artefact. Open 0900-1200 and 1500-1830 in summer, 1400-1730 in winter, closed Sun, entrance TD3.

The **Medina** is one of the best preserved and most authentic in Tunisia. Unlike the souks of Tunis and Sousse, it is primarily aimed at the locals, who do most of their shopping there. Many artisans and craftsmen still work here and earn a living in a traditional way. This all makes the medina very interesting for visitors, particularly as its walls are still intact and the difference in atmosphere between the old and new cities is clear.

Dar Jellouli houses the **Regional Museum of Popular Arts and Traditions** at 5 rue Sidi Ali Nour, off rue de la Driba. Set in a beautiful 17th century palace, the museum is extremely interesting and enables one to have a very good idea of life in Tunisia in the last century. On the ground floor the rooms are organized around a small courtyard. Each contains well-explained lifesize pictures of traditional Tunisian living. In one room is a kitchen complete with implements, in another living rooms with all the furniture and so on. On the 1st floor is a display of the traditional clothes and jewellery of each social class. A visit is definitely worthwhile and the setting is superb. Open 0930-1630, except Mon and public holidays, entrance TD3.

CLIMATE: SFAX

	Jan	Feb	Mar	Apr	May	Jun	Jul	Aug	Sep	Oct	Nov	Dec	Av/Tot
Max (°C)	16	18	20	22	26	29	32	32	30	26	22	18	24
Min (°C)	5	6	8	11	14	18	20	21	20	16	11	7	13
Rain (mm)	19	16	20	13	11	3	0	5	32	66	23	17	225

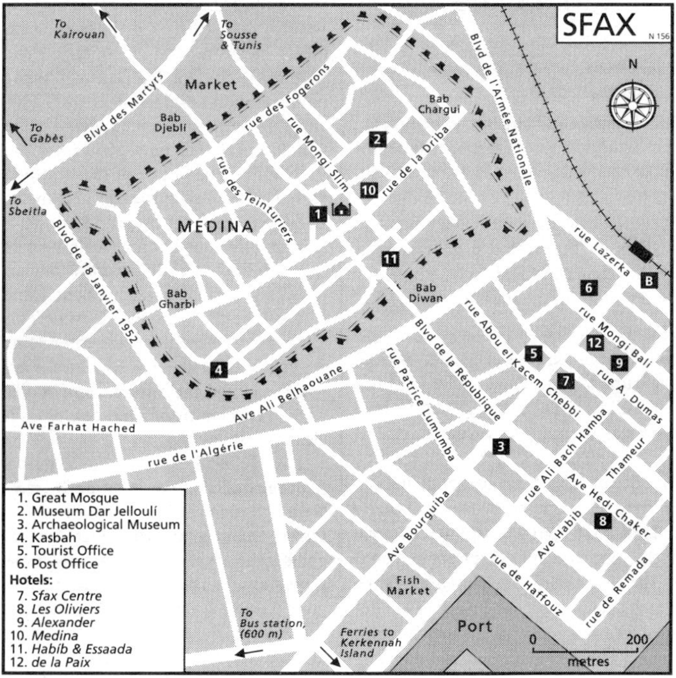

The **Great Mosque** was built in the 10th century, and from the outside the minaret, made of three superimposed towers in the same style as the Great Mosque of Kairouan, can be seen. Unfortunately, the interior is closed to visitors.

An interesting itinerary is to enter the medina by the main gate, **Bab Diwan**, and go up the road on the left, leading to the **Great Mosque**. Passing by, only glimpses of its interior, reputed to be very beautiful, can be seen since it is closed to visitors. Continue down rue des Teinturiers and enter the **souk**. Within the souks, one can find everything from clothes and meat to saddles for donkeys. At the end of this street are the city walls and the rue des Forgerons (ironmongers). Opposite is the **Bab Djebli**, a gate looking over a recently built market, where food is generally sold. This can be worth a visit. In the rue des Forgerons, artisans work in little workshops doubtless in the same way as they have for centuries. Go right up rue Mongi Slim. Again, this is the heart of the souks. Some buildings have superb façades. Follow rue de la Driba and on the left is the **Dar Jelloui Museum**. Without doubt, the best way to see the medina is to spend a few hours walking around, particularly as this is really one of the few authentic medinas left. Also of note is place de la Kasbah, to the W of Bab Diwan. The **kasbah** itself is of no great interest, but there is a beautiful private building on the square. In the streets leading into the medina from here notice the iron grilles on the 1st floors of most houses. Also notable is a beautiful 17th century private house on place Barberousse.

Local information

● Accommodation

A *Hotel Sfax Centre*, Ave Bourguiba, T 225700, 115 rm, 8 suites, brand new, very little character, all mod cons.

B *Novotel*, Route Soukra, T 243333, 127 rm, recommended to all travel agents.

C *Hotel Les Oliviers*, Ave Habib Thameur, new town centre, T 225188, charming, 50 rm, old style, good condition, pool.

D *Hotel Alexander*, rue Alexandre Dumas, T 221911, in new town, extremely well kept, 30 rm, clean, very good restaurant.

F *Hotel El Habib*, rue Borj Ennar, T 221373, in medina, 22 rm, clean, communal showers; **F** *Hotel Medina*, 53 rue Mongi Slim, T 220354, in medina (not surprisingly!), small, clean, pay shower; **F** *Hotel de la Paix*, rue Alexandre Dumas, T 221436, in new town, 30 rm, pay showers, very clean; **F** *Hotel Essaada*, rue Borj Ennar, T 220892, opposite *El Habib*, small, clean, communal showers.

● Youth hostel

On the road to the airport, T 243207, 126 beds, station 1 km.

● Places to eat

Le Baghdad, Ave Farhat Hached, very good restaurant, nice decor, but a bit expensive; *Le Corail*, T 227301, Ave Habib Maazoun, very comfortable restaurant, excellent seafood, expensive, but value for money; *Chez Nous*, rue Patrice Lumumba, good choice at a good price. *Restaurant Tunisien*, just inside Bab Diwan on the right, cheap, good food.

For a **drink** go to place de l'Indépendence and the surrounding streets, or to the medina. Try *Café Diwan*, on the left after the main gates following the walls.

● Banks

STB and **UIB**, Ave Hedi Chaker; **BIAT**, rue Salem Harzallah; **BT**, Ave Bourguiba; **BNT**, rue Taieb Mehiri; **UBCI**, rue Abou el Kacem Chebbi.

● Chemist

All night, *Rekik*, *Polyclinique Ettaoufik*, T 241105, 25 rue Alexandre Dumas; *Drira*, 109 Ave Farhat Hached.

● Hospital

Hôpital Hedi Chaker, route d'El Aïn, T 244422.

● Post office

Large building at E end of Ave Bourguiba.

● Telephones

Local code 04.

● Tourist Information

Place de l'Indépendence, in a little kiosk, T 224606.

● Travel agents

General Voyage, Ave Hedi Chaker, T 221067; *Tourafrica*, Ave Hedi Chaker, T 229089; *Univers Tours*, Ave Bourguiba, T 222029.

● Transport

Local: Car hire Avis, rue Tahar Sfar, T 224605; **Europacar**, rue du Commandant Béjaoui, T 226680; **Hertz**, 47 Ave Bourguiba, T 223553; **Locar**, rue Habib Maazoun, T 223738; **Rent a Car**, rue Habib Maazoun, T 227738; **Solvos**, rue Habib Maazoun, T 229882.

Ferry to the Kerkennah islands: summer (Jul-Aug) departures every 2 hrs 0600-2000. Winter 4 boats per day 0700-1700. Foot passengers 500 mills. The price for cars is TD5 and the crossing lasts just over 1 hr. For further information contact Sonatrak, Ave Hedi Khefacha, T 222216.

Air *Tunis Air*, 4 Ave de l'Armée, opposite the post office, T 228628; *Air France*, rue Taieb Mehiri, T 224847; *Tunisavia*, rue Habib Maazoun, T 222736. The airport is about 4 km SW on the road to Gafsa. Flights for **Tunis** Wed at 1700 and Thur at 2200.

Train Information on T 21999. Departures for **Tunis** (via Sousse) 0555, 1225, 1325, 1825, 0145; **Gabès** 1128, 0210; **Metlaoui** (via Gafsa) 0143.

Road Bus services for **Gabès, Djerba, Zarzis, Tataouine, Ben Ghardane** and **Tunis** leave from the bus station on Ave Bourguiba, by the train station. Information on T 22355. Departures **Djerba** (via Gabès) 0730, 1300, (via Gabès and Zarzis) 1100; **Tataouine** 1400, **Ben Ghadane** (via Medenine) 1530; **Tunis** 0800, 1200, 1500. Between midnight and 0200 there are 7 additional departures for Tunis. All other destinations are served from the bus station at the other end of Ave Bourguiba. **Louages**: leave from place de la République.

The Kerkennah Islands

There are 7 islands in the group with a total area of 15,000 ha made up of 6,000 ha of agriculture, 4,000 ha of palm trees and the rest uncultivated salt flats. The 2 large inhabited islands, Gharbi to W and Chergui to E, lie 20 km from the mainland. They are very beautiful, with wonderful, almost deserted, gently sloping sandy beaches, ideal for small children. The islands are almost flat (maximum altitude 13m) and covered in palm trees and with many lagoons. Historically they have been a place of exile, from Hannibal to Bourguiba. At the moment tourism is just developing with most of the hotels concentrated around the *zone des hôtels* in Sidi Frej, with a few in Remla.

The rest of the island is almost untouched, making it quite easy to 'get away from it all'. A good way to get around is to rent a bicycle from *Hotel Farhat*. Some of the beaches are difficult to get to without transport as the buses only go through the main villages. The inhabitants have the reputation of being the most hospitable in Tunisia. The people live largely off fishing and now tourism. The fishing is indeed an interesting event to watch as very unusual techniques are used. The traditional technique, known as *'sautade'*, resembles a hunt rather than fishing. The fishermen place baskets, made out of palm leaves, on the seabed and stand in the shallow waters surrounding the island, hitting the sea with palm tree fronds. The fish (mullet in this case) hide in the baskets and are consequently trapped. This is truly an interesting sight and can be viewed at very close range since many fishermen, for a small fee, will take a passenger with them. It is also possible to rent a *felouka* (traditional fishing boat) with a captain and go either for a day trip round part of the island and probably a quiet lunch out at sea, or for a week and a total tour of the island. Information for these trips at either El Attaya, a small fishing village in the N of the island, or at one of the 2 larger hotels, the *Grand Hotel* and the *Hotel Farhat*, in Sidi Frej.

Otherwise activity is restricted to lying on the beach and taking life easy! In Remla it is possible to visit a carpet factory, without the anxiety of sales pressure as here they don't sell, but ship them to the mainland for retail.

ACCESS Daily crossings from Sfax, 6 in summer, 4 in winter. Crossings take just over 1 hr. For information contact Sonatrak, Ave Hedi Khefacha, Sfax, T 222216. Most hotels in Sfax have timetables available. In Kerkennah the ferry lands at Sidi Youssef, on the island of Gharbi, about 20 km from the hotel zone. The 2 islands are linked by a Roman causeway. A minibus service is provided and will meet the incoming ferries, though this costs more than the service bus. A bus will go directly to the hotels, so be sure to take the right one! All buses go to Remla. For El Attaya, there are a few buses a day, but they tend to stop early, so check the times. Buses for the ferries leave about an hour before ferry departure time. Times can be checked at the bus station in Remla, right by the *Hotel el Jazira*. All other hotels should have this information. Otherwise, rent a bike, particularly as the islands are flat!

Things to see

Visit the museum in **Résidence du Salud du President Bourguiba** beyond El Attaya on the NE of Chergui. It commemorates Bourguiba's escape by boat into Libya in 1945 and contains the shack he hid in and some photographs. From Remla ½-day island tour TD13 or 'sea picnic' for TD20.

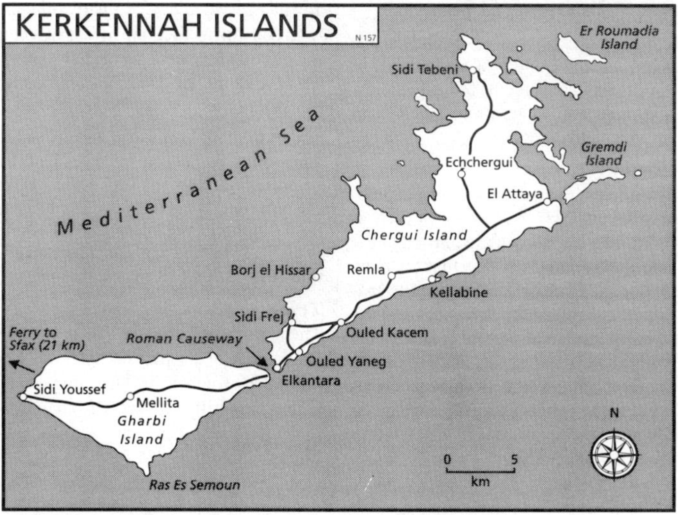

Local information

● Accommodation

Many hotels are closed in winter and those that remain open are often poorly heated. **C** *Grand Hotel*, Sidi Frej, T 281266, large hotel, 114 rm on 2 floors, half with sea view, a/c dining room, pool, tennis, organized watersports, cycle hire, nightclub, beach restaurant, open all year; **C** *Hotel Farhat*, Sidi Frej, T 281236, next to *Grand Hotel*, 308 rm, well decorated, pleasant, pool, tennis, beach virtually non-existent.

E *Hotel Cercina*, Sidi Frej, T 281228, very good, beach, half rm have bath, most rm are bungalows, some have sea view, restaurant has typical Kerkennian fish specialities.

F *Hotel el Jazira*, Remla, T 281058, well kept, small, 24 rm, communal bath/toilet, bar, good restaurant open all year but cold in winter.

● Youth hostel

Remla, just behind the stadium, T 281148, 80 beds, meals available, family rms.

● Camping

In El Attaya.

● Places to eat

Restaurant La Sirène by the bank in Remla, very good fish and seafood, alcohol available, shaded terrace; *Le Régal*, El Attaya, N of Remla, by the harbour, very good simple, cheap food, welcoming owner. Try the special Kerkennah sauce of tomato and garlic which is excellent on shellfish.

● Bank

UIB in centre of Remla, beside *Hotel el Jazira*.

● Chemist

In the centre of Remla, T 281074.

● Harbour

El Attaya has berths for 10 yachts, min-max draft 3-4m.

● Hospital

Remla, T 281052.

● Police

T 281053.

● Post Office

Centre of Remla. There are a few other branches, the closest to the hotel zone being in Ouled Kacem.

● Shopping

Best buys are olive oil and saffron.

● Sports

All water sports including windsurfing, horse and camel riding and tennis.

● Transport to the Kerkennah Islands

Ferry times: summer Sfax to Kerkennah 0730, 0900, 1130, 1400, 1630, 1800. Kerkennah to Sfax 0600, 0900, 1030, 1300, 1600.

El Djem (El Jem)

This is a small town of around 10,000 people in the middle of a plain full of olive trees that would be of little interest if it were not for its imposing Roman amphitheatre.

History

The ancient town of Thysdrus was probably founded by the Punics, but it was only under the Romans, in particular the rule of Hadrian (117-138), that the town prospered. Hadrian encouraged the continued cultivation of olive trees and the town became an important centre for the manufacture and export of olive oil. By the 3rd century the town reached its peak, as the ruins of luxurious villas testify. But, due to political rivalries within the Empire, El Djem's fortunes gradually decreased, and were finally brought to an end during the Arab invasion, when the olive groves were set on fire, definitively ending El Djem's commercial prosperity.

ACCESS The train station on main Tunis-Sousse-Sfax line is 5 mins E of the amphitheatre and the bus station is by the museum, 500m from the amphitheatre. In summer the buses are full and it is difficult to find a place. The louages terminate in a street by the station.

Things to see

The huge **Amphitheatre**, 148 m long by 122 m wide, has a perimeter of over 425 m. With seating for 35,000 it was the third largest amphitheatre in the Roman Empire. Construction, which is attributed to Emperor Gordien I (a keen follower of

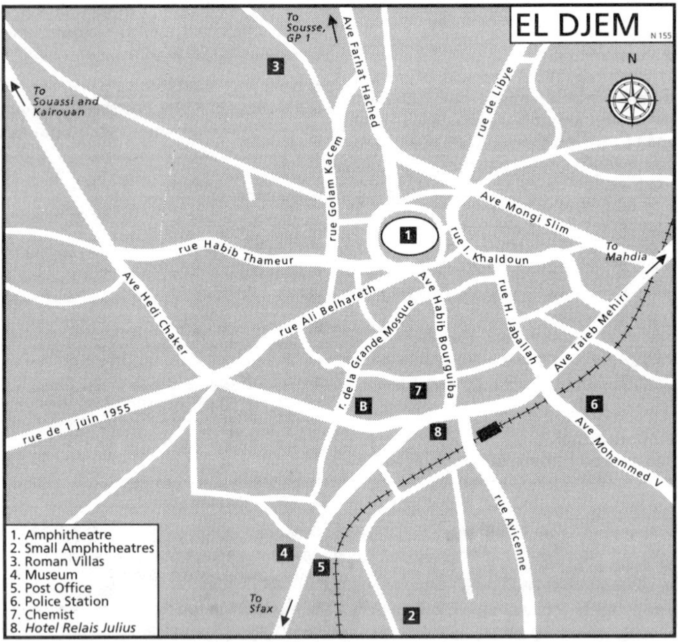

the kind of entertainment provided here), began in the 2nd century and when one considers that the nearest quarries were over 30 km away the task must have been enormous. It was never completed due to lack of funds and political instability. The stone was too soft for fine sculpture – hence the simplicity of the decoration.

Two smaller **amphitheatres** can be found on the other side of the road to Sfax. The older one from the 1st century was simply cut into the rock and the second one was built on top of it. Some 30 **Roman villas** have been excavated here, all of which indicate a considerable wealth. The dwellings, built round an inner courtyard and surrounded by a colonnaded gallery, were paved with colourful mosaics depicting mythological themes (most now in the nearby museum).

It was used throughout the centuries as a fortress or stronghold. In 1695, Mohammed Bey ordered a hole to be made in the amphitheatre's walls to prevent its use during any further uprisings. The theatre was thereafter used as a convenient supply of building stones by the inhabitants of the town. Nevertheless much of the original building remains and is very well preserved; it is a truly impressive sight. Open daily from dawn till dusk. Entrance TD4. Photography permit TD2 includes visit to museum.

The **Museum** is 500m from the amphitheatre on the road to Sfax, set in a replica of a Roman villa. It is very interesting, with magnificent mosaics. In the main room is the famous mosaic '*Orpheus and the animals*' while, particularly notable in the end room, are 2 mosaics, '*Lion devouring a boar*' and next to it '*Tiger attacking two wild asses*'. These were found in a villa which once stood behind the museum. Open 0730-1900 in summer and 1830-1730 in winter, entrance included with ticket to amphitheatre.

Local information

● Accommodation

E *Relais Julius*, off the main square by railway station, T 03 690044, simple, clean, cheap, 15 rm with bath round the courtyard.

● Places to eat

The cafés in front of the amphitheatre are expensive, prices reduce with distance from site. A meal at *Relais Julius* is better value for money.

● Transport

Train Departures for **Tunis** (via Sousse) 0649, 1316, 1416, 1825, 0145; **Sfax** 1020, 1620, 1726, 2043, 0035; **Gabès** (via Sfax) 1020, 0035; **Metlaoui** 0035.

Road Bus The bus station is by the museum. Frequent buses run to **Sfax, Sousse, Gabès** and **Tunis**. **Louages** By the train station, 5 min E of the amphitheatre.

THE DJERID

CONTENTS

MAPS

The Chott el Djerid gives its name to this low-lying region of salt lakes stretching from the Algerian border to the sea. Most of the oases lie on its perimeter. The Chott covers approximately 5,000 sq km, twice the size of Luxembourg and is mainly dry lake covered with a crust of salt. It is an impressive sight, especially from the P16 which links Tozeur and Kebili where mirages are frequent. The area has more on offer, however, than just the Chott. The oases, situated on the very edge of the desert to the W and E, are magnificent. Nefta and Douz, the doorways to the Sahara, are easily accessible and have a distinctive charm. The whole area abounds with fascinating landscapes and oasis villages and time should be spent here in order to explore thoroughly. In summer the temperatures reach 45°C and moving around becomes a slower and less comfortable process. The best periods to visit are spring and Nov when temperatures are more agreeable, the dates are being harvested and many festivals are held.

GAFSA TO TOZEUR

Gafsa

Pop 60,000 *Alt* 313m.

Gafsa is the capital of the region, the largest and most important oasis town in the Djerid. It stands at the junction of the P3, P14 and P15, the crossroads between the deep S and the N. This pink-walled town is built in a mixture of styles from both N and S. The large boulevards and modern buildings are reminiscent of the N, while the narrow streets close to the Piscines Romaines have a definite echo of the S.

Gafsa made the headlines in 1980 when a commando troop of 300 exiled Tunisians came from Libya and captured the city. It took the army 3 days to dislodge them. The reasons behind the seizure of the town remain something of a mystery.

The industrial basis of the town is phosphates and sections near the railway to the SE are to be avoided for that reason. Gafsa sees many tourists but pays attention to them only as a source of income and offers no real welcome. As a gateway to the S Gafsa is best passed through quickly.

ACCESS The railway station is 3 km E of town in the new suburb of Gafsa Gare. Buses and louages terminate in the main square, in front of *Hotel Gafsa*.

Things to see

The **Piscines Romaines** (Roman baths) are at the end of Ave Bourguiba and consist of 2 deep rectangular pools which overflow into a *hammam*. Open 0800-1200 and 1500-1900 in summer, 1930-1630 in winter, closed Mon, fee TD1. In the summer, youths jump from their side or from the top of a palm tree into the pools. Fun to watch but they will expect a tip! The surrounding square has recently been carefully redeveloped and

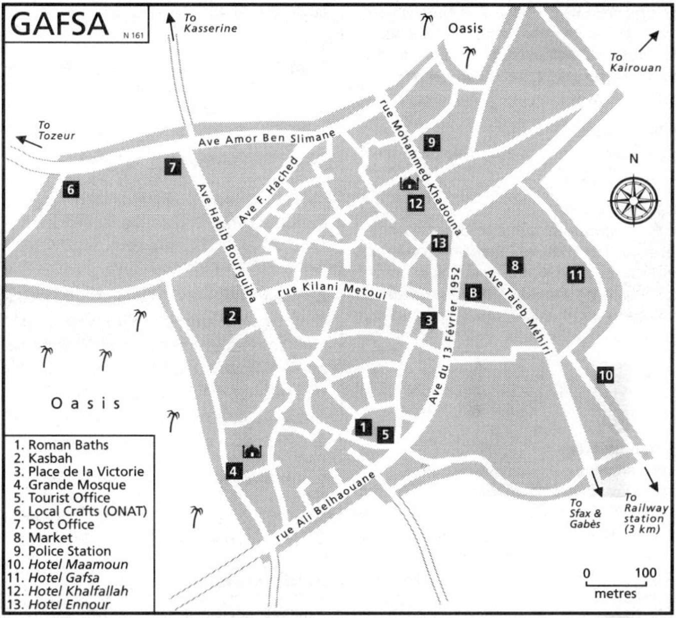

has a small café. The tourist information office is also here.

On the same street is the **kasbah**. From a distance the kasbah looks like a splendid pink fortress. It was built by the Hafsids and has been restored recently. A visit is of limited interest. The **oasis** starts just behind it, containing over 100,000 palm trees and numerous citrus trees. The main products are oranges and lemons which are better quality than the dates. For a typical oasis visit **Lalla** along the P15 SW to Gabès, turning left after crossing the railway at Gafsa Gare.

Local information

● Accommodation

B *Hotel Maamoun*, Ave Taieb Mehiri, T 222740, central, modern, relatively nondescript building, 46 a/c rm, restaurant used by tour buses, not very clean, indifferent service but all modcons.

C *Hotel Jugurtha*, 4 km W of town at oasis of Sidi Ahmed Zarroug, T 221467, impressive site, 78 rm, pool, tennis, its age is starting to show.

D *Hotel Gafsa*, on the main square in town centre, T 222676, modern, soulless, a/c.

E *Khalfallah*, rue Mohammed Khadouma, by police station, T 221468, clean, on a noisy road, rather expensive for what is provided.

CLIMATE: GAFSA

	Jan	Feb	Mar	Apr	May	Jun	Jul	Aug	Sep	Oct	Nov	Dec	Av/Tot
Max (°C)	14	17	20	23	28	33	36	36	32	25	20	15	25
Min (°C)	4	5	8	11	15	19	21	22	19	14	9	5	13
Rain (mm)	18	14	17	17	12	7	5	5	25	28	13	16	117

F *Hotel de la République*, Ave Ali Belhouane, T 221807, quite new, clean, 20 rm, probably the best of the cheap hotels; **F** *Ennour*, Ave du 13 Février 1952, T 220620, very cheap, outside showers.

● Youth hostel
2 km from station, T 220268, kitchen, meals provided, 56 beds.

● Places to eat
♦♦ *Restaurant Semiramis*, rue Ahmed Senoussi, T 221009, by *Hotel Gafsa*, one of the best places in town for French and Tunisian cooking, a bit expensive. ♦ *Restaurant de Carthage* on the main square, good, cheap, typical Tunisian food.

● Banks
BDS is on the main square, under *Hotel Gafsa*; **STB** nearby.

● Handicrafts
The craft centre is clearly signposted at the N end of Ave Bourguiba. This is a school set up by the ONAT to train people in the art of carpet making. Make a visit to the workshops. The best buys are the striped and geometrically patterned woollen blankets and woollen rugs and shawls.

● Post Office
Ave Bourguiba N of the kasbah.

● Tourist information
By Piscines Romaines at the end of Ave Bourguiba, T 221644.

● Transport
Train The station is rather inconveniently situated outside the town in the suburb of Gafsa Gare, along the road to Gabès. One train daily at 2026 goes on to **Tunis** (via Sfax and Sousse).

Road The bus station is by the main square. Information on T 221587. Frequent departures to **Tozeur** and **Nefta**, also buses to **Kairouan, Sfax, Sousse, Gabès** and **Sbeitla. Tunis** 1100, 2330. **Louages**: on the main square in front of *Hotel Gafsa*.

Around Gafsa are **Metlaoui** and, adjacent to it, **Phillippe Thomas**, named after the discoverer of the phosphate deposits which are mined here. The only real interest is the situation by the Seldja Gorge. Access by train, bus or louages all of which arrive in the centre of the town.

● **Transport to & from Metlaoui Train** The station is in the town centre, one train daily to **Tunis**, (via Gafsa and Sfax) at 1915; **Redeyef** at 1555; **Moulares** at 1505.

Seldja Gorges

These amazing gorges with 200m high sandstone cliffs are best seen from the train to Redeyef which departs daily from Metlaoui. This is a tourist train, the Red Lizard, and was once used to trans-

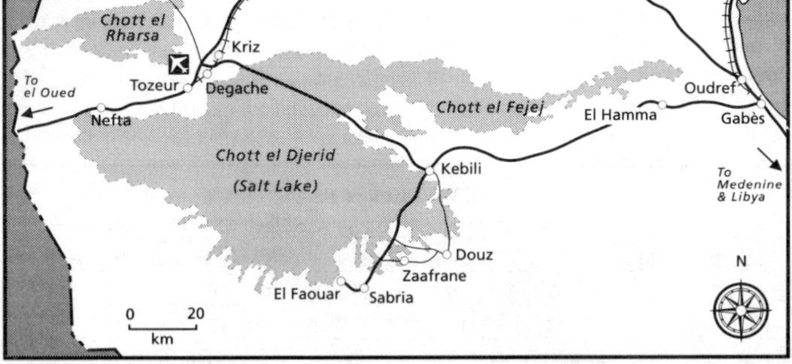

port the Bey. It comes complete with the original furniture and fittings which have seen better days. It does the journey in about 2 hrs and leaves daily at 1100. A fascinating trip, but some days full of tourists, which is only to be expected. Alternatively, take an ordinary train which is advertised to leave at 1500 to Moulares and 1555 to Redeyef. This is much cheaper but less appealing. Both trains return to Metlaoui at 1830. To travel the 5 km to the Gorges by car, take the track on the right at the end of Metlaoui going towards Tozeur. At the end of the track there are 2 tunnels. Walk through into the Gorges. It is best to do this in the morning before the temperature gets too high.

Redeyef is another phosphate mining town and is really very unpleasant. The oases of Tamerza, Chebika and Midès are well worth a visit from Redeyef or from Tozeur and could be combined with a visit to the Seldja Gorges making a circular tour.

Tozeur

A wonderful little town in an oasis in the middle of very dry, barren land. The town is famous for its oasis and more particularly its 200,000 or so palm trees. The oasis is a splendid place to walk, or take a swim in one of the tepid springs. The atmosphere is fresh, the vegetation is surprisingly dense and the area is large enough to be able to absorb the crowds. The old town is very beautiful and still untouched. Nevertheless, Tozeur is the well established political and commercial centre of the Djerid and with its new international airport is starting to develop an significant tourist industry. Tourism is still a relative newcomer, but hotels are going up everywhere in large numbers.

ACCESS The airport is 4 km out of town. The bus station on Ave Farhat Hached is used by buses from Tunis, Nefta, Gafsa and Kebili. The louage station is opposite.

Things to see

The old town is fascinating. Go down Ave Bourguiba, turn left before the market into Ave Ibn Chabbat. Down this street on the right, follow rue de Kairouan (signposted to the museum) which passes under an arch. This is the oldest part of the town with many archways and intriguing side streets. Some of the houses date back to the 14th century. They are wonderfully decorated with inscriptions from the Koran or with floral and geometric patterns, most of them built out of earthen bricks in an elaborate decorative style particular to this region. Notice that few houses have windows on to the street. They are organized in the traditional style with the rooms set round a central courtyard. The doors are also interesting, decorated with nails and bearing 3 door knockers. The one on the left is for women, on the right for men and the lowest for children. Each knocker emits a different sound, eg deeper for men, enabling residents to recognize who is at the door.

The small **Museum of Popular Arts and Traditions** in rue de Kairouan is very interesting, and clearly displayed, set in the old Mosque (Sidi Aissa). Everyday objects are on view giving a good insight into the daily life of people in Tozeur. The rooms contain such diverse objects as traditional clothes for celebrations, jewellery, oil lamps, cooking implements and weapons. Also on display are manuscripts written by Ibn Chabbat in the 14th century, setting out the complex water distribution system in the oasis. In the courtyard you can see one of the doors with the 3 knockers. This is a worthwhile visit, due to the simple charm of the museum and its setting. Open 0900-1200 and 1500-1800 in summer, closes 1700 in winter. Closed Mon.

The Oasis is the very reason for the existence of the town. It is beautifully fresh in summer, due to the large number of irrigation canals fed by more than 200

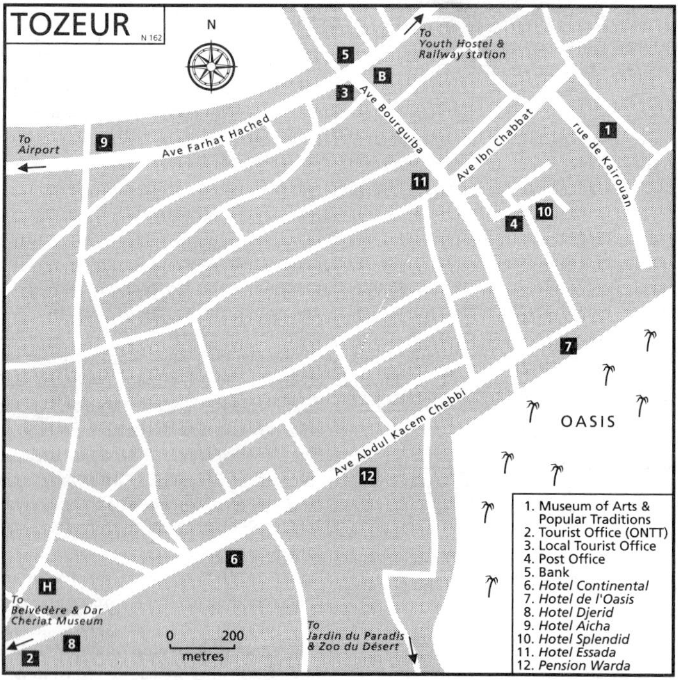

springs. Get there by following the signposts to the 'Jardin du Paradis' or take the road leading to the Belvédère, on the left after the Tourist Office. If the peace of the oasis is to be appreciated the well advertised tour by calèche is to be avoided.

The Belvédère is a large cliff by the side of the oasis where many of the springs emerge. Bathing in the hot springs has been recommended. The road to the Belvédère (3 km) goes through one of the most picturesque parts of the oasis. It is a long, but nevertheless very pleasant, walk starting on the left along Ave Abul Kacem Chebbi, beyond the Tourist Office, and following the river. From the top of the Belvédère the view over the Chott and the oasis is most impressive, particularly in the late afternoon.

Le Jardin du Paradis and **Zoo du Désert** are through the oasis (about 3 km), following the well signposted road which starts just before the *Hotel Continental*. It is a superb garden, with amazing trees and plants, particularly impressive in the spring time, and pleasantly fresh in the summer. Try the special, very refreshing drink, reputedly unique to the Jardin, with natural pistachio, banana, violet, rose or pomegranate flavourings. Next to the Jardin is the Desert Zoo with examples of many desert animals and reptiles including snakes and scorpions. A sorry place with many of the animals trapped in minute cages. Open daily from 0700 until dusk. Entrance TD1.

The **Dar Cherait Museum** past the Tourist Office is brand new, located in an imitation bourgeois Tunis house. The collection is, as usual, the reconstruction of traditional life in the previous century with rooms set up as kitchens, living rooms and even *hammams*. There are also many exhibits devoted to the life of the Beys and some of their weapons (more works of art than instruments of death), ceremonial clothes, jewellery and furniture including the Bey's bed. An interesting museum, perhaps a little too flashy, but nevertheless an impressive collection of many authentic works of art from recent Tunisian history. Open 0800-2400. Entrance TD2.5. Photography fee TD1.5. In addition to the museum, the Dar Cherait has a garden, no charge, with palm trees and amazing lighting, 2 restaurants (one with a floor show), good food and a Moorish café! Try their hot chocolate.

Local information

● Accommodation

B *El Hafsi*, on route Touristique, past the Tourist Office, T 450966, very pleasant, modern, restaurant, pool, 62 rm, being extended.

C *Hotel de l'Oasis*, on Ave Bourguiba, T 450522, 125 a/c rm, modern, tasteful, pool, garden; **C** *Hotel Continental*, Ave Abdul Kacem Chebbi, T 450411, conveniently situated adjacent to oasis, 150 rm, slightly rundown, pool, less expensive than *l'Oasis*.

D *Hotel Dar Ghaour*, rue de Kairouan, T 452782, near *Hotel Splendid*, opened 1993; **D** *Hotel El Djerid*, Ave Abdul Kacem Chebbi, T 450488, has definitely known better days, pool, 50 rm, clean, slightly over-priced.

E *Hotel Aicha*, rue Farhat Hached, T 450988, some rm with bath and a/c; **E** *Hotel Splendid*, opposite the post office, T 450053, faded charm, requires some attention, clean, most rm with bath, pool, restaurant.

F *Hotel Essada*, Ave Bourguiba, opposite the Market, T 450097, very simple, clean, noisy, communal bath/toilets; **F** *Pension Warda*, off Ave Abdul Kacem Chebbi, just before road to oasis, T 450597, very cheap, simple, very clean rm, very welcoming.

● Youth hostel

Ave de la République, close to the station, T 06 450235, 47 beds.

● Camping

At Degache, 10 km N of Tozeur on the C106. *Bedouin Camping*, down the track opposite the piscine municipale, clean facilities, food available, shady sites. TD5 for 2 people, 1 car and 1 tent – rates pro rata.

● Places to eat

Are all on or around Ave Bourguiba. ◆◆***Restaurant Le Petit Prince***, Ave Bourguiba, set in pleasant surroundings, very good, more expensive than the others; ◆ ***Restaurant du Paradis***, by the *Hotel Essaada*, off Ave Bourguiba, very good, cheap, a few pleasant tables outside, recommended; ***Restaurant de la République***, Ave Bourguiba, similar to *Paradis*, particularly good couscous; ***Restaurant El Faouiz***, Ave Bourguiba, very good, simple Tunisian food, cheap; ***Restaurant du Soleil***, Ave Abdul Kacem Chebbi, good atmosphere.

● Banks

STB and **BDS** on Ave Bourguiba, **BNT** and **BIAT** on Ave Farhat Hached.

● Bargains

There are many shops in Tozeur, but it is important to sort out the cheap imitations from the real bargains. Carpets and blankets are a very good buy, but be careful. In season the fresh dates are excellent.

● Hammam

1 min from *Hotel Essada*.

● Hospital

Hôpital Régional de Tozeur, Cité de l'Hôpital, T 450400.

● Police

T 450126, 1 km down route de Gafsa.

● Post Office

On the main square off Ave Bourguiba.

● Sport

Hot air ballooning.

● Travel agents

Rapide Voyages, T 450203; *Cartours*, T 450547; *Tunisie Voyages*; *Mehari Voyages* – all on Ave Farhat Hached.

● Tourist information

ONTT, Ave Abdul Kacem Chebbi, close to *Hotel Djerid*, T 450503. Local Tourist Office, place Ibn Chabbat, T 450034, organizes camel trips from Tozeur. There is an official price list for all excursions.

● Transport

Car hire all agencies on Ave Farhat Hached. **Avis**, T 450547; **Europacar**, T 450119; **Hertz**, T 450214.

Air *Tunis Air*, Ave Farhat Hached, T 452127; at the airport, T 450388. The airport is 4 km along the road to Nefta. Flights to **Tunis** Mon 0600, 0710, and 1145, Tue 0610, Sat 0630 and Sun 0600; **Djerba**, Thur 1700 and Fri 2150; **Paris**, Fri 1625. There are seasonal changes, always check.

Road Bus to **Tunis** 1300, 2300 and frequent buses to **Nefta, Gafsa** and **Kebili**. A few buses a day to **Gabès, Kairouan** and the N. Information on T 451557. **Louages**: opposite the bus station.

Around Tozeur

For those with transport there are 3 wonderful oases not to be missed, Chebika, Temerza and Midès, some 70 km NW from Tozeur. Take the track on the left after El-Hamma du Djerid. After 60 km of easy track Chebika is reached and Temerza is 15 km further along a very beautiful road. From Temerza it is 5 km to Midès. Return via Metlaoui to see the Seldja Gorges. A splendid ½ day excursion.

Chebika is a small oasis of palms and vegetables in a narrow gorge. It is very beautiful with an amazing landscape. The old, abandoned village appears to be hanging to the rocks while its residents have moved out to the new village. Walk up the gorge by the river to the small waterfall. Be prepared for some climbing. Above is the source of the river and further to the left there is a good view of Chebika.

Temerza is another beautiful village built along the top of the mountain. The old village has been abandoned but is worth a visit for the view. The new village is of no real interest, but a walk along the river bank is interesting. The area's only hotels are here, A *Temerza Palace*, T 448562, F 445214, probably the most beautiful of the new hotels, stunning views from terrace and pool overlooking old village, good restaurant; D *L'Hotel des Cascades*, T 445365, accommodation in 50 individual bungalows, outdoor restaurant, pool, beautiful location, excellent views at sunset, recommended. A cheaper and more pleasant alternative is to rent a tent from the locals at the entrance to the village (TD5 per person) and spend the night in the oasis by the river. This is not an official camping area.

Midès is 6 km from Temerza along a negotiable road. The landscape is amazing, with canyons and an oasis. Driving through at sunset is unforgettable. Surrounded by canyons on 3 sides, the village looks as though it is suspended in mid-air.

TOZEUR AND THE ROAD TO ALGERIA

Nefta

Nefta is a small oasis town 23 km W of Tozeur at the edge of the Sahara. The real desert is encountered just along the P3 towards the Algerian border only 36 km away. The oasis in Nefta has about 400,000 palm trees which produce some of the best dates in Tunisia and has the advantage of being visited by fewer tourists than Tozeur. The Corbeille, a wide, deep basin which originally had springs flowing from its sides, must be seen as well as the old town.

Nefta is known as the home of Sufism, an Islamic sect formed by ascetics who were concerned with trying to achieve communion with God by means of spiritual development rather than the study of the Koran. The participants are called *faqirs* or dervishes and only a few ever reach the end of the path, ie unity with God, at which stage they can be called a Sufi. Sufism was rejected by orthodox Islam but became quite popular due to the open-minded view it promoted, and the incorporation of local rites and traditions.

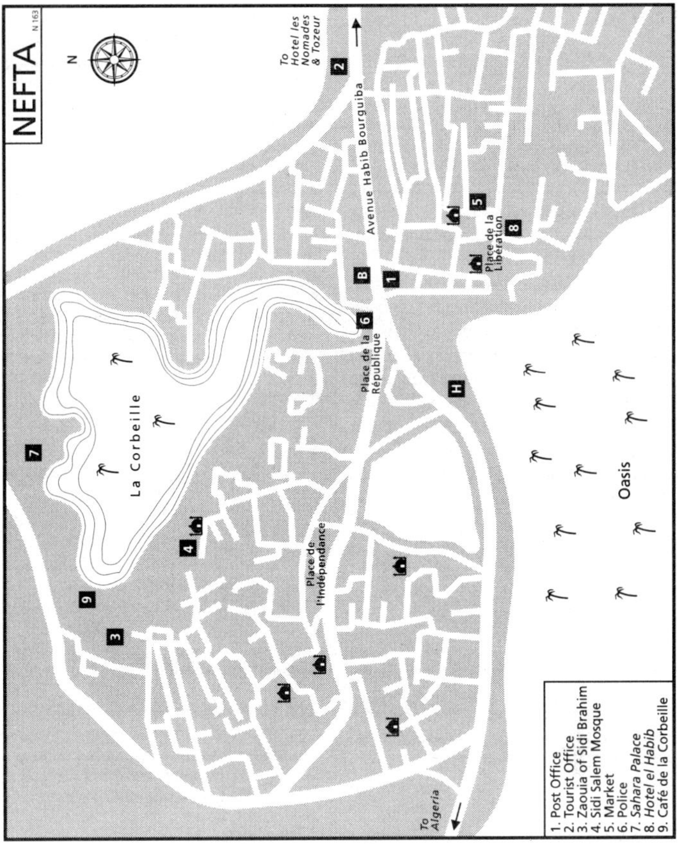

One of the visible peculiarities of Sufism in Tunisia is the importance of saints and their shrines. This partly accounts for the large number of *marabouts* in the S and in Nefta. In many cases, as with the *marabout* of Sidi Bou Ali, they became places of worship. According to legend, Sidi Bou Ali was the creator of Nefta and of Sufism. There are over 120 *marabouts* in Nefta! Every year, 3 days after the *Id el Kebir* (end of Ramadan) a large celebration takes place, attracting people from all over Tunisia. Many activities including music and dance take place in the courtyard of Sidi Bou Ali's *marabout* and in Nefta's main street. It is nevertheless basically a religious festival.

ACCESS The bus station is on the N side of the main street, Ave Bourguiba. The louages stop opposite.

Things to see

The **Corbeille** is a large depression situated to the N of Ave Bourguiba and from the ridge surrounding it there is an excellent view over the **oasis** below and towards the Chott el Djerid in the distance to the E. The best view is from the *Café de la Corbeille* which is reached by taking the road N from the Tourist Office or by foot through the old town N of the place de la République. Walk down into the oasis. Notice the numerous *marabouts* which are particularly beautiful at sunset. Children will want to act as guides but this is not necessary. The Tourist Office provides guides who are both competent and friendly.

The **old part of town** on the W side with its maze of narrow arcades is easily accessible from the Corbeille. It is recorded as having 24 mosques. The old town continues on the other side of the Ave Bourguiba and this is well worth strolling around, particularly as not that many tourists make the effort.

The **Zaouia of Sidi Brahim** (his tomb) is at the head of the Corbeille adjacent to *Café de la Corbeille*. Sidi Salem's Mosque, also known as the Great Mosque, is on the ridge above the Corbeille.

Local information

● Accommodation

A *Sahara Palace*, just behind the Corbeille, T 457046, 100 a/c rm and 9 suites, large, luxurious, Olympic size pool, disco, well situated overlooking the oasis, check renovations are complete before you book.

D *Hotel Marhala*, T 457027, brand new hotel, pool, restaurant, tasteful decorations.

E *Hotel Les Nomades*, at the entrance to town on the left, T 457052, typical rm with beds on the floor, all rm have bath/ toilet, original, very welcoming staff, pool, currently being renovated.

F *Hotel El Habib*, well situated in the centre of the old town, signposted, T 457497, clean and very basic, some rm with bath, rooftop restaurant.

● Places to eat

Restaurant du Sud, Ave Bourguiba, good, cheap Tunisian food; *Restaurant la Source*, by the Tourist Office on Ave Bourguiba, Tunisian specialities.

● Banks

BDS and **UIB** on Ave Bourguiba.

● Best buys

Desert Sand Roses, found a few metres under the desert surface, are unusual and attractive objects. They are formed due to evaporation from the mineral barites and are created in beautiful patterns. They make an excellent buy, particularly as they are not well known in Europe. The only problem might be transport as they come in all sizes, the biggest being really big. The market is about 10 km beyond Nefta on the road to Algeria. It is necessary to bargain as prices generally start 3 or 4 times higher than the actual value. The market is by the Chott and is very beautiful in the late afternoon or early morning light. You are also less likely to meet a bus load of tourists whose arrival would have the inevitable effect of increasing prices.

● Repairs & fuel

El Kaoui and Chkoba both on Ave Bourguiba.

● Hospital

Hôpital Local de Nefta, rue des Martyrs, T 457193.

● Police

T 457134.

● Post Office

Ave Bourguiba, 150m beyond the Tourist Office.

● Tourist information

The main office is on Ave Bourguiba, on the right as you enter the town, T 457184. It organizes horse drawn carriages and camel rides round the oasis. They also organize excursions into the desert and the dunes. Guides are available. Open daily 0800-1800.

● Transport

Road Bus: departures to **Tunis** 1030 and 2400 (takes 8 hrs); **Sfax** (via Gafsa) 1530; **Kairouan** 0530; **Gafsa** (via Tozeur) every hour from 0700-1600; **Hazoua** and the Algerian border 1000. Buses do not cross the border but taxis do, otherwise you are faced with a 5 km stretch of no-man's land to get to the Algerian border post. From the other side, it is an 80 km stretch to the first town, El Oued, but louages are available. **Louages**: depart frequently to **Tozeur** (takes 20 min). There is a service to **Hazoua** and the Algerian border (35 km).

Excursion Algeria is only 35 km W of Nefta and El Oued (see page 459) another 64 km. An interesting excursion for those with a visa.

TOZEUR TO KEBILI AND DOUZ

This is a worthwhile route to follow. It goes via the small oases of Degache and Kriz right through the centre of the massive salt lake, Chott El Djerid. It is a most impressive sight, a single black line of road cutting through the white salt deposits. Mirages and interesting optical illusions are frequent. Just after the Chott el Djerid, at Zaouia, 20 km before Kebili, is C *L'Hotel des Dunes*, T 05 99211, excellent, very well decorated, pool, entertainment includes *mecheoui* under tents with traditional dancing and music! **Menchia** has cafés for a rest en route. **Telmine** is another compact oasis reached before **Kebili.**

Kebili

This is a small regional town of military importance just W of the main road at the E end of the Chott el Djerid. One of the few interesting sights is the hot baths 4 km out of town towards Douz. There are 2 pools, one for the men and another further up the stream for women. An early morning bathe is very refreshing.

ACCESS The bus station is in the main street (the road to Douz) with buses to Douz, Gabès and Tozeur. The louages station is by the old military compound.

Local information

● Accommodation

C *Fort des Autruches*, signposted off the road to Douz, T 90233, 60 rm in an old fort, recently renovated, pool, bar on a terrace overlooking the oasis and the Chott, clean, a good place as stopover, but in summer it is advisable to book.

F *Ben Said*, Ave Habib Bourguiba, T 491573, on left of road to Douz, near centre of town and louage stop.

● Youth hostel

T 490835, 60 beds, meals provided, catch bus in town centre.

Djemma is noted for the water in the public fountain which, unlike most water in the area, is not brackish.

Douz

This really is the gate to the desert, where the oasis meets the sand dunes! Unfortunately the new hotels have not been positioned with consideration for anyone else's view. The village is compactly built with narrow streets in order to protect against the summer heat and keep the sand at bay. The fight against the sand is incessant and women sweep the sand away from the doorstep, only to repeat the process a few hours later. Douz is also the meeting point between the nomads and sedentary population. An increasing number of nomads are settling down. By the large hotels lies a small, modern village inhabited mainly by settled nomads. The desert is all around Douz and after a few km out of town the road is hemmed in by dunes. Douz makes a good centre from which to study the oases.

Things to see

The **Ofra Sand Dune**, one of the largest easily accessible sand dunes. Take the road towards the hotels and park by one of them or, alternatively, hire a camel by the Tourist Office. The official prices are posted in the Tourist Office. Particularly attractive at sunset.

Festival du Sahara is a 4 day festival including exhibitions on traditional ways of life, Arabic poetry, plays, and many competitions such as camel races, jumping and fights. The Festival takes place every year at the end of Dec. Check exact dates with the Tourist Office. At this popular period be sure to have booked a hotel room.

There is a **market** each Thurs attended by many nomads. There is also an animal market which sometimes has camels. Get there early if you want to buy one!

Douz is an important point of departure for many **desert trips**. One of the most interesting is a week's camping trip through the desert to Ksar Guilane by camel. For the less adventurous, trips in 4 wheel drive vehicles are a good way of seeing the desert. Remember that in summer the desert gets much too hot for these trips. If interested, contact Agence Abdel Moulah Voyage in Douz, 150m from the Tourist Office, T 95484, F 95366.

Local information

● Accommodation

C ***Mehari***, at the end of route Touristique, by the Ofra dune, T 495145, 125 rm, luxury with a/c, nightclub, 2 pools, a tower block provides excellent views for guests but spoils the view for everyone else. 3 new hotels also by Ofra dune are **C** ***Caravanserail***, T 470123; **C** ***Touareg***, T 470057, F 470313; **C** ***Sahara Douz***.

D ***Hotel Saharien***, on route Touristique, T 495337/9, accommodation in over 100 bungalows most with bath, very clean, pool, recommended.

E ***Hotel Rose du Sable***, route Touristique, T 495336, 45 rm, not quite as nice as *Saharien* but cheaper, all rm with bath, nearly all with a/c, being renovated, check they have finished before you book.

F ***Hotel 20 Mars***, next to the bus station, very basic, clean rooms are around a courtyard, with communal bath/toilet; **F** ***Hotel Bel Habib***, in place des Souk, T 495309, newly opened, clean, very cheap, welcoming owners, communal bath/toilet, large breakfast. **F** ***Hotel Splendid*** in town has been recommended. **F** ***Hotel de la Tente*** next to louage station, dormitories, bath with hot water, sleep on the roof in a bedouin tent for 2TD, manager very kind, recommended.

● Places to eat

El Khods, 100m from Tourist Office, good simple food, cheap; ***Restaurant Ali Baba***, in town, on the left on the road to Kebili, serves the 'best couscous in Tunisia'.

● Post Office

In the centre of the town.

● Tourist information

ONTT, route de Zaafrane, T 495350, is in the same building as the local tourist office. They are separated by a café. Local office, T 495341, open every day, all day. They organize excursions into the desert on camels.

● Transport

Road Bus from the station at the roundabout by the cemetery there are frequent buses to **Kebili; Tunis** 0600 (via Kairouan) and 2030 (via Gabès and Sfax); **Gabès** 1000, 1430; **Tozeur** 0630; **El Faour** (via Zaafrane) 1300. **Louages** are based opposite the bus station in the centre of town.

Excursions from Douz

Zaafrane is accessible by bus, louage or hitchhiking from Douz. Zaafrane really is a village in the desert. The old village has been abandoned and is slowly being covered by the sand. The surrounding landscape of endless dunes and sand with the occasional palm tree is very impressive. E *Hotel Zaafrane*, small, cheap hotel, clean and very simple, café. Excursions by camel are available TD25 per day, following a circuit around the water holes and eating biscuits cooked in the sand. A superb walk from Zaafrane back to Douz (3-4 hrs) via the sand sea. Navigate using Douz post office tower which is visible from the top of the dunes. Real desert environment including animal tracks in the sand. If a storm comes head N to the oasis and back to the road. Carry plenty of liquid and a compass.

El Faouar is also accessible by bus, louage or hitchhiking. This is the last village on the road. Try and see the **market** on Thur when any nomads and locals assemble. It is at its most interesting when dates are in season. Go early in the morning as many goods have disappeared by 1000. D *Hotel El Faour*, is virtually built in the desert with pool, a/c, restaurant. The hotel organizes camel trips (2-3 hours) in the desert and you can learn dune skiing! There is a direct route for 4 wheel drive vehicles from El Faouar to Kebili (54 km) via Blidet and Touiba.

SOUTHERN TUNISIA

Contents

Maps

This is where the N fringe of the Sahara begins. The architecture and landscape change noticeably as one goes S. There are few sites of historical acclaim but a great many interesting places to visit such as the unusual troglodyte dwellings in Matmata and the beautiful *ksour* of Medenine. The Sahara is the main attraction for visitors who want to see white desert sand dunes and palm tree filled oases, so the number of tourist centres is increasing with alarming speed but the distances are such that it is possible to avoid the crowds.

GABES TO MATMATA AND THE MOUNTAIN VILLAGES

Gabès

Pop 94,000 *Alt* 4m *Best seasons* Spring and autumn.

Gabès, 138 km S of Sfax, with its characteristic ochre buildings, is the first town along the route which gives a feel of 'the South'. It extends along the Oued Gabès which feeds the oasis and provides the harbour. The main attraction is the oasis which comes right down to the sea.

Gabès is a relatively new city, much of it having been rebuilt after WWII and the serious flood in 1962. Despite the long beaches and fine sand, the coast is not very appealing. A major industrialization programme in the area over the last 15 years means the sea is probably polluted, but it is nevertheless worth a stop to enjoy the coolness of the oasis (do not confuse this with village of same name near Tataouine,). Gabès is also an excellent centre for visits to the surrounding villages of Chenini and Matmata and a good stop over on the way to Kebili, Medenine and Djerba.

History

Thought to be of Phoenician origins, by 161 BC Gabès was part of Carthage, and a trading link with the S. It later came under Roman influence and was destroyed during the Arab invasion. The rebirth of the town is linked to the arrival of Sidi Boulbaba, the Prophet's compan-

Climate: Gabes

	Jan	Feb	Mar	Apr	May	Jun	Jul	Aug	Sep	Oct	Nov	Dec	Av/Tot
Max (°C)	16	18	20	22	24	28	31	31	30	26	22	17	24
Min (°C)	7	8	10	13	16	21	22	23	21	17	12	8	15
Rain (mm)	20	17	18	15	4	2	0	1	34	65	24	22	222

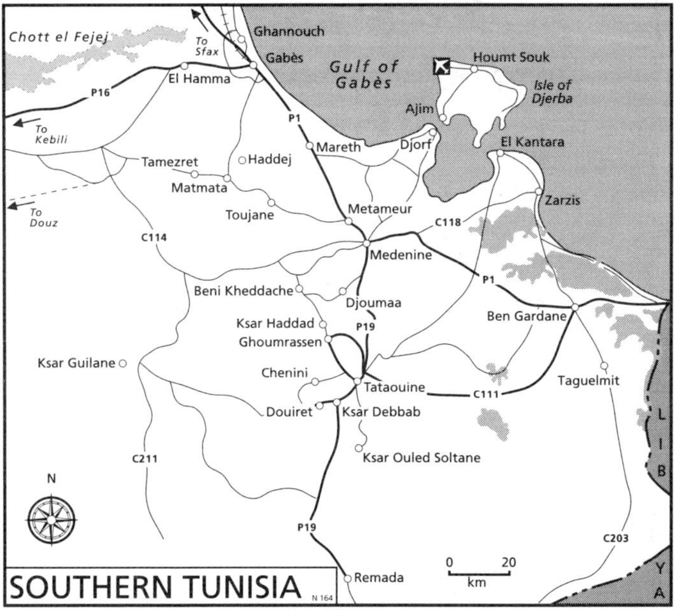

ion, in the 7th century. He is now revered as the town's patron saint. Gabès later became a *fondouk*, or halt on the way S. During WWII the Afrika korps settled in Gabès, using it as a strategic point on their supply lines to Libya. The town was finally liberated in March 1943 by British and French troops, but only after extensive damage had been done. Today, apart from traditional industries such as fishing and agriculture based on fruit from the oasis and the 200,000 palm trees, Gabès has become highly industrialized with a massive cement and brick factory, an oil refinery, harbour and projects for petro-chemical industries. Oil and gas wells have been drilled offshore in the Gulf of Gabès. Fortunately, though, the industries are dispersed over the surrounding suburbs, making them less conspicuous.

ACCESS The bus station is on the main street, Ave Farhat Hached, at the W end, after the roundabout, towards the oasis. Walk E to the town centre. Trains from Tunis and the coastal resorts, Gafsa and Metlaoui arrive at the station on Ave 1 Juin, right in the centre of town. The louages station is also on Ave Farhat Hached.

Things to see

The **Great Mosque** at the junction of Ave de la République and Ave Bechir Dzir was built in 1938 and in itself is of little interest, but the surrounding area has a souk and many shops selling handicrafts made of plaited palm fronds – everything from hats to baskets and mats. Shops also sell jewellery, food and spices, giving the whole market a colourful touch and interesting aroma. Both spices and plaited items are very good buys.

The **Oasis** is very large, covering 10 sq km, and has more than 300,000 palm trees which shelter hundreds of olive and fruit trees in addition to numerous vegetable gardens. To get to the more attractive parts of the oasis you can go by car towards the village of Chenini by taking the main road towards Sfax, turning left in the direction of Kebili, then left again, signposted Chenini. Alternatively go on foot from the other end of the oasis, by the bus station, crossing the little bridge. Following the road it is 7 km to Chenini, but it is not necessary to go that far since there are pleasant walks along the small, shaded paths between the palm trees, especially in summer. A

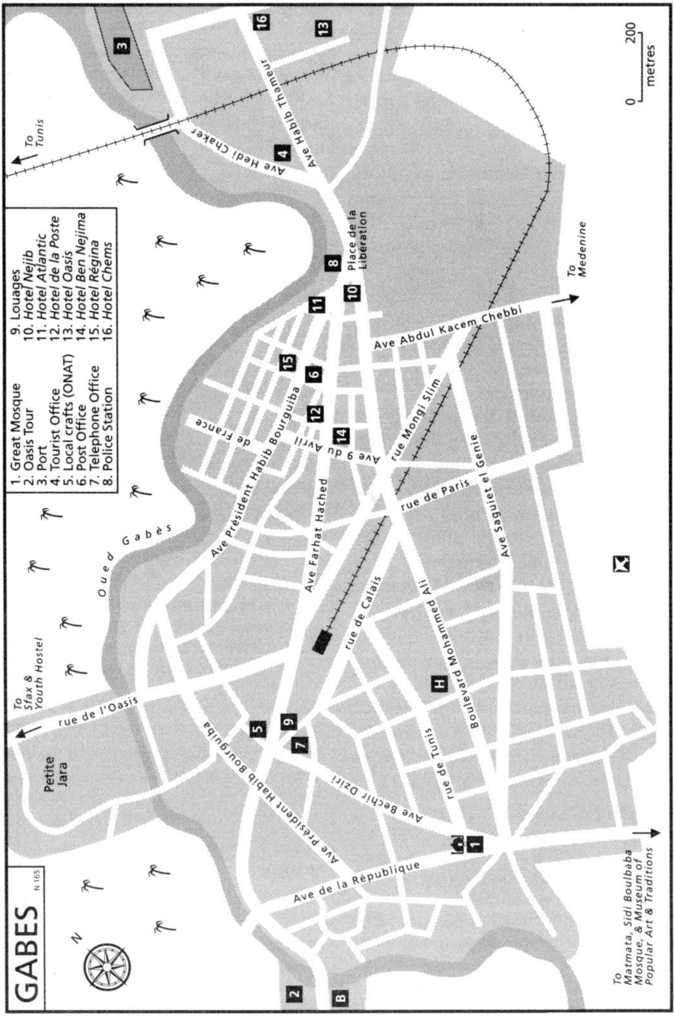

more picturesque way to see the oasis is to take a calèche (horse drawn carriage) from the end of Ave Farhat Hached. The price, TD7, is set by the Tourist Office. These are a tourist trap, strictly for the undiscerning as is the zoo complete with crocodiles and scorpions. At the end of the oasis, towards the source of the river, are located the **Sidi Ali el Bahoul Mausoleum** and a very small, but refreshing, waterfall. The region attracts a very high proportion of tourists but the oasis is large, and it is easy to get away from the crowds.

Mosque Sidi Boulbaba, one of the most important religious monuments in the area, is on the road towards Matmata, down the continuation of Ave de la République. This is the burial place of Sidi Boulbaba, who was the Prophet's barber after he came from Kairouan. The building is very elegant, with beautiful arcades. Only the inner courtyard is open to visitors.

The **Museum of Popular Arts and Traditions** is next to the Sidi Boulbaba mosque, set in an old *medersa* dating from the 17th century which has a simple but appealing architectural style. The museum has a collection of everyday objects demonstrating the traditional way of life in Gabès. The material is well displayed but unfortunately there is a disappointing lack of information. One very interesting room displays tools used within the oasis and behind there is a small garden with typical fruit trees. Open daily 0800-1200 and 1500-1900 in summer, 0930-1630 in winter. Closed Mon, entrance TD1, T 271111.

Local information

● Accommodation

C ***Hotel de l'Oasis***, at the end of Ave Habib Thameur, T 270782, on the right after the railway, 82 rm, no pool, beach, the best and most expensive hotel in town; **C** ***Hotel Nejib***, corner of Ave Bourguiba and Ave Farhat Hached, T 271686, modern hotel with little charm, 56 rm, all modcons, a/c, noisy due to main streets on both sides, slightly over-priced but very comfortable and convenient; **C** ***Hotel Chems***, end of Ave Habib Thameur on the right after the railway, T 270547, beach, over 200 rm, most parts tastefully decorated, each with a small terrace, some with sea view.

D *Chelah Club* (Village de Vacation), in Chenini in the oasis, T 270442, clearly signposted, accommodation in small wooden chalets, good situation, pool; **D** ***Régina***, 135 Ave Bourguiba, T 272095, only 14 rm all with bath, arranged around central courtyard, clean, restaurant, in summer dinner is served on the patio, best of the cheap hotels.

E *Hotel Atlantic*, 4 Ave Bourguiba, T 270034, old hotel retains some charm but needs decorating, clean, all 48 rm have bath, restaurant, good value, recommended.

F *Ben Nejima*, 66 rue Ali Djemel, near railway station, T 271062, clean and very simple, hot communal showers, rooms at front rather noisy, good restaurant; **F** ***Hotel de la Poste***, 116 Ave Bourguiba, T 270718, very cheap but not really very clean, communal bath and toilets.

● Youth hostel

Rue de l'Oasis, T 270271, in quarter called 'Petite Jara' N of the souk, 80 beds.

● Camping

On main road, follow sign opposite Agil petrol station. Cheap and adequate.

● Places to eat

Restaurant l'Oasis, 15-17 Ave Farhat Hached, T 270098, a very popular restaurant especially for locals at lunch time, evenings are quieter, more expensive than the others. Restaurant in *Hotel Ben Nejima* has good, well presented food. ***Restaurant Chez Amori***, 82 Ave Bourguiba, has good, simple Tunisian food, choose the fish before it is cooked, very friendly; ***Restaurant à La Bonne Table***, Ave Bourguiba, good, cheap food; ***Le Pacha***, Ave Farhat Hached, good, filling food, served by welcoming people. There are also several very small, very cheap restaurants beside the daily vegetable market off Ave Farhat Hached which serve Tunisian food.

● Banks

BIAT, Ave Farhat Hached; **BT, UIB** and **BDS** on Ave Bourguiba (0800-1200 and 1400-1700).

● Bargains

ONAT on Blvd Farhat Hached has a range of quality goods. Open 0900-1300 and 1600-1900 in summer; 0830-1230 and 1500-1800 in winter. Gabès is well known for its straw work which can be bought in the souk or the markets. Also recommended is the Berber jewellery. Gabès is the last town where you can buy a European newspaper, although it will probably be several days old.

● **Chemist**
All night, two in Ave Habib Bourguiba.

● **Crafts**
The ONAT school/workshop is worth a visit to see all the local handicrafts on display, closed afternoons on Fri and Sat. This is where the various craft techniques are taught. The course lasts 2-3 years for jewellery making, the majority of the young artisans opening their own shops on completing the course. There are courses, too, on palm frond weaving and carpet making and the demonstrations show how these skills are taught. The daily **vegetable market** gives a good insight into Tunisian life.

● **Harbour**
20 yacht berths min-max draft 2-4.5m.

● **Hospital**
Hôpital Universitaire, Cité M'Torrech, T 272700.

● **Post Office**
T 270544, Ave Bourguiba, opposite *Hotel Régina*.

● **Telephones**
Local code 05. On Ave Farhat Hached, opposite the ONAT Craft Centre.

● **Travel agents**
Sahara Tours, Ave Farhat Hached, T 270930; *Gabès Voyage*, Ave Farhat Hached, T 270797; *Carthage Tours*, Ave Bourguiba, T 270840.

● **Tourist information**
Place de la Libération, T 220254.

● **Transport**
Car hire **Avis**, rue du 9 Avril, T 270210; **Budget**, 57 Ave Farhat Hached, T 270930; **Hertz**, place de la Liberté, T 270525.

Cycle hire Enquire at the Youth hostel or at *Hotel de la Poste*.

Air (nearest airport is Sfax 137 km N or Houmt-Souk on Djerba 106 km E) **Tunis Air**, Ave Bourguiba, T 270697; **Tunis Avia**, route de Sfax, T 272501.

Train The train station is off rue Farhat Hached. Information on T 270944. Departures as follows: **Tunis** (via Sfax) 1525, 2242. For **Metlaoui or Gafsa** take the 2242 and change at Sfax for the 0140.

Road The bus station is at the end of Ave Farhat Hached, by the entrance to the oasis. Information on T 270008. Departures as follows: **Matmata** 0530, 0645, 0830, 0930, 1030, 1100, 1130, 1200, 1230, 1300, 1615, 1830; **Ben Gardane** (via Medenine) 0600, 0930, 1100, 1145; **Chenini** hourly from the corner of rue de la République and rue Haj Jilani Lahbib; **Djerba** (via Medenine and Zarzis) 0700 (via Djorf), 0945, 1030, 1515; **Gafsa** 0630 (via Kasserine) 0830, 1100, 1230 (via Kasserine), 1245, 1300 (continues to Tozeur); **Kebili** 0830 (continues to Douz), 1200, 1400, 1545 (continues to Douz); **Sfax** 0600, 0730, 0900, 1100, 1400; **Sousse** 0830, 0900, 1000, 1330, 2215; **Tunis** 0600, 0915, 0945, 1230, 1300, the 0915 is via Kairouan, the others via the coast. **Louages**: the louage station is opposite the ONAT on Ave Farhat Hached. It is possible to get a round trip visiting all the villages and the area surrounding Gabès. Tour operators offer a variety of options, including travel by 4 wheel drive vehicle with a group of 5-10 people (see Travel agents).

Matmata

Matmata is an amazing **troglodyte** village set in the mountains. The scenery round about is like a lunar landscape, with the houses being dug into the ground. See box, p 95. The only visible signs above ground are the TV aerials! There are also many very beautiful *marabouts* scattered over the mountainside. The village is inhabited by 3,500 people, but about half of them leave to work in the N or in Europe at some point in their lives, often setting up as bakers. Some who return, having earned sufficient money, build themselves a 'real' house in Matmata Nouvelle, 15 km down the road to Gabès. A section of the population still live in the underground dwellings, but their number is slowly decreasing. If you want to see the inside of one of the underground houses it isn't really necessary to take a guide, but doing so is one way of obtaining entry. The fee should be negotiated but is generally very reasonable, in the region of TD1-2.

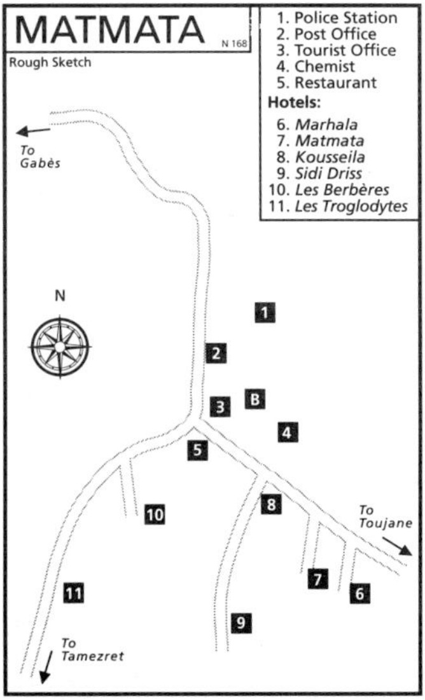

The Berbers, known as the Matmata, have been living in these houses for over 700 years. They originally constructed their homes underground in the soft rock to protect themselves from possible attacks and from the harsh climate. Habits are only now starting to change due to the exodus of the young people who set off to the large cities in the hope of finding work and an easier life.

There is little scope for agriculture in Matmata due to the harsh climate and the lack of water, which explains the tendency to migrate. However there is still some work to be found in the village, particularly in the ever-expanding tourist sector, and many locals make their money from the tourists who flock here during the day. Indeed it is worth staying overnight in Matmata in order to appreciate the village once the crowds have left and drive out to Zeraoua and Tamezret to see the sunset. Doing so, especially in one of the underground hotels, is quite an experience, although 2 new, above ground hotels are under construction and should soon be open.

ACCESS Ensure the buses from Gabès or the daily bus from Tunis drop you in the original Matmata, not Matmata Nouvelle which is 15 km down the road. A minibus runs between Matmata Nouvelle and Matmata costing 700 mills. It leaves when it is full.

Things to see

Underground dwellings On arriving in Matmata it is unclear where to go since nothing is visible, but walking around will reveal one of the 700 houses. It takes up to 7 months to build one of these, beginning with a hole 8m to 10m deep and about the same across. From this starting point the rooms are dug outwards with access to the house being provided either, in the most basic design, by a ladder or, more commonly, by a descending tunnel. Many of the houses can be visited in return for a small coin at the end of the tour.

Take the opportunity to see the living conditions. In summer, when temperatures reach 50°C, the rooms are remarkably cool while during the harsh and windy winters they are quite warm. In the centre of the 'courtyard' there is a small hole to collect rain water, this has the dual purpose of preventing flooding and providing drinking water. The rooms are not reinforced, the walls simply being painted or covered in lime. Most of the houses have up to 7 rooms, including the kitchen, bedroom, stable for the cattle and the grain store. In the grain store a hole in the ceiling communicates directly with the surface and the grain is poured straight down, loaded camels and donkeys being too large to enter the house. Even if you are not planning to spend a night in Matmata, go and visit a hotel, access being free, and see the labyrinth of tunnels leading from one courtyard to another.

Overlooking the village is a small fort which, unfortunately, cannot be visited since it is in a military zone.

Local information

● Accommodation

C ***Hotel les Troglodytes***, T 230062, F 230173, 1 km down road to Tamezret on left, above ground, pool, a/c rooms, opened 1992.

D ***Hotel Matmata***, T 30066, small, above ground (so no troglodyte charm), all rm have bath, a/c, comfortable, clean, pool, restaurant.

E ***Hotel Marhala***, T 230015, slightly out of the village, up the road towards the fort, probably the best of the 3 underground hotels, government owned, very clean, very basic (bed, door without lock, light bulb!), communal bath/toilet, quiet, good traditional restaurant, book in summer.

F ***Hotel Berbers***, T 230024, most recent and smallest underground hotel, communal bath/toilet, restaurant, book in season, a curious experience; **F** ***Hotel Sidi Driss***, T 230005, largest and most touristy, endless corridors and courtyards, communal bath/toilet.

● Youth hostel

'Berber City' grottoes, Old Matmata, 6070, 50 beds.

● Places to eat

For a decent meal it is best to eat in the hotels, although there are a few restaurants in the market place. ***Café Restaurant Ouled Aziz***, at the entrance to Matmata has good traditional Tunisian food and is quite cheap.

● Banks

These are situated in Matmata Nouvelle, 15 km along the road to Gabès.

● Post Office

In the centre of town.

● Transport

Road Bus Tunis 2030; **Sousse** 2215; **Gabès** 0530, 0730, 0900, 1100, 1230, 1330, 1400, 1600, 1730, 2000; **Tamezret** 1400.

Excursions

Matmata Nouvelle, 15 km away, is often ignored but a visit here will help explain the reasons why the villagers moved and give also some insight into the process of settlement of the nomads. By car there is a variety of places to visit. Going SE towards Médenine, take the track which goes via Toujane. This is shorter, but not necessarily quicker, and a very picturesque route (See Toujane, **see page579**). If you are travelling to Douz or Kebili or feeling adventurous, take the track to Tamezret. (See Tamezret below).

Haddej

To get to this village (Haddège on Michelin map), 6 km N of Matmata on the road to Gabès take the track to the right where the tourist shop and café are situated. Track not suitable for vehicles therefore very peaceful. Takes 1 hr to walk. Access is difficult without your own transport. Haddej is a very traditional village similar to Matmata but less involved with tourism. It is possible to see what Matmata must have been like before the tourist influx.

Tamezret

This beautiful Berber village lies 13 km W of Matmata. The bus leaves at 1330. The road here from Matmata has recently been surfaced with tarmac and is amazingly good. The scenery is quite extraordinary, a mixture of the moon and the Grand Canyon! The village is built on the side of a mountain. The houses built of dried earth blend in perfectly with the scenery. Stroll around the narrow, winding streets and walk up to the top of the village from where there is a marvellous view across the desert, particularly at sunset.

Toujane

No buses go along this road but it is possible to get a lift. By car it is a very worthwhile trip, mostly along a very easy track (be sure to have a spare tyre). Go S in the direction of Téchine and turn left after 6 km where there is a large white boulder indicating Toujane-Médenine. The track is steep and narrow and winds up to a fantastic view over the plain below and E towards the sea. On a bright and clear day it is possible to see Djerba! At the end of the track, go left and start the descent to Toujane which will suddenly appear, apparently clinging to the mountain side. It is a beautiful village on an exceptional site. Wander around and look at the carpets and the *kilims*, small smooth woven carpets with traditional designs originally used as prayer mats and in tents. They are all made locally and are cheaper here than in the main towns. Purchases can be made at Chez Laroussi on the road.

Towards Medenine
Continue on the road through the village. The first few km are tarmac and although the rest, about 30 km, is unsurfaced, it is neither difficult nor dangerous.

MATMATA TO DOUZ VIA THE DESERT TRACK

This journey can be done in a car which does not have 4 wheel drive (but don't tell the hire agency your plans!!!). It is an exciting experience and 60 km shorter than the route via El Hamma-Kebili, although not necessarily faster. Don't forget to take water and do not travel after rain as the vehicle will sink. (See Travel and Survival in the desert, p 40.) Take the black top road to Tamezret and follow the track W. Turn left at the junction after the pipeline, and about 2½ km further is the small *Café Djelili* where the food is excellent. Another 10 km will bring you to the *Café Sahara Centre* offering food, accommodation and selling 'Arab' headgear to tourists. Here you can sleep out in the open under an incredible star-studded sky. The road from here on is more or less a straight 43 km to Douz.

MEDENINE AND SOUTH TO TATAOUINE

Medenine

This is an important crossroads town. However it holds little interest for the visitor, having been extensively modernized with few traces of its past remaining. Medenine is at the centre of the **ksour** area. A *ksar* (plural *ksour*) is a fortified village built in a characteristic style with curved, whitewashed houses and the typical *ghorfas* (granaries). Originally the villages were not fortified, but with the Arab invasion and other dangers the Berbers were obliged to build defences. The *ksour* were generally built on the top of a hill, in an easily defensible position, out of dried earth which blends in with the colour of the landscape. Medenine is a good place for the start of excursions towards Metameur and the surrounding area where some *ksour* have been better preserved than in Medenine. This region is a frontier between two cultures, the nomads and the settled people. Once the area was totally controlled by nomads but today the tents have been replaced by small concrete houses and the camel by a Peugeot truck.

ACCESS The bus station is on rue du 18 Janvier and the louages station is in a small street opposite.

Local information

● Accommodation

D *Hotel Sahara*, Ave Bourguiba, T 640007, 20 rm, is a bit better than the others, fairly central, too pricey for what it offers.

F *Hotel Essaada* and **F** *Hotel Hana*, T 640690, both in Ave Bourguiba, quite noisy, but well placed, central.

● Youth hostel

On the road to Djorf, T 640338, 60 beds.

● Place to eat

Restaurant in *Hotel Sahara*.

● Banks

On Ave Bourguiba in the town centre.

● Police

T 640033.

● Post Office

Ave Bourguiba.

● Transport

Road Bus Information on T 640427. One bus to **Tunis** 2130; others to **Djerba**, **Tataouine**, **Zarzis**, **Ben Gardane**, **Gabès**, **Gafsa** and **Sfax**.

Around Medenine

Metameur can be reached by louage,

hitchhiking or a bus to the junction. Take the road to Gabès, turning left after 6 km to the village which is 1 km further up the road. Metameur is a beautiful village with *ghorfas*, which are still in relatively good condition, on the small hill.

• **Accommodation** **D** *Hotel El Ghorfa*, T 640294, 35 rm, a charming little hotel built in the ghorfas, a wonderful place if you want to get away from everything for a few days.

Djoumaa is situated 36 km SW of Medenine on the C113 to Beni Kheddache. There are buses here from Medenine at 0815 and 1000, returning at 1000 and 1400. It is worth a trip to this most attractive hill top village with splendid views. The *ksar* has only recently been abandoned.

Beni Kheddache, beyond Djoumaa, can be reached by the same buses from Medenine at 0815 and 1000. The village is of little interest in itself, but from here you can take the desert track S to Ksar Haddad and on to Tataouine.

Medenine to Ben Gardane

This 77 km of road is very busy as goods go into Libya this way. Getting a lift is easy. There are 3-4 buses daily. Stay in Ben Gardane at E *Hotel de l'Algerie*, rue 20 Mars, T 665279 or F *Baghdad*, rue de Zarzis, T 666123, next to bus station, clean, shared toilet facilities. A very good unofficial exchange rate for Libyan dinars is available here.

Medenine to Tataouine

With your own transport the most interesting route is via Beni Kheddache and S via Ghoumrassen. The track is not difficult and the landscape is fantastic. This is the area inhabited by the Haouia. Without transport, the quickest and easiest way is to do the 49 km by bus. For the more determined there is a bus from Medenine to Beni Kheddache and a bus from Ghoumrassen to Tataouine and it is possible to hitch a ride between the two villages.

Tataouine

The major town in the *ksour* area, Tataouine is a good place to start a circuit round the *ksour*. It is not a very interesting town, but more charming than Medenine. Especially lively and interesting is the market on Mon and Thurs.

ACCESS Buses from Medenine, Zarzis, Houmt Souk, Ghoumrassen and Tunis arrive at the bus station on rue du 1 Juin 1955. The louages station is on the same street.

Things to see

A very colourful **market** is held Mon and Thur on Ave Farhat Hached. There is a possibility of finding a bargain in the carpets, jewellery, straw goods, and particularly the materials from the bedouin women.

Local information

● **Accommodation**

The choice is very limited. **B** *Sangho*, T 860124, F 862177, 9 km S at the Douiret/Remada intersection turn right towards Ghoumrassen el Bled, clearly signed, spotlessly clean, tastefully decorated, pool, restaurant, opened July 1993.

D *La Gazelle*, Ave Bourguiba, T 860009, a/c, all 23 rm have bath, could be better looked after and cleaner, decent restaurant, 62 rm, definitely over-priced and not very welcoming, but unfortunately one of the few suitable hotels in town.

F *Hotel Medina*, rue Habib Mestaoui, T 860990, hot showers, restaurant, breakfast TD1; *Hotel Ennour*, Ave Bourguiba, T 860131, by the main road to Remeda, not very clean and quite noisy.

● **Transport**

Road Bus Information on T 862138. **Medenine**, 0530, 0630, 0800, 1000, 1430; **Gabès**, 0530; **Djerba** (via Zarzis), 1000; **Tunis**, 2130; **Sousse**, 0800, 2100.

Around Tataouine

Ksar Ouled Soltane is one of the best preserved *ksour* in Tunisia and has virtually no tourists. Take the road directly S of Tataouine, to the left of the main road to Remada, in the direction of Maztouria to the *ksar* of Ben Barka. From the terrace at the top there is a splendid view. Eight km after Maztouria turn left and the village is 2 km further on.

Ksar Ouled Debbab is about 10 km along the P19 on the road S to Remada. This beautiful hilltop *ksar*, now abandoned and falling into ruin, blends into the surrounding landscape. The people now live in the new town at the foot of the hill.

Douiret The road for Douiret, 9 km through land cultivated after the winter rains but barren in the summer, is W from the centre of Ksar Ouled Debbab. The old, almost abandoned village is perched on the hillside 2 km further along the track. It is very impressive, quite eerie, the place has a mystical touch. The white mosque attracts attention while the earth coloured houses tone in with the hillside. There is a small *marabout* on the left on the way into the village. Watch out for dogs. Notice the inscriptionless tomb stones. Douiret has the privilege of having so far escaped the tourists.

Roads from Douiret to Chenini

A possible route on to Chenini is via a scenic track N through the mountains. Take the usual precautions regarding water and spare tyres. It can be done in a Peugeot 205 or Citroen AX. Cross the new village of Douiret and take the track on to the W. It is best to check with one of the villagers to make sure the route is not closed by floods. The other road to Chenini is S of Tataouine, turn right after 2 km on the C207 to Ghoumrassen el Bled and 3 km further on keep straight ahead when the main route swings right. Total distance 10 km. There is no need to stop in the new town, rather follow the road round the hill to the only restaurant which serves excellent couscous.

Good news for walkers. Chenini is only 5½ km from Douiret over the top past the highest houses. Seek a guide as the only people en route will be girls herding goats.

Chenini

(Do not confuse with village of same name near Gabès, page 573). This is an amazing Berber village built on either side of a rock crest. The houses which are built into the rock have a small courtyard, where animals are kept. There are some *ghorfas* at the top of the village, but only a few of them are still in use. Chenini men are traditionally known as newspaper sellers. Visit the underground mosque with its particularly intriguing long tomb stones. Chenini has become part of the tourist route but, despite the crowds climbing up and down the village, it is worth seeing for the extraordinary setting. The streets here are just ledges, scarcely wide enough for 2 people to pass! The restaurant at the bottom of the hill has good, reasonably-priced food. At lunch service can be slow since many groups call in here. With a packed lunch and a drink you will have more time for seeing the sights.

Guermessa

About 4 km along the road to Tataouine, after the new town of Chenini, take a dirt track on the left. Follow the telephone poles. After 2-3 km the track forks, keep left still following the poles. At the end of this road you will come to the village of Guermessa. The new village is of no interest but behind, along a dirt track to the W, is the old village. It is similar to Chenini, but without the tourists. From the top (½ hr climb) the panorama of the surrounding area is breathtaking.

Ghoumrassen el Bled

Ghoumrassen is only 8 km further on to the W from Guermessa. The most interesting part is towards the centre of the town. Behind the town, to the N, you can see the old abandoned village clinging to the cliff topped by a small mosque, as if watching over the inhabitants. If you have the energy, it is worthwhile going up to the mosque. From here you will see the old *ghorfas* and the rest of the old town. This is a good example of how the inhabited area changes as circumstances alter.

Ksar Haddad

A quiet little village 5 km N along the road after Ghoumrassen el Bled. The only *ghorfas* left have been beautifully conserved and transformed into a hotel. The E *Hotel Ksar Haddad* is very cheap, simple rms, with bath/toilets which could be cleaner, restaurant serving good, traditional meals at reasonable prices. Even if the comforts are limited, a night in the hotel is an experience not to be missed.

Ksar Guilane

A very beautiful village, it is only accessible from Chenini with a 4 wheel drive vehicle, though it is preferable to take a guide. From Douz a normal car will do. This is a magnificent oasis in the middle of the desert and no opportunity to visit it should be allowed to slip by. It is quite out of this world! Unfortunately some tour agencies have 'found' this area and it is not now so peaceful.

ZARZIS AND THE ISLAND OF DJERBA

Zarzis

The town has long been associated with Djerba as a tourist resort, and is not without certain similarities. The architecture is quite similar and the landscape, with large olive groves and long, white beaches is indeed very reminiscent of Djerba. The town, originally the market town for the area, is highly developed for tourism and generally well organized. The main point of interest in the town, apart from the market on Mon and Fri is the Sponge Festival (from 15 Jul to 15 Aug) which is celebrated with traditional dances and music, fishing boat competitions and, of course, sponge fishing. Zarzis is the road access to Djerba, across the causeway which was originally built by the Carthaginians and later rebuilt by the Romans. The road as it stands today was rebuilt in 1953. The only other access to Djerba is by the Djorf ferry.

ACCESS Buses arrive some 100m from central square, by the Esso garage, and the louage station is next to the nearby Shell garage.

Local information

● Accommodation

D *Zita*, T 680246, 600 rm, a/c, adequate restaurant, coffee shop.

F *Hotel l'Olivier*, close to the bus station, T 680637, simple, clean, probably the best of the cheap hotels. All the others, used by package tours, are very similar, spread out along the beach to the N of the town and are expensive with at least 3 stars.

● Camping

Sonia site recommended.

● Youth hostel

40 beds, T 681599.

● Banks

STB, town centre; **BNT**, rue de Palestine; **BT**, rue de Palestine and rue d'Algérie; **BDS**, town centre. There are also bureaux de change along route Touristique, 100m beyond the Tourist Office. One takes VISA and Eurocheques.

● Hospital

In town centre, T 680302.

● Post Office

Is in rue Mohammed V. There is another Post Office/ telephone centre in the hotel zone, about 1 km N of the Tourist Office.

● Sport

Zarzis is a typical resort town with provision for water sports such as windsurfing and water skiing at all the large hotels along the beach. **Harbour** has 60 yacht berths, min-max draft 2-4.5m.

● Telephones

Area code 05.

● Travel agents

Agency Globus, T/F 668288; *Zarzis Travel Service*, route de Djerba, T 681072; *Zarzis Voyage*, route de Ben Gardane, T 680654.

● **Tourist information**
Route des Hotels, route du Port, close to the *Hotel Zarzis*, T 680445.

● **Transport**
Car hire Express, in *Hotel Oamarit*, T 680770; **Hertz**, in *Hotel Sangho*, T 680124; **Mattei**, next to *Hotel Sangho*, T 680124.
Road Bus Tunis 2100; **Sousse** 1300 (via Medenine); there are about 4 buses a day to **Medenine** and **Ben Gardane**, more frequent departures towards Djerba. Information on T 680661.

Beyond Zarzis The C109 follows the coast, skirts the salt lakes and reaches Ben Gardane 46 km away. You are now just 33 km from the Libyan border.

Island of Djerba

Djerba, with an area of 614 sq km, is a virtually flat island. Altitude reaches only 55m in the centre and it measures 29 km E-W and 28 km N-S. The island is surrounded by 130 km of white beaches, while the centre is covered by olive groves and palm trees. Djerba has a long history of independence and the architectural style, unique to the island, testifies to this. The number of settlements is small as, in general, the houses are spread around the countryside and Houmt Souk in the N is the only significant town. Unfortunately Djerba is well established in the tourist circuit and can be very crowded in summer. Nevertheless, the tourists tend to congregate in Houmt Souk or stay in their hotels, leaving the centre of the island relatively quiet.

History

Djerbian history began with Ulysses in the Odyssey. Homer wrote that Ulysses landed in Djerba and had great difficulty in leaving again, not least because of the attractions of the lotus flower he found

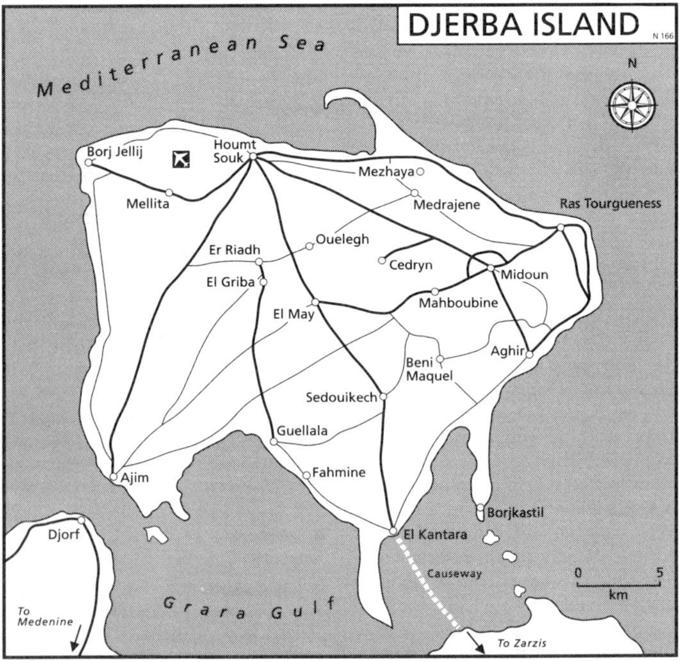

on the island. The island then became in turn Phoenician, Carthaginian and Roman. Known at the time as 'Menix' it went through a period of turbulence, as did most of Tunisia, due to the decadence of the Roman Empire and successive invasions. Djerba was finally conquered by the Arabs in 667, but was later involved in the rivalries between the Kharejite sect and the orthodox Muslims.

By the 15th century Djerba had become a den of pirates and various efforts were made to dislodge them, the most fateful being in 1560 when an attempt was made to fight off the pirate Dragut (see page617). This failed and Dragut built a tower with the skulls of the slain Christians. The tower was fortunately demolished in 1848! Since then, Djerbian history has been marked by French colonization. The Djerbians were actually quite happy to see the French come, fearing attacks from rebellious inland tribes.

Today Djerba's main resources are agriculture, fishing, handicrafts and, most importantly, tourism. Agriculture is difficult on the island due to the lack of water. There are many palm trees but they produce poor quality dates, due to the high salt content of the water. Olive trees are more successful and olive oil is an important industry. Fishing is an occupation that is slowly declining, due to the continued use of traditional fishing methods and the preference for employment in hotels, usually for a bigger salary. Crafts are still important, particularly catering for the large tourist market.

The people

Those living on Djerba have always been quite isolated from the mainland. The effect has been the development of a unique style of life and architecture. The population is now mostly Berber in origin but, until recently, there was also a significant Jewish population on the island, one of the oldest communities in the world, dating back to 566 BC and the fall of Jerusalem to Nebuchadnezzar. Now there are only about 1,000 Jewish people left here, a large number having emigrated to Israel. The Arab population, numbering over 100,000, belong to the Ibadite sect which derives from the rigorous and austere Kharejite sect, established shortly after the Arab invasion. It is said the Djerbians followed this branch of Islam so as to keep some independence from the mainstream Islam preached by the Arab invaders.

Today, the population is faced with the new problems of tourism and the influence of Western culture. Having lived for so long in isolation, they were perhaps less well equipped than other places for the large influx of tourists. The industry is having an adverse effect on the island's population and way of life since many of the traditional occupations such as agriculture and fishing are being abandoned for easier and better paid jobs in the tourist industry. Other residents have been forced to change jobs or leave due to the ever increasing cost of living, making Djerba an island with a very high emigration rate. In Tunisia and the Mediterranean region the word Djerba is synonymous with trader and grocer.

Architecture

Djerba is well known for its particular style of architecture. Houses, or *menzels* are found randomly scattered around the countryside, with no real village centres. The houses were organized in this way against the danger of attack and depending on the location of wells. Houmt Souk (the quarter of the souks) was until recently the only town and, in effect, the market place for Djerba. The striking white-painted, often single-storey houses are organized around central courtyards, with no external windows. They resemble small forts since each has at least one tower. Each house has a cistern to collect the precious rain water. There are also many small, fortified mosques (as many as 200) which add to the attraction of the scenery. Driving or cycling round the centre of the island is a discovery and a delight.

Houmt Souk

This is the only real town (40,000 inhabitants) on the island and therefore its capital. It has a certain charm when not taken over by tourists. Notice some of the houses are old *fondouks* where nomads rested for the night. Some have been transformed into hotels just as some houses in the small squares have been converted into cafés and restaurants. The town has nevertheless preserved a careful balance and has not been totally destroyed by tourism.

ACCESS By road is either from Zarzis across the 6 km causeway, or via the ferry from Djorf to Ajim. Coming from Gabès, the ferry saves a lot of time but in summer be prepared to queue. The crossing only takes 15 mins. The ferry runs every 30 mins until 2000 when it is hourly through the night. Free for foot passengers and motorbikes, TD1 for cars by day and TD1.5 at night. All buses arrive at the bus station in the centre of Houmt Souk. Djerba has its own international airport to the W of Houmt Souk receiving scheduled flights from Frankfurt, Lyon, Geneva, Zürich, Brussels and Paris, as well as regular internal flights from Tunis and Tozeur.

Things to see

The **souk** is in the centre of the town. The main souk, not to be missed, is covered and has many small shops selling mainly silver, brass, leather goods, shoes, material and clothes. Prices tend to be high, shop around for the best price. Don't forget to bargain! Djerba is noted for its straw mats, blankets, jewellery (most still made by the Jews) and pottery, particularly from Guellala. The typical Djerbian pottery has a special white colour obtained by the addition of sea water. The market is held around the souk every Mon and Thurs. The pottery and straw mats are sold on the main square, by Ave Bourguiba. Get there early.

Walking around the town will not take very long as it is quite small. Little streets lead on to charming squares with cafés. Notice the large doorways indicating an old *fondouk*.

On rue de Bizerte the **Zaouia of Sidi Brahim**, built in 1674, is particularly interesting with its multiple arches. Across the road is the **Mosque of the Stranger**, remarkable for the large number of small domes around the main one. The **Mosque of the Turks**, at the end of the Ave Abdelhamid el Cadhi, is interesting due to its splendid Turkish minaret. Unfortunately, all these monuments are closed to non-Muslims.

The Bordj el Kebir (the Great Tower) by the harbour is a 15th century Arab fort which was later reinforced by the pirate Dragut. Inside it is possible to see the ruins of an earlier fort built in the 13th century, though the site goes back further to Roman occupation. Open 0800-1200 and 1500-1900 summer, 0830-1730 winter, closed Fri. Entrance TD3. From the top of the fort is a wonderful view over the sea and harbour. Also very interesting is the **market** by the harbour held every Mon and Thurs. This is very typical with only a limited number of tourists, and goods are generally cheaper than in the main souk.

The **Museum of Popular Arts and Tradition** on Ave Abdelhamid el Cadhi is set in an old *zaouia* dedicated to Sidi Zitouni who used to come here and heal the mentally ill. The collection is very interesting and well labelled. The first room displays the traditional Djerbian costumes and jewellery and explains the history of the island. Another room shows a pottery workshop, the instruments used and the fabrication process. The last room is particularly special, as it was once a place of pilgrimage. This room is known as *quoubet el khyal* (the Ghost's Dome). Open 0800-1200 and

1500-1900 in summer, 0830-1630 in winter, closed Fri, entrance TD2.

Beaches
Close to Houmt Souk are not very pleasant. The nearest to be recommended is 6 km E along the road towards the hotels. Turn left along a track just before the *Hotel Ulysses*. There are other good beaches further along the coast.

Local information

● Accommodation

A *Hotel Ulysses*, T 657422, 300 rm all a/c, on

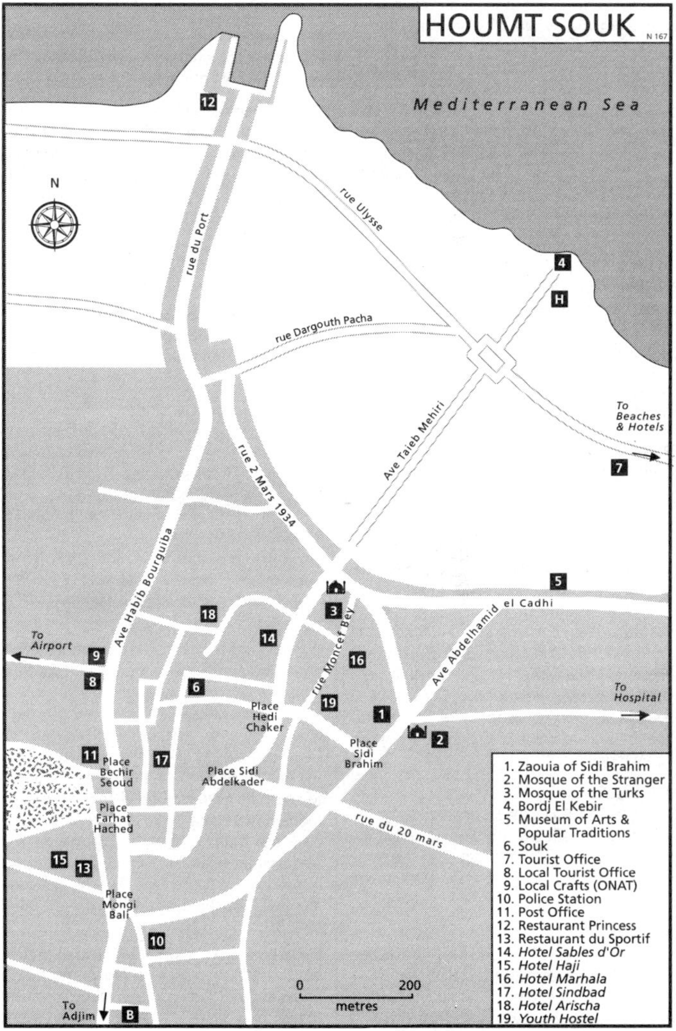

beach, pool, restaurant, night club, sports activities.

D ***Dar Faiza***, rue Ulysses, T 650083, pool, tennis, restaurant; **D** ***Hotel Sables d'Or***, rue Mohammed Ferjani, T 650423, charming old house transformed into a small hotel.

E ***Hotel Le Hadji***, off the main square, T 650630, modern, very clean hotel, all rm with bath; **E** ***Hotel Erryadh***, off place Hedi Chaker in rue Mohammed Ferjani, T 650756, an old *fondouk*, Berber style rm with bath arranged around a central courtyard, very clean, lots of charm, important to book in season; **E** ***Hotel Marhala***, beyond place Hedi Chaker on rue Moncef Bey, T 650146, small, beautifully decorated, clean and cheap, rm around attractive central courtyard, communal bath/toilets, recommended.

F ***Hotel Arischa***, on the street on the right opposite ONAT, at the bottom on the left, T 650384, converted *fondouk* with a central patio, clean; **F** ***Hotel Sindbad***, place Mongi Bali, T 650047, in town centre, opposite the post office, old *fondouk* with simple, clean rm, communal bath/toilet, one of the cheapest in Houmt Souk; **F** ***Hotel Essalem*** near market, recommended as cheap, clean and friendly.

● Youth hostels

11 rue Moncef Bey, T 650619, 120 beds.

● Places to eat

♦♦♦ ***Restaurant La Princesse d'Haroun***, T 650488, by the harbour, specializes in fish, cosy atmosphere and decor. Cheaper restaurants are: ♦♦ ***Le Mediterranéen***, 5 rue Moncef Bey, seafood and Tunisian food; ***Restaurant du Sud***, place Hedi Chaker, a bit touristy but the food is good; ♦ ***Restaurant Berbère***, place Farhat Hached, small, typical, good couscous; ***Restaurant Central***, Ave Bourguiba, good, cheap food; ***Restaurant du Sportif***, Ave Bourguiba, very good, cheap Tunisian food.

● Handicrafts

The main ONAT craft shop is on Ave Bourguiba, where the workshops and training centre are open for viewing. This is situated on the same road as the museum, a bit closer to the town, on the left.

● Banks

STB, place Farhat Hached; **BNT**, place Ben Daamech; **BT**, rue du 20 Mars; **BDS**, Ave Bourguiba. There are also many bureau de change offices around the town which accept credit cards and are open more flexible hours.

● Harbour

10 yacht berths, min-max draft 1-3m.

● Hospital

Main Hospital on Ave Bourguiba, T 650018.

● Post Office

Ave Bourguiba, after the main square.

● Telephones

Local code 05. International exchange on the side of the post office.

● Tourist information

The local office is on Ave Bourguiba, just before the post office, T 650157; **ONTT**, at the start of route Touristique, slightly out of town, T 650016, Tx 651956. Closed on Sat afternoon, Fri, Sun and public holidays.

● Tour companies & travel agents

Carthage Tours, centre of town, T 650308; ***Djerba Voyage***, Ave Bourguiba, T 650071; ***Malik Voyagec***, rue Habib Thameur, T 650235; ***Sahara Tours***, Ave Taleb Mehiri, T 652646; ***Tourafricac***, centre of town, T 650104.

● Transport on the island

Bus Djerba has a good public bus service to most parts of the island. There is a bus link with most major Tunisian towns. The bus station, through which all buses pass, is in the centre of Houmt Souk. Information on T 650076. Buses No 10 and 11 go hourly round the island, along the coast past the major hotels; No 12 goes to Ajim and the Djorf ferry; No 13 to Beni Maquel; No 14 to Guellala and No 16 to Sedouikech.

Car hire although cars can be rented they are expensive and there is a minimum 24 hour rental. However it is a good idea if you intend to go down to the S. Be careful in Houmt Souk when you park, as the Police have clamps (same problem as in Tunis: the difficulty is not the fine but finding the person with the keys to come and remove the clamp!). **Avis**, Ave Mohammed Badra, T 650151; **Budget**, rue du 20 Mars 1934, T 650185; **Europacar**, Ave Abdelhamid el Cadhi, T 650357; **Hertz**, Ave Abdelhamid el Cadhi, T 650039, highly recommended; **Topcar**, rue du 20 Mars 1934, T 650536.

Cycle hire: the island is small and flat making bicycles, which can be rented at most large hotels and in Houmt Souk, an attractive means of transport.

Moped From Location Cycles, Ave Abdelhamid el Cadhi, TD15 per day.

Taxis are a good way of getting around but can be hard to find, particularly at night. Taxi to airport costs TD3.

● Transport

Air Tunis Air, Ave Bourguiba, T 650586; **Air France**, Ave Abdelhamid el Cadhi, T 650461. The airport is currently being extended. It is 8 km from Houmt Souk, served by a bus from town, but be sure to check the times beforehand. Flight information on T 650233. New planes and lines are being put into service and will soon be in operation. Expect many more internal flights, including a service to Tozeur. In the summer there are many more flights in addition to those listed below. **Scheduled international flights**: **Frankfurt** Tue 0800; **Lyon** Fri 0925; **Geneva/Zurich** Sat 0800; **Brussels** Sat 0830; **Paris** Sat 0905 and Sun at 0905 and 1205. There is a daily internal flight to **Tunis** at 0725.

Road Bus The bus station is in the centre of Houmt Souk. Information T 652239. Departures to: **Sfax** (via Gabès) 1245; **Gabès** 0530, 0600, 1200, 1245; **Medenine** 0530, 0800, 1200, 1315; **Tataouine** (2½ hrs) 0800; **Zarzis** 0830, 1000, 1200, 1430, 1530, 1700; **Tunis** 0630, 1900, 2000. **Louages**: by the bus station.

Excursions

Midoun is the island's second largest town. A large black community, descendants of slaves brought from Sudan, exists here. It has a particularly good weekly market each Fri. To see an interesting olive press over 300 years old take the road towards Houmt Souk and turn right at the crossroads. It is a little further down on the left by the well. A mule or camel was used to turn the stone roller to crush the olives which were then transferred to a sieve where a large palm tree trunk squeezed out the oil into a jar underneath. All around are chambers once used for stocking olives.

Ajim is the island's main harbour and the departure point for ferries to Djorf on the mainland. It was once an important sponge fishing harbour. This profession is now virtually abandoned, due to the difficulties and dangers of the job. Today, Ajim is an important fishing port. The village itself is of minimal interest, but there are a few cafés and restaurants with large terraces.

El May has a typical Djerbian mosque with thick walls and a low, rounded minaret, resembling a fort. On Sat morning, a small local market takes place here.

Er Riadh In the village a signposted road on the left leads to the **El Griba Synagogue**. The original synagogue is said to have been built at the time of the first Jewish settlement in 586 BC. The present building was constructed in the 1920s and has become a spiritual centre for the study of the Torah. It is an interesting stop in an Islamic country. Inside the synagogue heads will have to be covered (head covers provided). In the first room, old men recite the Torah. The second room holds what is said to be one of the oldest Torahs in the world. Open 0700-1800 except Sat. A small contribution is appreciated.

Guellala is renowned for its **pottery**, particularly the typical Djerbian white coloured ware. The clay for the pottery comes from the small hill nearby, on the road to Sedouikech. Guellala has over 500 artisans making pottery, now mostly selling to the tourists. Indeed it has shops from one end of the village to the other. Fabrication de Poiterie in the main street will provide details on how the pottery is made.

The West coast is still untouched by tourism and is ideal for walks, or a trip along the coast. Unfortunately the coast is mainly rocky, but there are a few beaches. To get there, take the road to the airport and continue straight on towards Borj Jellij, until the road goes right. Here you should take the track to the left and follow it S, all the way to Ajim. A few km along the track, on the right, there are a few beautiful houses and a mosque by the sea.

The Northeast coast Here you will find the tourists and all the large hotels. There are lovely beaches kept clean near the hotels, but not elsewhere, with white sand but they get very crowded in summer. Surfboards can be rented and various other watersports are organized in all the major hotels. If you want some peace, go to the W coast!

The East coast There is an excellent walk, takes 2 hrs, from Aghir to Borj Kastil which is a fort falling into ruin. There are interesting views, especially S across the mainland and the causeway. A very primitive overnight stop, if necessary, is available at the fisherman's cottage at the end of the walk.

INFORMATION FOR VISITORS

Contents

Before you go

Entry requirements

● Visas

Passports Check all passport and visa requirements with your nearest Tunisian Embassy. For stays of over 6 months (US citizens 4 months) a residence visa is required. Tourist visas are not needed by nationals of EU, USA, Canada or Japan. At passport control you will be asked your hotel name. If you are undecided, give the name of any hotel in the town you plan to visit to avoid unnecessary questions.

For a private car you will need a driving licence, registration document (log book), and a Green Card valid for Tunisia. Stays of over 3 months are expensive as extension of vehicle permits is costly.

● Representation overseas

Algeria, 11 Rue de Bois de Boulogne, Algiers, T 601388; **Austria**, Chegastr 3, 1030 Vienna, T 786552; **Belgium**, 278 Ave de Tervuesen, 1150 Brussels, T 7621448; **Canada**, 515 O'Connor St, Ottawa, T 2370330, Tx 534161; **Egypt**, 26 Rue el Jazirah, Zamalek, Cairo, T 3412379; **France**, 27 Rue Barbet de Jouy, 75007 Paris, T 45559598; **Germany**, Godesberger Allee 103, 53 Bonn 2, T 228 376981; **Italy**, 7 Via Asmara, Rome, T 8390748; **Japan**, 292 Ichibabcho, Chiyoda-Ku, Tokyo 102, T 3534111, Tx 27146; **Jordan**, Ave el Aska, 4th Circle, Amman, T 674307; **Libya**, Rue Bèchir el Ibrahimi, Tripoli, T 30331; **Mauritania**, B.P. 681, Nouakchott, T 52871; **Morocco**, Corner of 6 Ave du Fes & 1 Rue d'Ifrane, Rabat, T 30576; **Senegal**, Rue el Hadj Seydou, Nourou Tall, Dakar, T 31261; **Spain**, Plaza Alonzo-Martinez 3, Madrid, T 4473508; **Sudan**, Rue No 18, Baladia Street, Khartoum, T 0024811/76538; **Syria**, 6 Jaddet al-Chaffi, Damascus, T 660356; **Switzerland**, 58 Rue de Moillebeau, 1029 Geneva, T 333023; **UK**, 29 Princes Gate, London SW7, T 071 5848117; **USA**, 1515 Massachusetts Ave NW, Washington DC 20005, T 202 8621850, Tx 248377.

● Tourist Information

Tourist offices in Tunisia are open Mon-Thur 0830-1745, Fri-Sat 0830-1330, Sun and public hols 0900-1200. They are open longer in summer.

Tunisian National Tourist Offices Overseas: **Canada**, 1125 Blvd de Maisonneuve Ouest, Montreal, T 514 985 2586; **France**, 32 Ave de l'Opera, Paris, T 75002; **Germany**, Dusseldorf Steinstrasse 23, 4000 Dusseldorf, T 84218; **Italy**, via Sardegna No 17, 00187 Rome, T 4821934; **Netherlands**, Muntplein 2111, 1012 WR Amsterdam, T 020224971; **Saudi Arabia**, BP 13582-Jeddah 21414, T 6534981, F 6534612; **Spain**, Plaza de Espana 18, Plaza de Madrid, Madrid 28008, T 2481435; **Sweden**, Engelbrektsgaten 19, 11432 Stockholm, T 00468 206773; **UK**, 77A Wigmore St, London W1H 9LJ, T (071) 224 5561; **USA**, contact embassy in Washington, T 2346644.

● Tunisian Hotel Associates

Is at 304 Old Brompton Road, London, SW5 9JF, T 071 373 4412.

● Specialist tour companies

Martin Randall Travel, 10 Barley Mow Passage, Chiswick, London W4 4PH T 081 9946477 – Roman and Islamic Cities; ***Branta Holidays***, 7 Wingfield St, London SE15 4LN T 071 6344812 – birdwatching winter visitors on Lake Ichkeul and Tozeur; ***Andante Travel***, Grange Cottage, Winterbourne Dauntsey, Salisbury, Wilts, SP4 6ER, T 0980 610555 – Art and Archeology; ***Prospect Music and Art Tours***, 454 Chiswick High Road, London W4 5TT, T 081 9952151; ***Discovery Cruises***, 47 St Johns Wood High Street, London NW8 7NJ, T 071 5867191 – sailing from Athens; ***Regency Cruises***, 2 Telfords Yard, 6 The Highway, London E1 9BQ, T0473 292222 – sailing from Nice.

When to go

● Best time to visit

The best season to visit is spring when the N is still green after the winter rains, the S is not yet too hot and the summer tourists have not arrived. The second best time is autumn when it is cooler, but tends to be very dusty. Summer can be extremely hot. Even in Tunis the summer temperatures can reach a maximum of 40°C while the S is even hotter. Despite this, it is the most popular time of the year for visitors. Winters are cold, very cold at some altitudes, and it can be damp in the N.

● Climate

There are considerable differences between the N and the S. Spring is a good period but it sometimes rains in the N. The summer is very hot, particularly inland and in the desert areas. On the coast the heat is made bearable by a light sea breeze. Autumn is the best period to visit the S and the oases. It is still warm, but can get very cold at night. Swimming in the sea is possible until Oct. In Nov it rains over most of the country, but never for very long. Winter is the ideal period for excursions in the Sahara, even though the nights are very cold the days are warm and the sky is blue.

● Clothing

Requirements depend on the time of year and the place. In summer it is necessary to be protected from the sun and to dress with consideration for the heat, bearing in mind that temperatures can fall very sharply at night in the desert. From Nov to Mar a warm coat is recommended and from Oct to May an umbrella or raincoat may be needed in the N.

Health

● Staying healthy

No vaccinations are necessary but a tetanus injection could make you feel more secure. The tap water in Tunis and most tourist centres is fit to drink but bottled water is easily available and may be better in the long run. Protection from the sun is essential. Most proprietary drugs are available over the counter from chemist shops in the main streets of even the smallest towns. Chemists can generally give advice on small problems. See regional sections for hospitals and chemists. Rabies is not to be lightly dismissed. While commonly associated with dogs, too many trusting tourists have been bitten by stray cats and had to undergo a series of very unpleasant injections.

● Further health information

Read the section on Health, see page19.

Money

● Cost of living

Tunisia can be lived in quite cheaply. It is much cheaper than Europe with a hotel costing as little as TD10-25 a night and food TD4-7 a day. Transport is cheap, too, making it therefore quite possible to live well on TD120 a week. Sample prices: bottle of water TD0.45; litre of milk TD0.45; bread TD0.30; cup of tea/coffee TD1/TD0.80; glass of beer TD1.80.

● Credit cards

Cards of various types are accepted by most banks. STB and BT accept Visa and most of their branches accept Mastercard. American Express is accepted in certain travel agencies and bureaux de change and in some branches of the BIAT. Obtaining money with a credit card is generally very easy and the wait very short, just the length of a phone call. Credit cards can be used in all major hotels, restaurants and tourist shops. For all money changes a passport is necessary.

Most hotels of 2 stars and over and most good restaurants accept Visa, Diners Club, American Express and Mastercard. Some shops in the souk will accept credit cards. AmEx office in Tunis is at Carthage Tours, 59 Ave Habib Bourguiba.

Credit cards are required for deposit when hiring cars.

● Currency

The monetary unit is the dinar TD1 = 1,000 millimes. Exchange rates are fixed daily by the

Central Bank. For rates for July 1994 see table, p 9. The exchange rate is fixed, with no black market price, and no need to shop around. Notes in circulation 5, 10, and 20 dinars. Coins in circulation 5, 10, 20, 50, and 100 millimes ½ and 1 dinar. Often prices over a dinar are still given in millimes which can be confusing. A taxi meter from the airport to central Tunis may say 3000 which is TD3. Be careful.

Tunisian dinars can only be obtained in Tunisia. You can take in as much foreign currency as you like. If you are carrying over £300 in foreign currency, complete a currency declaration so you can take it out again. No dinars can be taken out of the country. At the end of your stay you may change back up to 30% of the total value of foreign currency converted during the trip up to a maximum of TD100 dinars – so don't change more than you need at any one time and save all paperwork associated with financial transactions.

Crossing into Algeria it is mandatory to change some money (about AD1200). Sometimes they accept travellers' cheques. Be sure to save all the transaction slips as these may be checked.

Money can be changed at all border crossings. Eurocheques and travellers' cheques in European currencies and US dollars and are accepted at all banks and post offices.

● Taxes

There are no direct taxes levied on visitors. Indirect taxes are included in prices.

Getting there

● General note

There are no problems getting into Tunisia. Tourists are encouraged and visitors are made very welcome. Package holidays and tours are probably the cheapest way of seeing the country in some comfort. Individual travellers will find this the easiest country to move around within North Africa.

● Air

From Europe There are 6 international airports in Tunisia: Tunis, Djerba, Monastir, Sfax, Tabarka and Tozeur. In summer there are numerous charter flights from Europe, mostly to Djerba and Monastir. These can be very cheap, but generally have restrictions regarding length of stay and legally must include accommodation. In summer, book well in advance. For information on charter flights, contact the Tunisia National Tourist Office, 77a Wigmore Street, London, W1H 9LJ, enquiries, T 071 224 5561.

Tunis Air, GB Airways, and Air France (via Paris or Marseille) have scheduled flights to Tunis from London. The cheapest are GB Airways and Air France, from bucket shops. All major European airlines except British Airways fly to Tunis, including Iberia, KLM, Lufthansa, Sabena and Swissair, but may include time-wasting stopovers.

From the USA There are no direct flights. The best and cheapest way is to fly to London and get a charter or cheap scheduled flight from a bucket shop.

From North Africa Royal Air Maroc, Air Algérie and Egyptair fly into Tunis. Prices are generally reasonable and there are many scheduled flights. In summer finding places can be difficult.

Airfares Economy fares on scheduled flights, generally quite cheap, are more expensive in summer. Cheaper tickets can be purchased at bucket shops. Trailfinders in London T 071 937 5400 do cheap Gib Air and Air France tickets. Cheapest return fares quoted to Tunisia are TD260 but last minute bookings can be **much** cheaper.

Best deals are with charter flights and tour operators who fly into airports further S, contact the Tunisian Tourist Office (**see above**). Air fares from adjacent North African countries are generally cheaper. Single fares – Cairo to Tunis TD310 (4 hrs), Casablanca to Tunis TD225 (3 hrs), Algiers to Tunis TD75 (1 hr). Airport tax of TD2 is payable in Tunisia, but this is generally included in the ticket price.

● Train

There is a daily train from Algeria at 1900 entering Tunisia via Ghardimaou, return journey leaves Tunis at 1255. One way 2nd class fare TD20 for a 24 hr journey.

● Road

There are many road crossings to Algeria, the largest in the N at Ghardimaou and Barbouch are reached by local buses and louages. There are regular buses from Algeria and a daily bus to Annaba from Tunis at 0700. The main crossing in the S is at Hazoua beyond Nefta on the P3. Road crossings into Libya are at Ras Jedir on the coast and at Ghadames. The bus for Libya leaves Tunis on Mon, Wed, Fri and Sun at 0700. Where the bus service fails there is generally a taxi service to the border.

● Sea

There are regular car/passenger ferries from Marseille (France), Genoa (Italy) and Trapani (Sicily) to Tunis. From Marseille every 3 days in winter, daily in summer (takes 24 hrs). Contact Southern Ferries in London T 071 491 4968 who are agents for SNCM and CTN lines. Genoa: From Ponte Colombo Sat at 1700, 24 hr crossing. For information, contact Paris T 149242424. (No UK office). Trapani: Tue at 0900, crossing takes 7-8 hrs on Tirrenia line who also run to Cagliari. Their agent in UK is Serena Holidays, T 071 373 6548. In summer there is a jetfoil service between Trapani and Kelibia.

Sea travel from Marseille is very pleasant but can be expensive. Adult return economy fare TD260 (FF1,510), students and under 25's TD220 (FF1,340). Return rate for cars around TD560 (FF3,300) depending on vehicle length.

● Customs

Customs at the airport are slow as most bags (particularly those belonging to Tunisians) are searched. Be patient. Leaving Tunisia the customs officials are rarely in evidence.

Duty free allowances You may take into Tunisia 2 cameras of different types, 20 films, cassette player, 2 tapes, video camera (which will go down on your passport), portable typewriter, portable radio, binoculars, child's pushchair, sports equipment, 1 litre of spirits, 2 litres of wine, 400 cigarettes or 100 cigars or 500gm tobacco, ¼ litre of perfume, 1 litre of toilet water and gifts to value of £30.

Duty free goods to take out of Tunisia such as perfume, cigarettes, wine, spirits and gifts are available in varying quantity and quality in airport departure lounges, note Tunisian money is not accepted beyond passport control.

Import/export bans Weapons may not be taken in or out of Tunisia. Permits can be obtained for hunting weapons on organized visits. Possession of underwater weapons is a serious offence. The Tunisians are, understandably, strongly opposed to people exporting genuine pieces of their archaeological heritage.

Registration Other than the usual embarkation card filled in on arrival at a port or airport, no other formalities are necessary. Hotels register their guests. Informal visitors will need to register themselves with the nearest police station.

When you arrive

● Conduct

Clothing It is as well to remember that this is a Muslim country and you should dress casually but decently. There are strict rules for acceptable clothing for visiting a mosque. See the chapter on travelling in a Muslim country, (page 27).

Hammams Modest behaviour is expected in the hammam so cover yourself somehow.

● Electricity

The current is 220V on 2 pin plugs. Take an international adaptor plug. In the far S you may encounter 110V.

● Hours of business

Vary in summer, winter and Ramadan. These are minimum times: **Shops** between 0800-1230 and 1430-1800, Sat 0800-1300 but they open earlier in summer with one session 0730-1300. Shops in tourist areas are always open!!

Banks 0800-1100 and 1400-1700 Mon-Thurs, 0800-1100 and 1300-1500 Fri. Closed afternoons in summer. Ramadan 0800-1230. In Tunis, some banks are open outside these hours, and in most tourist resorts, money can be changed in large hotels at the aiports and in bureau de change establishments.

Government and Public Services 15 Jul-15 Sept 0730-1330. 16 Sept-14 Jul 0830-1330 and 1500-1745. Fri-Sat 0830-1330. During Ramadan opening hours are different and everything is generally closed in the afternoon.

● Official time

Tunisia is on Central European Time which is one hour ahead of GMT.

● Photography

Taking photographs is no problem in Tunisia, but be aware that some people object to being photographed and taking pictures of women is best avoided without their permission. However children love to be photographed – again and again! Avoid photographing military installations or risk losing your film, your camera or even gaining some hospitality in a police station. Film is readily available throughout the country, check the sell-by date. Bring your own specialist and video films.

● Safety

There is no threat to personal security in Tunisia. Normal vigilance is recommended against petty crime and basic common sense used with respect to personal property, especially money and passports.

● Shopping

A good range of crafts is available in Tunisia. You have the choice of buying them in tourist shops, the souks or in the Office National de l'Artisanat Tunisien (ONAT). It is a good idea to go to the ONAT first where the official prices are listed. Even though the prices are higher here than in the streets, the quality is guaranteed. The best place for shopping is undoubtedly the souk in the medinas. The prices are generally lower and bargaining is part of the fun. No prices are fixed and, as a general rule, the real price is 50% less than the price first given (but could be 90% less).

Carpets are made throughout Tunisia but best bought in Kairouan where the quality is superior and the prices cheaper. All carpets should have a sealed quality certificate. There are 3 main types:- the *Alloucha*, made with natural long wool; the *Zerbia* again with long wool but coloured (the colours used are generally artificial and not all natural as claimed) and the *Mergoum* made of short wool or silk. Don't forget to bargain. For advice on types and official prices go to ONAT.

Copper and brass goods vary in quality and price. The most common items are beaten copper plates, in different sizes. Some are still handmade, but most are mass produced.

Jewellery is either Berber or Arab in origin and sometimes a mixture of both. When buying gold or silver, be sure it has the official stamp on it: a horse head for 18 carat gold and a scorpion for 9 carat. A grape cluster is used for silver of 900 mills per gram. Anything without the stamps should be treated with care. Prices vary with the degree of craftsmanship and some items can be very expensive. A traditional design is the Hand of Fatima (the daughter of the Prophet).

Leather goods are of very good quality but not always cheap. Be sure to check the sewing as it is often of poor quality and the item may soon fall to pieces.

Perfumes many different types are available in various quantities, but the 'staying' qualities cannot be guaranteed.

Pottery is produced in large quantities, but good quality ware is found in both Nabeul and Guellala on the island of Djerba.

Straw goods are actually woven palm leaf fronds, mostly from Gabès and Djerba. They are cheap and range from simple baskets to touristy camels.

● Tipping

Service is included on bills in restaurants and hotels. If you intend to stay for a while at a café, or return to a hotel it pays to leave something. Tips of 5-10% are the norm in restaurants.

● Weights and measures

The metric system is used throughout. See conversion table on **p 17**.

● Worship

Anglican services in St Georges' Church, place Bab Carthage, Tunis each Sun at 1000, also each Sun in Sousse, at 0930, 16, rue de Malte. **French Protestant service** in Eglise Réformée, rue Charles de Gaulle, Tunis, each Sun at 1000. **French Catholic mass** in Jeanne d'Arc Chapel, Tunis and daily in the Cathédral Saint-Vincent-de-Paul 0815 and 1830, Sat 1800, Sun 0900 and 1100.

Where to stay

● Hotels

Hotels and hostels in Tunisia are all controlled by the Tourist Board, and divided into 5 categories. The top is 4 star luxury, the lowest one star. Each year the Tourist Board checks the hotels and renews their ranking, but it is often hard to understand their criteria as it is perfectly possible to find an unclassified (NC) hotel far cleaner and more pleasant than a 3 star one. The ranking also fails to take into account the level of service. The best way of judging a hotel is not to rely on the ranking, but to **ask to see a room**. The differences can be enormous. It must also be said that some hotels are really dirty with decrepit furniture. In this guide, we have tried to cover a range of hotels, all of them clean (well, fairly clean), but with a difference in comfort levels. It is also impossible to give a totally accurate description of a hotel as managements can change. Equally, you will be very surprised to find excellent, very clean small hotels in the medinas, with very friendly management. Quite a few hotels, which are generally still clean, have a distinctly 'past-it' look and urgently need refurbishment. All prices are posted in the reception and can be consulted. All official prices are per person and not per room. In all classified hotels, and even some unclassified ones, breakfast is included in the

Hotel Classifications

AL US$90+. International class luxury hotel. All facilities for business and leisure travellers are of the highest international standard.

A US$75-90. International hotel with air conditioned rooms with WC, bath/shower, TV, phone, mini-bar, daily clean linen. Choice of restaurants, coffee shop, shops, bank, travel agent, swimming pool, some sport and business facilities.

B US$60-75. As **A** but without the luxury, reduced number of restaurants, smaller rooms, limited range of shops and sport.

C US$40-60. Best rooms have air conditioning, own bath/shower and WC. Usually comfortable, bank, shop, pool.

D US$20-40. Best rooms may have own WC and bath/shower. Depending on management will have room service and choice of cuisine in restaurant.

E US$10-20. Simple provision. Perhaps fan cooler. May not have restaurant. Shared WC and showers with hot water (when available).

F under US$10. Very basic, shared toilet facilities, variable in cleanliness, noise, often in dubious locations.

price. It may be a good idea to request half board, as the difference in price is often very small. If travelling out of season check heating (some hotels have none) and number of blankets.

● Youth hostels

In Tunisia are part of the International Federation and accept YHA cards. In all there are 35 hostels. Hostels are located at Aïn Draham, Beja, Bizerte (2), Chebba, Gabès, Gafsa, Djerba, Hammamet, Jendouba, Kairouan, Kasserine, Kebili, Kelibia, Matmata, Médenine, Menzel Temime, Monastir, Nabeul (3), Nasrallah, Siliana, Sfax, Sousse, Teboursouk, Tozeur, Tunis (3), Zaghouan and Zarzis. Minimum age for unaccompanied children is 15, no maximum but priority is given to younger members. Open 0700-2300. Price per night TD3-4. Hire of bed linen and sleeping bags possible at all hostels for 500 mills per night. Use of kitchen 300 mills. Breakfast 700 mills, lunch and dinner TD3.

● Camping

Organized sites with full facilities are relatively few and far between but clearly signed when provided. Always ask permission of the landowner and/or local police before attempting 'casual' camping. None is allowed on tourist beaches. Camping is permitted at the Youth Hostels at Nabeul and Remel (Bizerte). The major camp sites are at Hammam Plage, Nabeul, Hammamet and Zarzis.

Food and drink

● Food

In Tunisia food is very good, quite varied and generally cheap. The small restaurants which do not serve alcohol are cheaper. Restaurants with alcohol are more expensive, even though the quality of the food and service is not necessarily better. Most local products are fresh and good quality. Food is cooked with spices but is never too hot. Along the coast and on the islands, fish is the main dish, and this is always fresh. Fish prices are often by weight, and you can have a nasty surprise if you haven't had it weighed before eating it. In most main towns you will find a large number of French restaurants which can generally be relied on for quality and price. Prices are not always indicated on the menu. Be sure to check before you order.

Specialities – Starters

Chorba – flavoured soup with lots of pepper.

Brik – deep-fried pastry containing egg and tuna, minced beef, lamb or vegetables, usually spinach, very popular.

Salade Michouia – cubed, mixed cooked vegetables with tuna and egg, can be very spicy, served cold.

Salade Tunisienne – Salade Nicoise with tomatoes, onions, tuna and egg.

Main Dishes

Keftaji – seasoned meat balls served with peppers.

Chakchouka – ratatouille with chick peas, tomatoes, peppers, garlic and onions, containing pieces of veal and served with a poached egg.

Couscous – steamed coarse semolina or millet served with vegetables and meat or fish. Typical dish eaten throughout the Maghreb.

Restaurant Classifications

Given the variations in price of food on any menu our restaurants are divided where possible into three simple grades:
♦♦♦ expensive, ♦♦ average and ♦ cheap.

Mechoui – grilled meat (usually lamb), very good.
Tajine – solid cheese quiche, with meat and vegetables, cooked in the oven.
Coucha – roast lamb with potatoes and peppers cooked in the oven, excellent.
Merguez – small spicy mutton or beef sausages, generally grilled.
Mermiz – stewed mutton with beans.
Soboku – steamed mutton with tomato sauce.

Fish: the best are the *Rouget* (red mullet), *Mulet* (mullet), *Merou* (grouper), *Lou de Mer* (perch) and sole; seafood is also very good.

Desserts

Like all Mediterranean countries, Tunisia has many varieties, all very sweet!
Baklava – puff pastry with lots of honey.
Makroud – semolina cake with crushed dates, baked in oil and dipped in honey.
Halva – very sweet cake made from sesame seeds.
Loukoum – Turkish delight.
Bjaouia – almonds, pistachio nuts and puffed rice in a cake mixture.

Fruit

Dates – the season for fresh dates is Oct. There are over 100 types but the best, the deglet nur, come from the desert oases, particularly Tozeur and Nefta.
Pastèque – watermelon, particularly refreshing in summer.
Grenade – pomegranates, served with sugar and sprinkled with jasmine flavoured water.

● Drink

The national drink is tea, generally mint tea. Try not to refuse if you are offered some as this may be seen as insulting! Tea is also served black with lots of sugar, or green tea TD1 per cup. Coffee is also widely drunk TD1 per cup. Two types are served, expresso and cappuccino. (In local bars coffee and tea is only TD0.5.) The most common and cheapest beer is Celtia (a Tunisian make) but Tunisian made Tuborg and Stella, as well as imported beers, can be found.

Wine The Tunisians have been making wine for over 2,000 years. Wines sold under certificate are under the strict control of the state. The **red wines** are more acidic than Western palates are used to and vary in quality. It is difficult to recommend any particular wine but for experience try one from the medium-priced *Maçon Rouge* to the cheaper *Vieux Thibar*. The **rosé** is by far the best bet. It can be drunk with anything and is rarely awful. Recommended are *Haut Mornag* and *Sidi Rais* and the more expensive *Château Mornag*. The **white wines** are generally dry – try *Sidi Rais*. Also considered worth a try are *Blanc de Blanc* and *Muscat sec de Kelibia*. Tunisian *vins gris* (untranslateable!) include *Gris de Tunisie* and *Gris de Bizerte*.

Other alcohol Tunisia also produces three types of very strong alcohol. **Boukha** is made from distilled figs, **Laghmi** is palm tree sap drunk immediately after it is collected and **Thibarine** is palm sap left to ferment for a while. Most imported alcohols are available generally in hotels and rarely in bars, but they are very expensive. Take your own alcohol to 'dry' restaurants.

Soft drinks are widely available. Bottled water is very good and is offered, but not free, with all meals. The larger 1.5 litre bottle costs about ½TD. The smaller, resealable plastic bottles are just right for taking on short journeys.

Cafés are an interesting experience. They are generally packed with men (no women) and intensely smokey and noisy! A good way to make contact with the locals is to try a Shisha. They are water pipes, but the tobacco is slightly different from cigarette tobacco, and flavoured with honey or sometimes apples. Stronger than cigarettes (but not the local Crystal cigarettes) it is nevertheless a good way to start up a conversation as somebody will invariably ask you if you like it.

Getting around

● Air

Flights Tun Inter (reservations via Tunis Air) run regular internal flights between Tunis, Monastir, Djerba and Tozeur. They are generally arranged so that travellers from other towns can spend the day in Tunis. Flights are not expensive but places are scarce. Tunisavia are flying smaller 72 seater planes on internal flights and have small planes for hire.

● Train

This is a good way of travelling in the main areas. The trains travel quite slowly so there is ample opportunity to see the scenery. From Tunis the lines go N to Bizerte (1 hr 50 mins) and Tabarka, W to Jendouba (3 hr) and Algeria and S as the 'Sahel Metro' to Hammamet (1½ hr), Sousse (2¼ hr), Sfax (4½ hr) and Gabès (7 hr) through all the coastal resorts. The TGM runs frequently from Tunis to Carthage and La Marsa stopping in all the suburbs. The only line inland goes to Metlaoui (11 hr), via Gafsa (10 hr). The service is quite efficient, nearly all trains leaving on time. First class trains with modern rolling stock, adjustable seats and refreshments are good but lack the atmosphere, interest and cheapness of the 2nd class. On a return ticket, 25% reduction cards can be obtained, valid 8 days. Timetables available from any station and most tourist offices in Tunisia and abroad.

● Road

Bus is the cheapest means of transport, and therefore the most popular. Virtually all towns and villages are on a bus route. Local buses can be a very interesting experience, as everything from fruit to chickens is transported. The inter-city lines are generally fast and comfortable. On most lines there are slightly more expensive a/c buses available, vital in summer, check the different companies for facilities available. Times available from bus stations and tourist offices. Advance booking is possible on most inter-city lines, very useful during summer. Arrive in advance, as buses are more likely to depart early than late.

Bicycles and motorbikes are a good way to see the country, depending on the terrain. Summer heat may make progress difficult, autumn or spring being a better choice. Bring essential spare parts, though if a problem occurs help is easily available as all towns and villages have mechanics. Spare parts for motorcycles may prove harder to find. Cyclists are advised to wear bright colours.

Car hire is probably one of the best ways of seeing the country, but prices are quite high as cars are expensive here. Expect to pay at least US$400 per week with unlimited mileage. There are a many agencies, everything from the large internationals (which tend to be the most expensive) to smaller local companies. The standard cars are generally Peugeot 205 and Citroen AX. Shop around as prices can differ and when comparing prices check the 17% VAT is included. It can also be cheaper to buy a package including flight and car in London or Paris. Try Nouvelles Frontières, 11 Blenheim St, London, W1Y 9LE, T 071 629 7772. International driving licences are normally required but a current European licence is usually sufficient. Be warned that hire is unlikely to include either the tyres or the windscreen and replacement can be extortionate. Read the

	Béja	Bizerte	Gabès	Gafsa	Kairouan	Mahdia	Nabeul	Sfax	Sousse	Tabarka	Tunis
Bizerte	107										
Gabès	390	430									
Gafsa	340	420	146								
Kairouan	180	215	210	205							
Mahdia	265	270	240	285	110						
Nabeul	170	131	325	320	114	160					
Sfax	315	330	136	195	136	105	225				
Sousse	205	205	265	260	57	62	96	127			
Tabarka	71	138	475	370	250	340	240	385	275		
Tunis	105	64	365	355	155	205	67	270	140	160	
Zarzis	480	565	138	285	350	380	465	275	400	615	505

Tunisia: distances by road between major cities (Km)

small print on the contract and check on the excess charge. Consider bringing your own car. Balance the hire charges against the ferry charge and greater flexibility.

Car breakdown You may be rescued by a patrolling Garde Nationale. Failing that, hitch to the nearest village for a mechanic or to ring the hire firm. Travellers intending to drive in the S are advised to read the section on travelling in the desert (see page40).

Driving in Tunisia is on the right. The roads are generally good but the number of cars on the road far exceeds the number of competent drivers. Be particularly careful when driving through villages, as children and animals have little road sense. Be very careful, too, of Peugeot pickups, which are more than likely to turn suddenly or stop without indicating. In town, the real danger is the pedestrians. Obey the speed limits, a strict 50 km in towns and 90 km on the main roads. There are numerous police controls, particularly by speed limit signs. If you are stopped, smile. It will make things easier. Safety belts are compulsory. Petrol is very cheap and there is no shortage of petrol stations. Avoid no parking zones in cities as illegally parked cars are clamped or towed away which is both tedious and expensive. Roads signs are French/International with Arabic translations.

Hitchhiking is easy, particularly going along the coast. Inland can be more difficult but is generally not a problem. Normally the ride is not free except in an emergency. Shared taxis are found on many routes and private cars and pickups will act in the same capacity, expecting payment as a matter of course. Foreign travellers may get a free ride. Remember drivers have a choice and may not choose heavily laden, unkempt passengers, especially not for a free ride.

While the editors appreciate that hitchhiking may be the only way to reach a given destination, travellers do so always at their own risk.

Louages, large taxis taking up to 5 or 6 people, are a very popular mode of transport and often the fastest. They leave as soon as they are full and have a station in virtually every town. They are excellent transport for a group or large family even though all children count full fare. Be sure to settle the price before leaving. They are generally a little more expensive than the train. The town indicated in the window of the louage does not indicate where it is going, but only where it is licensed! Be warned that some of the cars are old and slow, but some are brand new and travel fast (often too fast). In summer, it can be a good idea to travel in the evening, or at night, when it is considerably cooler.

Taxis should have meters and the meter should be turned on. If you hire a taxi for yourself, charges run at 200 mills plus 120 mills per km with an extra charge for luggage (sometimes for each piece of luggage). Higher fares after 2100.

Boat

Ferry services ply to Djerba and the Kerkennah Islands.

Walking

Is not usual but with a good map, adequate supplies and stout footwear it is possible. French series 1:50,000 maps, now out of date, are available in some parts of Tunisia, via France. Dogs can be a problem. Take a stout stick or an umbrella which can double as a sun shade!

Communications

Language

Arabic is the first language but virtually everyone has some French. In the tourist areas shop keepers and hotel staff speak 3 or 4 European languages, (**see page52**).

Postal services

Stamps are available from post offices, some shops, some kiosks and most hotels. Post offices open Mon-Thur 0800-1200 and 1400-1700, Fri-Sat 0800-1230. Summer opening 0730-1200 except Sun. During Ramadan Mon-Thur 0800-1400, Fri-Sat 0800-1200. Mail reaches the UK in one week, USA 2 weeks. Mail to Europe costs 350 mills, to USA 400 mills. Parcels about TD25 for 10 kg.

Telephone services

The telephone system is quite efficient and once you can get hold of a phone getting through should present no problems. Pay phones only take dinars. It costs about TD1 per minute to UK. Collect calls are possible but harder to make.

National calls can be more difficult, although the real problem is getting hold of a telephone. Public call boxes are generally in, or adjacent to, post offices. Queues can be huge and enough to deter all but the very determined. Calls from hotels are much more expensive with a minimum charge for 3 mins of

TD5-10, but much more comfortable.

Local codes

01 – Carthage, La Marsa, Tunis
02 – Bizerte, Hammamet, Zaghouan and Nabeul
03 – Monastir, Mahdia and Sousse
04 – Sfax and Kerkennah
05 – Gabès, Djerba, Medenine and Tataouine
06 – Tozeur, Gafsa and Sidi Bouzid
07 – Kairouan and Kasserine
08 – Tabarka, Le Kef, Aïn Draham, Jendouba and Béja.
09 – All car phones.

Entertainment

● Media

There are 3 daily newspapers in French, Le Temps, La Presse and L'Action. All international papers can be found in the main towns – usually the next day. Radio and TV is mostly in Arabic except for Antenne 2 (French) and RAI1 (Italian). There are no English programmes. BBC World Service can be picked up easily. For frequencies, **see page17**.

● Sport

Tunisia offers a variety of sports including:

Hunting and shooting of various game birds and wild boar. It is necessary to be part of an organized party for firearm permits during official hunting seasons.

Golf El Kantaoui Golf Course, Port El Kantaoui, T 03 31755, F 03 40506; Monastir Golf Course, Route de Ouardanine, T 03 61120; Hammamet Golf Course, Bir Bou Rekba, T 02 82722; Tabarka Golf Course, Montazah Tabarka, T 08 44321; Soukra Golf Course, near Tunis, route de la Soukra, T 765919. Average green fees TD30.

Riding on horses and camels. Horse racing at Kassar Saïd 10 km W of Tunis.

Tennis at most large tourist complexes.

Watersports including sailing, skiing, windsurfing, snorkelling, scuba diving, fishing and underwater fishing. Contact Centre Nautique International de Tunisie, 22 rue de Medine, Tunis.

Holidays and festivals

1 Jan: New Year's Day
18 Jan: Anniversary of the Revolution
20 Mar: Independence Day
21 Mar: Youth Day
9 Apr: Martyr's Day
1 May: Labour Day
1 Jun: Victory Day
25 Jul: Republic Day
13 Aug: Women's Day
3 Sep: Anniversary of PSD
15 Oct: Evacuation of Bizerte
7 Nov: New Era Day

● Local festivals

Many towns have festivals, some more interesting than others and some invented for the tourists. Interesting ones are mentioned in the text. Major ones include:

Apr *Ksar Festival* in Tataouine – Berber folklore and tradition; Nefta; Nabeul Fair, display of agricultural products; *Orange Festival* in Menzel Bou Zelfa (close to Hammamet), orange picking and folklore.

May *Sparrow Hawk Festival* in El Haouaria, hunting scenes and hawk displays; *Tunis fair* – alternate years.

Jun *Ulysses Festival* in Djerba, folklore of the island and simulation of Ulysses' arrival; *Dougga Festival* at Roman theatre; *Malouf Festival* in Testour – Andalusian folklore with Spanish performers.

Jul Carthage – events at Roman theatre; Monastir and Sousse both have *International Festivals* of music, dance and theatre.

Aug Sousse *Baba Aoussou Festival*; Hammamet *International Festival* of music, dance and theatre; Carthage – cinema of the developing countries; *El Djem Festival* of folklore and theatre in Roman Colosseum; *Béja* – wheat festival.

Sep *Wine Festival* at Grombalia – between Tunis and Nabeul; *Cavalry Festival* in Kairouan – Traditional Arab horse display.

Oct Carthage film festival alternate years.

Nov Tozeur *Sahara Festival* – oasis tradition and folklore.

Dec Douz *Sahara Festival*: Sahara folklore, camel races, cavalry and music – the best of the oasis festivals.

● Religious feast/fast days

These change every year as they follow the lunar calendar. Approximate dates for 1995:

1 Feb: Beginning of Ramadan (see page 30).
4 Mar: Aïd Esseghir celebrated by parties, music in the streets
31 May: Ras el Am Hejri (New Year 1416)
10 May: Aïd el Kebir
9 Aug: Mouled of the Prophet
4 Oct: Jewish feast of forgiveness in Djerba

● Market days

In every town in the country there is a market, some of limited interest, particularly in the main tourist areas. However the genuine markets are both interesting and colourful.

Mon Tataouine, Houmet Essouq, Kairouan, Aïn Draham, Mareth, Maktar, Kelibia, Mahres.

Tue Ghardimaou, Kasserine, Béja, Bizerte, Haffouz, Krib.

Wed Sbeitla, Nefta, Moknine, Sers and Jendouba.

Thur Gafsa, Teboursouk, Le Kef, Djerba, Bou Salem and Douz.

Fri Mahdia, Zaghouan, Tabarka, Mateur, Sfax, Nabeul, Zarzis.

Sat El Fahs, Ben Gardane, El Alia, Thibar.

Sun Sousse, Hammam Lif, El Djem, Enfida, Fernana.

Further reading

● Books

Anon, *Les Mosquées de Tunisie*, Tunis, 1973; Brett, M. (ed), *Northern Africa, Islam and modernisation*, Cass, London, 1973; Brown, L.C., *The Tunisia of Ahmed Bey*, University Press, Princeton, 1974; Douglas N., *Fountains in the Sand*, 1985; Hopkins, M., *Tunisia to 1993*, London, 1989; Kassab, A., *Etudes Rurales en Tunisie*, Tunis, 1980; Knapp, W., *Tunisia*, Thames & Hudson, 1970; Latham, J.D., *Towards a study of Andalusian immigration and its place in Tunisian history*, Cahiers de Tunisie, 1957; Lloyd, C., *English Corsairs on the Barbary Coast*, London, 1981; Messenger, C., *The Tunisian Campaign*, 1982; Sladen, D., *Carthage and Tunis*, London, 1906; Woodford, J.S., *The City of Tunis*, Menas Press Ltd, Wisbech, 1990.

● Guidebooks and Maps

Guide du Routard Tunisie, Algérie et Sahara edited by Hachette; *Guide Bleu Tunisie* edited by Hachette; *Stay Alive in the Desert*, K.E.M. Melville, edited Roger Lascelles.

The best map by far is Michelin 972, price £5. Map of Tunisia by Kümmerly and Frey, price £5, scale 1: million gives geomorphological details and a pictorial view worth studying before the visit. The Tourist Office will give you their free map which is good enough to pinpoint the main places but lacks detail.

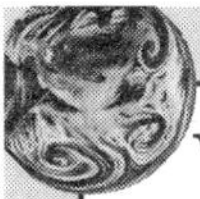

LIBYA

Contents

Introduction

Libya, the fourth largest state in Africa lies between latitudes 33°N and approximately 20°N and longitudes 20°E and 25°E. It lies in a transitional climatic zone between the Mediterranean and the Sahara Desert, having only a narrow cultivated strip in the north and more than 90% of its territory in the arid zone.

The two northern coastlands of Tripolitania and Cyrenaica have been associated throughout history with Mediterranean civilizations, notably the N African provinces of Rome and Byzantium. The Muslim invasion attached Libya to the Muslim and Arab worlds of the east, diversifying and complicating its affiliation to Mediterranean society and southern Europe. Libya came under the Ottomans and semi-independent local Turkish rulers or *bashaws* until the initial occupation of the country by Italy in 1911. Libya gained its Independence in 1951 as a monarchy under King Idris Senussi I. In 1969 a revolution saw the creation of a 'Jamahiriyah', or country of the masses, by Colonel Ghadhafi. Libya became increasingly an oil-based economy but after 1976 its economic and political relationships with other countries deteriorated, culminating in the severance of its worldwide air connections in 1992.

Basics

OFFICIAL NAME al-Jamahiriyah al-Arabiyah al-Libiyah ash-Shabiyah al-Ishtirakiyah (Socialist People's Libyan Arab Jamahiriyah)

NATIONAL FLAG Green.

OFFICIAL LANGUAGE Arabic.

OFFICIAL RELIGION Islam.

INDICATORS *Population* 4,500,000; *Urban* 76%; *Religion* Sunni Muslim 97%; *Birth rate* 44 per 1000 *Death rate* 9.4 per 1000, *Life expectancy* 59 men, 63 women; *GNP per capita* US$5,410.

Environment

Land

The state of Libya has an area of 1,759,540 sq km, 3 times the surface area of France. It has a 1,750 km seaboard with the Mediterranean stretching from Zuwarah in the W to Al-Bardia in the E. Most people live and work along the N coast. Elsewhere the country fades immediately inland into semi, then full desert S into the deep Sahara. The desert regions are lightly populated and support major routes often over 1,000 km in length where N to S transport tracks pass from oasis to oasis, ultimately linking with Chad, Sudan and Niger in Central Africa. For all its extent, therefore, Libya is a country where the ambitious traveller can see much of what exists simply by following the few key lines of communication.

Libya and North Africa

Libya is a cultural and geographic bridge firstly between Egypt and the Arabian lands to the E, the *mashreq* and the territory of the extreme Arab W, the *maghreb*. Secondly, Libya acts as a link between the Mediterranean/Europe and Saharan Africa. The Arabic spoken in Libya is gen-

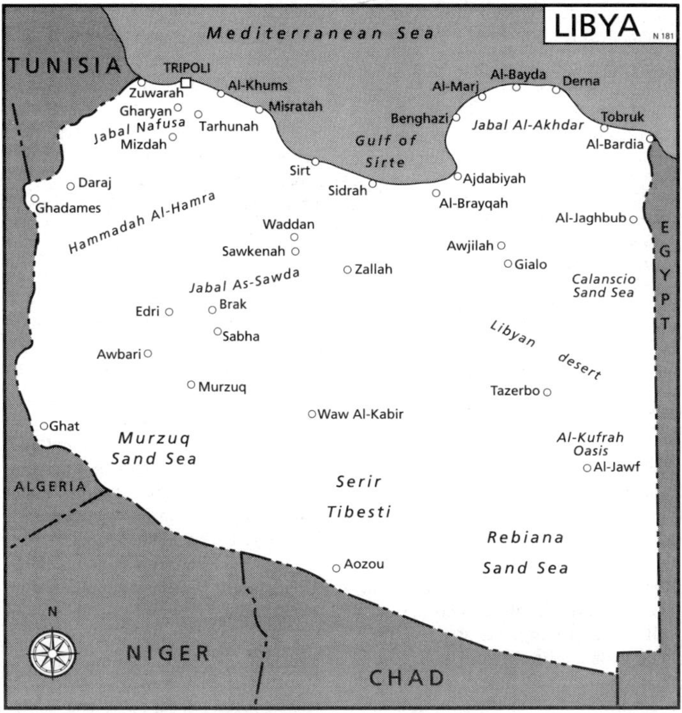

erally different from the Berberized and French-influenced Arabic of the Maghreb with its quite separate accent and dialect from the Arabic of the Nile valley. The coming of oil wealth profoundly affected the attitudes of small groups of an often bedouin population, barely one million in all, with their Libyan attitudes, way of life, and political structure. Apparently less culturally stable and profound, it is immediately different to the great Nilotic civilizations to the E, and to the more Mediterranean and French influenced societies to the W.

Libya and Europe

Although Libya was colonized by the Italians for a brief period (1911-1943) as its 'Fourth Shore' and was politically allied to Europe under the Senussi monarchy until 1969, since that time the country has become detached from European values. In contrast to the Maghreb, Libya will seem to be alien to the traveller from the W. Management and administrative systems are generally slow except in the new, small but flourishing private sector. The role of the state is much greater and impinges much further on people's private lives than in W Europe.

Borders

Libya is bounded to the W by Tunisia and Algeria. In the extreme SW, the border is not fully agreed and travellers are advised to keep to the main roads. In the E, the Libyan frontier with Egypt is for the most part agreed. Libya shares a border with Sudan in the SE. The entire S border is subject to dispute with Chad. The Uzu strip was bitterly fought over until 1990 when it was agreed to settle the matter by reference to the International Court of Justice. Travelling in the Uzu strip is not recommended and is disapproved of by the Libyan authorities.

Regions

Traditionally Libya was divided into 3 provinces – Tripolitania, Cyrenaica and Fezzan. Indeed, until recently, Libya was a united kingdom of these 3 provinces and Libyans still identify with these historic divisions. Recent political changes brought 4 new administrative districts including Tripoli, Benghazi, Sabha and Al-Khalij or 'Gulf'. Tribal territories are still observed in the popular culture of some districts.

Relief

A set of geographical districts naturally defined by relief features is recognized locally, the principal natural zones being the densely settled regions of the Jefara Plain, the Jabal Nafusa, Sirt, the Benghazi Plain, the Jabal Al-Akhdar, Fezzan and Al-Kufrah. In the centre and S very large scale features dominate. In the W the Hammadah Al-Hamra is a vast stony plain with no settlements and few lines of communication. Adjacent to the E of the Hammadah is the Jabal As-Sawda, the black mountains, a desolate and topographically broken area. In the S, Fezzan, is the great sand sea of Murzuq through which travel is feasible only via the few great *wadi* systems which traverse it. In the E, the settled zone of the Jabal Al-Akhdar is followed to the S by the Dahar, an extensive area of enormous sand seas, of which Calanscio is possibly the greatest. It is dangerous to travel off the few highways which link the small oases. Water holes are few and population numbers very thin. In the deepest SE lie the Tibesti Mountains, the land of the Tibu tribes, where security is unreliable and the traveller is advised to enter only when accompanied by an official courier.

Rivers

Libya has only one permanently flowing river, the Wadi Ki'am, in the W province between Al-Khums and Zliten. This is a tiny stream of no more than 2 km running from a spring source to a reservoir impounded in a lagoon adjacent to the seashore. Elsewhere the *wadis* run in spate after heavy rains but are dry for the rest of the year. *Wadis* in flood can fill at a dangerous speed. Among the major *wadis* of Libya are the Mejennin which runs through the W suburbs of Tripoli city. It is now mainly controlled through dams and diversion works in its upper reaches. The Wadi Soffejin drains much of S Tripolitania to the Gulf of Sirte, partly feeding the enormous natural salt marshes at Tauorga, located to the S of Misratah. In Cyrenaica the Wadi Derna is a rich area, its stream running for much of the year and providing irrigation water for a fertile oasis adjacent to the port. The generally waterless Wadi Al-Kuf runs through the hills of the Jabal Al-Akhdar in a steep, scenic gorge.

Climate

The Libyan climate is very varied. The Mediterranean coast has warm winters with an unreliable rainfall, though on average over 200 mm. Extended periods of poor rainfall are experienced even in this coastal zone. Summers are hot and often humid. Relative humidity in July can reach an uncomfortable 80+% for days on end especially in Tripolitania. The mountains of the Jabal Al-Akhdar attract considerably more reliable rainfall in winter and early spring, while in summer the heights are cooler than the surrounding plains. Further S the climate becomes increasingly Saharan. Low temperatures and occasional random rainfall are experienced in winter with a large daily temperature range from 15-20°C during the day to sub-zero at night. Cold nights also occur in early and late summer. Summers are hot and very dry in the S with highs of over 50°C but one can also feel cold in the night when a sweater is welcome. Al-Aziziyah, inland on the Jefara Plain behind Tripoli, has one of the world's highest recorded temperatures, 55°C.

The *ghibli* wind blows hot air from the Sahara across N Libya and carries a large amount of dust which severely reduces visibility. Relative humidity drops immediately at the onset of the *ghibli* to less than 15% and air temperatures rise rapidly. The wind is most noticeable in W Libya and is often associated with the spring solstice.

Flora and fauna

Outside the coastal plains, the Jabal Nafusah and the Jabal Al-Akhdar, the natural vegetation is dominated by tamarind, palm and fig trees. The acacia arabica, alfalfa grass, salt bush and a range of grasses grow thinly except after rain in the semi-desert. Other plants include the asfodel and wild pistachio. The dromedary was the principal animal of the region but is declining rapidly in importance. There is still a residual belief that the region was formerly, perhaps in Roman times, very rich and climatically more favoured than at present. Wall and cave paintings and graffiti of leopards, elephants, wolves and other animals of the Savanna suggest that this was so. There are antelope, gazelle and porcupine. Falcons, eagles, and other birds of prey are present in small numbers. During the period of bird migrations, many small migrant birds get blown into the Sahara and even the occasional exotic species strays into the oases. There are snakes, few dangerous, and scorpions which are to be carefully avoided. See also the introduction to North Africa, page 38.

Agriculture

Agriculture remains the main occupation of the Libyans despite the protracted existence and economic dominance of the oil industry. In good years rainfall turns the countryside green and the semi-desert blooms with a profusion of flowers, the Jefara Plain being particularly attractive at such times. Poor rainfall means thin crops from rainfed farming and a reliance on underground water resources lifted by diesel and electric pumps. A series of dry years causes the water table to fall dramatically and leads to the excessive use of pumps. Around Tripoli, salt water from the sea has been drawn into deep aquifers more than 20 km inland from the coast. Water for both agriculture and human use has become increasingly salty over the years.

The Jabal Al-Akhdar of Cyrenaica has a generally reliable rainfall of more than 300 mm per year but has only limited underground water resources. Here agriculture is rainfed and is mainly concerned with grain production. In the S areas of the country farming activity is limited to small oases where underground water occurs naturally in see pages for traditional farming or can be pumped in modern development projects. The traditional farms have successfully resisted extinction as the economy has been modernized, though many modern reclamation schemes, as at Al-Kufrah, have been abandoned as costs have risen and environmental limitations taken their toll.

In much of the broad zone of N Libya, including the semi-arid steppes and the inland *wadi* catchments, various forms of pastoral nomadism were important in the past. Tribal territories spread S from the coast to enable seasonal migrations of the nomads. In the central Jefara of Tripolitania, the fringes of the Gulf of Sirte and much of the S slopes of the Jabal Al-Akhdar, forms of full nomadism were practised. Other parts of the N were under types of semi-nomadism (family herding movement) or seasonal transhumance (movements of flocks by shepherds). The coming of the oil era, the imposition of firm boundaries between North African states and other processes of modernisation brought much of the nomadic activity to a halt. Some semi-nomadic shepherding of large flocks of sheep and goats still goes on in traditional pasture areas but on a minor scale, involving only small numbers of people.

Agricultural land use in Libya is concentrated on the coastal strip. Only 1.2% of the country is cultivated with a further 7.6% as pasture, rough grazing or forest. The only natural woodland, mainly evergreen scrub, occurs on the Jabal Al-Akdar, though this has been much reduced by clearances for agriculture. Total forested land is claimed at 0.4% of the land surface area.

The **land tenure** situation in Libya has evolved rapidly through the last 100 years. Communal, tribal land ownership was generally practised in Libya except in the settled oases. The Italian colonial period saw a great expansion of state-controlled lands which eventually devolved to the government of the independent state of Libya in 1951-61. Government intervention in all forms of ownership, ostensibly to socialize fixed assets in the country after the introduction of the Green Book decrees of 1973/75, led to more de facto nationalization of land. Small farmers are again being encouraged to remain in private ownership. In certain circumstances, individuals are also allowed to own more than one house. Some communal properties, mainly in the semi-arid steppes, are held by tribal groups. A gradual reassertion of private rights in land and other property began with the human rights decrees of 1977 and were reinforced by the privatization programmes implemented from 1989.

Economic potential

Libyan economic potential is greatly limited by the constraints of a harsh environment. No more than a fragment of the land receives rainfall adequate to support agriculture; underground water reserves are slight and declining. Even the costly movement of water from the S to the N by the Great Manmade River (GMR) projects inaugurated in late 1991 do little to mitigate the problem of water shortage. Other natural resources are scant. Oil, gas and some small chemical deposits occur. There is some potential for the development of the SW where yellow cake (low grade uranium) is found. Overall, however, the country is poorly endowed and its physical resources inevitably must restrict its future development.

People

The **population** of Libya was estimated at 4.5 million in 1992, 4.2% above the preceding year. There is great racial diversity. The original Berber population of W Libya gradually mixed with incoming Arab tribes after the 8th century BC, though some small groups of more or less pure Berbers from the Jabal Nafusa area of Tripolitania still exist. The peoples of E Libya are proud to be mainly Arab. Intermixture through marriage with slaves and other peoples of negro origin such as the Tibu from the Tibesti mountains of S Libya gives a further dimension to the racial variety. The coastal cities originally contained populations of Jewish, foreign Arab, Maltese, Greek and many others.

Tribal traditions are strong. Outside Tripoli the country was economically and socially structured on *qabila* (tribal) lines with *lahmah* (clans) and extended family sub-clans. Each tribe had a defined territory and a specific history of alliances and friction with adjacent groups. During Italian colonial rule, the legal and economic basis of society was changed, partly through systematic removal of Arabs from the land but also by the economic upheaval that came with colonial occupation and warfare. None the less, tribal affiliation has social importance in marriage, kinship and status, especially outside the major urban centres.

Some 95% of people are found in the narrow N coastal strip, with 70% of all Libyans crowded into urban areas. Many of those registered as rural in fact commute to work in nearby towns. Tripoli attracts long-distance daily commuters and there are few areas of the NW not dominated economically by the capital despite recent attempts to decentralize. There is an average of 2.5 persons per sq km, though in the coastal strip the densities are much higher.

It is estimated that about 47% of the Libyan population is less than 15 years old, 25% between 15 and 29 and a mere 3.8% above 60 years of age, a profoundly youthful population even by Third World standards. The balance between males and females is reported as 52% male and 48% female.

Religion

Libya is almost uniformly Sunni Muslim. Practice of Islam is normal for most people though, with some notable exceptions, Islam is kept as a way of life rather than a political force, in contrast to Algeria. Within Sunni Islam there is variation in attachment to different schools of ju-

The Tribes Of Libya

Libya remains a tribal society despite an attempt to undermine the system by the Italian colonial authorities, and strong forces for modernization since Independence especially since 1969. Perhaps the growth of an apparently all-powerful state control over the lives of ordinary people gave the tribal system the fillip it needed to survive. Caught up in a political regime many neither understood nor cared for, they turned to their traditional roots, the family, the extended family and the tribe. The genesis of the tribal system and its genealogies are all-important in giving strength to the tribes of the present day.

The tribes of Tripolitania are often of mixed Arab and Berber descent but might identify exclusively with one aspect of their ethnic origin. Geographically the tribes of different racial origin are in small areas so that there are few large confederations made up of a single ethnic source. In N Cyrenaica the tribes are exclusively Arab from the Obeidat of the Ulad Ali in the E to the Al-Magarba of Ajdabiyah and Sirt. All the tribes claim an individual or family as a common origin and it is not unusual for the pure Arab and Berber tribes to be able to establish long family trees. There are formerly saintly clans grouped around a *marabout* as a common ancestor. Some tribes claim their origins in a member of the family of the Prophet Mohammed. Other tribes have family trees which are suspect but which, nevertheless, serve to unite and bond the tribe. The still-practised custom of marriage between cousins brings a sense of closeness to those families involved.

Each tribe is made up of at least 4 different levels of organization, the nuclear family, the extended family, the large family group or sub-tribe and the tribe. The family and extended families are represented by the eldest male. The sub-tribe and tribe have a chosen or acknowledged head. Formerly the head or shaikh would act for his group in dealings with tribes or clans of a similar kind and with the outside world. This latter formality is less visible in modern society for since 1969 the government has not given recognition to the tribal units. An element of social support and economic backing comes from the tribe together with a feeling of a shared territory. A person's identity originates powerfully in his tribal and family name, which declares ethnic origin, historical status and possibly current political strength.

rists. Most Libyans are of the Malekite school, though Berber minority groups of Kharejite thought are also found.

Literacy

Rates are much improved in Libya from a very poor base level at Independence. By 1990, 74% of males and 50% of females were literate. The educational system has been the subject of constant interference by the authorities, and standards, especially in higher education, have fallen in recent years. Even so there are 40,000 persons each year in higher education with university levels, except in medicine and some other limited areas, approximating in most cases to those of European secondary schools.

Income

As an oil economy Libya generates an apparently high income per head at US$5,310. This figure can be misleading in the sense that the government controls and spends the greatest portion of national income which benefits the population at large. There is poor distribution of income, the isolated rural regions of the country being much worse off in real terms than the coastal cities. Between individuals, however, there is less visible difference in income than in other Arab states. Libyan participation in the workforce is low at 20% of the total population with only 8% of women taking part in paid employment. By far the majority of Libyans work for the government or its agencies, leaving foreign labourers to work in industry and perform other menial tasks.

History since Independence

British and French military administrations withdrew in 1951 when the state became independent as a United Kingdom of Cyrenaica, Tripolitania and Fezzan under the first Senussi monarch. The king kept close links with the British and Americans, permitting the retention of British land forces and American and British airforce facilities. Libya was economically poor at this period, having one of the lowest standards of living in the world. Foreign aid supported the state until an increasing volume of oil company expenditures in Libya on goods and services for exploration activity gradually improved the economy. Severe strains affected the Libyan nation as Arab nationalist and anti-Western ideology generated by Gamal Abdel Nasser in Egypt spread to Libya.

Oil was struck in commercial quantities in 1959 and oil exports began in 1961. Libya rapidly became financially independent and initiated sensible reforms in housing, health and education. Employment opportunities improved and a development programme for agriculture, industry and infrastructure was set in motion. Young Libyan technocrats were given scope to implement their policies and the country made rapid steps forward from a low economic base level. The king took little part in the management of the country. Politically the nation was concentrated in a United Kingdom of Libya in 1963, with a parliament of limited powers centred in Tripoli. The Palestine question and the spread of Nasserite ideas made Libya politically unstable.

A coup d'état by a group of young army officers took place on Sept 1, 1969. The leader of the coup was Mu'amar Ghadhafi who was a disciple of Gamal Abdel Nasser, overtly anti-Western and deeply convinced of the need to obtain full rights for the Palestinians. He banned alcohol and the use of foreign languages for official purposes. He closed down the remaining foreign military bases on Libyan soil. He abolished most private sector activities in the economy and promised a new Arab socialist society under the banner of the Socialist People's Libyan Jamahiriyah. He elaborated a set of philosophies encapsulated in his Green Book which set out his ideas on the nature of an Arab socialist state. He adopted the position of *qa'ed* (guide) and announced that democracy was untenable. Instead he set up people's committees in all administrative districts and work places as best representing the interests of the masses. Perhaps his greatest success was in threatening the assets of the foreign oil companies in Libya and in helping to force up oil prices in the early 1970s.

The Libyan role in favour of Arab unity and against Western interests was pursued through the creation of a vast and expensive military establishment, political activities abroad designed to frustrate Western interests and a solid pro-Palestinian stance. While oil revenues remained very high, Libya's international position gained some notoriety in Lebanon, Uganda and Chad. Military successes were denied the Libyan authorities and, as oil wealth declined first in the mid-1970s and then in the 1980s, Libyan foreign policy ceased to be significant in international affairs.

At home a series of economic plans promised rapid and integrated regional development of the country, but erratic implementation of projects, shortages of money and personnel and distraction abroad diluted the effort. Despite having a small indigenous population, Libya has never quite developed beyond oil as a productive and well-organized state with high personal incomes. In 1989 the socialist system of centralized national and economic management was abandoned piecemeal.

Political power is concentrated in the hands of Colonel Ghadhafi and, to a lesser extent, his close associates. An annual People's Congress permits some ventilation of other ideas and an apparent control system on spending of state revenues. In fact there have been few political changes to compare with the liberalization and privatization of the economy in recent years.

Despite official statements and propaganda images of Libya abroad, most Libyans are gentle and friendly, not least with foreign visitors who are clearly tourists and/or travellers.

Modern Libya

Government

The ideal of government was expressed in the Third Universal Theory, expounded by Colonel Ghadhafi in the early 1970s and enshrined in the **Green Book**, the first sections of which were published in 1976. Ghadhafi attempted to bring together strands of his own beliefs – Islam, freedom from foreign intervention, equality of people and the welfare of the greater Arab nation – within a unified philosophy. He was never taken entirely seriously in this ambition outside the country. Events were also to prove that Libya itself was resistant to his ideas. Despite the single minded expenditure of large sums on imposing socialism at home, including the devolution of bureaucratic powers to the 4 major regions – Tripoli, Sabha, Al-Khalij and Benghazi – and the removal of all private privileges of ownership of goods, property and even a fully private life, by 1987 the dream had to be abandoned. The structures he established persisted, however. A Basic People's Congress meets to manage the affairs of state, with Colonel Ghadhafi taking the position of 'guide' to the revolution. The congress acts officially through a series of appointed secretariats, which are now, for all practical purposes, ministries in the traditional mode. The revolutionary fervour, which characterized Libya in the 1970s and 1980s, has dimmed considerably and lives on only in the apparatus for security and military matters. Since he has these agents of political control in his hands, Colonel Ghadhafi effectively has the final say in decision-making in the country. There is no official opposition party and opponents of the régime have generally fled abroad.

Colonel Mu'amar Ghadhafi

Colonel Ghadhafi was born in the Gasr Bu Hadi area of Sirt on the coast of the Gulf of Sirte (Sidra) in 1942. His parents were from the Ghadhafa tribe, a mixed Arab-Berber group, which practised semi-nomadic herding of animals with some shifting grain cultivation in the arid steppelands surrounding the traditional tribal territories. He went to secondary school in Misratah before joining the army as an officer cadet. He graduated from the military academy and was eventually posted to Sabha in the Fezzan area. He briefly attended the University of Libya in Benghazi and undertook a short stay in the United Kingdom on a training course.

He rose to fame in Sept 1969 as the head of a group of revolutionary officers who overthrew the monarchy and set up an Arab republic ruled by a Revolutionary Command Council. The political programme introduced by Ghadhafi was simple and based mainly on the ideas of the Egyptian nationalist leader Gamal Abdel Nasser. Colonel Ghadhafi was anti-western, anti-Israel and in favour of a centrally controlled social and economic system within Libya. British and American military bases in Libya were closed down after the revolution. All public signs had to be written in Arabic and all foreigners, including any remaining Italian residents, were no longer made welcome.

Initially Colonel Ghadhafi was received by the Libyan people with acclaim. His simple creed of Arab nationalism fitted the mood of the day. In the early 1970s Libya became immensely rich in oil revenues as, aided by Libyan actions against the oil companies, the price of oil rose dramatically on the international market. At the same time, Colonel Ghadhafi issued his philosophy to guide the revolution, the so-called **Green Book**, preaching a form of Arab socialism. He also saw for himself a role as messianic leader of all the Arabs and a focus around which the Arab world could be united. At home, he entered into bold programmes for economic development, with expansion of agriculture, provision of state welfare schemes and investments in industry and infrastructure. Power was, at least in theory, devolved down to regional municipal assemblies which reported annually to a General People's Congress.

By the end of the 1970s Colonel Ghadhafi faced increasing difficulties. Abroad, Libya's attempts at Arab unity had failed. Libya had been unable to affect events in the Arab-Israel dispute despite a great deal of fiery rhetoric. Colonel Ghadhafi had also made an unsuccessful attempt to intervene in a war in Uganda to support the unpopular leader Idi Amin. Meanwhile Ghadhafi's political credentials were eroded by the rise of revolutionary Islamic movements in Iran and the Arab world. The collapse of oil prices after 1980 weakened the Libyan economy at a time when Colonel Ghadhafi became deeply embroiled in a territorial dispute with Chad over the Uzu strip, a band of desert lying between the 2 countries. Despite huge outlays in men and material, the war against Chad was lost and was taken to the International Court for arbitration. Suspicions that there was Libyan involvement in international terrorism came to a head in 1988 when responsibility for the destruction by a bomb of a Pan Am aircraft from UK to the USA at Lockerbie in Scotland was attributed to 2 Libyan officials. Libya eventually fell under a UN air transport embargo and was isolated from the international community as a pariah state.

In Libya, Colonel Ghadhafi lost some popularity as a result of these adverse changes but remained as the political guide of the country, defended by loyal echelons of the armed forces and without real rivals.

The secretariats which look after day-to-day administration are spread out throughout the country as part of a deliberate policy of regionalising management. Key ministries are in Sirt, though some scattered government offices also exist.

In foreign policy, Libya acted to harass the Western powers at whose doors Colonel Ghadhafi laid many of the ills of Libya and the Arab nation. While he could play off the West against the USSR and had access to considerable oil revenues, he successfully worked against the USA and EU states in propaganda and support for their opponents. The demise of the USSR as a world power in 1991, a massive fall-off in oil revenues in the mid-1980s and the rise of the conservative states as leading elements within the Arab world left him vulnerable to foreign pressures to accept international legal norms for state activities. This was signalled in Libyan problems in 1992 with US and British demands over the Lockerbie incident.

Economy

Libya is an oil-based economy. Oil was first exported commercially in 1961 and thereafter output rose rapidly so that at the end of the 1960s Libya was the fifth largest Opec producer of crude oil with more than 3 million barrels per day. This expansion was based geographically on the oilfields in the vast embayment of the Gulf of Sirte where small but prolific oilfields were found in the sedimentary rocks. While some oil was discovered by the major international oil companies such as Esso, Mobil and BP, there were also many small independent oil companies involved, for which Libya was the only source of traded crude oil. By the end of the 1960s a development of oilfields, pipelines and oil terminals had taken place in what had been a barren desert area lying between Tripoli and Benghazi. Following the revolution of 1969, economic policies were aligned towards making the country self sufficient.

Traditional agriculture

This was mainly self sufficient with small surpluses going to the many local occasional markets. The coastlands were comparatively rich agriculturally, favoured by adequate rainfall and available underground water for irrigation. Small fragmented farms were the rule on the coast, though many families had access to communal tribal lands for shifting cultivation and grazing animals to the S of the coastal oases.

Superimposed on this pattern of Arab farming and semi-nomadic herding is an Italian colonial structure established in the 1920s and 1930s but replicated since Independence by the Libyans themselves. The ex-colonial landscape is still a powerful feature of the country, especially in Tripolitania. Enormous areas of geometrically planted olive, almond and eucalypt plantations extend across the Jefara and parts of the Jabal Al-Nafusa, often in association with small colonial farmhouses. Although the Italian farmers have now gone, their legacy in the landscape, perpetuated by the local farmers who bought them out and by the government, remains and adds significantly to current output of olive oil and almonds.

The greatest single changes by Libyan farmers, though on a model mainly reminiscent of the Italians, is the introduction of citrus fruit orchards and the intensification of output through irrigation in what had originally been dryland or lightly irrigated Italian estates. The most important single field crop is fodder. Libyans prize their mutton enormously and sheep are kept by most farmers. There has also been an expansion of beef and dairy herding, which also requires abundant fodder production, mainly types of lucerne. On the Jabal Al-Nafusa, there is little irrigation and dryland crops are olives, figs and apricots. Grain of excellent quality is grown on the Jefara plain on lands owned by the Jabal tribes.

In E Libya, the Jabal Al-Akdar are used for dryland cereals, some fruit and a large area of fodder. In the S, Fezzan and Al-Khalij, oases survive using irrigation for intensive vegetable and fruit production. Libya's best dates come from the SW, the *deglet nur* being the most prized. (See also Algeria, **page 413** and Tunisia, **page 413**).

Modern farming

Contemporary agriculture other than the private sector activities already noted has until recently been mainly state managed. Underground water resources in the deep SE at Al-Kufrah, Tizerbu and Serir were developed for agriculture and new agricultural production units created in the SW at Sabha, Murzuq and other sites. Expensive imported technology was employed in these schemes and imported labour from Sudan, Egypt and elsewhere since Libyans were generally not prepared to move to these inhospitable regions. Despite the investment of very large resources, the majority of agricultural schemes in the S were abandoned or run down when Libya's oil revenues declined during the mid-1980s.

Libya's biggest and most spectacular development, the Great Manmade River (GMR), will carry water in a large diameter pipeline from wellfields in Al-Kufrah, Serir and Tizerbu to the coast and thence to Benghazi in the E and Sirt in the W. A second pipeline, it is projected, will transport water from the Murzuq Basin in the SW to the Jefara Plain adjacent to Tripoli. The movement of water to the N is at the cost of the closure of most major irrigation schemes in the S. Although the government has promised that the new water will be used in the coastlands for agriculture in addition to supplying industrial and urban areas, high costs of the water delivered there make its use in irrigation questionable. The need for new water illustrates the other great problem for farming in Libya – the falling water tables and intrusion of sea water into aquifers in coastal areas.

Oasis economies

In the oases of the deep S and the small towns at a modest distance from the coast, there is little industry. Here life revolves around earnings from agriculture and remittance income from employment on the coast. Construction of private villas and other housing is the most pronounced area of economic activity in the countryside, though farming is still a way of life for many Libyans outside the major coastal towns and involvement in transportation also absorbs a great deal of energy in these areas.

Petroleum

Provides the government with its principal foreign exchange income, usually US$9-10,000 million per year, the main source of general revenues in the annual budget (90%) and the most important single commodity for export (99%). The 2 areas of production are around the W borderlands and the Gulf of Sirt, the latter with export terminals at Sidrah, Ras Lanuf, Al-Brayqah and Zuwetina. The main oilfields are linked by pipelines to coastal terminals. Serir oilfield and its associated installations in the extreme SE are tied in to a terminal at Marsa Hariga near Tobruk (Tubruq), while a small line runs on a N-S axis in the W to Zaviyah oil refinery. An offshore field, Bouri, is sited on the Libyan continental shelf close to Tunisian waters in the NW. It was won from Tunisia in a judgment of the International Court of Justice in 1982. Libyan oil reserves are only moderate, rated at around 22,800 million barrels, which would last some 41 years at present rates of extraction. Libya produces approximately 1.5 million barrels per year and exports some three-quarters of its output, mainly to W Europe. The National Libyan Oil Co owns refineries in Italy and Germany.

Domestic refineries are found at Zaviyah, Al-Brayqah and Ras Lanuf.

Economic plans

The comparatively short life expectancy of Libya as a major oil exporter has given emphasis to the need to develop alternative sources of exports for the future. A set of economic development plans has been adopted by the government, the latest being a programme for 1980-2000 with aims to bolster self-sufficiency, create new jobs and lay the foundations for a future non-oil economy. Some successes were won, including an improvement in the country's transport infrastructure. Excellent road systems serve all parts of the country. New hospitals, hotels and schools have been set up so that even the most isolated settlements can offer good housing, health and educational facilities. Grandiose plans for a rail system to replace the old Italian lines closed in the 1960s have to be confirmed. A North African link through Libya from Morocco and Algeria to Egypt is under consideration, while a mineral and general purpose line from Brak (Brach) to carry iron ore to the Misratah steel plant is under consideration. Air transport in Libya is good but its growth has been impeded by USA sanctions against Libya which have limited the availability of new aircraft to Libyan Arab Airways, the national carrier.

Industry

Economic development outside transport and other infrastructure has been expensive and limited. Only petrochemicals, with large scale complexes set up at Ras Lanuf and Bu Kammash with a smaller operation planned at Sirt, have shown rapid growth, but they depend on the oil sector for raw materials, are highly polluting and employ few Libyans. The Misratah iron and steel mills began operations in 1989 and brought great prosperity to this old market town. How commercially viable the plants are remains to be seen. Elsewhere in industry the state agencies set up a variety of new concerns in food processing, soap making, aluminium and construction goods materials. As from the late 1980s, Libyan entrepreneurs were encouraged to begin work in industry on their own account, a move which saw the opening of many small scale workshops, stores and corner shop businesses.

Economic trends

The poor performance of the oil sector since the mid-1980s has dominated trends since that time. The late 1980s was a poor time for Libya and things have picked up only as better management of limited oil revenues and improved internal economic liberalisation has had an effect. The growth of private enterprise has been the main area of economic growth in the immediate past.

Economic Indicators US$bn

	1988	1989	1990	1991
Oil revenues	5.169	7.500	11.200	9.600
Exports	5.644	7.750		
Imports	5.753	5.497		
National income	19.000	19.500	20.500	21.100
Current account balance	-1.823	+2.253		
Inflation (%)	15	15		
Foreign debt	182			

Source: Economist Intelligence Unit

TRIPOLI

CONTENTS

MAPS

The climate of Tripoli is Mediterranean with hot dry summers, cool winters and some modest rainfall. Weather can be variable, influenced by the Sahara Desert and the Mediterranean Sea which moderates daily temperature ranges.

INDICATORS *Alt* Sea level. The population of Greater Tripolitania is 2,014,200. District populations are Tripoli 1,083,100, Gharyan 204,300, Nikat Al-Khums (Homs) 196,000, Zaviyah 326,500 and Jabal Nafusa 204,300. Growth of population is 4.5% per year. Literacy in Tripoli is higher than the national average though official figures of M 95% F 90% seem too good to be true. The labour force comprises Libyans 300,000 and immigrants 250,000. The average income per head is US$5,310, with inflation at 10%. Although the official language is Arabic, Berber is also common in the hill lands of Tripolitania, and English, French and Italian are also spoken.

The Capital

Tripoli, or Tarabalus Al-Gharb (Tripoli of the W in Arabic), is the major city and de facto capital of Libya. The removal of many government secretariats and faculties of the Tripoli, Al-Fatah, university has not changed the reality of Tripoli as the real political centre of Libya. The People's Congress meets in Tripoli and Colonel Ghadhafi is for the most part resident there. Plans continue to be talked about in government circles for the construction of yet another new capital which would be sited on neutral territory outside the 2 polarized traditional provinces of Tripolitania and Cyrenaica. Under King Idris Senussi, before the revolution of 1969, a new capital was set up at Al-Bayda in the Jabal Al-Akdar. It rooted itself well but political changes

CLIMATE: TRIPOLI

	Jan	Feb	Mar	Apr	May	Jun	Jul	Aug	Sep	Oct	Nov	Dec	Av/Tot
Max (°C)	23	24	30	36	39	41	40	40	41	36	28	24	34
Min (°C)	4	5	6	8	11	12	18	18	17	11	9	6	10
Rain (mm)	90	49	64	6	11	0	0	1	1	39	64	53	378

took away its role as capital. Colonel Ghadhafi and foreign consultants have proposed a new site for the capital on the coast of the Gulf of Sirte to act as a point of unity between the W and E regions. The fact that Colonel Ghadhafi has his tribal and close family links in Sirt adds to the attraction of this proposal.

Things to see

The old walled city of Tripoli, the **Medina**, is one of the classical sites of the Mediterranean. The basic street plan was laid down in the Roman period when the walls were constructed on the landward sides against attacks from the interior of Tripolitania. The high walls survived many invasions, each conqueror restoring the damage done. In the 8th century the Muslim ruler built a wall on the sea-facing side of the city. Three great gates gave access to the town, Bab Zanata on the W, Bab Hawara on the SE and Bab Al-Bahr in the N wall. Constant rebuilding means that few ancient commercial buildings remain and even the oldest mosque, Al-Naqah, was reconstructed in 1610. The **castle**, Al-Saraya Al-Hamra, occupies a site known to be pre-Roman in the E quadrant of the city and still dominates the skyline of Tripoli. The castle is made up of many distinct sections, formerly public and private quarters of the ruling family. The women were kept in a harem and a number of beautiful courtyards lie segregated from the alleyways which run through the castle. The upper walls afford a fine view to the sea and across the town.

The old city itself was made up of a series of separate quarters, 2 major parts of which were Jewish (*hara* is the name designating the Jewish areas of Tripoli). Narrow streets criss-cross the old city off which run blind alleys. Conventional wisdom suggests that the piece-meal development of the city gave rise to the impasses and that there is a chaos and randomness to the street pattern. This is only partly true. The blind alleys were often ways of sealing off areas controlled by single or extended families or ethnic groups so that attackers or casual passers-by would not intrude on family life, especially the lives of women. The through alleys in Tripoli old city are generally unroofed but with buttresses at intervals which help to hold up the walls on either side of the alley and provide some shelter from the sun. Walls facing onto the public alleys are for the most part plain with few windows, a device to increase privacy and deter curiosity. Doorways to houses and interior courtyards are remarkably ornate in contrast to the tall plain walls around them. Massive arches are used, displaying Roman or Islamic decorations while the doors themselves are often high, studded and provided with ancient locks.

Individual **houses** in the old city can be visited. Some still display their great cloistered courtyards and ornate tile, wood and plaster work. There are also several grand *serais* or *funduqs*, where merchants lodged their goods and animals around large courtyards. Generally less decorated than private houses, none the less they played an important role in the life of the city when the large traders organized and managed trans-Saharan caravans. The manufacturing and retail *suqs* of old Tripoli were carefully run by guilds of craftsmen and capitalists producing craft products for daily use. Pottery, metalwork, traditional clothing and jewellery were made in the various *suqs*. Some of the *suqs* still trade under vaulted brick ceilings, though very few goods are now manufactured in situ. Suq Al-Mushir is the popular tourist area of the old city situated immediately off Green Square adjacent to the castle. There are 7 **mosques** in the old city, containing a wealth of indigenous architectural detail (see map, **page 618**).

There was an exodus of the traditional families from the old city after

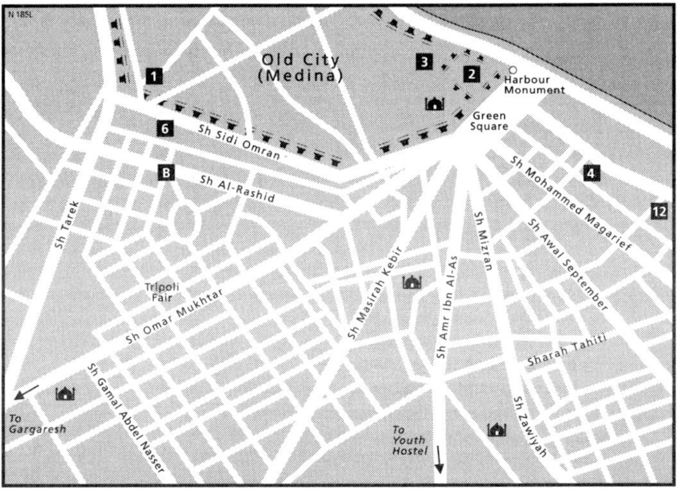

Independence in 1951. Families moved to occupy houses and apartments vacated by the departing Italians to take advantage of better sanitation, water supply and other facilities. By the mid 1970s the situation had deteriorated so badly that the majority of residents in the old city were immigrant workers from overseas. Neglect of the fragile buildings enabled damp to get into their fabric and many fell to ruin. The Libyan authorities determined to halt the rot and established a group to undertake restoration of key buildings and to write up the history of the city. In addition to the establishment of a research workshop and library in the old city, the main mosques, synagogues and consular houses have been restored in excellent taste.

Any tour of the old city should begin at the **castle**, entered from the land side near Suq Al-Mushir. It houses a library and a well organized museum and has excellent views over the city from the walls. This is one of the 2 principal **museums** in Tripoli, the other being in the medina, approximately 500m away. The **Castle Museum** is essentially concerned with the archaeology and ancient history of Libya. It covers the Phoenician, Greek and Roman periods well and has an expanding collection of materials on the Islamic period. Open weekdays 0800-1400, closed Fri. Entrance LD0.25. The main route through the citadel runs from the castle towards the sea, with the old French and British consulates, the Medina Museum and the Aurelian Arch all worthy of close attention. The old city has several key elements worth visiting. The old city walls are still standing and can be climbed. The **Harbour Monument** stands at the gates of the old city on the edge of the former corniche road adjacent to the castle. There are a number of restored houses, consulates and a synagogue in the narrow streets of the old city. The **Medina Museum** has a library with illustrated displays and helpful staff with a great knowledge of the medina area. Open weekdays 0800-1400, closed Fri. Entry is free and is from Bab Al-Jedid on the W side of the city walls at a point close to the sea not far from the taxi station. The main mer-

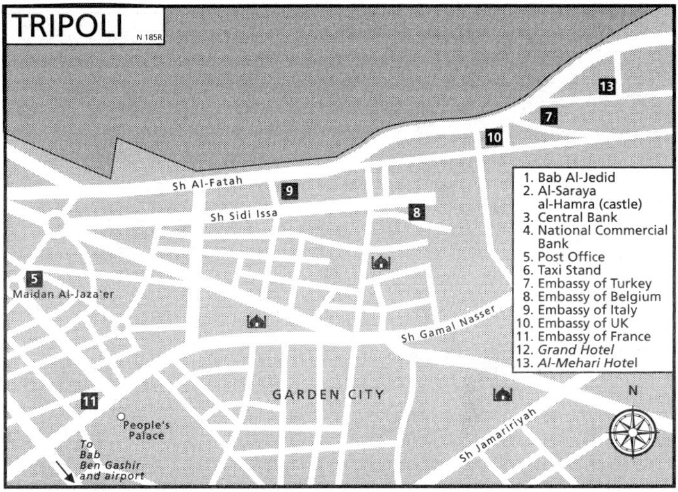

chant quarter is entered from the gate at Suq Al-Mushir. There are many separate small *suqs* such as the Suq Al-Attar (medicinal drugs), Suq As-Siiaja (goldsmiths), the remnants of which still operate though without their former Jewish workers and owners.

There are a number of interesting mosques including the **Karamanli Mosque**, the **En-Naqah Mosque** and the **Gurgi Mosque** both in the old town and adjacent to it. The En-Naqah mosque, the oldest of the Tripoli mosques, is called the camel mosque because it is said that the citizens of Tripoli met the great Arab conqueror Amr Ibn Al-As with a camel-load of valuables to buy the survival of the city. Amr Ibn Al-As refused to accept this gift and instead asked that a mosque be built. The present mosque is of various dates, the last major rebuilding dating from 1610/11 when it was called the 'Great Mosque'. The plan of the mosque is slightly irregular and aligned on a NW axis. The sanctuary makes use of columns of varied sources, some Roman. There are 42 brick-built domes comprising the roof of the mosque. The *mihrab* (a niche in the wall indicating the direction of Mecca) is in the middle of the *qibla* wall. There is a *mimbar* (low pulpit). A square minaret has a spiral stairway of palm wood and plaster.

Another interesting mosque is that of **Dragut**, the well-known Islamic admiral and scourge of shipping in the Mediterranean. He died during the great siege of Malta and was returned and buried in Tripoli in the large Dragut mosque, which was damaged during WWII but later restored. It has a square minaret and a small cemetery.

The **Al-Jami' Mosque**, the true 'Great Mosque' of Tripoli, contains interesting inscriptions to Othman Ra'is, who founded it in 1670 AD. The most magnificent mosque in Tripoli is the **Mosque of Ahmad Pasha Karamanli**, Governor of Tripoli in 1711 and founder of the Karamanli Dynasty. It is located a few metres from the castle near the main entrance to the *suq*. The mosque has an adjacent medersa in the W corner of the grounds, tombs and a cemetery. The centre point is a sanctuary with 25 domes

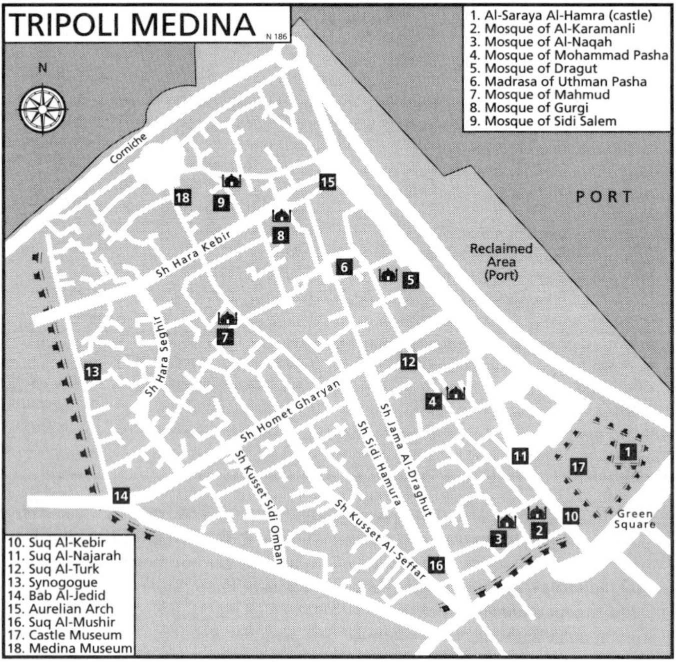

as a roof, the 2 domes over the fine *mihrab* being more elevated and carrying stucco work. The tombs of Ahmad Pasha and many of his family lie in a separate room with a large domed roof of spectacular design. The minaret is a very distinctive octagonal design in the Turkish style.

The best known of the Tripoli mosques is the **Gurgi Mosque** with its elegant architecture. It was built comparatively recently in 1833 by Yussef Gurgi (of Georgia in the Caucasus from which his family came) as an Islamic Hanifite establishment. It has a 16m square plan with 9 columns and 16 small domes, of which 4 over the main structures such as the *mihrab* and the *mimbar* are elevated. There are many delicately decorated areas of the mosque, especially around the *mihrab*. The octagonal minaret with 2 balconies is the tallest of the old Tripoli mosques. If the traveller wishes to view just one of Tripoli's mosques, the Gurgi Mosque is the one to choose.

Modern Tripoli spilled out from the tight confines of the old city as early as the 18th century and possibly before that. It is known from the letters of the European consuls such as Tully, resident in Tripoli during Karamanli times, that a thriving community existed on the flat lands immediately outside the old city known as the Menshia. Here the troublesome members of the traditional military class lived with farmers, traders and other individuals. The entire area was redeveloped by the Italians in the first half of the 20th century as a colonial city for Italian residents. They created a set of administrative buildings, many of which stand today, together with official residences and general residential areas. The garden city is still the most affluent and pleasant area of Tripoli, situated adjacent to the People's Palace. Straight streets were constructed, radiating from Green Square in front of the castle, together with a cathedral and a financial district adjacent to the *suq*, along what is now Sharah Omar Mukhtar.

This pleasing colonial urban form was broken by the revolution of 1969. In an attempt to diminish the apparent colonial heritage and European influence, all street names were changed, the cathedral closed and signs not in Arabic removed. Far more influential in changing the character of Tripoli, there was massive population growth during the post-revolutionary years combined with an influx of Libyans to Tripoli. Tripoli City grew fivefold in population size to stand at 600,000 by 1990. Extensive new suburbs grew up on all sides, many ill-planned so that Tripoli became a large metropolitan area in its own right spreading in all directions across the oases on its edge to reach out and encompass major satellite settlements such as Tajurah to the E and Zaviyah to the W.

The removal of some civil service personnel to other sites together with a fall in prosperity in the late 1980s eased some of the traffic congestion but expansion of the city continues, with people commuting 60-80 km into the city from outlying towns. At peak times, 0730-0900, 1330-1430 and 1800-1930, roads are choked and extra time must be allowed for travelling to appointments and particularly to the airport or bus station.

The main commercial streets lie in the centre. Most lead off Green Square in front of the castle. All street names are in Arabic but Libyans will assist in giving directions. The coast road, built over the former harbour area and adjacent to new wharves, is principally for vehicular traffic moving E. There are no buildings. The inner coast road from Green Square, Sharah Al-Fatah (originally Adrian Pelt, named after the UN official who sponsored Libyan Independence in 1951) is built up on its inland side with a number of public buildings and the main hotels. It travels on E along the corniche passing the major embassies of Italy, UK (currently operating as a 'British interests'section of the Italian embassy), Turkey and others. The road is planted with ornamental palms and has cafés and gardens along it. Sharah Mohammed Magarief, one of the capital's 2 main streets, runs from Green Square to the former cathedral. At its S end 500m S of the former cathedral is the People's Palace, built for the late King Idris and now in the service of the popular committees and the political activists supporting Colonel Ghadhafi. The French embassy faces it and on its NW corner is one of the oil company offices. The National Oil Company office is on Sharah Nasser, to the W side of the palace. Travelling up the E side of the palace leads to the Sharah Ben Ashur in the centre of a high class residential district, the garden city to the E and new properties to the W.

Walking around Tripoli centre is straightforward, though beyond the main business and shopping precincts there is little to see and walking, especially in the heat, is not recommended. For a **tour of the modern city** on foot begin in Green Square and travel W along Sharah Omar Mukhtar to see the private business district. Turn round at the Tripoli Fair building and return to Green Square from which go due S down Sharah Mohammed Magarief towards the post office and former cathedral. From the post office square (Maidan Al-Jaza'er) either turn directly right to Sharah Tahiti and thence right again into one of the commercial thoroughfares with small Arab lock-up shops or go on past the post office towards the People's Palace and thence right to the harbour front and back towards the

Green Square. This itinerary effectively shows the best of the modern city.

In Tripoli there are **war cemeteries** from WWII. The British & Commonwealth Cemetery is 2 km W of Tripoli and 364m S of the main road. There is also a British Military Cemetery.

Local information

● Accommodation

Price guide:			
L	US$90+	**D**	US$20-40
A	US$75-90	**E**	US$10-20
B	US$60-75	**F**	under US$10
C	US$40-60		

Tripoli is moderately endowed with hotels, adequate for a country with little development of commercial tourism but a large immigrant worker population. Business visitors are fairly well catered for with 5 or so luxury hotels in Tripoli centre. Cheaper accommodation is difficult to find when arriving in the evening, for example off the Benghazi bus, so book ahead. The newest hotel is the **A** *Al-Mehari*, Sharah Al-Fatah; **A** *Grand Hotel* (ask for *Funduq Al-Kebir*), also on Sharah Al-Fatah to the E, T 45940, very close to the medina, central, 2 restaurants, café, car hire.

D *Hotel Atlas*, top of Sharah Omar Mukhtar on a small square to the right, T 36815, simple but clean rm with bath; **D** *Hotel Lula*, seafront to the E of the medina, T 31013, clean, many rm with sea view, restaurant, café, rm with bath, breakfast included; **D** *Hotel White Sea*, off seafront E of the medina, T 606241, large, 200 rm, with bath, half a/c, roof terrace, clean but rather informal, breakfast included.

There are also small workers' hotels with shared facilities (category **E**) on the seafront beneath the walls of the medina, mainly clean but noisy. Outside Tripoli there are several tourist villages which can offer accommodation on request, but which are often very full in the vacation periods (see entries in Tripoli District section, pages 622).

● Youth hostels

Tripoli city for camping and dormitory accommodation, 69 Sharah Amr Ibn Al-As, T 45171, kitchen, 120 beds, family rms, 2 km from Green Square. **Gergarish** 5 km S of Tripoli, open 0700-2400, 200 beds, meals, family rms, laundry, airport 20 km, harbour 2 km, T 74755. Booking recommended at both hostels. **Ben Ghashir**, near Tripoli airport, 50 beds, kitchen, T (22) 30867.

● Places to eat

The main restaurants for Western visitors are in the principal hotels, all of which are open to non-residents. Some hotels such as the *Grand* and the *Al-Mehari* have more than one restaurant. They are all 'dry' but adequate. Popular eating places for the large numbers of non-Libyan Arabs are to be found in the city centre on or just off Sharah Omar Mukhtar and on the main roads immediately leading off to the S from the Green Square. They are cheap and offer Arab cuisine tending towards the rough and ready but generally hygienic. Outside the capital, eating is confined to the main hotel restaurants, their cafés or to popular eating houses which can be found near the centres of most provincial towns. Outside Tripoli, restaurant and popular café opening hours are limited. In the evening eat before 2100 or risk finding them closed. There is an excellent pizza restaurant (eat in or take away) just beside the post office. Recognize it by the 2 palm trees on either side of the door.

● Banks

Generally open 0800-1400, in the central shopping zone, with one conveniently on the roundabout adjacent to Green Square and others on the S main roads leaving the square. Go early for shorter queues. **Al-Umma Bank**, Sharah Omar Mukhtar, T 34031; **Central Bank of Libya**, Sharah Gamal Nasser, T 33591; **Jamahiriya Bank**, Sharah Mohammed Magarief, T 33553; **Libyan National Arab Bank**, Sharah 1st September, T20751-2; **National Commercial Bank**, Green Square, T 37191; **Sahara Bank**, Sharah 1st September, T 32771; **Wahhadah Bank**, T 34016.

● Bookshops

The main shop is ***Fergiani's*** near the roundabout off Green Square on Sharah 1st September. Books are otherwise available from official Libyan agencies which in the past acquired books exclusively by the state publishing organization. Most are in Arabic and/or are academic or somewhat propagandist.

● Chemists

In all shopping areas are normally marked with a red crescent or green cross sign. Chemists have a duty rota which is normally reliable, but travellers with special needs are advised to bring their own stores.

● Embassies

Tripoli is the diplomatic capital. **UK** citizens, for whom there is no embassy, should address themselves to the Italian embassy/consulate for assistance where there is a British affairs desk T 31191. Nationals of the USA, Venezuela and other countries suffer from periodic interruptions in diplomatic relations. Travel agents will have information on the current and constantly changing situation.

Algeria, 12 Sharah Kairouan, T 40025, 34631; **Belgium**, 1 Sharah Abu Obeidat Ibn Al-Jerah, T 37797; **Chad**, 25 Sharah Mohammed Sadeqi, T 43955; **CIS**, Sharah Mostafa Kamel, T 30545/6; **Czechoslovakia**, Sharah Ahmad Lotfi Al-Said, T 34959; **France**, Sharah Ahmad Lotfi Al-Said, T 33526-7; **Germany**, Sharah Hassan Al-Masha'i, T 30554, 33828; **Greece**, 18 Sharah Jellal Beyar, Tx 20409; **India**, 16 Sharah Mahmud Sheltut, T 41835-6; **Iraq**, Sharah Gurgi, T 70856; **Italy**, Sharah Wahran, POB 219; **Jordan**, Sharah Ibn Oof, T 32707; **Kuwait**, Sharah Amar Ibn Yasr, T 40281-2; **Lebanon**, Sharah Amar Ibn Yasr, T 33733; **Malta**, 13 Sharah Abu Bin Ka'ab, T 38081-4; **Mauritania**, Sharah Issa Wukuak, T 43646, 43223; **Morocco**, Sharah Bashir Al-Ibrahimi, T 41346, 34239; **Niger**, Sharah Tantawi Jowheri, T 43104; **Pakistan**, Sharah Khatabi, T 4084, 40072; **Saudi Arabia**, 2 Sharah Kairouan, T 30485-6; **Spain**, Sharah Al-Jaza'er, T 35462; **Syria**, 4 Sharah Mohammed Rashid Rida, 371955; **Tunisia**, Sharah Bashir Al-Ibrahimi, T 31051-2; **Turkey**, 36 Sharah Gamal Abdel Nasser, T 46528/9; **UAE**, Sharah Aljaza'er, T44146-8; **United Kingdom** c/o Italian Embassy, T 31191, when open Sharah Al-Fatah, T 31195, 31191.

● Hospitals

There are several large, well-equipped hospitals. The central civil unit is on the main road out to Sidi Mesri near the inner ring road. A secondary hospital is at Al-Khadra (the old military hospital).

● Post Office

This is found on the square opposite the former cathedral and has telecommunications facilities.

● Shopping

Sharah 1st September and Sharah Mohammed Magarief have shops with clothes and other consumer goods, travel agents, and an abundance of cafés. Two more streets fan out from Green Square and the adjacent traffic island. Sharah Mizran and Sharah Amr Ibn Al-As carry small scale commercial activity, bakers, general goods shops, traders and others.

Joining these streets to Sharah 1st September and Al-Fatah area are cross links, the most important of which is Sharah Tahiti. Sharah Omar Mukhtar leads off Green Square directly to the W. On the right is a red marble faced building, the Secretariat of Justice, with the rest of the street given over to trading houses, Arab restaurants, cafés and shops. On the right travelling W, the street opens up on the site of the **Tripoli Fair ground** used for international exhibitions. Sharah Omar Mukhtar ultimately gives access to the main western suburbs such as **Gurgi** and the former European villa area of **Giorgim Poppoli** with its supermarkets, beach clubs and tourist centres. Sharah Ben Ashur has dry cleaning, a pharmacy, a bakery and grocery stores. Throughout the central business and inner residential districts there are excellent doctors' surgeries, chemist shops, food stores, general goods shops, bakeries and small cafés. There are some popular restaurants, though these are almost entirely confined to the streets off and adjacent to the streets fanning out of Green Square. The poorer residential suburbs have small scale facilities and often no doctors, though pharmacies are common. The larger suburbs with pre-existing commercial centres such as Gurgi have a full range of facilities.

● Sports

There is a state-sponsored football team and some local football played. Dates and times of games are advertised in the Arabic press. The main opening for sport for visitors to Tripoli is swimming, snorkelling and scuba-diving in the sea along the coastline. For medium to long stay travellers it is worth joining a beach club, most are on the Gurgi side of the city. Each club is marked with a large board which, though in Arabic, makes it quite clear that it is a sports centre. It is advised that enquiries are made personally at the gate, through a state agency or, most easily, through a travel agent.

● Travel agents

Are in the shopping precincts in the main avenues leading from the Green Square. Highly recommended is the ***Libyan Travel & Tourist Co*** on Sharah 1st September headed by Salem Azzabi T 36222.

● Transport

Local Bus There are frequent, though in rush hour crowded, bus services across town on regular routes. The green/grey Tripoli service buses can be easily recognized with a destination board in Arabic but also a route number. The service can be rather erratic and breakdowns are common but the system is cheap. Buses run through the main bus terminal and other stops are clearly marked. There are no printed time tables and it is best to ask at your hotel before proceeding.

Taxis are very expensive with a price of LD5 for the shortest of trips but in the heat might be attractive to those with some distance to travel. Outlying parts of Tripoli can be reached by shared taxis at very reasonable rates. Otherwise, most travellers will be able to walk from point to point in the central area since the places to visit are concentrated around the city centre.

Air The main airport at Ben Ghashir/Suani Ben Yadim is some 24 km from the centre of Tripoli. A bus service is available to/from the main hotels and the bus station. Passengers with a deal of luggage are advised to face a charge of some LD25 for a private taxi rather than try the alternative. Uncertainties over transport to and from the airport are such that travellers should check well before the date of their flight with the airline, hotel or travel agent. Note must be taken of difficulties caused by the UN embargo on flights to Libya. It is now only possible to enter Libya by land and sea until the embargo is lifted. Most access under the embargo is by ferry from Malta or overland through Tunisia. The Libyan Airlines central office is located on Sharah Haiti.

Road Bus The terminal is in the street adjacent to the international departure station approximately 1 km W from the medina. For international links **see page 681**. Domestic timetables are very flexible. Departures from Tripoli leave early in the morning and passengers for small or distant Libyan settlements should be at the bus station not later than 0630 to be sure of a seat. Buses to **Benghazi** cost LD10 single with services daily using air conditioned coaches. Internal bus routes cover all towns and cities. **Taxi** These leave from stands between Sharah Omar Mukhtar and the sea. They ply for hire on a shared basis but, with haggling over the price, can be hired by an individual or private group.

TRIPOLI DISTRICT

Tripoli outside the city traditionally comprises the greater province and in this Handbook, the area defined by the Jefara Plain. The present administrative district of Tripoli is made up of the whole of the old province of Tripolitania taking in the Jabal Nafusa, Sirt and parts as far S as Jufra, Mizdah and Ghadames. The Great Jefara Plain covers the coastal lowlands from the Tunisian frontier in the W at Zuwarah to Misratah in the E and is bounded to the S by the line of the Jabal Nafusa as far as Al-Khums and thereafter as the 'Small Jefara' to Misratah in the E by a low range of hills. The district is a fertile and generally well watered zone except for the central area from Al-Assa to the S of Ajailat which is very arid. Rainfall comes in the winter months and causes flash flooding in the many *wadis*. Most water courses are now well controlled but it is wise to stay out of *wadi* beds in winter. Individuals are still carried away and drowned in flash floods.

The cultivated zone along the coastal strip is a narrow belt of palm oases. Cultivation here is very dense with multiple cropping in the spring and summer seasons. In its most sophisticated form, intercropping gives olives immediately below the palm canopy and other taller fruit trees, themselves standing clear of lower varieties such as pomegranates and apricot. Below the trees are tall vegetables such as peppers or maize and a final undercrop of wheat, barley or a vegetable such as broad beans. Cropping of this kind was labour-intensive but enabled a self-sufficient agriculture based on irrigation from shallow wells.

Animal herding is important on the Jefara Plain. Few black tents of the true nomads are now to be seen. Even the Sian nomads of the extreme W adjacent to Tunisia have become sedentary, but herds of sheep and goats can be seen throughout Libya particularly in the Jefara where herds are exceptionally dense. The sheep are Barbary fat-tailed varieties for the most part, with an ability to survive heat and short periods of drought. The animals are very valuable, being much prized for eating by the Libyans, each sheep fetching US$300 or more, depending on the animal and the season. Most herds are looked after by a hired shepherd.

The Jefara Plain drops from the foot of the Jabal very evenly and gradually to reach the coast in an often rocky and shallow shelf though there are excellent beaches well away from Tripoli city. Zuwarah and the W coasts are open, sandy and generally unpopulated except on Fri when they are crowded with people from Tripoli. Inland from the Arab oases are the former Italian farms with their regularly laid out orchards spreading deep into the interior. The Jefara Plain narrows considerably E until the Jabal reaches the coast in a low ridge at Al-Khums, separating the main Jefara from the limited coastal plain between Al-Khums and Misratah. The roads on the Jefara are wide, black topped and generally in good condition.

TRIPOLI TO AL-KHUMS AND MISRATAH

The main coastal highway runs from Tripoli to the E via Al-Khums and Misratah. The road links all the major coastal towns and passes through one of the richest agricultural zones of the country. The highlight of the route is Leptis Magna, the most imposing Roman ruin in N Africa.

This trip takes at least one hour. There is a choice of routes in the environs of Tripoli of either the old coast road or the modern highway. Buses and taxis leave Tripoli on the coastal main high-

OASIS CULTIVATION

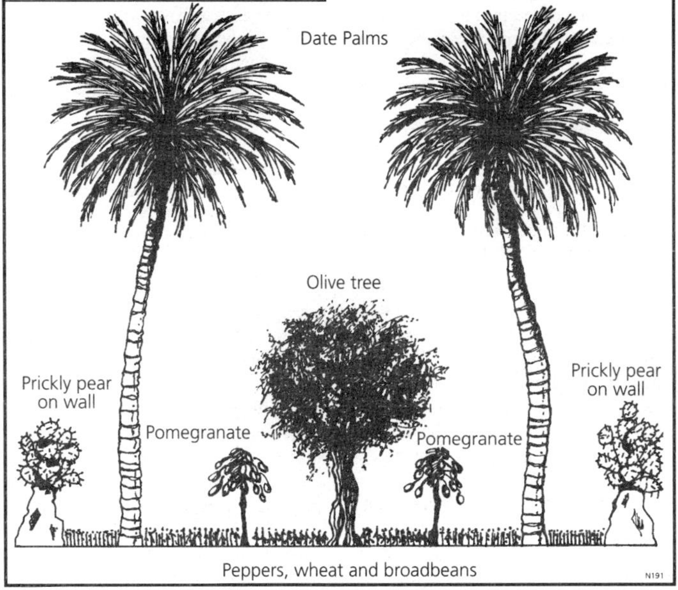

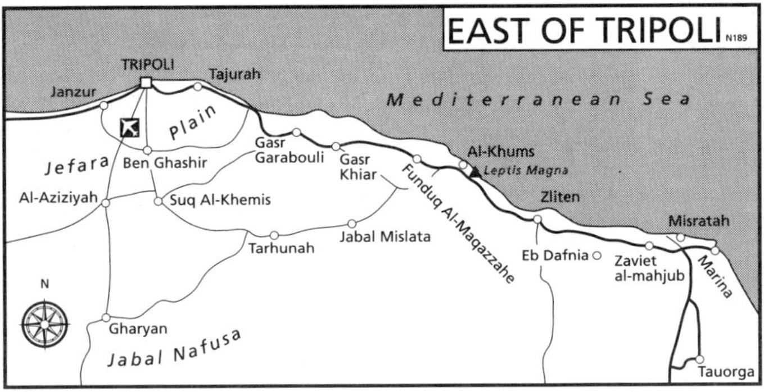

way. A dual carriageway leaves Tripoli city via Bab Ben Ghashir and travels through dense developments of villas and small houses, mainly expensive properties built on former oasis gardens. Architecturally the housing is very mixed – old square, single storey, whitewashed farmsteads interspersed with very modern villas of a slightly inferior finish. Occasional whitewashed small domed shrines, the tombs of *marabouts* or Islamic holy men, are visible, their titles being used for regional or topographical place names.

• **Accommodation E** *Madinah Siahiah Tajurah* (*Tajurah tourist village*) is located approximately 32 km E of Tripoli. Its surrounding beach is popular with Libyans on Fri but is otherwise clear for other tourists. Km 32 is its local name. The tourist village is an old development and open to all-comers.

Gasr Garabouli Km 60 from Tripoli lies on the old coast road and is now bypassed. Take the spur into town for petrol, police, shops and other services. There are small and mixed developments of shops, cafés and market places. The town area remains lightly wooded with some ex-Italian farms to be seen among dense, recent Libyan housing.

E from Gasr Garabouli there is open country with orchards and olives and almond plantations. At Gasr Khiar there are roadside shops on the main highway, cafés and petrol. Al-Khums is waymarked at Km 41 and Benghazi at Km 941. Along the main road other than in the smaller settlements there are plenty of roadside cafés. Small shacks of modern origin cater for travellers, especially on Fri and public holidays.

Telathin (literally Km 30 mark) is a tiny settlement providing chiefly a mosque, but with a shop and café adjacent. There is a fine area for swimming at the coast just N of the road. This is a highly recommended road in springtime when almond trees are flowering. In season succulent oranges are on sale at the roadside.

• **Accommodation D** *Funduq & Mat'am Al-Naqazzah* clean, 15 beds, restaurant and café, cooler in summer than the surrounding plains, hotel and restaurant of good contemporary design but now slightly run down, situated in an area of conifer trees just to the N of the main road. A good black top road runs to it then goes on to a rocky seashore 2 km below. Al-Khums town lies approximately 20 km to the E over the forested ridge.

Al-Khums

Al-Khums from the outside is not a very pretty sight. It contains low quality and incomplete dwellings in an apparently poor state of repair. The area has a very drab exterior with much accumulated rubbish around. The Al-Khums Fri market is held in the street leading to the old

The Delu Well Traditional Well Of Libya And North Africa

Water was always essential to life in North Africa. Given the scarcity of surface water, it was necessary for survival to lift water from underground. In traditional Libya – more or less until the 1960s – water was lifted from a shallow water table along the coast or from depressions in the desert by means of a device called a *delu*. The name is taken from the word for a goatskin, which is made into a bag, dipped into a well and drawn up full of water for both household and irrigation purposes.

The mechanism is simple and effective. A shallow one or 2m diameter well is hand dug to about 2 or 3m below the water table and lined with stone work or cement. Above ground an often ornate gantry is made of 2 upright stone or wooden pillars rising from the side of the wellhead. A cross beam between the top of the 2 pillars acts as an axle to a small pulley wheel which carries a rope tied to the mouth of the goatskin bag. The rope is drawn up or let down by the ingenious use of a ramp to ease the task of lifting water to the surface. An animal travels down the ramp when pulling up the goatskin from the bottom of the well and moves up the ramp to return the bag into the bottom of the well. Most *delu* wells have a secondary rope attached to the bottom of the goatskin bag which can be used when the full bag is at the top of the gantry to upend it and tip out the water.

The rate of water lifting by the *delu* method is obviously limited. The capacity of the bag is about 20 litres. Working from dawn to dusk, however, enough water could be raised to irrigate up to 3 or 4 ha of land – enough to feed a family and leave a small surplus for sale in the market. Most wells were equipped with a storage basin adjacent to the wellhead so that water could be raised and stored for household use and to give a reserve of water for irrigation.

The creak of the wooden pulley wheel of the *delu* was one of the characteristic sounds of the North African oases until the 1960s. After that time diesel and electric power pumps became available and the *delu* system fell into disuse. A few *delu* gantries remain as museum pieces and only the observant traveller in the deepest south of the Saharan oases will come across this splendid and environmentally friendly technology in day-to-day operation.

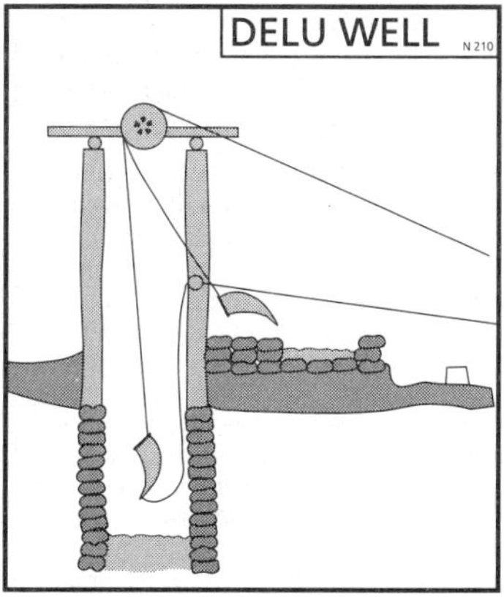

harbour. The main town has expanded considerably in recent years. Some Italian and British military and civilian landmarks are still to be found, with the army barracks as they were. The old market place next to the barracks is now the town taxi stand with transport available on a trip or day basis in private or shared taxi. There is an Arabic language cinema on the left of the street opposite the taxi ranks. Old Turkish houses have been demolished and replaced by a ghastly town council building just below the cinema.

ACCESS Care is needed when driving, especially on the outskirts of Al-Khums where slow moving vehicular and pedestrian traffic makes the main highway dangerous. Buses stop in the town centre near the taxi rank and on the main road at the *Al-Khums Hotel*.

• **Accommodation** At the junction of the main coastal highway and the first black top road after the *Naqazzah Hotel*, turn off to the **E *Khums Hotel***, cheap but noisy from close-passing traffic. The town's original hotel is still open for business as **E *Funduq Al-Khums Siahiah***. It is fairly run down but offers 18 rm, public telephone on site, restaurant and dingy café open 0600-2400. **Youth hostel** Sports City, 3 km SW of centre, T (23) 20888, 160 beds, meals, kitchen, laundry, family rms.

There is a vast extension to the town from the army barracks E along the coast towards the Wadi Lebda and between the coast and the by-pass built up solidly with mainly poor quality housing areas with few services for the traveller. Chalets have been built along the sea shore towards Leptis Magna. The modern port is located on the W of the town. There is some industry including a cement plant. Shared taxi from Tripoli costs LD5 to Al-Khums and LD1 to the site.

Leptis Magna

Open daily 0800-1730, 250 mills adult, 100 mills child. Shared taxi from Tripoli costs LD5 to Al-Khums and LD1 to the site. With museums, café and telephone this is a busy site. There are warnings that the ruins must not be touched nor artefacts taken away. These must be taken very seriously since successful prosecution can lead to imprisonment. The few sellers of items to be found on the site are operating illegally and should not be approached. There are guides available for a fee (LD5 seems to be a minimum) who speak the main European languages. Although Leptis Magna is an important archaeological site it is not complex since the best elements date from a fairly specific period. The information in this guide should enable most travellers to get a good overall view of the site. For specialists, an extended guided tour of the sites and the museums at Leptis Magna is recommended (see **page 631**). Guidebooks, maps and postcards of this site and others in Libya are available here.

ACCESS Travelling E from Al-Khums and Leptis Magna take the old road through the palm oases. The road is a single black top carriageway, often built up above the adjacent gardens. Beware of local traffic emerging abruptly from side roads and of the road surface in wet weather when the black top becomes notoriously slippery and vehicles can slide off into the palmeries. For cyclists the steep road embankment through this narrow route also has its hazards since 2 cars can pass only with difficulty. The old single track road has constant small scale road works. Children walk on the road and there is much local traffic from side roads. Motorists and others wishing to avoid the oasis route can take the new road which passes 1 km further inland between the palmeries and the main area of the former Italian La Valdagno agricultural estate to Wadi Ki'am. Buildings come right up to the new road.

For those with time the oasis route is to be preferred. After Leptis, the oasis, here called the Sahel Al-Ahmad, has dense mainly modern farmhouses. Farming continues in *suani* (small walled irrigated traditional gardens) but little effort is put into farming at present. The principal spring field crops in the gardens are wheat, barley and broad beans. The crops are mainly thin but the palm canopy remains for most part in good trim, providing welcome shade.

At **Wadi Ki'am**, Tripolitania's only flowing river, the long-established agricultural estate spreads out on both sides of the road. The original farm was a mere 120 ha of 2 ha plots fed by irrigation from the impounded stream of a spring source in the Wadi Ki'am. There is now an extension of reclaimed land under orchards and trees from Wadi Ki'am W to join up with old Sahel Al-Ahmad oasis and ex-La Valdagno.

Zliten

Zliten (37 km E of Al-Khums) is a thriving administrative and academic centre. Turn left into town for all main services. Zliten is surrounded by *marabout* tombs famous for their qualities of improving fertility, so inspiring pilgrimages. These tombs are best visited with a local inhabitant.

• **Youth hostel** Kashr House, Zliten, 20 beds, kitchen.

Misratah

The highway E from Zliten passes through poor grade lands with a slightly less reliable rainfall than areas further W. The coastal strip was thinly populated in the past and had only small and very discontinuous Arab oases. The Italians seized much of the coastal strip to set up estates for Italian farmers. The largest was Ed-Dafnia where the orchard groves of olives and almonds cover what was originally a mainly thin pastureland. The Italian effort at land settlement was added to by the Libyan Government after Independence with new areas reclaimed and ex-Italian estates taken over by Libyan farmers. Close to Misratah in the Zaviet Al-Mahjub district, a former private estate developed by the pre-Fascist Governor of Tripolitania, General Volpi, can be seen forming a fine garden and farmed area. However, the Italian farming estates which were so much the characteristic of Misratah oases have been reduced in importance by occupation by townsfolk who treat their holdings as amenity areas rather than as working farms.

The expansion of **Misratah** as an urban centre has also been prodigious. Population growth within the town has been much increased by mass migration from the rural areas. Misratah is the administrative and educational capital of E Tripolitania with most ministries having local offices. Schools, hospitals and colleges are located in the new town. Its layout is well organized and mainly rectangular. There seems to be less riotous self-build construction in progress than elsewhere.

Two events have strengthened the city. First, the construction of the 2 iron and steel mills in the settlement which have created employment and demand for local services so that there is a real sense in Misratah of growth and development. The power of the steel mill authorities is considerable and has helped to give a sense of unity to the town. Second, the old marina has been extensively redeveloped to take shipping coming to service the industrial plant with raw materials and other goods. The central business district provides a multitude of traditional shops, cafés and restaurants. A large number of immigrant managers and labourers live in the town and this is reflected in a fairly cosmopolitan atmosphere in the cafés. Many foreigners are housed on the steel mill residential site.

Things to see The most interesting items are the sand dunes on the W side of the town, some of the tallest sea dunes in the world. There is also the steel mill and the port.

• **Accommodation** The main hotel is large, modern and generally as well run as the larger hotels in Tripoli; booking is advised, rates as for those in the capital, large restaurant and other facilities. **Youth hostel** 4 km W of centre, T 24855, open 0700-2300, 120 beds, family rms, meals, kitchen, laundry, bus 400m, reservations recommended May-Sept.

• **Places to eat** You can eat in Arab cafés in the central business district. For a Western type menu use the main hotel.

Tauorga, some 40 km S of Misratah, is

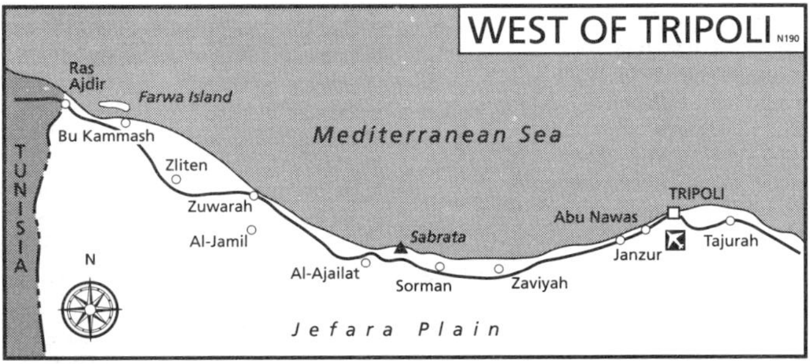

situated in the middle of a swamp formed by the great Tauorga salt lake and was reputed to be a refuge for escaping slaves. The town is located on a set of springs which provides water for agriculture, including a modern farm settlement set up by the government. Travellers would be better basing themselves in Al-Khums so that they can more easily get access to Leptis Magna and the beautiful mountain countryside of the Jabal Mislata to its hinterland. There is a basic 20-bed *Youth hostel* with kitchen facilities in Tauorga.

TRIPOLI TO FARWA AND THE TUNISIAN FRONTIER

W from Tripoli is the coastal road to Tunisia. Although heavily built-up with modern housing for many km on the fringes of Tripoli city, it eventually becomes open olive-growing country with many interesting tourist sites and the magnificent Roman ruins of Sabrata.

Leave Tripoli through Sharah Omar Mukhtar and Gurgi taking the main coastal highway W. The new highway is fast except during the rush hours and can be dangerous at major junctions. The dual carriageway road runs through palmeries and orchards as far as Zaviyah, thereafter its single track is more dangerous in an area subject to fog in spring. Undisciplined coastal traffic moves along this route to and from Tunisia. The main highway bypasses most of the coastal sites, however, and is recommended for car, caravan and motorcycle travellers. It ends at Zuwarah and the Farwa crossing point into Tunisia. Given a considerable flow of commercial traffic between the 2 countries now that there are only the barest of formalities for Arabs belonging to members of the United Maghreb Association, there can be long queues of cars and trucks at the frontier.

ACCESS Buses from Zaviyah and Zuwarah can be picked up or a shared taxi hired inside Libyan territory for those coming in from Tunisia. From Zuwarah both express luxury buses and ordinary interurban service buses can be caught to finish the journey to Tripoli. The border post has few facilities other than a petrol station and a small café on the Libyan side.

Farwa Island

The island of Farwa lies just offshore adjacent to the coast at the border post. Access to the departure point for Farwa Island is by road, though there is an airstrip nearby that could be used if upgraded. The island is approached either by a rough causeway built at the time of the construction of the nearby Bu Kammash petrochemical/refinery complex, or by ferry from a pier at Bu Kammash village to the W of the plant. The ferry, run by local fishermen, is an occasional rather than a regular service. There are sea police and customs officials at both the pier and the causeway to control movement and those at the pier can be helpful in retaining a boatman.

Things to see

The island, 12 km long and 2 km at its widest, is basically flat with dunes giving a slight elevation. Some 4,000 palm trees exist and have been tidied up in the central section of the island to look attractive. There is to be a tourist complex built on the island. The sand is fine grained and silver coloured. Other than the view of the petrochemical plant, the site is absolutely first class. In early spring it is mild/warm and extremely pleasant. Occasional storms are experienced but nothing severe. Arrangements can be made in Tripoli to view the island with Mr Gammoudi, Tourist Operations Department Manager, Farwa Tourist Co, Tripoli, POB 31479, T 44869, F 44919.

Tourism is now being taken seriously as an investment/development opportunity to diversify the national economy out of oil. Farwa company is under the control of the Secretariat of Planning. It was set up with state backing, with 6 state organizations as investors. As much as US$450 million will be invested in Farwa.

Planned facilities

A 5-star hotel with 300 beds is planned, but not yet constructed, together with bungalows/chalets of 500-bed capacity. A watersports centre, together with restaurants, floating restaurants, a disco and a small boat marina, desalination plants and sewage works with water reclaimed for garden use are also planned. A ferry link will be provided and a bridge on the E end of island. Availability of facilities at the site can be checked with the company managers as above or with Libyan Travel & Tourist Co, Salem Azzabi, Tripoli, T 36222.

Travelling back to Tripoli E, take the old road and travel into the main settlements along the coast. The road is slower than the main highway and often crowded, especially in the Tripoli suburb of Gurgi.

Zuwarah

This is an expanding town on the extreme W of the Tripolitanian coastal belt, approximately 100 km from Tripoli and 60 km from the border with Tunisia. The main employer is the petrochemical complex at Bu Kammash. Most commercial and municipal activity is concentrated in the centre of the town on the old road 1 km to the N of the new dual carriageway coastal highway. The town extends to the seashore. New villas mostly take up the coastal block.

Local information

● Accommodation

E *Zuwarah Esterah Siahiah* (*Zuwarah Tourist Resthouse*) in the middle of the town adjacent to the square, a cheap, small hotel used by Libyans.

● Camp sites

No camping facilities are reported, though along the coast there are plenty of good camping sites in woodlands or on the coast. Ask permission if possible before setting up camp.

● Places to eat

Zuwarah Esterah Siahiah (*Zuwarah Tourist Resthouse*) is the best restaurant and café and is in the middle of the town adjacent to the square. Full lunch costs LD3.50.

● First Aid

The Red Crescent clinic is on the old road.

● Petrol

There are 2 petrol stations to the E and W of town on the main highway.

● Post Office

This is near the clinic on the old road.

● Transport

Road The shared taxi/bus services to E and W along the coast road are very frequent. Costs LD7 Zuwarah to Tunis. LD10 Tripoli to Tunis. Express buses with a/c on Tripoli to Tunis run can be stopped in Zuwarah.

Sabrata

This is a 2-part town, one a modern residential centre and the other the archaeological site. There is a café and other services, including shops and cold drinks available at many main roadside shops. Sabrata town is rapidly expanding and some new industry has been set up. Many large villas extend down from the old coastal road towards the ruins. A new Faculty of Arts of Zaviyah University has been set up here. Shared taxi to Sabrata LD2. Taxi from town to ruins LD1.

Things to see

The Sabrata ruins (**see page 634**) are open Wed-Mon 0800-1700. Entry for adults is 250 mills and children 100 mills. The main **Sabrata Museum** and new **Punic Museum** keep the same hours. A café and shop are located inside the complex. The site is clean and well run.

Beach

At Telil there is a good sandy area with shallow water. It is popular with Libyan families. The beach is served by black top dual carriageway from the main road from junction W of Sabrata city.

Local information

● Youth hostel

160 beds, kitchen, meals, family rms, laundry, open 0700-2400, 1 km NW of town, T (24) 2821.

● Camp sites

Camping is banned in the woodlands around the archaeological site.

● Places to eat

There is a major restaurant at the ruins at the side of the large car park immediately outside the archaeological compound, which is open 0800-2200 winter and summer. The restaurant caters for Libyan and foreign visitors including large groups. The area offers a café and billiards.

● Petrol

There is a petrol station in the town and another at the road junction at Ajailat.

Janzur is on the old road as is the D *Janzur Tourist Village*, right on the coast, mainly new, with a wide range of accommodation – bungalows and apartments, excellent facilities, sailing, tennis, cinema, well equipped children's play room, shops, clinic, signposted in Arabic as *Medina Siahiah Janzur*; D *Abu Nawas Village*, another beach village in the Giorgim Poppoli area, old but cheap and open to all-comers at LD7 per night, close to shops, chemists and restaurants sited on the main street of N Gurgi; E*Old Janzur Tourist Village*, is further in towards the Tripoli boundary, comparatively run down, but convenient for shopping and facilities of what was Giorgim Poppoli estate.

Booking at these tourist villages is not easy from a distance since they are run by state organizations and are not essentially commercial in design. Persistence in seeing the on-site manager might be the best way to get accommodation. Their big disadvantage is their isolation from the city though bus or shared taxi transport is available on the old coast road 500m S of the beach club sites. Charges per night vary with the season and the quality of the complex between LD5 and LD20.

The old coast road into Tripoli is very crowded with shopping traffic and local people and should be avoided in the rush hours. Tripoli centre is only 5 km away but it can take 30 mins or more to complete the journey across the Wadi Mejennin bridge and then via Sharah Omar Mukhtar.

TRIPOLI TO THE JABAL NAFUSA AT GHARYAN

Directly S of Tripoli is the Gefara Plain, itself abutting the hills of the Jabal Nafusa. The Tripoli-Gharyan route gives an ideal cross-section of lands and climates through the Plain and the Jabal foothills.

Take the road S to Gharyan which now leads not only to the Jabal Nafusa but also from there to the deep SW at Ghadames and Ghat. The road is heavily built up in the long tentacles of the Tripoli suburbs. There are then dense farmstead settlements out to the Suani Ben Yadim turn off. The road is dual carriageway and busy with traffic, mostly local. Road signs, which in any case are only in Arabic, are painted out as a wartime precaution. After the Suani Ben Yadim and Ben Ghashir towns/oases, the highway runs through a countryside of trees and orchards. It is very green in spring, with uncultivated places forming rich pasture. The 2-lane highway is very fast from Suani Ben Yadim to Az-Zahra and onward to the main town of Al-Aziziyah.

Aziziyah has a petrol station, post office, hospital and several banks all situated on the main street or immediately adjacent in the few principal side roads. It is 221 km from Aziziyah to Nalut on the W end of Jabal Nafusa via the Wadi Hayyah route on the plain, via a single carriageway which is straight and fast.

Aziziyah to Gharyan

There are roadside stalls selling oranges in season. The wooded landscape thins rapidly with travel S. The road remains dual carriageway. The first sightings of the Jabal peaks can be had as the road approaches the scarp slope of the Jabal Nafusa. A few km S of Al-Aziziyah the landscape becomes open with very few trees. This is prime cereal-growing country in years of good rainfall. There is a large grain silo at Km 29 to Gharyan indicating this zone as a major contributor to Libyan wheat and barley production. At Km 25, the road begins the rise towards the Jabal. It is a slow climb through wooded terrain. Shortly afterwards the Bir Eyyad black top road is reached going W to Kikla and the fast route to Nalut. There is a quarry for tile making materials on the right as the main road climbs into the scarp face, then at Km 18 the sharp rise into the scarp face begins. There is a café at its foot on the left hand side of the road. On climbing the scarp the old Italian road to the left can be seen. Though it is no longer maintained it is a good alternative route for walkers and the more adventurous cyclists. At the top of the slope the roadside is built up increasingly with houses. There are olive trees mainly around the Guassem area of Gharyan, 11 km from the town itself. Approximately an hour from Tripoli centre you arrive at Gharyan. (For travel in the Jabal see page 635 – Jabal Nafusa and Ghadames.)

SITES TO VISIT IN THE JEFARA PLAIN

Leptis Magna

Leptis Magna is among the most complete and magnificent of the 3 towns (tripolis) of North Africa. It began as a Phoenician port of call on the trading route across the region, though it was ultimately administered in the 6th century BC, it is thought, from Carthage. The city grew up at the mouth of the Wadi Lebda where a small port was developed over the years, exporting important volumes of grain and olives. It joined Rome in 111 BC and enjoyed full rights as a *colonia* to Roman citizenship under the Emperor Trajan (98-117 AD).

The early Roman period saw the construction of basic harbour works and a forum close by the original Punic settlement. The city flourished under the rule and patronage of Septimus Severus (193-211 AD) who was born in Leptis Magna. Most of the major buildings at Leptis date from his time. The city spread W along the coast and inland. All the important buildings can be reached adjacent to or just off the main paved monumental road from the present entrance through the new parts of the site. A full inspection of the wealth of monuments requires at least a full day and rather longer for visitors with a specialist interest since Leptis Magna is well preserved and has an unequalled range of buildings from the classical period. In summer the site is very hot and justice can be done only by a series of visits when the heat is less oppressive.

A minimum tour begins at the **harbour** at the original Punic site and the adjacent ruins of the **Old Forum**. The newer harbour works undertaken during the reign as Emperor of Septimus Severus are also on view in this same area. An **aqueduct**, which originally brought in water to the city from 19 km inland, is a major feature of the site and the **triumphal arch** together with the new quarter along the 410m monumental road also date from this period. In the new quarter the key sites are the ornate arcaded porticoes, the circular **piazza** and **Nymphaeum**, the **Forum** and **Christian basilica**. Other areas to be seen include the magnificent **Amphitheatre** dating from 56 AD, among the most photogenic sites in North Africa. The **baths** constructed during the time of the Emperor Hadrian are also worth a visit.

Leptis Magna – an extended tour

Leptis Magna is a Roman city of great grandeur situated at the mouth of the Wadi Lebda immediately to the E of the town of Al-Khums. The origins of the town are not known with certainty. It is probable that a Berber settlement first existed at the site which was developed by Levantine trading groups from Tyre and Sidon that made use of the small natural harbour. Greeks also appear to have been at the site. In Carthaginian times the people at Lebda paid tribute of one talent per day, reflecting a certain prosperity based on a trading hinterland stretching deep into Tripolitania and Surt. By the time of the 3rd Punic War there were approximately 10,000-15,000 inhabitants in the city. In 107 AD Leptis set up formal relations with Rome and, despite the disruption caused by attacks from tribes from the desert interior, the city continued to develop.

The fortunes of Leptis Magna were greatly improved in 193 AD when Septimus Severus was made Emperor of Rome. He had been born at Leptis on April 11, 146 AD. He created a basilica at Leptis together with a great imperial forum. The prosperity of the city was considerable and the population grew to 60,000-80,000 people. Leptis suffered later from a decline in the Saharan trade and the silting of the mouth of the river. Attacks from Asturian groups beginning in 363 AD brought great problems for the city. In 455 AD the Vandals arrived and took Leptis, leaving it eventually in the hands of the Berber Zenata

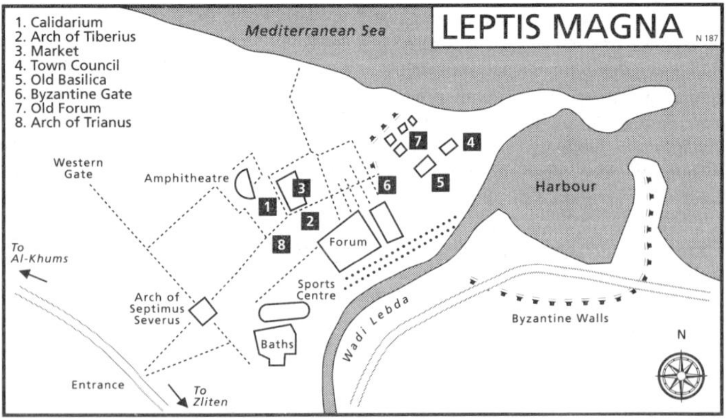

tribe until 533 when the Byzantines under Belasarius restored Roman rule. The Byzantines were put under heavy pressure from all sides and in Libya from attacks by the Zenata and finally the Arab invasions of 643-644 AD. The later incursions of the Beni Hillal and Beni Sulaim led to the completed abandonment of Leptis Magna in the 11th century. Coastal sand dunes overwhelmed the site, preserving it from destruction during the succeeding centuries.

The first of the antiquities at the site is the **Arch of Septimus Severus** which lies on the left at the end of a short avenue leading from the entrance. It has 4 facias. To the E of the arch is the **baths** (terme), an enormous construction covering with its ancilliary buildings approximately 3 ha and amongst the largest bath houses built outside Rome itself. The baths were put in place in 123-127 AD and improved and extended at various later dates. Excavations at the baths were begun in 1920 by Dr P. Romanelli. The baths are best approached through the Palestra, which is made up of a rectangular base with circular ends surrounded by a portico of 72 columns. There are 5 doorways into the baths, 2 on the N aspect leading from the Palestra. To the S 2 more doorways open onto a Corridor of 74.8m parallel to the fascia. Behind lies the Frigidarium a room of 30.35 x 15.40m. In the centre of the Frigidarium is a small monument dedicated to Septimus Severus, possibly commemorating the grant of full Roman rights to the city by that emperor. At the E and W sides of the Frigidarium are 2 highly decorated pools still showing their facings of black granite. Immediately S of the Frigidarium are 2 anterooms and connecting corridors together with a Tepidarium and its lateral pools. Further S lies the Calidarium in a room 22.15m x 19.90m. This room leads on by 2 doors to heated rooms, the Stufe or Sudatorium. Along the E and W sides of this blocks of rooms are parallel salons which give access to the main baths. Remarkably there is another set of baths at the site located close to the sea in the waterfront area of the city to the W of the Old Forum. These baths were never finished and are thought to have been under construction at the time of the Vandal invasions. The new baths are best approached from the E through a hexagonal domed hall, named by the British archaeologist Richard Goodchild the New Calidarium. To the W of the New Calidarium is the Old Baths made up of renovated Tepidarium and Calidarium from a previous period. Adjacent and to the N of the New Calidarium is a building of similar size which was used as an Apodyterium for an earlier bath system but later became disused. West again of these buildings is the New Frigidarium, which was constructed to be a vaulted hall with a plunge bath at each corner but which was not completed.

Among the other principal monuments at Leptis Magna which should not be missed are the Forum, the Old Basilica and the Colonnaded Street, the Old Forum, the port and the Circus. The Imperial **Forum** lies at the heart of Severan Leptis Magna. The Forum was constructed as a great wall of 92m backing on to the Basilica, with an inset arc. There is an entrance from the street on the SW side. It is a spectacular sight despite the ravages of time and looters. It abuts onto the Basilica in the N and forms a great trapezoidal shape with maximum dimensions of 132m x 87m.

The **Basilica** is 38m x 92m and built as a rectangle on the E side of the Forum. It has 2 semicircular recesses at its narrow ends. There are 3 lines of columns running the length of the church. The Basilica is surrounded by side galleries. Various dedications in Latin are found in the Basilica including an ornate inscription to Emperor Caesar Lucius Septimus. There is a great variety of sculptures and reliefs of mythical figures and animals.

The **theatre** at Leptis Magna is in excellent condition and commands views in all directions from the W side of the city. The theatre has a diameter of 70m and faces to the NE, heavily columned and with the stage and its entrances still clearly visible. The **Circus** at Leptis is on the extreme E side of the site, shaped as a great narrow horse shoe of 450m in length and 100m wide aligned parallel to the coastline. It is as yet not fully excavated but the starting gates are clearly to be seen at the city end, while the monumental arch and the circular terminus is at the E end. There are 2 tunnels at ground level carved apparently through solid rock. There are tiers of seats rising from the base around the arena. The **amphitheatre**, which lies immediately S of the Circus in the same complex, is thought to date from 56 AD and has been well excavated by Italian archaeologists. It is slightly elliptical in shape with circumferences of 100m x 80m.

The **port** at Leptis is in the form of a basin open to the E and fed with water from the Wadi Lebda. There is a small Doric **temple** at the site in Hellenistic style and a tower. The port has been studied by underwater archaeologists and some of the finds are shown in the main museum near the main site entrance. There are clear signs that the port suffered severely from silting, yet the historical record shows that Leptis port handled many thousands of tonnes of olive oil and food grain every year over many centuries as the centre of Rome's North African granary.

Shortly after the time of Septimus Severus, the Roman Empire had increasing difficulties in maintaining law and order in its domains in North Africa. In 263 AD Leptis was overrun by the Asturians and, despite some attempts at reconstruction under Byzantium rule, it never again flourished. The Arab invaders of the 7th century brought a final extinction of urban life to the site. Most of the excavations at Leptis were undertaken in the Italian period when the monuments, preserved from damage by encroaching sands, were unearthed.

Sabrata ruins

Like Leptis Magna, Sabrata began as a

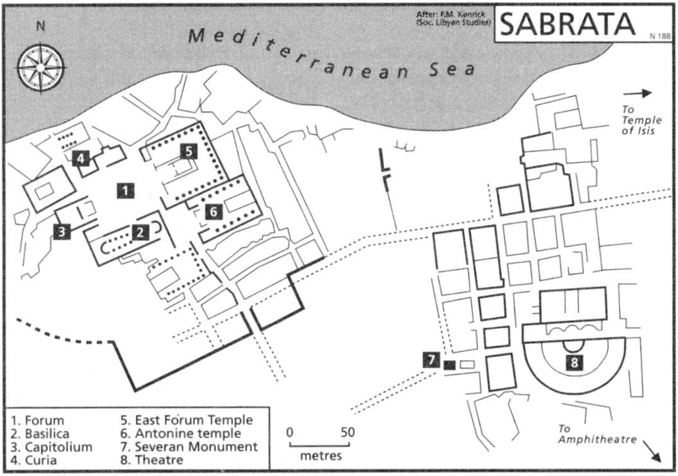

settlement to service the coastal trade of the Carthaginians. It was developed as a permanent site in the 4th century BC to act as a terminal for the trans-Saharan trade since it had a natural harbour on an otherwise long and unindented coastline. The site was later to become part of the 3 cities with Leptis and Oea (Tripoli). It was never favoured as much as Leptis Magna and has nothing to match its range and richness of buildings. Its coastal site is none the less impressive and Italian excavations and some reconstruction have made it well worth a visit. The main monument is the **Amphitheatre**, used in modern times as a theatre and concert hall. There is a variety of public baths, temples and fountains, with many first class **mosaics** both on site and in the adjacent **Museum**. Some Byzantine remains are on show to exemplify the revival after the Vandal invasions. The site was finally abandoned in the mid-7th century at the time of the Arab invasions. There appear to be no guides available but there are publications and artifacts on show at the museums.

TRAVEL IN THE JABAL NAFUSA

The Jabal Nafusa, geologically complex, is a long plateau which runs in broken foothills from Al-Khums on the coast in the E to the start of the Jabal proper at Al-Qusbat, some 20 km to the SW of Al-Khums and then further W into S Tunisia. It forms a scarp slope between 600m and 900m above the Jefara Plain. It drops in altitude only gradually to the S into a set of rough basins, the largest of which lies around the town of Mizdah. The Hammadah Al-Hamra, a vast level-topped plateau, is reached after climbing another scarp to the S of Mizdah.

The Jabal has a climate quite different from the Jefara. Rains are slightly less reliable than the northern plains and diminish rapidly from the crest of the scarp to the S. Most places have over 250 mm of rain per year. Winters are quite cold and snow and frost can be experienced. Air temperatures throughout the year are lower than on the Jefara. Both winter dress and sleeping bags need to be heavier and windproof. The evenings and nights in the summer are far more comfortable than in the plains. **Gharyan** is the main town of the Jabal Nafusa.

The Jabal economy has proved remarkably versatile. Agriculture survives in most areas though it has become increasingly concentrated on growing cereals and rainfed orchard crops. Figs and apricots are famous on the Jabal and it is often the Berber groups who farm the rich grain land of the Jefara under the shadow of their mountain homes. The greatest source of funds for the Jabal groups is, however, remittance income from members of the family living elsewhere, usually in Tripoli or in other coastal towns. Even permanent residents of Tripoli have houses in their tribal territories and a great deal of investment flows back to the Jabal villages in this way.

Berber history and culture

The culture of the Jabal Nafusa is for the most part Berber, though Arab tribes are interspersed within the main groups. Historically, the Berbers held the lands of the Jefara Plain with their main centre at Sabrata but they were driven back into the hills by the Arab invaders. The relative isolation of the Berber communities has meant not only a survival of their language and close kinship ties but also quite distinct urban forms and housing styles. In religion the Berbers are Muslim but follow the Ibadite branch of Islam, regarded by many Sunni Muslims as a heresy. The Berbers were aggressively separate from the Arabs on the Jabal Nafusa however much they intermarried with the Arab tribes elsewhere in Libya. The Berbers of the Jabal Nafusa participated in the revolts against Arab rule, the most ferocious of which took place in 896 AD.

More recently, the Berbers looked for the creation of a semi-autonomous Berber province. They had been a favoured group under the Italian occupation, making up important parts of the police forces in Tripolitania. On Independence it was hoped that Berber cultural separateness would be acknowledged and their language given equal status with Arabic. The rise of Arab nationalism at this time forestalled any chance that the small numbers of Berbers, less than an estimated 150,000 in all at that time, could make their voice heard. The revolution of 1969 set back Berber aspirations and for some time the government in Tripoli refused to admit there was any such group as the Berbers.

Despite the rapid economic changes that have taken place in Libya as a result of the spending of oil wealth, the Berbers still keep a sense of cultural separateness and even superiority.

Berber architecture

A distinctive feature of the Jabal Nafusa is troglodyte architecture. Buildings are excavated into the earth and rock to give only a slight external built up area. Both houses and mosques were constructed in this fashion which made them warm in the often bitter winters experienced on the Jabal and cool in the heat of summer. At Mizdah the troglodyte way of life was pursued until the 1970s so that families could escape the extremes of heat experienced in ordinary houses.

There is a doubt about the origins of some of the great ruined **castles** on the Jabal such as those at **Sharwas** and **Wighu**. They were the centres of the original Berber societies which were set up after the Berbers were driven into the hills by the Arabs and became the focus of revolt against the invaders during the bitter struggles of the 9th century. There is evidence that internecine strife between powerful Berber clans at Sharwas and Wighu in the 11th century resulted in extensive damage to their fortresses. The castles were eventually abandoned, Sharwas as late as the 16th century, but stand as bleak but recognizable ruins on the peaks of the Jabal E of Yafran.

The castles are quite different from the fortified granaries seen, for example at Nalut, Kabao and elsewhere in which small cells were created in the rock or built up one on top of another to accommodate stored grain and other items. These now mainly ruined buildings were surrounded by walls for reasons of defence. A third phase of abandoned dwellings can now be seen comprising the houses and quarters occupied until very recently in towns such as Jadu. The houses were built of loosely assembled stone with limited mortaring between joints and were clustered in tribal quarters and extended family dwellings incorporating areas for living, cooking and keeping the animals in safety at night. Prosperity in recent years has led many residents of the towns of the Jabal to move into private housing of the villa style situated in the open fields around the old settlements. The old quarters have been abandoned in many cases and are crumbling into ruin. This situation is causing rapid deterioration in towns such as Jadu.

JABAL NAFUSA – GHARYAN TO NALUT

The Jabal Nafusa road is narrow and slow but offers the prospect of visits to a variety of Berber centres. There are apricot and fig orchards as well as traditional terraced farmland to be seen as the highway carries the traveller W and S along the top of the scarp slope.

Gharyan

Pop 100,000 *Alt* 900m.

The centre of Gharyan shows signs of intensive rebuilding, reflecting the site's importance as a regional administrative centre. On climbing the scarp and traversing the olive groves where the road comes on to the summit of the Jabal, turn off right for Gharyan town, marked clearly but in Arabic script. Ask for '*al-markaz al-medinah*', the centre of the town. Note that the climate of Jabal is much cooler than the plain and even in spring can be several degrees colder on the ridge than on the Jefara.

• **Accommodation A** *Hotel Rabta*, brand new, in excellent condition, clean, run in a business-like way, working lifts, 68 rm, for the business traveller there are suites costing LD35 for single and LD45 for double occupation, well set up restaurant serves lunches and dinners at LD7.500 per person, modern café facing onto the street, film theatre, most modern facilities, owned by the Libyan Social Security Organization. **D** *Funduq Gharyan Siahiah (Gharyan Tourist Hotel)*, T 041 30105, very run down and seedy, 44 rm in use, modest price for Libya, small restaurant and café, open all the year. **Youth hostel** 120 beds, breakfast included, family rms, meals, laundry, kitchen and **camping** facilities in Gharyan at T (41) 31491. Information at the City Hall.

Leave Gharyan and travel W via the dual carriageway, passing through olive groves in rolling uplands. Shortly there is a road on the left to **Tigrinnah**, a former tobacco-growing area and now with fairly dense villa housing straddling it. Good views are to be had to the SW over broken country. The Jabal top is lightly wooded with olives and figs. After Tigrinnah, at a small settlement called Abuzeyan, the road divides with Mizdah 82 km and Sabha 700 km by road to the left.

After Tigrinnah the road on the top of the Jabal becomes a single carriageway. It passes through Assabah village with villas dispersed in farmlands. The village centre has a petrol station. Travel on 95 km to **Jadu**. The road traverses increasingly arid countryside with a light scrub covering to the hills. There are small occasional groups of houses such as Al-Gualith at Km 91 and Km 79. At Km 77 there is a mosque, a café and a petrol station. At Km 76 a turn to the right leads to **Kikla** 12 km away. On the main road, a green area under cultivation at Km 75-73 is an agricultural project run by the government. There are good places for picnics on sections of the old road visible from the new highway.

Turn right for **Yafran** off the main highway. This is classic old Berber town perched on the Jabal top and now much modernized but worth a visit. At Km 21 the black top road passes through fairly dense trees and cultivation. Note the good mainly reddish soils around Yafran. Reliable and heavy rains in late autumn and winter give the basis for a sound agriculture. There are fine views across the top of Jabal from the road towards Yafran. Also note the house decorations even on modern units, with complex ironwork doors, plaster work symbols such as butterflies and aircraft on house sides. Several small straggling villages lie along the roadside. A petrol station is located at **Qalah**, a village just before Yafran.

Yafran has been modernized. The old town and fortified grain storage towers and other ruins are still visible on the hilltops in the town. The new town spreads along the black top road. Culti-

CLIMATE: GHARYAN

	Jan	Feb	Mar	Apr	May	Jun	Jul	Aug	Sep	Oct	Nov	Dec	Av/Tot
Max (°C)	30	32	29	30	34	47	31	30	39	32	21	19	31
Min (°C)	8	1	2	5	7	13	12	11	14	9	6	4	8
Rain (mm)	67	73	136	51	31	2	0	0	5	77	33	48	500

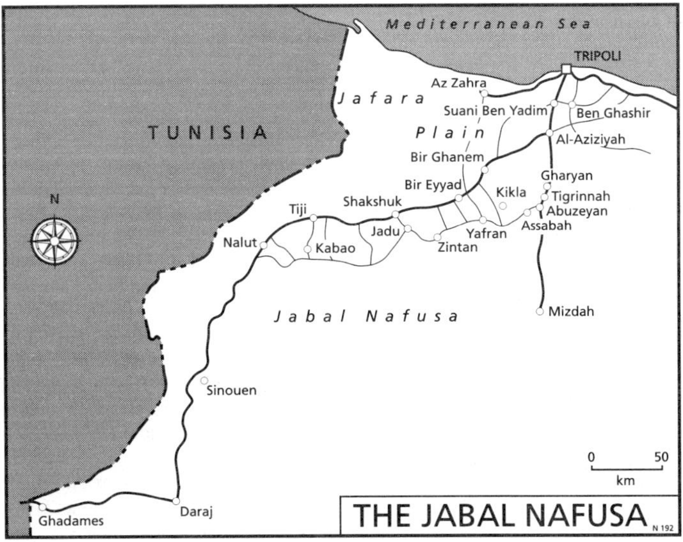

vation is still undertaken sporadically on terraces and scarp-top fields. The town is very scattered around a one-way traffic system through narrow streets. A new hotel is still under construction but no hotel is currently in use. The town has all services, almost all clustered in the main square and the streets immediately adjacent to it. There is a **Youth hostel** in the city centre, T 0421 2394, 45 beds, meals provided.

Leave Yafran and continue to **Al-Awenia** and **Aïn Rumia**. This road gives wide views across from the Jabal to the Jefara below. Some terraces cut into the Jabal face are still used for agriculture but many effectively have been abandoned. At 'Ain Rumia there is a café open only in summer. The spring at the site is no longer running since the water is being used for the water supply to the town. But the gardens there are flourishing with palm trees in the cultivated valley. This spot can be crowded on Fri and public holidays. Return to the main road where a signpost at the junction gives 66 km to **Nalut** and 24 km to **Zintan**. Travel on the Zintan road to return to Tripoli. Otherwise continue W along the top of the Jabal scarp. Pass through a further red soil zone with fruit tree cultivation.

Towards **Jadu** the rainfall decreases and the landscape is very arid, with few trees and little cultivation. At Km 10 turn right to Jadu. Arrive at Jadu passing through many new villas on the outskirts. The town gives the impression of a physical shambles since older communal and family stone constructed dwellings have been abandoned and new villas are randomly scattered across the landscape. In many ways Jadu has lost its old fashioned charm but is an important Berber town with notable tribes such as the Qabila Mizu there still. Berber is the main language in the households of the town. There is no hotel here.

• **Road Bus** services to both local and inter urban destinations run from just outside the town centre. **Taxi** station is sited on the side of the main road at the entry to town.

Leave Jadu to head for **Shakshuk** at the

foot of the scarp. There are 2 roads down the scarp, the newer one is better surfaced and better maintained. Shakshuk is a small settlement with animal pens and houses sited a short distance off the road. At the junction with the Jefara highway from Nalut there is a petrol station and small general shop which sells drinks and grocery items.

The traveller can either go on the fast road along the Jefara W or return to the mountain road which leads on a winding route to Nalut. The mountain road passes through arid landscapes and enables rewarding visits to the Berber settlements at Tmizda, Kabao, Wighu, Sharwas and other sites. Those keen to see indigenous Berber architecture should take the slow road on the scarp. Those not prepared to accept the very considerable Berber charms of Nalut would find the Jefara road far quicker.

Nalut is a small town with all public services near the centre. Work is proceeding to provide it with proper hotel facilities including a basic rest house for people coming up from Farwa on a desert tour. It is well provided with bus, taxi and other transport facilities, being the take off point for Ghadames and Ghat. It has car repair shops and garages. Expect work to be done slowly and at some considerable cost.

From Nalut and Jadu, as noted, there is access down the scarp to the Jefara single carriageway black top road returning to Tripoli. Roads off to the right lead back to the Jabal settlements at Kabao, Zintan, Yafran and most other settlements. There is a petrol station at Bir Eyyad and a roadside police control station. The control is not interested in tourists but have your passports ready in any case. On the left a road leads to Sorman, 110 km to the SW. At Bir Ghanem, the old stopping place on the Tripoli road, there is petrol, a café and shops. Carry on to the N passing through Sahel Jefara, again with a café and a small market. Another road to the left immediately after Sahel Jefara leads to Zaviyah, 78 km distant. Thereafter there is a slight increase in woodlands within government run agricultural projects and ex-Italian roadside trees. Some shifting grain cultivation is visible on the plain in spring. Increasingly dense cultivation indicates that **Al-Aziziyah** is being approached. Turn left at Al-Aziziyah and Tripoli lies 38 km to the N.

Ghadames

Pop estimated 7,500 *Alt* 500m. *Rainfall*: under 25 mm annually.

Ghadames is a very beautiful small oasis town located where the international frontiers of Libya, Algeria and Tunisia join. The residential area is divided into the old and new towns. The old town is situated within the oasis whereas the new town has been built on the dry slopes above the oasis. Since 1986 all but one family have moved out of the old town. The old traditional houses are not easily adapted to the fast-changing contemporary life-styles of the people of Ghadames. Fortunately, the old town has not been simply abandoned and still plays an important role in the life of the inhabitants. In effect, the old town is surrounded by small plots of farming land, still highly cultivated. In the high

CLIMATE: GHADAMES

	Jan	Feb	Mar	Apr	May	Jun	Jul	Aug	Sep	Oct	Nov	Dec	Av/Tot
Max (°C)	18	21	26	31	36	41	42	41	38	32	25	19	31
Min (°C)	2	4	7	10	15	19	18	19	18	14	9	4	12

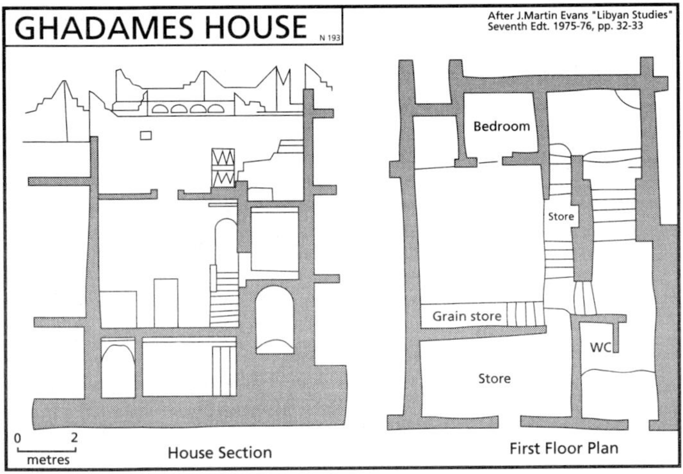

temperatures of the summer, the inhabitants of the new city return to their original town in search of coolness and protection. The old town with its Saharan architecture and great beauty is a uniquely preserved example of its kind.

History

The history of Ghadames is interesting. Paleolithic and Neolithic tools have been found in the surrounding region, but the first real documented information about Ghadames comes from the Romans who in 19 BC set up a garrison in what was then named Cydaus. Under the Byzantines, the town was set up to be an episcopate, under the tenure of a bishop, and some ruins from this period can be seen in the surrounding area. The Arab invasion in 667, led by Uqba Ibn Nefi, visited Ghadames before the Muslim forces continued on into Tunisia. By the 8th century, Ghadames was an important desert port of call for caravans and pilgrims but was also able to preserve its Independence. Until 1860, Ghadames was paying taxes to the Bey of Tunis. The second Turkish occupation of Libya in 1835 forced the town to recognize the authority of the Turkish Bey in Tripoli. When the Italians landed in Tripoli in 1911 it took them 3 years to reach Ghadames and even then their stay was of short duration. The Italians eventually returned on a permanent basis in 1924. They were great admirers of Ghadames and the area was treated sympathetically. New gardens were built and administrative offices set up there together with a small but pleasant hotel.

During WWII, Ghadames was occupied by the Free French Army led by General Leclerc and held under the Tunisian Protectorate until it was given up reluctantly at Libyan Independence in 1951. The last French troops left in 1955.

Ghadames suffered considerably with the development of less traditional sea-borne trade routes from West Africa. Situated in a very hostile environment even though there was water, trans-Saharan trade had been the main economic activity of the oasis. The people of Ghadames were trading and resident as far S as Timbuktu and on the Moroccan coast. The main trade consisted of caravans from the S bringing slaves, gold, leather and ivory in exchange for cotton, sugar and various products manufactured in Europe. By the start of the 19th century, trade had started to fall off due to the abolition of slavery. The decline was erratic and did not really end altogether until around 1910. Today, the inhabitants' only local sources of income are camel breeding and farming, the latter being very limited due to the lack of irrigation water and cultivable land, which is estimated at a mere 75 ha.

Architecture

The remarkable thing about Ghadames is the manner in which the people have been able to use all the resources available in a poor environment, together with their own traditions and architecture, to create perfect living conditions within this particular climate. The houses are built with mud, lime, palm tree trunks and fronds, the only available building materials. The result is impressive. Not only are the houses very elegant and beautiful, fitting perfectly into the environment, but they are also very practical. Built on 2 storeys, they have a central room on the first floor acting as a kind of courtyard with all the rooms leading out from it. The rooms are lit by an ingenious hole in the high ceiling, letting in sunlight that reflects off the white walls and provides quite sufficient illumination. The walls are made of mud and the upper floors are supported by palm tree trunks covered with fronds and mud. The interior of the house is decorated by the wife and tradition has it that this must be completed before the day of the marriage. The husband-to-be gives the key to his bride and she decorates their new home without his interference. The decorations are very simple, generally red patterns painted directly onto the white walls, with the addition of mirrors and a few small cabinets.

The roof is the domain of the women, the kitchen being on the roof. By tradition and due to the separation of sexes, the women were only permitted into the streets, either just after sunrise or just before sunset when the men are absent at the mosque for communal prayers. Otherwise in the old town they were confined to the house, especially the upper floors. However rather than hamper communication and freedom, this facilitated it, as most roofs touch and the women could easily move around from one roof to another. This is another remarkable feature of the architecture in Ghadames, possible because of the close intertwining of houses. All dwellings are physically linked together, to give shade from the sun and thus increasing the coolness of the settlement in the summer.

Within the houses there are some interesting features. One small room called the *koubba* is only used twice during the lifetime of the owners. First during the wedding ceremonies and second, if the husband dies, it is used by the widow to receive relatives and friends. The store room also has a clever system for preserving food. Due to climatic and other uncertainties, keeping a large stock of food was very important. Wheat would be stocked and a wall built with a small hole remaining open. A torch would be inserted in order to burn the oxygen and the hole quickly filled enabling wheat to be stored for years. When it was needed the walls would simply be demolished.

The streets also have charming characteristics. Small winding streets have covers for the most part, giving them a tunnel-like appearance and providing coolness with a few light wells between houses to illuminate the otherwise semi-dark streets. The roads lead to small public squares, some of which are covered. Most streets are lined with benches for the men to sit on.

Irrigation

An interesting feature of the oasis is the integration of the vegetation and cultivable land with the residential part of the town. The gardens are about 5m below

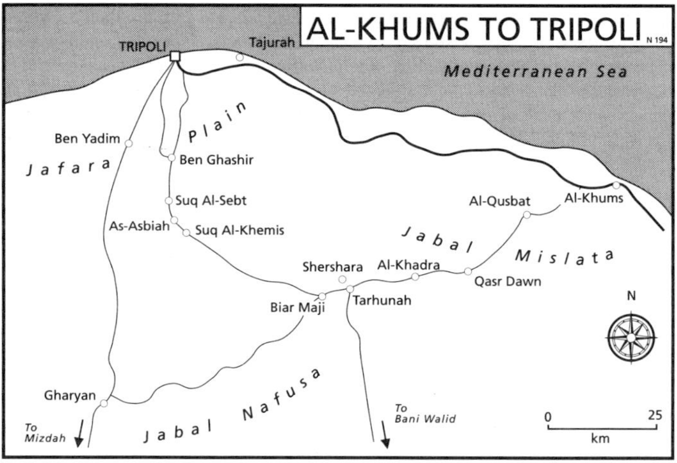

normal street level in order to be closer to the water table. Within the village there are 2 artesian wells operating in addition to Aïn Fares, the spring of the horses. Aïn Fares is said to have been discovered by Oqba Ibn Nefi, but this seems unlikely since the oasis pre-dates the Muslim invasion by a very considerable period. The sense of coolness given by the running water and the shade of the palm trees makes the heat bearable in the summer months.

Things to see

In the old town there is nothing specific to see because the beauty of the site is in the total harmony of the buildings and the small winding streets. In the old town situated behind the *Aïn Fares Hotel* there is a **House Museum**, a preserved Ghadames house. The interior is richly decorated with all the traditional furniture and implements of the oasis people. This is particularly interesting as it gives an insight into the traditional way of life in Ghadames earlier this century.

There is another 'Popular' **museum** at the entrance to the new town with a collection covering the popular and traditional aspects of life throughout the region, with clothes, weapons, tools and even desert animals. On the main square of the new town there is a large **market** every Tue and a small market every other day.

Local information

● Accommodation

The **C** ***Aïn Fares Hotel*** used to be an old Italian colonial style hotel, in need of some refurbishment, clean and agreeable, wonderful location right by the old town. A new hotel has been constructed slightly out of town.

● Youth hostel

T 2023, 120 beds, kitchen, only recommended if there is no where else to stay. However, its café is the young people's meeting point and gets very lively in the evenings.

● Travel agents

The recently opened *Ghadames Travel and Tourism*, T 0484/2307 will organize any trip in the surrounding area, including complete guided tours of the old town of Ghadames and trips into the desert down towards Ghat.

● Transport

Air Flights to and from **Tripoli** by Fokker 27 Tue, Thur and Sun. **Benghazi** Tue, Thur and Sun. **Sebha** and **Ghat** return flight Wed. Departure times change at short notice and travellers should check daily on the situation.

Road Bus There are 2 buses a day to **Tripoli**. Officially they leave at 0700 and 1100, but in reality they leave when full. Be at the terminal at least 90 mins before the official time as this is when the bus is likely to leave. All buses to Tripoli go via **Nalut**. There is a promise of luxury coaches being installed to run to Ghadames from Tripoli but no firm date has yet been given for the start of this service.

To the W of the town, the small village of **Tunine** is very similar and still inhabited, though it is much smaller and less attractive. Some very primitive forms of water lifting *delu* systems are still standing (see box, **page 625**). Further along the road after Tunine there is a large number of sand dunes. It is particularly satisfying to walk up to the top of the dunes and watch the desert sunset.

AL-KHUMS TO TARHUNAH AND TRIPOLI

The Jabal road back to Tripoli is well worth taking. The highway is occasionally narrow but this disadvantage is offset by a route through hill agriculture and breathtaking plantations of almond and olives.

The alternative to a direct route back to Tripoli from **Al-Khums** and **Leptis Magna** is to take the road through the Jabal Nafusa via Tarhunah. From Al-Khums travel W on the main highway to Tripoli but take the Tarhunah road at the first left hand junction. It is 67 km to Tarhunah from this junction. The road follows more or less the line of old road but is a good width of carriageway now. Take care on this road as it is dangerous, with mixed traffic and many curves as the road rises towards the town of **Al-Qusbat**.

Al-Qusbat is the central place of the Jabal Mislata (a sub-region of the Jabal Nafusa) and has been much extended in an undistinguished way, spoiling the former charm of the place. There are most facilities including a post office, clinic, petrol station and regional council office. A large hospital is being built. There is no hotel and travellers interested in walking across Mislata should stay in Al-Khums.

From Al-Qusbat take the road to Tarhunah. The road passes through scenic country in open landscape with ex-Italian olive and almond plantations at Al-Khadra and Qasr Dawn. Qasr Dawn has a hospital, police, school and shops.

At **Tarhunah** is the Faculty of Law of Al-Nasser University N of the town towards Shershara. Cinema, shops, Libyan Arab Airlines, an old hospital and a new one under construction are among the range of facilities in the town. This once beautiful town is now modernized to the detriment of its character. There is a hotel under construction but a dispute with the Turkish building firm has meant that it still has not been finished. The famous *Lady of Gharyan*, a wall painting on the barracks wall in the town painted by a US soldier in WWII, has sadly disappeared. Tarhunah's excellent wines are also no longer to be found on the open market. Leave Tarhunah towards Shershara.

- **Youth hostel** c/o Education Department, Tarhunah, T 3379, 20 beds, kitchen.

Shershara The much-visited spring at Shershara has practically stopped flowing as water has been diverted away and the local water table appears to have fallen. A small stream now comes in through a narrow upper valley with dense trees. It flows under the road which acts as an Irish bridge and there is a tiny fall of water on rocks below the roadway. The lower valley is green but very dirty with plastic and other rubbish. What was a very beautiful area is now slightly less than inspiring.

- **Places to eat** The hotel at Shershara, *Funduq Shershara*, is in a poor state: the rooms are not now used, but it has a restaurant and café. The staff do their best but the general effect is not very good. The hotel has no water from time to time. Arabic tea and a selection of cold soft drinks are available. Open 0800 to 2100.

Take the main road from Tarhunah out to the NW. A dual carriageway leads down to Tripoli. An alternative road leads W to Gharyan. The Tripoli road is fast but winding. There is a junction slightly N of Tarhunah which permits a direct link from the petrol station at Biar Maji to Bani Walid approximately 85 km to the S, and a second junction to Qatamah, 32 km from Biar Maji. It is a single carriageway road but good quality. Travellers can go directly via Mizdah to Sebha on black top without touching Tarhunah town. The road to Tripoli goes on to **Suq Al-Khemis**. Here there is a large roadside market, post office, police, shops and other basic facilities. At **As-Asbiah** is a junction with hospital, hospital-related housing but little else. Reaching **Suq Al-Sebt** there are more roadside shops, a petrol station and other services.

At **Ben Ghashir** the road leads off at a junction to the international airport link. Also from this point there is a dual carriageway to Tripoli. It is rather slow with lots of traffic. Roadside orange sellers are found in the spring season. Farm tractors and vehicles are plentiful on this dangerous road, mixing with fast airport and through traffic. Travellers can take the Tripoli-airport road with greater safety and speed.

BENGHAZI

CONTENTS

MAPS

Benghazi is the second largest town in Libya after Tripoli and as such is an important economic and administrative centre. The town acts as the main port for the E of Libya and has a number of food processing and packaging plants as well as other small and medium sized industries.

Pop 500,000 (estimated 1992) *Alt* Sea level. *Maximum recorded temperature* 40.1°C

The city has little to offer to the visitor as many of the older monuments have been destroyed, some during WWII but most through contemporary 'development' of the city. The present town is therefore relatively modern and charmless, except for areas in the old town and around the *funduq* market. Benghazi is nevertheless a good stopover point for trips to the E and into the Jabal Al-Akhdar.

The city enjoys a thoroughly Mediterranean climate with hot dry summers and warm winters with some rainfall. The Jabal Al-Akhdar region behind and to the E of Benghazi has a markedly heavier and more reliable winter rainfall of over 300 mm, with the scarp top attracting the larger rainfall total.

History

The town of Benghazi was probably founded around 515 BC, but no real information exists as to the precise date. The first settlers were most probably Greeks from Cyrene who had come down to the coastal plain. It is known that the first settlement was called Euesperides and was situated much further inland than the present city. In 249 BC, Ptolemy III of Egypt subjected Cyrenaica to Egyptian rule and married Berenice, the heiress to the Cyrenaican kingdom. A new site was found for the town of Euesperides, closer to the sea, probably because the old harbour had silted up, and the town was renamed Berenice. The situation of the ancient city is virtually identical to the present old town of Benghazi. The town then became part of the Roman Empire but once again little is known of its role. In the 6th century AD, the Byzantine Emperor Justinian made a number of repairs to the city after it had suffered an attack by the Vandals.

In 643 AD, the Arabs invaded, led by Omar Ibn el As, but they had little interest in Berenice. The 2 main cities at the time were Ajdabiyah and Al-Marj, due to their closer proximity to the main trans-African caravan routes. Very little is known of Berenice until the 15th century, when local tradition has it that merchants from Misratah and Zliten

CLIMATE: BENGHAZI

	Jan	Feb	Mar	Apr	May	Jun	Jul	Aug	Sep	Oct	Nov	Dec	Av/Tot
Max (°C)	23	26	31	34	39	38	33	33	34	34	31	26	32
Min (°C)	7	7	8	10	11	16	19	20	18	15	12	9	12
Rain (mm)	66	34	12	4	2	1	0	0	2	13	11	54	199

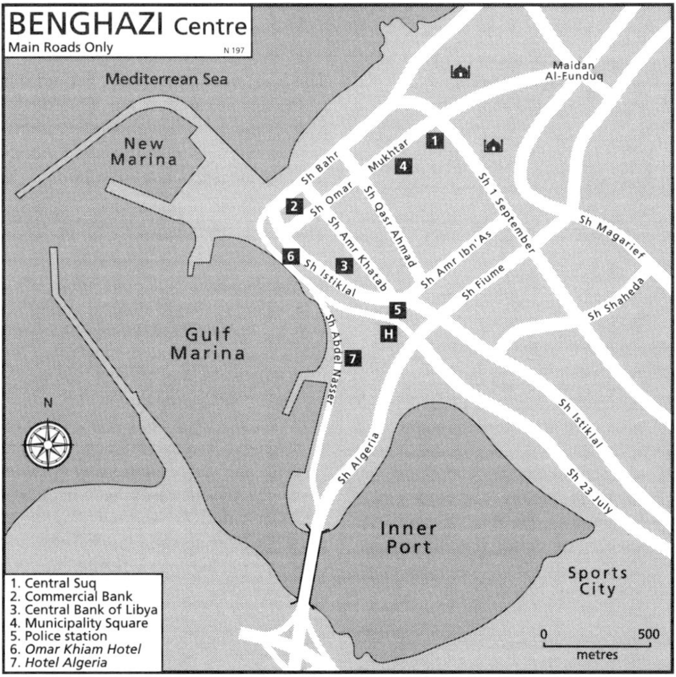

once again started using Berenice as a trading place. In 1579 the town was given the name Ibn Ghazi after a holy man of the city at that period. In 1648 the Turks, having previously settled in Tripolitania, advanced on Cyrenaica. By 1650 they held a position of strength in Ibn Ghazi, having built a fort. The town became the main centre for tax collecting. Because of this, few travellers or merchants came near it! In 1711, the Ottoman régime in Libya was interrupted by the Karamanli takeover and this once again plunged Benghazi into a period of stagnation. It was only under the second Ottoman occupation, beginning in 1835, that Benghazi again prospered.

In 1911, Benghazi was subjected to a siege by the Italian Navy, the city only surrendering after bombardment from the sea. The Italians then created a stronghold out of the city, building large walls encircling the centre. It took 20 years for the Italians to gain control of the surrounding areas, and only after 1931 were they in a position to start building up the city. The Italians poured large sums into urbanization projects and virtually managed to recreate an Italian city in North Africa. The real disaster for the town came during WWII when the city changed hands 5 times and was incessantly bombed by the Allies or the Axis. When General Montgomery finally liberated the city in November 1942, there was little left. Subsequently, due to the uncertainties as to the future of Libya, no major reconstruction works were carried out by the British Military Administration.

With Independence in 1951, the city

gained in importance as the regional capital and as the seat of the Federal Government, but developments were slow, particularly due to the government's lack of funds. In 1959, oil was found in the area around Sirt and the town became an important centre in the oil trade, particularly with the arrival of a large number of Europeans and Americans working in the oil fields. BP established its main office in Benghazi rather than Tripoli. Throughout the 1960s and 1970s, as oil revenues increased, the town developed rapidly. In the early 1980s the harbour was redeveloped in order to cater for large cargo vessels, new roads were built and small industries started to appear.

SOCIAL INDICATORS Benghazi is similar to Tripoli in per capita income (US$5,410), literacy (M 67%, F 50%) and life expectancy (61 years).

ACCESS There are frequent flights from Tripoli and other Libyan cities and, in normal circumstances, a few international flights. There is a bus service between the airport and central Benghazi (32 km). Taxis run into the town centre but make sure to agree a price before departure.

Things to see

Benghazi has few sites of any touristic value, but it is interesting to walk around the old town and see the myriads of small shops selling every imaginable type of merchandise. Particularly interesting is the **funduq**, a large market that mainly sells vegetables and fresh products. The atmosphere is typical of any Middle Eastern market and a worthwhile experience. The surrounding area is filled with stalls, particularly on Fri when traffic comes to a standstill. You will see trucks full of goods from Egypt, especially furniture, as well as a labour market where painters, electricians, carpenters, and so on stand by the side of the road waiting for an employer.

There are some **Roman remains** by the Regional Administration building on the seafront, but they are small and of only specialized interest. Otherwise there is the beach, either N or S along the coast. There are a number of good beach clubs, with restaurants and snack facilities.

The **Commonwealth Cemetery** in Benghazi is sited 6 km SSE of Benghazi on the inner ring road and in town there is a **Military Cemetery** containing 311 British war dead.

Local information

● Accommodation

AL *Tibesti Hotel*, T 92034, 274 rm, largest and newest, luxurious, *hammam*, impersonal.

B *Uzu Hotel*, very clean, modern, half the rm overlooking inner harbour.

C *Hotel Atlas*, Sharah Abdel Nasser, T 92314, not marvellous, acceptable for one night, being partially refurbished.

D *Hotel Omar Khiam*, Sharah Abdel Nasser, T 95102, 200 rm, once one of the best in Benghazi, has since become neglected, clean, welcoming, cheap, central; **D** *Hotel Al-Anis*, T 93147, rec, very simple, clean, good restaurant, welcoming, very cheap. *Tourist Village Garians*, T 96350, very cheap with good recreational facilities. **D** *Ghordabeia Hotel*, Sharah Abdel Nasser, T 97342/5, rm with shower, small hotel, friendly proprietor.

● Youth hostel

Sports City, T 95961, 200 beds, kitchen, meals, family rms, laundry, booking recommended May-Oct.

● Places to eat

Restaurant Al-Shallal, Sharah Abdel Nasser, by the *Hotel Atlas*; *Restaurant Ali Ayamama* Sharah Abdel Nasser, behind the *Tibesti Hotel*; *Ghordabeia Hotel* restaurant has a Kentucky Fried Chicken licence!! *Restaurant 23 July*, in the gardens by the inner harbour just before reaching the *Uzu Hotel*. Food and snacks are available at the various beach clubs near the city. Café in *Tibesti Hotel* open all day for snacks around LD5.

● Banks

Both the *Tibesti* and the *Uzu Hotels* have banking facilities. Otherwise the main banks are as follows: **Central Bank of Libya**, Sharah Abdel Nasser, T 91165; **Jamahiriya Bank**, Sharah Abdel Nasser, Tx 40008; **National Commercial Bank**, Sharah Omar Mukhtar, Tx

40012; **Sahara Bank**, Sharah Abdel Nasser, T 92766; **Umma Bank**, Sharah Omar Mukhtar, T 93377; **Wahhadah Bank**, Sharah Abdel Nasser, T 94527.

● **Chemist**
Sharah Gamal Abdel Nasser.

● **Consulates**
Most embassies and consulates are located in Tripoli to which ultimate reference for assistance must be made (**see page 621**). Among countries with consulates in Benghazi are: **Czechoslovakia**, T 92149; **France**, T 27566; **Greece**, Sharah Gamal Abdel Nasser, T 93064; **Italy**, Sharah Amr Ibn'As, T 92331/ 93484; **Poland**, Sharah Gamal Abdel Nasser, T 98363/92867; **Saudi Arabia**, Fuehat, T 20815.

● **Hospitals**
Benghazi has central hospital facilities and a modern complex on the outskirts of the town. While the air embargo remains in force, bear in mind that it is not easy to be repatriated from Libya in the event of an emergency.

● **Market**
The *funduq* offers an abundance of reasonably priced vegetables and other perishable products.

● **Post Office**
Sharah Omar Mukhtar. There is a smaller post office behind the *Tibesti Hotel* on Sharah Gamal Abdel Nasser.

● **Shops**
These are concentrated in the main street and the road leading from the centre W, Sharah Gamal Abdel Nasser, to the so-called Christmas Tree area. Some of the older suburbs have grocery and Arab lock-up shops selling a range of produce.

● **Sports**
There are several beach clubs not far from the city centre on the Ghar Yunis road towards the university campus. The bigger hotels, such as the *Tibesti*, have Arab baths. The ***Tourist Village Garians***, T 96350, 5 km to the S of the town, has a pool, tennis, bowling, snooker and other sports/recreational activities, facilities can be used by non-residents for a small entrance fee.

● **Telephone**
Local code 061.

● **Travel Agents**
Libyan Travel and Tourism Company is located at the start of Sharah Gamal Abdel Nasser, towards the harbour. This is a new agency specializing in organised tours. It can provide guides and transport. The company also issues tickets for all major airlines, T 93009. ***Libyan Arab Airways*** have an office on Sharah Gamal Abdel Nasser, behind the *Tibesti Hotel*. Both the *Tibesti* and the *Uzu Hotels* have travel agents that can issue tickets for all major airlines.

● **Transport**
Air – internal: from **Tripoli** there are 6 flights daily; flights per week **Ghadames** (3), **Ghat** (3), **Hun** (4), **Al-Kufrah** (1), **Misratah** (5), **Sabha** (5), **Sirt** (4), **Tobruk** (3).

Road Bus: **Faltco company**. The bus station is after the *funduq* on the right. Be sure to be there well in advance as buses tend to leave earlier rather than later than officially stated. Daily: **Tripoli** (4), **Cairo** (2), **Damascus** Wed and Sun 0800. **General Transport company**. Brand new bus station right next to the Funduq market. Daily: **Tripoli** 0730 (2 buses); **Al-Khums** 0700; **Misratah** 0800; **Al-Kufrah** 0730; **Sabha** Tue, Fri and Sun 0700; **Tobruk** 0730, 1100; **Derna 0800.**

Car hire: Tibesti Car Service is in the foyer of the *Tibesti Hotel*, T 92030, prices for 24 hours start at LD25. Local taxis are available for short or day-hire at expensive rates.

Taxi: All the intercity taxis leave from the Funduq area. They are all grouped by destination and leave when full. Slightly more expensive than the bus. Sample fare to Al-Bayda LD5.

TRAVEL IN THE JABAL AL-AKHDAR

The Jabal Al-Akhdar or Green Mountain range runs from Tocra to Derna. The highest point is close to Al-Bayda and reaches 880m. The Jabal is one of the few places where rainfall (about 300 mm per annum) is enough to sustain farming. The beauty of the landscape, the relative coolness in the summer as well as the important Greek and Roman remains make it an important part of any tour within Libya.

During the Greek Pentapolis period, the Jabal was reputed to be virtually the

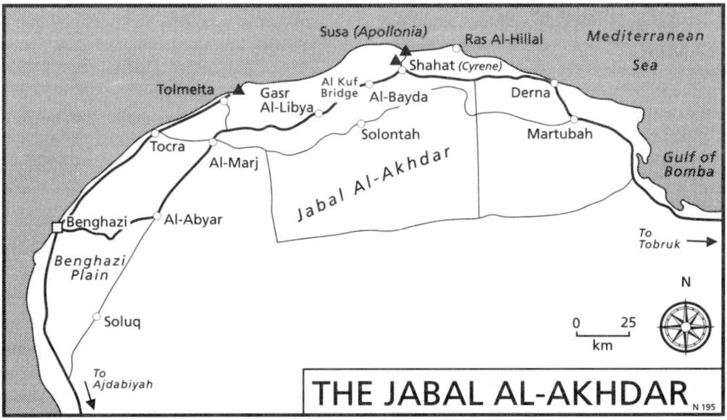

granary for mainland Greece and ever since has been seen, not entirely correctly, as a very fertile area. Recently, great efforts have been made to develop intensive farming using modern techniques and irrigation. An important underground water supply has made intensive irrigation farming a reality, particularly on the Al-Marj plateau. Production is still low and concentrated on fruits and vegetables, but some progress is being made. There are many new problems, particularly linked with overpumping and declining water tables, which are limiting development.

The Jabal peoples are historically independently minded and this area is not one that conforms easily with norms set by Tripoli. There was, for many years, difficulty with travel and access to certain areas within the Jabal. Given the ability of the local tribes to feed themselves and to sustain long periods of warfare, the region has been regarded with apprehension by outside groups. The Jabal Al-Akhdar has played a singular role in the history of Libya. It was the stronghold of anti-colonial rule and insurrection, giving great trouble to all would-be colonial rulers. Under the Senussi and Omar Mukhtar, the Cyrenaican tribes sustained many years of modern warfare in a one-sided struggle against the Italians. Today the Jabal is a major trade route to Egypt as well as having significant tourist potential.

Through Jabal Al-Akhdar

Tocra is a small town about 60 km from Benghazi. The new town is of little interest but the old part of town and the small central square with its **market** is worth a look around. Tocra has well-researched Roman ruins, though not all the workings are totally uncovered. Nevertheless, they are interesting and the small **Turkish fort** provides a good view over the plain towards the Jabal.

History

Teuchira, the original Greek name for Tocra, was founded around 510 BC. It became part of the Pentapolis. It changed names more than once and was called Arsinoe after the wife of Ptolemy II, and was briefly known as Cleopatris, the name of the daughter of Cleopatra and Mark Antony. There are still some surrounding walls built by the Byzantine Emperor Justinian in the 6th century and the Turkish fort, most probably built over the site of the Greek acropolis. From the ruins that have been excavated it is possible to deduce that the community at Tocra was poorer than the inhabitants of the other Pentapolis towns.

Al-Marj

The present Al-Marj is virtually a new city, the old town having been completely destroyed during an earthquake in 1963. The inhabitants were then relocated in the new town with a gigantic modern mosque that dominates the sky-line.

• **Accommodation** There is one hotel at Al-Marj which can be used as a good stop-over point. **D** ***Al-Marj Hotel***, T 067 2700, is situated near the centre of the new town, seems to have known better days, but is nevertheless clean, with a restaurant and cafeteria. **Youth hostel** T(67) 3669, 60 beds, breakfast included, meals, kitchen, family rms, bus 600m.

• **Transport Road** The bus and taxi station is about 500m in front of the mosque. There are no fixed times for buses, as they are only passing through, but they stop in Al-Marj in the morning between 0800 and 1000. Best to be there early. Otherwise there are shared taxis leaving throughout the day for destinations E and W.

Tolmeita (Ptolemais)

This site is of real interest for the Graeco-Roman ruins of the port of Ptolemais. The village itself is very small, but the situation on the coastal plain is magnificent. The scenery along the road from Al-Marj is very beautiful, particularly when driving down through the mountains towards the sea. The ruins are extensive and cover an area larger than in Cyrene, but remain largely unexcavated. Nevertheless, the site is worth a visit. Tolmeita is literally at the end of the road, for after early morning there are no buses. Transport back to Al-Marj or on to Tocra is by taxi if you can find one. The site surveyor (whose English is excellent) and the Chief of Police routinely ask visitors questions as Ghadhafi has a rest house down the coast. If relying on public transport visit Tolmeita then Tocra.

History

The ancient city of Ptolemais was named after Ptolemy II Philadelphus in the 3rd century BC. The town was actually founded earlier but only became of importance under the Ptolemy's rule as part of the Pentapolis. Ptolemais was originally the harbour for the inland city of Barce (Al-Marj), but later was of importance in its own right. After the Roman occupation the city was altered and buildings constructed, proving its continuing role as an important centre. From the 3rd century, both Apollonia and Ptolemais became the main cities in Cyrenaica. In the 4th century, Ptolemais became the seat of the bishop and the capital of a province and fortifications were increased against raids by Berber tribes, but were insufficient to prevent the Vandals in the 5th century from taking the city. Ptolemais fell into decay with the Arab invasion and its only use was in providing building material for the new village. The site was rediscovered in 1935 by the Italians who started excavations there and set up the museum.

Things to see

On the site there are several monuments that should not be missed. The **Street of the Monuments** is from the Roman period and was clearly an important place within the city, lined with porticoes, fountains, statues of people and deities, and inscriptions. The **Hellenistic Palace** is probably the largest and most interesting of excavated monuments dating back to the 1st century BC and altered in the 2nd century. From its size and elaborate decorations, it was clearly the house of a person of note. The house included large reception rooms with mosaic floors and traces of marble-panelled walls. There are 2 courtyards, one with an ornamental water tank, the other with Corinthian columns and traces of marble and mosaic floors. The house had 2 storeys, the basement presumably reserved for the servants. To the N of the building, one can see signs of the existence of private baths. On the N side, i.e. on the street, there is evidence that the front of the house had

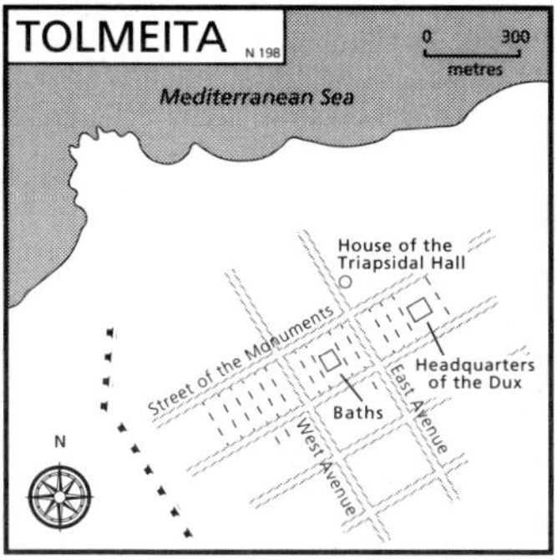

shops in it, a usual practice for private houses.

Not far from the palace, to the S, lies the **Forum**. This was rebuilt in the 1st century BC on the site of the Hellenistic Agora. The Romans built a large vaulted roof, a technique unknown to the Greeks. The entire structure covers 14 large reservoirs that were almost certainly fed by an aqueduct, traces of which can be seen by the Roman bridge that crosses over the *wadi* to the E of the site. The **Headquarters of the Dux** is a massive fortified building which presumably housed the garrison. Excavations of the **House of the Triapsidal Hall** indicate urban life continued here after the Islamic Conquest.

There are other worthwhile monuments to see but the excavations have not yet fully exposed the ruins and are thus not so immediately interesting as those mentioned above. To the W, remains of the walls that protected the city can still be seen. Close to the walls, a fully excavated **Basilica** dating back to the 5th century AD is well preserved. The church is original in that it was not an older converted building, a common practice during this period, and was built with defences. Vaults and arches replace the usual columns, but the nave was still roofed in wood. To the N of the basilica lies the **Amphitheatre**. Built by the Romans in the 1st century BC it was mostly used for gladiator fights and wild animal shows. Unfortunately today there is little to see. To the S, in the hillside, is the Greek theatre, probably built in the 2nd century BC. Once again little is visible. Finally, the ancient harbour was at the same place as the modern one. Some traces of buildings and their foundations can still be seen on the E side of the harbour, as can the location of some of the jetties.

There is a small museum located at the end of the road which passes through the village, by the harbour. The collection is small but interesting and mostly holds mosaics and sculptures from the Roman period. Some of the mosaics are very well preserved and are particularly of value, not for their great quality, but as an insight into life in Ptolemais, such as scenes with various wild animals, including lions and tigers.

Gasr Al-Libya

This small town is located on the road from Al-Marj to Al-Bayda. In itself it does not necessitate a visit but a fine old **Byzantine Fort** stands nearby. Coming from Al-Marj, take the road that goes to the left on entering the village. The site is 2 km down the road. The ruins date back to the 6th century and contain a well preserved **Byzantine Church**. The church was most probably fortified. The walls are still in perfect condition but the roof, originally made of wood, has been replaced. In the centre of the nave lies a large mosaic, which is in good condition. There is also a small museum that contains a set of mosaics. All the mosaics have been cut out of the floor of another building further down the hill. They are interesting because they give an account of what was clearly an important Christian community at the start of the 6th century. The rest of the ruins are dominated by a small **Turkish Fort** built as a stronghold and lookout over the surrounding countryside: it was later used by the Italians during their attempts to subdue the region. From the top of the fort there is a wonderful view.

Wadi Al-Kuf

On the road to Al-Bayda, there is an impressive new bridge crossing a deep gorge at Wadi Al-Kuf. The bridge is over 500m above the gorge and the view is breathtaking, definitely worth a stop. It is possible to take the road that goes along the bottom of the gorge. The cliffs in the side of the gorge are filled with small caves and quaint rock formations.

Al-Bayda

This is an important administrative regional centre. Once briefly the administrative capital of Libya in 1964, it is now the site of an important Islamic university. This is no coincidence since in 1843 Mohammed Ben Ali Al-Senussi established his radical Islamic movement in Al-Bayda, a movement that was to spread throughout Cyrenaica. In the 19th century the Turks had problems with the Senussi hold on the population and the leaders of the movement had to settle for safety in Jaghbub and Al-Kufrah. The Senussi led the rebellion against the Italians, finally leading Idris Al-Senussi to the throne and Libyan Independence in 1951. Today, Al-Bayda is a good stopover point and is very close to the major archaeological site of Cyrene.

Local information

● Accommodation

There is one good hotel in the main street. The **D** *Bayda Palace Hotel*, T 084 23455, run down, clean, rm with a/c.

● Transport

Road Bus There is a bus station on the main street, by the telecom tower. There are frequent buses to **Shahat** (Cyrene) every hour from 0800-1700. Other main line buses stop here, but there are no fixed timetables, except that the majority of the buses pass here in the morning.

Cyrene

Shahat (Cyrene) The modern city of Shahat is of little visual interest but the archaeological remains of Cyrene are very impressive and possibly the most worthwhile site in Libya after Leptis Magna. The situation of Shahat on the upper slopes of the Jabal Al-Akhdar is extremely fine, overlooking a high plateau leading to the sea. The site is as impressive as the actual remains of what must have been a very large city, but the combination of the 2 make it an absolute must for the traveller along the Cyrenaican shore. There is an hourly bus here from Al-Bayda. The last bus returns at 1700. Closed Mon and Fri. There is **no** public transport of any kind around the town so car-less travellers will need to rely on lifts from townspeople to reach the site in bad weather.

History

Cyrene goes back to the first half of the 7th century BC. The first settlers came from the island of Thera (Santorini) and the most plausible explanation is the over-population of the island and the necessity of finding an alternative outlet for settlement. The story has it that a young man named Battus went to Delphi to consult the Oracle, who told him to go and settle in Libya. He then left with an expedition, only to land on an offshore island. He later returned to see the Or-

CLIMATE: CYRENE

	Jan	Feb	Mar	Apr	May	Jun	Jul	Aug	Sep	Oct	Nov	Dec	Av/Tot
Max (°C)	19	21	26	30	353	37	36	34	32	30	27	23	29
Min (°C)	3	3	3	5	8	11	14	15	13	10	7	4	8
Rain (mm)	131	91	64	16	10	2	1	1	6	45	50	24	441

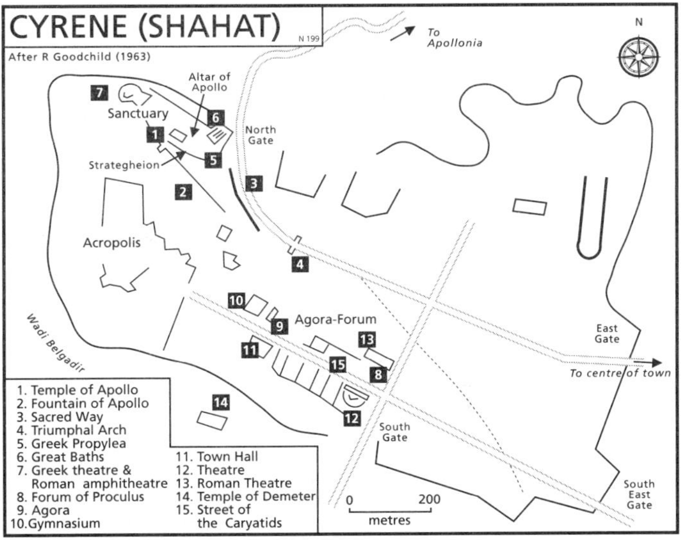

acle, who told him he had not been to Libya yet. He made another attempt and landed on the mainland, but not yet at the original site of Cyrene. It was only after a 6 year period that the colonists moved to the site of Cyrene and founded what was by the 5th century BC one of the largest cities in Africa.

Relations between the Libyans and the Greeks were friendly, both civilizations gaining from each other, and intermarriage between the 2 communities being permitted. When the city flourished, large numbers of Greeks came and settled in Cyrene: this gave rise to tensions and a small revolt by the Libyans in the 6th century BC. The city was ruled by Battus and his family until 331 BC and the coming of Alexander the Great. The Golden Age, from 450 BC until about 300 BC, saw Cyrene's prosperity increase. Due to the large number of crops obtained every year (up to 3), Cyrene was able to relieve famines in Greece and feed its own growing population.

The city also exported very valuable goods such as the silphium plant, now extinct, which was used as a laxative and an antiseptic. It was so important that the plant was depicted on the coins of the country for many centuries. Cyrene became part of the Pentapolis (Cyrene, Barka, Berenice, Tocra, Apollonia), a federation of 5 cities with agreements on trade, and joint coinage. This type of federation was quite common within Greek colonies until Alexander the Great attempted to unify all the cities.

On his death, the Greek Empire was split up and Cyrenaica came into the hands of the Ptolemy in Egypt. Cyrenaica passed into Roman hands when the illegitimate son of Ptolemy XI, who had inherited the Pentapolis, gave up his holding. In 75 BC, Cyrenaica was incorporated into the Roman Empire but, due to internal rivalries within the Empire, the Pentapolis was neglected. Emperor Augustus restored stability and gave a new span of life and prosperity to Cyrene. Various revolts broke out, the most serious by the Jewish community. In 115 AD Emperor Trajan ruthlessly suppressed the revolts but they brought about the inevitable decline of the city. Emperor Hadrian undertook large reconstruction works but the city never really recovered. By the 4th century AD the city was largely deserted and falling into decay. It was never again inhabited, except periodically by nomads.

Until the 19th century, very little attention was paid to Cyrene. One of the first expeditions was in 1838 by a British group and a few other outsiders followed in 1861 and 1864, but it was not until the Italian occupation that major excavation work was carried out. No real work on the site has been undertaken since the Italians and their successor under the British Military Administration, Professor Goodchild, left and much work still needs to be done.

Things to see

The site which is large and complicated to view, as much is obscured by more recent buildings and agricultural land use, can be divided into 2 main parts, the **Sanctuary of Apollo** and the **Agora-Forum Area**. The sanctuary is situated below the main part of the town, and contains the **Temple of Apollo** and the **Fountain of Apollo (Sacred Fountain)**. The main approach down the **Sacred Way** was through an arch which still stands. Pilgrims came from all over the African world of Greece to attend the ritual ablutions in the purifying waters of the sacred fountain and to venerate Apollo. Worship continued into Roman times, with the addition of the **Great Baths** built by the Emperor Trajan in the 2nd century. Once in the sanctuary, the pilgrims would congregate on the upper terrace and approach the temple through the **Greek Propylea**, 4 lofty pillars. These still stand and are of Doric style dating back to the Hellenistic period. Close by stands the **Strategheion**, built in honour of Apollo to celebrate the victory of 3 generals in the 4th century BC. It has since been restored and roofed.

The **Temple of Apollo** is certainly one of the oldest buildings in Cyrene, the rest of the sanctuary developing around it. The foundations of the original 7th century BC temple can still be seen, but it was later rebuilt and enlarged in the 4th century BC. Traces of blue paint still exist on the old Greek parts of the temple clearly showing that all buildings were painted, and often in bright colours. As a result of the Jewish revolts, the temple was burnt down and the Romans rebuilt a copy of the original Greek Doric temple. Later, during the Byzantine period, the temple was converted into a Christian chapel. Notice on either side of the entrance the inscriptions with the names of the Roman priests of Apollo, some being important Roman officials. In front of the temple to the SE stands the **Altar of Apollo** where the ceremonies took place. Traces of the channels which drained away the blood of the sacrificed animals can be seen, as can, between the altar and the temple, fragments of the metal ring to which the animals were tethered.

The **Fountain of Apollo** is situated by the cliff behind the Temple of Apollo. The water was used for purification and was said to have curative properties. Notice the seating inside the tank for people undergoing purification. This is one of the largest buildings in the **Great Baths**. The original building by Trajan in 98 AD was destroyed during the Jewish revolt and rebuilt by Hadrian in 119 AD. It is highly decorated, with marbled floors and walls and the baths looking, in their original form, quite superb. Most rooms had vaulted roofs and mosaic decoration. The **Calidarium**, or hot rooms, had raised floors and pipes in the walls for the passage of hot air from the furnace. In the **Great Hall**, a large cold bath is still in very good condition and fed by pipes coming from the Apollo fountain. The baths had more than just a hygienic role and were also highly important as a kind of social club, where all citizens would come and meet. Interestingly, before the reconstruction by Hadrian, mixed bathing was common, but a new law forbade this and 2 baths had to be built.

The **Theatre**, to the W of the site, is in fact a Roman theatre and not Greek as the building technique would suggest. The Greeks built theatres in hillsides, whereas the Romans generally built them on flat ground. In effect the theatre in the sanctuary is an amphitheatre, that is to say with a circular stage. Due to the sharp fall on one side of the building, seats were provided only on the hill side. Nevertheless, the Roman amphitheatre was probably built on the site of an earlier Greek theatre.

The **Agora-Forum** area is the real centre of the city and had all the conveniences of a metropolis. There were shops, theatres, baths, law courts and temples. The city had as its centre the **Agora**, equivalent to the Roman forum. Most of the main civic buildings were situated here. In the principal square is the **Tomb of Battus**, the founder of the city. This was a very special honour, as generally no tombs were allowed within the city walls. Close by are the remains of the supposed **Gymnasium**, the school for the elite youth where intellectual work was as important as physical exercise. In the square is the **Naval Monument**, probably erected in the 3rd century BC to commemorate a victory at sea. On the S of the square is the **Prytaneum**, or Town Hall. This building was the administrative centre of the town. The building resembled the plan of a private house, built around a central courtyard, with a sacred fire held in a niche to the E side symbolizing the communal home of the people. The officers of the Town Hall lived and worked within the building and invited privileged citizens and visitors to eat there. The Town Hall dates back to the Hellenistic period with only a few additions during the Roman times. The building was used until the Imperial officials from Rome took over the governing of the city.

On the E side of the Town Hall lies the **Capitolium**. The building dates to the end of the Hellenistic period and was converted by the Romans into the temple where Jupiter, Juno and Minerva were worshipped, symbolizing the Empire. The front has 4 white marble Doric columns and by the entrance are Greek inscriptions commemorating the gratitude of the city for the help Emperor Hadrian gave for the reconstruction of the town after the Jewish revolt.

To the E, going from the agora to the **Forum of Proculus**, is the **Street of Caryatids**. The road was originally lined on the N side with figures standing on pedestals (Caryatids) but they have all fallen over and are very damaged. On the S of the road is one of the most elegant houses in Cyrene, once belonging to Jason Magnus, a priest of Apollo. Built around the 2nd century BC by joining 2 houses, it is richly decorated, with mosaic floors, some well preserved. The larger of the 2 houses (on the higher level to the W) held the reception rooms. In the largest of the reception rooms remains of the magnificent marble floor can be seen. On the N, 3 small temples were incorporated into the house. One of the temples was the owner's private chapel. Both houses were built around a central courtyard. The second smaller house held the family's apartments.

Further E, the remains of a theatre are visible. This was probably built in the 3rd century BC and it is suggested that it was built as a replacement for the theatre in the sanctuary that had been converted into an amphitheatre. To the N of the Street of Caryatids, stands the impressive Forum of Proculus, probably built during the Hellenistic period, but later rebuilt by the Romans. The large central courtyard is lined with Doric colonnades, and in the centre lie the remains of an earlier temple, probably dedicated to Dionysius. Various fortifications were added to the forum during the 4th and 5th centuries when Cyrene was in constant fear of Berber attacks. To the NW of the forum lies a small **Roman Theatre**, which has been renovated and is sometimes used for performances. On the N side of the forum stands a **Basilica** built in the 6th century AD. Such buildings were used as an exchange for merchants or as law courts. The site extends for more than 3 km and this description has tried to give an account of the most interesting monuments, many of the others being in a poor state or still in need of excavation.

Particularly interesting is the **Necropolis** all around the site, making up an estimated 50 sq km. Tombs were not allowed inside the city walls and all tombs were thus situated on the surrounding lands and in particular in the side of the hill in front of the sanctuary. The tombs were dug out of the rock and formed small caves, often done in conjunction with quarrying, and the bodies placed directly into coffins carved out of the rock. The doorway was then sealed with a large stone. Due to the stones being movable, most of the tombs were broken into and even sometimes inhabited by nomads. It is strange that virtually all the bodies were actually placed within the tomb as, until the Christian period, cremation was commonly practised. Only a few lead urns containing ashes have been found. No clear explanation seems to have been found as to why interment was systematically practised. The shrine tomb was also a widely-used burial chamber. The tombs resembled small mausoleums or temples. These mostly date back to the Hellenistic period. The number of tombs may at first seem impressive, but one must remember that the period of occupation stretched from 700 BC to 400 AD.

Local information

● Youth hostel

Former Shahat Tourist Hotel, 200 beds, kitchen, meals, laundry, family rms, T (851) 2102, booking recommended Jun-Sept.

Susa (Apollonia)

This is a tiny settlement by the coast about 20 km from Shahat. The old town is very beautiful but falling into decay. The real interest of the town is the ruins of Apollonia, Cyrene's harbour. The site is by the sea, but a large part of the town and harbour have been submerged due to landslides. Susa can be reached by a road coming from Shahat, highly recommended because of the fine view over the coast and Susa itself.

Apollonia was founded at the same time as Cyrene and was named after the city's principal god. The harbour was at first a dependency of Cyrene, but later in the 2nd and 3rd centuries it gradually increased in stature, as the mother city declined, and finally became the capital of Upper Libya.

Approaching the site from the W, drive through the town square heading towards Derna and look for the track to the left leading up to the ramparts which leads to parking space on the beach. The first important monument encountered is the **Extra-Mural Church**. The **City Walls**, from which huge quantities of stone have fallen, continue up the Acropolis hill and turn N to the **Theatre** and the sea. Within the walls the **Cisterns** and the **Chambers** were both used for storage. The **Eastern Church** dating from the 5th century contains green marble columns from an earlier Roman building. The **Baths** to the left of **Main Street** now lie close to the sea, while on the hill top to the S are the extensive remains of the **Byzantine Palace**. The **Central Church** and **Western Church** are beyond to the W, the latter built up against the ramparts, making use of the wall in its structure. The **Western Gateway**, threatened by the encroaching sea,

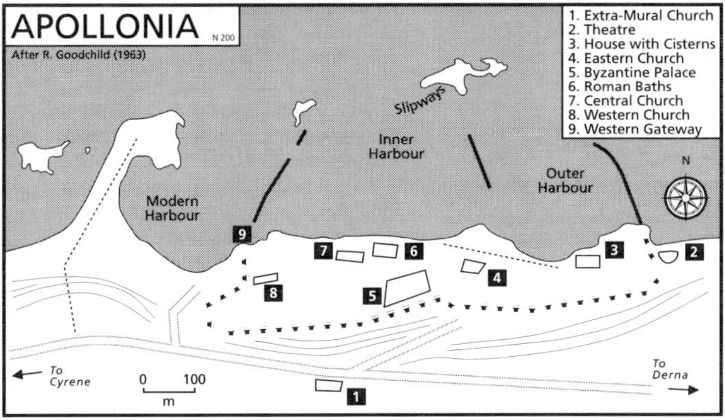

leads nowhere. Further remains lie submerged.

Even though there is nothing of any specific value, the site nevertheless gives an impression of life within the ancient port. Apollonia is also wonderfully situated and a walk around the site is worthwhile.

The **Museum** is situated in the centre of the old town. It is small with a collection of mainly Byzantine mosaics and sculpture. There are also a few Roman and Greek exhibits. The collection is not very rich, reflecting the small amount of work put into excavations at the site. Even so, there is an interesting room on traditional clothes, tools and crafts that provides an insight into the traditional way of life in this part of Libya.

The road from Susa to Derna

This is a very beautiful road following the coast, with the Jabal Al-Akhdar to the right. The coast is mostly rocky but the occasional beach provides a good spot to stop for a swim or a picnic.

Ras Al-Hillal (Crescent Headland) is a small but picturesque village by a rocky cape from which it takes its name. There are few small beaches along the coast from the town. In the town right on the beach there is a hotel, currently being refurbished. The hotel is more of a holiday village, with rooms and bungalows to rent.

Derna

Derna is an important town on the E side of the Jabal. Beautifully situated surrounded by the last hills of the Jabal with the *wadi* lying in the centre, Derna is a delightful town. The E part of the town is mostly new, but the old centre on the W side of the *wadi* is still very pleasing to the eye. From the central square, the covered *suq* goes N with many small streets leading to it. To the W of the *suq* lies the old town with its small streets occasionally leading to tiny squares, still very authentic because still inhabited. The new town has expanded around the old centre and not to the latter's detriment. All the shopping and activity still takes place within the *suqs* and old town. A good time to witness the thriving activity is on a Thur evening, when the entire population seems to congregate in the centre. This is an occasion to have a coffee in the café in the middle of the central square. Also on the square is the *Jabal Al-Akhdar Hotel*, one of the town's 2 hotels.

History

Derna was founded by the Greeks at the

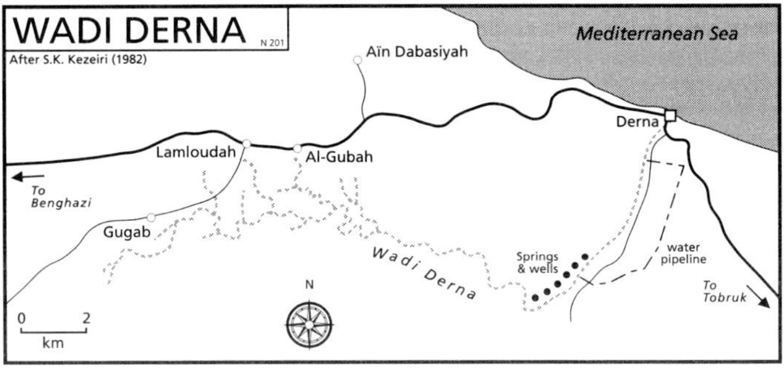

time of the Pentapolis. It was not an important town and never became part of the Pentapolis but did develop during the Ptolemaic period. In 96 BC it became part of the Roman Empire, and during the Byzantine period was the episcopate for the region. In 693 AD the Greeks attempted to land and take the region but were pushed back by an army led by Abu Shaddad Zuhayr, who was killed in the fighting and subsequently made a town hero.

Under the Arabs, Derna fell into decay. The harbour was less good than others in the region and situated too far N from the main caravan and trade routes that passed about 90 km S. It was only in the 15th century AD that Derna re-emerged with the arrival of Andalusians, mostly migrating from other North African countries where they had already settled. During this period, Derna was involved in rivalries with Benghazi over trade.

During the Turkish occupation, the Dernawis did not like being ruled from Tripoli, and in 1656 an expedition was sent to quell the inhabitants, resulting in large scale destruction of the town and its population. Under the auspices of the Governor Mohammed Ibn Mahmud in the 17th century, the town grew with the building of a Great Mosque and the initiation of irrigation works. In 1805, Derna was the scene of a curious event. The town was bombarded by the American Navy in an attempt to prevent pirate attacks against American ships. The Americans had already tried attacking Tripoli but had failed. An overland expedition left from Egypt heading for Tripoli, but never got further than Derna, when an agreement was finally made. During the second Turkish occupation, beginning in 1835, Derna was an important base for controlling the hinterland. Finally, during Italian colonization, the town was expanded and cleaned up, attracting many tourists. During WWII, the town changed hands a number of times and suffered from heavy bombing. Today, Derna is an important economic centre with an expanded harbour. It is also at the centre of an important irrigation project. Two dams have been built 2 km and 15 km upstream on the Wadi Derna and water is transported as far as Tobruk.

Things to see

In the town there is a small organization called *Haila* run by Mohammed Ahneid that concentrates on preserving the cultural heritage of the town. They have an interesting **museum** with rooms recreating the traditional homes which gives a very good insight into the traditional way of life. The organization will also arrange tours of the town and its principal sights as well as the surrounding area. There are a few excellent beaches E of Derna as well as caves in the cliff once inhabited by Christians seeking to escape persecution.

The centre of the town is the most interesting area. Walk around the old town and the *suqs*. The valley of the Wadi Derna is very beautiful. Take the road that follows the river. The road follows an impressive valley, green at the bottom, dry and rocky on the sides. The first of the 2 dams is at the outskirts of the town, the second about 15 km upstream. About 8 km after the first dam, water can be seen pouring out of the rock from an important spring. Continuing up the valley brings you to the last dam, where the landscape begins to look much less cultivable but the panorama definitely gains in beauty.

WWII Military Cemeteries The intensive fighting in the period 1940-43 in North Africa left large numbers of war dead on all sides. There are 2 Commonwealth war cemeteries, commemorating 6,124 souls, one 7 km E of Tobruk on the Alexandria/El-Adem road and the other, the Knightsbridge War Cemetery, Acroma, 24 km W of Tobruk on the S of the coast road. German war dead, numbering some 6,026, are interred near Tobruk at El-Adem S of the crossroads in a fort-like structure. The Italian war cemetery of the WWII period is across the border in Egypt at El-Alamein (see page 838).

Local information

● Accommodation

D/E *Jabal Al-Akhdar Hotel*, T 081 22303, very good, central, simple, clean, quite cheap.

E *Hotel Al-Bahr*, on the seafront, basic, clean, cheap, shared bath, good restaurant.

● Youth hostel

5 km W of centre, 200 beds, meals, kitchen, family rms, laundry.

● Transport

Road Bus There are frequent buses to towns all around the country. There are few fixed timetables, but most buses leave early in the morning. The General Transport Company has a bus to **Benghazi** at 0800. The bus from Benghazi to Derna leaves at the same time.

To Egypt

From Derna, the road E leads to Solum and the Egyptian border. Formalities at the Egyptian border are few but it is busy and can be very hot. There are few reliable facilities there so travellers should be prepared to be self-sufficient until they reach Marsa Matruh in Egypt.

FEZZAN

The third of the great historic provinces of Libya is Fezzan, a region spreading over some 684,280 sq km of desert lands in the SW of the country. The bulk of Fezzan is made up of uninhabited sand seas and deserts interspersed with gravel and stone plains. In the N and the E of Fezzan there are extensive areas of stone desert called *hammada*. Sabha, the capital, is the hub of the transport system in Fezzan and travellers can move to all key sites from there.

Sabha

Within the desert areas are a number of great *wadis* which give human access and have a modest availability of underground water. The 2 main dry *wadi* beds are the Al-Shatti and the Al-Ajal (Al-Hayyah). A shallow topographic basin around Murzuq also gives access to subsurface water at shallow depths.

There are dry salt lakes or *sabkhas* throughout the region, the greatest number being found in the Wadi Shatti and the Hofra-Sharqiya zone. The highest part of Fezzan lies in the Tibesti Mountain area, a huge uplifted massif in the Uzu region running to altitudes of 3,376m in the extreme SE of the system. Deeply incised *wadi* valleys are clearly vegetated and rich in animal and plant life. Lower elevations are reached in Jabal As-Soda, 840m and 1200m in the Jabal Al-Haruj Al-Aswad.

Climate

The climate of Fezzan is hot and dry. Everywhere is arid and desertic. Rainfall is slight and irregular at 8.3 mm per year, often falling as an occasional heavy downpour. Heavy rain storms bring chaos to transport and can lead to extensive damage to property with flash floods and disintegrating walls of traditional buildings. Temperatures are high during the day with no cloud cover, allowing rapid cooling at night. Daily ranges in temperature of 40°C are possible. Temperatures are higher in the summer with the Jun mean monthly temperature at 30.6°C in the regional capital, Sabha. Spring and particularly Jan is a better time to travel when average temperatures fall to 11.6°C. Winds can be severe in the desert, with westerlies dominating the winter and easterly/northerlies the summer. Fezzan experiences the *ghibli* wind in the form of a very hot, dry and uncomfortable blast of several days' duration. Transport can be disrupted during the *ghibli*.

Population

Human settlement was possible only where water could be reached easily by primitive technology in the Wadis Ajal and Shatti and in the Murzuq basin. Even here the densities of human populations were thin and villages widely scattered. Recent economic development has, despite enormous expenditures of cash and effort, made little difference to this underlying pattern. In 1980 the population was estimated at 190,265 of which only 165,245 were Libyan nationals. The popu-

CLIMATE: SABHA

	Jan	Feb	Mar	Apr	May	Jun	Jul	Aug	Sep	Oct	Nov	Dec	Av/Tot
Max (°C)	19	22	26	31	36	39	38	39	37	33	26	21	31
Min (°C)	5	8	11	15	20	23	23	23	22	18	12	7	16
Rain (mm)	1	1	1	1	2	1	0	0	0	1	1	1	10

lation was growing at 5.1% annually, mainly through inward migration by foreigners from countries such as Chad and Sudan. Non-Libyans represented 13% of the population of Fezzan at that time, a figure which has since gone up by at least 50%.

The indigenous peoples are dark-skinned but of Arab extraction. The Tibu and the Tuareg tribes have some Arab characteristics but are otherwise of separate origin. The Tuareg have their own, Berber-related, language of Tamashek. In recent years some have settled in towns. The Fezzanese are known as friendly and hospitable people. Only the Tibu, a tall and very dark group from the Tibesti, are unreliable in their treatment of strangers. A number of Europeans have been taken hostage in the Tibesti, though never within Libyan Tibesti. Great care is needed in travelling in Tibesti since it is isolated, difficult of access, bleakly inhospitable in its climate and unpoliced over very large areas.

Economy

The economy of Fezzan was traditionally dependent on oasis agriculture, some pastoral herding among the Tuareg and trans-Saharan trade. In recent years this has entirely changed as a result of oil revenues and the growing influence of the central authorities in Tripoli. Employment now depends on the state more than on traditional activities. No less than 80% of people rely on government generated services for a living. Agriculture employs a mere 7% and trade another 10%. Perhaps as much as 90% of all regional income comes from the government. The cause of the skew in the economy is directly related to the nature of oil income which is spent by the government. Investment by the government ran at US$7,000 per head of population in the region in the late 1970s and early 1980s, though it has since fallen significantly. Libyans have tended to give up active involvement in farming and employ foreigners. In services and construction foreigners make up over 80% of the work force.

Agriculture

This is known to have been practised in this region since the 5th century BC when the Garamantes used a form of irrigation in areas adjacent to Ghat. Agriculture was largely self-sufficient but was also designed to provide surpluses to feed passing caravan traffic. The main crops have always been barley and wheat in the winter and millet, sorghum and maize in the summer, together with vegetables and fruits in great variety. Forage crops were vital both for keeping animals on the farm and for providing food for the passing caravan trade. Farms are generally tiny and fragmented into small parcels. Including unused and unirrigated lands, average farm sizes at 7 ha were less than half of that for the rest of the country. Each irrigated plot is carefully levelled, provided with water and sheltered from the wind with palm frond hedges or mud walls. The main commercial field crops are tomatoes and onions, both of which are exported to the N. Fezzan produces more than two thirds of all dates in Libya at 86,523 tonnes per year from no less than 4,649,936 trees. Olives, grapes, figs and oranges are also grown among a vast range of fruits. Sheep and goats are the main animals kept, the richest grazing zone being the Wadi Shatti. The number of camels (dromedaries) is falling rapidly as they are no longer used for transport or ploughing. Some development of cattle herding for milk production is underway.

Modern agricultural estates have sprung up throughout the region and are easily recognized by their straight boundaries and regularly laid out facilities. The biggest projects include those at Maknusa and Wadi Aril which are principally designed to produce grain and fodder. They are basically agribusinesses run with large amounts of capital but few employees. Occasionally they have attracted local herders who make use of the fodder for their livestock. A second category of development estates is the settlement farm where small farms are set up within large estates run initially by government agencies. Farmers are recruited to take over the farms. There has been friction from time to time as locals have resented incoming farmers. The presence of estates means fresh water, electricity and telephones but not necessarily accommodation for the traveller.

Industry

By definition, industry in Fezzan is poorly developed. The resource base is weak but there are some oil and natural gas deposits in the extreme W and some iron ores in the Wadi Shatti. But these resources are most easily used in the N and at best will represent primary exports. Small workshops have grown up in Fezzan but they are mainly concerned with servicing government activities and construction, with mechanical workshops, building materials and food processing jobs dominating the sector. For the traveller it will be worthwhile looking out for the **local glass making plant** at Brak, the **handicraft centre** at Ghat and the **leather factory** at Traghan.

Access and travel in the province

Access to Fezzan is limited by the few international entry points. Most travellers will have to come through Tripoli, though there is the chance on some tours to enter directly from Niger and Algeria. Similarly, the internal access points are either via the airports at Sabha and Ghat or along the main roads to Sabha from the N of the country.

There are 2 main lines of road entry to Fezzan. The first is the traditional route from the coast at Bu Grayn via the Jufra region to Sabha and the second is the new road from just outside Gharyan via Mizdah. Significant resources have been expended in Libya to improve the road system and the main highways are by and large in good condition and constantly being supplemented by new spurs. The road system in Fezzan (see below) covers the main economic and strategic axes.

Road system of the Fezzan

Key Routes	Length (km)	Journey time (min)
Sabha – Traghan	128	100
Sabha – Obari	200	150
Edri – Brak – Ashkida	147	120
Murzuq – Zuwaylah	136	105
Obari – Ghat	370	300
Umm Al-Araneb – Qatrun	150	125

	Brak	Ghat	Murzuq	Obari	Sabha	Tripoli
Ghat	671					
Murzuq	833	544				
Obari	301	370	174			
Sabha	939	570	183	200		
Tripoli	939	1530	1143	1160	960	
Waddan	317	920	533	550	350	610

Fezzan: distances by road between sites (Km)

The main road system is fast and served by buses and taxis on regular scheduled/on demand routes. The buses are cheap but taxis can be expensive over long distances. The driving at times can be careless and even harrowing. Travel at cool times of day and use a/c buses when available. At present only the key routes between Sabha and Tripoli are served by super-express services. The bus services are important because the air link is crowded, infrequent and inconvenient. Buses give a cheap and easy way to continue a journey rather than put up with long stays in oasis towns.

The bus station in Sabha, the main transport hub for the area, is in the Jabeya district. Its facilities are very basic. Almost all long distance bus services run from Sabha usually on a once-a-day basis for major routes and alternate days or a lesser frequency for other services. The inter-urban taxi services are always available and are normally on, or adjacent to, the main street of each town.

Since travellers in Fezzan will find their lives dominated by the transport facilities, a distance matrix of main centres in the region is given below. The distances between centres are considerable and, even on the bus or in a taxi, you should take enough food, drink and clothing to manage through very hot and very cold conditions. A breakdown can cause long waits for which travellers should be well prepared, especially on some of the long inter-settlement roads in the S.

Things to see

Topography Fezzan offers endless but varied desert landscapes. A good relief map is essential to make the best of this experience. Secondly, there are a few small sites to visit, some living oases, others archaeological monuments or remains. The oases are best grouped into areas for visiting. The smaller ones should be visited with a guide if unwelcome attention or suspicion is not to be aroused especially by male groups. In the Wadi Al-Ajal (Al-Hayyah) there are still comparatively unspoiled villages such as Bent Bayah to the W where magnificent forms of traditional architecture are still in use. In Ghat there are still strings of small traditional settlements worthy of a half day visit with a translator. Similar villages exist as populated or recently abandoned sites throughout the province. The further they are from the developed centres, the more interesting the villages become, though some, like Umm Al-Araneb, have undergone a total population change in recent times.

The **architecture** in Fezzan is highly individualistic. Houses are built of sun-dried mud bricks in most regions, though near rocky outcrops flat natural stone can be incorporated into the buildings with mud rendering on both sides. Most houses are single-storey. The flat roofs are constructed with palm wood cross members covered with palm fronds sealed with a beaten mud coating. Ornamentation is provided on the roof corners by a triangular motif in which 2 flat bricks are leaned against each other above a horizontal brick or stone. This emblem is used in a variety of forms either as a single unit or in combination along the top of a wall. Doorways can be highly decorated, often with calligraphic or symbolic representations above the main door to the house. Some houses carry horn-shaped fixtures above their entrances, thought to be against the effects of the evil eye. Painting is rare except to highlight a doorway and it is usually the religious buildings which carry white or blue washes. Variations of style are noticeable throughout Fezzan.

The minarets of mosques in Fezzan are also distinctive and worth looking out for. They are often square-shaped and only slightly raised above the level of single-storeyed mosques, usually painted white. A complex and beautiful three-tiered mosque of this kind exists at Obari. Other fine mosques can be found, and **Zuwaylah** is worth calling at to see its **mosque** and the ruins of an associated **fort**. Some of the Turkish stone forts survive and the Murzuq fort can be seen in the centre of the new town.

The archaeological sites

Fezzan is rich in pre-historic sites where well-preserved cave paintings can be viewed. The main sites are: (1) **Akakus** and **Tashinat** where there are excellent wall carvings; (2) in the **Wadi Fuet** close to Ghat there are a number of coloured wall paintings; (3) **Zinkekra** in the W Garma area where there are rock carvings; (4) **Wadi Buzna**. The artwork depicting antelope, elephant and giraffe-like animals and human hunters dates from 6000-3000 BC.

Libya is famous for the **Garamantian** civilization of the Wadi Al-Ajal. The centre was **Garma**, established about 2000 BC, and only rediscovered in the 1960s. A series of ruins and sites are open for visitors to the Wadi Al-Ajal. The city of Germa is a clear attraction, lying close to Obari just off the Sabha road. Nearby are the tombs of Saniat Jebril and Ben Howaidi. Other tombs and cemeteries include the tombs of Ahramat Al-Hatiyah, the royal cemetery to the S of Jarma, the cemeteries at Bent Bayah and Budrinnah, and Al-Khareyk, the latter W of Garagra. There are the remains of forts at Al-Abiad and Al-Gullah. The full range of urban life is not yet known since excavations at the site have not been finished.

All Libyan monuments are open 0800-1700 and are normally closed on Tue. In Fezzan there is a certain informality over working hours and even the guardianship of sites. Local guides will see that you review the full extent of the known ruins but often travellers will be on their own. Care is needed to treat the sites well and not to take artifacts. Urban monuments, especially mosques, need a low key approach with permission asked before entering. Again, having a local Fezzanese with you can make a great deal of difference to your reception. Housing of interest will either be a prepared tourist site without a family in residence as at Bent Bayah or must be approached with care if there are women resident. There are rarely facilities of any kind at the Fezzanese archaeological sites.

Obari lakes

A strange site, signposted off the only main road to the N and well worth travelling a short distance to see is that of the Obari lakes. About 13 small lakes exist in the Obari sand sea sited between the great dunes of the system. The main lakes are **Mandara** 200-300m diameter, lake **Umm Al-Ma'**, which usually has water throughout the year, **Bahar Al-Daud** 300m diameter, **Tademsha**, **Umm Al-Hassan**, **Neshnusha**, **Bahar Al-Trunia**, **Frejia** and **Oudnei**. They are fed by ground water from the sand sea when the water table builds up in the dune systems. Most are very shallow, less than a metre, and many dry up during the summer. The water is very brackish in the lakes but water drawn from the dunes can be used in irrigation and for human consumption. There is a myth in Libya that the lakes area was populated by people who were 'worm-eaters', a belief arising from the local custom of eating shrimps taken from the lakes. Not surprisingly, local people do not take kindly to the 'worm-eating' story!

Excursions

A first approach to an area as widespread but thinly populated as Fezzan is to take the major geographical axes along the excellent road system. The main elements can be taken in using the following routes: **(1) Brak – Edri** along the Wadi Al-Shatti giving access to the old town of Brak, the S rim of the Hammadah Al-Hamra and the small traditional settlements of the valley; **(2) Sabha to Obari** along the line of the Wadi Al-Ajal taking in the traditional villages and the Garamantian sites; **(3)** the **Murzuq – Zuwaylah** road with more Garamantian remains, the fort at Murzuq, the mosque at Zuwaylah and the old and new towns at Umm Al-Araneb and **(4)** either by road or air, a visit to **Ghat and the SW corner of Libya**, one of the most unspoiled and rewarding areas of the country for the traveller.

In addition to this overall travel scheme, some specific **organized excursions** are available through the travel agencies, the most active for Fezzan as a whole being in the *Akakus Tours*, see page 666.

Fezzan tour includes trips to the old villages of Ghat and down to the Wadi Ayadar and to Takhakhori. The visitor travels through the desert of the Msak Mallat and Msak Satafet to look at the country and some ancient sites and also crosses one of the world's great sand seas, Erg Murzuq. The caravan then goes to the Wadi Matkhandus to look at wall engravings and to the Wadi Berjuj before arriving at Murzuq city. Zuwaylah and the sand dune lakes are visited. There is also a full scale visit to the ruins of Garma before returning via Al-Awenat to Ghat. The visit can be tailored to individual or group requirements to run between 7 nights to 13 nights under bivouac.

Teshuinat tour This takes the traveller in 4 wheel drive vehicles and under canvas through the Akakus mountains, and the immediately surrounding sand seas, to look in at Ghat, Al-Awenat and the extreme SW corner of Fezzan. The circuit lasts for between 3 and 5 nights and includes a visit to the cave painting sites of that region.

Discover Libya Tour offers a very varied set of packages of as short as 3 nights and as long as 17 nights. Again, travel is in 4 wheel drive vehicles and accommodation mainly in tents. It begins in Tripoli then moves along the Mediterranean coast through Leptis Magna and then Sabrata to the W borders to track down through Nalut on the western Jabal to Ghadames, a long cross-desert run to Sabha and on to the principal sites in Fezzan.

Central Saharan Expeditions Akakus have arranged with the authorities in

Algeria and Niger to take visitors across the international border to visit all the major central **Saharan cave painting sites**. The excursion is imaginative and unusual, taking in **Ghat** and **Tumu** in Libya, **Djanet** in Algeria and **Madama** and **Bilma** and **Agadez** in Niger. This is an exciting chance to see this previously difficult region in a 21 night tour which enters via Libya and leaves via Niger or vice versa. A more limited route through Libya and Algeria to the sites in those 2 countries takes between 7 and 17 nights depending on how many sites are taken into the itinerary.

Given the costs and administrative difficulties of setting up desert visits to this part of the world, ***Akakus Tours*** offer of desert expeditions is extremely attractive. Other tour operators are being set up. The largest in Tripoli is the ***Libyan Travel & Tourism Company***, T 21 48005/48011 F 21 43455. Their desert tours in Fezzan include a 15 day desert visit from Tripoli to the S flying from Tripoli to Sabha and thereafter by 4 wheel drive vehicle to Gabroun and Mandara sand dune lakes, and on to Garma and Wadi Berjuj. The itinerary goes to the Matkhandus prehistoric painting sites and then across the Murzuq sand sea to Gassi Ohabran, the Wadi Selfoufet in the Akakus and finally to Ghat, returning to Tripoli via Sabha by air.

Local information

● Accommodation

The tourist potential of Fezzan has been neglected almost entirely. The obvious attractions of desert travel, of the unique nature of the less 'developed' oases and of the archaeological sites were overlooked. Few hotel facilities exist in general, and very few have been constructed with travellers from overseas in mind. There are only 400 or less hotel beds of a satisfactory kind available in the whole of Fezzan. The main hotels are in Sabha and include a new Social Insurance Tourist Centre, **B** ***Hotel Al-Fatah***.

The **E** ***Al-Galah Hotel***, rather run down, 57 rm, 114 beds; **E** ***Mountain Hotel***, small, 19 rm, 38 beds. There are also rest houses in Sabha owned by official organizations to which access can only normally be obtained with the help of official letters of introduction from Tripoli. Other hotels include the new Hotel at Hun, where the old ***Tourist Hotel*** still functions, though parts of it seem to have been given over to foreign labourers. An 11-year-old hotel exists at Ghat and rest house facilities are available if not already occupied – ask for information at the Municipality building. It is best to telephone for a booking before arrival in Ghat to the energetic private ***Akakus Tours***, though they normally accommodate their guests in bivouacs. Small **guest houses** exist at Ghat, Traghan, Hun, Hammera and Garma but their facilities are limited and cannot be guaranteed to be available.

● Youth hostels

1) ***Sabha***, Gamal Abdel Nasser Street, T 27337, 160 beds, family rms, laundry, meals, kitchen. **2)** ***Ghat***, 40 beds, kitchen, meals, T (72) 32360. **3)** ***Hun***, 50 beds, kitchen, T (57) 3379. **4)** ***Brak***, People's Housing Project, 20 beds, kitchen, males only. **5)** ***Murzuq***, T 62, former *Murzuq Tourist Hotel*, 30 beds, kitchen. **6)** ***Umm Al-Araneb***, 120 km from Sabha, 90 km from Murzuq, 30 beds, kitchen. **7)** ***Fejeaj***, People's Housing Project, 60 km from Sabah, 40 beds, meals, kitchen, T (71) 28323.

● Camping

Is unlimited in the desert, though the security services do not look kindly on wild camping by foreigners unless supervised by a Libyan agency. Individual campers should either be discreet in their overnight stops, providing all their needs from their own resources, or ask permission from tourist agencies/local authority *baladiyah* offices in the nearest town. Often school or college facilities can be used by travellers.

There is a growth industry in camping in the S though this is under official auspices. In the SW, the small and efficient private ***Akakus Tours*** agency, T 0724 2804/2318, Tx 2938 Ghat, (General Manager, A Younis, home T 0724 2938) offers visits to the major archaeological sites of the region, especially Garma, under canvas. They will reserve travel to and from Libya, make hotel reservations in Libya, assist travel groups with handling arrangements on site. They offer a number of separate trips, one to Murzuq, Ghat, Obari, Al-Awenat over 8-13 nights, another through Teshuinat in the extreme SE of Ghat over 3-6 nights and another to a 21-night visit through the Libyan-Niger borderlands. Similar visits across into Algeria can be arranged. These desert circuits are designed for fairly rich and very fit Europeans and are an excellent introduction to parts of the Sahara which have been virtually closed to all but a few specialists for the last 20 years.

Places to eat

Eating out in Fezzan is a rather limited experience because local Fezzanese rarely eat outside their own homes. Restaurants and cafeterias do exist adjacent to the hotels and guest houses. In Sabha, Brak and Obari, the range of facilities is acceptable, with 2 or 3 eating places available. Cooking is basic and to local or Arab tastes with either rice or macaroni as its basis except in the few new hotels where forms of international cuisine can be found. In the summer heat, cooking is scarcely worthwhile and there is cold or tinned food available from the small private shops at a comparatively high price. The tourist agencies normally provide their clients with food cooked by their own staff. Eating in private homes is to be encouraged where invitations are received. Here the food is varied, wholesome and often interesting.

Banks

Few banking points in Fezzan deal with foreign exchange, especially any slightly unusual currency or travellers' cheques. Use the main banks in Sabha on the main street or, as a second and not always reliable best, the big hotels which usually have a small branch of a bank in-house.

Chemists

Most small settlements have pharmacies, but it is wise in Fezzan to travel with a comprehensive first aid kit and any personal medical drugs needed. Chemists shops are to be found in all centres and even small villages will have clinics of sorts with some medical drugs available. As elsewhere in Libya, people with special needs should ensure that they carry adequate supplies.

Entertainment

In Fezzan is limited to visiting friends' houses and having the occasional formal civic reception. Otherwise there are a few cafés and restaurants which stay open while customers remain. Most towns have a cinema with films in Arabic. Sports centres, nightclubs and other tourist attractions are altogether absent. For sport, the younger locals play volleyball and football.

Hospitals

Fezzan is well served by health centres, clinics and dispensaries. Hospital facilities are spread thinly, not surprising in a landscape of very distant settlements and low population densities. There are principal hospitals at Murzuq, Obari, Sabha, Al-Shatti and Sawkenah, that is in each district. Some of the smaller hospitals have limited staffing and facilities. On average Fezzan has half the health provision that other parts of the country enjoy. The traveller is warned that, together with a road accident rate far higher than the rest of the country, the overall record of which is very bad in any case, health repatriation insurance is more than usually important.

Shopping

In the Fezzan can be much more rewarding than in all other parts of Libya other than Ghadames. The leatherwork of the region, especially at Ghat, is excellent if at times quaintly crude in finish. The main traditional items are leather handled and sheathed knives, short spears/arrows and Arab slippers of ornate design. Woven date palm fronds are used to make a variety of matting products from fruit basins and rice trays to place mats. Tuareg and other ladies' ornaments are interesting and there is some glasswork. An attempt to resurrect the carpet industry is underway and some patterns are plain but effective.

Travel Agents

There are many **LAA** offices in Tripoli for travelling to Fezzan. The head office at Haiti St, POB 2555, Tripoli, Sales T 606833/36. In Fezzan, LAA has offices at Sabha T 071 23876, at Ghat T 0724 2035 and at Hun T 057 2456. In Ghat, **Akakus Tours**, T 0724 2804.

Local Transport

Bus Within the larger towns access can either be by bus or taxi. Distances are very short since no town is large except Sabha. All the town centres or hotels and the airports are served by bus.

Car hire Self-drive car hire is difficult though this can occasionally be arranged through a travel agent. More normally arrange for a car, preferably a 4 wheel drive vehicle if you are visiting sites off the road, with a driver. This can be expensive and rentals of LD100-LD200 per day are not uncommon. There are many mechanical workshops in the main towns which can repair and service vehicles. Some of the work is rough and ready but most makes of vehicle can be handled. Fuel is available in the main towns and most small villages. Drivers should always set off with a full tank and adequate spare fuel to reach the next large town rather than the next petrol station. Shortages of fuel do occur at individual stations from time to time.

Cycle hire Hire of cycles and motorcycles is not normal though some repair shops will lease them, but not cheaply or readily.

Taxi This can be expensive and prices should be negotiated in advance where possible.

● Transport

(See also Access and travel, **page 662**). **Air** There are regional airports at **Sabha, Ghat, Hun** and **Uzu**, though only Sabha has facilities for international flights. The airport is on the fringe of the town next to the old Turkish fort area. It has been rebuilt as a regional/ international airport. The passenger reception facilities are fair. Scheduled international air services to Sabha, when permitted, include flights from Accra, Alexandria, Casablanca, Damascus, Khartoum, and Ndjemena. Scheduled flights dominate, though some flexibility is now being shown as tourism develops in the S and the tourist authorities seek charter arrangements for direct flights or links through Tripoli. Flights into **Sabha** are mainly by Libyan Arab Airlines. There are 3 flights per day to/from **Tripoli** with supplementary flights on Sat and Sun. Sabha has direct daily connections with **Benghazi, Ghadames** on Wed, **Ghat** on Wed, Fri and Sat, **Hun** on Mon, **Misratah** on Fri and Sun, and **Sirt** on Tue, Thur and Sat.

Ghat: there is a bus from the town to the airport. Facilities here are good for a small site. There is a direct flight to **Tripoli** on Saturday. There are other connecting flights to **Tripoli** and **Benghazi** from **Ghat** to **Sabha** on Wed, Fri and Sat. The flights on internal airlines in Libya are cheap and busy. Booking well in advance is essential.

AL-KHALIJ

Contents

Maps

Al-Khalij (the Gulf) takes its name from the Gulf of Sirte. The province is an artificial creation of recent years and includes the Sirtican coastal embayment together with the routes to and from the entire SE quadrant of the country down to the Egyptian border S of 28°N and the Sudanese border E of 16°30'E. The area of the province is estimated at 730,960 sq km. The province was intended in the period after the coup d'état of 1969 to unite the centre of the country and give a political bloc strong enough to offset the traditional domination of Tripolitania and Cyrenaica. In fact, it has remained as an enormous no man's land around the Gulf of Sirte with a long tail S into the desert, the oases of which retain their individuality from the coastlands to which they were attached.

Climate

In this region the climate is in general Saharan. There are still inadequate data to give precise definitions of microclimate over this very large region. Extreme temperatures run at well over 50°C and lows of well below freezing are experienced, especially at night. Rain is very rare but can come occasionally in downpours inducing flash floods and surface erosion over limited areas. The coast, especially around Sirt, gets a rainfall of more than 100 mm, though this is very erratic and rare wet years are followed by many years of drought.

The Land

The Libyan Desert covers the territory between the 18° and 29° parallels N and the 18° and 28° meridians E. Its N limits are marked by the marginal settlement at Siwa in Egypt and Al-Jaghbub and Gialo in Libya. It comprises a vast sedimentary depression formed of limestones and marine origin clays. The area forms a flat platform with the strata tilted slightly to the N. The only high relief is in the Jabal Al-Awenat in the extreme SE where heights of 1,908m are attained at the Libyan-Egyptian-Sudanese border tripoint. The visible topography of the

Climate: Al-Khalij

	Sirt	Ajdabiyah	Gialo	Al-Kufrah
Mean annual minimum °C	8.6	7.3	6.3	4.8
Extreme minimum °C	2.4	0.0	-2.0	-3.3
Mean annual maximum °C	31.0	33.7	37.8	38.9
Extreme maximum °C	46.7	46.7	49.1	46.0
Relative humidity %	51-84	45-82	26-61	11-61
Mean annual rainfall mm	180.8	126.9	9.2	1.9
Maximum monthly rainfall mm	215.7	102.6	26.2	11.2
Maximum annual rainfall mm	429.5	227.6	50.3	11.9
Minimum annual rainfall mm	6.7	3.4	1.0	0.0

Source: *Speerplan*

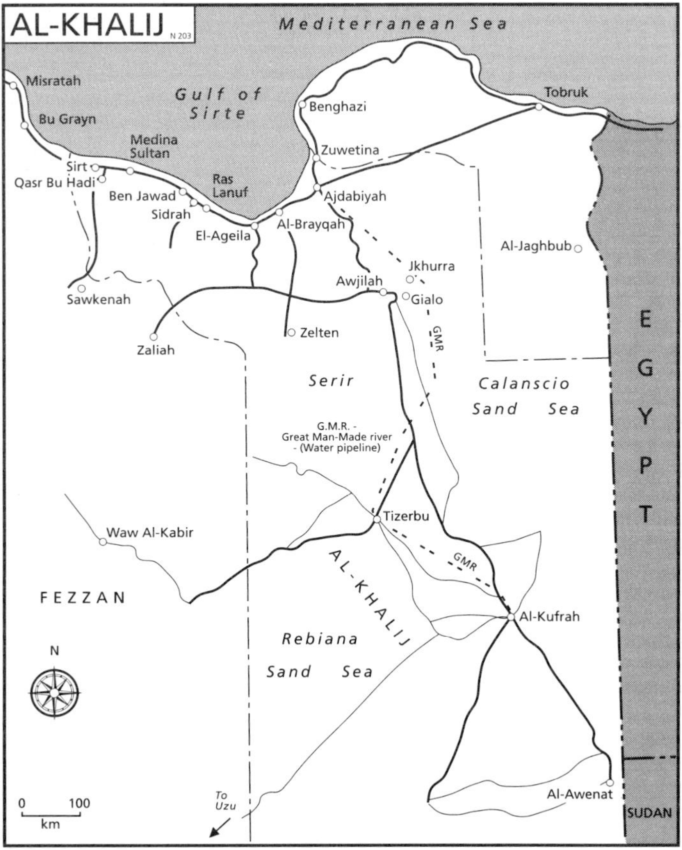

desert is dominated by sand, mainly in the form of dunes in the Jaghbub sand sea and elsewhere gravel desert such as the Serir Calanscio. Al-Khalij includes 2 other major sand seas, those of Calanscio, to the W of Serir Calanscio, and Rebianah, in the SW of Al-Khalij. The coast is also a desert, the Sirt desert made up of a low broken plateau.

The N coastlands are open to access from the sea and the sides. Southern Al-Khalij on the contrary has historically been, and still remains, difficult of entry from outside. Until the 1980s there was no permanent all-weather highway between the main settlement of the S, Al-Kufrah, and the N coast. Even now a single black top road acts as the link between the 2 very separate sections of the province, traversing 876 km from Ajdabiyah to Al-Kufrah.

Population

The Libyan population of Al-Khalij is very small, at best 175,000 and possibly as low as 165,000 in 1990 with a further 40,000-45,000 foreign migrant workers.

These estimates are very imprecise. Growth rates for the area have generally fallen according to UN data to about 3% per year, with the exception of the main coastal urban site at Ben Jawad, where 5.5% growth prevails. Overall, it appears that the country and inland areas of Al-Khalij are approximately maintaining their population size while losing many of their younger people to the coast and to the cities outside the region. The populations of the coastal sub-regions are very concentrated in the urban settlements. In the S the population is also clustered in small villages for security, except on modern farm estates where, incongruously, farms are laid out geometrically across the desert landscape in the teeth of regional social traditions.

Industry

The main towns of the province are the centres of the oil industry at Al-Brayqah, Ras Lanuf and Zuwetina. The only exceptions are Ajdabiyah and Sirt. The former is a route centre where the road from the S joins the coast. Ajdabiyah district contains approximately half the population of the Al-Khalij region, about 100,000 persons, by far the majority in the town area itself. Inland, the main towns are Al-Kufrah, Gialo-Awjilah and Tizerbu, all very small. The new coastal towns and the modern extensions to the S oases are dispersed and reliant on motor transport for communication between the different parts of the town. On the coast, the oil towns are well planned and the residential districts are made up of 2 areas, first the concentrated bungalow towns set up by foreign oil companies for their employees and second, modern towns built by the Libyan authorities at great expense for civil servants and other services. The oil towns are strung along and adjacent to the coastal highway.

The local economy

In Al-Khalij, this comprises agriculture and government services. Approximately 25% of the work force is employed in agricultural pursuits and perhaps 30% in government services. Agriculture is, for Libyans, a part-time activity. The males in Al-Khalij work with a government agency and also labour or manage their own farms in their, often generous, spare time. There are 42,500 ha under cultivation, of which about 11,000 ha is irrigated. Most dryland cultivation and livestock herding is concentrated along the coast, where the rainfall is slightly better and more reliable than the interior.

Inland farming is oasis-based in small fields with associated palmeries. Modern sector large settlement projects have been developed at great expense, the Al-Kufrah project running into several billions of US$. The units are capital intensive, based on water lifted from deep within the Nubian sandstones. The deep wells fed 100 x 100 ha circles of land with water through an automated mobile-rotating arm sprinkler system. They were used first for growing fodder for sheep. The costs were unsupportable and the project was turned over to grain production. Technical and economic problems continued and the units were eventually run down and many abandoned with water switched to supply the Great Manmade River Scheme (GMR).

A settlement scheme was also devised for Al-Kufrah, comprising 5,500 ha of hexagons each made up of 16 farms. The history of the settlement scheme is sad and expensive. Libyans by and large ignored the project and costs ran out of control against a small return in agricultural produce. Other production projects of a comparable kind were put in hand further N at Serir and were also beset by environmental and economic problems. Settlement schemes at Gialo and Tizerbu were also attempted. The residual areas of cultivation can still be seen in these various sites.

Private sector commerce was always important in the province, tied into participation in trans-Saharan caravan traffic. In the period since liberalization of the economy there has been a return by Libyans to shopkeeping, commerce and small-scale manufacturing.

However it is **oil** and **natural gas** which dominate the economy of Al-Khalij. Oil and gas fields are located in the N section of the province, the materials being pumped to the coast where they are exported as crude hydrocarbons or refined. There are many oil-related industries in the region. There is a gas processing plant and oil refinery at Al-Brayqah and another old small refinery at Zuwetina. New refinery capacity has been added at Ras Lanuf, while petrochemical units have been set up at Al-Brayqah, Ras Lanuf and Marada. Installations associated with the oil industry spread deep into the Sirtican embayment towards Waha, Mejid and Serir oilfields.

Al-Khalij's **water resources** are from 3 sources, groundwater, surface *wadi* flow and seawater desalination plants. The coastal zone has a limited and much depleted shallow aquifer. In the S there are very large deep aquifers in the Old Nubian sandstones within the 2 million sq km of the Al-Kufrah basin. The strength of these S reserves is uncertain and it is likely that extraction at present rates will be sustained for only 50 years or so. In the early 1980s it was decided to transfer water from the Al-Kufrah Basin to the N coastlands through a large diameter concrete pipeline, the Great Manmade River, costing some US$7 billion or more. The GMR runs from the S water fields to the coast near to Ajdabiyah and from there along the coast towards Benghazi and Sirt. The object of the line is advertised as principally for agriculture but it is thought by many experts that the bulk of water will only be utilized economically in urban water supply and for industrial end use. The GMR has been the largest development project in Libya for the last decade and the future of Libyan agriculture will rest on how the water is put to use.

Zuwetina is a small, formerly agricultural, centre now overwhelmed by the growth of the oil industry in its vicinity and the influx of foreign workers. The old settlement is sited off the highway to the N, where there are still farmed gardens and some fishing.

The **oases of the S** were never heavily populated. They acted as stopover points for the trans-Saharan caravans. Al-Kufrah was in fact a set of scattered palm grove villages in a large low plain in which water seepages occurred. Recent changes have resulted in considerable building activity both for new agricultural estates on the perimeter of the settlements and administrative, military and other buildings, often rather unsympathetic in architecture.

Tizerbu, see also page 676, has recently been developed, formerly being no more than a fuelling and water point on the route from the S and W Sahara to Al-Kufrah and Ajdabiyah. It now has most services including garages, fuel and a chemist together with urban services such as telephones, piped water, clinics and electricity. It is of little other merit. The **Gialo group of oases** are scattered around water holes some 250 km from Ajdabiyah. Originally very pretty with traditional farms and well laid out palm groves, Gialo-Awjilah has had some development of settlement farms and administrative services. It has fuel, water and limited urban facilities and is well worth a visit (see Things to see, page 675).

ACCESS Al-Khalij is reached mainly from adjacent provinces, though there are direct links in from Chad and Sudan, controlled by the military and not recommended both for that reason and because of the problem of finding safe transport overland. **Air** International flights come to Al-Khalij, mainly via Tripoli or Benghazi, although lateral entry is possible direct from Algiers or via Sabha or other airports when there are external links open for the entry of foreigners. On internal airlines, Sirt links

directly with Tripoli, Benghazi and Sabha, while Al-Kufrah links directly with Benghazi only.

Road access is from the N and still principally via the coastal highway coming in from Tripoli to the W and Cyrenaica to the E. Ajdabiyah is then the gateway S to Al-Kufrah. New roads have been built across the Sirtican embayment to support the oil industry, some pastureland developments and military/strategic objectives by providing a second land link between the 2 main parts of the country and reducing reliance of the exposed coast road. The main artery to the W comes in from Bu Grayn via Waddan and Zella through Marada eventually reaching Al-Brayqah and Gialo. A continuation of this road project continues E to Al-Jaghbub, hugging the N edge of the Libyan sand desert and thence leading N to Tobruk. A second road leads from Tobruk to the S of the Jabal Al-Akhdar the 400 km to Ajdabiyah via Bir Ghiymah. The traveller should be aware that there are a number of roads leading S from the coastal highway at Sidrah, Ras Lanuf and through Bir Zelten. These are private roads run by the oil companies for servicing their oil fields and facilities. They should not be used except with specific permission as trespass might be misinterpreted as a threat to the security of the oil fields.

Sea Theoretically, passengers from ships docking in the ports of Al-Khalij could enter by that route but, other than for sailors taking rare and limited shore leave, this is not open for most travellers.

Things to see

The great deserts of Al-Khalij have an attraction of their own, though they are at least over large areas heavily visited by commercial activities connected with oil and water developments. Even the extreme S is no longer terra incognita in that a major war between Libya and Chad was fought across this region in the period 1980-90. The very light human settlement of the province in past centuries has meant that there is little of human interest by way of monuments to see. Rather, there is a limited number of small oasis sites with a certain charm. Only the dedicated and highly inquisitive traveller can be encouraged to traverse vast distances in Al-Khalij to visit them.

Local information

● Accommodation

Facilities for travellers and tourists in Al-Khalij are minimal. This, after all, is the country's oil producing area and there are deemed to be few sights that a bona fide tourist would wish to see. Even the official tours run by semi-state agencies steer clear of this area. Provisions are for oil workers, workers in the water industry and for service personnel. Most accommodation, transport and entertainment is dedicated to a specific company workforce. There are some hotels but very few that cater for travellers. Ajdabiyah has a number of rest houses and cheap hotels for migrant Arab workers. They are basic but can be serviceable. The traveller to Al-Khalij must be adaptable and willing to accept hospitality where he/she can find it or get official hospitality from a secretariat or other official agency before entering the region. The modest privatization of the economy is opening up better prospects for the availability of accommodation but the easiest way for travellers is to ask at the *baladiyah* (local council) offices for a room in the school dormitory or the youth hostel.

● Youth hostels

Ajdabiyah, near the police centre on the coastal highway, bus 500m, 60 beds, kitchen, T 24017; *Sirt* on Sharah Sawadah, open 0700-2300, 120 beds, kitchen, meals provided, laundry, family groups, bus 1 km, airport 30 mins, T 2867.

● Camp sites

Camping is possible but in the oilfield area this should be done discreetly and preferably with the permission of the owner or the authorities. Elsewhere, camping in the oases can only be undertaken with permission but this is unlikely to be withheld.

● Places to eat

Eating out is difficult except in Ajdabiyah and Sirt where there are local cafeterias or restaurants providing often a limited service in range of meals and opening hours. Elsewhere, the coastal highway has small routestop cafés and cold drink stands where electricity is available. Catering is generally for institutions or households and the eating places are few and far between. Travellers should always have spare food and water, especially on the long inter-centre routes.

Sirt – the western entry to Al-Khalij

This small staging post on the coast road was used by the Italians as an administrative centre. It gained new life following the change of régime in 1969 since Colonel Ghadhafi came from the Ghadafha tribal area close by. Sirt was built up as a military centre and bastion for the government. Developments in communications, industry and agriculture there were given priority. The population of the town and its immediate hinterland is estimated at over 50,000. Development of the garrison and administrative centre has meant the emergence of a completely new, if not entirely well-integrated, town with all services but little of note for the visitor to see. Spreading from the town are a series of valleys and low hills where attempts have been made to develop agriculture, mainly orchards. Sirt has been connected by road to the Al-Jufra oases to the S by a good new 227 km black top road. Sirt has cafeterias, restaurants and hotel accommodation in addition to all services such as fuel, workshops, garages, PTT and medical facilities. Travellers should be careful when taking photographs not to include military installations.

Things to see

Close by Sirt is the unmarked battlefield of **Qasr Bu Hadi** where in WWI the Italians were beaten by the Libyans in a pitched battle. Along the coast is the site of **Medina Sultan** where the remains of a large mosque and Fatimid city have been discovered and partially excavated. Medina Sultan was set up at the point where a trans-Saharan route met the coast at a sheltered anchorage on the Gulf of Sirte coast. Fragments of pottery and inscriptions can be seen on the site.

Local information

● Transport to & from Sirt

Air Air services support the government central administration in the S and there are 2 daily flights from **Tripoli**. Departures from **Benghazi** to Sirt are Mon, Wed, Fri 1745, Sat. Sirt also advertises direct flights internally to **Sabha** Tue, Thur and Sat. A direct flight to **Algiers** runs when the embargo is not in force.

Road By shared taxi or bus along the coast road.

Ajdabiyah and the road to Gialo and Al-Kufrah

Originally a small Arab town, Ajdabiyah has now been developed to the S of the coastal highway as a residential centre for foreign workers and some Libyan staff associated with the oil industry and government services in the Al-Khalij district. It is mainly new but badly maintained with little sense of civic pride. Its utilities including water, telephone, fuel and electricity are good but other services such as hospitals and clinics leave a lot to be desired by modern standards. The concentration of low paid temporary foreign workers, mainly Sudanese, Egyptian and undenominated central Africans has done nothing to enhance the position of the town and, compared with Ras Lanuf new town and Al Brayqah, it has little to recommend it. Shops, mosques and fuel are all available close to the coastal highway and the road is now dangerous for driving given the unplanned, encroaching shops and housing built close to it.

Things to see

At Ajdabiyah there are a number of monuments worthy of a visit. A **10th century Fatimid mosque** existed here, highly regarded because of its external staircase and square block base originally carrying an octagonal minaret. The site is now in ruins. The mosque's courtyard is still visible. The sanctuary façade is composed of a series of niches and there is a single arcade surrounding the courtyard. There are small Roman remains in the form of rock-cut inscriptions, indicating that Ajdabiyah was a significant site long before the Arab invasion. Clearly, however, the Fatimid period was the one in which the city flourished.

● Transport

Road: Bus There is an excellent de-luxe and a regular bus service from **Tripoli** and **Benghazi** as well as intermediate points on the coast road. Buses start their runs early in the morning covering 161 km from Benghazi and 863 km from Tripoli.

Taxi Shared taxis run very frequently from Benghazi. Passengers from Tripoli can find their way to Misratah after having visited other Tripolitanian sites before catching the taxi or bus for the long run to Sirt (463 km from Tripoli and 561 km from Benghazi) and Ajdabiyah.

Gialo

History

Gialo is a centre in the Gialo-Awjilah groups of oases with Jkhurra, Leskerre and Bir Buattifel. The site is some 30m above sea level and lies in a shallow 30 km depression in the desert. Water is available from wells and in Awjilah there was formerly an important spring source. Awjilah was the main trading oasis taking advantage of the routes S and to the coast. It had the largest and most productive palmeries with some 50,000 trees. Gialo has in recent times tended to be the main town of the group because of its prominence on the main N-S routeway and its central position within the oasis cluster. Gialo consists of a number of smaller villages, the main ones being Lebba and Al-Areg. Gialo is renowned for the quality of its dates.

Things to see

Outside Gialo itself, the area is thinly populated and consists mainly of palmeries owned by people living in Gialo, Awjilah or absentee from the district. The rural population of the groups of oases at Gialo is some 20,000, of which about 3,000 are non-Libyans. The Libyan population is almost entirely of Berber origin. There is a unique **mosque** at Awjilah, **Al-Jami Al-Atiq**, built of a series of beehive domes of clay bricks and mud. The building measures approximately 30m x 21m and has been abandoned as an active place of prayer. The minaret has collapsed. On the minaret gallery below there is an inscription in Arabic, 'The witness is here deposited till judgment day, I testify that there are no gods other than God and that Mohammed is His Prophet. May the blessing of God be upon him by Abd Allah Ibn Abdulahmid Al-Qadi 1178 H (1764 AD)'.

Local information

● Transport to & from Gialo

Road Buses and **shared taxi** services run regularly to Gialo from the main station on the edge of Ajdabiyah or from the junction of the coast road with the S road to Al-Kufrah. The road to Al-Kufrah leaves on a clearly sign-posted road from the coastal highway at Ajdabiyah and cuts across the coastal hills and through a series of *wadis* and internal drainage basins to the settlement at Sahabi to Gialo at Km 250.

Al-Kufrah

Al-Kufrah is a group of oases long isolated in the Libyan desert by its very distance from the N and lack of wells on the formidable route to it. The site is made up of 5 major clusters, the main one originally Busaimah, in an enormous elliptical desert depression around the Wadi Al-Kufrah. The basin is on a 50 km axis NE to SW, and a 20 km axis NW to SE. The centre of the oasis is at 475m above sea level. The main oases are Al-Jawf, with 5 km x 3 km of cultivated land in gardens and palmeries. To the E of Al-Jawf is Busaimah made up of 2 small oases and Ez-Zurgh a former slave settlement.

History

Al-Kufrah was a quiet and rarely visited Tibu settlement until 1840 when it was overwhelmed by the Zuwaya tribe from Awjilah who converted the people to follow the Senussiya movement. Al-Kufrah became the centre of the Senussiya when Sayyid Mohammed Ali Al-Senussi moved there in 1894 to escape the influence of the Turkish governor of Cyrenaica. The Senussi thrived at Al-Kufrah and spread their influence deep into the Sahara, developing trade and communications links as they went. Al-Kufrah took on a considerable prosperity. The site was unvisited by non-Muslims until the Saharan explorer Rohlfs called there in 1879. The period from 1911 when the Italians invaded N Libya to their occupation of Al-Kufrah in 1931 was a difficult one. Al-Kufrah's trading base was cut off and the war in the N depleted the resources of the Senussi.

In the modern period, the Italians made a rough motor road link between the oasis and the N and provided landing strips along its route. Al-Kufrah was a staging post within the Italian colonial system linking with its E African possessions. Modern facilities were set up including an airbase, a garrison, a school, hospital and other facilities. WWII delivered a severe blow to Al-Kufrah. It was a base in early years for the Italians and then for the British Long Range Desert Group. The colonial subsidy was withdrawn. Trade never recovered and the place relapsed into a backwater until oil exploration began. The oil industry attracted the people of Al-Kufrah to act as guides and drivers in the desert and eventually a promise was made by Occidental Oil to assist in the development of the underground water at Al-Kufrah. Thus started a series of upheavals which entirely changed the oasis into a form of temporary boom town, overwhelmed local agriculture as a way of life and converted the site into a centre for military and civil government offices.

Things to see

The settlement and production agricultural complexes are still there and can be visited with 4 wheel drive vehicles. The water gathering systems for the Great Manmade River are also visible. Otherwise there is nothing of lasting architectural and historical interest to see. Travel around the outlying oases is interesting and some fragments of the original economy remain to be seen. **Al-Jawf** has all services, including guest houses. Hospitality is best gained from the town council offices if the traveller has not organized a family or official reservation in advance.

Local information

● Transport to & from Al-Kufrah

Air There are internal flights to Al-Kufrah from Benghazi on Mon at 1200 and the return the same day at 1430 connects to Tripoli.

Road Bus The road to Al-Kufrah leaves directly S from Gialo as a well maintained black top highway some 625 km in length. Shared taxis and buses run from Ajdabiyah to Gialo regularly. Visits further S can be arranged but there are less frequent departures. For those travelling from Ajdabiyah to Al-Kufrah via the Gialo-Awjilah groups of oases it might be easier to pick up transport in Gialo for Al-Kufrah. An express bus service is promised on the Benghazi-Ajdabiyah-Al-Kufrah route.

Other desert oases

In the S **Tizerbu** (see page 672), a palm grove oasis 600 km NW of Al-Kufrah is now served by black top road. Tizerbu is an elongated palmery almost 30 km long. It formerly had a tiny Tibu population the remains of whose fort, **Qasr Giranghedi**, can still be seen. Tizerbu has been modernized to manage agricultural development programmes in the oases

The Long Range Desert Group

During WWI the British army in Egypt developed a light car patrol system using Model T Fords and Rolls Royce armoured cars to penetrate the Libyan desert to protect their western flanks against attacks from Senussi armed groups. This activity was the direct military predecessor of the Long Range Desert Group (LRDG) established in June 1940 as the Long Range Patrols attached to the British army command in Cairo. The organization was the brainchild of R.A.Bagnold, who gathered an initial team made up of men with great experience of pre-war travel in the desert to harry the Axis forces behind their lines in the Saharan regions of Libya. Early recruits to the team were taken from the New Zealand Command and it was New Zealanders who remained an essential part of the LRDG.

Each patrol was originally made up of two officers and some 30 men supported by 11 trucks, with heavy machine and anti-aircraft guns, though this complement was later halved. The basic skills of the men of the LRDG were in signalling, navigation and intelligence-gathering. Map-making and the determining of routes through the desert were also important activities for the men of the LRDG. The LRDG patrols went out from Siwa in Egypt to Al-Kufrah in Libya, usually in the early days of the war to bring information of enemy movements in Uwainat, Jalu, Agheila and Ain Dua. On 1 March, 1941, the Free French General Leclerc captured Al-Kufrah from the Italians and the LRDG thereafter used this oasis as their base for the war in Libya.

During 1942 the LRDG was used in association with Major David Stirling's parachute raiders and other commando groups to attack Axis airfields and aircraft behind enemy lines. Its personnel were important in monitoring General Rommel's troop movements in the period leading up to the battle of El-Alamein in late 1942. After the defeat of the Axis army in Egypt at El- Alamein, the LRGD was engaged in attempts to cut off German forces retreating to Tunisia. Once the North African campaign moved into central Tunisia in 1943, the role of the LRDG came to an end.

and some settlement of Sudanese and others has proceeded in recent years.

Al-Awenat lies in the extreme SE of Libya, 325 km from Al-Kufrah, to be distinguished from Al-Awenat in the SW. The town is small and a security point for the Libyan authorities on the frontier with Sudan and Egypt. A new road into Sudan is under debate but nothing has thus far been accomplished. The town has basic telephone, health and other services. Visitors to Al-Kufrah by air should ensure that they have return bookings though there is an LAA sales office in the town, T 28701. Flights elsewhere in the S of Al-Khalij are for oil company purposes and are normally available only to company personnel.

Al-Jaghbub

An oasis lying 230 km inland from Tobruk, Al-Jaghbub is also connected by a new road from Gialo, 310 km away.

History

The oasis was important during the Senussi movement as a centre of resistance to the British and later the Italians. A large *zawia* or religious school was set up there, and the town flourished until the Senussi were forced to go further S to Al-Kufrah in 1895. The town is set in a large basin around Wadi Jaghbub and parts are below sea level forming closed sub-basins. Three main depressions exist, including the W one which is some 25 km in length, a central basin and an E basin. The traditional oasis gardens grow a wide range of irrigated crops such as peppers, tomatoes, potatoes and grain between palm trees. Natural vegetation is sparse with sage bush, and seasonal flora after rain. There is a rich variety of wildlife of the smaller rodents, mammals and gazelle.

Things to see

The town is small, its traditional, often 2-storey, houses made of natural rock and palm trunks. The main **mosque** contains the tombs of the Senussi leaders, Mohammed Ben Ali Al-Senussi, Al-Shattabi Al-Hasini Al-Idrisi el-Majiajhiri. The site of a small **traditional koranic school** can be found, part of the teaching establishment which at one stage in the 19th century made Jaghbub the second most active and famous Islamic religious centre in North Africa. Cars with drivers can be arranged to visit the more distant oases. The area remains slightly run down but still tranquil.

Local information

● Accommodation

Accommodation is difficult though there is provision for travellers at a rest house and the *baladiyah* will be helpful for short-stay guests.

● Transport

Road Buses and shared taxis come from the central public transport stand at Tobruk. Buses seem to run on a twice daily but irregular basis while fairly cheap, shared taxis are always available.

Warning: travel in Al-Khalij

Other than the detail given above on access and travel facilities in each of the small towns of the region, it must be emphasized that Al-Khalij is generally neutral or hostile to travellers and tourists. The desert is unforgiving to incompetence and bad planning. Very great distances separate the few settlements. The climate is increasingly extreme with travel S. Travellers should at all times stick to the black top roads. Off road travel is only for those with several all-terrain vehicles accompanied by a guide and with radio communication. Plenty of warm clothing, water and food should be carried. Travel in public transport during the cool but light hours of the day.

Al-Khalij is not tourist-friendly in other ways. As an oilfield and water source province of the country, it is run by either large commercial organizations, Libyan administrations or the military. The province is not structured for the normal traveller in either its transport or accommodation systems. To get round this, travellers should make arrangements to have their trip made 'official' by co-opting the help of the oil companies or a Libyan authority before arrival. If Libyan tourist companies offer passages through the area this should be used even by the hardened traveller since it will provide basic services from official sources. Local people can be friendly in this area and hospitality may be expected from the regional or town councils or individuals for a limited time.

There are very limited tourist facilities and guides to the area are few.

INFORMATION FOR VISITORS

Contents

● General note

Getting to Libya is not easy. Visa allocation is carefully controlled and mainly confined to those with bona fide jobs in the country. An invitation from a Libyan official agency or individual will perhaps assist the granting of a visa. Tourism is growing in importance for economic reasons, however, and there is a gradual relaxation of controls on this score. To take maximum advantage of this trend, travellers must take up a package from an officially recognised Libyan travel agency. Private visits to Libya can be made but access at frontier posts, for example, cannot be guaranteed except for residents of the Union of Maghreb States (Algeria, Morocco, Tunisia and Mauritania). The UN air embargo on international flights to Libya has added to the difficulties of all travellers.

Before you go

Entry requirements

● Visas

Travellers to Libya need a visa, normally issued at the People's Bureau, embassy or consulate overseas. Applications should be given 10 to 14 days in advance of travel since it is usual for the Libyan authorities overseas to check details with Tripoli before a visa is issued. It is possible to get a visa at the port of entry, though this carries risks of long delays or capricious acts by border officials. Those with Arab passports normally do not require visas. Non-Arabic passports must be stamped with an official Arabic translation of the personal details of the individual's passport. In the UK the Passport Office 7-78 Petty France, London SW1, T 071 279 3434 will do this as a matter of routine on presentation of the passport.

Visa extensions For extensions beyond the normal one-month visa period, the immigration police should be informed and the fact noted in the passport.

Registration Normally hotels register guests on arrival. If visitors are not staying in an official hotel, they should register themselves with the police otherwise they can be stopped and held. Worse, they can be delayed on departure, even missing flights if officials are convinced that malpractice rather than ignorance is the cause of the problem. Immigration and currency declaration forms are needed on arrival. The forms themselves are in Arabic but English translations are available from the airlines. Only the Arabic question form should be filled in with answers in English or French. Copies of the forms should be carefully retained since they will be requested on exit.

Departure Passengers leaving Libya should check that they have a Departure Date Tax Stamp (LD3) available from a marked kiosk in the departure hall and a completed immigration form which is available from the airline desk. At airports all luggage has to be identified by its owner before it is cleared by customs and placed on board the aircraft. There is also a currency control. Only small amounts of Libyan currency may be exported, preferably less than LD10. Any excess Libyan dinars should be changed back into hard currency before passing through the departure gate. Passports and boarding cards should be readily available since police and airline checks can be made up to a few minutes before departure.

Insurance For those travellers not already equipped with travel or other insurance, there are facilities available in Libya directly through the Libyan Insurance Co or the Libya Travel and Tourist Co shop in Tripoli, T 36222.

● Representation overseas

Belgium, 28 Avenue Victoria, 1050 Brussels, T 02 6492113; **France**, Paris, T 45534070; **Germany**, Bonn, T 0228 820090; **Italy**, Rome, T 06 8414518; **Spain**, Madrid, T 01 4571368. **UK**, London T 071 486 8250/071 486 8387, F 071 224 6349.

● Tourist information

Libya is only now awakening to the potential of tourism. Facilities are few and far between. Local tourist offices exist but are generally understaffed and ill-informed. They rarely have useful information, maps or guides. At present the best sources of help and information are the new private travel agencies springing up across the country. They have enterprise and initiative and understand the needs of foreign travellers. In Tripoli contact the Libyan Travel and Tourist Co T 36222 which has an office in Sharah Mizran close by the LAA head office. Other area offices are mentioned in the regional surveys within the Handbook.

When to go

● Best time to visit

The 2 coastal strips of Libya around Tripoli and N Cyrenaica together with the Jabal Nafusah and Jabal Al-Akhdar are all blessed with a Mediterranean climate which makes them pleasant in most seasons. The outstanding times to visit are in the spring after the rains when the ground is covered with flowers and other vegetation and the almond blossom is out. Autumn, too, can be most mild and attractive on the coast after the summer heat.

The ideal time to travel in the S is the period from Oct to Mar, when it is cooler. The summer in the S is absolutely to be avoided.

Health

● Staying healthy

Certified vaccinations against smallpox are no longer required, but prudence demands that anti-cholera and tetanus injections are received before entry. Travellers expecting to travel into the Libyan S might feel that a voluntary, yellow fever injection is worthwhile. Walkers and cyclists would also be wise to take up any anti-rabies protection that is safely available.

● Medical facilities

Libyan hospitals are fairly well equipped but are under-resourced in some critical areas. Travellers must take into account that, with a UN air embargo in place, it is difficult to be airlifted out in case of emergency. There are hospitals and clinics in most towns of over 25,000 population and emergency para-medical services exist to service the main motor traffic routes.

Most proprietary drugs are available over the counter in Libya and chemist shops are to be found in the main streets of all but the smallest of towns (see Chemist and Hospital sections for each of the regions).

● Further health information

See page 19, main health section.

Money

● Cost of living

Libya is an oil economy and it mainly imports its necessities from abroad. Prices tend to be high reflecting this external reliance, some inefficiency in the distribution system and the high level of mark-up by the merchants. Specialist Western foods and commodities like Libyan mutton are very expensive. Eating out is also far from cheap even in the small popular cafés if a full meal is taken. Otherwise fresh vegetables and fruit are moderately priced. Bread is very cheap and tasty. Pharmaceuticals, medical goods and imported high-tech items can be expensive. Personal services from plumbers to dry cleaners are expensive. Travel is comparatively cheap by air as well as land but hotels are few and the even fewer good quality hotels are very expensive. In general, assume that most things will be more expensive than in the USA or Western Europe, though this is offset by the generosity of the Libyans in rural areas in finding accommodation for visitors in public buildings.

● Credit cards

Cards can be used only in a small number of big hotels and in some of the larger travel agents. Cash is the normal medium of exchange and most shops are not equipped to handle credit cards of any kind. Credit cards at hotels are best if not of US origin, though generics such as Visa and Mastercard are normally suitable.

● Currency

The Libyan dinar is the standard currency which is divided into 1000 dirhams. Notes in circulation are LD10, 5, 1, 0.50; coins LD0.25, 0.10, 0.05 and 0.01. There are banks at Tripoli and Benghazi airports. Principal banks will exchange travellers' cheques and currency notes at the official rate of exchange. There is also a black market in foreign currency in which a variable rate is available. The black market is not active at street level and is best avoided.

All travellers should have US$500 in foreign exchange on entry. This regulation is rarely enforced. The Libyan Dinar is only convertible at the official rate inside Libya by official institutions. Travellers have to fill in a currency form on arrival and present it together with receipts of monies exchanged on departure. The system is not watertight or fully implemented but is best observed. Keep receipts from the banks. A sensible procedure is to make sure that you do not leave the country with either more than a few Libyan Dinars or more foreign currency than you arrived with.

For exchange rates at July 1994, see table on page 9.

● Taxes

Provided that travellers do not accept official employment in Libya, there are no direct taxes other than the LD3 exit tax payable at the airport before entering the departure gate. Indirect taxes are included in payments as you go.

Getting there

● Air

Libyan Arab Airlines is the main carrier. Air services to and from Tripoli, the main entry port for the entire country, have been difficult for some years. An embargo on the transfer of arms and strategic materials to Libya by the USA for its alleged involvement in state terrorism in the early 1980s led to a depletion in the Libyan aircraft fleet, which is ageing and inefficient. A number of foreign airlines do not visit Tripoli for political or commercial reasons. In April 1992, the UN Security Council introduced a ban on air traffic to Libya as part of a campaign to bring to book alleged perpetrators of the Lockerbie air disaster of 1988. In normal conditions foreign visitors by air are advised to have reserved firm flights for departure since it is not always easy to get return flights booked inside Libya. It is advised that all entries to Libya while the embargo remains in force should be by land frontier or by sea.

International flights In normal circumstances flights to Tripoli via LAA or other regular scheduled services from Europe arrive from Amsterdam, Athens, Belgrade, Brussels, Budapest, Frankfurt, Larnaca, Madrid, Malta, Moscow, Paris, Prague, Rome, Sofia, Vienna, Warsaw and Zurich. Most of the above are only on a one day a week basis. Alitalia, Lufthansa, Malta Airlines and Swissair are among the most frequent carriers to Libya. There are no direct flights to Libya from the USA, Canada or UK at the present time even when the UN embargo is not operative. Flights to Libya from African points of origin include Accra, Alexandria, Algiers, Cairo, Casablanca, Khartoum, Ndjamena, Niamey, Nouakchott and Tunis. Most Middle Eastern airlines have flights to Tripoli with the main scheduled flights in from Amman, Damascus, Dubai, Istanbul and Jeddah. The other incoming flight in normal times is from Karachi.

Fares The fare structure for flights, when they are in operation, is polarized. Swissair, for example, runs business class only flights to Libya. LAA is also expensive and not easy to get discounts for. Cheapest access by air is via Air Malta. Air Malta or airlines serving the Tunisian S such as Liberté to Monastir or Tunis Air/UK Air/Dan Air to Sfax are amongst the cheapest carriers during the embargo.

● Train

Libya's railways were gradually dismantled after WWII and there are no services within Libya. Libya can be approached by train from the Egyptian frontier as far as Marsa Matruh (**see Egypt, page 841**). On the Tunisian side there are trains from Tunis and the N as far S as Gabès from which travellers can go by bus or shared taxi to the Libyan frontier 188 km distant. Fares on both Tunisian railways CFT and Egyptian Railways are moderate (see page **597** for Tunisia and **page 887** for Egypt).

● Road

Bus These run from Cairo and Alexandria in Egypt and from Tunis and all major E coast towns in Tunisia to the Libyan frontiers. Passengers should cross the frontier on foot and then take advantage of Libyan domestic bus services (see Tunisia, **page 841** and Egypt, **page 593** for details of arrival at the Libyan border posts). Once in Libya, there are 2 main bus transport companies, one engaged principally in long-distance international services and the other plying between Libyan cities and towns.

When leaving Libya the traveller can use the Libyan International Bus Company which has an office behind the Tripoli medina off Sharah Omar Mukhtar to the W of the old citadel, in an area now being cleared of buildings and reconstructed. Buses tend to leave Tripoli very early in the morning, not later than 0800. Passengers should be at the bus station by at least 0700. The buses fill up rapidly, particularly while the air embargo is in operation and buses can leave as soon as all seats are taken. There are 4 main destinations, Benghazi, Alexandria, Cairo and Damascus. Fares are low. It costs LD10 to Benghazi, LD47 to Alexandria, LD52 to Cairo and LD78 to Damascus and equivalents in Egyptian or Syrian currency on return. Most services are run on a daily basis except for Damascus which leaves Tripoli on Tue and Sat only. The coaches used on international runs are of good quality, with a/c and all services provided. Coming into Libya, bookings can be made on Libyan bus lines in Cairo through travel agents. Times of departures can be variable. Otherwise it is as convenient and cheaper, if not so comfortable, to use internal Libyan services once through the international border.

Taxis Both local and international transport is as much in the hands of taxi drivers as the bus companies. In Tripoli, the taxis leave from large stands between Sharah Omar Mukhtar and the sea. They ply for hire normally on a shared basis but can be had for an individual or private group with suitable haggling over the price. On a shared basis they are normally cheaper than the luxury buses and far more frequent in their departures. Driving standards are variable among taxi drivers and good nerves are required of passengers! Travellers entering via land borders are advised that taking a shared taxi is easier and quicker than waiting for the bus. If a bus is preferred, take a shared taxi to the nearest town (Zuara in the W and Solum in the E) and take the bus from there in conditions of comfort.

● Sea

Air travellers can bypass the UN air embargo on Libya by flying to an adjacent country – Malta, Tunisia or Egypt and continuing their journeys by land, using buses or shared taxis or by sea on the regular ferry run from Malta.

Shipping Services The overnight ferry from Valetta in Malta uses modern vessels, usually the *MV Garnata* of 3,672 dwt, with other passenger vessels, the *MV Toletela* of 3,671 dwt and the *MV Garyounis* of 3,423 dwt. Sailing times change monthly and travellers should check with the General National Maritime Transport Co, Ahmed Elsherif St 2, Tripoli POB 80179, T 33155, F 34890, or via Seamalta in Malta on T 00356 23223019, Tx 1210 1321. There are agents for GNMTC in Tunisia, Morocco, Turkey, Italy, Germany, Belgium and Holland. Regular sailings run between Libyan ports and Alexandria and Izmir. Fares vary seasonally and annually and current levels can be checked with GNMTC agents.

● Customs

Duty free goods are available at the main airport departure lounge at Tripoli airport for foreign currencies only. A range of cigarettes, cigars, perfumes, watches and travel goods can be found. No other tourist facilities of this kind are available and offers elsewhere of duty free goods should be avoided as not worth the hassle.

Import-export bans Libya has a stringent ban on the import of alcohol of any kind. It is a pointless risk taking in beer, spirits, or indeed drugs. Severe penalties can be imposed and at the very least passengers can be incarcerated pending deportation. It is rather easier to carry books and newspapers into the country than formerly, though sensitivities remain and it is best not to carry literature which might be misunderstood or thought to be anti-Libyan. Firearms cannot be imported without special permission. Radio transmitters and electronic means of printing will attract official attention and should clearly be for personal use only.

On leaving Libya make sure that you have no antiquities. The Libyan authorities take unkindly to the illegal export of their ancient monuments and penalties for infringement can be ferocious.

When you arrive

● Airport Tax

Is LD3 is payable on leaving Libya. Only Libyan currency is accepted. At Tripoli airport, from which the majority of flights leave Libya, there is a special counter for buying the exit stamp before passing through to the passport and customs formalities. Without a stamp you will be sent back to start the entire process again. (See Documents, page 679).

Clothing

For general guidance, refer to the section on Travelling in Islamic countries on page 27.

There are 3 imperatives on clothing in Libya:

- Do not offend Muslim sentiment by wearing scanty clothing.
- Wear clothes which prevent sunstroke and sunburn;
- Wear clothes that enable you to keep your key documents on your person.

Libyan traditional workday dress, the *barakan*, is a vestige of the Roman toga made up in woven wool material of 5m length by 2m width which wraps round the head and body. This in a country with the world's highest recorded temperature! Scanty clothing is not regarded as sensible on grounds of either religion or practicality. Women should be careful not to leave arms and legs overly exposed. In a country where women dress well in public in both traditional and modern costume, to wear less could be seen as provocative or indicating moral slackness. In any case, outside the main hotels or private transport the need is to be sheltered from the sun, the sand and the glare. Desiccation problems effecting exposed areas of skin can come on quickly and harshly in the summer months for those who fail to look after themselves.

Electricity

Libyan electricity services use a standard 240V system for power. Take an international adaptor plug as socket sizes can vary. Electric power is available in all but the most isolated of settlements.

Hours of business

Working hours vary from summer 0700-1400 to winter 0800-1300 and 1600-1830 in private offices. Official agencies run on a basic day of 0800-1400, though it is always better to start communications with official offices and banks before 0900 since they can become busy or officials can be in meetings at later times. Shops open from approximately 0900-1400 and again from 1630-2030, depending on area and trade.

Official time

GMT -1.

Photography

The large sand deserts, arid rock formations and fine ruins of classical antiquity make photography in the excellent light conditions of Libya a great pleasure. Do not photograph military installations, and take care in photographing women: preferably if male do not photograph women at all. The camera still carries the feeling of intrusion and/or the evil eye in some areas. Film is generally available for 35 mm cameras and most other types of film can also be found in Tripoli. Kodak and Fuji brands are readily available in the capital. Check the 'sell by date'. For specialist and video film try to bring reserves from outside. Beyond Tripoli and Benghazi film supplies cannot be guaranteed.

Safety

This is very good in Libya. Occasional violence causes more noise than damage and walking through the streets is generally safer than in Europe. After dark, and indeed at all times everywhere, in Libya foreign nationals are advised to carry their passports. Libyans are used to foreigners in their midst but their visitors are almost exclusively male. European females need, therefore, to follow a sensible dress code and to act with suitable decorum, especially in Tripoli, to avoid arousing undue interest.

Women A woman travelling alone in Libya must appreciate that this is a totally segregated society, women sit apart and eat apart or after the men. On long distance buses the driver will organize space for the women. As no-one is prepared to speak it can be very lonely. The biggest problem is getting a room in a hotel without a male companion. The bus driver may feel obliged to introduce you to the hotel receptionist thereby giving some respectability, otherwise only the expensive hotels will accept women alone: take this into account when budgeting for a trip. One advantage of a woman being of no significance is the lack of problems at check points and compared with Egypt the lack of hassle. Travel alone in Libya by experienced female travellers can be recommended with the proviso that eventually the sheer masculinity of society and the feeling of isolation caused by the lack of communication makes leaving a welcome relief.

A special warning is necessary to travellers in the S Fezzan. This zone in the Uzu strip and to the S was a war zone until recently and its ownership is still unsettled. There are risks off the road in Uzu of offending the Libyan security officials. Travel in this area should only be with official knowledge. Any abandoned or scattered armament or ammunition should not be touched.

● Shopping

Best buys Libya is more of a consumer society than a producer of goods for export other than petroleum. In the SW of the country, especially in Ghadames and Ghat, craft goods of value are available. Leatherwork, woven palm frond articles and small rugs all have an individual charm. Stamp collectors will find a vast range of interesting stamps available from the main post offices in Tripoli and Benghazi where some small attempt is made to cater for the philatelist.

● Tipping

Is not widespread in Libya and is only expected by those giving personal services in hotels, cafés and restaurants. The normal rate is 10%. For small services in hotels use quarter and half dinar notes. At the airport only use porters if you are heavily weighed down with luggage then tip at half a dinar per heavy bag. Taxi drivers should, unless there is actually a working meter and then perhaps in any case, give a price before starting the journey. Tips for Libyan drivers are not the rule but will be accepted. Foreign drivers in Libyan employ tend to be more demanding of tips. Do not get drawn into bribing officials at any level since it is a sure way of bringing increasing difficulties and possibly severe delays.

● Weights and measures

Libya uses the metric system. See conversion table on **page 17**.

Where to stay

● Hotels

Libya is thinly provided with hotels, even in the populated N coastal area. This is mainly a result of years of state control when tourism was discouraged. The slow re-establishment of the private sector is making for a revival in the hotel trade at the bottom end of the market. Tripoli, the national capital, can boast only 3 or 4 top quality international hotels (*Al-Mahari*, *Funduq Al-Kebir*, and *Waddan*) of which only the *Al-Mahari*, is entirely first class in its services. Elsewhere standards are entirely variable and the regional comments on hotels should be read with care before setting out from the capital.

On the coast there are a number of often well-provisioned beach clubs with residential facilities. They are designed to cater for groups of officially approved visitors but can in certain circumstances be open to all travellers. They are best approached through a Libyan travel agent or a Libyan state organization for sports, youth or scouts.

HOTEL CLASSIFICATIONS

AL US$90+. International class luxury hotel. All facilities for business and leisure travellers are of the highest international standard.

A US$75-90. International hotel with air conditioned rooms with WC, bath/shower, TV, phone, mini-bar, daily clean linen. Choice of restaurants, coffee shop, shops, bank, travel agent, swimming pool, some sport and business facilities.

B US$60-75. As **A** but without the luxury, reduced number of restaurants, smaller rooms, limited range of shops and sport.

C US$40-60. Best rooms have air conditioning, own bath/shower and WC. Usually comfortable, bank, shop, pool.

D US$20-40. Best rooms may have own WC and bath/shower. Depending on management will have room service and choice of cuisine in restaurant.

E US$10-20. Simple provision. Perhaps fan cooler. May not have restaurant. Shared WC and showers with hot water (when available).

F under US$10. Very basic, shared toilet facilities, variable in cleanliness, noise, often in dubious locations.

● Youth hostels

Libya has a remarkable number of youth hostel facilities. They are basic but often available when hotels are not! The locations, numbers of beds and telephone numbers of Libyan youth hostels are given in all regional sections. Opening hours 0600-1000 and 1400-2300 unless otherwise stated. In all there are 27 youth hostels in Libya. The minimum age is 14. Overnight fees for members are LD1,000-2,000 including sheets, breakfast LD500, lunch LD2,500 and dinner LD2,000. The Libyan Youth Hostel Association is at 69 Amr Ibn Al-As St POB 8886, Tripoli, T 45171, Tx 20420 LYHA. Additionally, it is possible to stay in the dormitories of secondary boarding schools during holiday periods. This is best arranged officially in advance, otherwise through the local *baladiyah* (municipality offices).

● **Camping**
Is moderately popular in Libya, though as a mass organized venture through the state. Private camping is less usual except near bathing places on the Mediterranean shore. Here there are picnic sites which double as camping areas. They are crowded on public holidays but otherwise little used. Certain areas near to military camps and oil company installations are closed to all camping and any indications to this end are best complied with. Do not camp close to private farms or housing without an invitation to do so. Whenever possible seek permission from local farmers or land owners before setting up camp.

Food and drink

● **Food**
Eating out is limited to the major hotels. As Libyans prefer to eat at home, restaurants tend to be for foreigners and travellers. The exception is in the use of cafés in the towns where males, mainly younger males, gather for social purposes. On Fridays and holidays, Libyans picnic and buy food from beachside stalls. Libyan cuisine is a Mediterranean mixture with a strong legacy of the Italian period with pastas very popular, particularly macaroni. Local dishes include *couscous*, with a bowl of boiled cereal as a base carrying large pieces of mutton and some potatoes. The best traditional forms of *couscous* in Libya use millet as a cereal though now most meals come with wheat. *Bazin* is a Libyan speciality – hard, paste-like food made of water, salt and barley and is really not recommended except to the gastronomically hardy. *'Aish* is a similar food from the same ingredients but slightly softer and prepared differently. *Sherba* (Libyan soup) is delicious but highly spiced. For the rest, the range of meals is quite sophisticated as in Tunisia, with Italian influences being greatest in Tripolitania and rather more Arab dishes (less macaroni!) in Cyrenaica (see Tunisia, Information for Visitors, **page 596**). Family life is kept separate from public acquaintances, and invitations to dine in a Libyan home are rarely given. Any foreigner invited to a Libyan home should thus feel very favoured.

The offerings in cafés and restaurants will be very limited and mainly made up of various hot meat, chicken and vegetable stews either with potatoes or macaroni. In the main hotels, cuisine is 'international' and very bland.

Good dates and excellent oranges can be bought cheaply. There are olives of a slightly sour taste, apricots, figs and almonds in season, all of which are good value. The smaller varieties of banana are available at increasingly competitive prices.

Restaurant Classifications

Given the variations in price of food on any menu our restaurants are divided where possible into three simple grades:
♦♦♦ expensive, ♦♦ average and ♦ cheap.

● **Drink**
It should be emphasized that alcoholic drinks are banned in Libya. Offers of illegal liquor should be avoided even in private houses unless its provenance is beyond doubt. Local brews or 'flash' can be of questionable quality while traditional brews of *bokha* (a form of arak), or *laghbi* (beer), made from the date palm are illegal and lead to abuse of the date palm. Otherwise, Libyans drink local bottled mineral waters, most of which are not always reliable copies of lemonades, colas and orange drinks available worldwide. In season, real orange juice can be bought from stalls on the streets. These drinks are cheap and widely available. Take a bottle opener since most drinks are in glass bottles. The local tap water throughout much of Libya is slightly brackish. For personal use, buy bottled water such as *moyyah Ben Ghashir* (Ben Ghashir water).

Beverages include Libyan tea, which is heavy boiled thick tea, often with mint or peanuts in a small glass. If ordinary tea is wanted ask for *shay kees* (tea from a teabag) *bil leben* (with milk). Coffees include Nescafé (ask for Nescafé) with or without milk and Turkish (sometimes called Arabic) coffee. With the latter, specify whether you want it *bil sukar* (sweet) or *bedoon sukar* (unsweetened).

Getting around

● **Air**
There are connecting flights to the main cities – easiest access is from Tripoli. See separate towns for details. Book in advance as all flights are very busy – overbooking is common so arrive early. **NB:** the UK Foreign Office has advised travellers to Libya **not** to use internal airlines as a lack of spare parts prevents satisfactory safety standards.

Road

Bus The bus service is excellent including good quality air-conditioned intercity services and more interesting crowded local buses – see individual town entries.

Car hire Is possible in the principal luxury hotels. Availability, costs and contact telephone numbers are given in the regional sections (see Accommodation for Tripoli, **page 620** and Benghazi, **page 647**).

Cycling Travel by bicycle is unusual. Off the main track, cycling is extremely difficult in stony and sandy, albeit flat terrain. Cyclists are advised to be well marked in brightly coloured clothing. Puncture repair shops exist in the towns alongside the main roads at the point of entry, though they mainly deal with cars and light motorcycles rather than bicycles. In the countryside, repair of cycles will be difficult but the profusion of small pick-up trucks means that it is very easy to get a lift with a cycle into a settlement where repairs can be effected.

Hitchhiking Is used in Libya but not normally for a free ride except in emergencies. There are many shared taxis travelling the road and travellers usually make use of these on a paid basis. Private cars or pick-up trucks will act in the same capacity but will expect a small payment in the normal course. Foreign travellers might find themselves picked up for free for curiosity. In general hitchhiking is not to be encouraged since travellers in the S in particular will not be able to hitch reliably. Carry water and other safety supplies.

Motoring Great effort has gone into creating the road system and very few areas of the country are now inaccessible. Drive on the right of the road. Drivers are supposed to wear seat belts and these are checked by the police on entering and leaving Benghazi and Tripoli. Driving in Libya is poorly regulated and standards of driver training are very variable. The accident rate is high by international standards. Visitors should drive defensively for their own safety and to ensure that they are not involved in accidents, especially those involving injury to humans, for which they might be deemed culpable. Drivers can be held in jail for long periods and the settlement of law suits against drivers guilty of dangerous driving leading to death or injury of a third party can be protracted and difficult.

Care is needed in **off-road driving** since there are difficult sand dune areas and other regions where soft sand can quickly bog down other than 4 wheel drive vehicles. Even in far-flung parts of the Jefara Plain, the traffic is quite regular and people are never far away. In the central Jefara there are large areas of military installations which are best avoided. Petrol stations are fairly well distributed but only on the main through roads. Any off road travel should only be undertaken with a full tank and a spare petrol supply. Good practice is never to leave the black top road unless there are 2 vehicles available to the party. A reliable and generous water supply should also be taken. This is especially important in summer when exhaustion and dehydration can be major problems if vehicles need digging out of sand.

Fuel distribution is a monopoly of a state agency and there are petrol stations in every town and at most key road junctions. But, as noted in the regional sections of this Handbook, motorists should ensure that they fill up regularly rather than rely on stretching their fuel supply, since occasionally a station might be out of use for lack of deliveries or a cut in the electricity supply. Travel in the Saharan regions requires special precautions since running out of fuel can be fatal. There is no equivalent of Automobile Club services in Libya but passing motorists are normally very helpful. Drivers should always be aware of the enormous distances between settlements in S Libya and take defensive action to ensure fuel, water, food and clothing reserves at all times (see Surviving in the Desert, **page 40**). International driving licences are normally required though, in most cases, easily understood (English or Italian) foreign licences might be accepted.

Taxis **Individual taxis** are more expensive, more flexible and generally more comfortable over the same distance than the local bus. The taxis do have meters but these may not be in use. **Shared taxis** (larger) are a very popular mode of travel, leaving for a particular destination as soon as they are full. Be sure you have settled the price in advance. If in doubt check with the other passengers. These taxis look quite decrepit but generally get to their destination.

Walking

In Libya other than for point to point travel is not normal. Hiking is to be approached, therefore, in the knowledge that it may attract curiosity and possibly disbelief. Maps of good scale for walking e.g. better than 1:50,000 are very rare and thus travel has to be by sight lines, compass work and common sense. In many areas of the Jefara sighting to topographic markers on the Jabal can be used or lines on the taller minarets in the small towns are distinctive guides. Dogs are not a general problem in Tripolitania except near large farms where they are used for security purposes. Carry a stout stick and have some stones for throwing at approaching aggressive dogs, which is how the Libyans deal with this problem.

● Boat

There are no rental facilities for boats and only a limited few individuals own boats for pleasure purposes. There are small boat marinas at Tripoli and Benghazi for sailors bringing their own boats into port. It is occasionally possible to hire small fishing boats with their owners for the hour or day. Visits to Farwa, for example, near Zuara are only feasible by this means. The opening of new watersport tourist sites for foreign tourists such as at Farwa Island will make boat hire easier in the future.

Communications

● Language

Arabic is the official language throughout Libya. Given the Arab nationalist leanings of the government under Colonel Ghadhafi, Arabic is regarded with some pride as a cultural emblem. Immediately after the 1969 revolution or coup d'état, all foreign language signs were removed, including street names, shop names, signposts and indications on official buildings. The result is that it is difficult for non-Arabic speakers to make use of written signs. In normal circumstances Libyans are most helpful to foreigners and will point out routes and other destinations. Unfortunately, however, it is only the older generation who have colloquial English, French or Italian since the educational system is less good than formerly in teaching foreign languages and fewer Libyans travel abroad than previously. Tripoli City is the least difficult for the non-Arabic speaker followed by Benghazi. The answer to this problem, other than learning the Arabic script and some vocabulary before travelling, is to be very patient asking your way until help is volunteered by a source you can comprehend.

The private commercial sector is likely to be best aware of **English** and **Italian** since companies trade abroad so that calling in offices or agencies can locate assistance in an emergency. **French** is understood widely by the older generation in the SW of country in the areas of Ghadames and Ghat. Italian is still a used language in the Tripoli area. English is probably best used in Benghazi, Al-Khalij and the E where there are many oil industry workers who have rubbed shoulders with English speaking personnel. Language difficulties should not put off potential travellers in Libya since the Libyans themselves are helpful and patient. A few words or phrases in Arabic will ease the way considerably. (See key words and phrases, **page 52**.)

Berber is spoken as a first language in some rural areas, especially the Jabal Nafusah. Tamashek, related to Berber, is spoken by the few Tuaregs in the region of Ghadames. In the deep S around the Tibesti Mountains, the Tibu language is the lingua franca.

● Postal services

Independent Libya inherited a good postal system. Poste restante and post office box facilities are available in the main cities at the respective central post offices. The service to and from Europe, costing LD 350 for a letter, takes about 7 to 10 days in normal circumstances but, bearing in mind the international air embargo, long land transit for mail makes this a much longer and riskier process. Internal mail is cheap, and for in-city letters, fairly fast and efficient. Libya produces a great range of collectors' stamps and there is a philatelic counter in Tripoli main post office.

● Telephone services

PTT facilities exist in all towns and most villages. Internal calls are straightforward, though there can be some waiting time for a public line at the PTT office. International calls from all points can be difficult since there are restricted numbers of lines. The PTT offices in Tripoli and Benghazi are still quicker than trying international calls from private telephones. In-coming international calls, by contrast, are comparatively easy to get through. The **international code** for Libya is 218. Libya internal area codes are **Benghazi** 61, **Benina** 63, **Derna** 81, **Sabrata** 24, **Tripoli** 21, **Tripoli Int Airport** 22, **Zawiya** 23, **Zuarah** 25. Rates for calls are at standard international levels.

Fax and telex facilities are available from luxury hotels and the main PTT offices but suffer from the constraint on telephone lines. Late night automatic fax facilities in private offices are useful if available through friends of friends.

Entertainment

Media

Until very recently the Libyan media were powerfully controlled from the centre. This situation is changing only very slowly so that the media reflect the wishes of the régime. This does not make for good entertainment. Other than programmes in Arabic, which technically and in content leave so much to be desired that most Libyans watch videos or foreign stations via satellite especially CNN, not the regular local television, there is a news broadcast in French and English each evening for approximately half an hour each. There is an occasional sports programme, either Arab or international, shown on TV which is culturally neutral. The radio channel carries programmes of Western music from time to time. The state produces daily broadsheets in French and English together with Arabic language newspapers. Foreign newspapers can be bought though they are often very out of date even when the air system is working normally. BBC World Service news and programmes can be picked up easily in Libya (see frequency chart, 17).

Sport

Libya participates in the various Arab League sports tournaments but facilities for individuals are still very limited. Health centres exist for travellers at a few of the main hotels. Swimming is universally available in the Mediterranean or in the pools attached to the beach clubs in the main cities. Libyans themselves play volleyball for which there are plenty of facilities and football. Horse riding and trotting are also generally enjoyed. There is often a Tripoli Horse Show with international interest, now suspended. A Secretariat (ministry) of Sport exists but its activities are not given priority. The beach clubs near Tripoli and Benghazi have first class facilities for tennis, table tennis and canoeing and other sports. In the smaller towns the schools tend to be centres for sports while in industrial towns some of the companies have their own clubs with squash and tennis courts, for example.

Holidays and festivals

Libya, as Muslim country, observes all the main Islamic festivals as holidays (**see page 30** for details on Ramadan). Fridays are days of rest. In addition there are several national holidays.

- **2 Mar**: Declaration of the People's Authority
- **11 June**: Evacuation of foreign military bases
- **1 Sep**: Anniversary of the 1969 Revolution

Approximate dates for 1995:

- **1 Feb**: Beginning of Ramadan
- **4 Mar**: Aïd al-Fitr
- **10 May**: Aïd al-Aladah
- **31 May**: Islamic New Year 1416
- **9 Aug**: Prophet's Birthday

Further reading

Books and maps

There are few contemporary guidebooks to Libya. The Libyan tourist office is in the process of preparing maps and brochures but nothing was available at the time of going to press. The best available is Michelin Carte Routière et Touristique, *Afrique Nord et Ouest* at 1/4,000,000. Libyan maps of 1/50,000 are available for the main settled areas but are difficult to find except in the university library and the Secretariat of Planning. A very useful book is the Arabic/English language *Atlas of Libya*, available at the Fergiani Book Stores, Sharah 1st September, Tripoli.

There are a few books on Libya which are not essentially political. Of these the best are J. Davis's (1987) book *Libyan Politics: Tribe & Revolution*. On history J. Wright's (1982) *Libya: A Modern History* is a good review while J. A. Allan's (1981) *Libya: The Experience of Oil* deals with oil and agricultural development. On the disputed areas of S Libya books include M. Alawar, (1983) *Bibliography of Chad and the Libyan Borderlands* and J. Wright, (1989) *Libya, Chad and the Central Sahara*.

EGYPT

CONTENTS

INTRODUCTION

Egypt is among the most influential of Arab states, lying at the crossroads of Africa and the Middle East as well on the Mediterranean and Red Sea. This ancient country with a continuous history of over 6,000 years holds a tantalising attraction for travellers. The Pyramids, the Sphinx, the tomb of young Tutankhamen intrigue and enchant while the narrow green ribbon of the Nile cuts its way from S to N through the seemingly endless desert. This is however, only a small part of Egypt: and travellers are recommended to explore the small palm-sheltered settlements in the oases of the Sahara Desert or the empty expanses of Sinai where the coasts are fringed with teeming coral reefs. There is an additional 2,000 km of Red Sea and Mediterranean Sea coast, the former being promoted as an alternative or supplement to a Nile visit.

Basics

OFFICIAL NAME Jumhuriyah Misr al-Arabiyah (Arab Republic of Egypt)

NATIONAL FLAG Equal horizontal bands of red, white and black with a central emblem of Salah al-Din's golden eagle clutching a panel bearing the country's name in its claws.

OFFICIAL LANGUAGE Arabic

OFFICIAL RELIGION Islam

INDICATORS *Population* 57 million (1993), *Urban population* 44%; *Religion* Muslim (mainly Sunni) 90%, Christian 10%; *Birth rate* 32.2 per 1,000, *Death rate* 7.5 per 1,000, *Life expectancy* 59/60; *GNP per Capita* US$600.

Environment

Land

The overall area of the country is 1,002,000 sq km, which is just under half the surface area of Algeria and over twice the size of Morocco.

Egypt's location in NE Africa gives it great strategic importance because it is at the junction of the land routes joining Africa to the Near and Middle East and the sea routes from the Atlantic/ Mediterranean and the Indian Ocean/Red Sea. Its borders abut in the N on to the Mediterranean coast and for much of the E on to the Red Sea. These 2 coastal reaches are separated by the isthmus of Suez, a 150-km land bridge linking the eastern outliers of the Nile Delta with Sinai. The international frontier with Israel runs NW across the Sinai peninsula from the Taba strip at the head of the Gulf of Aqaba, to the coastal plain of the Negev with a deviation to take account of the Gaza strip.

Travellers going into Taba from **Israel** intending to stay in northern Sinai and people going to Israel from Taba only

need border permits. Travellers going from Israel into Egypt or vice-versa can expect 2 frontier checks at either end of the Taba strip. People intending to visit Arab countries should avoid passport stamps at either Egyptian or Israeli border posts here. The border area is clearly marked and the area is monitored by UN forces. Off-shore in the Gulf of Aqaba care is needed not to stray across undemarcated 'frontiers' because the Israelis are particularly sensitive about the possibility of terrorists crossing by sea from the 3 neighbouring Arab countries just across the water.

Egypt's 1,000 km S border is with **Sudan**, see page 811. There is a dispute over ownership of land and economic rights in the Halaib area immediately adjacent to the Red Sea which travellers should avoid. Egypt's 1,300 km long border with **Libya** (see page 835) on the W is one where there have always been periodic tensions. Nomads often smuggle goods across the border in the area between Siwa/Al-Jaghbub and the coastline in the territory of Ulad Ali tribe. The only easy and official crossing point is in the N on the coast road near Sollum. There is some dispute in the Egyptian-Libyan offshore zone about the alignment of the boundary but this does not currently affect either land or sea transport.

Main Regions

Egypt is correctly said to be the gift of the Nile and Egypt's 2 most important regions – the Delta and the Nile Valley – are both clustered close to its water supplies. The Delta lies N of Cairo and is a vast, low, flat triangle of land through which the tributaries of the Nile pass to the sea. South of Cairo the Nile is contained within a rich and fertile but narrow 2-3 km incised valley which eventually reaches Lake Nasser which is a 425 km ribbon of water extending up to and beyond the border with Sudan. The Delta and the Nile Valley contain almost 99% of the country's cultivated land and approximately the same proportion of the population. East of the Nile Valley is the Eastern Desert and the narrow Red Sea coastline. To the E of the Delta lies the formally isolated Sinai peninsula which now has international airports and harbours and is traversed by major roads. West of the Nile is the Libyan Desert which is often referred to as the Egypt's Western Desert. It is broken up by the occurrence of the Al-Uwenat Heights in the SW which extend in an elongated plateau towards the lowlands of Dakhla Oasis, which has larger parallel formations in the N as the Qattara and Siwa depressions which, together with Dakhla, form the eastern edge of the Sitican embayment. The long coastal plain between Alexandria and Marsa Matruh gets narrower towards the W as it approaches the Libyan frontier in the Gulf of Sollum.

Egypt is a country of lowlands and low-lying plateaux of which 60% is less than 400m above sea-level. The few areas of high relief are the Al-Uwenat Heights in the SW and in the Eastern Desert adjacent to the Red Sea coast where mountains rise to over 1,000m. The highest mountain in the country is Jebel Katrinah next to St Catherine's monastery (see page 853) which reaches 2,228m at its summit.

Egypt has the **River Nile** as its only but vital river. The total annual flow down the Nile, from the Blue Nile and River Atbara which both start in the Ethiopian highlands and the White Nile which begins in East Africa's Lake Victoria, is 55 cubic km. Under the 1959 Nile Waters Agreement, Egypt is entitled to take 37 cubic km but, because Sudan so far does not use its full allocation, has been able to take more. There is now growing pressure in all the upstream states for more water and another water crisis is looming.

Egypt has undertaken extensive engineering projects on the Nile over the centuries which reached a peak with work by the British authorities in the 19th and early 20th centuries. In the modern period the Aswan High Dam, (see page 804) which was designed to give Egypt both water storage facilities and hydro-electric power for its new industries, was built with Russian assistance in the 1960s. In fact the low level of the Nile in the late 1980s led to a major crisis and, if flows continue to remain low, there may not be enough water to drive the dam's turbines.

The construction of the Aswan High Dam also reduced the deposition of silt on Egyptian farmlands in the Valley and the Delta. This made necessary the use of large quantities of fertiliser and led to a decline in the offshore fishing production. Despite some initial success in the search for sub-surface water reservoirs under the deserts the River Nile remains the very lifeblood of Egypt. There are no other perennial streams, although wadis run elsewhere after heavy rain as brief but dangerous spates.

Climate

Egypt is a desert country. Even its frontage to the Mediterranean offers only a modest tempering of Saharan conditions in the vicinity of the coast in the Alexandria region. Here rainfall is at a maximum with an average of 188 mm per year with summer maximum temperatures averaging 30°C and diurnal ranges rarely more than 10°C. Moving inland brings a rapid decline in rainfall. Cairo, some 150 km from the sea, has an annual average rainfall of 25 mm, a maximum temperature of 35°C and average diurnal ranges of temperature of up to 15°C. Progression southwards brings even greater extremes. At Aswan rainfall drops away to 1 mm per year and average maximum temperatures rise to 37°C with a diurnal range of as much as 18°C. The profound aridity of Egypt outside the Nile Valley makes it absolute desert for the most part, relieved only where water occurs such as the Kharga, Dakhla and Siwa oases (see page 880, 879 and 841).

The **best time for travelling** everywhere except possibly the Alexandria region is the period Oct-Apr but best of all Nov-Feb. Travellers in Egypt in Apr-May should be prepared for the *khamseen* wind – the wind of 50 days – which blows sand and heat to the discomfort of those caught in the open. Relative humidity can be high (over 70%) on the coast and the Delta. Inland, humidity is not a problem with Aswan, for example, having averages of less than 50% for the whole year and a mere 30% in the summer months. At the height of the summer humidity falls in many places to less than 20%. Climate figures are given in regional sections.

Flora and Fauna

In the desert environment, annual plants have a very short life span, growing, blooming and seeding in a few short days, covering the ground, when moisture content permits, with a patchy carpet of low-lying blooms. Desert perennials are sparse, tough and spiny with deep root systems. Desert animals are rarely seen, being generally nocturnal and/or underground dwellers to avoid the heat. With water from the Nile, an oasis or precipitation in the S the plants are tropical and subtropical and the wildlife becomes more obvious in the form of small and medium size mammals like rats and the Egyptian mongoose with a tuft on the end of its tail. Bird life proliferates by the water, with roosting egrets, herons, kingfishers and hoopoes all very common. The birds of prey range in size from kestrels to black kites and Egyptian vultures. The number of Nile fish is decreasing but the coasts continue to teem with fish.

Agriculture

Agriculture is the basis of the Egyptian economy accounting for 20% of total national output and 43% of employment. Despite very rapid urbanization, farming and the rural community remains at the cultural heart of the country. Current land patterns show the vital importance of the Nile Valley and Delta because the rest of the country is little better than waste land. Unfortunately even this very limited arable area is being reduced by the encroachment of Cairo and other urban areas.

Land Use	**(%)**
Arable and orchards	2.6
Forests	0.0
Meadows and pastures	0.6
Desert, waste and other	96.8
Total	100.0

Source: FAO

Land tenure

Until the 1952 land reforms, 1% of Egypt's land owners possessed 90% of the farming land. The reform stripped the former royal house of its lands and the state took the estates of the great families who had controlled rural Egypt. In their place the revolutionary authorities established centrally controlled co-operatives which substituted civil servants for the former landlords, a move which did little to alter the agricultural system or indeed benefit the peasants. At the present time the peasantry is either landless or has tiny fragments of land which are mainly uneconomic. The average availability of land per cultivator is put at 0.35 ha. Attempts to reclaim land in the desert regions using underground water and high technology irrigation systems have, at best, been of marginal use in resolving Egypt's shortage of agricultural land. Many Egyptian farmers now emigrate to adjacent countries and travellers in North Africa will come across large numbers of Egyptian *fellahin* (peasants) working the land and undertaking manual labour in Libya.

Potential

Egypt's potential is hindered by its paucity of natural resources which, besides oil and natural gas produced in large enough quantities to meet domestic demand and some exports, are limited to iron, phosphate and a few other non-hydrocarbon minerals. The principal difficulty for Egypt, however, is its meagre area of fertile land and its reliance on the waters of the Nile. The growth of irrigation and hydro-electric schemes in the Upper Nile countries is putting Egypt's supply at risk and there is no available substitute. Industrialization has some scope for expansion but the past record here is not encouraging.

Ultimately it seems that Egypt will have to continue to rely on its current principal sources of foreign exchange – tourism, Suez Canal fees, and expatriate remittances – for its economic salvation. Unfortunately all 3 are dependent on stable political conditions in Egypt and the rest of the Middle East

The final problem for Egypt is that economic growth has to exceed its 2.5% annual population increase which implies no mean rate of development simply to stand still. For some years Egypt has relied, and will have to continue to rely, on predominantly US and European foreign aid for the 70% of food supplies needed annually from abroad to enable it to feed itself.

People

The Arab Republic of Egypt had a population of 56,984,000 in mid-1993. The growth rate of Egypt's population remains a sensitive matter given the difficulties of the government in providing jobs and feeding the people. It had seemed in the 1970s that the annual rate of increase was tailing off at 2.1% per year but there was a spurt again in the mid-1980s to 2.9% per year, which decreased the time in which the population will double to only 24 years. There are currently indications that the rate of increase has fallen back slightly with 2.3% as an estimate for 1993. In the recent past there were high levels of emigration to the oil-exporting states of the Persian Gulf but this diminished during the Gulf war and has not fully recovered. Meanwhile, the crude death rate has fallen over the last 25 years and life expectancy at birth has gone up thus adding to the growth of the population size.

Racial origins

Egyptians living in the Nile Valley between Aswan and the sea have ancient origins. It is speculated that the people of the Nile Valley were of Berber origin with some Arab and Negroid admixtures. The people of the Delta had a slightly different early history and thus had distinct racial origins in which Armedoid and Arab elements were fused with the other peoples of the Nile. Other racial additions were made from invasions from Libya, then from the desert lands of Arabia and Persia in the E, and finally the Mediterranean connections which is most graphically illustrated by the Alexandrine conquest and the Roman establishment in N Egypt. Present day Egyptians see themselves as having common racial and cultural origins which increasingly are not identified absolutely with the Arabs and Arab nationalism as a whole.

Distribution/density

The Egyptian population is concentrated in the Nile Valley and Delta where 98% of people are found. Average densities are put at 56 people per km sq but in Cairo and the irrigated lands densities of many thousands per km sq are recorded.

Age groups

The population is youthful with 42% under the age of 15, 52.5% in the working age group 15-59, and 5.5% over 60. Literacy is high at 48.4%, with males at 62.9% being better placed than women at 33.8% literate.

Income per head

Egyptian income is put at US$610 per head of population. UN sources suggests that there was a sprightly level of growth of 3.6% per year in real personal incomes in the 1980s, stimulated by inflows of earnings from workers abroad. This has probably not been sustained into the 1990s.

History

"*There is no country which possesses so many wonders.*"– Herodotus, 450 BC.

For tens of thousands of years the focal point of Egyptian life has been the River Nile. The availability of this vast supply of water permitted the creation of a society which produced the wonders of ancient Egypt. Today modern Egypt depends on the river to support its huge population. The Nile continues to be 'the lifeblood of Egypt'.

About 3100 BC, **King Menes** succeeded in uniting Upper and Lower Egypt into a single kingdom. His new capital at **Memphis**, about 15 km to the S of modern-day Cairo, was deliberately located on the border of Upper and Lower Egypt. Despite this the rivalry between the two parts of Egypt continued until the end of the Early Dynastic Period (3100-2686 BC).

The **Old Kingdom** (2686-2181 BC) began with the 3rd Dynasty by which time the sun-god Ra was the most revered deity. Until then it was common practice for leaders to be buried in underground mausoleums (*mastabas*). In the 27th century BC **King Zoser** and his chief architect **Imohotep** constructed the first **step pyramid** in Saqqara, the huge necropolis across the river from Memphis, and pyramids became the principal method of royal burial for the Pharaohs during the next millennium. The scale of organization required to mobilize the resources and manpower to build these phenomenal pyramids is testimony to the level of sophistication of this period. The three 4th Dynasty (2613-2494 BC) giant pyramids of Cheops, Chephren and Mycerinus erected on the Giza plateau still awe the world.

By the end of the Old Kingdom, the absolute power of the Pharaohs declined. Local leaders ruled their own *nomes* (provinces) and a second capital emerged at Heracleopolis. Few great monuments were built in this very unstable **First Intermediate Period** (2181-2050 BC).

During the 11th Dynasty **Menutuhotep II** reunited the country and created a new capital at **Thebes** (Luxor). Remains from this era, the **Middle Kingdom** (2050-1786 BC), demonstrate its prosperity.

During the 5 dynasties of the **Second Intermediate Period** (1786-1567 BC), central authority again disintegrated and Egypt was controlled briefly by Asiatic kings known as the **Hyksos** (foreign princes) rulers.

The **New Kingdom** (1567-1085 BC), spanning the 18th-20th Dynasties and based at Thebes, ushered in a period of unparalleled wealth and power. During these 400 years the Kingdom prospered and expeditions led to the creation of a huge empire. The temple complex of Karnak and the Valley of the Kings are but 2 of the astounding remains of the era. During this period (1379-1362 BC), Akhenaten renounced the traditional gods in favour of a monotheistic religion based on the sun-god Ra but his boy-king successor **Tutankhamen** immediately reverted to the former religion and its principal god Amun. In 1922 archaeologists discovered Tutankhamen's undisturbed tomb and its treasures are displayed in Cairo.

During the **Late Dynastic Period** (1085-332 BC), the succession of dynasties, some ruled by Nubians and Persians, became so weak that **Alexander the Great** had little difficulty in seizing the country. Although he did not spend long in Egypt his new capital city of Alexandria still flourishes. His empire was divided among his generals and Ptolemy established the Ptolemaic Dynasty (332-30 BC) which ended with the reign of Cleopatra VII (51-30 BC), the last of the Ptolemies, before Egypt became a province of the **Roman Empire**.

The division of power between Rome and Constantinople resulted in the virtual abandonment of Egypt. Egypt's autonomy led to the development of the **Coptic church** which was independent from both the Byzantines and the Romans, and whose calendar dates from 284 AD when thousands were massacred by the Roman emperor Diocletian.

The **Muslim** seizure of Egypt in 642 AD was, despite the introduction of Islam, broadly welcomed by the Copts in preference to remaining under the Byzantine yoke. Islam slowly prevailed as did the introduction of Arabic as the official language. Cairo became the seat of government and emerged as a new Islamic city. Whilst the seeds of Islam itself strengthened and blossomed there were centuries of political instability which led to the creation of countless dynasties, mainly ruled by foreign Muslim empires. The new faith was only fleetingly threatened when the Christian Crusader armies attacked Cairo and were repelled by Salah al-Din (1171-1193 AD).

The **Ottomans** absorbed Egypt into their Empire in 1517 and met with little resistance. The Mamlukes, a class of Turkic slave-soldiers, had already governed Egypt between 1250-1517 AD so Ottoman rule changed little. A significant proportion of tax revenues were remitted to Constantinople but day to day power remained in Mamluke hands. In the first centuries of Ottoman suzerainty of Egypt the nation flourished. Elaborate mosques were added to the already diverse cultural heritage. Later, as Britain and France sought to extend their empires, Egypt became subject to their designs.

After a vicious power struggle, Mohammed Ali (1805-1848) became Pasha. He sought to implement dramatic reforms which would drag Egypt from the Middle Ages into the modern world. Unfortunately economic mismanagement by his successors and the continuing Anglo-French rivalry over the country actually brought Egypt to her knees. The French-inspired Suez Canal linking the Mediterranean and the Red Sea, completed in 1869, bankrupted the country and led to its subsequent temporary control by Britain in 1882.

At the beginning of **WWII**, the potential vulnerability of the Suez Canal and the strategic implications of the Turkish-German alliance led **Britain** to increase its control over Egypt by declaring it a Protectorate. This led to the emergence, over the following 20 years, of both Arab and Egyptian nationalist movements which eventually procured semi-independent status for Egypt in 1936.

In 1952 the constraints of the **British Mandates** and the frustration following the defeat in the 1948 Arab-Israeli war led to the emergence of a new class of young army officers who staged a bloodless coup overthrowing King Farouk and ousting the remaining British troops. The new leader, Colonel Gamal Abdel Nasser, inherited a politically fragmented and economically weak state burdened with an ever-increasing demographic problem.

When the World Bank, at the behest of the USA, refused to help finance the construction of the new Aswan High Dam in 1956 Nasser nationalized the Suez Canal in order to raise the necessary revenues. This led to shock waves throughout the world and to the **Suez crisis** in which an Anglo-French force invaded and occupied temporarily the Canal zone. Nasser's dreams of development were hampered by Egyptian/Israeli tensions including the shattering Egyptian defeat in the 1967 war. He died

Dynasties In Egypt Up To 30 BC

(with rulers as mentioned in text)

Early Dynastic Period (3100-2686 BC)

Ruler	Date
First Dynasty	*3100-2890 BC (Memphis established)*
Menes	
Second Dynasty	*2890-2686 BC*

The Old Kingdom (2686-2181 BC)

Third Dynasty	*2686-2613 BC*
King Zoser	2667-2648 (Step Pyramid in Saqqara)
Huni	
Fourth Dynasty	*2613-2494 BC* (Pyramids of Giza)
Sneferu	
Cheops (Khufu)	
Chephren (Khafre)	
Mycerinus (Menkaure)	
Shepseskaf	
Fifth Dynasty	*2494-2345 BC*
Unas	
Pyramids of Abu Sir	
Sun Temples of Abu Gharub	
Sixth Dynasty	*2345-2181 BC*
South Saqqara necropolis	
Teti	
Pepi I	
Pepi II	

First Intermediate Period (2181-2050 BC)

Seventh Dynasty	*2181-2173 BC*

Middle Kingdom (2050-1786 BC)

Eleventh Dynasty	*2050-1991 BC*
King Menutuhotep II	Creation of Thebes (Luxor)
Twelfth Dynasty	*1991-1786 BC*
Amenemhat I	1991-1961
Senusert I	1971-1928
Senusert II	1897-1878
Amenemhat III	1842-1797
Queen Sobek-Nefru	1789-1786

Second Intermediate Period (1786-1567 BC)

Fifteenth Dynasty	*1674-1567 BC (capital Avaris)*

New Kingdom (1567-1085 BC) based on Thebes

Eighteenth Dynasty	*1567-1320 BC (Temples of Luxor & Karnak)*
Amenhotep I	1546-1526
Tuthmosis I	1525-1512
Tuthmosis II	1512-1504

Hatshepsut	1503-1482
Tuthmosis III	1504-1450
Amenhotep II	1450-1425
Tuthmosis IV	1425-1417
Amenhotep III	1417-1379
Amenhotep IV (Akhenaten)	1379-1362
Tutenkhamen	1361-1352
Ay	1352-1348
Horemheb	1348-1320
Nineteenth Dynasty	***1320-1200 BC***
Ramses I	1320-1318
Seti I	1318-1304
Ramses II	1304-1237
Seti II	1216-1210
Twentieth Dynasty	***1200-1085 BC***
Sethnakht	1200-1198
Ramses III	1198-1166
Ramses IV	1166-1160
Ramses V	1160-1156
Ramses VI	1156-1148
Ramses VII	1148-1141
Ramses IX	1140-1123
Ramses XI	1114-1085

Late Dynastic Period (1085-332 BC)

Twenty-second Dynasty	***945-715 BC***
Twenty-fifth Dynasty	***747-656 BC***
Shabaka	716-702
Twenty-sixth Dynasty	***664-525 BC***
Necho II	610-596
Twenty-seventh Dynasty	***525-404 BC (Persian occupation)***
Cambyses	525-522
Darius I	521-486
Thirtieth Dynasty	***380-343 BC***
Nectanebo I	380-362
Nectanebo II	360-343

Late Period (332-30 BC) (Macedonian Kings, capital Alexandria)

Alexander III (The Great)	332-323
Philip Arrhidaeus	323-317
Ptolemaic Era	***323-30 BC***
Ptolemy I	Soter 323-282
Ptolemy II	282-246
Ptolemy III	246-222 (Edfu Temple)
Ptolemy IV	222-205
Ptolemy V	205-180 (Kom-Ombo Temple)
Ptolemy VII	180-145
Ptolemy VIII	170-145
Ptolemy IX	170-116
Ptolemy XIII	88-51
Cleopatra VII	51-30

in 1970 and was succeeded by **Anwar Sadat**. Sadat was aware that Egypt could not sustain the economic burdens of continual conflict with Israel so, despite the partially successful Oct 1973 war which restored Egyptian military pride, sought peace with his neighbour. In 1977 he made a historic trip to Jerusalem and laid the foundations for the 1979 **Camp David Peace Accords** which enabled Egypt to concentrate on her own economic development. While he was applauded abroad he was considered a traitor in the eyes of the Arab world and Egypt was diplomatically isolated. His assassination by Islamic fundamentalists in Oct 1981 brought vice-president **Hosni Mubarak** to power.

Modern Egypt

Government

Egypt became a republic in 1952 with a presidential system of government. The current president is Hosni Mubarak who has effective control of the armed forces and the cabinet and can convene or dissolve the single People's Assembly virtually at will. President Mubarak is also head of the ruling National Democratic Party (NDP). There have been efforts to introduce an element of democracy into government with general elections for the People's Assembly. The cabinet is led by Atef Sedki but the principal influence on the membership of the cabinet is the president. The Assembly has worked well but, until recently, was seen as a puppet organization for the régime. The speaker of the Assembly was assassinated in Oct 1990. There was an attempt in 1991 to improve local administration with the appointment of a new minister. Regional government is carried out through 4 groups of administrations – the governorates for the Desert, Lower Egypt, Upper Egypt and the urban areas. Sub-districts operate from regional capitals and separately for the cities of Port Said, Alexandria, Cairo and Suez. The administration is very bureaucratic and slow. There have been generally fruitless attempts to reform the civil service but, with 22% of the work force in public administration and defence, progress has been slow. Travellers should not have high expectations of officials and official agencies, though there are some institutions, mainly military, which function well. Personal influence is a key element in making the system work.

The government is only partially representative of the people and there are major dissident groups whose activities could affect the traveller. The **Muslim Brotherhood** – a form of fundamentalist Islamic organization – has flourished in Egypt for many years. While the Muslim Brotherhood is now the leading opposition group and is tolerated by the government the more extreme splinter groups, which have resorted to terrorism, are not (**see page 32**). In addition to attacking members of the government, often successfully, the extremists are opposed to corrupt foreign influences, of which the excesses of the tourist industry, including the country's 20,000 belly dancers, are seen as a key part. Opposition groups are suppressed by severe laws such as the detention regulations and by an ever-present security service, the **mokhabarat**.

WARNING Travellers should bear in mind this aspect of security during their stay in Egypt and not act in ways that exacerbate local Muslim sensitivities.

Economy

Traditional agriculture

The great mass of Egyptian farmland is under traditional forms of agriculture and worked by the *fellahin*, the Egyptian peasantry. Farming is based on use of the waters of the Nile for irrigation which are now available, theoretically, throughout the year from Lake Nasser. In fact, approximately 65% of Egypt's agricultural land is under perennial cultivation and the remainder carries only one crop each year and/or is under a cultivation/fallow rotation. There has been a gradual increase in production of commercial crops but self-sufficiency is an important aim of small farmers. Wheat, melons, vegetables and fodder are the main crops, the latter to support the considerable number of draught (2.55 million buffalo), transport (2 million asses and 200,000 camels) and other animals (3.5 million cattle, 4.5 million goats, and 4.9 million sheep) kept mainly on farms. It is estimated that 5 million people are engaged directly in the traditional farming sector.

Modern Agriculture

Modern farming is principally a matter of the operations of the centrally managed co-operatives on 'reformed' land and the activities of the mixed farms on recently reclaimed land in the rimlands of the delta and the newlands in the desert interiors. The co-operatives are still managed with a large participation by the government, who control the crops within the central rotation and handle credit and technical matters. These farms have been turned over to commercial crops for the most part–cotton, sugar cane, maize and rice, some destined for export. The newland farms specialise in exploiting the opportunities for early cropping for the supply of fruit and vegetables to the European market. The new farms stand out in the landscape with their contemporary buildings and rectangular field patterns.

Agricultural Output	('000 tonnes)
Sugar Cane	11,095
Maize	5,270
Wheat	4,483
Rice	3,152
Tomatoes	1,592
Water melons	1,400
Sorghum	655
Dates	560
Onions	493

Source: FAO

Energy/Petroleum

Egypt has made major strides in the petroleum industry in recent decades without, however, joining the league of principal oil-exporters. Reserves of crude oil are put by the Egyptian authorities at 6,200 million barrels, about 0.6% of the world's total, and are given a life span of possibly 19 years. Production of crude oil ran at 925,000 barrels per day in 1992, approximately 1.5% of the world total. Crude sales abroad are important, accounting in 1991 for 52% of all exports. Natural gas resources are only slightly less significant than oil with reserves of 4,000 million cubic m and output at 8.8 million tonnes of oil equivalent in 1992. The oilfield areas are widely distributed among the Suez/Sinai zone to the E and the more recently discovered Western Desert fields. Western oil companies play a key role in oil development in Egypt. The Aswan High Dam supplies a sizeable proportion of the country's total electricity of 39,550 million kwh/y.

Economic Plans

Egypt was an early devotee of development planning, reinforced by the desire for a socialist centrally controlled economy under Gamal Abdel Nasser, the first president after the 1952 revolution. The plans were taken seriously and great efforts were made to use national resources to beat the twin difficulties of shortages of domestic natural resources and a burgeoning population. Some successes were won but the constant involvement of the country at the forefront of the Arab-Israeli wars diverted attention, funds and materials away from the economy. Under President Sadat the dedication to centralized control was gradually watered down and the plans became little more than indicative long-term budgets. Strategies were set at the top – development of the Suez Customs Free Zone under Sadat and privatization under Mubarak. The latest development plan for the period 1990/95, continued emphasis on growth of the private sector including the transfer to it of some state assets. The government has limited means at its disposal to promote economic expansion given the high costs of debt repayment at US$2.95 billion and defence US$2.07 billion, together representing 31.4% of the budget for 1992/93 fiscal year.

Industry

Since the time of the 1952 revolution, there has been a growing tendency to turn to industrialization as a means of achieving faster economic growth and providing for the needs of an expanding population. Most industries were then state-owned, carried very large workforces and were inefficient. The country did nonetheless lay the basis for iron & steel, automobile and petrochemical sectors. Industry was concentrated around Cairo and its outliers such as Helwan. In recent years Egypt has industrialized steadily through a growth of small, private and/or foreign funded plants producing consumer goods, textiles, arms and processed foodstuffs. These factories are often highly efficient. Egypt has still however to diversify effectively into industry. In 1990 oil, mining and manufacturing together accounted for 21.8% of the value of national output and employed 16% of the work force. The country was a long way from achieving its ideal of being the manufacturing centre for the Arab world.

Industrial output 1990/91	(tonnes)
Cement	16,650,000
Fertilizers	6,100,000
Iron	1,560,000
Sugar	973,000
Soap/detergent	383,000
Cotton yarn	305,000

Source: Encyclopaedia Britannica

Trends in the economy

Economic growth has been erratic, but mainly too low to enable the economy to reach a level of self-sustaining development. The most significant change in fortunes came in 1991 when its US$5.8 billion military debt to the USA was written off and a separate debt of US$7 billion owed to the Arab oil-exporters was also liquidated in acknowledgement of Egypt's positive role in the Gulf War, thereby removing at a stroke part of the heavy foreign debt burden on the economy. Egypt continues to borrow overseas and the trend towards external dependence has not been fully reversed.

Economic structure 1991	(%)
Trade & finance	24.0
Mining & manufacturing	21.8
Agriculture	19.6
Other services	15.8
Transport/communications	10.0
Construction	5.0
Utilities	3.8
Total	100.0

Source: IMF

Recent policies, enforced by the IMF, are designed to rid the state of its ownership of economic assets, to expand the private sector and remove distortions in the economy arising from subsidies and re-

Economic Indicators

	1989	1990	1991
GDP (E£ million)	45,419	47,911	50,177
Imports (E£ million)	24,831	34,300	21,849
Exports (E£ million)	5,715	9,900	8,606
Trade Balance (E£ million)	-9,228	-15,389	-10,932
Foreign Debt (US$ billion)	39.8	32.2	40.6
Inflation (1985=100)	221.5	247.0	295.9
Population (million)	51.8	53.2	53.6

Source: IMF

strictive practices. Domestic food production has risen but food output per head fell back in 1991 to the level of the 1980s. Tourism was badly affected by the Gulf War but income on this account recovered slightly in 1992 to some US$1.6 billion. The use of the Suez Canal continued to increase with income standing at a budget estimate of US$9.27 billion in 1992/93. Moderately good flows of water in the upper Nile catchment area improved the reserves in Lake Nasser and offer some certainty for agricultural output.

CAIRO

Contents

Maps

Cairo today is the result of many different cities which have been built on top of one another over the centuries and a cosmopolitan population with connections far beyond the Arab world. It is a teeming mega-city with an estimated 14 million people living in a fabric designed for 2 million. Standing at the crossroads of Africa and the Middle East it has dominated the region for centuries.

Population 6.5 million (1986). *Altitude* 75m.

History

Since the Arab conquest in 641 AD most Egyptians have called both the city and the whole country **Misr**, (pronounced Masr), which was the ancient Semitic name for Egypt and was also mentioned in the Koran. Having rejected Alexandria as the capital of his Egyptian province, because it was considered a Christian stronghold, the Arabs chose **Fustat** (encampment) in the middle of modern-day Cairo as their administrative and military capital. Consequently Cairo rapidly grew in size and importance and it is thought that the name Misr was used in order to distinguish the new city from the many other towns called Fustat in the Arab world. **Al-Qahira** (the Conqueror), which is the city's official but less commonly used name, is derived from Al-Qahir (Mars) because the planet was in ascendance when the Fatimids started the construction of their new city in 971 AD. **Cairo** was the Latin version of the name which was given to the city in mediaeval times and has since stuck.

Although the city of Cairo is younger than Alexandria the surrounding region has a very ancient and impressive past. **Memphis**, which lies 15 km S of Cairo across the Nile, was established as the capital in 3100 BC because of its geographical and symbolic position in controlling both Upper and Lower Egypt. It was during this period that the huge necropolis was developed across the river on the W bank first at Saqqara and then at the site of modern-day Giza where the largest pyramids were built (see Pyramids, **page 741**).

Memphis was temporarily eclipsed by the new capital of **Thebes** (Luxor)

Climate: Cairo

	Jan	Feb	Mar	Apr	May	Jun	Jul	Aug	Sep	Oct	Nov	Dec	Av/Tot
Av Max (°C)	19	21	24	28	32	35	35	35	33	30	26	21	28
Av Min (°C)	9	9	12	14	18	20	22	22	20	18	14	10	16
Av Rain (mm)	4	4	3	1	2	>1	0	0	>1	1	3	7	25

Source: UK Meteorological Office.

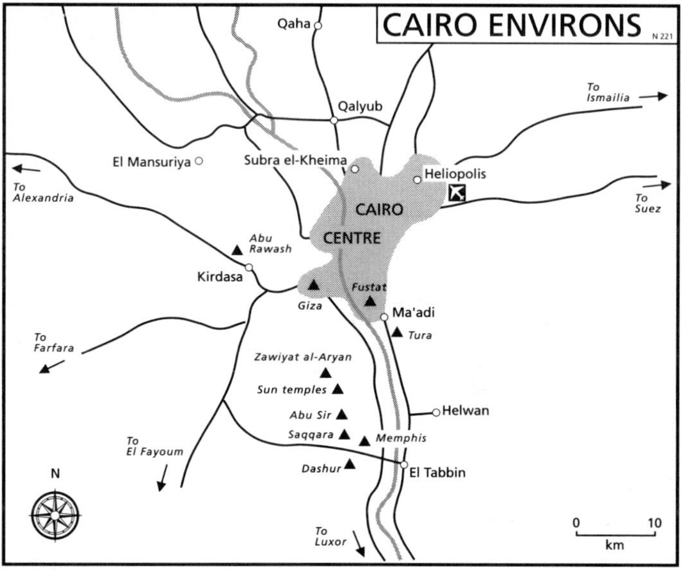

during the New Kingdom. Then another cult centre known as On, or **Heliopolis** to the Greeks and later Aïn Shams (Spring of the Sun) by the Arabs, was developed further N when a canal was cut between the Nile and the Red Sea. Although the gradual westward movement of the Nile left it stranded and miles from the river, a small E bank fortress which became known as **Babylon in Egypt**, was expanded during the Persian occupation (525-404 BC). At the time of the Roman occupation in 30 BC the fortress had been deserted and Memphis was still the country's second city after Alexandria. Recognising the strategic importance of the site, the emperor Trajan (98-117 AD) rebuilt and reinforced Babylon and a thriving town soon sprung up around its walls. During the subsequent Christian era Memphis was completely abandoned and never rose again, while Babylon became the seat of the bishopric and the W bank village of Giza grew into a large town.

When the **Arabs** conquered Egypt in 641 AD, they were given specific instructions by Khalifa Omar in Damascus to establish their administrative capital in Babylon rather than at the larger Alexandria. His general Amr Ibn Al-As built his encampment (or Fustat) in the middle of a deserted triangular plain on the E bank which was bounded by Babylon in the S, Aïn Shams (ancient Heliopolis) to the NE and Al-Maks (the Customs Point), which was the Arab name for Heliopolis' former port of Tendunyas and is now the site of Ramses Station, to the NW. The Amr mosque was the first of a number of new and permanent buildings which were erected as the plain filled up and the foundations of modern Cairo were laid.

Under successive Muslim dynasties additions were made to the area as new mini-cities, each to the NE of the previous one, were built. By the time the Fatimid heretical Shi'a invaders arrived from North Africa in 969 AD, under the military command of Gohar, only the S of the plain had been developed. He therefore chose to build a new walled city, (which included the Al-Azhar mosque, palaces, pavilions and gardens for the sole use of the Khalifa, his family and retainers), about 1½ km N of the Fustat complex and called it Al-Qahira. Two centuries later in 1168 AD calamity struck the Fustat area when, fearing occupation by the invading Crusaders, the Egyptian wazir Shawar set fire to the city. Over 54 days the fire almost totally destroyed Fustat whose inhabitants fled with most building temporary houses around Al-Qahira. Three years later the last Fatimid khalifa died and his wazir, the Kurdish-born **Salah al-Din**, assumed control of the country and founded the Sunni Muslim orthodox Ayyubid Dynasty (1171-1249 AD). He expelled the royal family from Al-Qahira which he opened to the public and it soon became the commercial and cultural centre of the metropolis.

Salah al-Din actually only spent 8 years of his 24 year reign in Cairo. Much of his time was spent fighting abroad where he recaptured Syria and finally Jerusalem from the Crusaders in 1187 and finally died in Damascus in 1193. He expanded the walls surrounding the Fatimid city and in the SE built a huge **Citadel**, which became the city's nucleus, on an outcrop of the Muqattam Hills. Under Mamluke rule (1250-1517 AD) the city grew rapidly to become the largest city in the Arab world. As the E bank of the Nile continued to silt up, the newly elevated areas provided additional space which could be developed to house the expanding population.

Under the **Ottomans** (1517-1798 AD) both Cairo and Alexandria were relegated to the position of mere provincial cities with little in the way of public building undertaken in the whole of the 17th and 18th centuries. This changed, however, with the combination of the arrival of the French in 1798 and the coming to power in 1805 of the Albanian-born Ottoman officer Mohamed Ali. As part of his ambitious plan to drag Egypt into the modern world by introducing the best that Europe had to offer, he embarked on a project which included a huge public building programme in Cairo which was turned into a large modern capital city.

The combination of very rapid population growth and extensive rural-urban migration to the city, particularly since **WWII**, has totally overwhelmed Cairo. It has totally outgrown its infrastructure and today a city, intended to house only 2 million people, is home to perhaps over 14 million. The result is that the transport, power, water and sewage systems are completely inadequate and hundreds of thousands live on the streets or wherever they can find shelter including the infamous 'Cities of the Dead' cemeteries. What is amazing is that, despite all its problems, this ancient city actually functions as well as it does and that in adversity the Cairenes are so good natured and friendly.

On arrival

As one of the world's most crowded and noisy cities, arriving in Cairo can initially seem a very daunting experience. Independent travellers, without the advantage of being met at the airport, have to cope with the problems of finding the way to their hotel and must fend off the unsolicited offers of cheap hotels and taxi rides. The best thing to do is to refuse all offers of help, except from official sources, having worked out in advance where you are going and how you are going to get there.

ACCESS Air Cairo International Airport, 15 km NE of Midan Tahrir (Tahrir Sq) in downtown Cairo, has 2 terminals which are about 3 km apart. The new Terminal 2 is used by most of the Western airlines while Terminal 1, which is the old airport, is used by Egyptair and all of the other airlines who cannot or

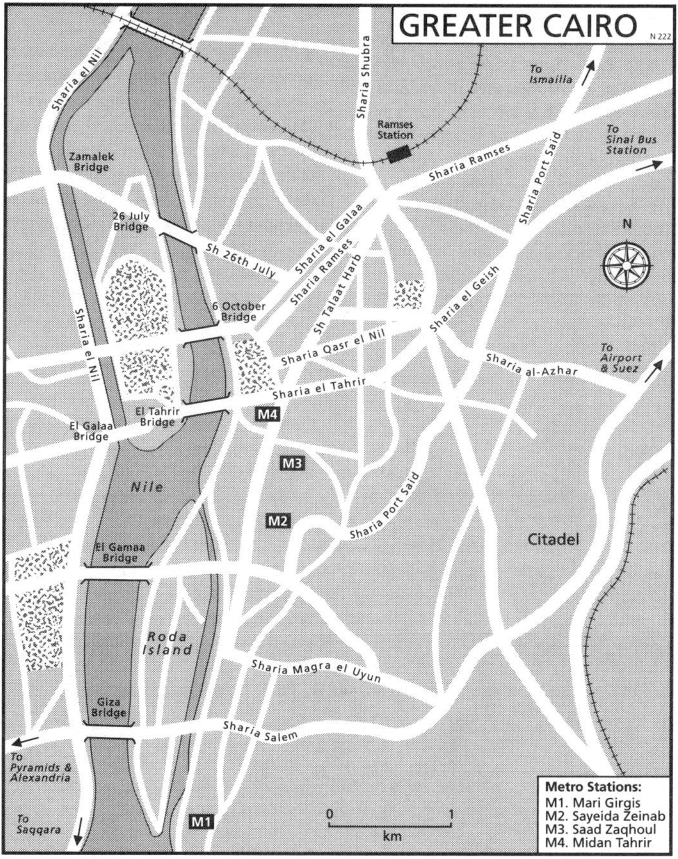

will not pay the higher landing charges. **Transport to town**: taxis are available immediately on exit from customs for E£30 (check current official fare from airline or airport official). A fixed price **limousine service** taxi at E£20 per head for a max of 4 people (check before you get in) leaves from Misr Travel's stand at Terminal 1. The **airport service bus** drops a minimum of 5 passengers at any central Cairo hotel at E£20 per head and E£25 for Giza. The cheaper and easier way, costing less than E£1, is **bus No 410** to Midan Ataba or the **No 400** bus every 30 min or **No 27** minibus every hour from Terminal 1 to the bus terminal at Midan Tahrir which is right in the centre of the city. From here one can get transport to everywhere else in Cairo.

Train: all trains arrive at **Ramses Station**, with different sections for Nile Valley and Delta tracks. It is at the N end of downtown Cairo about 2 km from Midan Tahrir which can most easily be reached by metro (2 stops) although bus (No 95) or taxi can also be taken.

Road Bus Long-distance buses arrive at **Sinai Bus Station**, also known as **Abbassiya Station**, about 5 km NE of Midan Tahrir which can be reached by the cheap

No 32 minibus or taxi from outside the terminal (expect to pay E£5 to get downtown). Buses from Luxor and Hurghada arrive at the **Ahmed Helmi Terminal** behind Ramses Station. The city's other 2 arrival points are the **Koulali Terminal**, in front of the Ramses Station, for buses from the Suez Canal Zone and the Delta while the **Al-Azhar Terminal** for those from the Western Desert, is about 450m E of Midan Ataba which is only one stop from both Midan Tahrir and Ramses Station.

Things to see

It certainly makes sense, if time permits, to visit the major sights of this area in chronological order. Therefore, rather than rushing to the large and exhausting Egyptian Museum, start outside the city at the pyramids and trace their development from the earliest in Saqqara to the splendours of Giza (see separate section **The Pyramids, page 741**). In Cairo city there are few remains from the pre-

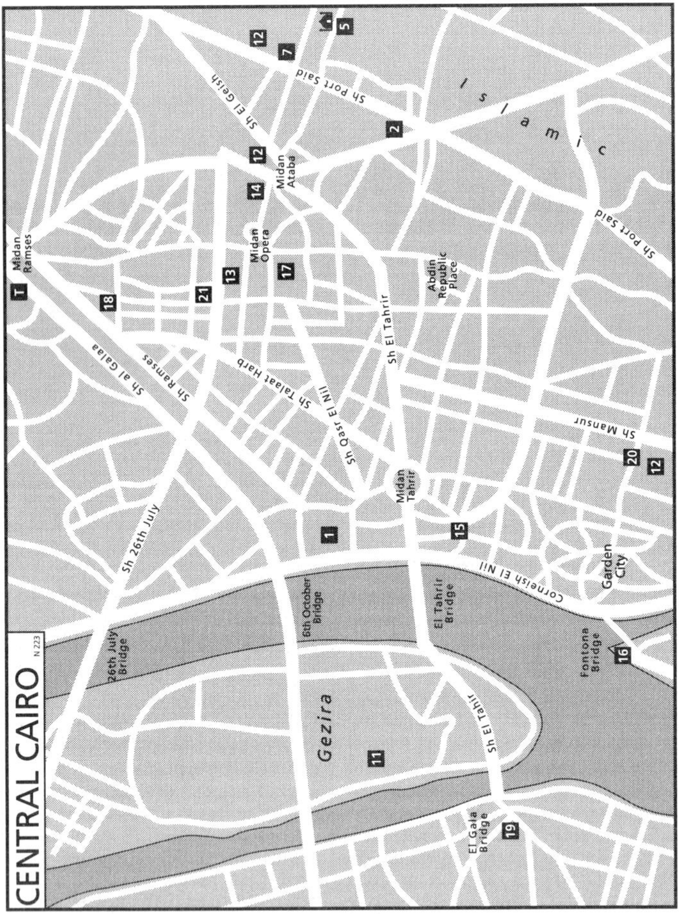

Christian era other than in the Egyptian Museum, so the logical sequence of visits would be – **Coptic Cairo** in the ancient fortress of Babylon-in-Egypt; the mosques, cemeteries and souks of **Islamic Cairo**; and the modern sites and museums of **Contemporary Cairo**.

Coptic Cairo

This settlement was constructed by the Persians in about 500 BC to guard the junction of the Nile and the canal linking it to the Red Sea. During the Christian period the fortified settlement of Babylon-in-Egypt grew into a large town. It was perhaps named by the fort's homesick building workers from modern-day Iraq or from the name for Gate of Heliopolis (Bab-il-On). Later the Arabs called it Qasr al-Sham'ah (Fortress of the Beacon). Whatever its

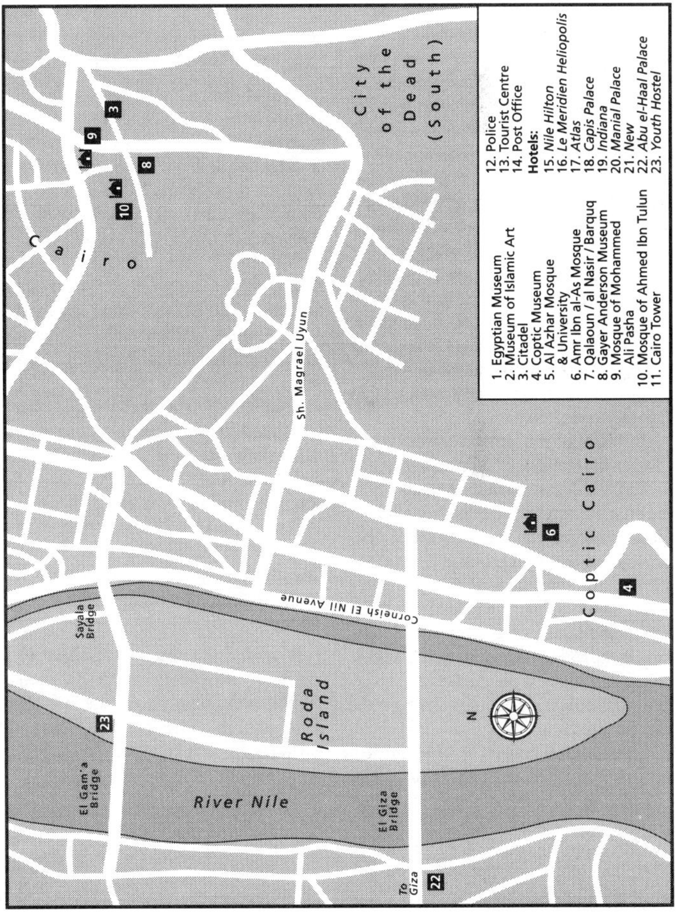

origins it is now known, not entirely accurately, as Coptic Cairo.

ACCESS Coptic Cairo is located on the E bank of the river about 5 km S of Midan Tahrir opposite the S tip of Roda Island to which it was connected by a pontoon bridge. From Midan Tahrir there are taxis and buses (Nos 92, 93, 134 & 140) and the metro (a better option) to **Mari Girgis** (St George), 4 stops in the Helwan direction.

Leaving the station, one is confronted by 2 circular Roman towers which comprised the W gate of the fortress built on what was at that time the E bank of the Nile and on foundations now smothered beneath 10m of Nile silt and rubble. Much of the original fortress was demolished as part of extensive alterations and today only its towers and gates have survived. The new **Church of St George**, built in 1904 and the only circular church in Egypt, is actually on top of the N tower and is part of the **Monastery of St George**, which is the seat of the Greek Orthodox Patriarchate of Alexandria, with the **Convent of St George**, the **Church of the Virgin** and the remains of the original fire-damaged **Church of St George** to the NW.

To the S of the Roman towers is the Church of the Virgin (Coptic masses held on Fri 0800-1100 and Sunday 0700-1000), is better known as the **Hanging Church** (Al-Mu'allaqah or 'The Suspended') because it stands on top of the three stone piers of the semi-flooded Roman **Water Gate** from where the Melkite bishop Cyrus, the last Byzantine viceroy, fled by boat as the Muslim army arrived. The gate below the church is reached via a stairway behind the piers, by buying a ticket for the Coptic Museum.

The original church built in the 4th century was demolished in 840 AD by Ali Ibn Yahya who was the Armenian Governor. It was rebuilt in 977 AD and modified several times, most recently in 1775. The church is approached though a wonderful narrow courtyard from which steps lead, via a 19th century vestibule, to the church's entrance. It is divided into 4 naves by 3 rows of columns. The 13th century iconostasis, (wooden screen supporting icons) which separates the congregation from the 3 haikals (altar areas) behind the marble pulpit is an incredible feat of fine woodwork and appears virtually transparent. To the right of the altar is a room which overlooks one of the towers while to its left and right, 2 secret passageways lead down to the foundations. These recent discoveries are thought to be escape routes used by the Christians during times of persecution.

Immediately to the W of the main Roman towers is the 5th century **Church of St Sergius**, dedicated to 2 martyred soldiers, St Sergius and St Bacchus. It was rebuilt after having been virtually destroyed in the 8th century. The architecture of the church, which contains many antiques recovered from ancient monuments, follows the style of a traditional basilica with 3 naves divided by 2 rows of pillars. The altar is separated from the main part of the church by a 13th century wooden screen which has fine encrustations and beautiful ornamentation. The partially flooded crypt, the only remaining vestige of the original church, is intriguing because it is claimed that the Holy Family sought refuge there during their flight to Egypt and the places where they sat are still visible. There are 2 smaller chapels on either side of the altar.

Just behind the church of St Sergius is the very similar 11th century **Church of St Barbara** standing on the site of an older church dedicated to St Cyrus and St John which was destroyed during an Arab assault. The 3rd century's St Barbara's relics were brought to the church and are now contained in a lovely little chapel to the left of the altar. The iconostasis (screen) is another fine example of encrustation work and the wooden panel linking the columns is an equally characteristic example of delicate Coptic architecture.

Just to the S of the Church of St Barbara is the **Ben Ezra Synagogue** in the former 6th century Church of St Michael the Archangel, which itself had been built on the site of a synagogue destroyed by the Romans. In the 12th century it was sold back to the Jews by the Copts in order to raise funds to pay taxes being raised to finance the Ibn Tulun mosque. The synagogue is built in the basilica style with 3 naves and an altar hidden by doors, which are wonderfully worked and encrusted with ivory. When the synagogue was extensively repaired in the 19th century, mediaeval Hebrew manuscripts, known as the **Geniza documents** and providing details of the history of the 11th-16th centuries, were discovered.

Beside the Hanging Church is the **Coptic Museum**, the other main tourist attraction in Coptic Cairo. It is closed on Sun but open Sat-Thur 0900-1600, Fri 0900-1100 & 1300-1600 but the old wing closes 30 min earlier and entry costs E£8. It was established in 1908 in an attractive building by a group of influential Coptic notables. Their aim was to display Egypt's rapidly decaying Christian heritage and to save the items from foreign collectors. Much of the beautiful and unique collection comes from ancient churches and houses but some is from private collections. The museum was enlarged in 1937 with the construction of a new wing. The collection gives a good insight into the evolution of Christian art between 300-1000 AD and into its influences on Islamic art and architecture. The gardens around the museum are very attractive and there is a pleasant café on the right of the building. The entrance is through the main door in the new wing. Start on the left and proceed in an anti-clockwise direction, following chronological order from Room 1.

You can follow the development from the pagan pre-Coptic period in **Room 1** through to the introduction of Christian symbols such as the cross and the fish in **Room 5**. Upstairs in **Rooms 10 to 12**, there are beautiful examples of the Coptic art of weaving. Other rooms contain icons, woodwork, metalwork and treasures from various churches and monasteries. The beautiful exhibits in **Rooms 22-30** in the Old Wing, which is reached via stairs from the sculpture garden, are laid out in a clockwise direction. Downstairs in the garden there are steps leading down to the Water Gate below the Hanging Church.

Islamic Cairo

As already noted in the history of Cairo (see page 703), the city was initially developed as a series of extensions and new walled mini-cities which radiated in a NE direction from the original encampment of Fustat outside the walls of the Babylon-in-Egypt fortress. There are literally hundreds of mosques in this Islamic city and it is difficult to know where to begin. Broadly speaking, however, the most important places to visit in Islamic Cairo are away from modern Cairo and the River Nile in a broad belt to the E of the main Sharia Port Said. The exception to this is the **Amr Ibn al-As Mosque**, the oldest mosque in the country which is just near Babylon-in-Egypt. It is recommended to visit this while seeing Coptic Cairo. The rest of Islamic Cairo can be visited by following a series of routes most beginning from the **Al-Azhar Mosque**.

SUGGESTED ROUTES (see map, page 710).

1. N via the concentration of buildings in the **Qalaoun/Al-Nasir/Barquq** complex, to the **Al-Hakim Mosque** at the N gates of the old city.

2a. S to the **Al-Muayyad Mosque** which stands at the **Bab el-Zoueila** gate at the S edge of the old city and the buildings on Sharia Darb al-Ahmar to the **Sultan**

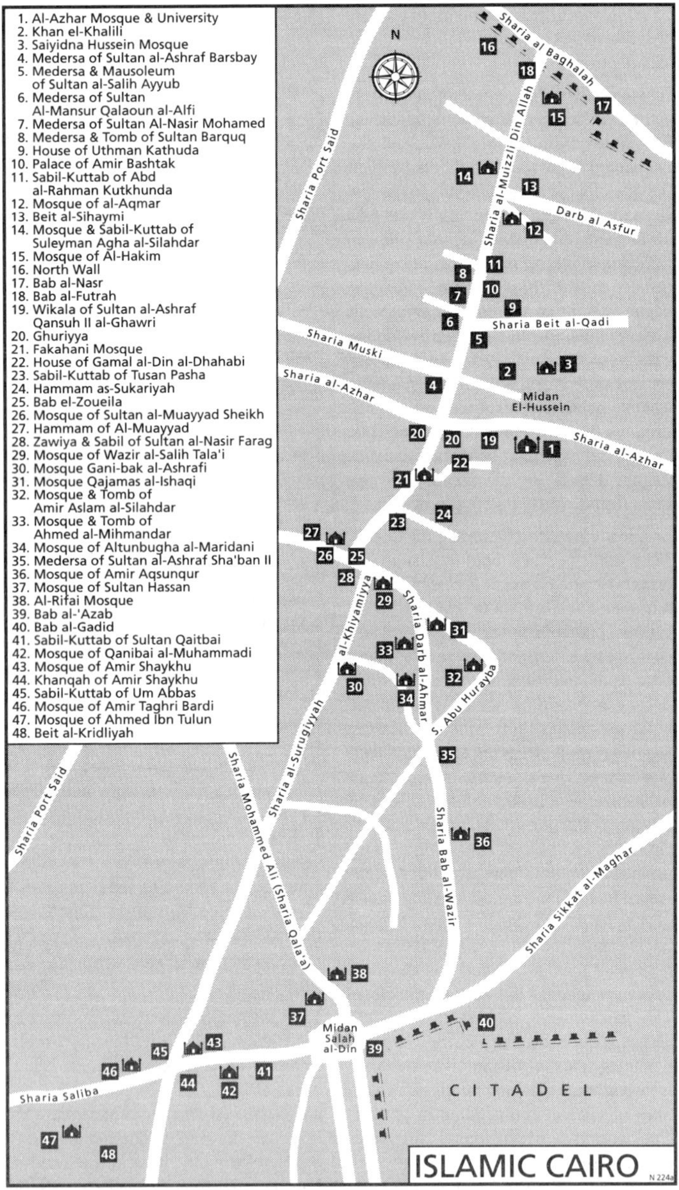
1. Al-Azhar Mosque & University
2. Khan el-Khalili
3. Saiyidna Hussein Mosque
4. Medersa of Sultan al-Ashraf Barsbay
5. Medersa & Mausoleum of Sultan al-Salih Ayyub
6. Medersa of Sultan Al-Mansur Qalaoun al-Alfi
7. Medersa of Sultan Al-Nasir Mohamed
8. Medersa & Tomb of Sultan Barquq
9. House of Uthman Kathuda
10. Palace of Amir Bashtak
11. Sabil-Kuttab of Abd al-Rahman Kutkhunda
12. Mosque of al-Aqmar
13. Beit al-Sihaymi
14. Mosque & Sabil-Kuttab of Suleyman Agha al-Silahdar
15. Mosque of Al-Hakim
16. North Wall
17. Bab al-Nasr
18. Bab al-Futrah
19. Wikala of Sultan al-Ashraf Qansuh II al-Ghawri
20. Ghuriyya
21. Fakahani Mosque
22. House of Gamal al-Din al-Dhahabi
23. Sabil-Kuttab of Tusan Pasha
24. Hammam as-Sukariyah
25. Bab el-Zoueila
26. Mosque of Sultan al-Muayyad Sheikh
27. Hammam of Al-Muayyad
28. Zawiya & Sabil of Sultan al-Nasir Farag
29. Mosque of Wazir al-Salih Tala'i
30. Mosque Gani-bak al-Ashrafi
31. Mosque Qajamas al-Ishaqi
32. Mosque & Tomb of Amir Aslam al-Silahdar
33. Mosque & Tomb of Ahmed al-Mihmandar
34. Mosque of Altunbugha al-Maridani
35. Medersa of Sultan al-Ashraf Sha'ban II
36. Mosque of Amir Aqsunqur
37. Mosque of Sultan Hassan
38. Al-Rifai Mosque
39. Bab al-'Azab
40. Bab al-Gadid
41. Sabil-Kuttab of Sultan Qaitbai
42. Mosque of Qanibai al-Muhammadi
43. Mosque of Amir Shaykhu
44. Khanqah of Amir Shaykhu
45. Sabil-Kuttab of Um Abbas
46. Mosque of Amir Taghri Bardi
47. Mosque of Ahmed Ibn Tulun
48. Beit al-Kridliyah
N
Sharia al Baghalah
Sharia al-Muizzli Din Allah
Sharia Port Said
Darb al Asfur
Sharia Beit al-Qadi
Sharia Muski
Sharia al-Azhar
Midan El-Hussein
Sharia al-Azhar
al-Khiyamiyya
Sharia Darb al-Ahmar
S. Abu Hurayba
Sharia al-Surugiyyah
Sharia Mohammed Ali (Sharia Qala'a)
Sharia Port Said
Sharia Bab al-Wazir
Sharia Sikkat al-Maghar
Midan Salah al-Din
Sharia Saliba
CITADEL
ISLAMIC CAIRO
N 224a

Hassan Mosque and the modern **Al-Rifai Mosque**.

2b. Continuing to the mosques and museums in the imposing **Citadel** and the huge ancient **Ahmed Ibn Tulun Mosque**.

3. To the mosques and tombs in the **City of the Dead** which lies in the 'Northern Cemetery' to the E of Islamic Cairo.

The original **Mosque of Amr Ibn al-As (Gama Amr)**, 500m N of Mari Girgis metro station, was built in 642 AD by Amr Ibn el-As commander of the Arab army which captured Egypt in that year. Built near both Babylon-in-Egypt and the Arabs' encampment (Fustat) it is the oldest mosque in Egypt and one of the oldest in the entire Islamic world. Because of the continual enlargements, which began in 673 AD only 10 years after Amr's death aged 93 and included major restoration work in the 15th and 18th centuries, nothing of the original mud-brick 30m by 17m thatched-roof mosque exists. Recently repainted and cleaned, its aspect today is virtually modern. As is often the case in the older mosques the interior includes many pillars taken from the ancient Egyptian monuments. As a result the whole mosque is a hybrid with parts of the fabric dating from before the conquest of Egypt until the 19th century alterations. In the N corner under the dome and surrounded by a bronze screen, on the site of Amr's house in Fustat, is the tomb of his son Abdullah who was born when Amr was only 13, became a Muslim before him and was a close companion of the Prophet.

The ancient **Al-Azhar Mosque (1)** and the nearby souks in the **Khan el-Khalili (2)** district are at the centre of modern-day Islamic Cairo. They are located SE of Midan Ataba (reached by taxi or No 66 bus from Midan Tahrir). You can either walk E from Midan Ataba beneath the flyover along Sharia al-Azhar or, better still, along the congested but fascinating Sharia Muski which, once across the tramlines of busy Sharia Port Said, becomes more attractive as you approach Khan el-Khalili.

Although it also refers to a specific street, the **Khan el-Khalili** (open daily except Sun) is the general name given to this district of Cairo which has a large number of individual souks. The Arab/Islamic system of urban planning has traditionally divided the souks by professions or guilds. While the system is less rigid than formerly there is still a concentration of one particular trade in a particular area. The Khan el-Khalili includes streets which almost exclusively sell gold, silver, copper, perfume, spices, cloth or any one of a number of particular products. Many of the products are manufactured within the souk, often in small workshops behind or on top of the shops.

The **Khan el-Khalili** has been the main souk in Cairo since 1382 when it was first created around a caravanserai by Amir Jarkas al-Khalil who was the Master of Horse to the first of the Burji Mamluke Sultans, Al-Zahir Barquq (1382-1389). The caravanserai attracted many foreign and local traders and expanded rapidly, to become a base for the city's subversive groups and was consequently frequently raided. Much of the area was rebuilt by Sultan Al-Ashraf Qansuh al-Ghawri (1501-1517) but it still maintained its role as Cairo's main area for traders and craftsmen. Today the main area of the souk is occupied by tourist shops but a few of the streets to the W are more authentic and much more interesting. Here you will find souvenirs including gold, silver, copperware, leather goods, perfume oils, alabaster, boxes, herbs and spices. **NB**: it is essential to bargain because the traders will always start at about double the price they actually expect.

Both Khan el-Khalili's Sharia Muski which is virtually a pedestrian precinct and the more congested Sharia al-Azhar lead E into Midan El-Hussein.

On the SW of the Midan El-Hussein, an underpass below the busy Sharia al-Azhar leads to the famous and very influential **Al-Azhar Mosque & University (1)** whose leader, known as the Sheikh al-Azhar, is appointed for life and is Egypt's supreme theological authority. It is open Sat-Thur 0900-1500, Fri 0900-1100 & 1300-1500, modest entry fee plus tip for any guides, no bare legs allowed, shawls provided for women.

The mosque was built in 970 AD and established as a university in 988 AD which, despite a counter-claim by Fes' Qarawiyin Mosque in Morocco (see page 286), may make it the world's oldest university. With the exception of the main E *liwan* (arcade), however, little remains of the original building because additions and modifications were made by successive rulers, including modern buildings to the N designed to house the university's administration block.

Initially during the Shi'a Fatimid era (969-1171), the university was used as a means to propagate the Shi'a faith in a predominantly Sunni city, but it fell into disrepair under Salah al-Din and his successor Ayyubids (1171-1250) Sunni Muslim rulers before being reopened by the Bahri Mamlukes (1250-1382) and eventually became a bastion of Sunni orthodoxy. Later during the rise in Arab nationalism in the late 19th and early 20th centuries, Al-Azhar became a stronghold for independent thinkers. It is no coincidence that in 1956 Nasser made his speech against the Suez invasion in the university.

The entrance to the mosque is through the Barber's Gate (where students traditionally had their hair shaved), which was built in the second half of the 15th century by Qaitbai (1468-1496). This opens out on to the 10th century Fatimid *sahn* (central court) which is 48m by 38m and is overlooked by 3 minarets. With the exception of the Mamluke *medressa* (theological schools) surrounding the *sahn* (courtyard), most of the buildings date back to the Fatimid period. The carpeted E *liwan* is particularly impressive with a great number of ancient alabaster columns. The *mihrab* is strangely placed in the middle of the *liwan*, with no *qibla* wall behind it. An extension of the *liwan* by Sultan Abd el-Rahman in 1751 left the *mihrab* in this unusual position. Take the opportunity to climb one of the 5 minarets for an excellent view over the surrounding area.

Immediately to the S of Al-Azhar is an area known as **Butneya** once notorious as the base for Cairo's underworld where drugs were openly traded by powerful and locally popular gangsters. After a major crack-down in 1988 most of them left but the area is still home to minor local gangs who tend to prey on shops, restaurants and middle-class Egyptians rather than on tourists who should be perfectly safe.

Route 1: N from Al-Azhar

The area with the greatest concentration of historic buildings in Islamic Cairo lies N from the Al-Azhar complex and the Khan el-Khalili to the N gates of the old city. On the N side of Midan El-Hussein is the **Saiyidna Hussein Mosque (3)**, Cairo's official mosque where President Mubarak and other dignitaries worship on important occasions, closed to non-Muslims. This mosque is named after and contains the head of the Prophet Mohamed's grandson Hussein. He was killed at Karbala in 680 AD at the climax of the struggle which led to the early and continuing schism in the Muslim world between the orthodox Sunni (followers of the way) and the Shi'a (party) followers of Ali. Hussein, because of his marriage to Mohamed's daughter Fatima, was the father of the Prophet's only direct descendants, who revere Hussein as a martyr and a popular saint like his sister

Zeinab. His mosque is the focus of his annual *moulid*, one of the city's most important festivals which is held over a fortnight climaxing in Sep, and a number of other religious festivals. Walk back 200m NW along Sharia Muski to Sharia al-Muizzli Din Allah. Note on the SW corner of the crossroads the **Medersa of Sultan al-Ashraf Barsbay (4)** (1422-1437). This liberal and enlightened Mamluke Sultan, originally from the Caucasus, financed his capture of Cyprus in 1426 by turning the spice trade, which in Cairo is based just to the S of the *medersa*, into a state monopoly. Turn right at the crossroads and head N along Sharia al-Muizzli Din Allah passing some of the many goldsmiths and coppersmith shops. These are concentrated in the alleys to the right including the actual Sharia Khan el-Khalili. Although its façade is largely hidden by shops, at the right hand side of the street, on the site of the former slave market, is the **Medersa & Mausoleum of Sultan al-Salih Ayyub (5)** (1240-1249) who was the last of the Ayyubid Sultans and who was the first to introduce the foreign Mamluke slave-soldiers. The *medersa* was special because it was the first built to include all 4 of Egypt's schools of law while the tomb is the first example where it is placed next to the *medersa* of its founder.

Opposite, with a wonderful unbroken 185m long façade, stands an amazing complex of 3 ***medressa*** founded by 3 of the most influential mediaeval sultans, Qalaoun, Al-Nasir and Barquq. This section of the street is known as Bayn al-Qasrayn (between two palaces) because of the Fatimid period's magnificent Great Western Palace and Eastern Palace which stood on either side.

The earliest and most impressive *medersa* is the **Qalaoun (6)** complex built by Sultan Al-Mansur Qalaoun al-Alfi (1280-1290). Like so many other Mamlukes ('possessed') slave-soldiers he was a Kipchak Turk who used the name Al-Alfi because he was originally bought for the high price of 1,000 (or alf) dinars. He subsequently diluted the influence of his own Kipchaks amongst the Mamlukes by importing Circassians whom he billeted in the Citadel. These Burgis Mamlukes (*burg* = tower) were rivals to the Bahri Mamlukes (1250-1382) stationed on Roda Island and eventually created their own dynasty (1382-1517). Qalaoun was constantly fighting the Crusaders and eventually died of a fever in 1290 aged 79, on an expedition to recapture Acre.

The complex was built in just over a year in 1284/85 on the site of the Fatimid's Western Palace and includes a *medersa* and mausoleum to the left and right, respectively, of the entrance with a *maristan* down a now closed 10m high corridor to the rear of the two linked buildings.

The 20.5m by 17m *sahn* of the *medersa* has only 2 *liwans* while the NE wall has 3 storeys of tunnel-vaulted alcoves which were used as student rooms. Of particular interest is the *qibla liwan* and the *mihrab* arranged into 3 aisles with a glass mosaic around the *mihrab*.

On the N side of the corridor is the beautiful mausoleum (open 0900-1700) which is a 21m by 23m rectangular room with 4 pillars and 4 piers arranged in an octagon below an 11.5m diameter 30m high dome built in 1903 to replace the original wooden dome which was demolished in the 18th century. The rose granite pillars have Corinthian capitals and the ceilings are finely carved. The walls are decorated with beautiful marble and mosaics topped by a frieze. The 7m high horse-shoe shaped *mihrab* is particularly outstanding with columns on either side and covered with rich mosaics and marble. The tomb of Qalaoun and his son Al-Nasir Mohamed is in the middle of the room surrounded by a beautifully sculpted wooden rail.

The *maristan* is now reached via an

alley along the SW wall of the *medersa*, but little remains of the original hospital except for one of the *liwans* and the remnants of a marble fountain. Since 1910 it has been the site of a modern eye clinic.

To the N is the **Sultan Al-Nasir Mohamed (7)** complex which was started by Sultan Kitbugha in 1295 and finished by Al-Nasir during his second reign in 1304 which is commemorated by over 30 mosques and other public buildings throughout the city. Qalaoun's eldest son Khalil (1290-1294), was assassinated in 1294 and his 9 year old brother Mohamed (1294-1295) was elected Sultan. He was deposed the following year by the Mongol regent Kitbugha (1295-1297) who in turn was soon forced into exile. Kitbugha was replaced by Lajin (1297-1299) but he was assassinated after a short reign while playing chess. Following this chapter of 'accidents', Mohamed was restored to the throne, but was kept in terrible conditions by his regent until he escaped to Jordan 10 years later. He eventually returned with a large army the following year, executed his enemies, and ruled happily for another 30 years until his death in 1341.

The complex (open 0900-1600) consists of a mosque, *medersa* and tomb. Although restoration work is still in progress it is worth trying to get in to see the *qibla* wall which still has its original decoration and Kufic inscriptions. The *mihrab*, although incomplete, is also interesting because it is one of the last stucco *mihrabs*. Little remains of the mausoleum and parts of the walls have been removed to the Museum of Islamic Art. It was originally built for Al-Nasir but he was buried next door in his father's mausoleum and the 2 tombs here belong to his mother Bint Suqbay and Anuq, his favourite eldest son who died the year before his own death. The 3 storey minaret is very beautiful with a richly ornamented Andalusian style first storey and the other 2 storeys surmounted with delicate stalactite cornices. The main door is Gothic and was brought back from the Church of St George in Acre during a campaign against the Crusaders.

This is followed to the N by the *medersa* and tomb which make up the **Sultan Barquq (8)** complex which was built in 1384-1386. The marble entrance and the silver-encrusted bronze-plated door are very impressive and lead into a corridor to the *sahn* which has 4 *liwans* arranged in a cruciform shape. The *qibla liwan*, to the E is divided into 3 aisles by 4 ancient columns which support beautifully carved and painted ceilings. Upstairs there are cells for the Sufi monks who once inhabited the building. To the N of the *medersa* a door leads to the mausoleum where Sultan Barquq was originally buried before being transferred to the mausoleum specially built by his son Al-Nasir Farag (1399-1405 & 1405-1412) in the city's northern cemetery (see below).

Sultan Al-Zahir Barquq (1382-1389 & 1390-1399) reigned twice and was the founder of the dynasty of Circassian slave-soldiers who became the Burgis Mamlukes rulers of Egypt. He was reportedly an enlightened Sultan, who admired piety and intelligence and surrounded himself with learned scholars, before dying of pneumonia aged 60 in 1399.

Besides the Qalaoun/Al-Nasir/Barquq complex which is on the W side of Sharia al-Muizzli Din Allah there is a number of other interesting, if less important buildings on and near the E side of the street on the route N to the Al-Hakim mosque. This area, which is heart of Islamic Cairo, is definitely worth exploring for a full day.

Directly opposite the Qalaoun complex is Sharia Beit al-Qadi and 40m down on the left hand side is the modern looking house No 19 which is marked with a green plaque where visitors should knock to be shown around in return for a little *baksheesh*. This is the remains of a palace built in 1350 but better known as the **House of Uthman Kathuda (9)** who restored it during the 18th century.

Further N opposite Barquq's complex are the beautiful if neglected remains of the 5-storey **Palace of Amir Bashtak (10)** (Al-Nasir's son-in-law) built in 1334-1339. The warden is usually to be found at the nearby **Sabil-Kuttab of Abd al-Rahman Kutkhunda (11)**. There used to be many of the these Ottoman-influenced *sabil-kuttab*, which combine a water supply for the public at street level and a Koranic school in the building above, throughout Cairo. This example, built in 1744 by a powerful amir seeking absolution for his former sins, stands on a triangular piece of land where 2 roads meet.

About 75m further N on the right up the main road is the roofless and dilapidated **Mosque of al-Aqmar (12)** which was built in 1121-1125 by the Fatimid wazir of Khalifa al-Amir (1101-1131). Take the next right hand turn for a brief detour to No 19 Darb al-Asfur which is 50m along the left hand side of the street. This is the **Beit al-Sihaymi (13)** (open 0900-1600), actually two houses, built in 1648 and 1796 and inhabited until 1961, and probably one of the finest examples of a luxurious Mamluke mansion in the whole of the city. It has a lovely courtyard and a *haramlik (harem)* for the women including a domed bathroom.

Returning to the main street and continuing N, one reaches the **Mosque and Sabil-Kuttab of Suleyman Agha al-Silahdar (14)**, built in 1837-1839 by one of Mohamed Ali's ministers who also built many other *sabils* throughout the city. The style of the building is very much influenced by the contemporary style in Istanbul including the minaret with an Ottoman style cylindrical shaft and conical top.

Continuing to the N end of street is the giant **Mosque of Al-Hakim (15)**, (open 0900-1600, E£10 plus a tip for both your guide and minder in the mosque), which abuts the **North Wall (16)** of the old city of Fustat/Cairo between the **Bab al-Nasr (17)** and **Bab al-Futrah (18)** gates and commemorates its most notorious ruler (see box, page 716). It was begun in 990 by the Shi'a Muslim Fatimid Khalifa Al-Aziz (975-996) and was eventually finished some 23 years later by his son who took the name **Al-Hakim bi-Amr Allah** (Ruler by God's Command) and ruled between 996-1021.

Possibly having a Christian wife was the reason why his reportedly tolerant and humane father Al-Aziz had been more forbearant towards Christians and Jews than towards the indigenous Sunni Muslim population. In contrast his son was very intolerant to everyone. With such a colourful history, the large 122m by 115m mosque itself is actually rather plain. It is organized around a large central *sahn* and built of bricks with a large porch in the traditional Fatimid style. It has been restored many times throughout the centuries, notably after the major earthquake in 1302 and by Sultan al-Hassan in 1359. After the 14th century it was converted to house Crusader prisoners-of-war, then as a stable by Salah al-Din, during the French occupation as a fortified warehouse, and in the mid-19th century to store items destined for the **Museum of Islamic Art** which opened in 1896. Since 1980 the mosque has been restored by the Indian based Bohra sect of Ismaili Muslims who claim direct spiritual descent from the Fatimid imams who they worship. Its twin minarets have been reinforced by stone carvings and from these and from the roof there is a wonderful view over Cairo.

Route 2a: S from Al-Azhar

The route S from Al-Azhar mosque has

a number of very interesting buildings including the **Mosque of Al-Muayyad** at the mediaeval **Bab el-Zoueila**. Further to the S of Fustat is the **Sultan Hassan Mosque** and the much more modern **Al-Rifai Mosque** which stand side-by-side below the mighty **Citadel** (see page 720) and its various mosques. One can then head W to the huge and very old **Mosque of Ahmed Ibn Tulun** and the nearby **Gayer-Anderson Museum** before returning to the river. Allow a minimum of half a day to take in all of the sites on this tour of the S part of Islamic Cairo.

Immediately to the S of the Al-Azhar complex are a few of the 20 remaining *wikalas*, hostels for merchants which were usually above a bonded warehouse for their goods, which numbered over 200 in the 1830s. The wonderfully preserved **Wikala of Sultan al-Ashraf Qansuh II al-Ghawri (19)**, which was originally built in 1504, is just off the SW corner of

AL-HAKIM – THE VANISHING DESPOT

In 996 AD at the age of 11 Al-Hakim succeeded his father as the second Egyptian Fatimid Khalifa and began a despotic reign. At the age of 15 he had his tutor assassinated and started his extremely cruel and relentless persecution of Christians, Jews, Sunni Muslims, women and dogs. He prohibited any Christian celebrations and had the Church of the Holy Sepulchre in Jerusalem demolished. He also prohibited Sunni ceremonies and tried to established Shi'a Islam as the only form of Islam. Women were forbidden to leave their homes and, in order to enforce this, cobblers were not permitted to make or sell women's shoes. At one time all of Cairo's dogs were exterminated because their barking annoyed him. Merchants who were found to have cheated their customers were summarily sodomized by his favourite Nubian slave whilst Al-Hakim stood on their head. Wine, singing, dancing and chess were also prohibited and the punishments for disobeying this laws were very severe and usually resulted in a gruesome death.

His erratic rule, with laws often changing overnight, led to tensions within Fustat/Cairo, particularly between the various religious communities. In 1020, the news that Al-Hakim was about to proclaim that he was a manifestation of Allah provoked serious riots to which he responded by sending in his Sudanese troops to burn down the city where they clashed not only with the civilians, but also the Turkish and Berber soldiers. An alternative story is that one particular quarter of Fustat was torched because he thought that was where his favourite sister Sitt al-Mulk (Lady of Power) took her lovers, but when she was proved to be a virgin by the midwives he examined the ruins and asked "who ordered this?". Whatever the truth, he then sent his chief theologian Al-Darazi to Syria for safety where he is believed to have originated the theology of the Druze who consider Al-Hakim to be divine.

Despite his ruthless public acts Al-Hakim's personal life was very abstemious and he was a very generous alms-giver. He took to riding around the city and surrounding countryside on a donkey with only a couple of servants but disappeared in Feb 1021. Following the discovery of his knife-slashed robe, it is believed he was murdered, possibly on the instructions of his Sitt al-Mulk with whom he apparently argued because of her refusal to begin an incestuous marriage with him. The fact that his body was never discovered led the Druze to believe that he had retreated from the world to return at a later date, whilst the Copts believe that he had a vision of Jesus, repented and became a monk.

Al-Azhar: it now houses a permanent exhibition of desert life and is also used as workshops for artisans. Traditional handicrafts for sale. Open daily (except Fri) 0900-1700 or 0900-1100 and 1400-1600 during Ramadan, entry E£3.

50m to the NW back on Sharia al-Azhar just near the footbridge, is the **Ghuriyya (20)**, the magnificent complex of **Sultan al-Ashraf Qansuh II al-Ghawri** (1501-1517), which is bisected by a continuation of Sharia al-Muizzli Din Allah. The complex, made up of his domed mausoleum to the E of the street and his mosque and *medersa* to the W, was built in 1504-1505 and was the last great Mamluke public building before the Ottoman conquest. He died of a stroke in 1516, aged about 76, during a battle near Aleppo against the Turks who then immediately invaded and captured Egypt and began their long rule which lasted from 1517 to 1805. Because Al-Ghawri's body was never found, he was not buried in this magnificent and hugely expensive tomb.

Sharia al-Muizzli Din Allah between the 2 buildings, originally roofed, was the site of the exotic silk market. Today mainly household goods are sold in the shops. Each section of this main thoroughfare, Islamic Cairo's main street, was named after the merchandise sold in that particular stretch. For example the fruit-sellers had their own mosque, the **Fakahani Mosque (21)** (built in 1735), about 200m down the street on the left hand side. Make a detour by walking left from its NW corner and then left again where, 70m to the E at No 6, is the **House of Gamal al-Din al-Dhahabi (22)**, Cairo's richest gold merchant in 1637 when this beautiful house was built. It is used as a documentation centre and open to visitors (daily 0900-1400 except Fri). Back to the S of the mosque, is the ornate **Sabil-Kuttab of Tusan Pasha (23)**, built in his name by his father Mohamed Ali Pasha in 1820. From here the S gates of the ancient city are just ahead. Before going through the gates turn left or E at the *sabil-kuttab*. About 75m along the side street is an old 18th century mens' bath-house known as **Hammam as-Sukariyah (24)** which was originally owned by a rich woman who also owned the nearby *wikala* and *sabil* of Nafisah Bayda. Although like the other remaining bath-houses in the city it is no longer a den of vice, it is still an interesting place to visit and relax. Today it helps the local community by allowing its fire for heating the water to be used to cook *ful mudammas* (beans) for the locals' breakfast.

Bab el-Zoueila (25), built by Badr al-Gamali in 1092 when Fatimid fortifications were being reinforced, was one of the 3 main gates in the city walls. It is named after mercenaries from the Al-Zoueila tribe of Berbers who were stationed in the nearby barracks. The gate was soon inside the city following the successive expansions and Salah al-Din's construction of larger walls further out from the centre. Cairo was in effect divided into 2 with the inner walls still in existence and both sets of gates locked at night.

Bab el-Zoueila also has a more popular history linked to the caravans departing both to Mecca and the S. It was not only the location of street performers including snake-charmers, story tellers and dancers, but after the 15th century it also became the site of public executions. Common criminals were beheaded, garrotted or impaled, while cheating merchants were hanged from hooks or rope. Defeated Mamluke Sultans, including the last one in 1517, were hanged and sometimes nailed to the doors. Even today the 20m high Bab el-Zoueila, which comprises a 4.8m wide multi-storey arch between 2 solid stone towers, is still an impressive sight particularly from the S.

Immediately to the W of the gate is the **Mosque of Sultan al-Muayyad Sheikh**

(26) (1412-1421) built on the site of the old Kazanat al-Shamaii prison. Al-Muayyad had been incarcerated here on a number of occasions because of his love of alcohol when he was a Mamluke slave-soldier. On being released after one particularly long and unpleasant stretch, he vowed to replace the prison with a mosque which he began in 1415 after becoming Sultan.

The mosque, which is sometimes known as the Red Mosque because of the colour of its external walls, was one of the last to be built in the ancient large enclosure style before the Turkish style was adopted as the norm. The superb bronze-plated wooden entrance doors leading to the mosque were originally intended for the Sultan Hassan Mosque but were purchased by Al-Muayyad for his own mosque. The entrance leads into a vestibule with an ornate stalactite ceiling. From the vestibule, the door on the left leads to the Al-Muayyad's mausoleum and marble tomb with Kufic inscription, while nearby is the tomb of his son, Ibrahim, who died in 1420.

From the mausoleum a door leads to the E *liwan* which was restored at the beginning of this century and gives an impression of the mosque's past splendour. Many of the columns were taken from ancient monuments but the most exceptional sight is the *mihrab* and the surrounding wall because of the perfect harmonization of the coloured marble stucco. The *minbar* is an example of fine woodwork, but has also been restored. The courtyard is now planted with shrubs and palm trees. From the top of one of the 2 minarets, there is an excellent view over the surrounding area and the adjacent Bab el-Zoueila.

From here a 20 min walk or 5 min ride on bus No 75 to the W of Bab el-Zoueila along Sharia Ahmed Maher brings you to the **Museum of Islamic Art** (see page 724).

En route immediately next to the mosque is a large and elegant building which looks like a small palace but is in fact the **Hammam al-Muayyad (27)** bath-house which has fallen into disrepair and is now often flooded. The area between the two is known as the Bab el-Khalq after a mediaeval gate which has long since vanished.

From the S of Bab el-Zoueila there are 2 routes you can take to reach the **Sultan Hassan** and **Rifai mosques** which stand N of the Citadel. One is to continue SW along what is officially known as Sharia al-Muizzli Din Allah but which, like so many other long roads, changes its name in different sections and at this point is also known as Sharia al-Khiyamiyya (Tentmakers) because of its bazaar. After about 1 km you reach a major crossroads where you should turn left or SSE along Sharia al Qala'a which leads to the rear of the 2 mosques. A much more interesting route includes a few nearby sites on Sharia al-Khiyamiyya before heading E along Sharia Darb al-Ahmar, after which the whole area is named, towards the Citadel.

Immediately S of the gates are 2 buildings which are bisected by Sharia al-Khiyamiyya. To the W is the *Zawiya* (Sufi monastery) and *Sabil* (public fountain) of **Sultan al-Nasir Farag (28)** (1405-1412) who was Barquq's son and successor. To the E is the much more magnificent **Mosque of Wazir al-Salih Tala'i (29)** which was both the last Fatimid mosque and, when it was built in 1160, was the country's first suspended mosque resting on top of a series of small vaulted shops which, with the rise in the street level, are now in the basement. Tala'i reportedly died regretting the construction of the mosque because, being located directly outside the walls of the city, it could be used as a fortress by an enemy.

Further S down the street is what is probably the city's best preserved example of a roofed market which, because of the multitude of coloured printed fabrics sold here, is known as the **tentmakers bazaar**. Further on are the small **Mosque of Gani-bak al-Ashrafi (30),** built in 1426 and named after the favourite amir of Sultan al-Ashraf Barsbay (1422-1437) but who was poisoned by rivals when he was only 25 years old, and what little remains of the nearby **Souk al-Surugiyyah** (saddle-makers market).

Returning to Bab el-Zoueila and turning right (E) into Sharia Darb al-Ahmar (Red Rd) there is an interesting 1¼ km walk to the Citadel. The street gets its name from the incident in May 1805 when the Mamlukes were tricked into going to discuss their grievances with Mohamed Ali Pasha (1805-1848). He had them slaughtered as they travelled 'Between the Two Palaces' and their heads sent to Istanbul as a demonstration of his power and independence. In March 1811 he did a similar thing again on the same street when 470 Mamlukes and their retainers were persuaded into going to a banquet at the Citadel to celebrate his son's imminent departure to fight the Wahabis in modern day Saudi Arabia. They were slaughtered on their return near Bab el-Zoueila.

About 150m after the Mosque of Wazir al-Salih Tala'i the road bends towards the S and on the corner of the fork in the road is the beautiful late-Mamluke era **Mosque of Qajamas al-IshaqI (31)** who was Sultan Qaitbai's Viceroy of Damascus where he died and was buried in 1487. Although the mosque was built in 1480-81, it is now known locally as the **Mosque of Abu Hurayba** after the 19th century sheikh who occupies the tomb.

At this point you can could make a detour off the main road E up Sharia Abu Hurayba where the left hand fork leads 250m to the **Mosque & Tomb of Amir Aslam al-Silahdar (32)** built in 1344-45 and then follow the road around SW and back to the main Sharia Darb al-Ahmar.

Alternatively you can forget about the detour and just continue S from the Mosque of Qajamas al-Ishaqi along Sharia Darb al-Ahmar. About 50m on the right is the **Mosque & Tomb of Ahmed al-Mihmandar (33),** built in 1324 but restored in 1732, but much more interesting is the beautiful, relaxing and very peaceful **Mosque of Altunbugha al-Maridani (34)** (1339-40) which is 100m further along the street. Another 200m further S past a small Turkish mosque, by which time the road is now called Sharia Bab al-Wazir in memory of the Gate of the Wazir which once stood there, is the large **Medersa of Sultan al-Ashraf Sha'ban II (35)** (1363-1378). It was built in 1368 when he was only 10 for his mother, who was one of al-Nasir Mohamed's (1310-1340) concubines, which is why it is known locally as *Umm Sultan Sha'ban* ('mother of Sultan Sha'ban') but he died before her and is buried there.

The final major building on the road S is the **Mosque of Amir Aqsunqur (36)** who was the son-in-law of al-Nasir Mohamed and later became Viceroy of Egypt. It is sometimes known as the **Mosque of Ibrahim Agha** by locals and the **Blue Mosque** by Europeans because of both the exterior's blue-grey marble and the beautiful indigo and turquoise tiling of the *qibla* wall. In the 1650s Ibrahim Agha usurped the mosque started in 1346 and decorated it with imported tiles. From here the road slopes up to the left to meet the approach road to the Citadel but we continue right to the 2 imposing mosques.

Directly below the Citadel are 2 adjacent mosques. The **Sultan Hassan Mosque (37)** (Entry E£6) was started in 1356 and finished 6 years later during the second reign of Sultan Hassan (1354-1361). The building is a masterpiece of Islamic art and is of incomparable simplicity and beauty. The main entrance is through a large, impressive doorway decorated with stalactites and finely sculpted ornaments. This leads into an antechamber connected to the main courtyard. The magnificent cruciform courtyard has an ablutions fountain at the centre covered by a large dome which was originally painted blue. Each of the vaulted *liwans* served as a place for the teachings of one of the 4 doctrines of Sunni Islam. The *liwan* containing the *mihrab* has richly decorated marble lined walls and a Koranic frieze in Kufic writing. Its height is accentuated by hanging lamp-chains.

From here an ornate bronze door with gold and silver motifs leads to Sultan Hassan's tomb. The room is dominated by a large 21m diameter dome which was actually built later during the Turkish period. The 3-section 86m minaret by the mausoleum is the highest in Cairo, with each new section richly decorated at its base with numerous stalactites. Another much smaller 55m minaret on the E side of the mosque was built in 1659 to replace the existing one which was decaying. The building also contains 4 *medressa* with one for each of the four – Malaki, Hanafi, Hanabali and Shafi'i – Islamic schools of law. Each *medersa* forms a virtually autonomous part of the building. The ground floor is used as a place for teaching, meditation and praying and the first floor as lodgings for the students.

Despite its appearance, the **Al-Rifai Mosque (38)** (entry E£6), directly to the E of Sultan Hassan Mosque, was only started in the late 19th century and was actually finished in 1912. However the mosque, which is named after Sheikh Ali al-Rifai who was the founder of the Sufi Muslim *tariqa* bearing his name and who was originally buried there, blends remarkably well into the surroundings. It was built over and expanded by the Dowager Princess Khushyar, the mother of Khedive Ismail who died in 1885 before it was finished, and was intended to contain the tombs of her descendants. Besides Al-Rifai and herself it contains the tombs of Khedive Ismail (1863-1879), his sons Sultan Hussein Kamil (1914-1917) and King Ahmed Fouad I (1917-1936) but not King Farouk who died in exile and is buried in the southern cemetery. It is also the last resting place of the last Shah of Iran, (Mohamed Reza Pahlavi) who died in exile in 1980 and, on President Sadat's instructions, was buried with great ceremony in a tomb made of green marble imported from Pakistan.

Route 2b: The Citadel

The magnificent **Citadel** reached direct from Midan Tahrir by taking a No 82 bus, is also known as Al-Qala'a al-Gabal (Citadel of the Mountain) or Al-Burg, is open daily 0830-1600 (except 1130-1300 on Fri), entry E£10, but entrance into the museums ends at 1530. Enter via **Bab al-Gadid (40)**.

It was built by Salah al-Din (1171-1193) as part of a very ambitious general fortification plan which included enclosing the whole city with a new wall which could be controlled from the Citadel. The original fortress and remaining fortifications were strongly influenced by the architecture of castles built in Palestine and Syria by the Crusaders. It was built in two walled enclosures, linked by their shortest walls, with the military area to the NE and the residential quarters in the SW. Every 100m or so along the walls there is a tower and there are numerous gates. The whole complex is still under military control and there are large areas which are closed to the public.

Later the Citadel was abandoned until the Mamlukes' arrival, when it became the Sultan's residence and the *Burji Mamlukes* (1382-1517) took their name from their base in the Citadel. In the 14th century Sultan al-Nasir Mohamed (1310-1340) added a number of buildings including a mosque and later, because of the development of warfare and the use of canons, the Turks undertook major reinforcements. The most recent modification to the Citadel was by Mohamed Ali Pasha (1805-1840) who built an impressive mosque on the site of the original palaces. Today the most interesting features of the Citadel are the **Mosque of Mohamed Ali Pasha,** which provides an amazing view W over Cairo and the restored **Sultan al-Nasir Mohamed Mosque**.

The **Mosque of Mohamed Ali Pasha** (Entry E£10, E£5 students) was started in 1824 but only finished 8 years after his death in 1857. The architecture was strongly influenced by the Turkish mosques of Istanbul with the characteristic high minarets and an imposing dome which had to be rebuilt in the 1930s. The marble floored courtyard is very finely proportioned, with a beautiful central ablutions fountain. To the NW is a small square tower for a clock which was a gift from King Louis-Philippe of France in 1846 in exchange for the obelisk now sited in Paris' Place de la Concorde, but the clock has never worked. The mosque is covered by a large dome with 4 half domes on each side. Once inside, it takes some time to become accustomed to the dim lighting. The white marbled tomb of Mohamed Ali is on the right of the entrance, behind a bronze grille.

To the S of the mosque is the **Qasr al-Gawharah** (Palace of Jewels) which was built in 1824 as the first of 2 palaces with French-style salons that Mohamed Ali built in the Citadel. Having been the residence of Egypt's rulers since the 12th century he predicted that his descendants would rule Egypt as long as they lived in the Citadel: sure enough, Ismail's move to the Abdin Palace foreshadowed the decline in their fortunes.

The **Sultan al-Nasir Mohamed Mosque** was built between 1318 and 1335 and now looks quite desolate because the marble that once paved the courtyard has gone. The *mihrab* is still in good condition and the survival of a number of granite columns suggests the prior existence of a dome. The unusual bulbous tops of the minarets are probably due to Persian influence.

To the S of the mosque is **Bir Yusef** (Joseph's Well), built by Crusader prisoners-of-war in the 1170s, which spirals down in a 10 sq m shaft to a depth of about 90m to the level of the Nile where water which percolated through the rock was collected and carried by donkey to the surface.

From Midan Salah al-Din to the W of the Citadel and in front of the Sultan Hassan Mosque make your way W along Sharia Saliba. On the left is the highly decorated **Sabil-Kuttab of Sultan Qaitbai** (1477) (41). This is another *sabil* and *medersa* but has, unusually, no connection to a larger religious foundation. Continue W past the small **Mosque of Qanibai al-Muhammadi** (**42**) to the imposing architectural buildings with matching minarets which face each other across the Sharia Saliba. On the right, N, is the **Mosque of Amir Shaykhu** (1349) (**43**) and on the left, S, the **Khanqah of Amir Shaykhu** (1355) (**44**). Amir Shaykhu was the Commander in Chief of the Mamluk army during the reign of Sultan Hassan. The *khanqah* had small cells for up to 70 *sufis* around the inner courtyard and in the NE corner of the arcaded prayer hall is Amir Shaykhu's tomb. Go straight ahead at the cross roads, with the **Sabil-Kuttab of Um Abbas** (**45**) on the corner, passing the small but impressive **Mosque of Amir Taghri Bardi** (1440) (**46**) with a carved stone dome. While the external structure of this building follows the E-W line of Sharia Saliba the interior is aligned SE to Mecca.

The largest mosque in Cairo and the oldest one which retains its original features is the **Mosque of Ahmed Ibn Tulun (47)** (open daily 0900-1600) which is located about 15 min walk W of the Citadel along Sharia Saliba on the way towards the river. Alternatively it can be reached from Midan Tahrir by bus No 72 or minibus No 54 which go to the Citadel via the Saiyida Zeinab area and then past the mosque. Although the Saiyida Zeinab metro station is only 2 stops from Midan Tahrir it is probably a 30 min walk from there to the mosque.

It was built between 876-879 by Ahmed Ibn Tulun, the son of a Turkish slave who became governor of Egypt but who then declared independence from the Baghdad-based Abbasid Khalifas. He thereby became the first of the Tulunids (868-905 AD), at the new town of Al-Qata'i (the Concessions or the Wards) NE of Al-Askar which, in turn was NE of Fustat, and near the foothills of the Muqattam Hills. When the Abbasids regained power in Egypt in 905 AD they destroyed much of the town except for the mosque which fell into decay until it was restored in 1296 by Sultan Langin who had hidden there after he was implicated in an assassination attempt against his predecessor.

The mosque was originally built in 876 by a Syrian Jacobite Christian architect which probably explains the presence of many designs and motifs inspired by Coptic art. Despite the extensive restoration work by Sultan Lagin, but apart from the addition of a spiral minaret with a outside staircase which appears to be a copy of the one at Samarra in Iraq, no major changes were made. Despite its huge size, which is 140m by 122m and a 92m square courtyard, the overall impression is of harmony, simplicity and sobriety. The walls have been plastered but the ornamentation is sculpted and not moulded. Note the long Kufic script inscriptions, almost 2 km long, of about 20 per cent of the Koran which circle the mosque several times below the roof. The marble plated *mihrab* is surrounded by an elegant glass mosaic frieze. Directly above is a small wooden dome. The *minbar*, presented by Sultan Lagin in 1296, is a fine work of art. The view from the top over the surrounding area is excellent and worth the climb.

The **Gayer-Anderson Museum**, entrance E£8, (open 0900-1600, Fri 0900-1100 & 1330-1530), which is also called **Beit al-Kridliyah (48)** (House of the Cretan Woman), abuts the SE corner of the mosque. It is contained in 2 houses, the one on the W dating back to 1540 and the one to the E to 1631, on either side of a small alley called Atfat al-Gami which originally belonged to the Al-Kiridhi family. The houses were sold to the government which in 1934 gave them to Major Robert Gayer-Anderson (1881-1945), a retired doctor and member of the Egyptian Civil Service, when he expressed a desire in restoring them and refurnishing them with Ottoman furniture and fittings. A tour of the houses give a good insight into the decoration and organization of a house during the Ottoman rule.

The area to the W of the giant mosque is known as **Saiyida Zeinab** after the Prophet Mohammad's granddaughter Zeinab (628-680 AD) who settled in Fustat/Cairo in 679 with her 5 children and the son of her brother Hussein who was murdered at Karbala in the Sunni-Shi'a conflict. Because of her position as closest kinswoman to the martyred Ali and Hussein the area has become a site of pilgrimage for foreign Shi'a Muslims. This is focused on the mosque built and continuously rebuilt over her tomb which is located off Sharia Bur Said but is closed to non-Muslims. Her moulid (saint's day) between 13-27 Ragab (Dec 1994) attracts up to half a million revellers who come to watch the wild Sufi parades and evening festivities.

Route 3: The Cities of the Dead

The **Cities of the Dead** is the name given by Europeans to Cairo's 2 main cemeteries which spread from the Citadel. The S cemetery is older and spreads to the SE but there are few monuments to see. The

N cemetery, which is known locally as Qarafat al-Sharqiyyah (the Eastern Cemetery) because it was E of the old city, is much more interesting and has been the burial place of the sultans since the 14th century. It contains a number of interesting mausoleums including those of Barquq and Qaitbai.

ACCESS The easiest way to the S cemetery is to turn left off Sharia Saliba, about half way between the Sultan Hassan and Ibn Tulun mosques, and head S along Sharia el-Khalifa for about 1 km. The easiest way to the N cemetery is either by taking a taxi direct to Qarafat al-Sharqiyyah or by walking E along Sharia al-Azhar from the Al-Azhar mosque for about 15 min until you reach the roundabout junction with the N-S dual carriageway of Sharia Salah Salam and then N for 250m. Then cut into the cemetery and head for the dome and minaret which are clearly visible.

WARNING This area is densely populated by Cairenes who live in or near the tombs. In Egypt there has long been a tradition of living close to the dead but the very large numbers are a relatively recent trend caused by an acute scarcity of housing. Consequently the people who live in the cemeteries tend to be comparatively poor and, although certainly not dangerous, it is obviously advisable not to flaunt your wealth, dress modestly and remember that this is where people live.

In the Northern Cemetery the **Mausoleum of Sultan al-Zahir Barquq** (1382-1389 & 1390-1399) was built over a 12 year period in 1398-1411 by his son Al-Nasir Farag (1399-1405 & 1405-1412). It was the first royal tomb to be built in this modern necropolis after Barquq had expressed a wish to be buried alongside a number of pious Sufi sheikhs who were already buried there. Therefore his body was moved from the *medersa* on Sharia al-Muizzli Din Allah once the 75 sq m complex had been completed. It is square with 2 minarets symmetrically placed on the façade. The entrance in the SW corner leads along a corridor to the *sahn* which has an octagonal fountain in the centre and is surrounded by 4 *liwans*. The N and S *liwans* have one aisle whereas the W has 2 and the E 3. The E *liwan* has 3 very simple *mihrabs* and an extraordinarily finely sculpted stone *minbar*. Doors lead from either side of the *liwan* into mausoleums. The N mausoleum contains Barquq's own marble cenotaph which is richly decorated with Koranic inscriptions, together with the tombs of an unknown person and another intended for Farag whose body was left in Damascus after he had been assassinated on a military campaign in Syria. The mausoleum to the S holds the tombs of Barquq's wife and two granddaughters.

A little to the S is the **Medersa & Mausoleum of Sultan al-Qaitbai Mosque** (1468-1496), built in 1472-1474, which is a magnificent example of 15th century Arab art and possibly one of Egypt's most remarkable monuments from the Arab era. From the outside the building has very harmonious proportions with the dome finely decorated with polygonal motifs. The minaret is also remarkable because it has with a square base, octagonal middle section and a cylindrical top tier. The mosque is reached by climbing 17 steps to the entrance which leads into the SE *liwan*. The cruciform *medersa* has side *liwans*, and a relatively small covered *sahn* with an octagonal roof lantern. The superbly decorated coloured marble floors are somewhat damaged but still attractive. The *liwans* are very narrow but the E *liwan*, which has a modern ceiling, still has a very well preserved and finely encrusted *minbar*. A door in the S corner of the *qibla liwan* leads to the mausoleum which is decorated with the same sort of marbles as the *medersa*. Its high dome is simply decorated, in contrast with the highly ornate walls. Sultan Qaitbai's tomb is enclosed behind an elaborate wooden *mashrabia* while the other tomb is that of one of his sisters.

Contemporary Cairo

Contemporary Cairo has developed further W on both sides of the river into a modern and increasingly Europeanized capital. Although residential suburbs spread outwards in all directions any visit to Cairo should include the **Egyptian Museum**, the **Museum of Islamic Art**, the **Manial Palace** on Roda Island and, provided it is a clear day without too much pollution haze, the **Cairo Tower** on Gezira Island.

The **Egyptian Museum** is open daily 0900-1600 (Fri 0900-1115 & 1330-1600). Tickets cost E£10 or E£5 for students, E£10 cameras, E£100 amateur videos, no flash photography. Additional E£30 for entry to Mummy room, reopened March 1994. It is worth purchasing a detailed guide to the rooms (E£5) before you go into the museum. There is a souvenir shop outside on the right of the entrance and a café and restaurant on the first floor. Allow at least 4 hrs for a full visit to appreciate everything properly or about 2 hrs for a rushed visit, so either pace yourself or go twice.

It is one of the world's truly great museums. It takes up the whole of the N side of Midan Tahrir and is right in the centre of the city. Established in 1857 by Auguste Mariette the museum was initially located in Giza but, because there were so many wonderful archaeological discoveries, the building became too small and it was transferred to the current site in 1902. The growing chorus of complaints about its crowded and poorly displayed layout and the current problems of preservation have led to ambitious but necessary plans to construct a modern new purpose-built museum for the estimated 100,000 exhibits near the Pyramids of Giza. Until then, however, despite its problems the existing museum, which houses an amazing collection covering most of the Pharaonic period, remains is an essential key to understanding Egypt's fabulous past.

Ideally, you should aim to be there early in the morning or during the afternoon because the tour groups arriving during the middle of the morning quickly make viewing more difficult. This is particularly important if you want to visit Tutankhamen's Treasure because access is limited and queues form. In general the upper floor, reached via the stairs from **Room 50**, is the most interesting section. To follow the history in chronological order you should start in **Room 47** and follow a clockwise route.

A few of the many items worth noting are the statue of the obese Queen of Punt in **Room 12**; the statues of Nakhtmin and his wife in **Room 15** which are a very fine example of 18th Dynasty art at its best; the Decree of Canopus in 3 languages used by Champollion in deciphering hieroglyphics in **Room 34**; the many sarcophagi from different periods, including those of Seti I and Ramses II, in **Rooms 46-47**; the realistic Fayoum Portraits in **Room 14** which were painted on wax while the person was still alive and were later affixed to the mummies; and the Mummies in **Room 52**, reopened March 1994, having been closed since 1981 because the display was considered offensive to many Egyptians.

The largest part of the upper floor is dedicated to **Tutankhamen** and the highlight is the treasure in **Room 4**, including the fabulous funeral mask, but be prepared to queue for this one! More artifacts discovered in the tomb are on display in the E gallery including life sized statues of Tutankhamen in **Room 45** and in **Room 20** his trumpet which was last played in 1930 and is still in good working order.

The **Museum of Islamic Art** (open Sat-Thur 0900-1600, Fri 0900-1100 and 1330-1600, Entry E£10, ticket is also valid for Gayer-Anderson House – see above), is ideally located on the junction of

Sharia Port Said and Sharia Qalaa about equidistant between Midan Ataba and the Bab el-Zoueila.

It was originally established in the courtyard of the Al-Hakim Mosque (see above) in 1880 but it was moved to the present building, containing over 75,000 exhibits from various Islamic periods, in 1903. The dates indicated in the museum's exhibits are AH (After the Hegira), which is the starting point of the Islamic Calendar in 622 AD when Mohamed is thought to have fled from Mecca. The rooms follow a chronological order through from the Umayyads to the Abbasids, Fatimids, Ayyubids, Mamlukes and Ottomans. Of particular interest are – **The Fatimid panels** in **Room 4** which depict animals and birds because, unlike the Sunni Muslims, the Fatimid Shi'a have no objection to portraying living things; the doors to **Room 6** which were originally from the Al-Azhar Mosque; the reconstruction of an 18th century Ottoman patio in **Room 10**; the Mamluke astrolabe used by Muslim navigators in **Room 11**; the glassware in **Room 21** and the Persian art in **Room 22**.

Argricultural Museum, adjacent Ministry of Agriculture in Dokki at end of 6th Oct Bridge. Oldest agricultural museum in world, stuffed animals, Egyptian farming practices, open 0900-1400, closed Mon, entrance 10 piastres.

Cotton Museum, next to Agricultural Museum, survey of cotton growing in Egypt, open 0900-1400, closed Mon and Fri afternoon, entrance free.

Railway Museum, next to Ramses station, automated display, coaches for Khediv Ismail's private train, open 0900-1400, closed Mon.

The **Manial Palace** and gardens on Roda Island in the middle of the Nile are an oasis of tranquillity in noisy Cairo and are well worth visiting. Entry is E£5 for foreigners and E£2.50 for students. There is also a fee for normal cameras (E£10), video cameras (E£100). Open daily 0900-1600.

The palace, which was built in 1903 and is now a museum, was the home of King Farouk's uncle Prince Mohamed Ali and comprises a number of buildings in various styles including Moorish, Ottoman, Persian, Rococo and Syrian. The first is the Reception Palace at the gate which is beautifully decorated with polychrome tiles and stained glass. Upstairs are a number of luxurious rooms, of which the Syrian Room is the finest, and a mother-of-pearl scale model of Sultan Qaitbai's mausoleum. To the right is a mosque with a tall mock Moroccan minaret and then a revolting Trophies Museum with tatty and poorly stuffed animals including a hermaphrodite goat and a table made of elephant's ears. Much more interesting is the royal residence in the middle of the garden which is a mixture of Turkish, Moroccan, Egyptian and Syrian architectures and contains a number of rooms, nearly all of which are decorated with blue earthenware tiles. The Throne Hall behind the residence is of little interest but the Private Museum, which includes a very varied collection of Korans, manuscripts, carpets, plates and glassware, is fascinating.

Having been satiated with mosques, mausoleums and museums it is probably worth visiting the top of **Cairo Tower** to get a bird's eye view of the city before treating yourself to a relaxing mini-cruise along the Nile and away from the noisy traffic. The 87m tower (open daily 0900-2400, £E5), is located on Gezira Island and its lotus-shaped top is one of the city's most visible landmarks. It was built with Soviet help in 1957-1962. Although the restaurant and cafeteria are OK it is the viewing platform that is most important. Providing the pollution is not too bad, which it often is, you can look E across the modern city centre to the minarets and mosques of Islamic Cairo and the Muqattam Hills beyond; W beyond the residential areas to the Pyramids and the edge of the desert; N towards Zamalek and beyond; or S upstream to Roda Island and the original pre-Coptic settlement of Babylon-in-Egypt where this teeming mega-city first began almost 2,000 years ago.

Gardens

There are several spacious gardens for the visitor to find some tranquillity from the city bustle. These include the **Zoological Gardens** in Giza, The **Andalusian Gardens** overlooking the Nile, The **Manial Palace Gardens** on Roda Island, The **Fish Gardens** in Zamalek, The **Japanese Gardens** in Helwan, The **Meryland Gardens** in Heliopolis, The **International Garden** in Nast City and the **Kanater al-Khaireya Gardens** (the Good Barrage) abut 25 km from the capital.

Local information

Price guide:

AL	US$90+	**D**	US$20-40
A	US$75-90	**E**	US$10-20
B	US$60-75	**F**	under US$10
C	US$40-60		

● Accommodation

As the largest city in Africa and the Middle East and one of the world's great tourist destinations it is not surprising that Cairo has hundreds of hotels ranging from deluxe accommodation, often run if not owned by the major international chains, to some really unpleasant places. The listing below, which has sought to avoid the worst, provides a wide range to suit every budget.

AL *Baron Hotel Heliopolis*, 8 Sharia Ma'ahad el-Sahara, off Sharia el-Uraba (also known as Airport Rd), PO Box 2531, El-Horriya, Heliopolis, T 2915757, F 2907007, 126 rm and 14 suites, 226 beds, located in Heliopolis overlooking palace, a good businessman's hotel, clean and comfortable, if unspectacular, decent food and good service, banqueting rm for 700 people, 2 restaurants, 24 hr coffee shop, bar, ballrooms and discotheque, unfortunately staff in business centre are surprisingly rude, 150 rm extension almost complete; **AL** *Cairo Heliopolis Movenpick*, (also known as *Movenpick Concorde*) Cairo International Airport Rd, El-Horriya, Heliopolis, T 2470077, F 2919400, 412 rm, one of best hotels in Cairo, located next to the airport, used by transit and business passengers; **AL** *Cairo Jolie Ville Movenpick*, Desert Rd, PO Box 1, Giza, T 3852555, F 3835006, 240 rm, located near the Pyramids, lovely gardens and excellent food; **AL** *Cairo Marriott Hotel*, Sharia Saray el-Gezira, Zamalek, T 3408888, F 3406667, 1147 rm, 1634 beds, built around a lavish 19th century palace, located in the heart of the city, has own sporting facilities – tennis court, health club, etc, beautiful gardens; **AL** *Cairo Ramses Hilton*, 1114 Corniche el-Nil, Maspero, T 5754999, F 5757152, 900 rm, on the Nile near Midan Tahrir, has the *Felafa* nightclub; **AL** *Cairo Sheraton*, Midan Gala', Dokki, Giza, T 3488600, F 3489051, 660 rm, 1211 beds, located just S of the Gala' bridge, views of Nile, Sheraton high quality service; **AL** *El-Gezira Sheraton*, Gezira Island, PO Box 264, Orman, Giza, T 3411555, F 3405056, 520 rm, opposite the *Cairo Sheraton*, circular tower on the S tip of Gezira Island is one of the Cairo's most distinctive landmarks, *El-Samar* restaurant nightclub and *Regine's* discotheque; **AL** *Forte Grand Pyramids*, Desert Rd, T 3830383, F 3831730, 523 rm, recently renovated, near the pyramids; **AL** *Heliopolis Sheraton*, Sharia el-Uraba, PO Box 11361, Heliopolis, T 2902027, F 2904061, 90 rm, 162 beds, located near airport, currently only the front building is in use; **AL** *Helwan Shepheard*, Corniche el-Nil, Garden City, T 3553900, F 3557284, 281 rm, 536 beds, S end of Gezira Island, good Nile view, glory is fading; **AL** *Le Méridien Heliopolis*, 51 Sharia el-Uraba, PO Box 2928 El-Horriya, Heliopolis, T 2905055, F 2918591, 302 rm, pool, good hotel located only 10 min from airport; **AL** *Le Méridien Le Caire*, Corniche el-Nil, Garden City, T 3621717, F 3621927, 275 rm, very well-managed French hotel, located by the Nile on N tip of Roda Island, with excellent service and restaurants; **AL** *Mena House Oberoi*, Pyramids Rd, El-Ahram, T 3833222, F 3837777, 520 rm, very attractive old style hotel, excellent view of Pyramids, set in 16 ha of gardens, superb nightclubs and restaurants, discotheque, casino, largest outdoor pool in Cairo, tennis, a nearby 18 hole golf course, horse and camel riding with experienced instructors; **AL** *Nile Hilton Hotel*, Corniche el-Nil, Midan

Tahrir, T 5780444, F 5780666, 434 large rm, 822 beds, located on the Nile, adjacent to Egyptian Museum, recently modernized but showing its age; **AL *Pullman Ma'adi Towers Hotel***, 29 Corniche el-Nil, PO Box 217, Ma'adi, Cairo, T 3506092, F 3506209, 176 excellent rm, 308 beds, good view of the Nile, excellent service, located at S end of Corniche and a long way from downtown Cairo; **AL *Pyramids Park Sofitel***, Desert Rd, T 3838666, F 3839000, 481 rm including 31 duplex suites, 962 beds, good service, located 2.5 km outside Cairo near the Pyramids, facilities include 4 restaurants, nightclub with oriental floorshow, banqueting and conference centre for up to 400 delegates, pool, health club, gym, sauna, tennis, and nearby golf course and horse-riding clubs; **AL *Safir Cairo Hotel***, Midan El-Misaha, PO Box 138 Orman, Dokki, T 3482424, F 3608453, 280 rm, 502 beds, located relatively close to but without view of the Nile, offers good group discounts; **AL *Safir Zamalek Hotel***, 21 Sharia Mohamed Mazar, Zamalek, T 3420055, F 3421202, 104 rm, 412 beds, expensive but pleasant hotel with a good view of the Nile from the NW end of Gezira Island; **AL *Semiramis Inter-Continental***, Corniche el-Nil, Garden City, T 3557171, F 3653020, 840 rm, 1181 beds, an ugly building and very expensive, is possibly the best hotel in Egypt with excellent service and a good view of Nile overlooking the SE end of Gezira Island; **AL *Sonesta Hotel***, 4 Sharia el-Tayaran, Nasr City, T 2628111, F 619980, 210 rm, located half way to the airport just off Sharia el-Uraba in Nasr City (Madinet Nasr) just E of the main stadium; **AL *Swissotel Cairo el-Salam***, Abdel Hamid, Sharia Badawi, Heliopolis, T 2455155, F 2455755, 323 rm, 580 beds located in wooded site in Heliopolis a taxi ride away from downtown Cairo.

A *Atlas Zamalek Hotel*, 20 Mohandsseen, T 3465782, F 3476958, 74 rm, 236 beds; **A *Dreamers***, 5 Sharia Jeddah, Dokki, T 709540, Tx 92073, F 3600665, 84 rm; **A *Europa Cairo***, 300 Pyramids Rd, T 621100, F 2907077, 250 rm, 450 beds; **A *Flamenco Hotel***, 2 Sharia el-Gezira el-Wasta, Abu el-Feda, Zamalek, T 3400815, F 3400819, 132 a/c rm (33 singles and 77 twins and suites), 236 beds, new hotel, located on quieter but less scenic NW corner of Gezira Island, high standard and spotlessly clean, restaurant, 24 hr café, cocktail bar, conference rm for 30-40 people, ballroom, take-away shop, tea rm, shops, bank, business centre; **A *Ma'adi Hotel***, 55 Sharia Misr Helwan, PO Box 196, Ma'adi, T 3505050, F 3518710, 145 rm, 219 beds, a long way from downtown Cairo in the S suburb of Ma'adi; **A *Novotel Cairo Airport***, PO Box 8, Cairo Airport, Heliopolis, T 2474772, F 2914794, 209 rm, 415 beds, an unspectacular airport version of the Novotel 4 star chain, almost all the guests are transit and business passengers; **A *Siag Pyramids Penta Hotel***, 59 Mariuteya, Saqqara Rd, PO Box 107, Ahram, T 3856022, F 3840874, 352 rm, large hotel located near, and with a good view of, the Saqqara pyramids, good rm service reportedly better than eating in the restaurant.

B *Alnabila Cairo Hotel*, 4 Sharia Gamiat ad-Duwal al-Arabia, Mohandsseen, T 3461131, F 3475661, 170 rm, 364 beds; **B *Belair Cairo Hotel***, Mokattam Hill, PO Box 996, T 916177, F 922816, 276 rm, 550 beds, good view of the Citadel, badly located for downtown Cairo; **B *Green Pyramids***, 13 Sharia Helmiat, El-Ahram, T 537619, F 537232, 84 rm, 166 beds, on the main road to the Pyramids; **B *Holiday Sphinx***, Cairo/Alex, Desert Road, T 854930, 182 rm, 378 beds, out of town; **B *Kaoud Delta Pyramids***, end of King Faisal Road, El-Ahram, T 3833000, F 3830957, 140 rm, 210 beds, pool, double room E£200, a room with view of Pyramids also suffers from traffic noise; **B *Manial Palace (Club Mediterranee)***, Kasr Mohamed Ali, El-Manial, T 846014, F 3631737, 190 rm, 360 beds, an oasis of peace and tranquillity in exquisite gardens of Manial Palace on the N end of Roda Island, half board only, discotheque open from 2300-dawn; **B *Oasis Hotel***, Cairo/Alex Desert Road, PO Box 44, Pyramids, T 3831777, F 3830916, 260 rm, good motel style hotel near Pyramids, large clean pool and a 24 hr restaurant; **B *Residence***, 11th Road 18, PO Box 418, Ma'adi, T 3507189, 28 rm, 90 beds.

C *Atlas*, Sharia Mohamed Roushdi, Midan Opera, T 3918311, Tx 92564, 110 rm, a decent 3 star downtown hotel but is noisy because it is next to a large mosque; **C *Beirut Hotel***, 56 Sharia Beirut, Heliopolis, T 662347, Tx 22115, 91 rm; **C *Cairo Uncle Sam***, 54 Sharia Abul Mahasen El-Shazli, Agouza, Cairo, T 3465377, Tx 20147, 150 rm, family-run, on W bank, just behind the *Atlas Zamalek*; **C *Chateau des Pyramides Hotel***, 10 Sharia Sadat, PO Box 167, Cairo-Alexandria Desert Road, T 3871342, F 3838545, 75 rm, very good; **C *Concorde Hotel***, 146 Sharia el-Tahrir,

Mummy Come Home

An elegant new tomb has been constructed, its pillars supporting a deep blue ceiling studded with gold stars. This is an attempt by the Egyptian Museum in Cairo to recreate the ambience of Thebes in around 1300BC and provide a final resting place for some of its most famous pharoahs.

The mummies have suffered many indignities. Take Merneptah, grandson of Seti I. Having survived a spectacular first burial with all the pomp and splendour due to Egyptian royalty, tomb robbers flung his mummy aside and 21st Dynasty priests rewrapped him and placed him with 8 other displaced persons in a side chamber in the Tomb of Amenhotep II. Rediscovery in 1898 was followed by transport to Cairo where he was put on view. Queen Nedjemet, another resident was slashed by the knives of those who unwrapped her. The great Ramses II unwrapped in public in 1886 in an unseemly 15 minute strip has also found a decent home here. In 1946 public display of mummies was banned as improper. But in March 1994 the special tomb tastefully displays these bodies neatly wrapped once again, complete with dimmed lighting and dehumidifiers to protect the desiccated remains. Among the eleven who have found, hopefully, a final resting place here beside Queen Nedjemet, Merneptah and Ramses II are Merytamum his queen and his father Seti I.

Dokki, T 708751, F 717033, 72 rm, on main street running W from the Gala' bridge; **C *Egyptel***, 93 Sharia el-Merghani, Heliopolis, T 2907444, Tx 93987, 78 rm, 174 beds, near the *Baron Hotel*; **C *Horriya Hotel***, 14 Sharia el-Horriya, Heliopolis, T 2903472, Tx 94332, 57 rm, budget hotel near *Baron Hotel*; **C *Marwa Palace***, 11 Sharia el-Khatib, Dokki, T 3433380, Tx 23000, 28 rm, very noisy but clean; **C *Pharaoh Egypt Hotel***, 11 Sharia Ahmed Orabi, Mohandsseen, T 3471619, F 3474196, 138 rm; on W bank; **C *Pharaohs***, 12 Sharia Lutfi Hassuna, Dokki, T 712314, Tx 93383, 96 rm, friendly, very clean, family-run hotel with good service but a poor breakfast, located in a street parallel to the Nile and NNW between the Gala' and 6th October bridges; **C *President Hotel***, 22 Sharia Dr Taha Hussein, Zamalek, T 3400718, Tx 93655, F 3413195, 119 comfortable, clean rm, very good well-run hotel, provides good value for money, quiet and convenient location in the middle of the N end of Zamalek, restaurant with good food and excellent service, slow and inadequate lift; **C *Pyramids Hotel***, 198 Sharia el-Ahram, El-Ahram, T 3875100, F 3874974, 84 rm, located on the main road to the Pyramids, caters for budget groups; **C *Raja Hotel***, 34 Sharia Mohyi ad-Din Abul'izz, Dokki, T 3604297, 66 rm, 150 beds, near the Shooting Club in Dokki; **C *Saqqara Country Club & Hotel***, Saqqara Road, Abu el-Nomros, T 852282, 20 rm, located outside the city near the Saqqara pyramids, very highly recommended, well run with good food and excellent horse-riding facilities, temporary club membership available.

D *Abu el-Hoal Palace*, 161 Sharia el-Ahram, El-Ahram, T 856043, 20 rm, 43 beds, located on way to the Pyramids; **D *Arabia***, 31 Sharia Abdel Aziz al-Saud, El-Manial, T 841444, 16 rm, 40 beds, family run hotel on Manial Island which specialises in budget groups; **D *Cairo Crillon***, 19 Sharia el-Montaser, Agouza, T 3477570, 38 rm, 76 beds, very good hotel in the W bank area of Agouza; **D *Cairo Inn***, Sharia 26 Syria, Mohandsseen, T 3490661, 25 rm, 46 beds, off Midan an-Nasr; **D *Carlton***, 21 Sharia July 26th, Azbakia, T 755323, Tx 20734, 60 rm, family-run,located on a noisy downtown street; **D *Caesar's Palace Hotel***, 45 Sharia Abdel Aziz Fahmi, Heliopolis, Cairo, T 2457241, F 2457240, 60 rm, 112 beds, family-run hotel near the main Heliopolis Hospital; **D *Cosmopolitan***, 1 Sharia Ibn Tahlab, Kasr el-Nil, T 3923845, F 3933531, 84 a/c rm including 6 suites, located in centre of downtown Cairo in a relatively quiet side-street in an elegant building, restaurant which serves reasonable food, bars, café, nightclub, excellent laundry service; **D *El-Kanater Chalets***, El-Kanater Gardens, Kalioubeya, T 958328, 24 rm, 70 beds, good location but a long way from downtown Cairo; **D** *El-Manar*, 19 Sharia Abdel Hamid, off Sharia Lutfi, Mohandsseen, T 709299, Tx 94004, 85 rm, 170 beds, caters for budget groups; **D** *El-Nil Hotel*, 12 Sharia Ahmed Raghab, Garden City, T 3542800, Tx 93284, F 3552878, 272 rm, rather dark and dreary; **D** *El-Nil Zamalek*, 21 Sharia Maahad, Sharia el-Swisri, Zamalek, T 3401846, 38 rm, 60 beds; **D** *Fontana*, Midan Ramses, T 922145, 93 rm, 181 beds, cheap hotel with pool, located near the very noisy and crowded Ramses station; **D** *Heliopark*, 100 Sharia el-Hegaz, Heliopolis, T 2451346, F 2459789, 96 rm; **D** *Horus House Hotel*, 21 Sharia Ismail Mohamed, Zamalek, T 3403977, F 3403182, 35 rm, 58 beds; **D** *Indiana*, 16 Sharia el-Saray, Dokki, T 714422, F 3493774, 115 rm; **D** *Jasmin Hotel*, 29 Sharia Geziret el-Arab, Mohandsseen, Cairo, T 3472278, F 3421907, 65 rm, 112 beds, off Midan an-Nasr; **D** *Kanzy*, 9 Sharia Abu Bakr el-Siddik, Mohandsseen, T 709461, 57 rm, 109 beds; **D** *Kemet Hotel*, Midan Abbasiya, PO Box 46, Abbasiya, T 824018, Tx 93256, 96 rm, 216 beds, poor location halfway between Heliopolis and downtown Cairo but good hotel; **D** *King Hotel*, 20 Sharia Abdel Rahim Sabri, Dokki, T 710939, Tx 22393, 90 rm, family-run hotel; **D** *Longchamps*, 21 Sharia Ismail Mohamed, Zamalek, T 3409644, 30 rm, decent well located hotel run by a very helpful and friendly family; **D** *New Star*, 34 Sharia Yiyha Ibrahim, Zamalek, T 3401865, Tx 23000, 28 rm; **D** *Odeon Palace Hotel*, 6 Sharia Abdel Hamid Said, Kasr el-Nil, T 776637, Tx 21708, 30 rm, 48 beds, modern hotel with a roof garden in a noisy but central location; **D** *Saqqara Palm Club*, Saqqara Road, Badrashin, T 200791, Tx 23646, 21 rm, clean, excellent pool, set in beautiful gardens, excellent hotel but located right outside Cairo; **D** *Salma Hotel*, 12 Sharia Mohamed Kamel Morsi, Mohandsseen, T 700901, F 701482, 54 rm, good view of Cairo from the roof-top bar and on a clear day you can see pyramids, good and friendly service, an English pub, bar, restaurant with good food and cheap drinks; **D** *Sheherazade*, 182 Sharia el-Nil, Agouza, T 3461326, F 3460634, 160 rm, budget hotel with a good view of the Nile overlooking the Gezira Island; **D** *Sweet Hotel*, 39 Road 13, Ma'adi, T 3504561, 6 rm, in the S suburbs; **D** *Tonsi Hotel*, 143 Sharia el-Tahrir, Dokki, T 3484600, 37 rm, 70 beds; **D** *Vendome*, 287 Sharia el-Ahram, El-Ahram, T 538904, F 854138, 60 rm, clean and comfortable family-run hotel on the way to the Pyramids; **D** *Victoria*, 66 Sharia el-Gumhorriya, Midan Ramses, T 918766, 105 rm, 200 beds, located in noisy, crowded area near Ramses station, has large a/c rm, restaurant, bar; **D** *Windsor*, 19 Sharia Alfi Bey, T 915277, F 921621, 55 rm, 101 beds, recommended as best 3 star hotel in downtown Cairo, well run, one of the nicest bars in the city, Michael Palin stayed here while going round the world in 80 days – not very reliable plumbing!

E *Amun*, Midan Sphinx, Agouza, T 3461434, 40 rm, noisy hotel a the busy W end of the 26th July bridge; **E** *Cairo Commodore*, 10 Sharia Fawzi Ramah, Mohandsseen, T 3460592, 25 rm; **E** *Caroline Crillon*, 49 Sharia Syria, Mohandsseen, T 3465101, Tx 23158, 38 rm, 110 beds; **E** *Gabali Hotel*, 221 Sharia el-Higazt, Heliopolis, T 2455224, Tx 23568, 68 rm; **E** *Grand Hotel*, 17 Sharia July 26th, Azbakia, T 757700, F 757593, 99 rm, 180 beds, located in a crowded downtown area, has much of its original Art Deco fixtures and furniture; **E** *Green Valley*, 33 Sharia Abdel Khalek Sarwat, Kasr el- Nil, T 3936317, 28 rm, 46 beds, a decent budget hotel near the noisy Opera Square; **E** *Kinow*, 382 Sharia el-Ahram, El-Ahram, T 859260, 36 rm, located on way towards the Pyramids; **E** *Lotus Hotel*, 12 Sharia Talaat Harb, T 750627, F 921621, 50 rm, clean, comfortable and friendly budget hotel in very central location, reception is on the 7th floor and is reached via the Malev Airlines arcade; **E** *New Hotel*, 21 Sharia Adli T 3927033, F 3929555, 65 rm, 107 beds; **E** *Oasis Hotel*, 15 Sharia Abdel-Wahab el-Kadi, Kolleyet el-Banat, Heliopolis, T 2917312, F 2907912, 60 rm, 135 beds; **E** *Omayad Hotel*, 22 Sharia July 26th, T 755044, 72 rm, 120 beds, noisy downtown location; **E** *Rose*, 6 Sharia Iran, Midan Dokki, T 707059, 40 rm, located just off Dokki's Sharia el-Tahrir; **E** *Sphinx*, 8 Sharia Magles el-Sha'b, Abdin, T 3557439, 80 rm, 200 beds, located in a tower block on the S side of the Peoples' National Assembly (parliament); **E** *Tiab House Hotel*, 24 Sharia Mohamed Khalaf, Dokki, T 709812, 33 rm, 60 beds; **E** *Zayed*, 42 Abul Mahasen el-Shazli, Agouza, T 3463318, 40 rm, 96 beds, near Midan Sphinx and the W end of the 26th July bridge to Zamalek.

F *Anglo-Swiss*, 14 Sharia Champollion, T 751479, charming 1930s style downtown *pensión* run by a friendly Greek couple with very clean shared bathrooms, good service and drinks but no food except breakfast; **F** ***Aviation Hotel***, PO Box 2688, S. Fatima, Heliopolis, T 2450393, 29 rm, 46 beds, used almost exclusively by foreign air crews; **F** ***Big Ben***, 33 Sharia Emad el-Din, T 908881, 37 rm, 82 beds, near Ramses Station, reception is on the 8th floor; **F** ***Blue Nile***, 4 Sharia el-Hokama, off Manshiet el-Bakri, T 291078, 27 rm, 50 beds, located between downtown Cairo and Heliopolis; **F** ***Cairo Palace***, Sharia el-Gumhorriya, Midan Ramses, T 906327, 24 clean rm, located in the very noisy area outside Ramses Station, roof-top restaurant and a friendly staff; **F** ***Capsis Palace***, 117 Sharia Ramses, Midan Ramses, T 754219, 72 rm, 114 beds, clean and comfortable, located in crowded and noisy area; **F** ***Ebeid House***, 179 Sharia Gesr el-Suez, Heliopolis, T 2454079, Tx 23251, 40 rm, 115 beds; **F** ***Garden City***, 23 Sharia Kamel el-Din Salah, Garden City, T 3544969, 38 rm, 75 beds, 1930s style *pensión* hotel located behind *Semiramis*, some rm have Nile view; **F** ***Gresham House Hotel***, 20 Sharia Talaat Harb, T 759043, F 762298, 45 rm, centrally located downtown; **F** ***Happy Town***, 10 Sharia Ali el-Kassar, Emad el-Din, T 928600, 66 rm, 113 beds; **F** ***Helio Cairo***, 95 Sharia Abdel Hamid Badawi, Heliopolis, T 2450682, Tx 20327, 41 rm, 112 beds; **F** ***Hotel Des Roses***, 33 Sharia Talaat Harb, Cairo, T 758022, 32 rm, 51 beds, clean and comfortable, centrally located, make sure you get one of the refurbished rm; **F** ***Kasr el-Nil***, 33 Sharia Kasr el-Nil, T 754523, 62 rm, central location, noisy disco; **F** ***Lido Hotel***, 465 Sharia el-Ahram, El-Ahram, T 727373, Tx 93661, 90 rm, on road to the Pyramids; **F** ***New Helwan***, 29 Sharia Sherif, Helwan Hamamat, T 784508, 31 rm, on main industrial area; **F** ***New Riche***, 47 Sharia Abdel-Aziz, Midan Ataba, T 3900145, 37 rm, cheap hotel located equidistant between the downtown area and the Islamic section with a sympathetic female proprietor; **F** ***Radwan***, 83 Sharia Gawhar el-Kaaid, Midan Azhar, T 901311, 45 rm, 80 beds, noisy, not advisable for single women; **F** ***Safa Inn Hotel***, Sharia Abbas el-Aqqad, Madinet Nasr, Cairo, T 2619022, F 2619022, 50 rm, 85 beds, located far from centre; **F** ***Scarabee***, Sharia 16 July 26th, Azbakia, T 3939675, F 3930170, 76 rm, 140 beds, rather noisy; **F** ***Select***, 8th Floor, Sharia Adli, highly recommended downtown budget hotel located on 8th floor, breakfast included; **F** ***Tourist Palace Hotel***, 12 Sharia el-Baidak, El-Muski, T 915126, 51 rm, near noisy and crowded Midan Ataba; **F** ***Tulip***, 3 Midan Talaat Harb, T 766884, 22 rm, good location on 3rd floor and above an office block in the heart of downtown Cairo, clean and comfortable; **F** ***Viennoise***, 11 Sharia Mahmoud Bassyouni, Kasr el-Nil, T 751949, Tx 94285, 26 rm, atmospheric downtown hotel which retains its turn of the century character.

● Youth hostel

2 km S of city centre, **135 Sharia Abdel-Aziz al-Saud**, El-Manial, near University Bridge, T 2 840729, 204 beds, kitchen, meals available, family rm, laundry, overnight fee E£5, station 3 km. Book 1 month in advance. **Egyptian Youth Hostel Association (EYHA)**, 7 Sharia Dr Abdel Hamid Said, Marouf, Cairo, T 2 758099.

● Camping

Because there are so many hotels there is little demand for camping. One of the very few is called ***Salma Camping*** which can be reached by turning off from Harraniya village on the road between the Pyramids and Saqqara. It offers both cabins, a camping ground, hot showers, a buffet and a bar.

● Places to eat

Price guide:
♦♦♦Expensive; ♦♦average; ♦cheap.

The numerous high quality hotels can be relied upon to serve good, anxiety-free meals and usually have a range of expensive and average meals. Cheap meals are available in the many *fuul* restaurants (see Information for Visitors, **page 887**).

♦♦♦ *Cairo Tower*, Sharia el- Guezira, T 3474122, stunning views; ***Tokyo***, 4 Sharia el-Maahad el-Swissry, Zamalek, T 816610 interesting Japanese food, excellent service, if this is what you came to Egypt for; ***Starlight***, in *Baron Hotel*, international food, panoramic views; ***Al-Saraya***, in *Heliopolis Movenpick*, seafood specialities and gourmet menu, open 1800-2400; ***Movenpick***, Cairo International Airport, Swiss and Far Eastern specialities; ***Al-Adin***, in *Cairo Sheraton*, Lebanese and Middle Eastern specialities from 2000-0100; ***La Mamma***, in *Cairo Sheraton*, serves Italian food with live entertainment 1200-2400; ***Justine's***, 4 Sharia Hassan Sabri, Zamalek, at The Four Corners, T 3412961, excellent service, high quality French food, the place for a special meal; ***Moghul Room***, *Mena House Oberoi*, authentic Indian food, live Indian entertainment every evening; ***Le Chalet***, Swissair Restaurant, El Nasr Building, Nile St, Giza, T 3485321, Swiss, French specialities, good service; ***Chin Chin***, at The Four Corners, high quality Chinese food, beautifully presented.

♦♦***Roy's***, in *Marriott Hotel* serves Mexican food from 1200-2400. ***El-Dar*** Saqqara Road, T 852289, Western/Egyptian food; ***Felfela***, 15 Sharia Talaat Harb, T 742751, open 0700-0100, one of downtown Cairo's most famous and popular tourist restaurants, serves good decent food and beer but its fame has allowed it to rest on its laurels and put up its prices, now over-rated, toilets are far too close to the end tables particularly when the restaurant is full; ***Ali Hassan el-Hati***, 8 Sharia July, T 918829, open 1100-2200, fish and kebab both recommended; ***Le Rendezvous***, in shopping arcade of *Hotel Ramses* for quick service, open 1000-2200; ***Cellar***, at *The President Hotel*, Western/Egyptian food in a convivial bar setting, popular socially with young affluent Egyptians; ***La Piazza***, at The Four Corners, reliable, tasty Egyptian/Western food, speedy service; ***Silver Fish***, 39 Mohy El Din, Sharia Abu El Ezz, Dokki, T 3492272, good seafood in a relaxed setting.

♦***Andreya***, 59 Mariuteya Canal, T 851133, specialities are chicken /pigeon, eat out of doors; ***La Rose***, 58 Sharia Mariuteya Canal, T 855712, clean surroundings, tasty food; ***Zamalek Restaurant***, 118 Sharia 26 July for *fuul*; ***El Omda***, 6 Sharia El Gazzor, Mohandiseen, next to *Atlas Zamalek Hotel*, famous for Egyptian specialities, especially *koshan*.

Floating Restaurants *Nile President*, good efficient service, clean, well maintained, excellent and varied food,

● Airline offices

Air France, 2 Midan Talaat Harb, T 743300; **Air India**, 1 Midan Talaat Harb, T 3922529 (Airport T 966756); **Alitalia**, *Nile Hilton Hotel*, T 743488 (Airport T 655143); **British Airways**, 1 Sharia Abdel Salam Aref, T 762914 (Airport 963456); **Egyptair**, 9 Sharia Talaat Harb, T 3932836 or *Nile Hilton* (Airport 697022); **Iberia**, 15 Midan Tahrir, T 749955; **KLM**, 11 Kasr el-Nil, Cairo, T 5740999; **Lufthansa**, 6 El-Sheikh el-Marsafi, Zamalek, Cairo, T 3420471; **Quantas**, 1 Sharia Kasr el-Nil, T 749900; **Royal Air Maroc**, 9 Sharia Talaat Harb, T 740378; **Swissair**, 22 Sharia Kasr el-Nil, T 741522 (Airport 669537); **Tunis Air**, 14 Talaat Harb, Cairo, T 769726.

● Banks

Bank of Alexandria and **Egyptian Central Bank** in Sharia Ksar el-Nil; **National Bank of Egypt** 24 Sharia Sherif; **Bank of America** 106 Sharia Kasr el-Ainy, Garden City; **Barclays International Bank** 1 Sharia Latin America, Garden City; **American Express**, 4 Sharia Syna, Mohandiseen; **Citibank**, 4 Sharia Ahmed Pasha, Garden City; **Chemical Bank**, 3 Sharia Ahmed Nessim, Giza; **Hong Kong Egyptian Bank**, 3 Sharia Abu El Feda, Zamalek.

● Bookshops

Those selling books and periodicals in European languages. ***Academic Bookshop***, 121 Sharia el-Tahrir, Dokki open 1000-2000; ***Al-Ahram***, 165 Sharia Mohamed Farid, Downtown in *Nile Hilton*, open 0830-2200; ***Al-Arab Bookshop***, 28 Sharia Faggala, T 908025, open 0900-1400, 1700-2000, closed Sun; ***Alexandria Bookshop***, 134 Sharia Omar Ibn el-Khatab. **Heliopolis**: ***American University in Cairo Bookstore***, on main campus; ***Anglo-Egyptian Bookshop***, 165 Sharia Mohamed Farid, Downtown, open 0900-1330 and 1630-1930; ***Baron Books***, *Méridien Heliopolis Hotel*; ***Dar ek Shark***, Sharia Brazil, Zamalek, open 1000-1400 and 1700-2000, closed Fri; ***Lehnert & Landrock***, 44 Sharia Sherif, books in German and English. Open 0930-1330 and 1530-1930, closed Sat afternoon and Sun.

● Casinos

Found in the following hotels: ***Cairo Heliopolis Movenpick, Cairo Marriot, Cairo Sheraton, El Giza Sheraton, Mena House Oberoi, Nile Hilton, Ramses Hotel, Semiramis Intercontinental, Shepheard Hotel.***

● Chemists

24 hr service: ***Old Cairo airport***, T 2903964; ***New Cairo airport***, T 2446032; ***Ataba Pharmacy***, Midan Ataba, T 920831; ***Isa'f Pharmacy***, Sharia Ramses, T 743369; ***Helwan Pharmacy***, 17 Sharia Ahmed Anas, T 38018; ***Magsoud***, 29 Sharia Mahmoud Shahk, Heliopolis, T 2453918; ***Zamalek Pharmacy***, 3 Shagaret El Dor, Zamalek, T 3402406.

● Cinemas

Karim I/Karim II, rue Emad Al-Dine; ***Cine Al Tahrir***, 122 Sharia al Tahrir, Dokki; ***Metro***, in *Swissotel el-Salam*.

● Embassies in Cairo

Algeria, 14 Sharia Brazil, Zamalek, T 3418527; **Canada**, Sharia Mohamed Fahmi el-Sayed, Garden City, T 3543110/9; **France**, 29 Sharia el-Nil, Giza, T 3415694/7; **Germany**,

8A Sharia Hassan Sabri, Zamalek, T 3418153; **Libya**, Sharia el-Saiobh, Zamalek; **Morocco**, 10 Sharia El Din Ayoub, Zamalek, T 3409677; **Spain**, 25 Sharia Gamal el-Din Abu al-Mahasen, Garden City, T 3547069; **Sudan**, 3 Sharia El Ibrahimi, Garden City, T 3549661/3545043, letter of recommendation required; **UK**, 7 Sharia Ahmed Raghab, Garden City, T 3540852/9; **USA**, 5 Sharia Latin America, Garden City, T 3557371.

● Hospitals
Coptic Hospital, Sharia Ramses, T 904435; *Anglo-American Hospital* behind Cairo Tower, T 3406162; *El-Salam International*, Maadi, T 3507592; *Damascus Hospital*, 1 Sharia Damascus, Mohandiseen, T 3470194; *Shaalan Surgical Centre*, 10 Abdel Hamid Loth, Mohandiseen, T 3605180.

● Nightclubs/Discos
All with live entertainment and most with belly dancer: ***Abu Nawas***, in *Mena House Oberoi Hotel*, open 2000-0300, T 3833444; ***Aladin***, open air, and ***Alhambra***, in *Cairo Sheraton Hotel*, summer only, T 3488600; ***Belvedere***, in *Nile Hilton*, open 2000-0230, closed Tue, T 767444; ***El-Samar***, in *El-Gezira Sheraton Hotel*, T 3411555; ***El-Torero***, in *Pullman Maadi Towers*, T 3506092; ***Haroun el-Rachid***, in *Semiramis Intercontinental Hotel*, closed Mon, T 3557171; ***La Belle Epoque*** in *Le Méridien Cairo Hotel*, T 3621717; ***Tent***, in *Heliopolis Sheraton Hotel*, closed Mon, T 2455155; ***Ya Salam***, in *El-Salam Hotel*, closed Mon, T 2455155, extn 7003.

Most popular **discos** with young and affluent Egyptians and expatriates: ***Tamango*** in *Atlas Zamalek Hotel*, T 3466567, open 2200-0300, entrance E£30; ***Saddle*** at the *Mena House Oberoi*, open 2200-0400, closed Sun, entrance, E£30; ***Atlantis*** at *Shepheard Hotel* open 2300-0400, entrance E£50; ***Borsalino's***, 15 Sharia Rustum Basha, Garden City, open 2300-0300, entrance E£20, for a more basic club playing African influenced pop and reggae.

● Post Office
Cairo's main post office is on Midan Ataba. Major hotels can possible provide the same services without the crowds.

● Religious services
Anglican/Episcopalian, 5 Sharia Michel Lutfalla, Zamalek T 3418391, services Sun at 0800, 1030 and 1930; **Christian Science**, T 3929032, 3 Midan Mustafa Kamel, Sun and Wed at 1930; **Coptic Church**, T 821274; **Roman Catholic**, *Holy Family Church*, T 3502004, Maadi, daily Mass at 0830, Fri at 0930 and 1800, Sun at 1800; *St Joseph's Church*, T 3408902, 2 Sharia Bank Misr, Downtown, Mass (English) Sun at 1630; *St Joseph's Church*, 4 Sharia Ahmed Sabri, Zamalek, Mass (English) Sun 1800; **German Evangelical**, Sharia Galaa, Boulaq, T 3478549; **Quaker**, alternate Sat at 1900, T 3539692.

● Shopping
Among the most attractive areas to shop is the ***Khan el-Khalili Bazaar*** and ***Sagh*** comprising an array of shops dating from the 14th century. Renowned for craftsmanship in silver and gold, embroidered cloth, copper ware, leather and ivory inlaid goods. (Remember that the import of ivory is forbidden into most Western countries.) The Kerdassa village, E of Giza, is noted for its embroidered cotton and silk dresses *galbeyas* and other hand-made goods while Haraneya, W of Giza, is the main centre for quality carpets.

● Sound and Light
Two performances daily at the Sphinx and Pyramids, Giza: at 1830 and 1930 in Winter, and 2030 and 2130 in Summer. Entrance E£30. Information T 3852880.

Mon	English/French
Tue	French/Italian
Wed	English/French
Thur	Arabic/English
Fri	English/French
Sat	English/Spanish
Sun	French/German

● Sports
Yacht Club Maadi, T 3505169; **Shooting Club** Dokki, T 3498479; **Horse Riding** Guezira, T 3405690. **Swimming** use the pools at the hotels: those in the five star establishments cost more. Heliopolis, Giza and Gezira Sporting Clubs have pools, daily and weekly membership available. Public pools are to be avoided. **Keep fit** includes gymnasia at *Nile Hilton*. **Golf** There is a public golf course at the foot of the pyramids. Also *Mina House Oberoi* and *Pyramid Park Sofite*. Tennis courts can be booked at the *Marriott Hotel*.

● Spectator sport
Horse Racing weekends from 1300 in winter at the Guezira race-course and weekends mid Oct to end of May at Heliopolis race-course. **Football** at the stadium in Heliopolis week-

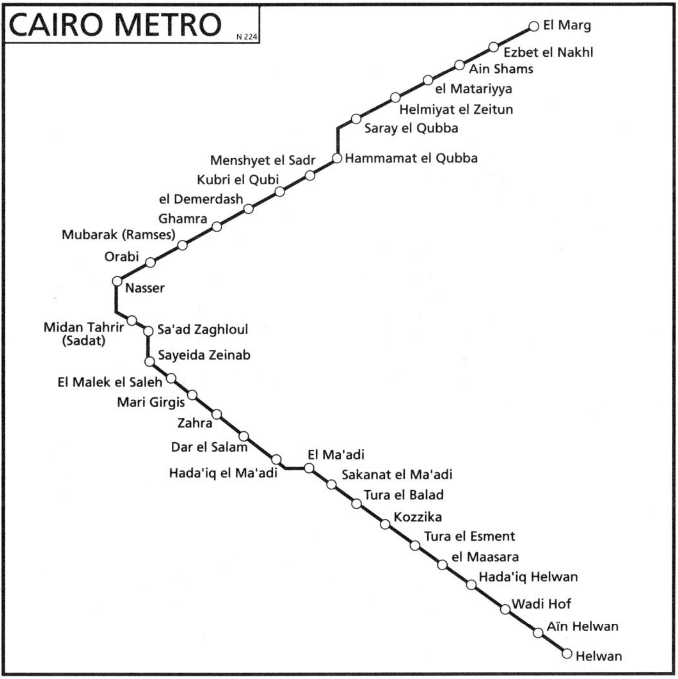

ends at 1500. **Rowing** races each Fri on the Nile.

● Telephone

Local code: 02. **Emergency numbers**: Police, T 122; Accident, T 123; Fire, T 125; Tourist Police, T 926028; International collect call 146. **Major Polices offices**: Railway Station, Cairo Airport, Midan Tahrir, Sharia 26 July/Mansour Mohamed. There are International telephone, telex and fax services at all major hotels.

● Theatres and Cinemas

Current information for theatre and cinemas performances is given in the *Egyptian Gazette* and *Egyptian Mail* as well as the monthly *'Egypt Today'* publication. The 7-storey ***Opera House***, T 3420601, in the Gezira Exhibition Grounds has a main hall with 1200 seats for opera, ballet and classical music performances, a second hall with 500 seats for films and conferences and an open air theatre. Advance booking is recommended. Men must wear jacket and tie. ***The National***, in Azbakiah T 917783; ***Al-Gumhorriya***, in Sharia Gumhorriya, T 919956; ***Mohamed Farid***, in Sharia Mohamed Farid, T 741204; ***Balloon***, Sharia el-Nil near al-Zamalek Bridge, T 810503; ***Puppet Theatre***, Azbakiah T 910954. Apart from the *Opera House*, all performances are likely to be in Arabic.

● Travel agents

Abercrombie and Kent, 5 Sharia Bustan, Tahrir, T 761324; ***Academy Tours***, 95 Sharia el-Herghani, Heliopolis, T 345050; ***American Express***, 21 Sharia Giza, Nile Tower Building, T 3703411; ***Astra Travel*** 15 Sharia Demashk, Mohandsseen, T 3446445; ***Egyptian Express*** 8 Sharia Kasr el-Nil, T 750620; ***Etam Tours*** Egyptian Tourism and Medical Services, 3 Sharia Kasr el-Nil, T 754721, F 5741491, ask for Dr Bishara, along established firm offering specialized handling of handicapped visitors; ***Gaz Tours***, 7 Sharia Bustan, T 752782; ***Hermes Travel***, 1 Montaser Bldg, Sharia Sudan, Sahafeyeen, T 3451474; ***Isis Travel*** 48 Sharia

Giza, Orman Bldg, T 3494326; ***Karnak Travel and Touristic Services***, 12 Sharia Kasr el-Nil, T 750600; ***Mena Tours***, El-Nasr Bldg, Sharia el-Nil, Giza, T 3482217 and 14 Sharia Talaat Harb, T 740955; ***Misr Travel***, 1 Sharia Talaat Harb, T 3930010, ask for Mr Mohamed Halawa; ***Seti First Travel Co*** 16 Sharia Ismail Mohamed, Zamalek, T 3419820, F 3400855; ***Thomas Cook Overseas*** 12 Midan El-Sheikh Youssef, Garden City, T 3564650.

● Transport

Local: Buses in Cairo are only for the strong and the brave. They are very crowded. They tend to slow down rather than stop which requires some agility. One enters at the rear and leaves by the front which means pushing the length of the bus. The main bus station is in Midan Tahrir. Bus No 900 goes to the pyramids and No 400 (hourly) to the airport.

Calèche for a tourist ride. This is expensive but an experience.

Car Hire Avis, 16 Sharia Ma'amal el-Soukkar, Garden City, T 3547081, also at *Hotel Méridien, Nile Hilton Hotel, Hotel Jolie Ville* and *Sheraton Hotel*; **Bita**, 15 Sharia Mahmoud Bassyouni, T 746169; **Budget**, 1 Sharia Mohamed Ebeid, Heliopolis, T 666027, also at *Marriott Hotel*; **Hertz**, 195 Sharia July 26, Agouza, T 3474172, also at *Ramses Hotel, Sonesta Hotel, Maadi Hotel* and *President Hotel*.

Metro In addition to the Heliopolis Metro connecting Midan Ramses to Heliopolis, Nasr City and Mattareya there is the Helwan Metro from Helwan, stopping at 14 stations including Old Cairo and Maadi, operates daily every 6 minutes from 0530-2400 (summer 0530-0100). (**See page 733** for map.) Don't lose your ticket and don't smoke. There are separate 'women-only' carriages on all trains.

Taxis Ramshackle but the best way of getting around. Check current prices with locals or at your hotel. Best not to ask the price first or to bargain but just pay the current price at the destination and don't ask for change.

Train Sleeping cars T 753555/3484633. To **Alexandria** 17 daily; to **Luxor** 0100,1200,1400; to **Aswan** 0730, 1545, 1900, 1915, 1930, 2000, 2030, 2100; to **Port Said and Ismailia** 0620, 0845, 1240, 1425, 1830; to **Beni Suef and Assuit** 0700, 1000, 1240, 1410, 1600.

Road: **Bus** For destinations outside Cairo – Middle Delta Bus Co T 946286; East Delta Bus Co from Midan Abbassiya, T 824753; West Delta Bus Co, T 759701.

CAIRO ENVIRONS: THE PYRAMIDS & EL-FAYOUM

CONTENTS

MAPS

Ever since the Greek and Roman era, if not earlier, the Pyramids at Giza just to the W of Cairo have been one of the world's great tourist attractions. Although there are other pyramids in Egypt, the ones at Giza are almost certainly the largest, most imposing and best preserved ancient monuments in the world. In order to see the development from the simple underground tomb to the audacious concept and awesome majestic splendour of the Pyramid of Cheops it is undoubtedly worth visiting Saqqara before going on to Giza

Memphis

The oldest known imperial city on earth, was founded in the 1st Dynasty (3100-2890 BC) at the start of the Early Dynastic Period (3100-2686 BC), and lies 15 km S of Cairo. It was established sometime around 3100 BC by Menes who may have actually been several successive kings rather than a single person. It was the Pharaohs' capital city throughout the Old Kingdom (2686-2181 BC) and was inhabited for 4 millennia, until it was eventually abandoned by the Moors, and returned to the Nile silt from which it was originally constructed. Sadly all that remains today is a limestone Colossus of Ramses II (1304-1237 BC) and a giant alabaster sphinx weighing 80 tonnes, both of which may have stood outside the huge Temple of Ptah, and the remains of the Embalming House, where there are several alabaster tables, weighing up to 50 tonnes, which were used to embalm the sacred Apis bulls before burial at Saqqara. Beyond these its former glories can only be imagined.

SAQQARA

ACCESS To reach **Saqqara** (open daily 0900-1600, entry fee E£10 or E£5 for students with cards, camera fee E£5 or E£25 for video cameras) by public transport take the No 121 bus from Giza Pyramids to Badrashin (E£0.25) and then Badrashin to Saqqara village (E£0.30) after which it is a 3 kms walk. Giza to Saqqara by camel costs E£150 per person and takes 4-5 hrs or E£100 and 2 hrs by horse. Because of the hassle of public transport and the fascinating information an informed tour guide can provide about the area it is probably best to spend E£40-E£50 to go with a reputable tour group. All guides will expect *baksheesh* (small tip) of a few E£ at the end of the tour but only give it if you genuinely feel that they have been good. On the journey between Saqqara and Giza most tour coaches will stop at some of the numerous carpet schools.

Saqqara, which faces Memphis across the Nile from the W bank, was the enormous necropolis for the first pharaohs. It extends for over 7 sq km. With many tombs believed to be still undiscovered it is currently Egypt's largest archaeological site. From its inception it expanded W into the desert until the 4th Dynasty (2613-2494 BC) when the Giza plateau superseded it. At the end of the 5th Dynasty (2494-2345 BC) a more systematic construction of pyramids and *mastabas* began which resulted in many splendid monuments around Saqqara. In 1883 a Middle Kingdom (2050-1786 BC) necropolis was found to the E but it was not until the New Kingdom (1567-1085 BC) that Saqqara is thought to have regained its importance as a burial ground.

Zoser's Funerary Complex

This complex, the largest in Saqqara, is an example of some of the world's most ancient architecture. The whole complex, including but not confined to the **Step Pyramid**, was designed and built by Zoser (2667-2648 BC), the 2nd king in the 3rd Dynasty, under the control of his chief architect Imhotep who some regard as the world's first architect. At its heart is the Step Pyramid, the first of its kind, which can be seen as a prototype for the Giza Pyramids. This marked the evolution of burial tombs from *mastabas* with deep shafts for the sarcophagus to imposing elevated mausoleums. It was constructed in steps building up from the traditional *mastaba*. The original tomb was initially expanded to a 4 step and then to a 6 step pyramid. Although the external white limestone casing has disappeared over time this step structure is still clearly visible. The pyramid eventually reached a height of 62m which, although small by comparison with those at Giza, is still an amazing feat because of the primitive building techniques. The advances represented by Zoser's Pyramid were not in the building techniques or materials, which were already established, but the concept, design and calculations involved which made such a monument possible.

In accordance with the traditional *mastaba* technique, the Royal Tomb lies 28m underground at the bottom of a vertical shaft. The shaft was then sealed with a 3 tonne granite block but this did still not prevent the tomb from being looted. Another 11 shafts were found, 32m deep, under the E side of the Pyramid, which lead to the tombs of the queens and royal children. Unfortunately these are no longer open to the public.

The whole funerary complex was completely surrounded by buttressed walls which were over 544m long, 277m wide and 10.4m (20 cubits) high. Although 14 fake doors were built, only the one in the SE corner, which leads into the colonnade **Hypostele Hall** actually gives access to the site. It is thought that the area was walled in order to deter intruders and thieves, and to provide space for the Pharaoh's *Ka* (spirit) to live in the after-life. Before entering the Colonnade, observe the fake door complete with hinges and sockets in the Vestibule on the right. The Colonnade leads through to the **Southern Court**, on the S side of which there is a frieze of cobras. This represents the fire-spitting goddess of destruction Edjo who was adopted as the Uraeus, the emblem of royalty and of protection, which was worn on the pharaonic head-dress.

Further along this S wall is a deep shaft at the bottom of which lies **Zoser's Southern Tomb** which some believe held the King's entrails. More importantly there is a relief, depicting the King running the Heb-Sed race, which illustrates the purpose of the surrounding buildings and monuments. The buildings in the funerary complex, some of which are mere façades like a Hollywood film-set, simply represented a pastiche for the after-life of this crucial ceremony. Their intended purpose was to eternalize the symbol of the unification of a greater Egypt and the power of the pharaoh even in death.

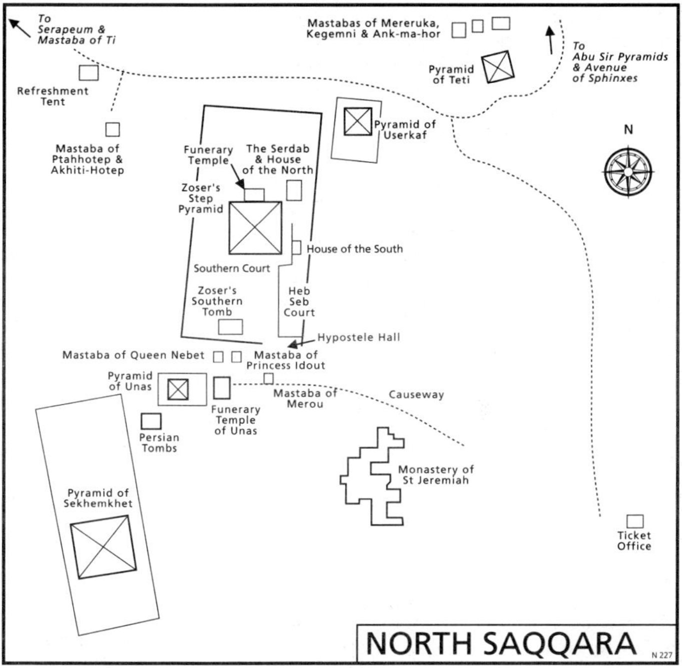

This symbolism is echoed in the lotus and papyrus capitals on top of the columns fronting the **House of the South** and the **House of the North** which represent the heraldic emblems of Upper and Lower Egypt, respectively. The **House of the South** is interesting because its columns, which are precursors of the Greek Doric style, and its New Kingdom graffiti offer a fascinating reminder of the continuity of human civilization.

On the N side of the Step Pyramid there is a stone casket, known as the **Serdab** (cellar), containing a copy of a life-size statue of Zoser. The original is in the Egyptian Museum in Cairo. The Serdab has 2 cylindrical holes to enable the statue to communicate with the outside world and to preserve the Pharaoh's *Ka*. To the W of the Serdab the **Funerary Temple** is in ruins but some of the walls and the entrance can still be seen. A tunnel originally linked it with the royal tomb.

S of Zoser's Funerary Complex

The Pyramid of Unas, which was built for the last pharaoh of the 5th Dynasty (2494-2345 BC), appears from the outside to be a heap of rubble but the inside is still very well preserved and contains some beautiful hieroglyphs. As always, the entrance is from the N side down a passageway leading to the Burial Chamber. This is largely undecorated except for the star-covered ceiling and the sarcophagus which is made from a single block of black basalt and bears no inscriptions. The most interesting inscriptions are in the passageway, painted in green and organized in vertical lines. The hieroglyphs are magic formulae and prayers for the Pharaoh to help his passage into the after-life. They were the first to be found inside a tomb and formed the basis for the *Book of the Dead* (see **Valley of the Kings, page 781**). To the E, a few remnants of the **Funerary Temple** can be seen. Beyond this the remains of a causeway linking the **Funerary Temple** to the Valley Temple 700m away have been discovered. The pyramid was excavated and opened as a tourist attraction in 1881 by the director of antiquities Gaston Maspero with financial sponsorship from Thomas Cook & Son.

To the N of the Pyramid the **Mastaba of Queen Nebet**, who was Unas' wife, is also fascinating and well preserved. It is divided into 3 rooms of which the second is most interesting because it contains some rare scenes of Nebet in the women's quarters, or harem, in the palace. From here, a door leads to a gallery with beautifully decorated walls.

Opposite, to the NE, is the **Mastaba of Princess Idout**. The tomb is divided into 10 rooms but only 5 are decorated. The wall paintings give us a glimpse of life in Idout's day with the many tableaux of rural and domestic scenes. Two rooms are dedicated to the offerings to the Princess and are designed to provide for her in the after-life.

Slightly to the E is the **Mastaba of Merou** containing some exceptionally well preserved paintings. In the **Grand Offerings Room** the paint scarcely seems to have faded thereby giving a good idea of the original splendour of these tombs.

S of the Pyramid of Unas a stone hut covers the access to 3 small **Persian Tombs** 25m underground and composed of 2 shafts. In order to lower the heavy sarcophagus, an ingenious system was devised involving the use of an additional smaller shaft. The main shaft was dug out, then filled with sand. The sarcophagus was then placed on top of the sand which was gradually removed from below via the smaller shaft. The tombs dating from the 27th Dynasty (525-404 BC) are interesting because they have very similar inscriptions to those found in Unas' Pyramid constructed over 2,000 years earlier.

To the SW are the remains of the **Pyramid of Sekhemkhet** which was at the centre of an unfinished and unused funerary complex, very similar to that of his predecessor Zoser, which was only discovered in 1950 and to which there is no public access.

To the E of the Pyramid of Sekhemkhet can be seen the remains of the **Monastery of St Jeremiah** which was founded in the 5th century but destroyed by the Arabs 5 centuries later. Following its discovery in 1907 many of the paintings and other items of interest were removed and are now on display in the Coptic Museum in Cairo.

Dash For The Altar – The Heb-Sed Race

The Heb-Sed race took place during the festival held to mark the 30th anniversary of Zoser's reign. He would sprint between two altars, which represented Upper and Lower Egypt, thereby not only re-enacting his coronation in both parts of the country and symbolising the unification of the two lands but also demonstrating his continuing vigour.

NE of the Funerary Complex

The **Pyramid of Teti**, the founder of the 6th Dynasty (2345-2181 BC), was discovered by Mariette in 1853 but is now little more than a pile of rubble in constant danger of being submerged by sand. It is entered via a steep pathway leading to the funerary chamber in which the ceiling is decorated with stars.

Mastaba of Mereruka To the N are a

number of well preserved *mastabas*. The most outstanding is that of **Mereruka**, who was Teti's vizier, an important person in 6th Dynasty society. This is one of the largest Old Kingdom *mastabas* to have been found. Its 32 rooms are divided into 3 parts for Mereruka (21 rm), his wife (6 rm) and his son (5 rm). In the main entrance passage Mereruka is depicted painting the 3 seasons which leads to the next room containing some interesting hunting scenes. Particularly worth noting is the indication of the types of animal that they hunted and the techniques being used. Scenes of everyday life are beautifully depicted throughout the tomb giving a valuable insight into contemporary life. The largest room, with 6 pillars, has a statue of Mereruka to the N and some unusual mourning scenes on the E wall. On the left are scenes of Mereruka carried by his son and surrounded by dwarfs and dogs. To enter Mereruka's wife's rooms go back to the main entrance and take the door on the left.

To the E, the **Mastaba of Kagemni** has some excellent reliefs and paintings of a much a higher standard, but unfortunately less well preserved, than those in Mereruka's tomb. Further E is the **Mastaba of Ankh-ma-hor**, the vizier and overseer of the Great House in the 6th Dynasty, which is also known as the Doctor's Tomb because of the paintings depicting circumcision and an operation on a toe! The other rooms are interesting and show the usual scenes of the preparation and transportation of the offerings and various representations of hunting and daily life.

NW of the Funerary Complex

Situated about 200m S of the road to the refreshment tent is one of the finest of all the *mastabas*. The **Double Mastaba of Ptah-Hotep & Akhiti-Hotep** contains some of the finest Old Kingdom art and some fascinating unfinished work which demonstrates the techniques used in painting reliefs. Ptah-Hotep was a priest of Maat in the reign of Djedkare, who was Unas' predecessor: his son Akhiti-Hotep was vizier, judge, and the overseer of the treasury and the granaries.

The entrance leads into a long corridor decorated with unfinished agricultural scenes. The red paint indicates the preliminary drawing before the wall was carved and painted. The outstanding masterpiece, however, is in the **Sanctuary** dedicated to Ptah-Hotep. On the walls behind the entrance Ptah-Hotep is seated watching a concert while his servants wash and manicure him. Other walls bear scenes of Ptah-Hotep receiving offerings. On the left wall, which is the most interesting and impressive, the figure in the first boat is being given water by a boy. The inscription describes him as the Chief Artist, who is thought to have been Ankhen-Ptah, and this scene may well represent the first known example of an artist's signature.

The Serapeum was a burial place for the sacred Apis Bulls which were believed to be manifestations of Ptah's blessed soul and were identified with Osiris after his death. They were given full honours in a ceremony worthy of any Pharaoh or important noble and were then embalmed and the mummified body placed in a sarcophagus and buried in the Serapeum. The sarcophagus was then sealed off from the main gallery by means of a richly decorated wall. The high priests would then start searching for the new Apis Bull within the sacred herd. The cult was a significant one and the Serapeum represents an important funerary complex which, besides the tombs themselves, included the priests' quarters, schools and inns catering for passing pilgrims. The cult of the Apis Bulls lasted well into the Ptolemaic period.

The Serapeum is situated 300m to the NW of the refreshment tent and is one of the most impressive sites in Saqqara.

It is reached via a long, sloping path, at the bottom of which a door leads to the 3 galleries. Only 2 are accessible, and the 24 surviving sarcophagi are set in small galleries on either side of the main one. Only 3 of the enormous basalt or granite sarcophagi bear inscriptions, and these are marked with the cartouches of different pharaohs. The Serapeum was discovered in 1851 but, with the exception of one tomb, most had already been looted. The artifacts discovered are now displayed in the Musée du Louvre, Paris.

The **Mastaba of Ti** is one of the wonders of the Old Kingdom, and its beautiful reliefs provide some interesting insights into life during that period. Ti was a 5th Dynasty royal hairdresser who married well and became steward of the sun temples of Neferikare and Nyuserre and whose children later bore the title of 'royal descendant'.

The *mastaba* stands 400m N of the refreshment tent, very close to the Serapeum, and is centred around a square courtyard which is surrounded by columns. The entrance is through a vestibule with portraits of Ti on the 2 entrance pillars. The reliefs in the courtyard have been damaged but their representations of daily life – breeding birds (N wall left), Ti on his litter with dogs and dwarfs (E wall, centre), and Ti with his wife (W wall centre) – are still worth seeing. In the centre of the courtyard an undecorated shaft leads to the tomb. A corridor leads from the SW corner through to the main shrine. On the left of the corridor, just after the door, servants are depicted bringing offerings while on the right are musicians and dancers. Further on, to the right, is a false door bearing a representation of Ti's wife.

Further down the corridor on the right is a storage room and then the main hall of offerings and shrine which has a number of scenes depicting the offerings ceremony, the brewing of beer and the baking of bread. The main shrine is remarkable for its abundance of scenes depicting daily life including one illustrating boat construction. Note the extreme simplicity of the tools used.

The S wall holds the **Serdab**, where a copy of Ti's statue, the original being in the Cairo Museum, can be seen through the slit. Around the 2 slits there are scenes of daily market life, carpenters, tanners, and various other artisans. Around the second slit, Ti is entertained by musicians while servants burn incense. These paintings should be taken on one level as literal depictions of Egyptian life but it is also important to realize the importance of symbolism and allegory. The N walls show Ti in a boat observing a hippopotamus hunt in the Delta region. The hippopotamus was symbolic of evil so there is probably more to the picture than meets the eye.

The **Pyramids of Abu Sir** are situated 2½ km further NE of the Mastaba of Ti. The site originally contained 14 5th Dynasty pyramids but only 4 are still standing. When arriving from the main Saqqara complex the **Pyramid of Neferefre** is the first to be encountered. It was never finished and is now in very poor condition. The next also unfinished pyramid to the N was built for **Neferikare** and towering over the others is, at 68m, the tallest of the group. To the NE, the **Pyramid of Nouserre** is worth noting for its **Funerary Temple** which, although originally built for the Neferikare, was used by Nouserre because of Neferikare's premature death. About 100m to the NE lies the tomb of **Ptah-Cepses**. The *mastaba* is not in good condition but is worth seeing for the columns with lotus capitals which are the oldest so far discovered.

The remaining one, **Sahure's Pyramid**, is directly N and its **Funerary Temple** is not too severely damaged. Excavation work around it has led to the discovery of the remains of a 240m ramp which connected it to the **Valley Temple**. The Funerary Temple was originally walled with reliefs, some of which have been removed and placed in museums, but a few remain and are quite well preserved.

The Sun-Temples of Abu Ghurab, built in the 5th Dynasty when the solar cult had been declared the State religion, are about 1 km NE of Sahure's Pyramid. Unlike earlier temples their purpose was solely devotional and the pharaohs who built them were not buried in them. There were twin temples but only the **Sun-Temple of Nyuserre** remains with the **Sun-Temple of Userkaf** being little more than rubble. Fortunately because they were identical little is lost.

At the Western end of an enclosed courtyard a massive 70m obelisk once stood. The obelisk was the symbol of the primordial mound, the sun's resting place at the end of the day. An alabaster altar stands in the centre of the courtyard which would have been at the Eastern side of the obelisk's base. Animals were sacrificed at the NE corner of the courtyard from which channels cut in the paving carried the blood to ten alabaster basins, nine of which survive.

South Saqqara

This completely separate necropolis, founded by the pharaohs of the 6th Dynasty (2345-2181 BC), is situated about 1 km S of the Pyramid of Sekhemkhet which is the most southerly of all the pyramids in North Saqqara. It has a few interesting tombs, based on the Pyramid of Unas as an architectural model, but sadly has been plundered by unscrupulous stone-masons or their suppliers. The pyramids of **Pepi I** and **Merenre** are in ruins.

To the E of the latter lies the **Pyramid of Djedkare**, known in Arabic as the Pyramid of the Sentinel, which is 25m tall and is open to visitors. The entrance is on the N side through a tunnel leading into the funerary chamber but there is comparatively little to see.

The most important and interesting tombs are further S. The **Pyramid of Pepi II** is surrounded by an entire funerary complex. The inside chamber is decorated with stars and funerary inscriptions. Within the complex are a number of other smaller pyramids belonging to his queens. They are all based on the same design as Pepi's pyramid and contain a miniature funerary complex. The **Pyramid of Queen Neith** is interesting and has some wonderful inscriptions and decorations.

To the E is the **Mastaba Faraoun**, the tomb of **Shepseskaf**, the last Pharaoh of the 4th Dynasty (2613-2494 BC). The inside is interesting but undecorated and the walls are made from large blocks of granite. From the outside the tomb looks like a gigantic sarcophagus and the exterior was originally covered in a thin layer of limestone. About 1 km further S are two more pyramids. The first is the brick **Pyramid of Khendjer** which has a funerary chamber made out of quartzite. The second is larger, but unfinished, and bears no inscriptions or signs of use. It has impressive underground white stone chambers and a quartzite funerary chamber.

THE PYRAMIDS OF GIZA

Of the Seven Wonders of the ancient world only the **Pyramids** remain. Those at **Giza** outside Cairo are by no means the only ones in Egypt but they are the largest, most imposing and best preserved. When **Herodotus**, chronicler of the Ancient Greeks, visited them in 450 BC they were already more ancient to him than the time of Christ is to us today! That the huge blocks were quarried, transported and put into place demonstrates how highly developed and ordered the Old Kingdom was at its peak. Herodotus claimed that it would have taken 100,000 slaves 30 years to have constructed the great **Pyramid of Cheops**, but it is more likely that the pyramid was built by peasants, paid in food, who were unable to work the land whilst the Nile flooded between July and Nov. Happily, the high waters also made it possible to transport the casing stone from Aswan and Tura, virtually to the base of the pyramids. The enormous Pyramid of Cheops, built between 2589-2566 BC out of over 2,300,000 blocks of stone with an average weight of 2.5 tonnes and a total weight of 6,000,000 tonnes to a height of almost 140m, is the oldest and largest of the pyramids at Giza. The **Pyramid of Chephren** and **Pyramid of Menkaure** date from 2570 BC to 2530 BC.

A breakdown in the structure of society, and the reduction of wealth, have been proposed as reasons why other pyramids were not constructed on the same scale later in the Old Kingdom. The first thefts from tombs occurred relatively soon after the Pyramids' construction. A couple of centuries, or so, is not long when one considers that they have been standing for 4,000 years! This was undoubtedly an important factor in the preference for hidden tombs, such as in **The Valley of the Kings**, by the time of the New Kingdom.

ACCESS One of the first things that visitors to the Pyramids will notice is their unexpected proximity to Cairo. Giza itself is now little more than a suburb. Naturally the picture-postcards do not emphasize this fact! It costs E£10 per person to enter the area and the second pyramid, (but an additional E£10 to enter the Pyramid of Cheops), plus E£10 for cameras inside the pyramid but no flash photography is allowed. All the official guides demand a tip but most have already been tipped by the tour operator so don't give much. It is difficult but possible to avoid amateur guides who then demand money. The café has a minimum charge and should be avoided so make sure that you take water with you The hassling camel owners will demand much more but don't pay more than E£10 for a short ride and make sure you agree the price first and don't pay until you are back on the ground. The whole complex can be fairly busy at peak times and very dusty. Claustrophobics should avoid the inside of the pyramids.

Pyramid of Cheops (Khufu)

Very little is known of Cheops. His tomb, which could have provided some answers, was looted long before the archaeologists arrived. He is believed to have been the absolute ruler of a highly stratified society and his reign must have been one of great wealth in order to afford so stupendous a burial site. Although he was buried alone his wives and relations may have merited smaller *mastabas* nearby.

Originally the 230m x 230m pyramid would have stood at 140m high but 3m has been lost in all dimensions since the encasing marble was eroded or removed. The entrance, which was at the centre of the N face, has been changed in modern times and access is now 15m lower via an opening created by the plundering Khalifa Ma'mun in 820 AD. From this entrance a tunnel descends steeply for about 25m until it reaches a point where it is met by an ascending corridor which climbs at the same angle.

If one were to continue down the very long, narrow and steep descending shaft, which is closed to ordinary visitors and is definitely not for those who are either unfit or claustrophobic, one would eventually reach a lower unfinished chamber which lies 20m beneath the bedrock of the pyramid's foundations! Even though the chamber is empty, except for a deep pit where the sarcophagus would have been lowered, the sensation of standing alone under 6 million tonnes of stone blocks is overpowering. Despite the speculation that the chamber was unfinished because of a change of plan by either Cheops or his architect the later pyramid of Chephren follows an identical pattern.

Going up the 36m long ascending corridor, which is 1.6m high and has a steep 1:2 gradient, one arrives at the start of the larger 47m long **Great Gallery** which continues upward at the same incline to the **King's Chamber** 95m beneath the pyramid's apex. The gallery, whose magnificent stonework is so well cut that it is impossible to insert a blade into the joints, narrows at the top end to a corbelled roof which is 8.5m high.

At its beginning of the gallery there is a second horizontal passage, 35m long and 1.75m high, which leads to a room misleadingly known as the **Queen's Chamber**. In fact no queen was buried there and the small room, measuring 5.2m by 5.7m with a 6.13m pointed roof, is more likely to be the Serdab which contained the icon of the Pharaoh. In 1872 two triangular holes were made by a British engineer in the chamber's N and S walls in order to discover the location of the ventilation shafts.

The walls of **The King's Chamber** are lined with polished red granite. The room measures 5.2m by 10.8m by 5.8m high and contains the huge lidless Aswan red granite sarcophagus which was all that remained of the treasures when archaeologists first explored the site. It was saved because it was too large to move along the entrance passage and, therefore, must have been placed in the chamber during the pyramid's construction. Above this upper chamber there is a series of 5 relieving chambers which are structurally essential to support the massed weight of the stones above and distribute the weight away from the burial chamber. A visit to the collapsed pyramid at Maidoum (see Fayoum, page 750) will illustrate why this was necessary! As in the Queen's Chamber the N and S walls bear air shafts but in this case they are the original ones.

Around the Cheops Pyramid

In accordance with the Pharaonic custom, Cheops married his sister Merites whose smaller ruined pyramid stands to the E of his together with the pyramids of two other queens, both of which are attached to a similarly ruined smaller sanctuary. Little remains of **Cheops' Mortuary Temple** which stood to the E of the pyramid. It was connected by a causeway, which collapsed only in the last 150 years, to the Valley Temple which stands near the modern village of **Nazlat al-Samman**. The temples and causeway were built and decorated before Cheops' Pyramid was completed.

W of the Cheops Pyramid is an extensive Royal Cemetery in which 15 *mastabas* have recently been opened to the public after having been closed for over 100 years. A 4,600 year old female mummy, with a totally unique internal plaster encasement unlike that seen anywhere else, was discovered at the site.

The **Boat Pits and Museum** (open daily 0900-1600) is located at the base of the S face of the Cheops Pyramid where 5 boat pits were discovered in 1982. The boat, which is encased in the stones, is amazingly intact and was held together with rope with no nails being used at all. The exact purpose of these buried boats is unclear but they may have been regarded as a means of travelling to the after-life, as can be seen in the 17th to 19th Dynasty tombs at Thebes, or possibly as a means of accompanying the Sun-God on his diurnal journey. One boat has been located but has not yet been excavated though an excellent reconstruction of a boat can be seen in the museum. It is best to avoid visiting the sun ship at prayer time because you cannot get in.

Pyramid of Chephren (Khafre) Built for the son of Cheops and Hensuten the Pyramid of Chephren, or Khafre as he is sometimes known, stands to the SW of the Great Pyramid of Cheops. Although,

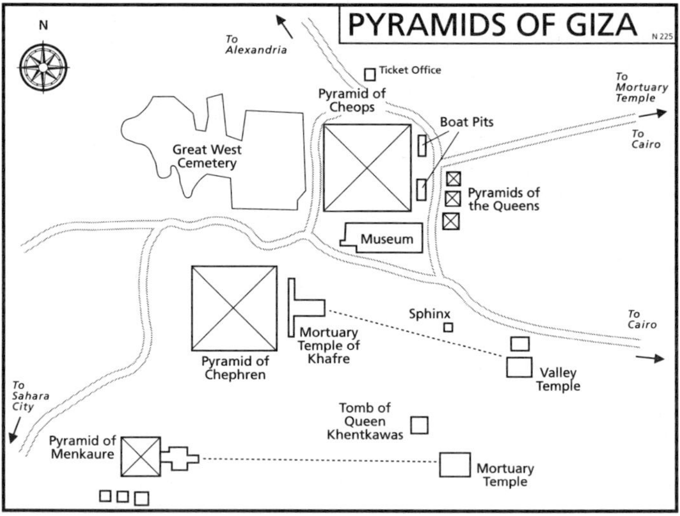

at 136.5m high, and an estimated weight of 4,880,000 tonnes, it is actually a few metres smaller than the Cheops Pyramid. The fact that it was built on a raised limestone plateau was a deliberate attempt to make it appear larger than that of his father. The top of the pyramid still retains some of the marble casing that once covered the entire surface, thus providing an idea of the original finish. The entrance to the tomb was lost for centuries until 1818 when Belzoni located and blasted open the sealed portal on the N side. Although he believed that it would still be intact, he found that it had been looted many centuries earlier. As with the Pyramid of Cheops there is an unfinished and presumed unused chamber below the bedrock. The passageway now used to enter the burial chamber heads downwards before levelling out to the granite lined passageway that leads to the chamber. To the W of the chamber is the red granite sarcophagus, built into the floor, with the lid lying nearby.

The **Mortuary Temple of Khafre** lies to the E of the pyramid and is more elaborate and better preserved than that of his father. Although the statues and riches have been stolen, the limestone walls were cased with granite which is still present in places. There are still the remains a large pillared hall, a small sanctuary, outhouses and a courtyard.

A 500m causeway linked the Mortuary Temple to the **Valley Temple** (open daily 0900-1600) which is better preserved than any other because it lay hidden in the sands until Mariette rediscovered it in 1852. It is lined with red granite at roof height which protects the limestone. Two entrances to the Temple face E and lead to a T-shaped hall supported by enormous pillars. In front of these stood 23 diorite statues of Khafre. The only one which has remained intact can be found in the Egyptian Museum. Side chambers lie off to the S of the hall. A passage which joined the causeway is now closed off.

The Sphinx is next to Khafre's Valley Temple to the NE. We are extremely lucky that it still exists because it was built of soft sandstone and would have disappeared centuries ago had the sand not covered it for so much of its history. Yet it is equally surprising that it was ever carved because its sculptor must have known that such soft stone would quickly decay. The Arabs call it *Abu'l-Hawl*, the awesome, or terrible one. Nobody can be certain who it personifies but it is possibly Khafre himself. Some say that it was hewn from the remaining stone after the completion of the pyramid and that, almost as an afterthought, Khafre set it, as a sort of monumental scarecrow, to guard his tomb. Others claim that the face is that of his guardian deity rather than Khafre's own. The Sphinx was first uncovered by Tuthmosis IV (1425-1417 BC) thereby fulfilling a prophecy that by uncovering the great man-lion he would gain the throne. Recent efforts to conserve the Sphinx are now complete but the rising water table threatens to accelerate its decay. Earlier attempts to restore it caused more harm than good when the sandstone was filled, totally inappropriately, with concrete. The Sphinx is incomplete. The 'beard' is exhibited in the British Museum.

The Pyramid of Menkaure (Mycerinus) is the smallest of the 3 Giza Pyramids and marks the beginning of a steep decline in the standards of workmanship and attention to detail in the art of pyramid-building. At the time of the death of Menkaure, who was Chephren's successor and was later known by the Greek name of Mycerinus, it was unfinished and the granite encasement was never completed by his son Shepseskaf who completed the pyramid. It stands at only 66.5m high, considerably lower than the earlier pyramids, and also differs from those of Khufu and Khafre in that the lower chamber was used as the burial tomb. The walls are lined with granite hewn into the rock below the level of the Pyramid's foundations. The sarcophagus was discovered but unfortunately lost at sea en route to Britain.

E of the Pyramid of Menkaure lies the **Mortuary Temple** which is relatively well preserved. The walls were not encased with granite or marble but with red mud bricks and then lined with a thin layer of smoother limestone. It is connected to the Valley Temple via a 660m mud-brick causeway which now lies beneath the sand.

Subsidiary pyramids

S of the Pyramid of Menkaure are 3 smaller incomplete ones. The largest, to the E, was most likely intended for Menkaure's principal wife. The granite sarcophagus of the central tomb was recovered and was found to contain the bones of a young woman.

The Tomb of Queen Khentkawes, who was an obscure but intriguing and important figure, is situated to the S of the main Giza pyramids. Although she appears to have been married to Shepseskaf, who was the last 4th Dynasty pharaoh, she subsequently married a high priest of the sun-god Re at a time when the male dynastic line was particularly weak. By going on to bear a number of later kings who are buried in Saqqara and Abu Sir, she acted as the link between the 4th and 5th Dynasties. Her tomb is an enormous sarcophagus and is linked to a Mortuary Temple cut out of the limestone.

The Zawiyat al-Aryan Pyramids are roughly halfway between Giza and N Saqqara and one has to ride through the desert to see them. A visit would probably only be rewarding to the devoted Egyptologist. There are 2 pyramids of which the southernmost one is probably a 3rd Dynasty (2686-2613 BC) step pyramid. The granite of the more northerly suggests that it is 4th Dynasty (2613-2494 BC) but it would appear to have been abandoned after the foundations had been laid. The **Pyramids of Abu Sir** and **The Sun-Temples of Abu Ghurab** are about 3 km further S (see Saqqara, page 741).

EL-FAYOUM AND LAKE QAROUN

After the noise, crowds and pollution of Cairo the **El-Fayoum** oasis, which includes **Lake Qaroun**, is literally a breath of fresh air. It offers both Egyptian and foreign visitors a relaxing break from city life, a day at the beach and a chance to see oasis life without having to venture too far. It has few ancient monuments. A relaxing day or two in El-Fayoum is strongly recommended for those in Cairo who are beginning to feel claustrophobic.

ACCESS The Bahr Yusef canal bisects Fayoum and trains, buses and taxis from Cairo all terminate close to the canal in the centre of town near one of the city's 8 tourist offices. Negotiate the price then take one of the *hantours* (horse-drawn carriages) to your destination. Local buses and service taxis serving the oasis can be obtained from the Al-Hawatim terminal to the S of the Bahr Yusef.

Fayoum City

The main town in the oasis is located 85 km SW of central Cairo, 75 km from Giza Pyramids and 105 km from Cairo airport. Its name is probably derived from *bayoum* meaning water. Although usually described as an oasis El-Fayoum is not fed by underground water, like the Western Desert oases further SW, but by water from the Nile which is transported to this natural triangular depression by a series of canals. Having irrigated the oasis the water runs into Lake Qaroun which, despite having dramatically shrunk over the past few thousand years, is at about 215 sq km still Egypt's largest natural salt-water lake.

About 70,000 years ago the Nile flood first broke through the low mountains which surround the large Fayoum depression and formed Lake Qaroun and the surrounding marshes. This is believed to be one, if not the first, site of agriculture in the world as plants which grew around the lake were collected, land was fenced in, and dry and guarded storage areas were built. Even today Fayoum is still famous for fruit and vegetables and its chickens. To describe food as *fayoum* means delicious.

The 12th Dynasty pharaoh Amenemhat I (1991-1962 BC) first drained part of the marshes to develop the area for agriculture and also dug a large canal from the Nile controlled by a regulator at El-Lahun to the NW of Beni Suef. The result of this and further developments by Amenemhat III (1842-1797 BC), who showed great interest in the area and built a pyramid at Hawara (see page 749), was Lake Moeris (Great Lake), twice the present size and teeming with fish, and an agricultural area to the S renowned for its rich and varied crops.

The Romans, who called the area **Crocodilopolis** (because of the crocodiles!) changed Fayoum's previous system of crop rotation and forced the area to supply grain exclusively to the Roman market. Muslims believe that the prophet Joseph developed the area during his captivity in Egypt through the canalization of the Bahr Yusef river and by building the world's first dam. Although Fayoum's national strategic importance diminished with the canalization of the Nile Delta it remains one of the most productive agricultural areas in the country.

The water level in Lake Qaroun had been falling for about 2,000 years as it received less and less water until the construction of the Aswan High Dam led to far greater stability in the level of the Nile. By mediaeval times the lake had become far too salty to sustain freshwater fish and new species were introduced. The shrunken lake now lies 45m below sea level and 40m lower than its original level of 70,000 years ago. It is now appears that the water table is rising again as houses and fields at the lakeside have been flooded in recent years.

Despite its stagnant and polluted water the beach resorts around Lake

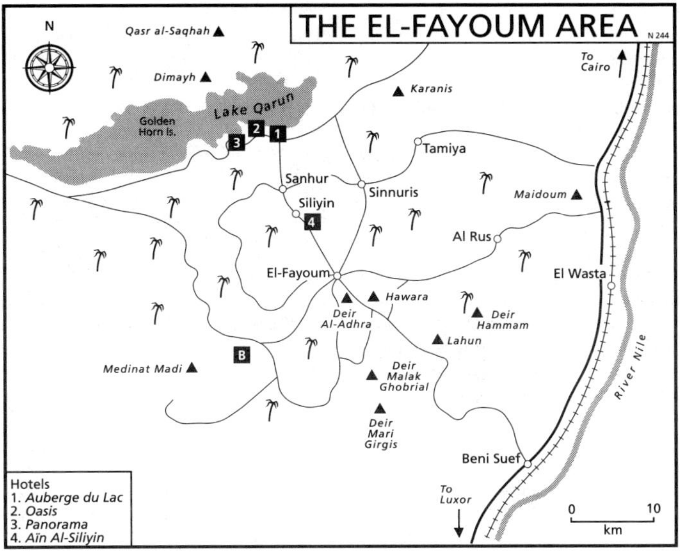

Qaroun still attract the more affluent visitors to the region. The number of visitors is increasing and while half are Egyptian about a third are European. The season runs all year round but from Jan to Apr it is considered too cold to swim. The highly ambitious regional government is now studying new tourist desert sites to the N and W of Lake Qaroun, a wildlife park and conservation area, and infrastructure is being developed. A conference hall is being built together with museums showing monuments, fossils and civilisation. As part of its efforts to persuade tourists to visit areas outside the Nile valley the Egyptian Tourist Association is trying to encourage tours from Cairo, via Fayoum and the Middle Egypt sites, to both the Red Sea coast and Upper Egypt which would undoubtedly be a wonderful and fascinating tour.

The city of El-Fayoum, or Fayoum, in the centre of the depression, is the province's capital and the largest of its 5 small cities. The majority of the oasis' population of 1.45 million people are not Nile Valley Egyptians but a Berber people who are related to the Libyan Arabs. Although few reminders of its ancient past have survived it is still a relatively attractive town though visitors are not advised to stay in the city for long but rather to enjoy the peace and tranquillity of the oasis' gardens and the lake.

Things to see

There is comparatively little to see in El-Fayoum City itself although the covered souk and the adjacent street of goldsmiths, **es-Sagha**, found across the 4th bridge to the W of the central tourist office, are worth a visit. A little further W along the S side of the Bahr Yusef is the attractive **Mosque of Khawand Asal-Bay** believed to have been built in 1499, or earlier, making it the oldest in Fayoum. It was built by the Mamluke Sultan Qaitbai (1468-1498) for Asal-Bay who was not only his favourite concubine but also the mother of his assassinated successor Mohamed IV (1496-1498), sister of Qansuh I (1498-1500) and wife of Janbalat (1500-1501) who were both deposed and murdered. When, however, Tumanbay I (1501-1501) married Qaitbai's official wife Fatima he insulted and disgraced Asal-Bay but he was soon deposed and exiled. Remains of its former impressive structure, most of which fell into the Bahr Yusef in 1892, include the dome supported by ancient pillars and the teak gilded *mihrab* elaborately inlaid with ivory. Other mosques worth visiting in town, particularly during the **moulids** are the **Mosque & Mausoleum of Ali er-Rubi** and the so-called **Hanging Mosque** built above 5 arches next to the Bahr Yusef on the way back to the tourist office.

The locals are particularly proud of their water-wheels, first introduced by the Ptolemies and used now as the official symbol of El-Fayoum province. There are over 200 to see in the region. Besides the 4 large ones behind the tourist office on the main Sharia Gumhorriya the most famous are the series of **Seven Water-wheels** about 3 km N along the Bahr Sinnuris.

Local information

● Accommodation

B *Auberge du Lac-Fayoum*, T 700002, 77 rm, 162 beds, located on Lake Qaroun. King Ibn Saud and Winston Churchill met here in 1945 and the elegant lounge, bars and snooker room still maintain the 1940s style. The a/c rm with bath in the main building and chalets are comfortable rather than luxurious; 4 restaurants, discotheque, tennis, squash, 2 pools, water sports, duck shooting, a small poorly equipped gym and health club, facilities for the handicapped.

D *Panorama Shakshouk*, Shakshouk, T 701314, 34 rm, 60 beds, plus a 34 chalet extension and holiday village.

E *Palace Hotel*, on Sharia Horriya, central, 35 clean a/c rm and a friendly owner who others have claimed is a real shark so beware, plans to upgrade, cars, motorbikes and bicycles for hire.

F *Aïn al-Siliyin*, currently 24 rm, plans for upgrade and 6 more rm, good gardens and a mineral water spring; **F** *Oasis Tourist Village*, Qaroun Lake, T 701565, 28 rm, 60 beds, lakeside location, gardens, restaurants, private beach, plans for upgrading; **F** *Honey Day Hotel*, Sharia Gamal Abdel Nasser, Fayoum Entrance, T 321205, 25 rm, 40 beds, spacious and clean with 1970s decor and friendly staff, 25% discount for groups; **F** *Geziret el-Bat*, Manshiet el-Sadat, Lake Qaroun, T 749288, 22 rm, 42 beds, lakeside location; **F** *El Montazah*, Sharia Ismail el-Medani, Fayoum City, T 324633, 40 beds, located next to the Bahr Sinnuris canal to the N of the town centre, run by Copts; **F** *Queen*, Sharia Menshat Luftallah, Fayoum City, T 326819, 32 beds, reasonable and newish hotel.

● Youth hostel

Flats No 7 & 8, Housing Block No 7, Hadaka, 48 beds, T 323682, station 3 km, overnight fee E£3.

● Camping

Aïn al-Siliyin Hotel and the *Kom Abu Muslim* camp site.

● Places to eat

♦♦♦The *Auberge du Lac-Fayoum* has 4 restaurants – ***Le Rois, La Brasserie, Green House*** and ***La Pasha*** provide good quality food which is a little expensive for outside Cairo (ie continental breakfast E£8.60, American breakfast E£10.10, Oriental breakfast E£11, lunch E£22.50 and dinner E£29.10.). ♦♦*El-Felucca*

The Groaning Water-Wheels Of El-Fayoum

Because the land in the El Fayoum oasis varies from +26m to -42m in three main steps, self-powered water-wheels were essential and the construction of one particular type, which is exclusive to Fayoum, began in pharaonic times. There are often whole series of these *'sawaqih al-Hadir'* (or 'roaring water-wheels'), which produce a perpetual groaning noise and can last 10 years if they are properly maintained, and there are over 200 in the oasis which has adopted the water-wheel as its official symbol.

restaurant in *Louloua el-Fayoum* beach complex at Qaroun Lake about 2 km from *Auberge du Lac-Fayoum* serving Western food. ***Cafeteria el-Medina*** near the four water-wheels. ♦***Mokhimar*** 100m W of the central tourist office.

● Banks

National Bank of Egypt, Banque Misr, Banque du Caire and **Bank of Alexandria** in town centre. You may have to try all for exchange facilities.

● Post Office

Central post office is on the other side of the Bahr Yusef canal opposite the central tourist office.

● Telephone

Local code: 084; **Police**: T 24048; **Ambulance**: T123.

● Tourist information

There is a particularly active and helpful local tourist administration, which is run by the excellent director of tourism Nabil Hanzal, which can be contacted at the office (T 22586) in the centre of town on Sharia Gumhorriya.

● Transport to & from El-Fayoum

By bus: to Cairo's Ahmed Helmi and Giza stations buses leave every 30 min between 0630-1830 from the main bus station in the centre of town on Sharia el-Hadqa. There are also regular buses S to Beni Suef which has connections S up the Nile Valley. **Service taxis**: are quicker but more hair-raising than buses and leave the depot next to the bus station for Cairo's Midan Giza, and thence on to central Cairo, and for Beni Suef. **By train**: these are so slow and inefficient that they are not worth taking, except to El-Wasta and Beni Suef.

Excursions from El-Fayoum

Outside town at **Aïn al-Siliyin**, 9 km N of the city towards Lake Qaroun, is a popular beauty-spot and park which has natural springs and a stream but is very overcrowded on Fri and holidays. Further N is **Lake Qaroun** which, despite the stagnant and salt encrusted water, is a favourite beach resort of Cairenes. Although it is empty and calm as a mill-pond much of the time in winter, it is reported to be quite rough and teeming with ducks and geese which brings the hunters to the lakeside hotels. Qaroun means 'Lake of the Horn' and it is possible to negotiate a price to get a row boat from the *Auberge du Lac* to the barren **Golden Horn Island** or to the N shore.

Kom Aushim

To the E of the lake and 30 km from the city on the main road towards Cairo, Kom Aushim is the site of the ancient city of **Karanis**. The results of excavations carried out in the 1920s by the University of Michigan are displayed, together with exhibits from other sites around the Fayoum, in a small museum, open Tue-Sun 0900-1600. The most interesting exhibits are the carefully restored pottery and glassware. The remains of 2 temples dating from 1st century BC have also been found, apparently built on the foundations of earlier temples. Mud brick houses have also been discovered although little remains of these. Trips to **Qasr es-Saghah** and the ruins of the Ptolemaic settlement of Soknopaiou Nesos, which used to be on the lakeside but is now 11 km away and 65m above the current lake, can be arranged at the museum and it is strongly recommended to take a guide.

There are 4 separate pyramid sites in and near the Fayoum depression: the main ones at **Hawara**, **Lahun** and the collapsed **Maidoum** pyramid are all near the main road from Fayoum to Beni Suef.

The **Pyramid of Amenemhat III** (1842-1797 BC), which is also known as the **Hawara Pyramid**, is a 3 km walk across the Bahr Yusef and into the desert from Hawara which is 6 km SE of Fayoum. Contrary to normal practice the entrance of the pyramid, of which only the mud-brick core remains, its external limestone cladding having long since disappeared, was situated on the S face in an unsuccessful attempt to confuse looters. When archaeologists opened it up they found that Amenemhat's body had been removed and destroyed and his sarcophagus was missing. It was discovered next to that of his daughter Queen Sobek-Nefru, who was the last 12th Dynasty ruler and had completed her father's pyramid after his death, when her own fully-intact tomb was discovered in 1956. The apex of this easily climbed pyramid, offers excellent views.

To the S of the pyramid is the **Mortuary Temple of Amenemhat III**, which was known as the **Labyrinth** in classical times when it greatly impressed Herodotus who considered that it far surpassed the pyramids as a building. It was half carved into the interior of rock and was composed of over 3,000 rooms but unfortunately today it bears few traces of the original spectacular construction and is little more than a huge pile of debris.

Another 9 km along the road to Beni Suef is **Lahun**, 'mouth of the lake', where the Bahr Yusef carries the Nile waters into the Fayoum depression. It is the site of the latest of a series of water regulators built by successive generations including those of Amenemhat III in the 18th century BC and the Qantara of Sultan Qaitbai around 1265 AD.

About 6 km off the main road SE of Lahun is the ruined **Pyramid of Senusert II** (1897-1878 BC) built by Amenemhat III's grandfather. It was built on a rocky outcrop on which limestone pillars were constructed and then covered over with mud-brick and finally encased in stone. A 'sponge' made of sand and flint was placed around the base in order to prevent any flooding. Once again the unusual S facing entrance did not deter the tomb robbers who looted Senusert's sarcophagus but left some wonderful jewellery which is now in the Egyptian Museum and New York's Metropolitan Museum. The walled pyramid complex also include the ruins of a subsidiary pyramid for the queen, the mortuary temple and the mastaba tombs of other members of the royal family.

Although not officially located in Fayoum the collapsed **Maidoum Pyramid**, located to the NW of El-Wasta on the Nile, is most easily reached from there by a 1 hr early morning train journey followed by a 15 min taxi ride to the village of Maidoum and a short walk. Originally it was 144 m square and 42m high but over the centuries the imposing pyramid, which is built on the edge of an escarpment above the cultivated area, has collapsed leaving only a central layer of stone which looks rather like a mediaeval fort. The difficult entry is up a 30m stairway on the N side from which visitors descend into a long 57m sloping passage which levels out to reach a short vertical shaft leading to the limestone-lined and corbel roofed burial chamber which is on the same level as the pyramid's foundations.

While it is generally agreed that the Maidoum Pyramid housed the first 4th Dynasty (2613-2494 BC) pharaoh Sneferu, because he also had 2 other pyramids at Dashur, it is now believed that it was started by his father Huni and completed by Sneferu. The theory as to why it collapsed is that, unlike the pyramids at Giza which distributed the stresses inwards, the incorrectly calculated outward stresses in this progression from the early step-pyramid to the later standard pyramid caused its collapse.

The remains of the **Valley Temple** at the edge of the cultivation, which was linked to the pyramid by a roofless causeway, have never been excavated because of high water levels and there are no plans yet to begin the project.

The monasteries of El-Fayoum

Saint Anthony (251-356 AD) acted as an inspiration for hermits and there were soon numerous monasteries throughout the country including in the Fayoum depression. A number are still standing today and, although perhaps only for pilgrims and those with a specialist interest, are worth visiting. The 12th century **Deir al-Adhra (Monastery of the Virgin)** just off the road to Beni Suef about 6 km outside Fayoum City is the most accessible. Further S is the beautiful 7th century **Deir Malak Ghobrial (Monastery of the Angel Gabriel)** which is located on the desert escarpment above the cultivated lowlands. **Deir Hammam**, which was originally built in the 6th or 8th century, is 6 km NE of Luhun and **Deir Mari Girgis (Monastery of St George)** can be reached by boat from Sidmant al-Gabal which is 15 km SW of Luhan. Even more isolated is **Deir Anba Samwail (Monastery of St Samuel)** which is about 30 km S of the rim of the Fayoum depression and can only be reached by pack animal or 4 wheel drive vehicle.

THE NILE VALLEY
MIDDLE EGYPT (CAIRO TO LUXOR)

Contents

Maps

Although most tourists tend to concentrate on Cairo and the splendours of Luxor and Aswan in Upper Egypt, the area stretching along the Nile between Cairo and Luxor, termed Middle Egypt, should not be missed. There is a number of very interesting sites and the slower provincial pace of life is most acceptable after the noise and hassle of Cairo.

WARNING Middle Egypt in general and the towns such as Beni Suef, Assuit and Qena in particular are Islamic fundamentalist strongholds. Christian Copts, some 20 per cent of the region's population, have been the target of intimidation, extortion, arson and even murder by small and unrepresentative terrorist groups who have also, on occasion, targeted tourists in an effort to harm the government's largest source of foreign currency.

The threat should not, however, be exaggerated or be allowed to deter tourists from visiting Middle Egypt provided they take precautions. In order to minimise the risks it is probably best for independent travellers to avoid staying in Beni Suef, Assuit and Qena which, besides any potential threat, are unpleasant towns with little or nothing to see. Instead most sites can be seen on trips from the attractive and peaceful provincial capital of **Minya** (see pages 753) while the wonderful temples at Abydos and Dendera can be visited on long but worthwhile day trips from Luxor or Sohag rather than staying nearby in less pleasant circumstances.

Beni Suef

130 km S of Cairo, with a population of 86,000, Beni Suef is the northernmost provincial capital in Middle Egypt but is best avoided (see above) if possible and the few nearby sites can be seen on day trips from Cairo or the Fayoum Oasis.

Things to see Besides the **Maidoum Pyramid**, which is best seen on a trip from the Fayoum Oasis or even Cairo, there is little to see in Beni Suef except the ancient and very poorly preserved cities of **Heracleopolis** and **Oxyrhynchus**. They are located 15 km W of Beni

Suef and 9 km W of Beni Mazar on the route to Minya.

Excursions can be made from here to the monasteries of St Anthony and St Paul (see page 872 and 873).

• **Accommodation F** *Semiramis*, Sharia Safir Zaghloul, Midan El- Mahat, T 322092, 30 rm, 52 beds, a poor quality hotel in an unpleasant city.

• **Post Office** Located opposite the *Semiramis hotel* in Midan El-Mahat.

• **Telephone** Local code: 082.

• **Transport Train** It is easy to make a quick getaway from Beni Suef because almost all express and slower trains travelling up and down the Nile Valley stop at the station in the centre of the city. **Road Buses** can be caught from the bus station, just E of the railway station, every 30 min to Cairo or Fayoum. Less frequent direct services go to Alexandria and some of the Delta towns. **Service taxis** N to Cairo, W to Fayoum, S to Minya and E to Zafarana on the Red Sea coast can be caught from the depot W of the bus and train stations.

Minya

Minya, 110 km S of Beni Suef and 245 kms from Cairo on the W bank of the Nile, could not be more different and is still one of the nicest, friendliest and most relaxed towns in the whole country, although recent reports indicate some apathy to visitors. At night, half its population seem to be promenading through the streets or picnicing on the grass between the long and beautiful flame-tree lined Corniche and the river Nile. The tranquil atmosphere and the view at sunset, of cattle being herded across the half submerged island in the middle of the Nile by a farmer in his row-boat, is hard to equal. Rather than missing it by rushing through the town it is better to use Minya as a base for a few days to see Middle Egypt's main archaeological sites which are within a 50 km radius.

The centre of Minya is bounded on the E by the river Nile which here runs SE-NW, and the parallel railway line and Ibrahimiya Canal to the W. Beyond to the W is agricultural land. The N end of the town, where the *Nefertiti* and *Lotus* hotels are situated is the most pleasant.

ACCESS Train At the train station exit, across a colonial looking square, is the town's main street called Sharia Gumhorriya which runs NE to the Corniche and the river front about 1 km away. **Road** The main service taxi depot and the bus terminal are both 5 min walk to the right of the railway station exit along the parallel Sharia Sa'ad Zaghloul. The service taxi depot for Abu Qirkus, the jumping off point for Beni Hassan only, is 250m further S just across the railway and the canal bridge. Two buses a day from Alexandria to Assuit stop at Minya, cost E£17. Picking the bus up for return is difficult.

Things to see

Beni Hassan, which is named after an ancient tribe, is about half way between Minya and Mallawi. It is the site of a neat row of 11th and 12th Dynasty (2050-1786 BC) tombs which were dug into the rock face of hills overlooking the Nile. The tombs are important because they are the first to show illustrations of sports and games as well as the daily life of the people.

ACCESS Reach Beni Hassan by service taxi to the small town of Abu Qirkus on the main Minya to Mallawi road, cross over the canal and walk about 1 km straight down its main street until the road forks from where you can take a E£0.25 pick-up to the banks of the Nile. The efficient little ferry across the river costs E£4.50 return but this also includes the short minibus ride to the tombs. Entry is permitted to 4 tombs, open daily 0800-1600 costs E£6 or E£3 for students. Although the regional Ministry of Tourism is now reviewing the policy, which is set by the national rather than provincial authorities, it still costs E£10 to take photographs in each tomb which, given their simplicity compared with the wonders of Luxor's Valley of the Kings, is both a rip-off and a disincentive for tourists to visit the region.

HERMOPOLIS – THE CITY OF THOTH

Hermopolis was the city of Thoth, the gods' scribe and vizier, the reckoner of time, the inventor of writing and, following his association with Khonsu, a moon-god with mastery of science and knowledge. Thoth is depicted either with a man's body and the head of a sacred ibis or as a white and very well endowed baboon. Although his cult originated further N in the Nile delta, its greatest following was in Middle Egypt.

In the city's complex creation myth, known as the Hermopolitan cosmogony, the chaos before the world's creation was thought to have had 4 characteristics – water, infinity, darkness and invisibility – each represented by a male and a female god who collectively are known as the Hermopolitan Ogdoad (company of eight). A primordial mound and the cosmic egg arose from the chaos and hatched the sun god who then began to organize the world from the chaos. While most people believed that the Ogdoad itself produced the cosmic egg Thoth's devotees alone credited him with having laid it and therefore having been connected with the creation of the world. A modern interpretation of the link between his representation as a baboon and his role in the Creation is associated with the habit of baboons shrieking at sunrise thus being the first to welcome the sun. The baboon is also connected to the moon and there are often statues of baboons with moons on their head. This is probably because of the ancient Egyptians' love of puns and word-play because the word for "to orbit" was apparently similar to that for "baboon". Although by the New Kingdom this Hermopolitan version of creation myth had been supplanted by the Heliopolitan cosmogony, Thoth's cult continued until the later Ptolemaic era.

The tombs are interesting because they mark a stage in the evolution of tomb design from the lateral Old Kingdom (2686-2181 BC) style *mastabas* to the deep New Kingdom (1567-1085 BC) royal tombs of the Valley of the Kings (**see page 782**). At Beni Hassan some of the earlier tombs have no vestibules and consist only of a simple chamber carved in the rock while the later ones contain a vestibule and a more intricate arrangement of the chamber. Another interesting feature is that they were not royal tombs but were built for regional rulers and military leaders. Their illustrations tend to be more personal and to depict feudal or military life rather than those of offerings and magic formulae for reaching the after-life which are more commonly associated with the royal tombs. Of the 39 tombs only 12 were decorated and only 4 can currently be visited.

Tomb of Amenemhat (No 2) He was the regional governor and commander-in-chief at the time of Senusert I (1971-1928 BC) and his tomb has a columned portico facade and a lintel bearing a list of his titles. The texts inside the door relate to his numerous military campaigns S to Kush and praise his administrative skills. Particular reference is made to a year when there was heavy flooding of the Nile but taxes were not increased. The main chamber has a vaulted roof which is supported by 4 columns and decorated in a chequered pattern. To the back of the chamber the niche once contained a statue of Amenemhat. The chamber walls are finely decorated with a cooking scene on the right of the S wall. In the middle Amenemhat is seated during an offering ceremony while the N wall has scenes of hunting and military preparations. On the E wall there are pictures of wrestling, an attack on a fortress and boats sailing towards Abydos.

Tomb of Khnumhotep (No 3) This

tomb is very similar and is that of Amenemhat's successor Khnumhotep who was also governor of the Eastern Desert. The façade has a proto-Doric columned portico leading into a central chamber with a niche for his statue at the far end. Inscriptions of great historical importance about feudal life in the 12th Dynasty were discovered in the tomb. Clockwise around the tomb there are scenes of ploughing, the harvest and his voyage to Abydos. Below the next scene of desert hunting on the N wall is the lower register showing the arrival of an Asian caravan which offers gifts to the governor which is all shown in minute detail. This is followed by Khnumhotep and his wife who are shown fishing and fowling in the marshes on the left and harpooning fish from a punt on the right of the niche for the statue. On the S wall he inspects boat-building and then sails to Abydos while other registers show dyers, weavers, carpenters and other artisans.

Tomb of Baqet III (No 15), who was governor of the Oryx Nome, is much simpler than the others and dates back to the 11th Dynasty (2050-1991 BC). In the chamber are 2 columns with lotus capitals. On the N wall are scenes of a desert hunt with 4 mythological animals in the midst of the normal animals including copulating gazelles. On the E wall there are illustrations of 200 wrestling positions while the S wall illustrates scenes from Baqet's turbulent life including an attack on a fortress.

Tomb of Kheti (No 17), who was Baqet's son and heir, is quite similar to that of his father. The same wrestling scenes are to be found on the E wall and there are very similar representations of craftsmen and desert hunts. On the S wall Kheti is shown watching agricultural scenes and receiving offerings from under a sunshade attended by his servants and a dwarf.

Today little remains of the ruined 7th Dynasty (2181-2173 BC) city of **Hermopolis Magna** and its necropolis at nearby **Tuna el-Gabel** which are located to the NW of **Mallawi**, about 50 km S of Minya. Mallawi was replaced by Minya as the regional capital in 1824 since when it has deteriorated sharply. Today its dirty streets and open drains make it a town to avoid particularly because Minya is just up the road. Although Mallawi is an awful town the fact that there are a number of important archaeological sites has persuaded the regional tourist authority to plan to new 3 or 4 star hotel. Located besides the Nile, mercifully outside the town, it will have berthing facilities for 9 tourist boats while the chalets will be able to accommodate 404 tourists. This remains at the planning stage.

Mallawi

Mallawi is not a place to stay. The atmosphere is very uncomfortable as the residents simply ignore visitors. Use it as a stepping-off place only.

ACCESS from Minya is possible with patience. The minibus which fills up slowly and the bus which leaves very early in the morning both cost E£1 and take the same time. From Mallawi, it is very difficult to reach the sites by public transport: having to change pick-up truck twice and then walk 6 km from the village of Tuna el-Gabel to the sites might seem to be more trouble than they are worth. Unless you are part of an organized tour of the sites from Minya, which is undoubtedly the most relaxed way to see them, the independent traveller is strongly recommended to hire a taxi for a few hours from Mallawi to Tuna el-Gabel and back. Private hire of pick-up costs E£10 for round trip to sites from Tuna el-Gabel village. Tourist police may check the agreed price and the driver's permit.

Hermopolis Magna as it was known in Ptolemaic times, was the ancient city of Khmunu the capital of the Hare Nome, and had a dual function as a secular and religious centre and was ruled by the High Priest. It was once quite large, extending to both sides of the Nile's banks, with a temple surrounded by a 15m thick wall at its centre. The town regained importance under the Ptolemies who associated Thoth with their god Hermes and gave the town its name. At the same time a vast necropolis, now known as Tuna el-Gabel, was established W of the town. Today, however, little remains of the city except a large mound of rubble and mud-bricks and 24 rose granite columns.

The **Tuna el-Gabel Necropolis**, (open daily 0900-1700 E£7) is 6 km W across a very hot and empty desert road from the small town of that name and 6 km SW of Hermopolis. To the right of the sand-blown entrance site where the road ends, is a tree-lined government rest-house. The café has closed since tourist numbers dropped so take your own water. To the left are the administration and accommodation buildings. There is comparatively little to see above ground because most of the tombs lie below the sand dunes which would soon cover the whole site if it were not for the workers' constant efforts to keep them at bay.

The **Sacred Animal Necropolis** is to the right of the entrance and is set in catacombs, which may stretch as far as Hermopolis, but only a small area is now open to the public. Mummified baboons and ibises, which were sacred animals because they were the 2 representations of Thoth, were buried in these catacombs. A large number of mummified animals were found but the best have been removed to museums and the remaining ones are poorly preserved.

A few hundred metres to the S is the main part of the **City of the Dead** which was modelled on a real city with streets and some tombs which resemble houses. Egyptians traditionally went to visit their dead relatives and took a meal or spent the night in the mausoleum. Some of the tombs therefore have more than one chamber and a few have an additional floor or even a kitchen. The City of the Dead's most interesting building is the tomb-chapel of **Petosiris** who was the High Priest of Thoth at Hermopolis and whose coffin is in the Cairo Museum. It was built in 300 BC and is strongly influenced by Hellenistic art as illustrated by the Greek clothes. The mausoleum was a family tomb divided between the vestibule, which is decorated with scenes with scenes of traditional crafts such as metalwork, wine and brick making and woodwork, and the inner shrine. On either side of the door to the shrine are offering and sacrifice scenes. In the shrine are colourful illustrations from traditional Egyptian funerary texts with the E wall depicting a funerary procession. The actual burial chambers, where 3 generations of high priests were buried, is 8m below the shrine.

Another interesting 2 storey tomb-chapel is that of **Isadora** which dates from 120 BC and still contains the well-preserved mummy of the young girl. Because she drowned in the sacred Nile this led to the brief establishment of a cult for her. Also worth a visit is the tomb known as the **House of Graffiti** which has been restored and contains a kitchen, various rooms and a chamber where the deceased was exposed before being buried in the funerary shaft.

Tell el-Amarna

12 km S of Mallawi, Tell el-Amarna is the E bank city which was founded by Pharaoh Amenhotep IV (1379-1362 BC), who is better known as **Akhenaten**, after he had left Thebes (Luxor) to establish the totally new and heretical monotheistic religion. Although little remains today because most of the temples and palaces were destroyed by subsequent pharaohs who reverted back to the previous polytheistic religion, the site still has plenty

REVOLUTIONARY ART: AKHENATEN AND NEFERTITI'S NEW DESIGNS

The new settlement of Akhetaten was not only revolutionary in its religion but also in the arts. A number of excellent craftsmen and artists were recruited to work on the decoration of the new city. Rather than focusing almost exclusively on the theme of resurrection and the after-life they also depicted daily life and nature in greater detail than before. There were 2 main art styles with the first depicting Akhenaten with an elongated face, protruding stomach, and female-style thighs, as demonstrated by the famous colossi from his temple at Karnak which are now in the Cairo museum, while the later style is much less distorted. It has been suggested, although not proven, that the earlier distortions were partly due to the difficulties that the artists had in radically altering their style. Alternatively it may have been that the decoration was undertaken too hastily using inferior limestone and varying quality carvings.

It has been suggested that Akhenaten intended that the depictions of himself and his family, which appear in the shrines of private houses in Tell el-Amarna, should be worshipped and that only he could directly mediate with the god. The Aten disc is only shown when he or the Royal family are present. While the pharaoh was always, at least nominally, accepted as a god or the gods it appears that Akhenaten may have been particularly literal about this convention.

Very unusually, in scenes of royal dinners both the pharaoh and his wife were depicted and the presence of both their cartouches almost as co-rulers demonstrated the difference in Amenhotep IV's approach. Wives had never previously been portrayed as equal to the pharaoh and their names had never appeared side by side.

of atmosphere. There is another school of archaeologists who believe that, far from introducing a radical new monotheism, Akhenaten chose to ignore a religion which through a multiplicity of myths and images was able to present a surprisingly complex view of the world.

ACCESS In order to reach Tell el-Amarna, (open daily 0700-1700), drivers should head S from Mallawi to the village of Deir el-Mawas and then E to the ferry crossing, E£1 return. The river can easily be reached by catching any southbound bus or pick-up from the depot just S of the Mallawi train station at the bridge between the canal and the railway tracks or taking a private taxi. Pick up costs 25p. The Nile can be crossed by car ferry, motorboat or *felucca* to the rather unpleasant E bank village of El-Till, where you will be greeted by hassling adults and children hawking basketwork and other handicrafts. The ticket kiosk is just to the left of the landing stage and there is a little café to the E of the village. On arrival independent travellers will be expected to pay a 'local tax' of a few E£ to keep El-Till functioning. Alternatively there is also a small car ferry from nearby Beni Amar to the nicer village of Hagg Qandil, to the S of El-Till, but the only tickets and transport are at El-Till. Note that neither ferry can be relied on to carry cars after 1600. The tractor ride to the Northern Tombs costs E£8, expensive but the only realistic option, plus E£6 (students E£3). Make sure the guide includes Tomb 6 in the itinerary. The Northern Palace costs a further E£5 to visit.

Things to see

The huge site is made up of a number of different areas – the **city ruins** to the S of El-Till; the **Northern Tombs** 5 km to the E and up an 80m escarpment for which a donkey or tractor-driven trailer is almost essential; the **Royal Tomb** 5 km further away up a hidden valley; the rarely visited **Southern Tombs** 14 km from El-Till; and the **Northern Palace** near the riverbank to the N of the village. At least half a day is required for the site and a full day if the Southern Tombs are to be included.

Amenhotep IV was the son of Amenhotep III (1417-1379) BC and his dark-skinned and possibly Nubian 'chief wife' Queen Tiy who may have ruled jointly for 12 yrs with her son after he ascended the throne in 1379 BC. The cult of Aten, which was one aspect of the sun-god, had been mentioned in earlier texts and shown as a human being but may have been a private and personal royal belief during his father's reign. Amenhotep IV, however, espoused it very strongly at the expense of Amun and the other gods very early in his reign which naturally upset the high priests of Amun in Thebes (Luxor).

Therefore, in the 5th year of his reign in 1374 BC, he and his wife Nefertiti moved the capital to Akhetaten ('horizon of Aten') half way between Thebes and Memphis at Tell el-Amarna in order to make a clean break with previous traditions. For those of a romantic disposition the large gully or river wadi cutting through the eastern cliffs have been likened to the Egyptian symbol for the horizon. It has been suggested that it was because the sun rose from behind these cliffs that Akhenaten chose this as the site for his new city of Akhetaten.

On arriving in Akhetaten he changed his name to Akhenaten or 'servant of Aten' while Nefertiti became Neferneferuaten or 'beautiful are the beauties of the Aten'. In the 12th year of his reign he adopted a more confrontational approach to the old cults and his decision to close down all the old temples probably led to unrest because of the detrimental economic effect caused by the temple being closed. There is some evidence that Akhenaten was criticized for not defending Egypt's borders and for jeopardising the territories previously won by his expansionist father.

How Akhenaten's reign ended is still a mystery. One theory is that Akhenaten rejected his wife Nefertiti and made his son-in-law Smenkhkare the co-regent. Some have interpreted the fact that the 2 men lived together and some of their poses in the murals as proof of a homosexual relationship. Smenkhkare, who was both the husband of Akhenaten's eldest daughter and his half-brother, is thought to have continued ruling for one year after Akhenaten's death in 1362 BC but soon died himself. The other, more contentious, interpretation of events is that, far from splitting up with Nefertiti, the pharaoh actually made her co-regent and his equal. She may then have adopted Smenkhkare as her official name and been illustrated in a different way. However only the cartouches can be used to identify the figures which makes the theory a suitably interesting alternative. The reality is that no-one knows the truth which may be very dull compared with these stories.

Worship of Aten did not long outlive its creator. In 1361 BC Smenkhkare was succeeded by Tutankhamen (1361-1352 BC), another of Amenhotep III's sons and therefore Akhenaten's half-brother, who returned to the Thebes-based cult of Amun. He and his successors attempted to eradicate all traces of Akhenaten and the city of Akhetaten was subsequently destroyed and completely pillaged by Seti I (1318-1304 BC) so that nothing was known of the city or its cult until the second half of this century.

Apart from the romantic story of Akhenaten, the importance of the city lies in its short history. Although about 5 km long, the city was built and occupied for no more than 25 years. When abandoned a record of life in the late 18th Dynasty was left which ranged from peasants in small houses to the official buildings and palaces. Most urban sites in Egypt have either been lost under modern towns and villages or have been badly damaged so that Tell el-Amarna offers a unique record.

The Northern Tombs, which are the most interesting site at Tell el-Amarna, was the necropolis for the nobles many of whom were not originally from Thebes but were elevated to their position by Akhenaten once he arrived at Akhetaten. Most of the tombs also devote more space and decoration to Akhenaten himself than to the occupant. It is advisable to carry a torch but there is now electric lighting in the Northern Tombs.

Tomb of Huya (No 1) Huya was the Superintendent of the Royal Harem and Steward of Akhenaten's mother Queen Tiy and may have died during her visit to Akhetaten in 1367 BC. At the entrance he is pictured praying next to a hymn to Aten and on either side of the door are highly unusual scenes of Queen Tiy drinking wine with Akhenaten, Nefertiti and princesses. On the left wall is a scene showing Akhenaten in a procession being carried on his litter towards the Hall of Tribute where ambassadors from Kush and Syria await his arrival. To the left and right of the entrance to the shrine are somewhat damaged scenes of Huya being decorated by Akhenaten from the Window of Appearances with the sculptor's studio below. On the right hand wall Akhenaten leads Queen Tiy to see the temple he has built for his parents while the staff who worked on the temple are displayed below. The shrine is undecorated but the niche has some scenes of funerary offerings, mourning, and a curious representation of the funerary furniture.

Tomb of Mery-Re II (No 2) This tomb of the Royal Scribe, Overseer of the Two Treasuries and Overseer of the Harem of the Great Royal Wife Nefertiti was started during Akhenaten's reign but finished by Smenkhkare and follows a similar plan to Huya's tomb. After the now destroyed Hymn to the Aten at the entrance, Mery-Re is shown worshipping the Aten and then to the left Nefertiti offers Akhenaten a drink next to 3 young princesses. Further along the upper register depicts Mery-Re receiving a golden collar from Akhenaten while foreigners look on and then being acclaimed by his household. Further along the right wall Akhenaten, Nefertiti and their daughters are at the centre of a scene divided into 3 subjects. The first shows black slaves, with their faces painted red, carrying gold bars and coins. The tables are heaped with piles of gold and a number of slaves are shown carrying their children. In the second scene, Asian people pay homage to Akhenaten and bring him treasures and a number of female slaves. The last scene shows a double procession with the empty royal litter and the royal guard while treasures are offered to the Pharaoh. The rest of the tomb was never finished except for a defaced scene on the back wall of Mary-Re being rewarded by Smenkhkare and his wife.

Tomb of Ahmose (No 3), who was Akhenaten's fan bearer and therefore had the right to a noble's tomb, is with another group of 4 tombs just beyond the next valley. The tomb was unfinished and some of the scenes are damaged. Most of them depict aspects of the palace including the throne room, the royal apartments and some of Akhenaten's army preparing for battle.

Tomb of Mery-Re I (No 4), the High Priest of the Aten and the father of Mery-Re II, has 3 chambers and is probably the best of all. On the entrance wall he is shown in adoration before the Aten while in the columned and flower decorated vestibule Mery-Re and his wife Tenro are shown in prayer. On the left hand wall of the main chamber, which now only has 2 of the original 4 columns, Mery-Re is invested with the High Priest's gold collar by Akhenaten. The royal family and escorts are then portrayed in an important scene, because it shows the height of the buildings, leaving the palace for the Great Temple in chariots. There are hymns to the Aten and offering scenes above the entrance to the unfinished inner chambers. On the right of the main chamber Akhenaten, accompanied by Nefertiti and 2 of their daughters, is in the Great Temple making sacrifices to the Aten. Other scenes show Akhenaten after the sacrifice with his daughters playing musical instruments while beggars await alms in the corner. Below is a scene which has given archaeologists a rare insight into the original appearance of the city. Mery-Re is seen showing the Pharaoh the stocks in the temple with views towards the port, a stable and the royal boats on the Nile.

The nearby **Tomb of Pentu (No 5)**, the royal scribe and chief physician, is badly disfigured and it is better to see the **Tomb of Panehsi (No.6)** which is 500m S. This High Priest's tomb, which has 4 columns in each of the 2 chambers, was later transformed by the Copts into a chapel but many of the original decorations are still in place. In the first chamber are scenes of Akhenaten decorating Panehsi. On the left hand wall, the royal family worship the Aten in front of their household. There are further scenes of Akhenaten including one on the far wall on the left behind a Coptic baptistery and one by the stairs leading down to the funerary chamber, showing him with Nefertiti and their daughters in their chariots surrounded by troops. The rest of the tomb is either unfinished or has been damaged.

The **Royal Tomb**, which is located in a secret valley 5.5 km E of the main plain, has been closed since 1934 and cannot normally be visited although if really keen it is possible to arrange a visit beforehand with the antiquities department at Minya. Although there are electric lights, because there is no source of power, it is necessary to take your own generator. It is a very rough ride, best undertaken by tractor, because it will damage all but the strongest of 4 wheel drive vehicles.

People with their own transport can see the **Northern Palace** about 1.5 km N of El-Till which was re-cleared several years ago by the Egyptian Antiquities Service. Although it is only really for enthusiasts it is possible to walk around and enter this large mud-brick ruin where a section of mosaic can still be seen. There is a temple to the S called Kom el-Nana which is being excavated by a British mission but it is not accessible or currently open to the public.

The **Southern Tombs**, which are located 14 km away, are spread over 7 low hills in two groups but only about 5 of the 18 tombs are of any possible interest. They include the **Tomb of Ay** (1352-1348 BC), who was Akhenaten's maternal uncle and vizier to Amenhotep III, Akhenaten and Tutankhamen whom he succeeded as pharaoh when he died. There are unproven theories either that his wife Tey was Nefertiti's wet-nurse or that the couple conceived Tutankhamen. Despite this, possibly because they do not justify the effort of getting there, the southern tombs are rarely visited by tourists.

ACCESS Visitors to the southern tombs usually travel on the N-S road along the edge of the cultivated area which almost exactly follows the ancient 'royal road' which linked all Akhetaten's official buildings.

Leaving El-Till one passes the remains of the massive **Great-Aten Temple** on the right which is now partly covered by the modern cemetery. There are then the vague ruins in the sand of a mixture of administrative and residential buildings until one reaches the **Small-Aten Temple** which is currently being preserved and re-excavated by the Egyptian Exploration Society. Although it is not yet open to tourists a good view of the temple can be had from a local tractor-trailor.

Just before the temple there is a large mud-brick structure on either side of the road. This is the remains of the **Bridge** which crossed the road and connected the **King's House** to the E with the so-called **Great Palace** to the W which runs along and partly under the cultivated area. This area including the palace, temple and ancillary buildings is the **Central City** which was the administrative and religious centre of the ancient city.

Local information

● Accommodation

A *PLM Azur Nefertiti & Aton*, Corniche el-Nil, T 086 331515, F 326467, river-side location about 2 km N of the town centre on both sides of the beautiful tree-lined corniche, opened 1986 and recently expanded, 96 rm (30 decent rm in main building, 24 satisfactory garden chalets without a river view, and 42 chalets adjacent to the Nile), 3 restaurants (La Palma, Banana Island and Darna), a bar, tea and coffee shops, pool, tennis, sauna, small gym, efficient and very friendly staff, reduction in tourist trade has resulted in some of the facilities being closed.

E *Beach Hotel el-Shata*, 32 rm and 2 suites a/c with bath, good location.

F *El-Shatek*, 31 Sharia el-Gumhorriya, T 322307, 32 rm; **F** *Lotus*, 1 Sharia Port Said, T 324541, F 324576, 42 extremely clean rm with rather noisy a/c and bath, 92 beds, Nile 1 km, station 1 km, pleasant hotel, run by a friendly Copt called Sobhey Mena who provides good service, top floor restaurant serves beer (a rare find); **F** *Ibn Khassib*, 5 Sharia Ragab, T 224535, 20 rm, 38 beds.

● Youth Hostel

Has dormitory beds and a pool, 1.5 km out of town near the stadium.

● Places to eat

Besides restaurants in the *PLM Azur Nefertiti* and *Lotus* hotels, which offer different standard but reasonably priced good quality food, the *El-Fayrouz* restaurant on the Corniche about 150m N of Sharia Gumhorriya provides excellent meat dishes and juices. The *Ali Baba* cafeteria is not recommended. Good **cheap** food can be bought at many of the other local cafés such as *Cafeteria Ali*.

● Banks

There are two banks, open Sun-Thur 0830-1400 and 1700-2200, next to the tourist office on the Corniche.

● Post Office

In the main square called Midan Sa'a directly outside the railway station and open Sun-Thur 0830-1400 & 1700-2200.

● Shopping

While the more up-market shops are on Sharia Gumhorriya the best and main shopping streets bisect it about half way between the station and the river. There has been a Monday market since Ottoman times.

● Telephone

Local code: 086.

● Tourist information

The Minya provincial government is very keen to promote tourism and the tourist information office (open daily 0800-1400 & 1700-2200, T 320150) on the Corniche is very helpful and is well worth a visit.

● Transport

Train Most inter-city trains stop at Minya so it is possible to travel easily N to Cairo (4 hr, E£20 first class) via Beni Suef or S to Luxor via Assuit and Qena.

Road Bus Almost hourly buses from the terminal on Sharia Sa'ad Zaghloul to Cairo (5 hr) or S to Assuit. **Service taxis** which are quicker but still cheap can be caught to the same destinations from the nearby depot under the railway arch. Those for Abu Qirkus (30-45 min), the jumping off point for Beni Hassan, can only be caught 250m further S just across the railway and the canal bridge.

Assuit

Assuit, 109 km S of Minya and the largest city S of Cairo (375 km), is well worth missing. Not only is it a noisy, aggressive and unpleasant city but, as one of the Islamic fundamentalist strongholds, it has also been the scene of some of Egypt's worst communal violence during the past decade (see **Political Risks, see page 30**). Having almost nothing to offer the tourist except a few fairly decent hotels, fast trains out of town and the main road to the Western Desert oases which is 12 km N of the city it is probably best avoided. For those who have the misfortune to be stuck in the city here are a few of the essential details.

ACCESS The train, bus and service taxi stations are all located on Sharia el-Geish and most of the best hotels are situated on or near the same street. Roads in front of the stations run to the Nile while those behind the railway station lead to the souks. The airport 10 km NW of the city has no bus connection.

Things to see

There is comparatively little to see in Assuit itself although the **Nasser Museum** in the village of Beni Marr just to the S of the city and the very large **Convent of the Virgin** (Deir el-Adhra), where Copts believe the Holy Family sought refuge from Herod in the caves at Dirunka 12 km W of Assuit, are worth a visit. Every year in Aug icons are paraded around its cave-church during the **Moulid of the Virgin**. Further afield, 5 km out of El-Qusiya which is 42 km N of Assuit, is the **Burnt Monastery** (Deir el-Muharaaq) which gets its name from its location on the edge of the burning, roasting desert but which, given the attacks on Coptic churches by the area's Islamic fundamentalists, is a particularly apt name. It is better to visit Tell el-Amarna from Minya and Abydos from Sohag rather than from Assuit.

Local information

● Accommodation

If you have to stay in Assuit the decent hotels are near the train station, but there are also some really unpleasant places. **D** *Badr Touristic*, Sharia el-Thallaga, T 329811, F 322820, 44 rm, 103 beds, comfortable hotel where tour groups are usually accommodated; **D** *Casa Blanca*, Sharia Mohamed Tawfik Khashaba, T 324483, F 321662, 50 rm, 90 beds.

E *Reem Touristic*, Sharia el-Nahda, T 326235, F 329102, 40 rm, 73 beds; **E** *Happy Land*, Sharia el-Sawra, T/F 320444, 52 rm, 96 beds; **E** *Akhenaten Touristic*, Sharia Mohamed Tawfik Khashaba, T 327723, F 321600, 35 rm, 58 beds.

F *El-Salam*, Sharia Thabet, T 332256, 40 rm, 68 beds; **F** *YMCA*, Sharia Gumhorriya, T 323218, located about 10 min walk from the train station, clean, cheap a/c rm, pool.

● Youth hostel

Building 503, El-Walidia, Assuit, T 324841, 40 beds, kitchen, 2 km from station, overnight fee E£3.

● Camping

It is possible to camp near the Assuit barrage (built by the British in 1898-1903 and carries a wide road) at the Officers Club (T 323134) and the Sporting Club (T 233139) or on Banana Island where there are no facilities.

● Places to eat

All the better hotels have restaurants which offer decent food as do the various clubs which usually admit better-dressed tourists. There are a number of good cheap and cheerful restaurants between the back of the station and the souk in the main commercial district. The **cheap** ones include ***Express Restaurant*** and ***Mattam al-Azhar*** as well as others along Sharia Talaat Harb and Sharia 26th July.

● Banks

There are a number of banks, including the Alexandria Bank (Open Sat-Thur 0830-1400 & 1800-2100, Fri 0900-1230 & 1800-2100) in the commercial district around Talaat Harb.

● Post Office

Near the railway station and open Sun-Thur 0830-1400 & 1700-2200.

● Telephone

Local code: 088.

● Tourist information

It is best to ask for information at the better hotels.

● Transport

Air Internal flights to Cairo and Kharga from the airport 10 km NW of the town.

Trains run 12 times a day to Cairo (7 hrs) via Mallawi (2 hrs) and Minya (3 hrs), but less frequently to Luxor (6-7 hrs) via Sohag (2 hrs) and Qena (4-5 hrs).

Road Bus 7 daily buses Cairo (7 hrs), 5 to Kharga Oasis (5 hrs) which go on to Dakhla (8-9 hrs), and 4 to Qena (4 hrs), as well as buses every 30 min between 0600-1800 N to Minya (2 hrs) and S to Sohag. **Service taxis**, which are quicker than buses, run to every town between Minya and Sohag, as well as to Kharga (5 hrs), and are easy to catch from the depot in the mornings but are less frequent later in the day.

Sohag

A small agricultural and university W bank town, 97 km S of Assuit along the Nile, Sohag has a large Coptic community amongst its 90,000 population. Although it has few minor sites it is not really geared to tourists but it does have the advantage of being relatively close to the beautiful temple at Abydos and within half a day's journey from Dendera.

ACCESS Directly outside the train station on Sharia el-Mahata (Station Rd) are the only hotels in the town while N and S bound service taxis are at either end of the street 5 min from station. Over the bridge across the railway tracks is the main road to the river Nile.

Things to see

The small **White Monastery** (Deir al-Abyad) and **Red Monastery** (Deir al-Ahmar), at 10 km and 14 km S of Sohag are of interest. On the way S the beautiful temple at **Abydos** is an absolute must and better visited from here than from Qena.

Abydos is 10 km SW of El-Balyana and halfway between Sohag and Qena and can be reached by service taxi from Sohag to El-Balyana (E£2) and then on to Abydos (E£0.5). It was the holiest town of all for the ancient Egyptians and pilgrims were making the journey to Abydos from the 7th Dynasty (2181-2173 BC) until well into the Ptolemaic era (323-30 BC). Site open 0700-1800, entrance E£6.

It was the cult-centre for **Osiris**, the god of the dead who was known as 'Lord of Abydos', because according to legend either his head or his whole body was buried at the site. (see Temple of Isis, Aswan, page 805). Abydos was considered the door to the after-life which looked out over the W Desert where the gates were thought to be. Initially, in order to achieve resurrection it was necessary to be buried at Abydos but the requirement was later changed to a simple pilgrimage and the gift of a commemorative stele.

There are cemeteries and tombs scattered over a very wide area in Abydos but there are only a few buildings left standing. They do, however, include the **Temple of Seti I**, the **Osirieon** and the **Temple of Ramses II** which are open daily 0700-1800 (Entry E£6 & E£3 for students).

Next to the ticket booth is an excellent little café with green tables which is cheap and clean and serves very welcoming cold drinks.

The Temple of Seti I, was built by Seti I (1318-1304 BC) as an offering in the same way that lesser individuals would come on a pilgrimage and make a gift of a stele. Most of the work on the temple and its convex bas-reliefs, which are amongst the most beautiful of all New Kingdom buildings, was carried out by Seti I but when he died his son Ramses II (1304-1237 BC) completed the courtyard and façade. This can be seen from the quality of workmanship which changes from Seti I's beautiful bas-reliefs to Ramses II's much cruder, quicker and therefore cheaper sunken reliefs. It is a very unusual temple because it is L-shaped rather than the usual rectangular and because it has 7 separate chapels rather than a single one behind the hypostele halls. This may have been because of the water table or the presence of the older Osirieon behind the temple.

The temple was originally approached via a pylon and 2 forecourts, built by Ramses II below the main temple so that the concept of the temple sloping upwards from the entrance to the inner sanctuary was maintained, but they have now been largely destroyed. The temple's front is now the square-columned façade behind 12 rectangular pillars decorated with Ramses welcoming Osiris, Isis and Horus. Originally there were 7 doors through the façade which led on to the 7 chapels but Ramses altered the construction and only the central one is now unblocked.

The theme of the 7 separate chapels is evident in the **First Hypostele Hall**, built and decorated by Ramses II's second-rate craftsmen, where the columns with papyrus capitals depict Ramses with the god represented in the corresponding sanctuary. In the much more impressive **Second Hypostele Hall**, built by Seti, the first 2 rows of columns also have papyrus capitals but the last row have no capitals at all. On the right-hand wall Seti is pictured before Osiris and Horus who are pouring holy water from vases and making offerings in front of Osiris' shrine as 5 goddesses look on. The quality of the work in this hall contrasts sharply with the rougher decoration in the outer hall which was probably because Ramses had ordered all the most skilled craftsmen to concentrate on his own temple!

Behind the inner hypostele hall there are 7 separate **Sanctuaries** or chapels which are dedicated to the deified Seti I, the Osiris triad of Osiris, Isis and Horus, and the Amun triad of Amun, Mut and Khonsu. Many of the wonderful bas-reliefs are still coloured, which gives a good idea of the temple's original decoration, but some of the finest are unpainted and show the precision and great artistry used in the moulding. The sanctuary to the left is dedicated to Seti and contains a beautiful scene of the Pharaoh being crowned by the goddess of Upper and Lower Egypt.

Each of these sanctuaries would have contained the god's barque as well as his stele placed in front of a false door. The sanctuary was locked and only High Priests had access because the Ancient Egyptians believed that the gods lived in their sanctuaries. The daily rituals which were carried out included a sacrifice as well as the dressing and purification of the stele. Unlike the others, the **Sanctuary of Osiris** does not have a false door at the back of the chapel but connects with the pillared **First Osiris Hall**. It is decorated with scenes from the Osiris myth and has 3 shrines on the W wall dedicated, with magnificent and incredibly vivid paintings, to Seti, Isis and Horus. The Mysteries of Osiris miracle play would have been performed in the hall and in the unfinished and partially destroyed **Second Osiris Hall** which is reached through a narrow entrance on the opposite wall.

Back in the Second Hypostele Hall the temple changes direction on the left-hand or SE side with 2 entrances leading to a number of other halls. The nearest is the 3-columned **Hall of Sokar & Nefertum**, northern deities subsequently integrated into the Osirian cult, with the separate **Chapel of Sokar** and **Chapel of Nefertum** at the back. Through the other entrance is the narrow star decorated **Hall/Gallery of Ancestors/Lists** which, very usefully for archaeologists, lists in rows the names of the gods and 76 of Seti's predecessors although, for political reasons, some such as Hatshepsut, Akhenaten and his heirs are omitted. The gallery leads on to the **Hall of Barques** where the sacred boats were stored, the **Hall of Bulls** used as the slaughterhouse for the sacrifices, and other store-rooms: they are currently closed to visitors. Instead it is best to follow the side **Corridor of the Bulls**, where Ramses II is shown lassoing a bull before the jackal-headed "opener of the ways" Wepwawet on one side and driving 4 dappled calves towards Khonsu and Seti I on the other, before climbing the steps to the temple's rear door and the Osirieon.

The **Osirieon**, built earlier than the main temple and at water level which has led to severe flooding, is sometimes called the Cenotaph of Seti I because it contains a sarcophagus. Although it was never used by Seti I, who is actually buried in the Valley of the Kings in Luxor, it was built as a symbol of his closeness to Osiris. Many other pharaohs built similar 'fake' tombs, which were modelled on the tombs at Luxor, in Abydos but were eventually buried elsewhere. The Osirieon is the only remaining visible tomb but is unfortunately inaccessible because of the inundation of sand and the flooding caused by the rise in the water table.

The small **Temple of Ramses II**, near the village 300m NW from the Temple of Seti I across soft sand, is naturally an anticlimax after the scale and sheer beauty of the Temple of Seti I. It was originally a very finely built shrine which was erected in 1298 BC for Ramses' *Ka* or spirit in order to give him a close association with Osiris. The workmanship is better than in most of Ramses II's monuments because it was probably decorated by craftsmen trained in his father's era. Although the temple was reportedly almost intact when first seen by Napoleon's archaeologists, it has since fallen into ruin except for the limestone walls which are still brightly coloured.

Local information

● Accommodation

There are 4 hotels directly outside the railway station of which the best is **F** ***Andolous*** which is a clean but noisy budget hotel which mainly caters for Egyptian train travellers. There are fans in each rm but only an inadequate shared shower and toilet on each floor.

● Youth hostel

5 Sharia Port Said, T 324395, 28 beds, kitchen, parking, station 1.5 km, overnight fee E£5 includes breakfast.

● Places to eat

There are a number of small **cheap** restaurants and cafés in the streets around the railway station including ***El- Eman*** to the N of Andolous.

● Telephone

Local code: 093.

● Transport

Train To all regional destinations, but those to Cairo and Luxor (4 hr) are much slower than buses or service taxis and are not worth taking.

Road Bus 5 daily buses N to Minya and Cairo and S to Luxor, as well as much more frequent ones to Assuit (2 hr), El-Balyana (for Abydos) and Qena (3 hr), which can be caught from the bus depot 5 min to the left of railway station.

Service taxis run N as far as Assuit and S to Qena via El-Balyana and Nag Hammadi.

Qena

Although not as bad as Beni Suef or Assuit, the town of Qena, 147 km S of Sohag and 58 km N of Luxor, is another place which is best avoided. It is an unfriendly, dirty town with difficult transport connections and problems of Islamic fundamentalism (**See political risks, page 30**. The only reason for stopping in the town is to see the magnificent temple at Dendera about 8 km from the centre of town.

ACCESS From the train station and the southbound service taxi depot, which are on either side of the main canal, yet another Sharia el-Gumhorriya leads SE to a major roundabout and the town's main street, to the W end of which is the bus station and the northbound service taxi depot.

Things to see

Visitors should immediately head for Dendera. Because Qena's transport terminals are so far apart the easiest way of getting there is to forget about the cost, which in Western terms is still very modest, and take a taxi direct from Qena to the temple and thereby avoid a long hot walk or misdirections and total confusion. Alternatively service taxis between Qena and Sohag which can be caught next to the bus station will drop you at Dendera village which is only a 1 km walk to the temple.

Dendera was the cult-centre of Hathor since pre-dynastic times and there are signs of earlier buildings on the site dating back to Cheops in the 4th Dynasty (2613-2494 BC). Hathor, who is represented as a cow or cow-headed woman, was the goddess associated with love, joy, music, protection of the dead and, above all, of nurturing. Her great popularity was demonstrated by the huge festival held at Edfu (see page 795) when her barque symbolically sailed upstream on her annual visit to Horus to whom she was both wet-nurse and lover. As they reconsumated their union the population indulged in the Festival of Drunkenness which led the Greeks to identify Hathor with Aphrodite who was their own goddess of love and joy.

The **Temple of Hathor** (Open daily 0700-1800, Entry E£6 or E£3 for students), which was built between 125 BC and 60 AD by the Ptolemies and the Romans, is only the latest temple on the site with the first being built by Pepi I in the 6th Dynasty (2345-2181 BC). The huge well preserved temple dominates the walled Dendera complex which also includes a number of smaller buildings. Even although it was built by non-Egyptian foreign conquerors it copies the earlier pharaonic temples with large hypostele halls leading up, via a series of successively smaller vestibules and store-rooms, to the darkened sanctuary at the back of the temple. There are also 2 sets of steps leading up to and down from the roof sanctuaries.

At the front the pylon-shaped façade is supported by 6 huge Hathor-headed columns and reliefs showing the Roman emperors Tiberius and Claudius performing rituals with the gods. Through in the **Hypostele Hall** the 18 Hathor-headed columns, organized into groups of 3, are identical to those on the façade. The ceiling, which is illustrated with an astronomical theme showing the mystical significance of the sky, has retained much of its original colour. It is divided between day and night and illustrates the 14 day moon cycle, the gods of the 4 cardinal points, the constellations, the zodiac, and the elongated goddess Nut who swallows the sun at sunset and gives birth to it at dawn.

The next room, which is known as the **Hall of Appearances** and is supported by 6 columns, is where the goddess 'appeared' from the depths of the temple as she was transported on her ritual barque for the annual voyage to Edfu. On either side of the doorway there are scenes of offerings and the presentation of the temple to the gods.

Around the Hall are 6 small rooms. The first on the left was the laboratory, used for the preparation of balms and the 9 oils used to anoint the statues, which has several inscriptions with the recipes and instructions for their preparation. The next 2 rooms were used as store-rooms for offerings such as flowers, beer, wine and poultry. On the right of the hall's doorway is the Treasury which has scenes on the base of the walls representing the 13 mountainous countries where the precious minerals were found. The second room called the Nile Room, has river scenes and an exit to the back corridor and the well outside.

Next is the first vestibule which was known as the **Hall of Offerings** because it was there that the priests displayed the offerings for the goddess on large tables. The food and drink was then divided among the priests once the gods had savoured them. On the left a stairway leads to the roof sanctuary. Note that all the rooms are lit by sunlight from holes in the roof. The second vestibule called the **Hall of the Ennead** contained the statues of the kings and gods which were involved in the ceremonies to Hathor while her wardrobe was stored in the room on the left.

This leads on to the **Sanctuary of the Golden One** which contained Hathor's statue and her ceremonial barque which would be carried to the river each New Year to be transported on a boat upstream to the Temple of horus at Edfu. The S and N walls of the independently roofed sanctuary depict the Pharaoh in various phases of the ceremony. The so-called **Corridor of Mysteries** around the outside of the sanctuary has 9 doors which lead to 11 small shrines with 32 closed crypts below the back shrines including crypt where the temple's valuables would have been store.

The walls of the stairway from the left of the Hall of Offerings to the **Roof Sanctuaries**, which unlike anywhere else have been completely preserved at Dendera, depict the New Year ceremony when the statue of Hathor was carried up to the roof to the small open **Chapel of the Union with the Disk** pavilion to await the sunrise. The scenes on the left of the stairs represent Hathor going up and those on the right going down. In the NW corner of the roof terrace is **Osiris' Tomb**, where ceremonies commemorating Osiris' death and resurrection were carried out. In the E corner there are 2 rooms with the outer one containing a plaster-cast copy of the original **Dendera Zodiac** ceiling which was stolen and taken to the Louvre in Paris in 1820. The Zodiac was introduced to Egypt by the Romans and, although Scorpio's scorpion is replaced by a scarab beetle and the hippo-goddess Tweri was added, this circular zodiac held up by 4 goddesses is virtually identical to the one used today.

Back downstairs in the temple enclosure there are a number of small ruined buildings surrounding the main temple. At the back is the small **Temple of Isis** which was almost totally destroyed by the early Christians because of the fear that the worship of Isis as the universal Egyptian god might spread. At the front of the main temple to the right is the **Roman Birth House**, or Mammisi, which has some interesting carvings on its façade and S walls. It was built to replace the older 30th Dynasty **Birth House of Nectanebo** (380-362 BC) which was partially destroyed when the Romans built a wall around the temple. The **Sanatorium** between it and the main temple was where pilgrims, who came to Dendera to be healed by Hathor, were treated and washed in water from the stone-lined **Sacred Lake** to the SW of the main temple which is now drained of water. Between the 2 birth-houses is a ruined 5th century **Coptic Basilica**, one of the earliest Coptic buildings in Egypt, which was built using stone from the adjacent buildings.

This site is spoilt by the unusually large number of 'guides' who hang around wanting payment for helping you up a step or round a corner.

Local information

● Accommodation

The only semi-decent hotels are: **E** *Aluminium*, Aluminium, Naga Hammadi, Qena, T 581320, 72 rm, 150 beds.

F *Dendera*, Dendera, T 322330 also called *Happy Land* is on the junction of the main road to Sohag and the turnoff for the temple 1 km away and is probably a much better bet than Qena's grubby hotels; **F** *New Palace*, Midan Mahata, Qena, T 2509, 75 rm, 120 beds, behind the Mobil garage near the train station.

● Camping

Located next to the *Hotel Dendera* the camp site has hot showers, electricity and a kitchen.

● Places to eat

There are a few small **cheap** restaurants, including the ***El-Prince***, ***Hamdi*** and ***Maradona*** in and around town, but none of them is particularly good.

● Post Office

Open Sat-Thur 0800-1400 & 1800-2000 is at the canal end of the main street.

● Telephone

Local code: 096.

● Transport

Unfortunately the transport terminals are very spread out and it may be best to take a *calèche* from one to the other provided your bargaining is pretty good.

Train: 6 daily trains from the station next to the canal both N to Cairo (11-12 hrs) via Sohag, Assuit, Minya and Beni Suef, and S to Luxor (2 hrs) and Aswan (6-7 hrs).

Road Bus Although they are slower and less convenient than service taxis, there are buses to Assuit, Sohag and Cairo, from the bus station on the main street, but the 6 daily buses to Hurghada on the Red Sea coast may be of more use.

Service Taxis The quickest way to Luxor (1 hr) and other points S is by service taxi from the square just across the canal behind the railway station: 500m away there are taxis to Safaga and Hurghada. Northbound service taxis along the W bank to Sohag via Nag Hammadi and El-Balyana, can be caught from the depot which is next to the bus station but one should be prepared for a long wait except in the early morning.

THE NILE VALLEY
LUXOR AND THE WEST BANK

CONTENTS

MAPS

The area around Luxor, which was the capital of the New Kingdom (1567-1085 BC), has the largest concentration of ancient tombs and monuments in the country and has been the focus of Upper Egypt's tourist industry for more than a century. It is more dependent on tourism than any other town in Egypt and its fortunes have therefore fluctuated in recent years as a result of the Gulf War and the threat of Islamic fundamentalist terrorism.

Luxor

Population: 40,000. *Altitude:* 89m.

History

On the site of the small present-day town of Luxor, (676 km S of Cairo, 65 km S of Qena and 223 km N of Aswan), stood the ancient city which the Greeks called Thebes and which was described in Homer's *Iliad* as the 'city of a hundred gates'. Later the Arabs described it as 'el-Uqsur' or 'city of palaces' from which it gets its current name.

The town and the surrounding limestone hills had been settled for many centuries but during the Old Kingdom (2616-2181 BC) it was little more than a small provincial town called Waset. It first assumed importance under Menutuhotep II who reunited Egypt and made it his capital but it soon lost its position. It was during the 18th-20th Dynasty of the New Kingdom (1567-1085 BC) that Thebes reached its zenith when, except for the brief reign of Akhenaten (1379-1362 BC), it was the capital of the Egyptian empire which stretched from Palestine to Nubia. At its peak the population reached almost 1 million. Besides being the site of the largest and greatest concentration of monuments in the world it was, for the ancient Egyptians, the prototype for all future cities.

When the capital later shifted elsewhere it remained a vibrant city and the focus for the worship of Amun ('the Supreme Creator'). Although there is no

CLIMATE: LUXOR

	Jan	Feb	Mar	Apr	May	Jun	Jul	Aug	Sep	Oct	Nov	Dec	Av/Tot
Max (°C)	23	25	29	35	39	41	41	41	39	35	30	25	34
Min (°C)	6	7	11	16	20	23	23	24	22	18	12	7	16
Rain (mm)	<1	<1	<1	<1	<1	0	0	<1	<1	<1	<1	0	<1

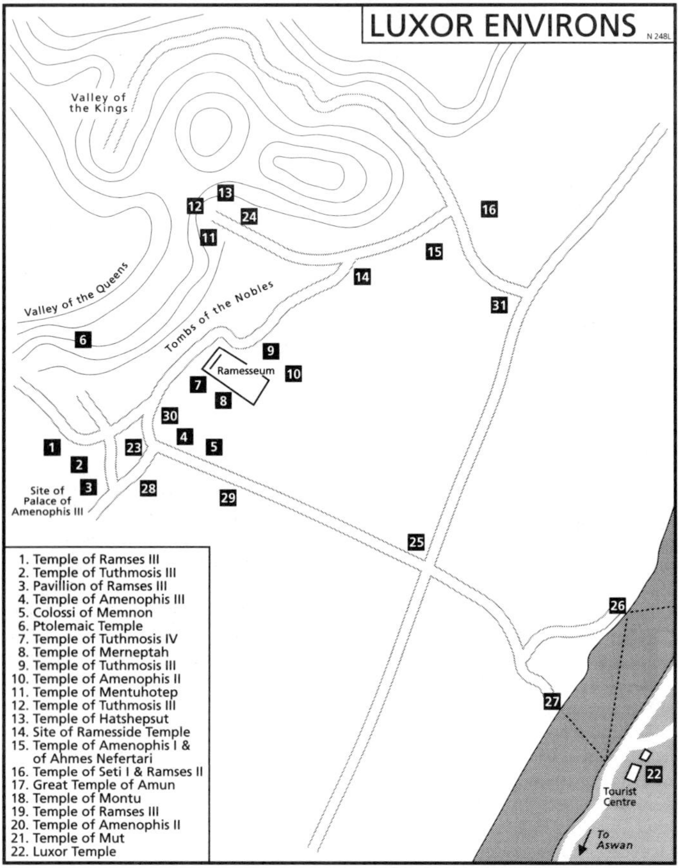

obvious connection with the Greek city of Thebes the name was subsequently given to the city by the Greeks. It was a shadow of its former self during the Ptolemaic (323-30 BC) and Roman (30 BC – 640 AD) periods but, unlike ancient Memphis to the S of Cairo, it was never abandoned and it became an important regional Christian settlement.

After the Muslim conquest in 640 AD, the town continued to decline and it was not until the beginning of the 19th century, during Napoleon's expedition to Egypt, that its historical importance began to be recognized. The display of some of its treasures in Paris' Louvre museum sparked off considerable interest from the world's archaeologists who still continue to explore the area almost 200 years later. Since 1869, when Thomas Cook took his first party of travellers to Egypt for the opening of the Suez Canal, Luxor has become the most important tourist destination in Upper Egypt. Today, although it has become an important administrative town, the eco-

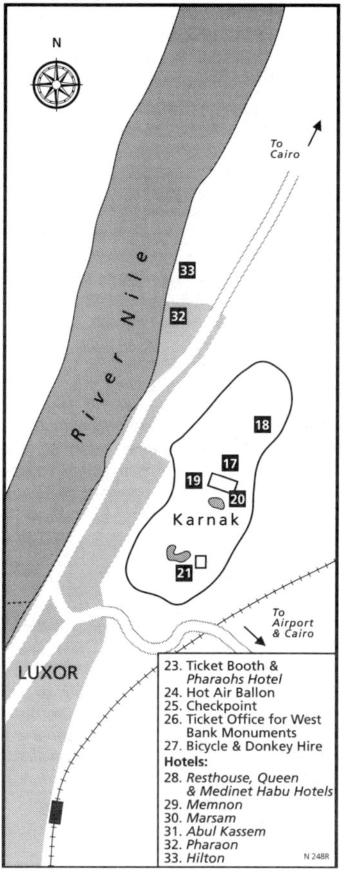

nomic livelihood of Luxor is, as the sudden collapse in business during the 1990/91 Gulf war demonstrated, almost totally dependent on the tourist industry.

ACCESS Air The airport is 7 km E of the town centre which can be reached by taxi (E£15) or bus. **Train** Those arriving at the railway station can take a *calèche*, a taxi or walk the 500m along Sharia al-Mahata into town. **Road** The bus terminal is on Sharia Television about 10 min walk from the centre of town, while the service taxi terminal is just off Sharia el-Karnak about 1 km from both Luxor town centre and Karnak temple. The majority of the tourist hotels and shops are located near the river Nile along the Corniche and the parallel Sharia el-Karnak.

Things to see

There is so much to see in Luxor that it is best to plan your itinerary carefully. In and around the town on the E bank of the river the **Luxor Temple** (see page 775), **Luxor Museum** (page 776) and **Karnak Temple** complex (page 777) are essential stops. Although the W bank is dominated by the **Theban Necropolis** (page 782) and the **Valley of the Kings** (page 782) there are also important temples and monuments to see above ground and the W bank is certainly worth two days. See separate details below.

Local information

● Accommodation

Price guide:			
AL	US$90+	**D**	US$20-40
A	US$75-90	**E**	US$10-20
B	US$60-75	**F**	under US$10
C	US$40-60		

Because Luxor attracts so many tourists there are over 35 hotels, with thousands of beds, covering the widest range of accommodation. Most hotels are located on or close to the river although some are a short bus ride S of the town. Rooms are cheaper if booked as part of a package. In normal circumstances, during the peak season in Nov-Feb there are no spare rooms but during the hottest months there are plenty of cut-price deals to be had if you shop around.

AL *Movenpick Jolie Ville Luxor*, Crocodile Island, T 374855, F 374936, 320 rm in 20 bungalow pavilions, the only tourist village in Luxor, beautiful location 4 km S of Luxor, connected to mainland by bridge and to town centre by free hourly ferry, under 16s can sleep free in their parents' rm, good restaurants – Movenpick, Jolie Ville, Garden Terrace, Sharazade Nile Terrace, Crocodile Bar, and the Sobek Hall for banquets, functions and conferences, good pool; **AL** *Luxor Hilton*, New Karnak, T 374955, F 376571, 261 rather small rm, located to N of town with free courtesy bus, unprepossessing exterior hides an excellent interior with reportedly the best hotel management in the town, sleep may be disturbed by cruise liners which moor alongside and run engines all night, excellent food; **AL** ***Luxor Sheraton Hotel & Resort***, Sharia El-Awameya, PO Box 34, T 374544, F 374941, 298 rm, 435 beds, well managed, caters for tour groups which receive reduced rates.

A ***Isis Hotel Luxor***, Sharia Khalid Ibn el-Walid, T 373366, F 373923, the largest hotel in Upper Egypt with 500 large, clean, well decorated rm and 150 more planned, located to the S of town, courtesy bus, 2 pools, non-residents can swim for E£15, main Italian and seafood restaurants plus 3 specialists restaurants, excellent facilities but slow service.

B ***Akhetaten Village***, Sharia Khalid Ibn el-Walid, T 580850, F 5808079, 144 rm, run by Club Med with its unique and stylish atmosphere; **B** ***Etap Luxor Hotel***, Corniche el-Nil, T 580944, F 373316, 306 quality rm with bath, located in town centre on river front, attractive atmosphere, very well run, 2 restaurants with live entertainment, 24 hrs coffee shop, most guests are tour groups who are mainly British in summer and German in the winter high season when the hotel is always full; **B** ***Luxor Hotel***, opposite Luxor Temple, T 580018, F 580623, 86 rm, standard hotel; **B** ***Novotel Luxor***, Sharia Khalid Ibn el-Walid, Tx 23748, F 580972, new hotel run by Accor group, 180 rm, emphasis on friendly service, 2 restaurants (1 floating), conference and fax facilities. Most guests are tour groups with predominantly British, German, French and Scandinavian guests in winter and Italian, Swiss, Japanese and Americans in summer; **B** ***PLM Azur Egotel***, 10 Sharia Maabad Luxor, T 373521, F 580817, 89 rm, caters mainly for tour groups, reportedly has excellent food; **B** ***Winter Palace Hotel***, Corniche el-Nil, T 580422, Tx 92160, F 374087, 110 rm in the old building and 260 in the new, 700 beds overlooking the Nile, the oldest and most famous luxury hotel in Luxor whose guests have included heads of state, Noel Coward and Agatha Christie. The old style rm are unusual but rather basic, 2 restaurants, terrace bar in splendid position overlooking Corniche and river, shared pool (in which some people have slipped and fallen).

C ***New Windsor Hotel***, Sharia Nefertiti, T 374306, F 373447, 40 rm, biggest and probably the best 3 star hotel in town, located just behind the Corniche, roof garden has river view, rm in the new extension around the small pool are better choice, bar, discotheque below the restaurant, a bank and 2 international telephone lines, food good but unspectacular.

D ***Arabesque***, Sharia Mohamed Farid, T 372193, F 372193, 36 rm, new; **D** ***Flo-Pater***, Sharia Khalid Ibn el-Walid, T&F 374223, 40 rm, new; **D** ***Paula Hotel***, El-Takhit, Sharia el-Eklimy, T 580551, F 580552, 40 rm, good, clean budget hotel; **D** ***Pharaon***, New Karnak, T 374924, F 376477, 50 rm, located near Nile, service reportedly not particularly good; **D** ***Emilo Hotel*** and ***New Emilo Hotel***, Sharia Yusef Hassan, T 373570, F 374884, in town centre, 111 a/c rm with bath and TV, 2 restaurants, 3 bars, disco, pool, small shop, exchange, international phone lines, friendly service, main guests are German and British tour groups; **D** ***Philippe Hotel***, Sharia Dr. Labib Habashi, T 372284, F 580060, 40 rm; **D** ***Savoy Hotel***, Corniche el-Nil, PO Box 83952, T 580522, F 580526, 108 rm, cheapest of Luxor's classic Victorian hotels; **D** ***Shady***, Sharia Television, T 581377, F 374859, 50 rm, 115 beds, new hotel conveniently located near the bus station; **D** ***St Joseph***, Sharia Khalid Ibn el-Walid, T 581707, F 581727, 55 rm, 109 beds, new.

E ***Marwa Palace***, Sharia Television, T 580040, 40 rm, 85 beds, convenient for bus station; **E** ***Santa Maria***, Sharia Television, T 372603, 48 rm, 88 beds, convenient for bus station; **E** ***St Catherine Hotel***, 2 Sharia St Catherine, T 372684, 60 rm, 104 beds; **E** ***Windsor***, Sharia Nefertiti, T 372847, F 373447, 112 rm, clean, family run budget hotel joined to the *New Windsor Hotel*.

F ***Abu el-Hagag (4 Seasons)***, Sharia Maabad Luxor & M Farid, T 372958, 15 rm, 33 beds, one of the cheapest hotels in town mainly frequented by long-stay budget travellers, located adjacent to Luxor Temple with excellent views from the top floors; **F** ***Beau Soleil***, Sharia Salah al-Din, T 372671, 22 rm, new; **F** ***El-Aref***, Sharia St Catherine, T 372557, 33 rm, 63 beds, new; **F** ***El-Mustafa Hotel***, Sharia Television, T 374721, 20 rm, new, near bus station and the *Marwa Palace* and *Santa Maria* hotels; F ***Horus***, Sharia el-Karnak, T 372165, 25 a/c rm, 71 beds, highly recommended, centrally located but rather noisy budget hotel with friendly staff, clean a/c rm, hot showers and a good breakfast; **F** ***Mina Palace***, Corniche el-Nil, T 372074, 40 rm, one of the best cheap hotels, excellent location, some rm overlook

Nile/Luxor Temple; **F *Nefertiti***, Sharia el-Karnak, T 372386, 27 rm, very cheap; **F *Nile Hotel***, Sharia Labib Habashi, T 372859, 48 rm, 102 beds, near Corniche with *calèche* drivers always parked on the street outside; **F *Nobles***, Sharia Yusef Hassan, Midan Ahmose, T 372823, 40 rm, 85 beds, very cheap; **F *Nour Home***, Sharia Mohamed Farid, highly recommended quiet budget hotel with worn but clean rm but no daily clean linen, helpful owner; **F *Pyramids Hotel***, Sharia Yusef Hassan, T 373243, 20 rm, 50 beds, cheapest in town located near *Nobles Hotel*; **F *Ramoza***, Sharia Sa'ad Zaghloul, T 372270, Tx 23604, 48 clean a/c rm, hot showers, near railway station but about 1 km from the river; **F *Sphinx***, Sharia Yusef Hassan, T 372830, 33 rm, 73 beds; **F *Venus***, Sharia Yusef Hassan, T 372635, 23 clean, basic rm with fans or a/c and bath, one of the best small downtown budget hotels, good laundry service, planned new roof-top bar and restaurant to serve meals and alcohol, popular with young German tourists.

● Youth Hostel

Clean, spartan 275 bed IYHF Youth Hostel halfway between Luxor and Karnak Temples at 16 Sharia Karnak Temple, T/F 372139, 275 beds, meals available, family rooms, laundry, overnight fee E£5-10. Although it is cheap, there are many cheap hotels which offer more comfortable and convenient accommodation without the 1000-1400 lockout and 2300-0600 curfew.

● Camping

Opposite the youth hostel, the permanently guarded camp site (T 382425), which mainly caters for noisy Egyptian families, offers space for tents and hot showers.

● Places to eat

Price guide:
♦♦♦Expensive; ♦♦average; ♦cheap.

While the majority of the better hotels have expensive good quality restaurants, which serve standard international hotel food, and in some cases interesting Egyptian food, there are no excellent independent restaurants. There are, however, a number of comparatively **cheap** restaurants which are concentrated around the tourist shops on Sharia el-Karnak behind Luxor Temple. Away from the shops the ***Maharba Restaurant***'s rooftop terrace above the town's tourist office on the Corniche commands an excellent view of the Nile and serves decent food and beer.

♦♦♦Cruising restaurants provide a splendid meal in a spectacular setting, either a day cruise with lunch to Dendera or a dinner. ***Le Lotus*** from *Novotel Luxor* with bar and disco; ***M S Africa*** from *Movenpick Hotel*; ***Luxor Sheraton*** from *Sheraton Hotel*.

● Balloon flights

In British built hot air balloons. Leave your hotel at 0500, total excursion time is 4 hrs, flight 45-90 mins, breakfast served in desert or leave you hotel at 1430 and return after a desert 'sundowner buffet'. Insured by Lloyds of London and full refund if weather conditions prevent flight, T 386515/581584.

● Banks

National Bank of Egypt (open Sat-Thur 0830-1400 & 1700-2000, Fri 0830-1100 & 1700-2000) just S of the Old Winter Palace Hotel, **Banque Misr** (Sun-Thur 0830-2100) on Sharia Nefertiti, and **Bank of Alexandria** N of Sharia Nefertiti and Sharia el-Karnak intersection.

● Nightlife

Although most of the major hotels have music and floor shows they are generally mediocre compared with Cairo. Nightlife is largely restricted to promenades through the town and along the Corniche with stops for soft drinks, a water-pipe *sheesha*,and backgammon *thowla*. The Sound & Light show at Karnak is over melodramatic but certainly worth a visit. Rather than buy an expensive all inclusive 'tour', which can cost E£40 or more, arrange your own transport for a few E£ and pay the normal E£18 entrance at the kiosk.

● Sound & Light at Karnak

Shows daily at 1800 and 2000 as follows:

Mon	English/French
Tue	French/English
Wed	English/German
Thur	Arabic/English
Fri	French/English
Sat	English/French
Sun	French/German

● Discos

Aladin in *Isis Hotel* open from 2100; ***Rababa*** in *Luxor Hilton* open 2000-0200; ***Sabil*** in *Etap Hotel* and ***Sukkareya Club*** in *Sheraton Hotel*.

● Post Office

Main post office (Sun-Thur 0800-1400) is on Sharia el-Mahata on the way to the railway station. Hotels sell stamps.

● Religious Services

Roman Catholic 16 Sharia Karnak Temple, holds Mass in Latin with multilingual readings each Sun at 0900 and 1800 and Mass in Arabic Sun at 0730.

● Shopping

Luxor shops are mainly divided between those for tourists found in the hotels and in the main central tourist bazaar, and the local markets. For the independent traveller good quality fruit and vegetables can be bought in the ***Sharia Television market*** on Tues. Generally the further away from the river the lower the prices and the less the hassle. Foreign newspapers are sold in a kiosk in the middle of the street outside the *Old Winter Palace* hotel.

Bookshops At *Hilton* and *Sheraton*, also ***Aboudi Books*** (0800-2000) and ***Gaddis Books*** (0800-2130) in Tourist Bazaar beside *Winter Palace*.

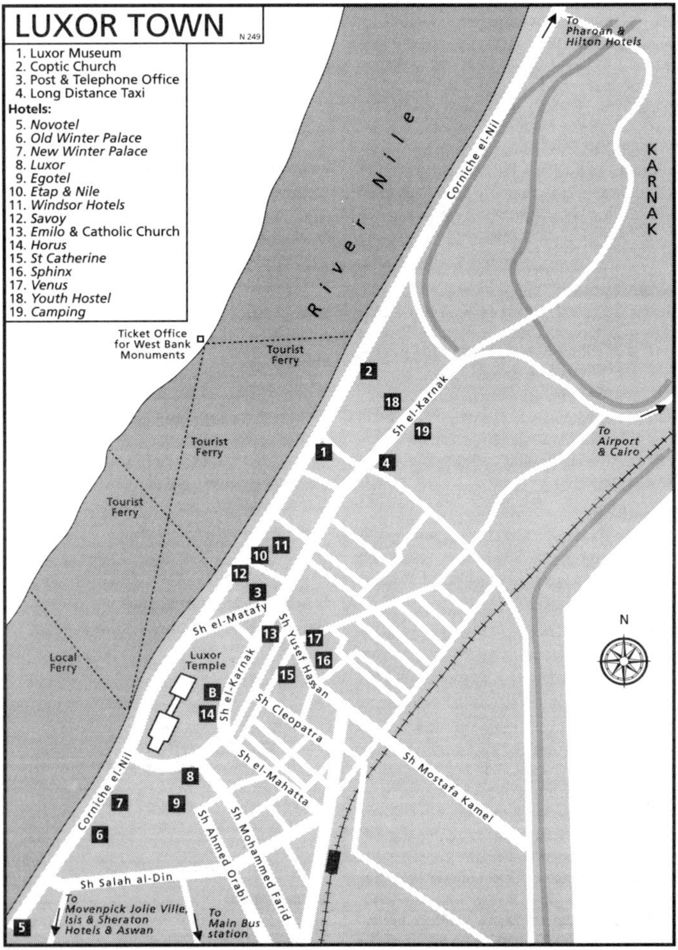

● **Sport**

Besides swimming pools, the main hotels have the best sporting facilities including tennis, sailing and a wide range of indooor games. This section of the Nile is used for international rowing championships.

● **Telephone**

Local code: 095.

● **Travel agents**

Those in the main hotels are generally very good and can arrange tickets for almost anywhere in the country. The town's travel agents include ***Eastmar Travel***, Corniche el-Nil, *Old Winter Palace*, T 382151, F 382151 and ***Kuoni Travel***, *Sheraton Hotel*, T 384544. ***Egypt Air***, T 580581.

● **Tourist information**

The official and very helpful Egyptian Tourist Authority (ETA) office, T 382215, open daily 0800-2000, is on the Corniche between the Luxor Temple and the Old Winter Palace Hotel. It is worth a visit to check the current official prices for everything including *calèches*, taxis and other services. The tourist police are in the same building but also have branches at the airport and the railway station.

● **Transport**

Local: Cycle hire from *Hilton Hotel* or *Egotel* for E£5 per hour. Cheaper and fairly roadworthy cycles can be hired from El-Hussein behind Luxor Temple.

Air There are frequent daily flights particularly in the winter high season to Cairo, Aswan and Abu Simbel and less frequently to Hurghada. Egyptair and the privately-owned ZAS charge identical rates for their flights. There is an increasing number of charter flights to/from European cities.

Train From the station on Sharia al-Mahata there are 6 daily a/c trains to Cairo (12-14 hrs) and slower ones to Aswan (5 hrs). The 1st class service on the Cairo trains is good and it is a pleasant way to see the Egyptian countryside. It is essential, particularly in the high winter season, to reserve your seat at the station a few days before you travel.

Road: **Bus** From the Sharia Television bus terminal it is possible to catch 3 daily express buses to Cairo (10 hrs); 3 to Hurghada (4 hrs) via Qena (the left-hand seats are cooler in the Eastern Desert); and frequent slow southbound ones every few hrs to Aswan via Esna, Edfu and Kom Ombo.

Service taxi From the terminal just off Sharia el-Karnak, half way between the Luxor town centre and Karnak temple, these are quicker and more convenient than trains or buses but only go as far N as Qena (1 hr). Change taxis there to go on to Esna (45 min), Kom Ombo (2-3 hrs) and Aswan (4-5 hrs).

Private taxi Sample charges E£100 to Aswan, E£160 to Hurghada, E£13 to airport.

Sites in Luxor and on the E bank

Luxor Temple

The temple, in the centre of town on the Corniche, is open daily 0700-2100 in winter, 0700-2200 in summer and during Ramadan 0800-1100 and 2000-2300. Entry E£10 and E£10 for cameras.

Like the much larger Karnak Temple it is dedicated to the 3 Theban gods Amun, Mut and Khonsu. **Amun** is usually depicted as a man wearing ram's horns and the feathered Atef crown. His wife **Mut** was considered to be the mistress of heaven and **Khonsu** was their son who was believed to travel through the sky at night assisting the scribe god.

Because it is smaller, more compact and fewer pharaohs were involved in its construction, Luxor Temple is simpler and more coherent than Karnak Temple a few km away. Although the 18th Dynasty (1537-1320 BC) pharaoh **Amenhotep III** (1417-1379 BC) began the Temple, his son **Amenhotep IV**, who changed his name to **Akhenaten** (1379-1362 BC) by which he is better known, concentrated instead on building a shrine to Aten adjacent to the site. However **Tutankhamen** (1361-1352 BC) and **Horemheb** (1348-1320 BC) later resumed the work and decorated the peristyle court and colonnade. **Ramses II** (1304-1237 BC) completed the majority of the building by adding a second colonnade and pylon as well as a multitude of colossi. The Temple subsequently became covered with sand and silt which helped preserve it although salt encrustation has caused some damage. Because the ground level has risen 6m since its construction the temple now stands at the bottom of a gentle depression. An avenue of sphinxes, a 30th Dynasty (380-343 BC) addition, lines the approach. This avenue once stretched all the way to the Karnak Temple complex.

The **First Pylon** gives an impression of how awe-inspiring the Temple must have looked in its prime. The 22.8m 2nd Obelisk, which was given to France by Mohamed Ali Pasha in 1819 and was re-erected in the Place de la Concorde in Paris, and 3 of Ramses II's 6 original colossi have been removed. The reliefs on the First Pylon depict Ramses' victory at the Battle of Kadesh with later embellishments by Nubian and Ethiopian kings.

Passing through the pylon, the **Peristyle Court** is set at a slight angle to the rest of the Temple and encompasses the earlier shrine of **Tuthmosis III** (1504-1450 BC) which is also dedicated to the Theban triad. The E end of the court has not been excavated because it is the site of the **Mosque of Abu el-Haggag**, the patron saint of Luxor and, although another mosque with the same name has been built nearby, this one is still preferred by locals. While most of the mosque is 19th century the N minaret is much older. At the S end of the court, the portal flanking the entrance to the colonnade supports 2 black granite statues bearing the name of Ramses II but the feathers of Tutankhamen.

The **Colonnade** of 14 columns with papyrus capitals was built by Amenhotep but decorated by Tutankhamen and Horemheb. Beyond it is a **Court of Amenhotep III**, which is the second peristyle court with double rows of columns flanking 3 of the sides. It was built by Amenhotep III for the deity Amun who he claimed was his father. None of the original roof remains, but the columns are well preserved. It leads to the **Hypostele Hall** with 32 papyrus columns which were taken over by **Ramses IV** (1166-1160 BC) and **Ramses VII** (1148-1141 BC) who took no part in their erection but still added their cartouches!

Look out for the chamber which was converted into a **Coptic church** during the 4th century. The Pharaonic reliefs were plastered over and early Christian paintings covered the whitewash although little of these remains today. In a few places the stucco has crumbled away and some of the original reliefs are revealed.

Beyond is a smaller second vestibule, the **Offerings Chamber**, with its 4 columns still in place. Further on, in the **Sanctuary of the Sacred Barque**, the doors were made of acacia and inlaid with gold. **Alexander the Great** (332-323 BC) rebuilt the shrine in accordance with Amenhotep III's original plans. The E passage leads to the Birth Room built because of Amenhotep's claim that he was the son of the god Amun, who is depicted as entering the queen's chamber disguised as Tuthmosis IV (1425-1417 BC) and breathing the child into her nostrils. The furthest hall has 12 poorly maintained papyrus bud columns and leads on to the small **Sanctuary** where the combined god Amun-Min is represented.

Luxor Museum

The Luxor Museum, located on the Corniche half way between Luxor and Karnak temples, is open daily – winter 0900-1300 and 1600-2100 (last tickets 1230 and 2030) summer 0900-1300 and 1700-2200 (last tickets 1230 and 2130). Prices E£8 and E£10 for New Hall, 50% discount for students.

The few exhibits in this modern museum are tastefully displayed, centred around a small garden, with a large ground floor and a smaller upper gallery. The most important are the statues which were found in a cache at Karnak in 1989 but the exhibits range from pharaonic treasures to the Mamluke period (1250-1517 AD).

Of the statues on the ground floor the most striking are the large pink granite head of Amenhotep III (1417-1379 BC), an alabaster crocodile-headed Sobek, and 2 memorable busts of Akhenaten. A few choice exhibits from Tutankhamen's tomb are also displayed including a gold-inlaid cow's head of the goddess Hathor, a funerary bed and 2 model barques. The prints showing how the sites looked in the 19th century are also interesting.

Karnak Temple

The Karnak Temple complex, 2.5 km N of Luxor town, is the largest pharaonic monument in the country after the Giza Pyramids and covers almost 25 ha. Open daily winter 0700-1700, summer 0700-1800, entry E£10 and E£10 for cameras. The site can just about be covered in 2 hrs. The evening Sound and Light Show (E£18) is good with a somewhat

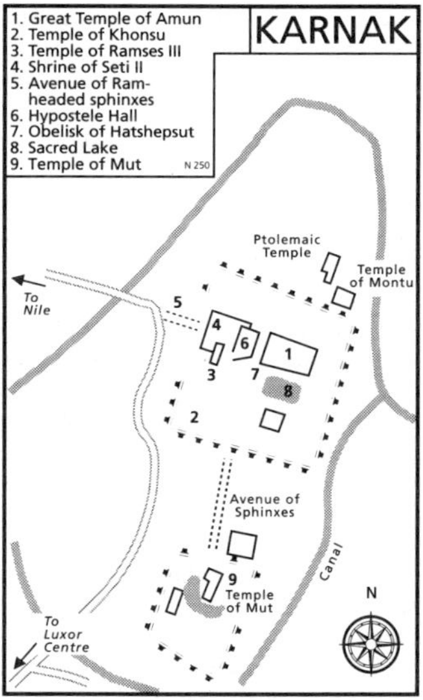

overdramatic commentary. See Sound & Light, page 773. *Calèches* and service taxis from Luxor town should officially cost about E£1 but you can expect to have to pay more and the ride along the Corniche is very pleasant.

Known in earlier times as **Iput-Isut** 'the most esteemed of places', the extent, scale and quality of the remains is astonishing. The complexes' numerous temples vary greatly in style because they were constructed over a period of 1,300 years. Their only common theme is worship of Amun, Mut and Khonsu who make up the Theban Triad of gods. In order to see as much of the site as possible, aim to arrive very early or just before sunset when it relatively cool and less crowded.

At the heart of the complex is the enormous **Temple of Amun (1)** which was altered and extended by successive pharaohs. For example although the heretical **Akhenaten**, who converted to the world's first monotheistic religion and moved the capital from Thebes to Tell el-Amarna (see page 756), replaced the images of **Amun** with representations of **Aten**, these were later erased by his successors and Amun's images were restored! Surrounding the main temple are numerous smaller but magnificent ones including the **Temple of Khonsu (2)**, the **Temple of Ramses III (3)** and the smaller **Shrine of Seti II (4)**.

The **Temple of Amun** is approached via the **Avenue of Ram Headed Sphinxes (5)** which used to link it to the Temple at Luxor. The imposing **First Pylon** is 130m wide and each of the 2 unfinished towers are 43m high and, although incomplete, nothing else matches its enormous scale. Dynasty after dynasty added to it and one might speculate about which ruler oversaw each of the various sections. Moving towards the inner core of the temple, which is the oldest section, one is moving back in time through successive dynasties. The entry towers are thought to have been constructed by the Nubian and Ethiopian Kings of the 25th Dynasty (747-656 BC) while recent work has revealed that several levels were built during the later Greek and Roman eras. For a little baksheesh it may be possible to climb the stairs up the N tower and marvel at the fantastic view it offers of the complex.

Arriving through the First Pylon, you come to the **First Forecourt** which was begun in the 20th Dynasty (1200-1085 BC) but completed somewhat later. Immediately on the left is the very thick-walled rose coloured granite and sandstone **Shrine of Seti II** (1216-1210 BC) which was a way-station for the sacred barques of Amun, Mut and Khonsu as they were taken on ritual processions. The W wall had to be subsequently rebuilt because it collapsed when the First Pylon was under construction. The outer façade portrays Seti II making offerings to various deities. In the middle of the First Forecourt are the 10 columns of Taharga which once supported a 26.5m high kiosk or small open temple.

To the right of the forecourt is the small **Temple of Ramses III** (1198-1166 BC) which would have stood in solitary splendour in front of the **Second Pylon** when it was first built in honour of Amun. Like the Shrine of Seti II, it was used as another way-station for the sacred barques. Part of an inscription in the interior reads: "*I made it for you in your city of Waset, in front of your forecourt, to the Lord of the Gods, being the Temple of Ramses in the estate of Amun, to remain as long as the heavens bear the sun. I filled its treasuries with offerings that my hands had brought*".

To the left of the **Second Pylon** is the 15m high **Colossus of Ramses II** (1304-1237 BC) with his daughter Benta-anta standing in front of his legs. On the right of the pylon is the **Bubastite Portal** named after the 22nd Dynasty (945-715 BC) kings from the Delta town of Bubastis. Through the Second Pylon is the immense 5,000 sq m (102 x 53m) and spectacular **Hypostele Hall (6)** which is probably the best part of the whole Karnak complex. Its has 134 giant columns, which were once topped by sandstone roof slabs, of which the 12 largest making up the central processional way to the other chambers are 23m high and 15m round. The other 122 smaller columns, which have papyrus bud capitals and retain some of their original colour at the higher levels, cover the rest of the hall. They are decorated by dedications to various Gods, but particularly to the many different guises of Amun and the Theban Triad, and are also inscribed with the cartouches of the pharaohs who contributed to the hall. The S side was decorated by Ramses II with vivid but cheap and simple concave sunk-reliefs, whilst the N is attributed to Seti II whose artists painstakingly carved delicate convex bas-reliefs on the walls. Ramses is shown, on the S side of the internal wall of the Second Pylon, making offerings before the gods and seeking their guidance, while on the left is a beautiful representation of Thoth inscribing Seti's name on a holy tree.

Seti II is depicted on both sides of the **Third Pylon** but the S wall running along the right of the hall was mainly decorated by Ramses II. He is shown being crowned by Horus and Thoth and then being presented to Amun while the Theban Triad is also pictured.

The **Third Pylon** was constructed by Amenhotep III (1417-1379 BC) on the site of several earlier shrines which were moved to the Luxor Museum and the Open Air Museum within the walls of Karnak. On the inner E face is a text of tribute and a scene showing the gods' sacred boats. Amenhotep III built a small court to enclose 4 **Tuthmosid Obelisks** in the narrow gap between the Third and Fourth Pylon which at that time represented the entrance to the

Temple. Of the 4, only one pink granite obelisk (23m high, weighing 143 tonnes and originally tipped with electrum) built by Tuthmosis II (1512-1504 BC) now remains and the stone bases and some blocks from 2 other obelisks built by Tuthmosis III (1504-1450 BC) are scattered nearby.

Moving towards the earlier centre of the temple is the limestone faced sandstone **Fourth Pylon**, built by Tuthmosis I (1525-1512 BC). Texts describing later restorations are recorded on both sides by Tuthmosis IV (1425-1417 BC) to the left and Shabaka (716-702 BC) to the right. Just inside is a small **Transverse Hall** which was originally a hypostele hall before the Temple was extended outwards. Only 12 of the original papyrus bud columns and one of two 27m and 340 tonne rose-granite **Obelisk of Hatshepsut (7)**, which once stood at the entrance, now remain. In the 16th year of the reign of Hatshepsut (1503-1482 BC), the only woman to rule Egypt as pharaoh, the obelisks were transported from Aswan where a third unfinished one was discovered (**see The Unfinished Obelisk, page 804**). The tip of the second obelisk, which fell to the ground, is now lying near the Sacred Lake. The surviving erect obelisk is decorated along its whole length with the following inscription – "*O ye people who see this monument in years to come and speak of that which I have made, beware lest you say, 'I know not why it was done'. I did it because I wished to make a gift for my father Amun, and to gild them with electrum.*" Her long frustrated and usurped infant stepson Tuthmosis III (1504-1450 BC), who had plotted against her during her reign, took his revenge by hiding the obelisks behind walls almost to the ceiling which actually preserved them from later graffiti.

The E wall of the Transverse Hall is the **Fifth Pylon** which has been attributed to Hatshepsut's father Tuthmosis I. Beyond is another hall and then the badly damaged sandstone **Sixth Pylon**. The world's first imperialist Tuthmosis III inscribed it on both sides with details of his vanquished enemies and his victory at the Battle of Megiddo or Armageddon. Past the pylon is a **Vestibule** which is flanked by 2 courts and is dominated by 2 granite pillars with carvings showing Tuthmosis III being embraced by Amun, and the lotus and papyrus symbols of Upper and Lower Egypt. A seated statue of Amenhotep II (1450-1425 BC) is against the W wall and on the N side are 2 colossi of Amun and Amunet, although their faces resemble Tutankhamen (1361-1352 BC) who had had them built. The Vestibule leads to the **Granite Sanctuary** built by Alexander the Great's moronic half brother and successor Philip Arrhidaeus (323-317 BC). The ceiling is covered with golden stars on a dark base while the walls depict scenes of Philip with the god Amun. The exterior walls are decorated in a similar fashion.

N of the Sanctuary beyond the granite door is a series of small chambers built by Hatshepsut but later altered by Tuthmosis III. Some of the rooms were walled up by her son to conceal Hatshepsut's influence and consequently the bright colours have been very well preserved although Hatshepsut's face has been cut away whenever it appeared.

Further to the E is Tuthmosis III's **Festival Hall** which, with its central tentpole-style columns symbolising the tents used during his campaigns, is unlike any Egyptian building. It was built for his jubilee festivals which were intended to renew the pharaohs' temporal and spiritual authority. Access is via a small vestibule which leads to the central columned hall. The columns in the central aisle are taller than the side ones and would have supported a raised section of the roof thereby permitting sunlight to enter. The hall was later used as a Christian church and early paintings of the saints can still be seen on some of the columns.

Off to the SW is a small chamber where the original stele, or standing block, known as the **Karnak Table of Kings** minus Hatshepsut was found. The original is in the Louvre in Paris, the one on display being a replica. The series of interconnecting chambers beyond is dedicated to the Theban Triad and further N is an attractive chamber known as the **Botanical Vestibule**. Its 4 columns have papyrus capitals and are carved with the unfamiliar plants and shrubs discovered by Tuthmosis III during his Syrian campaign. Surrounding the small chamber on the far E wall is the small and badly decayed **Sanctuary of Amun**, built by Hatshepsut and originally decorated with 2 raised obelisks on either side of the entrance – only the bases now remain. The nearby **Chapel of Sokar**, which is dedicated to the Memphite god of darkness, is better preserved.

To the S of the main temple is the **Sacred Lake (8)** (200m x 117m), which has been restored to its original dimensions but has become stagnant since the inundation which used to feed the lake by underground channels from the Nile ceased after the construction of the Aswan Dam. Today the lake is totally uninteresting but it has the Sound & Light Show grandstand at the far end and a café on the N side. A Nilometer is attached to the lake and there is a statue of a giant scarab beetle which childless women walk around 5 times in order to ensure that they soon bear children.

While the main temple runs from W to E there is a secondary axis running S from the area between the third and fourth pylons. It begins with the **Cachette Court** which received its name after the discovery of 17,000 bronze statues and 780 stone ones which had been stored in the court during the Ptolemaic period and the best of which are now in the Cairo Museum. The reliefs on the outside wall of the Hypostele Hall, NW of the court, depict Ramses II in battle. On the E walls, close to the **Seventh Pylon**, is a replica of a stele now in the Egyptian Museum which shows the only reference to Israel during Pharaonic times. The Seventh Pylon was built by Tuthmosis III and shows him massacring his prisoners before Amun. In front of the façade are parts of 2 colossi of Tuthmosis.

Although restoration work continues on the nearby **Eighth Pylon** and others further along, it may be possible to have a quick look in return for a small tip to the guard. The Eighth Pylon was built by Tuthmosis II and Hatshepsut and contains extensively restored reliefs and cartouches. As in so many other places, Hatshepsut's name has been erased and replaced by Tuthmosis II's name while Akhenaten's name was systematically erased by Seti I. The S side of the pylon has 4 of the original 6 **Seated Colossi**, two of which are Tuthmosis II and one is Amenhotep I.

The **Ninth Pylon** and the **Tenth Pylon** were built by Horemheb (1348-1320 BC) using materials from the demolished Aten Temple. The Tenth Pylon has 2 colossi of Ramses II and his wife Nefertari usurping the original colossi of Amenhotep III. On the S side of the pylon there are 2 quartzite colossi of Amenhotep III. The pylon is part of the outer enclosure and marks the start of the sphinx-lined road to the southern enclosure. This includes the **Temple of Mut**, and the small temples of Ramses III and Amenhotep III, but virtually nothing is left except numerous diorite stone statues of the goddess Sekhmet.

Back in the main central enclosure in the far SW corner are 2 fairly well preserved temples, but they of limited interest. The **Temple of Khonsu** was built by Ramses III and Ramses IV and dedicated to the son of Amun and Mut. Many of the reliefs show Herihor, high-priest of Amun, who ruled Upper Egypt after Ramses XI

(1114-1085 BC) moved his capital to the Delta and delegated power to the high-priest. In the courtyard Herihor's name is inscribed on every pillar and all the scenes depict him venerating the gods and making offerings to them. The **Temple of Optet**, the hippopotamus-goddess, is of little interest and is normally closed to the public.

On the N side of the central enclosure, the **Temple of Ptah** leads on to Karnak's northern enclosure which includes the small temples of Montu and Amun, the Chapels of Amenortais and the Avenue of Sphinxes. However, after the splendours of the main temple complex what is left in this northern enclosure is hardly worth the effort and is only for the real enthusiasts.

The **Open Air Museum** is situated to the NW of the complex. It contains 1,300 blocks from the foundations of the Third Pylon and 319 stone blocks reassembled into Hatshepsut's **Sanctuary of the Barque**. Another barque sanctuary built by Amenhotep I is also on display, but the most beautiful monument is the lovely 12th Dynasty (1991-1786 BC) **White Chapel** built by Senusert I (1971-1928 BC) which is divided into 4 rows of 5 pillars and includes some wonderful convex bas-reliefs and an interesting geographic list of the Middle East. The rest of the chapel is dedicated to offerings to a phallic Amun-Min who is embraced by Senusert. Open daily 0700-1800 summer, 0700-1700 winter. Entrance E£5, tickets sold at museum entrance.

THEBAN DEATH RITES AND THE BOOKS OF THE DEAD

The order to fully appreciate the Theban Necropolis in the soft limestone hills opposite Luxor on the West Bank of the Nile it is important to understand a little about the celebration and rituals of death in Ancient Egypt.

The ***Books of The Dead*** feature 2 main gods, Re and Osiris, who play the most important role in the journey to the after-life. The oldest written references to this passage from one life to the next are found on the walls of pyramids constructed during the 5th-7th Dynasties (2494-2170 BC). Later the text and descriptions of the rituals which were involved were written on the actual coffins. Eventually lack of space on the sarcophagi led to only the ritual prayers and offerings being listed. When papyrus began to be used during the New Kingdom (1567-1085 BC) written texts were enclosed in the coffin and they became known as the *Books of the Dead*. Many copies of the writings, including the *Book of the Caverns* and the *Litany of Re*, were subsequently discovered.

The ancient Egyptians believed that at sunset the sun-god Re descended into the underworld and voyaged through the night before emerging at dawn to sail his barque (boat) across the heavens until sunset when the whole cycle began again. This journey was believed to be replicated by the dead pharaoh who descended through the underworld and whose heart, which was believed to be the centre of intelligence, would be weighed in the **Judgment of Osiris** to determine whether or not he would be permitted to continue his journey to the after-life.

The burial ceremony was elaborate with priests performing all the necessary rites, including sacrifices, in order to ensure that the deceased had a rapid passage to the next life. The tomb, together with everything the pharaoh might need including slaves, was then closed, plastered over and stamped with the royal seal. In order to protect the royal tombs from grave-robbers, they were fitted with false burial chambers and death-traps which unfortunately did not work.

The West Bank and Theban Necropolis

NB: TICKETS It is very important to note that tickets for all of the sites on the W bank of the Nile **must** be bought in advance at the main kiosk, where the river ferry from the *Etap Hotel* (E£2 single) arrives from Luxor, although students with identification can buy half-price tickets at the kiosk near the Colossi of Memnon. Both kiosks, which also sell non-refundable photograph permits at E£10 per tomb (flash photography is strictly forbidden because it damages the pigment), are open from 0600-1600. Sites are open 0700-1800 summer, 0700-1700 winter. The prices of the individual tickets changes from season to season but are required for the Valley of the Kings, Deir el-Bahri (Hatshepsut's Temple), Madinet Habu (Temple of Ramses III), Ramesseum, Asasif Tombs, Tombs of Nakht & Mena, Tombs of Rakhmire & Sennofer, Tombs of Ramoza, Userhat & Khaemhat, Deir el-Medina, Workers' Village, Valley of the Queens, Temple of Seti I and the Tomb of Oabhasa. Some tombs are individually priced at E£6, others E£6 for two or three tombs. A taxi can be hired here for the day for E£40.

The Valley of the Kings

One of many necropoli in the limestone hills on the W bank of the Nile, the area

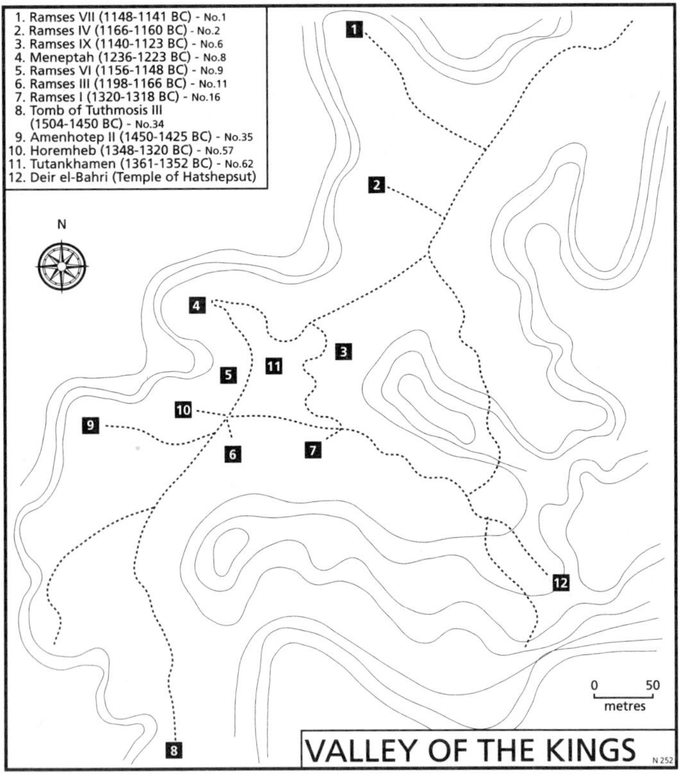

MUMMIFICATION

The ritual of Mummification reached its zenith during the New Kingdom at the same time as the Luxor and Karnak temple complexes were built. It was developed because the Ancient Egyptians believed that in order for a person to reach their heavenly aspect or **Ak** in the after-life, it was essential that both their name and body survive thereby sustaining their cosmic double or **Ka** which was transported from one life to the next. In order to achieve this, the mummification ritual developed into an extremely complex means of preserving bodies. The dead were placed in tombs together with any food and utensils thought necessary to accompany the pharaoh's Ka for the journey to the underworld. Although we know the most commonly used New Kingdom mummification methods, others are still being revealed. For example a recently opened princess' tomb in Giza revealed that the body had been hollowed out and lined with very fine plaster. However the most common mummification method found in and around the Valley of the Kings is described below.

The brain was removed through the nose and was discarded because the heart was thought to be the centre of intelligence. The entrails and organs were then extracted and stored in jars while the corpse was soaked in natrun salts for 40 days until it was dehydrated, when the embalming process began. In an attempt to recreate its original appearance the body was packed and then painted red for men and yellow for women, artificial eyes were inserted and the face was then made up before the body was wrapped in gum-coated linen bandages and placed in its coffin.

first became a burial site during the New Kingdom rule of Tuthmosis I (1525-1512 BC) in the hope that the tombs would be safe from looters. The kings' tombs are not actually confined to the single valley and it is believed that there may be others still waiting to be discovered. Those already discovered are numbered in the chronological order of their discovery rather than by location. Although some are simple and comparatively crude the best are incredibly well preserved, stunningly decorated and illustrate their intricate craftsmanship.

The tombs generally follow 2 designs. The early 18th Dynasty (1567-1320 BC) tombs are a series of descending galleries followed by a well or rock pit which was intended to both collect any rain water and deter thieves. On the other side of the pit there were sealed offering chambers and then the rectangular burial chamber built at right angles to the descending galleries. The later tombs, from the late 18th to the 20th Dynasties (1567-1085 BC), were built in the same way but the galleries and burial chambers were on the same axis being cut horizontally but deeper straight into the rock face.

VISITING THE TOMBS Although so far a total of 62 tombs have been opened many, including some of the most remarkable such as that of Seti I (1318-1304 BC) (No 17), closed to the public because they suffered so badly from mass tourism that they have had to be resealed for restoration work. The combination of long queues and the hot and stuffy atmosphere in some of the most popular tombs make it impractical to try and visit all of the tombs on one visit. In order to avoid the heat and the rush it is best to go as early as possible, particularly during the summer, take a bottle of water and a torch both because there are occasional power cuts and the lighting in some of the tombs is inadequate. There are some poor quality rip-off tours offered by some companies and individuals in Luxor and, unless already part of a tour group, it is probably best to rely on the recommendation of other visitors. The entry fee for the Valley of the Kings is E£10 for three tombs plus E£5 for cameras for each tomb.

Ramses VII (1148-1141 BC) (No 1) (1) This later style, single horizontal plane, and poorly preserved tomb lies in a small valley before the entrance gate and is seldom visited by tourists. Above the outer door Ramses VII's names are displayed with a scabbard and disc. The walls are lined with scenes from the *Book of Gates*. The most interesting area is the Burial Chamber with its granite sarcophagus still in place. The picture on the ceiling portrays the constellations and calendar of feasts while the sky goddess Nut spans the area. The inner chamber contains scenes of Ramses making offerings to the gods.

Ramses IV (1166-1160 BC) (No 2) (2) Nearer but still outside the main gate, is the looted tomb but not the body of Ramses IV, although his coffin was reburied in Amenhotep II's tomb. Do not be discouraged by the Coptic and Greek graffiti because the colours of the inner tomb are truly fantastic. The first 2 corridors contain poorly preserved reliefs of the *Litany of Re*, while the Hall and Burial Chamber are decorated with parts of the *Books of the Dead* and Nut spans the ceiling. The sarcophagus lid shows Ramses IV protected by Isis and Nephthys and the pink granite coffin is inscribed with magical texts. This is the only tomb for which the original plans, now in the Turin Museum, still survive.

Ramses IX (1140-1123 BC) (No 6) (3) Situated immediately to the left of the barrier, it is of the typical later long deep style which became the established style by the end of the New Kingdom. The reliefs on the corridor walls depict Ramses before the gods and this is followed by 3 chambers. The 4 pillared Offerings Chamber leads to the richly decorated Burial Room but the sarcophagus is missing. The ceiling depicts a scene from the *Book of the Night* with jackals, watched by Nut, drawing the barque through the skies to the after-life.

Meneptah (1236-1223 BC) (No 8) (4) Set back against the cliff face on the other side of the road is a long steep 80m tomb with a wonderfully preserved false Burial Chamber. The ceilings of the 5 corridors are decorated with flying vultures and other forbidding reliefs. Looters abandoned the sarcophagus lid, which portrays scenes taken from the *Book of Gates* and the *Book of Am-Duat* similar to those in the hallway, in the antechamber. Steps lead down to the Burial Chamber where the pink granite inner sarcophagus lies, decorated with intricate designs from the *Book of Gates*.

Ramses VI (1156-1148 BC) (No 9) (5) The discovery of this tomb, which was usurped and enlarged from his predecessor Ramses V (1160-1156 BC) and is one of the longest in the valley, shed light on some aspects of pharaonic beliefs which were not previously understood. The corridor displays reliefs from unknown and long since lost *Books*. Egyptologists were fascinated at their revelation of Pharaonic concepts, more usually associated with India, of reincarnation birth into a new life. One does not, however, have to be an expert to appreciate the graphic designs and the colours beyond the graffiti drawings in the first 2 corridors.

The themes on the corridor ceilings are predominantly astronomical while the walls are largely devoted to the *Book of Gates* and the *Book of Caverns*. In the Offerings Hall there is a relief of Ramses making libations before Osiris. The pillars are devoted to the Pharaoh making offerings to other gods including Amun. Descending deeper within the tomb the passage leading to the Burial Chamber is guarded by serpents of Nekhbet,

Neith, Meretseger and Selket. Further on illustrations from the *Books of the Dead* predominate. Just before the entrance to the Burial Chamber, cryptographic texts adorn the ceiling. The Burial Chamber is supported by 4 pillars but 2 are damaged. Astronomical scenes from the *Book of Day* and the *Book of Night* cover the ceiling and the sky goddess Nut observes from above. The sarcophagus, shattered by grave robbers centuries ago, lies broken in the centre of the room

Ramses III (1198-1166 BC) (No 11) (6) This particularly beautiful tomb is unusual because, unlike those of most Pharaohs, it illustrates scenes from everyday life as well as a wonderful scene of 2 harpists from which the tomb's other name is derived. It was originally intended for Sethnakht (1200-1185 BC), but the angle of digging was such that it coincided with another tomb and it was abandoned. Later Ramses III restarted the work by digging into the rock face from a different angle. The lintel with a disc and Re shown with a ram's head accompanied by Isis and Nephthys can be seen at the entrance. Ten side chambers – 5 to the left and 5 to the right – which were for storing objects that the Pharaoh would require after his death, lead off from the entrance corridor. One section of the tomb is closed because of a collapsed ceiling.

Ramses I (1320-1318 BC) (No 16) (7) Despite being the founder of the 19th Dynasty, his short reign meant that this Ramses did not merit a larger tomb but it still has beautifully ornate and sophisticated designs which are preserved on the blue-grey foundation. The granite sarcophagus is decorated with yellow while the wall relief depicts scenes of the Pharaoh with local deities and divisions from the *Book of Gates*.

Tomb of Tuthmosis III (1504-1450 BC) (No 34) (8) Hidden away high up a side valley furthest from the main gate this is one of the oldest tombs. Its simple design is balanced by the interesting layout because, after the first steep corridor, it veers sharply to the left at the antechamber. The walls are lined with lists of 741 deities who are portrayed as tiny stick figures. The walls of the tomb chamber, entered by a set of unusually oval shaped steps, are dominated by sections of the *Book of Am-Duat* with an abridged version also inscribed on 2 pillars. The Pharaoh is depicted on one of the pillars with his mother standing behind him in his boat. A beautiful carving of Nut, effectively embracing the mummified Tuthmosis with her outstretched arms, lines the inside of the red granite sarcophagus.

Amenhotep II (1450-1425 BC) (No 35) (9) Over 90 steps lead down to the Burial Chamber which is in one of the deepest tombs in the valley. Here for once the tactics of building false chambers and sunken pits actually worked and the mummified body was found in the sarcophagus, together with another 9 royal mummies which had been removed from their original tombs for safety's sake, when the tomb was opened in 1898. Amenhotep's mummy was originally kept in the tomb but after a nearby theft it was removed to the Egyptian Museum in Cairo. Steep steps and a descending corridor lead into a pillared chamber where the tomb's axis shifts 90° to the left, after which the walls and ceiling are decorated. Further steps and a short passage lead to the enormous Burial Chamber. The delicate blue-grey of the roof is covered with clustered stars and adorned with the *Book of Am-Duat* as well as images of the Pharaoh before the gods. The sarcophagus is still in place in the centre of the pillared chamber.

Horemheb (1348-1320 BC) (No 57) (10) After the long, steep and undecorated descent is the Well Room where the reliefs begin. Colourful scenes portray General Horemheb, who despite lacking royal blood was the effective regent during Tutankhamen's short rule and leader of the Theban counter-revolution against Akhenaten's mono-theistic religion, being introduced to Isis, Osiris, Horus, Hathor and Anubis. The scenes are repeated in the antechamber in front of the Burial Room in which the *Books of the Dead* are recounted anti-clockwise around the chamber which is dominated by the huge red granite sarcophagus.

Tutankhamen (1361-1352 BC) (No 62) (11) The tomb owes its worldwide fame not to its size or decoration, which is small and ordinary, but to the multitude of fabulous treasures that were revealed when it was opened in Nov 1922. The scale of the discovery was so vast that it took 10 years to fully remove, catalogue and photograph all of the 1,700 pieces.

The short entrance corridor leads to 4 chambers but only the Burial Chamber, which is the second on the right, is decorated. Around the room from left to right murals display Tutankhamen's coffin being moved to the shrine by mourners and officials after which his successor Ay (1352-1348 BC) performs the ceremony of the Opening of the Mouth and makes sacrifices to sky-goddess Nut. Tutankhamen is then embraced by Osiris and is followed by his black-wigged Ka or spirit. A scene from the *Book of Am-Duat* on the left hand wall depicts the Pharaoh's solar boat and sun-worshipping baboons. The quartzite sarcophagus is still in place, with its granite lid to one side, and inside is the outermost of 3 coffins.

Deir el-Bahri

Meaning 'northern monastery' in Arabic, it derives its name from the fact that during the 7th century the Copts used the site as a monastery. It is now used as the name for both the temple and area around the magnificent **Temple of Hatshepsut (12)**, (entry E£6). The Valley of the Kings is hidden, away from Luxor on the W side of the imposing limestone hills with virtually nothing above ground. By contrast crossing back E towards river over the hills, which is either a 30 min hike worth it for the view from the top or 10 min by road, one arrives at a natural amphitheatre with the beautiful temple, surrounded on 3 sides by the hills, imperiously looking down on Luxor across the Nile.

Queen Hatshepsut was not only the only female Pharaoh to reign over ancient Egypt (1503-1482 BC) but also one of its most fascinating personalities. She was Tuthmosis I's (1525-1512 BC) daughter and was married to his successor Tuthmosis II (1512-1504 BC) but was widowed before she could bear a son. Rather than give up power to the son of one of her husband's minor wives she assumed the throne first as regent for the infant Tuthmosis III but then as queen. Tuthmosis III, who later hugely expanded the Egyptian empire and was the first imperialist, was only able to

THE CURSE OF TUTANKHAMEN

Tutankhamen tomb's fame and mystery was enhanced by the fate of those who were directly connected with its discovery. The expedition's sponsor Lord Carnarvon, who had first opened the tomb with his chief archaeologist Howard Carter, died shortly afterwards in April 1923 from an infected mosquito bite. A subsequent succession of bizarre deaths added weight to novelist Marie Corelli's totally unproven and unhistoric claim that "dire punishment follows any intruder into the tomb". Such alleged curses have, however, done nothing to deter the tens of thousands of visitors who still visit the site despite the fact that most of the treasures are now in the Egyptian Museum!

assume office when Hatshepsut died 21 yrs later in 1482 BC. He naturally resented her usurping his position and removed all traces of her reign including her cartouches. Consequently the truth about her reign and the temples she built both here and at Karnak was only fully appreciated by archaeologists relatively recently. As a woman she legitimized her rule by being depicted with the short kilt and the false beard worn by the male pharaohs.

Hatshepsut's imposing temple was designed and built in the Theban hills over an 8 year period between the 8th-16th year of her reign, by **Senenmut** who was her architect, steward, favourite courtier and possibly the father of her daughter Neferure. The temple's 3 rising terraces, the lower 2 terraces lined with fountains and myrrh trees, were originally linked to the Nile by an avenue of sphinxes which was aligned exactly to Karnak. A pair of lions stood at the top and another at the bottom of the ramp which leads from the ground level 1st terrace over the 1st colonnade to the large 2nd terrace.

The scenes on the restored left hand S side of the 1st colonnade columns depict the transportation of the 2 obelisks from Aswan to Karnak temple. Behind its columns on the right hand N side is a relief defaced by Tuthmosis III in which Amun can be seen receiving an offering of 4 calves from Hatshepsut whose face has been erased. The original stairs from the second terrace to the second colonnade have now been replaced by a ramp. Hatshepsut's famous voyage to **Punt**, which was known as "God's Land" by the ancient Egyptians, and various texts to Amun are depicted on the left hand or S side of the 2nd colonnade. Voyages to Punt, now believed to be modern-day Somalia, had been undertaken since the Old Kingdom (2686-2181 BC) in order to find the incense and myrrh which was required for temple rituals.

Further to the left is the large **Chapel of Hathor** where the goddess is depicted both as a cow and as a human with cow's ears suckling Hatshepsut. This area was badly damaged because Tuthmosis removed most but not all traces of Hatshepsut and Akhenaten later erased Amun. The reliefs on the colonnade to the right hand or N side of the ramp portray Hatshepsut's apparent divine conception and birth. She claimed that her father was the supreme god Amun who visited her mother Ahmose disguised as Tuthmosis I just as Amenhotep III (1417-1379 BC) made similar claims later on (see **Luxor Temple, page 775**). Further to the right is the fluted colonnade and the colourfully decorated shrine of Anubis, who is portrayed in the customary way as a man with a jackal mask, but the images of Hatshepsut are once again defaced.

The ramp leading to the smaller and recently restored upper terrace is decorated with emblems of Upper and Lower Egypt with vultures' heads guarding the entrance. There are suggestions that this was originally a Hypostele Hall and not a terrace. The columns were originally round but were squared off by Tuthmosis III in an attempt to replace her name with his own and that of his father Tuthmosis II. Beyond the Osiride portico to the left is the **Sanctuary of Hatshepsut** with its enormous altar and to the right is the **Sanctuary of the Sun**. In the middle at the back of the whole temple is the **Sanctuary of Amun** which is dug into the cliff-face and is therefore connected to the Valley of the Kings which lies on the other side of the hill. Hatshepsut's burial chamber lies underneath but it is unclear whether she was actually ever buried there.

Tombs of the Nobles

While the pharaoh's tombs were hidden away in the Valley of the Kings and were dug deep into the valley rock those of the most important nobles were ostentatiously built at surface level overlooking the temples of Luxor and Karnak across the river. Their shrines were highly decorated but the poor quality limestone made carved reliefs impossible so the façades were painted on plaster. Freed from the restricted subject matter of the royal tombs the artists and craftsmen dedicated less space to rituals from the *Books* and more to representations of everyday life and their impressions of the after-life. Because, unlike the royal tombs, they were exposed to the elements many of the nobles' shrines have deteriorated badly over time. Although some were subsequently used as store rooms and even accommodation others are still in relatively good condition and give a clear impression of how they must originally have looked.

Tomb of Nakht (No 52) Nakht was Tuthmosis IV 's astronomer, vineyard keeper and chief of his granaries. He and his wife Tawi were buried is this small shrine with its well preserved and colourful transverse room which depicts the harvest in intricate detail. On its W wall is the stele illustrating what is known of Nakht's life together with the goddess of the W. On the left of the far wall is a depiction of a funeral banquet is which Nakht, his top half having been badly defaced, is shown seated beside his wife with a cat eating a fish at his feet while being entertained by harpists and dancing girls. Opposite the stele on the E wall, peasants are shown treading grapes while empty wine jars await filling and the ceiling is brightly decorated with designs representing woven mats. In the inner chamber there is a small niche with a replica of a statue of Nakht bearing a stele with a hymn to Re. Unfortunately the original was lost in 1917 when the SS Arabia, which was transporting it to the USA, was torpedoed by the Germans in the Atlantic. There is a deep shaft leading to the inaccessible burial chamber.

Tomb of Ramoza (No 55) Ramoza was Vizier and Governor of Thebes at the beginning of the Akhenaten's heretical rule in 1379 BC and the tomb illustrates the transition in style between the worship of Amun and Aten (see **Tell el-Amarna, page** 756). The impressive and excellent quality workmanship of the shrine is probably because it was built by Ramoza's brother Amenhotep who was the chief of works at the family's home-town of Memphis. This is one of the few tombs where the forecourt yard is still preserved and the central entrance leads into a broad hall with 64 columns. On the wall to the right are depictions of Ramoza with his wife and opposite on the back wall Akhenaten and Nefertiti stand at their palace windows giving a golden chain to Ramoza. On the left hand wall are scenes of Ramoza and his wife worshipping Osiris. Beyond is an undecorated inner hall with 8 columns and the shrine at the far end. Within each hall are the gated entrances to dark and dangerous tunnels which end with a 15m drop to the burial chamber.

Tomb of Userhat (No 56) Userhat who, in the reign of Amenhotep II (1450-1425 BC), was a royal tutor and scribe was buried in a small but pinkishly decorated tomb which was partially damaged by early Christian hermits. Note the interesting representation of rural life on the left on the way into the hall, the façade of the snake-headed harvest goddess Renehat on the right of the back wall, and a realistic hunting scene on the left of the inner hall.

Tomb of Mena (No 69) This tomb has been undergoing restoration and, although Mena's eyes have been gouged out by rivals, the paintings are in good condition. He was an 18th Dynasty scribe or inspector of the estates in both Upper and Lower Egypt. On the left in the first hall is a scene of field workers while the other walls show Mena and his wife preparing and laying offerings before Osiris. The ceilings are brightly coloured and represent woven cloth.

Tomb of Sennofer (No 96) At the time of Amenhotep II (1450-1425 BC) amongst other positions Sennofer was Mayor of Thebes, overseer of the granaries and gardens, and chief vintner. The ceiling is covered in vines and the tomb is known locally as the "Tomb of Vines". The antechamber is rough and irregular in shape. Within the 4 pillared hall Sennofer is shown making offerings to the deities and on his journey into the after-life he is accompanied by his wife. A double figure of the jackal-headed Anubis looks down on the whole chamber from above the entrance.

Tomb of Rekhmire (No 100) This crucifix-shaped tomb should not be missed because its highly decorative paintings and inscriptions reveal some of the secrets of Egypt's judicial, taxation and foreign policy. Rekhmire, who came from a long line of viziers and governors, was the vizier at the time of Tuthmosis III's death in 1450 BC when he then served his successor Amenhotep II. Walking left or clockwise around the whole tomb from the entrance wall of the transverse hall one sees – Egyptian taxes, Rekhmire being installed as vizier, foreign tributes being received from Punt, Crete, Nubia, Syria and Kush, then along the main corridor the inspection of the various workshops, the voyage to Abydos, the various gods of the dead, and the end niche which would have contained a statue of Rekhmire. On the way out along the other corridor wall are pictures of the after-world and then, back in the transverse hall, illustrations of hunting and fowling, wine-making, Rakhmire's wives and ancestors, and finally more taxes being collected.

Valley of the Queens

Like the Valley of the Kings, the Valley of the Queens, which is about 3 km S from the tombs of the nobles, can be reached via another road which cuts NW through the main NE-SW escarpment. It was once known as the 'Place of Beauty' and was used as a burial site for officials long before the queens and their offspring, who had previously been buried with their husbands, began to be buried there in the 19th Dynasty (1320-1200 BC). It contains more than 80 tombs but many are still unidentified. The tombs are generally quite simple with a long corridor, several antechambers branching off and the burial chamber at the end. The most famous tomb is that of Ramses II's wife Nefertari but it is currently indefinitely closed to the public.

Prince Khaemweset (No 44) Although the tomb is dedicated to one of Ramses III's (1198-1166 BC) young sons who died of smallpox, it is dominated by the pharaoh himself. The reliefs depict the young boy being led to the underworld by his father who is offering sacrifices and helping his son through the underworld and the judgment of Osiris to the Fields of Yaru.

Queen Titi (No 52) was the daughter, wife and mother of a succession of the 20th Dynasty (1200-1085 BC) pharaohs called Ramses but it is uncertain which one she was married to. Although the tomb is open to the public the reliefs are faded and damaged. A corridor leads to a square shrine which branches into 3 antechambers with the badly preserved burial chamber on the left being dedicated to the 4 sons of Horus and Osiris. The central chamber features the Queen before the gods and the shrine is dominated by animal deities with pictures of jackals, baboons and guardian lions. The right hand chamber is the best preserved and depicts the tree goddess and Hathor as a the cow goddess rejuvenating the Queen with Nile water.

Other temples and sites

The Ramesseum While most tourists confine themselves to the two valleys and Hatshepsut's temple there are a number of other interesting W bank ruins closer to the river. Of these amongst the most impressive was the Ramesseum, a 19th century name for what was effectively a state cult-temple, on the opposite side of the road near the tombs of the nobles. Today only scattered remains and faded reliefs suggest the great temple which once stood there and reportedly rivalled the splendours of the temples at Abu Simbel.

The vain-glorious Ramses II (1304-1237 BC) built this mortuary temple, on the consecrated site of Seti I's (1318-1304 BC) much smaller but collapsing temple, in order to impress his subjects but he failed to take account of the annual flooding of the Nile. The result was that this enormous tribute to Amun and himself was less eternal than he expected!

The first 2 pylons collapsed and only a single colonnade remains of what would have been the First Courtyard. On its S side is a palace where Ramses stayed when he attended religious festivals on the W bank. In front of the ruins of the Second Pylon is the base of the enormous colossus of Ramses which was originally over 17m high but it is now much eroded and various parts of his anatomy are scattered throughout the world's museums. The forefinger alone measures more than 1m in length. The upper part of the body crashed into the second court where the head and torso remain. Three smaller colossi stood next to the 3 stairways leading to the Hypostele Hall but only one fragmented one now remains.

Although it is now roofless, 29 of the original 48 columns still stand in the Hypostele Hall. The centre of the roof would have been higher than the sides in order to allow shafts of sunlight to enter the hall. To the left of the entrance is the famous relief of the Egyptian victory over the Hittite city of Dapur in the battle of Kadesh. Around the base of the W walls some of Ramses' many sons are depicted. At the far end of the hall a central door leads into the Astronomical Room renowned for its ceiling which is illustrated with the oldest known 12 month calendar. Because the temple was dedicated to Amun it is thought to represent a solar year. Two other vestibules, a library and a linen room, lead to the ruined sanctuary which is the temple's highest point.

The Mortuary Temple of Ramses III, (1198-1166 BC), which lies W of the Colossi of Memnon and S of the Valley of the Queens at a place known in Arabic as **Madinet Habu**, was modelled on that built by his forefather Ramses II (1304-1327) near by. It is second only to Karnak in terms of its size and complexity and within the enormous enclosing walls are a palace, a Nilometer and several smaller shrines with some pre-dating the temple itself.

When Thebes was threatened, such as during the 20th Dynasty's Libyan invasions, the enclosing walls sheltered the entire population. Although Ramses III named his temple the 'House of a Million Years', the smaller shrine that already occupied the site next to the S enclosure walls was in use long after the main temple shrine had fallen into disuse.

The small temple, which was constructed by Hatshepsut but later altered by Tuthmosis III who erased her cartouche, was built on a platform from which there are good views in all directions. Until the 18th century a grove of acacia trees led to the Colossi of Memnon. The site, known as Jeser Ast or 'Sacred Place', was venerated because it was thought that the waters of chaos had divided and the primeval mound erupted here. During Akhenaten's rule, Amun's images were destroyed but they were later replaced by Horemheb and Seti I.

The whole temple complex is entered via the 3 storey SE gatehouse which is built like a fortified Syrian pavilion and

The Singing Colossus Of Memnon

The northern gigantic sandstone colossus was broken off at the waist by the earthquake in 27 BC after which it was reputed to sing at dawn. This phenomenon, which was most likely caused by the wind or the expansion of the broken stone in the morning sunlight, attracted many visitors including the Roman emperors Hadrian in 130 AD and Septimus Severus (193-211 AD). The latter decided it should be repaired, after which time it never sang again.

was originally 22m high. Arriving through it into the large forecourt one sees the small temple to the right, the huge main temple directly ahead, and the small Chapels of the Votressess, dating from the 25th Dynasty (747-656 BC) kings of Kush, just to the left.

The remarkable homogeneity of the main temple's structure reflects the fact that it was designed and built by Ramses III alone rather than being expanded and altered by successive pharaohs. The immense and wonderfully preserved First Pylon, which is 65m long by 27m high, was originally dedicated to Amun but was also used by Ramses II as a memorial to his Libyan and Asiatic campaigns. It would originally have been larger than the one at Luxor, standing 27m high and 65m long, but now the N corner and cornice are missing. The images on the left of the Pylon show Ramses slaying Nubian prisoners watched by Amun and Ptah while Syrians are slain on the right hand side. Although the illustrations are based on genuine wars Ramses III never actually fought either nation!

On the left of the entrance way through the first pylon, before arriving in the large 48m x 34m first court, Ramses III is shown worshipping the deities Ptah, Osiris and Sokar. The W of the great court is flanked by 8 columns and the E by 7 Osiride pillars. On the Second Pylon the Pharaoh is depicted marching rows of prisoners, the third row being Philistines (or Palestinians) wearing feathered head-dresses, towards Amun and Mut. The second court is also made up of a combination of Osiride pillars and columns. Eight pillars line the back and front of the hall while the sides are flanked by 6 columns. One scene depicts the Feast of Sokar while the lower register of the back wall is dedicated to the Ramses III's sons and daughters. At the far right end of the hall is a small entrance which has 2 interesting illustrations. One shows the Pharaoh before Seth, but this was later defaced to change him into Horus, while above the door Ramses is shown kneeling on the symbol of the united Upper and Lower Egypt.

The W door connects to the ruins of the severely damaged Hypostele Hall. Above the door the Pharaoh can again be seen kneeling over the symbol of Upper and Lower Egypt and at the base of the entry wall are 13 princesses and 10 princes. The central aisle of the hall would have been raised, in the same way as at Karnak, to allow Re's sunlight to enter.

A multitude of side rooms would originally have led off from the hypostele hall but little now remains because of the severe damage caused by the major earthquake in 27 BC. The best preserved room is the Treasury to the N where the walls are adorned with scenes of the Pharaoh making offerings of gold to Amun. Another small room shows the Pharaoh wearing the Osiride symbols of the Atef feathered crown, a crook and flail.

The outer walls are better preserved and some of the reliefs are clearly visible. At the far end of the S wall is a calendar of religious feasts which is believed to be the longest such inscription. Further along is a portrayal of all the benefits with which Ramses III was blessed by Amun. The rear W wall is dedicated to the Pharaoh's victories in battle. In the NE corner of the enclosure near the small temple is a small sacred lake where childless women came to bathe at night and pray to Isis that they might conceive. Close by stand the remains of the Nilometer that was originally fed by a canal which branched off from the Nile.

Colossi of Memnon (See box) These 2 gigantic sandstone colossi, which are located on the main road 1.65 km from the river and next to the student ticket kiosk, represent Amenhotep III (1417-1379 BC). They once stood in front of his mortuary temple which collapsed and was plundered for stone long ago. Although the faces and crowns have been eroded the 2 colossi make a strange spectacle seated in splendour in the midst of the desert and are well worth a visit.

THE NILE VALLEY LUXOR TO ASWAN

CONTENTS

MAPS

Although the majority of tourists travel non-stop from Luxor to Aswan there are a number of interesting and beautiful temples en route of which Edfu and Kom Ombo are well worth visiting. What is so extraordinary about the generally unspectacular road journey is the fact that the strip of cultivated land between the Nile and the desert is so narrow. On one side is lush vegetation and the river and on the other the harsh and arid desert.

The main road follows the Nile along its E bank from Luxor, past Edfu (115 kms) which is on the W bank about half way to Aswan, before continuing via Kom Ombo (176 kms) to Aswan (216 kms). There is an alternative less crowded but less scenic route along the W bank from the Valley of the Kings to Esna (55 kms) and Edfu before having to cross the river to continue the journey along the E bank to Aswan.

Increasing numbers of visitors are now making this journey by river in one of the many floating hotels which moor at the sites along the way. Egyptian village life, which is often obscured from the road and cannot be appreciated from the window of a speeding car, can be seen on this relaxing journey which is thoroughly recommended.

Esna

This small market town lies about 55 km S of Luxor on the W bank of the Nile which, besides its **Temple of Khnum**, is mainly known for the sandstone dam across the river. This was built in 1906 at about the same time as the first Aswan dam and today cruise ships and barges usually have to queue for a number of hours for their turn to pass through its locks. The town and the temple are certainly worth a couple of hour's visit.

ACCESS Service taxis and buses stop about 10 min walk from the temple which is in the centre of town. Walk to the river and then S along the Corniche to the ticket kiosk. The railway station is in the centre of town and is a short *calèche* ride to the temple.

Things to see

The **Temple of Khnum**, open daily 0700-1800, entrance E£4, lies partially exposed in a deep depression in the centre of town. The excavation began in the 1860s but did not continue because the area above was covered in houses. Over the centuries since its construction the annual Nile flood has deposited 10m of silt over the temple site so that all that is visible today is the **Hypostele Hall**. The part of the temple that can be seen today is Ptolemaic/Roman and was built on the foundations of a much older shrine which was also dedicated to the ram-headed deity Khnum. He was believed to have created man by moulding him from Nile clay on a potter's wheel. Later, when Amun became the principal deity, Khnum's image changed and, in conjunction with Hapy, he came to be regarded as the guardian of the source of the Nile.

The hypostele hall's **Outer Façade** is decorated from left to right with the cartouches of 3 Roman emperors Claudius (41-54 AD), Titus (79-81 AD) and Vespasion (69-79 AD). Above the

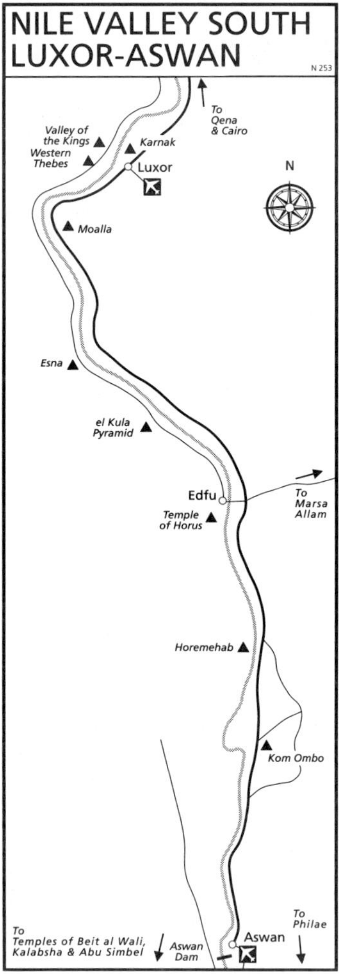

entrance, on the lintel, is the winged sun disc. Inside the tall hall 18 columns support the **Astronomical Ceiling** which, although once a beautiful and complex spectacle, is barely visible today because it was blackened by the wood fires of a Coptic village which was once housed within the temple. In places various deities and animals, including winged dogs, two-headed snakes and the pregnant hippo-goddess Tweri, can be seen intermingled with signs of the zodiac. The hall's columns are decorated with crocodiles and rams and are inscribed with texts detailing the temple's various festivals. On the rear wall the Roman emperors Septimus Severus, Caracella and Geta make offerings to Khnum. Around the N outer walls at the back of the temple are texts of Marcus Aurelius (161-180 AD) while Titus, Domitian and Trajan slay their Egyptian enemies on the E & W outer walls.

Local information

● Accommodation

The town's only hotel is the **F** ***Haramin*** about 1 km S of the ticket kiosk along the Corniche but it is best avoided unless stuck in town at night.

● Places to eat

There are a few cafés and stalls in the central square but there are no restaurants.

● Banks

One bank open Sat-Thur 0830-1400 & Sun 1800-2100 & Wed 1700-2000. 1000-1330 during Ramadan.

● Telephone

Local code: 097.

● Transport

Train To Luxor and Aswan stop at Esna but only very slow and crowded 2nd and 3rd class service.

Road: **Bus** N to Luxor or S to Edfu, Kom Ombo and Aswan are frequent but crowded in the morning. **Service taxis**: to Luxor (1 hr), Edfu (1 hr) and Aswan (2-3 hr) are quicker but marginally more expensive than the buses.

Edfu

Edfu, which is 60 km S along the W bank and almost equidistant between Luxor (115 km) and Aswan (106 km), is the site of the huge, well preserved Ptolemaic cult **Temple of Horus** which, as the most complete in the whole country, is certainly worth a visit.

ACCESS The temple is W or inland from the river along Sharia al-Maglis and can be reached by *calèche*, many of which are

Horus – The First Living God-King

Horus who was originally the Egyptian sky-god and falcon-god was later identified as the son of Osiris and his sister Isis. He subsequently avenged his father's murder by his uncle Seth in an epic fight at Edfu in which Horus lost an eye and Seth his testicles. It was not until Isis intervened that Horus prevailed as good triumphed over evil. Osiris pronounced his judgment by banishing Seth to the underworld and enthroning Horus as the first living god-king. Each Pharaoh claimed to be an incarnation of Horus and the annual Festival of the Coronation, at Edfu's now destroyed Temple of the Falcon in front of the main temple's grand pylon, followed by a crowning ceremony in the temple's main forecourt, symbolized the renewal of royal power.

drawn by emaciated and badly treated horses, or taxis which await the arrival of the tourist cruise ships. Taxis and pick-ups to the temple can be caught from the train station, which is just across the Nile bridge, while the service taxi terminal at the town-side W end of the bridge is a 20 min walk or short ride to the temple. Inter-city buses drop their passengers on Sharia Tahrir or the parallel Sharia Gumhorriya about half way between the bridge and the temple.

Things to see

Edfu Temple, open daily 0700-1800, entry E£10 and E£10 for cameras, is the name given to the enormous **Temple of Horus** which was the focus of the ancient city of Djeba. It was begun in Aug 237 BC by Ptolemy III and took 25 years to complete, with the decoration taking another 5 years. Because of a revolt in Upper Egypt it was not until Feb 176 BC that the opening ceremony took place under Ptolemy VII, but there were further additions until Ptolemy XIII. Like Esna's **Temple of Khnum**, it was completely buried except for its huge pylons under silt and sand and its top was covered with houses until the 1860s but, unlike Esna, the whole site has been excavated. It had been severely damaged by the town's inhabitants and it was not until 1903 that the excavation work was finally completed.

The whole complex is entered from the ticket office in the NW corner at the rear of the main N-S axis temple, which one walks along to reach the entrance at its S end. Just to the SW is the small E-W axis birth house called the **Mammisi of Horus**, which was built by Ptolemy VII and VIII. Each year there is a performance of the miracle play which represents Horus' birth at the same time as the birth of the divine heir to the throne of Egypt. At the SW corner of the birth house there are reliefs of Isis suckling Horus and an erect Amun.

The main **Temple of Horus** is entered through the huge **Grand Pylon**, which was originally protected by an enormous hawk which has been moved to the N end of the **Court of Offerings** guarding the entrance to the **Hypostele Hall**. On the outer wall of the pylon Ptolemy XIII (88-51 BC), who was also known as Neos Dionysus and had usurped the pylon from its original builder Ptolemy IX (170-116 BC), is shown killing his enemies before Horus. On its inner wall Horus travels to Edfu on his barque and Ptolemy makes offerings to Horus and Hathor.

The giant **Court of Offerings** is lined with 32 columns behind which on the W side Ptolemy IX makes offerings to Horus, Hathor and Ihy and on the right Ptolemy X appears before the same three. At the N end of the court is the **Hypostele Hall**, built by Ptolemy VII (180-145 BC), with its 18 once brightly painted columns supporting the roof, each with a different capital. At the entrance to the Hypostele Hall is the small Chamber of Consecrations changing room to the left and a small Library, where the names of the guests for the day's festival would be kept, to the right.

Leading N from the hall is a smaller 12 slender columned hypostele hall, known as the **Festival Hall**, the oldest part of the building dating back to Ptolemy III (246-222 BC) and completed by his son, where offerings entered the temple and were prepared. These were then carried through into the **Hall of Offerings**, or first vestibule, where the daily offerings would have been made at the many altars and tables bearing incense, juices, fruit and meat. From here there are steps to the E which were used for the procession up to the roof where a **Chapel of the Disc** once stood. The stairs are illustrated with pictures of the priests carrying the statues of the gods to the roof to be revitalised before returning down a separate staircase to arrive back on the W side of the Hall of Offerings. Today all the roof offers is an excellent view of the surrounding area.

The Offerings Hall leads to the inner vestibule called the **Sanctuary of Horus**, where engravings show Ptolemy IV (222-205 BC) making offerings to the deities while others show Horus and Hathor in their sacred vessels. The sanctuary is virtually a separate temple within the main temple and is surrounded by a series of 10 minor chambers of which the most attractive is the **New Year Shrine** which contains a relief of Nut spanning the roof. These chambers, many of which originally served as vestries and store rooms, are better examined with a torch. On the dimly lit NE wall of the outer corridor are the remains of a Nilometer. (See Aswan, **page 801**) Horus' defeat of Seth, who is portrayed as a hippopotamus, is illustrated in the middle of the W wall of the main temple.

Local information

● Accommodation

There are no good hotels in town and most tourists are either only passing through or are staying on cruise ships which moor on the river bank from where caléches take them to the temple. There are a few cheap hotels including the relatively clean **F** ***Dar es-Salaam*** near the temple, the fairly awful **F** ***Semiramis*** and **F** ***El-Magdi*** further down Sharia al-Maglis, and the friendly but shabby **F** ***El-Medina*** just off the main roundabout on Sharia Gumhorriya.

● Places to eat

The ***Happy Land*** restaurant is on the Corniche between the bridge and Sharia al-Maglis where the ***Zahrat el-Medina*** restaurant is located: neither of these **cheap** restaurants are very good.

● Bank

Sharia Gumhorriya in the centre of town is open Sun-Thur 0830-1400.

● Post Office

Located near the temple on Sharia Tahrir on the S side of the main roundabout.

● Telephone

Local code: 095.

● Transport

Train To Luxor and Aswan stop at Edfu but only very slow and crowded 2nd and 3rd class service.

Road Bus N to Esna and Luxor or S to Kom Ombo and Aswan, caught from Sharia Tahrir half way between the bridge and the temple, are slow but very cheap. **Service taxis**: N to Esna (1 hr) and Luxor (1 hr), or S to Kom Ombo (45 min) and Aswan (90 min, E£3.50) can be caught from the W end of the bridge.

Kom Ombo

Kom Ombo, 66 km S of Edfu and only about 40 km N of Aswan, is a small E bank town known today for its sugar refinery which processes the cane grown in the surrounding area. It is home for many of the Nubians who were displaced by the flooding which followed the construction of the Aswan High Dam. Kom Ombo was the ancient crossroads where the '40 Days Road' caravan route from western Sudan met the route from the eastern desert gold mines. It was also the site of the training ground for the war elephants used in the Ptolemaic army. Most tourists stop here to visit the **Temple of Sobek and Horus**, which stands on the banks of the Nile 4 km from the town.

ACCESS To reach the temple, leave the service taxi to Aswan at the turnoff 2 km S of Kom Ombo town from where the signposted 'tembel' is only 1.5 km away. In the town itself both buses and service taxis stop on the N-S Sharia 26th July but 300m apart. Cheap pick-ups to the temple can be caught from behind the white mosque which is one block away from the Luxor-Aswan road on the E-W axis Sharia Gamhorriya. These days the vast majority of visitors arrive by coach or by cruise ships which dock on the river bank directly below the temple itself.

Things to see

Kom Ombo Temple, open daily 0600-1800 (entry E£4 or E£2 for students and E£10 for commercial photography permit) is the more usual name given to the small but beautiful **Temple of Sobek and Horus**. It faces the Nile at a bend in the river. The temple is unusual because it is dedicated to two gods rather than a single deity. Sobek was the crocodile god which, given the fact that the nearby sandbanks were a favourite basking ground for crocodiles until the construction of the Aswan Dam, was particularly appropriate. On its right hand side Sobek-Re, who is identified with the sun, his wife in another form of Hathor, and their moon-god son Khonsu are honoured. The left hand side is devoted to a form of Horus the Elder or Haroeris known as the 'Good doctor', his consort Ta-Sent-Nefer ('good sister') and his son Horus the Younger who was known as Pa-Heb-Tawy ('Lord of the Two Lands'). A healing cult developed and pilgrims who came to be cured would fast for a night in the temple precinct before participating in a complex ceremony with the priest of Horus in the heart of the temple.

The present temple, like many others along this stretch of the Nile, is a Greco-Roman construction, built of sandstone and completed by Ptolemy V (205-180 BC). Its proximity to the Nile was a mixed blessing because, while its silt assisted in preserving the building, the flood waters eroded the First Pylon and Forecourt which were falling into the Nile before they were strengthened by the Department of Antiquities in 1893.

Like so many others the temple lies on a N-S axis with the main entrance at the S end. In front of it to the W on the riverbank itself is the **Mamissi of Ptolemy VII** (180-145 BC) which has been virtually destroyed by flooding. To the E of the main temple is the **Gate of Neos Dionysus**, who is believed to have been Ptolemy XIII (88-51 BC) and the father of Cleopatra, and the tiny two-room **Chapel of Hathor** which is now used to display mummified crocodiles found near the site.

With the Pylon and much of the **Forecourt** now destroyed by water erosion, one enters the main temple at the forecourt which was built by Tiberius (14-37 AD). Unfortunately only the stumps of the colourful columns, with a high-water mark clearly visible at about 2.5m, and a few pieces of its walls now remain. Continuing the theme from the rest of the temple the twin deities are divided so that the left-hand columns are dedicated to Horus the Elder and the right-hand ones to Sobek-Re. In the centre of the forecourt is a huge altar which is flanked by two granite basins set into the paving. At the N end is the double entrance of the **First Hypostele Hall** with one door for each deity. The capitals are brightly decorated with floral arrays while the base is decorated with lilies. The reliefs on the lintel and door jambs show the Nile gods binding Upper and Lower Egypt together.

The 5 entrance columns and the 10 columns inside the Hypostele Hall and its wall reliefs are attractively decorated and the curious mixture of the 2 deities continues. Part of the roof has survived on the E side of the Hall and flying vultures are clearly depicted on the ceiling. The rear walls leading to the older **Second** or **Inner Hypostele Hall**, which has 2 entrances and 10 columns, show Ptolemy VII holding hymnal texts before the Nile gods. Inside he is shown offering sacrifices to the gods and on the N side of the Inner Hypostele Hall, between the 2 doors, is a text detailing the temple gods' various festivals. The most striking relief is adjacent on the left of the N wall where Horus the Elder presents the *Hps*, the curved sword of victory to Ptolemy VII, while Cleopatra II and Cleopatra III, his wife and sister respectively, stand behind him.

This is then followed by 3 double **Entrance Vestibules**, each progressively smaller and higher than the last, also built by Ptolemy VII. The outer vestibule shows the goddess of writing Sheshat measuring the layout of the temple's foundations, while the middle chamber served as an **Offering Hall** to which only priests were allowed entrance. Two small side rooms originally served as the Library for the sacred texts and the other as a vestry for the altar clothes and the priests' robes. As in Edfu, a staircase originally led to the now destroyed Chapel of the Disk on the roof.

The inner vestibule has 2 doors leading to the 2 separate **Sanctuaries of Horus and Sobek** and between the doors the gods give a Macedonian cloaked Ptolemy a notched palm branch from which the Heb Sed, or jubilee sign displaying the number of years of his reign, is suspended. Khonsu, who is wearing a blue crescent around a red disk, is followed by Horus in blue symbolising the air, and Sobek in green representing the water. Just as at Edfu to the N of the sanctuaries there is a **New Year Shrine** with a poorly preserved illustration of the Sky Goddess Nut on the ceiling. The sanctuaries, built by Ptolemy XIII (88-51 BC), are in a bad state and are much smaller than those at Edfu. Within each was an altar upon which a portable shrine would have stood. Beneath the sanctuary are the crypts which are empty but, unusually, are open to the public.

On the right inner wall of the outer corridor is the first known illustration of medical instruments, including bone-saws, scalpels, suction caps and dental tools, which date from the 2nd century AD and show that complex surgery was carried out over 1,800 years ago. Nearby the temple corridor floor is marked with graffiti which were drawn by patients and pilgrims as they spent the night there before the next day's healing ceremonies.

In the NW corner of the temple complex is a large circular well which has a stairway, cistern and rectangular basin which are believed to be connected in some ways with the worship of the crocodile god Sobek.

Local information

● Accommodation

The cheap and clean **F** *Cleopatra Hotel* is located near the service taxi depot on Sharia 26th July.

● Places to eat

Besides the small stalls which serve '*ful*' (beans) there is the **cheap** and clean *El-Noba* restaurant just to the S of the white mosque on the main Luxor-Aswan road.

● Bank

Next to the mosque, open Sun-Thur 0830-1400 but 1000-1330 during Ramadan.

● Telephone

Local code: 097.

● Transport

Train to Luxor and Aswan stop at Kom Ombo station just across the highway but only the very slow and crowded 2nd and 3rd class service.

Road Bus N to Edfu, Esna and Luxor or S to Aswan, leave the bus terminal on Sharia 26th July about 350m S of Sharia Gumhorriya. **Service taxis**: N to Edfu (1 hr) or S to Aswan (45 min) can be caught from the terminal on Sharia 26th July just S of Sharia Gumhorriya.

THE NILE VALLEY SOUTH TO ASWAN AND ABU SIMBEL

CONTENTS

MAPS

For many visitors to Egypt the highlight of their trip is Aswan and Abu Simbel which, after the noise and crowds of Cairo and the over-commercialization of Luxor, is wonderfully relaxing. The combination of the magnificent sites, the breathtaking sunsets and the friendliness of the indigenous Nubian population make Egypt's deep south an experience which must not be missed.

Aswan

Population: 90,000. *Altitude:* 193m.

Aswan, Egypt's southern frontier town, in its delightful river setting is the highlight of any Nile cruise. It is stunningly beautiful, charmingly romantic, and wonderfully relaxing, an escape from the over-commercialization of **Luxor's** hordes of tourists and vendors.

Aswan's indigenous inhabitants are the ethnically, linguistically and culturally distinct **Nubians** who are undoubtedly African rather than Arab. Despite being frequently invaded and conquered by their northern Egyptian neighbours, the Nubians actually controlled Egypt during the 25th Dynasty (747-656 BC). Cleopatra was a Nubian from the modern-day Sudanese town of Wadi Halfa. Indeed, the term Nubian is equally applicable to the Sudanese who live along the Nile as far S as Khartoum. The later Nubian kingdom of Kush, whose capital was the Sudanese town of Merowe and which included Aswan, remained largely independent from Egypt. Having been the last region to adopt the Christian faith Nubia became a sanctuary for Coptic Christians fleeing the advance of Islam and it remains a Christian stronghold today.

For many centuries a sleepy backwater, Aswan assumed national importance when it became the headquarters for the successful 1898 Anglo-Egyptian reconquest of Sudan. With the 1902 construction of the first **Aswan Dam** the town became a fashionable winter resort for rich Europeans who relished its dry heat, luxury hotels and stunning views, particularly from the *feluccas* sailing on the Nile at sunset. With the completion of the **Aswan High Dam** in 1970, the Nubian villages to the S of Aswan were submerged by the rising waters of Lake Nasser and many of those who were displaced joined in swelling the population of that ever expanding town. Despite the subsequent construction of a number of heavy industries in Aswan, to

CLIMATE: ASWAN

	Jan	Feb	Mar	Apr	May	Jun	Jul	Aug	Sep	Oct	Nov	Dec	Av/Tot
Max (°C)	24	26	30	36	40	42	42	42	40	37	31	26	35
Min (°C)	10	10	12	14	17	21	23	23	22	19	16	12	18
Rain (mm)	0	0	0	0	1	0	0	0	0	0	0	0	1

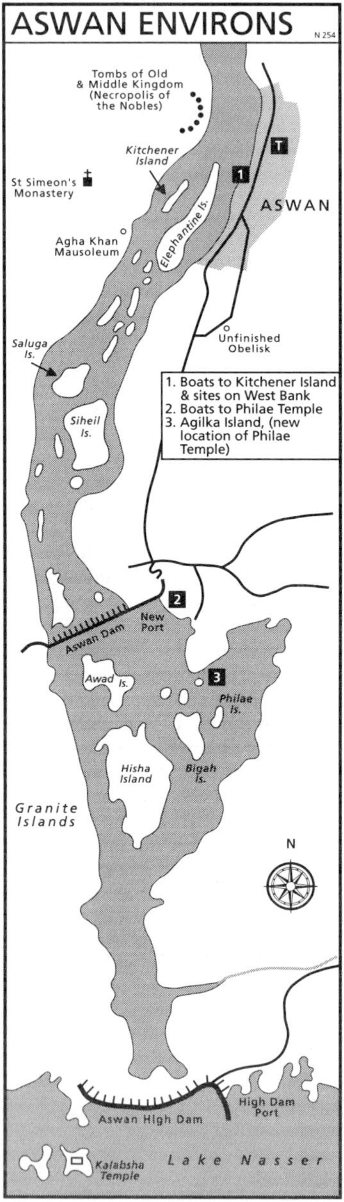

take advantage of the cheap hydro-electric power generated at the dam, the town has retained its attractive charm and relaxed atmosphere.

ACCESS The railway station is at the N end of the town, about 5 min walk from the Corniche where most of the tourist hotels are found. The inter-city taxi depot is nearby, just one block to the S of the railway station. The inter-city bus station is even more conveniently located in the town centre behind the Corniche on Sharia Abtal el-Tahrir and *feluccas* and cruise boats moor at many places along the Corniche. Aswan's desert airport is 24 km S of the town. There is no bus service connecting the airport and town. A hired taxi will cost about E£30 but bargain like mad.

Things to see

In the town itself, besides watching the beautiful sunset either from the **Corniche** or from the terrace of the **Old Cataract Hotel**, it is well worth visiting the exotic **souk** which, with the exception of Cairo, is probably the best in the country. Running parallel to the Corniche there are stalls selling food and a wide range of fresh produce, best bought in the morning, as well as jewellery, textiles and a host of oriental herbs and spices which are best bought after sunset.

Opposite the Corniche and only a short ferry ride away in the middle of the Nile is **Elephantine Island**. Measuring 2 km long and 500m at its widest point the island which gets its name from the large black rocks off its S tip which look, perhaps, like bathing elephants, is worth visiting. Public ferries run every 15 min between 0600-2400 from the landing dock opposite the Egyptair office and dock just next to the island's **Aswan Museum**, like the *feluccas* which can be hired at negotiable rates (see Transport below). **NB**: the free ferry to the *Oberoi Hotel* does not give access to the rest of the island.

The region's first inhabitants lived on this island long before Aswan itself was occupied. It was reputed to be the home of Hapy, the god of the Nile flood, and the goddess of fertility Satet, who were both locally revered, and the regional god Khnum, who was represented by a ram's head. The **Temple of Khnum** once accounted for over two-thirds of the island's 2 sq kms fortress town of **Yebu**, the word for both elephant and ivory in ancient Egyptian and which for centuries was the main trade and security border post between Egypt and Nubia. The ruined temple, at the S end of the island boasts a gateway portraying Alexander II worshipping Khnum which suggests that the Greeks added to this temple complex. The island has a number of less impressive ruins, and temples have been built here for 4 millennia.

The **Roman Nilometer**, which was rediscovered on the SE tip of Elephantine Island in 1822, was designed to measure the height of the annual Nile flood. This enabled the coming season's potential crop yield to be estimated and the level of crop taxation to be fixed. Besides Roman and very faint pharaonic numerals, there are also more recent Arabic ones, on the 90 walled stairs which lead down to a riverside shaft.

The **Aswan Museum**, was established in order to display relics salvaged from the flooded areas behind the Aswan dams, which is ironic because the villa and gardens originally belonged to Sir William Willcocks, the designer of the first Aswan Dam. Its brief was subsequently expanded to act as a museum of the region's heritage and eventually to include a permanent exhibition of Nubian history, however, a *New Museum of Nubian History* is now almost complete to the S of the town. The ground floor is arranged in chronological order with items from the Middle and New Kingdoms, including pottery, combs and some jewellery, while the basement displays a series of human and animal mummies and an impressive gold sheathed statue of Khnum. Open daily 0800-1700, E£10 entrance and E£10 for camera.

Besides the museum, Nilometer and temple ruins in the S and the *Aswan Oberoi Hotel* in the N, there are also 3 small typical **Nubian villages** in the middle of Elephantine Island. Although it is suggested that the villagers prefer not to become a tourist attraction, visits are organized for foreigners including hospitality in the houses.

Kitchener's Island which lies N of the larger Elephantine Island, originally known as the 'Island of Plants' has a magnificent **Botanical Garden**. The beautiful island was presented to Lord Kitchener, who had a passion for exotic plants and flowers from around the world, in gratitude for his successful Sudan campaign and the gardens have been maintained in their original style. The atmosphere on the island, which is almost completely shielded from the bustle of Aswan by Elephantine Island, is very relaxed and its lush vegetation, animals and birds make it an ideal place to watch the sunset. There is an expensive café at the S end of the island. Open daily from 0800 until sunset, entrance E£5. Can only be reached by *felucca*, start bargaining at E£5 return.

The beautiful **Agha Khan Mausoleum**, which is situated on a hill on the W bank of the Nile opposite the town, was built of solid marble for the 3rd Agha Khan (1877-1957) who was the 48th Imam of the Ismaili sect of Shi'a Muslims. He was renowned for his wealth and was given his body-weight in jewels by his followers for his 1945 diamond jubilee. As an adult he visited Aswan every winter for its therapeutic climate, having fallen in love with its beauty and built a villa on the W bank. His widow, who still lives in the villa every winter, erected the mausoleum on the barren hill above the villa. Its is a brilliant white marble building, closely resembling a miniature version of

The Nile – The Lifeblood Of Egypt

Although it has since become a cliché, the Nile really is 'the lifeblood of Egypt' and the combination of a restricted area of agricultural land and an ever expanding population has necessitated the very careful management of what limited water is available. The theory behind the construction of the Aswan dams was that, rather than years of low water levels, drought and famine being followed by years when the Nile flooded and washed half the agricultural soil into the Mediterranean, the flow of the Nile could be regulated and thereby provide a much more stable flow of water. Unfortunately, although the 2 dams did control the Nile and thereby boost both hydro-electric-power and agricultural production, the mushrooming population outstripped the gains and Egypt now imports over half of its cereal requirements. At the same time it is now recognized that the High Dam was planned and built when the level of the Nile was particularly high. Whether it is because of climatic change or simply part of an apparent 20-30 year cycle the volume of water reaching Aswan is decreasing and if the trend continues it may be necessary to pipe natural gas from the Gulf of Suez to generate the electricity at the giant 2,100 mw power station at Aswan.

The original **Aswan Dam** was built by the British between 1898-1902 and was then raised twice in 20 years to make it the largest dam in the world. Although no longer used for storage or irrigation the dam, which is crossed by the road to the airport, is now mainly used to provide local power. After the 1952 Revolution, the new leaders recognised that massive population pressure meant that a more radical solution was required both to control the waters of the Nile and generate sufficient electricity for the new industrial sector and bring power to every Egyptian village. To finance the construction of the planned High Dam, following the withdrawal of a World Bank loan under US pressure, Nasser nationalized the Suez Canal and persuaded the USSR to help build the dam. Construction started in 1960 and was completed in 1971 after Nasser's death in Sept 1970.

Although it took a number of years to fill, the most visible effect of the dam was the creation of **Lake Nasser** which, covering an area of about 6,000 sq kms and being over 180m deep in places, is the world's largest reservoir. This has enabled Egypt, unlike Sudan or Ethiopia, to save water during times of plenty and have an adequate strategic reserve for times of shortage. The extra water from the dam significantly increased the area of land under permanent irrigation and allowed over one million feddans (about 400,000 ha) of desert to be reclaimed. In addition, the extra electric power facilitated the expansion of the industrial sector not only around Aswan but throughout the country.

There were, however, major environmental implications of the dam's construction because the rise of Lake Nasser flooded the homeland of the Nubians who were forced to migrate N to other towns and cities: to date they have been offered negligible compensation. Another drawback is that the lake accumulates the Nile's natural silt which used to fertilize the agricultural land downstream from Aswan. Consequently farmers in Lower Egypt are now having to rely heavily on chemical fertilisers which destabilises the whole food chain. In view of its expanding population, however, Egypt would be in an absolutely hopeless situation without the dams.

the Fatimids' mausoleums in Cairo, with virtually the only hint of colour the fresh red rose placed daily on the sarcophagus. Outside, the views of the desert and of Aswan across the Nile are particularly breathtaking at sunset. There is free entry to the mausoleum for respectably dressed tourists and pilgrims on Tue-Sun 0900-1645. Can by reached by ferry E£1 return or *felucca*, start bargaining at E£5 return.

The **Necropolis of the Nobles** is located further N along the W bank of the Nile, W being the world of the dead and E the world of the living. The riverside cliff is lined with tombs from various periods which have been discovered during the last century. These tombs, open from 0800-1600, entrance E£5, can be reached by ferries, E£1 return, from the Corniche near Seti Tours which run every 30 min from 0600-1800 and every hour from 1800-2100. Just above the water-line are the Roman tombs, a little higher are earlier ones and in the highest more durable rock are those of the Old and Middle Kingdoms. The majority of the dead are believed to have been priests or officials responsible for water transport between Egypt and Nubia. Most of the tombs are numbered in ascending order from S to N with the more interesting ones including the following:

Mekhu (No 25) This 6th Dynasty tomb, which was built by his son Sabni, is crudely carved and decorated into the rock face with its chamber being supported by columns and with a false door in a recess on the back wall.

Sabni (No 26) oversaw the construction of both his own tomb and the adjacent one containing his father Mehu, whose body he recovered in an expedition to Nubia, and the 2 tombs are very similar. There are small obelisks at their entrances and painted scenes of fishing and fowling in Sabni's chapel.

Sirenput II (No 31), who was governor or Guardian of the South at the height of the Middle Kingdom, has the largest, most elaborate and best preserved tomb. An entrance corridor leads into a hall in which Sirenput II is clearly portrayed on the columns. In a small recess at the rear of the tomb there is an elaborate relief portraying him with his wife, son and mother in a beautiful garden.

Harkhuf (unnumbered, alongside No 32) This 6th Dynasty tomb belonged to another Guardian of the South and caravan leader. A small pillared hall leads to the burial chamber. The delight of this tomb is the account in hieroglyphics, which are now badly eroded, of the expedition Harkhuf made into Nubia and the gifts, including incense, ebony and a dancing dwarf, that he presented to the pharaoh Pepi II upon his return.

Sirenput I (No 36), the grandfather of Sirenput II in No 31, was both Guardian of the South and also the overseer of the priests of Khnum and Satet during the 12th Dynasty (1991-1786 BC). The tomb is one of the largest but unfortunately the reliefs are badly decayed. The pillared court was roofed with an ornate façade, but little remains of this either. Scenes in all the chambers portray Sirenput I with his family during rituals and leisure activities such as hunting, fishing and watching a bullfight.

The ruined desert **Monastery of St Simeon**, which lies on the W bank inland from the Agha Khan's Mausoleum, open daily from 0900-1600, entrance E£5, was built and dedicated in the 7th century to a 4th century local saint Anba Hadra. Following an encounter with a funeral procession on the day after his own wedding he decided, presumably without consulting his wife, to remain celibate. He became a student of St Balmar, rejected urban life and chose to become a desert hermit. The fortress monastery stands at the head of a desert valley looking towards the Nile and from where the dramatic sunsets appears to turn the sand to flames. Until Salah al-Din destroyed the building in 1173 it was used by monks, including Saint Simeon about whom very little is known, as a base for proselytising expeditions first S into Nubia and then, after the Muslim conquest, N into Egypt.

Although the monastery is uninhabitable its main features, the lower stone storeys and upper ones of mud-brick, have been preserved. Visitors are admitted through a small gateway in the E tower which leads to a church with a partially collapsed basilica but the nave and aisles are still accessible. There is a painting of the ascended Christ surrounded by angels near the altar recess. The walls of a small cave chapel, which can be entered via the church, are richly painted with pictures of the Apostles which were partially defaced by Muslim iconoclasts. The cave chapel leads to the upper enclosure from which the living quarters can be entered. Up to 300 monks lived in simple cells with some hewn into the rock and others in the main building to the N of the enclosure, with kitchens and stables to the S.

Back on the E bank of the Nile on the outskirts of Aswan about 2 km along the highway S, is the **Unfinished Obelisk** in the quarries which provided red granite for the ancient temples. The huge obelisk, which would have weighed 1,168 tonnes and stood over 41m high, was abandoned before any designs were carved when a major flaw was discovered in the granite. It was originally intended to form a pair with the **Lateran Obelisk**, the world's tallest obelisk which once stood in the Temple of Tuthmosis III at Karnak but is now in Rome. When it was discovered in the quarry by Rex Engelbach in 1922 the unfinished obelisk shed light on pharaonic quarrying methods, including the soaking of wooden wedges to open fissures, but shaping and transporting them remains an astounding feat. For those having seen the other wonders of ancient Egypt the unfinished obelisk, open daily 0600-1800, entrance E£5, is a little disappointing and it is probably better combining it with a trip to the Aswan Dams or the Philae Temple. Hire a taxi to the High Dam for E£35.

There are in fact 2 **Aswan Dams** but it is the so-called High Dam, just upstream from the original 1902 British-built Aswan Dam, that is Egypt's pride and joy and which created Lake Nasser, the world's largest reservoir. In fact the High Dam is so big – 111m high, 3,830 km long, 980m wide at its base and 40m at its top – that it is almost impossible to realize its scale except from the observation deck of the lotus-shaped Soviet-Egyptian Friendship tower or from the air when landing at nearby Aswan airport. To help appreciate the scale and consequences of the dam's construction the visitors' pavilion, which includes a 15m high model of the dam and photographs of the relocation of the Abu Simbel temple, is worth a visit. Occasionally, crossing the dam is prevented for security reasons. There is comparatively little to see except the fish processing factory and it can be a very hot and somewhat disappointing visit. It costs E£2 per person to cross the High Dam between 0700-1700 and it may be necessary to show your passport to prove that you are not a Israeli spy. Photography of the snap-shot variety is permitted. A taxi here from Aswan will cost E£30 return.

For many tourists the most beautiful and romantic monuments in Aswan, if not in the whole of Egypt, are the **Philae Temples** which were built in the Ptolemaic era (332-30 BC) as an offering to Isis. In fact, the **Temple of Isis** and the rest of the monuments were moved to the neighbouring Aglika island by UNESCO in 1972-1980 when the construction of the High Dam threatened to submerge Philae forever. They were then reconstructed to imitate the original as closely

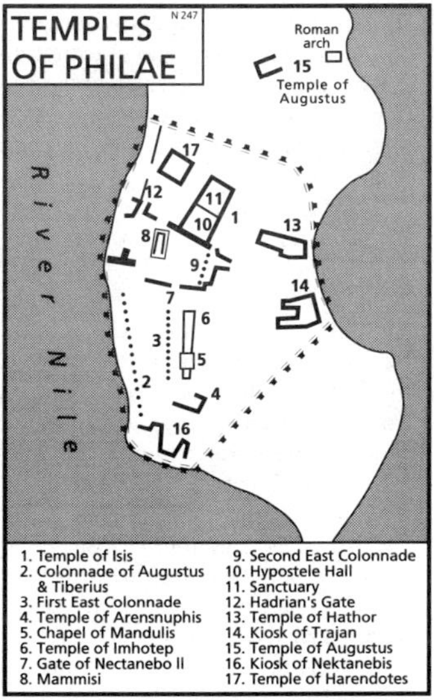

as possible but the new position no longer faces neighbouring Bigah island, one of the burial sites of Osiris and closed to all but the priesthood, which was the whole raison d'être for the Temple of Isis being on Philae island.

ACCESS Although it is possible to catch a bus and then walk 2 km to the lakeside motorboat dock, unless on a organized tour the island is most easily reached by taking a E£5 taxi ride from Aswan to the dock and a motorboat across to the island. They seat 8 people and cost E£2 per person or E£16 per boat for the return journey including a 1 hr wait at the temple although 90 min is preferable. Entrance E£10.

Although there are other smaller temples on the island it is dominated by the **Temple of Isis (1)**. She was the consort of her brother Osiris and eventually became the "Great Mother of All Gods and Nature", "Goddess of Ten Thousand Names", and represented women, purity and sexuality. Isis is attributed with reconstructing Osiris' dismembered body and creating his son Horus who became the model of a man and king. In the 3rd-5th century the worship of Isis became Christianity's greatest rival throughout the Mediterranean. There have even been claims that the early Christians developed the cult of the Virgin Mary to replace Isis in order to attract new converts.

Different parts of the Temple of Isis, which occupies over a quarter of the new island, were constructed over an 800 year period by Ptolemaic (332-30 BC) and Roman (30 BC – 395 AD) rulers. At the top of the steps where the motorboats arrive is a Roman colonnaded court which leads to the main temple. On the W or lakeside side of the court the **Colonnade of Augustus and Tiberius (2)** is well preserved and contains 31 columns with individual capitals. There are still traces of paint on some of the columns and the starred ceiling. On the right is the plainer **First East Colonnade (3)** behind which are first the foundations of the **Temple of Arensnuphis (4)** (Nubian God), the ruined **Chapel of Mandulis (5)** (Nubian God of Kalabsha) and the **Temple of Imhotep (6)** (the architect of Zoser's step pyramid at Saqqara who was later deified as a healing God).

The main Temple of Isis at the end of the court is entered through the **First Pylon of Ptolemy XIII Neos Dionysus** which show him slaying his enemies as Isis, Horus and Hathor look on. The pylon was originally flanked by 2 obelisks, since looted and transported to the UK, but today only 2 lions at the base guarding the entrance remain. The **Gate of Ptolemy II Philadelphus**, just to the right of the pylon's main **Gate of Nectanebo II (7)**, is from the earlier 30th Dynasty (380-343 BC). On its right is graffiti written by Napoleon's troops after their victory over the Mamlukes in 1799.

Arriving in a large forecourt to the left is the colonnaded **Mammisi (8)**, used for mammisi rituals, which was originally built by Ptolemy VII and expanded by the Romans which explains why images of Isis with Horus as a baby are intermingled with the figures of contemporary Roman emperors. In the inner sanctum of the Mammisi itself are historically important scenes of Isis giving birth to Horus in the marshes and others of her suckling the child-pharaoh. On the opposite side of the forecourt from the Birth House is the late Ptolemaic **Second East Colonnade (9)** behind which are a number of attractive reliefs and 6 small function rooms including a library.

The axis of the temple is changed by the **Second Pylon**, set at an angle to the first, which was built by Ptolemy XIII Neos Dionysos and which shows him presenting offerings to Horus and Hathor on the right tower but some of the scenes on the left tower were defaced by the early Christians. Beyond the Pylon a court containing 10 columns opens onto the **Hypostele Hall (10)**. These have retained few traces of their original colour although the capitals are better preserved. The ceiling in the central aisle has representations of vultures which were symbolic of the union of Lower and Upper Egypt. The rest of the ceilings have astronomical motifs and 2 representations of the goddess Nut. On either side of the wall, backing onto the Second Pylon, Ptolemy VII and Cleopatra II can be seen presenting offerings to Hathor and Khnum. From the entrance at the far end of the Hypostele Hall is a chamber which gives access to the roof. The interconnecting roof chambers are all dedicated to Osiris and lead to his shrine. Vivid reliefs portray the reconstruction of his body.

Continuing upwards and N from the chamber, linked to the Hypostele Hall, are 3 rooms decorated with sacrificial reliefs representing the deities. The central room leads to a further 3 rooms linked to the **Sanctuary (11)** in which is a stone pedestal dedicated by Ptolemy III which formerly supported the holy barque (boat) of Isis. Reliefs portray Isis and her son surrounded by Nubian deities. The temple's exterior was decorated at the direction of the Emperor Augustus.

Hadrian's Gate (12), which is W of the Second Pylon, has some very interesting reliefs. The N wall on the right depicts Isis, Nephthys, Horus and Amun in adoration before Osiris in the form of a bird. Behind is the source of the Nile which is depicted emerging from a cavern and Hapy, a Nile god, is shown pouring water from 2 jars, indicating the Egyptians' knowledge that the Nile had more than one source. The S wall depicts a mummified Osiris lying on a crocodile together with another image of the reconstructed Osiris seated on his throne with his son Horus.

Smaller shrines can be seen throughout the island dedicated to both Nubian and local deities. East of the temple of Isis is the small **Temple of Hathor (13)**. Two columns depict the head of Hathor at their capital while, in a famous relief, the local deities play musical instruments. The **Kiosk of Trajan (14)** further S has 14 columns with floral motifs. Only 2 walls have been decorated and these depict Osiris, Horus and Isis receiving offerings from the Emperor Trajan. It is thought that the Kiosk originally had a wooden roof. At the NE end of the island is the ruined **Temple of Augustus (15)** and the **Gate of Diocletian** which were next to a mud brick Roman village which was abandoned by the archaeologists when Philae was moved because the water had already caused such severe erosion.

Although it is wonderful to visit Philae in the late afternoon, when the light is most attractive, many tourists attend the **Sound & Light Show** which involves a 1 hr floodlit tour through the ruins. As in Karnak and the Cairo Pyramids the visual beauty of the place is more impressive than the historically informative but melodramatic soundtrack. Tour companies, obviously keen to sell you a package deal including transport to and from the show, can provide full details of the times of each show which is in a different language. Inclusive charge from Aswan E£50.

Sound & Light Shows daily at 1800 and 2000 as follows:

Mon	English/Italian
Tue	French/English
Wed	English/Spanish
Thur	Arabic/French
Fri	English/French
Sat	English/French
Sun	French/German

By comparison with Philae the **Kalabsha Temple**, open 0600-1800, which was also relocated when the High Dam was built and is now semi-marooned on an island or promontory (depending on the water level) near the W end of dam, is rarely visited by tourists. The easiest way to reach the temple is by taxi from Aswan or possibly as part of a half-day tour which would include the Unfinished Obelisk, the Aswan Dams and Philae. Negotiate with the boatmen if the waters of the lake cover the pathway from the shore. Pay at the end of the return trip after about an hour on the site.

The original site of the temple, which was built in the 18th Dynasty (1567-1320 BC) in honour of Marul (Greek =Mandulis) a Nubian fertility god, was about 50 km S of Aswan at Talmis which was subsequently renamed Kalabsha. Over the centuries the later **Temple of Mandulis**, a Ptolemaic-Roman version of the earlier one, developed a healing cult as did those of Edfu and Dendera. It was moved from Kalabsha to its present site in 1970 by West German engineers in order to save it from the rising waters of Lake Nasser.

Leading up to the First Pylon is an impressive 30m causeway, used by pilgrims arriving by boat, but it is not known why the causeway and first pylon are at an angle to the temple. In order to align the structure, the first court is in the shape of a trapezium, with the pillars on the S side grouped closer together.

The left portico, beside the entrance to the Hypostele Hall, portrays the pharaoh being purified and anointed by Thoth and Horus, while on the right is inscribed a decree from Aurelius Besarion who was Governor of Ombos and Elephantine ordering the expulsion of pigs from the temple precincts. The Hypostele Hall has lost its roof, but the 8 columns are still in good condition. The capitals are ornate and flowered, some paintings having been preserved with their original colours, though not all are complete. On either side of the doorway leading to the vestibule is a relief of Trajan making offerings to Isis, Osiris and Marul.

Beyond the hall are the inner vestibules each with 2 columns and S access to the roof. Most of the decoration has survived and on the entrance wall the pharaoh can be seen offering incense to Marul and Wadjet, and milk to Isis and Osiris. The S wall depicts the emperor making libations to Osiris, Isis, Horus, Wadjet and Marul. The statue of Marul has long since vanished, though he is pictured on the walls amongst the other deities.

Local information

● Accommodation

AL *Aswan Oberoi*, Elephantine Island, P.O. Box 62, T 323455, F 323485, Tx 92120, 160 rm with balcony, 38 suites and 16 villas, excellent location in middle of river Nile, reached by a free ferry which runs to/from the *Isis Hotel*, stunning views particularly at sunset, restaurants offering Indian, Egyptian and continental food, coffee shop, bar, night club, health spa, gym, also tennis and pool which non-residents can use; **AL** *P.L.M. Azur New Cataract*, Sharia Abtal el-Tahrir, T 323377, F 323510, 144 rm, 280 beds, an unfortunate slab of a building overlooking the Nile about 5 mins walk S from town centre, connected by a series of gardens to and shares many facilities including the pool with the *Kalabsha Hotel*, and the famous *Old Cataract Hotel*, choice of restaurants, 24 hr coffee shop, bar and discotheque. **AL** ***Pullman Cataract Hotel***, Sharia Abtal el-Tahrir, T 323434, F 323510, 144 rm, 280 beds, Edwardian Moorish-style hotel, universally known as the *Old Cataract Hotel*, located opposite Elephantine Island about 5 mins walk S from town centre, connected to *New Cataract Hotel* and *Kalabsha Hotel*. Opened in 1899, is one of Egypt's oldest and most famous hotels, large a/c rm, some with river view, friendly service but faults due to age are reported, full range of facilities include classic *1902* restaurant; **AL** ***Amun Tourist Village***, P.O. Box 118,

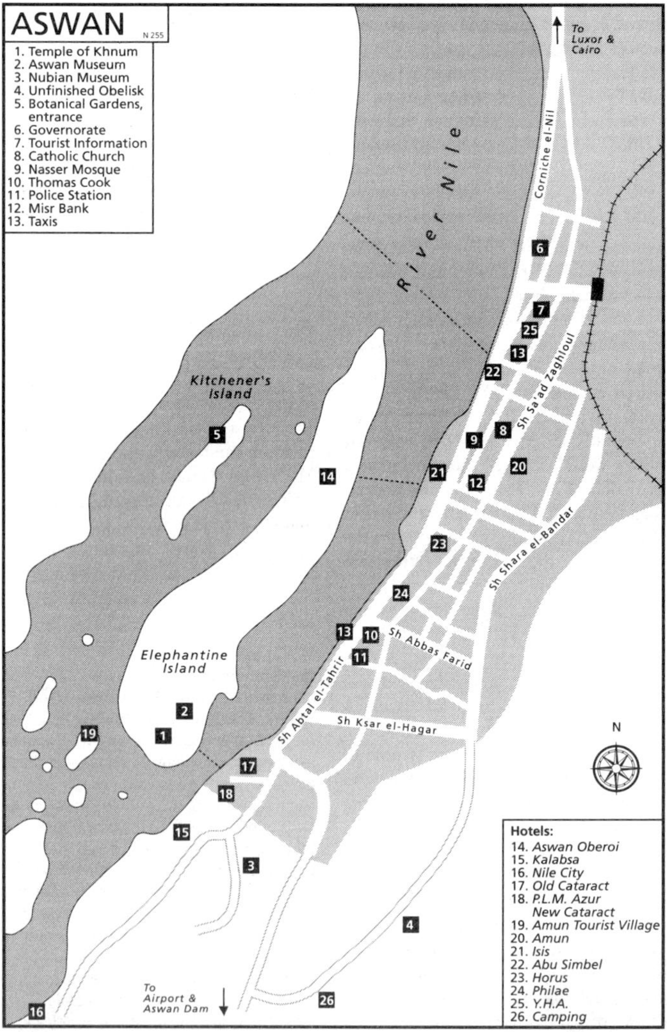

Sahara City, T 480438, F 480550, 252 rm. Located near airport about 18 km from the attractions of Aswan and the Nile, less busy in low season, restaurants, pool, tennis.

B ***Isis Hotel***, Corniche el-Nil, T 324905, 100 rm, excellent location between river and Corniche next to *Hotel Oberoi's* landing stage, a/c bungalows, pool, river-side terrace and restaurant.

C ***Kalabsha Hotel***, Sharia Abtal el-Tahrir, T 323434, F 325974, 120 rm, on hill overlooking the Nile about 5 mins walk S from town centre, shares many facilities with *PLM Azur New Cataract* and *Old Cataract Hotel*. Built in 1963 for Russians working at the High Dam, good reception and public rooms, poorly decorated bedrooms, starkly furnished restaurant serves a good breakfast, friendly and helpful service but barking dogs can be disturbing at night; **C** ***Amun***, Amun Island, T 322555, F 322555, 56 rm, excellent location on its own lush island in the middle of the river Nile opposite *Old Cataract Hotel*, free ferry operates to/from the Egyptair office, a Club Mediterranée resort with excellent standard of food, service and facilities.

D ***Cleopatra***, Sharia Sa'ad Zaghloul, Aswan, T 314001, F 326381, 130 rm, 250 beds, located downtown near bus station and souk, pool on top floor, restaurant and juice bar; **D** ***Oskar Tourist Hotel***, Sharia Abbas Mahmoud el-Akad, T 326066, 54 rm, 123 beds. Despite its name it is not a tourist hotel and is located in a crowded downtown area with Egyptian life all around it.

E ***Horus***, T 323323. Located on Corniche S of the *Isis Hotel*, pleasant a/c rm, with balconies overlooking the Nile, daily clean linen and a relaxed atmosphere; **E** ***Philae***, Corniche el-Nil, T 322117, 34 small rm with bath, small fan or a/c, view of the Nile; **E** ***Ramses Hotel***, Sharia Abtal el-Tahrir, T 324000, 112 rm with bath, unspectacular but comfortable, small balconies overlooking Nile, friendly staff serve breakfast in the basement restaurant also bar and discotheque.

F ***Abu Simbel***, Corniche el-Nil, T 322888, renowned for its reasonable prices, near bus station, 66 a/c rooms have a good view of the Nile, restaurant, bar, discotheque, laundry, bank, garden, oriental dancing and night club; **F** ***Continental***, Sharia Abbas Farid, T 322311, located near the main police station and close to the Corniche overlooking the Nile is the oldest, cheapest and one of the most infamous fleapits in town. The hotel and café in front are a rendezvous for budget travellers; **F** ***Happi Hotel***, Sharia Abtal el-Tahrir, T 322028, 60 rm, 126 beds, located in town centre near the Corniche behind the Misr Bank, Nile views from the rather cramped single and more spacious double rm with bath on higher floors, has good reputation and serves decent food.

● Youth hostel

96 Sharia Abtal el-Tahrir, 80 beds, T 322313, 3 min from railway station, overnight fee E£3, free kitchen.

● Camping

Official site with guards is located outside town near the **Unfinished Obelisk**, rather inconvenient without your own transport. Compound has showers and toilets but almost no shade. At E£5 per car and E£3 per person per night but it is probably far more sensible to stay at one of the cheaper hotels unless you are determined to camp out.

● Places to eat

♦♦♦***Tower Restaurant*** in *Aswan Oberoi* has international cuisine with the most spectacular views over Aswan and the Nile. ***Orangerie*** in *Aswan Oberoi* varied buffet, excellent choice. ***Darna Restaurant*** in *New Cataract Hotel* excellent Egyptian meal served buffet style in restaurant designed as an Egyptian house. ***1902 Restaurant*** with classic decor in *Old Cataract Hotel* offers international food spiced with Nubian dancers. While in Aswan even the most budget conscious visitors should treat themselves to tea or a drink at sunset on the terrace of the *Old Cataract Hotel*.

♦♦ Besides the hotels there are a number of relatively cheap restaurants which serve good food including fresh fish and some of the local Nubian dishes. They include but are not limited to the ***El-Gumhorriya*** and ***Darwish*** near the railway station, the ***Aswan Moon***, ***Restaurant Shatti*** overlooking river opposite *Hotel Continental*, ***Bonarama*** and ***El-Nil*** on the Corniche and the ***El-Medina*** near the tourist office.

● Banks

Besides the major hotels which change money, there are numerous branches of most of the Egyptian banks on the Corniche and elsewhere in Aswan. Open Thur-Sun 0830-1400 with some also open from 1700-2000.

Nightclubs
There are nightclubs in the *Kalabsha, New Cataract* and *Oberoi* hotels amongst others which offer Nubian and Western floorshows. In many ways, however, it is both preferable and certainly cheaper to spend the evening promenading along the Corniche and souk visiting the riverside restaurants and cafés. During the winter except on Fridays there are nightly performances (2130-2300) by the Nubian Folk Troupe at the Cultural centre T 323344, at the N end of the Corniche.

Post Office
Located in the road behind the *Philae Hotel* open 0800-1400 except Fri. Post restante Sat-Wed 0700-1100 and 1700-2000, Thur 0700-1100, Fri 1700-2000. It is best to post outgoing mail from the major hotels because they seem to get priority.

Religious services
Roman Catholic church, 89 Sharia Abtal el-Tahir, near *Hotel Abu Simbel* one block behind the Corniche has services Sat 1800 and Sun 1900.

Shopping
Aswan is now a large city and it has shops of every description but the souk, which runs parallel to the Corniche probably still has the best selection and the most competitive prices and is much more fun than the tourist shops near the major hotels and cruise ships. There is a departmental store on Sharia Abtal el-Tahrir. Books shops in *Oberoi* and *Isis* arcades.

Sport
The major hotels have good sports facilities but remember that with temperatures as high as 50°C (122°F) in the summer Aswan is not the place to be engaging in very active sports, particularly in the middle of the day. Water sports are available at the Rowing Club on the Corniche above the *Isis Hotel*. Horse riding on a short or long term basis can be arranged. Try at the large hotels for the safest mounts.

Telephone
Local code: 097.

Travel agents and Airlines
There are numerous travel agencies and guide companies throughout the town who are all touting for your booking. ***Eastmar Travel***, Corniche el-Nil, T 323787; ***Misr Travel*** one block behind Corniche on way to railway station, adjacent to Tourist Information; ***Egypt Air***, T 22400.

Tourist information
Located behind the gardens towards the N end of the Corniche next to Misr Travel. The Tourist Authority office is manned by the wonderfully helpful Shoukry Sa'ad and his excellent staff who are the nicest, most polite and well informed officials you will meet in Egypt. Although the official opening times are 0830-1600 and 1800-2000 during the high season it is manned from 0800-2000.

Transport
Local: Bicycles are becoming very popular for short distances. There are many hire shops. Try on the Corniche near Misr Bank at E£5 per hour.

Air For those who can afford it the easiest, if not the most adventurous, way to leave Aswan is by air. (Taxi to the airport E£15). There are regular daily Egyptair and ZAZ flights both to Luxor and Cairo which take about 30 and 90 mins, respectively. Single fare Aswan to Luxor E£250. Allow plenty of time. Don't expect any flight announcements. When the gates open for a flight push forward, if it is not your flight you will be turned back.

Train For long distance travel to Luxor (5 hrs), Cairo (17 hrs) and Alexandria (approx 24 hrs) train is the most comfortable method. Trains range from the deluxe first class sleeper service to crowded and dirty 3rd class cattle trucks. The a/c night train from Aswan to Cairo is highly recommended as being safe and comfortable and providing a meal and drinks service and an early breakfast. The cabins, which have large windows with blinds, are small but easily turn into rm with bunks, a sink and table, and there are clean communal toilets along the corridor. Departures to Cairo at 0700, 0800 (with a/c 1st class coaches), 1500, 1745 and 1920 (these 3 have sleeping compartments), 2030 and 2230. Tickets cost about E£216 for dinner,bed and breakfast; E£40 1st class and E£23 2nd class.

Road: **Bus** Very regular slow buses and less frequent express buses, stopping only at Kom Ombo (E£1), Edfu (E£2) and Esna, go to Luxor (E£5) which takes 4 hrs. There are also 3 daily buses of very varying quality and price to Cairo but, given the distance, the train is a more comfortable option. There is now also a daily a/c bus to Hurghada on the Red Sea coast which continues to Cairo via Suez which is a good stopping off point for travellers to Sinai.

Service Taxi Usually quicker than bus or

train can be picked up from the stand S of the railway station. Places served include Kom Ombo (E£1.50 per person), Edfu (E£2.50) and to Luxor which takes 3½-4 hrs and costs E£6. The 220 km road to Luxor is good in places!! The speed limit is 90 kms/hr and petrol costs E£14 per gallon. Taxi travel can be a heart-stopping experience and with some drivers it is difficult not to close your eyes and start praying.

Felucca Official prices, regulated by the government, for 1-10 passengers including waiting time from the Corniche are: *Kitchener Island and Agha Khan Mausoleum*, E£20, 2 hrs; *Kitchener Island, Elephantine Island, and Agha Khan Mausoleum*, E£25, 2½ hrs; *St Simeon's monastery and Nobles Tombs*, E£35, 3 hrs; *St Simeon's monastery, Kitchener Island and Agha Khan's Mausoleum*, E£50, 3 hrs; *Nubian village*, E£40, 2½ hrs; *Elephantine Island only*, E£15/hr, 1½ hrs; *Elephantine Island and the Nobles' Tombs*, E£50, 4 hrs; *Elephantine Island and St Simeon's monastery*, E£50, 4 hrs; *Elephantine Island, St Simeon's monastery and back via Kitchener island*, E£40, 3 hrs. Alternatively a 1 hr tour around the islands costs E£18. Hire your own *felluca* for E£25 per hour and go where you like. The per person prices for **long distance feluccas** from Aswan, which carry a minimum of 6 people and where the group pays for and buys their own food and pays the E£5 per person required to obtain permission to travel are as follows – *Kom Ombo*, E£25, 1 day and 1 night; *Edfu*, E£45, 2 days and 2 nights; *Esna*, E£50, 3 days and 3 nights; and *Luxor*, E£60, 4 days and 4 nights. The Tourist Office should be able to recommend the best captains and is often a place to meet potential fellow passengers.

Abu Simbel

Sometimes a trip to Abu Simbel is offered as an 'extra' on a tour or an excursion from the hotel in Aswan. Do not miss the opportunity to see this amazing site.

Abu Simbel, which lies 280 km S of Aswan and only 40 km N of the Sudanese border, (virtually closed to all traffic) is the site of the magnificent **Sun Temple of Ramses II** and the smaller **Temple of Queen Nefertari**. With the exception of the temples and the homes of tourist industry employees, there is almost nothing else in Abu Simbel.

ACCESS For tourists arriving by plane there are free buses from Abu Simbel airport to the site of the temples while the coach tours from Aswan go direct to the site.

Things to see

Temples of Abu Simbel Open 0600 until the departure of the last plane. The two temples, which were rediscovered in 1813 completely buried by sand, were built by the most egotistical pharaoh of all, Ramses II (1304-1237 BC) during the 19th Dynasty of the New Kingdom. Although he built a smaller temple for his queen Nefertari, it is the 4 gigantic statues of himself, which were carved out of the mountainside, which dominate Abu Simbel. It was intended that his magnificent and unblinking stare would be the first thing that travellers, visitors and enemies alike, saw as they entered Egypt from the S. Behind the statues is **Ramses II's Temple of the Sun** which was originally built to venerate Amun and Re-Harakhte but really dominated by and dedicated to the pharaoh-god Ramses II himself.

Although it had become the highlight of the trip for the relatively few intrepid travellers who ventured so far S, it was not until the monuments were threatened by the rising waters of Lake Nasser that international attention focused on Abu Simbel. UNESCO financed and organized the ambitious, costly (US$40 million) and ultimately successful 1964-1968 operation, to reassemble the monuments 61m above and 210m behind their original site.

The imposing façade of the main temple (35m wide by 30m high) is dominated by the 4 seated **Colossi of Ramses II**. Each was originally 20m high but one lost its top during an earthquake in 27 BC. There are smaller statues of some of the members of the royal family standing at Ramses' rather crudely sculptured feet which contrast with the ornately chiselled and beautiful faces of Ramses. There are graffiti, written by Greek mercenaries about their expeditions into Nubia, on the left leg of the damaged statue. The sides of the huge thrones at the entrance to the temple are decorated by the Nile gods entwining the plants representing Upper and Lower Egypt around the hieroglyph "to unite". Below are reliefs, called the Nine Bows, of bound Asiatics on the N side and the Nubians to the S representing Egypt's vanquished foes. Lining the façade, above the heads of the 4 Ramses, is a row of baboons. There are 2 small chapels at either end of the façade.

At the entrance into the temple's rock **Hypostele Hall** is a door bearing Ramses II's cartouche. Having entered the temple the eye is immediately drawn to 8 statues of Ramses, 10m high and clad in a short kilt typical of the Nubian Osiride form, which are in front of the 8 enormous square pillars which support the roof. The 4 statues on the right bear the double crown and those on the left the white crown of Upper Egypt. Each pillar depicts the kings presenting offerings to the gods. The hall's ceiling is crowded with vultures and the reliefs on the walls are colourful and well preserved. The N wall is the most dramatic with 4 different scenes depicting the Battle of Kadesh against the Hittites in 1300 BC which, despite the scenes on the wall, was not an unqualified Egyptian success. The depictions of chariots and camps are particularly revealing of ancient battle methods but, more interestingly, Ramses's double arm lancing a Libyan may have been an attempt at animation.

There are also side chambers, probably originally used to store vases, temple linen, cult objects and Nubian gifts, branching off from the hall. Their walls are lined with reliefs of sacrifices and offerings being made by Ramses to the major gods including Amun.

The **Inner Hall** has 4 columns depicting the pharaoh participating in rituals before the deities. On the far left, Ramses can be seen standing up before Amun. Two sandstone sphinxes, which originally stood at the entrance to the hall, are now in London's British Museum.

Further in and in front of the inner sanctuary is the transverse vestibule where offerings of wine, fruits and flowers were made. The **Sanctuary** itself, which was originally cased in gold, has an altar to Ramses at its centre behind which are now, unfortunately mutilated, statues of Ramses together with Amun, Re Harakhte and Ptah who were his patron gods. Before the temple's relocation the dawn sunrays would shine on all but Ptah, who was linked with death-cults, on Feb 22 and Oct 22 which were Ramses' birthday and coronation day. A sacred barque (boat) would have rested on the altar and the walls beside the door portray the barque of Amun and Ramses.

Despite its magnificence and beauty for many visitors to Abu Simbel there is a slight tinge of disappointment because of the the combination of a sense of familiarity and artificiality. The latter is heightened when at the end of the official tour one is led through a door and into the hollow mountain on which the temple was reconstructed when it was moved. At the same time, however, the combination Ramses' egoism and the scale of the magnificent feat of saving the temple from the rising waters of the Nile make the trip from Aswan worthwhile.

The **Temple of Queen Nefertari** is situated 120m N of Ramses II's Temple. Although dedicated to the goddess Hathor, like that of her husband, the temple virtually deifies the human queen Nefertari. Unsurprisingly it is much smaller than that of the egotist Ramses but is nevertheless both imposing and very very beautiful. The external façade is 12m high and lined with 3 colossi 11.5m high on either side of the entrance. Nefertari stands with her husband and their children cluster in pairs at their knees. Just within the entrance are the cartouches of Ramses II and Nefertari. There is one simple **Hall**, with 6 pillars depicting the pharaoh and queen making their offerings to the gods. The ceiling bears a well preserved dedication inscription from Ramses to Nefertari. The reliefs on the hall walls are rather gruesome with the pharaoh slaying his enemies while Nefertari and the god Amun look on. The walls backing the entrance depict Ramses killing a Nubian and a Libyan.

Three corridors lead from the rear of the hall into the **Vestibule**, the central one passing directly into the **Sanctuary**. The back walls of the Vestibule portray reliefs of Ramses and Nefertari offering wine and flowers to Khnum and Re-Harakhte on the right and to Horus and Amun on the left. Vultures protect the Queen's cartouche on the door above the sanctuary which is dominated by the figure of Hathor in the form of a cow watching over Ramses. On the left wall, Nefertari can be seen offering incense to Mut and Hathor whilst on the opposite side Ramses worships the deified images of himself and Nefertari.

Local information

● Accommodation

B *Nefertari Abu Simbel*, T 324836, F 2825919, 110 a/c rm, built in 1960s, located near the temples, best hotel in town but has few guests because most tourists only spend 2 hours in Abu Simbel before returning to Aswan. There is sometimes a problem over the limited choice of food in the restaurant, offers pool and tennis.

C *Nobaleh Ramses Hotel*, T 324735, F 3484821, 32 rm, good but spartan hotel which sometimes has problems with the limited choice of food.

● Camping

The **Nefertari Abu Simbel** has a campground where tents can be pitched but camping at the temples is illegal.

● Places to eat

Because of Abu Simbel's position in the middle of the desert, most supplies come from Aswan and consequently there are often problems with the range of foods available. Indeed, with the exception of the hotels, there are few if any places to eat and only a few poorly equipped stores.

● Shopping

Because there are only a few poorly stocked stores it is essential to bring your own supplies if intending to stay in Abu Simbel.

● Sport

Swimming and tennis at the *Nefertari Abu Simbel*.

● Telephone

Local code: 097.

● Transport

Air Numerous daily services to Abu Simbel from Cairo (2 hr) via Luxor (1 hr) and Aswan (30 min) during the winter high season and about 3 during the summer low season. It is absolutely essential to book a ticket as early as possible. Most tickets are sold on the assumption that you will return the same day but it is possible to include overnight stopovers. Seats on the left hand side of the aircraft usually offer the best views as it circles the temples before landing at Abu Simbel.

Road Bus Although most tourists travel by air or coach tour there is a service from Aswan which leaves at 0800 and arrives at around 1130, returning from the *Nefertari Abu Simbel* hotel at 1330-1400. It is best to buy a ticket at least a day in advance from the Aswan bus station with the ticket for the return journey being bought on board the bus.

Coach There are a number of companies which operate daily luxury return coach services from Aswan to Abu Simbel. Details and schedules can be obtained from the tourist office in Aswan.

Service taxi Some of the Aswan hotels organize taxi tours to Abu Simbel but groups of travellers can make their own arrangements the day before with a driver. The taxis normally leave very early arriving at Abu Simbel before 0900 and returning at around 1400. The boring 3-4 hr return journey over baking featureless desert is particularly hot and uncomfortable.

THE NILE DELTA

CONTENTS

MAPS

North of Cairo, the two main distributaries of the Nile continue NNE and NNW to meet the Mediterranean near Damietta and Rosetta, respectively. On either side and between the two branches the very flat, green and fertile land fans out to create, with the help of some of the world's oldest and most efficient irrigation systems, the Nile delta, Egypt's agricultural heartland and most heavily populated region. The fertility of this region has enabled this scorched desert country, with under 4% of its land cultivatable, to support a huge population and to export large quantities of fruits and vegetables, albeit while having to import huge volumes of cereals. Confusingly, because of its position N rather than S of Upper Egypt, this area was known as Lower Egypt. Because of the lack of hard stone and the very high population density, successive generations plundered old buildings for stone and built new ones on top of ancient sites. As a result there are no monuments to match the splendours of Upper Egypt. This is no reason, however, for visitors to ignore the region which personifies Egypt's calm and relaxing but industrious village life and is the region of many *moulids* or popular religious festivals.

The branching of the Nile divides the Delta into 3 interlocking areas. The best pharaonic ruins including Tanis and Bubastis are in the E Delta. The central Delta includes El-Mahalla el-Kubra and Tanta which are Egypt's 4th and 5th largest cities, while Tanta is the location of Egypt's largest *moulid*. If heading for Alexandria, in preference to the more direct desert route, take the more scenic 'agricultural route' on highway H1 from Cairo through the cotton growing region of the W Delta which includes the coastal town of Rosetta. Although technically in the central Delta the small coastal resorts of Gamassa and Ras el-Bar can be reached more easily from the E Delta coastal town of Damietta.

Eastern Delta

The main road (H1) from Cairo to **Damietta** runs N through the central Delta via **Tanta** before striking NE through **El-Mansura** but there are other routes which offer more interest to the traveller. Turning E in **Benha**, a road goes through **Zagazig** to the ancient sites of **Nabasha** and **Tanis** from which a minor road continues to the coast or N through the intensive cultivation to El-Mansura. Damietta gives access along the coast either E to **Port Said** (**see page 849**) at the N end of the Suez Canal or W to the coastal resorts of **Ras el-Bar**, **Gamassa** and even the isolated **Baltim**.

The main road is normally very busy with a mixture of agricultural traffic and vehicles bound for the ports. On Fri and holidays it can be even busier with private cars. Shamut Oranges between Tukh and Benha is a very popular spot for picnics. Pigeon towers of varying designs are common in the delta region. The pigeons provide free fertiliser and are the main ingredient in 'pigeon sweet and sour', a speciality dish.

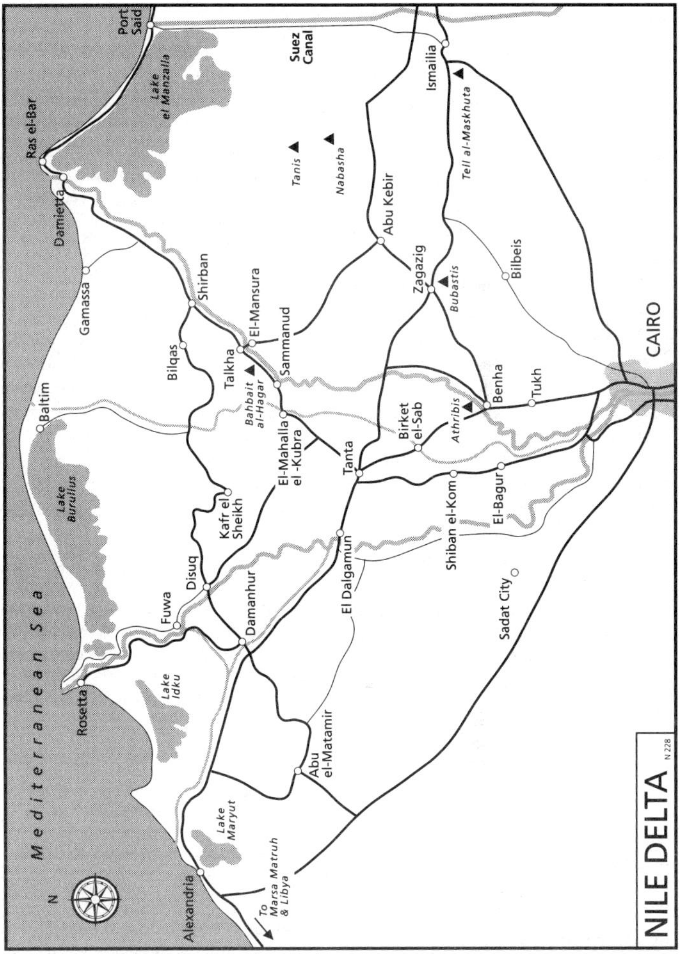

Benha

48 km N of Cairo and the first major town on the H1 highway, can be reached by bus which runs every 30 min from Cairo's Koulali Terminal (0600-2100). Close by lie the remains of the ancient town of **Athribis** which was once the capital of the 10th Nome and associated with the worship of the black bull. Although it pre-dates the Greeks, its greatest importance was during the Roman period. Its orderly layout, like that of many Delta towns, was built around 2 intersecting roads. Little remains of the town today except traces of 18th-26th Dynasty temples and an extensive Greco-Roman cemetery. A cache of 26th-30th Dynasty silver ingots and jewellery from the site is now in the Egyptian Museum in Cairo.

Zagazig

The provincial capital, 36 kms N of Benha and 80 kms from Cairo, was founded in 1830 and was the birthplace of the nationalist Col Ahmed Orabi who led the 1882 revolt against the British. It can be reached by bus or service taxi from Cairo and trains to Port Said stop at the local station. The small **Orabi Museum** (open daily 0900-1300 except Tues) contains some interesting archaeological exhibits. Most visitors stop in Zagazig to see the large ruins of Bubastis which lie 3 km SE of the town.

Bubastis

This was the capital of the 18th Nome of Lower Egypt and was known to the Ancient Egyptians as Pr Baset (House of Baset). The name is derived from the worship of the Egyptian cat goddess Baset who was believed to be the daughter of the sun-god Re. During the Old Kingdom she was originally associated with the destructive forces of his eye and she was symbolized as a lion. Later, during the Middle Kingdom, this image was tamed and she was represented with a brood of kittens and carrying the sacred rattle. The ancient Egyptians worshipped cats and mummified them at a number of sites including Bubastis because they believed that they would be protected by Baset.

The town was begun during the 6th Dynasty (2345-2181 BC) with the granite **Temple of Baset** which was enlarged over the centuries until the 18th Dynasty (1567-1320 BC) and was excavated in the 19th century. Later Herodotus described it as the most pleasing in the whole of Egypt but also criticized the antics of up to 700,000 pilgrims who attended the licentious festivals. Near the site an underground **cat cemetery** can be visited where many statues of Baset have survived.

El-Mansura

About 55 km N of Zagazig, El-Mansura is an attractive Nile city which was founded comparatively recently (1220 AD) by the great Salah al-Din's nephew Sultan al-Kamil (1218-1238 AD) during the Siege of Damietta by the Crusader forces during the 6th Crusade. Despite its name, which means 'the victorious', the Crusaders reoccupied Damietta in 1249 and then, following the death in El-Mansura of Kamil's son Sultan Ayyub (1240-1249), which was concealed by his widow in order not to demoralize his troops, the Crusaders captured the town. However when the Crusaders were weakened by a vicious bout of food poisoning, the Muslims counter-attacked and captured not only El-Mansura but also France's King Louis IX before he was eventually ransomed for the return of Damietta.

• **Accommodation** There are a few cheap and simple hotels in El-Mansura including: **F** *Cleopatra*, 13 Souk Toggar, El-Gharby, T 341234, 44 rm; **F** *Marshal*, Midan Om Malsoum, T 3243890, 57 rm; **F** *Mecca Touristic*, Sharia el-Abbas, Corniche, T 349910, 54 rm, 113 beds; **F** *Abu Sham Hotel*, Sharia Bank Misr, T 354227, 20 rm.

• **Telephone** Local code: 050.

• **Transport Road** There are very frequent **Buses** and **Service taxis** to/from Zagazig and Cairo to the S and Damietta to the N and links to various towns in the E and central Delta.

Tanis

While most travellers from Zagazig head N to El-Mansura, those going E towards the Suez Canal might make a detour to the ruins of an Old Kingdom city better known by its Greek name of **Tanis (Djane)**. It is located near the modern village of San el-Hagar, 167 km from Zagazig, and once lay alongside and got its name from the now dry Tanite branch of the Nile. In the Second Intermediate Period (1786-1567 BC) Asiatic settlers to the region, known as the Hyksos kings or 'princes of foreign lands', established the 15th Dynasty (1674-1567 BC) until they were expelled from Egypt and chased back to Asia by indigenous Theban kings from Luxor.

Until earlier this century it was believed that Tanis was Avaris which was the capital of the Hyksos kingdom but Avaris has now been discovered further to the SW at the modern day site of Tell el-Dab'a. Instead Tanis was the birth place of Ramses I (1320-1318 BC) an ambitious local prince who become pharaoh and founded the 19th Dynasty (see **page 785**.) The area is dotted with ruins, scattered and broken statues and stones which are the only remnants of the **Temple of Amun**. To the S of the temple is the **Royal Necropolis** which is closed to the public.

Tell al-Maskhuta

Another ruined site on the eastern edge of the Delta is **Tell al-Maskhuta** which lies just S of the main Zagazig (70 kms) to Ismailia (11 kms) road. It has been identified as the site of the ancient town of Tjehu which was the capital of the 8th Nome of Lower Egypt and was often known by its Biblical name of Pithom. Archaeological excavations have revealed the foundations of the ancient city, a temple structure and brick chambers for single and multiple burials together with children's bodies buried in amporae. A well preserved sphinx and a statue of Ramses II were also uncovered and are now in a museum in Ismailia.

Damietta

Back near the Nile the easiest way N from El-Mansura is to cross the river to the central Delta town of Talkha and head up the main H8 highway to the coastal town of **Damietta** (or **Dumyat**). It is located on the E bank almost at the mouth of the Damietta branch of the Nile and is 191 km from Cairo, 122 kms from Zagazig and 66 kms from El-Mansura.

The town is in many ways similar to Rosetta, 50 km E of Alexandria (see **page 821**). Indeed Damietta flourished as a trading port throughout the Middle Ages but suffered greatly during the Crusades. The Christian forces occupied the town in 1167-1168 and again in 1218-1221 when St Francis of Assisi accompanied the invaders. Sultan al-Kamil's attempts to recapture it followed. (See El-Mansura, **page 816**). Worse was yet to come, for the Mamlukes destroyed the city in 1250 and made the river impassable as a punishment for suspected disloyalty and to prevent further invasions. The Ottomans revived the town and, as in the case of Rosetta, many of their attractive buildings are still in good condition. The last Ottoman Pasha here surrendered to the Beys in 1801 before the time of Mohamed Ali. Although the construction of the Suez Canal shifted trade to Port Said, 70 kms to the E, Damietta is still a small and successful port although it has little to attract visitors.

What to see Besides its Ottoman buildings there is little to see in Damietta itself. Out of town, however is the huge **Lake el Manzalla** which in winter teems with migrating birds including flamingoes, spoonbills and herons. On the other side of the branch of the Nile there are 3 beach resorts, **Ras el-Bar**, **Gamassa** and **Baltim** which, although technically in the central Delta, are most easily reached from Damietta.

- **Accommodation** The only government registered hotel is **F** *El-Manshi Hotel*, 5 Sharia el-Nokrashy, T 323308, 20 rm, 42 beds but there are a few other cheap hotels along the Corniche.

- **Telephone** Local code: 057

- **Transport Trains** Although they are slower, there are trains to Cairo, Alexandria, Tanta and Zagazig. **Road** There are hourly **buses** and **service taxis** to Cairo either down the main H8 highway via Tanta and Benha or the E route via El-Mansura and Zagazig. Port Said, 70 km E along the causeway which divides the lake from the Mediterranean, is

Moulids – Festivals In The Delta

Officially, *moulids* are festivals in commemoration of a specific saint when pilgrims obtain their *baraka* or blessing by visiting their shrine. There is usually a parade of devotees, carrying banners and dressed in turbans and sashes in the colours of their saint, which is followed by chanting and dancing that goes on for hours. In addition, however, the most important *moulids* are like a giant mediaeval fair where pilgrims meet their friends and eat, drink and have fun together. They stroll amongst the stalls and rides watching the magicians, jugglers, acrobats, snake charmers, animal trainers and other traditional entertainers.

only easily reached by service taxi.

Ras el-Bar

Located on the W bank of the Damietta branch of Nile only a few km N of the city at the point where the river meets the sea. It is a favourite resort for middle-class Egyptians who want to get away from Cairo's summer heat. It can be reached very easily either from Damietta or by special a/c buses direct from Cairo's Koulali bus station or service taxis.

• **Accommodation** There a lots of cheap beach hotels which cater for the Egyptian tourists. They include **E** *Beau Sejour*, 40 Sharia 67, T 528368, 36 rm, 88 beds, despite being more expensive than most of the others this is only graded as a 1 star hotel; **E** *El-Mina Hotel*, end of Sharia 61, El-Shatee, T 529290, 53 rm, 165 beds is the most expensive 2 star hotel in the resort. **F** *Abu Tabl*, 4 Sharia 17, T 528166, 26 rm, 68 beds; **F** *Balboul Hotel*, El-Souk el-Amoumey, T 527420, 20 rm, 54 beds; **F** *El-Madina el-Monawara*, 1 Sharia 29, T 527261, 34 rm, 90 beds; **F** *El-Mobasher*, 1 Sharia 56, T 527097, Tx 63104, 34 rm, 94 beds; **F** *El-Salam*, 6 Sharia 44, First Area, T 528156, 37 rm; **F** *El-Foyer*, 33 Sharia 47, 45 rm, 105 beds; **F** *El-Home*, 4 Sharia 10, T 528015, 56 rm, 111 beds, **F** *El-Mogharbel*, 23 Sharia 51, T 528697, 56 rm, **F** *El-Riad*, 4 Sharia 47, T 5280919, 20 rm; **F** *El-Shatee*, 39 Sharia 63, T 528029, 48 rm; **F** *Marine el-Nil*, 1 Sharia el-Mohafza, T 528006, 49 rm, 96 beds; **F** *Marine Ras el-Bar*, 4 Sharia el-Mohafza, T 528728, 32 rm, 59 beds; **F** *Mira Hotel*, 2 Sharia 33, T 529868, 21 rm.

Gamassa

Further W along the coast about 20 km from Damietta, Gamassa is another quiet and beautiful beach resort. It can be reached, either by bus from Damietta or directly from Cairo. Alternatively catch a train to El-Mansura or Shirban from where a bus can be caught.

• **Accommodation** There are a number of hotels which range from those detailed below to unofficially registered ones with cabin-like chalets. **D** *Amun*, El-Souk area, Gamassa, 82 rm, located on the beach, best in town.

F *Beau Rivage*, Gamassa, T 805268, 56 rm, 172 beds; **F** *Hannoville*, Shagaret el-Dor Area, Gamassa, T 805750, 51 rm.

Baltim

The most inaccessible and quietest of the 3 resorts, is actually about half way between Damietta and Rosetta and, although it can be reached from Damietta it may be easier by direct coach from Cairo.

• **Accommodation** There are two officially registered hotels but neither have many Western visitors and mainly cater for Egyptian summer tourists. **F** *Baltim Beach*, El-Narguess Area, Baltim, T 501541, 30 rm, 52 beds. **F** *Cleopatra Touristic*, Baltim Beach, Baltim, 28 rm, 60 beds.

Central Delta

There are fewer sites in the central Delta but it does include 2 of Egypt's largest cities and has some of the largest annual *moulids*. Assuming that most tourists to the northern beach resorts will probably either travel to Damietta or take special coaches direct from Cairo it is probably best for visitors to the central Delta region to base themselves in the centrally situated, large but charming town of **Tanta**, which has excellent communications, and then from there make day trips to the various sites.

Tanta

This town maintains its rural atmosphere despite being the 5th largest city in Egypt with a major university. It is located 94 km N of Cairo and 130 km SE of Alexandria on the main agricultural route between the 2 cities. The H1 highway from Cairo to Benha crosses the Damietta branch of the Nile and continues NW via Birket el-Sab to Tanta. In late Oct the biggest *moulid* of all, attracting up to 2 million visitors (**see page 818**) is held here.

Things to see Although it is an interesting city, which is worth visiting to soak up the atmosphere of modern life for most Egyptian without the glories of past eras and masses of tourists, there is little or nothing to see in Tanta itself for most of the year. It really comes alive, however, in Oct at the end of the cotton harvest during the 8 day festival or **Moulid of Sayid Ahmed el-Badawi** when the population swells to over 2 million as pilgrims pour in from throughout Egypt and the Muslim world.

Sayid Ahmed el-Badawi (1199-1276 AD) was the founder of one of Egypt's largest Sufi *tariqas* (brotherhoods/orders) which is known as the Badawiya. Born in Fes in Morocco he emigrated to Arabia and then travelled to Iraq where he joined the Rifaiyah brotherhood. He was sent to Tanta in 1234 as its representative but then received permission to establish his own *tariqa* which soon flourished. Although the mosque built by his successor and containing his tomb was demolished in the mid-19th century a large, new, rather undistinguished one was built by pasha Abbas I (1848-1854 AD) and is the focus of Badawi's annual *moulid*.

• **Accommodation** There are few facilities for Western tourists here but, unless you are visiting specifically for the *moulid* when it is essential to book well in advance, there should be no problem in finding a room. Although there are many other small establishments there are only 2 officially registered hotels. **D** *Arafa Hotel*, Midan Station, First Tanta, Tanta, T 336952, F 331800, 43 rm, 79 beds, directly outside the station; **D** *Green House*, Sharia el-Borsa, Midan Gumhorriya, Tanta, T 330761, F 330320, 30 good a/c rm, restaurant, splendid central location, parking, opened 1988, recommended.

• **Youth hostel** Sharia Mahala el Kobra, T 337978, 24 beds, parking.

• **Places to eat** There are numerous **cheap** food stalls during the moulids, otherwise eat at the restaurant in *Green House*, which is clean and comfortable.

El-Mahalla el-Kubra

The 4th largest city in Egypt, is 25 km NE of Tanta and 120 km N of Cairo. The only decent hotel isF *Omar el-Khayyam*, Midan July 23rd, T334866, 36 rm. To the W of the nearby riverside town of **Sammanud** is the remains of the red and black granite **Temple of Onuris-Shu** which was rebuilt by Nectanebo II (360-343 BC) for Tjeboutjes which was the capital of the 12th Nome of Lower Egypt. Further NE some 10 km from Sammanud along the main H8 highway towards **Talkha** there is the modern town of **Bahbait al-Hagar** and what little remains of the great **Temple of Isis** in the ancient town of **Iseum** or **Pr-Hebeit** as it was known to the ancient Egyptians.

Continuing further along the H8 highway 25 km past Talkha, is the town of **Shirban** which has a bridge to the E bank of the Rosetta branch of the Nile. Leaving H8 and travelling 12 km W along H7 is **Bilqas** where, 3 km to the N, is the **Monastery of St Damyanah** (Deir Sitt Damyanah). Normally it is isolated and difficult to reach but during the annual **Moulid of Damyanah** between 15-20 May, which is one of the country's largest Christian *moulids*, thousands of

High Noon At Damyanah – Martyrs' Calendar

Damyanah, who was the daughter of Rome's regional governor in the time of **Diocletian** (284-305 AD), chose celibacy rather than marriage and took refuge with 40 other virgins in a palace built for her by her father. When her father renounced the worship of the Roman gods and converted to Christianity both he and all of the women were executed on the orders of Diocletian. His persecution of the Christians was so great that the Copts date their era, known as the Martyrs' Calendar, from the massacres of 284 AD. The first shrine to Damyanah is believed to have been built by St Helena who was the mother of emperor Constantine (306-337 AD).

pilgrims flock to the four 19th and 20th century churches on the site in the hope of being healed.

The only claim to fame of **El-Bagur**, which lies at the extremity of the central Delta to the S of **Shiban el-Kom**, is that it is President Mubarak's small home town. The only place to stay is E *Nice Tourist Village*, El-Bagur Minufiya, T 384073, 25 rm. Mubarak's predecessor President Anwar Sadat, who was assassinated by Islamic fundamentalists in 1981, came from the nearby village of **Mit Abu el-Kom** which is close to Quweisna on the main Benha-Tanta highway.

- **Telephone** Local code: 040.

- **Transport** The central Delta region is well served by public transport and there are **buses** and **service taxis** between all the major and most of the minor towns. From Tanta there are very frequent services to Cairo and Alexandria while the **train** journeys take 90 min and 2 hrs, respectively. Although they are less frequent there are also train services from Tanta to the other major cities but a service taxi may be easiest given the comparatively short distances.

Western Delta

The main H1 continues on to Alexandria and there are many clean roadside restaurants catering for the weekend travellers – strangely there are more on the N bound carriageway. On the outskirts of Tanta going N try the *Pearl* café (where the waiters wear bow ties) for tea or Turkish coffee and a clean toilet.

Across the wider Rosetta branch of the Nile is the **Western Delta** which has fewer ancient remains than either the E or central Delta. The main attractions are the port of **Rosetta** and a couple of *moulids* held in and around the town of **Damanhur**. This route, like most in the delta, goes through an interesting mixture of scenery: fields of cotton, sugar cane and pocket-sized areas of vegetables, tiny clusters of houses, old fashioned water lifting devices (see delu well, page 625) and the whole area is busy with carts, donkeys, and men and women working in the fields. It is an ever-changing scene of rural Egypt, absolutely fascinating, yet most travellers rush straight on to Alexandria. The taming of the Nile in the late 19th century, changing the water supply from uncontrolled annual flood to perennial irrigation, enables the cultivation of 3 or 4 crops a year in this extremely fertile region.

Damanhur

Mid-way between Tanta and Alexandria, Damanhur lies in the middle of the W Delta, 160 km NW of Cairo. This sleepy provincial capital and textile town, which was once the site of the ancient city of Tmn-Hor dedicated to Horus, normally has nothing to offer the visitor. In Nov, however, there is the **Moulid of Sheikh Abu Rish** which follows the more important one in Tanta. Extending over

2 days in Jan is Egypt's only **Jewish moulid** at the shrine of a 19th century mystic called **Abu Khatzeira**. Because of the security problems, non-Jewish Egyptians are kept out of the festival by the police and most of those who attend are Europeans and Israelis who bring sick relatives or bottled water to be blessed at the shrine.

- **Youth hostel** 9 Sharia el Shaheed Gawad, T 324056, 30 beds, kitchen, station 2 km, overnight fee E£3.

Rosetta

50 km E of Alexandria on the H18, Rosetta (Rashid) is famous for the discovery, in 1799, of the **Rosetta Stone**, which was the key to our understanding of Hieroglyphics and, consequently, much of what we know of Egypt's ancient civilization. The stone is inscribed, in Greek, hieroglyphics and demotic Egyptian with a proclamation by Ptolemy V Epiphanes. Today the stone is in the British Museum in London. Like many towns in Egypt that can claim a flourishing and varied past, there is relatively little to see in Rosetta today. Since ancient times its fortunes have been linked with the ebb and flow of those of it's neighbour Alexandria. When one waxed, the other would wane. Mohamed Ali's Mahmudiya Canal project linking the Nile to Alexandria marked the end of Rosetta's significance as a port. Whilst Alexandria is now Egypt's second city, Rosetta is little more than a fishing village.

The H11 Desert road is a fast dual carriageway and the distance from Cairo to Alexandria (224 km) can be covered easily in 3 hrs. Express coaches of the W Delta Bus Co follow this route (**see page 734**). It is not busy as most drivers begrudge the E£1.5 toll per car. There is plenty of fuel available and accommodation: try the *Sahara Inn Motel* 117 km before Alexandria for a long or a short rest. Agriculture along here is large scale, comprising huge developments of bananas, dates and deciduous trees all dependent on underground water supplies. There is a large new town, **Sadat City**, off the road to the E. Unfortunately the Coptic St Macarius Monastery signed N of Sadat City is no longer open to visitors.

ALEXANDRIA AND THE MEDITERRANEAN COAST

CONTENTS

MAPS

Alexandria (El-Iskandariya), 224 km NW of Cairo, is Egypt's second largest city. It extends 20 kms along Egypt's northern coast at the western edge of the Nile Delta. From Alexandria, the Mediterranean Coast stretches 500 kms W to the Libyan border, passing the city's local beach resorts of El-Agami and Hannoville, the site of the huge WWII battle at El-Alamein, and the new beach resorts of Sidi Abdel Rahman and Marsa Matruh from which a road leads inland to the Siwa oasis, before finally arriving at the Libyan border near Sollum.

FOR DETAILS on El-Agami and Hannoville see **El-Alamein** (page 835) and for the Siwa oasis which is accessible only from the coast see **Marsa Matruh** (page 838).

Alexandria

Population: 3.5 million. *Altitude:* 7m.

History

Having conquered Egypt by 332 BC, **Alexander The Great**, who was then only 25 years old, commissioned his architect Deinocrates to construct a new capital city on the coast. He chose a site near the fishing village of Rhakotis for its natural harbour and its proximity to his native Macedonia, that had significant strategic and commercial advantages over Memphis (near modern-day Cairo). It was the first Egyptian city to be built to the Greek design, with the two major roads running N-S and E-W intersecting in the city centre, and the rest of the town built around them in rectangular blocks, as can be seen in almost any modern North American city. A causeway linking the city to the island of **Pharos** created 2 huge harbours and Alexandria became a major port.

Alexander never saw his city. He travelled to Asia after instructing his architects and 8 years later he was dead. The priests at Memphis refused him burial, so his body was sent to Alexandria instead.

After Alexander's death his whole Empire was divided amongst his various generals. **Ptolemy I Soter** (323-282 BC) started the Ptolemaic Dynasty (323-30

CLIMATE: ALEXANDRIA

	Jan	Feb	Mar	Apr	May	Jun	Jul	Aug	Sep	Oct	Nov	Dec	Av/Tot
Max (°C)	19	20	21	24	27	29	30	31	30	28	25	21	25
Min (°C)	10	10	12	14	17	21	23	24	22	19	16	12	16
Rain (mm)	46	24	13	3	1	0	0	1	1	11	37	51	188

BC) in Egypt, and Alexandria became a major centre of Hellenistic culture, attracting many of the great and good, acquiring significant social, historical, and commercial importance throughout the Graeco-Roman period.

The Greeks integrated well with the Egyptians and created a new hybrid religion known as the cult of Serapis. The Romans, however, were more reserved. The influence of later Ptolemies declined steadily and they relied on the Romans for support. **Cleopatra VII** (51-30 BC), the last of the Ptolemies, seduced first Julius Caesar and then his successor Mark Anthony in order to retain her crown. Mark Anthony and Cleopatra held sway in Egypt for 14 years until they were deposed by Octavian who became the Emperor Augustus.

Tradition has it that the Gospel was first preached in Alexandria by Saint Mark in 62 AD. Whatever the accuracy of this date, **Christianity** was certainly established around this time and Alexandria remained the centre of its theology for 3 centuries. However, its presence was still sufficiently threatening to the Muslim conquerors 3 centuries later to make them move their administration and theological capital inland to Cairo. Although Alexandria was still important as a centre of trade it's decline as a city was inevitable when the power base, along with the customary baggage of wealth, learning and culture went S.

With the 16th century discovery of America and the sea route around Africa to India and the Orient, which made the land route via Egypt virtually redundant, Alexandria lost its former magnificence. The decline during the Ottoman period was so great that while Cairo continued to flourish, the population of Alexandria fell to a mere 5,000 people by 1800.

Just in time, a saviour was found in the shape of **Mohamed (Mehmet) Ali** (1805-48). He organized the construction of the **El-Mahmudiya Canal** starting in 1819 and linked the Nile and Alexandria's W harbour, reconnecting the city with the rest of Egypt, whilst simultaneously irrigating the surround-

SEEING THE LIGHT – ANCIENT ALEXANDRIA

The Mouseion, from which the word *museum* is derived, meaning Temple of the Muses, was a vast centre of learning standing at the main crossroads of the city. As well as laboratories, lodgings and a refectory for hundreds of scholars, it housed the famous library which by Caesar's day contained nearly a million papyrus volumes. Tragically, it was sacked and burned by Christian mobs in the 7th century AD. Recently, however, the international community has pledged US$64 million to build a new one and the phoenix of the Alexandrine Library is scheduled to rise gloriously from its ashes sometime in 1995.

The Lighthouse of Pharos The fire from this immense lighthouse could be seen from 55 km across the open sea. It was 135 m high and stood at the mouth of the E harbour where Sultan Qaitbai's fort now stands. It was still in use at the time of the Muslim invasion over 900 years after its construction. The idea for the lighthouse may have come from Alexander the Great but it was actually built in 279 BC by Sostratus, an Asiatic Greek, during the reign of Ptolemy II (284-246 BC). According to popular myth an immense mirror lens made it possible to view ships far out at sea while the fuel to feed the fire is said to have been hydraulically lifted to the top of the lighthouse. The great earthquakes of 1100 and 1307 destroyed the ancient foundations and the stones lay abandoned until the Ottoman Sultan Qaitbai decided to build the fort on the site in 1479 AD.

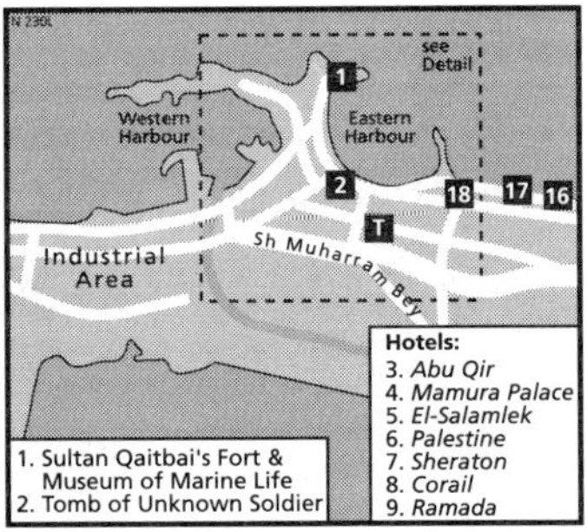

ing land, which had been badly neglected. With a trade route open, the city prospered once more and now it is only surpassed by Cairo itself. Foreign trade grew at a pace with the Egyptian merchant fleet and was later maintained by the British. Being further N and nearer to the sea, the city is cooler than Cairo in summer and each year the administration moved to the coast during this hot season. The British invested in many building projects including, true to the Victorian obsession, a sea-front promenade. If you half close your eyes, and use a bit of imagination, you could be in an English sea-side resort!

Population growth and industrialization have altered Alexandria since **Nasser's** revolution (see **History of Egypt, page 695**) in 1952. Today it is a modern city with much to recommend it. Although the outer areas have suffered from too rapid rural-urban migration, the busy central area is small enough for the visitor to walk around and become familiar with the main squares and landmarks. Having the coast to the N makes orientation easy. Although Alexandria's opulent heritage is no longer so obvious, the atmosphere of the town which inspired such literary classics as Durrell's *Alexandria Quartet* still remains.

Alexandria is a thin ribbon-like city which is 20 km long but only a few km wide because the residential areas are still largely bound by the El-Mahmudiya canal. At the city's W end is the El-Anfushi peninsula which now links the mainland and the former island of Pharos and divides the giant functional W harbour and the beautiful sweeping curve of the E harbour and its Corniche. To the E is a series of beaches which stretch to the Montazah Palace and on to Ma'mura beach and eventually Abu Qir which was the site of Nelson's 1798 victory over the French fleet. The city's main downtown area, its main transport terminals and many of the hotels are in the blocks around Midan Sa'ad Zaghloul in El-Manshiya which is in the W end of the city just inland from the E harbour.

ACCESS The airport is about 10 km from the town centre which is reached by bus No 307 or No 310 to Midan Orabi or No 203 to the nearby Midan Sa'ad Zaghloul. Inter-city buses to Alexandria stop in the heart of the downtown area in Midan Sa'ad Zaghloul while buses from the Delta towns sometimes stop 1 km further S at the huge Midan El-Gumhorriya outside the main Masr railway station. Service taxis stop at either of the two squares or at Midan Orabi which is 750m W of Midan Sa'ad Zaghloul. Traffic flow directions change on the Corniche depending on the time and the day. Follow police instructions.

Things to see

Historical remains in Alexandria today are such pale shadows of their former glories, chief amongst which were the **Mouseion** and the **Lighthouse of Pharos**, one of **the seven wonders of the ancient world**. For a city with such a magnificent past history there is, unlike Cairo, comparatively little to see today because the modern city overlies the ancient one. Most visitors come to Alexandria for its Mediterranean beaches and cool and cosmopolitan atmosphere.

The description of places of interest begins in Central Alexandria at the harbour and works S and E.

Sultan Qaitbai's Fort, built in 1479 by Sultan Qaitbai (1468-1496 AD) on the

ancient site of, and probably with the stones of, the Lighthouse of Pharos stands at the far end of the E harbour as one of a series of coastal forts. It is one of the city's major landmarks and is now the property of the Egyptian Navy. The keep houses a small mosque which, unusually for the Delta region, is built in the shape of a cross. The fort's greatest attraction is the view from the battlements back over the open sea toward Alexandria. It can be reached from downtown Alexandria by taking the No 15 tram from Raml tram station. Open Sat-Thur 0900-1600, Fri 0900-1200 and 1400-1600, Ramadan daily 1000-1430. Entrance E£6, students E£3, camera E£10 and video camera E£50. Its **Naval Museum** contains artifacts from Roman and Napoleonic sea battles which are likely to appeal more to specialists than to the casual tourist.

The **Marine Life Museum** and Hydro-Biological Institute near Sultan Qaitbai's Fort on Anfushi Bay houses a rare collection of fish and marine life. Open daily 0900-1600.

The **Fish Market** further W on Anfushi Bay is easy to find, just follow your nose. Go early to see this small area teeming with fish and people.

The **Anfushi Tombs**, (open daily 0900-1600, Fri 0900-1130 and 1300-1600, entrance as above) are located to the W of the fort near the sweep of the small Anfushi Bay. The necropolis' chambers which are cut into the limestone date from 250 BC with some later Roman additions. The entrance passage forks at the bottom of the steps into 2 main chambers. The main hall, from which a multitude of smaller chambers branch off, is decorated with stucco resembling marble tiles. Some of the chambers are very spacious with high, decorated ceilings and benches where you can rest to contemplate the surroundings which vary in design from mythological ornamentation to the immortalized doodling of Greek workmen from the 3rd century before Christ.

Further W along the peninsula are formal gardens and then **Ras el-Tin's Palace** (Cape of Figs Palace) which overlooks the W harbour but which is now the Admiralty Headquarters and is unfortunately closed to the public. It was built so that Mohamed Ali (1805-1848) could review his fleet and was reconstructed in the European Turkish style by Fouad I (1917-1936) to serve as the government's summer seat. It was therefore ironic that his son King Farouk signed his abdication at the palace on 26 July 1952 before boarding a yacht bound for exile in Italy.

Inland from the peninsula towards the city centre is the old Ottoman area of Anfushi and some of the most important mosques including the **Mosque of Abu al-Abbas al-Mursi** N off Sharia Ras el Tin. Ahmed Abu al-Abbas al-Mursi (1219-1287) was an Andalusian who came to Alexandria to join and eventu-

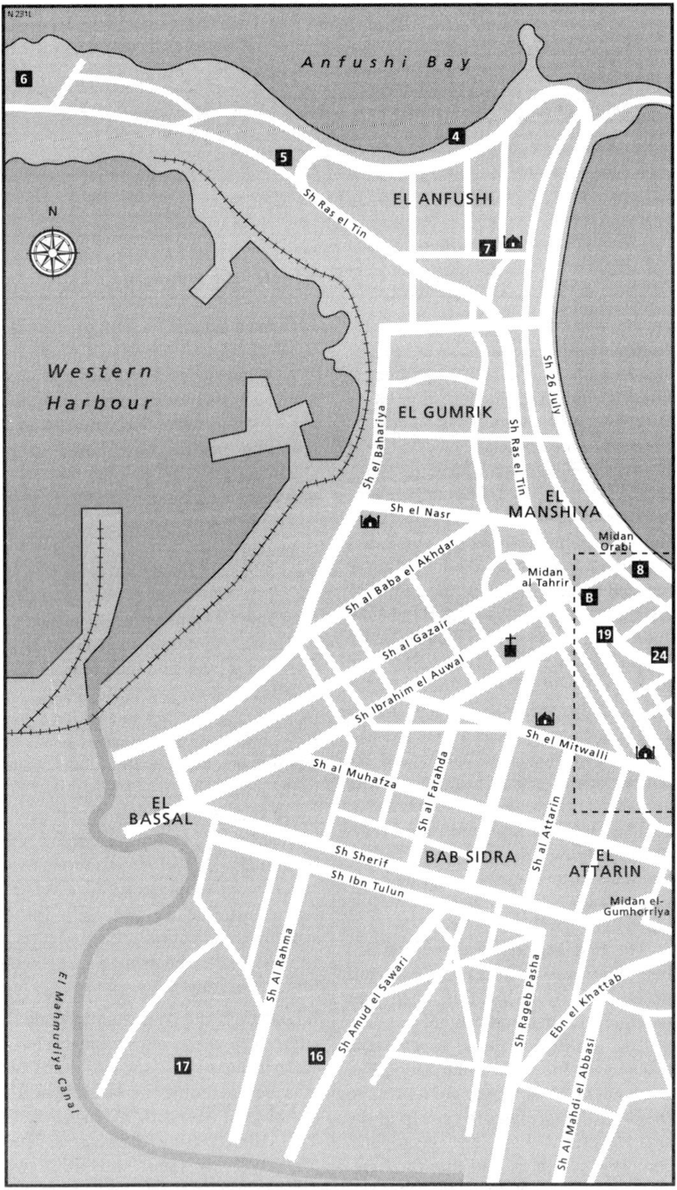

Anfushi Bay
6
4
5
EL ANFUSHI
Sh Ras el Tin
7
N
Western Harbour
Sh 26 July
EL GUMRIK
Sh el Bahariya
Sh Ras el Tin
EL MANSHIYA
Sh el Nasr
Midan Orabi
Sh al Baba el Akhdar
Midan al Tahrir
8
B
19
24
Sh al Gazair
Sh Ibrahim el Auwal
Sh el Mitwalli
Sh al Muhafza
Sh al Farahda
EL BASSAL
Sh al Attarin
Sh Sherif
BAB SIDRA
EL ATTARIN
Sh Ibn Tulun
Midan el-Gumhorriya
Sh Al Rahma
Sh Amud el Sawari
Sh Rageb Pasha
Ebn el Khattab
Sh Al Mahdi el Abbasi
El Mahmudiya Canal
17
16

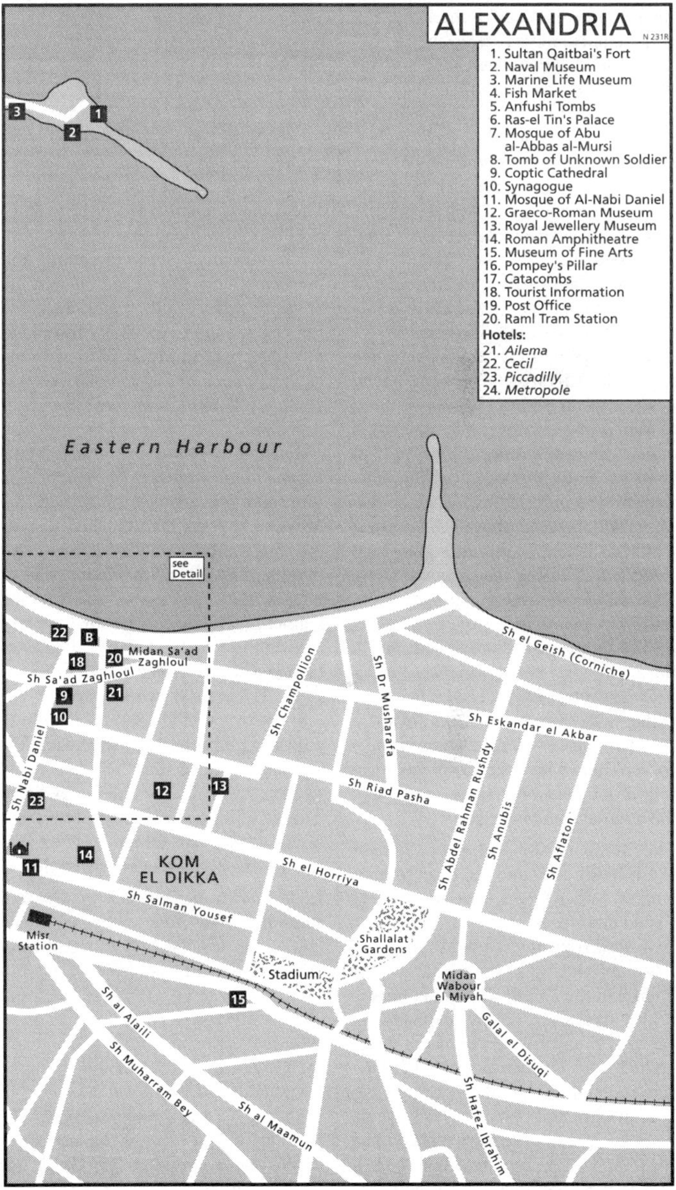
ALEXANDRIA
N 231R
1. Sultan Qaitbai's Fort
2. Naval Museum
3. Marine Life Museum
4. Fish Market
5. Anfushi Tombs
6. Ras-el Tin's Palace
7. Mosque of Abu al-Abbas al-Mursi
8. Tomb of Unknown Soldier
9. Coptic Cathedral
10. Synagogue
11. Mosque of Al-Nabi Daniel
12. Graeco-Roman Museum
13. Royal Jewellery Museum
14. Roman Amphitheatre
15. Museum of Fine Arts
16. Pompey's Pillar
17. Catacombs
18. Tourist Information
19. Post Office
20. Raml Tram Station
Hotels:
21. *Ailema*
22. *Cecil*
23. *Piccadilly*
24. *Metropole*
Eastern Harbour
see Detail
Midan Sa'ad Zaghloul
Sh Sa'ad Zaghloul
Sh el Geish (Corniche)
Sh Champollion
Sh Dr Musharafa
Sh Eskandar el Akbar
Sh Nabi Daniel
Sh Riad Pasha
Sh Abdel Rahman Rushdy
Sh Anubis
Sh Aflaton
KOM EL DIKKA
Sh el Horriya
Sh Salman Yousef
Misr Station
Shallalat Gardens
Stadium
Midan Wabour el Miyah
Galal el Disuqi
Sh al Alaili
Sh Muharram Bey
Sh al Maamun
Sh Hafez Ibrahim

ally lead the Shadhali brotherhood. His mosque and tomb were renovated in 1775 by a rich Maghrebi merchant but was then demolished and rebuilt in 1943. The current layout is octagonal with Italian granite supporting the roof arches, 4 decorated domes and the slender 73m minaret rising in tiers which gives the modern mosque a pleasing weightless aspect. This is one of Alexandria's foremost religious buildings and is well worth a visit but visitors are advized that women are only permitted entry into a room at the back of the mosque.

Further S in this Ottoman part of the city is the **Al-Tarbana Mosque** which is situated on Sharia Farnasa to the E of Sharia al- Shahid. It has undergone major alterations since it was built in 1685 by Hajji Ibrahim Tarbana. The minaret is supported by 2 antique columns which stand above the entrance whilst a further 8 columns support the ornamental ceiling. The original Delta style façade is almost completely obscured by plastering.

The **Ibrahim al-Shurbaji Mosque**, to the E of Sharia al-Maydan, was built in 1757. The internal layout is similar to that of the Al-Tarbana Mosque. A courtyard to the rear creates a pleasant impression of space. There have been many modifications, but the *mihrab* is still decorated with the original Kufic inscriptions.

The **Tomb of the Unknown Soldier**, about half way round the Eastern Harbour on Midan Obari, is worth noting as a good landmark.

Turn S from the sea to Midan Sa'ad Zaghloul and walk down Sharia Nabi Daniel to the **Coptic Orthodox Cathedral**. This is a very recent establishment (1950-87) and presented as a large arched vault is a fine example of ecclesiastical architecture. It is dedicated to 5 saints, in particular St Mark whose head is reputed to be buried at this site together with the remains of early patriarches of the Egyptian church including St Menas, see page 837. A sunken chapel beyond an interesting recent mosaic of incidents in the life of St Mark gives access to their tombs. Entry welcome – leave a small donation. Nearby at 69 Sharia Nabi Daniel is the main **Synagogue**, over 145 years old. The previous building was destroyed by Napoleon. The synagogue which serves the remaining 90-100 Jews who live in Alexandria is not normally open to the public and the security guards are quite off-putting: but with gentle, polite persistence one can get through to the lady curator and into the ornate building. Ask to see some of the 50 ancient 500 to 1000 year old Torah scrolls held in worked silver cases in the arc.

Further S down the street is the French Cultural Centre where the Mouseion once stood and then the **Mosque al-Nabi Daniel** which is near the main Masr railway station. Although popular myth claims that it houses the remains of the prophet Daniel it actually contains the tomb of a venerated Sufi sheikh called Mohamed Danyal al-Maridi who died in 1497. Excavation works around the tomb have revealed another tomb from a 10th or 12th century Muslim cemetery and also revealed that the site is likely to have been that of the Great Soma Temple which was erected over the tomb of **Alexander the Great**. New excavations of the crypt area are scheduled.

In downtown Alexandria is the **Graeco-Roman Museum**, (open daily 0900-1600, Fri 0900-1130 and 1330-1600, during Ramadan daily 0900-1500, entrance E£8), in Sharia Amin Fikri and Tariq Abdel Nasser. It contains an interesting collection of around 40,000 items, mainly taken from local tombs dating from about 300 BC to AD 300, of relics from the Graeco-Roman period. The most significant cult was that of Serapis which was a hybrid of the Greek god Dionysus and the Nile god Osiris. The

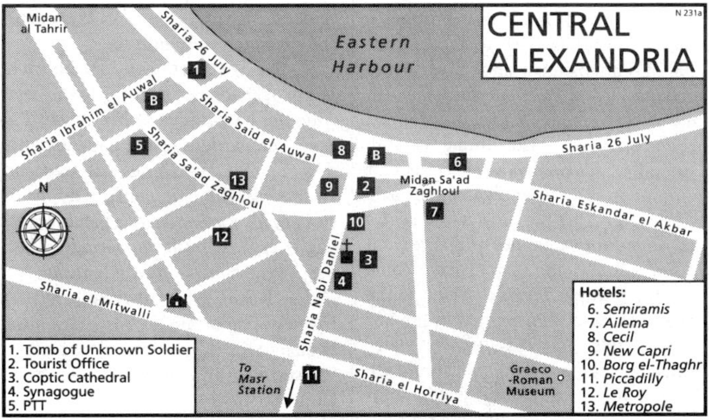

Serapis was depicted as a bull and is directly associated with the ancient Egyptian cult of the Apis bull. There is a number of well preserved mummies of which the 2 most interesting are a crocodile from the Roman Sobek cult and a human mummy with a cross on its neck which was found in Fayoum. The exhibits in the other rooms are mostly statues or busts of Roman emperors including excellent busts of Julius Caesar and Augustus. Also on display is a number of smaller objects including a collection of Christian antiques, coins, figurines and lamps in the shape of the Pharos Lighthouse.

Royal Jewellery Museum, 21 Sharia Ahmed Yehia Pasha, Gleem, T 5868348, (behind the Governor's residence), houses a glittering collection of treasures from the time of Mohamed Ali through to King Farouk. The mansion in which these are housed is almost of equal interest. Lift your eyes from the jewels to admire the ceilings. Open daily 1900-1600, Fri 0900-1130 and 1330-1600, entrance E£10.

Cavafy Museum, 63 Sharia Alexander the Great, Ahzarita (in Greek Consulate) has a collection of books, manuscripts and household furniture once belonging to the Greek Alexandrian poet. Open 1000-1300, entrance free.

To the E of the mosque and to the N of the Misr railway station is the Kom al-Dikkah (Hill of Rubble), thought to be the ancient site of the Paneion ('Park of Pan', a hilly pleasure garden), which has been excavated since 1959. Instead a small semi-circular 700-800 seat **Roman Amphitheatre**, (open Sat-Thur 0900-1600, Fri 0900-1130 and 1330-1600, Ramadan daily 0900-1500, entrance E£6), was discovered with 12 rows of marble seats focussing on a columned stage which still has the remains of its mosaic flooring. A **residential quarter** with Roman baths is being excavated to the N. The site is one of the few in Alexandria to indicate the wealth of the city's heritage and it is well worth a visit. An annex of the Graeco-Roman Museum displays local discoveries.

Fine Art Museum, (open 0900-1300 and 1700-2000, closed Tue, entrance free) is located at 18 Sharia Menasce. On the ground floor there is a permanent exhibition of 20th century Egyptian painting while the upper floor is dedicated to temporary exhibitions which are generally of modern Egyptian art. Film club meets here every Wed.

Further SE on the way to the El-Mahmudiya Canal and Lake Maryut in an area of cheap markets is **Pompey's Pillar** (open daily 0900-1600, closes at 1500 in Ramadan, entrance E£6), just to the E of Sharia al-Rahman which is a 27m high column of red Aswan granite topped by an impressive Corinthian capital. This pillar, Alexandria's tallest ancient monument, is a rather bizarre spectacle and its origins are the subject of speculation. It certainly does not originate from Pompey and is thought to have come from the **Sarupis Temple** (40 km to the W) and to have been erected in honour of **Diocletian** (AD 284-305). Extensive archaeological excavations surround the site. See the 3 sphinxes and some underground cisterns to the W of the ridge.

Nearby in an area where many of the houses are 120-200 years old are the **Catacombs of Kom el-Shoquafa** (Mounds of Shards), (open daily 0900-1600, closes 1500 in Ramadan, entrance E£6 plus E£10 for camera), originally 2nd century private tombs which were later extended in order to serve the whole community. They have been extensively excavated since their rediscovery in 1900 but sadly, water has flooded the lowest level and caused some deterioration. A large spiral staircase serves as the entrance to the tombs, below which passages lead to interconnecting tomb shafts. Immediately to the left of the entrance is a corridor leading to the more recent tombs. The main passage from the stairwell runs into a large rotunda with a domed roof. Branching from this is a banqueting hall for those visiting the deceased! A burial chamber leads off the rotunda opposite the dining area. Within the chamber are many niches in which one or more bodies were sealed. A fourth passage leads to another stairway from which further ornate chambers branch off. In places red paint can be found below the niches bearing the name of those encased within. The eerie atmosphere is intensified by the ornate serpents and medusa heads that lurk above doorways and passage entrances. Also on the site is a **Hypogeum** containing over 30 murals.

To the E of downtown Alexandria lie 17 km of beaches stretching to the beautiful 140 ha gardens of **Montazah Palace**, (see gardens, page 830) which is now a state guesthouse. It was constructed in the 19th century by the visionary Mohamed Ali as a palace for the engineers who built the barrages which are so important for the irrigation of the Delta. It was later inhabited by King Farouk. The original construction had been halted, and was completed later in the century, on a grander scale, by Sir Colin Scott-Moncrieff.

Further to the E and 5 kms along Ma'mura Bay is **Canopus** which bears few traces of the Delta's chief port which flourished before the development of Alexandria. The motivation for building a city in the area was the Canopic branch of the Nile which has long since dried up. The city is claimed to have been built by Menalaeus' pilot Canopus on his return from the Trojan wars who was venerated by the local population after his death from snakebite. Today little remains of the site. The destruction is a recent phenomenon, apparently mainly caused by British occupation during WWI and WWII. The ancient remains which have survived, including several statues of Ramses II, are now in the Graeco-Roman Museum in Alexandria. Two abandoned forts to the E of Canopus can be explored.

Gardens

The **Montazah Palace Gardens** cover almost 160 ha. A welcome respite from the bustle of the city. Open 24 hrs, entrance E£4. **Nouzha Gardens and Zoo**, Sharia Smouha, Smouha has many interesting birds and animals in the zoo. Adjacent gardens have picnic areas. Entrance to zoo 15pt and gardens 15pt. Both open daily 0800-1600. The **Antoniadis Gardens** are near the El-Mahmudiya Canal and the zoo. Well maintained gardens and walkways, several Greek statues, open daily 0800-1600, entrance 25pt. **Shallalat Gardens** to E of city centre, varying levels, waterways, lovely.

The Yacht Club beside Qaitbai's Fort hires boats, so why not end your tour of Alexandria by seeing it from the sea?

Local information

● Accommodation

Price guide:			
AL	US$90+	D	US$20-40
A	US$75-90	E	US$10-20
B	US$60-75	F	under US$10
C	US$40-60		

Alexandria is Egypt's second largest city and the major domestic resort for Egyptian tourists and has hotels to suit every taste. Besides the main downtown hotels there are others E along the coast to the exclusive El-Montazah area and beyond. **Note** that all hotels on the Corniche suffer from traffic noise – day and night. They include but are not limited to the following officially registered hotels:

AL ***Palestine***, Montazah Palace, El-Montazah, T 5474033, F 5473378, 210 rm, located in the grounds of the Montazah Palace with a lagoon, beautiful gardens and an excellent beach nearby, E£250 for double rm, no breakfast; **AL** ***Pullman Cecil***, 16 Midan Sa'ad Zaghloul, T 4837173, F 4836401, 86 rm, 158 beds, guests have included Churchill, Noel Coward and Lawrence Durrell, located in town centre, close to the E harbour, 5 restaurants and casino 2000-0400; **AL** ***Montazah Sheraton***, Corniche, El-Montazah, T 5480550, F 872848, 305 rm, 570 beds, probably the best in Alexandria, located outside the grounds of the walled Montazah Palace, with excellent sea-views, private beach; **AL** ***Ramada Renaissance***, 544 Sharia el-Geish, Sidi Bishr, T 5490935, F 5497690, 29 suites and 150 very comfortable double rm, located on coast road 12-15 kms from town centre, try excellent restaurant with panoramic view of the Mediterranean.

A ***Plaza***, 394 Sharia el-Geish, Zizinia, T 5862723, F 5875399, 180 rm, 276 beds, good standard, modern, sea view; **A** ***Pullman Romance Egotel***, Sharia el-Geish, Saba Pasha, T 5876804, F 5870526, 64 rm.

B ***El-Salamlek San Giovanni***, Montazah Palace, T 860585, F 5464408, 33 rm, 110 beds, built like an Alpine chalet for the Khedive's Austrian mistress, currently being renovated, E£150 double rm with breakfast; **B** ***Landmark***, 163 Sharia Abdel Salam Aref, San Stefano, T 5877850, F 5869470, 150 rm, 211 beds, located about half way between downtown Alexandria and the Montazah Palace.

C ***Alexandria***, 23 Midan El-Nasr, El-Manshiya, T 801041, F 4823113, 108 rm, 179 beds, family run downtown hotel with good personal service; **C** ***Delta***, 14 Sharia Champollion, Mazarita, T 4829053, F 4825630, 63 rm; **C** ***Desert Home***, Sharia Omar el-Mokhtar, King Mariout, T 981315, F 4914939, 14 rm, cosy; **C** ***Ma'mura Palace***, El-Ma'mura, T 5473108, 80 rm, 180 beds, good standard, modern, good views, located in the exclusive El-Ma'mura area to the E of the Montazah Palace; **C** ***Mecca***, 44 Sharia el-Geish, Camp Caesar, T 5973925, F 5969935, 120 rm, 270 beds; **C** ***San Giovanni***, 205 Sharia el-Geish, Stanley, T 5467774, F 5464408, 30 rm, 55 beds, beach hotel located about half way between downtown Alexandria and the Montazah Palace; **C** ***Venezia***, 21 Sharia el-Nasr, El-Manshiya, T 802322, F 4824664, 120 rm, good value for money.

D ***Amun***, 32 Midan el-Nasr, El-Manshiya, T 807131, 120 rm; **D** ***Metropole***, 52 Sharia Sa'ad Zaghloul, Raml Station, T 4821466, F 4822040, 82 rm, all with phones and TV, 120 beds, worth staying for the wonderful Art Deco and Art Nouveau decor; **D** ***New Swiss Cottage***, 346 Sharia el-Geish, Gleem, T 5875830, on coast road about halfway between downtown Alexandria and the Montazah Palace, next door to the original *Swiss Cottage*; **D** ***San Stefano***, Sharia Abdel Salam Aref, San Stefano, T 5863587, F 5865935, 120 rm, on beach; **D** ***Semiramis***, 80 Sharia el-Geish, Raml Station, T 4830824, 64 rm, many with sea view, roof-top restaurant.

E ***Deauville***, 274 Sharia el-Geish, Stanley, T 5454804, F 5454806, 41 rm, 96 beds, on beach; **E** ***King Mariout***, Sharia Pharaana, PO 3058, El-Manshiya, King Mariout, T 981424, F 980293, 26 rm.

F ***Abu Qir***, 30 Sharia Gawhar el-Kaed, Abu Qir, T 865000, 30 rm, 66 beds, on Abu Qir bay; **F** ***Admiral***, 24 Sharia Amin Fikri, Raml Station, T 4831787, 68 rm, 120 beds, generally clean, some rm with bath, good value, breakfast included; **F** ***Ailema***, 21 Sharia Amin Fikri, Raml Station, T 4837011, 38 rm, rather faded Greek-run downtown hotel; **F** ***Borg el-***

Thaghr, Sharia Safeya Zaghloul, Raml Station, T 4924519, 33 rm, 69 beds; **F *Cleopatra***, 160 Sharia el-Geish, Cleopatra, T 852409, 60 rm, on beach at Cleopatra bay; **F *Corail***, 802 Sharia el-Geish, El-Mandara, T 5480996, 28 rm, 52 beds, beach hotel just to W of Montazah Palace; **F *Dubai***, 13 Sharia Hehia, Camp Caesar, T 5961139, 50 rm, 113 beds, on beach; **F *El-Mehrek***, 133 Sharia el-Geish, Sporting, T 854513, 99 rm, just N of the Alexandria Sporting Club; **F *Holiday***, 6 Midan Orabi, El-Manshiya, T 8014559, 44 rm, 80 beds, comfortable; **F *Hyde Park House***, 21 Sharia Amin Fikri, Raml Station, T 4835667, 58 rm, 119 beds, rather run down, one floor above the *Ailema hotel*; **F *Jeddah***, 137 Sharia el-Geish, Sporting, T 857643, 69 rm, 125 beds, just N of the Alexandria Sporting Club; **F *Le Roy***, 25 Sharia Talaat Harb, Raml Station, T 4833439, 65 rm, rather shabby, a shadow of its former Art Deco self; **F *New Capri***, 23 El-Mina, Sharia el-Sharkia, Raml Station, T 809310, 32 rm, downtown hotel located in tourist police building, reportedly unsympathetic management; **F *Philip***, 236 Sharia July 26th, Mazarita, T 4829620, 27 rm, overlooking E harbour; **F *Piccadilly***, 11 Sharia el-Horriya, El-Nabi Daniel, 32 rm, 60 beds, a 6th floor cheap hotel; near the railway station; **F *Union***, 164 Sharia July 26th, Raml Station, T 807771, 36 rm, good standard, clean, located in town centre on the Corniche, avoid the 6th floor disco by getting a rm on the 4th floor; As a cheaper alternative a group of visitors can hire an apartment from Menatours in Ma'mura beach to the E of the Montazah Palace.

● Youth hostel

32 Sharia Port Said, Shatbi, Raml, T/F 5975459, 2km NE of city centre, 200 beds, meals available, train 3 km, ferry 5 km, overnight fee E£5.

● Camping

At Sharia Bahr al-Mait in Abu Qir which is about 20 km from downtown Alexandria about 5 km E of the Montazah Palace.

● Places to eat

For the greatest concentration of restaurants and cafés, try the area bounded by Sharia Sa'ad Zaghloul, Raml station and E Harbour by Midan Sa'ad Zaghloul. The restaurants in the higher grade hotels are reliable and serve Western and Egyptian cuisine.

Price guide:
♦♦♦Expensive; ♦♦average; ♦cheap.

♦♦♦***Alexander's*** at the *Ramada Renaissance*, 544 Sharia el-Geish, Sidi Bishr, T 866111, elegant service, excellent fish food, has a panoramic view of the Mediterranean; ***Santa Lucia*** T 4824240, 40 Sharia Safeya Zaghloul, excellent seafood, serves wine and beer, open 1200-1600 and 1900-0100; ***San Giovanni***, on Corniche in Stanley, excellent fish, sea views, from E£30 per head.

♦♦ ***Tikka Grill*** T 805119, near Al-Mursi's Mosque, views overlooking E Harbour, beautifully served, spicy Indian food, salad bar, open 1300-1700 and 2000-0200, from E£40 per head; ***New China Restaurant*** in *Corail Hotel*, T 5470996, 802 Sharia el- Geish, Chinese food, spicy shrimps and beef served in lovely setting, alcohol, open 1200-1600 and1800-2300; ***Elite*** 43 Sharia Safeya Zaghloul, T 4823592, opposite *Santa Lucia*, large helpings, alcohol, open 0900-2400; ***Denise*** Sharia Ibn Bassam, off Raml tram station, T 4830457, select your own fish from the freezer, alcohol, open 0900-0100; ***Seagull***, Sharia el Agami, T 4455575, highly recommended but way out of town to W in industrial area.

♦***Cafeteria Asteria*** T 4822293, next door to *Santa Lucia* in Sharia Safeya Zaghloul, serves a range of tasty, cheap meals, open until 2400; ***La Pizzeria*** T 4838082, 14 Sharia el-Horriya, filling rather than fancy; ***Taverna Restaurants*** T 4928189 at Raml station, Greek owned tasty fish dishes and pizzas with salad bar, open 0730-0200, recommended; ***Fuul Mohamed Ahmed*** T 4833576, a block E of Midan Sa'ad Zaghloul, beyond Bank of Alexandria and a block S of Sharia Safeya Zaghloul, very cheap, very tasty, open 0600-2400. For those lacking in initiative there are 3 Kentucky Fried Chicken and 2 Pizza Huts.

● Coffee Houses

Coffee, 24 hr service in better hotels including *Sheraton*, *Ramada Renaissance*, *Plaza*, *Landmark* and *San Giovanni*. Good atmosphere at *Cecil Hotel* by bus station, minimum charge E£8 per person, mouthwatering pastries;. ***Trianon***, T 4828539, E end of Midan Sa'ad Zaghloul by station under *Hotel Metropole*, elegant, pricey, excellent coffee; ***Délices***, T 4825657, 46 Sa'ad Zaghloul, faded charm; ***Pastroudis***, T 4929609, 39 Sharia el-Horriya behind Roman amphitheatre, enjoy the atmosphere, watch the crowds and try the excellent cakes; ***Athineos*** by the station, classical decor, gets noisy in the evenings; ***Brazilian Coffee Shop*** by the Tourist Office on

Sharia Sa'ad Zaghloul, open 6300-1500, excellent coffee and pastries.

● **Banks**

There are branches of most domestic banks. The downtown branches of **Bank of Alexandria**, 1 Sharia Mahmoud Azmy, 59 Sharia Sa'ad Zaghloul and 6 Sharia Salah Salam are open Sun-Thur 0830-1400 and 1030-1300 during Ramadan. **Bank Misr**, 9 & 18 Sharia Talaat Harb, T 807429 & 807031 and *Pullman Cecil*; **Banque du Caire**, 16 Sharia Sisostris and 5 Sharia Salah Salam. Foreign banks include **Bank of America**, T 4921257 on Sharia Lomomba, **Chase Manhattan**, 19 Sharia Dr Ibrahim Abdel el-Said; **Citibank**, T 806376, 95 Sharia 26th July; and **Barclays**, T 4921307 at 10 Sharia Fawoteur, takes all Visas and Mastercard, as well as money changing outlets in most of the major hotels.

● **Bookshops**

Book Centre, Sharia Sa'ad Zaghloul, has best choice of books in English, French and German; Dar el-Mostakbal 32 Sharia Safeya Zaghloul, books and magazines in English, French and German; Al-Ahram 10 Sharia el-Horriya; ***Nile Christian Bookshop***, 4 Sharia Anglican Church, Attarine; ***Book Bazaar*** in *Ramada Renaissance* open 0900-2300 daily.

● **Chemist**

Open late, Khalid near bus station in Sharia Sa'ad Zaghloul, T 800772.

● **Consulates**

France, 2 Midan Orabi, T 807518, Sun-Thur 0900-1400; **Germany**, 5 Sharia Kafr Abdu, Roushdi T 845443; **Netherlands**, 35 Sharia el-Shaheed Salah Mustafa, T 4823999; **Spain**, 101 Sharia el Horriya, T 4838346; **Sudan**, Silsila Bldg, Sharia 26th July, Azharita, T 483920; **Switzerland**, 8 Sharia Mokhtar Adbel-Hamid Khalifa, T 5872978; **UK**, 3 Mena Kafr Abdu, Roushdi, T 847166, open Sun-Thur 0800-1300; **USA**, 110-111 Sharia el-Horriya, T 4821911, Sun-Thur 0900-1200. Please note Libyan consulate is for Arab nations only.

● **Emergency**

Ambulance, T 123; **Fire**, T 180; **Tourist police**, T 807611; **Police**, T 122.

● **Hospital**

Sharia el-Horriya, T 4212886 or the *Medical Care Advisory Team 97 Sharia Abdel Salam Aref*, Glym Beach, T 5862323; *Italian Hospital*, El-Hadarah, T 4921459; *Coptic Hospital*, Moharam Bey, T 4921404.

● **Nightclubs**

Most of the large hotels have some evening entertainment, though not with the style of the capital. Try ***El-Phanar*** at the *Montazah Sheraton Hotel* open 2230-0300 except Mon; ***Dolphin Night Club*** at *Palestine Hotel* open 2200-0330; ***Palace Suite*** at the *Plaza Hotel* open 2200-0430; ***Queen's Hall Night Club*** in the *San Giovanni Hotel*; ***Monte Carlo***, 34 Sharia el Geish or ***Crazy Horse***, Midan Sa'ad Zaghloul.

● **Passport Office**

28 Sharia Talaat Harb, T 4824366, for registering arrival and renewing visas, open Sat-Thur 0830-1400, Fri 1000-1300 and 1900-2100.

● **Police – Tourist**

On Midan Sa'ad Zaghloul, T 5473814 and in grounds of Montazah Palace, T 863804.

● **Post office**

Open daily 0800-2000 at Midan Raml, Misr station which has an express mail service, and Sharia Iskander al-Akbar with a post restante service. **American Express**: (C/o Eyeress Travel, 26 Sharia el-Horriya, Mon-Thur 0830-1300 & 1730-1800, Fri & Sat 0830-1300) also does post restante.

● **Religious services**

Anglican/Episcopal in *All Saint's Church*, Stanley Bay, services Sun 1900 and Fri 1030, prayers Wed, Thur, Sat and Sun at 1830; **Protestant** interdenominational worship, Schutz American School, Fri 1030, T 857525; **Catholic** at *Sacred Heart Convent* opposite Lord's Inn, Roushdi, Fri 1700 and Sat 0830; **Synagogue** 69 Sharia Nabi Daniel, Fri pm and Sat am, T 4821426.

● **Shopping**

Alexandria has a wide range of shops but lacks the famous specific souks of Cairo. The main area is S and W of Midan Sa'ad Zaghloul. Leather goods including shoes are of good quality and recommended as best bargins. Look also for silk and cotton material and clothes.

● **Sport**

Beach and water sports facilities are available at all major hotels. Non residents can, with permission, use pools at major hotels like *Sheraton* and *Ramada Renaissance*. ***Alexandria Sporting Club*** has golf, tennis, bowling and horse riding. ***Alexandria Yacht Club***, adjacent Sultan Qaitbai's Fort, gives sailing lessons and holds an annual regatta each Nov, boats available for hire. ***Delta Harriers*** run or jog each Fri evening, T 849344.

● Telephone

Local code: 03. **International calls**: from the exchange at Midan Raml, open 24 hrs. International calls from hotels are trouble free but slightly more expensive. Cheaper calls 2000-0800.

● Travel agents & Airlines offices

Atlantic Tours, 40 Sharia Safeya Zaghloul, T 4821109; **Egyptian International Travel**, 16 Sharia Talaat Harb, T 4825426; **Fayed Travel**, 7 Sharia el-Fath, Wezarah Station, Fleming, T 5870579; Misr Tours, 33 Sharia Salah Salem, T 4825025, F 4829617; **North African Shipping Co**, 63 Sharia Nabi Daniel, T 4830050; **Passant Travel**, 164 Sharia el-Horriya, Camp Caesar, T 5966091; **Sporting Tours**, 178 Sharia Omar Lutfi, Sporting, T 5952778. **Thomas Cook**, 15 Midan Sa'ad Zaghloul, T 4827830 and in hotels *Pullman Cecil, Palestine, Metropole* and *San Stephano*. **Air France**, 22 Sharia Salah Salam, T 4836311; **Air Maroc**, 15 Midan Sa'ad Zaghloul, T 4816638; **British Airways**, 15 Midan Sa'ad Zaghloul, T 4821565; **Egyptair**, 19 Midan Sa'ad Zaghloul, T 4828937; **Lufthansa**, 6 Sharia Talaat Harb, T 4835983; **Sudan Airways**, 6 Sharia Talaat Harb, T 4824834.

● Tourist information

Open daily 0800-1800 but 0900-1600 during Ramadan, located right in the city centre on SW corner of Midan Sa'ad Zaghloul, T 4807611. There are also tourist offices at the Misr railway station (T 4925985), the airport (T 852021) and the port (T 803494). For practical advice visit Misr Tours.

● Tourist Friends Association

Offers all services needed by tourists, introduces them to local customs, provides multilingual guides. T 5962108/5866115.

● Transport

Local: Car hire Avis, T 807532 in *Pullman Cecil*; **Budget**, T 5971273, 59 Tariq el-Geish. A/c Fiat costs E£125 per day including tax and insurance, deposit of E£300 required.

Service taxis run quick and relatively cheap services from Midan El-Gumhorriya, which is next to the Misr railway station and about 1 km S of the Corniche, to most places within a few hundred km radius. Drivers call out their destinations.

Taxis & Calèches Metered black and orange city taxis can be caught throughout the downtown and many other areas but a tip will be expected. E£25 to ride full length of Corniche. A ride in a horse-drawn *calèche* along the Corniche or from outside the Misr railway station for a pre-negotiated price is an alternative.

Trams and city buses From Raml station just to the E of Midan Sa'ad Zaghloul there are very cheap but crowded trams from dawn until 2400 including – E to Sidi Bishr beach (No 1-No 4), W to the Maritime Station (No 6) in the W Harbour, N to Qaitbai Fort (No 5) via El-Gomruk and El-Anfushi, and S from Midan Orabi which is W of Midan Sa'ad Zaghloul to Karmous and Pompey's Pillar (No 5 & No 15). As a general rule blue trams to middle class areas and yellow to poorer areas. Local buses, which are fast but very crowded and dirty, operate throughout the city from the main squares. The main services include the following – Midan Sa'ad Zaghloul to the airport (No 203); Midan Orabi to the airport (No 307 & No 310), Montazah & Abu Qir (No 129); Raml to Pompey's Pillar (No 209), along the Corniche to Montazah (No 120, No 220 and No 300), Ma'mura (No 725), Abu Qir (No 729), or to El-Agami and Hannoville beaches (No 455 or No 500); Misr station to the Zoo (No 41).

Air The airport, which is SE of the city on land reclaimed from Lake Maryut off the main Delta road to Cairo, has regular daily flights to Cairo, Athens (4 a week) and Paris (1 a week). For information T 420202.

Train The main Misr station in Midan El-Gumhorriya has inter-city services S to **Cairo** via Sidi Gaber, Damanhur, Tanta and Benha (11 a day, 2½-3 hrs) and some a/c which go onward to **Luxor** and **Aswan**. Although less frequent, there are trains W to El-Alamein and Marsa Matruh. For information T 4923207.

Road The main terminal at Midan Sa'ad Zaghloul operates very regular a/c express Superjet buses to Cairo (3 hrs), T 482439, and a twice daily service to Ismailia (5 hrs), ***West Delta Buses***, T 809685. There are also 3-4 daily services from Midan El-Gumhorriya, which is next to the Misr train station and about 1 km S of Midan Sa'ad Zaghloul, including the express service to Marsa Matruh (4 hrs) and Siwa (7 hrs) and the regular non-express bus which goes to Marsa via El-Alamein. Seats for these services, however, have to be booked at Midan Sa'ad Zaghloul. Non-scheduled buses E along the coast to Rosetta and Damietta can

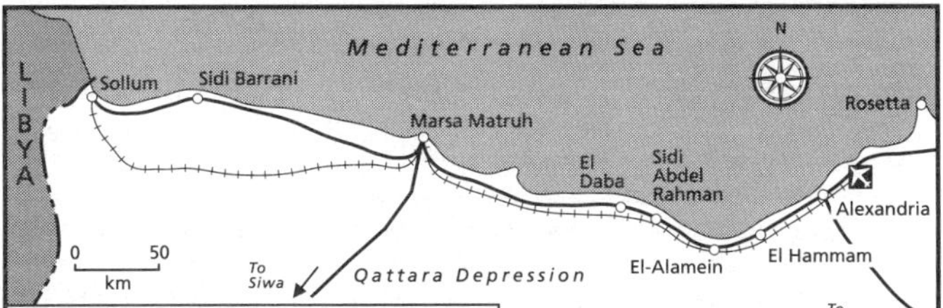

MEDITERRANEAN COAST N 229

be caught from near the Roman Theatre in Midan El-Gumhorriya. International departures from outside *Cecil Hotel* to Tunisia, Libya, Syria and Abu Dhabi. Payment on these superjet services required in hard currency. Where *West Delta Buses* have equivalent departure this can be paid for in local currency.

Sea There are sailings on Adriatica Lines (main office 33 Sharia Salem) from the Maritime Station to Piraeus and Venice via Crete every 8-12 days. Bookings should be made in advance with Menatours (T 806909) in Midan Sa'ad Zaghloul. *Alexandria Navigation Agencies*, 71 Sharia el Horriya, T 4837113/5. For information at port T 802909.

West to Libya

The **Mediterranean Coast** stretches 500 kms W to the Libyan border passing through Alexandria's local beach resorts of **El-Agami** and **Hannoville**, and the new beach resorts of **Sidi Abdel Rahman** and **Marsa Matruh** from which a road leads inland to the **Siwa** oasis, see page 841, before finally arriving at the Libyan border near Sollum.

The first few km are the worst as the road W out of Alexandria is complicated and very badly signposted. There are 2 roads going W: it is best to take the more scenic coastal route. For the first 30 km a series of developments, more attractive to stay in than to look at, lie between the road and the sea. Petrol is easily available.

El-Alamein

106 km W of Alexandria, owes its fame to what was, until the 1967 Arab-Israeli war, the largest tank battle in history. In July 1942 the Allies under Field Marshal Montgomery halted the German-Italian advance towards the Nile and, in British eyes if not in those of the Soviet troops at Stalingrad, turned the course of WWII. Winston Churchill later wrote, not entirely accurately that, "Before Alamein we never had a victory. After Alamein we never had a defeat". (See The North Africa campaign, see page 836.) Unless you are a military historian or have a personal interest in the battle, there is little to see and it is probably best to combine a visit here with other sights on the journey from Alexandria to El-Alamein.

ACCESS El-Alamein is only a short car or bus ride away from Alexandria but the trains are slow and it is a 2 hr return journey and then a 2 km walk N from the station to the town. The buses and taxis doing the journey between Alexandria and Marsa Matruh stop at *Alamein Rest House*.

Things to see

El-Agami and **Hannoville**, 20-25 kms W of Alexandria, are beach resorts which are packed at weekends and during the high season with the result that litter and pollution are a growing problem. They can be reached both easily and cheaply from Alexandria by bus (No 455 from Midan Sa'ad Zaghloul or No 760 and No 600 from Misr Station and Midan Orabi); service taxi; or micro buses which leave El-Gumhorriya every 10-30 min.

Abu Sir is further along the coast halfway between Alexandria and El-Alamein. In the Ptolemaic period a string of beacons

THE DESERT WAR 1940-1943

Italy, the colonial power in Libya at the outbreak of WW II, invaded Egypt in the closing weeks of 1940 thus beginning a long period of fighting between the Axis powers and Great Britain in North Africa. Italian and later German strategic plans were the displacement of Britain from Egypt, destruction of Britain's imperial communications links through Suez and the opening up of the Middle East oilfields to Axis penetration. The local Arab and Berber peoples of North Africa played a remarkably small role in events, though royalist Libyan troops joined the British in the final liberation of their country. The damage and disruption of the war were considerable and their negative effects persisted long after the end of hostilities.

The Italians were soon expelled from Egypt and much of eastern Libya but were powerfully reinforced in Tripolitania in Feb 1941 by the arrival of German troops and armour which rapidly drove the British back to the Egyptian frontier by Apr. The German formations were led by Rommel with skill and audacity. Air power favoured the joint German-Italian armies in the earlier part of the campaign. Rommel's eastward advance was slowed by the protracted resistance of the garrisons, first Australian then British and Polish, at Tobruk. Meanwhile, the main armies fought pitched battles around the Libyan-Egyptian border until Rommel withdrew temporarily in Dec 1941. He used his improved lines of communications in the W to prepare a counter attack and pushed E again as far as Gazala, near Derna, in Jan and Feb 1942 and, after a pause, into Tobruk and deep into Egypt in June though his advance was finally held at El-Alamein after a fierce battle. Rommel made a final attempt at Alam Halfa, E of El-Alamein, to push aside British and Commonwealth forces and break through to the Nile Valley in Aug 1942 but failed in the face of a strong defensive effort and his own growing losses of men and equipment.

The balance in the desert war was changing in mid-1942 as the Allies gradually won superiority in the air and had more freedom of movement at sea. The Germans and Italians began increasingly to suffer from shortages of equipment, while the health of Field Marshal Rommel gave rise for concern. On the Allied side General Montgomery took over leadership and began a build-up of the Eighth Army sufficient to overwhelm the well trained and experienced Afrika Korps. Montgomery opened his attack at El-Alamein on 23 Oct 1942 and after 11 days of hard fighting the Axis army was beaten back and retreated by rapid stages to the W to make a last stand in Tunisian territory.

The German attempt to hold on in North Africa was made difficult by sea and airborne landings by Allied, including American, troops in Morocco and Algeria in Nov 1942. These 2 countries were liberated with ease when French Vichy units, formerly collaborating with the Germans, were brought round to supporting the invasion. German and Italian reinforcements were rushed to Tunis and a battle began to stop the advance of allied units from the W as they fought their way in from Algeria and from the S through Libya. German attacks in the Battle of Kasserine in the hills N of Gafsa during Jan and Feb 1943 almost succeeded in halting Allied progress but when Rommel's final assault on Mongomery's advancing Eighth Army arriving from Libya failed in early Mar, the Axis forces retreated northwards behind the Mareth Line on the Gulf of Gabès before being outflanked and being forced to withdraw by Montgomery's troops. A final set of battles in northern Tunisia saw the Allies push through the Medjerda Valley to Tunis and Bizerte in May 1943, effectively ending Axis resistance in North Africa.

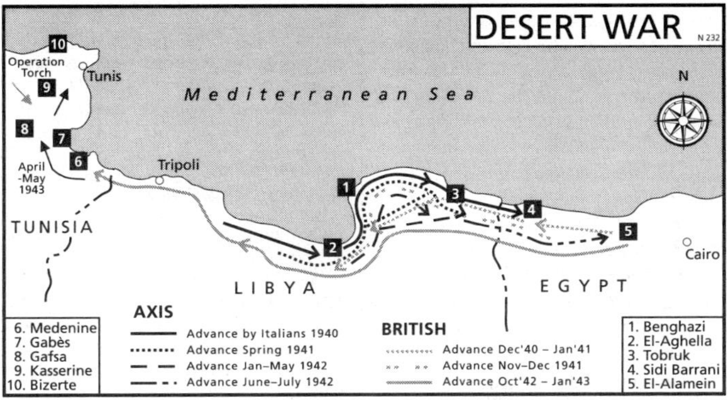

lit up the coast from Pharos in Alexandria to Cyrenaica in Libya. The **Burg al-Arab** (Arab Tower) just to the E of Abu Sir, is the sole survivor. The **lighthouse** has the same three-tier construction as Pharos but is a tenth of the size. The cylindrical top has collapsed but it does give an accurate impression of the appearance, if not the scale, of the Wonder at Pharos. W of the Burg al-Arab are a few remains of a temple of Osiris. Abu Sir was once an important coastal town, surrounded by great walls which have long since crumbled, so now only the gates remain. From the top there is a beautiful view over the Mariout marshes to the sea.

Abu Mina lies 48 km WSW from Alexandria and about 15 km inland from Abu Sir, beyond the new town of Mobarak. It is black top all the way. It was once the most important destination in the E for Christian pilgrims as **Deir Mari Mina** is one of the largest Coptic monasteries. St Menas, who was an Egyptian-born Roman legionnaire, was martyred in Asia Minor in 296 AD for refusing to renounce Christ. He was buried here when the camel carrying his body would go no further towards his home. When miracles occurred at the site of his tomb the news travelled across Christendom, via the camel trains, that the tomb of Abu Mina and the Holy Waters nearby could cure sickness and suffering, and his sanctity was assured. Successive emperors built temples and basilicas around the shrine but when the waters dried up in the 12th century the town fell into decay. Excavations have revealed the remains of the basilicas and shrines and much of the surrounding pilgrim town. Saint Menas's day is now celebrated on Nov 11 and the town is the site of an austere concrete Coptic monastery which was built in 1959, easily recognised by its two white towers.

El-Alamein was the site of the battle between Germany's Afrika Korps and the Allied Eighth Army which turned WWII in the latter's favour and marks the closest that the Axis forces got to the Nile valley. The results of the encounter can be seen adjacent to the town in the huge **war cemeteries**. The Greek war memorial is passed first. The **Commonwealth cemetery** (entry free, open daily 0700-1630 but books of remembrance not available Fri) lies to the E of the town to the S of the road. Through the arch and beyond the gardens sombre lines of over 7,000 white headstones commemorate those who fought and died supporting the Allied cause. The **German cemetery** lies about 4 km to the W of the town between the road and the sea. Here in a sand coloured building resembling a castle there are 4,200 graves. The man with the key will see you coming. He lives nearby. The **Italian cemetery**, the only one in North Africa, lies a further 6 km W of the town on seaside. Just walk in.

A **museum** to the W of the settlement contains maps of the campaign and some of the uniforms and weaponry used in Egypt by both sides. A clever map/model display with lights and commentary (choose your language) explains the North Africa campaign. There is also information here about the war between Egypt and Israel in 1973. Open daily 0800-1800, 0900-1500 in Ramadan, entrance E£5 plus E£5 for camera.

• **Accommodation** **B** *El-Alamein*, Sidi Abdel Rahman, El-Dabaa Center, T 4921228, 209 rm and villas with own sea-side barbecue, very good standard, located on the beautiful white sands of the isolated up-market resort of Sidi Abdel Rahman about 25 km W of El-Alamein, early reservations essential, open Apr-Nov; **B** *Atic Hotel*, Km 90 Alexandria to Marsa Matruh road, T 4921349, F 4938313, 64 double rm, located 16 kms E of El-Alamein, good standard of service, pool, private beach, mainly Egyptian guests; **B** *Aida Beach*, Km 77, Alexandria to Marsa Matruh road, T 90851, F 990867, 249 rm, good standard, located 30 km E of El-Alamein with a private beach and many sports facilities. **D** *Agami Palace*, Al-Bittash Beach, El-Agami, T 4330230, F 4309364, 56 rm, located 20 km W of Alexandria, tasteful decor, pool; **D** *Hannoville*, Hannoville Beach, El-Agami, T 4303258, 157 rm, 300 beds, located on rather polluted and crowded Hannoville beach about 25 kms W of Alexandria, day-trippers from Alexandria flock here every weekend; **D** *Summer Moon*, Betach Beach, El-Agami, T 4330834, 96 rm, 264 beds. **E** *New Admiral*, Hannoville, El-Agami, T 4303038, 44 rm, on beach. **F** *Alamein Rest House*, Km 105, Alexandria to Marsa Matruh road, El-Alamein, T 4302785, 8 rm, 35 beds, small, mainly Egyptian guests, serves decent meals, including such local specialities as armadillo eggs; **F** *Costa Blanca*, Sharia Hannoville, El-Agami, T 4303112, 36 rm, on beach, see comment for *Hannoville Hotel*; **F** *Menas Agami*, Agami Beach, El-Agami, T 4300150, 55 rm; **F** *Monoco*, Abu Talaat, Km 25 Alexandria to Marsa Matruh road, T 4321100, 33 rm, 90 beds on beach; **F** *New Talaat* Hannoville, El-Agami, T 4891039, 25 rm, 39 beds, see comment for *Hannoville Hotel*.

• **Camping** There are no specific camp sites but the *El-Alamein Hotel* has a tourist camp equipped with all necessary services. **WARNING**, as with the Red Sea coast, large parts of the coast and the desert are fenced off because they are still littered with unexploded mines and shells. It is **ESSENTIAL** to obey signs, use common sense and keep to the main roads and beaches.

• **Places to eat** These are tiny places and except for the hotels there are few restaurants in and around El-Alamein. 8 km beyond the Italian cemetery, turn right at roadblock for a good coffee stop at *El-Alamein* hotel.

• **Telephone** Local code: 03.

• **Transport** Besides private transport there are regular buses and irregular trains from El-Alamein either E to Alexandria or W to Marsa Matruh.

Marsa Matruh

Marsa Matruh, (178 kms W of El-Alamein, 288 kms W of Alexandria and 512 kms NW of Cairo), has been transformed from a sleepy fishing village and minor port into a popular, low grade, summer resort for domestic tourists with a plethora of tatty beach side tented areas belonging to trade and government groups. Despite the government's attempts it has not, and is unlikely to be, turned into the new mass tourist Mediterranean beach destination for European tourists. Although there are some good beaches in the area and the lagoon has potential if correctly developed, the dull little town with a population of around 25,000 has few of the holiday facilities and nightlife that tourists expect.

ACCESS Marsa Matruh's streets are on a grid pattern with most of the hotels being located on the streets behind and

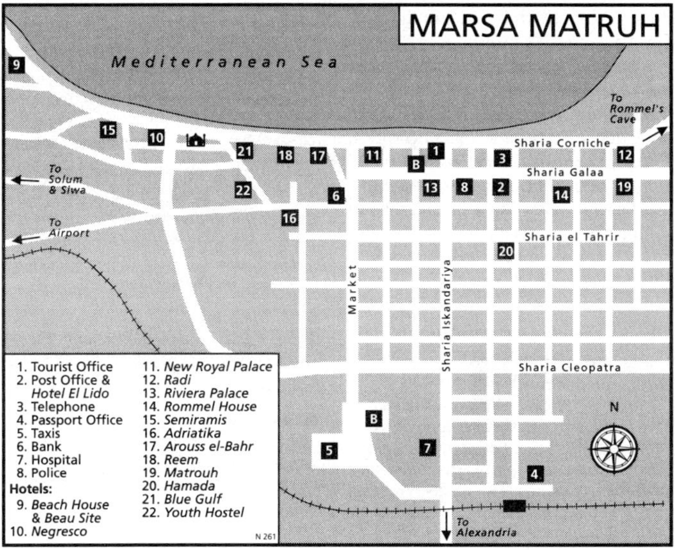

parallel to the Corniche. Buses and service taxis stop at Sharia Cleopatra about 1 km S of the beach and the hotels which can be reached by one of the *carettas*, cheap donkey carts, which are the main type of transport within the town. Airport close to S of town.

Things to see

There are really only 2 reasons for visiting Marsa Matruh, either to travel to the magnificent desert oasis at Siwa (see Siwa, page 841) or a rest enroute to Libya. The area's much advertised beaches are a severe disappointment. Except for the *Beau Site* hotel's private beach, almost all beaches are public. Western women can still experience problems from both voyeurs and exhibitionists who are more used to seeing fully-clothed Egyptian women swimming and sunbathing, although the situation is improving as the locals become more used to visitors. No serious attempt has been made to solve the major litter problem on those beaches closest to town.

The beaches in the town's bay are protected by 2 sand spits which will eventually meet and form a lagoon. The water is shallow and stagnant, NOT a place to swim. **Lido Beach** and **Beach of Lovers** curve around the bay to the W of the town while in the other direction **Rommel's Beach** and its small museum are beyond the small port and are almost facing the town on the landward side of the E spit. The approach, past rusting pipework which once served as the naval pier, is depressing even in the sunshine. **The Rommel Museum** (open summer 0930-1600) gives details of this famous field marshal in the WWII campaign. Offshore from the beach is a red buoy, 25m beyond which is a sunken German U-boat, which can be seen if you have suitable underwater swimming gear.

The better and cleaner beaches are those to the W of the town: in order they are **Cleopatra's Bath** (7 km) which is surrounded by cliffs and gets deep very suddenly; **Al-Nasr City Beach** (10 kms); **El-Obeid Beach** (20 kms) and **Agibah**

Beach (28 kms) which is set in the middle of a cove.

The nearby beaches can be reached from town by hiring a bicycle for 24 hrs from the hire shop (open 0600-2400) E£10 or by donkey cart for a negotiated price. Donkey carts carry 2 people and cost E£3 out to Rommel Museum. The more distant beaches to the W can be reached in summer by service taxi, microbus or Tuf-Tuf which shuttle back and forth (0800-1700) from near the bus station. In the winter the seaside areas are dead but the town life continues as normal.

Local information

● Accommodation

Many hotels are closed in winter. Hotels may have a problem of fresh water supplies. There are no really first class hotels and it is best to avoid the very cheap ones near the bus station. This leaves, in addition to a number of cheap and cheerful hotels to the S, away from the beach, a wide range of officially registered hotels in and around Marsa Matruh including the following: **A** ***Badr Tourist Village***, El-Obeid, T 945348, F 730443, 130 rm, 250 beds, large hotel located on El-Obeid beach about 20 km W of town, currently under renovation; **A** ***Beach House Hotel***, Sharia el-Shatee, T 945169, F 943319, 30 suites, 136 beds.

B ***Beau Site***, Sharia el-Shatee, T 932066, F 2599484, 90 rm, open May-Oct only, highly recommended, located 2 kms W of Sharia Iskandariya on the Corniche, full board is compulsory, but the food is reported as excellent, also rents out chalets for 3-8 persons.

C ***Negresco***, Corniche, T 934492, 24 rm, 64 beds, breakfast included.

D ***Miami Hotel***, Corniche, T 935891, F 935892, rather large with 200 rm; **D** ***New Royal Palace***, Corniche, T 933406, 170 rm; **D** ***Radi***, Corniche, Old Port, T 934827, F 934828, 72 rm, disco in summer, pleasant staff, lots of hot water, food ok; **D** ***Riviera Palace***, Sharia Galaa, Market Area, T 943045, 32 rm, a downtown hotel, good restaurant, no alcohol, closed in winter; **D** ***Rommel House***, Sharia Galaa, T 945466, 60 rm, 107 beds, good café, a good standard; **D** ***Royal Palace***, Corniche, T 944295, largish with 130 rm; **D** ***Semiramis***, Corniche, T 944091, 64 rm, good standard.

E ***Adriatika***, Sharia Galaa, T 945195, 60 rm with bath and balcony, good, located just N of the tourist office, closed in winter, inexpensive, yet facilities include 24 hr rm service, laundry, bar, cafeteria and TV; **E** ***Arouss el-Bahr***, Corniche, T 942419, 19 rm, 44 beds, some bungalows for 4 persons, small hotel, sea views, helpful staff, restaurant.

F ***El-Khalig el-Azrak***, Corniche, T 942981, 57 rm, 96 beds, recently expanded; **F** ***Reem***, Corniche, T 943605, 58 rm, very cheap, good value; **F** ***Shatek el-Gharam*** Lido Area, T 944387, 32 rm, 62 beds.

● Youth hostel

Behind 4 Sharia Galaa, Sollum Rd, T 932331, 60 beds, kitchen, overnight fee E£5, train 2 km.

● Camping

It is essential to obtain permission to camp on the beach from the Military Intelligence Office on Sharia Galaa because they patrol the beaches at night. There is camping on the beach at *Badr Tourist Village* and on El-Obeid beach.

● Places to eat

Besides the hotel restaurants including those at the *Beau Site* and *Riviera Palace*, there are a few cheap downtown restaurants near the Corniche including the ***Mansour Fish Restaurant***, ***Alexandria Tourist Restaurant***, ***Restaurant Panayotis*** which serves cheap beer and salads, and the bargain ***Hani el-Onda***. Choose carefully remembering the fresh water problems....

● Banks

Most of the town's banks are W of the Egyptair office and are open daily 0900-1400 and 1800-2000. The **Banque du Caire** branch, located E of the main N-S Sharia Iskandariya is open 0830-1430 and 1800-2100. **National Bank of Egypt** to W of town. There are no banks in Siwa so make sure that you have enough or change your money in Marsa Matruh.

● Nightclubs

There are nightclubs in the larger hotels and discotheques at the *Beau Site* and *Radi* hotels, in summer.

● Post Office

On Sharia Galaa to E of Sharia Iskandariya, open daily 0900-1500. 24 hr telephones are just opposite the post office on Sharia Galaa.

● **Telephone**
Local code: 094.

● **Travel Agents and airlines**
Egyptair: Sharia Galaa, near Tourist office.

● **Tourist information**
On Sharia Galaa open daily 0900-1400 and 2000-2200 has limited material. You are advised to get information from one of the better hotels.

● **Transport**
Air There are 3 flights a week by Egyptair from Marsa Matruh to Cairo. Book in advance during the summer high season.

Train Although in summer there is a daily train service to Cairo (5-15 hrs) it is very slow and is not really worth the effort.

Road: **Bus** local transport to the beaches of Cleopatra, El-Obeid and Agibah leave every 15 mins during daylight. The best long distance services are the 3 daily Golden Rocket buses to Alexandria (3-4 hrs) and Cairo (8 hrs) which should be booked in advance. There are also slower blue buses to Alexandria (5 hrs) which stop at Sidi Abdel Rahman and El-Alamein, E£8. There is an early morning non-stop 5 hr a/c daily service to Siwa, E£10, which is better than the afternoon service which, because it originates in Alexandria, is usually very crowded by the time it reaches Marsa Matruh. **Service taxis** are quicker and cheaper but less comfortable than the express buses to Alexandria. Taxis to Siwa (5 hrs) leave early morning or in the afternoon to avoid the midday heat. It is difficult but not impossible to take one of the service taxis, which carry Egyptian expatriate workers, to the Libyan border (230 kms E of Marsa Matruh) via Sidi Barrani (150 kms) and Sollum (220 kms) but it is essential to have a Libyan visa.

Siwa Oasis

Siwa Oasis is 82 kms long E-W and 20 kms N-S at its widest point and includes a number of large lakes. It is 300 km SW from Marsa Matruh, a journey by car of 4 hrs along a black top road built in 1986. Traffic is sparse. The half-way stop for tea or coffee is the Badwy "hotel". Scenery is limited until the escarpment is crossed and the trees of Siwa, 300,000 date palms and 70,000 olive trees come into view. This magnificent oasis is recommended for those who want a break from the beach and want another type of sand. Comparatively few travellers visit the oasis because of its isolation and very limited facilities, but with the improved road and the encouragement of tour companies, the sense of 'away from it all' has been lost. Siwa is further from the Nile Delta, the source of Egyptian civilization and the point of contact with those civilizations which superseded it, than any of the oases along the Great Desert Circuit. With Siwa's customs unchanged for centuries, untouched by the world

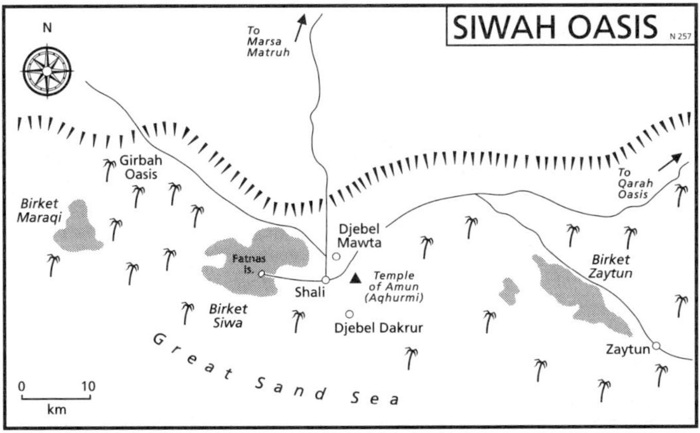

> **SEXISM IN SIWA**
>
> Female donkeys are not allowed in Siwa oasis.

around, and its position on the shores of the Great Sand Sea, it is geographically and culturally remote, and the closest to every romantic's notion of what a *real* desert should be like. It is not surprising then that there is a potential clash of cultures and visitors would do well to respect local customs by dressing modestly. Women are requested to keep legs and upper arms covered. Alcohol and affection are forbidden in public!

Siwans, currently numbering 30,000, have always been fiercely independent, in fact this oasis only officially became part of Egypt in the 19th century. It has been inhabited, with reliance on the 200 or so fresh, salt, warm and cold springs, since Palaeolithic times.

S from Siwa the Sudanese border lies across 700 km of desert. Of this 400 km is **The Great Sand Sea**, which like a frozen storm with waves 100m high, has rolling sand dunes in every direction. Legend tells of a **lost oasis,** but it has never (obviously) been found. Perhaps the descendants of Cambyses live on! (See box).

The main settlement is **Shali**, until recently straddling two low hills within the depression, but now abandoned. The ruins of the old town established in 1203 are still impressive. The minaret of the 17th century mosque remains. The mud brick walls and towers are floodlit at night, a splendid sight. New stone dwellings, mainly single storey, have been constructed. They are certainly not so attractive but probably much more comfortable. The new mosque of Faud I, a solidly built structure of stone in the pleasant style of the late 19th/early 20th

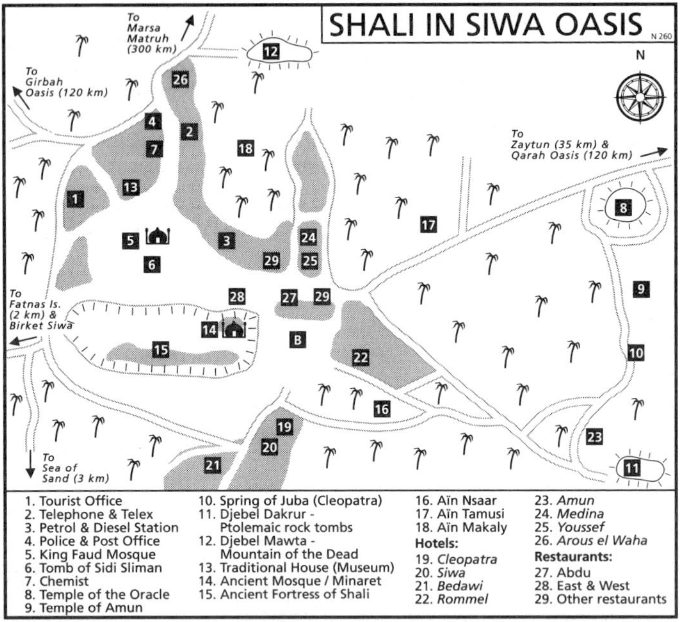

1. Tourist Office
2. Telephone & Telex
3. Petrol & Diesel Station
4. Police & Post Office
5. King Faud Mosque
6. Tomb of Sidi Sliman
7. Chemist
8. Temple of the Oracle
9. Temple of Amun
10. Spring of Juba (Cleopatra)
11. Djebel Dakrur - Ptolemaic rock tombs
12. Djebel Mawta - Mountain of the Dead
13. Traditional House (Museum)
14. Ancient Mosque / Minaret
15. Ancient Fortress of Shali
16. Aïn Nsaar
17. Aïn Tamusi
18. Aïn Makaly

Hotels:

19. *Cleopatra*
20. *Siwa*
21. *Bedawi*
22. *Rommel*
23. *Amun*
24. *Medina*
25. *Youssef*
26. *Arous el Waha*

Restaurants:

27. Abdu
28. East & West
29. Other restaurants

century, is the natural centre of the new town. Adjacent to it is the tomb of Sidi Sliman, a local saint.

The economy is based on agriculture, dates and olives. The Sa'idi date is preferred for eating. Water supply is from natural springs. No pumping is necessary but the springs are capped to provide some control. Surplus water is a serious problem and the water level is rising at about 9 mm annually. New land is taken into cultivation if demand increases, the olives bearing fruit in 5 years and the date palms in 10 years. Quarrying, transport, trade (and smuggling?) are also important with increasing revenue from tourism. Labour costs are high as labourers have to be brought in and need food and accommodation.

ACCESS Permits are no longer required. The bus station and taxi halt are in the S of the town only a short walk from the centre.

Things to see

Siwa is such a wonderful place that rather than going to see anything specific most tourists visit Siwa simply to soak up the experience and the atmosphere of life in the oasis which is totally surrounded by the majesty of the desert. Its isolation from the rest of Egypt is increased by the fact that the inhabitants speak Siwa, which is a Berber dialect, rather than Arabic, and have their own festivals and customs.

Birket Siwa salt lake and **Fantis Island** reached by a newly built causeway are a popular picnic spot and on all itineraries. Recommended for an afternoon swim and later for the spectacular sunsets. Take precautions against the many mosquitoes.

Temples of Amun There are two temples to Amun here, both at the deserted village of Aghurmi 3km to E. The **Temple of the Oracle** (see box) is built on a large rock amidst the remains of the village. The ascent is quite steep and in summer when temperatures reach 44 °C almost impossible. The Temple which dates back to the 26th Dynasty is fairly well preserved and some attempts have been made to clear the debris and reveal the original façade. Views to the adjacent Temple of Umm 'Ubayda, Gebel Matwa and across the palm groves to the shimmering salt lakes. The site of the second temple **Umm 'Ubayda**, from the 30th Dynasty, is marked by an area of fallen blocks in which one wall, carefully inscribed, still stands.

Juba's Spring, also called Cleopatra's Pool although it has nothing at all to do with the lady, was mentioned by Herodi-tus. It is supposed to change temperature during the day but the reality is the relative difference between air temperature and the temperature of the person dipping in, and many people do... On a practical note, the spring produces enough

The Oracle Of Amun

It was **The Oracle of Amun** which brought Siwa to the attention of the world, from the 26th Dynasty (664-525 BC) onward. **Alexander the Great** is known to have consulted the Oracle in 331 BC after wresting control of the country from its Persian rulers in order to ask it if, as he suspected, he was indeed the son of Zeus. His arrival with a large party of friends and an even larger number of soldiers must have caused quite a stir in sleepy Siwa. Unfortunately posterity does not record the Oracle's response. Nearly 200 years earlier, Egypt's Persian ruler Cambyses (525-522 BC) is said to have carelessly lost an army of 50,000 men who were dispatched from Aïn Dalla near the Farafra Oasis to Siwa in order to destroy the Oracle. The army was simply never seen again having been either buried by a sandstorm or snatched by aliens.

water to irrigate 121 ha every 14 days.

Tombs of Gebel Mawta or Mountain of the Dead is a conical hill about 1½ km from the centre of Shali. It is honeycombed with tombs varying from small chambers to large composite excavations complete with columns and wall paintings. Anything worth stealing has long since been removed. During 1940 many items were 'sold' to the visiting troops by Siwans who had moved into the tombs for security. Splendid views from the summit, open 0900-1400, closed Fri. No photographs allowed inside.

Traditional Siwan House, exhibition financed by Canadians, shows in great detail the artefacts and decorations used until very recently in the houses of the oasis. Open 0900-1200 on request – best to give some notice – visitors book is almost as fascinating as the house. No fee, just a tip.

Siwa Festival in Oct just before date harvest, lasts 3 days and over 3,000 people come to celebrate with prayers and sing some religious songs.

Olive press This old press, driven by donkey power, is in operation only at end of the olive season around the first week of Dec. Arrangements can be made at the Tourist Office. No fee but do tip as it is the man's livelihood.

Siwa water bottling plant is run by an Italian company on the outskirts of Shali. An excellent way to exploit an area with too much water.

Sulphur Springs and **Oasis Garden** in desert, contact Ahmed in *Café Abdou*. Cost E£35 day trip.

Local information

● Accommodation

There are 8 small cheap hotels in Siwa. Price for double rm give range of comfort. All basic facilities, tiled floors, a/c of sorts. Ask to see the room. ***E Arous el Waha***, all rm bath and balcony, hot shower, E£20; ***Cleopatra***, front view with shower, E£15-20, rear view with shower, dormitory E£5 each, roof E£1, hot showers, clean spartan rooms, friendly staff, recommended; ***Youssef Hotel***, E£10; ***Amun Hotel***, E£8; ***Bedawi Hotel***, hot showers, E£6; ***Siwa Hotel***, E£6; ***Medina Hotel***, E£6; ***Rommel Garden Hotel***, under construction.

● Camping

This is a sensitive area close to the Libyan border, so despite the good relations, don't camp out without permission from the tourist office. Hotels are so cheap camping is really unnecessary but is allowed at the springs called Cleopatra's Baths. *Hotel Cleopatra* permits sleeping on the roof for E£1 per night.

● Where to eat

The only places to eat in town are 2 or 3 small cafés in the area around the market and new mosque in the centre of town. ***Abdou***, which is cheerful and welcoming, is considered 'one of the best' but there is not much competition. Prices cheap, omelette and chips with pepsi E£2.

● Banks

There is no bank in town.

● Market

Every Fri.

● Post Office and telephones

Located with the police station just S of the *Arouss el-Waha hotel*.

● Tourist information

Located to the W of the new mosque, the tourist office run by English speaking Mahdi Mohamed Hweti (open sat-Thur 0900-1300, Fri 1800-2000) is a very helpful first stop for any information. A guide for the main sites of Siwa will cost around E£25. Try Mohammed Ali Herdi on T 6033.

● Transport

Local Most places are within cycling distance – *Youssef Hotel* and *Cleopatra Hotel*, hire cycles at E£3 per hour or E£5 per day. *Abdou* Café or your hotel can organise a donkey cart.

Road Besides a reliable private car, the only way to and from the oasis are the 2 daily **buses** from Siwa to Marsa Matruh at 0630 and 1300, costs E£6, goes on to Alexandria (extra E£6.50), a/c bus to Alex from Siwa Sun, Tue and Thur, E£20, leaves at 1000, book the night before travelling and wait next to the new mosque. There are **service taxis** back to the coast which leave mid-morning and late afternoon.

THE SUEZ CANAL ZONE

Contents

Maps

Although the Suez Canal Zone may not be the most attractive or interesting region in Egypt, it is certainly worth a detour to Ismailia when crossing between Sinai and the rest of Egypt. We may live in an age when it is difficult to be impressed by something as mundane as a canal but it should not be forgotten that the Suez Canal was as great a feat of engineering in the 19th century as the Pyramids were in their day.

Most visitors who head E from Cairo cross the desert and go under the Suez Canal through the Ahmed Hamdi Tunnel, 12 km N of the town of Suez. From there they go into the Sinai peninsula, ignoring not only Suez itself which is not a pleasant town but also the relatively tedious journey N past the Great Bitter Lakes to Ismailia and Qantara and to Port Said on the Mediterranean. Although these towns may not have the attractions of either Cairo or the Sinai resorts, the route is used by those travelling overland to Israel or to catch the ferry to Cyprus and Greece.

Suez

Suez, at the S end of the Suez Canal, was known as Klysma during the Ptolemaic period and as the walled city of Qulzum it was an important spice and pilgrim port in mediaeval times. It was almost totally destroyed during the 1948 and other wars with Israel, after which it was rebuilt with Gulf funds. Today it is an important industrial centre producing cement, fertilisers and petrochemicals using domestic oil from the offshore fields in the Gulf of Suez. Besides a new ferry terminal for pilgrims bound for Mecca it is also linked to Port Tawfik and its other docks and ferry terminals.

ACCESS Buses and service taxis arrive at the Arba'in Terminal just off the main Sharia el-Geish which leads left to the nearby railway station and right to the main hotels and then the causeway to Port Tawfik.

Things to see

There is very little to see in Suez, but a stroll along Sharia el-Geish then across the causeway to Port Tawfik's NE corner where there are 4 captured US-made Israeli tanks is quite pleasant.

Excursions are organised from here to the Monasteries of St Anthony and St Paul. See page 872.

Local information

● Accommodation

D *Green House*, Sharia Port Said, T 223337, Tx 66102, F 223330, 48 rm, like most of the hotels in Suez the majority of the guests are Egyptians and oil company workers; **D** *Red Sea Hotel*, Sharia 13 Riad, Port Tawfik, T 223334, Tx 66074, F 227761, 81 rm; **D** *Summer Palace*, Port Tawfik, T 224475, 77 rm.

F *White House*, 322 Sharia el-Geish, T 227599, Tx 66102, 45 rm; **F** *Misr Palace*, 2 Sharia Sa'ad Zaghloul, T 223031, 30 rm.

● Youth hostel

Sharia Tariq el-Horriya (near sports stadium), PO 171, Suez, 100 beds, kitchen, station 2 km, T 21945, overnight fee E£5.

● Places to eat

There is a decent fish restaurant on Sharia el-Geish near the bus station. Beer can only be found in one or two of the hotels and the **average** *El-Magharbel* restaurant near the *White House* hotel. Try also the **cheaper** *El-Tayib* on Sharia Hoda Sharawi.

The Suez Canal

Since its completion in 1869 the **Suez Canal**, which at 167 km is the third longest in the world, has enabled ships to pass from the Mediterranean to the Indian Ocean via the Red Sea without sailing around the southern tip of the African continent. There had been many previous attempts to build a canal including those in the 26th Dynasty by Necho II (610-595 BC) and the Persian Emperor Darius I (521-486 BC). Napoleon's engineers vetoed their own plan to build the canal after calculating (incorrectly) that the sea level in the Red Sea was 10m lower than in the Mediterranean. Although it was the British who discovered their error in the 1840s it was **Ferdinand de Lesseps**, a young French vice-consul in Egypt, who finally persuaded the Khedive Said Pasha (1854-1863), son of the great Mohamed Ali Pasha, to begin work at the N end of the canal in 1859. Thousands of the workers died before its eventual completion in 1869 during the rule of his successor the Khedive Ismail whose name is given to Ismailia midway along the canal.

The lavish opening ceremony was attended by many European dignitaries and a party of tourists organized by Thomas Cook who travelled in their wake, but things soon began to go wrong. Given Britain's constant opposition to the project it was ironic that it was to her that the bankrupt Ismail was forced to sell his 44 per cent holding in the Suez Canal Company for £4 million, the amount loaned to Disraeli's government by the Rothschild bankers, before the much more enthusiastic France could make an offer. The canal, the main route between Europe and India, soon produced very significant profits which were remitted to Britain rather than being ploughed back into Egypt. In the 1920s and 1930s the strategically vital Canal Zone was one of the world's largest military bases.

Since 1945 the canal has been the subject of both important political disputes and serious armed conflicts. Britain reluctantly agreed to remove its troops in 1954 but refused to give a larger share of the revenues to Egypt. The West vetoed World Bank loans to help finance the construction of the Aswan Dam because of the Soviet Union's offer to rearm Egypt after its 1948 defeat by Israel. In reply Colonel Gamal Abdel Nasser nationalized the Suez Canal on 26th July 1956. Britain and France used the pretext of an agreed and pre-planned Israeli invasion of Sinai in Oct 1956 in an attempt to reoccupy the Canal Zone but were forced to withdraw when the US, opposed to imperialism but wanting to break Britain's stranglehold on the Middle East and get a slice of the action in the region itself, threatened to destabilize the British economy.

The Six Day War with Israel in 1967 caused new damage to the recently rebuilt canal cities and the canal itself was blocked by sunken ships. Egyptian forces briefly broke through the Israeli's Bar-Lev Line on the E bank of the canal during the Yom Kippur war of Oct 1973 before being forced back and it was not until 1982 that the Israelis withdrew from the E bank and the canal could be reopened.

With access via the canal denied, super-tankers were built to carry vast quantities of crude oil around Africa. These huge vessels are unable to pass through the reopened Suez Canal which, in order to face increasingly fierce competition from other routes, is now to be widened. It will accommodate vessels up to 180,000 dwt and 20m draft compared with the current 150,000 dwt and 19m draft. In 1992 canal receipts brought in US$1.9 billion, (37% of which was from oil tankers), making it one of the largest sources of foreign currency after tourism, oil and expatriate remittances.

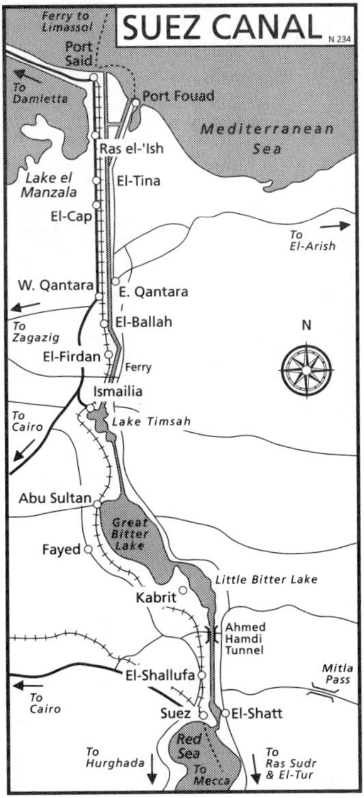

● **Banks**
There is a bank on Sharia el-Geish just near to the bus station.

● **Post Office**
On Sharia Hoda Sharawi which is one block away from the main Sharia el-Geish, near the causeway to Port Tawfik. Open Sat-Thur 0830-1400.

● **Telephone**
Local code: 062.

● **Tourist information**
There is a **Tourist Friends** booth at the bus station manned by friendly volunteer students who want to be helpful while improving their English.

● **Transport to & from Suez**
Buses: leave the terminal every 30 min between 0600-2030 for the 2 hr journey for Cairo and N along the canal to Ismailia and Port Said. Other buses include: 2 a day E to Sharm el-Sheikh and Dahab, St Catherine's monastery and Nuweiba, and Taba; and N to Alexandria; 5 a day S along the Red Sea coast to Hurghada and on to Luxor. **Ferry**: the vehicle ferry service, taking 2-3 days, from Port Tawfik to Port Sudan is supposed to be weekly but because of both operational and political problems it is often less frequent. During the Hadj season, the ferries shuttle instead to and from Jeddah in Saudi Arabia. **Service taxis**: from the main Arba'in terminal off Sharia el-Geish these travel to all of the same destinations as the buses. Besides the very frequent services to Cairo and N along the canal, travellers going E and S to more remote destinations must split the pre-arranged cost of the journey. **Trains**: run to Cairo but it is better to take the direct express (3 hrs) train which runs 4 times a day rather than the much slower ones via Ismailia.

Fayed

This small beach resort is located just to the W of the Great Bitter Lakes about 60 km N of Suez and 30 km N of Ismailia.

• **Accommodation B** *Helnan Morgan Village*, Km 54, Ismailia/Suez Road, Fayed, T 661718, F 661719, 124 good rm, 262 beds, excellent views, good pool and beach. **E** *Shamoussa*, Km 59, Suez Canal Rd, Great Bitter Lakes, T 661525, 36 rm, poor standard.

• **Transport Road** Buses and service taxis running between Suez and Ismailia stop at Fayed.

Ismailia

Ismailia is 90 km N of Suez and 85 km S of Port Said, is the largest and certainly the most attractive of the 3 main Canal Zone cities. It was built as a depot by the Suez Canal Company in 1861 on the W shore of Lake Timsah (Crocodile Lake). It is divided by the railway track with the attractive and calm Garden City, which was built for the company's European employees to the S towards the Sweetwater Canal and the lake, and the poorly constructed apartment blocks, which were financed with Gulf money, and slums to the N. The Sweetwater Canal

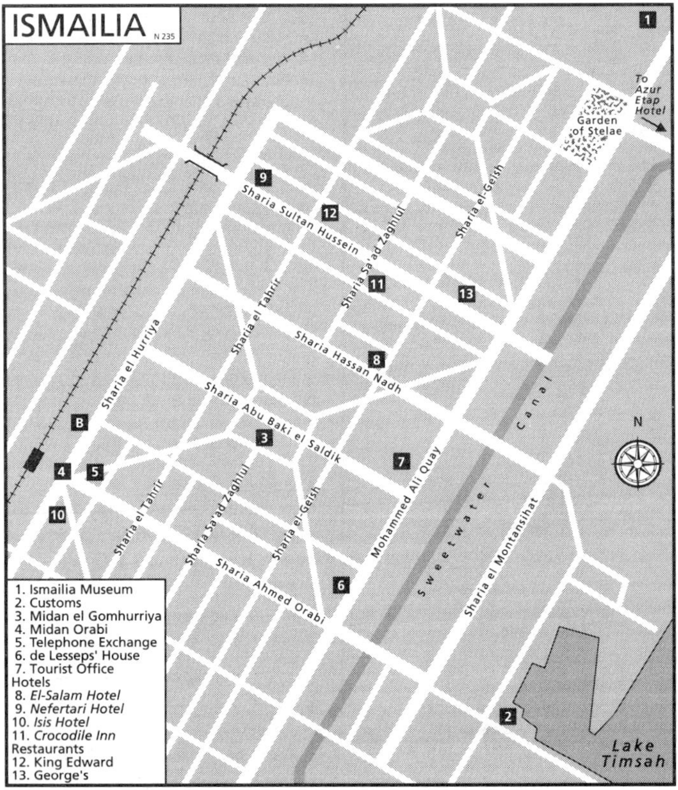

was dug from its source in Lake Timsah to provide fresh water during the construction of the Suez Canal. Desert weary travellers find the gardens and trees a delight. There is very little night life but blissful days can be spent sitting on the beach on Forsan Island watching the ships go by.

ACCESS Travellers arriving by public transport from the Canal Zone and the Delta will be dropped at the depot on Sharia Gumhorriya on the wrong side of the railway tracks. Cross the line to reach the decent end of town and head for the railway station on Midan Orabi. Sharia Ahmed Orabi outside the station runs straight down to the lake and most of the hotels are to be found to the N or left of the street in the Garden City area.

Things to see

Located in the attractive Garden City are a number of minor sites which, although comparatively unimportant, are worth visiting while in town.

The **Ismailia Museum** near Fountain Park in the N of the Garden City is open 0900-1600 on Sat-Thur, 0900-1100 & 1400-1600 on Fri, and 0900-1400 daily during Ramadan. Although it has some minor ancient Egyptian pieces it is the mosaics and other pieces amongst its collection of 4,000 Graeco-Roman artifacts which are the museum's highlights. There is also an interesting exhibit illustrating the construction of the Suez Canal.

Left off Sharia Ahmed Orabi on Mohammed Ali Quay next to the Sweetwater Canal is the **House of Ferdinand de Lesseps** which, although officially a museum, open Wed-Mon 0900-1600, is sometimes used as a government guest house at which times it is closed to the public.

About 7 kms N of the city is the main car-ferry across the Suez Canal to Sinai and the **Bar-Lev Line** which is the impressive 25m high embankment built by the occupying Israelis to stall any Egyptian advance across the canal and into Sinai. Although Egyptian forces managed to break through the line at the beginning of the Oct 1973 war, by using the element of total surprise and high pressure water hoses, the Israeli counter-attack across the Great Bitter Lakes virtually succeeded in surrounding the Egyptian army and, under pressure from the super-powers, both sides were forced to the negotiating table.

Local information

● Accommodation

B ***PLM Azur Etap Forsan Island***, PO Box 77, T 765322, F 222220, 152 rm, 287 beds, the best in Ismailia, located on the lush Forsan Island to the NE of town, good views of Crocodile Lake, private beach, tennis and watersports, a lunchtime buffet on Fri and Sat and a nightly barbecue, all facilities available to non-residents for E£15 per day, excellent value.

C ***Palma Abu Sultan Village***, Abu Sultan, T 400421, F 400862, 98 rm.

F ***Crocodile Inn***, 179 Sharia Sa'ad Zaghloul, T 222724, 39 rm, 86 beds; **F** ***El-Salam Hotel***, Sharia el-Geish, PO Box 50, T 224401, 50 rm, 90 beds, has not received much praise; **F** ***Isis***, 32 Sharia Adli, Midan Station, T 227821, 51 rm, 100 beds, façade more impressive than service, favoured by Egyptian honeymoon couples; **F** ***Nefertari***, 41 Sharia Sultan Hussein, T 222822, 32 rm, excellent value with good rm and facilities; **F** ***Hotel de Voyageurs***, 22 Sharia Ahmed Orabi, T 228304, 25 rm, atmospheric but cheap colonial style hotel.

● Youth hostel

Sea Scout's building, Temsah Lake, Ismailia, T/F 322850, 200 beds, meals available, family rm, kitchen, laundry, parking, station 5 km, overnight fee E£5-12.

● Places to eat

Although there are many other places to eat, besides the hotels, the best restaurants are the ***King Edward*** on Sharia Tahrir just off Sharia Sultan Hussein which is the site of the ***Nefertari*** and ***George's***. At the other extreme are the kebab and other food stalls around the bus terminal but there are also a few cheap restaurants such as the ***El-Gandool*** off Sharia Sultan Hussein.

● Post Office

Located beside the railway station, it is open Sat-Thur 0900-1500.

● Telephone

Local code: 064.

● Tourist information

The tourist office open Sat-Thur 0800-1400 is near the Sweetwater Canal on Mohamed Ali Quay.

● Transport

There are regular **Buses** and **Service taxis** to towns in the Canal Zone and Delta which can be caught from the depot in Sharia Gumhorriya to the W of the railway tracks. Those to Cairo (every 30 min), Alexandria 2 per day (E£10/4½ hrs) and El-Arish on the Sinai coast can be caught from outside the railway station. There are 7 daily **trains** to Cairo (3-4 hrs).

Port Said

Port Said, 225 km from Cairo and 85 kms N of Ismailia at the Mediterranean end of the Suez Canal, was founded in 1859 and named after Said Pasha (1854-1863) who began the construction of the canal. It used to be synonymous with smuggling, drugs and every vice under the sun but today it is a slightly seedy beach resort, predominantly for Egyptians, and free port. Although it has almost no sites, because of the lack of Western tourists it is a relaxing place to sit on the beach for a few days.

ACCESS Most visitors arrive either at the bus terminal in the centre of town near Ferial Gardens or at the railway station and service taxi depot near the Arsenal Basin. The city's main streets are Sharia Filistine (Palestine) along the water-front and the parallel Sharia Gumhorriya which are only a few mins walk from either transport depot.

Things to see

Like the other Canal Zone cities there is comparatively little to see compared with the major tourist attractions. The many Egyptian and few Western visitors stroll around the main shopping streets by day and promenade along the canal and seafront in the evening. There is a free ferry across the canal to Port Fouad and its yacht basin on the E bank which is quieter than the main city.

The **Port Said National Museum**, open Sat-Thur 0900-1600, Fri 1200-1400, is located near *Nora's Floating Restaurant* on Sharia Filistine in a brand new and cool, uncrowded building. Its decent collection ranges through Egyptian history from 2 well-preserved pharaonic mummies through to the coach used by Khedive Ismail at the inauguration of the Suez Canal in 1869.

The **Military Museum**, open daily 0800-1500, is located on Sharia 23rd July near the Corniche and displays exhibits from the various conflicts fought along the length of the Suez Canal. These have included not only the 1956 Suez crisis, but also the successive wars with Israel: the 1973 storming of the Bar-Lev line receives pride of place.

Local information

● Accommodation

B ***Helnan Port Said***, El-Corniche, PO Box 1110, T 320890, F 223762, 70 good rm, private beach overlooking the Mediterranean.

B ***Nora's Tourist Village***, El-Corniche, T 329834, Tx 63404, F 239978, 192 rm, 768 beds, the first tourist village in Port Said and still the best.

D ***Holiday***, Sharia Gumhorriya, PO Box 204, T 220713, F 220710, 81 rm, 147 beds; **D** ***New Concorde***, Salah Salam & Mustafa, Sharia Kamel, T 235341, Tx 63521, 68 rm, 130 beds; **D** ***New Regent Hotel***, 27 Sharia Gumhorriya, T 223802, Tx 63174, F 224891, 36 rm; **D** ***Palace Hotel***, 19 Sharia Ghandy, T 239990, Tx 63534, F 239464, 72 rm, near the governorate building just off the main coast road and the beach.

F ***Abu Simbel***, 15 Sharia Gumhorriya, T 221595, 45 rm, 93 beds; **F** ***Crystal***, 12 Sharia Mohamed Mahmoud, T 222961, Tx 53159, 70 rm, 154 beds; **F** ***La Poste***, 42 Sharia Gumhorriya,T 224048, 46 rm; **F** ***Riviera***, 30 Sharia Ramses, T 228836, 48 rm, 91 beds; **F** ***Savoy Tours Hotel***, Sharia Mohamed Ali, El-Shohada, T 222197, 30 rm, 59 beds, **F** ***Akry Hotel***, 24 Sharia Gumhorriya, T 221013, 26 rm, 48 beds; **F** ***New House***, 128 Sharia Orabi, T 220515, 40 rm, 102 beds; **F** ***Regent***, 27 Sharia Gumhorriya, T 223802, 16 rm, 48 beds; **F** ***Suez Canal***, 10 Sharia el-Taamim, Port Fouad, T 235584, 37 rm, 66 beds.

● Youth Hostel

Sharia el-Amin and Kornaish (near sports stadium), T 226433, 210 beds, family rm, kitchen, meals available, parking, train 2 km, bus 3 km, overnight fee E£5 includes breakfast.

● Places to eat

There are numerous restaurants serving decent if unspectacular Western food with the best being on Sharia Gumhorriya and the Corniche coast road, such as the ***Seahorse*** which serves good seafood. The reasonably priced lunch and dinner cruises on the ***Nora's Floating Restaurant***, which operates from Sharia Filistine in front of the National Museum, provide a good view of the Canal. The most fashionable place in town is the ***Pizza Pino***, serving standard Italian fare, which is nearby just behind the National Museum on Sharia Gumhorriya. Further S along the street is ***Popeye's Café***, which is really a burger bar, past which is ***Reana House*** which serves large helpings of Korean food.

● Banks

There are numerous banks by the canal, or **Thomas Cook** on Sharia Gumhorriya, open 0900-1800.

● Post Office

The main post office, open daily 0700-1700, is on the corner of Ferial Gardens near the bus station.

● Shopping

As Port Said is a free port visitors, excluding ship passengers, are supposed to pass through customs when entering and leaving and it is therefore necessary to declare all valuable items on arrival to avoid being charged a hefty tax when leaving.

● Telephone

Local code: 066.

● Tourist information

The tourist office is at the S end of Sharia Filistine, T 23868.

● Transport

Trains There are 5 slow and dirty trains a day to and from Cairo which take 4-5 hrs via Ismailia. Buses and service taxis may be preferable.

Road Bus There are both regular express and normal a/c buses from the bus station at Ferial Gardens to Cairo (3 hrs) and Alexandria (7 hrs). There are also buses S along the canal, W to the Delta and E to El-Arish.

Service taxis Regular and quick service taxis can be caught to Cairo and Alexandria from the depot near the railway station as well as to other destinations in the Canal Zone, Delta and across the canal to El-Arish.

Sea A weekly ferry service to Limassol in Cyprus usually leaves Port Said on Tues while its sister ship sometimes goes on to Athens via Rhodes.

THE SINAI PENINSULA

CONTENTS

MAPS

Although some hardy travellers wish to encounter the isolation of the harsh but stunning landscapes of the desert interior, most tourists come to the Sinai peninsula to visit the remote St Catherine's Monastery and experience some of the world's finest diving and snorkelling grounds off the Gulf of Aqaba coast around Sharm el-Sheikh. Since the area reverted to Egyptian control in 1982 and the chance of yet another war with Israel receded, the government has succeeded in encouraging the private sector to invest in the area and it is now Egypt's major tourist destination outside the Nile Valley.

Sinai is a very sparsely populated 62,000 sq km desert peninsula which throughout history has acted as both a land bridge linking, and a hostile but spectacular wilderness dividing, Africa and the Middle East. It was the route by which the Israelites reputedly reached the Promised Land and Islam arrived in Africa. It is divided from the rest of Egypt both literally, by the geographical barrier of the Suez Canal and Gulf of Suez, and metaphorically, by successive Israeli occupations between 1948 and 1989 when the dispute over the ownership of the Taba enclave was finally resolved in Egypt's favour. While many tourists still travel overland, either from Cairo or Israel, or by ship from Hurghada or Jordan, the majority now fly to Sinai direct to Sharm el-Sheikh airport.

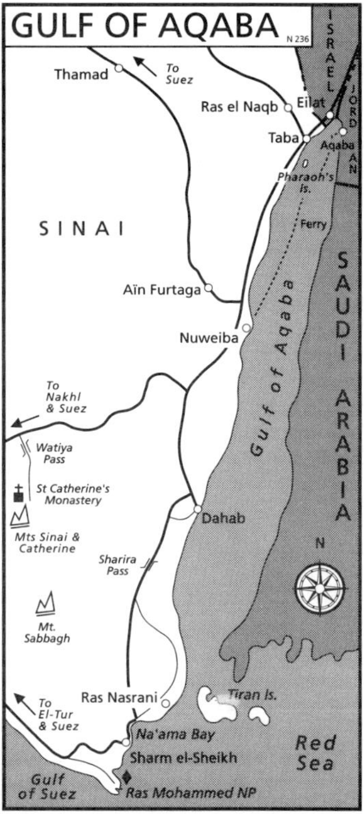

THE EAST COAST

The E coast of Sinai from Ras Mohammed to Taba boasts the most attractive shoreline coral reefs in the northern hemisphere. The climate, tempered by the sea, varies from pleasant in winter to hot but bearable in summer. There are white sand beaches, rugged cliffs and views E to Saudi Arabia and Jordan while to the W lies the barren interior.

Sharm el-Sheikh

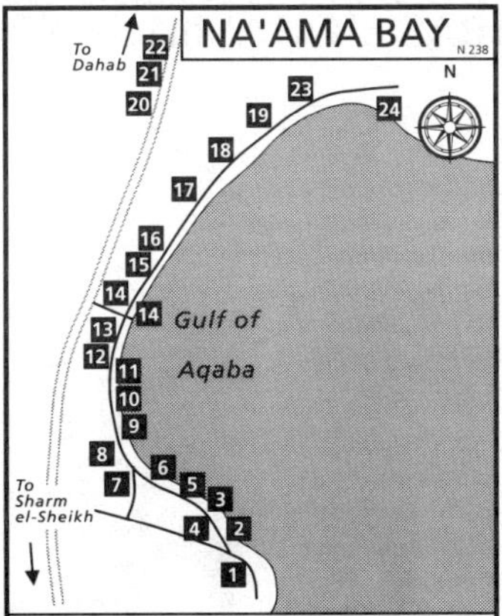

1. Halumi Al Nugum
2. Tourist Police
3. Red Sea Divers
4. Helman Marina Sharm
5. *New Tiran Hotel*
6. Cataract Layalina
7. *Tiran Hotel*
8. Camel Dive Club
9. Red Sea Divers College (Sultana)
10. Sharm Shopping Mall
11. *Kanabesh Hotel*
12. *Sanafir Hotel*
13. Shamandoura Shopping Mall
14. *Movenpick Hotel*
15. *Ghazala Hotel*
16. *Hilton Farouz*
17. *Pullman PLM Azur*
18. *Bastan Village*
19. *Gaffy Land*
20. *Tropicana Hotel*
21. *Pigeon House Hotel*
22. *East Oasis Hotel*
23. *Sonesta Beach Resort*
24. *Oonas Divers Inn*

This is the usual name given for the twin resorts of Sharm el-Sheikh and Na'ama Bay (some 7 km further N) which lie about 470 km from Cairo. The latter has developed rapidly in recent years. Sharm itself, which existed pre-1967 as a closed military zone was used by the Israelis. This small town, which is rapidly shedding its previous dilapidated image, has a bus station, docks, 3 banks, post office, telephone exchange, hospital, police station, supermarket, poorly stocked local shops, a couple of seedy cafés, 2 garages with welding facilities, a row of souvenir shops, a sports club and the rather run down Tentoria Dive Club which is popular with Israelis in the summer season. Although most tourists stay in adjacent Na'ama Bay, Sharm has a youth hostel, a couple of cheap hotels, the excellent *Fayrouz Residence* hotel belonging to the Hilton chain and the 5-star *Seti Sharm Beach Hotel*.

Purely a tourist resort, **Na'ama Bay**, which gets its name from the Arabic for 'God's Blessing', is much more attractive than Sharm and has an excellent sandy beach, good quality modern hotels and some of the best diving facilities in the world (see sports, page 856). There are restaurants and shops for divers and other tourists but little or no indigenous Egyptian life. Indeed the vast majority of the hotel workers come not from Sinai but from elsewhere in Egypt.

ACCESS Package tours lay on a bus to the hotel from Sharm el-Sheikh airport, about 10 km N of Na'ama and 17 km N of Sharm, but individual travellers must rely on service taxis (around E£20) into town. Buses from Cairo (470 km) to Sharm via Suez (336 km) and the rest of Sinai can be caught from Cairo's Sinai Bus Terminal in Abbassia, (T 824753) and terminate in Sharm opposite the market. Buses to Sharm call at Na'ama Bay afterwards while S bound buses from Dahab (98 km), Nuweiba (167 km) and Taba (231 km) stop on request at some of the major Na'ama hotels. There are also frequent cheap bright-coloured minibuses called Tuf-Tufs which run between the two resorts. Ferries from Hurghada arrive at Sharm el-Sheikh port, 1 km from the bus station.

Things to see

There is very little to see in Sharm el-Sheikh or Na'ama Bay and tourist life revolves around the diving and typical beach life. See Sinai's desert interior by taking an organized day trip to **St Catherine's Monastery**, which is breathtak-

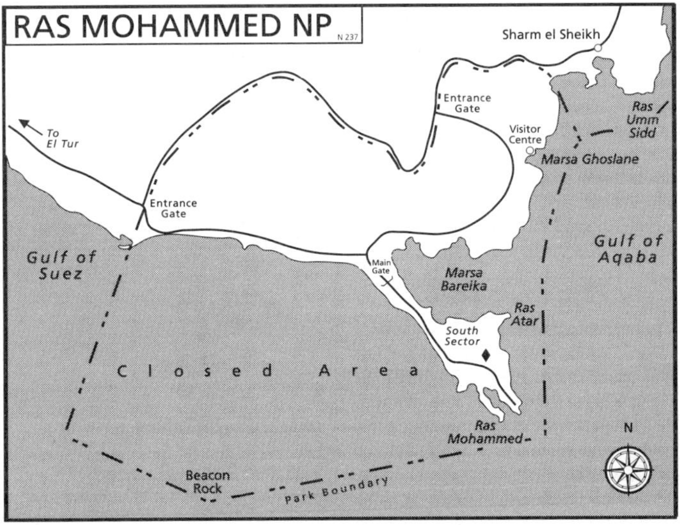

ing, or a desert safari which includes a camel ride and possibly supper under the stars at a bedouin encampment. The Tourist Scene centre at *Sanafir Hotel* offers a selection of package deals including a 1 day safari $55, St Catherine's $49, Camel sunset including dinner $35. A helicopter or a glider can be rented for a tour of the area from the Siag Travel Agency offices in Sharm, T 600860, (helicopter, $70 an hour), or through the *Movenpick Hotel*, (glider). Best Tours, office in *New Tiran Hotel*, offers short tours to Aqaba, Petra and Amman by plane from Sharm airport. Spring Tours, office at Sharm port, offer daily boat trips, except Fri, between Sharm and Hurghada, E£65. Visits to the **White Stork Sanctuary** in the desert near Sharm can be arranged through the *Sanafir Hotel*.

A visit to nearby **Ras Mohammed National Park** to see the marine life from the shark observatory is well worth the effort. Ras Mohammed is a small peninsula which juts out from Sinai's most southerly tip and is the point where the waters of the shallow (95m) Gulf of Suez meet the deep waters (1,800m max) of the Gulf of Aqaba. The result is that, while the land is barren desert, the waters teem with exotic marine life. Besides the huge variety of brightly coloured fish which live on the coral reef normally deep water species such as sharks, tuna, barracuda and turtles come to the reef to feed. Ras Mohammed has clean, shallow beaches, some sheltered but others very windy, from which the snorkelling is excellent.

Taxis to Ras Mohammed from Sharm el-Sheikh cost E£40 one way but it is advisable to keep the taxi for the day – around E£100 – as there are no taxis at Ras Mohammed. Vehicles pass through UN checkposts. Passports are scrutinized at the Egyptian checkpost where Israelis or any non-Egyptians without a full tourist visa, (not just a South Sinai one) are turned back. Beyond deserted Israeli trenches are the gates of the the national park and nature reserve, entrance fee US$5 equivalent plus US$5 per car. The National Park is open from sunrise to sunset while the visitors centre, which includes a restaurant, audiovisual presentations, first aid, shops and toilets, is open from 1000 to sunset. There is very limited water so bring your own bottles from Sharm el-Sheikh.

Local information

● Accommodation

There is accommodation to suit all pockets. Most of the hotels are in Na'ama Bay and it is advisable to make advance bookings for all but the winter season. Rooms are much cheaper if they are booked as part of a package.

The hotels in **Sharm el-Sheikh** itself are: **AL** *Hilton Residence*, T 600266-8, F 770466, 150 rm, now has own beach and sports facilities, buses run to *Fayrouz Hilton* every ½ hr, reported as too quiet in the low season, good *Wadi* restaurant. **A** ***Seti Sharm Beach***, T 600670-3, F 600147, brand new, 231 rm, 7 suites, beach location, 2 swimming pools, tennis courts, water sports and diving centre.

C ***Cliff-Top Hotel***, T 600251, F 600253, 30 rm, part of Sinai Hotel & Dive Club; **C** ***El-Baraka Village***, T 770550, Tx 55092, F 770550, 77 rm, 268 beds.

D ***El-Kheima Village***, T 600167, F 600166, 33 rm of which 20 double rm have a/c, near harbour.

Hotels in Na'ama Bay include: **AL** ***Movenpick Hotel Jolie Ville***, T 600100, F 600111, Tx 66038 Oasis, 210 rm, huge, brand new, excellent service, modern facilities but soulless and not in sympathy with its environment, beach location.

A *Hilton Fayrouz Village*, T 600137-9, F 770726, 150 double a/c bungalow rm, in lovely gardens, beach location, bar, restaurant, excellent meals, first class water-sports, yacht, glass-bottom boat, pool, tennis, minigolf, volley ball, horse riding, massage, aerobics, discotheque, games rm, play area for children. Bus (E£1) to and from Na'ama Bay every hour until midnight; **A** ***Ghazala Hotel***, T 600150, Tx 66037 Gazal, F 600155, 168 a/c rm, smart modern hotel, restaurants, beach location.

B ***PLM Azur Aquamarine Hotel***, T 600175, Tx 66045 Pazur, F 600177, 152 rm, brand new, beach location, *Al Dente* restaurant, dive centre.

C ***Marina Sharm Hotel***, T 600170-1, F 600170, 150 rm, the first hotel here, beach location, good sea views, helpful and efficient staff, bar service, clean rm, buffet; **C** ***Tiran Village***, T 600221, Tx 66013 Tiran, F 600220, currently 75 a/c clean rm with bath, 155 beds, extensions underway, 150 seat restaurant open to non-residents, bank, shops, diving centre, snack bars, pleasant open air areas, mainly European tourists in winter and Israelis in summer.

D *Red Sea Diving College Sultana* run by the Sinai Hotel & Dive Clubs, has 12 double a/c rm with bath, fridge and phone; **D** ***Gafi Land Tourist Village***, T 600210, F 600210, 45 rm, 135 beds, beach restaurant open to non-guests, special dinners, loud disco, relaxed, friendly, clean, welcoming, credit cards accepted, plans for pool; **D** ***Kanabesh Hotel***, T/F 600185, 64 double rm with a/c and bath, restaurant, café, snackbar, bar, live music, small kiosks, travel agent, dive club (**see sports, page 856**); **D** ***Sanafir***, T 600197, F 600196, 90 rm/huts, 150 beds, all creditcards accepted, highly recommended by all the guests of whom about 80% are divers, relaxed, friendly authentic Egyptian atmosphere, *Divers Den* bar, Egyptian, fish and South Korean restaurants, snackbar, own private beach.

● Youth hostel

Sharm el-Sheikh, PO 46619, T/F 600317, 105 bedsin a/c dormitories, with double bunks, no lockers, open 0600-0900 and 1400-2200, kitchen, food available, laundry, parking, members E£5 per night, includes breakfast.

● Camping

Safety-Land, large, cheap camp site next to Sharm el-Sheikh's *Tentoria Diving Centre*. Is particular popular with young Israeli tourists. Divers should be warned that, although cheaper than the Na'ama Bay clubs, the diving safety record is generally not so good at Sharm el-Sheikh. 38 bungalows for 2-4 people at about E£25 per person for half board and 60 large army tents sleeping 4 at the same price, an indoor winter and outdoor summer restaurant with a E£5 breakfast and a E£12 lunch/supper. Nearby ***Sharks Bay*** camp, cost E£30 per night, good for diving, very popular with Israelis, run by Bedouin, staff friendly, good snorkelling, recommended for budget travellers.

● Places to eat

♦♦♦ Pick from the multitude of restaurants, which cater for all pockets and tastes, both along the Na'ama Bay beach-front and in all the major hotels which are open to non-residents. Most serve huge buffet meals. ***Wings and Things***, at the *Sonesta Hotel* for a special occasion meal.

♦♦***Viva Restaurant*** beach location, friendly, new and spacious a/c restaurant and bar which serves good quality French food; ***Wadi*** restaurant in *Hilton Fayrouz Village*, lunch E£40, restaurant dinner E£46 with belly dancer at 2100. ***Al Dente*** restaurant in *Azur Aquamarine Hotel* open 1200-1600 and 1800-2200 also does take-aways. ***Yong Jong*** South Korean restaurant at *Sanafir Hotel*; ***Franco Pizzaria***, at *Ghazala Hotel*, serves good Italian food; ***Viva La Vista*** at the *Divers College* (Sultana) serves reasonably priced, no nonsense, food.

♦In addition there are beach-front stalls serving most varieties of take-away food. The ***Tam Tam*** is recommended.

● Banks
At the top of the hill near the *Hilton Residence* in Sharm el-Sheikh there are 3 banks (Mon-Sat 0800-1400 and 1800-2100, Sun 1000-1200). Most hotels have banking facilities exchanging money at the normal rate.

● Medical
There is a decompression chamber located at the entrance of Sharm el Sheikh (nr MFO checkpoint) operated by **Dr Adel Taher**, T 600922/3, F 601011 or at the *Hilton Residence*, rm 2012. The Multinational Force Observers and the Egyptian Army have provided help in the past for serious cases by flying them to Eilat or Cairo, but this requires special clearance.

● Pharmacy
In Sharm Mall – ***Towa Pharmacy***, T 600779; In Sharm town – ***Dr Sherif Pharmacy***, T 600388.

● Ambulance
Sharm, T 600425.

● Nightclubs
Oriental floorshows, which are open to nonresidents, are largely confined to the major hotels but new independent bars and restaurants are being opened all the time in Na'ama Bay. Most popular nightclubs are the ***Bus Stop*** at the *Sanafir* and the ***Cactus Disco*** at the *Movenpick*.

● Photography
Hire an underwater camera at *Hilton Fayrouz Village*. Kodak have a shop in *Sanafir Hotel* where film can be developed within 1 hr.

● Post Office
At the top of the hill near the *Hilton Residence* in Sharm el-Sheikh there is a post office (Sat-Thur 0800-1500) but all the major hotels have mail services.

● Shopping
Most shops in Na'ama Bay are linked to the hotels and are small but well stocked with provisions for a beach or diving holiday. Two shopping malls offer a variety of fashionable shops including Adidas and Naf Naf. There are no souks and, except for a few near the bus station in Sharm el-Sheikh, there are comparatively few normal Egyptian shops.

● Sport
Water sports In general, and diving in particular, are the main attractions in S Sinai. The reefs off the Gulf of Aqaba coast are acknowledged as some of the best in the world with incomparable coral reefs and colourful marine life. The main dive centres, which are based in Na'ama Bay but which organize dive trips to all of the region's major reefs, include the following:

Aquamarine PLM International Diving Center, Na'ama Bay, T 600276, F 600176, is hidden away in the *Aquamarine PLM Azur Hotel* from where its 9 instructors operate friendly PADI, NAUI and CMAS diving courses using 4 boats.

Aquanaute Diving Center, T 600187, located in Na'ama Bay next to the *Kanabesh Hotel*, comes **very** highly recommended by our correspondents. Eleven instructors, 3-6 boats, good underwater photo facilities. Aquanaute has lots of return customers. Back packers are welcome and helped with accommodation while booked groups receive discount rates. Specimen all inclusive prices: 1-day 2-dive package US$40, 5-day 10-dive package US$195, 5-day course for PADI licence US$285, 2-day advanced diver course US$210. Bookings in England through Regal Diving, Station Rd, Sutton in the Isle, Ely, Cambridgeshire CB6 2RL, T 0353-778096, F 0353-777897.

Camel Dive Club, Na'ama Bay, T 600700, F 600601, which claims to be the largest in town, slick and friendly service. In winter the majority of the divers are Italians, Swiss and Germans while British and French predominate in summer. The club runs 4-7 boats, has 10 European instructors who provide a flexible

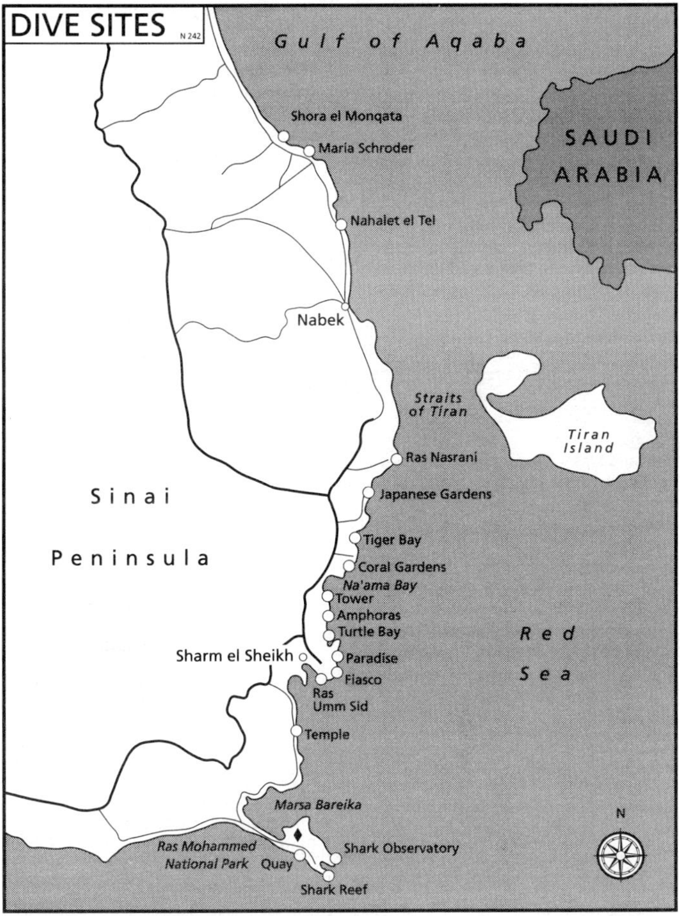

range of CMAS, PADI and NAUI courses. Provides free camping for divers who should bring their tents and sleeping bags. Operates dive safaris to Sudan for a maximum of 12 passengers at US$140 a night.

Oona Diving Centre, Na'ama Bay, T 600581, F 600582. Residential diving club whose guests only come via tour operators, accommodates up to 48 divers in self-catering rm over diving centre, which has full equipment and repair facilities, at about US$20 a night. Oona runs land safaris in 2 Mercedes trucks at US$90 a day and sea safaris for 6-8 people at US$100 a day. Mainly European instructors and divers. Egyptian office at 32 Sharia Baron, Heliopolis, Cairo, T 02 668747, F 02 674153, overseas bookings can be made through Oona Divers UK, 23 Enys Rd, Eastbourne, Sussex, T 0323-648924

Red Sea Diving College, Na'ama Bay, T 600145, F 600144, located in the centre of the beach next to *Kanabesh Hotel*, is a PADI five star fully equipped IDC centre joint project between Sinai Hotels & Diving Clubs, and

Scubapro Europe. Opened 1991, 10 multi-lingual PADI instructors from a good purpose built facility. Courses which includes all the gear but excludes certification fees are US$40 for an introductory dive, US$265 for a standard open water course, US$360 for a 3 day underwater photography course and US$550 for a dive masters' course. The college caters for up to 40 divers including British (35%), German (30%), Italians and other Europeans.

Sinai Divers Club, Na'ama Bay, T 600150-4, F 600158, Gazal UN. Claims to be the largest diving centre in Na'ama Bay and handles 40-110 divers on 2 dives a day. Germans make up half the divers in summer (May-Oct) while about 60% of the winter divers are British. Book in advance in the winter high season. Sinai runs 8 day boats and 2 live aboard boats, has 10 qualified instructors, runs a full range of courses, has daily excursions and dive cruises for the keen diver with everything under one roof and trips to all the major reefs.

Colona Dive Club at the *Kanabesh Hotel* caters for 40-50 people from beginners to experienced divers and rents all equipment for snorkelling, glass bottom boats, jetski from private beach. 95% of guests come through tour operators mainly from Western Europe. T 600184.

For **non-divers** there are many other water sports. On the beach outside the *Marina Sharm Hotel* you can rent masks and fins (E£16/day), windsurf board (E£31.5/day), jetski (E£150/hr, E£75/30 min, E£40/15 min), glass-bottom boat E£20 for ½ hr.

At *Fayrouz Village* snorkelling equipment E£15, motor boat E£30 for 15 min, windsurf board E£30 per hr, pedal boat or canoe E£15 per hr. Glass bottom boat trip E£20 for ½ hr.

The *Sanafir* offers horse riding excursions including sunset rides. Lessons E£10 per hr; hire E£20 per hr and E£70 per day.

● Telephone

Local code: 062; **Fire**: T 600633 **Ambulance**: T 600425.

● Travel agents

There are travel agents attached to almost all the major hotels, as well as a few independent ones, which can book transport, hotels, sightseeing and other excursions.

● Tourist information

The Egyptian Tourist Authority (ETA) office is at the top of the hill near the youth hostel in Sharm el-Sheikh, T 768385. In addition all the major hotels can provide detailed tourist information.

● Transport to & from Sharm el-Sheikh

Local Car hire Europe Car from *Fayrouz Hilton* or *Ghazala* hotels. **Hertz** from *Movenpick Hotel*. **Taxi** T 600357.

Air Ras Nasrani Airport, T 600314, 600543, is further along the coast 10 km N of Na'ama Bay with direct flights to and from an increasing number of European cities as well as internal flights to Cairo (daily at 0645), Hurghada and St Catherine.

Road The bus station Sharm, T 600660, is at the bottom of the hill in Sharm el-Sheikh. Buses to Cairo cost E£25-E£50 depending on which you take, go at 0700, 1000, 1300, 1630, 2330 and 2400, and take 6 hrs. Other destinations include Zagazig E£15, 1200, 7 hrs; Suez E£12, 0900, 1100, 5 hrs; Mansura E£27, 0900, 1100, 8 hrs; Taba E£10, 0900, 3.5 hrs; St Catherine's Monastery E£10, 0800, 4 hrs; Nuweiba E£7, 0900, 2.5 hrs; and Dahab E£5, 0900, 1.5 hrs.

Sea Daily ferry to Hurghada (except Sat), takes 5-15 hrs, costs E£60.

NORTH FROM SHARM EL-SHEIKH

The road journey N from Sharm el-Sheikh to Dahab (98 km) takes 60-90 min and passes the airport before turning inland through beautifully rugged scenery past a bedouin school, a water drilling camp, a manganese quarry, the tomb of an Israeli general and the remains of his bombed out car before entering Dahab.

Dahab

98 km N of Sharm el-Sheikh, 82 km from Sharm el-Sheikh airport, 133 km from Taba and 570 km from Cairo, Dahab made its name which means 'gold' in Arabic, as Egypt's hippy capital after Israeli troops started visiting the bedouin village for rest and recreation on its golden beaches in the 1960s. Although it is a rather commercialized shadow of its past it is still a primary destination for would-be hippies and beach bums. In recent years the government has tried to clean

up Dahab's image, by cracking down on drugs and discouraging back-packers and turn it into a more conventional resort to cater for 'normal' tourists.

Dahab can be divided into 3 distinct areas. About 1 km inland from the beach is the dull little administrative town of Dahab which seems covered in wind-blown rubbish from the local tip. Bedouin village, Asla, 3 km up the coast, is where the hippies hang out in the beach campgrounds and restaurants. Meanwhile the impressive new and totally self-contained holiday village on the beach is deliberately isolated from the 2 other parts of the town.

ACCESS There are daily buses N from Sharm el-Sheikh and S from Taba and Nuweiba, or shared taxis can be hired from anywhere along the Gulf of Aqaba coast. Because of Dahab's split site, make sure you know where you want to be set down. A taxi from one section of town to the other will cost as much as the bus fare from Sharm el-Sheikh.

Things to see

On land there is little or nothing to see in Dahab itself, but camel trips can be organized to one or two bedouin villages in the beautiful interior. Jeep and horse-back safaris can be taken into the mountains.

Local information

● Accommodation

There are really only 2 accommodation options in Dahab, either the tourist holiday village or the numerous campgrounds along the beach in the bedouin village. **B** ***PLM Azur Dahab Holiday Village***, Dahab Village, P.O. Box 23, Dahab, T 600403, F 600890-3, 142 rm with private terrace, including 40 divers' cabanas, 1 two-bedroom suite and 4 one-bedroom suites. Brand new, spotlessly clean, very attractive, excellent beach, best beach in Dahab, 'A' rm are on the beach, 'B' rm in the middle of the village and 'C' rm at the back, restaurant, café, bar, discotheque, bank, the **Inmo Diving Centre**, windsurfing, a glass boat, pedalos, canoes, tennis courts, free bicycles, volley ball, horseback riding, safari and desert trips, shops, satellite TV. Non-residents can enjoy the facilities for E£40.

● Camping

The contrast could not be greater than with the multitude of cheap campgrounds, which have names like ***Fighting Kangaroo***, ***Crazy House***, and ***Lazy Days Camp***, along the beach-front in the nearby bedouin village. For the sake of security it is best to opt for thatched-roofed but stone-walled huts which can be padlocked while avoiding the baking tin-roofed shacks. Most have showers, sinks, primitive toilets, but no electricity. Like the ***Hilton Camp*** most charge around E£4 a night or about E£15 for full board. While some campgrounds, such as ***Reef & Coral***, ***Mohamed Ali***, and ***Star of Sinai***, are more popular than others and some should be avoided, they change from year to year and it is probably best to ask around and see which ones are recommended. More hygenic, if more expensive, is the ***Sheikh Ali and William Camp***, E£10 a night, which still retains its original Bedouin simplicity and beauty.

● Places to eat

In the *Dahab Holiday Village* restaurants are: ♦♦♦ ***Zeitouna*** main restaurant. ♦♦ ***Lagoon*** beach café; ***Aqamarina*** diving centre cafeteria; ***Bar-A-Cuda*** bar; ***Bedouin Corner***; ***Tota*** in Asla, is the most highly recommended eaterie in Asla, easily recognised by its boat shaped façade, good quality, and almost the only place selling beer. In addition there are lots of beach-front restaurants in the Bedouin village including: ♦***Hard Rock Café***, ***Scorpions Restaurant***, and the Australian run vegetarian ***Fighting Kangaroo***. In Asla ***Ali Baba***, which includes vegetarian dishes, a Chinese and a Korean restaurant; ***Neptune's***, decent food, sparkling clean, cost E£15 each.

● Banks

Bank of Egypt, (open daily 0830-1400 and 1800-2100) near the bus station, in Dahab town accepts travellers' cheques. There is also a bank in the holiday village.

● Nightclubs

Besides the holiday village's ***Where-Else*** discotheque and bar, nightlife mainly revolves around the restaurants and cafés in the bedouin village which are open until around midnight. Most popular by far, is the ***Black Prince Disco*** in the *Gulf Hotel*. A shuttle bus to the camp sites is provided by the hotel free of charge.

● Post Office
In Dahab town centre is open Sat-Thur 0830-1500.

● Shopping
In Dahab town and a few very small supermarkets in the bedouin village which are open 0730-2400 and stock most of the basics including bottled water. ***Hano's Madness*** in Asla is the only tattoo parlour in Egypt.

● Sport
Although the reefs are not as good as in Na'ama Bay there are diving centres in the holiday village and in the bedouin village which rent equipment and run PADI diving courses. Overnight trips to see the nocturnal lobsters at the Blue Hole, 2 km N of the village, and possibly eat one the next day are recommended. The holiday village also offers a wide range of sporting activities including the **Inmo Diving Centre**, windsurfing, a glass boat, pedalos, canoes, tennis courts, free bicycles, volley ball.

● Telephone
Local code: 062.

● Tourist information
There is no tourist office in town. Drivers should be warned that there is only one petrol station on the 81 km route between Dahab and Sharm el-Sheikh which also has the nearest hospital.

● Transport
Road: **Bus** The bus station is outside the Bank of Egypt in Dahab and there are a number of daily buses S to Cairo via Na'ama Bay and Sharm el-Sheikh, N to Nuweiba and Taba, and E to St Catherine. **Taxis** are a necessary expense for getting between Dahab town and the beaches and unfortunately tourists are usually charged more than Egyptians.

Nuweiba

This town, 69 km N of Dahab and 64 km S of the Israeli border at Taba, and its Moshav or cooperative village used to be a major destination for Israeli tourists during its occupation, but it has long since been surpassed by Na'ama Bay and has now lost most of its tourist business. Nuweiba is divided between the tourist village and the small town around the port, 8 km S, which ferries Saudi Arabia bound Egyptian expatriate workers and pilgrims to the Jordanian port of Aqaba. From Nuweiba you can see Saudi Arabia across the water as the Gulf of Aqaba narrows towards the N. There can be strong southerly winds but not sandstorms for a few days in Jan, Feb, April and Oct.

ACCESS All the buses arrive at Nuweiba port and most continue on to the tourist village or vice versa.

Things to see
Apart from the beachlife there is little to see or do in Nuweiba which is a boring little town. Enterprising locals, however, organize camel treks and jeep safaris from the resort to the magnificent Coloured Canyon and elsewhere in the interior. Many take short trips to Petra in Jordan via the ferry to Aqaba.

Local information
● Accommodation
Nuweiba has a number of mid-range to cheap hotels and camp sites mainly in the tourist village but also in the port and further along the coast towards Taba. **A** ***Nuweiba Hilton Coral Village***, T 520320-1, F (02) 771689, new 5-star hotel with 200 rm, 6 suites, 20 'superior' bungalows, spread over 115,000 sq m of beach front, watersports, horseback riding, safaris; bicycles, tennis, children's facilities, 2 pools, diving centre.

B ***Nuweiba Holiday Village***, Nuweiba, T 770393, F 3922228, 172 rm, Egyptian run, 60% of guests are on package tours, clean, comfortable a/c chalets with bath, beach location, shuttle bus to/from Nuweiba, restaurant, sports facilities.

C ***El-Sayadeen Touristic Village***, Nuweiba, T 757398, Tx 92634, 66 a/c twin bed chalets with bath, poorly located near (but outside) the port, adequate but rather old and spartan, restaurant, pool, pebbly beach with windsurf boards and pedalos, European guests in winter and locals in summer.

D ***Bawaki Beach Hotel***, km 18 N of Nuweiba, T 770825, F 3526123, 36 rm, 108 beds, beach location 1 km from Nuweiba-Taba road and 47 km from Taba, attractive, well built chalet hotel, friendly and helpful staff, cheap restaurant, bar, beach café, seawater pool, mainly European guests in winter and locals in summer, some problems with fresh water, power and telephone facilities, hire of fishing boat, cruise boat (E£100/hr), speed boat for water skiing (E£40/hr), windsurfing, and good snorkelling with submerged coral reef just offshore.

E *Barracuda Hotel*, Nuweiba, T 771611, F 762298, 24 rm, simple hotel next to the port, main guests are expatriate Egyptian workers travelling to/from Jordan and Saudi Arabia; **E** *El-Salam Village*, Nuweiba, T 3928830, Tx 93939, 100 rm; **E** *Sally Land Tourist Village*, Taba-Nuweiba Road, Nuweiba, T 743689, located off coast road half way between Nuweiba and Taba (36 km), highly recommended, tastefully planned, 32 attractive chalets, beautiful white sandy beach, courteous and efficient staff, mainly European guests, restaurant, café, bar, shop and beach snack bar, snorkelling and windsurfing equipment for hire.

● Camping

Nuweiba Camping located next to *Nuweiba Holiday Village*, simple huts with 3 beds, a mirror, cupboard, table and chairs (E£24 per person), E£12 to pitch your own tent or E£3 to sleep on the beach, large clean communal cold showers, self-catering facilities and also near to a range of restaurants, cheerful staff who will organize camel and other trips.

● Places to eat

♦♦The **Nuweiba Holiday Village's** main restaurant provides adequate but unspectacular breakfast (E£8), lunch (E£21) and dinner (E£23) as well as a special barbecue (E£25), and fish restaurant dinner (E£23). At **Bawaki Village** restaurant the prices are slightly less. Besides the hotels there are a number of places to eat such as the **average** ***Macondo's*** fish restaurant next to the Holiday Village and the **cheaper** ***Sharkawi*** which is one of 3 **cheap** restaurants near the former Moshav and along the beach towards the village of Tarbeen, 2 km N of the resort.

● Banks

There is a bank inside Nuweiba port, but you need your passport to get into the port, and the tourist village will change cash.

● Nightclubs

Nightlife in Nuweiba is very limited and revolves around the hotel beach bars. *Pool Cave Bar* with live music and darts at *Nuweiba Hilton Coral Village* is the most popular.

● Post Office

In the tourist resort.

● Shopping

There are a few small stores and bakeries in and around Nuweiba town and the tourist resort.

● Sport

Although the Holiday Village has some facilities including tennis courts, sports are otherwise limited to water sports with equipment being hired out at the hotel. The ***Nuweiba Diving Centre*** is run by good European divers who are recommended as being particularly helpful for beginners. Nuweiba itself is not the best site on the coast for diving but, because it is quiet, it is ideal for beginners and a 45 min introductory course costs US$40 while a full diving course costs US$240 per person. Trips to other and better dive sites can also be organized.

● Telephone

Local code: 062.

● Travel agents

There are no travel agents in Nuweiba.

● Tourist information

Only at the hotels.

● Transport

Road Bus There are various daily buses from Cairo, Suez, Sharm el-Sheikh and Taba which call at the port and the tourist village.

Service Taxis, with passengers sharing the cost of the journey, are available from Nuweiba port to Taba and other towns in the region and prices should be negotiated before setting off.

Sea There are 2 ferries a day between Nuweiba port and the Jordanian of port of Aqaba which is 4 hrs further up the coast. Although there are some tourists the service is mainly used by Egyptian expatriate workers and also pilgrims who have to queue for hours outside the port during Ramadan, when a third sailing is often added to the schedule. Having checked their passports, foreigners are usually encouraged to jump the queue and proceed into the port to the ticket office and through customs. Two week or one month Jordanian visas are issued on board or immediately on arrival in Aqaba, although it is slow process, with charges varying according to nationality. You will not be allowed to disembark if there is any evidence of a visit to Israel in your passport including a Taba entry stamp.

Taba and the Realigned Border Post

Taba is an enclave of land of no more than 1 sq km on the Gulf of Aqaba seized by the Israelis in the war of 1956 but, unlike the rest of Sinai, never returned to Egypt. Assuming that the Taba strip would be forever Israeli, an international hotel complex was built there (now the *Taba Hilton*). In 1986 agitation by Egypt for a final settlement of the international border at Taba led the dispute being put to an arbitration panel of three persons.

The arbitration revealed that the border post at Ras Taba, one of fourteen put in place after the 1906 Anglo-Turkish agreement, had been moved by the Israeli side. This was discovered from searches made by specialists from the **School of Oriental & African Studies, London University**, of the Ottoman archives in Istanbul and through evidence taken from the notes of the original British survey team in the early part of the 20th century.

In one of the oddest of cases concerning the delimitation of an international border this century, it was found that the Israeli army had cut away part of the hill at Ras Taba to enable Israeli artillery to have a good sweep of the Sinai coast road as it approached the port of Eilat. At the same time the Israeli military engineers removed the border post which rested on the top of Ras Taba. This gave the Israeli government the excuse to claim that, despite Israeli maps to the contrary, the old border had always run S of the Taba strip. In 1989 the arbitrators returned Taba to Egypt, though it remains virtually an enclave with border posts on all sides.

Taba

This town has a special place in the hearts of most Egyptians because, although it is only tiny, it was the last piece of territory which was occupied by the Israelis. The fact that the luxury *Sonesta hotel*, one of Israel's best and most popular hotels, was located in the Taba enclave no doubt complicated the dispute. Despite having to pay compensation to the Sonesta's owners, before handing the hotel over to the Hilton group to manage and despite the very small size of the area in dispute, Cairo had been determined to retrieve every centimetre of Egyptian land and was satisfied at the outcome.

Besides the hotel there is little else in the tiny enclave except barracks and facilities for the border guards and customs officials. There are, however, major plans for the area and a danger of too much development. Land is very cheap at only E£5 per square metre to be paid over a 10 year period. The result is that a huge and ugly 3 storey concrete development is now being built 9 km SW along the coast from Taba. Having won Taba back from Israel, the government is now concentrating tourist development in the region and is building power stations and other infrastructual facilities to support the planned tourist influx.

Climate: Taba

	Jan	Feb	Mar	Apr	May	Jun	Jul	Aug	Sep	Oct	Nov	Dec	Av/Tot
Max (°C)	21	23	26	31	36	38	39	40	37	33	28	23	31
Min (°C)	10	11	14	18	22	24	26	26	25	21	16	12	19
Rain (mm)	2	8	8	5	2	0	0	0	0	2	2	8	37

ACCESS The easiest way to reach Taba, which is 390 km from Cairo and 260 km from Sharm el-Sheikh, is via Israel's Eilat airport which is only 15 km across the border. Taxis and buses run to the border and the hotel is just a few steps on.

Things to see

Sightseeing in Taba is limited to trips to the beautiful interior, **Pharaoh's Island** with the ruins of Salah al-Din's (Saladin's) fortress, and across the Israeli border to Eilat. A visit to the island, which is a short boat ride (400m) from the *Salah el-Din* hotel, is well worth the trip especially around sunset when it is particularly beautiful. The fortress was originally built by the Crusaders to guard the head of the Gulf of Aqaba and protect pilgrims travelling between Jerusalem and St Catherine's monastery: it was also used to levy taxes on Arab merchants travelling to and from Aqaba. Although Eilat, which is Israel's main holiday resort has many obvious attractions, it should be remembered that a visit could cause passport problems in other Arab countries (**see transport into Israel, page 864**). There are helicopter rides available from Taba (also Dahab and Sharm el-Sheikh), max 5 passengers, range 600 km. For information Siag at *Taba Hilton*, T 771414 or T 771309, also Sharm el-Sheikh, T 600860.

Local information

● Accommodation

AL ***Taba Hilton***, Taba Beach, Taba, T 771888, Tx 63552, F 771461, (address via Israel which is far more efficient is PO Box 892, Eilat 88107, Israel, T 059 79222, F 059 79660), 10 storey hotel with 251 double rm, 53 twin bed rm and 12 suites, private beach, pool, water sports, a 150 hp motorboat, a diving yacht with 14 berths for extended trips, 5 floodlit tennis courts, volley ball, table tennis, billiards rm, games rm, and video games, use of facilities at the sister hotel *Club Inn* just across the border in Eilat. There are 5 restaurants and 3 bars – the ***Taba Lounge, Papo's Pub, Fantasy Island***, pool bar and ***Nelson Village*** bar. In addition there is the ***End of the World*** nightclub and a gambling casino attracting cross-border business from Israel, a variety of shops, bank, travel agency and car rental service.

C ***Salah el-Din Hotel***, Taba, T 771345, Tx 21472, F 3564005, 50 double well equipped chalets, located 5 km S of Taba, view of Pharaoh's Island, large portions of simple food, friendly staff.

● Camping

F ***Basata Camping***, at Ras al-Bourg, T (02) 3501829, beach location 42 km S of Taba, peaceful, well run, caters for a maximum of 300 people in single/double/family huts but 80-90 is normal, especially popular with Germans, Israelis, Egyptians, Dutch, British and French including many diplomats from Cairo embassies, strict policy of no drugs, alcohol or loud music, only natural food, no diving which would damage the coral, communal evening meal (E£7-E£10), clean and well run communal kitchen. Facilities include a small desalination plant, showers, snorkelling, safari trips by camel and jeep, and 2 taxis for hire.

● Places to eat

Expensive in the *Taba Hilton* restaurants – ***Palm Court, Marhaba Oriental, Casa Taba Italian, Surfer's Deck***; **Average** at the *Taba Hilton* outdoor ***Nelson Village Grill*** and **cheap** and cheerful meals in the ***Salah el-Din***: breakfast E£6, lunch E£14 and dinner E£16.

● Banks

Taba Hilton in Taba open 24 hrs, only bank in Egypt that changes Israeli money.

● Nightclubs

The ***End of the World*** and gambling casino at *Taba Hilton*. ***Nelson Village Disco*** under the stars, also at *Taba Hilton*.

● Post Office

Use *Taba Hilton* which sends mail via adjacent Eilat rather than distant Cairo.

● Shopping

Except for a few local food shops the only other ones are in the hotel.

● Sport

See *Taba Hilton* above.

● Telephone

Local code: 062.

● Travel agents

In *Taba Hilton* are very efficient and can arrange onward travel.

● Tourist information
Available at hotels.

● Transport
Air Nearest airport is Eilat (15 km) with direct daily flights to major European cities. (No problem at Egyptian border but customs officials at airport are very thorough). By comparison the local Ras el-Naqb airport 39 km away only has a few flights a week from Cairo.

Road Bus There are daily buses to and from Cairo, Sharm el-Sheikh via Nuweiba and Dahab, and Eilat across the border in Israel.

● Transport into Israel
Although the checkpoints are always open it is better to cross between 0700-2100 and to avoid crossing on Fri just before the Israeli sabbath when almost all businesses close and transport ceases. Free one-month Israeli entry visas are available for most Western tourists. **NB**: make sure that your **entry card** and **not** your passport are stamped because an Israeli stamp, and even an Egyptian entry stamp from Taba, disqualifies you from entering most other Arab counties. Once on the Israeli side of the border you can catch a service-taxi or much cheaper No 15 bus into Eilat.

Excursions from Taba

The Ahmed Hamdi Tunnel The road journey across the centre of the Sinai peninsula from Taba to the Ahmed Hamdi tunnel under the Suez Canal takes about 4 hrs. Due to repairs, the tunnel is no longer open 24 hrs but only from 0600-2000. The turnoff just to the S of Taba is the main road, which is good except for the first 17 km which is very steep and suffers from regular flooding, to the tunnel 270 km away. Ras el-Naqb airport, 20 km further on, serves Taba and Nuweiba which is 80 km away but only has a few flights a week from Cairo. From the airport the road proceeds onto a flat plain and to both UN and Egyptian checkpoints. About 190 km from the tunnel there is a small, dirty site which includes a petrol station, mosque, restaurant, radio mast and semi-finished houses. Further along the route there are pillboxes, burnt out trucks from the fleeing Egyptian army in 1967, and lots of road building. At **Nakhl** there is a petrol station, police post, garage, mosque, as well as cafés and stalls which have fresh fruit. At a crossroads 126 km from the tunnel there are turnoffs to El-Arish (151 km) and El-Hasana (63 km). The maximum speed limit is 90 km/hr for cars and 80 km/hr for buses. About 70 km from the tunnel there is turnoff for Ras Sudr one way and El-Hasana the other way. Further on is the **Mitla Pass** and its trenches, pillboxes and other war debris, which was the site of one of the largest tank battles in history. Closer to the tunnel there are turnoffs for Ras Sudr, Wadi el-Giddi, El-Tur and Qantara. The tunnel under the Suez Canal costs E£1.50 for cars and E£3 for buses.

Immediately after the Ahmed Hamdi Tunnel there is a crossroads to Ismailia, Suez and Cairo where there are some dirty cafés and a petrol station. The road to Cairo across a empty featureless desert plain passes lots of quarries, a coal stockpile and army camps, including one with candy striped huts, and follows the railway line from Suez to Cairo. After a major traffic police checkpoint the dual carriageway is a very good road. About 100 km from Cairo there is a Red Crescent station. The E of Cairo has some very large industrial works and the air becomes noticeably more polluted.

THE INTERIOR

St Catherine's Monastery, (Cairo 450 km, Sharm el-Sheikh, Dahab 140 km, Nuweiba 110 km, Taba 188 km, Ras Sudr 260 km), despite its location in the heart of the Sinai wilderness, is one of the most important tourist sites in the country. The monastery located at the base of **Mount Sinai**, where God is believed to have revealed the Ten Commandments to Moses, has attracted pilgrims and visitors for centuries.

The **Burning Bush**, through which God is said to have spoken to Moses, holds religious significance for Jews,

Blazing Bushes And Catherine Wheels

Mount Sinai marked the half way point of the flight of the Jews from Egypt to the 'promised land'. Moses was clearly an inspirational leader for the incident of the burning bush led him to return to Egypt to lead his people to the land of milk and honey. Despite calling down from God the 10 plagues (frogs, lice, locusts, hail and fire among them), he failed to persuade the Pharaoh to release them from their slave labour. Finally the 80-year-old Moses asked God to strike the Egyptians with the passover when the Jews marked their houses with lamb's blood and were spared the massacre of all first born children. As a result, the Pharoah banished the 600,000 Israelite men, women and children from Egypt. Their epic journey is related in the Book of Exodus in the Bible. They were pursued by the Egyptians (drowned after the Red Sea divided to allow the Israelites across), faced starvation (rescued with manna from heaven) and thirst (saved when a spring flowed from a rock Moses had struck with his staff) and defeated an attack by the Amaleks.

On Mount Sinai, Moses received the wisdom of the Ten Commandments which have formed the code of practice for human behaviour for centuries.

The supposed site of the burning bush was developed into a monastery and in the tenth century named after Saint Catherine. According to legend Saint Catherine, who was born in AD 294 and was from a noble family in Alexandria, was a Christian convert who was martyred in the early 4th century for refusing to renounce her faith. She herself converted hundreds of people to Christianity and accused Emperor Maxentius of idolatry. When he tried to have her broken it was claimed that she shattered the spiked (Catherine) wheel by touching it, so Maxentius resorted to having her beheaded in Alexandria. Her body was alleged to have been found centuries later at Egypt's highest point on top of Mount Catherine (2,642m), where angels were said to have laid it, but others believe that the myth was created by mediaeval Western Catholicism.

Christians and Muslims and in 337 AD **Empress Helena**, mother of **Constantine**, decreed that a sanctuary was be built around what was thought to be the site of the bush. It became a refuge for an increasing number of hermits and pilgrims who sought the wilderness of the Sinai Valley over the following centuries. Between 537 and 562, **Emperor Justinian** expanded the site considerably by building fortifications to protect the residents and adding the **Church of the Virgin** and the **Basilica of the Transfiguration**. The monastery and its community which then, as today, was controlled by the Byzantine Church was tolerated by the subsequent Muslim conquerors. The number of pilgrims dwindled until a body, claimed to be that of the Egyptian born St Catherine, was 'discovered' in the 10th century and was brought to the monastery which attracted many pilgrims during the period of Crusader occupation (1099-1270). The numbers of both pilgrims and monks, who are now restricted to Greeks mainly from the Mount Athos area, subsequently waxed and waned until today there are only 17 monks, but the thousands of international pilgrims and tourists actually make the monastery too crowded in the high season.

The road journey from Dahab to St Catherine, which is generally very good with little traffic, takes about 1½ hrs. On the way, at the top of a very steep hill there is a breathtaking view over the desert. The coaches and taxis stop here and bedouins attempt to sell fossils, sand-roses and other souvenirs. You then pass through one UN and then 2 Egyptian checkpoints. There is a small run down cafeteria 55 km from St Catherine, trenches (25 km), the *El-Salam hotel* (15 km), Green Lodge camping and restaurant and Masr petrol station (10 km), Morganland camping (8 km) and a bedouin village and encampment just before arriving in St Catherine.

ACCESS While all of the organized tours to St Catherine stop at the monastery itself, the normal buses services stop in the small village of St Catherine about 2 km below the monastery. **NB**: **climate** St Catherine's is very cold in winter with a metre of snow a few times a year and snow sometimes until March but it is very hot in summer. Despite the environment there are no problems with water or electricity.

St Catherine's Monastery

Entry to the monastery, which is open Mon-Thur & Sat 0900-1200 but closed Fri, Sun and public holidays is free. Visitors to the interior of the Monastery must dress modestly. Shorts are not allowed – for either men or women. There is no dress code for outside visiting. Although an official tour guide, who will explain the history and symbolism of each part of the monastery, is a bonus he is not essential if you buy the monastery's guide book in the small bookshop near the entrance.

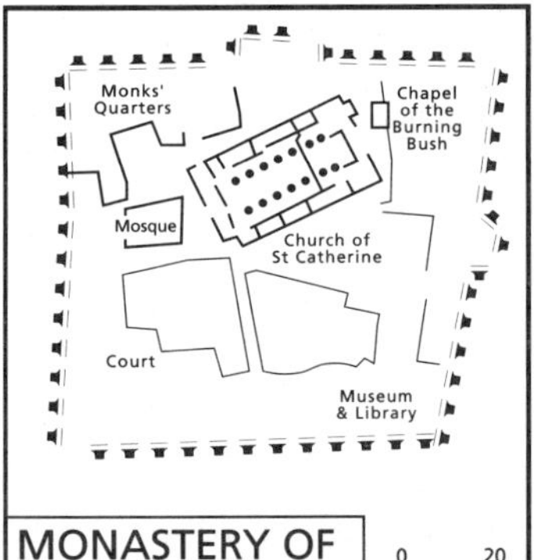

MONASTERY OF ST. CATHERINE

The highlight of the walled monastery, which includes the monks' quarters and gardens which are not open to the public, is the highly decorative and incense-perfumed **St Catherine's Church** which includes the **Chapel of the Burning Bush**. The church was built between 542-551 AD in memory of **Emperor Justinian**'s wife. Its 12 enormous pillars are decorated with beautiful icons representing the saints which are venerated in each of the 12 months of the year. A candle is lit below the relevant icon on each saint's day. The walls, pillars and cedar-wood doors of the church are all original. At the far side of the N aisle is the **Chapel of the Burning Bush** which, although it was the site of the original sanctuary, was not included in Justinian's original building but was only enclosed later on. A silver plate below the altar marks the site where the bush is supposed to have stood.

W of the church is a small 11th century **Mosque** which was apparently built in order to placate the Muslim invaders and to encourage them to tolerate the monastery. Significantly, however, the church steeple is considerably taller than the minaret of the mosque.

The **Library**, which is unfortunately closed to most of the public, is one of the monastery's most unique features with an almost unrivalled collection of precious Greek, Arabic, Syrian, Georgian, Armenian and Slavonic manuscripts reputedly second only to that of the Vatican.

The monastery's small **Museum** contains a collection of the gifts presented to the monastery over the centuries. The treasures were randomly scattered throughout the monastery until their accumulated worth was calculated by Friar Pachomius who then carefully gathered and preserved them in one place but many of the more interesting items have been lost over the ages.

Because the monastery's **Cemetery** in the gardens was so small the custom was developed of storing the overflow of monks' bodies in the **Charnel House** which is in the monastery gardens. When a monk died his body was buried in the cemetery place of the oldest body which is then removed to the Charnel House. Visitors can visit this rather macabre room which is full of skeletons and skulls.

Immediately to the right of the monastery's main entrance at **Kleber's Tower**, which is about 15m high and 3m thick, is **Jacob's Well** which it is claimed has never dried up. It is supposed to be the site where the 40 yr old Moses, who was fleeing from Egypt, met one of Jethro's seven daughters called Zipporah whom he subsequently married. Just around the corner to the left of Kleber's Tower is a rather unimpressive overgrown thorny evergreen bush which is claimed to be a transplanted descendant of the **Burning Bush** from which God allegedly spoke to Moses.

Mount Sinai

If time permits, climb Mount Sinai (Jebel Musa), 2285m, where Moses is alleged to have received the Ten Commandments. The view is particularly spectacular at sunset and sunrise (see Camping above). The stiff walk up the steep camel track, which takes about 2½ hrs, is quite rough and stout shoes and warm clothing are essential. Although there are refreshment stalls on the way up, which get more expensive nearer the summit, it is advisable to take at least 2 litres of water per person if making the ascent during the day but it is best to start the ascent at about 1700, or earlier in winter, in order to arrive at the summit at sunset.

A summit meeting of Christians, Jews and Muslims is planned here in 2000. Go now and avoid the rush.

Mount Catherine

At 2642m Mount Catherine or Jebel Katrinahth is Egypt's highest peak. It is about 6 km S of Mount Sinai and is a 5-6 hr exhausting climb. On the summit there is a small chapel with water, a 2 room hostel for overnight pilgrims and a meteorological station.

Local information

● Accommodation

AL *St Catherine Tourist Village*, Wadi el-Raha, St Catherine, T 770221, Tx 21472, F 770221, in the Wadi el-Raha or "Valley of Repose", unrestricted views of the monastery 2 km up the road, 130 clean twin-bed chalets of local stone the shape of a bedouin tent, mainly European, US and Japanese guests who stay one night, normally full in high season, restaurant, coffee shop, gift shop, library, video hall, tennis, billiards, and table-tennis.

C *El-Salam*, St Catherine Airport, St Catherine, T 771409, Tx 92634, 35 rm, 135 beds, expensive 2 star hotel.

D *Danielli*, T/F 749772, St Catherine, nice grounds, simple, comfortable but not enough blankets in winter.

● Hostel

The hostel at the monastery, E£30+ a night for a bed in a simple and cramped dormitory, communal showers, includes simple breakfast. Reserve a room by asking at the monastery between 1700-1900.

● Camping

There is no specific camp site at St Catherine but it is possible to spend the night on Mount Sinai to see the sunrise but, because of the altitude, its sub-zero night-time temperatures for much of the year make a torch, sleeping bag and warm clothing absolutely essential.

● Places to eat

Besides the more expensive hotel restaurants like ***El-Safsafa*** at *St Catherine's Tourist Village* there are two cafés serving decent food in town and the El-Monagah snack bar.

● Banks

Bank Misr branch on the main street in St Catherine town is open daily from 1000-1400 and 1800-2100.

● Post Office

Is opposite the bank in town and open Sat-Thur 0800-1400.

Shopping
In the town there is the ***Supermarket Katreen*** and another supermarket, a grocery store, bakery, bazaar and petrol station.

Sport
Mainly limited to tennis and a few indoor games at the tourist village.

Telephone
Local code: 062. There is an international telephone exchange in town open from 0800-2400 near the post office.

Transport
Air Reservations must be made well in advance for the direct Air Sinai flights between St Catherine airport, 15 km from the town, and Cairo (2 flights a week), Hurghada and Sharm el-Sheikh which offer in addition spectacular views of the Sinai peninsula.

Road Bus There are direct buses for the 8 hr journey between St Catherine town and Cairo's Sinai terminal via Suez and others to Dahab, Nuweiba and Sharm el-Sheikh. **Service taxis**: travellers can share the cost of hiring a 7 seat service taxi to Dahab, Sharm el-Sheikh, Taba, Suez or other towns in the peninsula, but the prices almost double once the last bus has left St Catherine.

THE WEST COAST

The W coast of Sinai on the Gulf of Suez is far less attractive than the Gulf of Aqaba coast. It has been spoilt by the oil industry which, while being one of Egypt's sources of foreign exchange, has transformed this region into a mass of oil rigs and gas flares and made it unsuitable for another foreign exchange earner – tourism. The largely featureless coast has become polluted with oil industry debris and is far more interesting to the industrialist than to the tourist.

El-Tur

Although it is the administrative capital of S Sinai the seedy and dilapidated coastal town of El-Tur, which is 108 km from Sharm el-Sheikh and 170 km from Suez, has little to commend it. The best hospitals are located here as it was the quarantine stop for pilgrims from Mecca.

• **Accommodation** **E** *Jolie Valley Hotel*, by Port El-Tur, Tur Sinai, T 771111, 43 rm, 140 beds; **E** ***Lido Hotel***, Moon Beach, Tur Sinai, T 771700/Cairo 2906496, F 771780, 35 rm, 86 beds.

• **Places to eat** Only the restaurants in the hotels can be recommended.

• **Telephone** Local code: 062.

• **Transport Road Bus** The most important information about El- Tur is how to get out of town. There are daily buses to Sharm El- Sheikh and Suez.

Ras Sudr

Cairo (190 km), Sharm el-Sheikh (290 km), Nuweiba (365 km), Dahab (385 km), St Catherine's (250 km), Taba (433 km), near the northern end of the Gulf of Suez is both an oil company town and the site of a noxious oil refinery but also a destination for middle class Egyptian tourists.

Things to see Nearby sites include **El-Shatt point** (41 km), **Oyoun Moussa** (31 km), the 494m high natural pyramid at **Hammamat Pharaoun** (50 km), and the rock temple at **Sarabit el-Khadem** 'Heights of the Slave' (130 kms).

• **Accommodation** **C** *Ras Sudr Tourist Village* 12 villas with 40 beds, 100 chalets with 400 beds, and a 20 rm hotel with 60 beds, 2 restaurants, shops, water sports, tennis,

CLIMATE: EL-TUR

	Jan	Feb	Mar	Apr	May	Jun	Jul	Aug	Sep	Oct	Nov	Dec	Av/Tot
Max (°C)	21	22	24	28	31	34	35	35	32	30	27	23	29
Min (°C)	9	10	13	17	20	23	24	25	23	19	15	11	17
Rain (mm)	1	1	1	0	0	0	0	0	0	0	0	5	8

squash and volley ball, childrens' playground, video hall, billiards, chess and table tennis. Information/reservations from Misr-Sinai Tourist Company, Misr Travel Tower Building, Abbassia, Cairo. T 02 821061, F 2 830242, Tx 93565.

D *Sudr Beach Inn*, PO Box 119 Cairo, Ras Sudr, T 770752 or Cairo T 2828113, F 770752, 20 rm with bath and balcony (12 double and 8 triples), good accommodation overlooking the Gulf of Suez, restaurant and gift shop.

F *Daghash Land Tourist Village*, Ras Sudr, T 777049 or Cairo 605884, 84 rm, located 19km from Ras Sudr, often space available, restaurant, café, table tennis, video hall and private beach with 2 bars. Information/reservations from the Daghash Company, 8 Ahmed Fouad, Sharia Nassim, Nasr City, Cairo, T 609672.

• **Places to eat** Only the restaurants in the hotels are recommended.

• **Sport** Some facilities at the tourist village.

• **Telephone** Local code: 062.

• **Transport** By bus: the daily buses between Suez and Sharm el- Sheikh stop at Rus Sudr.

NORTHERN SINAI

Although the majority of tourists only visit the Gulf of Aqaba coastline and St Catherine's Monastery, the northern part of the peninsula has a number of attractions both in El-Arish and along the 210 km Mediterranean coastline which stretches from Port Said to the Israeli border at Rafa. Unfortunately, while the region is beginning to be appreciated by Egyptian tourists, most foreigners only see the area from the bus window as they speed to or from the Israeli border.

El-Arish

This town 180 km E of the Suez Canal is the governorate capital of N Sinai and is noted for its 30 km of palm-lined beach. From the bus station in Midan Baladiya it is a 2-3 km walk or minibus ride along the main road N to the beach which is the site of most of the hotels. This area is very popular at weekends.

Things to see You can visit **El-Arish Castle**, which is located on a plateau to the SW of the town on the remains of an ancient pharaonic castle. Otherwise life in town revolves around the beach. Out on the Rafa road there is a small **museum** of handicrafts and stuffed Sinai wildlife but its opening hours are very irregular and the exhibits disappointing. Thurs market (Souq el-Khamees) bedouin market in the oldest part of town selling N Sinai embroidered cloth, plants, produce, bedouin handicrafts.

• **Accommodation** Hotels along the beach range from the luxurious **A** ***Hotel Egoth Oberoi***, T 351321/7, F (02) 3837777, sports and recreation facilities including health spa, tennis and squash courts, windsurfing, pedal boats, private beach, which is the only place in town which sells alcohol and the **A** ***Al-Baron***, T 668701, to a number of more simple tourist hotels. During the July-Sept high season it may be difficult to find a room without booking.

• **Camping** It is possible to camp on the beach with permission from the police. ***El-Arish Camping***, about 7 km W of the town has two-man tents or you can pitch your own.

• **Places to eat** Besides the hotels there is an outdoor restaurant near the *Egoth Oberoi* and a number of cheap restaurants and sheesha (water-pipe) cafés in and around Baladiya Square such as ***Aziz*** or there is ***Maxim's*** on the beach.

• **Banks** Misr Bank T40036, National Bank of Egypt T40414, Bank of Alexandria T40169 and Sinai National Bank for Development T40952 in town and the main hotels will also change money.

• **Nightclubs** Besides the main hotels there is almost no nightlife except the cafés in Baladiya square.

• **Post Office** The post office and the international telephone exchange are located off Sharia 23rd July between the *Sinai Sun Hotel* and Baladiya Square.

• **Shopping** There are some rather sleazy tourist shops on Sharia 23rd July but for quality items it is better to bargain at the bedouin market on Thurs.

• **Telephone** Local code: 068.

• **Travel agents** *Misr Travel Office*, T 41241/41049.

• **Tourist information** There is an Egyptian General Authority for the Promotion of Tourism office in El-Arish T 41016 in the same office as the Tourist Police station T 41016 which is located just before the beach on Sharia Fouad Zakry. The main police station and hospital are on Sharia el-Geish on the way to Rafa.

• **Transport Air** There are 2 Air Sinai flights a week from Cairo on Sun and Thur. The airport is along the Bir Lahfan road to the S of the town. **Road Bus** There are frequent daily buses between El-Arish and Cairo (6 hrs), which should be booked the day before, and others to the Suez Canal cities of Qantara and Ismailia. **Service taxis** leave El-Arish in the morning and drop passengers off at Koulali Square in Cairo.

• **Transport into Israel** There are very frequent buses and service taxis E to the international border with Israel at **Rafa**, 41 km from El- Arish, open winter 0900-1700 and summer 1000-1800. It is best to avoid crossing on Fri. Whenever you cross it is advisable to leave El-Arish in the morning to avoid getting caught in the Gaza Strip during the 2000-0400 curfew. There is a free one month Israeli visa for most Western tourists. **NB**: make sure that your **entry card** and **not** your passport are stamped because an Israeli stamp, and even an Egyptian entry stamp from Rafa, disqualifies you from entering most other Arab counties. Occasionally there are major luggage searches of tourists but this is usually reserved for Arab travellers. Once on the Israeli side of the border you can catch a service-taxi into the Israeli side of the divided town of Rafa and then on to Khan Yunis and Gaza City's Palestine Square from where there are service taxis to Jerusalem and Tel Aviv.

THE RED SEA COAST & EASTERN DESERT

Contents

Maps

The EasternDesert lies in a belt between the Nile and the Red Sea which stretches for about 1,250 kms from the southern end of the Suez Canal to the Sudanese border. The slowly widening major fault line running along the whole length of the Red Sea has created the Red Sea Mountains, including Jebel Shaayib el-Banat (2187m), which are the highest in Egypt outside the Sinai peninsula. Most visitors simply traverse this scorchingly hot, inhospitable and virtually uninhabited region to get to the Red Sea Coast which is one of the fastest growing tourist regions in the country.

The Ministry of Tourism is trying to encourage tourists to visit not just Cairo, Luxor and Aswan but also other regions of the country. This will reduce the burden, particularly during the high winter season, on the overloaded infrastructure of the main tourist centres and spread the financial benefits of the tourist industry more evenly throughout the country. For this reason the ministry is promoting the Sinai peninsula, which is already a major tourist destination, the Western Desert and, above all, Hurghada on the Red Sea coast.

Hurghada

529 km SE of Cairo, 395 km S of Suez and 299 km NE of Luxor, Hurghada lies on the Red Sea coast about half way between Suez and the Sudanese border. In some ways it is an ideal location for a new tourist development because it is in a virtually uninhabited region and a long way from the Islamic fundamentalist strongholds. This means that the hotels and their guests do not overburden the local infrastructure or offend the sensibilities of the local population. Instead hotels and holiday villages have been built which, with the exception of fresh water which is supplied from the Nile valley, are largely self-contained. They employ workers from the major cities. Unfortunately, although there are some very good hotels, in its dash for growth the government has allowed the 'get-rich-quick' private sector to erect some appalling shoddily-built concrete boxes. The area has been developed too quickly and without adequate controls and has thus repeated the mistakes of some resorts on the N Mediterranean shores. While Hurghada's facilities undoubt-

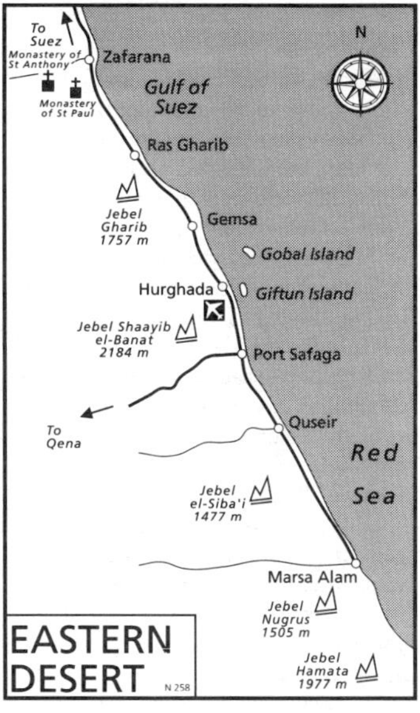

edly offer good cheap beach holidays it has been partially achieved by removing any trace of local Egyptian culture. The Egyptian government has pledged $130m to create further leisure facilities here.

ACCESS Most visitors arrive at Hurghada from the airport, which is 6 kms SW of the town which can be reached by taxi, or by bus or service taxi which stop on the main N-S "highway" at the S end of the town. The main town and most of the hotels lie to the W and N of the area's main physical feature, a barren rock outcrop known as Ugly Mountain to the E of which is the public beach and the Red Sea. About 2 km S along the main highway is Hurghada's port after which is a number of the major holiday villages.

Although it is easy to walk around the relatively compact town it is necessary, when trying to get to the port or the holiday villages to the S of town, to take cheap local buses and minibuses or the town's taxis which are amongst the most expensive in the country. Alternatively cars and bicycles can be hired from some of the hotels.

Things to see

In Hurghada life revolves around the beach, water-sports and nightlife. All-day boat excursions to **Giftun Island**, now often overcrowded with boats anchored offshore, are available from most hotels which usually add a 20%-25% commission to include rental of snorkelling equipment. The same operators, including Flying Dolphin Sea Trips, Nefertiti Diving Centre and Sunshine Sea Trips also organize longer boat trips including 3 day trips to **Gobal Island**, overnight excursions to Giftun, and expeditions to the deeper reefs such as the **House of Sharks** (20 km S) where the experienced divers can see hammerheads and tiger sharks and other exotic marine life. To view marine life and keep dry there is the Finnish-built a/c 44 seat **Sinbad Submarine** offering a 2 hr round trip including 1 hr underwater for US$50 which should be booked the day before. **Marine Museum** (5 km N), open 0800-1200, E£3.50. **Aquarium**, 6 Sharia Corniche, adjacent Three Corners Village, open 0900-2200, E£5.

Much further afield, back N towards Cairo on highway H44, are 2 neighbouring isolated monasteries (also on itineraries from Beni Suef or Suez.) Pilgrim tours to these monasteries are organized by the Coptic church in Cairo, T 821274 or YMCA T 917360, and from Minya, Assuit and Luxor. Day tours there with lunch are offered by a number of Hurghada travel agents including Misr Travel. Otherwise a group can negotiate a single price with a local taxi in Hurghada. Provided it is not too hot and you take enough water and only light luggage it is also possible to get out of a Beni Suef to Zafarana service taxi or the Hurghada to Cairo or Suez bus at the turn offs for the monasteries of St Anthony and St Paul, respectively, and then hitch the remaining 15 kms in each case.

St Anthony's Monastery (open daily 0900-1700 except during Lent and between Nov 25-Jan 7), known locally as Deir Amba Antonyus is the more important. St Anthony, (251-356 AD), became a hermit after he was orphaned at 18 just before the height of the persecution against the Christians by emperor Diocletian (284-305 AD). By 313 AD not only was Christianity tolerated but it had also been corrupted by becoming the state religion. This led to increasing numbers of hermits following Anthony's example and seeking isolation in desert retreats (see St Catherine's monastery, page 853 and El-Fayoum, page 746). After his death, at the reported age of 105, the location of his grave was kept secret but a small chapel became the foundation of the monastery shortly after his death. St John the Short sought refuge at the monastery 200 years later and died there.

In the course of its history it has been subject to attacks from the bedouin tribes in the 8th and 9th centuries and the Nasir al-Dawla who destroyed it in the 11th century. It was restored in the 12th century by monks from throughout the Coptic world, only to be attacked again in the 15th century when the monks were massacred and the buildings badly damaged by rebellious servants. Syrian monks were sent to rebuild it in the mid-16th century and it was then inhabited by a mixture of Coptic, Ethiopian and Syrian monks. Its importance rose and many 17th-19th century Coptic patriarchs were chosen from amongst its monks: by the 18th century it was receiving increasing numbers of European visitors. The result has been that the 5-church monastery has developed into a large and virtually self-sufficient modern village which draws water from an ancient spring and grows most of its own food.

St Anthony's Church, parts of which date back to the 13th century, is the oldest church in the complex. It consists of a central nave, 2 side chapels and an antechamber. While inside try to identify the apostles in the picture on the S wall! There are 4 other churches in the complex. **St Mark's Church** dates from 1766 and is reputed to contain the relics of St Mark the Evangelist in a chest on the N wall.

The whole complex is enormous with the outer walls spanning 2 km. In addition to the churches and chapels there is a library, a large garden, flour mills and a bakery.

Cave of St Anthony, 276m above and 2 km NE of the monastery, is a steep 1-2 hr walk but the view alone from the cave, 690m above the Red Sea, justifies the climb. The cave, where St Anthony is supposed to have spent the last 25 years of his life, consists of a terrace, chamber, tunnel and balcony. The decorations on the walls are mediaeval graffiti often complemented by more recent additions in the shape of supplications stuck into the cracks of the walls by visiting pilgrims.

The smaller **Monastery of St Paul**, (open daily 0900-1700 except during Lent and Nov 25-Jan 7), which lies to the SE of St Anthony's monastery and is reached via the main coastal road, was built around the cave where St Paul the Theban (228-348 AD) spent his life. Although the dates do not actually match, he is supposed to have fled the persecution of **Decius** (249-251 AD) and arrived in the E Desert from Alexandria at the age of 16. He is the earliest hermit on record and was visited by St Anthony to whom he gave a tunic of palm leaves. St Paul apparently acknowledged him as his spiritual superior and St Anthony's Monastery has always overshadowed that of St Paul both theologically and architecturally.

The larger of the 2 churches is dedicated to St Michael and there are 2 sanctuaries. The S one is dedicated to St John the Baptist where a strange 18th century gilded icon depicts the saint's head on a dish. The **Church of St Paul** contains the actual cave where he lived and what are claimed to be his relics which were preserved during the many raids on the monastery. On the third floor of the keep is the **Church of the Virgin** which is unfortunately closed to the public because its wooden floor is dangerous.

Local information

● Accommodation

There are many officially registered hotels and many other non-registered ones and new ones are being erected all the time. Although most visitors pre-book their accommodation as part of a package with their flight there should be no problem, except during the winter high season, for independent travellers to find a room. All of the hotels have roof tanks to store fresh water which is piped in from the Nile Valley but, depending on their capacity and electricity supplies, there can be problems with the water provisions at certain times. If the promised tourist developments along the coast towards Safaga do go ahead it will be necessary to build at least one desalination plant because the water supply is the main obstacle to any major expansion in tourist numbers in the area.

Although there are numerous small and unregistered hotels and fleapits, the registered hotels with the address Hurghada, Red Sea, are as follows: **AL** ***Hurghada Sheraton***, T 40785, Tx 92750, F 442033, 130 rm, 250 beds, to S of town, 8 km from airport, 65 rm in distinctive circular main building, 19 poolside cabanas and 10 two-storey 4 room chalets on the beach, all luxury facilities, 3 restaurants, bars, large pool, tennis, water sports, boat cruises, fishing trips and barbecue; **AL** ***Sonesta Beach Resort***, PO Box 18, T 764633, Tx 93242, F 443660, 153 rm, 300 beds, new, private beach, guests are 80% German and 20% British tour groups, Sonesta Diving Centre with 8 instructors.

A *Coral Beach Village*, 22 Km Hurghada-Safaga Rd, T 443577, F 443577, 178 rm.

B *Magawish Tourist Village*, Magawish, T 763284, F 440255, 314 rm, excellent standard, private bay and beach to S of port, offers all the normal facilities plus a wide range of water sports and children's activities; **B** *Mashrabia Village*, Sheraton Road, T 443602, Tx 20021, 140 rm, very good Moorish style 4 star hotel, located to S of port, 3 pools, para-sailing and excellent water sports, guests 75% German.

C *Arabia Beach Tourist Village*, T 441790, F 441792, 348 rm, 700 beds, very large, well equipped, new, mainly German guests, pools, tennis, squash, courts, jetski and water-skiing, fitness centre, Nautico Diving Centre with 6 instructors; **C** *Giftun Village*, T 440665, F 442666, 282 rm, 584 beds, good, comfortable, German-run, to S of port, private beach; **C** *Jasmine Holiday Village*, 6 km airport, T 441442, Tx 20735, F 442441, 430 rm, 1,000 beds, good standard, so large that it is a long walk from the main building to the beach, the beach restaurant, inconveniently, only accepts cash.

D *Gezira*, Sharia el-Baher, T 441708, 30 good rm built around a courtyard, located in NE of town near the poor public beach, restaurant, bar and discotheque; **D** *La Bambola* Corniche, T 44085, 56 en suite rm with balconies, clean, good, up-market, highly recommended budget hotel, located in town centre, 200m from beach, restaurant, roof-top bar, pool, barbecue, discotheque; **D** *Moon Valley*, Sheraton Road, T 440074, 30 rm, former backpackers retreat which moved up-market, located to S of port, private beach, diving courses around a small coral reef; **D** ***Princess Club/Palace***, T 443100, F 443109, 160 rm, 2 separate parts directly opposite one another about 3 kms S of town, *Palace* offers better accommodation than the cheaper *Club*, both offer good service, cool, relaxing atmosphere, restaurants, bar, shops, squash, pool, private beach, water-sports; **D** *Shedwan Golden Beach*, T 441044, 152 rm, reasonable standard, town centre location, restaurant, bar, disco, banking, private beach, pool, tennis, squash, dive centre, guests mainly French, Belgian and German; **D** *Three Corners Village*, 2 Corniche, T 447816, F 447514, 132 rm, well run, lively, welcoming, downtown beach-front hotel, Dutch manager, good facilities, 2 restaurants, bars pool, ideal for families, winter guests mainly Dutch, French, German and Austrian with British visitors in summer.

E *Dolphin House*, T 446977, 26 rm with bath, (10 with a/c), small, friendly but rather jerry-built hotel, close to the beach, use of private beach (E£5 per day), rooftop restaurant with sea view, and bicycle, motorcycle and car hire. **E** *Friendship Village*, T 443100-2, F 443109, 104 rm, 260 beds, budget hotel, use of facilities at *Princess Palace*, large open-air restaurant, pizzeria, shop and laundry service, clean rooms, problems with smelly drains and mosquitos; **E** *Mena House*, 20 rm, budget hotel which caters mainly for students, restaurant, bar, oriental cabaret and belly dancing, private beach, windsurfing, diving with multilingual instructors, and day trips to Giftun Island; **E** *White House*, Sheraton Rd, very clean, up-market budget hotel, German owned, large a/c rm with bath and balconies, decent restaurant, TV lounge.

F *New Ramoza*, Hurghada, 43 rm with a/c or fans and balconies, good value, popular with students, small private beach, TV lobby, and discotheque. ThE ***Old Ramoza*** just next door has 24 rm with fans, communal showers, guests are students or Egyptians; **F** *Sunshine Hotel*, T 441463, located off main road near minibus stand, cheap and tatty but clean community style hotel with shared kitchen and showers, restaurant and diving centre, has been highly recommended.

● Youth hostel

New Tourist Centre, T 442432, 45 beds, kitchen, overnight fee E£5 includes breakfast.

● Camping
There are so many cheap hotels that camping is unnecessary. The site most recommended is the *National Youth Camp* 5 km N of town. **BEWARE if camping on the coast, large areas of shoreline are still mined, enter fenced-off areas at your peril.**

● Where to eat
Besides the hotels there are a number of places to eat in Hurghada. ♦♦♦*Lacost de Mirette* beach restaurant. There are lots of ♦restaurants, cafés and food stalls in the centre of town of which the best are probably the ***Red Sea Restaurant*** for good fish dishes and ***Columbo Restaurant*** at the S end of Sharia Abdel Aziz Mustafa.

● Banks
Banque Misr (Sun-Thur 0830-2100, Fri & Sat 0900-1330) and **National Bank of Egypt** are almost adjacent on main street.

● Nightclubs
As a major tourist resort there is less concern about offending Islamic sensibilities. As a result, besides the main hotel restaurants which serve beer, there are many discotheques in town including the ***Cha Cha Disco*** which is open until 0300, and those at the major hotels.

● Post Office
Is located next to the tourist police on Sharia al-Centeral to the S of the new mosque. It is quite easy to make international telephone calls from most hotels.

● Religious services
Coptic Church, Fri and Sun 1000.

● Shopping
Hurghada has very few local shops although all of the major hotels and holiday villages have shopping arcades which cater for the tourists' requirements.

● Sport
Deep-sea fishing in the particularly rich fishing grounds of the Red Sea is very popular with rich European and Japanese businessmen but it is also comparatively expensive.

Diving Visitors come to Hurghada for the water sports and all the major hotels either have an affiliation to one of the main diving centres or have their own.

Most of the diving centres offer similar facilities and it would be difficult to detail them all. As an example, one of the best is the ***Red Sea Scuba Diving School***, T 443101, F 443109. It was the first PADI and BS-AC school in the country. Its multi-lingual instructors operate from the school, located at the *Princess Village* hotel, which has its own training pool, classrooms, equipment room, shop and boats. Once students qualify they can dive with the associated dive centre in the *Princess Village* which is one of the best in the resort. In 1994 the PADI Open Water Course or BS-AC Novice II course costs US$220. Bookings for all grades of courses can be made in England through Regal Diving, Station Rd, Sutton, Ely, Cambs, CB6 2RL, T 0353 778096, F 0353 777897.

Watersports At the *Mashrabia Village Hotel* non-divers can hire **jetskis** (E£160/hr), **waterskis** (E£170/hr) and 6-8 man boats for fishing trips from E£600, while its Mistral windsurfing centre hires up to 150 boards. Similarly the Giftun Village Hotel has the well-equipped ***Barracuda Club*** for diving and windsurfing.

Windsurfing is particularly good at Hurghada because of the gusty winds and equipment can be hired from a number of outlets.

● Telephone
Local code: 065.

● Travel agents
Besides the independent travel agents there is at least one in each major hotel.

● Tourist information
(Open daily 0900-1400) is in the same building as the tourist police, on the main street between the telephone exchange and the Egyptair office. Given the intense competition between travel agencies and dive centres, there is probably little additional information that the office can provide.

● Transport
Air There are regular daily Egyptair flights (T 22400 in town and at airport T 84088300) and ZAS flights from Hurghada airport to Cairo (1 hr) daily at 0715 and 1600 plus additional flights during the week, and 3 times a week to Luxor. Egyptair (open 0800-2000, T 440788) and ZAS (open 1000-2100, T 440019) have offices almost next to each other in the square with the new mosque. Air Sinai has weekly flights to Sharm el-Sheikh and St Catherine's monastery.

Road: **Bus** The new bus station is on the main N-S road to the S of the main town. Regular daily buses N go to Suez (6-8 hrs) and Cairo (6-12 hrs depending on the service), and SE to

Luxor (4-5 hrs) and Aswan via Qena (7-8 hrs) which are very full in the winter high season.

Service taxis (quicker but more expensive than buses), can be caught from either the minibus stand on the main road or the square next to the old mosque. Go early in the morning for the 7-seat taxis to Suez (4 hrs) and Cairo (5-7 hrs) or Luxor (4 hrs) and Aswan (6 hrs). Group hire of a taxi to Sharm el-Sheikh (700 km about 10-14 hrs) avoids the 18 hrs bus journey with a long wait in Suez.

Sea Daily ferry (except Sat) to Sharm el-Sheikh on the Sinai peninsula (5-15 hrs depending on the weather and the boat), costs E£70. Early booking essential. Take food and water for the journey.

Safaga

60 kms S of Hurghada, this town stands where the coastal road meets the main road across the Eastern Desert to Qena. Its small port exports phosphate from the local mine and imports grain, much of it US food aid, which is currently trucked inland to the Nile Valley although a disused freight railway line to Qena may soon be reopened.

Hurghada developed rapidly but is unable to cope with the tourist pressure during the winter high season. In addition, lack of planning control has allowed large, ugly hotels to create a concrete eyesore. To escape these problems, new self-contained holiday villages are being built to the S of Hurghada and to the N of Safaga. These include a huge project on the **Abu Soma peninsula** outside Safaga. In a few years time, if the pace of development continues, there will probably be a ribbon of holiday villages stretching between the 2 towns.

Things to see

Most tourists simply pass through on their way between Hurghada and the Nile Valley. There is very little to visit other than a small ancient fort which overlooks the town and offers good views. More adventurous visitors continue to **Quseir** 85 kms S along the Red Sea coast. This was once the most important Muslim port on the Red Sea and was the main transit point for Egyptian pilgrims bound for Mecca. In the 10th century it was superseded first by Aydhab, which is the ancient name for the Halaib in the currently disputed triangle on the Egyptian-Sudanese border, and then by Suez after the canal was opened in 1869. It fell into disuse until it was recently reopened as a phosphate export terminal. The road inland from Quseir to Qift, which is just S of Qena, follows the ancient pharaonic road which was built at a time when almost 100 small but very rich gold mines operated in the region. Many of these mines have been reopened using modern technology.

Local information

● Accommodation

The officially registered hotels all addressed as Safaga, Red Sea, are: **C** ***Menaville Village***, T 451761, F 451765, 152 rm, pleasant atmosphere, our choice; **C** ***Safaga Paradise Village***, T 451631, F 451630, 244 rm, similar to *Menaville* but larger and less cosy.

E *Cleopatra Hotel*, T 451544, 48 rm, 126 beds, more than adequate.

F *Seeland Village*, Sharm el-Naga, T 3545756, F 3545060, 15 rm, 45 beds, value for money.

● Places to eat

This resort is so new that only restaurants in hotels are established.

● Sport

There is one diving centre at Safaga for studying the nearby larger fish and hammerhead sharks but the sea is too rough for other than experienced divers. The further S one goes in the Red Sea the larger and better the fish. The Sudanese coast is reported to be the best of all.

● Telephone

Local code: 065.

● Transport

See Hurghada above.

THE WESTERN DESERT AND THE GREAT DESERT CIRCUIT

CONTENTS

MAPS

This section concentrates on the journey along the 'great desert circuit' rather than on individual towns, because it is the journey itself and not the oases towns which is of greatest importance.

"It is not easy to conceive the sterile grandeur of the scene...I may truly say, I never enjoyed myself more, despite the thermometer at 105 degrees, and the numerous petty inconveniences I was necessarily obliged to submit to. Certainly, no fine lady, who could not do without her everyday luxuries and comforts, should attempt the desert ... but I was born under a wandering star..."

Anne Katherine Elwood 1830.

Wherever you are in Egypt, the desert is not far away, and its presence can always be felt. The Western Desert alone constitutes two-thirds of Egypt's total area. Its significance in any travel itinerary depends upon how much of a traveller you are and how much a tourist. Desert travel presents its inconveniences and its hazards, but the rewards are beyond measure.

Depending upon the time available and personal preference there are various choices. They range from a day trip from Cairo to **El-Fayoum** (see page 746) or **Wadi Natrun**, which technically are not true oases because they are fed with water from the Nile, to **The Great Desert Circuit** of **Bahariya, Farafra, Dakhla** and **Kharga Oases**, or **Siwa** (see Marsa Matruh, page 838) and **The Great Sand Sea**. Although it is undoubtedly part of the Western Desert, the wonderful oasis of Siwa is dealt with in the section on Alexandria and the Mediterranean because it is only accessible from Marsa Matruh and is not linked to the Great Desert circuit.

Many areas in the vicinity of the oases are set aside for military use, so for detours from the main road a **permit** is usually necessary. For trips around the Great Desert Circuit, permits can either be obtained from the oases themselves or, for routes spanning more than one military district, from The **Travel Permits Department** (T 3556301/ 3548661) at the Ministry of the Interior in Cairo in the Abdin district which is open Sat-Thur 0900-1400. In order to get your permit, which can take anything from 1-7 days, it is essential to take photocopies of the first 3 pages of your passport and the Egyptian entry stamp and 2 passport photos.

Spring is the best time to visit the desert, when the daytime temperatures are still bearable and the nights are cool

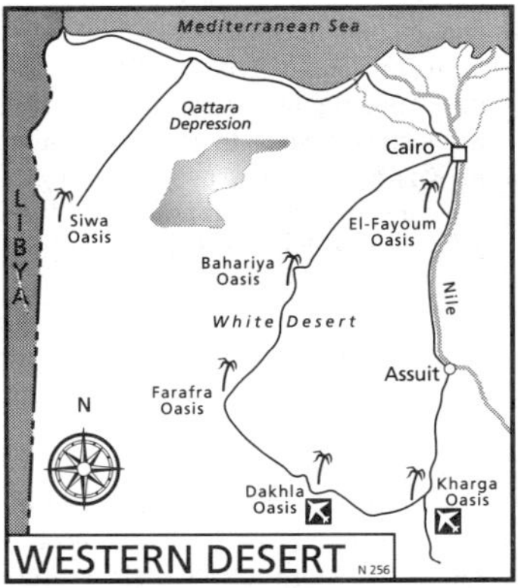

but not cold, and the summer desert winds and sand storms, which can be very uncomfortable, have not yet arrived. Take enough money with you. Credit cards will *not* do, indeed, you will be lucky to find a bank. When planning a drive NEVER underestimate the potential dangers of the desert. It is said that in 524 BC Cambyses, the Persian conqueror of Egypt, managed to lose an entire army of 50,000 men without a trace! Always carry more than enough fuel, food and water. There are no service stations between towns. You need the right type of vehicle, and the necessary driving skills to handle it in this terrain. **See Travel and Survival in the Desert, page 40** and read further on the subject before you throw yourself into a potentially lethal environment. Other options include service buses and organized desert safaris. The latter could be the most rewarding if you are anything but meticulously prepared and equipped.

The Great Desert Circuit

The Great Desert Circuit became accessible in the 1980s, when a road was built linking the oases of **Bahariya**, **Farafra**, **Dakhla** and **Kharga**. These are all situated on a dead branch of the Nile, and depend, for their livelihood on the massive fossil water reservoirs beneath the Libyan Desert. The area was designated as the **New Valley** in 1958 with a scheme to tap this subterranean water-source and relocate landless peasants from the overcrowded Nile Valley and Delta. However the lack of resources and a reassessment of the long-term viability of the water supply led to the virtual abandonment of the project and to the area's inevitable stagnation.

Coming from Cairo, the natural choice is an anti-clockwise journey round the circuit beginning by going into the desert past the Pyramids at Giza on Route 341. This gives the option of a refreshing last leg of your journey back down the Nile. Driving conditions are not ideal, with pot-holed roads and few opportunities for petrol, food or water. You may have to stand for hours on crowded buses, and accommodation along the route is pretty basic. Lacking the time or the inclination for all this you can fly direct from Cairo to New Valley Airport at Kharga, where you can get a taste of the desert, but you will be missing far more than you experience. It may be true that Kharga has more interesting monuments than some of its neighbours, but the desert itself is the star of this piece and Kharga, with it's sprawling modern town, is undoubtedly a disappointment.

Bahariya

The journey to Bahariya, 360 km W along Route 341 from Cairo past the Pyramids of Giza, takes about 6-7 hrs by bus, with a stop en route, or 5-6 hrs by service taxi. Running parallel to the road is a private railway line which takes iron ore from the country's most important mine, which lies just to the NE of the main oasis, to the giant Helwan steelworks near Cairo. This was the catalyst for Egypt's industrial development in the 1950s. Until the New Valley Development scheme the water level here in the oasis was falling but by tapping into the subterranean aquifers, water availability has increased, albeit, not as much as the government had hoped. The recent developments of the oasis' towns have been carried out with greater care than in Kharga city, thereby preserving the pleasant and lively atmosphere of the area despite the industrial and agricultural innovations.

Throughout their history the people of the oasis have prevaricated between Independence and co-operation with the current régime. They converted to Islam soon after the Muslim invasion but returned to a Berber Emirate during the 10th century before being incorporated once more into the Islamic state by the Fatimids a century later. In the last few centuries they have co-operated fully with the ruling régimes but have maintained a slightly independent stance. They are generally very welcoming to visitors.

Bawiti

The capital of the Bahariya oasis, Bawiti covers an area of 2000 sq km although very little is cultivatable. Don't be too depressed when you arrive because it gets a lot better further on up the road when you enter the mud brick built **Old Quarter** and, further still, **Al-Qasr**, it's old sister village, beneath which lies Bahariya's ancient capital. Here you will see stones from a 26th Dynasty (664-525 BC) temple re-used for house building and the remains of a Roman triumphal arch which stayed intact until the 19th century.

Before moving on from Bahariya, drivers must fill up with fuel and water as the nearest service station is in Dakhla which is 490 km away. The 180 km road SSW between Bahariya and Farafra passes through what is known as the **White Desert** where many travellers stop for a night. By moonlight, the eerie wind-blown landscape has been likened to an Arctic wasteland, and sunrise here might be the highlight of your trip.

Farafra Oasis

This is the smallest and most isolated of the oases in the Western Desert but the deep depression in which it lies suggests that it was once larger. To the NW steep cliffs rise dramatically out of the desert whilst to the S there is a gentle incline. In spite of its isolation the residents of the region, who now number about 2,500 and are mainly from two extended families, have been involved in trade and contact with the Nile Valley since earliest times. The village of Qasr el-Farafra had a large 116 room mud brick *qasr* (fort, or castle) from which it got it's name. This was used by all the villagers when they were under attack until it collapsed in 1958. The village is generally pleasing with palm-lined roads and decorated houses, although some less attractive concrete buildings are now being constructed.

Dakhla Oasis

Population: 70,000. *Altitude*: 111m.

Moving on SSE from Farafra, the much larger **Dakhla** oasis, with a population of around 70,000 in 14 settlements, is 310 km from Farafra, and buses make the journey in 4-5 hours. Set in a striking landscape the capital, **Mut**, is pretty in a shabby and faded way. Of interest to the sightseer is the **Museum of Inheritance** (open 0800-1400 and 1800-2100, Entry E£4). It displays the rapidly disappearing traditional village life of Dakhla although some of the customs depicted still remain. Clay figures are used to illustrate typical activities such as meals, marriage, pilgrimages and deaths. Mut is a good base for day trips to the surrounding areas.

Excursions from Mut

Al-Qasr and the **Al-Muzawaka Tombs.** On the road in from Farafra, about 35 km NW of Mut along an arm of the oasis, is the charming little town of Al-Qasr. It was a Roman settlement and Dakhla's

Climate: Dakhla Oasis

	Jan	Feb	Mar	Apr	May	Jun	Jul	Aug	Sep	Oct	Nov	Dec	Av/Tot
Max (°C)	22	24	28	33	37	39	38	38	36	33	28	23	32
Min (°C)	4	6	10	14	19	22	23	22	20	17	11	6	14
Rain (mm)	0	0	0	0	0	0	0	0	0	0	0	0	0

mediaeval capital and its old quarter's tiny interconnected streets reflect the antiquity of the area. The names of former inhabitants can be traced in ancient Kufic (ancient Arabic) script above the doorways. Today very few of the houses are occupied. 5 km further W a hot (45°C) sulphurous spring flows by a sandstone temple dedicated to the triad of Theban gods, Amun, Mut and Khonsu. The site is well preserved and may have been rebuilt during the reigns of Nero (54-68 AD) and Titus (79-81 AD). The Al-Muzawaka Tombs (Hill of Decoration), one of Petosiris and the other of Sadosiris, are nearby and both have murals depicting contemporary myths relating to the after-life.

Bashendi is about 40 km SE from Mut towards Kharga. It is an attractive village where the houses are decorated with floral paintings. The 1st century BC **Tomb of Kitnes** lies in the desert nearby. The walls of the 4 chambers are ornamented with engravings and frescoes portraying Kitnes entering the after-life.

Kharga Oasis

Kharga Oasis is a further 197 km along the same road, which bears round now more to the E. Pre-industrial Kharga was very different from the city of today. At that time the water level was considerably higher and the route was vital for the caravan trade. The New Valley scheme has converted this attractive oasis into a modern concrete town thereby removing almost all traces of its former charm. Nevertheless, 2 sites of interest remain in the surrounding area.

The **Temple of Hibis**, about 2 km to the N of the town, was erected in 510-490 BC at the beginning of the Persian occupation, and is one of the few remains from that period. Unfortunately it was built on clay and suffers from subsidence. Several attempts have been made to restore the planks and reinforce the foundations. It is relatively well preserved from the **Third Pylon** onwards. The remains demonstrate the prevailing influence of the Pharaonic era on the later Empires. The ornamentation and designs within the temple are mainly animals, showing vultures, dogs and serpents intertwined with Persian and Egyptian deities.

The **Necropolis of El-Baqawat**, approximately 5 km N of the town, can be reached by taking a dirt track from the Hibis Temple road through a palm grove and a short distance into the desert. Hundreds of baked brick tombs, originating from an early Christian burial site, lie crumbling in the desert. Small chapels cover some of the tombs. The most interesting features of the burial ground are the vivid wall paintings of biblical scenes. Some are fairly crudely executed and others were defaced by the ancient Greeks. The illustrations are mainly of Old Testament scenes depicting Adam and Eve, Noah's Ark, Abraham and Isaac. From the New Testament the Virgin Mary and St Paul feature most often. Some of the best preserved paintings are in locked chapels but, by negotiating with the guard, you may be allowed in to see them.

Local information

● Accommodation

Accommodation along the Great Desert Circuit is rather primitive. There are two very adequate 2 star hotels in Kharga – **F** *El-Kharga Oasis*, El-Kharga, El-Wadi Guedid, T 901500, Tx 93766, 30 rm and **F** *Hamadalla Hotel*, El-Kharga, El-Wadi Guedid, T 900638, 54 rm with a/c. Cheap unregistered hotels include the ***Alpenblick*** and ***Oasis*** in Bahariya, ***Dar al-Wafden*** in Dakhla, and ***Waha*** in Kharga. Alternatively there are government **resthouses** in all of the oases which offer very variable accommodation and facilities. For information T 900728.

● Camping

Nasser Wells S of Kharga is in a beautiful site. Although there are only a few official camping there is no problem camping along the route. Indeed one of the highlights of the trip, albeit for properly equipped campers with sufficient water, is a night spent under the stars in the White Desert between Bahariya and Farafra.

● **Places to eat**
Besides the hotels and the few usual cafés there are a few **cheap** restaurants along the route but none is particularly good and the choice is limited. There is the ***Popular Restaurant*** in Bawiti, ***Sa'ad's*** in Farafra, ***Hamdy*** and ***Abu Mohamed*** in Mut, and the ***New Oasis*** in Kharga.

● **Banks**
There are branches of the **Misr Bank** open Sun-Thur 0830-1400, Fri & Sat 0900-1300 in Mut on Sharia Wadi Jedid and near the *Waha Hotel* in Kharga.

● **Post Office**
In Mut the post office, open Sat-Thur 0800-1400, is in New Mosque Square but international calls can only be made from the exchange near the *Dar al-Wafden Hotel*. The Kharga post office is 500m E of the *Waha Hotel*.

● **Telephone**
Local code: 088.

● **Tourist information**
There are tourist offices in Mut's New Mosque Square and Kharga's Sharia Nasser near the *Kharga Oasis Hotel*.

● **Transport**
Air There are direct flights 2 days a week to Cairo from the airport which is 5 km NE of Kharga on the main road to Assuit.

Road Bus It is possible to travel around the Great Desert Circuit by bus from Cairo to Assuit but is not always a comfortable or easy journey depending on the time of year and type of bus. It is necessary to book seats about 2 days beforehand and thereby avoid having to stand. The times of the inter-oases buses which do not start from Cairo vary from month to month and it is important to check locally for the current timetable. There are 2 daily buses at 0700 and 1200 from Cairo's Al-Azhar terminal to Bahariya which takes 6-7 hrs with those on Mon, Thur and Sat continuing on to Farafra and Dakhla. From Farafra's Resthouse Two there are 6 buses a week to Dakhla which is also served in the opposite direction by 3 daily buses from Cairo via Assuit. There are frequent daily buses from Mut's New Mosque Square in Dakhla to Kharga's bus station in Midan Showla near the old mosque. Most of the buses continue on to Assuit which is just as well for those who want to avoid the least attractive of the oases towns.

Service taxis Usually caught from near the bus station are marginally more expensive than the bus but are quicker taking 5 hrs to Assuit. Some only travel at night when it is cooler – this means missing the searing heat and the magnificent scenery which are the two things which make the Great Desert Circuit the great experience that it is!!!!

Assuit

Arriving back in the Nile Valley at **Assuit** one can either continue the circuit back to Cairo via the relaxed charm of Minya or take the opportunity to travel S via the Abydos and Dendera temples to the wonders of Luxor and the Valley of the Kings.

● **Transport from Assuit** is certainly no problem. **Air** There are direct flights to Cairo and Kharga from the airport 10 km NW of the town. **Trains** run 12 times a day to Cairo (7 hrs) via Mallawi (2 hrs) and Minya (3 hrs), but less frequently to Luxor (6-7 hrs) via Sohag (2 hrs) and Qena (4-5 hrs). **Road**: **Bus** There are 7 daily buses Cairo (7 hrs) as well as buses every 30 min between 0600-1800 N to Minya (2 hrs) and S to Sohag. **Service taxis** run to every town between Minya and Sohag and are easy to catch from the main depot in the mornings but are less frequent later in the day.

INFORMATION FOR VISITORS

Contents

Before you go

Entry requirements

● **Visas**

Passports are required by all and should be valid for at least 6 months beyond the period of intended stay in Egypt.

Visas are required by all. Tourist visas cost around US$20 equivalent. In UK this is £15 for a single entry and £18 for up to three entries. Business visas cost £53 and £91 provided a business letter is provided. Payment must be by cash or postal order, cheques are not accepted. Visas are valid for 3 months from date of issue and 1 month from date of arrival and cannot be post dated.

Emergency visas may be granted at the point of entry other than Sinai. Visas are not required for nationals of Ghana, Guinea and Malta and most Arab countries. Entrance without a visa is permitted for visits of up to a week to South Sinai and St Catherine when entering through Sinai entry points of Taba, St Catherine and Sharm el-Sheikh airports, Nuweiba and Sharm el-Sheikh seaports. Do not permit officials to stamp your passport at these entry points.

Visas for Libya available only from their embassy in Cairo: their consulate in Alexandria deals only with Arab nations. At present visas are issued on an individual basis. A letter of recommendation is required from the traveller's own embassy (£27.50 from UK embassy in Cairo). The Sudanese embassy also requires a letter of recommendation. Presenting the application in modest dress and a courteous manner aids the process.

● **Vaccinations**

Vaccinations are not required unless travelling from a country where yellow fever or cholera frequently occurs. You are advised to be up to date with polio, tetanus and hepatitis protection. (**See Health page, 19**.)

● **Representation overseas**

Embassies Australia, 1 Darwin Avenue, Yarralumla, ACT Canberra, T 062 734437; **Austria**, Kreindll Gasse 22, Vienna 1190, T 361134; **Belgium**, Avenue Leo Errera 44, 1180 Brussels, T 3455015; **Canada**, 454 Laurier Avenue East, Ottawa, Ontario, K1N 6R3, T 613 234 4958; **Denmark**, Nyropsgade 47, 3rd Floor, DK-1602 Copenhagen V, T 3312 7641; **France**, 56 Avenue d'lena, 75116 Paris, T 47209770; **Germany**, Kronprinzenstr, Bonn 2, T 228 364000; **Israel**, 54 Rehov Basel, Tel Aviv, T 5464151; **Libya**, Al Fondok Al Kabier, Tripoli, T 45940; **Morocco**, 31 El Gazaer Street, Sawmaat Hassan, Rabat, T 731833; **Netherlands**, Borweg 1, 2597 LR The Hague, T 70 354 2000; **Norway**, Drammensveien 90A, 0244 Oslo 2, T 200010; **Portugal**, Av. D. Vasco Da Gama No 8, 1400 Lisbon, T 3018374; **Spain**, Velazquez 69, Madrid 28006, T 5776308; **Sudan**, El Gamaa Street, Elmakran, Khartoum, T 72836; **Sweden**, Strandvagen 35, Stockholm, T 468 6603145; **Switzerland**, 61 Elfenauweg, 3006 Berne, T 448012; **UK**, 26 South Street, London W1Y 6DD, T 071 499 2401, F 071 355 3568; **USA**,

2310 Decatur Palace N.W., Washington D.C. 20008, T 202 234 3903.

Consulates Canada, 3154 Côtes-des-Neiges, Montreal H3H 1V6, T 514 937781; **UK**, 19, Kensington Palace Garden Mews, London W8, T 071 2298818, open 1000-1200 Mon-Fri for visas; **USA**, 1110 Second Ave, New York, NY10022, T 212 7597120; 3001 Pacific Ave, San Francisco, CA 94115, T 415 3469700.

● Tourist information

Egyptian State Tourist Offices: **Austria**, Elisabeth Strasse, 4/Steige 5/1, Opornringhof, 1010 Vienna, T 587 6633; **Canada**, Place Bonaventure, 40 Frontenac, PO Box 304, Montreal, T 514 8614420; **France**, 90 Ave Champs Elysees, Paris, T 00331 45629442; **Germany**, 64A Kaiser Strasse, Frankfurt am Main 6, T 252319; **Greece**, 10 Amerikis St, Athens 134, T 3606906; **Italy**, 19 Via Bissolati, 00187 Rome, T 00396 4827985; **Japan**, 19 Akasaka, 2-Chome, Minato-ku, Tokyo, T 5890653; **Kuwait**, 5 Omar Ibn el-Khatab St, Safat, Kuwait 13133, T 2403104; **Spain**, La Toree de Madrid planta 5, Oficina 3, Plaza de Espana, 28008 Madrid, T 5781732; **Sweden**, Drottnin 99, Atan 65, 11136 Stockholm, T 102548; **Switzerland**, 9 rue des Alpes, Geneva, T 022 329132; **UK**, 170 Piccadilly, London W1V 9DD, T 071 4935282, F 071 408 0295; **USA**, 630 Fifth Ave, New York 10111, T 212 2466960 and 323 Geary Street, Suite 608, San Francisco, Ca 94102, T 415 7817676.

● Tours and Travel Agents

Travelscope Worldwide, (Gaz Tours), PO Box 158 Guildford, Surrey GU2 6PU, UK, T/F 048369453. An excellent independent travel company, which has been in business since 1972, and which arranges individual and group tours not only to classic sites in Cairo, Luxor and Aswan but also to the oases. Special tours for Christian groups can follow the Holy Family's flight from Egypt, while tours to Sinai cover all the major sites to the Israeli border. The service is excellent because the company specialises in providing a personalized service to each and every client. Dr Sadek has direct access to the Egyptair computers and can therefore make and confirm flight reservations. ***Egyptian Encounter*** part of Misr Travel, 51 Brookley Rd, Brockenhust, Hants, UK, T 059022992, F 059024025. ***Explore Worldwide***, 1 Frederick St, Aldershot, Hants, GU11 1LQ, T 0252 319448, for hotels/camping in oases of Siwa and Western Desert. ***Twickers World***, 22 Church St, Twickenham TW1 3NW, UK, T 081 8928164 offers desert tours.

When to go

● Best time to visit

Climate The sun shines the whole year round and rainy days are the exception. The temperature increases as one travels S with Luxor being about 10°C warmer than Cairo. The high summer temperatures in the desert will be of greatest concern for visitors. **See page 691** and individual climatic statistics in the text.

Each section has at least one climatic table with the best season(s) shaded for easy reference.

● Clothing

Cotton clothes in summer, warmer garments for winter and desert evenings. Egyptian cotton garments are good value. Trousers and long sleeved shirts provide protection from the sun. A wide brimmed hat or sun glasses will offer protection from the glare of the sun. Comfortable shoes are necessary for sightseeing. Open sandals let the sand and dust in. Egypt is a Muslim country and scanty clothing can cause offence. Speedy and efficient laundry services are provided by most hotels. See section on clothing (**see page 27**).

Health

● Staying healthy

Mosquitoes and flies can be a problem in certain areas. Buy a fly spray, take good repellent creams and antihistamine cream if you are prone to bites. Raw food is best avoided unless you can wash it or peel it. The sun is hot all year round so take adequate precautions.

● Water

Bottled water is safer to drink, but cleaning your teeth with tap water will not be harmful.

● Further health information

Read the section on Health, **see page 19** and be prepared for some stomach upsets due to heat and change of diet.

Money

● Banks

There are 5 national banks and more than 78 branches of foreign banks. Banking hours are 0830-1400 Sun-Thur.

● Cost of living

Egypt is very cheap. Depending on the standards of comfort and cleanliness one is prepared to accept for accommodation, food and travel, it is possible to survive on as little as E£15-20 per person per day. Petrol (super) 100 piastres per litre.

Credit cards
Access/Mastercard, American Express, Diners Club and Visa are accepted.

Currency
E£1 =100 Piastres. Notes are in denominations of E£1, E£5, E£10, E£20, E£100 and 5, 10, 25 and 50 Piastres. Coins are 1, 5 and 10 Piastres.

Regulations and money changing
Visitors can enter and leave Egypt with a maximum of E£10,000. There are no restrictions on the import of foreign currency provided it is declared on an official customs form. Export of foreign currency may not exceed the amount imported. All cash, travellers cheques, credit cards and gold over E£500 must be declared on arrival.

Travellers' cheques
There is no difficulty changing travellers' cheques. US$ denomination cheques are more widely used and understood. Bring some cheques for small amounts for changing at the end of your stay.

Getting there

Air
Egypt's international airports are Cairo International (CAI) 22 km NE of the city (travel time 30 mins); Alexandria Airport (ALY) 5 km SE of the city; Luxor Airport (LXR) 5.5 km from the town. The national airline is **Egyptair**. Flight times to Cairo: from London about 4 hr 40 mins, £240 return; from Paris 4 hr 30 min; from Athens 2 hrs; from Tunis 1 hr 45 mins.

There are regular flights from & to **USA**: New York (4) and Los Angeles (2). Flights from & to **Asia**: Tokyo, Karachi (2). Flights from & to **Europe**: Paris, Rome, London (daily), Barcelona, Madrid (3), Berlin (1), Copenhagen, Milan (2), Frankfurt (5), Geneva, Zurich (4). Flights from & to **Middle East/North Africa**: Abu Dhabi, Amman, Dubai, Jeddah, Kuwait (daily); Bahrain, Beirut, Tunis, Tripoli (2/3 per week); Khartoum, Algiers (1); Casablanca (3).

Air Sinai operates return services: Cairo-Tel Aviv; Cairo-El-Arish, Cairo-St Catherine-Eilat; Cairo-Ras el-Nakab-Luxor-Sharm el-Sheikh. Details from *Nile Hilton Hotels*, T 760948/776893.

Train
There is no international rail link either E to Israel or W to Libya (Libya has no railway) and only a ferry connection across Lake Nasser between Aswan and Wadi Halfa in Sudan.

Road
Bus and taxi For coaches to Israel contact **Travco Travel Agency**, T 403448; The **East Delta Bus Company** (Sinai International Station) runs a/c buses daily except Sat to Tel-Aviv. Contact Sinai International Station, T 824753 or East Delta Buses, 14, Sharia Mustafa Abu Hef, Cairo, T 743027. Service taxis run between Marsa Matruh and Sollum on the Libyan border. Reach Marsa Matruh by bus (a/c or service) from Midan Sa'ad Zaghloul, Alexandria. Arab Union superjet buses leave from Midan Almaza, Cairo at 0200 for Amman, Jeddah, Damascus, Kuwait, Bahrain and Qatar; at 0700 for Libya. Regular departures from Alexandria to Benghazi (15-20 hrs) and Tripoli (30 hrs). The Benghazi costs US$34 or E£90.

Motoring Vehicles drive on the right in Egypt. Road signs are international with Arabic script.The main international road W goes to Libya and to the E over the Suez Canal and via El-Arish to Israel. Other international routes are along the Nile Valley or along the northern Sinai and the Red Sea coasts. Entry for private cars requirments – a Carnet de Passage en Douane and an International Driving Licence. Contact Egyptian Automobile Club, 1 Sharia Kasr el-Nil, Cairo, T 743355. Vehicles must be petrol, not diesel and 4 wheel drive vehicles require permission from the Ministry of Defence. Extra vehicle insurance may be required at the border.

Sea
The main coastal ports are Alexandria, Port Said and Suez. Ferries operating in this area can be contacted in UK at: Viamare Travel, Graphic House, 2 Sumatra Rd, London NW6 1PU, T 071 431 4560 or CTC Lines, 1 Regent Street, London SW1Y 4NN, T 071 930 9962.

For connections to Italy, Greece, Cyprus contact Adriatica's representive at Mena Tours Agency, 14 Sharia Talaat Harb, Cairo, T 740955/740864; 28 Sharia al-Ghorfa al-Tigariya, Alexandria T 809676.

For connections with Jordan, from Nuweiba to Aqaba contact Egyptian Shipping Co., Cairo T 758278.

Nile steamers connect with Sudan, from Sadd el-Aali to Wadi Halfa.

Ferries ply between Suez and Jeddah in Saudi Arabia via Aqaba, contact **Mena Tours Agency**, 14 Sharia Talaat Harb, Cairo, T 740955 or **Misr Travel**, 1 Sharia Talaat Harb, Cairo, T 3930010.

● Customs

Departure Confirm airline flights at least 48 hrs in advance. Have all currency exchange receipts easily available. Before passing into the departure lounge/area it is necessary to fill in an embarkation card. To add to the complications, it will be necessary to have the personal details on this card translated into Arabic at a desk which may or may not be clearly visible. Only a limited amount of currency can be reconverted before you leave. This is a tedious process and is not possible at Luxor airport. Sometimes suitable foreign currency is not available. It is better to budget with care, have no excess cash and save all the trouble.

Duty free allowances Goods may be **imported** into Egypt as follows: 200 cigarettes or 50 cigars or 250 gm of tobacco, 1 litre of spirit, 1 litre of perfume or toilet water, gifts up to the value of E£500. **Duty free export** of purchases can be arranged through the larger shops and tourist agencies.

Entry into Israel, Libya and Sudan With the appropriate visas entry is comparatively straight forward.

Insurance Comprehensive travel insurance is essential. Consider one which offers immediate repatriation for illness or accident. Claims for lost or stolen items must be backed by evidence of reporting the matter to the police.

Prohibited goods include drugs and firearms. Permits can be obtained for hunting guns through the hotel/tour organiser. It is forbidden to take into UK – ivory, crocodile, snake or lizard skin. It is forbidden to take from Egypt genuine Egyptian artifacts.

Registration All visitors to Egypt must register with the police within one week of arrival. This is generally done by the hotel. Independent travellers are responsible for their own registration.

When you arrive

● Airline offices

British Airways, 1 Abdel Salam Aref, Cairo, T 759977, at airport 671741; **Air France**, 2 Talaat Harb, Cairo, T 5743300, at airport 661028; **Air India**, 1 Talaat Harb, Cairo, T 3934873; **Alitalia**, Nile Hilton Commercial Complex, Cairo, T 5743488, at airport 665143; **Iberia**, 15 Midan Tahrir, Cairo, T 3910828; **KLM**, 11 Kasr el-Nil, Cairo, T 5740999, at airport 662226; **Lufthansa**, 6 El-Sheikh el-Marsafi, Zamalek, Cairo, T 3420471, at airport 666975; **Royal Air Maroc**, 16 Bustan, T 3934574; **Swissair**, 22 Kasr el-Nil, Cairo, T 3937955, at airport 669537; **Tunis Air**, 14 Talaat Harb, Cairo, T 769726.

● Electricity

220 volts AC. Sockets take standard continental 2 round pin plugs. Continental adaptors are useful.

● Hours of business

Government offices from 0900-2100 every day except Fri and national holidays; **Banks** are open 0830-1400 Sat-Thur; **Shops** are open 0900-1230 and 1600-2000 in summer and 0900-1900 in winter. Hours on Fri and Sun will vary.

● Maps and town plans

Michelin map No 154 covers Egypt. The Oxford Map of Egypt by Oxford University Press is very good. Several maps of the whole of Egypt and of the major towns are available from the the Egyptian Tourist Board.

● Official Time

GMT + 2 hrs.

● Photography

Egypt's fine weather, clear skies and varying scenery gives opportunities for spectacular pictures. However, photographs of military areas, airports, radio stations and other public utilities are prohibited. Photography is also prohibited in tombs. Some sites make an extra charge for cameras. Flashes are not permitted in the museum in Cairo nor for delicate relics such as the icons in St Catherine's Monastery. Taking photographs of any person without permission is unwise, of women is taboo and tourist attractions like water sellers, camels/camel drivers etc will require payment. Even the goat herder will expect a tip for providing the goats.

Most types of film are available. Check the sell by date and purchase from shops that appear to have a rapid turnover of films. Bring specialist films with you.

Video cameras must be declared at the customs on arrival in Egypt. Always check that use of a video camera is permitted at tourist sites and be prepared to pay a heavy fee (E£20+) for permission.

Safety

The level of petty crime in Egypt is no greater than elsewhere. It is unlikely that you will be robbed but take sensible precautions. Leave your valuables in a hotel deposit box and never leave valuables or money around. Avoid carrying excess money or wearing obviously valuable jewellery when sightseeing. There will be pickpockets in crowded places. It is wise not to walk around at night away from the main thoroughfares.

Egypt is a Muslim country and Fri is the day of rest when offices and many shops are closed. The Christians celebrate Sun as their sabbath when many of their shops are closed. As the Islamic year is shorter than the Western year the dates of their religious holidays change (**see page 841** in Introduction). The Christian Coptic calendar gives a third set of variable dates. It has 12 months of 30 days with the extra 5 days added every 4th year.

Security The increase in attacks on tourists by religious extremists is unfortunate and is a cause for concern but has news value because Egypt is normally a very safe place. The national and local security services have been much augmented to protect tourists and are very visible at all major tourist areas. The danger to life and limb is very low indeed despite the country's current problems. Ironically as the more timid tourists are dissuaded from travelling here, access to museums, monuments and other attractions is very much easier.

Shopping

Places to shop The most interesting shopping is in the bazaars. This takes time but bargains can be found. The main bazaar in Cairo, ***Khan el-Khalili***, has a wide selection of ethnic items. By contrast the smaller ***Aswan bazaar***, parallel to and one block behind the Corniche, has less hassle and more time to ponder on the purchases.

Best buys Jewellery (sold by weight) and precious stones – particularly lapis lazuli, perfumes, spices, carpets, copper and brass ware, inlaid wooden boxes with intricate designs and cotton garments.

Tipping

Usually 10% is added to hotel and restaurant bills but an extra tip of about 5% is normal. Taxi drivers expect between 5-10%. In hotels and at monuments tips will be expected for the most minimal service. Rather than make a fuss have some very small coins handy. Tips may be the person's only income.

Weights and measures

Egyptians use metric measurements. **See page 17** for conversion tables.

Where to stay

Hotels

As tourism is one of Egypt's major industries, accommodation is available at the main sites and in all the major cities. This varies from deluxe international hotels to floor or roof space for a sleeping bag – at prices to suit all pockets. Tax and a service charge will be added to the bill. Always ask to see the room first.

It should be noted, however, that, while price is a reasonable reflection of the type of hotel and service you can expect, some hotels are expensive but very ordinary while there are some wonderful hotels which are real bargains. If you are unsure about whether a cheap hotel is any good, only book in for one night, leave your baggage there and then go and explore the other choices.

Hotel Classifications

AL US$90+. International class luxury hotel. All facilities for business and leisure travellers are of the highest international standard.

A US$75-90. International hotel with air conditioned rooms with WC, bath/shower, TV, phone, mini-bar, daily clean linen. Choice of restaurants, coffee shop, shops, bank, travel agent, swimming pool, some sport and business facilities.

B US$60-75. As **A** but without the luxury, reduced number of restaurants, smaller rooms, limited range of shops and sport.

C US$40-60. Best rooms have air conditioning, own bath/shower and WC. Usually comfortable, bank, shop, pool.

D US$20-40. Best rooms may have own WC and bath/shower. Depending on management will have room service and choice of cuisine in restaurant.

E US$10-20. Simple provision. Perhaps fan cooler. May not have restaurant. Shared WC and showers with hot water (when available).

F under US$10. Very basic, shared toilet facilities, variable in cleanliness, noise, often in dubious locations.

● Youth hostels

Information from **Egyptian Youth Hostels**, 7 Sharia Dr Abdel Hamid Said, Marouf, Cairo, T 43799. There are 15 hostels located in Egypt's main historic and tourist towns which are open all year round, closed 1000-1400 and 1300-0700. Minimum age 6 years. Overnight fees range from 350-750 piastres including breakfast. Visitors may stay more than 3 consecutive nights if places are available. Although cheap meals are available (breakfast is included, lunch 250 piastres, dinner served from 2000-2100, 250 piastres), all the big hostels have a member's kitchen where guests can prepare meals for themselves (use of the kitchen is free). Holders of membership cards can obtain significant reductions on train journeys. Those who do not already have cards can obtain them from any of the hostels in Egypt. The rules include no alcohol or gambling, single sex dormitories, lights out between 2300-0600. Groups must make advance bookings at least 2 weeks before their arrival.

● Camping

There are only a few official camp sites with good facilities and guards. Sites of varying quality exist in Aswan, Luxor, Cairo, Giza, Sharm el-Sheikh and Marsa Matruh. Hotels are very cheap and are probably a more comfortable option.

Food and drink

● Food

The national dish is *fuul*, beans in a thick spicy sauce. This is a cheap meal at most Egyptian cafés. Egyptian soups too are thick and spicy and with bread (which is delicious when fresh) can be filling. Kebabs, lamb pieces grilled over charcoal on a skewer, and *kufta* minced lamb are normally very well done. Pigeon and chicken are the main meats. The fish food, from the Red Sea and the Mediterranean is good, try the Red Snapper but mind the bones. There are many fresh vegetables which are, after bread, the main part of an Egyptian diet (Egyptian potatoes are sold in Europe) and a wide selection of fruit in season. Try the pomegranates, figs and dates. The desserts are sweet, sticky, fattening and delicious.

RESTAURANT CLASSIFICATIONS

Given the variations in price of food on any menu our restaurants are divided where possible into three simple grades:
♦♦♦ expensive, ♦♦ average and ♦ cheap.

● Drink

Although Egypt is a Muslim country, alcohol is available in bars and good restaurants. 'Stella' beer is most popular and sold in litre bottles with a stronger version sold in smaller bottles. Egyptian wines are a reasonable price. Try *Omar Khayyam* (best buy) and *Pharaon* reds, *Ptolomee* dry white or *Rubis d'Egypte* rosé. Quality varies and addition of bottled water may be necessary!! Local spirits are rather rough. The local rum is *Zattos*. Imported spirits and wines are VERY expensive.

The usual soft drinks are on sale. Tea, prepared with mint, is very popular and will be served at the slightest pretext. Instant coffee and thick Turkish coffee are also available. Bottled water is sold widely, just check the bottle has not been refilled.

● Where to eat and drink

The better hotel restaurants serve international cuisine of a high standard and often have speciality Egyptian restaurants. From there the price but not necessarily the standard falls down to the street stalls which perhaps are best avoided for hygiene reasons. See entries under separate town sections.

Getting around

● Air

There are daily flights between Cairo, Alexandria, Luxor, Aswan, Abu Simbel, New Valley and Hurghada and less frequently to Marsa Matruh. Contact Egyptair T 922444. There are regular flights from Cairo to St Catherine, El-Arish and Sharm el-Sheikh. Contact Air Sinai at *Nile Hilton* T 760948.

Flight times: Cairo to Luxor 1 hr; Cairo to Aswan 2hr; Aswan to Abu Simbel 40 mins; Cairo to Hurgarda 1 hr; Cairo to St Catherine's Monastery 50 mins.

● Train

The rail network extends W to Sollum on the Libyan border, S along the Nile from Alexandria and Cairo to Luxor, Aswan and Abu Simbel. There are links to Port Said and Suez. There are several luxury a/c trains with restaurants to Luxor and Aswan with sleeping accommodation. Contact International Sleeping Cars, T 761319. Inclusive tickets with reduced hotel charges in Luxor and Assan can be negotiated. Reductions on train tickets are available for students (see Tourist Office in nearest town) and members of the YHA (see Youth hostels below). Cheaper student and group tickets are available. Contact T 753555.

Approximate journey times from Cairo by train

Alexandria	$2\frac{3}{4}$ hr
Aswan	15 hr
Luxor	12 hr
Port Said	$2\frac{1}{2}$ hr

● Road

Bicycles and motorcycles Bicycle hire is becoming widely available although the mechanical fitness of the machines is often dubious. Traffic conditions can make cycling a dangerous sport. Motorcycles can also be hired. Comments above regarding cycles apply also to motorcycles – but more so.

Bus Local buses are cheap and vary in comfort. They keep to timetable within reasonable (Egyptian) limits. There are a/c intercity buses, slightly more expensive. For bus services see information for individual towns.

Car hire The main car hire firms are **Avis**, **Hertz** and **Budget**. See entry for each town. International Driving permit required. Own country driving licence often accepted. Remember driving on the right is the rule in Egypt. Petrol (super) E£1 per litre.

Approximate journey times from Cairo by road:

Alexandria	3 hr
Aswan	16 hr
Luxor	10 hr
Port Said	3 hr

Hitch hiking Rides are often available on lorries and in small open trucks but payment is always expected. Hitch hiking has a measure of risk attached to it and is not normally recommended, but in out of the way places is often the only way to travel.

Taxi Taxis with meters are available to all the larger cities. Long distance shared taxis (service taxis) are quite cheap. It is always possible to negotiate and if more comfort is required the extra places can be purchased.

● Boat

The traditional Nile sailing boats *feluccas*, can be hired by the hour but are not recommended for travelling between towns. The Sudanese railway operates a steamer service from Aswan to Wadi Halfa. Regular Nile cruises operate between Luxor and Aswan and sometimes between Cairo and Aswan for 5 days (standard tour), 7 days (extended tour) and 15 days (full Nile cruise). The leading Nile cruise companies are Seti, Sheraton, Hilton, Presidential, Sphinx, Pyramid and Eastmar.

A new steamer route from the Aswan Dam to Abu Simel is advertised. It will be even slower than the road journey and the scenery only slightly more interesting. (Go by plane!)

Communications

● Language

The official language is Arabic, however many Egyptians are proficient in foreign languages, in particular English and French.

● Postal services

Local services: all post offices are open daily except Fri and the Central Post Office in Cairo is open 24 hrs. Airmail letters cost E£0.80 and local letters E£0.10. Postage stamps can be purchased from cigarette kiosks and from hotels where mail can be posted too. Mail services are unreliable so away from the capital do not expect a quick service.

International telegram services are available at the main post offices in Cairo, Alexandria, Luxor and Aswan. **Parcels** for abroad may only be sent from a main post office. Do not seal it until it has been seen. Shops will arrange to send items you purchase. Receiving a parcel may involve import duty.

● Telephone services

Country code: 20. **Internal area codes** are: **Cairo** 02, **Alexandria** 03, **Aswan** 97, **Luxor** 95, **Hurghada** 62.

Cheapest time to telephone is between 2000-0800. Local calls can be made from coin operated machines in shops (tip the shop keeper), cigarette kiosks and hotels (which normally add a premium in any case). Long distance and international calls can be made from telephone offices and the better hotels. For International calls dial 00 before country code and subscriber's number. The telephone office has a circular dial sign rather than a handset. Most large towns have a 24-hour service. The system is overburdened and you will require immense patience.

Entertainment

● Media

The *Egyptian Gazette* is a daily paper in English. The most influential Egyptian daily is *Al-Ahram*. The BBC World service wave lengths are given on **page 17**. Reception quality varies greatly: as a general rule lower frequencies give better results in the morning and late at night and the higher ones in the middle of the day. *Cairo Today*, a monthly publication in English gives up-to-date information.

● Sport

Sport opportunites range from riding horses or camels in the desert to under-water swimming over coral reefs, from floating in balloon over the temples to a leisurely sail in a *fellucca* on the Nile in addition to the more usual golf, tennis, swimming etc. See entries under individual towns.

Holidays and festivals

1 Jan: New Year's Day
Sham al-Nessim (Sniffing of the Breeze, or the first day of Spring) is celebrated 2nd Monday after the Coptic Easter Day with family picnics.
25 April: Liberation of Sinai
1 May: Labour Day
18 Jun: Evacuation Day – the day the British left Egypt
23 Jul: Anniversary of 1952 Revolution
26 Jul: Alexandria National Day
6 Oct: Armed Forces' Day – parades and military displays
13 Oct: Suez Day
23 Dec: Victory Day

Approximate dates of Islamic festivals in 1995:
1 Feb: Beginning of Ramadan
4-5 Mar: Eïd al-Fitr
11 May: Eïd al-Adha
31 May: Ras al-Sana – Islamic New Year
9 Aug: Moulid al-Nahl (Prophet's birthday) – street celebrations in main towns

Approximate dates of Coptic celebrations in 1995:
7 Jan: Christmas
19 Jan: Epiphany
13 Mar: Annunciation
Easter: moveable feast
4 June: Penticost
19 Aug: Transfiguration

● Other events

Jan Cairo International Book Fair; National Tennis Championships; Rowing regatta in Cairo.

Feb Abu Simbel Festival (22nd), birthday of Ramses II; International Fishing Festival in Hurghada; International Tennis Championships; International Bridge Tournament.

Mar Cairo International Fair; Annual Spring Flower Show, Andalucía Gardens, Cairo; International Marathon (Cairo-Alexandria).

Jul National Fishing Festival Hurghada.

Aug Nile Festival – Wafaa el-Nil.

Oct Abu Simbel Festival (22nd) coronation of Ramses II; Commemoration of Battle of El-Alamein, 24 Oct; International Folk Festival, Ismailia.

Nov Duck Shooting Festival, El-Sharkia; Egyptian Arabian Horse Event; International Yacht Regatta, Alexandria.

Dec International Rowing Races, Luxor and Aswan; International Film Festival.

Further reading

● Books

Durrell, L. *Alexandria Quartet*, Faber & Faber: London; Heikal, M. (1975) *Autumn Fury* and *The Road to Ramadan*: London; Hirst, D. & Beeson, I. (1981) *Sadat*: London; Murnane, William J. *A Penguin Guide to Ancient Egypt*; Pick, Christopher *Egypt: A Travellers Anthology*, John Murray Publishers Ltd; Seton, M.V. *A Short History of Egypt*, Rubicon Press; Steindorff, G & Seele, K.C. *When Egypt Ruled the East*, University of Chicago Press; Stephens, R. (1971) *Nasser – a Political Biography*: London; Vatikiotis, P.J. *The History of Modern Egypt: From Mohammad Ali to Mubarak*, Weidenfeld & Nicolson: London; Waterbury, J. (1983) *The Egypt of Nasser & Sadat*: Princeton; Fakhry, A. (1990) *Siwa Oasis*, American University of Cairo Press.

The *Shire Egyptology* series: Shire Publications Ltd., Princes Risborough, Bucks, UK, have a fascinating series £3.50 each including Egyptian Coffins, Food and Drink, Mummies, Painting, Pyramids and Household Animals. *Common Birds of Egypt*: American University in Cairo Press, helps to sort out some of the less usual birds. Brown and Rachid *Egyptian Carpets*, American University in Cairo Press E£10.

Egypt Focus, a monthly newsletter published by Menas Associates Ltd, PO Box 513, London E17 6PP, T 44-(0)81-520-8067, F 44-(0)81-520-1688.

SUDAN

Contents

Maps

Introduction

At present travelling in Sudan is difficult because of the civil war. The result is that the whole of southern Sudan is totally unsafe and travellers are **strongly advised not** to attempt to travel to or through the region. At the same time large parts of far western Sudan are also insecure.

It is currently **unsafe** to travel much further S than 13°N or W of 32°W. As the régime actively discourages internal travel here it is almost impossible to obtain the essential official permission to travel in these regions.

For these reasons this edition concentrates on the ***Three Towns*** area of Khartoum, Khartoum North and Omdurman and places easily accessed from there. It is hoped that the situation will change in the coming years and that future editions will include much more of this wonderful country.

Basics

OFFICIAL NAME Jumhuriyat as-Sudan (Republic of Sudan)

NATIONAL FLAG Rectangular, with a green equilateral triangle with one side adjacent and parallel to the flagpole imposed on 3 equal horizontal bands of red, white and black.

OFFICIAL LANGUAGE Arabic.

OFFICIAL RELIGION Islam.

INDICATORS *Population* 30 million (1992); *Urban* 22%. *Religion* Sunni Muslim 73%, traditional beliefs 17%, Christian 8%. *Birth rate* 44 per 1000; *Death rate* 13 per 1000; *Life expectancy* 52 (men)/54 (women). *GNP per capita* US$650.

Environment

Land

The Republic of Sudan is the largest country in Africa and the ninth largest in the world, covering 2,503,890 sq km. As such it is larger than all the countries of the European Union put together, or as large as the part of the USA which lies E of the Mississippi River. Greatest distances from N to S 2,050 km, and from E to W 1,850 km.

Borders

Sudan has 2 great difficulties in respect of its territorial integrity – first, from neighbouring states which harbour claims against it, and, second, from the internal cleavage between the N and S regions. There are 644 km of coastline while elsewhere there are complex borders inherited from the colonial past. In the N a line runs E-W through the latitude of Wadi Halfa, leaving that town in Sudan. The easterly extension of this border zigzags to the Red Sea coast at Bir Shalatain where there are complicated

rights shared for territorial and economic purposes between Sudan and Egypt. Sudan's Red Sea offshore boundary with Saudi Arabia is unusual in that the central block running down the spine of the sea is kept in joint Sudanese-Saudi control. In the SE the border is with Eritrea/Ethiopia. In general Sudan has the lowlands and Ethiopia the highlands The southern border touches the mountains of Uganda before turning N and W on the rough watershed between the Nile and the Congo rivers. Sudan's Northern Darfur includes the Darfur mountain zone N of which the international boundary swings N and E on longitude 24°E to the 20°N parallel and thence along longitude 25°E to join the Egyptian-Libyan tripoint near Aïn Zuwwayah.

Main regions

This huge country is a vast patchwork of different peoples and regions and loyalties tend to be much stronger to family, tribe and region than to the concept of the nation state. Sudan can broadly be divided into a number of specific regions. In political terms **southern Sudan** refers to the 3 old provinces of Bahr el Ghazel,

Equatoria and Upper Nile, which have since been divided and renamed so many times that it is difficult to keep track, while **northern Sudan** refers to the rest of the country.

While the geographical term **southern Sudan** refers to the same area, the N has traditionally been divided into a number of regions. In its limited sense **northern Sudan** refers to the narrow strip of irrigated lands along the Nile to the N of Khartoum and the harsh desert on either side. The area around the capital, which is usually referred to as **Khartoum** or the **Three Towns**, includes the area in and around not only the capital itself but also across the Blue Nile in Khartoum North and the White Nile in Omdurman.

Western Sudan describes the mainly pastoral nomadic central and western provinces of Kordofan and Darfur which are a mixed area of extensive sand dunes, scrub, semi-desert and the Nuba Mountains of Southern Kordofan. **Central Sudan** is the area to the S of Khartoum including Blue Nile province and the **Gezira**, a huge irrigated area which is bounded by the Blue and the White Niles and forms a triangle with Khartoum, Kosti and Sennar at its N, W and E corners, respectively. **Eastern Sudan** is divided between the claylands around Gedaref and Kassala, the country's main granary, the drier areas to the E of the main Nile, the Red Sea Hills and finally the narrow coastal strip on the other side.

Relief

Sudan is rather like an amphitheatre and is surrounded by mountains to the E, S and W and, for so large a country, has remarkably few mountain massifs. In the extreme S adjacent to Uganda are the **Imatong Mountains** including **Jebel Kinyetti** (3,187m), Sudan's highest peak. In the W in Darfur the mountains rise to over 3000m and include **Jebel Marra** (3,088m) a dormant volcano. **Jebel Hamoyet** (2,736m) is the highest peak in the Red Sea Hills. In Southern Kordofan the **Nuba Mountains** have several peaks over 1,000m of which the highest is **Jebel el-Dayer** (1,375m). Almost 75% of Sudan lies below 1,000m and most of its central portion is a vast clay plain broken by isolated hills.

Rivers

The Nile traverses the entire length of the country from Nimule to Wadi Halfa on a winding 3,614 km course. The **White Nile** rises in Lake Victoria and enters Sudan near Nimule from where it flows swiftly to Juba. It then enters the huge flat perennial swamplands of the 8,000 sq km **Sudd** which increases to over 19,000 sq kms in the wet season. Just to the S of Malakal it is joined first by the **Bahr el Ghazel** river which drains the SW province of the same name and then the Sobat which drains much of Ethiopia's SW highlands. Further N at Khartoum the White Nile meets the Blue Nile and becomes the main Nile river.

The **Blue Nile**, which provides the greatest water flow in the Nile system, rises in Ethiopia's Lake Tana crossing the border S of Roseires. It is joined by the **Dindar** and seasonal **Rahad** rivers before it meets the White Nile at Khartoum, just to the S of the 6th cataract between the city and the Egyptian city of Aswan. The main Nile is joined by the River **Atbara** at the town of Atbara and then flows in a huge S-bend through 1,100 kms of desert to **Lake Nasser** (**Lake Nubia**) (see page 804) which filled the valley behind the Aswan High Dam.

Climate

With the exception of the Red Sea coast which has its own Mediterranean-like micro climate, the climate of Sudan is layered from N to S in broad zones. Northern Sudan lies for the most part in the Saharan climatic zone with negligible rainfall, 22 mm per year at Wadi Halfa for example. Khartoum lies astride the junction between the date growing

Sudanese Measurements: Confused? Now Read On ...

Length

1 diraa or pik baladi = 24 kirats = 0.58 m
1 qadam = 1 foot (imperial)
1 busa = 1 inch (imperial)
River lands are measured in ud where 1 ud = 4 diraa

Height

1 ragil is the distance between fingertips when both arms are outstretched = about 1.666m. This is used for measuring wells but 1 ragil Bergdawi = 2.5m which can be confusing...

Weight

The unit of measurement here may depend on what is being weighed:
1 green sunt = 400 kg (used for green wood)
1 dead sunt = 350 kg (used for dead wood)
12 wagia = 1 rotl = 450 gm and a sack contains about 125 rotls
1 kantar = 100 rotls = 45 kg. This is a measure used for cotton, but where cotton is grown under irrigation 1 kantar = 315 rotls

Cereals are measured in ardeb where 1 ardeb = 12 kelas = 2 sacks but the number of rotls to the ardeb varies: for sesame = 264 rotls, wheat 360 rotls, maize 336 rotls and groundnuts 160 rotls.

Dry volume

1 ardeb = 198 litres
1 keila = 16.5 litres
1 rubu = 8.25 litres
1 malwa = 4.1 litres
1 qadah = 2 litres
1 nus qadah (½ qadah) = 1 litre

Liquid measure

1 girba = 40 cu cm
1 rotl liquid = 4.5 cu cm

Area

1 feddan = 4,200 sq metres

areas of the Sahara and the Baobab tree vegetation area (or the 'Sudan' climatic zone) with its Savanna grassland and, in its S, scattered trees in tall Savanna grasses. Adjacent to the Ethiopian Highlands the pattern becomes complex with interwoven areas of Savanna and subtropical forest. Similarly the climate S of the Sudd becomes in part tropical, with rain forest along the S flowing river systems of Bahr el Ghazel.

Two winds play an important role: the Northerlies which bring cool, dry weather in winter and heat in summer dominate the desert regions of the dry N; the Southerlies which carry rain from the S in Jan and reach their extreme in Aug.

Agriculture

Out of an estimated potential arable area of 84 million ha only about 14.8% was utilized in 1989 and only 2% was under irrigation. A further 46.5 million ha was believed to be forested but desertification is continuing to reduce this total. Until Independence cultivated lands were heavily concentrated along the Nile in general and in the huge Gezira irrigated agricultural scheme in particular. Besides the subsequent development of a number of large irrigated agricultural projects such as Rahad and Khashm el Girba, mechanized agriculture was begun over huge areas of rich claylands around Gedaref and Kassala. To the W of the Nile, however, most of the land has remained a grazing zone for nomadic and semi-nomadic pastoralists.

The problems of agriculture in the E are varied and challenging. People talk of pest infestations, the difficulty of finding seasonal labour to harvest crops and fuel shortages added to the normal run-of-the-mill problems such as drought, salination and erosion. Not a pretty picture at the moment. There are rumours of serious food shortages in the W, which, given the current situation in the capital itself, must mean it's fairly desperate.

Land Use 1990	(%)
Arable and orchards	5.4
Forests and woodland	18.9
Meadows and pastures	46.3
Desert and other waste	29.4

Source: Encyclopaedia Britannica (1993)

Land tenure

Sudan officially has few of the land tenure problems experienced by other North African states because land ownership is vested in the state rather than in individuals. In practice, however, the country has very serious difficulties. The vast territories outside the Nile valley are under traditional occupation by tribal groups whose sense of communal ownership is undiminished by the niceties of law in the capital city. Bitter land disputes persist between new settlers from outside and local tribes. On modern agricultural schemes, created for single commercial crops such as cotton, including the Gezira, complex sub-letting and share-cropping goes on despite rules to the contrary. Outside the wet and fertile S, land takes its value from the availability of water and the stock carrying capacity of the ranges rather than from the extent of the surface area. Political stability or otherwise also plays an important role in the value of land and resources. Large areas in the S have been devastated by persistent civil war over many decades and basically are unproductive.

Potential

The comparatively low density of population and the apparent availability of large amounts of water from the Nile and its tributaries led to highly ambitious plans in the 1970s to turn Sudan into the *'bread basket for the Arab World'* but there are a number of long-term problems which have to be overcome before Sudan can reach its full and undoubtedly excellent agricultural potential.

Not only has there been a gradual decline in rainfall and the associated problems of desertification in Sudan but also, under the 1959 Nile Waters Agreement with Egypt, it is only permitted to take 18.5 cu km of water out of the supposed 74 cu km which flow through to Egypt. By 1990, however, Sudan was already using 17.1 cu km despite its low standards of irrigation, hydro-electric and urban water consumption. In the near future Sudan will need to make major steps in water conservation if it is to keep its present level of water use per head of population.

No less than 45 cu km of water are lost through evaporation and seepage in the Sudd swamps which could be reduced by as much as 4 billion cubic metres by the construction of the **Jonglei canal** to speed river flow. Construction on a first phase of the Jonglei scheme was abandoned because of the civil war and even when peace finally comes it will be very difficult and expensive to restart. Although dry farming is possible provided the environmental consequences are considered, without attention to enhancing its water supply and conservation the outlook for Sudan's agriculture is relatively bleak.

The immense transportation problems need to be resolved before real potential can be revealed. Despite operating 4,725 km of mainly narrow gauge single track, making it one of the longest in Africa, the railway system is dilapidated and inefficient. Sudan's only black top road is between Khartoum and

THE PROBLEMS OF SOUTHERN SUDAN

Sudan continues to suffer from what has been called 'a forgotten war' in its southern territories. The S of Sudan is a vast area of land the size of France, comprising Equatoria, Bahr el Ghazal and Upper Nile provinces which are occupied by black peoples who are mainly Nilotic, animist or Christian but infrequently Muslims. This contrasts with the N where the population is to a greater extent Semitic and Muslim. The S is equatorial in climate, well watered for the most part and rich in soils and other natural resources.

The history of relations between N and S Sudan is one of exploitation of the S by northerners. Until the arrival of the British colonial authorities, the Muslim N traded and raided in the S to get slaves for the traffic initially to Egypt and then the Arabian Gulf. There was deep resentment of this activity which succeeded in creating what has become a permanent wedge between the two communities. Under the British, who deliberately separated N from S, Christian agencies were allowed to work in the S exacerbating Muslim distrust by their missions.

Sudan became independent in Jan 1956 but an inability by the political parties in the N to accept that S Sudan was an equal partner in nation-building led to a mutiny in the S which eventually became a fully fledged rebellion. Despite an attempt at national reconciliation in the 1970s the differences between N and S came to the fore again as a result of the insensitive introduction of basic Islamic *sharia* law to all areas, including many that were non-Muslim, in 1983. In Sep 1989 there was a coup d'état by Muslim fundamentalists in Khartoum which heralded an escalation of the civil war in the S which had been ongoing since 1983. The Sudanese People's Liberation Army (SPLA) continues to fight for regional autonomy and as time goes on for complete independence from Khartoum. The Sudanese government has received some limited military assistance from Iran but so far has been unable to break the continuing rebellion in the S.

The human and economic costs of the war have been terrible, with the occurrence of drought and the inflow of refugees at various times from conflicts in neighbouring countries making the situation worse. Development of economic resources including the Jonglei canal scheme for straightening the course of the River Nile and the exploitation of oil reserves have been suspended. Food supplies in the war torn areas of the S are often inadequate and travellers will have problems in finding foodstuffs and clean water supplies sources or adequate transport. Although a few courageous missionary and aid agencies are at work there, there is great insecurity and personal safety cannot be guaranteed. The visit of the Archbishop of Canterbury to S. Sudan in 1994 caused a diplomatic storm. Most international organizations will not send their staff to Sudan because of the war and the unacceptable activities of the central government in Khartoum.

In general, independent travellers are advised to approach visits to Sudan, other than Khartoum, with great caution. Always refer for advice to your embassy in Khartoum before planning to go up-country.

Port Sudan, thus large areas of the country are cut off from Sudan's capital and only port throughout the rainy season. This obviously creates severe transport and distribution problems which must be overcome before the currently peripheral regions of western and southern Sudan can be developed.

There is also the overriding matter of internal political stability. Currently, therefore, Sudan's potential for economic positive change is low and it will remain a deficit economy dependent on external financial and humanitarian aid.

People

Population

Although there are no accurate figures, Sudan's population given as 30 million in 1992 has an annual growth rate which slipped slightly from about 3.0% between 1965-80 to about 2.7% between 1980-1990 and in 1991 was again 3%. The average population density is about 12 per sq km but there are significant regional variations and about 50% of the population live on just 15% of the land.

Main towns with population estimates

The Three Towns	6 million
Port Sudan	1 million
Wad Medani	1 million
Atbara	500,000
Kassala	500,000
El Obeid	250,000
Juba	250,000

The combination of the presence of foreign refugees (estimated at over 1 million) and the widespread internal migration caused by the drought and civil war has caused very rapid rural-urban migration. It is now estimated that about 6 million people live in and around the capital.

Fertility

Total fertility rates are put at 6.4%, one of the highest in the world. The population is youthful in structure. In 1990 45.2% of the people were 14 years of age or under against 52.2% in the economically active group from 15-64 years.

Literacy

Literacy rates are still very low at only 43% and 12% for men and women respectively. It is estimated that 59% of boys and 41% of girls in the relevant age group attend primary school while for secondary school attendance the respective rates were 23% and 17% in 1986-1988.

Income per head

This can only be guessed at but is put by UN sources at approximately US$650 per man, woman and child which is equivalent to standards in Upper Egypt. Personal incomes vary considerably depending on region and the rainfall régime of the year in question, not to mention the degree of maladministration and disruption of the economy by war.

History since Independence

When Sudan became Independent on 1st January 1956, areas that had little or no common history were united in a single country.

Sudan's post-Independence politics were initially dominated by the political parties of the 2 principal Sufi Muslim *tariqahs* or brotherhoods. The **Umma Party** is the political arm of the *Ansar tariqa* which is led by the Mahdi's descendants including his 2 times prime minister great-grandson Sadiq El-Mahdi. The Mirghani family has been the traditional leaders of the *Khatimiyya tariqa* and its **Democratic Unionist Party** (DUP). In this case Unionist refers to its now-defunct aim of unifying Sudan and Egypt. By contrast the Umma Party has traditionally been more nationalistic and has had strained relations with Egypt.

Between 1956 and 1969 there were 7 coalition governments, as well as a 6 year military régime which were characterized by inter-party rivalry and instability. A minor mutiny in the S was allowed to escalate into the bloody and tragic first civil war which lasted until 1972 and which, directly and indirectly, is believed to have been responsible for the deaths of over 500,000 people. Eventually it was ended by the 1972 **Addis Ababa Agreement** which gave the 3 southern provinces a large measure of regional autonomy in the newly created Southern Region.

During the mid-1970s it seemed as if Sudan was entering a phase of relative stability when it could concentrate on its considerable economic potential. Despite its many faults the Nimeiri government was generally seen as a stabilizing influence on the country. Unfortunately this was largely thrown away as President **Nimeiri** (1969-1986) became increasingly autocratic and despotic, particularly after the coup attempts in 1975 and 1976. The 1977 National Reconciliation policy led to the return of leading northern opposition politicians including the Muslim Brotherhood which, in turn, led to the increasing role of Islam in Sudanese politics which alarmed both southerners and other non-Muslims. Despite the secular 1973 constitution a form of Islamic *sharia* law was introduced in Sept 1983. Between May and Sept 1984 there was a 5 month State of Emergency when '*courts of decisive justice*' handed out draconian punishments, including public floggings, 56 amputation of limbs and a number of executions, to Muslims and non-Muslims alike.

The euphoria of the Addis Ababa Agreement had long since evaporated because of the increasing mismanagement, corruption and inter-tribal rivalries in the S. At the same time there was increasing southern opposition to Khartoum's perceived theft of southern natural resources. The giant Jonglei Canal project, which was designed to reduce the water loss in the Sudd swamp and thereby transport more water to northern Sudan and to Egypt, was also opposed because of the environmental damage that it was expected to cause. Meanwhile the proposed project to export crude oil from the newly discovered southern oil fields via a pipeline to Port Sudan was criticized by southern politicians.

These and other factors led to a revolt by 3 southern garrisons in Jan 1983 who, together with other southerners from the army, police, prison and game warden services, formed the **Sudanese Peoples' Liberation Army (SPLA)** under the leadership of Col John Garang. This small guerrilla army, which did not initially represent a threat to the government, received a major fillip with the introduction of Islamic *sharia* law in Sept 1983. It soon expanded and became a large guerrilla army which plunged Sudan into a second major civil war. Almost a decade later it shows no real sign of ending and the civil war remains the most intractable problem facing the country.

President Nimeiri was overthrown in Apr 1985 in a broad-based revolution and was replaced by a Transitional Military Council (TMC) which governed the country together with a civilian non-political cabinet until the Apr 1986 elections. This led to the formation of an Umma/DUP grand coalition government, under Prime Minister **Sadiq El-Mahdi**, which won 162 of the 264 seats which were contested. By its very nature the coalition government proved fragile and indecisive and it collapsed and was reformed a number of times. While the northern politicians squabbled over power, the war in the S was allowed to escalate. Just when the government finally appeared ready to ignore the opposition of the fundamentalist National Islamic Front (NIF) and signed a peace treaty with the SPLA which had the support of the army high command, there was a successful military coup on 30th June 1989 and civilian rule came to an abrupt and tragic end.

Modern Sudan

Government

The new **Revolutionary Command Council** (RCC) for National Salvation led by Lt-Gen Omar Hassan Ahmad al-Bashir is linked politically with the NIF, the real power behind the throne. During the past 4 years the régime has accelerated the **Islamization** of Sudanese society and those who have opposed it have been subjected to an appalling catalogue of human rights abuses. While creating a climate of fear and repression in N Sudan in order to change fundamentally the previously tolerant society, the régime has escalated the war in S Sudan in a vain attempt to defeat the SPLA by military rather than political means. Although the SPLA is split on tribal lines between those military commanders wanting the S to secede and Garang who is still aiming for the increasingly impossible goal of a united secular decentralized Sudan, the status quo is simply untenable. The next few years will determine whether Sudan remains a single country or breaks into at least 2 parts possibly with an Islamic fundamentalist state in the N and an African animist/Christian state to the S.

The country is divided into 26 states, 17 of which are new, added since the recent federal structure of Sudan was inaugurated in 1991, after the present régime came into power. These new arrangements, says the minister at the Bureau of Regional Affairs, 'will enhance chances of peace since they are *universally welcomed by people in the South*'.

Economy

Economic development projects have always been concentrated in the heartland rather than in the peripheral provinces. The 1920s Gezira cotton scheme acted as a magnet for both people and projects. Later the eastern claylands around Gedaref became the focus of new mechanised farming. Other regions have had comparatively little development. The result has been a relatively prosperous heartland in a sea of absolute poverty.

Agriculture

Accounts for 36% of the national output, provides a livelihood for over 80% of the population, employs over 60% of the labour force and generates 95% of total exports. There are four distinct sub-sectors in Sudanese agriculture – modern irrigated farming, mechanized rain-fed crop production, traditional rain-fed farming and livestock. The first two account for over 65% of agricultural production.

Modern irrigated farming is dominated by the 880,000 ha **Gezira** scheme with over 100,000 tenant farmers. By far the greatest proportion of cultivated land is rain-fed with the modern sector in the E around Gedaref particularly important for producing sorghum and other cereal crops. The traditional rain-fed and livestock sub-sectors are mainly subsistence agriculture and tend to be relatively inefficient.

Traditionally irrigated long-staple cotton from the Gezira is Sudan's main export (the country produces more than a third of the world total), followed by gum arabic (in which Sudan leads the world), sesame, groundnuts and sorghum. Wheat is grown as a second crop in the irrigated areas to cater for the growing urban demand for white bread, millet is the main crop in the traditional rain-fed sector but sorghum from the mechanized rain-fed areas dominates cereal production. Sugar-cane for home consumption is also grown in irrigated areas.

Livestock is very important for both settled and nomadic communities. The drier regions of the N support goats, sheep and camels while cattle are kept in the wetter centre and S. It is estimated that in 1991 there were 21 million cattle, 21 million sheep, 15 million goats, 2.7 million camels, 692,000 donkeys and horses, and 30 million chickens. These numbers have fluctuated sharply over the years and the combination of the civil war, drought and desertification killed a significant proportion during the past decade.

Industry

The state-dominated manufacturing sector is still relatively small and, together with mining, only contributed about 8.2% of GDP in 1990. It employs about 267,000 people representing about 4% of the total labour force. Manufacturing is closely linked to the agricultural economy with cotton ginning, textiles, flour and sugar processing, and the production of vegetable oils, soap and leather dominating the sector. It is highly inefficient because of the shortages of power, qualified management, technical resources and imported spare parts.

Sudan's potential mineral resources could be very considerable but little of the country has been explored and the continuing political insecurity makes this impossible over large areas of the country. The politically stable Red Sea Hills, which have the advantage of being close to Port Sudan, have small but rich gold reserves and chromite is produced in the Ingessana Hills in Blue Nile province. High transportation costs and the inaccessibility of the rest of the country is likely to hinder further foreign investment in other areas and the industry will remain small scale for the foreseeable future.

Energy

In 1991 Sudan consumed 1.33 bn kW/hr of energy, of which fuel wood, charcoal and other biomass constituted 79% and oil 20%. Rural households consume 93% of the biomass which is mainly used for cooking. In 1980 transport accounted for 58% of total petroleum product consumption followed by industry (15%), agriculture (10%) and power generation (8%) but the latter is increasing rapidly. **Hydro-electric power** schemes are currently limited to the dams at Sennar (15 MW), Khashm el Girba (12 MW) and Roseires (250 MW). Consequently the majority of the new power stations have to rely on unreliable imported oil.

Chevron discovered significant oil reserves in the 1970s near Bentiu just inside Upper Nile province. If these are developed the prohibitive 1,400 km distance from Bentiu to the Red Sea coast will probably confine the oil to domestic consumption. Meanwhile the available woodland resources in the N are being severely depleted because of the lack of a cheap alternative energy supply.

Trends in the economy

The economy is in a dreadful mess with a spiralling debt crisis from which Sudan has been unable to extricate itself. The decision to grow wheat in the irrigated areas reduced the traditional export cotton crop. Although more rain-fed cotton is now grown it has not compensated for the loss in the irrigated area with the result that cotton exports, which usually account for over half of the total, have declined sharply. The result is that total exports have fallen from US$427 million in 1988 to under US$300 million in 1992. Imports have remained at around US$950-US$1,150 million in the same period.

This increased trade deficit has been made worse by a fall in the level of expatriate remittances and foreign aid. Consequently the current account deficit has increased from US$358 million in 1988 to around US$1,652 million in 1991 thereby making it even harder to repay the outstanding foreign debts which now total over US$16 billion.

The régime's **economic transformation programme** includes – reducing government expenditure including consumer subsidies on basic commodities and fuel; increasing taxes; the privatization of most state owned companies' assets; the unification of exchange rates; interest rate liberalization and other measures. Although it is determined to continue its programme until it bears fruit, it has led to massive inflation and devaluations which are hurting the weakest members of society. Because of the régime's hostility towards its most important former aid donors these hardships are not being cushioned by international financial assistance.

Economic structure 1990	(%)
Agriculture	30.1%
Industry	15.3%
of which manufacturing	8.6%
Services	50.5%

Source: EIU

Economic Indicators

	1988	1989	1990	1991	1992*
GDP in S£ billion	40.3	73.6	104.0*	117.9*	158.6
Imports US$ million	949	1,051	649	1,138	975
Exports US$ million	427	544	327	303	275
Balance of trade	-522	-507	-322	-835	-700
Inflation (%)	65	64	96*	200	250
Foreign debt (US$ billion)	12.0	13.9	15.4	15.9*	16.2

* estimates (Source: EIU)

KHARTOUM

CONTENTS

Currently the Three Towns of Khartoum, Khartoum North and Omdurman are the only places easily accessible to visitors. Even here movements are restricted and although the strict curfew has been lifted it is definitely recommended to be indoors between midnight and 0500 (taxis to the airport are an exception). The people have become so used to the curfew that the streets are deserted after 2300. There are random checkpoints set up and at bridges the checks are particularly severe. However, opportunities for sightseeing are available.

Population 6 million *Alt* 380m.

History

Khartoum was established in 1821, became the capital of Sudan in 1834 and grew on the miseries of the slave trade. The horrific slaughter of General Gordon on the palace steps and the wholesale massacre of the inhabitants in 1884 by the Mahdi is well chronicled. Omdurman was set up across the river by the Mahdi and still retains Islamic characteristics. The Sudanese capital was captured in 1898 by General Kitchener and his army after the so-called Battle of Omdurman which more accurately should be called the Battle of Karari. Kitchener enacted Britain's revenge for the murder of General Gordon both by the virtual sacking of Omdurman, the wholesale slaughter of much of its population, and the rebuilding of a new capital in the shape of the British Union Jack flag across the river in Khartoum.

Situation

The name in Arabic means 'elephant's trunk', reputedly the shape of the narrow tongue of land on which it is built at the confluence of the Blue and White Niles. Another version of the name comes from the time of the Roman conquest of Egypt when an expedition coming up the Nile discovered the sunflower seed called *ghartum* in Arabic. The oil from the seed was used to cure the wounds of soldiers. By and by the name was changed from Ghartum to Khartoum.

Although the area of the Three Towns is quite large, and is expanding all the time, **downtown Khartoum** which includes all the main government buildings and company offices is only about 10 sq km in area. The majority of western expatriates live in the **New Extension** (Amarat) which was built to the S of 'Khartoum Two' (also known as Souk Two) which was Khartoum's small original southwards extension. The numbers of the New Extension's streets, which run E-W between Africa/Airport Rd and Cemetery Rd, get progressively higher going S so Street One is closest to the city centre and Street 61 at the edge of the city. The shanty towns which surrounded the city have been removed.

ACCESS Khartoum Airport is located just off Africa Rd (also known as Airport Rd) about 5 km to the SE of the city centre. The new departure terminal is functioning well, the arrival terminal is under construction. From here it is very easy to get a taxi (S£1,000-S£2,000 by day and S£3,000 at night) to your hotel. Trains from Port Sudan, Atbara and Wadi Halfa arrive in Baheri (Khartoum North). The old, centrally located, Khartoum railway station (destinations S and

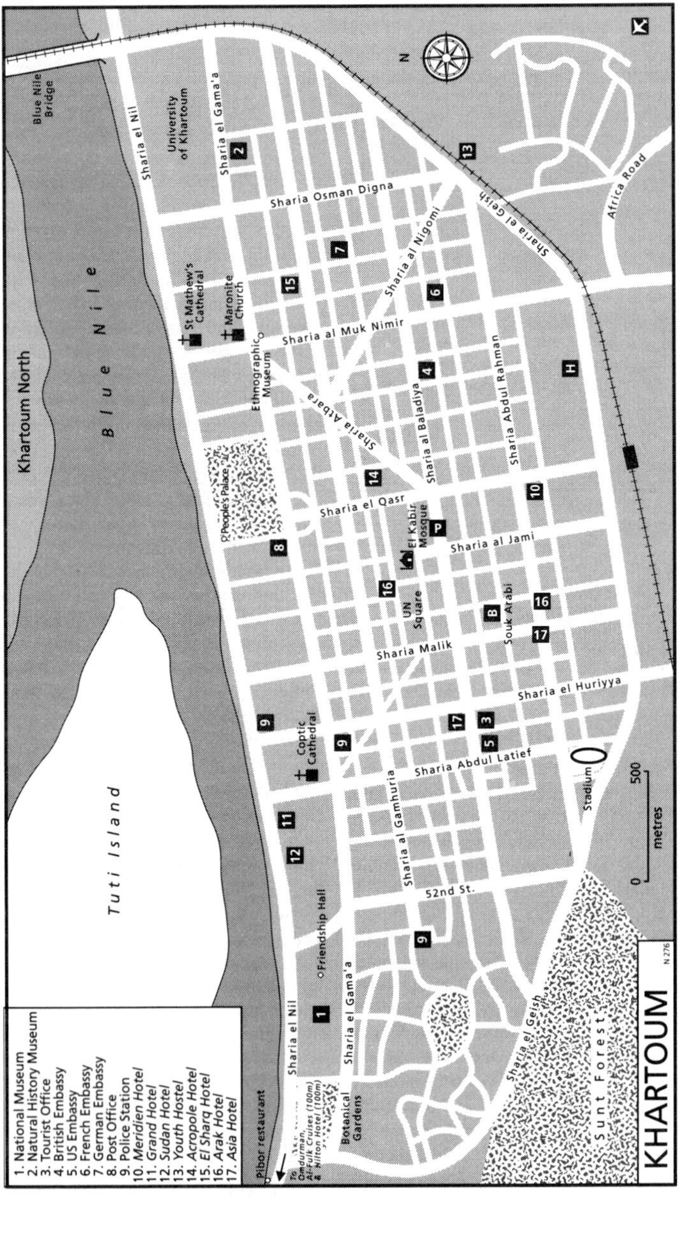
KHARTOUM
1. National Museum
2. Natural History Museum
3. Tourist Office
4. British Embassy
5. US Embassy
6. French Embassy
7. German Embassy
8. Post Office
9. Police Station
10. Meridien Hotel
11. Grand Hotel
12. Sudan Hotel
13. Youth Hostel
14. Acropole Hotel
15. El Sharq Hotel
16. Arak Hotel
17. Asia Hotel
Khartoum North
Blue Nile Bridge
Blue Nile
Tuti Island
University of Khartoum
St Mathew's Cathedral
Maronite Church
Ethnographic Museum
People's Palace
El Kabir Mosque
UN Square
Souk Arabi
Coptic Cathedral
Friendship Hall
Botanical Gardens
Sunt Forest
Stadium
Sharia el Nil
Sharia el Gama'a
Sharia Osman Digna
Sharia al Nigomi
Sharia al Muk Nimir
Sharia Atbara
Sharia al Baladiya
Sharia Abdul Rahman
Sharia el Qasr
Sharia al Jami
Sharia Malik
Sharia el Huriyya
Sharia Abdul Latief
Sharia al Gamhuria
52nd St.
Sharia el Geish
Africa Road
Pibor restaurant
To Omdurman, Al-Fulk Cruises (100m) & Hilton Hotel (100m)
0
500
metres
N
N 276

W) is at the S end of Sharia el Qasr (Palace Rd) at the other end of which, about 2 km away, is the People's Palace which stands on the banks of the Blue Nile.

Travel around Khartoum itself has become either incredibly arduous (if you take the buses), very expensive (if you take the taxis) or simply dependent on the goodwill of those fortunate enough to have a vehicle and the petrol sufficient for a return journey. (Private cars are rationed to 1 gallon per week.) Travel by night, even though the curfew is lifted, is restricted by the numerous checkpoints. Driver's ID must be produced, and possibly that of the passenger and great care should be taken to look out for these checkpoints which are not 'lit up' as such. Driving through inadvertently will turn you into a 'Swiss cheese' as one unfortunate Chinese diplomat found out.

Things to see

Khartoum

In 1898 Khartoum was rebuilt by General Kitchener in the shape of the British Union Jack in order to both make it easier to defend and to stamp Britain's authority on the capital.

The **National Museum** is located on Sharia el Nil to the E of Friendship Hall and is open Tues-Sun 0830-2030 but from 0830-1200 & 1530-2030 on Fri. It provides an interesting introduction to Sudan's long history with a particularly good section on the ancient kingdoms of Kush and Napata. Queen Hatshepsut's (1503-1482 BC) small Temple of Buhen and the Semna West Temple, which was built by Tuthmosis III (1504-1450 BC) were rescued from the waters of Lake Nasser (Lake Nubia) and have been reconstructed in the museum's garden. There is also a selection of Christian art and artefacts dating from 7th-11th centuries.

The exhibits in the smaller **Ethnological Museum** (supposedly open Sat-Thur 0830-1330 & Fri 0830-1230) further E on the corner of Sharia al Muk Nimir and Sharia el Gama'a. It is interesting as a quick introduction to the diversity of Sudan's ethnological heritage. The display includes musical instruments and weapons from Sudan's various regions. Further E along the street towards the Blue Nile Bridge is the small **Natural History Museum** which has the same opening hours. It contains an impressive collection of stuffed birds. Models of Sudanese fauna are displayed in replicas of their natural habitat. A reptilery contains crocodiles, snakes and tortoises. Supporting text is poor and identification confusing.

Tuti Island, which is in the centre of the Blue Nile and can be reached from ferry near the National Museum, is a haven of tranquillity from the city and is a favourite picnic site.

Confluence of the Niles Most of the major hotels either operate or can organize river cruises on Fri and Sat. When the Blue Nile is in full spate there is a most remarkable natural phenomenon as the dividing line between the white and blue waters can be clearly seen. On Fridays there are boat/ferry trips up the Blue Nile to see the spectacular views, returning at sunset. Tea and soft drinks included.

Camel Market 5-6 km E of the airport is a fascinating scene for Westerners.

Saha al-Khadra (Green Field), site of the government's parade ground and where the Pope preached to around 250,000 people. In many eyes this is a monument to the régime's folly, huge, wasteful of energy (lit up at night) and normally empty except for the odd horse or camel grazing on the lush irrigated grass.

Khartoum North

On the N bank of the Blue Nile and to the E of the main Nile is Khartoum North, also known as **Khartoum Baheri**,

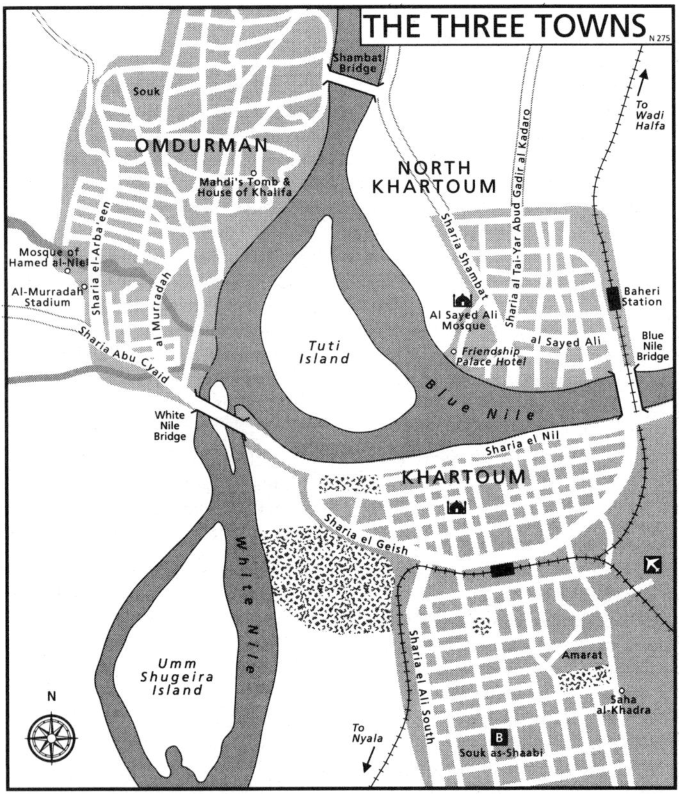

which is the country's industrial capital. There are few if any things to see or do in Khartoum North although the view of Khartoum back across the river from the *Friendship Palace Hotel* is wonderful.

Omdurman

Lying on the W bank of the White Nile and main Nile river, Omdurman was Sudan's traditional capital until Khartoum was developed as the administrative capital by the British after the Battle of Omdurman in 1898.

The **Mahdi's Tomb**, which is in a large yellow silver-domed mosque just across the main bridge from Khartoum, is closed to visitors. The original mosque and tomb, which were built after the Mahdi died of typhoid in June 1885, were destroyed by the British in 1898. In order to prevent it once again becoming a site of pilgrimage the Mahdi's body is said to have been burnt in the furnace of one of the Nile steamers and his ashes scattered into the Nile. The mosque and tomb were not rebuilt until 1947. The **museum** next door, which used to be the **House of the Khalifa**, Abdullahi Tour Shain who succeeded El Mahdi and developed Omdurman as his capital, is open Tues-Sun 0830-2030 and Fri 0830-1200 &

1530-2030. Its interesting collection of relics from the Mahdi's era include banners and guns, suits of armour from the 1898 Battle of Atbara, the 1902 Arrol car of Governor Wingate, and General Marchand's steel boat used to reach and occupy Fashoda. It also exhibits some photographs taken at the turn of the century, the Khalifa's gigantic bathroom and his bedroom dominated by his huge bed.

The **Omdurman Souk**, which can be reached from outside the Omdurman bus station by the *Arak Hotel* in Khartoum, by 'box' or bus or taxi (S£200) is a traditional Arab souk and the largest in the country. Besides food, spices and household goods there are also craftsmen working with gold, silver, ebony, ivory, animal skins and leather. (It is forbidden to import ivory and certain skins into most Western countries).

An hour before sunset, about 1530, every Fri the **Whirling Dervishes** gather in front of the **Mosque of Hamed al-Niel** who was the 19th century head of one of the Sufi Muslim *tariqas* (religious order or brotherhood). The mosque can be reached by bus from the *Arak Hotel* in Khartoum to al-Murradah Stadium on Sharia el-Arba'een (40 St) from where it is a 10 min walk to the W. The dervishes, who are dressed in brightly coloured patchwork *jallabah*, circle a pole while whirling themselves into a frenzy to the sound of drums and chanting in a ceremony known as a *dhikr* which lasts until they collapse or darkness comes.

Birdwatching There is good birdwatching along the Nile, especially when the birds are migrating. Make sure you use your binoculars with discretion and have a camera permit, see page 914.

Local information

● Accommodation

There are comparatively few hotels in Khartoum and even fewer really good ones. Most visitors opt for the *Hilton* and *Meridien* or the older but refurbished *Grand* because they are almost the only islands of 'Western standards' in the country with a/c or coolers and often private bathrooms. There are also a number of cheap but clean and comfortable hotels and much more basic *lakondas* (traditional cheap hotels with basic facilities) where *angrebs* (rope-woven beds) are put on the roof or courtyard on hot nights. Due to inflation, the current prices of most hotels are unknown and therefore, with the exception of those specifically mentioned, they have been put into three categories – expensive, middle, and cheap. Make reservations well in advance. A 20% government tax and a 10-12½% service charge is added to all restaurant and hotel bills. Bills in the expensive hotels must be settled in hard currency.

AL ***Hilton***, PO Box 1910, Mogran, Khartoum, T 74100, F 75793, Tx 22250, 285 rms, the best hotel in the country, located at the confluence of the Blue and White Nile rivers, about 10 min from the city centre and 6 km to the airport, wonderful views from upper floor facing N/NE and S/SW, TV, good pool, tennis, indoor bowls, sauna, health club, business centre and conference room for up to 500; **AL** ***Meridien***, Sharia el Qasr, PO Box 1716, Khartoum, T 75970, F 79087, 100 rms, high quality downtown hotel, slightly cheaper than 'Hilton', but more central position, 5 km from the airport, 2 restaurants, pool, sauna, TV, gym, and business centre

A ***Friendship Palace Hotel***, PO Box 148, Khartoum North, T 78204, built by Chinese in 1970s, pool, magnificent views across the water of Khartoum in general and of the Peoples' Palace in particular, on the steps of which General Gordon was killed in 1885; **A** ***Grand***, PO Box 516, Sharia el Nil, Khartoum, T 72782, Tx 22436, on banks of Nile overlooking the E end of Tuti Island, as its name implies was the country's first large luxury hotel, now extensively refurbished with modern facilities, still maintains its old-style charm, suffers from delusions of grandeur as the official government 'first class' hotel—but does have satellite TV in all rms, pool (quality unreliable), toilets unpleasant.

B ***Acropole***, downtown Khartoum, T 72680, Tx 22190, even before it was bombed by the Abu Nidal terrorist group in mid-1988 this was probably the most famous and best loved hotel in Khartoum amongst the international aid agencies. Located between Sharia Zubeir Pasha and Sharia el-Baladaya it is run by a Greek called George who is renowned for his friendly assistance with the result that, although it does not have facilities to match the more expensive hotels, the *Acropole* was almost always full during the famine crisis years. Current prices half those of 'Meridien'. Booking recommended. A number of hotels, which used to be amongst the best on offer before the big international standard hotels were built, are still operating but it is unknown what the standard or prices are like today. They included the ***Sudan*** on Sharia el Nil, T 80811, next to the *Grand*, and the ***Arak*** on Sharia el Qasr. The ***Asia Hotel*** on Sharia el-Baladaya near the tourist office is popular and clean with rooms on the roof for sunbathing. ***Africa Hotel***, Airport Rd near Street 30, clean and cheap, breakfast included.

There are a number of extremely cheap hotels to the W of United Nations Sq near the railway station. The standard and prices vary greatly but one which has been recommended is the traditional ***Port Sudan Hotel*** on Sharia Kulliyat el-Tibb which has beds in the courtyard. Try also the ***Hotel Mona*** in Souk al-Arabi which is OK. **E** *Sahara Hotel* and **E** *Falcon Hotel*, located near the ***Acropole***, are basic, cheap and clean, breakfast included. The ***Youth Hostel***, which is also known as the ***Student House***, is on 47th Ave next to the railway line and the American Club about 1 km E of the railway station.

● Places to eat

There are a number of good hotels and restaurants which serve excellent but very expensive food and the huge set-price eat-all-you-can buffets are very good value. Besides its excellent other food the *Hilton's* ***Ivory Room*** has such a buffet for Fri lunch. As might be expected the *Meridien* has good quality French food while the *Grand Hotel* and *Friendship Palace Hotel's* ***Tuti Café*** are well known for their excellent meat and fish club sandwiches for non-residents. The food in most of the other hotels is OK but not particularly inspiring.

Other decent restaurants include the following: The ***Korean Restaurant*** in the *Africa Hotel* and the ***Chinese Restaurant*** at the airport end of Street 15. On the bank of the Blue Nile, extending from opposite the Hilton to the confluence, there is a string of reasonable restaurants selling fish, chicken, kebabs and *tahina* or *babganush* with chips and a soft drink. It is very romantic to sit at sunset and watch the Nile flow by. Recommended is the ***Pibor Restaurant*** with friendly staff and good food costing about $2,000 per head.

Khartoum also has a number of very rudimentary restaurants, cafés and juice bars which serve a wide variety of delicious and exotic freshly-squeezed fruit juices. Of the latter the ***Athenae Café*** in Athenae Sq, is one of the most popular and the nearby ***Casa Blanca*** serves wonderful ice cream.

● Airline offices

Air France, T 76606; **Alitalia**, T 80526; **British Airways**, T 74577; **Egyptair**, T 70123; **Gulf Air**, T 75334; **Japan Airlines**, T 77685; **KLM**, T 74066; **Lufthansa**, T 71322; **Sudan Air**, T 73240/76341; **Swissair**, T 80208; **TWA**, T 80903.

● Banks

There are a number of commercial banks, which are open 0830-1200 Sat-Thur, and are mainly near the post office on Sharia el Gama'a. **Bank of Sudan**, T 78064; **National Bank of Sudan**, T 78153; **Citibank**, T 452423; **Bank of Khartoum**, PO Box 1008, T 81071; **Sudanese French Bank**, T 71831; **Habib Bank Ltd**, PO Box 159, T 81497.

● Cinemas

This is a very popular form of entertainment. All the cinemas are outdoor except the one in Friendship Hall, T 72223. Language will vary, the majority being in English, Arabic or Hindi with subtitles in other languages.

● Cruises

Al-Fulk on river bank opposite *Hilton Hotel*.

● Cultural centres

French, T 72837, open 0900-1300 Sun-Thur; **German**, T 78331, 1730-2030 Mon-Fri; **British Council**, T 80817, 14 Sharia Abu Sinn, open 0900-1230 and 1730-2030 Sat-Thur; Goethe Institute, T 77833.

● Embassies and consulates

France, T 77619; **Germany**, T 77990; **UK**, Sharia Zubeir Pasha, T 70760; **USA**, Sharia Abdul Latief, T 74611.

● Hospitals

Khartoum, T 79500, in Hospital St, opposite the railway station; **Khartoum North**, T 32841; **Omdurman**, T 52716.

● Night club

Gordons, once notorious for alcohol and dancing girls, has a traditional Sudanese evening each Fri—cost US$10 for entrance and food. Once a month has a Western style evening.

● Photography

Passport photographs from ***Sahara Photographer*** underneath the *Arak Hotel*, Sharia Zubeir Pasha, cost S£800 for 4 in black and white.

● Post Office

The main post office is located next to the People's Palace on Sharia el Gama'a. Open 0730-1300 & 1730-1830 Sat-Thur. The overseas postal service is quite reliable and fast but the domestic postal service is almost non-existent and parcels will almost certainly get lost or stolen. Letters to be collected using the Poste Restante service should be clearly addressed in the following way – Surname and initials, Poste Restante, Main Post Office, Sharia el Gama'a, Khartoum, Sudan. **Courier services**: TNT Skypack, T 446883; DHL, T 84590.

● Religious services

Anglican: Street 1 New Extension, Sun 0730, 0930 and 1700; **Coptic**: Street 15 New Extension, Sun 0600 and Fri 0800; **Evangelical**: Sudan Interior Mission, Khartoum Two, Sun 0900 and 1900; **Roman Catholic**: St Matthew's Cathedral, Sharia el Nil, Sun 0700, 0930,1800; **Moslem**: Grand Mosque adjacent to the Arabic Souk.

● Sports

Although there are very few public facilities there are a number of clubs which have some sports facilities. ***Khartoum Yacht Club***, opposite University by the Blue Nile, organizes races and teaches sailing. Visitors welcome. Water skiing on Blue Nile near Yacht Club S£6,000. The ***American Club*** T 70114 near the Youth Hostel has a larger pool and tennis courts. In the New Extension there are also the German, Italian, Hellenic, Syrian and Armenian clubs.

● Telephone/Telex

Code for Sudan is 249. In general telexes are much more reliable than fax messages. **Local code for Khartoum**: 011. International calls can be made from almost all the major hotels at the rate of S£450 per minute. **Emergency numbers**: **Police** T 73333, Fire T 74444.

● Tourist information

Although Sudan does not really have a tourist industry at the moment there is a tourist office (open 0830-1430 Sat-Thur) on the corner of Sharia el-Baladaya and Sharia el Huriyya to the W of United Nations Sq. It is probably easier to get accurate information, however, from your hotel.

● Travel Agents

Thomson Travel, T 440524/446883; ***Nile Safaris***, T 80718/73538. ***Speedbird Travel***, Sharia Barlaman, PO Box 1464, Khartoum, three blocks down from Sharia el Qasr, T 70594, F 70209, Tx 22130, very helpful, fast and reliable. Manager Huda Abdalla on hand to facilitate the travel arrangements. ***George Bernard Shaw*** of British/Irish extraction whose company repairs generators and installs satellite communications is the best contact in Khartoum, he and Polly his Ugandan colleague can arrange trips inside and outside of Khartoum and provide sensible advice, T 451663/451490.

● Transport

Local: Box-taxi These converted and covered pick-up trucks carry 8-10 passengers and are cheaper than taxis and more expensive, faster and less crowded than buses. Each plies the route between a specific area of town and the area around United Nations Square but those to Omdurman leave from the corner of Sharia al Gamhuria and Sharia el Huriyya to the W of the main mosque. Coloured bands along the side are intended to indicate the route but in practice the route is shouted out by the conductor. Listen carefully. Fares around S£20.

Car hire **Afro Elephant**, T 72355, **'5M'** T 440438. Where the road is wide enough, vehicles travel on the right. Roads are of varying quality; so is the driving.

Yellow taxi These operate throughout Khartoum and, although prices are increasing sharply all the time as the petrol shortages get worse, they are still relatively cheap but cost more than buses and boxes.

Air At Khartoum Airport – flight information T 77162 and general enquiries T 80370. There are flights to a number of major European cities as well as to Sudan's neighbours and the Gulf. The exit and foreign currency regulations have changed so frequently in recent years that it is essential to check the current situation before making plans to leave. Sudan Airways and a number of other airlines are notorious for over-booking flights so it is essential to arrive early for your flight. Air France, Egypt Air, Lufthansa and KLM fly into Khartoum once or twice a week. Other carriers on a regular basis are Ethiopian Airlines, Balkan, Saudi and Kenya Airways. Sudan Airways are using their new

A300 airbuses for the daily flight to Cairo. There is a S£500 airport tax. **See page 914** for flight information.

Internal services Sudan Airways operate internal services with return journeys to Khartoum on the same day flying Fokker 50s. The following times are quoted but have been described as a figment of the imagination so check carefully. Delays and cancellations due to fuel shortages are becoming more frequent.
Mon to **Nyala** 0300, **Wadi Halfa** 0300, **El Obeid** 0800, **El Gedaref** 0900, **Dongola** 1130.
Tue to **Nyala** 0300, **El Obeid** 0330.
Wed to **El Gedaref** 0300, **Atbara** 0400, **Merowe/Port Sudan** 1730, **Dongola** 0900.
Thur to **Nyala** 0300, **Wadi Halfa** 0300, **El Obeid** 0800, **El Gedaref** 0900, **Merowe** 1130.
Fri to **Nyala** 0300, **Dongola/Port Sudan** 0300, **Kassala** 0530, **El Obeid/El Gedaref** 0930, **Merowe** 1200.
Sat to **Nyala** 0300, **El Gedaref** 0400, **Atbara/Port Sudan** 0900, **Dongola** 0930.
Sun to **El Gedaref** 0300, **Dongola/Port Sudan** 0300, **El Obeid/Port Sudan** 0830, **Merowe** 1200, **Kassala** 1230. Sample fare Khartoum to Dongola S£15,000.

Khartoum to Port Sudan or Wadi Halfa takes 80 mins and costs S£6,000. Airport tax at the provincial airport is S£75. A number of relatively efficient charter airlines operate: **Sasco**, T 80718; **Nile Safaris**, T 80718; **Air Taxi**, T 73307.

Train For arrivals and departures, T 72381/75388, for fares T 72769. The main railway station is in Baheri (Khartoum North) for trains to N. Trains to S and W leave from the old railway station about 1 km from the town centre at the S end of Sharia el Qasr. Both stations sell tickets and provide information. Although there are trains, albeit very slow and inefficient, in all directions from Khartoum the timetable is notoriously inaccurate with not only the times but also the days of the service being changed. It is best to go to the information office to the left of the ticket desk a few days before your intended departure to get the latest information. The trains are very crowded and a reservation is not a guarantee of a seat, so it is advisable to arrive at the station some hours before departure. Be warned, however, that trains often leave very late and you could be stuck on a hot and crowded stationary train for hours before it actually leaves Khartoum. The one train a week to Wadi Halfa leaves on Sun at 0800 (perhaps) takes 24-30 hrs, costs S£8,000 first class, and S£6,000 second class. This links with the weekly ferry from Wadi Halfa to Aswan. Trains to Atbara leave from Baheri, take 7 hrs and cost S£5,000 second class and S£3,000 third class; to Karima, leave Fri 0800, take 24 hrs (who knows how many really....) cost S£4,000 first class and S£3,290 second class; to Port Sudan, Tue 0800, take 19 hrs cost S£5,500 first class and S£5,000 second class. Trains also (apparently) run W to Nyala and El Obeid.

Road: Bus These are cheap but extremely crowded. Most buses arrive/leave from United Nations Square in the centre of town, costs S£10 to suburbs. Buses to Omdurman, S£20, leave from Sharia el-Taiyar Zulfu, outside the *Arak Hotel*. Frequent buses run daily from Souk Es Shaab to Wad Medani, takes 2-3 hrs and costs S£700, to Kassala takes 8 hrs and costs S£3,000, to El Obeid takes 1-2 days and costs S£4,000, to Dongola on Sat at 0600, takes 24 hrs, costs S£4,000, goes on to Wadi Halfa.

NB On all overnight journeys a sleeping bag is recommended. Modern a/c bus to Port Sudan each day takes 20-24 hrs and costs S£6,000.

When travelling out of town it is possible for the hardy (foolhardy?) to take a place on the bus roof. This offers an excellent view, is rather fun, particularly after the event, and not really more uncomfortable than the cramped interior. However, do not take a place up there until the police checkpoint outside of Khartoum is passed as here they monitor the number of travellers and are likely to haul down any roof-top passengers.

Ferry to Tuti Island from Sharia el Nil opposite the National Museum.

General comment On the whole the most reliable form of transport is the bus while the train is best avoided at all costs, except as an experience.

Excursions

Djebel Aulia reservoir, 40 km S (1 hr drive) of Khartoum on the White Nile is a popular picnic spot. A well preserved dam, topped by very period-piece street lamps holding back this huge expanse of shallow water, was built early this century to increase water supplies in Egypt.

Now it is redundant as a reservoir of water but is said to be a great reservoir of Nile crocodiles!!

Sabaluka game reserve, about 60 km N of Khartoum, after Djebel Qerri on the main Nile.

Sixth Cataract, also known as the Sabaluka Cataract, about 50 km N with some magnificent white water.

Meroe, a prosperous agricultural and industrial centre in 500-400BC. Its ruins of temples and pyramids are accessible by road and rail. Alight at Kabushiya from Khartoum (200 km) and negotiate local transport to the Royal City.

Shendi, for the ruined Meriotic Temples of Musawwarat and Naqa. There are buses and trains to Shendi from where local transport must be hired.

BEYOND KHARTOUM

Khartoum to Wad Medani

Buses for Wad Medani, 187 km SW of Khartoum, leave each morning from Souk as-Shaabi, reached initially by box or yellow taxi from Souk al-Arabi. This journey takes 3-4 hrs depending on traffic and the condition of the vehicle. This is the busiest road in Sudan and the scene of some very creative driving. The black top surface is just about wide enough for two buses to pass. Beyond Khartoum to the E of the road stretches the huge expanses of the Gezira irrigation scheme (see page 898) with occasional cotton ginning factories along the way. The road follows closely the course of the Blue Nile which can be glimpsed from the bus, while to the W the belching chimneys of Sudan's second largest sugar factory at Gunaid often cloud the horizon. Beyond Gunaid buses stop en route near Hasaheisa or Rufaa. Here stalls and restaurants sell refreshments, mainly *fuul* sandwiches (S£40), kebabs (S£100), tea (S£20) and soft drinks (S£50).

The closer you get to Medani, the greater the intensity and variety of agricultural production. However, in 1993 the many desiccated carcasses of cattle by the roadside bore testimony to the fragile subsistence agriculture practised by many agro-pastoralists who survive on the fringes of the Gezira scheme but who are far removed from its rigid system of production.

Wad Medani's main recommendation is its situation by a scenic stretch of the Blue Nile. Its major disadvantage is the endemic malaria and although it is the main town of the Gezira, some of the agricultural service businesses are considering relocation of personnel to Khartoum for health reasons. The bus will drop you at the small souk not far from E *Hotel International*, PO Box 213, T 392, rm with (smelly) bath, service not good, limited menu of fish, *taamaya*, salad and eggs served in an austere dining room with lurid wall friezes. **D-E** *Hotel Yugoslavia* is perhaps slightly more expensive while there are other, smaller hotels alongside the river which, although more picturesque, are even less well equipped.

Wad Medani to Kassala

Buses from Wad Medani for Kassala, E of Khartoum, leave from the souk in town. The road to Kassala is black top and has recently been upgraded. After crossing the river Rahad, more of a trickle in the dry season, and its namesake irrigation scheme and canal, the bus trundles across the flat plains of rain-fed dura and maize crops, passing the occasional craggy outcrop, until **Gedaref** is reached. This is a dirty town best known for its sesame seed auctions. Here the children will hawk their cold *karkade* (hibiscus drink), lemon drink, bananas, peanuts and other less recognizable snacks. About 70 km NE of Gedaref, the road drops down to the Atbara Gorge. The Khashem el Girba Dam, which is not visible from the main road, was constructed to serve the Halfa Jedida (New Halfa) irrigation scheme, built for the resettlement of the Nubians displaced by the building of the High Aswan Dam. The reservoir is silting up and is said to have only a life span of a further 10 to 20 years. The scheme was also responsible for excessive erosion which reduced the palmeries and the livelihood of the locals.

Now the distant mountains of **Kassala** begin to grow on the horizon like milk teeth, until eventually they dominate the town. The bus station is outside the town so share a box for about S£20 each to the souk in the town centre. Kassala is immediately prettier and quieter than Wad Medani and, with the spectacular hills as a backdrop and the riverside gardens, is a fascinating place to stay and popular with Sudanese honeymooners. The gardens are beside the River Gash, which is a seasonal stream feeding into the great outwash of the Gash Delta irrigation scheme.

Local information

● Accommodation

The hotel by the bus station is very basic, water supply intermittent, be very careful with your belongings.

● Places to eat

Restaurants beside the main souk serve familiar Sudanese food, although it is most likely to be served by Eritreans who seem to staff most of the restaurants.

● Shopping

Kassala souk is interesting for its crafts from E Sudan, daggers, swords, leatherwork and other artefacts. Silver jewellery of the local tribes is a good buy. Fruits including citrus, dates, bananas and water melons (S£200 each) are on sale.

● Banks

Don't rely on being able to change money here quickly or efficiently, although the banks purport to provide the service.

● Transport

Road Buses leave for Port Sudan (8 hrs), Atbara (1 day), Asmara (1½ days) and Eritrea leave at sunrise.

North to Egypt

Khartoum to Atbara

Buses take approximately 7 hrs and cost S£2,500 one way. The road is black top to Shendi heading NE from Khartoum: for short stretches it follows the course of the Nile, jockeying for position with the railway. The journey through wide, flat expanses of desert, scrub, thorn trees and wandering camels, with the occasional small irrigated plot or a woman riding a donkey, can be very uncomfortable and it is wise to try and secure seats at the front as far away from the rear axle as possible. Take ample provisions as the bus only stops once for refreshments.

Trains also go to **Atbara**, which is the main hub of the Sudan railway network, such as it is. Trains to Port Sudan, to Karima and the express to Wadi Halfa all stop at Atbara. The flight time is 45 mins for a bumpy but scenic journey with fine views of the River Nile. Reconfirm and confirm again your booking.

Atbara to Wadi Halfa

The train from Atbara follows the course of the Main Nile for 209 km before striking out at Station 10 just after Abu Hamed, across the barren Nubian Desert for a further 369 km. Take plenty of provisions for the journey although, almost miraculously, people appear along the route, including the middle of the desert, selling *karkade*, *fuul* sandwiches and other refreshments.

The hotels in **Wadi Halfa** are situated near the souk which is opposite the railway station. Hotel accommodation is cheap and very basic, catering for travellers onward-bound for Egypt, usually an interesting mixture of Sudanese, Egyptians and assorted other African nationalities.

The ferry port is 15 min drive from the souk but tickets must be bought in advance in the souk. The ticket sales office is easily distinguished from the other whitewashed buildings by the queue that forms there from very early in the morning. Last minute souvenirs and snacks can be bought at the ferry port but food is available on the boat and the ticket price includes a meal.

Getting the requisite stamps and pieces of paper is tedious but don't be put off. The hassle is worth it when you are under full steam on Lake Nubia and the sun sets. Next morning as the sun rises the boat is approaching the Aswan High Dam. Getting off the boat can take several hours as the Egyptian authorities are meticulous in their scrutinization of disembarking passengers.

Khartoum to Dongola

The route from Khartoum to Debba (386 km) and on W to Dongola or E to Karima is plied by **boxes** (Toyota pickups) which are faster but more expensive than buses. They cover the Karima to Dongola section in 2 hrs compared with the bus taking 7 hrs. To rent a box for the same journey will cost S£3,000, or a fraction thereof, depending on how many wish to travel.

A domestic **flight** from Khartoum to Dongola costs around US$45.

A **steamer** from Dongola to Karima, in theory, departs Thur (very flexible time schedule) and takes 3 days, depending on the level of the Nile. Operates only between Sep and early Jan.

Bus from Dongola to Karima leaves Sat from ferry terminal on E bank, takes 7 hrs, S£2,500. Karima to Dongola leaves Mon.

INFORMATION FOR VISITORS

Contents

Before you go

Entry requirements

● Visas

It is impossible to visit the country without a visa and, although they are officially issued from Sudanese embassies in Western Europe within 48 hrs, expect to wait 5-6 weeks in the normal course of events. All applications are referred back to Khartoum by telex which explains the delay. The régime sometimes delays or refuses to issue visas to anyone in general, and journalists in particular, who is thought to be opposed to its policies. With the exception of Egypt, which used to be very quick when bilateral relations were better, trying to get a visa from one of the Sudanese embassies in the Middle East or Africa can also take weeks. An Israeli stamp in your passport will make it difficult, if not impossible, to obtain a Sudanese visa. To obtain a visa from a Sudanese embassy it is usually necessary to have a return airfare and 'sufficient funds' to support yourself while you are in the country.

A visa, costing £53 in UK, when obtained, is usually valid for 1 month, but the period of stay may be extended if you ask. Passports must be valid for at least 3 months from the date of issue of the visa. Travellers continuing their journey in other countries requiring visas are advised to have these organized before they travel to Sudan. An exit visa is not required.

Travel Permits The régime does not discourage internal travel for foreigners in areas away from the war zone. Travel permits are no longer required, except for the S (and they won't be granted anyway).

Registration Visitors staying for more than 3 days in any one place must register at the Alien's section of the Department of Passports, Immigration and Nationality on Sharia Osman Digma. This is to the left of the impressive Arab Authority for Agricultural Investment Co building and near the FAO building. A good hotel might do this for you, otherwise start off with 1 photograph, a letter from the Tourist Department/Business organization giving reason(s) for visit, fill in two forms and expect to spend about 1 hr there.

● Vaccinations

Entering and leaving the country you may be asked for a valid **cholera** certificate. Visitors wishing to travel to the S must have a valid vaccination certificate for **yellow fever**. Visitors wishing to enter Egypt from Sudan (and anxious to avoid being held in quarantine in Egypt) must produce a valid vaccination certificate for yellow fever or a *location certificate* showing they have not been in a yellow fever area. These are obtained from the Khartoum Municipality 24 hrs before departure.

● Representation overseas

France, 56 Ave du Montaign, 75008 Paris, T 1 422 55573; **Germany**, Bonn, T 49 228 36 3074; **Switzerland** (Consulate), Geneva, T 22 733 2560; **UK**, 3 Cleveland Row, London SW1A 1DD, T 071 839 8080; **USA**, 2210 Massachusetts Avenue NW, Washington DC, T 202 3388 565.

When to go

● Best time to visit

The best season for visiting Khartoum is from early Oct to mid-Apr. After that the weather becomes exceedingly hot and strong desert winds, *haboobs*, bring sandstorms. The temperature drops when the rains begin and humidity soars. See main section on climate, **page 892**.

● Clothing

Lightweight clothing of natural fibres is recommended. A coat or sweater will be needed in the winter months and protection from the rain in the wet season from May to Aug. Women should dress with extreme modesty in a country where the majority follow the Muslim code of behaviour and men are not normally seen in shorts in public. On any long journey women will find it more convenient to wear a long skirt as toilet facilities do not exist.

Health

● Staying healthy

Protection against malaria is **essential** and treatment must begin 2 or 3 weeks before the journey begins. Also before leaving for Sudan, visitors are recommended to have vaccinations against cholera, typhoid, tetanus, meningitis and infectious hepatitis while one for yellow fever is mandatory for travellers coming from infected areas. Immunization against cerebral meningitis (A and C), more common here than elsewhere in North Africa, though not essential, provides a high degree of protection. The medical facilities even in the capital leave much to be desired and your first aid kit should include disposable needles and sterile dressings. Salt tablets are recommended.

● Water

The water in the capital is safe enough for cleaning your teeth but not for drinking without boiling or using purifying tablets. Outside the capital treat all water with suspicion.

● Further health information

Read the section on Health, **see page 19** with particular care.

Money

● Cost of living

Sudan is currently suffering from virtual hyperinflation of around 250% per year and the value of the Sudanese Pound has fallen like a stone from S£4.5/US$1 in 1990 to over S£120/US$1 in 1993 and S£340/US$1 in 1994. The result is that while almost everything is expensive for the local population, visitors changing hard currency will find many things very cheap. Because S£ prices are constantly changing it is impossible to provide accurate details of any prices.

Prices at the beginning of 1994: Petrol S£400 per gallon (official), S£2,500 free market; cigarettes – Sudanese brand S£200, imported brand S£250 for packet of 10; bread S£7.50 per loaf (official), S£10 free market; sugar S£900 per kilo; meat (beef) S£500 per kilo; meat (lamb) S£600 per kilo; fish S£200 per kilo; apples S£2,000 per kilo; oranges S£30 each; tomatoes S£200 per kilo; onions S£400 per kilo; bananas S£80 per kilo; passport photographs (black and white) S£800 for 4; tablet of soap S£75; Pepsi/Coke S£50 per bottle in shops, much more in hotels; cup of tea S£30; cup of coffee in *Hilton Hotel* S£700.

● Credit cards

The major hotels accept American Express, Visa and Diners Card. Travellers' cheques are also accepted in the capital.

● Currency

The Sudanese Pound (S£ in this text) is divided into 100 piastres. For exchange rate July 1994, **see page 9**. Due to inflation a new denomination has been introduced – a Sudanese Dinar 1SD = 10S£. Notes in circulation are £S100, 50, 20, 10. There is an illegal black market with a 15% premium above the official rate but visitors are advised to avoid this despite the financial attractions and to do all transactions through banks or hotels. It is illegal to import or export Sudanese currency. Changing money can take 30-40 mins. Ask for dinars or you will get handfuls of old denomination notes.

● Currency restrictions

Currently all travellers are permitted to enter and leave Sudan with whatever currency they carry without restriction, but all foreign currency bank notes and travellers' cheques have to be declared on entry and departure. Your form will be looked at on departure but no-one with a calculator is likely to add it all up! Be prepared for these regulations to change.

● Taxes

There is a government tax of 20% and a service charge of 10-12½% added to most bills. Bills in international hotels must be settled in hard currency.

Getting there

The best way to reach Khartoum is by air. Journeys by bus and rail are difficult but not impossible. There are timetables but these change frequently and are unreliable.

Air

Airport, located just off Africa/Airport Rd, is about 5 km to the SE of the city centre. It is very easy to get a taxi from your hotel. Check in and clearance of customs and immigration are quite quick and efficient at the new departure terminal building. The arrivals hall is now being expanded.

Flights from Khartoum Frankfurt and **London**, Fri and Sun at 1200; **Cairo and Rome**, Sun at 1100; **Cairo**, Mon at 1100, Mon and Sun at 0700; **Jeddah**, Tue, Thur and Fri at 1600, Wed and Sun at 2030; **Addis Ababa**, Sun at 0530; **Asmara**, Mon, Tue, Fri and Sun at 0530; **Nairobi**, Sun at 0330; **Kano**, Wed at 0830; **Abu Dhabi**, Tue, Thur and Sun at 0800 Mon at 1700; **Muscat**, Thur at 0800; **Sharjah**, Tue at 0800; **Damascus**, Sat at 1600; **Doha**, Mon and Thur at 0800; **Amman**, Mon at 2000; **Dubai**, Sun at 0800.

Flights into Khartoum **London**, Mon and Sat at 1600 leaving **Frankfurt** at 1930; **Rome**, Sun 2000 leaving **Cairo** at 0030; **Cairo**, Tue and Thur at 1730; **Jeddah**, Tue, Thur and Fri at 2010; **Addis Ababa**, Sun at 0830; **Asmara**, Mon, Tue, Fri and Sun at 0900; **Nairobi**, Sun at 0820; **Kano**, Wed at 1345; **Abu Dhabi**, Tue,Thur and Sun at 1630, Mon at 2330; **Dubai**, Sun at 1445; **Muscat**, Thur at 1440; **Sharjah**, Tue at 1445; **Damascus**, Sat at 2015; **Doha**, Mon and Thur at 1300; **Amman** Mon at 2350.

Immigration Foreigners do not require exit visas. However, to travel by a carrier other than Sudan Air, Egyptair or Ethiopian—ie Air France, Lufthansa or KLM—any passenger has to get permission from the Civil Aviation Authority. For Air France, the ticket must be paid for into a special account at the Sudanese-French Bank. Permission and payment can be arranged by the travel agent, but expect the whole process to take 2 hrs.

Airport Tax There is an airport tax of S£500.

Ferry and train

There is a weekly ferry from Aswan in Egypt, across Lake Nasser to Wadi Halfa, linking with the weekly train from Khartoum. First, second and deck classes available.

Road

Buses to Asmara, Eritrea leave from Souk Es Shaab, take 3 days and cost S£6,000.

Customs

Travellers may bring in 200 cigarettes or 50 cigars or 400 gm of tobacco for their own use, 5 kg food, gifts up to US$500. It is strictly forbidden to import, sell or deal in any way with alcoholic drinks (see below).

When you arrive

Electricity

Is 240 volt single phase AC. Plugs are mainly 2- and 3-pin round. The voltage is very erratic and supplies are subject to very frequent interruptions.

Hours of business

Fri is the weekly holiday. **Shops** are open 0800-1330 and 1730-2000 Sat-Thur. **Government offices** 0730-1430 Sat-Thur. **Banks** 0800-1230 Sat-Thur. Hours in Ramadan are generally shorter. In the S the official weekly holiday is Sun.

Official time

GMT + 2.

Photography

You will need a Photography Licence – available from the Sudanese Tourism Corporation on Sharia Baladiya or the Ministry of Information and Culture on Sharia Gama'a. This will reduce the hassle – a little. The Sudanese are very sensitive and photography should not be attempted of anything that could be considered strategic like broadcasting stations, bridges, dams and public utilities like water, gas, or electricity works, railways, air transport and military establishments which can be easily recognized by the huge bilingual signs prohibiting photography! They are also sensitive about photographs being taken of slum areas and beggars. Avoid taking photographs of women and be very discreet at all times. All photography must be for private use.

Safety

Physical violence to persons is very unusual. Petty theft, however, is very common both by pickpockets and also, unfortunately, in the hotels. Be very careful to keep all important papers next to your skin, keep a small amount of spending money separate from your main cash, and keep your hand firmly on your money in any crowded place.

Shopping

The main markets are Omdurman Bazaar and Khartoum Souk where locally made goods are sold. The main shopping centres around Sharia al Gamhuria in Khartoum open 0800-1500. There are small shops inside every major hotel in Khartoum. Remember that many items made from hides, skins and ivory are forbidden entry into Western countries.

Tipping

Taxi drivers do not expect a tip on a negotiated fare – but will rarely be able to find change for large notes! Elsewhere tipping is not expected but gratefully received.

Weights and measures

Sudan generally uses the metric system. **See page 17** for conversion tables. They also have their own system of measurement (**see box, page 893**).

Where to stay

Hotels

Accommodation is not a problem in Sudan but there are very few hotels, even in Khartoum which are up to Western standards with private bath/shower, a/c and a decent restaurant. Many are run down with an irritating lack of reliability. The cheaper hotels may be as comfortable and the basic *lakondas* just as clean. (See Accommodation, page 905).

HOTEL CLASSIFICATIONS

AL US$90+. International class luxury hotel. All facilities for business and leisure travellers are of the highest international standard.

A US$75-90. International hotel with air conditioned rooms with WC, bath/shower, TV, phone, mini-bar, daily clean linen. Choice of restaurants, coffee shop, shops, bank, travel agent, swimming pool, some sport and business facilities.

B US$60-75. As **A** but without the luxury, reduced number of restaurants, smaller rooms, limited range of shops and sport.

C US$40-60. Best rooms have air conditioning, own bath/shower and WC. Usually comfortable, bank, shop, pool.

D US$20-40. Best rooms may have own WC and bath/shower. Depending on management will have room service and choice of cuisine in restaurant.

E US$10-20. Simple provision. Perhaps fan cooler. May not have restaurant. Shared WC and showers with hot water (when available).

F under US$10. Very basic, shared toilet facilities, variable in cleanliness, noise, often in dubious locations.

Food and drink

The Sudanese are not renowned for their cuisine which tends to be very basic but very varied and tasty. For the majority of the population it consists of *fuul* (Fava beans) and rather poor stews which are eaten with unlevened bread and washed down with black tea, so sugary you can stand your spoon up in it. If you are lucky enough to enjoy Sudanese home cooking you can expect a variety of salads, *bamia*, *molokhia*, fish, liver, *fuul*, *taamaya*, cheese, cakes, pastries, lamb, *fasoulia*, peppers, *mashi*, with bread, rice or *kisra*. Coffee and soft drinks such as Pepsi, Sprite, Fanta, Coke and Vimto at around S£50 per bottle are also available and *karkade*. Even in the capital, on the banks of one of the world's great rivers, there is, with the exception of bony but delicious Nile perch, surprisingly little fish in the diet. Although the Nimeiri government was comparatively lenient towards expatriates found with alcohol and used to turn a blind eye to the embassies smuggling it in for their own consumption in the diplomatic bag, the current régime is far less tolerant and, although some people brew alcohol at great risk if they are caught, Sudan is now a 'dry country', avoid therefore any peddlers or black marketeers with this commodity. Being drunk in public is a punishable crime.

Sudanese food explained:

Babganush: an aubergine dip.
Bamia: vegetable, better known as okra or ladies' fingers.
Fasoulia: white beans in tomato sauce
Fuul: stewed Fava beans.
Karkade: hibiscus drink
Kisri: unleavened bread.
Mashi: stuffed vegetables.
Molokhina: a vegetable, somewhat like spin-

RESTAURANT CLASSIFICATIONS

Given the variations in price of food on any menu our restaurants are divided where possible into three simple grades: ♦♦♦ expensive, ♦♦ average and ♦ cheap.

ach, but with the consistency of egg white when cooked. Served with lamb or chicken.
Taamaya: fried balls of sesame paste with chick peas and other ingredients.
Tahina: a sesame paste usually served with green salad.

Getting around

Taxi drivers cannot be relied upon to know other than major places in town. Few streets are named and fewer properties numbered. Taxis are less frequent due to petrol shortages.

For internal travel by air, bus and train, see Transport to & from Khartoum, **page 907**.

Communications

● Language

Arabic is the official language although most Sudanese speak one of the great many tribal languages as a first language. English is the most widely spoken foreign language.

● Postal services

Main post offices 0730-1300 and 1730-1830 Sat-Thur. Stamps for stamp collectors are available at main offices. Fax and Telex available throughout day in central office or Friendship Hall. Also in major hotels. Telegraph services at main and local offices.

● Telephone services

Making international calls from Sudan is not easy. Be prepared for a long wait until you get a line which will then be very bad. Calls to Egypt have to go through the operator. Sending a fax from Sudan is not to be relied upon. Most important documents now go with the courier services.

Entertainment

● Media

Radio: **see page 17** for BBC World Service wave bands. **Television**: there is one TV station with programmes in Arabic.

Holidays and festivals

When an official holiday falls on a Fri, the Sat is normally taken as a public holiday with banks and businesses closed. The 28 days of fasting in Ramadan are certainly not the best time to visit Sudan or any Muslim country (**see page 30**).

1 Jan: Independence Day
6 Apr: Popular Uprising
30 Jun: National Salvation Revolution
21 Oct: October Revolution

Approximate dates in 1995:

1 Feb: Beginning of Ramadan
4-8 Mar: Eid el Fitr (end of Ramadan)
10-15 May: Eid el Adha (Qurhan Bairam)
31 May Islamic New Year (Anno Hegira 1416)
9 Aug: Prophet's Birthday

Further reading

Sudan Update offers the best news on Sudan, T 071 833 4924, Box CPRS, London WC1N 3XX, UK. Annual subscription £25.

Asher, Michael, *A Desert Dies (The demise of the Kababish tribe of Sudan)*, Viking (1986); Asher, Michael, *In Search of the Forty Days' Ride*, Viking (1986); Churchill, Winston *The River Wars* (historical); Khaled Mansour, *The Government they Deserve* (contemporary account, biassed); Niblock, Tim, *Class and Power in Sudan* (analytical); Waterbury, John, *The Hydro-Politics of the Nile Valley*, New York (1979).

GLOSSARY

A

Agora	Market/meeting place
Aïd/Eïd	Festival
Aïn	Spring
Affanes	Woollen slipper used by nomads
Abbasids	Muslim Dynasty ruled from Baghdad 750-1258
Aghlabids	Orthodox Muslim Dynasty in Tunisia and eastern Algeria 800-909
Alaouite	Present rulers of Morocco since 1666
Alcázar	Royal Palace
Alcazaba	Fortress
Almohads	Islamic Empire in North Africa and Spain 1130-1269
Almoravids	Islamic Empire in northwestern Africa and southern Spain 1054-1147
Andalucía	Moorish Spain
Arabesque	Geometric pattern with flowers and foliage used in Islamic designs
Azulejos	Tiles

B

Bab	City gate
Bâches	Converted pick-up truck
Bahri	North/northern
Baladiyah	Municipality
Baksheesh	Money as alms, tip or bribe
Baraka	Blessing
Barakan	Woollen wrap 5m by 2m to cover entire body
Barbary	Name of North Africa 16th-19th centuries
Barboushe	Soft, flat leather slipper
Barrio	Section of a town
Basha	see Pasha
Basilica	Imposing Roman building, with aisles, later used for worship
Bazaar	Market
Bedouin	Nomadic desert Arab
Beni	Sons of (tribe)
Berber	Indigenous tribe of north Africa
Bey	Governor (Ottoman)
Bidon-ville	Shanty town
Bodegas	Wine cellars
Borj	Fort
Bour	Depressions in sand down to water table for cultivation
Burnous	Man's cloak with hood – tradional wear

C

Caid	Official
Calèche	Horse drawn carriage
Calidarium	Hot room
Capital	Top section of a column
Caravanserai	Lodgings for travellers and animals around a courtyard
Cartouche	Oval ring containing a king's name in hieroglyphics
Ciudad	Town
Chaouia	Berbers of the Aurés
Chechia	Man's small red felt hat
Chotts	Low-lying salt lakes
Cobijas	Triangular shawl
Colossus	Gigantic statue
Correos	Post
Corrida	Sequence in bull fight
Couscous	Steamed semolina with lamb

D

Dar	House
Darj w ktaf	Carved geometric motif of intersecting arcs with superimposed rectangles
Dechra	Earth coloured terraced hamlets topped by fortress silos
Deglet Nur	High quality translucent date
Delu	Water lifting device at head of well

Dey	Commander (of janissaries)
Djebel	Mountain
Djemma	Main or Friday mosque
Dólmenes	Prehistoric cave
Dour	Village settlement

E

Eïd	see Aïd
Erg	Sand dune desert

F

Faqirs	Muslim who has taken a vow of poverty
Fassi	A person or item from Fes
Fatimids	Muslim dynasty 909-1171AD claiming descent from Mohammed's daughter Fatimah
Felucca	Sailing boat on Nile
Feria	Fair
Fiesta	Feast/holiday
Flamenco	Traditional dance of Andalucía
Foggara	Underground water channel
Fondouk/ Funduq	Lodgings for goods and animals around a courtyard
Forum	Central open space in Roman town
Ful/Fuul	Beans

G

Gare Routière	Bus station
Garrigue	Mediterranean scrubland – poor quality
Ghibli	Hot dry wind from south
Ghorfa	Granary or storehouse/ room/temporary dwelling
Ginan	Small garden or tree embayment
Gymnasium	Roman school for mind and body

H

Habous	Religiously endowed land in Morocco
Hafsids	Berber dynasty 13th-16th century in present day Tunisia and Algeria
Hamada	Stone desert
Hammam	Bath house
Hara	Jewish quarter in Tripoli
Harem	Women's quarters
Harira	Soup
Harmattan	Mauritanian hot dry wind from east that raises temperatures and reduces humidity
Hassi	Well
Huerta	Area of oasis gardens

I

Idrissid	Dynasty founded by Moulay Idriss I 788AD
Imam	Muslim religious leader

J

Jabal	see Djebel
Jallabah	Outer garment with sleeves and a hood – often striped
Jami'	Mosque
Janissaries	Elite Ottoman soldiery
Jarapas	Rough cloth made with rags
Jebel	see Djebel
Jihad	Holy war by Muslims against non-believers

K

Ka	Spirit
Kasbah	Castle/Fort
Kilim	Woven carpet
Kif	Hashish
Kissaria	Covered market
Koubba	Dome on tomb of holy man, also special room in houses in Ghadames
Ksar (pl Ksour)	Fortified village

L

Levante	Strong easterly wind
Liwan	Vaulted arcade
Locutorio	Building containing numerous public telephones

M

Mahboub	Coins worn as jewellery
Maghreb	Western Arab world – Morocco, Algeria and Tunisia
Malekite	Section of Sunni Islam
Maquis	Mediterranean scrubland – often aromatic
Marabout	Muslim holy man/his tomb
Marinids	Berber dynasty 13th-15th centuries, strongest in Morocco
Maristan	Hospital
Mashrabia	Wooden screen
Mashreq	Eastern Arab world
Mastaba	Tomb
Mausoleum	Large tomb building
Mecheoui	Moroccan meat dish (mutton)
Medersa (pl Medressa)	School usually attached to a mosque
Medina	Old walled town, residential quarter
Mellah	Jewish quarter of old town
Menzel	House
Meseta	Plateau
Mihrab	Recess in wall of mosque indicating direction of Mecca
Mimbar	Pulpit in a mosque
Minaret	Slender tower of mosque from which the muezzin calls the faithful to prayer
Mirador	Viewing point
Mosque	Muslim place of worship
Moulid/ Mouloud	Religious festival – Prophet's birthday
Moussem	Religious gathering
Muezzin	Priest who calls the faithful to prayer
Mullah	Muslim religious teacher
Murabtin	Dependent tribe

N

Nasrids	Muslim Dynasty in Spain 1238-1492
Necropolis	Cemetery

O

Oasis	Watered desert gardens
Obelisk	Tapering monolithic shaft of stone with pyramidal apex
Ottoman	Major Muslim Empire based in Turkey 13th-20th centuries
Oued	see Wadi
Ouled	Tribe
Outrepassé	Horse-shoe shaped arch

P

Parador	State run hotel chain in Spain
Pasha	Governor
Pensiones	Low grade hotels
Phoenicians	Important trading nation based in eastern Mediterranean from 1100 BC
Piscine	Pool
Pisé	Sun-baked clay used for building
Piste	Unsurfaced road
Plasticultura	Horticulture under plastic
Pylon	Gateway of Egyptian temple

Q

Qibla	Mosque wall in direction of Mecca
Qasr	see Ksar

R

Rabbi	Head of Jewish community
Ramadan	Muslim month of fasting
Reconquista	Christian campaigns to recapture Iberian territory from Muslims
Refugio	Mountain hut
Reg	Rock desert
Ribat	Fortified monastery

S

Saadian	Moroccan dynasty from 1541
Sabil	Public water fountain
Sabkha	Dry salt lake

Saggia	Water channel
Sahn	Courtyard
Sarcophagus	Decorated stone coffin
Sahel	Coast/ coastal plain
Salat	Worship
Sebkha	see Sabkha
Semana Santa	Holy week leading up to Easter
Serais	Lodging for men and animals
Serir	Sand desert
Shahada	Profession of faith
Shergui	Hot, dry desert wind
Sidi	Mr/Saint
Sierra	Peaked mountain range
Souq	Traditional market
Stele	Inscribed pillar used as gravestone
Suani	Small walled irrigated traditional garden
Sufi	Muslim mystic
Suq	see Souq
Sunni	Orthodox Muslims

T

Tagine/Tajine	Stew
Taifa	Sub-tribe
Talgo	Fairly fast train
Tamashek	Language of Touareg
Tapas	Bar snacks
Tariqa	Brotherhood/Order
Tizi	Mountain pass
Touareg	Nomadic Saharan dwellers, noted for men's blue face covering
Troglodyte	Underground dweller

V

Vandals	Empire in North Africa 429-534 AD
Venta	Roadside restaurant/café
Visir	Governor

W

Wadi	Water course – usually dry
Wikala	Merchants' hostel
Wilaya/Wilayat	Governorate/district

Z

Zaouia/Zawia	Shrine/Sennusi centre
Zayyanids	Berber dynasty NW Algeria in 13th century
Zellij	Geometrical mosaic pattern made from pieces of glazed tiles
Zeriba	House of straw/grass

INDEX

INDEX OF TINTED BOXES

INDEX OF MAPS